GunDigest® Book of

CLASSIC
COMBAT
HANDGUNS

Dan Shideler

Published by

World Publications Group, Inc.
140 Laurel Street
East Bridgewater, MA 02333
www.wrldpub.com

Cover photography courtesy Chip Morton Photography, morton.chip@gmail.com, www.chipmortonphoto.com, 951-699-7873

ISBN-13: 978-1-4643-0277-0
ISBN-10: 1-4643-0277-4

Cover Design by Tom Nelsen
Designed by Dustin Reid
Edited by Corrina Peterson and Dan Shideler

Printed in China

Contents

Introduction

Welcome to the *Gun Digest Book of Classic Combat Handguns*!

I t might have been quite a job for editor Dan Shideler to select the chapters for this book, but then again it was also a pure labor of love. Dan, who passed away April 3, 2011, probably savored every moment he spent combing through his collection of *Gun Digest* annuals dating all the way back to the inaugural 1944 edition.

Gun Digest was an integral part of Dan's life from the time he was a teenager. He was named editor of the *World's Greatest Gun Book* in 2009, just in time to start work on the 2010 edition. In the introduction to that volume, Dan wrote:

"I was raised on *Gun Digest*. Once a year, in the long-gone Indiana of the 1960s and 1970s, my father brought home the new edition, which my brother Dave and I eagerly devoured. I mean we read it literally from cover to cover, absorbing whatever wisdom and insight that could be found in its pages. I still have some of those 40-year-old volumes, nearly all of them showing pencil marks in their catalog sections where we, with boyish enthusiasm, checked guns that we would surely buy someday …

"And now, forty-some years later, I am the editor of that same book. Karma? The inscrutable workings of Fate? Call it

Dan Shideler
1960 - 2011

what you will, I will say simply that it is an honor ‹ for me, it's the stuff that dreams are made of."

Even though Dan is no longer with us, the literature he chose to represent some of the most memorable combat handguns of all-time is testament to great guns and great gun writers.

The content herein spans 1949-1999. Topics range from the obvious (Model 1911, Luger, Glock) to instructional ("Rating Handgun Power") to historical ("Early Rivals of the 1911") to just plan ol' food for thought ("Too Many 45s?").

Once available only to those few collectors who owned a complete set of *Gun Digest, Gun Digest Book of Classic*

Combat Handguns represents the cream of the crop from the most enduring gun annual of all time. We hope you enjoy reading this compilation as much as Dan enjoyed putting it together.

Sincerely,
Corrina Peterson
Editor
Gun Digest Books

Handgun Facts

■ Major Charles Ashihs, Jr.

THE FIRST revolver was patented by young Samuel Colt in 1836. Since then there have been no less than 156 manufacturers of revolving handguns. The Army and Navy, since that time, have adopted 44 different revolvers and 9 different pistols, made by 32 separate manufacturers, ranging in calibers from 32 to 58. The earliest model was accepted in 1842, the last in 1911. While Colt invented the first firearm which successfully employed a cylinder containing separate charges of powder and ball, it remained for another soon-lo-grow-famous New Englander, Douglas Wesson, to adapt his newly perfected 22 rim fire cartridge to an equally successful and new revolver. His revolver, puny and low powered, was quite popular with Union officers during the War between the States. This revolver, a seven-shot breech loader, was the Model of 1855.

From their crude beginnings in 1836, the Colt and contemporary revolvers were what is known as the single action type — the hammer must be eared back each time a shot is fired. About 1877 the double action revolver made its appearance. This gun was a considerable refinement over the original as it merely necessitated pulling the trigger strongly to make the hammer rise and fall. In addition, of course, the weapon could be employed as a single action any time the shooter desired. As may well be appreciated, the double-action feature made it possible not only to fire the first shot quicker and more accurately, but also to get off the following shots with greater speed. Today, all revolvers are of the double action type save three. The original Colt Peacemaker (discontinued) is still sold in quantities, as well as two inexpensive semi-target revolvers.

MAJOR CHARLES ASKINS, JR. is undoubtedly the country's foremost handgun authority. Not only is he a ballistic and arms expert, but also a world renowned shooter who has won every major handgun championship at one time or another.

Service Type Revolvers

As revolvers were improved, three definite types emerged. The first of these was the service type handgun. This is a revolver of 38, 44 or 45 caliber with a large frame, considerable weight, not less than a 4 to 6 inch barrel with fixed sights, a large grip, and characterized by great sturdiness of construction, rugged reliability and long life. Both Colt and Smith & Wesson make such guns in several models and calibers:

Colt New Service (Discontinued)
Colt Official Police
S & W Military and Police
S & W 38-44 Heavy Duty
S & W 1926 Model 44 Military
S & W 357 Magnum
S & W 1917 Army (1949 Production)

Utility or Pocket Type Revolvers

We have a second and much larger group of handguns which may be classed as general utility or pocket weapons. These models are not nearly as big or as heavy as the service type revolvers and are almost invariably of smaller caliber and shorter barrel length, lighter in weight, and have been designed essentially for stowing in the pocket or concealing beneath the coat. They may be grouped as follows:

Colt Police Positive Special
Colt Police Positive (Not in Production)
Colt Detective Special
Colt Banker's Special
(Not in Production)
Colt Pocket Positive
(Not in Production)
S & W Military and Police
S & W Terrier (1949 Production)
S & W Hand Ejector (1949 Production)
S & W Regulation Police
(1949 Production)
I. J. Protector (Not in Production)
Iver Johnson Hammerless
(Not in Production)

Target Type Revolvers

The major class of revolvers is the target handguns. These models have seen more development and refinement than either the service or utility types due to the fact that target shooters are a more vocal group than any other class of revolver users; as a consequence, they have demanded, and obtained in some measure, those improvements which they desired.

Colt Officers Model
Colt Police Positive Target
(Not in Production)
Colt Shooting Master
(Not in Production)
S & W K-22 Masterpiece
S & W 22-32 Target (1949 Production)
S & W 22-32 Kit Gun
(1949 Production)
S & W 38-44 Outdoorsman
S & W 1926 Model 44 Target
Harrington & Richardson Sportsman
Iver Johnson Supershot Sealed Eight
I. J. Champion (Not in Production)

Automatic Pistols

At various times during the past, auto pistols have been made by Savage, Remington, Harrington & Richardson, Smith & Wesson, and other companies since gone out of existence. Today, only Colt and High Standard survive.

Colt automatic pistols are a result of the inventive genius of the world's greatest firearms designer, the incomparable John Browning. The weapons range from the tiny 22 caliber to the 45 ACP. In Europe, the Fabrique Nationale d' Armes de Guerre, at Herstal, Belgium, manufacture the Browning auto pistols which are the same as the Colt product. The FN Company, however, produces only the 25, 32, and 380 Auto, and, so far as is known, have never attempted to manufacture a 22 similar to the Colt Woodsman. The 45 Colt Automatic is the property of the U.S. Government and, consequently, was never considered for manufacture by the Belgium firm.

Service automatic pistols used by the military and police, as well as outdoorsmen, are the following: Colt 45

Here is the author with his handy shooting case made by Buchanan. This versatile carrying case holds a battery of handguns, supports the spotting scope on the folding lid, and provides plenty of space for ammunition, cleaning gear and other essentials.

Automatic Model 1911 and the Colt 38 Super Automatic.

Very recently High Standard has designed for future production an entirely new automatic pistol chambered for the 38 Special cartridge. This pistol will be a big gun with a weight of 40 ounces and will utilize one of the finest all-purpose cartridges in the book. It will offer strong competition to the 45 and the 38 Super.

Among the utility or pocket type automatics, Colt had three little guns identical in action but differing slightly in weight, frame, and barrel length. These models were made up for the 25 Auto, 32 Auto and 380 Auto cartridges. High Standard also makes an automatic for the 380 Auto cartridge.

Automatic Target Pistols

Automatic pistols intended for use as target handguns represent the most tangible progress in the improvement of hand weapons during recent years. Credit for this improvement lies largely with High Standard. Some 25 years ago this company, newly organized, designed a 22 auto pistol that was roughly

finished but possessing many virtues. It had a 6¾ inch barrel, good sights, considerable weight, fair balance, and reliability — plus a very reasonable price. As a result of the success of this model, the company developed a line of target guns which incorporated longer stocks, greater weight, heavier barrels, improved trigger pull, adjustable sights, and outside hammers. As a result of these improvements the High Standard auto pistol is today as good as any firearm made. The improved High Standard guns especially constructed for target shooting (before World War II) were:

Model A	weight 36 ozs.	Hammerless
Model H-A	weight 36 ozs.	Hammer
Model D	weight 40 ozs.	Hammerless
Model H-D	weight 40 ozs.	Hammer
Model E	weight 42 ozs.	Hammerless
Model H-E	weight 42 ozs.	Hammer

Of these, only the H-D Military is now in production.

Colt, under the prodding of their energetic competitor, brought out the Match Target Woodsman in 1937. This was a great improvement over the original Woodsman. It had a much heavier barrel which eliminated the shimmy at the front end and made possible an increase in weight (36 ozs.) of the entire piece. This pistol was an instantaneous success and champion handgunners promptly established an entirely new set of 22 caliber records with it.

In 1948 Colt further improved the Match Target Woodsman to the extent that it is practically a new gun. The Match Target now has a weight of 41 ounces, a still heavier barrel, click adjusting rear sight, a newly designed receiver with a grip long enough and large enough for a man's hand, a splendid target trigger pull with a built-in trigger stop, a disconnector so that the weapon cannot double (fire several shots with one pull of the trigger) and a slide latch with a new clip release.

These mechanical advancements, beneficial though they are, shrink to somewhat insignificant proportions when viewed against the really outstanding improvements of this splendid new Woodsman. The truly great accomplishment of the Colt engineers is the remarkable degree of balance achieved in this arm. Here, unquestionably, is the best balanced, best feeling, and most natural pointing handgun ever manufactured! The balance is an incomparable thing. So cleverly has the weight been distributed, that so comfortable does the grip feel, and so naturally does the gun hang, that it practically aims itself. Great things are predicted for this brilliant new Colt.

The new High Standard 38 Special auto pistol, when it makes its appearance, will be somewhat of a sensation. It will eclipse, in my opinion, the dominant target firearm in the center fire category today, which is the 38 revolver. In match shooting the revolver must necessarily be cocked for each shot discharged in the timed and rapid fire stages. This process takes a lot of time and hurts the score. With the arrival of the High Standard, 38 automatic, this undesirable feature will be eliminated. As a consequence, the gunner will have more time to aim and squeeze each shot.

The Colt National Match 45 Automatic, a great favorite in match shooting, is to be replaced by a new and lighter caliber automatic pistol now under consideration by the Army.

The revolver is obsolescent. With the appearance of a first class self-loading pistol, it will be completely eliminated as a target proposition. High Standard also intends to produce a companion pistol in 22 caliber.

Two years ago. an interesting new 22 single shot pistol, the Tompkins, was put into very limited production in this country. This weapon has a trigger mechanism superior to any yet seen on American handguns. This mechanism contrives to cam the sear out of the hammer notch. This camming action permits a trigger which has no perceptible movement — at least to the eye — and makes possible an exceedingly light, adjustable pull. Further, the Tompkins has a rather unique type of action. It resembles nothing so much as the old Springfield Model 1870 ride. Other than these features, the pistol has little to recommend it. It is too light, The grip is ill-shaped, the barrel is on the waspy side, and the rear sight is startlingly crude. Slow fire pistol shooting is not popular in the United States. Consequently, a single shot weapon can never hope to attain popularity.

Foreign Handguns

A veritable flood of war-prize handguns has reached the U. S. These pistols are almost entirely of automatic type and are either 7.65 mm (32 ACP) or 9 mm Luger calibers. They are, for the most part, roughly machined and badly finished, although those which come from Germany are superior in design to the best which American manufacturers now produce.

The Walther P-38, firing the 9 mm Luger cartridge, was the standard German military sidearm and is excellent though roughly machined. Nonetheless, it is a weapon with numerous superior improvements in design. It has a double action feature which precludes the necessity of cocking the weapon in order to fire the first shot, and it is possible to get off the first shot faster than conventional automatics. It has a safety of novel design, is quickly and easily disassembled without tools, utilizes the powerful 9 mm Luger cartridge, and has an indicator which reveals at all times whether or not there is a cartridge in the chamber. The P-38 is muzzle light, a serious fault for precision shooting, and the trigger pull is not especially good (this latter fault may be rather easily corrected, however).

Luger and Mauser pistols were brought home by our returning veterans in somewhat smaller numbers. Both pistols are well known here because of regular importation for many years prior to the war. Both are out-of-date and while they fire excellent cartridges from a ballistic standpoint, the guns themselves possess so many faults as to be undesirable. The Walther pistol in Models PP and PPK, calibers 7.65 and 9 mm Korto (380 ACP), as well as the Mauser HSc Model, and the Sauer Double Action auto pistol are excellent pocket automatics incorporating the double action feature of the P-38.

The Austrian Steyr, Italian Beretta and Glisenti, and the Japanese Nambu automatic pistols, as well as a score of others, are interesting souvenirs, but due to a lack of proper ammunition or because of poor workmanship, inferior materials, badly designed sights, or an abominable trigger pull, are hardly worthy of consideration for any sort of serious handgun work.

Air Pistols

During recent years, we have developed some exceedingly interesting air pistols. These pistols are entirely out of the small boy's air gun class — are indeed man-sized and powerful. Instead of utilizing the conventional BB pellet, these new guns fire a flanged slug which is pointed at the forward end and has a sort of lead skirt at the rear. This acts as an obturator to the air blast and assists materially in accurately guiding the projectile.

Best known of these air pistols are the Hy-Score, Crosman, Apache, and Benjamin. The Hy-Score is a direct adaptation of the old German Haenel air pistol and has much of the feel and appearance of the Luger. It employs a powerful spring that actuates a piston which, when released by the trigger, moves within a tight cylinder building up air pressure which is vented into the barrel. The barrel has a firing chamber and is rifled exactly like a conventional handgun. Calibers are 177 and 22. The 177 caliber develops a velocity of 367 feet per second and approximately 3 ft. lbs. of muzzle energy. The 22 caliber, with its heavier pellet, travels 273 feet per second and has an energy at muzzle of 3 ft. lbs. These are somewhat trivial figures when compared with the 22 Short cartridge with its 54 pounds of energy. Nevertheless, the air pistol will consistently kill rats, sparrows, mice, and starlings and is a remarkably efficient practice weapon for the marksman who wants to keep in trim during the winter months. The accuracy of these pistols is very good. At 30 feet the Hy-Score pistol will shoot into a 1-inch ring with regularity. Plenty of weight, excellent adjustable patridge sights, man-sized stocks, fair trigger pull and passable balance place it in the target class. They are definitely of training value to the target marksman.

Custom Built Accessories

Unfortunately, when a handgun is made, whether revolver or auto pistol, the grip must conform to a single rigid pattern. Quite often this means a poor fit. The need for custom built handgun stocks was seen a dozen years ago and as a result, we have a half-dozen manufacturers who turn out some excellent made-to-measure stocks. Foremost among these are the Southwest Cutlery and Manufacturing Co., Mershon Co., Walter Roper, and King Gun Sight.

In addition to the special stocks which are a boon to most marksmen, we have a select coterie of pistolsmiths who do precision rebuild jobs on the old 45 auto as well as short actions for our 38 revolvers, cockeyed hammers, broad triggers, trigger stops, click adjusting sights, ventilated ribs, and innumerable other jobs aimed at improving the shooter's score. Our leading pistolsmiths are Buchanan, Pachmayr, King and Harpe.

It is exceedingly interesting to note that the precision work of leading pistolsmiths was incorporated as standard manufacture by Smith and Wesson as of the latter part of 1948. The new Masterpiece line of K22, K32 and K38 revolvers now boast such improvements as a fast-falling hammer with a 33% shorter throw than formerly, wide hammer spurs, ribbed barrels, adjustable trigger stops, micrometered click adjusting rear sights, and increased weights. The 38 Military and Police also has incorporated in it the Masterpiece Short Action and the same hammer profile; other models of the S&W line which will shortly undergo much needed changes are the 357 Magnum, 38/44 Outdoorsman, and 1926 Model.

Match Shooting

Match pistol shooting is organized excellently in this country. It is fostered by several thousand clubs and claims many members. Local, state, and national matches are fired annually and these contests have developed shooters second to none throughout the world. Matches are fired with 22, 38, and 45

caliber pistols; the distances are divided between 25 yards and 50 yards. One-third of the shooting is slow fire, two-thirds is timed and rapid fire. Scores run phenomenally high and competition is keen. About two decades ago the law enforcement peoples became interested in improving the shooting skill of their officers, and today, if you should select the ten ranking pistol men in this country, you would find seven were policemen, two civilians, and one soldier. Shooters are classified as marksmen, sharpshooters, and experts so the tyro does not have to compete against the shark to earn his prize.

How to bag crows with a Colt 22 automatic is illustrated, by Charley Askins.

Hunting with Handguns

Service type handguns as well as all the target models make excellent hunting weapons. Game may be killed with any caliber from 22 to 45. It is simply a matter of not overmatching the cartridge against the game. To kill varmints successfully a handgun of hefty proportions, patridge sights, a barrel of not less than 4½ inches, (6 inches is preferable), a trigger pull of not more than 4 pounds, (3 lbs. is better), a well fitting and comfortable grip, plus sufficient wallop in the cartridge to perform good execution is needed.

As an example, the 22 long rifle will do a very satisfactory job on sparrows, squirrels and cottontails but it will not kill jackrabbits, larger hawks, or coyotes consistently. The best of our handguns for game taking is the 357 Magnum. This is the most powerful handgun cartridge in existence. It develops 1510 foot seconds of muzzle velocity and 800 ft. lbs. of muzzle energy. By comparison, the old 45 auto has a velocity of 860 foot seconds and a muzzle energy of only 378 ft. lbs. The 357 usually will kill such game as fox, hawks, coyotes, rabbits, woodchucks and a variety of similar varmints. With all its power the 357 is not recommended for such game as deer (although deer have been killed with the weapon) since deer are usually shot at comparatively long range, yet it is potent enough for mountain lion — generally killed at long range.

The handgun which ranks as an odds-on favorite with the police is the 38 Special. Smith & Wesson has long claimed that their Military & Police Model 38 Special revolver is used by more city police departments than any other. Be that as it may, the 38 Special is the gun usually chosen. The New York State Police are armed with the Colt New Service 45 caliber, the Royal Canadian Mounted Police use the same weapon in a 455 caliber (of somewhat lesser power than the 45 Colt), the US Border Patrol carry the New Service in 38 Special caliber, and the Texas State Police pack the same weapon nickelplated in order to eliminate the nuisance of rust and to aid them in seeing their hardware quicker when taking a fast shot at night. The FBI has a variety of weapons, the most popular of which is the S&W 357 Magnum.

Just before the war, the various ammunition companies developed and loaded a variety of powerful new 38 Special ammunition. Remington-Peters brought out the 38 Special High Velocity which developed 1115 foot seconds (158 grain standard bullet) as against the old standard velocity of 870 foot seconds. Subsequently, Western-Winchester developed the 38 Special Super-X which had a velocity with a 150 grain bullet of 1175 foot seconds. These new loads were available with two types of ball: (1) lead bullet, (2) copper nose cap and a lead core.

For individuals who feel the necessi-

A good holster is as necessary as a fine gun. Here is a representative assortment of some of the best and most practical types as manufactured by S. D. Myres Saddlery Co. of El Paso, Texas.

ty of keeping a gun for protection, such excellent guns as the Colt Detective Special, (38 cal, 2-inch barrel), S&W Military & Police (38 Special 2-inch barrel), S&W 357 Magnum with 3½ inch barrel, or the Iver Johnson Hammerless revolver (38 cal, 3¼ inch barrel, not currently in production) are suggested. These revolvers are short, compact, light and yet possess full sized grips, point naturally, and are quite reliable. Among automatics, the Colt 38 automatic, the Walther, Mauser, or Sauer 7.65 mm auto pistols are ideal for the purpose. These latter guns have the double action feature which makes them exceedingly fast to get into action.

Future of the Handgun

The revolver has been with us, substantially unchanged, for more than one hundred years. The automatic pistol represents the logical evolution from this obsoleted powder burner. I have not the slightest doubt but that in the not too distant future the automatic will relegate the revolver to the museum shelf.

The ideal pistol has not yet been built. However, it is most assuredly coming and will incorporate among other improvements these and other advancements:

Barrel and action will be so low as to extend in prolongation of the forefinger. Such a pistol would develop little or none of the objectionable "turning motion" during recoil, so common in present day handguns. Such recoil as did occur with this new weapon would be readily absorbed, due to the barrel being in direct prolongation of the wrist-and-forearm axis. Present handgun sights are deplorably crude. Recently, however, I saw an encouraging indication of what is coming. This was a new handgun sight looking exactly like the Lyman 48 receiver sight for rifles. This sight has micrometered click adjustments for windage and elevation. Faster falling hammers are badly needed. The hammer on the revolver falls too far, too slowly, and strikes so hard the gun is actually moved by the impact. The mechanical principle upon which the sear operates is another hundred-year-old relic much in need of modernization. The Tompkins is the only handgun made in this country with a truly modern trigger system. That this system, or one of similar good characteristics, will be adapted to our coming crop of automatic pistols is consistent with the progressive trend in the handgun field.

45 Auto Pistol

▌ Robert A. Burmeister

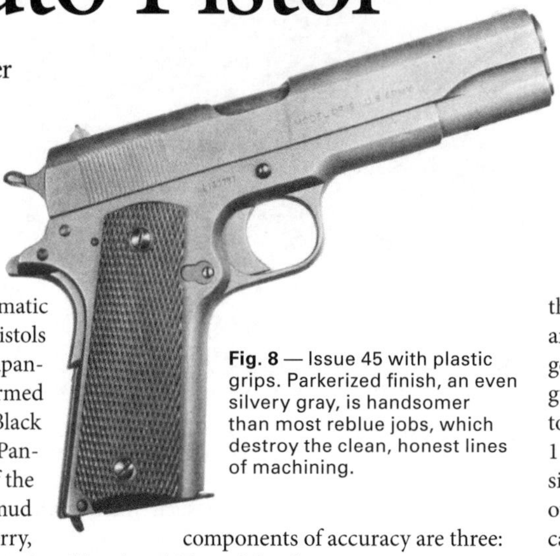

Fig. 8 — Issue 45 with plastic grips. Parkerized finish, an even silvery gray, is handsomer than most reblue jobs, which destroy the clean, honest lines of machining.

THE 45 automatic — enigma of pistols — sturdy companion of our armed forces from the days of Black Jack Pershing hot after Pancho Villa in the deserts of the Southwest, and to the mud and fury of Chateau Thierry, to the shell holes of Anzio beachhead, to the volcanic dust of Iwo Jima, to the frozen night patrols at Pork Chop Hill in Korea. Sometimes carried and not used; sometimes a last defense in some far corner of the world; the choice of FBI man Purvis, nemesis of Dillinger; and the choice of many another law man. Universally admired for pure perfection in engineering, for its flawless functional design, for its brutish power, but always about it one sad doubt — accuracy?

The difficulty of shooting the 45 automatic with passable accuracy has been written about many times. Ex-servicemen will often make appropriate caustic comments. Target shooters, usually, enjoy only partial or intermittent success with this old war horse, yet the factors or components of accuracy that are responsible for this curious situation are seldom evaluated realistically. Another aspect which confuses and misleads is the all-too-common comment that most of the better handguns will shoot closer than any shooter can hold. True enough, of course, but a lamentable distortion that only conceals a most important fact — that fact is that whatever inaccuracy exists for ammunition or gun will further enlarge the group a shooter is capable of holding, and in the case of the 45 the enlargement may be prodigious. The components of accuracy are three:

1) That of the shooter.
2) That of the ammunition.
3) That of the gun.

These components are cumulative, that is, whatever group size a shooter is capable of making with perfect ammunition and a perfect gun will be enlarged by any inaccuracy of the ammunition and will be further enlarged by the inaccuracy of the gun.

This is shown graphically for one 45 automatic in fig. 1. The largest circle represents a 17.9" group at 50 yards, which is attainable by a shooter who is capable of shooting into a 3.5" group at 50 yards with a perfect gun and perfect ammunition but who in this instance has ammunition capable only of a 3.8" group at 50 yards, and a gun capable only of a 10.6" group at the same distance. The shortest arrow "A" in fig. 1 represents the radius of a 3.5" diameter group and shows how far a bullet can diverge to the right of aiming point due solely to optical error of aim by shooter (for simplicity of treatment it is assumed that the shooter makes no error due to erratic gripping, flinching, or poor trigger release). Arrow "B" represents the radius of a 3.8" diameter group and shows additional possible divergence to the right because of error of ammunition. Arrow "C" represents the radius of a group of 10.6" diameter and shows yet another possible divergence to the right because of error of gun, thus the three arrows accumulate to make a group size of 17.9". While fig. 1 shows only divergences to the right, similar divergences could occur in any other direction. Also divergences can cancel one another in whole or in part. Nevertheless the accumulation in one direction such as shown in fig. 1 expresses the worst that can happen.

Statistical analysis will quickly point out that such an accumulation of errors, all in the same direction, does not happen often. Quite true, but it happens often enough to account for many a poor score. It should be remembered that the foregoing is based on the premise that there is no error due to erratic gripping, flinching, or poor trigger release, etc., which in effect are complementary to "A," the optical error of aim, and if these were included the maximum group size would be still larger.

Values for fig. 1, namely 3.5" for optical error of aim of shooter, 3.8" for error of ammunition and 10.6" for error of gun were obtained as follows:

Error of Shooter

Individual shooting skills vary considerably, but every shooter's performance depends on:

a) How well he can align his sights with the target, which we'll call optical error of aim.

b) When sights are aligned how well he can pull the trigger without disturbing alignment (and, of course, how well he resists flinching, accommodates recoil and muzzle blast, etc.).

c) How uniform his grip or hold is from shot to shot.

d) How accurately he can adjust his sights with due regard for ballistics, range, and his hold.

As stated before, items such as (b), (c), and (d) are not treated in this article but item (a), optical error of aim, is considered here as a basic component of accuracy — a principal and assessable error of the shooter. The War Department Basic Field Manual FM 22–35, Automatic Pistol Caliber 45, M1911 and M1911 A1, contends that a shooter should be able to make a dime-sized group at 30 feet (equivalent to 3.5" at 50 yards) by use of a special fixed rest for the pistol and an aiming test called a sighting exercise. In this "triangulation" test the pistol is held motionless in the fixed rest and an assistant moves a bull's-eye on a blank target until the shooter, looking over his sights, declares alignment has been attained. The position of the center of bull's-eye is then marked and the test is repeated. After three trials the marks should make a dime-sized group. A seasoned target shot will do better than the criteria specified but the average shooter will do well to equal it. As an interesting comparison the aiming tests made as above and reported by Donald E. Fischer in the March, 1961 The American Rifleman showed that his best 5 "shot" groups with a Hammerli free pistol at 50 meters (54.7 yards) were approximately ¾" in diameter. Since this free pistol has about double the sighting radius of the 45 automatic, plus precision sights very much superior to the crude military sights of the 45 auto, it is apparent that

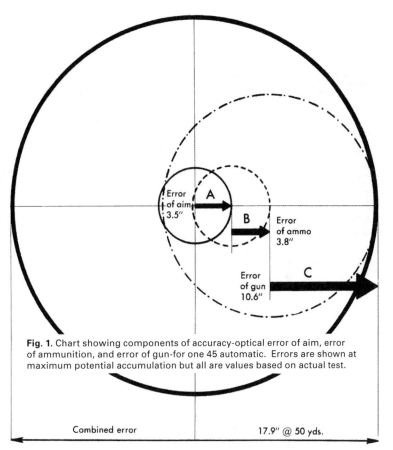

Fig. 1. Chart showing components of accuracy-optical error of aim, error of ammunition, and error of gun-for one 45 automatic. Errors are shown at maximum potential accumulation but all are values based on actual test.

Combined error — 17.9" @ 50 yds.

the criteria of 3.5" at 50 yards for optical error of aim is realistic.

Error of Ammunition

In an excellent article entitled "National Match 45" by Colonel Jim Crossman, U.S.A., and Major Bill Brophy, U.S.A., which appeared in the August 1959 issue of The American Rifleman, the following table appears:

Fig. 2. Accuracy of various lots of ammunition.

Groups were obtained by using a special heavy barrel in a rifle action and firing from a machine rest — hence shooter's error is absent, likewise error of gun is virtually nonexistent. Note variations in group sizes of various lots of ammunition even though these lots (except handloads C and D) were

Fig. 4 — Pre-war commercial 45 has King sights and belt clip (arrow).

Fig. 5 — Government issue hybrid 45 auto. Springfield receiver, Colt slide and barrel; assembled at Rock Island Arsenal. Has low mounted ⅛" Micro sights.

TABLE A

Groups fired from a single accuracy weapon; range 50 yds.; size of 10-shot group measured from center to center of widest holes; selected ammunition lots.

Ammunition	Average Group Size for 3 ten-shot groups
Commercial "A"	0.9"
Handload "A"	1.7"
Service ball, lot 1887	2.4"
Service ball, lot 1806	2.5"
Handload "B"	2.5"
Service ball, lot 18407	3.4"
Service ball, lot 18451	3.4"
Commercial "B"	3.5"
Service ball, lot 1885	3.8"
Handload "C"	7.9"
Handload "D"	8.9"

Same, except 3 groups fired from each lot from each of 3 accuracy weapons.

Ammunition	Average Group Size
Service ball, lot 1854	2.4"
Service ball, lot 6445	2.7"
Service ball, lot 18258	3.0"
Service ball, lot 1686	3.1"

TABLE B

Number of guns tested	Type of gun	Average of 3 groups of 10 shots		Average of all guns, fired 3 ten-shot groups per gun
		Worst gun	Best gun	
106	1959 NM	5.3"	3.3"	4.3"
12	1956 NM	5.7"	3.3"	4.4"
10	1955 NM	6.2"	3.6"	4.7"
8	Gunsmith A	5.7"	3.4"	4.8"
21	Gunsmith B	6.2"	2.8"	4.9"
4	Gunsmith C	8.2"	3.5"	5.6"
21	Gunsmith D	8.7"	3.9"	5.8"
9	Gunsmith E	8.6"	4.2"	5.8"
14	Gunsmith F			6.4"
5	Gunsmith G	9.7"	4.6"	6.6"
5	Gunsmith H	8.4"	5.8"	7.0"
13	Gunsmith I	11.7"	4.4"	7.2"
21	Gunsmith J	10.5"	5.1"	7.5"
6	Gunsmith K	10.8"	4.4"	7.7"
5	Gunsmith L	13.6"	5.1"	8.8"
6	Gunsmith M	15.9"	5.0"	9.5"
15	Gunsmith N	16.3"	4.8"	10.6"

Fig. 3. Accuracy of various guns.

selected for accuracy. Service ball lot 1885, which gave a group size of 3.8" at 50 yards, was chosen for fig. 1.

Error of Gun

In the previous sections it has been shown that at the 50-yard range the optical error of aim and the error of ammunition can account for 3.5" and 3.8"respectively. Error of gun for fig. 1 was derived as follows: Crossman and Brophy tested 5 government issue 45's for accuracy and found that with ammunition rated at 3" the group sizes for the 5 guns were 7.1", 11.8", 6.5", 5.1", and 13.6" respectively. Taking the poorest of these at 13.6" and subtracting ammunition error of 3" the gun is therefore capable of 10.6", the value used for fig. 1. Note that the best of these guns — the 5.1" one, is quite accurate.

Fig. 3 gives the results of the Crossman and Brophy tests on National Match and other accurized guns — of the 281 guns tested the worst was 16.3" and the best was 2.8".

It is apparent that there is a large variation in accuracy among 45 automatics! This is readily appreciated inasmuch as there have been eight different manufacturers of them in the past 50 years. As to commercial models my first experience was with the one depicted in fig. 4 — a pre-war model. After putting several thousand rounds through this gun (mostly government ammunition) I wrote to the late J. H. Fitzgerald, Testing Engineer for Colt's, telling him that I could do much better with my re-

volvers than with the 45 automatic and wondered whether I already "shot out" my 45 or whether it was basically inaccurate. His reply sums up the situation admirably!

He stated: "The life of the 45 barrel, for extreme accuracy, is between 5 and 6 thousand shots. In the case of the revolver, the writer has one that has been fired over 150,000 shots, and fired it over 100,000 accurately and without any new parts being installed since the arm left the factory. Extreme accuracy in the 45 automatic requires a match barrel and also a proper fitting bushing that will fit perfectly both slide and outer surface of the barrel. A tight link and link-pin is also necessary. The lower part of the link should correctly fit the slide stop of the pistol. The wear on these parts will, of course, correspond to the wear on the inner surface of the barrel after approximately 5000 shots. For extreme accuracy, they should then be replaced. Trigger pull of not less than 4½ lbs. is recommended by the factory, because

after wear the pull may change to about 4¼ lbs."

Fig. 5 shows an issue 45 (equipped with new sights, of which more later); note that in comparing the fit of slide to receiver (fig. 6) of this gun with that of the commercial model (fig. 4) there is a marked difference. Yet the GI 45 of fig. 5 is quite accurate, even with its relatively loose slide.

What to do About Your Issue 45

About this time the reader may want to check out his own 45 to determine how much work may be necessary to improve accuracy. The first step is to run an accuracy test. This is best accomplished by using a machine rest, but if such is not available an improvised forearm rest may be used. An economical and effective rest may be made by constructing a special raised arm rest on a heavy wood lawn chair, or, a bench rest may be utilized. The use of such rests combined with suitable padding, a two-handed hold, and good weather

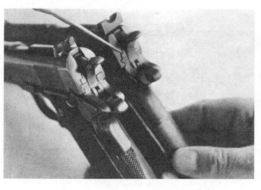

Fig. 6 Rear view of guns shown in figures 4 and 5. Note close fit of slide to receiver on pre-war gun at left compared to loose fit (pointer) of slide to receiver on government issue hybrid Springfield-Colt on right. This looseness of fit is not as important as fit of barrel, link, link pin, bushing and slide.

will give results comparable to the machine rest. Testing must be done with ammunition of known accuracy such as commercial target ammunition or high grade custom handloads. (I have found a good load available locally at $3.00/50 having a 185 gr. H&G semi-wad-cutter cast bullet and 3.5 grains of Bullseye powder. There are equally good loads offered in your area, I'm sure.) Don't waste your time with the usually erratic "hard ball" surplus GI ammo or by shooting offhand; the latter will only confuse you as you will be testing a combination of yourself and the gun.

Typical tests of two 45's are plotted in fig. 7. Note that at 20 yards one 45 gave a tight five-shot 1½" group, all in the black, whereas the other spread three shots over 6". The first gun is the one shown in fig. 5; it has ⅛" low-mounted Micro sights with front sight staked and silver soldered in place by a custom pistolsmith who also reduced trigger pull to a smooth 4¼ pounds. In other respects this gun is as issued, no "accurizing" as such, so it is suitable for field and target work. The second gun, fig. 8, an issue 45, is obviously not in the same accuracy class as the first and is therefore subject to an "accurizing" job involving new barrel, new bushing, link, link-pin and possibly tightening slide, in addition to new sights and trigger pull reduction.

Fig. 9 — Details of belt clip. Grip is hollowed to accommodate clip.

Ratings of these guns were based on not one target as shown but also on repeat tests which confirmed results. By testing a gun in this fashion the shooter can determine just how much "accurizing" and improving is desirable. Sometimes a lot of work is necessary, but fortunately some pistols are accurate enough as issued. The writer regards a 45 capable of 2" groups at 20 yards or 5" groups at 50 yards as entirely satisfactory for field work.

New sights are an absolute must on issue 45's, for the old military sights are much too small for accurate sighting. Similarly the trigger pulls on most issue 45's are atrocious — rough, grating and running between 5½ and 7½ pounds. Even an expert cannot shoot such guns

well, and it is amazing how much better a 45 will shoot if ⅛" sights are installed and the trigger pull is reduced and smoothed. (Of course target ammunition must be used.) The sight and trigger pull work referred to above for the fig. 5 gun cost $22.50; that included the furnishing and installing of ⅛" Micro sights, the rear sight low-mounted in milled recess, the front staked and silver soldered in place; trigger pull was reduced to 4¼ pounds. This work, done by a custom pistolsmith, is beyond the capability of most home workshops.

For some field work, and as a substitute for a holster, a belt clip may be used as shown in fig. 9. Note that no alteration of the gun is required except for hollowing out the underside of the right grip. The clip is made of 16-gauge steel, shaped and bent as shown. The clip is not as secure as a holster but on the other hand it takes less room, thus preserving one of the salient features of the 45 — its handy, compact, functional design. The writer abhors any alteration of a 45 which clutters it up or makes it unhandy — alterations such as huge, high-mounted sights, ribs, front sights on forward protruding bars and monstrous "anatomical" grips. Maybe these do help in raising the score — but they look like hell and destroy the practicality of the weapon.

Take another long look at your old war horse — it may be better than you think.

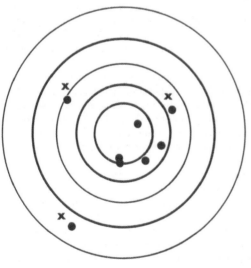

Fig. 7 — A test target showing difference in accuracy of two 45's. One (fig. 5) gave a tight 5-shot 1½" group, all in the black, the other 45 (fig. 10, a strictly issue model), spread 3 shots over 6" (these three marked X). Range 20 yards, forearm bench rest used.

Oddball Hardballs

For well over a half-century we have been blessed — or bemused — by the 45 ACP, so there's little left to say about it, right? Wrong. This collector describes in detail a number of unusual GI 45s, guns few shooters know exist. ∎ Mason Williams

This Remington-UMC pistol has no serial number and is without any inspector's stamps, assembler's stamps or other markings — a real "lunch pail" pistol.

I N SHOOTERS' parlance "hardball" refers to the GI cal.-45 Colt automatic pistol that fires GI ammunition — loads with full metal jacket bullets. Usually these handguns are pretty much as-issue jobs, or else they are the finely finished Match Target pistols available from the Director of Civilian Marksmanship via the National Rifle Association. Seldom has a better dollar value been offered the American handgun shooter. This article, however, is not about match target handguns, regardless of their capabilities. Rather, I would like to ramble on about some of the goofed-up 45 ACP pistols that I have run into.

In most businesses it takes a lot of brains and initiative to foul up on a production piece, and when such happens the result is customarily sold at a premium price as a "one in a million" item. The rate of goof-ups in the arms industry, I believe, ranks as one of the highest in the world, particularly during wartime when the primary object of production lines is to get as many pistols as possible into the hands of our men. When the scrap is all over, Ordnance sits down and sorts through those which remain, then picks out the unusual items and does something with them. Now and then one gets through them, though, and that is what this article is all about.

Now, I'm sure that somewhere among my readers there lurks an overzealous policeman or Federal officer who wants to get a Medal of Commendation. Let me state for the record that all the oddballs mentioned here are strictly — but strictly — legitimate. So relax and forget about the medals. Also, at this point, a word to collectors. None of these is for sale. If anyone has a real oddball I sure would like to hear about it. I'm not an avid collector but when an unusual Model 1911 cal. 45 ACP comes my way, I buy it if it will add to my basic collection and to my over-all knowledge of 45s. Many 45s that have been reblued, altered, etc., have no value to me. I am interested only in the more unusual "as-issue" oddballs. The thing that fascinates me is how these pistols get through the countless Government checks, inspections, etc., to finally fall into the hands of the American shooter. A lot of these pistols are simply curiosa, while others are genuine collector's items. Often it is

difficult to draw the line. I will not attempt to do so.

I must be vague about certain details here, because the entire history and background of the 45 ACP pistol is filled with grey areas. Records no longer exist or have been lost. Many of the men who worked on the original 45s are no longer with us. Much of the information is secondhand. So please do not be too critical if I appear to sluff off some details. Most of the time I will come right out and say I just don't know. Bear with me and let's have some fun trying to figure out some of the goofs that I know about.

Rem-UMC

Let's start off with one I purchased from the Director of Civilian Marksmanship. Now the DCM is about as official an agency of the Government as one can find — and anything that is officially an agency of the U.S. Government dislikes anything that does not fit the prescribed specifications. Let me try to trace — theoretically of course, because no one really knows — the origin of this particular 45 Model 1911 and/or Model 1911A1.

Way back around 1917 the U.S. Army needed 45s, so among other contractors they authorized Remington-Union Metallic Corp. to manufacture as many 45s as they could. Remington-UMC was given a block of serial numbers entirely separate from the regular run of numbers. These commenced with number 1 and ended with number 21,676. This much is known.

The frame of this 45 meets every requirement as one of the Remington-UMC frames, starting off with the inspector's initials, "EEC," just above the magazine release on the left side of the receiver. The

The Savage Arms "slide" pistol, rarely seen today. To the author's knowledge, Savage Arms did not produce complete pistols.

tially over and partially below the "No." preceding the serial number. Directly below these ordnance bombs and a bit to the left is stamped 10210, in slightly smaller numerals. This is the only instance I have ever run into of a firearm carrying two numbers. The interesting point is that both numbers fall well within the numbering series assigned to

THIS IS THE ONLY INSTANCE I HAVE EVER RUN INTO OF A FIREARM CARRYING TWO NUMBERS. THE INTERESTING POINT IS THAT BOTH NUMBERS FALL WELL WITHIN THE NUMBERING SERIES ASSIGNED TO REMINGTON-UMC BACK IN 1917

phrase "United States Property" is in the correct place (for this specimen) on the left side of the frame ahead of the trigger guard. So far all is well.

The numbers on these pistols should be stamped just above the trigger on the right side of the receiver. Mine has No. 1545 all right, which is correct for a Remington-UMC. Two Ordnance bombs are stamped side by side par-

Remington-UMC back in 1917.

My thought on this double numbering is that this receiver came off the line for issue, and then for some reason was held out and possibly used as an instruction control receiver. This could well have been the case because the low number 1545 shows this was one of the first production receivers off the line. Later on, pressure for more and more pistols could

have forced the company to re-number the receiver and re-issue it for service. This is all guesswork. I don't know. I have examined all the stampings under a glass and they appear to be of the same approximate vintage. This receiver came to me completely equipped as a Model 1911 frame with the short safety spur, flat mainspring housing and every indication that it was original throughout.

If you think one error is plenty for one pistol — hold on to your hats. The slide is standard, of Colt manufacture, and meets all specifications of the Model 1911A1 slides. On the other hand, all slide parts appear to be Model 1911 type. The left side carries all the correct stampings for such a slide, but there is absolutely nothing on the right side of the slide — not even serrations, despite the fact that the left side does carry serrations. I have miked the slide and it meets specifications. Obviously someone failed to put this slide through the

Right side of the double-numbered pistol, grips removed to better show double numbers and the two Ordnance bombs, the latter stamped in the correct location. The two numbers fall within the numbering block assigned to Remington-UMC.

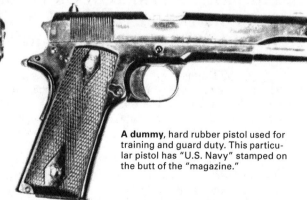

A dummy, hard rubber pistol used for training and guard duty. This particular pistol has "U.S. Navy" stamped on the butt of the "magazine."

The X-number 45. Such pistols were machined and rebuilt at Government arsenals. Williams believes that all rebuilt pistols carry the eagle over S17 just above the magazine release on the left side of the frame of the pistol.

final stamping on the right side, but how the serrations were left off remains a mystery. It's a weird looking pistol viewed from the right side.

This pistol was obviously brought in after World War II for rebuilding. The finish, a relatively new and perfect parkerizing, is clean, light and unused. Plastic grips were added. How such an odd combination ever got through without someone picking it up I don't know. As I mentioned above, this pistol was purchased by an NRA member from the DCM just a couple of years ago. No other pistol that I own has so many oddball things wrong with it.

years in the Navy during the Second World War and I saw just one of these pistols. It was kept by the Executive Officer for training purposes. Every now and then some fortunate seaman would be permitted to drop it into his empty holster and go on guard duty. I have heard men speak of these dummies, and I understand many were used for hand-to-hand combat training during the war. As far as I am concerned these dummies are so realistic that if the lights were low or visibility bad I certainly would not argue with a man shoving one at me. Despite the fact that they cannot fire they make an

off during the breaking up of the Indian charge. Since then it has been carefully protected. Being martially marked it will remain in my collection of 45 ACPs.

Lunch Pail 45

I now come to a real fouled-up 45 ACP — one that I have named my "lunch pail" 45. This pistol also started out in life as a Remington-UMC handgun — at least to the best of my knowledge. The slide meets every requirement of that brand, including all component parts of the slide assembly.

The odd thing about this pistol is the receiver. It has the customary "United States Property" stamping on the left side of the receiver, ahead of the trigger guard, but that is the only mark on the frame. No serial number, no inspector's initials, no marks of any kind appear. Again the receiver has been assembled with parts that meet the specifications of a pistol of that manufacture and age.

The outside shows considerable holster wear, a police officer having carried it for nearly 30 years. I doubt if it has been fired more than a hundred times. The inside parts show little or no wear and they all appear to be original.

The slide and the receiver assembly appear to have been together for a good many years — in my opinion they are the original assembly. I can't be certain, of course, but I imagine this receiver was "borrowed" from the line after completion but prior to final acceptance and stamping. The parts were probably also brought home piecemeal in the lunch pail every evening. With the millions of parts then coming off the line each day it's a wonder more of this style don't turn up. If you ever run into one I suggest you take it to a local authority and ask them to assign it a number; then you will be in the clear. A lot of these pistols — so I am told — were given to foremen and heads of departments after the war as a token present or as a momento so don't assume that every one was stolen.

> AS FAR AS I AM CONCERNED THESE DUMMIES ARE SO REALISTIC THAT IF THE LIGHTS WERE LOW OR VISIBILITY BAD I CERTAINLY WOULD NOT ARGUE WITH A MAN SHOVING ONE AT ME

45 Dummy

Compared to this one-in-a-million pistol let's look at another weird 45. To confuse the issue even more, this 45 is not a pistol at all. What is it? It's a dummy 45 pistol made of hard rubber, plus solid lead, to give it weight so that it duplicates the hang and feel of the conventional 45 ACP. The butt is stamped U.S. Navy. I spent four full

excellent blackjack or pacifier. I would hate to be clobbered by one. One of my friends back from China in 1947 gave it to my son to play with. One day he and a friend were repulsing Indians — the odds were something like 6000 to two — and he threw it at the screaming savages. I happened to witness this and, on picking it up, realized what it was. Unfortunately, the hammer broke

One of the original 1911 pistols with the short spur used before the Cavalry re-designed the hammer. Note location of the serial number. Only the first few pistols had the number in this place, Williams believes. By serial number 10,000 the number was back over the trigger.

Savage 45

Another oddball that you will run into occasionally is the "Savage" variation of the Model 1911 45 pistol. Now this has nothing to do with the Savage Arms Corp. in Westfield, Mass. In 1917–1918 the demand for 45 pistols was so great that the government gave contracts to any firm which could produce them. The records are a bit fuzzy but it appears that the A. J. Savage Munitions Co. of San Diego, Calif., was given a contract to manufacture complete Model 1911 pistols. From what I can find out they only made slides before the contract was cancelled in 1919. It would appear that these slides, or at least some of them, were accepted by the government so that, after the war, these slides were incorporated into rebuilt pistols. You can identify these Savage slides by the lettering, all in one block, on the left side of the front part of the slide. This reads:

PATENTED DEC. 19, 1905
FEB. 14, 1911, AUG. 19, 1913
COLT'S PT. F. A. MFG. CO.

Directly to the rear of this lettering is a flaming bomb with a large S inside the bomb circle. The right side of the slide carries the standard stamping "Model of 1911 U. S. Army." While this variation may factually be considered a "production" model they are seldom encountered. Few people have ever seen one.

X-Number 45s

Another seldom-seen variation is the X number pistol. As I understand it these pistols were brought back into certain government armories, stripped down and rebuilt. From what I can determine all of the receivers were machined flat and cleaned on both sides to remove all lettering and numbers. After blueing the receivers were stamped on the right side with an X followed by a new serial number. Those serial numbers I have seen were low, mine being 1923. This new number is found above and behind the trigger. Above the number is the phrase "United States Property."

On the left side of the receiver — at least on my pistol — is a sitting eagle. Below this is S17. The eagle and the lettering are quite small and you need a good glass to make out the details. They are located directly above the magazine release, slightly higher than the spot where the regular inspector's initials are customarily found.

I have seen these pistols with the receivers machined so much that the naked eye can readily see the difference between the thickness of the X frames and a new frame. If you run into one of these X numbered 45s, examine the slide for machining — it might well be original and legitimate.

Low Number 45s

Every now and then you will see one of the original low number Model 1911 pistols. The first 50,000 or so were superbly finished. They stand out like a flashlight among candles. The very early ones, carrying numbers down around 10,000 or lower, are beauties — too good to shoot, in my opinion. So far I've seen only one with a misplaced serial, that one number 6324, so-stamped far ahead of the trigger guard. This on the right side of the receiver, of course, directly opposite the legend "United States Property" stamped on the opposite side.

I have run into quite a few of the old World War I pistols carrying serial numbers that date them back to 1916, 1917, 1918 and 1919, which have been entirely re-finished, parkerized and given new inspector's initials. I don't know when this was done, but from the looks of the finish I'd guess sometime after World War 2. Those I've examined closely show little signs of wear, indicating that the work must have been done fairly recently — or the pistols released lately. These are good buys for the man who wants a rugged handgun.

In conclusion I'd like to point out that many 1911 and 1911A1 pistols may be found in variations that add considerably to their value for collectors. If you find one of these oddballs ask a collector about it — it may be of some worth.

All Purpose Defense Gun:
Colt 45 Auto Or Charter 44 Bulldog?

Apart from their considerable recoil, the choice of a defense sidearm propounded here covers two vastly different handguns — and mandates a serious, sustained program to master either.

▌ Richard Allen

IF YOU MAKE no secret of your interest in guns you may, like me, be occasionally asked which handgun is best for self defense. Since I live in a city the question pertains to self defense in cities, against people. Self defense for woodsmen, against dangerous animals, say, is another matter, and one I know little about.

Of course I have an answer to this question: the Colt Gov't Model 45 automatic — or another gun so chambered. The list of virtues is too well known to bear repeating here. (If you are new to guns, get The Complete Book Of Shooting, edited by Jack O'Connor and read the handgun section by Jeff Cooper. Also see Cooper On Handguns, by Jeff Cooper. However, the latter book was written more for informed handgunners than for beginners. James D. Mason's excellent new book Combat Handgun Shooting, published by Chas. C. Thomas, Springfield, Ill., offers much information to the novice shooter.*See our Arms Library pages for source information, etc.

For most cases the obvious answer is the right one, but there are situations where another model deserves serious consideration: the Charter Bulldog 44 Special, which has three advantages: concealability, price and safety.

Let's consider a gun to be carried on the person. Its two major requirements are stopping power and hide-ability. Unfortunately, these are conflicting requirements; powerful guns tend to be big. Some of you will think about having several models: a big 45 auto for use at home or in the store; a Charter Bulldog when the 45 can't be concealed; a 5-shot 38 when the Bulldog can't be hidden; a Hi Standard Derringer when anything else would be too big.

It's only natural for us to think that way, but remember the person who asks your advice will usually want only one gun. He or she is unlikely to want or to be able to afford several handguns or the trouble and expense of learning to shoot so many different models. He should have a spare, in case his gun needs repairs, but he may not. If he does it should be as much like his main guns as possible. Those of us who own several guns rarely have two alike, which certainly applies to me. But the man who isn't interested in guns as

such has the advantage. Having learned to shoot on a particular model he can simply get a spare just like it.

Despite the thickness of the Bulldog's cylinder, the smaller grip makes the Charter easier to hide, and it can be made even more concealable. The smaller grips of the Charter Undercover 38 Spl. can be used on the 44. True, felt recoil is increased and, unless the shooter has small hands, the smaller grip will be awkward and practical accuracy may suffer.

Colt 45 ACP with minimum alterations — safety from Armand Swenson, sights from King Gun Works. The Bulldog has the smaller Undercover grip, for greater concealability — and possibly more awkwardness in handling.

Here is the major advantage of the Bulldog: it may be carried when the big 45 — if any — has been left home because it's too big. As noted above, that reasoning can be carried further, but somewhere you have to draw the line. At some point you have to say, "This is the smallest gun suitable for all-round self defense. If I may at some time need a smaller gun I'll have to get two guns to defend myself adequately."

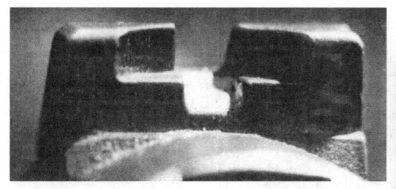

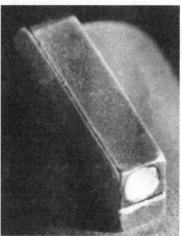

There is, of course, no hard and fast place to draw the line. It may be argued that nothing less than a 45 auto is really good enough, that anything less is a desperation measure. It can also be argued that the small-frame 38s actually belong on the big gun side on the line. I choose to draw the line right under the Charter Bulldog.

Stopping Power

Why there? Stopping power. Stopping power is the ability to put a man out of action immediately — not kill. It will do you no good if your attacker dies two days after you shoot him, or even if he bleeds to death two minutes after being shot. Jeff Cooper (op cit) estimates the chances of downing a man with a solid body hit at 19 times out of 20 with a 45, 50–50 with a 38. The 44 Bulldog is somewhere in between.

Where in between? Mr. Cooper can estimate, from the teachings of experience, about how good the 45 ACP and the 38 Spl. are. The 3" barrel 44 Spl. is relatively new, so we don't have much experience yet. The best estimate we can make is by using the Hatcher Scale of Relative Stopping Power or other similar formulas.†See GUN DIGEST, 30th/1976 ed. for Ken Walters "Handgun Stopping Power" (p. 260)

The Speer Reloading Manual, No. 9, gives the muzzle velocity of the factory 44 Spl. with 246-gr. bullet from a Bulldog at 689 foot seconds (fs). The 44 Spl. bullet's true caliber is .429", say .43". The Hatcher scale gives the Bulldog 88% of the 45 Auto's stopping power. The 2" barrel 38 has less than half the 45's stop-

ping power. As best we can estimate the Bulldog is "almost" as good as the 45. The small-frame 38s are only a little easier to hide than the Bulldog, yet their stopping power is obviously a lot less.

Stopping power is also why I considered the Colt 45 and the Charter 44 in the first place. Guns with less recoil may be easier to master — but provide only an illusion of effectiveness. The heavy recoil does make proper handling more important. A good instructor would be nice, but most people must learn to shoot without one. The books mentioned above are the best substitutes I know of.

So much for S.P. and concealability. What other differences are there between the 44 and 45? Safety, problems in proficiency, price and firepower.

Safety Factors

It is generally felt that revolvers are somewhat safer in the hands of a semi-trained man, yet the man or woman who takes the trouble to really master a gun can handle an automatic safely. Regrettably, there are too many who buy a gun, fire a few shots, and put it away in a drawer. No gun is really likely to do that kind of owner much good, but he is less likely to shoot someone — or himself — accidentally with a revolver. Another point for the Bulldog.

Price and learning problems are related, since the gun's "cost" should include learning to shoot it. This includes ammo and, possibly, a 22 rimfire substitute for cheaper training.

Here we face a small difficulty. The

prices I quote will probably have gone up when you read this, but the proportions should remain about the same.See our catalog pages for various makes and their current prices.

Colt 45 Auto

The Colt 45 ACP (various versions) retails for about $213 today — mid-1976 — but that's just the beginning. The gun isn't ready for use as purchased, and there are all sorts of recommended alterations to consider. For minimal self defense I consider two indispensable: a new thumb safety, and new sights.

The regular thumb safety is too small, I feel. When you have to grab the gun and thumb the safety off in a hurry there is too great a chance you'll fumble the job. After years of experience I usually hit the issue safety OK, but I'd hate to stake my life on it. Furthermore, the fear of fumbling is a temptation to thumb off the safety whenever something goes bump in the night That's how accidents happen. A good thumb safety is made by Armand Swenson (Box 606, Fallbrook, CA 92028) at $20 for a right-handed type or $32.50 for the dual form (ambidextrous), plus $15 for your local gunsmith to install it.

Recent developments in the art of combat shooting have taught us the val-

Charter Arms Bulldog with the Charter 38 Undercover. The Undercover seems a lot smaller when you handle both guns, but it is only a little easier to hide — and it has a lot less stopping power.

sity. 500 rounds of 22 ammo (Long Rifle) go for about $14, thus adding $132 more to the $322, or a new total of $454.

The 22 kit is the reason I haven't mentioned the Commander Model. The Commander is only a little bit easier to hide than the Gov't Model, but it suffers a major disadvantage — it won't take the 22 unit.

Note that I have considered only the cheapest possible outfit. A left-handed man will need the ambidextrous safety. One who suffers from hammer bite may need a Commander hammer installed. Spare magazines? Any trouble will be settled with the first 8 shots or not at all. No trigger job, and no money allotted for fixing the defects that can show up in any brand new gun. (Factory warranties are worthless unless you are willing to wait several months for the gun.)

The big Colt — as with most other auto pistols — takes down quickly, and the owner who will familiarize himself with his autoloader can easily manage replacement of various component parts. Not so with the revolver.

The Charter 44 Bulldog

The Charter is simpler. All it needs is an action job, say $15 a gun (as with the Colt, there are other extras — grip filler, trigger shoes, custom grips). The 22 substitute is the Charter Pathfinder which, though the frame is smaller, has the same grip frame and sight picture as the 44. The "feel" of the gun is close enough. Since the 22 and 44 are issued with different grips, you must buy one extra pair. Total cost is:

Bulldog	$138
Pathfinder	114
Grips	15
Two action jobs	30
100 rounds 44 ammo	22
500 rounds 22 ammo	14
Total	$333

A few points warrant further explanation: I allowed only 100 rounds of 44 ammo. A revolver is less prone to intermittent failure than an automatic, hence needs less checking out.

ue of a quick sight-pickup, even at close range. After extensive practice good shooting may be done by merely looking over the top of the gun, but we're considering the beginner. Sights suitable for quick line-up in dim light are essential.

The best I know of are the King Combat Sights (King Gun Works, 1837 W. Glenoaks Blvd., Glendale, CA 91201). Again, the King sights must be installed at extra cost on the 45 Colt. The King sights are better than the issue sights on the Charter but it would be impractical to put such sights on the 44 Spl. King sights are $20, say $10 for gunsmith installation.

Ammunition

Now, ammo. Two hundred factory rounds through a new automatic are a minimum for checking out the gun and for a minimal training program as well. Four boxes of 50 at $11 each, $44.

Some of you may have access to reloaded ammo, which can be found sometimes for $5 or so per 50. Such loads are fine for further training, but the gun must be checked out with full power, self defense ammo.

Our cost so far is:	$213
Swenson Safety, installed	35
King Sights, installed	30
200 rounds 45 ammo	44
Total	$322

For further training the Colt 22 Conversion Kit ($118.50) is almost a neces-

Charter Arms Bulldog (below) and its 22 understudy, the Pathfinder, out of the box. The grips are interchangeable. Although frame sizes differ, and only the Pathfinder has adjustable sights, sight pictures are identical and the "feel" of the two guns is similar enough.

Gunsmithing on the Charters, though cheaper, can be tricky. Some gunsmiths, asked to smooth the action, cannot resist lightening the trigger pull so much the gun doesn't always fire. You can only tell him that it is a self defense gun, that you would rather it go off every time than have a light pull, and hope the smith listens. Someone with a knack for double action shooting might consider going without an action job. Unfortunately, the Charter out-of-the-box action isn't as good as we could hope for.

With the Colt I totalled the 45 gun and ammo first, then added the 22. The idea was that a new shooter could buy the 45 stuff first, do his preliminary training on that, and save the 22 kit for later.

However, the recoil of the Charter Bulldog is very severe, about the same as a steel-frame S&W Chiefs Special with high speed loads. Relatively few new shooters, or experienced shooters for that matter, will want to practice extensively with the Bulldog. Even preliminary training will probably require the 22, though I could be wrong. There may be some who can put 50 rounds through a Bulldog in one afternoon and not be bothered. Others may be so sensitive to recoil they must buy a 22 kit for preliminary training with the 45 Colt.

No matter, I've done enough on costs to give you the general idea of how to make cost comparisons. You can add up the costs yourself for any combination of circumstances that interests you.

Conclusions? As of mid-1976, a Bull-dog, with 22 substitute costs about $121 less than the equivalent setup with the Colt, and $2 less than the Colt 45 setup alone. It seems silly to make a life and death decision over $121, but that's a lot of money to some people. Furthermore, I have given only the minimum cost for both brands. You could get stuck with the cost of fixing up a lemon — and I won't guess which brand this is more likely to be. Then there is the matter of spare guns: $153 for the Bulldog; $278 for the Colt.

Mastering the Gun

Now we come to a big point for the Colt and against the Charter: difficulty in learning to shoot. Shooting double action is harder than shooting an automatic. How much harder? At the beginning of World War II, William Fairbairn and Eric Stykes, formerly of the Shanghai police, wrote training books on handguns, knives, and hand-to-hand combat. Their gun book, really ahead of its time, was recently reprinted (Shooting To Live) from Paladin Press, Box 1307, Boulder, CO 80302). The desirability of automatics over revolvers was stressed — more than 20 years before that idea was general knowledge in this country. It was stressed that traditional bullseye shooting has no relation to combat shooting.

Comparing training with revolvers and automatics, the authors said that the revolver requires thrice the time and double the ammunition costs to achieve the same proficiency. Of course, this was long before Jack Weaver taught us all to use a two-handed grip for close-range shooting. Michael Harries, a handgun instructor, pointed out a danger I was unaware of — almost anyone can be taught to shoot single action, he told me, but some people never do get the hang of DA shooting. Someone, then, who buys a revolver runs the risk of investing a lot of time and money in a gun he never will be good with.

This risk is not to be taken lightly, but I am without a hard and fast answer to these conflicting points.

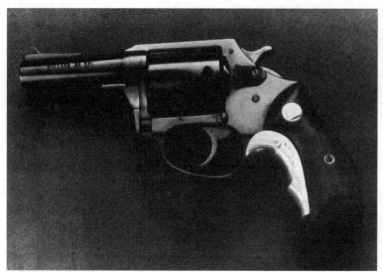

Charter Arms handguns may be fitted with grip fillers (for the small grip). The expense is slight and — in my hand — it makes a difference. Shown is the Tyler T-Grip filler, from Melvin Tyler, 1326 W. Britton Rd., Oklahoma City, OK 73114. These are available in black, polished aluminum or gold.

The extra ammo expended in mastering a revolver doesn't cost much, since most practice will be with the 22. The 500 rounds I've already added in make a good training program, even for a revolver. How much value to put on the extra time is up to the individual shooter.

Firepower

Another point in favor of the Colt is firepower. The Charter holds 5 rounds, the 45 Colt 8: two spare magazines hold 14 more. It takes a couple of seconds to change magazines in the Colt; considerably longer to reload a revolver. I can't manage it in less than 30 seconds, but it's not something I practice.

How important is firepower? It can be argued that our beginner can't hope to stand off the whole Symbionese Liberation Army single handed. At best he can hope to down one or two people, and he can do that with 5 shots if he can do it at all.

There have been plenty of reports of policemen emptying their revolvers in action. However, these cases usually involve stopping failures or panic sprays. Stopping failures are more likely with police 38s than with the Bull-

dog. As for panic sprays, if a man can't keep his head enough to aim well, what good will additional shots do him? In one recent gun fight four California Highway Patrolmen fired a total of 50 shots without one hit.

But we can find a few individual cases to support almost any argument. What are the chances that the difference in firepower will make the difference between life and death? I just don't know. Still, the Bulldog gives 5 shots more than the Colt 45 that isn't with you because it's too big.

There are some cases where people need a small, inconspicuous gun sometimes but want more firepower at other times. The usual answer is two different guns, but here's another — if one Bulldog holds 5 shots, two Bulldogs furnish 10.

Two Bulldogs can be kept next to each other in store or home, and two weigh you down no more than one 45. Two Bulldogs answer the question of holstering the gun for the F.B.I, draw (fastest standing up) or the cross draw, fastest if you get caught sitting down. Too, and important, the shooter saves the trouble and expense of mastering two different guns.

Sure, the idea of wearing two guns has a juvenile ring to it. We are used to thinking of two guns as comprising a belt gun and a hideout gun, but two guns smack of Matt Dillon or some other movies cowboy.

Another point for the Colt is durability. Some of them, I've heard, have shot 100,000 rounds or so. It's a gun to outlast most shooters. The Bulldog, very light for its cartridge, probably wouldn't last that long. Still, since most Charter practice will be with a 22, that isn't really an issue.

What happens if the gun is dropped or otherwise roughly treated? (Yes, I know you're not supposed to do that, but it does happen.) The Colt auto is very hard to damage. Revolvers are more vulnerable.

Reliability? I don't know. The Bulldog hasn't been around long enough.

As I review what I've written, I seem to have come down heavily on the side of the Charter. Perhaps, but I feel the Charter is under-rated today and needs to be better known. Now let me sum up what's been said.

The Colt has more stopping power; it's the easier one to shoot; it allows more practice with business ammo since it doesn't have the Charter's demoralizing recoil; it has more fire power and it's probably more durable. It is the best combat handgun available. All others, including the Bulldog, are meant for those occasions when circumstances prohibit using the big Colt.

Model 1911 Colt: Six Decades Of Service

"It stands quite alone as a standard of excellence among military pistols" ▌ Dennis Riordan

I N THE PASSING years since the adoption of the Browning/Colt Model of 1911, the development of military pistols has been influenced by three major factors: advances in firearms design, gradual changes in military requirements, and the introduction of new materials and manufacturing methods. All of the Colt's contemporaries have long since disappeared from the martial arsenals of the world, but the 1911 still retains its position as the standard service pistol of the United States. The only military handgun in history to compare with this record was Britain's 455 Webley revolver, which passed through 6 Marks and broached the transition from black to smokeless powder in its long and stormy career. However, even the great Webley has been far outstripped by the Browning/Colt, both in length of service and in actual battle use.

The reasons for the Colt automatic's longevity are various and complex. Unquestionably the basic excellence of the gun and of its unique cartridge have always been paramount, but many other contributory factors may also be cited, whose total leverage has proved irresistable.

A historically related series of events began in 1892, when the Double Action 38 New Army Revolver replaced the 45 Single Action Army, which had been standard issue since 1875. The new revolver appeared to hold great potential, since its swingout cylinder offered si-

U.S. Service Pistol, Model 1911-A1. Original M1911 is distinguished by flat mainspring housing, short grip safety tang, slightly longer trigger, and lack of finger clearance cuts in receiver.

multaneous ejection and fast reloading, its double-action mechanism increased the rate of fire, and the greatly reduced level of recoil made the gun pleasant to shoot. Whatever the good qualities of the revolver, however, the 38 Long Colt cartridge proved woefully inadequate in battle. This became evident during the close-quarter encounters of the 1899 Philippine Insurrection, where quantities of 45 Single Action Colts were hastily reissued to supply the stopping power that the newer handgun patently lacked.

In 1904, the Army's Ordnance Department assigned Col. (later Brigadier-General) John T. Thompson of Ordnance and Col. La Garde of the Medical Corps, to conduct an investigation into the hitherto shadowy subject of stop-

ping power. The Thompson-La Garde Committee determined the nature of wounds and shock effect by the empiric method. Exhaustive shooting trials were conducted, initially with human cadavers, later with live steers at the Chicago stockyards. Several then-current revolvers and pistols were used for the tests, including the 7.65mm and 9mm Parabellum, and Colt automatic pistols in 38, 45, and 476 caliber, using various types of ammunition.

Operation of firing mechanism. Upper left: ready position. Upper right: instant of discharge. Lower left: disconnection of sear. Lower right: return to battery — disconnector will move to ready position upon release of trigger. Notice relationship between sear and disconnector throughout.

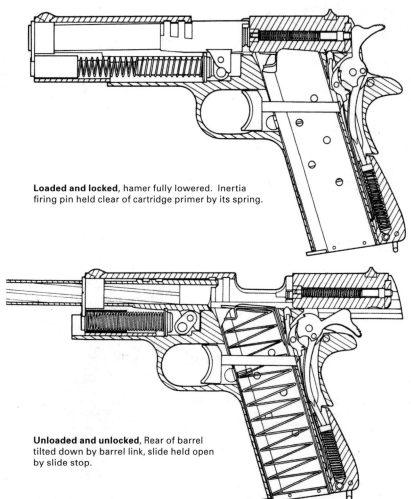

Loaded and locked, hamer fully lowered. Inertia firing pin held clear of cartridge primer by its spring.

Unloaded and unlocked, Rear of barrel tilted down by barrel link, slide held open by slide stop.

Author's Note

When I once did some drawings on the derivative Model B Star, I began to see the strong points of the basic Model 1911 design. The features of the Star that I disliked, the extractor, firing pin, and disconnector, were departures from the original concept, which began to look very good indeed. This chain of thought was confirmed when I finally obtained a specimen 1911-A1. I then reviewed every objection to the gun that I could find in my files, and found precious little substance in any of them. On the contrary, I found a gun that stands quite alone as a standard of excellence among military pistols.

and field trials that were to proceed intermittently from 1906 to 1911.

Both Colt and Smith & Wesson presented 45 caliber revolvers for evaluation, but during these years the automatic pistol was coming into its own, and the military advantages of the new firearm type were so compelling that the revolvers had little chance of acceptance.

Colt's 45 automatic was designed by John Browning and was, from the very beginnings of its development, intended as a military pistol. Each element of its construction was chosen for that specific purpose, and all compromises were resolved in favor of military use. Nonetheless, as the pistol went through the Army's gruelling tests in competition with rival designs, weaknesses and inadequacies appeared within the prototypes, and changes were made as the trials went on. Since the tests were conducted in peacetime, the Army proceeded in leisurely fashion, insisting upon extremely high standards of reliability and strength. No inherent weakness remained in the final version of the big Colt, which passed the last 6000-round endurance test without a stoppage or broken part. The selection board adjudged the Colt as a clearly superior design and recommended its adoption; shortly thereafter, in early 1911, it became the standard service pistol. The true extent of the Colt's superiority has only become evident with the passage of time.

Momentous Decisions

The Committee's findings were of great significance in several areas. Recommended as the most effective manstopper was the 45 caliber, with a blunt nosed bullet of at least 230 grains and a minimum initial velocity of 800 feet per second. The 9mm Parabellum was found to be relatively ineffective as a manstopping cartridge. It was noted that this small caliber, relatively high velocity bullet inflicted small, clean wounds that were easily healed. Frequently the body was completely penetrated without instantaneous damage, and apparent damage was occasionally delayed for hours. The tests proved conclusively that the often quoted muzzle energy fig-

ure (kinetic energy of the bullet, derived solely from its mass and velocity and expressed in ft. lbs.) has no direct bearing on the relative stopping power, since it does not consider the cross-sectional area of the bullet (frontal area) nor the factor of bullet shape. (Stopping power is also influenced by expanding bullets, but these have been outlawed for military use since the Second Hague Conference of 1907).

On receipt of the Thompson-La Garde report the Ordnance Department determined to adopt a new service pistol in accord with the Committee's recommendations. Manufacturers were invited to submit 45 caliber pistols for the lengthy series of comparison tests

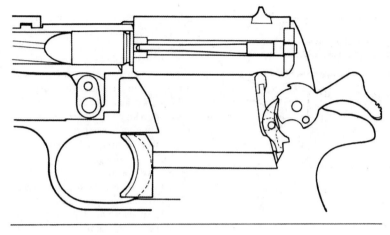

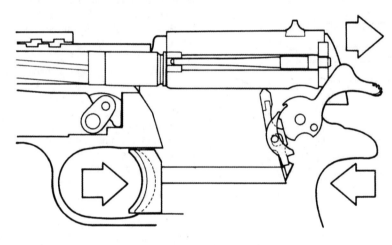

To battery - disconnector will move to ready posistion upon release of trigger. Notice relationship between sear and disconnector throughout.

The 45 Government Automatic Cartridge was adopted simultaneously with the Colt pistol. This round, carrying a full-jacketed 233-gr. bullet, was developed at Frankford Arsenal from an original Browning design. Although considerably smaller in case capacity than the old 45 Colt revolver cartridge, the 45 Automatic was nearly as powerful, since it was designed for maximum efficiency with smokeless powder.

First Major Test

The new pistol/cartridge combination was used in a series of skirmishes along the Mexican border, and carried into Mexico during the punitive expedition against Pancho Villa's raiders, but the first large scale battle test of the arm followed America's entry into World War One, when U.S. troops arrived in the trenches of Belgium and France. Here, under actual field conditions, the 1911 established its reputation as a rugged, reliable handgun, and also as a dependable man-stopper, despite the rarity of documented enemy casualties that could be attributed to it. Most officers and NCOs were armed with the Colt, however, and no rumors of failure, either of arm or ammunition, ever surfaced.

Criticism of the 1911 did arise during the WW I period, and as a result, certain modifications were later undertaken at Springfield Armory to improve the pistol. These consisted of a widened front sight to better the sight picture; an enlarged spur on the grip safety to prevent pinching of the thumb web during recoil; a shorter trigger and finger cutouts in adjacent receiver areas, to accommodate soldiers with small hands and generally improve trigger control; and a curved mainspring housing, to benefit the pistol's pointing characteristics and afford a superior grip. In 1926 these changes were approved, and the modified pistol was accepted as the M1911-A1. All service pistols manufactured since that date have conformed to the A1 specifications, and the older guns were gradually modified as they were returned to military arsenals. It should be noted that the improvements effected in the A1 version were entirely external in nature; no mechanical changes have ever been made.

The 30-M1 Carbine, adopted upon the very eve of World War Two, was conceived as a replacement for the pistol in the hands of combat troops. In the event, this did not occur. Both weapons were manufactured in huge quantities and equally distributed to U.S. forces in all war zones. The relative value of each was not difficult to assess, since WW II was a long war, and the best documented in history. Combat reports and wound statistics proved the carbine an effective aggressive arm, while the pistol was revealed as a primarily psychological weapon. Times were changing; as shoulder arms became self-loading or fully automatic, the melee was becoming rare. Again, as in WW I, enemy casualties inflicted by the pistol were far flung and few, but its contribution to morale was strong.

The introduction of the German assault rifle during the course of WW II had broad repercussions in the postwar years. The Germans retained full power ammunition for the machinegun and the sniper rifle, but the basic weapon for the infantryman became a short, light,

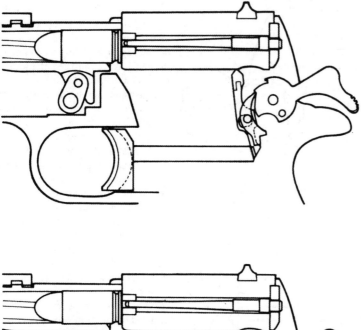

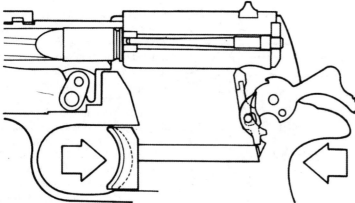

Unlocked slide: Should the slide fail to lock completely (upper), disconnector prevents discharge (lower).

pistol and submachinegun use. Therefore, a list of requisites was established for a handgun of similar type, including a limitation in bore size of 30 to 35 caliber. Upon Army invitation, several strictly commercial designs were submitted for evaluation, as well as the T3 pistol, developed by the High Standard Company under direct Army contract. A number of these submissions were double action designs, and most were chambered for the 9mm Parabellum. The situation seemed strikingly reminiscent of that which had been obtained in 1892; single versus double action, 45 vs 38 (i.e., 9mm) caliber. The guns and the ammunitions were actually a far cry from those which had figured in that elder challenge, but the findings of the Thompson/La Garde Committee had never been discredited, although they appeared about to be ignored. However, trials were still in process when the decision was announced to retain the 1911, and the pistol testing was abruptly terminated. The reason for this decision has never been publicly revealed, and the preliminary findings of the tests themselves are still classified.

Certainly, a pertinent circumstance was the fact that the nation's armories retained an enormous stock of 1911 pistols produced during the WW II period, even beyond those at present in service in Korea and throughout the world. To replace these existing and battle-proven pistols with a handgun of new design would have required a major expenditure of funds, and this in face of a marked de-emphasis on the role of the pistol as a military arm.

Existing WW II stocks of M3-A1 submachineguns may also have clouded the issue, but only marginally. While these were also chambered for the 45 pistol cartridge, their design permitted conversion to 9mm Parabellum, and their number was not particularly large. Use of submachineguns by U.S. forces had been extensive only among paratroop units, and their future utilization was uncertain.

Naturally, the design of the 1911 and its 45 caliber cartridge were prime fac-

selective-fire rifle, firing a shortened 8mm cartridge of intermediate power and range. This single compromise weapon was intended to replace the full power rifle, the submachinegun, and, it was hoped, the pistol as well.

Russia embraced this concept without reservation, and the power and prestige of the U.S.S.R. carried the idea throughout the Communist World. The pistol could not be eliminated in any of these nations, but its role was downgraded and, in Russia itself, smaller, less powerful handguns were adopted.

With the usual exception of France, the powerful western nations reluctantly followed the lead of the United States in the acceptance of the 7.62 NATO car-

tridge. This round is a shortened, updated version of the 30-06 that differs only slightly in ballistics; a full power cartridge for rifle and machine gun. Our new infantry rifle became the M-14, and the carbine and pistol remained in service.

Successor Rejected

During the 1950s, the U.S. Army explored the possibility of a new handgun. Germany's P-38 seemed to hold the answers to many of the complaints that had been leveled at the 1911 over the years; that it was too bulky and heavy, too powerful, too slow to get into action. In addition, the 9mm Parabellum cartridge had already become the universal choice of the other NATO countries for

Unloaded and locked, hammer at full cock. Magazine not shown.

The 1911 pistol itself was and is much too good to discard unless a prospective replacement could offer irresistible improvements. No pistol has ever surpassed the Colt for utter reliability. It has operated under the most extreme conditions of nature and endured the roughest treatment without failure, and has digested ammunitions of greatly varying chamber pressure without trouble. Any modern military pistol must be capable of field stripping without tools, but the 1911 goes much farther than this. It can be completely disassembled without the use of any tool, excepting only the grips, whose removal is never required. These are attached by four screws and bushings, the only screwed parts used in the gun. Breakage or loss of either or both grips has no effect on the gun's operation, and does not permit the escape of any other part, since all pins are mechanically retained within the pistol independently of the grips. This is an important feature; many of today's military pistols would be put out of action by grip failure.

The pistol's controls are intelligently located for convenience of operation. The hammer is easily thumb cocked, and its contour affords an excellent gripping surface. The safety lies directly above the thumb and operates with great ease. The pushbutton magazine release allows disengagement and ejection of the magazine using only the shooting hand, making this pistol one of the fastest of all automatics to reload. The slide stop works efficiently to signal an empty gun and hasten reloading, and it also permits locking the slide open manually at any time. The Colt's balance is good, and the gun handles well. The weight of the piece and its long sighting radius contribute to steady holding and accurate fire. The presence of the grip safety requires the use of both hands to lower the hammer from full cock. Since manual decocking is the single most dangerous operation necessary to the employment of an automatic pistol, the added control afforded by the mandatory second hand raises the level of safety proportionately.

tors in the question of replacement. Gun and cartridge were inseparable, since a caliber change would almost certainly have resulted in a new pistol. The 45 U.S. automatic pistol round had been the center of controversy ever since its introduction. The heavy weight of its bullet creates an inordinate amount of recoil, and this characteristic has always caused unsettlement and even fear in military recruits undergoing their ordinarily rather superficial training with the 1911 pistol. The girth of the cartridge also reduces the magazine capacity below that of comparable 9mm pistols, and practically eliminates the possibility of staggered loading that the smaller caliber allows. The superior penetration of the 9mm Parabellum has often been cited as cause for change, since the 45 comes into difficulties against obstructions which the Parabellum pierces with

ease. Penetration is of advantage to the submachine gun, an arm of offense, but with the exception of military police duty, the pistol had not been employed as an aggressive weapon since WW I. The role of the pistol had declined to one of a purely defensive arm, whose function consisted of stopping the advance of a determined opponent at close quarters. Stopping power and reasonable accuracy are the primary requirements of a weapon of defense, and these qualities the 45 possessed in full measure. A good man-stopper inflicts instant and massive bodily damage sufficient to break off an attack (not necessarily to kill), and the 45 will almost always achieve this result with a solid hit anywhere in the torso. No military cartridge came near the 45 in this respect, certainly not the Parabellum.

As a mechanism, the 1911 abounds in excellent features. Its tilting barrel lock remains one of the strongest and simplest of locking systems, and its dual barrel lugs both contact recesses in the top of the slide, dispersing recoil forces over a large surface area. The tilting barrel also brings its breech into close proximity with the incoming round from the magazine, and this, plus the barrel tang, affords almost flawless feeding. It is true that a cam system such as Browning used in his later High Power pistol is slightly stronger and more efficient, but this superiority is in degree only; it certainly does not obsolete the swinging link of the 1911.

Abounds in Excellence

There is no finer extractor in any pistol. It is located entirely within the slide, fully protected against injury or the ingress of foreign matter. Since it does not pivot on a pin and acts as its own spring, it cannot become frozen by rust or hardened lubricant. The design of the feed mechanism is such that the rims of incoming rounds are forced upward behind the extractor, rather than requiring the extractor to snap over them, prolonging the life of the part. However, the extractor is sufficiently flexible to jump the rim of a hand-loaded round as the slide is slam closed upon it. Damage or loss of the magazine does not completely disable the big Colt, since its slide stop, large ejection port, and lack of a magazine disconnector allow handloading and firing in the total absence of the magazine.

The firing pin is an inertia type, affording safe carry with the hammer fully forward over a chambered round. Its long, tapered tip is highly resistant to breakage, while its symmetrical design allows the pin to turn freely, distributing wear. Dry firing is not injurious to the firing pin, because its forward movement in dry fire is arrested by the full compression of its spring, not by a retaining pin.

The firing-pin stop is also a fine feature of the 1911, locking the extractor as well as the firing pin, and affording easy

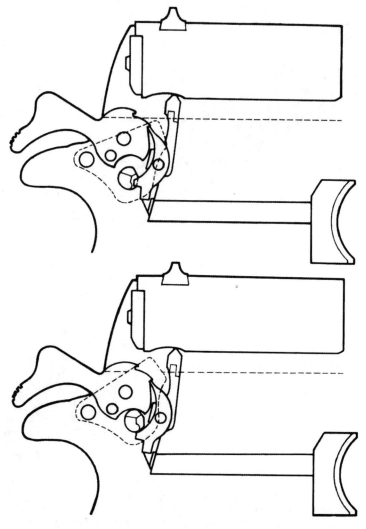

Action of manual safety. Upper: fire position. Lower: safe position — safety nose raised into slide recess, locking it closed. Separate surfaces of internal boss lock hammer and sear, preventing movement of either.

disassembly of both parts.

Some criticism has been directed at the Colt's sliding, stirrup type trigger, because of its vertical play. This play is detrimental only in match shooting; the fact that the trigger does not pivot on a pin is actually of advantage to a military pistol. Neither rust nor any accumulation of debris is likely to affect the trigger's movement, and its operation cannot sweep mud or dirt into the receiver. The trigger and its bar are incorporated into one simple part, the trigger bar being entirely enclosed within the receiver.

No other trigger/trigger bar system is simpler or more foolproof.

The safety mechanisms of the 1911 are also very good. Separate surfaces of the manual safety lock the hammer, the sear, and the slide.

The disconnector is completely enclosed by the receiver and operates within a rounded notch on the underside of the slide to prevent automatic fire and discharge with an unlocked slide. Should the gun be assembled without the disconnector, it cannot be fired.

The hammer's safety notch inter-

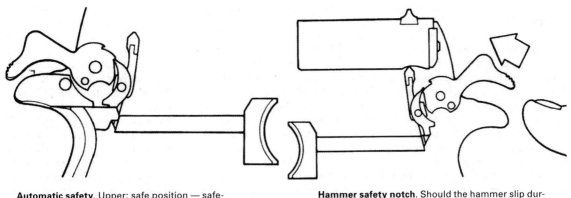

Automatic safety. Upper: safe position — safety nose contacts rear of trigger bar, blocking its movement. Lower: fire position — safety disengaged by pressure on grip.

Hammer safety notch. Should the hammer slip during thumb cocking (upper), it is intercepted by the sear (lower) which moves into the hammer's safety notch before the firing pin can be struck.

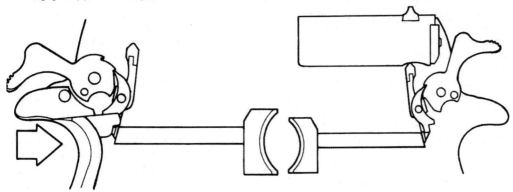

rupts hammer fall in any circumstance that does not originate from trigger release. The sear enters this notch if the hammer slips in thumb cocking, or the slide moves forward after partial withdrawal, either manually or through an accidental fall upon the muzzle. If the sear loses contact with the hammer's full-cock notch through a jar, the safety notch allows the hammer's recapture before it can complete its stroke. The hammer safety notch is not a half-cock position and should never be so employed, because a blow upon the hammer in this attitude could fracture the sear or hammer notch and discharge the gun.

The grip safety blocks movement of the trigger unless the pistol is held naturally in the hand. Its location at the rear of the grip allows the safety to function without conscious thought, and reduces the danger of accidental self-inflicted wounds.

The Colt's magazine floorplate is permanently attached, in contrast to several more recent designs, whose detachable magazine floorplates allow easy takedown and cleaning of the assembly. Actually, the Colt pattern is preferable from a military standpoint, since this magazine cannot become accidentally disassembled and parts lost, yet its follower and spring may be removed from the top.

The sights are simple, effective, and strong. That they are nonadjustable is advantageous, since their height is calculated for service ammunition at predetermined range, and they are factory set for windage zero. These sights have no small parts to loosen or break, and they cannot be tinkered out of adjustment. Their very low profile and rounded contours easily clear holster surfaces. Both sights may be replaced in case of damage, or target sights substituted for

match shooting.

Few Faults

The 1911 has no really bad features, but it is less than ideal in several areas. The gun is large and heavy in weight, both factors owing to the cartridge it fires. Any reduction in weight would increase the difficulties of recruits in mastering the arm.

The grip safety was incorporated into Browning's prototype 45 at Army request, while the pistol was undergoing its pre-adoption trials. At this time, pistols were carried fully armed in the advance by infantry officers and noncoms, and employed in like manner by mounted cavalry troops. Compared to a shoulder arm, the pistol is difficult to control in a stumble or fall; its small size allows it to turn in the hand and endanger its bearer. An automatic safety reduces such risks, since it tends to engage as the wrist is twisted into an unnatural position. However, the new defensive role of the service pistol largely invalidates this consideration, and the grip safety is at present of small practical value in a military pistol having both an external hammer and a positive manual safety. The Colt's automatic safety causes few problems in its operation, but the safety's inclusion in the design requires a goodly number of additional parts, expensive machining operations, and an additional receiver opening, affording entry to water and dust.

A left-handed shooter encounters handling difficulties with the manual safety, but this is unfortunately true of almost all military automatics.

The external location of the safety plunger-tube exposes the safety and slide-stop plungers to water and dirt. The malfunction of either plunger would not put the gun out of action and they are easily serviced, but the arrangement is not ideal. Also, the tube is riveted to the receiver, and any looseness that should develop in these rivets cannot be serviced in the field.

The slide stop does not extend sufficiently rearward to afford good leverage, nor an easy reach for the thumb.

Field stripping of the 1911 is not difficult, but it is rather slow, fairly complicated, and results in more loose parts than could be desired. It should be noted, however, that there is no hazard of kinking the recoil spring during this operation, and that the gun cannot be improperly assembled in a dangerous condition.

The 1911 is not as safe as others whose design affords a mechanical means of decocking the hammer, and is theoretically inferior to a double action pistol, which may be cocked and fired by the application of a long pull on the trigger.

In practice, double-action trigger mechanisms tend to be delicate and complicated. It is doubtful if any such system offers the complete inter-changeability of parts enjoyed by the 1911 Colt, and none can match its reliability of function.

For reasons of safety, army regulations require that the Colt pistol be carried with its chamber empty in non-combat areas. Under such restrictions, there is no advantage to a double action pistol, since either type requires manual cycling of the slide before discharge is possible. In combat zones, the Colt is carried loaded, either with safety off and hammer fully down, or with hammer cocked and safety engaged. The first condition requires thumb cocking of the hammer before the gun can be fired, and is slower than the long trigger pull of a double-action pistol. In the second condition only thumb release of the safety is necessary; this operation may be performed and the gun discharged in about the time required to fire a double action design.

An often stated advantage of the double action automatic is its ability to quickly deliver a second blow to a reluctant primer. This may be a valid argument, but it seems equally likely that a soldier would prefer to manually reload the piece immediately upon a failure to fire.

On the whole, the supposed superiority of the double-action pistol is largely illusory. The idea has psychological value but, as a practical matter, an external hammer single-action automatic such as the 1911, having a positive safety properly located and contoured, is no less efficient.

Changes Since Last Trials

In the years that have passed since the abortive pistol trials of the 1950s, significant changes have been made in U.S. infantry weapons. The venerable B.A.R. and the Browning 30 caliber machineguns have been withdrawn from service and quietly replaced by the excellent 7.62mm M60 General Purpose Machinegun, derived from the German FG-42 and MG-42 of WW II design. The jungle fighting in Vietnam called for a high rate of fire and a short, light weapon of intermediate power, a class of arm that fell midway between the M-14 and the M-2 Carbine. Caught in a pinch, the tail wagged the dog, and the services were forced to employ and eventually accept the previously rejected AR-15,

with its untried gas system and unconventional design. Deficiencies arose in the field and manufacturing changes were made to counter them; the corrected version was adopted as the M16-A1, a good and serviceable weapon.

Withdrawal of American troops from Vietnam found the U.S. in the position of possessing large quantities of modern service rifles of both full and intermediate power, a luxury enjoyed by no other major nation on earth. The future employment of each has yet to be determined. What proved to be the ideal weapon for Vietnam may not suffice in more open country and under more conventional methods of warfare. In any case, the 30 Carbine and the 45 submachinegun would seem on the verge of obsolescence, and there is apparently no longer any possibility of adopting a 9mm submachinegun.

The nature of the war in Vietnam worked greatly to increase the status of the service pistol. Guerrilla activity in the cities meant that there were no safe areas in the country, and rearechelon personnel were often dependent on the pistol as a means of personal protection. Carrying it openly reduced chances of attack, and pistols were in great demand, whether authorized or not. Such lessons are not quickly forgotten; the position of the 1911 pistol seems more secure today than it did 20 years ago. The career of Browning's 45 is far from ended. It is as good as it ever was, and that is very good indeed.

The 45

This soldier had a 45 autoloader better than Colts Model 1911- or so it worked for him. ∎ Robert Skiles

ONE FATEFUL DAY in 1926 in Denver, Colorado, a woman raised a 45-caliber automatic pistol, aimed it at her husband, pulled the trigger and blew him to Kingdom Come. I have that pistol today, and it is one of my most valued possessions because it is a very special firearm.

At the time, my father was on the Denver Police Department and responded to the homicide call. Later, he told me she told him she had thrown the gun into the overhead flush box of a chain-pull toilet. He fished it out of the water, cleaned it and turned it in to the Police Custodian who, I presume, retained it for evidence in a murder trial.

The woman's fate is buried, but Dad liked the pistol and was able to obtain it from the Custodian when no one claimed it after the standard time. This was commonly done in those days and some policemen and detectives accumulated sizeable gun collections.

They were not necessarily looking for valuable guns, but were interested in a variety of light and heavy caliber pistols, rifles and shotguns, sometimes for curios and sometimes for utility. Dad told me that he liked the 45 automatic because it was light and thin. He could carry a big wallop in a relatively small holster in his hip pocket.

Denver policemen, even off duty, were required to be armed at all times and prepared for immediate call. To my knowledge, Dad never used the pistol in the line of duty, but he did en-

joy firing it. When I was a boy, he and I would go east of Denver into the open plains where I could shoot my 22 rifle and Dad would unlimber "the 45" at tin cans.

After the outbreak of World War II, I was commissioned in the artillery and Dad gave me "the 45." The issue Model 1911 45-cal. automatic pistol was more awkward to handle, so I carried mine exclusively. It was lighter weight because it is very simply constructed and of thinner metal. It has no such feature as the grip safety. In fact, the only safety on it is the half cock. A disadvantage was that the clip was not interchangeable with the 1911, so I had to keep my own supply.

Also, my pistol could not use the steel-cased ammunition that was issued during the war. If a round was in the chamber it would fire, extract and eject satisfactorily, but would not prop-

erly pick up the next round from the clip and seat it in the chamber. Nevertheless, there was always some brass-cased ammunition to be found, and I didn't suffer.

I had a shoulder holster made for the pistol in the U.S. and while in Europe I wore it all the time.

Once in Italy after firing the pistol I noticed the front sight had fallen off. It could not be found, but I was not concerned because a short-range handgun was rarely aimed, and, further I thought the sight might interfere with a rapid draw from the shoulder holster and never replaced the sight.

A few months later I was in Berlin with the Army of Occupation. The U.S. forces had been having trouble with Russians taking jeeps from our troops. Two or three Russian soldiers would stop a jeep on the street, take it away from the American at rifle point, and drive away. Very simple. Our enlisted troops were not armed unless on guard duty, but all Russians carried their weapons everywhere. Some Americans had been badly beaten or shot when resisting.

The U.S. command decided that the losses had to stop. Certainly the Russian command was not going to take action. Orders came down that anyone who lost a jeep under any circumstances would have the value deducted

The Colt 1905 was built for a 200-gr. bullet at 900 f.p.s., so author's experience with 230-gr. GI load is understandable. NRA photo.

"....I WATCHED THEM CAREFULLY AND SAW THEM BEGIN TO UN-SLING THEIR RIFLES..."

from his pay. If my memory serves me correctly, that was about $700.

One cold day in January or February of 1946 I was driving toward Templehof Airport when I was stopped by two Russian soldiers standing in the middle of a quiet, isolated street.

They were carrying their rifles innocuously slung across their backs and, to all outward appearances, I was completely unarmed. They came to my side of the vehicle and said something, I guess in Russian. I told them in English that I could not understand. Of course, that went over their heads. By then I was highly suspicious and had slowly begun to unbutton my Eisenhower jacket.

One of the Russians then began to tell me in very halting German that they wanted the "yeep." In an equally halting German, I told them that they could not have it. They then moved to the front of the jeep for a conference. I watched them carefully and saw them begin to unsling their rifles as they separated toward either side of the jeep.

Immediately I jumped out and jerked the 45 out of my shoulder holster. When I leveled it at them the matter was settled! They turned around and walked away.

After the war the pistol was retired to closets or trunks for quite a few years. At regular intervals it was cleaned and oiled, but it was not until one of my sons became interested in guns that we began to fire it occasionally.

One day after we had returned from the range I noticed a small crack in the slide near the retaining pin. I thought that it was probably due to metal fatigue and was afraid to shoot it anymore. It seemed that the best solution would be a new slide.

After searching unsuccessfully through many gun catalogs I wrote to Colt in Hartford, Connecticut and received the following reply: "The patent dates indicate your pistol to be the Model 1905 .45 automatic pistol. This is the direct predecessor of the Model 1911. The development of the 45 ACP

cartridge and the subsequent appearance of the Model 1911 pistol cut short the Model 1905 production at just over 6000 made over a brief span of six years. We regret that its short production and long obsolescence exclude the possibility of parts being available from Colt. According to Colt's production records (your) serial number 1205 was manufactured in 1906."

I next attempted to have the slide repaired and a sight mounted on it. I found that to be impossible, at least in my part of California, because gunsmiths have been the victims of heavy lawsuits if their repairs failed. The slide cannot be replaced or repaired.

So, after 72 years of life, "the 45" has been put on the shelf. Nevertheless, I still enjoy cleaning it, handling it and remembering.

Shooting The 1911's Spanish Cousins

A little pitting doesn't really hurt. ■ WM. Hovey Smith

I TOOK CAREFUL aim with the Llama, squeezed off five shots, and was relieved to see the bullets grouping satisfyingly in the black. Considering the first time I shot the pistol only half struck the 25 yard target and many of those hit sideways, I thought this relatively tight group something of an accomplishment. It was not so much the fault of the pistol that it shot the hot plus-P 38 Super loads so badly nor was this poor performance due to any lack of accuracy of the Remington factory ammunition. The problem was the pistol's barrel was so pitted it had more than

passing resemblance to a rusted sewer pipe with barely discernible rifling.

After writing the Llama factory in Spain for a new barrel, I was informed they had no replacement parts for the 50-year-old pistol. This disappointing news prompted me to work up some handloads that would enable me to use the pistol which was in relatively good condition except for the bad barrel.

Several years before I reloaded for a 45-60 '76 Winchester with a pitted bore and found reduced velocity loads with jacketed bullets gave best accuracy. I decided to use the same approach to see if

The author testing loads with the 38 Super Llama Extra. One hundred percent reliability was easily obtained with the Llama, but the Star balked with soft point and some jacketed hollow point bullets.

I could concoct some reasonably good loads for the Llama and an old Star military.

Both the Llama and Star might be called the 1911's cousins because they have more than passing resemblance to the Government Auto. Certainly, the Llama Extra and Colt 45 Auto are very similar. The Llama incorporates the shorter trigger, milled frame, and arched

The Llama is chambered for the 38 Super-9mm Largo and is marked on the slide "CAL 9 m/m 38" to distinguish it from similar pistols chambered for the shorter 9mm Luger. It has a slightly longer barrel, slide, and frame than the M1911.

The Star is designed for the 9mm Largo and is slimmer and shorter than either the Colt or Llama. It is also simpler, without, for instance, a grip safety.

This is the original, but good 45's aren't cheap anymore, which is why Smith took up with its Spanish cousins. The M1911 is the standard, but not the only pistol worth shooting.

housing of the Model 1911 A-1, but has a longer barrel, frame, and slide. Because of the similarity of size, shape, and function of Colt and Llama parts, they might be thought to be interchangeable. Most are not. The Llama was designed in 1931 and introduced in 38 Super Auto-9mm Largo. Later it was offered in 45 ACP, 9mm Luger, and in scaled down versions for 380 ACP, 32 ACP, and 22 Long Rifle.

Star pistols differ from the Llama and Colt in that several simplifications have been made. The most obvious is that the various Stars have no grip safety and the trigger is pinned at the top and pivots rather than slides.

The present Stars even more closely resemble the Colt Government Auto than does the old Star military featured in this article. Besides offering smaller versions in 380 and 32 ACP, Star chose to produce two frame sizes for the 38 Super. This caliber is available in the same size frame as the 45 ACP, which was the method chosen by Colt, and also in a slightly smaller version chambered for the 9mm Luger and 38 Super. The Star military was designed for the 9mm Largo cartridge which resulted in its being slimmer and lighter than the 45 Colt Auto. The Star proved to be a good military handgun and was used by the Spanish Civil Guard. When this pistol was replaced by the present Star Super large numbers were sold as surplus.

Thousands of Star and lesser numbers of Llama pistols were sold by mail order (then quite legal) during the 1950s. These guns were priced at between twenty and forty dollars. Along with these guns large quantities of 9mm Luger, 9mm Bergmann-Bayard (9mm Largo), and 9mm Steyr ammunition were imported. Most of this ammunition was corrosively primed, and resulted in many of these pistols developing badly pitted barrels.

In addition to these military surplus arms, new Llama and Star pistols were sold by Stoeger and other importers. The smaller versions in 380, 32, and 22 Long Rifle proved quite popular. The fact that these pistols closely resembled the Government Auto, and that most disassembled in exactly the same manner added no small amount to their sales appeal. The larger 9mm Luger, 38 Super, and 45 ACP versions did not sell as well. At the time, GI 45s were selling in good to excellent condition for about forty dollars, and many potential customers chose to buy one of these rather than the Spanish imports.

This sales resistance was because decades ago many shoddy copies of Colt and Smith & Wesson guns were made in Spanish workshops. Some were downright dangerous, and cast doubts on the safety of any Spanish-made handgun. However, pistols made by Bonifacio Echeverria (Star) and Gabilondo Y. Cia (Llama) have been of at least fair quality and many good to excellent models have been produced since 1930. Some feature hand-fitted actions and target sights.

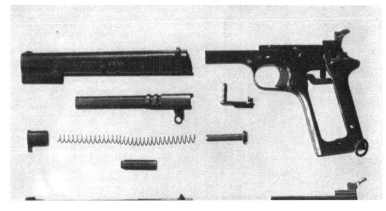

From left — 9mm Luger, 38 Super, and 45 ACP. The 38 Super when loaded to full velocity has more muzzle energy than the other two cartridges. The reduced velocity loads developed by the author to use in pistols with worn barrels are accurate and reliable, but do not compare with factory 38 Super loads.

Llama and Star handguns are becoming increasingly desirable as the price of new and used Colts continues to climb. The possibility of buying a powerful well-made handgun for less than half the price of a comparable Colt is appealing to many potential buyers. The only reservation many people have is that these pistols are often chambered for the 9mm Largo cartridge.

The 9mm Largo is the Spanish name for the 9mm Bergmann-Bayard cartridge which was introduced into Spain with the Bergmann pistol. It is quite similar and will interchange with the 38 Super. At one time it was thought almost any 9mm, including the 9mm Luger and 380 ACP, would work in guns chambered for the 9mm Largo. This issue was definitively put to rest by the late George C. Nonte Jr. in his article in the 1971 GUN DIGEST. In brief, he found these shorter cartridges would fire and sometimes function the mechanism if they were caught and held against the firing pin by the extractor. If they were pushed into the chamber ahead of the extractor and fired, case heads often separated. He concluded that using these shorter cartridges, particularly the powerful 9mm Luger, in 9mm Largo chambered guns was foolhardy and dangerous.

For the American shooter, the most reasonable substitute for the 9mm Largo is the 38 Super Auto. This cartridge is among the most powerful of pistol cartridges. In comparison with the shorter 9mm Luger it uses a bullet that is four grains heavier at a higher velocity (130-grain bullet at 1280 feet per second vs. a 124-grain bullet at 1110 feet per second for the Luger). This difference gives the 38 Super a muzzle energy of 475 foot pounds which is 136 foot pounds more than the 9mm Luger, and a 140 foot pound advantage over the 45 Auto.

The 38 Super uses the same case and bullet as the older 38 ACP, but is loaded to higher pressure. The warning that the Super 38 is not to be used in the 1900,1902, and 1903 model Colt automatics is valid as this cartridge is intended for a slight modification of the much stronger 1911 Colt 45 Auto.

Despite the impressive ballistics of the 38 Super it is not outstandingly popular. This lack of interest is no fault of the cartridge's ballistics, but lies squarely with the fact that, except for a period prior to World War II, only full jacketed bullets were available in this caliber. While such bullets give good penetration they do not have the killing power of soft or hollow pointed projectiles. This reduced the popularity of the 38 Super for sporting use.

The answer for increasing the effectiveness of the 38 Super is not by increasing its velocity, but by loading more effective bullets. This need has now been met by Remington who markets a 125-grain jacketed hollow point loading, and by independent bullet makers like Speer, Sierra, and Hornady who offer hollow and soft point bullets in weights of from 88 to 130 grains. These developments considerably enhance the usefulness of pistols chambered for the 38 Super — particularly for the reloader.

Since these pistols might be described as "poor man's Colts," I decided to work up some handloads as cheaply as possible. I purchased a box of 125-grain Speer soft points for $6.50, a Lee Loader in 38 Super for $11.25, a box of primers for $1.10, and used some Unique I had left over. Excluding the cost of the powder and a powder scale I already owned, I reloaded 100 rounds for $18.60 compared to the cost of 100 factory cartridges at $22.10.1 realized a savings of $3.50 for the first 100 rounds including the cost of the new reloading equipment.

I had never used a Lee Loader, but quickly became resigned to the fact that patience is a virtue. The Lee is slow, slow, slow; but it gets the job done. The first step is decapping which consists of knocking out the fired primer with a rod. The next is resizing where the lubricated case is driven into the sizing die with a plastic mallet. This was where the work started, and after I sized 100 cases that

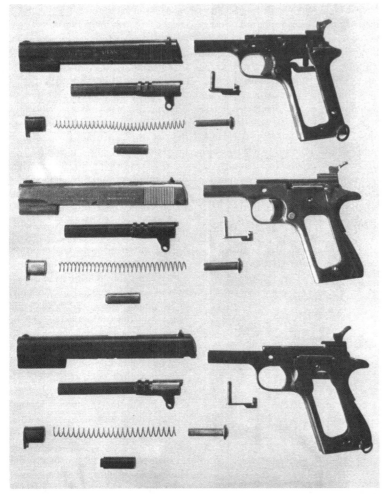

Star military (top), Colt 45 Automatic (middle), and Llama Extra (bottom) field stripped. The similarity of the three pistols is apparent. All use the basic Browning design. The Star differs from the Colt and Llama in that its hammer spring is directly below the hammer instead of being housed lower in the grip. The Star also uses all coil springs, has a simplified thumb safety, and does not have a grip safety.

a spire point.

Of the first 50 rounds, three were so deformed they were discarded, 16 had off-center bullets, and 31 were sufficiently uniform to expect some sort of accuracy. Some sort of accuracy — damn poor — was all I did achieve, and I realized I would have to make some changes in loading techniques and bullets to obtain reasonable results.

I bought a box of Remington 124-grain metal cased bullets which would resist deformation during reloading. I would have preferred the 130-grain bullet Remington loads in 38 Super, but had to settle for the lighter 124-and 100-grain 9mm Luger bullets because they were the only full metal cased 9mms carried by the distributor. If I could obtain reasonable results with these, there was some possibility of developing good hollow point loadings using a variety of available bullets.

To solve the bullet seating problem, I purchased a woodworker's vise to use as a press and mounted it on a heavy plank. Better bullet seating was obtained, but I still had bullet alignment problems. At the start, I chamfered the case mouths with a pocket knife, but found that a $7.50 deburring tool gave much better results.

Using the vise, the deburring tool, and the metal cased bullets helped tremendously, and both the Llama and Star shot the new loads reasonably well. After some experimentation with different charges of Unique, I found 5.4 grains gave good accuracy and functioned well in both pistols. This load is 1.1 grain less than the 6.5 grains Speer recommends as the starting load for the 38 Super in their manual. The historic tendency with reloading the 38 Super has been to concentrate on loads at the high velocity end of the scale, but for worn barrels reduced velocity loads gave much better accuracy.

This is one case where less definitely gives more.

Reduced velocity loads, target loads, and small game loads are often considered one and the same. They are

was all I cared to do that night. Unlike revolver cartridges which are often only neck sized for target loads the 38 Super must be full-length resized to insure positive function.

The next evening I reprimed the sized cases. Lee would have the user reprime as he is knocking the case out of the resizing die, but I found a better feel is obtained if repriming is done separately.

Bullet seating proved to be the most exasperating operation. To seat the bullet, the primed and powder-filled case is placed back into the sizing die, the die placed on the decapping base, and the bullet pounded into the case using the mallet and bullet seating rod. This rod is attached to the priming chamber and is adjustable for bullet seating depth. The three pieces have to be held and aligned with one hand while pounding with the other. The problem is to keep the base aligned with the sizing die to prevent bullets from canting. Canted bullets could be pounded until the soft lead nose resembled a wadcutter, but they would not enter the case. Even when the bullet seated easily, the cone-shaped end of the seating rod deformed the bullet nose into

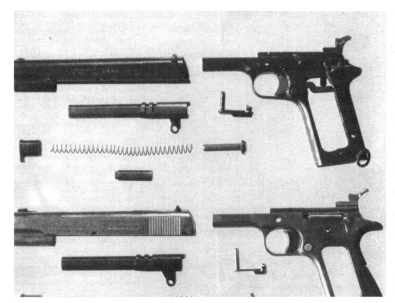

From left — Colt 45 magazine, Llama magazine, and plated magazine of the Star. The Llama's magazine has indentations on both sides to adapt it to the 38 Super, the same method used by Colt. The modified magazine and modifications to the frame and slide gave Colt a new cartridge and pistol at a fraction of the cost of an entirely new design. The Star's magazine was designed for the 9mm Largo and did not require modification.

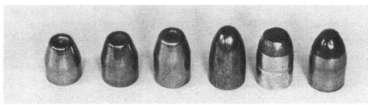

From left — 88-gr. Speer jacketed hollow point, 100-gr. Speer jacketed hollow point, 115-gr. Sierra jacketed hollow point, 124-gr. full metal cased Remington 9mm Luger bullet, 125-gr. Speer jacketed hollow point, and 125-gr. Speer jacketed soft point.

usually assembled with lead bullets, have velocities between 700 and 800 feet per second, and have as their chief virtues high accuracy and low recoil. The loads listed below differ in that full jacketed or nearly full jacketed bullets are used and many are hollow pointed. This approach was used to reduce leading which would have otherwise been a serious problem in the badly pitted barrels, to promote better feeding, and to make the loads as effective as possible on small game. There is no hope of obtaining reliable expansion at these velocities, but the jacketed hollow points did promise to be non-leading and better killers than jacketed round nose bullets.

Unique and 700-X powders were chosen because they represent a fast and moderately fast powder commonly used in shotgun and pistol reloading. Unique is an extremely versatile powder that works well with heavier bullets in many pistol calibers, and 700-X does nicely with lighter bullets.

A selection of bullets ranging in weight from 88 to 125 grains was obtained. Most of the bullets are made by Speer, and the jackets on the 88- and 100-grain bullets extend very slightly beyond the edge of a large hollow point cavity. These proved to feed bet-

ter, particularly in the Star, than heavier bullets where lead extended beyond the jacket.

Starting loads were selected by reducing the powder in increments from the lowest charge listed in the Speer tables. When the lightest loading was reached that would reliably function the guns the charge was increased until best accuracy was obtained.

Loads were considered accurate when they would group within the 5½-inch 9 ring of the 25-yard pistol target. Pistols designed for target use are expected to group within the 1¾-inch X-ring at 25 yards, but for issue pistols with bad barrels consistent 5½-inch groups are acceptable. The Llama with the 124-grain Remington bullet often produced 4-inch five-shot groups at this range with occasional clusters of three shots grouping within 1½ inches.

The Llama proved to be an easy pistol to work with, and digested soft point and hollow pointed bullets without a hitch. The Star was another story. It would only function reliably with the 100- and 124-grain full metal cased round nose bullets and the long jacketed Speer hollow points.

Although the loads charted are low velocity loads, some cautions need to be observed. All of the listed loads have a total length of 1.280 inches. If bullets are seated deeper the charges of 700-X need to be reduced to prevent potentially dangerous pressures.

While loads ranging from 5.1 to 5.7 grains of Unique gave no indications of high pressures when used with the 124- and 125-grain bullets, changes of a few tenths of a grain of 700-X are significant. This powder, like Bulls-eye, should only be used with reduced velocity loads, and no attempt should be made to use 700-X with bullets heavier than 100 grains in 38 Super or to assemble high velocity loads. Excessive pressures may well be reached before the 1200 feet per second velocity level is obtained. No indications of high pressures were seen in the loads listed in the table.

Resizing with the Lee Loader. A woodworker's vise made full-length resizing the 38 Super cases much easier. The vise is attached to a four inch thick block of wood about a foot square which is braced between the feet when cases are resized.

Reduced Velocity Loads For 38 Super

Bullet	Bull. Weight grains	Powder	Charge grains	Notes
Remington FMC .354	124	Unique	5.4	Best functioning and most accurate load.
Hornady FMC .355	100	Unique 700-X	6.0 4.2	Functions well, but not as accurate as FMC.
Speer JHP .355	125			Bullet nose deformed so much during reloading loads could not be developed.
Speer JSP .355	125	Unique	5.4	Bullet nose deformed during reloading and when being fed from magazine. If bullet bases were lubricated during reloading better loads resulted.
Sierra JHP .355	115	Unique	5.8	Functioned well in Llama, but often failed to feed from Star's magazine.
Speer JHP .355	100	Unique 700-X	6.0 4.2	Best JHP loading in Star and Llama. Difficult to seat bullet without canting in Lee Loader.
Speer JHP .355	88	700-X	4.5	Almost impossible to reload without canting these short bullets. Load functioned well in Llama and Star.

FMC—Full metal cased bullets. JSP—Jacketed soft point. JHP—Jacketed hollow point.
　All loads have an over-all length of 1.280 inches.
　All loads assembled in Remington plus-P cases and used CCI 500 small pistol primers.
　Base of hollow point and soft point bullets lightly lubricated with Lyman bullet lubricant to promote easier bullet seating.
　These loads worked safely in the author's pistols; however, no responsibility can be accepted for handloads assembled by others.

Reduced velocity loads, rough bores, and jacketed bullets can theoretically lead to bullets sticking in the barrel or jackets separating from bullet cores. Neither problem was observed during testing, but charges should not be reduced to the point that the pistol fails to function.

After shooting 1000 rounds through the Llama Extra and perhaps half that number through the Star, I had some definite opinions about the pistols. The Llama was easier to shoot because of its larger grip, wide Patridge sights, heavier weight, and longer sight radius. The smooth backstrap of the Star became slippery when my hand sweated in the 95 degree temperatures of the summer shooting sessions. I found myself doing most of the load testing with the Llama not only because it was easier to load for, but simply because it felt better to shoot.

I have little doubt that Star introduced the present Star Super, which even more closely resembles the Colt 45 Auto, to overcome this handicap. That they succeeded in significantly improving the pistol is attested by the fact that the new Star Super was adopted by Spain's military forces.

Even though both pistols were made some 50 years ago, there were no mechanical failures. Considering that they digested loads ranging from the hot Remington plus-P ammunition, which exceeds the 9mm Largo's ballistics by a considerable margin, to reduced velocity loads without any problems proved they are not the worthless pieces of Spanish junk some think them to be.

During all this, half a dozen cottontails, one red fox, and a feral house cat have been taken with the Llama using reduced velocity loads. All were killed with a single shot, and confirmed that I had restored a pistol to useful life by crafting some handloads that would shoot well in its badly pitted barrel.

The Uncolts: U.S.-Made Pistols Of 1911 Pattern

■ J.B. Wood

IF JOHN MOSES Browning were alive today, he might be pleased to see how his design of 75 years ago has lasted and, in recent years, proliferated. In his own time, he saw his 1911 U.S. Government Model pistol produced in a commercial version by Colt, and made for military use by Colt and several other government contractors. In Norway, a slightly-modified version was made under license as their Model 1914, and numerous unlicensed copies were made in Spain and elsewhere. A licensed copy was also later made in Argentina for military use.

Down through the years, the Colt company has continued to make the pistol. Along the way, they have made several modifications to the original design, but the basic pattern has been unchanged. In addition to the original 45 Auto chambering, the pistol was made available in 38 Super, and later in 9mm Parabellum. A shortened version in all three calibers was offered as the Commander, with a choice of frames in steel or lightweight alloy. A target model of the full-sized gun, the National Match, later evolved into the excellent Gold Cup.

Inside, the Colt engineers have made some subtle changes. Lately, a collet-type muzzle bushing grips the barrel for more consistent positioning, and the introduction of this feature gave the pistol a new designation, "Mark IV/Series 70." More recently, the addition of an automatic internal fir-

ing pin block safety system created the "Mark IV/Series 80." Last year, Colt introduced their "Combat Grade" model, with special sights and ejection port, a wrap-around Pachmayr rubber grip, a longer trigger, and a beveled magazine entry, among other features.

Meanwhile, since the basic design has long been out-of-patent, others have wisely decided to make their own versions of the old war-horse. These range from virtually identical copies to very innovative extensions of the pattern. One stainless-steel copy, the Vega, was short-lived, but the rest are doing quite well. Over the past few weeks, I've tried seven of them, and all are a credit to the original Browning concept.

AMT

The first successful stainless-steel version, Harry Sanford's AMT Hardballer, is presently offered in both a standard size and a Long Slide, the latter with seven-inch barrel. Other features of both models are extended safety and slide latch levers, fully adjustable rear sights, and skeletonized triggers with adjustable stop screws. The grip is a wrap-around rubber type by Supreme. A raised and ribbed sighting plane runs the full length of the slide top.

The mainspring housing is straight, with vertical serrations, the one favored by many serious shooters. Firing the Long Slide model was, for me, an interesting and educational experience. Up to

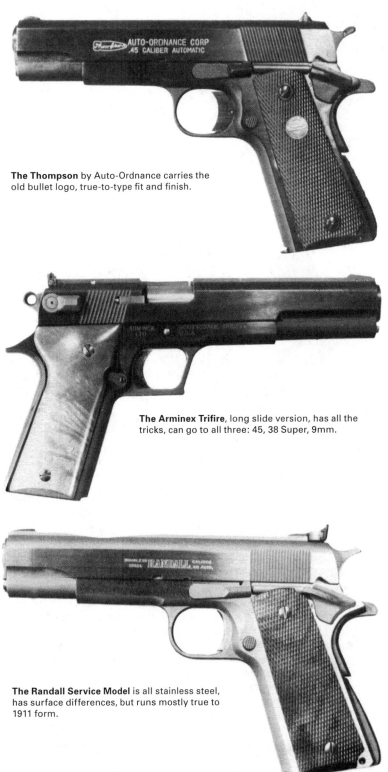

The **Thompson** by Auto-Ordnance carries the old bullet logo, true-to-type fit and finish.

The **Arminex Trifire**, long slide version, has all the tricks, can go to all three: 45, 38 Super, 9mm.

The **Randall Service Model** is all stainless steel, has surface differences, but runs mostly true to 1911 form.

now, seeing photos of some of the custom long slide pistols, I had always wondered … well, now I know. The recoil and muzzle whip are reduced, and the sight picture, because of the extended radius, is enhanced. The extra two inches of barrel length give a slightly higher velocity, and the accuracy is absolutely deadly. Finally, I expected the handling to be a bit awkward, and it wasn't.

The AMT guns have matte finishes on all surfaces except for the side flats of the slide, the magazine, the barrel, and the plug and bushing. The overall fit and finish are excellent. At the range, the functioning was perfect.

(I'll note here that I fired all of the guns with regular 45 full-jacket rounds by Federal and Hornady/Frontier. I was firing them for functioning and accuracy, and not as combat pieces, so I didn't try hollow points. Remarkably, even though most of these guns were in-the-box new, there was not a single incident of misfeeding or incomplete ejection — tribute to Mr. Browning's design, and good ammunition.)

Detonics

Another stainless-steel entry has been around for a while in abbreviated form — the Detonics. The finely-made small guns have now been joined by the Scoremaster, a full-sized 45 that has several special features. Starting from the top, there's a fully-adjustable Bo-Mar rear sight, and a double-pinned ramp front sight with an inset orange "T" in its rear face. The barrel is pure Detonics design, with a coned front section that is hand-fitted to the slide interior, so there's no bushing. The buffered recoil spring system is also of Detonics design.

A graceful full-beavertail extension tops the grip safety, to eliminate any chance of hammer-bite. The manual safety is of standard design, but is ambidextrous, and the opposite unit on the right side is a beautiful piece of engineering. The grip is wrap-around rubber by Pachmayr, and the rear of the straight mainspring housing is also checkered rubber. The magazine entry is beveled, and the release button is high-profile.

The new Detonics Scoremaster is the firm's first full-size 1911. Barrel and allied parts are different.

The MS-Safari Arms Enforcer is the small one; they make them big, too, with a wide array of options.

The slide and frame are by Essex, the rest from assorted sources; it works really well, Wood says.

The vertically-grooved trigger has an Allen screw for stop adjustment.

This pistol was obviously designed for serious competition, not casual shooting, and my range-testing methods sometimes border on plinking. Even so, it performed beautifully. The unique "coned" effect at the muzzle results in an external diameter of .695", a little over 11/16 of an inch, and this gives the effect of a "bull barrel" — a slight muzzle heaviness and reduced whip during recoil. Accuracy was outstanding. The fit and finish are up to Detonics standards — impeccable.

Randall

A newcomer to the stainless-steel 1911 group is the Randall, and from the start this California firm has concentrated on one of the old design's main points, reliability. This is not to say, though, that they have neglected other important features. The Randall is made 100% of stainless steel, a special alloy, and the barrel has ten-groove rifling. A solid recoil spring guide is used. The ejection port is opened, and the magazine entry is beveled. The gun is available with either fixed combat-style sights (stainless, but black-finished), or with fully-adjustable Millets. Long or short triggers are optional, and both have a stop-screw.

On the Service Model, Randall stays very close to the original pattern, except for the special recoil spring guide and a combat safety that is slightly extended at the front of the lever. The Randall has the arched mainspring housing of the 1911A1, with vertical grooving. The finish is satin, slightly brighter on the sides, but still not highly reflective. The grips are checkered walnut, and on my Randall they have a nice grain pattern. The fitting of the steel parts is precise, and all lines and flats are very clean.

At the range, I found that the Randall performed as well as it looked. I didn't fire from a rest at formal targets with any of the pistols, but some of my casual targets were smaller than the standard center bull, and the pistol hit them with regularity. Later, when there's time and the weather is better, I'm going to find

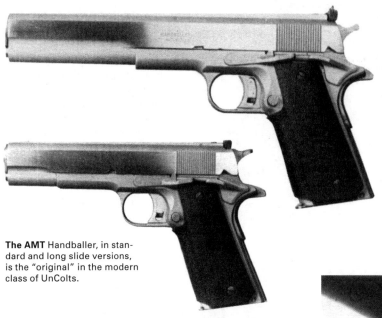

The AMT Handballer, in standard and long slide versions, is the "original" in the modern class of UnColts.

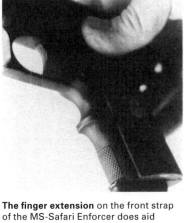

The finger extension on the front strap of the MS-Safari Enforcer does aid control.

out if that ten-groove barrel is as superior as they claim. For now, it's enough to say that it will consistently nail a soft-drink can at 25 yards, and that's very good. In addition to the Service Model, there are five others, including lightweight and shortened versions, and this year they introduced a true mirror-image left-handed model.

Although of Spartan design, the Auto-Ordnance pistol has a long trigger with an adjustable stop.

The safety lever on the Randall Service Model is slightly extended; the sight is by Mitchell.

Auto-Ordnance

Moving out of the stainless-steel group, there's a pistol that probably comes closest to the military-issue Government Model, and it's the Thompson by Auto-Ordnance. If the name is familiar, it's because they're also the makers of the modern-day version of the famed Thompson Submachinegun and the Thompson SemiAuto Carbine. In fact, the pistol carries the well-known bullet/signature trademark on its slide and on the grip medallions. The Thompson is supposed to be a Spartan, no-frills gun, and it costs somewhat less than the others, but there are a few surprises.

As standard equipment, it has a long-style trigger that is screw-adjustable for over-travel, and an arched, checkered mainspring housing. The hammer is the old, comfortable wide-spur model with fine checkering, and I'd swear that the

smooth magazine is original military issue from a high-quality supplier. For a pistol that's intended to be utilitarian, the fit and finish are surprisingly good. The surface is a nice blue, matte on the top and undersides, and a medium polish on the sides of the slide and frame.

The sights are the standard fixed military type, and on my pistol they were perfectly aligned for a center hold at 25 yards. For those who are afflicted with World War II nostalgia, the Thompson will have a magical effect — it feels exact-

ly like a GI-issue 45, and to a great extent also looks like one. It does, however, shoot much better than most of them did. Auto-Ordnance also offers the same gun in 9mm Parabellum and 38 Super.

Essex

The next one on our list is not available as a finished pistol. The Essex Arms Corporation of Island Pond, Vermont, makes a nicely-finished frame and slide, for the shooter who prefers to build his own gun. A while back, a friend gave me an Essex frame and slide, and over a few months time I gradually put together a 45 Auto that has proved to be both dependable and accurate. The fin-

The ambidextrous safety on the Detonics Scoremaster is especially well-designed.

The slide latch and the safety are both extended on the Hardballer.

ish on my Essex is either a matte blue or very smooth Parkerizing, I've never established which. A wide raised solid rib extends the full length of the slide top, and it has five deep grooves.

The front sight cut and aperture were there, but the rear of the rib was left uncut, to allow the individual to decide what type of rear sight was wanted. I chose an MMC combat-style with white outline, and a matching bar-cross front blade. An old-style wide-spur hammer was installed, and a standard safety. All of the smaller internal parts were standard, either U.S. surplus or Colt. The stainless magazine originated from the now-departed Vega.

Rubber wrap-around grips from Pachmayr were used. The barrel bushing, recoil spring unit, slide latch, and one-piece solid backstrap were from Arminex, Ltd. I beveled the magazine entry. Except for that and the mounting of the sights, no other gunsmithing was done. By fortunate accident, the safety and the sear engagement were perfect as installed, and the barrel required no fitting. When one of these Frankenstein jobs is assembled, that's not always the case. By now I've probably put at least a thousand rounds through my Essex, and it has given me no problems with any type of factory ammo.

MS-Safari Arms

Long before I actually fired one, I looked at the photos of the MS-Safari Arms Enforcer, and wondered about the "hump" on the frontstrap, between the second and third fingers. Was it comfortable? Did it have any real purpose? Now that I've fired an Enforcer exten-

sively, I have the answers: Yes, and Yes.

MS-Safari makes several models, including full-sized and special target/competition versions, but the one I have is their smaller gun. The barrel is 3 15/16 inches, and the height is 5¼ inches, with the shortened magazine holding six rounds.

On an MS-Safari pistol, you can choose the features you want, such as an extended slide latch, ambidextrous safety, or other items. My gun has both these. The fully-adjustable rear sight is similar to a Smith & Wesson revolver sight, but somewhat heavier. The trigger is long-style, stop-adjustable, and the grips are rubber with a pebbled surface.

The handling qualities are excellent, and the reliability and accuracy were above reproach. I found that the "hump" on the frontstrap gave a more secure grip, and it was a definite help in controlling muzzle whip.

Arminex Trifire

I will admit to a certain amount of non-objectivity in regard to the Arminex Trifire. When it was just in the planning stages, I had many long conversations about it with my good friend Jim Mongello and, by suggestion at least, I had a small part in its design. When it emerged, the Trifire had several distinctive features. As its name suggests, it is convertible from 45 Auto to 38 Super and 9mm Parabellum, without changing the slide.

While it has the "classic cosmetic configuration" of the Government Model, it abandons the frame-mounted sear-block safety in favor of a slide-mounted

firing pin block type that does not drop the hammer. The firing pin can be manually locked during loading, and the pistol can be carried cocked-and-locked. It can also be dryfired forever with the hammer never touching the firing pin.

The Trifire has an Arminex self-contained recoil spring unit and a solid one-piece backstrap. Both are available as separate accessories for use on other 1911 pistols. The solid backstrap has a subtle shape that is exactly right, and the absence of a grip safety is welcome.

A fixed combat-style rear sight or a fully-adjustable target sight installs in the same milled space at the rear of the slide, and the retaining cross-pin is extra heavy. The ramp-style front sight is double-cross-pinned to the slide rib. The rib is low and wide, with lengthwise grooving. The hammer is a ring-type, and the slide latch is slightly extended. An ambidextrous safety system is available.

The trigger is beautiful. Wide and glass-smooth, it's made of beryllium alloy. At the range, the Standard Trifire performance and handling qualities were outstanding. The externally-mounted pivoting extractor and wide ejection port put the fired cases neatly in a group for retrieval.

I was favorably impressed with all these pistols. Once, more than 30 years ago, I spent an afternoon shooting a government-issue 45 at reasonably-sized targets, and my abysmal scores engendered a long-lasting dislike for the 1911 design. If that pistol had been one of the modern versions described above, it would have been a different story.

Early Rivals of the Model 1911 45 Automatic

It was a well-attended race, but most of the entrants were also-rans. ▮ John Malloy

PERHAPS no single automatic pistol is better known or has had more influence on automatic pistol design than the Browning-designed Colt Model 1911 45. It dominated the big-bore pistol scene of this century to such an extent that little memory is left of its early rivals. Yet these pistols, also-rans in the race against the Colt, should not be forgotten, for their influence still lives today.

Most people with an interest in firearms know that the Colt 1911 45 automatic was chosen, after some of the most extensive testing ever conducted, in a series of trials that spanned the 4-year period between 1907 and 1911. Then, in 1917, only 6 years later, the United States entered World War I. Battle experience proved the merits of the new pistol. In every instance, the 1911 gave a good account of itself when called upon. In some cases, such as its use in the hands of Corporal Alvin York, its performance became legendary.

The pistol was so good that, hardly more than a decade after the war, copies and modifications of the Colt-Browning design were being made all over the world.

It was so good that its early rivals — pistols that offered different ideas in the 1907-1917 decade — were soon all but forgotten.

The events leading up to the 1907 test trials, which gave the Colt its start to prominence, are of interest. And in those events is the story of the also-rans.

The 45-caliber Colt Single Action

Having its 1905 45 pistol already in commercial production before the test trials gave Colt a decided advantage over its rivals.

Army revolver had been replaced in Army hands by Colt's 1892 double-action design of 38-caliber. During the Philippine insurrection of 1899-1901 and continuing encounters with Moro tribesmen, it was found necessary to rush the obsolete Single Actions out of storage and back into service, and a quantity of 45-caliber 1878 Colt double actions were purchased. The stopping power of the old 45s proved to be far superior.

Thus, the search for a new sidearm began in the early 1900s with the consideration that it be of 45-caliber. Although semi-automatic pistols were coming into use, the cavalry firmly favored the revolver. The stage was set that any "automatic" considered must have reliability equal to that of the revolver and be of 45-caliber.

In anticipation of the tests, Frankfort

Arsenal had designed two cartridges — a rimmed one for revolver use, and a rimless one for the automatic pistols.

The rimless version was very similar to a commercial round produced by Winchester Repeating Arms Co. for Colt since the spring of 1905. The WRA cartridges were made for Colt's new 45 automatic pistol, introduced in the fall of 1905. The Army round differed primarily in having a slightly longer case (.911- over .898-inch) and a slightly heavier bullet (234 over 200 grains.)

With the benefit of hindsight, it is difficult to understand why the Army, which had certainly been aware of Colt's development work, felt it needed a special round. Indeed, problems developed with the Frankfort Arsenal cartridges, and commercial ammunition (with a heavier 230-grain bullet) was used during much of the testing.

Invitations to submit pistols for testing were sent on January 31, 1906, to over 20 companies and individuals believed to be interested in developing military sidearms. The invitations included cartridge specifications (for the Frankfort cartridges) and offered to furnish a supply of ammunition to assist in preparing the pistols.

When the board convened on January 15, 1907, eight applicants had submitted nine general designs. Three were revolvers and six were automatic pistols. The revolvers are of interest themselves, but do not concern us here. The automatic pistols, at this early stage of history, represented a variety of concepts in competition for the first time.

The Colt was clearly the front-runner. The others were:

1. The Bergmann
2. The Knoble (actually two versions; one double action, one single action)
3. The White-Merrill
4. The Luger
5. The Savage

Three of the entries — the Bergmann, Knoble and White-Merrill pistols — were rejected early in the tests.

The fate of the Bergmann was sealed with this rather terse excerpt from the Board's report:

"An attempt was then made to fire 20 rounds to observe the working of the pistol, but it was found that the blow of the hammer was not sufficient to discharge the cartridges, and the test was discontinued."

There is an air of mystery surrounding the unbelievably poor showing of the Bergmann 45. It seems incredible that a pistol that had obviously not been testfired with the required ammunition should arrive for these important trials without any representative, to be tested by persons unfamiliar with its operation.

Theodor Bergmann was a German inventor and industrialist, with a factory complex in Gaggenau, in southwest

Because specimens are often on public display, the Savage 45 is probably the best known of the early rivals. This one is in the Metzger collection at Texas A&M University.

Germany. Largely through the efforts of his employee, Louis Schmeisser, the Bergmann pistol had become one of the first successful automatic pistols.

Always desiring a chance for military contracts, Bergmann had requested U.S. Army trials of his pistols as early as 1899. In 1903, he requested a test of his latest pistol. The caliber was 11.35mm, using a cartridge similar to the later 45 ACP. Apparently, no such test took place.

In 1905, the 9mm Bergmann pistol was adopted by Spain. Bergmann had subcontracted his pistol manufacture to the Schilling firm of Suhl. Schilling, however, was bought out by Krieghoff, which ended pistol production for Bergmann just as the Spanish contract was negotiated. Bergmann had a contract and no way to fulfill it.

To justify new expanded firearms facilities at his Gaggenau plant, Bergmann needed to obtain other contracts. He got a delay for the delivery of the Spanish pistols, and submitted a 45-caliber pistol to the U.S. Ordnance Department in June, 1906. In January, 1907, the pistol was tested at Springfield, with the dismal results mentioned.

Adoption of the Colt 1911 by the Army halted development of most of its early rivals.

In the hands of World War I troops, the Colt performed so well our military had no reason to consider other designs.

After World War I, the superiority of the Colt was firmly established. The pistol is here carried at a 1923 training camp. The young man on the left will later become the writer's father. (Courtesy of Harold F. Malloy)

> WHY, WITH SO MUCH AT STAKE, DID BERGMANN SEND A GUN TO AN IMPORTANT TEST WITHOUT BEING SURE THAT IT WOULD FUNCTION WITH THE APPROPRIATE AMMUNITION? WHY, WITH COMPANY AGENTS IN BOTH GERMANY AND THE U.S., DID NO BERGMANN REPRESENTATIVE ATTEND THE TRIALS TO DEMONSTRATE THE PISTOL? AT THIS DISTANCE IN TIME, THESE QUESTIONS MAY NEVER BE ANSWERED.

Why did the Bergmann pistol fail so miserably? Why, with so much at stake, did Bergmann send a gun to an important test without being sure that it would function with the appropriate ammunition? Why, with company agents in both Germany and the U.S., did no Bergmann representative attend the trials to demonstrate the pistol? At this distance in time, these questions may never be answered.

Bergmann, disappointed with this failure, decided it was not economically sound to continue pistol manufacture. The Spanish contract was taken over by the Pieper firm, of Herstal, Belgium, who added their trademark "Bayard." The Bergmann-designed 9mm cartridge remains popular in Spain to this day. Denmark adopted the Bergmann-Bayard pistol in 1910; it remained the official Danish side-arm until 1946.

Theodor Bergmann retired from automatic pistol development just as that type of arm was coming into its own. One can only speculate as to what might have occurred had the Bergmann pistol made a satisfactory showing at the 1907 trials.

Faring little better than the Bergmann test pistol were the two pistols submitted by W.B. Knoble of Tacoma, Washington. The 1907 report states, "… several efforts to fire these weapons showed that they were so crudely manufactured as to render any test without value …"

Knoble began working on automatic pistol designs about 1904 and made several prototypes. For the 1907 tests he prepared both double-action and single-action versions in 45-caliber. The double action is of special interest; it was a very early use of that feature in a semi-automatic pistol.

Knoble's plan was to have his pistols represented by von Lengerke & Detmold, New York outfitters. However, that firm dropped Knoble in order to demonstrate a planned 45 pistol by Mauser. The Mauser design, however, was never submitted. And when Mauser withdrew, so did von Lengerke & Detmold.

Knoble's pistols were tested without anyone who knew enough about them to keep the roughly-fitted prototypes functioning. The failure of his designs discouraged Knoble from further work with pistols. Although he retained his interest in firearms, his later efforts were all shoulder arms, and none gained prominence.

The White-Merrill pistol fired 211

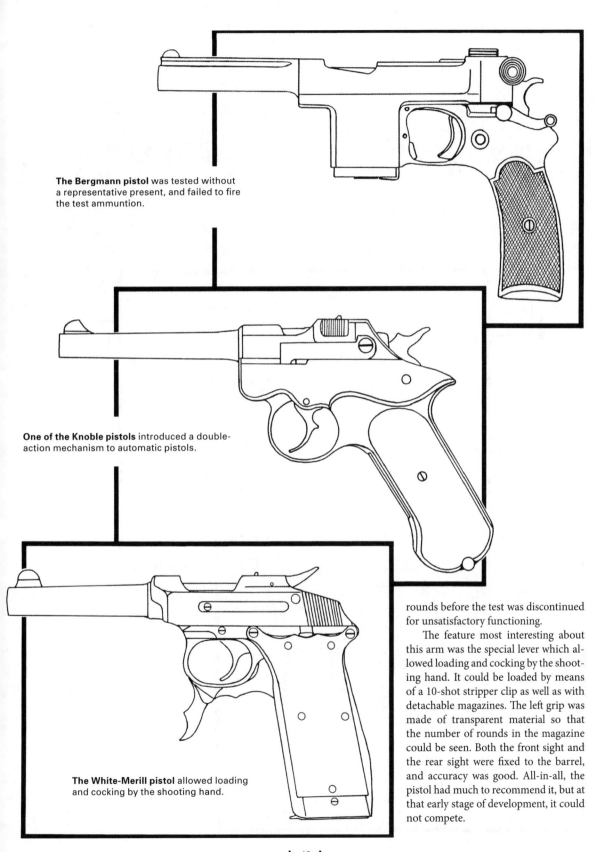

The Bergmann pistol was tested without a representative present, and failed to fire the test ammuntion.

One of the Knoble pistols introduced a double-action mechanism to automatic pistols.

The White-Merill pistol allowed loading and cocking by the shooting hand.

rounds before the test was discontinued for unsatisfactory functioning.

The feature most interesting about this arm was the special lever which allowed loading and cocking by the shooting hand. It could be loaded by means of a 10-shot stripper clip as well as with detachable magazines. The left grip was made of transparent material so that the number of rounds in the magazine could be seen. Both the front sight and the rear sight were fixed to the barrel, and accuracy was good. All-in-all, the pistol had much to recommend it, but at that early stage of development, it could not compete.

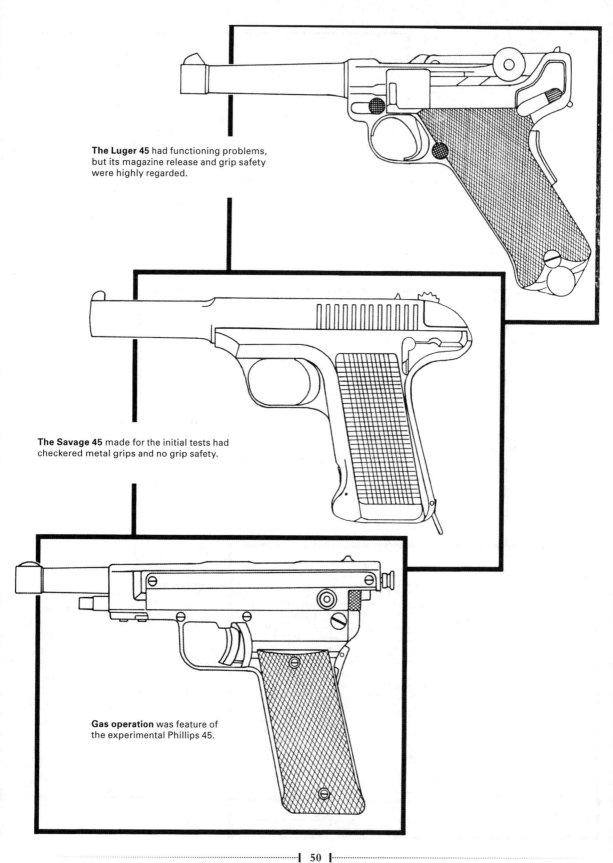

The Luger 45 had functioning problems, but its magazine release and grip safety were highly regarded.

The Savage 45 made for the initial tests had checkered metal grips and no grip safety.

Gas operation was feature of the experimental Phillips 45.

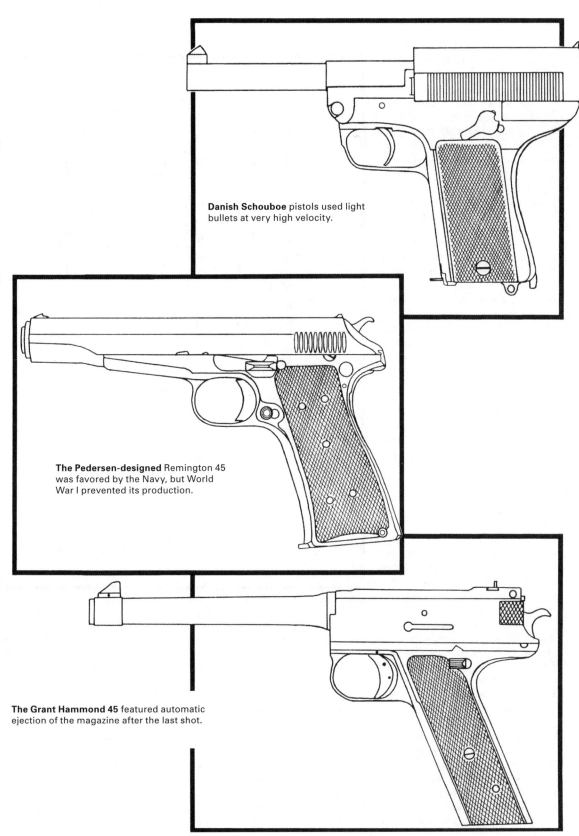

Danish Schouboe pistols used light bullets at very high velocity.

The Pedersen-designed Remington 45 was favored by the Navy, but World War I prevented its production.

The Grant Hammond 45 featured automatic ejection of the magazine after the last shot.

Joseph C. White and Samuel Merrill, the co-inventors, had formed a corporation in Boston, Massachusetts, in order to promote their designs, and had patented at least one other method of one-hand cocking. After their 45 entry had been rejected, they discontinued further work on it. They worked on two quite different pistols of 38-caliber, but by 1910 they seem to have given up pistol work and turned their efforts to automatic rifles. None of these achieved any success.

The 45-caliber Luger pistol was an enlarged version of the 30-caliber 1900 Parabellum pistol which had found favor in Germany and elsewhere. It was the only test pistol submitted that had a grip safety, and one of only two that allowed ejection of the magazine by the shooting hand. These features were viewed favorably by the board and, indeed, the final victor — the Colt 1911 — incorporated both of them.

The main objection to the Luger was that the toggle-joint action closed by the momentum of the moving parts, and not by positive spring action. This design required ammunition of high pressure level. Luger brought with him a supply of German-loaded cartridges, and at his request, the special ammunition, as well as that supplied by Frankfort Arsenal, was used in the tests. A total of 1022 rounds was fired. The Luger cartridges did not function appreciably better than those the Arsenal supplied, and most malfunctions related to feeding and final closing of the breechblock.

The opinion of the Board was:

The Luger automatic pistol, although it possesses manifest advantages in many particulars, is not recommended for a service test because its certainty of action, even with Luger ammunition, is not considered satisfactory …

However, the Luger 45 was to be given another chance. The Board authorized the purchase of 200 each of Colt and Savage pistols for field tests. Colt readily accepted, but Savage was unwilling to tool up for such a relatively small production run. Whereupon, the contract was offered to Luger.

DWM apparently accepted the con-

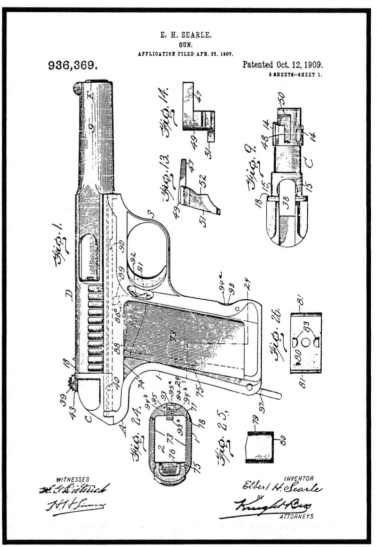

Searle's patent illustration shows a pistol that was essentially the Savage 45 of the initial tests. Note the large butt opening for the staggered-column magazine.

tract, then backed out shortly after acceptance. The 45 was probably enough different in size and contour so that existing machinery could not be used, and, like Savage, the firm may have been reluctant to redesign production facilities for a small contract. They may also have felt certain of the acceptance of their new 9mm pistol by the German government and wished to devote attention to preparations for its production. That pistol was indeed adopted in the following year as the P.08.

The failure of DWM to supply Lugers for the service tests gave Savage a chance to reconsider. Their pistol had been judged almost the equal of the established Colt, and lucrative future contracts might be awarded — a powerful incentive to the small company, then just 12 years old.

Savage Arms Company had been formed in 1894 by 37-year-old inventor Arthur Savage to produce his hammerless lever-action rifle. By the turn of the century, the company was looking for ways to expand its product line. About 1905, the company was approached by

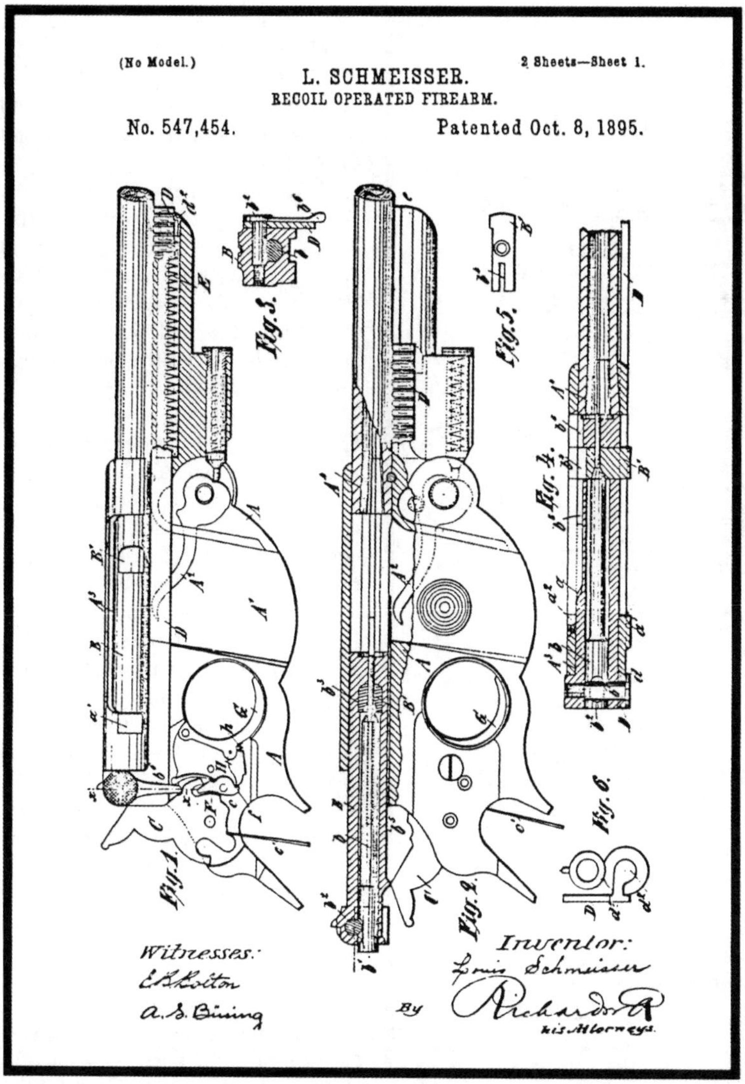
(No Model.)
2 Sheets—Sheet 1.
L. SCHMEISSER.
RECOIL OPERATED FIREARM.
No. 547,454.
Patented Oct. 8, 1895.
Fig. 1.
Fig. 2.
Fig. 3.
Fig. 4.
Fig. 5.
Fig. 6.
Witnesses:
Inventor:
By
his Attorneys.

This 1895 patent, assigned to Bergmann, suggests that Louis Schmeisser was responsible for the basic Bergmann pistol design.

Elbert H. Searle of Philadelphia and his financial partner William D. Condit, of Des Moines, concerning a new automatic pistol invented by Searle. An arrangement was made whereby Savage would develop the pistol, and Searle would work with Savage for that purpose.

When the test trials were announced, Savage and Searle produced a 45-caliber specimen. The pistol had a rotating barrel which was held to the slide by a lug through a very small rotation of about 5 degrees. Rotation was supposedly resisted by the inertia of the bullet passing through the rifling.

The actual mechanics of this system have inspired considerable discussion. It seems safe to say that the barrel and slide are indeed locked at the instant of firing, but they unlock very rapidly. For all practical purposes, it was a delayed blowback system, with attendant heavier recoil than true locked-breech designs.

Containing only 34 parts, the Savage pistol was noted for its simplicity. The simple design enabled it to function well following the dust and rusting tests, and its overall functioning was actually slightly better than that of the Colt. Like the Luger, the magazine could be released by the shooting hand. The position of the latch on the lower front grip frame allowed release by the little finger of either hand. The innovative staggered magazine held eight rounds in a relatively short grip.

It has been reported that one or more of the original 1907 prototypes was lost or stolen during return to the factory after the tests. If this is so, it may have been partly responsible for the company's initial rejection of the field trial contract. Without the original test guns to examine, planning improvements would have been difficult.

Certainly, theft played a large part in the history of the Savage 45. The original shipment of 200 field trial pistols arrived at Springfield five short. Contemporary rumors credited the shortage to theft by foreign agents. Savage shipped five replacement pistols within a few weeks. However, many of the pistols developed problems with the magazines feeding improperly or unlatching prematurely. The 200 guns were shipped back to the factory for modification. This time, 72 of them were lost or stolen in transit. One can imagine Savage's frustration, but the company built more pistols, and the full number was tested in troop tests during 1910–1911.

The heavy recoil of the Savage worked against it. One Ordnance tester was reported to have said that 500 rounds from the Savage was equivalent to 2000 rounds from the Colt. The recoil was not only uncomfortable for the shooter, it was harder on the pistol's own internal parts.

The end came during the final 6000-round endurance firing between the Savage and the improved Colt, in March, 1911. Both pistols fired 1000 rounds without problems, but the Savage's recoil began to take its toll.

The Colt, with inventor John M. Browning — then 56 years old — looking on, fired through the entire 6000 rounds without a problem.

The Savage would have outperformed most pistols, then or now, but it could not match that performance. In

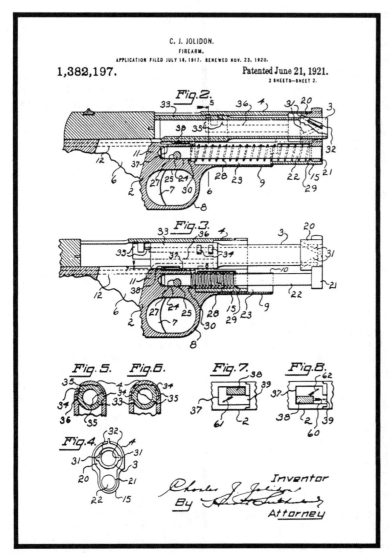

C. J. JOLIDON.
FIREARM.
APPLICATION FILED JULY 14, 1917. RENEWED NOV. 23, 1920.

1,382,197.

Patented June 21, 1921.
2 SHEETS—SHEET 2.

Charles Jolidon's pistol was a rotating-barrel modification of the Colt 1911. It functioned satisfactorily, but was not adopted.

the final 1000 rounds, the Savage malfunctioned 31 times and five parts developed defects.

With the completion of the trials, Savage concentrated on its line of sporting rifles and the Searle-de-signed pocket pistols in 32 and 380 calibers. These scaled-down pistols were selling well, whereas the big 45, having lost the trials, was of relatively little interest to the general public.

There is some question as to how many Savage 45 pistols were made. Only a few prototypes were apparently made

for the 1907 trials. Two-hundred had been ordered for the troop trials, but replacement of the stolen guns would have pushed that number to at least 277. It is logical that Savage, with the machinery ready to make a basically good pistol, would have made at least some for civilian sales. Various authorities have estimated the number of such additional guns at between 100 and 300.

The Savage pistol deserves a great deal of credit. Without the tough competition it offered Colt, there would not have been the need to refine the

1911 pistol to the peak of perfection it finally attained.

These trials and the subsequent adoption of the Model 1911 put an end to military efforts to develop a pistol on their own.

In the years between 1907–1909, the recoil-operated Pearce-Hawkins pistol was developed at Springfield Armory. The subsequent competition between the Savage and Colt pistols overshadowed all other weapons, and work on the Pearce-Hawkins was brought to a close.

The Phillips, also developed at Springfield Armory, was a departure from other designs in that it was gas-operated. At least one specimen was completed and tested, but it was not considered for service. The superiority of the new Colt design left little chance for such new developments.

Still, in 1912 another pistol was submitted for U.S. Army trial that had no possibility of serious consideration, but was of interest. From 1904, small quantities of the Danish Schou-boe pistol had been produced in a special 11.35mm cartridge. The pistol was manufactured at the Dansk Re-kylriffel Syndikat (DRS), Copenhagen, which produced Madsen machine guns. The pistol's inventor, Jens Schouboe, was Chief Engineer at DRS, and was able to keep the pistol in production in spite of its limited popularity.

Schouboe had started with a 7.65mm pistol in 1903. He wanted to make a large-bore military pistol but was faced with the limitations of his simple blowback system. He found that an extremely light bullet at high velocity would keep pressures within the limits of his design.

The 11.35mm Schouboe pistol was about the same caliber as the U.S. 45, but used a very different cartridge. The case was much shorter than that of the 45 ACP, but the big difference was in the design of the bullet. A cupronickel jacket covered a core of pine wood, protected at the base by a plug of aluminum. Weight was only about 63 grains. A heavy charge of powder pushed this light bullet at over 1600 fps. Accuracy was not particularly good, but was considered adequate for close-range military use. Penetration was surprisingly good.

Several variations of the 11.35mm Schouboe pistol were made, and it is not certain which one was tested by the U.S. Army at Springfield. The pistol functioned satisfactorily, but interest was focused on the high-velocity round it fired.

With the extensive testing of 1907–1911 just past, there was no chance for the Schouboe, but after its test, the Ordnance Department made up a lot of 45 ACP cartridges with wood-core bullets. Fired from the 1911 pistol, accuracy was very poor, and such experimentation stopped.

The Schouboe was never popular, even in Denmark. It was, however, the only native Danish pistol. For a time, the pistols were awarded as marksmanship prizes for Army officer cadets.

When Jens Schouboe retired from DRS in 1917, production of his pistols ended. In all probability, no more than 500 to 600 11.35mm pistols had been made.

As world war spread across Europe after 1914, there was renewed interest in military arms, and other pistols were offered for consideration.

Remington Arms Company had developed a 45-caliber pistol designed by John D. Pedersen of Jackson, Wyoming, and submitted it for U.S. Navy tests in 1917. The Remington pistol was favorably received by the Navy and contract negotiations were in progress. Then, on April 6, 1917, the United States entered the war.

The national interest lay in getting the greatest number of weapons possible into the hands of troops. Machinery to build the Colt pistol was already in operation. Instead of producing the Pedersen design, Remington was given a contract for 1911 pistols. The firm thus became one of the three manufacturers of 1911 pistols during World War I, the other manufacturers being Colt and Springfield Armory. There were 21,676 Remington 1911s made.

The Remington 45, the Pedersen design variously noted as the Model

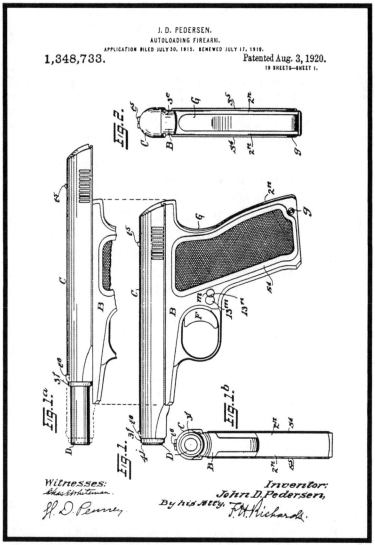

J. D. PEDERSEN.
AUTOLOADING FIREARM.
APPLICATION FILED JULY 30, 1915. RENEWED JULY 17, 1919.

1,348,733.

Patented Aug. 3, 1920.
10 SHEETS—SHEET 1.

Witnesses:
Inventor:
John D. Pedersen,
By his Atty.

Pedersen's excellent pistol design, although not produced in 45-caliber, went on to become the popular Remington Model 51 pocket pistol.

1917 or Model 53, was never produced. The single existing specimen became resident in the Remington museum.

Pedersen gained fame as the inventor of the World War I "Pedersen Device." He continued his interest in semi-automatic arms, and developed both rifles and pistols. In the post-war years, Remington used the Pedersen design in a successful pocket pistol, the Model 51, which was offered in 32 and 380 calibers. Although the two firms had been competitors since cap-and-ball days, Remington never again

challenged Colt in the field of big-bore military sidearms.

U.S. entry into the war had dashed Remington's chances of a contract for their new design, but the growing need for arms raised the hopes of other inventors during the wartime period.

In the summer of 1917, a new 45 pistol, the Grant Hammond, was submitted. Hammond, of Hartford, Connecticut, had been working on automatic pistol designs since about 1913. Around 1915, he concentrated his efforts on a relatively simple recoil-operated design which is sometimes referred to as the "Liberty" pistol.

His design seemed to studiously avoid any characteristics of the Colt 1911, and used a long exposed barrel, a hollow receiver and a cylindrical bolt. In many respects, the pistol is similar to a late White-Merrill prototype, and it is possible Hammond may have known ofthat earlier pistol.

based on the 1911 and his trial specimen was made from a commercial 1911, but modified to use a rotating barrel.

Jolidon's design actually decreased the number of parts needed and simplified some of the machining. The specimen provided apparently performed satisfactorily in an Ordnance test, but there was never any real possibility of production. The time spent to retool for a new design would have more than offset any gains the simplification would have provided.

reappeared later in different forms.

The double-action feature, introduced by the 1907 Knoble, was used three decades later in some German pistols. Now, most new designs have double-action mechanisms.

The increased capacity of a detachable staggered magazine appeared with the 1907 Savage. After several decades, it reappeared with the 1935 Browning and now seems almost mandatory for any new centerfire automatic.

The push-button magazine release was introduced by the Luger, quickly adapted to the Colt, and has been almost universal for big-bore automatics. The first attempt at an ambidextrous release came with the Savage.

Different methods of loading and cocking by the shooting hand were introduced by the early White-Merrill pistols. Several European designs appeared between the wars, but were short lived. Just recently, new concepts of one-handed cocking have gained acceptance with the Heckler & Koch P9S and P7 pistols.

Gas-operated pistols — the Wildey and the Eagle — have recently appeared, recalling the Phillips pistol of Springfield Armory experiments.

With the emphasis on speed of reloading found in modern action shooting competition, we may even someday see reintroduced the magazine-ejecting feature of the 1917 Grant Hammond.

The Colt 1911 design lives on, and remains essentially unchanged. It is still considered by many to be the best pistol in the world. The also-rans are all gone, but some of their features influence modern design.

> BY THE END OF THE 1907–1911 TEST TRIALS, THE 1911 COLT EMERGED AS THE MOST THOROUGHLY-TESTED, MOST RELIABLE AND MOST POWERFUL SEMI-AUTOMATIC PISTOL IN THE SERVICE OF ANY COUNTRY. BY 1918 IT HAD BEEN PROVEN IN BATTLE, WAS FAMILIAR TO MILLIONS AS A MILITARY ARM, AND WAS AVAILABLE COMMERCIALLY. THERE WAS LITTLE INCENTIVE FOR ANYONE TO INTRODUCE A COMPETING BIG-BORE AUTOMATIC.

The most interesting feature of the Grant Hammond pistol is the automatic ejection of the magazine after the last round has been fired. As the last round is fed, the magazine follower sets a spring-powered ejector mechanism. Then, as the action recoils from firing the last shot, the magazine catch is mechanically released and the magazine is ejected from the butt.

Aside from that novel feature, Hammond's pistol could not offer any challenge to the Colt. It was not considered for service.

During the 1930s, Hammond became associated with High Standard Manufacturing Company. The experimental 45-caliber High Standard pistols ofthat period show some similarities to his 1917 pistol.

If the Colt 1911 could not be replaced, perhaps it could be improved? At least one inventor felt that if the 1911 could be simplified, it could be made faster and greater numbers could be produced.

Charles J. Jolidon, of Hartford, submitted a new design in 1917. Jolidon had had an uncertain relationship with Colt as an inventor and was familiar with the Colt pistols. His design was

When the war ended, there was little reason to consider this design further. Jolidon worked on a series of blowback pocket pistols, none of which attained any success.

If there is any negative feature about the 1911, it is that it discouraged development of alternate concepts.

Automatic pistol development in the early stages at the turn of the century was closely related to the quest for military contracts. By the end of the 1907–1911 test trials, the 1911 Colt emerged as the most thoroughly-tested, most reliable and most powerful semi-automatic pistol in the service of any country.

By 1918 it had been proven in battle, was familiar to millions as a military arm, and was available commercially. There was little incentive for anyone to introduce a competing big-bore automatic.

Still, the Colt's early rivals had influences. The rejected pistols represented a variety of concepts. Many were suppressed by the Colt's superiority, but

Colt's 455 Model 1911:
The First Variation

▌ John Malloy

T HE COLT MODEL 1911 Is Probably The Most Widely Copied Pistol Ever Designed. Outright Copies And Numerous Variations Have Been Made Throughout The World.

The traditional caliber has been the original 45 ACP, but variations have been made for a number of calibers down to 22 Long Rifle. Only once has the 1911 design been produced for a cartridge larger than 45. During World War I, Colt manufactured their pistol for the 455 Webley Automatic cartridge.

This self-loading pistol was adopted by Great Britain, giving the British military a substitute standard side-arm actually more reliable than the one it replaced. It was the first caliber variation of Colt's then-new automatic, and turned out to be — by a small margin — the largest caliber for which the 1911 was ever chambered.

With the benefit of hindsight, World War I was almost inevitable. The event that sparked it was the assassination of Archduke Ferdinand of Austria/Hungary by a Serbian. Within a month Austria, supported by Germany, declared war on Serbia. The alliances that had been developed to prevent war served only to drag in other countries once it began.

Czarist Russia, allied with Serbia and also with democratic France, began to mobilize. Germany issued ultimatums to both Russia and France, apparently attempting to frighten those countries into a neutral position. This strategy failed,

and Germany planned to defeat France before the huge but poorly organized Russian army could be made ready for action. The German army swept into neutral Belgium to attack France.

England was pledged to uphold Belgian neutrality and, at any rate, could not afford to have France's channel ports fall under German domination. British forces went to war against Germany.

The British were poorly prepared for war. The British War Department began programs to increase armament production. One of the actions taken was to arrange for the manufacture of large quantities of small arms in the United States.

Among these contracts, semi-automatic pistols were ordered from Colt's Patent Firearms Manufacturing Company of Hartford, Connecticut. These pistols were to be chambered for the British 455 Webley Automatic cartridge, which had been adopted by the Royal Navy just a year or so before the outbreak of hostilities.

The United States was officially neutral at that time, but American sympathies were with Britain and France. Under the policy of neutrality, manufacturers could supply arms to any country. However, the

The 455-caliber Colt Model 1911 can be distinguished by the "Calibre 455" slide marking and the "W" prefix to the serial number.

British blockade, begun in November, 1914, prevented any great amount of material from going to the Central Powers.

Thus, the pistols were manufactured by Colt and delivered. They saw service in the hands of the Royal Navy and possibly other units. Following the defeat of Germany in November, 1918, they were recalled by the British War Department. Subsequently reissued to the Royal Air Force in the early 1920s, the 455s remained in British service until after World War II. They were then declared surplus and sold, primarily to American buyers.

The cartridge for which these pistols were chambered is known variously as the 455 Eley, 455 Webley & Scott or 455 Webley Automatic. It has a straight, semi-rimmed case, similar in general dimensions to that of the later 45 ACP. Its blunt, 224-grain bullet at 700 fps was considered an effective man-stopper.

The cartridge was developed much earlier for use in the Webley 1903 self-loading pistol, of which only a few experimental pieces were made. A year or so later, the Webley Model 1904, in caliber 455, did reach production and a small number were sold. This pistol was a real pioneer. If we do not consider the 45-caliber Mars and the 11.35mm Bergmann, which were essentially experimental arms, the

Webley 1904 was the first commercial self-loading English pistol and the first large-caliber semi-automatic pistol ever produced anywhere.

The 1904 was beautifully made, but was large, heavy and expensive, and relatively few were sold. Nevertheless, it was one of the first serious attempts to compete with the big-bore stopping power of the revolver. Development continued, with other versions appearing in 1906 and 1909.

By 1912, Webley & Scott had developed what they considered a satisfactory 455 semi-automatic pistol. Opening of the breech was delayed by vertical displacement of the barrel through a system of inclined grooves on the barrel and receiver. The pistol was much lighter and more compact than the 1904. Under the designation "Pistol, Self-Loading, .455, Mark I," it was placed in service in 1913 as the sidearm of the Royal Navy. It was issued to all naval units and to the Royal Marines. The Army retained the 455 Webley revolver. The 1913 pistol, with its 5-inch barrel, weighed a reasonable 39 ounces, and was only 8½ inches long.

From the left view, markings were the same as contemporary 45-caliber pistols, prior to additional markings by the British.

However, the precision machining of the inclined tongue-and-groove locking system did not lend itself to reliable functioning under adverse conditions. Foreign material such as sand or dirt in the mechanism could put it out of commission. It was thus suitable for service at sea, but not well suited for landing parties. For land use, this questionable functioning made it inferior to the Webley service revolver and the recently adopted pistol of the United States, the 1911 Colt.

The Webley pistol had other drawbacks. The hammer location made cocking difficult. With the shooting hand, the straight angle and protruding grip safety gave the 1913 grip an awkward feel; it did not "point" naturally. The V-type recoil spring under the right grip was a poten-tial source of trouble — if the brittle grip were broken, the spring could be lost, putting the pistol out of service. Nevertheless, under favorable conditions the pistol functioned well, was accurate, and handled a cartridge with good man-stopping characteristics.

By August, 1914, when England entered the war against Germany, fewer than four thousand of these pistols had been made. Webley factories could not increase production of both the Army revolver and the new Navy self-loader; they concentrated on revolver production.

A spur to this decision may have been the fact that, by this time, the new pistol's problem with reliability had begun to show up. During sustained firing, stoppages could be caused just by the powder residue from previous rounds.

The War Department supplemented the Naval pistol supply by obtaining Colt Model 1911 pistols, modified to take the 455 Webley Automatic cartridge. And the choice proved a good one. The Colt pistol was thoroughly reliable, well-suited to handle a large and powerful military cartridge.

Colt introduced the big-bore semi-automatic pistol to the United States in the form of their Model 1905. The cartridge introduced with this pistol was to become known as the 45 Automatic Colt Pistol (45 ACP). The 45 ACP is rimless, slightly shorter and slightly more powerful than the British 455 Webley Automatic round. Still, considering their independent development, the cartridges are surprisingly similar.

Colt's 1905 pistol utilized the Brown-

Parts of the 455 are the same as those for a 45, but there are a number of small dimensional differences.

ing double-link locking system that had been introduced with its 38-caliber pistol of 1900. Designed by John M. Browning, locking and unlocking was accomplished by vertical displacement of the barrel. This movement was accomplished by parallel links at the front and rear of the barrel.

The 45-caliber 1905 pistol was the first large-caliber semi-automatic pistol to be commercially manufactured in the United States. With its 5-inch barrel, it was only 8 inches long and weighed about 33 ounces. Light, flat and compact, it was powerful and generally reliable, and stayed in production until replaced by the Model 1911.

The 1905 Colt and the 45 ACP cartridge formed the basis for the 1907 U.S. Army test trials.

These Army trials, which began in 1907 and ended in 1911, were a milestone in the development of the semiautomatic pistol. The end result was the most reliable large-caliber pistol in the world.

The program of tests had been drawn up to determine the type of side-arm best suited to military service. Both revolvers and automatics were subjected to the most extensive testing that had been done to that time. As a result, a 45-caliber revolver was adopted as an interim measure, but field trials continued with Colt and Savage automatics. During these trials, modifications and improvements were made. Both companies submitted redesigned versions for a final series of tests in 1911. John M. Browning made design changes on the new Colt and attended the final tests in person. When the grueling schedule was over, the new Colt had completed the tests, including a six-thousand-round endurance test, without a malfunction. The Colt was adopted on March 29 as "Pistol, Caliber .45, Model 1911."

As adopted, the pistol had a 5-inch barrel and weighed about 38 ounces. The unlocking was still accomplished by downward movement of the barrel, but the barrel had only one link at the rear, with the muzzle supported by a barrel bushing. It had both thumb and grip safeties. For better pointing characteristics, the grip-to-bore angle had been changed

Those Colt 455s issued to the Royal Air Force were handstamped R.A.F. or RAF on the frame forward of the slide release. (Courtesy of Howard J. Nickel)

from 84 degrees to 74 degrees. The 1911 was offered by Colt to the commercial market, replacing the 1905.

Probably no other pistol had ever been so thoroughly tested or had such a deserved reputation for reliability. It was the obvious selection for manufacture in 455-caliber when the British began looking for supplementary supplies of pistols.

The similarity in dimensions between the 45 ACP and the 455 Webley Automatic cartridges allowed the Colt 1911 pistol to be readily modified to the British round. In general size and shape, the 455 cartridge resembles the 45 ACP. However, it is semi-rimmed, not rimless. The bullet is blunt and more flattened at the point than that of the 45. The case of the 455 is only slightly longer, but in overall length, the 455 cartridge is actually slightly shorter, due to its flatter bullet. Case body diameters are essentially the same.

In power, the two cartridges were similar. The 455's 224-grain bullet left the muzzle at about 750 feet per second, while the contemporary loading of the 45 used a 230-grain bullet with a muzzle velocity of about 800 feet per second.

The similarity in dimensions and power permitted relatively straightforward production of the 1911 pistol in 455-caliber.

External dimensions remained the same. Visually, the 455 pistol can be distinguished from the 45 only by markings. Legends are generally the same as contemporary commercial 45s, with the exception of the caliber designation "CALIBRE .455" on the right slide and a "W" prefix to the serial number on the right frame. The magazine is marked "CAL .455 ELEY" on its base. Most specimens are found stamped with the broad arrow of

the British War Department on the frame. Those issued to the Royal Air Force have "R.A.F." or "RAF" on the left side of the frame.

That portion of the barrel exposed in the ejection port may be unmarked, or may bear only a proofmark, or the ".455" caliber designation. One observed specimen, however, had this informative legend:

.455" SL .923

6 GRs NPP 10

225"-BULLET

Mechanically, the differences are subtle but are more numerous than might be imagined. Comparison of a 455 pistol with a World War I 45-caliber 1911 revealed these points:

The barrel is the obvious difference, as it must handle the British cartridge. The bore and groove diameters are, respectively, .451-inch and .458-inch, much larger than the corresponding .444-inch and .451-inch of the 45 barrel. The six-groove, left-twist rifling is of the style of the 45. To accommodate the longer case of the 455, the chamber is deeper with less forward shoulder. A groove in the hood allows the cartridge to headspace on the rim. The feed ramp is broader, to accommodate the blunt British bullet.

The barrel is about .005-inch larger in outside diameter, in keeping with its larger bore. Strangely enough, though, the diameter over the chamber is about .005-inch smaller than that of the 45. Another surprise is the width of the link-attachment lug on the underside of the barrel, which is .007-inch smaller than the lug of the 45 barrel. The slide is a close fit to this lug, and a 45 barrel will not go into the 455 slide. These subtle dimensional differences may have been planned by Colt to prevent a 45 barrel being installed into a 455 slide when both were assembled concurrently. Of course, 45 barrels were later installed in some surplus 455s; a small amount of file work would probably allow this.

Except for the narrow slot for the barrel lug, the slide exhibits little difference. Either assembled slide will go onto the other frame. The 455 extractor has a different arc because of the larger rim diameter.

The magazine is wider, due to the larger diameter of the cartridge rim. Thus, a larger magazine-well cut was required in the frame. A 45 magazine will fit loosely in the 455 frame, but a 455 magazine will not go into the 45 frame. The clearance between the frame opening and the widest part of measured magazines turned out to be .012-inch for both the 455 and the 45.

The exact number of 455-caliber Colt 1911 pistols made has not been completely resolved. Likewise, the numbering system used is in some doubt.

For some time, it was thought that all the Colt 455s were in a special serial number range with a "W" prefix, beginning with W100001 and running to about W110000. This indicated a total of about 10,000 pistols produced. The reason for the choice of the "W" prefix is not known. It has been suggested that it represents "Webley," for the developer of the original 455 cartridge. Correct or not, it is easy to remember. There was some speculation that the serial numbers duplicated numbers assigned to military 45 production. If so, this would place manufacture during late 1914 and 1915. Some authorities, perhaps noting the intriguing similarity of the military serial numbers, have stated that production took place "about 1915." An idea that the "W" number replaced corresponding numbers in

Colt's commercial series production does not seem to be correct.

At any rate, information from British firearms historian Jim Stonley indicates that Colt 455 pistols were in use by British troops by the end of 1916.

Perhaps the most extensive research on the subject for the time was done by Donald F. Bady, author of Colt Automatic Pistols (1956, revised 1973). Bady reported that Colt records indicated a total production of 13,510. The first 1500 pistols were reportedly made on Colt commercial frames and numbered within Colt's "C" series, C29001-C30500. (This would indicate production during the year 1916.) After this initial run, the "W" series pistols were shipped, in the range W100001 to about W110700. Thus, the total delivered during the war years would have been about 12,200. Another British contract was supposedly negotiated near the end of the war. If total production of 13,510 is correct, then approximately

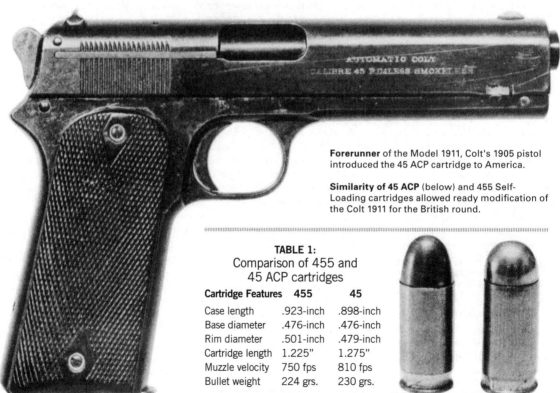

Forerunner of the Model 1911, Colt's 1905 pistol introduced the 45 ACP cartridge to America.

Similarity of 45 ACP (below) and 455 Self-Loading cartridges allowed ready modification of the Colt 1911 for the British round.

TABLE 1:
Comparison of 455 and 45 ACP cartridges

Cartridge Features	455	45
Case length	.923-inch	.898-inch
Base diameter	.476-inch	.476-inch
Rim diameter	.501-inch	.479-inch
Cartridge length	1.225"	1.275"
Muzzle velocity	750 fps	810 fps
Bullet weight	224 grs.	230 grs.

1300 pistols may have been delivered from this later contract, probably after the war. Bady points out that a single pistol in the W124000 range may indicate that the numbers were not continuous with the earlier series, but may have continued after a gap.

The number of postwar pistols may be greater. A collectors' publication recently reported this notation from a Colt shipping book for March/April 1919: "455 Autos 5000 shipped."

As recent collector interest in the 455s increased, other numbers — primarily lower numbers — have come to light. Pistols observed by the writer and reported by collectors include numbers in these series:

The Webley & Scott 455 Mark I pistol introduced the 455 Self-Loading cartridge into British service in 1913. (Courtesy of Robert C. Blackstone)

W19000
W29000
W40000
W60000-W69000
W71000-W78000
W92000-W99000

Suggestions to account for these lower numbers include early production for trial purposes and early purchase by the British for colonial service. A possibility exists in the later assignment of low numbers to fill gaps in previous series.

At any rate, the dates, the total number and the numbering system of the 1911 455s remain open to some speculation. The subject is of continuing interest to collectors, and information may yet be uncovered that will clear up the uncertainty that still surrounds the numbering of the 455 pistols.

Whatever the number, the pistols were ordered to re-

place the Navy's 1913 Webley and were, logically, used by the Royal Navy. There have been reports that some British and Canadian army units were issued these pistols. While this is possible, it does not seem likely — primarily because of the limited production of the ammunition, which was distributed through naval supply channels. In addition, the Canadians were already using Colt pistols in 45-caliber, and preparations were under way to manufacture 45s under contract in Canada.

There does seem to be documented use of the 455s by the Royal Flying Corps prior to its 1918 reorganization into the Royal Air Force. After World War I, most of the Colt 455s were turned over to the Royal Air Force during the early 1920s, probably beginning in 1923. Most specimens thus have "R.A.F" or "RAF" stamped on the left side of the frame, forward of the slide stop. The stamping was done by hand on a local basis, and may be somewhat irregularly done. No RAF-stamped pistols seem to have been reported in publications with serial numbers under W100000. This may have led to the early idea that numbers began there.

The ammunition for these pistols essentially became obsolete between the wars. Most cartridges in collections are

TABLE 2:
Comparison of 455 and 45 Pistol Dimensions

Barrel:

Bore diameter	.458-inch	.4515-inch
Groove diameter	.451-inch	.444-inch
Outside diameter	.579-inch	.574-inch
Width over chamber	.683-inch	.688-inch
Width of lug	.355-inch	.362-inch

Slide:

Inside, at chamber	.725-inch	.731-inch

Frame:

Magazine well	.573-inch	.559-inch

Magazine:

Max. width	.561-inch	.547-inch

Magazines for the 1911 455 are stamped "CAL 455" above the lanyard loop and "ELEY" below. The magazine is wider than that of a 45.

dated as World War I production. Stories have been told that RAF personnel were sometimes issued 45 ACP ammunition to be used in their 455s. The 455 ammunition was actually reintroduced in 1940, but the use of 45 cartridges in the 455 pistols is a real possibility. During the World War II years, the British military had large stores of 45 ACP ammunition acquired for their Thompsons.

The pistols remained in RAF service through the early part of World War II. Stonley reports that they were transferred to Air/Sea Rescue units about 1942. After the war, they were declared surplus, along with large quantities of other British military equipment.

In 1957, the FN Browning 9mm pistol was adopted, and surplus pistols were sold off. The first ad noted that offered the Colt 455s for retail sale was in the March, 1960, American Rifleman. The price was $39.95. When the 455s arrived on these shores, 455 Automatic ammunition was not readily available. To spur sales, some local sellers priced them lower than 45 Automatics, and ads proclaimed that the 455s "will shoot 45 ACP."

Shooting any cartridge other than the one for which the gun is chambered is not a practice to be generally recommended. The shooter of an old firearm is the custodian of a bit of history and should take care to preserve it. Still, no less an authority than the late Gen. Julian S. Hatcher reported extensive shooting of 45 ACP ammunition in a 455.

Before considering such a practice, it is wise to examine the relationship of the cartridge to the mechanical parts of the pistol.

The 455 round positions its semi-rim in a groove in the barrel hood to maintain proper headspace. Because the cartridge feeds from the magazine at an angle, there is a large clearance between the breech face and the extractor hook. In firing position, the extractor hook is well forward of the semi-rim, making no contact.

When a 45 ACP round is inserted into the 455 chamber, the rimless round slides forward of the hood groove. It would be expected that the shorter case would be held by the extractor against the firing-pin blow, with resulting strain on the hook. However, the case is only .025-inch shorter than that of the 455. In the pistol examined, the clearance between breech face and extractor hook is an even .100-inch, enough to let the 45 cartridge position on the case mouth in the normal manner. The firing pin can easily reach the primer and the case will, of course, move back against the breech face when the cartridge fires. These relationships can be seen from the underside of the assembled slide.

Still, it is something of a surprise to find that 45 ACP cartridges work so well. Both military loads and several varieties of cast-bullet handloads fed and functioned perfectly. Even blunt wadcutters such as Lyman's 452389 and 452309 gave no trouble. The broad feed ramp of the 455 barrel apparently aids the feeding of such bullets.

Accuracy is not particularly good. This is no surprise, considering that the .452-inch bullets are passing through a

Visually indistinguishable from a 45, the 455-caliber 1911 is seldom seen at firing ranges.

The 455 cartridge (left) can be approximated by a careful handloader using cases made from 45 Colt, 45 Auto Rim or 451 Detonics brass.

.458-inch bore, barely riding the tops of the lands. Yet, groups at twenty-five yards proved good enough for informal plinking or emergency short-range defense. "Tipping" of one or more bullets in each five-shot group was evident. Also, three or four shots might form a fairly close group, with the remainder wide. Translated to fifty yards, only three or four shots could be counted on to hit the paper of a conventional fifty-yard bullseye target.

It is possible that erratic ignition may result from different positions — some forward, some rearward — of the cartridges in the chamber. This could add to the detrimental effect of the oversize bore on accuracy.

Accuracy should certainly be better using original 455 cartridges. However, such rounds are now collector's items. Most specimens observed date back to World War I and might not even fire.

It is possible to make ammunition that is close to the original specifications. Modern 45 Colt and 45 Auto-Rim cases can be converted to the semi-rimmed configuration of the 455. In each case, the rim must be turned to .500-inch diameter and an extractor groove cut. Readily done on a lathe, it can also be accomplished in the ordinary home workshop. Inserting a 45-caliber jacketed bullet into a case will keep the walls from collapsing, and it can be chucked into a ½-inch drill. Carefully filing with a three-cornered file while turning the case will allow thinning the rim and cutting the groove.

The 45 Colt case will be too long and must be trimmed to .923-inch. The 45 Auto-Rim case will be slightly too short, but will headspace on the semi-rim.

Loading is easily accomplished with 45 ACP dies. Among common shell-holders, one made for the 45 Colt will be a bit loose but will work.

Another possibility is the use of 451 Detonics Magnum cases. These cases, obtained from Detonics Manufacturing Corporation of Bellevue, WA, are of the general dimensions of the 45 ACP, but are .94-inch long. They can be easily trimmed and used without further modification. Although not semi-rimmed, the case will headspace on the mouth for firing, and will feed and extract reliably.

In order to appeal to American shooters, ads for surplus 455s proclaimed that they could be used with 45 ACP ammunition.

A 45 ACP shell-holder can be used, and the cartridge will function through either 455 or 45 magazines.

It is difficult to obtain bullets of the proper diameter. I was fortunate to have access to a mould that cast semi-wadcutter bullets at .457-inch diameter. These bullets were lubricated by hand and used as cast for reloading the modified cases. Groups were noticeably improved. Hollow-base bullets should work well, but a single test with Lyman's 450229 was disappointing.

However, with some experimentation, it should be possible for a careful handloader to produce ammunition that will give excellent accuracy in the Colt 455. Being realistic, though, the exercise is probably academic.

The Colt 1911 455 is a collector's item of some historical interest. Most existing specimens will never be shot, and if they are in mint condition, they probably ought not to be. As with any other collectible firearm, wear and tear will detract from the value. For those owners who just want a few shots to try out a less-than-perfect specimen, 45 ACP cartridges will work well enough.

Considering that their history of production is still indefinite, it is even more difficult to speculate on how many Colt 455s remain in existence. Certainly an appreciable number must have been lost in service during the two World Wars.

Model 1911 455s are occasionally seen at gun shows and in collection displays. Should you get a chance to examine one, you will be looking at an interesting and seldom-recognized pistol. Produced because of wartime need, it has the distinction of being both the first caliber variation and the largest caliber variation of the Colt Model 1911 series.

SELECTED BIBLIOGRAPHY
Bady, Donald F.
Colt Automatic Pistols.
Alhambra, CA: Bordon, 1973.

Ezell, Edward C.
Handguns of the World.
Harrisburg, PA: Stackpole, 1981.

Goodman, Roy G. "The .455 Webley & Scott Pistol."
American Rifleman,
Vol. 110, No. 5 (May, 1962), pp. 40–43.

Hatcher, Julian S.
Hatcher's Notebook.
Harrisburg, PA: Stackpole, 1962.

Hill, Bob. "Webley's Amazing Autos."
Guns & Ammo,
Vol. 18, No. 3 (March, 1974), pp. 26–29, 82.

Remling, John. "The Webley & Scott .455 Auto Pistol."
Guns,
Vol. XIX, No. 3–6 (June, 1973), pp. 37–39, 64–67.

Smith, W.H.B. and Joseph E. Smith.
Book of Pistols and Revolvers.
Harrisburg, PA: Stackpole, 1968.

Stonley, Jim. "The .455 Automatic Pistol in the British Services, Part One — The Webley .455 Automatic."
Guns Review,
Dec. 1978, pp. 728–732.

Stonley, Jim. "The .455 Automatic Pistol in the British Services, Part Two — Ammunition Troubles and Colt Automatic Purchases." Guns Review,
Jan. 1979, pp. 20–24.

Stonley, Jim. "The .455 Automatic Pistol in the British Services, Part Three-The Colt .455 Automatic."
Guns Review,
Feb. 1979, pp. 90–92.

Stonley, Jim. "Observed/Reported 'W' Prefix .455 Colt Auto Pistols.": Auto Mag,
Vol. XIX, Issue 5 (Aug, 1986), p. 105.

Stonley, Jim. ".455 Automatic Pistols in World War I — British Government Contracts."
Guns Review, March, 1987, pp. 188–190.

Williams, Mason. "Collecting 45s."
Shooting Times, Vol. 7, No. 4 (April, 1966), pp. 24–29.

Wilson, R.K.
Textbook of Automatic Pistols.
Plantersville, SC: Small Arms Technical Publishing Co., 1943.

Wilson, R.L.
The Colt Heritage.
New York: Simon & Schuster, 1979.

Wood, J.B. "Webley Automatic Pistols."
Shooting Times, Vol. 10, No. 1 (January, 1969), pp. 44–47, 53–54.

Tricks & Treats For Your 45

Drop-ins that might make a difference ▌ W.E. Sprague

I CAN THINK OF no other handgun that pistolsmiths have tuned, rebuilt, and modified to suit more goals and purposes than the M1911 45 ACP. The 45 automatic, as it's commonly called, reigns supreme in the realm of conventional bullseye shooting, dominates freestyle combat matches, is a potent contender in the sport of metallic silhouette shooting, and has only the 44 Magnum double-action revolver as a practical rival in bowling-pin competitions. And, of course, it has long since been accepted as the one to beat in the area of self-defense.

As a result of its widespread use, more modifications, adaptations and accessories have probably been devised for the M1911 than for any other handgun in history. Judging from the number of ads in the various shooting magazines, it's probably safe to say that more such modifications, adaptations and accessories exist for the 45 than for all other handguns combined. And though many of these require the services of a gunsmith, what are commonly called "add-on" or "drop-in" parts comprise the bulk of the trade and hold the greatest interest for the largest number of shooters. These are accessories of a type that can be installed at home with very little trouble, and range from simple, redesigned replacement parts on up through such major components as frames, slides and barrels.

Where barrels are concerned, the 45 owner can choose from a generous menu of replacements, including extended barrels that can be ported, or fitted with compensators, to help reduce recoil and promote faster follow-up shots. But whether extended or standard length, perhaps the most popular are corrosion-resistant stainless steel barrels.

While offered by many suppliers, these were pioneered back in the early 1970s by Bar-Sto Precision Machine, and today Bar-Sto offers them for virtually every pistol on the market, including, of course, the 45. With prices starting at about $135, Bar-Sto barrels are superbly finished, held to close dimensional tolerances, and include refinements such as radiused chamber mouths to help eliminate feeding problems. And, while their match-grade barrels must be professionally fitted, their standard barrels, for either the Government Model or Commander, can be had as drop-in units, providing the pistol is a genuine Colt. Barrels for clones and copies, Bar-Sto warns, may or may not require fitting; it depends on how faithful the copy is to the Colt.

A number of suppliers now offer stainless steel barrels that come with their own compensator units. Brownells, for example, widely known as a primary source for gunsmith tools and supplies, also offers a wide assortment of brand-name gun parts and accessories, including a dozen or so different "comp kits," as these barrel/compensator units are commonly called. The installation of most of them requires the services of a gunsmith, but several can be had as true drop-in units for either competition or self-defense guns.

One such is the Quadra-Comp II, developed by Centaur Systems. Priced at about $269.95, and available either directly from Centaur or through Brownells, it consists of a 5.5-inch bushingless tapered stainless barrel with a radiused chamber mouth; a dual-ported, dual-chambered compensator; a buffered, captive recoil spring with full-length recoil guide rod; and Centaur's exclusive adjustable slide stop system.

This latter piece is perhaps the most unusual feature of the Quadra-Comp II. The slide stop — which comes with a small roller, a specially dimensioned barrel link, and several shims of varying thickness — has a groove milled into the

This otherwise stock 45 has no less than ten drop-ins and add-ons from as many different suppliers.

Pioneered by Bar-Sto, stainless steel barrels are now offered by countless suppliers. Except in genuine Colts, they may require some fitting.

Lightweight replacement triggers, such as this ultra-light from Wilson, are available from many different suppliers.

Whichever — straight, standard, checkered, not — mainspring housing, it's there today.

Replacement grip safeties are made with a broad extension to keep the web of the hand from being pinched by the hammer.

Extended magazine catches — these from Ed Brown Products — provide a more positive magazine "drop."

top of its link pin contact area. By "stacking" the proper selection of shims in the groove (initially, a matter of trial and error), then topping them with the roller, consistent lock-up, and so greater accuracy, is achieved by a camming action that forces the chamber end of the barrel up against the rear of the slide, while forcing the muzzle end down against the front in sort of a V-block fashion. Extra shims, supplied with the system, can be used to compensate for wear.

This same slide stop system is part of another drop-in offering from Centaur. Called the Quadra-Lok "T" and priced at $179.95, it includes a stainless barrel (without a compensator) and a so-called universal bushing — which the latter, according to Centaur, fits any 45 slide, providing solid muzzle support and making the entire unit transferable to any M1911. Meant to enhance the accuracy of Tactical Class IPSC competition pistols, it will, of course, do the same for plain-vanilla 45s.

A far less costly means of improving the accuracy of a stock-barreled 45 is the Wilson-Dwyer Combat Group Gripper, a modified recoil spring guide from Wilson's Gun Shop. Retailing at around $26.95 for either the Government Model or the Commander, it has a special barrel link with a cam on its leading edge that engages a leaf spring in the rear of the guide; thus, as the slide moves forward into battery, the link is forced up and forward by the spring, which in turn forces the barrel up into the locking lugs in the slide. The result is a more consistent lock-up and greater accuracy than might be obtained in a standard production gun. In fact, according to many experts, the Gripper can provide a greater increase in accuracy than can be achieved with any other drop-in or accessory.

With the 45 that's fired a lot, it's a very good idea to protect it from the recurrent rearward impact of its slide, which, over time, can result in a cracked frame. So, for years now, several different suppliers have offered recoil buffers designed to do just that. Typical of these is the type made by Bar-Sto. Priced at

Designed to promote consistent lock-up, the Wilson-Dwyer Group Gripper seems to do more to improve the accuracy of a stock 45 than any other drop-in or accessory.

Precision made magazines, (below) such as these from Wilson, have special followers, extra-power springs and pads or bumpers to aid rapid magazine change.

Full-length recoil guide rods — this from Ed Brown Products — keep the recoil spring from kinking or binding.

$30 for either the Government Model or Commander, and made from the same quality stainless that Bar-Sto uses in its barrels, it consists of a standard recoil spring guide fitted with a strong spring-loaded plunger that extends beyond the forward end of the guide to contact the slide during recoil. When compressed by the moving slide, the plunger slows the final part of its rearward travel, thus easing the blow when it strikes the usual arresting surface. In addition, as the slide moves forward into battery, the plunger spring accelerates its closing, often improving feeding by supplying more energy to carry the cartridge forward.

Yet another way to offset the effects of the recoiling slide is Wilson's Combat Shok-Buff kit. With a price tag of only $6.75, the basic kit consists of a heavy-duty recoil spring and two injection-moulded poly fiber buffers, one of which is meant to be sandwiched between the spring and the pistol's recoil spring guide. Of the same shape and approximate thickness of the metal stop at the rear of the guide itself, the poly fiber buffer, good for 1000 rounds of hardball, absorbs the final impact of the rearward-moving slide. The poly fiber buffers, in packs of six, can be had without the heavy-duty spring for the same modest price, while at the top end of the price

scale ($36.95) is what might be called the deluxe version of the kit. This consists of six poly fiber buffers, an extra-power firing pin spring, a heavy-duty recoil spring, a "softball" target spring, and a full-length recoil guide rod and plug.

Full-length recoil guide rods, meant to take the place of the standard recoil spring guide, are in themselves popular drop-in items. These help to promote smoother functioning and longer recoil spring life by keeping the recoil spring from kinking or binding against the slide, which can slow the movement of the slide, and thus the cycling rate, whenever the gun is fired. They come with their own specially designed spring plugs and, often as not, are two-piece affairs joined by fine precision threads for ease of assembly. Typical of these is the two-piece unit designed by Ed Brown, renowned gunsmith and head of Ed Brown Products. At a cost of about $27.50, it's available for either the Government Model or Commander.

Some suppliers offer full-length recoil guide rods that incorporate additional features. Wilson's, for example, has a two-piece rod, priced at $39.95, that includes their aforementioned

Group Clipper as part of its design, thus affording the standard 45 with a factory barrel the advantages of a full-length rod plus the consistent lock-up and improved accuracy of the Group Gripper.

Consistent lock-up and improved accuracy are also added features of a full-length guide designed by Accu-Systems and available either directly or from J.P. Enterprises. Called the Dual Action Buffer Spring System, this $69.95 drop-in is really a two-piece rod with the pieces permanently joined in overlapping sections by a stout roll pin, and with a secondary spring contained within the breech-end section. This, in combination with its heavy-duty recoil spring and a head designed to match the curves and angles of the barrel link and lug, applies upward tension on the barrel and keeps the slide from slamming against its stop.

(Left) **Pioneered** by Pachmayr, wrap-around grips are now a standard. These from Hogue offer a slightly softer rubber, finger grips and the "pebble" finish.

(Right) **For those who prefer** them, Hogue offers replacement grips in a wide variety of exotic woods.

(Left) **King's Speed Grip** has ambidextrous palm swells, built-in magazine well, dual thumb guards and full lenght non-slip checkering.

(Left) **The Safariland 1911** Auto Combat Grip forms a "lip"or extension that forces the shooter's hand up against the trigger guard for increased stability and control.

Wilson's grip adaptor provides an inexpensive alternative to having the frontstrap checkered or stippled for a more solid hold.

Because of its adjustable slide stop system, the Quadra-Comp II from Centaur Systems is one of the few drop-in comp kits that requires no gunsmith fitting whatsoever. (Bilal photo)

Richard Heinie's comp kit (below) is a true drop-in for 99 percent of all Colts. Clones and copies, though, may require some fitting.

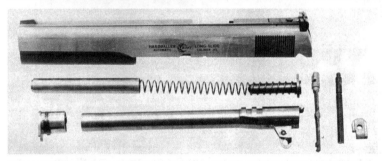

The Long Slide Kit from AMT, which includes a 7-inch stainless barrel and slide, replaces the entire upper assembly of a stock 45, providing a greater sight radius and thus improved accuracy.

Yet another "added-feature" full-length guide rod is one designed by master gunsmith Richard Heinie and available from his company, Heinie Specialty Products. Priced at $65, it's made from heavy tungsten steel and, replacing the .5-ounce factory spring guide, adds 3.5 ounces of weight to the front of the pistol, thus reducing felt recoil and muzzle flip.

Two other popular items are redesigned replacements for the standard grip safety and mainspring housing. The former, another drop-in offered by virtually everyone in the trade, is made with a broad — or sometimes upswept — extension at its upper rear that sets back over the web of the hand to keep it from being pinched between the hammer and the tang of the standard safety. Often called a "beavertail" grip safety, it also helps position the gun more firmly in the hand.

Although many of the upswept versions require fitting and frame contouring by a competent gunsmith, the other type can usually be owner-installed quite easily, especially those made by King's Gunworks. Over the years, I've installed no less than a dozen of King's #203 grip safeties ($33 for the Colt Series 70, $35.50 for the Series 80) without any fitting whatsoever. At comparable prices, King's also offers a model to fit the Springfield frame, and one that's notched to allow the use of a Commander hammer with the Colt Government Model pistol.

Two reasons for replacing the factory mainspring housing would be that the 45 owner either wants one that's checkered or one that's flat (and checkered), rather than arched, because it affords a more comfortable hold. If the pistol is a genuine Colt — clones and copies might need a bit of fitting — several suppliers can oblige. Wilson, for one, has deeply checkered steel housings, either flat or arched, at a cost of $36.95 in blue and $39.95 in stainless. Pachmayr, for another, offers drop-in housings covered in checkered rubber at either $18.95 or $19.95, depending on the style.

Lightweight replacement triggers, with either plastic or aluminum finger pieces — and most with adjustable screw-type trigger stops — are available from several different sources. Pachmayr has one with a self-lubricating nylon finger piece at a cost of $14.95, while Wilson offers one at $17.95 with an alumi-

Characterized by a familiar white "Y" rear-sight outline, Millet sights offer a wide variety of popular replacements for the M1911.

Low light sights, like Millet's Tritium Night Sight, utilize a minuscule amount of a radioactive isotope, allowing them to be seen even in total darkness.

For the pistol owner who uses different bullet weights and loads, an adjustable rear sight, like this one from Pachmayr, is a highly desirable replacement.

King's "arsenal-type" front-sight staking tool can be used by almost anyone with the ability to handle a file and mallet, and with it, a profusion of both fixed and adjustable sights becomes available to the 45 owner.

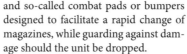

Lighter and less expensive than other red dot sights, the "epc" is chemically bonded to the gun, thus doing away with the need for a separate mount.

num finger piece that's further lightened by a trio of holes drilled through it.

Replacement magazines of plain steel in both standard and increased capacity are available from several vendors. Generally, though, anything over a ten-round length tends to make the gun cumbersome. Far more popular are standard length and eight-round magazines in stainless steel. Precision-made, they usually incorporate such features as specially designed followers meant to eliminate feeding failures, extra-power springs to resist "spring set,"

and so-called combat pads or bumpers designed to facilitate a rapid change of magazines, while guarding against damage should the unit be dropped.

Worthy of special mention is the magazine made by Eagle International. Priced at $31.50, and available in either natural or blackened stainless steel, it holds nine rounds, instead of seven, without increasing its overall length beyond that of a seven- or even eight-round magazine equipped with a combat pad. Its secret seems to be a unique constant force spring that takes up very little space inside the body, thus allowing it to hold two more rounds than a standard type with its conventional spring

compressed at the bottom. In any case, with one round in the chamber, the 45 equipped with an Eagle mag has more than a 42 percent increase in immediate firepower.

Another popular item offered by several suppliers is the extended magazine catch. Designed to be more accessible to the shooter's thumb, it generally consists of a standard catch to which extra length is added by way of a "button" attached to its protruding end with a screw that sets flush to the surface of the button after installation. Typical examples are those available from Ed Brown Products at a cost of $29.95 for either a blued or stainless steel version, or $31.95 for a hard

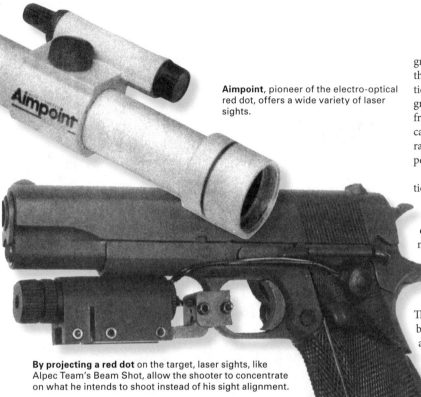

Aimpoint, pioneer of the electro-optical red dot, offers a wide variety of laser sights.

By projecting a red dot on the target, laser sights, like Alpec Team's Beam Shot, allow the shooter to concentrate on what he intends to shoot instead of his sight alignment.

chromed stainless model.

The item most often replaced by the 45 owner would seem to be the pistol's factory grips. Accordingly, there seems to be an almost unlimited assortment of available replacements in exotic woods, rubber and various plastics, making a proper choice a matter of knowing exactly what the owner wants from his replacements.

For the shooter who wants a well-balanced blend of beauty and function, a fine line of quasi-custom grips is offered by David Wayland, longtime master craftsman and grip designer, whose business name is Wayland Precision Wood Products. Called Classic+ Grips, they follow the factory shape, but are made a bit fuller, incorporating subtle changes that improve the hand-to-gun fit. A basic set in tropical wood with smooth finish and a German silver oval inlay (suitable for engraving) set in the right-hand panel costs $34.95, with hand-cut checkering, if desired, adding another $24 to $70, depending on the grade of checkering desired (deluxe, presentation, extra fine, etc.) and the number of lines per inch.

Similar replacements are available from Hogue Grips, a firm best known for its unique revolver Monogrip. The Hogue grips, though, more closely replicate the 45's original style, with the exception of one type that comes with finger grooves designed to enclose the pistol's front strap. Available in Pau Ferro, Goncalo Alves and comparable woods, they range in price from $34.95 to $42.95, depending on the style and kind of wood.

For those more interested in function than appearance, the choice is often a set of so-called wrap-arounds. Made of a tough synthetic rubber, or in some cases, a proprietary elastomer, they consist of a single piece, the center section or web of which completely encloses the smooth front strap of the grip frame, providing a positive, nonskid hold. The only problem confronting a would-be buyer would seem to be a confusing array of choices.

Pachmayr, for example, who introduced the concept back in 1974, now offers three different styles for the Government Model or Commander, each with slightly different features, and each at a cost of $30.50. Like all Pachmayr grips, they're made of tough neoprene rubber that affords positive contact with the shooter's hand and fingers. Further augmenting this contact, they are checkered to about 20 lines per inch.

Comparable wrap-around grips are offered by other suppliers, including Hogue. The Hogue grips, though, priced at $19.95, seem to be slightly larger in girth and are made from a slightly softer rubber. They're also made with finger grooves that force the hand up against the trigger guard for better recoil control. Instead of checkering, they have Hogue's customary "pebbled" finish.

A unique offering from Michaels of Oregon is a three-piece grip for the Colt Government Model and its various clones and siblings. It uses a separate center section or web, incorporating finger grooves, that locks into the cutouts of the grip frame by way of thin, integral "slabs" that approximate the size and shape of the cutouts, after which it's secured by the grip panels. At a cost of

The 45 is perhaps the first handgun in history for which independent makers have produced major components such as this frame from Essex Arms.

$17.95 a set, they're precision-moulded reproductions of hand-carved hardwood masters and are made of a specially formulated elastomer that's both lighter in weight and firmer than rubber.

If wrap-around grips have any particular failing, it's that many 45 owners find their ubiquitous black to be aesthetically lacking. In an effort to offset this, Radical Concepts (formerly R. J. Renner Co.) offers one-piece wrap-around grips in color. Aptly named "Radical Grips," and priced at $19.95 each, they're made of a proprietary elastomer that's virtually immune to chemical attack from oils and solvents. They also offer their wrap-arounds with the choice of a center section featuring a "grid" of fourteen evenly spaced 5mm holes, into which the shooter's fingers are firmly compressed each time the gun is gripped, virtually locking the hand in place.

But, "grid grip" or plain, the most obvious feature is, of course, color. Besides the usual black, they come in a smoky gray that complements stainless steel, as well as in a veritable rainbow of other colors: royal blue, coral, lime and yellow. One might wonder about the virtue of colors, aside from aesthetics, that is, but there are some practical aspects. For example, some owners maintain a "wardrobe" of grips, changing them whenever they grow a bit bored with those on their guns. And some few others literally color-code their otherwise identical pistols according to caliber, permitting a quick selection.

There is yet another practical aspect that, hopefully, none of us will ever have to discover the hard way. According to at least one legal expert, if ever the day should come that you find yourself in court, defending yourself for having used deadly force to stop a malicious intruder in your home, a set of colored grips could work to your advantage. It's not uncommon these days for a prosecutor (or a plaintiffs attorney in a civil case) to try to convince a jury that defendants in such cases are monsters of some kind

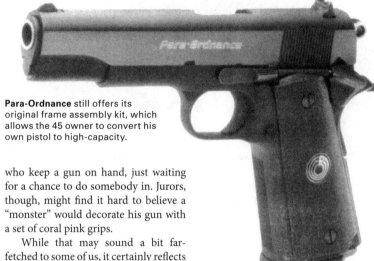

Para-Ordnance still offers its original frame assembly kit, which allows the 45 owner to convert his own pistol to high-capacity.

who keep a gun on hand, just waiting for a chance to do somebody in. Jurors, though, might find it hard to believe a "monster" would decorate his gun with a set of coral pink grips.

While that may sound a bit far-fetched to some of us, it certainly reflects one of the major purposes behind Radical's introduction of colored grips. As a company spokesman put it, "we want to make handguns look more like the sport equipment they are, and not the tools of crime that the media like to paint them."

Though not exactly wrap-arounds as such, there are two replacement grips for the 45 that accomplish much the same thing, and in one case, even more. One is King's Speed Grip, and the other is Safariland's 1911 Auto Combat Grip.

Flared slightly forward at the bottom, the Safariland grip wraps around the lower end of the front strap, forming a lip or extension that forces the shooter's hand up against the trigger guard for increased stability and control. Made of a proprietary plastic, it's embossed with checkered panels and comes in black for $19.55, or in brown simulated wood burl for only a dollar more.

Costing $49.95, the King's Speed Grip, made of a hard, black polymer, follows the same basic design, but incorporates several additional features, such as ambidextrous palm swells, a built-in magazine well, dual thumb guards, and full-length non-slip checkering. The swells provide a more hand-filling hold for either a right- or left-handed shooter, while for the shooter who prefers a high thumb hold, the twin guards prevent ejection failures caused by friction between the thumb and the rearward-moving slide.

For shooters who favor factory stocks, or those of similar design, the smooth front strap of the 45 is often a source of irritation, promoting, as it does, a slippery hold, especially in hot and humid climates or if the hand is wet or oily. And while having the frontstrap checkered seems an obvious cure, it's also quite expensive. A much less costly cure, priced at $14.95, is offered by Wilson's Gun Shop in the form of a special adapter. Available for either blued or stainless steel guns, it consists of a thin steel overlay, stamped with a check-

Replacement slides are also among the major components produced by independent makers such as Essex Arms.

Thought by some to be the Rolls Royce of frame kits, the Modular 1911 from Chip McCormick combines space-age polymer parts with steel parts.

ered design, that completely encloses the frontstrap, and is held in place by the factory-design stocks.

Replacing the 45's original sights is a virtual "must" where many owners are concerned, but owing to the way in which the front sight is attached, installation generally calls for a gunsmith's services. King's, however, offers an "arsenal-type" front sight staking tool priced at $19.95. Of simple design, it can be used by almost anyone with a modicum of mechanical aptitude and the ability to handle a file and mallet; with its use, a profusion of both fixed and adjustable sights becomes available to the 45 owner.

King's offers several front/rear combinations, including a "target" version of the popular three-dot system priced at $39, and a "combat" version costing $32. Other outstanding sights can be had from other suppliers too numerous to individualize here; suffice it to say that the Brownells catalog devotes a good five pages to 45 replacement sights, all at comparable prices.

Popularized by competition shooters, the electro-optical "red dot" sight is yet another item finding favor with more and more non-competition shooters. It's fairly expensive, though, with Aimpoint, who pioneered the concept, charging $229.95 for its least expensive sight, the Model 3000, plus the cost of a suitable mount which adds another $59.95. A far less pricey red dot is the epc (all lower case letters, please) from Electro Prismatic Collimators at a cost of $149.50, with further savings affected by the fact that it doesn't require a mount. Considerably smaller and lighter than competitive red dot sights, it uses a unique chemical

bonding system that attaches the sight directly to the slide — which means it can also be used with virtually any firearm.

For those who decide it's worth the price, the complex mating of optics and electronics that goes into this type of sight all but guarantees a hit by generating the illusion of a bright red dot on the target, obviating the need for the usual sight alignment, proper focusing of the eye on the front sight, and so forth. The same is true of laser sights, which have the added advantage of allowing the shooter to fix on the target instead of the gun or its sight, since that's where it actually puts its dot. Laser sights, though, are also fairly expensive. The Beam Shot from Alpec Team, for example, retails for $159, but the price includes a mount.

The M1911 is one of the few guns in history for which independent makers have produced major components. Essex Arms, for instance, offers both frames and slides, with a matte blue frame costing $125.80 and a matching slide $130.66. Still other suppliers offer major components, among them AMT (Arcadia Machine & Tool) which offers its Long Slide Kit (an entire upper assembly that includes a 7-inch stainless barrel and slide) for $259.99, or its Hardballer Kit (a comparable upper assembly, but in standard length) for $245.95.

Yet other suppliers offer the 45 owner a way to upgrade his seven-rounder to a high-capacity pistol holding thirteen rounds or more. Para-Ordnance, for example, sells a selection of three so-called frame assembly kits, two in steel and one in alloy. Each consists of a high-capacity "wide body" frame and compatible magazine, along with a recoil spring and

guide, and a redesigned trigger and magazine release. Priced at $269, the alloy kit accommodates thirteen rounds, as does one of the steel kits, priced at $375. The remaining steel kit, priced at $385, holds fifteen rounds.

Another fifteen-rounder, considered by some to be the Rolls Royce of frame kits, is one designed and manufactured by Tripp Research and available from Chip McCormick. Priced at $665 (which price, at least in part, might account for the Rolls Royce comparison), it's called the Modular 1911 Frame Kit — so named because it is, in effect, a two-piece affair. It has a fully checkered grip and squared-off trigger guard made from a space-age polymer, and a slide-rail upper portion machined from a solid steel billet. The two materials, though, are bonded in such a way as to produce, in effect, a one-piece frame that's 42 percent lighter than even a standard 45 frame.

With such components available, it's possible for a 45 buff to assemble his own custom pistol, mixing and matching a choice of frames and slides along with the other parts mentioned here, producing a wide array of special features never made by Colt, nor imagined by John Browning.

Still other modified parts and accessories are available for the 45, including a good many more from the suppliers and manufacturers mentioned here, but space prohibits listing them all. A good idea is to send for their catalogs, or even better, the Brownells catalog ($3.75 to non-dealers), since it seems to give the best overview of what's available from almost everyone in the trade. Where any accessory is concerned, a closing word of caution is in order: Over the years, I've learned the wisdom of avoiding any accessory that requires a major alteration of the gun; should the accessory ever break, replacing it with a Colt or a GI part could be your only recourse, but one that's unavailable if the gun is substantially altered. With that said, there are endless tricks and treats awaiting your 45.

Too Many 45s?

■ Lee Arten

THE PISTOL THAT started it all is an old Colt 45ACP with a World War I-vintage trigger, a flat main-spring housing and 'MODEL Of 1911' stamped on the slide. It sports a World War II-style hammer, and a thinning coat of gray Parkerizing.

I was just out of high school in 1969 when I talked my father into buying the pistol for $75, and later transferring it to me. The man who sold it to Dad had intended to make a target pistol out of the 45, so a set of Micro sights, a target bushing, three magazines and a Dwyer 'Group Gripper' came in the original deal. It wasn't long before I had a local gunsmith add the target sights and bushing to the pistol. I installed the 'Group Gripper' myself — it has been in the gun and working for 31 years.

I added black rubber Pachmayr grips in the 1980s but didn't have anything else done to the pistol until I started to shoot bullseye matches later that decade. The first few matches were shot indoors with a Colt 22 conversion kit installed on the gun. It took about two matches for me to decide the military trigger wasn't going to suffice. Shooting two-handed, I was able to manage the heavy trigger. One-handed match shooting was something else again, so I took the 45 to another gunsmith and had the trigger smoothed, and lightened by a pound or so.

Two or three years later, I was at the 1988 Second Chance Combat Shoot. I competed that match for the next 10 years and used the old 45 in about half of those matches. Even after I got a new custom 45, it came along as a backup gun.

At the 1988 match, the old 45 developed a dislike for the Blazer ammunition

I brought. I remember thinking factory ammo would be a better bet than reloads but I shot poorly and cut myself on the rear sight clearing stoppages. As soon as I stopped the bleeding, I took the 45 down to the Cylinder & Slide trailer near the end of Commercial Row and gave it to gunsmith Bill Laugh-ridge from Fremont, Nebraska. He did a throating job on it and I fired my second event with reloads and without any jams. I had Bo-Mars put on the gun when the sharp-edged Micro sights fell apart several years later.

The 5 shots below the pistol in the nine- and ten-ring on this silhouette target were fired from 50 feet. The 5 in the five-and six-ring above the pistol were fired more quickly from seven yards. The author was happy with the perfomance of the Officer's ACP and his hardball-equivalent loads. Isaac Arten photo

The author's 45-caliber handguns include (from the top) the Model of 1911, a Model 1927, and Officer's ACP, an Ashabell Cook underhammer blackpowder 45, a Model 1991A1 Commander, the pin gun, a hybrid ported pistol with a Caspian slide and a Para Ordnance frame, and the target gun, a utilitarian bullseye pistol. These are just a good start, according to the author.

Ammunition on hand for the author's 45s includes Winchester hardball, and Federal, Black Hills and CorBon hollow points. The factory loads are backed up by lots of reloads, usually made with FMJs or LRN bullets.

(Above) **The pin gun** with a target shot from 50 feet. The 'eight' was the author's fault, not that of the gun. Isaac Arten photo

(Left) **The pin gun** has a Para Ordnance frame, and a hybrid slide and barrel from Caspian. The barrel has five ports that make compensated perfromance possible in a standard-size gun. The system controls recoil of heavy pin loads well, helping to cut time between shots in steel plate or bowling pin matchs.

I can't begin to guess how many thousands of rounds have gone through the old 45. At first, I didn't shoot it much since ammo was expensive and I didn't reload. In the early 1980s, after I got dies and a cheap box of bulk bullets, my 45 ACP consumption rose steadily. Practicing to shoot pin matches, I used to shoot up a hundred rounds one night, reload them the next and shoot them up again the night after. Later, I went on reloading binges every two or three months. By then, I had more brass and was making ammo for two 45s.

My standard 45 ACP load has become 5.8 grains of Unique and a 230-grain lead round-nose bullet, or the same amount of powder with a 230-grain full metal jacket slug. The load is accurate enough for pin shooting, International Defensive Pistol Association (IDPA) matches, steel matches, and plinking. I even used it in

one 2700 match when I ran out of time to load target ammo. Accuracy was no problem but the brass bounced a long way down the range after being ejected from the Pin Gun. During breaks in the centerfire and 45 stages, other shooters would come up to me and ask, "What are you using in that thing ?"

I've also used 4.0 grains of Bulls-eye for target loads with 200-grain lead semi-wad cutters. Other loads I've tried have either been less accurate than my Unique or Bullseye loads; or they haven't functioned as well in my guns.

My second 45ACP handgun was a revolver. I'd come across a copy of Shotgun News and one of the display ads showed a Smith & Wesson 1917. In 1989 or '90, the Brazilians sold as surplus — at good prices — the revolvers they acquired from S&W in 1937 or '38. I'd always been fascinated by the S&W and Colt 1917 revolvers and so had a local dealer order me one of the returned Smiths from

The Target 45 with an 'X,' two tens, and a nine showing. The author hadn't shot bullseye for more than a year, but at least the gun remembered how.

The long and the short of the author's 45s. At the top is the custom Para/Caspian P-14 with the larger grip, which accepts high-capacity magazines. Below is the Officer's ACP. It is about as accurate as the larger gun, but easier to conceal because it is smaller and thinner.

Southern Ohio Gun. I bought 100 full-moon clips from Ranch Products, and was ready to go.

The old revolver had a rough bore, skinny, oily stocks and a lot of holster and storage wear. It looked a little better after I wiped it down and cleaned the bore with FP10 and a lot of patches, and it shot much better than it looked. I put the old factory grips in a box and slipped rubber Pachmayr grips onto the gun. A few months later I added an Evans 'Wonder sight' to the frame that allowed me to adjust the point of impact without having to resort to a file.

Later, after winning a certificate for some gun work at Second Chance, I had Cylinder & Slide check over and refinish the 1917. I had to send the gun to them for the work, instead of getting it done at the match. The old '17 came back in a few weeks with a report that said the cylinder gap was slightly enlarged, but the revolver had passed the hammer push-off test. The 1917 also sported a new coat of black Parkerizing, looked handsomer than it had for many years — and shot just as well, too.

The old N-frame has served as a house gun, a backup gun in revolver events at pin matches, in PPC-type matches at local clubs and for small game hunting. I like to take it out at the end of small game

season (if the snow has melted enough) and sneak around looking for cottontails or snowshoes. I once thought of cutting it down, but decided I liked it just as it was. Chronographing loads fired from the old S&W showed that, with the same loads, it produced higher velocities than my old 1911. It has almost a 1/2-inch longer barrel than my Government Model 45, but I had assumed the cylinder gap would drop velocities below those from an autopistol.

Although I did some conventional target shooting with rifles and pis-

Dillon's LTD holster nicely fits the author's carry 45s, the Officer's ACP and the 1991 Commander. It has carried both in matches. The Officer's ACP has ridden in it in the woods while the author was trout fishing.

tols then, the biggest thing on my shooting calendar in the early 1990s was bowling pin shooting. Richard Davis, head of the Second Chance Body Armor Company, ran a very interesting and eclectic match. There were custom revolvers and autopistols made to suit almost any taste, and some of the people with the tricked-out guns could shoot them well, too. Carbines, shotguns and submachine guns were also in evidence and you could even try 30-and 50-caliber machineguns, and pay by the belt. My nearly stock 1911 sometimes looked like a Model A Ford at a modern drag race.

After meeting Charles Wooley and shooting his hybrid 45 on the practice range at Second Chance, I went into full plot-and-scheme mode. By 1992 I had a Para-Ordnance P-14 frame mated to a hybrid-ported Caspian slide. It was a slick setup, with a great trigger, and it would stack round-nose 230-grain bullets one on top of the other at eight yards, the distance from the firing line to the bowling pin tables. After I got some loading problems worked out, I posted my best pin shooting times ever with that gun. Trivia was still my best event, but the Para definitely helped me improve in Five Pin.

I shot the Para in two steel matches at my club during the last two years, and managed to win both of them. The matches went by very quickly, but what

(Left) **The six 45 ACP** handguns in the author's collection surround a 30-round group shot by the author's son Isaac. Isaac is left-handed and tends to shoot to the right with revolvers and the smaller semi-automatics. One shot was off the paper, but some groups from individual handguns weren't too bad.

(Below) **Uncle Mike's Sidekick #3** holster fits the Model 1917 quite well. It has carried the old revolver on rabbit hunts, in PPC-type matches, and in revolver stages at bowling pin matches.

stayed with me afterward was how the Para seemed to float smoothly from one 12-inch plate to another — and then go off at just the right time. After shooting pins, the plates seemed large and easy to hit. I knocked 12 plates off their steel racks in about 13 seconds. That isn't really fast, but it was fast enough to win that day.

The Para is heavy, too high-tech for IDPA matches, and I haven't hunted with it. It was fired in a few 2700 matches some years ago. In one, I posted the only 98 rapid-fire target I've managed to shoot in centerfire competition so far. (The gun would have let me clean the target too, but I pulled one shot down into the eight ring.) I haven't been able to make any bowling pin matches for the past two years, so I've been considering shooting the Para in the 'Centerfire' stage of bulls-eye again.

The Para/Casp is my most custom-ized gun, but the next 45 I acquired is a close second. A friend told me that The Northwoods Trading Post in Hancock, Michigan had a target 45 for sale. Northwoods, run by a former cop, is one of my favorite gun stores so I was only too glad to stop by. When I got nose-to-nose with the handgun case, however, the target gun I thought I was looking for immediately took a back seat to a carry 45 that was also in the case.

The gun was a stainless Officer's ACP. (Please don't call it an Officer's Model, which would make it a target 38 revolver.) The ACP had a checkered front strap, a trigger job and a custom trigger, probably a Videki. It also had the best standard sights I'd ever seen on a 45. They were higher than the minuscule sights on my original 45, and sported white dots front and rear. I could have lived without the dots, but the high-visibility sights lined up quickly and impressed me.

I bought the Officer's ACP in the fall of 1994. The following June, in the Second Chance Trivia competition, I managed to come up with another certificate for gunsmithing. Using that, I had the factory bushing exchanged for one with less of a history of breaking and flying down-range at inopportune moments.

I intended to use the Officer's ACP as a concealed-carry piece, but found the custom trigger a bit light. I haven't had the trigger redone yet, and may not. In the meantime, I've used the little pistol in practical pistol matches, carried it in the open while fishing, and shot it at gongs and silhouette targets just for fun. It seems to be almost as accurate as the Para, and it is a favorite .45.

In 1996, for my 45th birthday, my wife gave me a target 45, complete with an old Aimpoint scope, an Elliason rear sight and rib, and extended front sight. The pistol appeared to have been made by a military armorer and is utilitarian, rather than decorative. The front-strap was harshly stippled, and the frame and slide showed some wear. The old Aimpoint was usable but not much of a sight anymore, so I replaced it with a Tasco Pro-Point. This gun has been sitting, awaiting my return to bullseye competition. That return was "temporarily delayed" several years ago but the gun is ready, even if I'm not. With 4 grains of Bullseye and a locally cast 200-grain SWC, it would shoot slightly elongated one-hole groups at 25 yards when I was in training, or when shooting from bags.

The last 45 I got my hands on arrived in 1998. It is a stock Colt 1991A Commander that my brother, Jon, had before me. It has a matte black finish, high visibility sights and black plastic grips. It appears to have had a factory throating job and has usually been very reliable with hardball, hardball-equivalent reloads and target SWC reloads. It has also been accurate enough to hit a quart oil jug out to 60 yards.

The only time the gun has been unreliable was during an IDPA match. Because of a brain fade while packing my gear, I was short of magazines and had to shoot the match with one of my 10-round mags and one borrowed 8-rounder. The "Stage From Hell," as my squad quickly named it, started by requiring us to shoot right-handed around the left side of a barricade — and went downhill from there. One guy had his pistol jam so solidly he could barely work the action. Another shooter barked his knuckles severely and bled on the floor. I was lucky and just had a consistent second-to-last round stoppage with my 10-round magazine, and an occasional random stoppage with the borrowed one. The next week — same range, same gun, same ammo - but different magazines - I shot strong hand, weak hand, and from a barricade — with no stoppages at all.

I might have a little trigger work done on the 1991A1, but I don't think I'll do anything else to it. Except for that ill-fated IDPA match I haven't done any competition shooting with the 1991A1. I've done a little plinking and have considered it for a carry gun and a house gun. Some authorities on self-defense say that customized guns should not be used for self-defense. Unscrupulous attorneys have been known to paint owners of customized handguns as 'Rambo' wannabes or vigilantes. The 1991A1 is a stock gun's 'stock' gun, so I suppose it would be safe to defend myself with it.

I have another 45, a replica blackpowder 45-caliber under-hammer pistol. (Early American gunsmith Ashabell Cook designed the original pistol.) This replica was made in the 1980s by the Italian gunmaking firm of P. Bondini. I use a fired 45 ACP case filled with Pyrodex to load it.

The under-hammer design is supposed to be altogether American and that gives me a patriotic reason to like the Bondini replica. Another is that it is fun to shoot, and cleans up a lot easier than my other black-powder firearms.

In my collection of 45 ACP pistols I have one for nostalgia: my 'starter' pistol, the 'MODEL Of 1911.'

There is a gun for bowling pins, steel shoots and some target shooting: the PARA/CASP P-14. It is my only real custom pistol and I'm very glad I got it before 1994, when high-capacity magazines were available and fairly cheap.

The S&W Model 1917 is available for PPC-type shooting, home defense, small game hunting and plinking.

When plinking palls, I have the utilitarian target 45 with the red-dot scope. I know that gun is going to make a good showing in bullseye someday; I just don't know when.

I also have two good carry guns. The Officer's ACP is one: stainless, small, powerful for its size and accurate. The 1991A1 Commander is the other carry piece. It is just 1/2-inch longer in barrel, slide and butt than the Officer's and can use the same holsters as all my other 45s with iron sights.

To remind me of how good 45 semiautos really are, I have the under-hammer blackpowder single shot.

I think I've covered the 45ACP waterfront pretty well, but you never know what might turn up at Northwoods, or one of the other 'firearms emporiums' I frequent. The only 45 I'm actively seeking is a used Smith & Wesson 625. A modern 45 ACP revolver that uses full moon clips and loads as fast as my slightly tired 1917 would be just the thing for some of my shooting.

When I find a 625 on the same day I have the money, I will have eight 45s in the collection. That can be thought of as a lot of guns in one caliber — or just as a nice start. As the guys I shoot with like to say, "You can't have too many 45s."

One of the pin gun's best qualities is that it takes high-capacity magazines. Here it is with "not quite enough" 14-rounders.

The Luger Pistol

Model 1900 Luger Sporting Carbine with checkered walnut fore-end and buttstock. ∎ Fred A. Datig

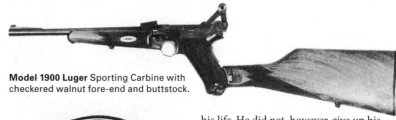

Model 1900 Luger Sporting Carbine with checkered walnut fore-end and buttstock.

A special condensation for THE GUN DIGEST of the author's book of the same title. See the Book Review pages for price and further details.

FOR GENERATIONS the most famous name in pistols has been Luger. There is no country however small or insignificant in which that name, or its foreign counterpart, Parabellum, is unfamiliar. To make the statement that it is the world's finest, most accurate, well designed or generally the "best" pistol would merely be expressing an opinion, but what are the reasons for its popularity? Why has it been accepted as the "best" and what is the story behind its phenomenal success?

To relate the tale from the beginning we must go back to a well known arms designer of his day, Hugo Borchardt, a naturalized American citizen. Borchardt was a mechanical genius of some note, for he not only entered the inventing profession at an early age but also developed many diversified types of mechanical devices.

The earliest record we have of Borchardt, as applied to the weapons field, is a letter written in his own hand to Mr. E. G. Westcott, President and Treasurer of The Sharps Rifle Co. of Hartford, Conn., dated March 18, 1875, when Borchardt was applying for the position of Superintendent of that company:

"... I took the superintendency of a shop in the worst condition at Trenton (New Jersey), designed the tools and finished a contract for 5,000 guns to the entire satisfaction of the Co. Mr. Meecham, who was treasurer of The Pioneer Breechloading Arms Co., hesitated at first in placing confidence in me, owing very likely to my age, I was 24 years old. There were about 60 hands employed. I afterwards had a foremanship in Singer (Sewing Machine Co.?) and several other places...."

His first patent, for a bullet grooving machine, was issued on July 21, 1874. This was followed by a bullet patching machine in 1875, a breech-loading firearm (Sharps-Borchardt) in 1876, a gun sight in 1877, another breechloading firearm, a shirt neck shaper, a magazine; rock driller; wire straightener; recoil magazine pistol (Borchardt Pistol, 1893), and numerous others.

Borchardt was versatile indeed, but it appears that his many patents added few coins to his coffers, for he was constantly changing jobs and addresses. His part in developing the Sharps-Borchardt rifle was his greatest achievement before forsaking his adopted country for Europe, where he remained for the rest of his life. He did not, however, give up his American citizenship.

Georg Luger was born in Steinach in Tirol in 1849. Originally an officer in the Austrian Army and with a decided liking for mechanical things, he became acquainted with Herr Mannlicher, inventor, among countless other designs, of the Austrian Infantry Ordnance Rifle. Together these two wizards produced an automatic, army rifle, (Luger's military career was at an end) opening the door to a new vocation, one that was to make Luger world renowned.

In 1891 Luger held a position with the firm of Ludwig Loewe of Berlin, from whence he was sent shortly thereafter to exhibit yet another military rifle in the United States, and where he more than likely first met Hugo Borchardt.

It is known that Borchardt left the United States and took a position as director of the Hungarian Arms Company, but he soon had a disagreement with the Hungarian War Minister, General Fejervary, and undoubtedly through the influence and persuasion of his new friend, Georg Luger, was offered a job with Loewe, which he accepted.

The next we hear of Herr Luger is in the year 1894 when he is once again exhibiting a new weapon before the United States Naval Ordnance Board. That new design was a semi-automatic pistol named after its creator, Borchardt!

The Borchardt Pistol was patented in all of the major countries between 1893 and 1896. Sometime in 1893 the "Automatic Pistol, Borchardt Patent" was offered for sale on the commercial market to the world at large. It was of the finest precision workmanship and only the very best materials were used in its construction. The pistol carried a beautiful, glossy satin finish. The barrel was approximately caliber 30, using a special bottlenecked cartridge. This cartridge was the forerunner of (and interchangeable with) the well known caliber 30 (7.63mm) Mauser round. It is also almost identical to the 7.63mm Mannlicher Pistol cartridge, Model of 1896.

The Borchardt was sold in the United States for $30.00 — that price included a wooden shoulder stock with detachable cheekpiece, leather holster, 3 spare magazines, a wooden dummy magazine which included tools, ramrod and oiler and an instruction manual. For an extra $5.00 a fitted leather case was included. Unfortunately, few of these complete outfits remain intact today although they may be encountered from time to time in some of the larger collections.

The Borchardt Pistol was originally marketed by the Loewe firm but soon after the weapon was placed on the market, that company absorbed the Deutsche Metallpatronenfabrik of Karlsruhe, forming a company thereafter known as the Deutsche Waffen and Munitionsfabriken of Berlin-Karlsruhe (January 1, 1897). After that date all weapons were manufactured at the DWM plant in Berlin, and only ammunition was made at the Karlsruhe subsidiary.

On November 22, 1894, the Boston Herald printed a glowing report about Borchardt and his new pistol, noting that Georg Luger exhibited the new gun before a U. S. Navy small arms board at Providence, R. I. on November 21, and "that it had a great future before it." The account went on to say that the "exhibitor fired 24 shots in 43¾ seconds … range 110 feet, and all were hits." The magazine was described as holding "eight cartridges, with nickel jacketed bullets," and these were "the Luger rimless type."

Georg Luger 1849-1923

It is interesting to note that it was Georg Luger and not Hugo Borchardt who brought the pistol to this country for these tests. Notice that the cartridge is indicated as being of the "LUGER rimless type" which leads us to believe that Georg Luger might have had more to do with the marketing of the pistol than is generally believed. Also of interest is the fact that although the press gave it an excellent notice the U. S. Navy failed to follow up the tests with any further trials of the Borchardt Pistol.

The U. S. Army also tested the Borchardt, for the Chief of Ordnance ordered a board of officers to meet at Springfield Armory on October 20, 1897 "to make a thorough test of, and report upon, a Borchardt Automatic Pistol Carbine." This test was not pursued further so it may be assumed that the pistol did not meet with the complete approval of the officers on the board.

Georg Luger was more than an employee of the new firm of DWM. He re-

ceived a handsome salary, could patent all of his inventions at company cost and had all of his traveling expenses cared for by the firm. Having no definite office hours, he was more of a partner with a fixed salary and a lengthy contract. After five years his salary was doubled and his contract extended. A point of interest which should be interjected here is that Luger spelled his name exactly that way … LUGER, and not LUEGER or LEUGER as has been erroneously quoted. His personal signature, as early as 1896, bears this out, and members of the Luger family do not recall the name ever having been spelled any other way.

According to close friends and relations, Borchardt and Luger were the best of personal friends though they often had their differences at the factory. Years after the deaths of their husbands the two widows were constant companions. Luger had a son, Georg, Jr., who lives today in Berlin at the age of 81, and who has been of invaluable assistance to the author in bringing to light many of the facts concerning the Luger Pistol and its famous inventor. Herr Luger, Jr. was a famous pistol shot, with a Luger, of course, though he modestly disclaims any outstanding ability. His life was spent with much larger and more complicated weapons than those produced by his sire, namely torpedoes.

Excellent though it was, especially in relations to the other pistols of its day, the Borchardt left a great deal to be desired. The inventor believed his gun to be perfect, though, and so steadfast were his refusals to redesign even the smallest component that DWM, the manufacturers, called upon Herr Luger to make the desired changes. This he did in the following manner. The strong and sturdy action of the Borchardt was retained along with many other of the original features, some being altered slightly and others quite radically. The barrel, though shortened, maintained its long, slim appearance. The grip was inclined at an angle to the receiver and the recoil spring was incorporated in the grip, thereby doing away with two major problems, the angle of the grip and the bulky, protruding, recoil spring housing. The trigger and trigger cover were altered, the latter now completely concealing the rollerpin of the sear and partially covering the sear itself. The position of the ejector was changed from beneath the breechblock to the right side of the receiver, while the extractor remained unchanged. The lanyard ring was moved from the left side of the receiver to the rear, just above the grip safety, a new feature. Buttstock and toggle-knob were completely done away with and all screws, with the exception of the ones holding the wooden grips to the frame, were replaced by pins. The sights remained unchanged.

In the latter part of 1898, November 24 to December 8, a series of pistol trials were held at Bern, Switzerland by a board of army officers. Other pistols entered were: Mauser with 10-shot magazine, Mauser with 6-shot magazine; Bergmann with 10-shot magazine; Borchardt-Luger with 8-shot magazine; Roth with 10-shot magazine; Mannlicher with 7-shot magazine.

Explanation, assembly and firing of 50 rounds followed; then timing per firing of each weapon; target shooting, 3 frames each at 50 meters; endurance of 400 rounds without cleaning or cooling, etc. The Borchardt-Luger was the only weapon in the endurance test to perform satisfactorily. Then followed dust and water tests, and the firing of 20 rounds in each weapon. Again the Borchardt-Luger was the only weapon without malfunction. The point of greatest interest is the fact that the pistol is referred to as the "Borchardt-Luger." This was a transition piece, a true cross between the Borchardt and the Luger which was to evolve from this and a later Swiss test.

A second series of tests were conducted by the Swiss. They were held at Thun on May 1 to 3, 1899. The Mauser, Bergmann, Roth and Mannlicher Pistols of the previous trials were retested. New models of the Mauser, Hauff and Browning were listed as were the new Mannlicher and a new Borchardt-Luger — these latter two having been modified according to the wishes of the Board. The 1899 tests were conducted in a manner similar to those of the previous year. The Borchardt-Luger of the latter tests was described as "made lighter in weight and fitted with a new safety." It is more than coincidental that the United States patent on this piece was applied for two days before the start of these tests!*The patent for the first of the true Luger pistols was filed on March 17, 1900 (British Patent 4399 #x2014; March 7, 1900) but was not granted in the United States until March 1, 1904 (75,414). This was a remarkably lengthy patent — 7½ pages of text and 10 pages of drawings and diagrams! Georg Luger wanted to be absolutely certain that no one would swipe the slightest detail of his new design.

In contrast to the Borchardt, the "Pistole Parabellum," or "Parabellum Automatic Pistol, Borchardt-Luger System, Swiss Model 1900," was all that had been expected of it. The weight had been decreased from 40 to 30 ounces, the barrel length from 7¼ to 4¾ inches and the overall length from 14 to 9 inches. Also, because greater accuracy could now be got from the pistol, the buttstock was no longer necessary and thereby lessened the weight by another 15 ounces.

The Model 1900 was the first weapon to bear the famous scrolled DWM, trademark of the Deutsche Waffen und Munitionsfabriken of Berlin, where all earlier models were made.

A note of interest is the origin of the

Original Borchardt automatic pistol, Model 1893, cal. 7.65mm Borchardt. Weight 40 oz., overall length 14".

name "Parabellum," thought to derive from a Latin phrase, Si Vis Pacem Para Bellum. Translated into German this became Bereite Den Krieg vor Parabellum, or in English, "If you Want Peace, Prepare For War." Consequently, as the pistol was intended as a military weapon, the "For War" or "Parabellum" name came to be coined.

It is known throughout the world today by that name. In mentioning the name "Luger" to a European, with the possible exception of the English, do not be surprised to be met with only a blank stare! The name "Luger" was first applied to the pistol by Hans Tauscher, first representative for the Borchardt and Luger Pistols in the U.S., and later, after World War I, was registered by the post-war importer, A. F. Stoeger; consequently, the name "Luger," although not an American name has become an American term! In some instances the name "Borchardt-Luger," "Borchardt-Luger Parabellum" and designations such as "P.08" (meaning "Pistol, Model 1908," the year the Germany Army first adopted the Luger), "M943," the Portuguese military title, "Pistole 1900," the Swiss version, etc. may be encountered.

The Model 1900 became a success overnight. On April 2, 1901, the Swiss "Bundersrate," or governing body, officially became the first to adopt it by placing an order with DWM for 3000 pistols. On April 16, 1901, the Commanding Officer of Springfield Armory was officially directed to purchase 1000 Lugers for test by troops of the United Stales Army! Rock Island Arsenal was directed to fabricate a sufficient quantity of russet or black leather holsters and hardened steel combination tools. The 1000 pieces purchased by the U.S. were marked with small ordnance-bomb proofs, and most of the holsters carried the familiar "U.S." on the flap. These pistols were the original "American Eagle" type, being so marked over the chamber. As far as can be determined these marks were unofficially stamped, and later commercial types carried on with the identical crest. Because these pistols and holsters were issued to and used by U.S. troops, they are considered by some to be U.S. martial weapons!

The Swiss and Americans were not the only ones to test the Model 1900 for in 1903 and 1904 at Rosenburg, Sweden, extensive government trials found the Luger and the Model 1903 Browning in the semi-finals. Although the Swedish report favored the Browning it noted that the Swiss were issuing the Luger to mounted troops. Similar reports indicate that the Parabellum was issued to German officers for use in the Boxer Rebellion in 1901. Other countries to test the Luger in those early days included Austria, Spain, Canada, Russia, Brazil, Luxemburg, Holland, Bulgaria, Norway, Portugal, Chile and several others.

Between 1901 and 1906 rapid advancement was made in making the Luger a better gun, with both military and commercial markets in mind. The first modification of the original was offered in 1902, and was designated the model of that year. Few of these were produced — the type is quite scarce today — but they'll be remembered for one outstanding reason; they were the first weapons to chamber the 9mm Luger cartridge! Now, half a century later, it is by far the most popular and widely used cartridge in the world. This was an unusual situation — the pistol itself was not successful but the cartridge flourished. Probably an accident — or could it have been planned that way?

The first model to be officially adopted by the German Government was the "Marine Modell 1904," or what has become known as the "Navy" Luger. Thus it was the German Navy and not the Army who first realized the merits of the Luger. The Naval Luger has a 6-inch barrel with a 2-position rear sight situated on the extreme rear of the rear togggle link. Caliber was the new 9mm.

One of the most interesting, different, costly and coveted variations of the Parabellum is the "Luger Carbine," which was introduced about 1904 in an attempt to compete with similar weapons marketed at that time by Mauser, Mannlicher and Bergmann. With a barrel too long to be practical as a pistol and too short to meet the requirements of a rifle, it was more nearly the equivalent of a "brush gun." The Luger Carbine is actually a Model 1900 with a heavy 11¾-inch barrel recoiling within a checkered walnut fore-end, and detachable walnut

DWM Lugers with various barrel lengths; left to right: 3 , 4 , 4¾ , 6 , 7 , and 8 .

shoulder stock. The 100 to 300 meter rear sight is mounted on the barrel just in front of the chamber. Despite the many rumors of special specimens with assorted differences, all Luger Carbines of the factory production lot are identical and were only produced in caliber 7.65mm Luger. A special cartridge containing one-seventh more powder and having a blackened case was developed for use in the Carbine models.

The German Kaiser, Wilhelm II, because he had difficulty in handling a full sized hunting rifle due to the deformity of his left arm, was extremely fond of hunting deer on his many estates armed with his Luger Carbine. When, prior to the First World War, the President of the United States, Theodore Roosevelt, paid a visit to Germany, he was a guest of the German emperor on at least one of those hunting excursions and was presented with a Luger Carbine by the Kaiser. This gun bears a plaque denoting the presentation, and may be seen today at Roosevelt's home in New York on display with his many other weapons.

The year 1906 brought what was to become known as the "New" Model. This is a colloquial designation, not necessarily an official factory term. The part that was new in the "New" Model was the replacing of the old laminated flat recoil spring with one of coiled type. As all Lugers after 1906 have the coiled spring, they are all designated as "New Models," and consequently all models with the flat recoil spring are called the "Old" Model.

Of even greater historical interest than the U.S. Army Tests of 1901 were the trials that took place in the spring of 1907. These were the tests which led to the adoption by the U.S. Government of the Colt Automatic Pistol, caliber 45, but not before it had successfully competed and won out against the caliber 45 Luger! Records indicate that two, pos-

Disassembling the Luger: remove the magazine (J) and make sure the chamber is EMPTY. With the right hand, grasp the pistol as shown, pulling the barrel and receiver (E) rearward firmly. Rotate the locking bolt (D) 90° downward; the trigger plate (C) will now fall out. The barrel and receiver may be slid forward off frame (A). The breechblock and toggle linkage (F) may be separated from the receiver by pushing out the connecting pin (H). The trigger (B) and the locking bolt may also be removed if desired. To assemble, reverse operations — make sure that the coupling link (G) does not hang into magazine well but drops behind it and in line with link lever (K).

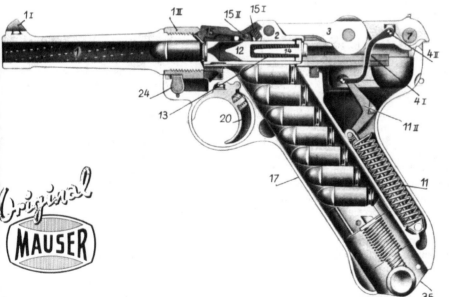

Original **MAUSER**

1—barrel.
1'—front sight.
1"—receiver.
2—breechblock.
3—front toggle link.
4'—coupling link.
4"—coupling link pin.
7—connecting pin.
11—mainspring.
11"—coupling link lever.
12—firing pin.
13—firing pin spring.
14—breechblock end piece.
15—extractor.
15'—extractor spring.
15"—extractor pin.
17—grip frame.
20—trigger.
24—locking bolt.
35—magazine.

sibly three, of these large Lugers were personally produced by Georg Luger and brought by him to the United States for the Army Tests. Prior to his arrival, Frankford Arsenal supplied him with 5000 rounds of caliber 45 ammunition with which to experiment. Luger pulled the bullets and, with his own special powder, loaded 11mm Bergmann cases which thereby formed the 45 Luger cartridge. The tests were originally planned for the year 1906 but Luger was ill and the tests were postponed until the following year!

The 45 Luger is merely an enlarged version of the 9mm Model 1902/06 with slight modifications necessitated by the use of the larger cartridge. The only specimen known to exist today bears the serial number "2" and is truly a fine example of Luger workmanship. The initials "GL" appear on the rear toggle link while the absence of proof marks corroborates the fact that this was a super special experimental pistol never intended for sale.

As mentioned earlier, the German Army adopted the Luger in 1908, a move which insured its success for decades to come. The grip safety was omitted from the Model 1902/06 and the first specimens were produced without any accommodation for a "holdopen device." No stock attachments appeared on these early "P.08's."

With the adoption came large orders which could not be filled in the time allotted by DWM. Consequently, the Royal German Arsenal at Erfurt was appointed co-manufacturer. Many thousands of Lugers were turned out of that great establishment, all bearing the insignia of the arsenal, a large crown surmounting the name "Erfurt," stamped on the forward toggle link instead of the DWM trademark. Almost all DWM and Erfurt Lugers produced for the military will bear the date of manufacture and acceptance stamped into the receiver ring. A new system of numbering was initiated wherein the block of numbers never exceeded 9,999. Once that figure was reached a letter was added beneath the numbers beginning with "a" and

so on through the alphabet. This letter becomes as much a part of the serial number as the numbers themselves, a point to remember when recording serial numbers on Luger pistols. Without the inclusion of the letter, hundreds of Lugers would carry the identical number and the difficulties which might arise may well be imagined.

In 1914, Germany entered the Great War armed with two basic Lugers, the military Model of 1908/14 and the Naval Model of 1904/14. The military or Army Model is almost identical to the Model 1908. All types have a 4-inch barrel, stock lug, holdopen device and a letter of the alphabet following the four digit serial number. All are caliber 9mm and will have the date of manufacture over the chamber. According to unofficial sources, approximately 2 million 4-inch barrelled Military Models were produced by both manufacturers, DWM and Erfurl, during the First World War period. In addition to this staggering figure, about 50 million replacement parts were supplied. The majority of these pistols and parts were of DWM manufacture.

Like the military Model, the Naval Model was also exactly the same as the earlier Navy Model of 1908 (1904/08), except for having a wartime date over the chamber. All had the 6-inch barrel, stock lug, 2-position rear sight, and a letter following the serial number. Not nearly as many Navy Models were produced due to the much smaller demands of the junior service.

In 1914, a new model was introduced, "new" consisting of the fitting of an 8-inch barrel to the standard Military Model, and the elimination of the rear sight from the rear toggle link. The caliber was 9mm and the back sight, of tangent type, was on the rear of the barrel just forward of the barrel flange. In this respect, it is similar to that on the Luger Carbine, but the sight itself was not the same. It is adjustable from 100 to 800 meters in 100-meter graduations. One unusual thing about this sight is that it has built-in drift allowance to the left. In other words, when the sight is elevated,

it not only moves upward but also to the left to compensate for the drift of the bullet over long ranges. Some front and rear sights are adjustable by means of a tiny set screw on the front sights of Naval models. The Model 1914, or "Long Barrelled Model" as it is sometimes called, was issued complete with a long holster, a shoulder stock and a 32-round helical, or snail, drum. It is claimed that these were issued especially to artillery troops, to machine gun units, and to auxiliary cruisers or "Z" boats in place of a rifle or carbine. The reasoning behind this move was, undoubtedly, that a lighter, smaller and more compact sidearm than the rifle was needed — one that could easily be converted into a pistol-carbine for long range firing, and be much handier for the man who had to serve larger weapons. These "Long Barrelled Models" are quite handy and extremely accurate, and all in all, are a pleasure to fire. The loaded drum makes for a rather bulky weapon but not really as bad as one might think.

After World War I

If there is any period in the complete history of the Luger where almost every rule is broken regarding models, variations, serial numbers, or anything on which a definite conclusion may be based, it is found in the post-World War I period. Perhaps the most important influence upon Luger production after that war was the Treaty of Versailles. This Treaty limited production to calibers not larger than 8mm and barrels no longer than 100mm, or 3 15/16 inches. These restrictions did not require a complete retooling by Luger manufacturers, however, as the pistol is so designed that by merely changing the barrel, and no other parts, the Luger is transformed from one caliber to the other! Because the standard military issue barrel was 4 inches, or 1/16th-inch longer than the terms of the Treaty would allow, the barrel had to be shortened in order to conform. The Germans chose a barrel with a length of 3⅝ inches or approximately 98mm. This model became known as the post-War Model, or the Model 1923.

Model 1902 Luger, first to use the 9mm Parabellum cartridge. Note heavy 4 bbl. and magazine cartridge counting strip.

A. F. Stoeger Luger imported by that firm in the 1930s. (Photo courtesy Sidney Aberman.)

(LEFT) **Swiss Model 1929** (06/29) Luger, cal. 7.65mm, 4¾ bbl. Note stepped receiver ring, the "S" above thumb safety, the straight line of the grip, and the grip safety.

(LEFT) **ERMA 22** conversion unit fitted to Luger.

The rare 45 cal. Luger, serial #2, submitted for U. S. Army test in 1907. (Photo courtesy Sidney Aberman.)

Model 1900/06 American Eagle Luger. Note LOADED on the extractor instead of the more common GELADEN. Cal. 7.65mm.

For all practical purposes, the Model 1923 was a Military Model of the 1908/14 type with the two differences of the shorter barrel and smaller caliber. Strangely enough, this Model 1923 was produced almost exclusively for export outside of Germany. The Germans themselves, theoretically restricted by the Treaty of Versailles, continued not only to use the 4-inch barrelled 9mm weapon but also to manufacture them for military and police use inside Germany.

Also under the terms of the Treaty, Germany was permitted to retain an army of 100,000-man strength. These men had to be armed and they assuredly were. In the days immediately following the war, regular Military Models of 1908/14 were issued to this army. These were pistols that had either seen service during the war or were assembled from parts that had been finished but never issued. The only distinctive marking of these particular guns was a new date of issue added to the one already marked over the chamber. Consequently, we find the "two-date" model. (For example, a Luger that already had the date "1918" over the chamber now had "1920" above the "1918," not superimposed upon it. Both dates may be easily distinguished.) These pistols were quickly relegated to the police, however, for whom the "second rate" weapons would suffice, and this double-dating became an outmoded practice very rapidly. In a very few instances, the "two-date" Model may be found with police or military markings on the forward part of the frame, just below the trigger guard.

By 1920 the Germans had begun to manufacture or assemble (probably the latter), "as new" Lugers for the Army. These, too, were EXACTLY like the Model 1908/14 except that they were dated "1920," "1921" or "1922." As I recall, I have never seen any with dates other than these three years. These Lugers were of very fine workmanship, for this period, and appear to have been made entirely of new parts.

Somehow the German Navy benefited by this "stretching" of the limits of the Treaty of Versailles, as Naval Model Lugers have been seen, precisely 1908/14 specifications in all respects, also dated "1920," etc. and with no other date. Almost all of these types were caliber 9mm! A few have been encountered in caliber 7.65mm, however.

About 1922 the old, established arms firm of Simson & Co. of Suhl, Germany was given a contract to supply Lugers to the 100,000-man Reichswehr. According to reliable sources, they were the only official suppliers of pistols for the 10-year period 1922 to 1932. These Simson & Co. Lugers were assembled from surplus parts left over in large quantities from World War I. In some cases, the receivers were dated. The only date so far seen on Simson & Co. Lugers, however, is that of 1918; the majority of them have the date ground from the receiver ring, leaving it without markings. A few such pieces have been noted chambered for the 7.65mm Luger cartridge. It is more than likely that such pistols were intended for the commercial market, as were possibly a few of those chambered for the 9mm cartridge. Simson & Co. Lugers are identical with the standard Military Model of 1908/14 type, except for markings. All examples observed have 4-inch barrels, stock lug, holdopen, etc. Instead of the DWM trademark, the words "Simson & Co., Suhl" appear on the forward link of the toggle. Lugers assembled by Simson are relatively uncommon but they can hardly be considered "rare"; let's call them "scarce."

Great numbers of ex-military issue Lugers were "rejuvenated" and heaped upon the commercial market. Some of these were rebarrelled with "as new" surplus military barrels and others were not rebarrelled at all. Almost all had the dates ground from the receiver ring. Original proof marks were often ground away also and replaced by commercial proof marks of that period. In some cases, the old marks were left on, and one or two commercial ones were added.

An extremely interesting and unusual piece, whether it is of this period or not, is the so-called "Baby" Luger chambered for the 7.65mm Browning, or .32 ACP, cartridge! This strange experimental pistol is reported as "smaller in the overall" than an ordinary Luger, or approximately in the same relation to a standard Luger as the "Baby" Nambu is to a large Nambu Pistol. Very few of these pieces were produced, the number reportedly not more than a dozen. One example has been reported as bearing the serial number "8" and with the DWM trademark on the toggle. No other specifications have been forthcoming.

Another experimental Luger, certainly worthy of special note, is the "5-shot" or "Pocket" Luger, consisting of a shortened (possibly 2-inch) barrel, normal action and shortened frame, housing a 5-cartridge capacity magazine. The "5-shot" was one of extremely limited production, no more than one or two examples having been produced.

Even before the machine pistol, or sub-machine gun as it is known in this country, first emerged as an accepted military weapon, attempts were made to convert the Luger from semi-automatic to fully automatic fire. Though many attempts were made, none went beyond the experimental stages. This was, undoubtedly, due to the delicate trigger mechanism of the Luger and also to the fact that even in normal semiautomatic firing the ammunition used in a Luger must be fairly well standard in power or the various stoppages common to the Luger will occur.

One very unusual Luger is a Model 1908 of World War I vintage, with a 4-inch barrel and a 12-inch silencer about 1½ inches in diameter. A threaded metal disc is permanently attached to the barrel in about the same position as the front sight, which has been removed; the tube, or body, of the silencer screws onto the disc. It is assumed that the tube was filled, at intervals, with rubber or composition baffles and possibly steel wool or some comparable material.

Experiments were conducted at the factory in an attempt to perfect a silencer for the Luger. These tests called for removing "0.36 gram of powder (from the cartridge) and replacing it with only

Model 1914 Military Luger, 8 barrel with tangent sight, wooden holster-stock, and 32-shot drum. Caliber 9mm.

0.25 gram of powder." This charge reduction was necessary because the bullet velocity had to be reduced below the speed of sound (1126 feet per second at 68 degrees Fahrenheit) or the silencer could not function efficiently. To further insure the lower velocity the weight of the bullet was increased. However, one problem remained — the silencer functioned as desired, but the pistol would fire only as a single shot. This was because "a Luger with silencer does not function automatically due to the heavier bullet and lesser powder charge, the gas pressure being too small to allow sufficient recoil for normal functioning of the action." No record of further similar tests has been uncovered.

By 1930 the confusion and restrictions of the post-war period had begun to relax and standardization again became the order of the day. Once more DWM changed hands, finally becoming a member firm of the same holding company that controlled the famous Mauser-Werke at Oberndorf on the Neckar. On May 1, 1930, 800 machines, tools and technicians were transferred from the Berlin branch of the DWM factory to the Oberndorf location. DWM then concentrated on the production of ammunition and Mauser became the foremost supplier of Lugers from that time until production was finally halted in 1942.

While the changeover from DWM to Mauser was taking place, Simson & Co., continued to supply all Lugers to the German government. Their contract with the military was terminated in 1932, however, and no more Lugers were produced by that firm thereafter.

About 1933, when Adolph Hitler rapidly ascended to power, steps were taken to legally sidestep most of the restrictions placed upon Luger production. The point was argued, and won, that as cylinders of revolvers were not considered to be a part of the length of the barrel, neither then should the chamber of the barrel on an automatic pistol be considered when measuring barrel lengths.

It was a small task to completely throw off the remaining restrictions and return to the old proven and desired ways of Luger production without the annoying regulations.

Mauser continued to use the old DWM trademark until late in 1934 but in that year secret code names were given to the major producers of war material, and Mauser was assigned the code name "S." The "S" was replaced almost immediately by "S/42." At the same time, the commercial Mauser Banner trademark first appeared on Luger Pistols. There was a definite reason behind the using of both the code name "S/42" and the commercial Mauser Banner. The former were elements of secret production, employed to confuse the manufacturer's identity. The latter was marked on arms supposedly intended for commercial sales, and a few of them actually reached the commercial market. Most, however, were destined for the rapidly growing German military forces of the early and mid-thirties. To doubly insure their carefully guarded secret from being discovered, pistols were not only marked with the code name but also with a code date of manufacture. Consequently we find "S/42" Lugers carrying the letters "K," indicating manufacture in 1934, and "G," indicating those made in 1935. Production under these circumstances did not get under way until late in 1934, so few pieces bearing the "K" designation will be encountered. Those marked with the letter "G," or 1935, were in much greater evidence. By the beginning of 1936, the cloak of secrecy was thrown off and Lugers of "S/42" and "Mauser" manufacture, which were in reality one and the same, were marked with the actual dates in numbers over the

chamber. It should be noted that the "K" and "G" markings appeared over the chamber in the exact place where the date would normally have been. The names "S/42" and "Mauser" were placed on the forward link of the toggle where the scrolled DWM trademark had previously been encountered. Those few Lugers intended for commercial sale carried only the "Mauser" marking, and were without dates or other stampings over the chamber. Examples were produced in both 7.65mm and 9mm calibers. All had barrels 4 inches long.

Mauser, however, was not the only supplier of Lugers in the 1934–35 period — during that time another name was added to the growing list of Luger producers. It has been said Herman Göring, Marshal of the German Air Force, had a personal interest in weapons produced by the Heinrich Krieghoff Waffenfabrik of Suhl. For one reason or another, Göring decided that his Luftwaffe would be supplied with Lugers produced by that firm. In those days, however, demand far exceeded ability to supply, and the only manner in which any sizable quantity of Lugers could be obtained in a relatively short time was through the assembly of the millions of spare, or replacement parts left over from World War I. Krieghoff acquired the necessary parts, doubtless through his powerful political connections, and began to assemble the Lugers requested by Göring Like the Mausers, these were marked with a code date, but not with a code name. Because their full production did not begin until 1935, Krieghoff Lugers are to be found bearing only one code date, an "S," indicating the year 1935, stamped over the chamber. As Krieghoff's capacity to produce was on a much smaller scale than that of Mauser, and also because he too marketed a small portion of his total output commercially, it was evidently not deemed necessary for the Krieghoff Lugers to employ a code name. Consequently, as did DWM, Krieghoff marked all of his Lugers with his commercial brand. The trademark of Krieghoff was an anchor, the upright body of which was formed by a dagger pointing downward, the letter "H" on the left side of the anchor and the letter "K" on the right. Directly below was the wording, in two lines, "Krieghoff" and "Suhl." Some examples, however, bear only the word "Suhl," the "Krieghoff" having been omitted.

ture, Krieghoff Lugers do not have a letter following the serial number, though with this one exception, they are numbered in the military system. A few examples may be encountered bearing dates of "1936" and "1937" which do not conform to the proper serial number range. These were pieces assembled from already numbered surplus parts at those later dates.

Some of the Mauser-made Lugers will be found bearing not only the commercial Mauser Banner but also carrying a date-stamp over the chamber. Such arms were originally intended for commercial sale, but when the German military forces demanded more Lugers than normal Mauser production could supply, pistols

by the Wehrmacht, the German Armed Forces, who had the power to dispose of any surplus as they saw fit.

In 1945 and 1946 a small quantity of Lugers were assembled from surplus parts left over from 1942, the year in which official production of the Luger was superseded by that of the Walther "P.38." These were put together at the direction of the French Occupation Forces, in whose zone of occupation the Mauser factory was situated. Exact amounts produced and specifications thereof are not known. Krieghoff, too, assembled a few hundred Luger pistols, in the period following the war, for American occupation troops. It was among these latter that the unusual pieces bearing no date and no name were found.

After exactly 30 years of Army service in Germany progress finally caught up with the Luger when that Government adopted the Walther "Heeres Pistole," or "P.38" (Pistol Model 1938), though production continued through necessity until 1942. Switzerland, which since 1924 had produced its own Luger, followed suit in 1948, when the Neuhausen replaced it. The loss of World War II by Germany was the coup de grace for the Luger. Countries that had been dependent upon Germany for their supplies of the pistol were forced to turn in other directions when their orders could no longer be filled by the Mauser Werke.

Regardless of the fact that it is no longer produced, the Luger is not a "has been" by any means. Over a period of 40 years literally millions were produced, most of which are today in the hands of the military the world over. There are thousands of soldiers, marksmen and gun fanciers to whom it will never lose its value as a weapon for defense, shooting, or as a collector's item.

Quite possibly Luger production may never again be resumed. Should this prove to be true, all Lugers, especially the rarer ones, will increase in value and the demand will grow. No matter which course the armies of the world pursue, the Luger is now and shall always remain one of the greatest handguns in history.

REGARDLESS OF THE FACT THAT IT IS NO LONGER PRODUCED, THE LUGER IS NOT A "HAS BEEN" BY ANY MEANS. OVER A PERIOD OF 40 YEARS LITERALLY MILLIONS WERE PRODUCED, MOST OF WHICH ARE TODAY IN THE HANDS OF THE MILITARY THE WORLD OVER

Others, some of which are marked only with the word "Suhl" and still others with both words, are found with the added markings "Heinrich Krieghoff Waffenfabrik, Suhl" in two lines on the left side of the frame. Pieces so marked will usually have a letter "P" preceding the serial number. Those Krieghoff Lugers having the letter "P" before the serial number, may not necessarily have the wording on the side of the frame, however. Guns with the "P" are examples of the few commercial Krieghoff Lugers placed for sale in both 7.65mm and 9mm. Areas over the chamber will be unmarked on these commercial pieces. The trademark is, of course, stamped on the forward link of the toggle. Beginning in 1936 Krieghoff, like Mauser, dated his products with the year of manufacture in numbers. Those Krieghoff Lugers with the code date "S," or 1935 over the chamber were probably not serial numbered higher than #5,000. Pieces dated "1936" have been observed from the #5,000 series to the #7,000 series. Unlike those of Mauser manufac-

previously set aside for the commercial market were merely stamped with a date and accepted by the Army as regular issue weapons.

In 1936 the secret code names were augmented. Mauser was assigned the code number "42" in addition to the "S/42" already in use. It is not unusual, then, to find Lugers bearing the code name "S/42" and, for example, the date "1936," and also to encounter "42" pieces having the same date. To add to the confusion, pieces were also produced bearing the same date, "1936," and inscribed with the commercial Mauser Banner.

In 1941 yet another code name was given to Mauser, in this case "byf." Most examples of "byf" Lugers will have black plastic grips, a semi-successful experiment. These "byf" Lugers were in addition to and did not replace the "S/42", "42" and "Mauser" types.

According to reliable sources none of the Luger producing firms were permitted to sell their pistols commercially after 1940 or 1941. All production was claimed

MARS
Automatic Pistols

▌ Larry S. Sterett

(Top) **The Mars Model 1899.** The second known model and probably the first weapon produced by Webley & Scott in an attempt to refine the crude Mars design. Locking by revolving lugs was retained, but an outside hammer was provided. An experimental model, it was soon replaced by a less cumbersome design. Overall length, 12½" with a 6" bbl. Weight, with empty 8-round magazine, 54 ozs. Completely finished, it is marked on the bbl.: MARS AUTOMATIC PISTOL (Cal. .36); on the breech-bolt: MARS AUTOMATIC PISTOL (Cal. .36) MADE BY THE WEBLEY & SCOTT REVOLVER & ARMS CO. LTD. There is no serial number.
(Below) **The first known Mars pistol**, the one submitted to T. W. Webley in May, 1898. The pistol was completed by Gabbett-Fairfax in Apr., 1898, and patents 9066–9068 were granted for its design. 12½" long overall with a 6" bbl. Weight, with empty 8-round magazine, 53 ozs. Cal., 360. Never completely finished, tool marks are visible, and it's still in the white. No markings or serial numbers.
Both of the above are in the Webley & Scott, Ltd., collection in Birmingham.

A LTHOUGH automatic pistols have never replaced revolvers as being the most suitable handguns for all purposes, feeling at the close of the 19th century was that they might. Several automatic pistol designs had appeared on the continent of Europe, and were receiving wide acclaim, among them the Mauser, the Borchardt, and the Pieper. About this time an Englishman, Hugh W. Gabbett-Fairfax, came forth with his design for the ultimate in autoloading handguns. By combining a locked breech of great strength with a cartridge of high velocity, he intended to produce a weapon which would be limited only by material strength — and the strength of the user!

The first actually known Mars pistol appeared in April, 1898, and was submitted to Mr. T. W. Webley, of Webley & Scott Revolver & Arms Co. Ltd., in May of that same year. Public feeling and Mr. Webley's reaction to this English designed pistol is recorded in the following brief passage from Webley history:[1]

"An article in the Daily Chronicle dated Feb. 2nd, 1899, drew attention to several automatic pistols which were being marketed. They were the Mauser, Borchardt and Pieper. The article went on to say that it looked as though the revolver was going to be replaced by the automatic and that Birmingham was doing nothing to replace the business it was about to lose. It accused the British manufacturer of being too conservative and too slow."

Countering this report, Mr. Webley gave an interview to a reporter of the Birmingham Daily Post (Apr. 2, 1899), disclosing that, as noted above, Gabbett-Fairfax's pistol design, in crude form, had been submitted to Webleys.

"Mr. Webley formed so high an opinion of the Mars that the Company undertook to work out the details at their own expense and take sole license for manufacture when completed.

"It was a very heavy pistol and took a large charge of cordite or nitro powder. Several models were made but the pistol was not produced in quantities."

Although there were other weapons and pistols preceding the 1898 pistol, dating from 1895 and 1896, none survived. They were of a different design from the four-lug, rotating breech-bolt 1898 model and later versions. The 1898 design, granted British patent 9067, was chambered for a bottleneck 360 caliber cartridge. The magazine was located in the grip, but instead of the cartridges being fed directly into the chamber, they were shoved onto a lifter, located forward of the magazine and above the trigger guard. This lifter was then forced upward by spring action and the cartridges fed into the chamber.

The first known model of the Mars made by Webley appeared in late 1899. It used the Model 1898 method of locking and feeding, and was the same 360 caliber. The only major change was an outside hammer to facilitate cocking.

Under the direction of Gabbett-Fairfax and one W. J. Whiting[2] the Webley concern produced about 12 specimen pistols, in calibers 8.5mm, 9mm, 360, 10mm, and 45 Long, these supposed to have been marked with Roman numerals from I to XII. A few of them were modified at a later date, such modifications being indicated by a letter F following the Roman numeral.

In 1900 the Mars pistol became, more or less, standardized. Patent 14,777 (Aug. 17, 1900), was for a weapon using the same method of locking as the previous models, but with a much shorter breech-bolt and an entirely different method of feeding. Instead of the cartridges being fed forward out of the magazine, they were now pulled backward out of the magazine, tilted upward, and then fed into the chamber.

In 1901 the Mars Automatic Pistol Syndicate, Ltd., of Birmingham, was

Hugh W. Gabbett-Fairfax

formed to promote the sale of the pistols. About this same time Webley lost interest in the Mars and stopped further development, turning the pistols over to the inventor. The Syndicate intended to outfit a factory for the manufacture of the Mars, but never did so. Instead, the pistols were made by small gunmakers in Birmingham and in London, with the design and improvement work being done by one Col. Johnstone and a Mr. Brown, coworkers of Gabbett-Fairfax. Beginning with a new number 1, Syndicate specimens went to at least number 56. The calibers available were the 8.5mm, 9mm, 360, 45 Long and 45

Short. The 10mm cartridge was dropped and 472 caliber, on which the inventor had begun working in March, 1901, was also dropped when even the 450 Long proved too powerful. Pistols were made with barrels as long as 12 inches, some had a provision for a shoulder stock.

The British government had, for some time, been considering the possibility of adopting the automatic pistol as a service weapon. A Committee was appointed to study the weapons available, and on Jan. 7, 1901, the War Office had opened the first file, relating to the Mars automatic pistol. The first firing trial of the Mars did not take place until late March of 1901, but the Committee met on March 11, 1901, with reference to the Mars. The minutes of this meeting follow:

Minute No. 416/11.3.1901 W.O. Paper 84/H/3494 Subject U9./6. Automatic Pistols "MARS"

Director General of Ordnance submitted, for the consideration of the Committee, the following description of the above pistol:

"The 'Mars' pistol is loaded, cocked, and the fired cartridge ejected automatically. The cartridge is inserted into the barrel of the pistol, whereby the entire force of the powder gas is utilized, and large charges of slow-burning smokeless powder can be used.

"The revolver, on the contrary, must be cocked after each discharge, and the powder is not consumed in the barrel, but in a separate detachable chamber at the rear of the barrel, a large proportion of the propelling power of the gas being thereby wasted. Smokeless powder can be used in the revolver in very limited charges only.

"It will be possible, when the plant necessary for production in quantities has been laid down, to place upon the market a thoroughly reliable automatic pistol at a cost no greater than that of a first-class self-extracting revolver; its weight and length do not exceed that of the latter; the working parts are not so numerous, and the 'Mars' automatic pistol is not more complicated than any self-extracting revolver.

2

The Mars Model 1899 -disassembled. Note the three locking lugs on the rotating breech bolt and the conventional magazine.

Calibre		Charge	Cordite	Projectile	Weight
XI.	10mm or 0.394"	12 grains	Flake	175 grains	2 lbs. 14 ozs.
X.	9mm or 0.354"	12 "	"	160 "	2 lbs. 13 ozs.
III.F.	8.5mm or 0.335"	10 "	"	150 "	2 lbs. 9 ozs.
VI.	0.360"	12 "	"	156 "	2 lbs. 10½ ozs.
VII.	0.360"	12 "	"	156 "	2 lbs. 15 ozs.

Length of barrel, 9.2"; number of shots in magazine, 10. N.B.
These pistols are shorter over all than revolvers with 7½" barrel, except No. VI, which has a barrel 12" long.

"The following are the standard models of 'Mars' pistols:

"With any of these pistols very accurate shooting can be made at 300 yards without rest or stock. With the detachable stock and 12" barrel the shooting is good at 600 yards. The 'Mars' pistol, is, in fact, from its very high velocity and great power, a small and very compact rifle. Long and short barrels can be supplied with any model, and all parts of the pistols interchange where the model is the same.

"A practically continuous fire can be maintained with the 'Mars' firearms, as the cartridges are fed into the weapon in magazine clips which are instantaneously inserted, and which are made to contain as many as twelve cartridges.

"The 'Mars' rifle can be retained in the firing position at the shoulder, and will fire when the trigger is pulled, eject the fired cartridge, and reload automatically. The magazine contains ten cartridges. In the sudden rush of a. numerous body of enemies, or when in pursuit of dangerous game, the immense advantage thus possessed by the bearer of a 'Mars' rifle is apparent. Automatic rifles on the 'Mars' system will be produced about as cheaply as any high-class non-automatic military or sporting rifles.

"Automatic shotguns[3] on the 'Mars' system, superior in many respects and equal in all, except as regards finish, to the very best London hand-made double-barrel shotguns, will be marketable (with a handsome profit) at about 20 per cent of the cost of the latter.

"The 'Mars' is the only automatic firearm in which the recoil is completed and the barrel and breech block move forward together in their return movement to the normal position before the breech block

The upper pistol is marked MARS PISTOL 9mm = 354 on top of the barrel rib. 11" overall with an 8¾" bbl., weight with an empty 10-round magazine is 52 ozs. The numbers 93/647 are scratched upside-down on the receiver. Similar numbers appear on other models. What they signify is not known.

The lower pistol is marked MARS PISTOL 8.5mm on top of the barrel rib. Also 11" overall with 8¾" bbl., with empty 10-round magazine it weighs 49 ozs. 93/648 is scratched upside-down on the left side of the receiver.

A pistol similar to the lower pistol is in a Washington, D.C. collection. It carries serial number 19. The left side of the receiver is engraved: PISTOLET MARS, Brevette S.G.D.G., A. Guinard, 8 avenue de l'Opera Paris. (See footnote 8.)

Still in its original case, along with a box of 8.5mm Mars cartridges, spare mainspring and an extra magazine, it is believed to be the only complete Mars outfit in existance.

The two pistols illustrated above are in the collection of the Imperial Chemical Industries, Ltd., in Birmingham.

is unlocked from the barrel. Therefore, the 'Mars' system ensures absolute safety, as the breech block is not unlocked until the gas from the discharged cartridge has left the barrel. Nor can the 'Mars' weapon be discharged until the breech has been entirely closed.

"Mr. Gabbett-Fairfax and Lieut. Col. Johnstone attended [the meeting] and explained the mechanism of the pistol.

"(The) Secretary (is) to arrange for Mr. Gabbett-Fairfax and Lieut. Col. John-

stone to take the pistol to Enfield Lock and make a firing trial. The Supt. R.S.A. F.[4] to furnish a report of the result."

On March 13, 1901, Fairfax wrote to the Director General of Ordnance, "I shall be prepared with an automatic magazine pistol to fulfill the following conditions, viz.: Magazine to contain eight cartridges. Projectile, 250 to 260 grains. Muzzle velocity not less than 1,000 f.s.," and he added that such a pistol would be ready for trial by the 1st of June.

This pistol, owned by R. Alexander Montgomery of Philadelphia, is 11½ overall with an 8¾ bbl. It weighs 52½ ozs. with empty magazine. The top of the barrel rib is marked MARS PISTOL 0 "450 , and 93/646 is scratched upside-down on the receiver. There are several other numbers on this weapon: 195 on the right side, forward of the right hand cocking knob; 19 on the right, forward of the hammer pin; 79 on the bottom of the butt, forward of the magazine, and 8 on the magazine itself.

Left — Mars cartridges in the H. P.White Co. collection: left to right — 8.5mm, 9mm, 450 Long and 45 Short.

The D.G.O., on March 20, 1901, forwarded Mr. Fairfax's letter to the Committee and requested that they make a recommendation with reference to his proposal.

On March 25, 1901, the Committee met to discuss the Mars firing trial, which had been held at Enfield Lock the preceding week. The minutes of this meeting follow:

Minute No. 427/25.3.1901 W.O. Paper 84/H/3502 Subject 119/6. Automatic Pistols "MARS" Previous Minute 416/11.3.1901

Supt. R.S.A.F. 16.3.1901, reported as follows on firing trial of above pistol:

"Mr. Fairfax and Col. Johnstone came here on the 12th instant, and tried various experiments with the 'Mars' pistol.

"The pistol, with 7-in. barrel, was fired with a charge of 10 grains cordite (the proper charge of 12 grains could not be obtained in time for the experiment.) Weight of bullet, 155 grains, .35-in. diameter.

a) It penetrated 18½ in. deal boards 1-in. apart, as against the Service Webley of 10 boards. Range, 12½ yards.

b) The enclosed shows the diagram obtained by Mr. Fairfax at 15 yards.No "diagrams" were found with the records.

c) Captain Wallace and myself fired the pistol, which worked well, and without excessive jar on the wrist.

d) Owing to the charge not being sufficient, there were one or two failures, but fire was immediately resumed by pulling back the breech mechanism.

e) As with all automatic pistols, the mechanism is rather complicated, but still it seems to work well, and appears worthy of a further trial.

f) Mr. Fairfax said he was prepared to produce a pistol with a .47-in. bullet, giving a muzzle velocity of 1,000 (f.s.). This, it seems to me, would suit Service requirements as to man-stopping power."

Following this report, the Committee recommended that two pistols of Fairfax's design, but with a .45-in. bore, be obtained for further trials.

These were ready for trial in late October. On Nov. 11, 1901, the Committee met, following receipt of the D.G.O. report of the firing trial. The minutes of this meeting follow:

Minute No. 55¾.11.1901 W.O. Paper 84/F/1770 Subject 119./6. Automatic Pistol "MARS" Previous Minute No. 450/6.5.1901

D.G.O. forwards W.O. Paper 84/F/1770 containing the following report

on the firing trial with the above pistol:

Chief Inspector of Small Arms to Director General of Ordnance, 1 Nov. 1901.

"Mr. Fairfax attended and delivered two 'Mars' pistols and 450 rounds .45-bore ammunition. Fifty rounds were fired without any mishap. The velocity at 90 ft. was 1,137 f.s.; the penetration at 25 yards was 16 to 18½-inch deal boards one inch apart.

"The accuracy at 25 and 100 yards range was good. The pistol handled comfortably, but the recoil was heavy. The weight of the pistol with magazine empty is 3 lbs. 1 oz.; with magazine full, 3 lbs. 9 ozs.

"The pistol was stripped, and required the use of tools to do so. The parts were numerous and complicated, and the pistol would require a good deal of training on the part of the armourers to strip and reassemble.

"Next day I fired 31 rounds. At first round an empty case caught in the mechanism, and at the last round the connecting piece broke, preventing the pistol from firing. The ejection is straight to the rear, and sometimes the empty cartridges strike one in the face.

"The magazines, which are inserted and withdrawn through the bottom of the stock, hold eight rimless cartridges, firing 11.57 grains of finely cut cordite and a 216-grain bullet covered with a stout nickel envelope.

"Return of the pistols to Mr. Fairfax to lighten the pull-off and to remedy the defect of the cartridges striking the face on extraction.

"When the pistols are returned by Mr. Fairfax one should be forwarded to C.S.O.F. to be fired to ascertain its man-stopping power in comparison with the Borchardt pistol, Minute No. 534/7.10.1901, and then sent to Commandant, Hythe, for accuracy trial and report as to the general working of the mechanism.

"The other pistol should be sent to the Captain H.M.S. 'Excellent' for trial and report. 100 rounds of ammunition to be supplied for trials at Hythe and H.M.S. 'Excellent' and 50 for trials at Woolwich."

On Nov. 23, 1901, representatives of the press were invited by Mr. Fairfax to witness a demonstration of the Mars pistol. A full report of the demonstration appeared in the Dec, 1901, issue of Arms & Explosives.[1]

"...Apart from the fact of its British origin, the 'Mars' has various other features entitling it to favourable criticism. Hitherto there has been a somewhat distinct dividing line between the automatic pistol and the revolver in respect to calibre, the ammunition of the former being, with one exception, of relatively small calibre, and in no way comparable in actually shock-producing effects with the larger, heavier, and slower-moving bullet of the revolver. Reasons for this difference are not far to seek. The tendency of the day towards high velocities and long ranges needs no elaboration or explanation. Therefore, the fact stands that in the leading and successful types of automatic pistol now in use the calibre rarely exceeds .300 in., or the weight of bullet 100 grains, while the muzzle velocity ranges between 1,000 and 1,400 ft. per second, as against the .455 calibre, 265-grain bullet and 700 ft. per second velocity, which are adopted in the Service revolver.

"...the inventor of the 'Mars' pistol

has turned his energies in the direction of producing a weapon which should combine the shock-producing qualities of the Service arm with the superior ballistics and the more rapid manipulation of the automatic pistol, and it is interesting to notice how the development has been brought about, and how far successfully accomplished. At the present time there are three calibres of the 'Mars' in existence, advancing by steady degrees from a minimum of 8.5mm, or .3346 in., to .360 in. and .450 in. It will be noted that even the smallest calibre is larger than the average of the other automatic pistols...The largest calibre is approximately that of the British Service revolver, but the ballistic qualities of the two arms are of a very widely-removed character.

"...the cartridge for the .450 calibre 'Mars' pistol is of distinctly up-to-date design, weighing approximately 363 grs., of which the empty shell contributes 130 grs. The nickel-coated bullet is of 220 grs. weight, and is propelled by from 12 to 14 grs. of cordite, the latter amount only having been quite recently adopted. This cartridge gives a muzzle velocity of about 1,250 ft. per second, corresponding to an energy of about 760 ft.-lbs. In other words, it gives a muzzle energy practically 2⅔ rds greater than that obtained with the Service ammunition. Superior relative results are also obtained from the smaller calibres, the 8½ mm pistol with its 140-gr. bullet and 1,750 ft. per second velocity, showing a muzzle energy of 950 ft.-lbs., and the .360 calibre, with a bullet weighing 160 grs., and a muzzle velocity of about 1,640 ft. per

second, developing about 960 ft.-lbs. of energy. The ammunition...is supplied by Messrs. Eley Bros., Ltd....By the way, the 8½mm and .360 cartridges are of the bottle-neck pattern, while that of the .450 calibre is straight-tapered, all being provided with a rim groove. Each calibre of bullet has two cannelures, and the inventor of the 'Mars' pistol may take some credit to himself for the neat and practical design of his ammunition. There is no projecting shoulder where the cartridge case ends, but the metal is bevelled off and then compressed all round into the top cannelure of the bullet, thus making a very efficient junction of the two components of the complete cartridge.

"...Unfortunately, Mr. Gabbet-Fairfax was not able to give extended displays of the rapidity of fire possible with his pistol, owing to the fact that he had not received the expected supply of ammunition, and had very few cartridges available. But he was able to demonstrate the ease and rapidity of working of all calibres of the 'Mars' up to the full extent to which speed of fire would be desirable, in so far as it would be possible to take aim in shooting. And beyond that, he was able to give a very practical trial of the ballistic qualities of his pistol, as compared with others, by means of a series of tests for penetration:

Although all three Mars calibers

Pistol	Calibre	Weight of Bullet	Charge of Powder	Muzzle Velocity	Penetration of 1 in. Deal Boards
	ins.	grs.	grs.	ft. per sec.	No.
Colt Revolver	.455	265	18	700	6
Colt Automatic	.360	105	7.8	1,260	8½
Mauser	.300	85	7.75	1,400	10
Mars	.450	220	12	1,250	10½
"	.450	220	12	1,250	11
"	.360	160	12	1,640	12
" (8½ mm.)	.334	140	10	1,750	16½

To indicate the capacities of the pistol for long-range shooting, the inventor showed one of .360 calibre fitted with a 12 in. barrel and a neat detachable stock for firing from the shoulder, but it was impossible at that time and under the circumstances to make a detailed trial. Even under disadvantages, however, it was seen that the pistol could make fair practice at over 100 yards..."

5

6

(LEFT) **This pistol** is marked .450 MARS PISTOL on top of the barrel rib. 11¾ overall with an 8¾ bbl., it weighs 50 ozs. with empty magazine. 53 appears on the front base of the butt and on the base of the magazine. Photograph courtesy Sidney Aberman.

(Right) **This pistol**, from the Pattern Room of the Royal Small Arms Factory at Enfield Lock, is marked on top of the barrel THE MARS PISTOL .450. 11½ overall with a 9½ bbl., weight with an empty 8-round magazine is 50 ozs. Serial No. 52. The magazine shows clearly that the cartridges must be extracted rearward, instead of in the conventional manner of being pushed forward.

were demonstrated at this public exhibition, the main pistol used was of 360 caliber, with a 10-shot magazine. Barrel length, from muzzle to breechblock was 8.7 in., or to the back of the latter, 9.5 in. Overall length of the pistol was 11.5 in., its weight 2 lbs. 10 ozs.

On 28 Apr., 1902, the Committee again met to discuss further trials of the Mars pistols and make recommendations. The minutes of this meeting were as follows:

Minute No. 615/28.4.1902 W.O. Paper 84/F/1805
Subject Further Trials of "MARS" Pistols of .36-inch and .45-inch Calibres
Previous Minute No. 603 III./17.3.1902

D.G.O., 25.4.1902, forwards W.O. Paper 84/F/1805 containing the following report on pistols as above. The inventor states that one of the .45-inch pistols submitted is of an improved type; the other is one of those previously tried, but converted to the pattern of the former.

Chief Inspector of Small Arms to Director-General of Ordnance, 24 Apr. 1902.

"A representative on the 21st instant brought down a .45 and a .36 inch 'Mars' pistol, which were stated to have had the mechanism altered and simplified. They were first fired for velocity:

.36-inch gave 1,470 f.s., 90 feet from the muzzle.

.45-inch gave 1,142 f.s., 90 feet from the muzzle.

"When fired to test the penetration, the .36-inch at 25 yards' range perforated the entire apparatus used for testing, viz., 22½-inch planks 1 inch apart, and the back of the box 1 inch thick. It was fired again with bullets with special thin envelopes. One bullet passed through 17 and one through 20½-inch planks. The bullets have the points flattened. Samples forwarded.

"The .45-inch at 25 yards' range perforated 18 and 19½-inch planks set 1 inch apart. Bullets forwarded.

"The pistols were fired for accuracy, and to compare the recoil with a Webley pistol. The accuracy was decidedly good (see diagrams),No "diagrams" were found with the records. but the recoil was much heavier than with the Webley, and the pull-off was heavy and rather grating. The certainty of action was not very good, for with the .36-inch there were three cases of insufficient recoil and two miss-fires; the latter were partly accounted for by deep-set caps.

"With the .45-inch there were two miss-fires; which exploded on second trial.

"Fine sand was then blown over the pistols; the .36-inch in eight rounds missed fire twice, and twice the breech had to be closed by hand.

"Total rounds fired:

.36-inch, 34 rounds — .45-inch, 44 rounds

"The .36-inch bore 'Mars' pistol will be sent to Superintendent, R.L.6, as soon as the makers send a further supply of ammunition.

"The recoil of these pistols is very severe. Mr. Fairfax should be asked whether he could alter the .45-inch pistol so as to give a velocity not greater than 1,000 f.s., and as much less down to 800 as he could arrange for. Also whether an uncoated hard lead bullet, similar to the Webley Mark II. bullet, or a bullet of a softer character than those recently tried, could be supplied for use with this pistol."

In Oct., 1902, the Mars Automatic Pistol Syndicate, Ltd., issued their first and only catalog, from 29/35 Whitehouse St., Aston, Birmingham. In it were listed pistols of the 1901 model, available in calibers 8.5mm, 360, and 450 Long. The following data, taken from the catalog, compare these three calibers with three other handguns of similar calibers:

In Oct., 1902, the trial aboard the "Excellent," which had been discussed

Pistol	Caliber	Bullet weight, grs.	Powder charge, grs.	Muzzle vel., fps	Muzzle energy, ft.lbs.
Colt Revolver	455	265	18	700	287
Colt Automatic	360	105	7.8	1,260	364
Mauser	300	85	7.75	1,400	379
Mars	450	220	12	1,250	760
"	360	160	12	1,640	969
" (8½ mm)	335	140	10	1,750	950

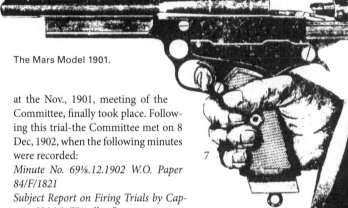

The Mars Model 1901.

at the Nov., 1901, meeting of the Committee, finally took place. Following this trial-the Committee met on 8 Dec, 1902, when the following minutes were recorded:

Minute No. 69⅛.12.1902 W.O. Paper 84/F/1821

Subject Report on Firing Trials by Captain, H.M.S. "Excellent"

Previous Minute No. 635 11⅓3.6 1902

D.G.O., 22.11.1902, forwarded the following for consideration and report, and notified that the inventor would attend the meeting to explain the working of the pistol. Mr. Fairfax attended.

Director of Naval Ordnance to Director-General of Ordnance, 23 Oct., 1902.

"Please see following report of Captain of 'Excellent,' with which I concur. The results confirm those obtained at the previous trial of this pistol at Whale Island.[7]

"Sample cartridges received with 'Excellent's' report are forwarded.

Captain, H.M.S. "Excellent," 20 Oct., 1902:

"Extended further trial has now been carried out. 'Mars' pistol and 500 rounds of ammunition were received 27.9.1902 (a); another 500 rounds of ammuntion

were received 13.10.1902 (b); 122 rounds of (a) and 18 rounds of (b) have been fired by five officers and four men.

"The pistol has jammed several times, the last time necessitating stripping before it could be made safe. The cause of this jam was apparently the canting of the cartridges in the magazine. The ammunition has been improved since former trial; there were no miss-fires due to ammunition.

"On two occasions the last cartridge in the magazine was telescoped (samples forwarded).

"No one who fired once with the pistol wished to shoot with it again; several of those who fired are good shots and in the 'Excellent's' pistol team.

"Further trial I consider quite unnecessary. Its disadvantages are as follows:

1. Liability to jam.
2. Weight.
3. Unwieldy shape.
4. Difficult to hold steady. The handle being between the sights, any shakiness

of the hand becomes amplified.

5. The fired cartridges constantly strike the firer in the face.

6. Mechanism complicated and would, in the hands of men not thoroughly acquainted with it, be a dangerous weapon.

Opinion.

"That this pistol is quite unsuitable for adoption in Navy.

"Mr. Fairfax called at the War Office on 4 Nov., 1902 and explained the many difficulties in preparing a satisfactory design of automatic pistol to fire a heavy bullet, and that it would be of great assistance to him if trials might be made in the presence of a representative.

"D.N.O., 13.11.1902, did not think any further trials in the presence of Mr. Fairfax's representative were necessary in view of Captain of 'Excellent's' reports.

"The Committee defer consideration of this question pending receipt of report of trials at Hythe, and of replies from the makers of the Borchardt, Roth, Bergmann, Browning Andrews, and Colt pistols, as to whether they can supply a pistol with a calibre of not less than .4-inch, and firing a bullet of a weight not less than 200 grains."

Apparently the reports from the trials at Hythe were not encouraging, for the Committee did not immediately recommend the ordering of any Mars pistols.

On Feb. 2, 1903, the Committee again met to consider some letters received from Fairfax concerning reimbursement for expenses incurred in developing the Mars, an requesting permission to give another exhibition of the pistol's abilities. In the minutes of this meeting, no recommendation was made of reimbursing him.

Minute No. 719/2.2.1903 W.O. Paper 84/F/1856

Subject: 119.6. "Mars"

Previous Minute No. 707v./12.1.1903

D.G.O., 23.1.1903, forwarded the following letters and asked for a report on the pistols:

Mr. Gabbett-Fairfax to Director-General of Ordnance, 20th Jan. 1903.

"I have the honour to submit to you that the cost of experiments necessary to

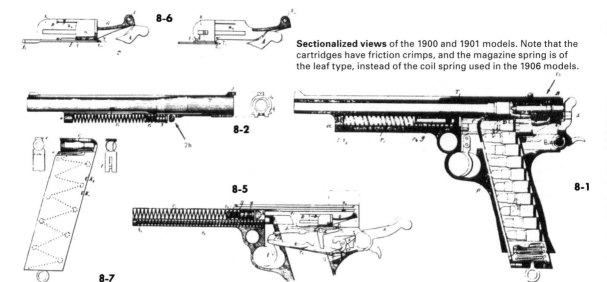

8-6

Sectionalized views of the 1900 and 1901 models. Note that the cartridges have friction crimps, and the magazine spring is of the leaf type, instead of the coil spring used in the 1906 models.

8-2

8-5

8-1

8-7

the production of the 'Mars' pistols, calibre .450-inch, recently supplied to H.M.'s War Department, and of the ammunition therefore, amounts to over £2000. It appears that the objection to this model is that it is too powerful, giving too great a shock to the hand.

"I now have the honour to advise you that, while I am anxious to provide an arm which shall in all respects conform to the requirements of your Department, I cannot undertake further experiments to that end at my personal expense. I would therefore suggest, sir, that a grant of £1000 be made to me from the Public Funds for the production of a pistol to conform to your specification."

Mr. Gabbett-Fairfax to Director-General of Ordnance, 27th Jan. 1903.

"Referring to previous correspondence with your Department on the subject of 'Mars' automatic pistol, I would respectfully suggest that I be permitted to give an exhibition of the shooting of the 'Mars' pistols furnished to your Department at such time and place as you may appoint.

"In order that I may be enabled to make a pistol which would completely satisfy and conform to all requirements of your Department, I would ask that I should be supplied with a complete written statement setting forth the results of the various trials and stating clearly in what respects the pistol is considered unsatisfactory.

"I feel confident that due consideration will be paid to the fact that, in bringing the pistol to its present perfected form, I have incurred the expenditure of a large sum of money; and, therefore, in the event of further modifications being considered necessary by your Department, I would ask that such a sum be granted to me as will, in my opinion, be required to carry out such modifications.

"If an arrangement of this kind could be made, there appears to me to be no difficulty in producing a pistol which would meet with your requirement.

"The Committee recommend that Mr. Gabbett-Fairfax be asked if he could give an exhibition of shooting in London,

and if so, when he would be ready. If the 16th February be convenient some members of the Committee would probably attend."

Whether the 16 February trial, or other trials, ever took place is not known, as all War Office files (except an old correspondence register) on the subject were destroyed. According to the register a file was opened on 19 June, 1903, on the subject "Mars Automatic Patents transferred to Mr. Sanders and Mr. Cartland," and on 22 June, 1903, the interest of the War Office in the Mars pistol ceased to exist.

Disaster faced Gabbett-Fairfax. Although he held patents for such items as engines, power-transmission mechanisms, etc., profits from these inventions apparently weren't enough to cover losses on the Mars. In the Oct., 1903, issue of Arms & Explosives, under the heading "Round the Trade," the following note appeared:

"The usual bankruptcy notice has been issued with reference to the affairs of Mr. H. W. Gabbett-Fairfax. The cause

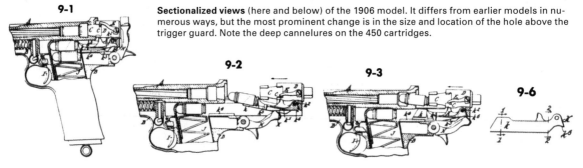

9-1

Sectionalized views (here and below) of the 1906 model. It differs from earlier models in numerous ways, but the most prominent change is in the size and location of the hole above the trigger guard. Note the deep cannelures on the 450 cartridges.

9-2

9-3

9-6

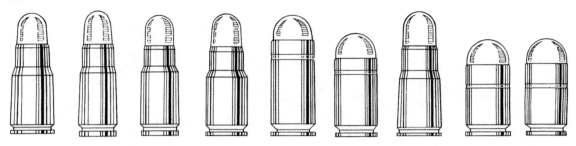

of failure is attributed to delays incidental to obtaining order of assurance from H. M. War Department, leading to the seizure of the patents by the mortgagees. The statement of affairs seem to show that the debtor mainly carried on his experiments with the aid of borrowed money, and no practical results were forthcoming. The losses incurred are mainly attributed to the difference between the amount at which the patents were formerly valued and the sum for which they were mortgaged."

Following seizure of the patents the Mars Automatic Pistol Syndicate, aided by Clement Brown, the former associate of Fairfax, continued work on the Mars, possibly hopeful still of interesting the British and French governments. Although a rumor has long existed that French trials of the Mars were held, only recently was the author able to verify this.[8]

On Dec. 9, 1905, the Mars Syndicate, then of 37 Newhall St., Birmingham, and Clement Brown, Engineer, of 154 Trinity Road, Aston, Birmingham, applied for a patent on an improved version of the 1900 model. This improved model was manufactured by various small Birmingham

The complete line of Mars cartridges. Left to right: 360, the first known Mars caliber; 8.5mm early type; 8.5mm late type; 9mm 450 Long; 472; 10mm; 450 Short, early type; 450 Short, late type. All cases are drawn to scale, using dimensions taken from actual cartridges, with two exceptions — the 472 and 10mm. Samples of the last two have been unobtainable, so the drawings represent only the author's conception on what they may have looked like. For ease in comparing, all cartridges have been given the same type of rim, though the actual rims were more like fig. 10. The larger calibers have been given one type of crimp, while the smaller calibers have been given another type, only two of the many variant forms of crimps used on Mars cartridges.

gunmakers and placed on the commercial market in 1906. It never became a sales success and by the end of 1907 it was no longer being made. The few pistols remaining on hand were disposed of through small dealers. Thus, within a decade, the "world's most powerful handgun" hit the limelight and passed into oblivion.

The Mars Pistols

It is extremely difficult to give the Mars pistols model designations, because of the variant forms and the lack of designation on actual weapons. The author has, therefore, attempted to classify them by comparing actual weapons with dated patent specifications and photographs. While the possibility of other versions cannot be overlooked, there appear to have been three main types — the Mod-

els 1900, 1901, and 1906. Figs. 3 (lower), 4, 5, and 8-1, are of the Model 1900. Figs. 3 (upper), and 8-5, are of the Model 1901. Fig. 6 is of the Model 1906.

The basic action of the Mars pistol is one of the strongest and most peculiar designs ever applied to a selfloading handgun. Peculiar, not so much for its unusual method of locking as in its method of feeding. The normal feed-system in a selfloading handgun is for the breechblock, as it moves forward, to shove a cartridge up out of the magazine into the chamber. In the Mars the manner of feeding is entirely different. As the breechblock recoils backward, two fingers below the bolt proper withdraw a cartridge backwards from the magazine. Then the cartridge is tilted upward at an angle of about 30°, the empty case is ejected, and eventually

[1]Webley 1790–1953, by C.W.T. Craig and E. G. Bewley, F.C.I.S., Webley & Scott Ltd., Birmingham 4, England, p. 25.
[2]W. J. Whiting served as the mechanical brains to Fairfax, while the Mars was under development at Webley. Later, when Fairfax elected to continue on his own, Whiting designed the first of a series of Webley automatic pistols, beginning in 1903 with an experimental model chambered for the 455 cartridge.
[3]Fairfax intended to make, at a later date, automatic rifles and shotguns, but none were ever produced.
[4]Royal Small Arms Factory.
[5]The 'Mars' Automatic Pistol." Arms & Explosives, 1, Arundel St., Strand, London, W.C., Vol. IX, pp. 190–192.
[6]Royal Laboratory, Woolwich.
[7]Whale Island is of nearly 90 acres, on the east side of Portsmouth Harbor. This island forms the great Naval Gunnery School. Those in charge of this school are, in the quaint phraseology of the Navy, said to be commissioned to H.M.S. "Excellent," which has no floating properties, and is merely an alias for Whale Island.
[8]The following letter (one of five discovered) has been translated from the French original, and probably refers to an 8.5mm caliber pistol. No report of the actual trial has been located.
The other four letters concern the importation of 2000 rounds of Mars ammunition, possibly of 450 caliber.
Archives de 1 Artillerie

13 Sept. 1901
Monsieur Gabbett, who is the manufacturer of the pistol sent by Mr. Guinard (8, avenue de Opera), came on the 13th at 11:30, accompanied by the latter, and was astonished that we have had functioning difficulties with the weapon. He attributed it to a defective lot of cartridges (weak rim), but has not had any difficulties elsewhere. He would like to return with another weapon of larger caliber, which he would shoot before the service officers. He could return after the 25th, depending on the advice of Mr. Guinard, who will accept the date chosen by Col. Pralin.
These gentlemen have refused to consider for the time being the weapon sent.
Signed: V. Leleu
[9]Complicated action design made the Mars pistol extremely expensive to manufacture, since much detailed machining was necessary. Too, all observed models, with the exception of the inventor's model, have been very well finished, which did not lessen the cost. Just how many Mars pistols were manufactured is not known; probably less than 100, including all variant forms.
[10]1906 models have four tapered locking lugs spaced 90° apart around the bolt-head. 1900 and 1901 models have three tapered locking lugs spaced 120° apart, which rotate approximately 75° to unlock. In all three models the extractor is close beside the topmost lug.
In the 1906 model the loading tray was redesigned for improved efficiency — see fig. 8-6 for the 1900 and 1901 loading tray, and fig. 9-6 for the 1906 loading tray.

(footnotes continued on page 99)

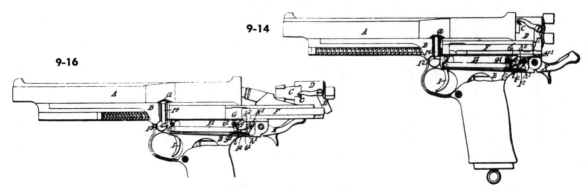

chambering takes place.

A simplified version of the sequence of action of the M1906[10] Mars pistol is as follows:

Fig. 9-14 shows the pistol with a cartridge in the chamber and the hammer cocked, ready to fire. In fig. 9-1, the hammer has fallen and the cartridge discharged. Barrel and breechblock now recoil backward a full 3 inches, compressing the heavy recoil spring and the two lighter breechblock return springs." At this same time the loading tray is pulling a cartridge backward out of the magazine (note opening back of magazine in fig. 9-2). When the barrel and breechblock have reached the full limit of recoil, still locked together, they begin to move forward under the impulse of the three compressed springs. After about one-fourth inch of forward movement a small wedge in the frame causes the actuating bar F (fig. 9-16), to strike the end of the bell-crank lever E, causing it to revolve and rotate the pin C (an integral part of the bolt-head) 45°, unlocking the barrel; the barrel then continues to move forward.

The extractor, near the top lug of the bolt-head, holds the fired case, which is ejected upward by the pressure of the loading tray below; the loading tray having been forced upward by the pressure of the hammer below it (fig. 9-2).

At this point, in all models, no further movement takes place until the finger pressure on the trigger is released (fig. 7), upon which the breechblock moves forward (fig. 9-2). The loading tray releases the fresh cartridge into the path of the moving breechblock, which slams it into the chamber. At the same instant, a strong spring under tension inside the breechblock (fig. 8-r5) is released, causing the bolt lugs to rotate to the right, locking the action closed. As the breechblock moves forward the hammer strikes the tip of the loading tray (k[6], fig. 9-3), camming it back into place under the barrel, ready to pick up another cartridge.

By following this sequence of action, the reader can see that the Mars pistols did not automatically fire, eject the empty case, and chamber a fresh cartridge, for each pull of the trigger in the usual manner. Instead, pulling the trigger only fired the cartridge and ejected the empty case. Then everything stopped.[12] Only after the trigger was released was the fresh cartridge chambered.

Judging from the comments made by individuals firing the various caliber Mars pistols, during the government trials and afterward, they were not the most pleasant weapons to shoot. The pistols, even with long barrels, were well balanced statically, because most of the weight was above the grip, but when the hammer was cocked and the trigger squeezed, things began to happen. The center of gravity suddenly and violently shifted 3 inches to the rear, causing the pistol to literally stand on its tail. This was most alarming when firing the .450 Mars Long cartridge. Even some of the most seasoned shooters were willing to stop after firing a couple of rounds. In the small calibers, however, it was found that with sufficient practice reasonably accurate shooting could be done.[13]

Today, the scarcity of the pistols, coupled with the unusual design, has made the Mars a most desirable collectors item, causing it to be ranked among automatic pistols as the Colt Walker is in the revolver field.

Mars Ammunition

The Mars cartridges were first made by a small brass-working firm in Birmingham, whose name is now lost, but which might have been the predecessor of the Birmingham Metal and Munitions Company, Ltd., or King's Norton Metal Company, Ltd., both of these companies being cartridge manufacturers a few years later. The first quantity lot of Mars cartridges was made by F. Joyce and Co., Ltd., Waltham Abbey, Essex. This company, well-known then as cartridge manufacturers, was taken over (in part) in 1903, and finally entirely, by Nobel's Explosives Company, Ltd. Possibly Joyce and Co. also did some of the earlier work on Mars cartridges.

From about late 1898 to 1901 Mars cartridges were made by Kynoch, Ltd., at their Witton factory. The first recorded firing of Mars ammunition by Kynoch was in March 1899, using the 450 Mars Long cartridge.

Following Kynoch came Eley Brothers, Ltd., London, who were, at this time,

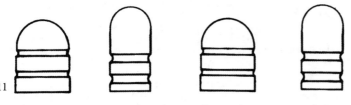

11

45 and 9mm Mars bullets, showing the two crimping cannelures. Full jacketed in cupronickel, the round-nose shape was apparently adopted to gain maximum bullet weight with minimum bullet length, and maximum stopping power with a bullet which would still function through the action.

manufacturing over 400 different varieties of cartridges at their Edmonton factory.

There are literally hundreds of variant forms of the Mars cartridges — some headstamped with the maker's name and caliber, some with the caliber only, some unmarked — depending on how the Mars pistols were performing and who was manufacturing the cartridges. Early cartridges were made with crimped bullets and sometimes a reeded cannelure, with deep set copper Berdan primers. Later, the cartridges were made with one deep cannelure, then with two deep cannelures in the larger calibers, and with flush primers. The clanature also changed — see fig. 10. The cartridges were never adapted to any weapons other than Mars pistols.

The Mars bullets have cupronickel jackets with hemispherical noses. With one known exception — a 360 Mars cartridge headstamped Eley, with 160-gr. hollow point bullet — all bullets are of the full patch or solid variety. The hard lead bullets asked for by the British government were apparently never manufactured. At least no records exist of such bullets, nor does the author know of any Mars cartridges containing unjacketed lead bullets.

Some of the variant forms of Mars cartridges are listed below. Where recorded velocities are shown, the reader must bear in mind that, with the exception of Col. Wilson, who did his own testing, the figures quoted are from old records, and that the velocities were obtained under varying conditions. In general the powders used were of two types, pistol Cordite (a cord form) and flake Cordite. Just what Webley Cordite was is not known. Beginning sometime in 1902, all Mars cartridges were loaded with a "Special Mars Powder," made by Nobel Explosives Co., Ltd. This may have been another name for the Ballistite flake powder — the first nitroglycerine smokeless powder invented by Nobel — listed as being used in the 450 Mars Short cartridge.

Caliber	Bullet weight, grs.	Powder weight, grs.	type	Muzzle Vel. f.s.	Source
8.5mm	140	11.5	P. Cord.	1550*	Kynoch
8.5mm	139			1660†	Pollard
8.5mm	139	10.0	" "	1748†	Pollard
9mm	154	10.0	F Cord.		
9mm	155	12.5	P. Cord.		
9mm	156	12.0	" "	1400*	Kynoch
9mm	156	12.5	" "	1600†	Wilson
9mm	158			1650†	Pollard
360	155	10.0	F. Cord.	1470**	Bady
450 Long	216	11.57	" "	1140**	Bady
450 Long	219			1211†	Pollard
450 Long	220	8.0	Web. Cord.	753***	Bady
450 Long	220	9.0	" "	833***	Bady
450 Long	220	10.0	" "	957***	Bady
450 Long	220	11.0	P. Cord.	1200†	Kynoch
450 Long	220	12.25	F. Cord.		
450 Long	222	12.5	P. Cord.	1222†	Wilson
450 Long	250	10.0	F. Cord.		
450 Long	220	11.4	Nobel		
450 Short	220	9.0	"		
450 Short	220	9.5	P. Cord.		
450 Short	220	9.5	Ballis.		
450 Short	220	9.5	Nobel		

Magazines carry from 8 to 11 cartridges, depending on caliber, and are held in place by the stop P (fig. 8-1). Note in fig. 8-7, and also in fig. 6, that the magazine has two retaining notches, K1 and K2, in which the stop P will catch. When the magazine is caught in the K1 position the pistol is ready for magazine fire; when in the K2 position only one shot at a time can be fired, with the weapon being reloaded manually for each succeeding shot.

[11]All models have a heavy recoil spring located beneath the barrel, with smaller breechblock return springs located on each side and slightly below. A buffer-spring assembly is contained at the rear of the recoil spring. The large pin, seen above the forward part of the trigger guard just below the barrel in all photographs, and in fig. 8-2h, keeps the buffer assembly from moving farther, and takes up part of the shock.

[12]When firing the Mars it was natural to grip it very tightly. The barrel would have then returned to its forward position before the trigger was released, allowing the breechblock to move forward. Only by strict concentration, could the trigger be released before the barrel was in battery. To prevent any such premature movement of the breechblock, due to the release of the trigger, the 1906 model incorporated a lock consisting of a recess in the barrel (fig. 9-16a), a vertical pin I4, and an arm on the trigger [13]. If the barrel is in its forward position, the pin rises into the recess and allows the trigger to return to its normal position. If, however, the barrel is not fully forward, the pin cannot rise in the recess. Thus, even though the finger pressure has been released, the trigger cannot return to its normal position and release the breechblock.

[13]An interesting comment appeared in the U.S. Naval Intelligence's 1902 report, "Information from Abroad, Notes on Naval Progress," to the effect that a Mars pistol, 18 inches long, with correct sight, fired from a rest, would keep all its shots on a 4-foot square target at 1000 yards.

Notes and References

The American Rifleman, Apr. 1956.
R. K. Wilson, Textbook of Automatic Pistols, Plantersville, S. C, 1943.
The Gun Collector, No. 24, Sept. 1948.
Illus. 1 and 3 from the Museum of Science & Industry — Crown copyright.
The author would like to thank the following people and organizations for their help in making this story possible: Eric Bewley of Webley & Scott, Ltd.; Keith Dunham of the Birmingham City Museum; R. L. Lees of the Birmingham Proof House; the British War Office Records Centre; Col. Watts of the Royal Small Arms Factory; Col. H. du Lattay and the bureau "Armements et Etudes;" Imperial Chemical Industries, Ltd.; Mr. Donald Bady; R. Alexander Montgomery; Sidney Aberman; Fred Mullet.

Military Handguns for Sporting Use

■ Frank C. Barnes

LARGE quantities of surplus military handguns have been imported and sold on the American market, usually at low prices compared to new sporting or self-defense weapons. Many purchasers know little about such pistols or revolvers and even less about the cartridges they fire. Acquisition is motivated almost entirely by the low cost. Some of these guns are old, obsolete models of value only as conversation or collection pieces. However, the majority are relatively modern and in good shooting condition, having been retired only because of change in caliber or type. Western European military establishments have standardized on the 9mm Parabellum (Luger) cartridge and various semi-auto pistols. This has released older models as surplus and eventually most of them show up here; due in part to the fact the United States is the only country in the world where large scale ownership of handguns by the civilian population is permitted. It is also one of the few places where handguns are popular for all phases of sporting use, including big game hunting. In fact, handgun hunting has emerged as one of our major gunsports, a development increasing at a rapid pace. For this reason, the adaptability of military side arms to field use is of interest to a large and growing segment of the shooting fraternity. As with most other things, the value and usefulness of a military handgun depends to a large extent on the buyer and what he intends to use it for.

Before discussing the individual weapons and cartridges, it might be well to establish something as to the general performance required of a sporting handgun. In reading through literature on the subject, one gets the impression American handgunners are involved in a continuous series of gun fights and grizzly bear hunts. Gun writers appear heavily preoccupied with the man-stopping, bear-killing potential of such weapons. The author's grandfather, father and two uncles are retired police officers and not one of them ever had a shoot-out of any kind, even in 25 or more years of service. The truth is that 98% of all pistol shooting is against inanimate objects such as cans, bottles and targets, or small game and varmint type animals. Only a mere handful of big game animals are killed each year with the handgun and most of these are deer. It is necessary to mention this because the weapon and cartridge required to incapacitate an armed assailant or down a bear is vastly different from what is needed for ordinary handgun shooting. Another fallacy is the idea that most handgun hunting is at ranges of 100 yards and beyond. In reality, the average range

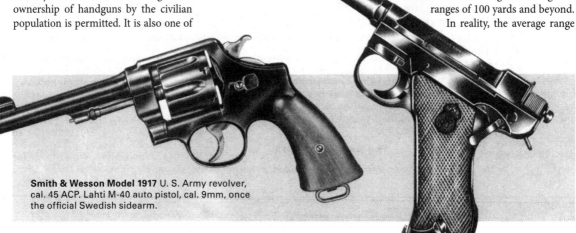

Smith & Wesson Model 1917 U. S. Army revolver, cal. 45 ACP. Lahti M-40 auto pistol, cal. 9mm, once the official Swedish sidearm.

is not over 25 yards or so and 50 yards taxes the ability of all but a few experts. We are referring here to the potential of the usual iron sights. The new scope sights will extend this somewhat. Military handguns are condemned almost solely on the grounds they are unreliable against armed men or bears (armed or unarmed) and lack the accuracy to hit small targets 200–300 yards away. This may be true, but it's of little concern to the average user. For plinking or shooting small animals within practical ranges, very few handguns are completely inadequate.

To keep the record straight, it would be ridiculous to claim surplus military handguns are superior, or even equal, to modern magnum pistols for field use. Magnum handguns were designed specifically for sporting purposes, and nothing else is quite as good. No military handgun, regardless of caliber, can be considered fully adequate for big game. However, most military weapons can be adapted to at least limited sporting use by one method or another. We'll discuss here how to do just that, plus outlining the physical characteristics of individual models and cartridges. Most arms likely to be encountered in surplus military stores are covered, but information of special or historical interest has also been included.

Early Handguns

As a practical military weapon, the pistol was introduced sometime in the mid-14th century. By 1500 they were well known, but in limited use, mostly by mounted troops. Evolution closely paralleled shoulder arms through the matchlock, wheel-lock, flintlock and percussion periods. Pistols apparently didn't come into popular use in America until about the time of the Revolutionary War. Old records indicate that "the shot heard round the world" at Lexington in 1775 may have been fired from a pistol. Almost the minute the United States began its westward expansion, the handgun became a popular auxiliary weapon. Samuel Colt patented the first successful commercial revolver in 1835–36, and a few

of the early Paterson-made models were used on the western frontier. There they established a reputation that dispelled all doubts as to the efficacy of a multifiring weapon. The exploits of the Texas Rangers and the U.S. Army during and after the Mexican War established the revolver as a military weapon. It became the principal side arm of our own and other military establishments until the automatic pistol was successfully developed between 1893 and 1900. At the present time every military power has officially adopted the automatic pistol. However, large stocks of revolvers are held in reserve by some countries and would see service in any major conflict.

Weapons

The United States has adopted a larger variety of military handguns and cartridges than you might think. Beginning about 1860, the metallic cartridge was developed here, the rimfires evolving into the centerfire cartridge as we now know it about 1870. In 1867 the navy adopted the 50 cal. Remington single shot pistol and cartridge, and in 1871 the army adopted a slightly different version of the same. This pistol was based on the famous Rider rolling block design. From 1870 the army used a quantity of Smith & Wesson American revolvers and the outside lubricated 44 S&W American CF cartridge. In 1873 the first Colt Single Action Army revolvers in 45 Colt caliber were ordered, and this model continued in service until 1892. The 45 Smith & Wesson Schofield, single action, hinged frame revolver was adopted for alternate use in 1875. The cylinder of the S&W revolver, too short for the 45 Colt cartridge, used a

British 455 Webley revolver makes a good field weapon in original caliber, or converted to 45 ACP/45 Auto-rim. Handloaded ammo with hunting type bullets is about all one needs to make the transition from military to sporting weapon.

shorter version called the 45 S&W. After 1875 the government loaded the 45 S&W cartridge exclusively as it could be fired in either make revolver. In 1892 the army adopted the double action, swing out cylinder Colt Army & Navy revolver and the 38 Colt Long cartridge. A few S&W Military & Police revolvers in this caliber were used also. The 38 Long proved so unsatisfactory in combat it was replaced from 1909 to 1911 by the Colt New Service revolver; the cartridge used was the 1909 type 45 Colt, identical to the original 45 Colt except for a wider rim. In 1911 we adopted the Browning-designed autoloading pistol, using a new, shorter and rimless 45 caliber cartridge which, with minor modifications, is still in use. During the First World War the army used the Model 1917 Colt and Smith & Wesson revolvers chambered for the

45 Auto cartridge (45 ACP) via special three-shot, half-moon clips. This was necessary because of the shortage of 45 auto pistols. After the war these revolvers were sold as surplus and the Peters Cartridge Co. introduced a rimmed version of the 45 ACP to eliminate the need for the unhandy clip. These were commonly called the 45 Auto-Rim.

Until about 1940–42, most obsolete American military handguns were common, but today only a few late models are plentiful. The 38 Long Colt, 45 Colt and 45 ACP are the last of the military rounds commercially loaded. However, there

Left to right — Two 380 ACP; three 9mm Luger; two 9mm Steyr, and two 45 ACP.

ought to be plenty of 38 Colt DA Army & Navy revolvers around. One of the first centerfire revolvers the author owned was one of these, with surplus ammo plentiful and cheap up to about 1940. After the supply was exhausted I traded it off for a 38 Special, since the cost of commercial ammunition was about the same. Incidentally, you can shoot 38 Longs in any 38 Special revolver, but the reverse is not possible. The 45 Govt. auto pistols and 1917 revolvers are in plentiful supply. These arms are so well-known and so familiar that no discussion is needed here.

The British, rather conservative in the matter of military hardware, clung to the revolver longer than anyone else. They adopted the 455 Webley top break revolver in 1890 and were using virtually the same gun in World War II. In the mid-30's they changed to a smaller, lighter-frame version firing the 380/200 (38 S&W) cartridge. These are well-designed, sturdy and thoroughly reliable arms. Before WW II, Webley pistols were a rare item in the U.S., but tens of thou-

Standard Ballistics of Military Handgun Cartridges, Modern and Obsolete

Cartridge	Bullet grs.	MV fs	ME fp
7.62mm Russian Nagant	108	1100	294
7.62mm Russian Tokarev	87	1390	365
7.63mm Mannlicher	85	1025	201
*7.63mm Mauser	86	1410	375
*7.65mm Browning (32 ACP)	71	960	145
*7.65mm Luger	93	1220	307
7.65mm Long, French MAS	85	1120	240
7.5mm Swiss, Revolver	102	725	120
7.5mm Norwegian	104	725	121
8mm Roth-Steyr	116	1100	315
8mm Rast-Gasser	124	750	154
8mm Nambu	102	950	209
8mm Lebel, Revolver	120	625	104
*9mm Luger	116	1165	350
9mm Steyr	116	1200	370
9mm Bayard	125	1115	348
*9mm Browning Short (380 ACP)	95	955	192
9mm Browning Long	110	1110	300
9mm Russian Makarov	94	1115	262
*38 Long Colt	150	770	195
*380/200 British	200	630	176
10.35 Italian	177	735	212
10.6 (11)mm German	262	700	288
11mm French	180	795	252
44 S&W Russian	246	770	324
44 S&W American	205	687	212
44 Colt	210	660	206
*45 Colt	255	855	405
45 S&W Schofield	250	710	283
*45 ACP	230	855	405
455 Webley Revolver	265	600	220
455 Webley Auto	224	700	247
50 Remington Army	300	600	240

Various other loads are or have been available for most cartridges listed. Those given are the most common.

* Loaded in U. S. at present time.

Standard Loading Data for Military Handgun Cartridges

Cartridge	Bullet grs.	Powder type	Load grs.	Vel. fs	Remarks
7.62mm Nagant	115	No. 5	3.0	800	Lyman 311441 GC
7.62mm Nagant	100	B'eye	3.5	1000	Speer 30 "Plinker"
7.62mm Tokarev	Use same data as for 7.63mm Mauser				
7.63mm Mannlicher	77	Af'eye	2.2	980	Lyman 311252
7.63mm Mauser	100	B'eye	4.7	1250	Speer 30 "Plinker"
7.63mm Mauser	93	Unique	5.3	1345	Norma 30 Luger SP
7.65mm Luger	100	Unique	4.8	1210	Speer 30 "Plinker"
7.65mm Luger	93	Unique	5.0	1250	Norma SP
7.65mm Long French	77	Unique	3.6	1100	Lyman 311252
7.5 Swiss Rev.	105	B'eye	2.0	720	Lyman 31133 HP
8mm Roth-Steyr	95	B'eye	2.5	970	Lyman 313226
8mm Rast-Gasser	95	B'eye	2.2	800	Lyman 313445
8mm Nambu	83	Unique	3.0	950	Lyman 32362
8mm Lebel Rev.	115	No. 6	3.0	765	Lyman 32359
7.5mm Norwegian	115	No. 6	2.0	720	Lyman 32359
9mm Steyr	116	Unique	6.7	1250	Norma 9mm SP
9mm Bayard	116	Unique	7.0	1280	Norma 9mm SP
9mm Browning Long	75	Unique	5.0	1078	Lyman 358101
38 Colt Long	150	No. 6	3.0	770	Lyman 358477
380/200 (38 S&W)	135	B'eye	3.0	830	Lyman 358480
380/200 (38 S&W)	115	Unique	5.0	980	Lyman 358345
10.35mm Italian Rev.	225	B'eye	3.0	695	Lyman 421183
11mm German Rev.	205	5066	5.2	780	Lyman 42798
11mm French Rev.	200	B'eye	3.1	725	Lyman 42798
44 S&W Russian	250	B'eye	5.7	700	Lyman 429336
44 S&W American	205	5066	5.5	800	Lyman 429478
44 Colt	210	5066	5.0	650	Lyman 429185
45 S&W	250	5066	6.0	700	Lyman 454424
45 Colt	250	Unique	8.0	810	Lyman 454424
455 Webley Rev.	250	B'eye	3.5	710	Lyman 454424
	200	Unique	6.2	775	Lyman 452460

Above load combinations will enhance the sporting potential of the arms involved, but emphasis is on maintaining standard pressure and performance levels. Load information was gathered from various sources, and about 90% of these loads were actually fired and tested by the author. All should be safe in the proper weapon if in first class condition.

Four 32 ACP loaded with hunting type bullets.

sands of them, sold as surplus, are now widely distributed. A few of the unique 455 Webley-Fosbery automatic revolvers, now a collector's item, have been sold, too. The barrel, cylinder and receiver form a separate unit that slides back and forth in a groove in the frame or handle. The grooved cylinder is rotated by a stud fastened to the frame. The revolver is cocked in a conventional manner for the first shot, after which all the work is accomplished by recoil until the last shot is fired. Of top break design, they're loaded the same as the standard Webley revolver. In 1912 the British navy adopted the Webley auto pistol and a semi-rimmed 455 cartridge that resembles the 45 ACP. They retained the cartridge, but dropped the pistol in favor of the Colt automatic. A small number of these Webley auto pistols have been sold, but too few to merit serious consideration here. The 455 caliber is not ideal for sporting purposes, but some improvement in performance is possible, as will be discussed further on. Many of the 455 Webley revolvers were converted to shoot the 45 ACP (with clips) or the 45 Auto-Rim. This works quite well and, from the American point of view, makes a more satisfactory field weapon.

The British also used the S&W Military and Police model in 38 S&W (380/200) cal. and the S&W Model 1917 in 455 cal. These are both excellent weapons. Revolvers chambered for the 38 S&W cartridge cannot be altered to handle the 38 S&W Special. Not only is the chamber of the 38 S&W too large in diameter, but so also is the barrel. Very poor accuracy would attend any such mis-conversion.

Russia has used more modern and advanced military small arms than we have been led to believe. In 1870 the Russians adopted the Smith & Wesson 44 Russian top break revolver, at the time one of the best military handguns available. This was replaced in 1895 with the gas sealing 7.62 Nagant revolver. When the hammer is cocked the cylinder pushes forward, the chamber mouth slipping over a bevel on the end of the barrel. The case, extending beyond the bullet, enters the barrel to further minimize gas escape. The system works all right, but complicates manufacture and is of doubtful value. In 1930 Russia adopted the Tokarev TT-30 semi-auto pistol of 7.62mm caliber, and later improved it as the Model TT-33. The 7.62mm Russian auto cartridge is practically identical to the bottlenecked 7.63mm Mauser. After WW II Russia designed a new 9mm pistol-round and adopted the Makarov semi-auto and Stechkin selective-fire pistols.

44 S&W Russian revolvers, military or civilian, are no longer common. The German firm of Ludwig Loewe made copies of this revolver, but thus far not many of them have shown up either. Fair numbers of the Nagant revolver and 7.62mm Tokarev auto pistols have been sold from time to time. Russian small arms are usually crude by our standards, but nevertheless are well-designed and quite sturdy. Some people refuse to believe a gun with a rough finish can function and shoot just as well as one with a fine polish. None of the late model 9mm pistols have been sold to date; the Stechkin, being capable of full automatic fire, probably never will be.

Germany has used a variety of modern and well-designed military handguns. In 1904 the navy adopted the 9mm Luger pistol and cartridge, and the army followed suit in 1908. The Mauser auto pistol in 9mm and 7.63mm caliber was

Special Hunting Loads for Military Semi-auto Pistols

32 ACP (3¹/₁₆" bbl.) — Bullet diameter .308"

Bullet grs.	Powder type	Charge grs.	Vel. fs	Remarks
77	B'eye	2.2	968	Lyman 311252
85	Unique	3.1	985	Lyman 311419 GC
100	Unique	2.8	876	30 cal. Speer "Plinker"

380 ACP (5" bbl.) — Bullet diameter .355"

Bullet grs.	Powder type	Charge grs.	Vel. fs	Remarks
75	Unique	5.0	1067	Lyman 358101 sized .355"
105	Unique	4.6	972	Home swaged, ½-jacket
116	Unique	4.1	910	Norma 9mm Luger SP

9mm Luger (3⅞" bbl.) — Bullet diameter .355"

Bullet grs.	Powder type	Charge grs.	Vel. fs	Remarks
105	Unique	7.0	1316	Home swaged, ½-jacket. Hot load!
116	Unique	6.0	1030	Norma 9mm soft point
124	Unique	6.0	1010	Harvey Prot-X-Bore, zinc base
125	Unique	6.3	1165	Lyman 356402. Hot load!

45 ACP (5" bbl.) — Bullet diameter .452"

Bullet grs.	Powder type	Charge grs.	Vel. fs	Remarks
185	2400	14.0	865	Lyman 452389 or any lead semi-wadcutter of 180 to 185 grains
185	Unique	8.0	1050	Very good hunting load
190	Unique	7.6	1024	Harvey Prot-X-Bore, zinc base
200	Unique	7.5	970	Lyman 452460
215	Unique	7.4	935	Speer cast lead

NOTE—All combinations above are heavy hunting loads for military type automatics. They are not recommended for casual plinking or target practice. All were field tested and chronographed by the author without damage to the test guns used. However, it is advisable to start from 0.30- to 0.50-grain below the load listed and work up from there. If at any point the slide appears to recoil more violently than normal, back off one or two tenths of a grain. It is a good idea to reduce 32 and 380 ACP loads by about 0.20-grain if they are to be used in lightweight pocket automatics.

also used as were a variety of pocket type automatics in 7.65mm (32 ACP) caliber. In 1938 the Germans adopted the advanced Walther P-38 of 9mm Luger caliber. The post-war West German army also uses the P-38 pistol. All of the German service automatics have been sold in large numbers along with Spanish-made copies of some models. Luger, Mauser and Walther pistols are too well known to require additional description or comment here. Prior to adoption of the Luger automatic, Germany used an 11mm (43 caliber) service revolver. A few of these have been sold as surplus, but are obsolete, designed for black powder and hardly constitute first class field weapons. The various auto pistols are extremely well-made and can be adapted to sporting use by nothing more complicated than using hunting type bullets.

France now uses the M-50, 9mm automatic, similar to the Belgian Browning Hi-Power. A well-designed pistol, but very few, if any, have appeared on the surplus market. During World War II the French official side arm was the M-35 auto in 7.65mm Long (MAS) caliber. Moderate quantities of these have appeared at odd times. French officers also carried various 7.65mm (32 ACP) caliber automatics such as the Spanish-made Ruby and Star pistols. Fair numbers of the 1892 French Ordnance or Lebel revolvers of 8mm caliber have appeared as surplus. French military handguns can be adapted to sporting use, but 7.65mm Long and 8mm Lebel pistol ammunition is not easy to find.

Other European countries used pistols of their own design or bought those offered by established arms plants. As a matter of national pride, each had to have something a little different. The Austro-Hunga-rian cavalry adopted the 8mm Roth-Steyr automatic in 1907, then in 1912 Austria changed to the more powerful 9mm Steyr pistol. Prior to adopting the automatic, Austria used the 8mm Rast-Gasser solid frame, rod-ejector revolver. All of these arms have been sold as surplus in varying quantity. They show good manufacture, but are obsolete and ammunition in shooting quantities is a problem. A few years ago the Danish Model 1910 Bergman automatic for the 9mm Bayard cartridge made a brief appearance — now they're more of a collector's item than anything else, but the cartridge has ample power for field use. The 7.5mm Swedish and Swiss Nagant revolvers have been in plentiful supply, and both military and commercial ammunition has been available. Many of the Swedish models were converted to 22 Long Rifle by lining the cylinder and barrel. These are extremely well-finished inside and out.

Belgium has been a major arms manufacturing center since the 1800's and their products are among the world's finest. Fabrique Natio-nale d'Armes de Guerre, S. A., of Herstal, Liege (or F. N., as it is more generally known), turns out both sporting and military small arms. John M. Browning, the great American arms designer, was associated with the F. N. organization for years. They held the European rights to many of his patents. F. N. Browning pistols have been very widely used as military side arms. In 1935 they began manufacture of the latest Browning design, known as the "F. N. Hi-Power 9mm," a modification actually of the 1911 Colt 45 Gov't. automatic. Quantities were manufactured in Canada during World War II after the Germans overran Belgium. Many of these pistols were brought back as souvenirs by returning GI's and a few have turned up as surplus. A sporting or civilian model made by Browning is available through sporting goods dealers. Magazine capacity is 13 rounds, enough to keep one going a long time in a survival situation. The F. N. Browning hammer-less automatic in 9mm Browning Long or 9mm Browning Short (380 ACP) was another popular military side arm in Europe. The Swedes adopted it in 1907 and used it until they changed to the 9mm Luger cartridge and the Lahti pistol in 1940. Many of these Swedish 380 pistols have been sold in surplus arms stores. The variety of Belgian pistols in 32 and 380 ACP caliber is too great for detailed discussion here. The same can be said for the many Italian and Spanish made pistols of the same caliber.

Ammunition

The only thing really wrong with most military handguns as sporting weapons is the bullet they use. Soft point or expanding bullets of any type have been outlawed under international agreement. In combat the idea is to put a man out of action so he can no longer participate in the engagement, not cripple him for life. Dead soldiers are of no value, but they are also no burden. Wounded men are not only of negative value, but in addition they constitute a considerable problem because they have to be transported and cared for. When hunting, though, we don't want to merely wound an animal; our object is to both stop and kill as quickly as

Soap block test illustrates the difference in destructive power between standard and hunting type bullets.

possible. This is best accomplished with bullets designed to shatter and tear up the maximum amount of bone and tissue. Years ago handgun hunters found out that round nose, hard alloy or jacketed bullets did a very poor job on anything at the velocity possible with such weapons. This prompted men like Elmer Keith, the late Phil Sharpe and Jim Harvey, plus many others, to develop more effective bullets. It has been well-proven that, at velocities of from 600 to about 13–1400 fps, the flat point, sharp-shouldered Keith-type bullet is the most effective on game. The half-jacketed, pure lead type designed by Jim Harvey and further tested and developed by Kent Bellah, is as good or better in stopping and killing power,

but not as accurate. The latest half-jacket-et bullets, made with the jacket material riding up over the ogive, can now be driven at speeds in keeping with a jacketed bullet — they can't lead, and they are more accurate. The big factories have these now in 357 and 44, and Shooters Service & Dewey, Inc., Clinton Corners, N. Y., also has them for the handloader. Unfortunately, modern hunting bullets work fine in revolvers, but don't function very well through the automatic, and military handguns are predominantly of the latter type.

The author has conducted all kinds of experiments with an impressive number of automatic pistols to improve them as sporting weapons. Handloading with hunting bullets made an

immediate and marked improvement in killing power regardless of caliber, but created severe feed and function problems. While it is true that a malfunction could bring on a slight case of rigor mortis in a gunfight, it's just an inconvenience in the field. It is possible, with some guns and loads, to achieve almost 100% efficiency, but it invariably requires a certain amount of fitting to the individual gun. Here are the most important factors affecting the feed and functioning of lead bullets in the automatic: Bullet hardness, bullet shape, seating depth, crimp, headspace and general shape and smoothness of the feed ramp. Of course, the powder load used will also have an effect, but this is the easiest item to adjust.

Dimensions of Military Handgun Cartridges

Cartridge	Case Type	Bullet Dia.	Neck Dia.	Shoulder Dia.	Base Dia.	Rim Dia.	Case Length	Cartridge Length
7.62mm Russian Nagant	B	.295	.286	—	.355	.388	1.53	1.53
7.62mm Russian Tokarev	C	.307	.330	.370	.380	.390	0.97	1.35
7.63mm Mannlicher	D	.308	.331	—	.347	.347	0.82	1.12
7.63mm Mauser	C	.308	.332	.370	.381	.390	0.99	1.36
7.65mm Browning (32 ACP)	H	.308	.336	—	.336	.354	0.68	1.03
7.65mm Luger	C	.308	.322	.374	.388	.391	0.75	1.15
7.65mm Long, French MAS	D	.309	.336	—	.337	.337	0.78	1.19
7.5mm Swiss Revolver	B	.317	.336	—	.354	.407	0.89	1.29
8mm Roth-Steyr	D	.318	.346	—	.347	.347	0.74	1.14
8mm Rast-Gasser	B	.320	.333	—	.336	.374	1.04	1.41
8mm Nambu	G	.320	.338	.388	.408	.413	0.86	1.25
8mm Lebel Revolver	B	.323	.380	—	.384	.400	1.07	1.44
7.5mm Norwegian	B	.325	.328	—	.350	.406	0.89	1.35
9mm Luger	D	.355	.380	—	.392	393	0.76	1.16
9mm Steyr	D	.355	.379	—	.383	.384	0.90	1.30
9mm Bayard	D	.355	.380	—	.388	.383	0.91	1.33
9mm Browning Short (380 ACP)	D	.356	.373	—	.373	.374	0.68	0.98
9mm Browning Long	H	.356	.380	—	.382	.404	0.79	1.10
9mm Russian Makarov	D	.363	.384	—	.389	.396	0.71	0.97
38 Long Colt	B	.357	.377	—	.378	.433	1.03	1.32
380/200 British (38 S&W)	B	.359	.386	—	.386	.433	0.78	1.20
10.35mm Italian Revolver	B	.422	.444	—	.451	.505	0.89	1.25
11mm German Revolver	B	.426	.449	—	.453	.509	0.96	1.21
11mm French Revolver	B	.425	.449	—	.460	.514	0.94	1.15
44 S&W Russian	B	.429	.457	—	.457	.515	0.97	1.43
44 S&W American	B	.434	.438	—	.440	.506	0.91	1.44
44 Colt	B	.443	.450	—	.456	.483	1.10	1.50
45 Colt ACP	D	.452	.476	—	.476	.476	0.898	1.17
45 S&W Schofield	B	.454	.477	—	.476	.522	1.10	1.43
45 Colt Revolver	B	.454	.476	—	.480	.512	1.29	1.60
455 Webley Revolver	B	.454	.476	—	.480	.535	0.77	1.23
455 Webley Auto	H	.455	.473	—	.474	.500	0.93	1.23
50 Remington Army	A	.508	532	.563	.565	.665	0.57	1.24

Unless otherwise indicated, all dimensions are in inches.

CASE TYPE:

A—Rim Bottleneck   C—Rimless Necked   G—Semi-rim Necked

B—Rim Straight   D—Rimless Straight   H—Semi-rim Straight

Nation	Weapon	Caliber	Type	Cap.	Bbl.	Wgt.	Remarks
Argentina	Ballester Molina	45 ACP	S-A	7	5	40	Modified Colt 45 auto design
Austria	Steyr M-12	9mm Steyr	S-A	8	5	34	Top loading
	Roth-Steyr M-07	8mm R-S	S-A	10	5.1	34	Top loading
	Rast-Gasser	8mm R-G	R	8	4.5	33	Solid frame revolver
Belgium	Browning Hi-Power	9mm Luger	S-A	13	5	32	Very good sporting weapon
	FN Browning	9mm Br. Long	S-A	7	5	30	Same as Colt Pocket Model, longer
Britain	Enfield	380/200	R	6	5	28	Top break, 38 S&W revolver
	Webley	455	R	6	4-6	38	Top break
	Webley-Fosbery	455	R	6	6	40	Top break automatic revolver
	Webley auto	455 auto	S-A	7	5	36	Used by British navy, obsolete
Czechoslovakia	Cz M-52	7.62mm Russ.	S-A	8	4.7	25	Original design, very good pistol
	Cz M-50	7.65mm Br.	S-A	8	3.8	24	Mod. Walther PP, shoots 32 ACP
	Cz M-47	9mm Luger	S-A	8	4.6	33	Double action, hammer
	Cz M-27	7.65mm Br.	S-A	8	3.5	25	Uses 32 ACP and 380 ACP types
Denmark	Bergmann M-10	9mm Bayard	S-A	6-10	4	36	Very sturdy and well-made
France	M-1950	9mm Luger	S-A	9	4.4	29	Similar to Browning Hi-Power
	M-1935A & S	7.65mm Long	S-A	8	4.3	26	Mod. Colt 45 auto design
	Lebel M-92	8mm Lebel	R	6	4	31	Solid frame, swing out revolver
	Service M-73	11mm French Serv.	R	6	4.2	39	Quick, hinged takedown
Germany	Walther P-38	9mm Luger	S-A	8	4.8	34	A most modern design
	Luger M-08	9mm Luger	S-A	8	4-6	30	Toggle joint lock, Maxim-type
	Mauser M-96	7.63mm Mauser	S-A	5-10	5.3	45	A few also made in 9mm Luger cal.
	Walther PP & PPK	7.65mm Br. & 380	S-A	8-7	3.8	23	
	Service M-79	10.6 (11)mm	R	6	5	37	Var. models, all black powder
Hungary	Model 48	7.65mm Br.	S-A	8	4	24	Mod. Walther PP design
	Frommer M-39	7.65 & 9mm Br.	S-A	7	3.3	22	Var. models of 32 & 380 ACP
Italy	Beretta M-51	9mm Luger	S-A	8	4.5	31	Very good. Available in U.S.
	Beretta M-34	9mm Brown.	S-A	7	3.5	24	Similar model sold in U.S.
	Glisenti M-10	9mm Luger	S-A	7	4	32	Not safe with standard 9mm Luger
	Service M-72	10.35mm Ital. Serv.	R	6	6.3	33	
Japan	Nambu Type 14	8mm Nambu	S-A	8	4.5	30	
Mexico	Obregon	45 ACP	S-A	7	5	39	Mod. Colt 45 auto design
Poland	Radom M-35	9mm Luger	S-A	8	4.8	30	Improved Browning design
Spain	Star	45 ACP	S-A	7	5	38	Colt-Browning system
	Astra M-400	9mm Bayard	S-A	8	5.5	32	Straight blow-back type
Sweden	Lahti M-40	9mm Luger	S-A	8	5.5	36	Short recoil type
	FN Browning M-07	9mm Brown. (380)	S-A	7	5	32	Similar to Colt Pocket auto
	Nagant M-87	7.5mm	R	6	4.5	28	Solid frame revolver
Switzerland	Neuhausen M-49	9mm Luger	S-A	8	4.7	34	Available in U.S.
	Army Model 1882	7.5mm	R	6	5	30	Solid frame, DA revolver
Russia	Makarov M-PM	9mm Makarov	S-A	8	3.8	26	Mod. Walther PP
	Stechkin-APS	" "	S-A	20	5	30	Full auto. fire selector
	Tokarev TT 30 & 33	7.62mm Rus.	S-A	8	4.5	33	Simplified Browning design
	Nagant M-95	7.62mm Nagant	R	7	4.5	28	Gas-seal cylinder
United States	Colt M-1911	45 ACP	S-A	7	5	39	Military & civilian models
	Colt M-1917	" "	R	6	5.5	40	Colt and S&W revolvers both
	S&W M-1917	" "	R	6	5.5	37	Requires 3-shot clip for 45 ACP
	Colt New Service-09	45 Colt 1909	R	6	6	40	In use only two years
	Colt Army & Navy-92	38 Colt Long	R	6	6	34	Not satisfactory in combat
	S&W Army M-1875	45 S&W	R	6	7	38	Schofield model, top break
	Colt SA Army 1873	45 Colt	R	6	7.5	40	Solid frame, rod ejection

NOTE—Only the principal or official model is listed. Most governments used a variety of alternate types and officers often used non-official makes. The latest model is always listed first, older models in order.

S-A=Semi-auto   R=Revolver
Cap.—Cylinder or magazine capacity

Bbl.=Barrel length in inches
Wgt.=Weight in ounces

Ballester Molina

Steyr M-12

Roth-Steyr M-07

Browning Hi-Power

FN Browning

Rast-Gasser

S&W 380/200 revolver

Enfield

Cz M-27

Webley

Webley-Fosbery

Webley Auto

M-1950

Bergmann M-10

Lebel M-92M-1935 A&S

Lebel M-92

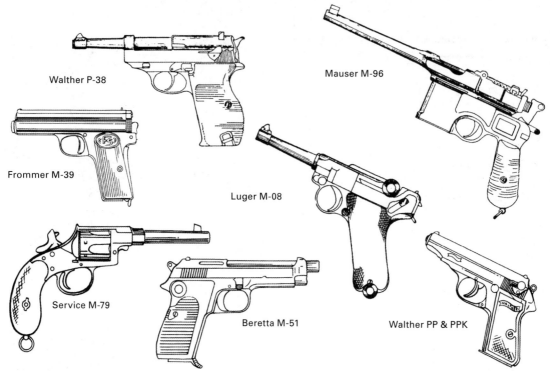

Walther P-38

Mauser M-96

Frommer M-39

Luger M-08

Service M-79

Beretta M-51

Walther PP & PPK

A round nose or tapered cone will ordinarily feed and function better than a flat, blunt one. Many hunting bullets have a sharp shoulder that often hangs up as the cartridge chambers. If the shoulder is seated even with the shell mouth, this leaves only a tapered cone protruding from the case and improves feed in some instances. However, there are other factors that enter into this; a straight rimless case is stopped in its forward motion by the case mouth butting against a shoulder in the chamber. Such cases should not be roll-crimped — if heavily crimped, the cartridge might not fire as the firing pin will only drive it further into the chamber. This can be corrected by allowing the bullet to protrude beyond the case sufficiently to support the entire cartridge. A soft alloy bullet may have to protrude a little further than a hard one. Straight semi-rimmed cases are supported by the rim and bottlenecked cases by the shoulder, but even these can sometimes be improved by adjusting the bullet seating depth just so. As a general rule, if the bullet is seated friction tight without crimp, it should be seated deep enough to prevent any portion from contacting the end of the chamber or rifling lead. If the bullet protrudes too far the action can't close properly, which will certainly cause

malfunction. As little as .01" difference in seating depth can affect functioning.

It is sometimes possible to improve the operation of an automatic with home loads and lead bullets by polishing or altering the chamber mouth or the feed ramp. A slight grinding operation to reduce the angle is all that is necessary. It is better to trust this to a gunsmith as overdoing it might ruin the barrel entirely. Most Browning designed or imitated guns have a simple groove to act as a feed ramp. It is easy to extend the radius slightly and polish out any rough spots. If the pistol shoots a semi-rimmed cartridge exercise caution so as not to remove the rim support. Some pistols have the feed ramp cut in the top of the magazine well, the barrel lug or some other place. Usually you can't do much to these except polish them. I polished the feed ramp and chamber mouth of a 45 automatic, then sent the barrel to Marker Machine Co. and had it hard chrome plated inside and out. This made quite a difference in the handling of lead bullets.

Automatic pistols are adjusted to handle recoil within rather narrow limits. For this reason, published loading data is usually for loads of equal or less power than standard factory ammunition. This keeps everyone out of trouble, because if extra

heavy loads are used, the slide will slam back too hard and eventual damage may result. Heavy military pistols will handle full charges better than lightweight pocket guns, but there is a limit to what any of them will stand. If you want to get higher than standard velocity the only way to do it is with lighter than standard bullets. Heavier bullets must be driven at reduced velocity. Loading data for this article was worked out and tested mostly in heavy frame military pistols and none of the test guns was damaged in any way. If you use the data for light pocket pistols reduce all top loads by 0.20-gr. or so, especially if the slide of your pistol appears to recoil more violently than usual. Individual guns vary in performance with the same load and this must be considered. Any of the standard pistol powders can be used for loading military handgun cartridges. Standard loads are listed by the powder companies for all but a few of the European calibers. Hercules Unique appears to give the most satisfactory pressure-velocity ratio for top loads in the auto pistol. As long as you stick to a standard bullet weight and velocity you are not likely to get in trouble.

32 ACP (7.65mm Browning)

It is difficult for Americans to realize the 32 ACP is a military and police cartridge. It has been quite popular in Europe and is still used by many police organizations on the continent. Here it is regarded as something useful only to frighten old ladies or kill sparrows. Regardless, it is one of the most popular pistol cartridges ever designed, mostly because of the small, light, handy weapons that fire it. For hunting it is entirely a small game number. Commercial, full jacketed bullets will do a fair job on such things as cottontail rabbit or birds without ruining any edible meat. However, good bullet placement is important. It can be improved to a satisfying degree by handloading. Most loading tables give bullet diameter as .311" but this is wrong. It is actually 30 cal. and uses .308" or .309" bullets. Larger diameter bullets will bulge the case and the cartridge won't chamber or feed properly.

Lyman's 313445 (95-gr.) is a good semi-wadcutter for target or hunting if you prefer cast bullets. The best bullet I have found for loading the 32 ACP is the 100-gr. 30-cal. "Plinkers" made by Speer or Hornady. Seat them with the slight shoulder even with the case mouth and don't crimp. They will function to near perfection. The Norma 93-gr. 30 Luger soft point will also work well, but expansion is a sometimes thing at permissible velocity. Any of these bullets will turn the 32 ACP into a fine small game or pot gun, one much more effective than the 22 Long Rifle.

7.65mm Long, French (MAS)

French military cartridge used in the 1935A pistol and some submachine guns. Sort of an elongated 32 ACP, the case is rimless rather than semi-rimmed. It is also similar to the 8mm Roth-Steyr except for the slightly shorter case length and difference in bullet diameter. Any of the bullets listed for the 32 ACP can be used for loading as bullet diameter is .309". A little more powerful than the 32 ACP, but not enough to qualify it for anything the smaller cartridge won't handle.

7.63mm Mannlicher

A straight, rimless cartridge for the 1900 and 1901 Mannlicher military automatics. It is another elongated 32 ACP type like the French 7.65mm Long. It is slightly more powerful than the 32 ACP, but still effective only for small game. Use any of the bullets listed for the 32 ACP.

7.65mm (30) Luger

Introduced in 1900 as the original cartridge for the Luger pistol. Commercial ammunition is loaded in the U.S. This is another true 30 cal. using .308g bullets. Norma makes a 93-gr. soft point bullet for this cartridge or one can use the 100-gr. 30-cal. swaged rifle bullets. Lyman's 311419 85-gr. cast gas check bullet is a good one for field use. With its 1220 fps muzzle velocity, the 7.65mm Luger shoots rather flat, but doesn't have sufficient knockdown ability for anything but small game. The 100-gr. Speer "Plinker" makes this a much more effective hunting round than the standard metal cased bullet.

7.63mm (30) Mauser

Designed by the American, Hugo Borchardt, in 1893 for the first successful commercial auto pistol. The Borchardt automatic was later redesigned as the famous Luger pistol. The cartridge has been used  mainly in Mauser automatic pistols and various copies manufactured in Spain and China. The 7.63 Mauser was the high velocity champion of the pistol world until the 357 S&W Magnum edged it out. 1410 fps is good handgun velocity even though the bullet weighs only 86 grains. Lyman 311419 85-gr. gas check bullet can be used for very satisfactory hunting loads. The swaged 30-cal. rifle bullets of 100-gr. weight are also quite good, even at slightly reduced velocity. With proper hunting bullets the 7.63 Mauser will do for such larger animals as coyote, bobcat and the like. I've also heard of deer being taken with the 30 Mauser pistol, but it is not an entirely adequate cartridge for animals of this size.

7.62mm Russian Tokarev

Adapted by Russia in 1930 for the Tokarev automatic pistol. It is so similar to the 7.63mm Mauser that most Mauser ammunition can be used in the Russian pistol. Bullets and loading data would be the same.

7.62mm Nagant Revolver

Cartridge for the Russian Nagant revolver with gas-seal cylinder and similar types. Ammunition is currently available in many of the surplus stores, but  won't last forever. When the supply is exhausted, satisfactory cases can be made by using 32-20 brass. It isn't as long as the Nagant case, but will work. Bullet is of 30 cal. and one can use the 100-gr. 30-cal. rifle bullets mentioned earlier. Lyman's 311316 110-gr. gas check bullet for 32-20 rifles works well if properly sized. In power, the 7.62 Nagant is very similar to the 32-20 when fired in the revolver. It isn't a bad small game number at all.

8mm Roth-Steyr

Cartridge for the 1907 Model Austro-Hungarian cavalry pistol used in WW I. Another elongated 32 ACP type, it uses a little larger diameter bullet (.319"). At first glance it is difficult to distinguish it from the French 7.65mm Long. Lyman 313226 or 313445, both of 95 grains, can be used for loading if properly sized. Ammunition is scarce and something of a collector's item at the present time. Ammunition could probably be made from 7.65mm Long brass, but then this is not very plentiful either.

8mm Nambu

Official Japanese handgun cartridge used in WW II. It was adapted in 1914 for the Nambu auto pistol of the same year and also used in the modified 1925 model and the odd looking 1934 model. Quite a few pistols for this cartridge were brought back by returning servicemen, but not many

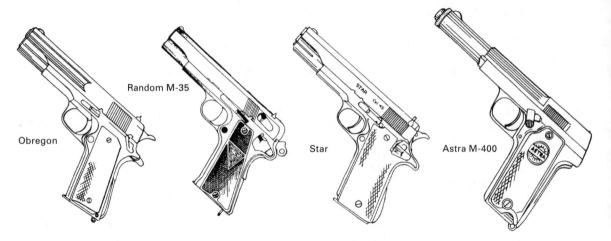

Obregon

Random M-35

Star

Astra M-400

have been sold in surplus stores. The cartridge resembles the 7.65mm Luger, but it has a semi-rimmed case and a larger diameter bullet (.320"). About the same class as the 7.65 Luger, it is only slightly less powerful. Any bullet of 80 to 110 grains can be used if sized to the proper diameter.

8mm Lebel, Revolver

This is a straight rimmed cartridge for the 1892 French Ordnance revolver. In appearance it resembles the 32-20 and  one can make ammunition by cutting off 32-20 brass and reforming it. The old Lyman 32359 115-gr. bullet can be used or any other 32 revolver bullet sized to .323". In power it is in about the same class as the 32 S&W Long.

7.5mm Nagant

Both the Swedes and the Swiss used a revolver of practically identical caliber. The sample rounds in the author's collection differ in bullet type. The Swedish cartridge has an outside lubricated bullet of .325" diameter and the Swiss version has an inside lubricated bullet of about .317" maximum. I have fired the Swiss cartridge in the Swedish revolver and they shoot with acceptable accuracy. I don't know how the Swedish cartridge works in the Swiss revolver. Both versions are currently available and Norma loads smokeless commercial ammunition for the Swedish Nagant. You can make brass for either one by cutting off 32-20 cases.

The old Lyman 32359 115-gr. bullet is about the only one of proper diameter. However, smaller 32 S&W or 32-20 bullets will work and give satisfactory hunting accuracy. In power they are in the same class as the 32 S&W Long.

8mm Rast-Gasser

Cartridge used in the 1870 Rast-Gasser revolver, by Austria and to some extent by Italy. It closely resembles the 8mm French Lebel, but has a smaller diameter bullet of .320" It also looks somewhat  like the 32 S&W Long, but with a longer case. I have been told that you can shoot the 32 S&W Long in these revolvers, but have never actually tried it. They are of practically the same power.

9mm Browning Short (380 ACP)

A well-known cartridge that has been loaded by American companies ever since Colt introduced the Browning pocket automatic in 1910. It was first introduced in Europe by FN in 1908. At one time or another it has been the official military cartridge of Czechoslovakia, Italy and Sweden. It is also a favorite with many European police departments. So many pistols have been chambered for the round it would be impracticable to try to list all of them. It is actually quite a good small game cartridge, though not considered a sporting round in the U.S. The author has used it with both factory ammo and handloads for shooting all kinds of small game — for which it is a better cartridge than the

32 ACP. Bullet diameter is .356" and any 9mm bullet up to 115 grains will work all right. Home swaged, half-jacketed bullets of 105 grains are very good for hunting, but don't function as well as might be desired. Lyman's 358242 95-gr. bullet works well, but is round nosed and doesn't add much to the killing power.

9mm Browning Long

A longer version of the 380 ACP, popular in Europe, but never used in the U.S. It was designed for the FN Browning 1903 pistol which is similar to the Colt Pocket Model made here. Several other pistols were also made for it, including the Webley & Scott New Military and Police Model. Belgium used the 9mm Long Browning as a military weapon up to 1935. It is somewhat more powerful than the 380 ACP, but not much. Ammunition is not available in the U.S. and the caliber is seldom used here for any purpose.

9mm Parabellum (Luger)

The 9mm Luger is undoubtedly the world's most popular military handgun cartridge. It is at present the official caliber of all the NATO powers except the U.S. It was introduced in 1902, but was not highly popular in the U.S. until recent years. It is much more widely used now because of the many surplus 9mm weapons sold. Loaded with hunting type bullets, the 9mm Luger is actually quite an effective small-to-medium game cartridge. Any .355" diameter bullet from 95 to 130

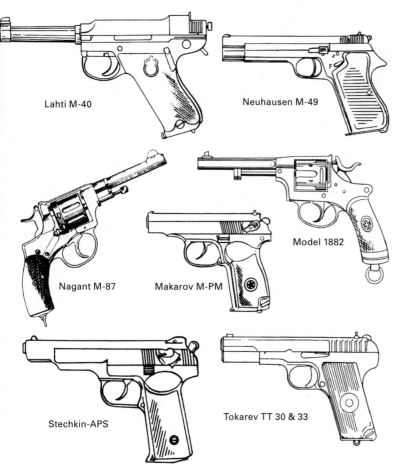

Lahti M-40

Neuhausen M-49

Model 1882

Nagant M-87

Makarov M-PM

Stechkin-APS

Tokarev TT 30 & 33

is very similar to the 9mm Steyr, only longer. The Astra Model 400 pistol designed for the 9mm Bayard will also handle, without adjustment, the 9mm Steyr, 38 Colt ACP and the 9mm Luger. In a pinch it will also digest the 9mm Browning Long. It is the only pistol capable of this, and obviously there must be a similarity in many dimensions of these cartridges to make this possible. The 9mm Bayard is a fairly potent round and makes a good field cartridge.

9mm Makarov

This is the current Russian pistol cartridge. Neither guns nor ammunition have been available so there is no use discussing its sporting potential. In power it is between the 380 ACP and the 9mm Luger.

380/200 Mk II (38 S&W)

The British adopted this cartridge to replace the 455 Webley. It is the same as the old 200-gr. 38 S&W "Super Police" load discontinued some years ago. It is a good short range, small game round, but has a rather curved trajectory. It can be improved a little by handloading, but is not a very versatile cartridge for field use.

38 Colt Long

Obsolete American military revolver cartridge. It is still loaded commercially and makes a satisfactory small game number at short to moderate ranges. Its performance can be improved quite a bit by using swaged or Keith type cast bullets. The old revolvers won't stand modern high pressures so don't try to exceed factory velocity by very much.

44 S&W Russian

This obsolete, black powder, Russian military revolver cartridge was also popular in the United States. Both the gun and cartridge are collectors' items. In its day the 44 Rus-

grains can be used. Norma 115-gr. soft point bullets improve field performance and so do pure lead-zinc base or swaged half-jacketed bullets. Many shooters report excellent results using the Harvey 124-gr. Prot-X-Bore bullets seated about .120" out of the case mouth and uncrimped. Lyman's 356402 is a good cast bullet of 125 grains. Many cast and swaged commercial bullets are available for the 9mm Luger. The number of European pistols made for the 9mm Luger is too long to list here: In the U.S. both Colt and S&W currently manufacture auto pistols of this caliber.

9mm Steyr

Austrian military cartridge for the. Model 1912 Steyr auto pistol. Using standard 9mm or .355" bullets, it is longer than the 9mm Luger, but of about the same power. Loading data for the Luger cartridge can be used for the 9mm Steyr, a straight, rimless case with dimensions practically identical to the Colt 38 ACP. The difference is that the Colt cartridge is semi-rimmed and .008" shorter. You can make 9mm Steyr cases from 38 ACP brass by turning down the rim, resizing, then seating the bullet out of the case far enough to adjust the difference in headspace.

9mm Bayard Long

Official Danish cartridge for the 1910 Bergmann-Bayard automatic. The Spanish also used the same combination and in addition the Astra pistol and various Browning copies made in Spain were chambered for the round. The cartridge

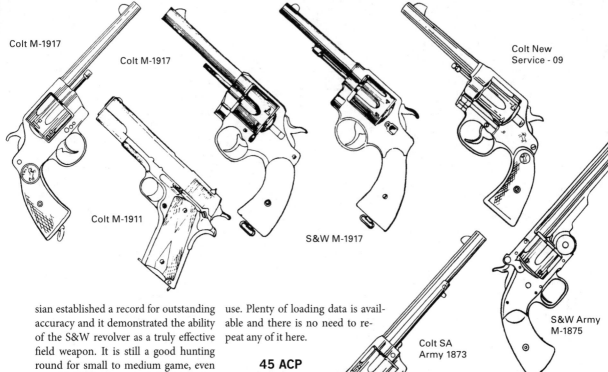

Colt M-1917

Colt M-1917

Colt New
Service - 09

Colt M-1911

S&W M-1917

S&W Army
M-1875

Colt SA
Army 1873

sian established a record for outstanding accuracy and it demonstrated the ability of the S&W revolver as a truly effective field weapon. It is still a good hunting round for small to medium game, even with black powder. Ammunition can be made by trimming 44 S&W Special brass back to the proper length. Only light smokeless loads should be used as these old break-open revolvers were designed strictly for black powder pressures.

455 Webley Revolver

British military cartridge used in both world wars. It was adopted in 1879 to replace a slight-

ly different round originally used in the Webley revolver. It is a good short range hunting cartridge, but is limited by its curved trajectory. It can be improved by using lighter bullets at increased velocity. Any .454" or .455" diameter bullet will work, which means you can use 45 Colt bullets. When 455 revolvers are converted to fire the 45 Auto-Rim, accuracy with the factory load is usually poor because of the .452" diameter bullet. Handloading with bullets of proper diameter will make a big improvement.

45 Colt

One time American military cartridge, still loaded and popular for target and hunting

use. Plenty of loading data is available and there is no need to repeat any of it here.

45 ACP

United States military cartridge since 1911 for the Colt Gov't. Model auto pistol, it is also used by Mexico and many South American countries. Although popular for match shooting because of its military position, the 45 ACP is not ordinarily considered a hunting round. However, when loaded with 180- or 200-gr. bullets at increased velocity, it is very effective on all small to medium game. Cast and swaged hunting bullets can be made to function extremely well. Lyman 452389 (185-gr.) and 452460 (200-gr.) bullets are both good hunting bullets. A variety of commercial semi-wadcutter and hollow point bullets are available for the 45 ACP. The 180-gr. bullet at over 1000 fps is very deadly on game and also increases the range potential of the 45 automatic.

In conclusion, a few points worthy of mention. Practically all military handguns can be used for sporting purposes as issued. Expensive remodeling is not necessary, and anyway they don't lend themselves to much alteration. Smoothing up

the trigger pull or adding new sights is about all one can do. However, because these weapons are all sighted for a specific bullet weight and loading, changes in ammunition can make a big difference in point of impact, usually making the gun shoot higher or lower than desired. This can be corrected by adjusting the height of the front sight accordingly. Before you start for the field, be sure and sight in with the load to be used as this will save ammunition and disappointment. A set of adjustable target sights is often a good investment if you expect to do much shooting under varying conditions. Any military handgun is a potential sporting weapon if the ammunition can be loaded with modern hunting type bullets. The general usefulness is determined primarily by this factor. For plinking or target practice, military ammunition is quite satisfactory. Those individuals not addicted to gun fights or grizzly bear hunts will find most military handguns entirely adequate as well as instructive and entertaining to shoot.

The Luger Myth

For generations shooters have spoken of the Luger pistol in hushed and reverent tones, overawed by its deadly appearance, it's world-wide reputation. Is this idolatry justified or... ∎ R.A. Burmeister

O F ALL THE PISTOLS that have crossed the military, police and sporting scene in the past few decades three loom out above all others — the Luger, the Colt 45 Automatic, and the 357 S&W Magnum. Each has its own peculiar claim to fame; the Magnum because of its power, accuracy, and versatility, the 45 Auto because of its rugged reliability and because it is the official side arm of our armed forces, the Luger because of its sleek, functional appearance and its aura of utter efficiency. That this latter reputation is undeserved is largely the substance of this article.

The reliability of the revolver is well known — it is fully capable of handling low-grade ammunition and a wide variation in load intensities, and a half-century of use has shown it to be thoroughly dependable, hence the matter of reliability becomes largely a comparison of the Luger to the 45 Automatic.

30-caliber American Eagle Luger has 4 5/8″ barrel and gold bead front sight.

Feed System

The 45 Auto is an unusually reliable pistol characterized by a simple, posiitive cartridge feed system. The tip of the bullet of the top cartridge in the magazine is ⅛″ back of the barrel, and the upward and forward movement of the cartridge is well-guided by a suitable groove cut in the frame ahead of the magazine well. Prolonging the path thus set is another similar groove or chamfer at the bottom of the chamber at the breech end of the barrel. Since the barrel breech is in its lowest, most rearward position at the time of cartridge feeding and stays that way until the cartridge is in the chamber, there is practically no chance for a malfunction in feeding.

In the Luger the tip of the top cartridge in the magazine is 5/16″ back of the barrel, and this cartridge literally must chase the barrel during its forward movement; for as this cartridge is pushed forward out of the magazine, the barrel, too, is moving forward. The chamfer on the barrel is steeper than on the Colt, offering more chance of snubbing the tip of the bullet. This can be demonstrated by operating the Luger action slowly by hand — the bullet will follow the barrel, and its nose will touch the steep slope of the barrel chamfer momentarily before going forward into the barrel. Because of the steepness of the slope and the length of travel, the bullet does not enter the chamber as surely and smoothly as in the Colt. The feed system is a weak feature of the Luger.

Closure of Breech

The final ¼" movement of the slide of the 45 Auto is powerful and reliable while the Luger breechblock has little snap left to it in its last ¼" of travel. This is because the knee action camming system of the Luger — smooth and efficient in handling the powerful recoil forces on the back stroke — is correspondingly weak at the end of the fore stroke because the recoil spring exerts a small indirect force at this part of the cycle. Consequently Luger ammunition must be loaded to full power as there is little reserve energy available on the fore stroke of the breechblock. This is in marked contrast to the 45 Auto, where the recoil spring acts in a straight line with breechblock and consequently has a powerful closing force of straight spring tension — thus a bit of dirt in the chamber or on breech face or a slightly deformed cartridge case which would jam the Luger is not likely to jam the 45 Auto. An interesting and illuminating comparison of the two pistols can be made by handloading for them, starting with a full load then reducing the powder charge (Bullseye) a 1/10 of a grain at a time. It will be seen that the 45 will function with loads so weak that the empty cases barely clear the ejection port, seeming to just fall out of the gun. The Luger will show distress long before this, and with only a few tenths reduction in powder charge malfunctioning will occur. I have extensively tested about a dozen Lugers, all especially

Colt 45 auto of pre-WW II vintage has King gold bead front and adjustable rear sights-Note carrying clip pointed to by pencil.

Smith & Wesson 357 Magnum, 6"barrel. For the author, this gun proved faster in delivering first aimed shot than any of the automatics tested.

selected for high quality, and speaking now only of commercial ammunition, I have never had a Luger that did not jam. Some in the first 50 shots, some later, but no Luger ever fired 500 shots without a jam — including a high grade American Eagle model.

Cartridge Case Ejection

The ejection of the empty cartridge case in the 45 Auto is more positive than that of the Luger. In the 45 the extractor is situated on the right side of the gun and the ejector diametrically opposite on the left. As the empty case is drawn back by the extractor the ejector bumps the case head at 9 o'clock (as viewed from the rear) which throws the case to the right and di-

rectly out of the port at 3 o'clock.

In the Luger the extractor is at 12 o'clock, the ejector is at 4 o'clock and the ejection port is at 12 o'clock, thus the case is thrown to the left against the frame and from there is caromed or bounced upwards and out of the port at the top. I checked this feature by placing a small mark of red fingernail lacquer on the Luger cartridge case, then carefully chambered the cartridge so that the mark was uppermost at 12 o'clock. Examination of cases so marked and fired invariably showed a deformation at the mouth of the case on the left side at 9 o'clock. Sometimes the deformation consists only of a slight flattening but usually the case is abraded as well.

Incidentally, contrast the Luger with the Colt Woodsman 22. In this pistol ejection is remarkably positive and one big reason for this is that the entire area in the rear of the barrel is open at the time of ejection and the ejected shell has plenty of room in which to travel — no bouncing and no small port to find. Incidentally, I have had fewer jams with a Woodsman (prewar) than with the Luger. I keep the Woodsman action clean by wiping and brushing out every 200 rounds. This fine performance is a testimonial to the brilliant Browning design features of this pistol, handicapped as it is by having to handle a flanged cartridge which must be held low enough in the magazine so that the breechblock may pass over the flange. (Modern gun designers seem to have difficulty in appreciating this factor in gun design.)

Handiness and Carrying Safety

Just a glance at the table (Handiness and Carrying Safety) will show that because of the complexities of the mechanisms involved there are subtle variations in speed even when safety is the same, and conversely there are subtle variations in safety when the speed in getting off first shot is the same; for example, considering the four principal classes of pistols:

45 Automatic

Double action automatic (S&W M39 Walther P38)This class is included here because it presumably obsoleted older designs. It is moot, however, whether this class is as advanced as it is supposed to be for few of these pistols are being sold.

Luger

Double action revolver (such as S&W Combat Magnum)

All of these can be carried at their fastest condition of speed (condition F, cartridge in chambers, hammer or striker cocked, no grip safety on) but because of the unique and efficient grip safety of the 45 auto, it is safer than its competitors. When these four pistols are carried with what is generally regarded as practical and common sense safety we then have the 45 automatic with cartridge in chamber and hammer down (condition B), the S&W M39 and Walther P38 with cartridge in chambers and hammer down (condition E), the Luger with cartridge in chamber, striker cocked, thumb safety on (condition C) and revolver with hammer down, but here the S&W M39 and Walther P38 and revolver have a big advantage in speed over the 45 and the Luger. But, many disagree with this equating of safety, feeling that the 45 should be compared when in condition D (hammer cocked, grip safety on), and then its speed is markedly superior to the Luger but only equal or less in speed than the revolver or double action automatic. However, there are many who feel that even this comparison is not realistic because the 45 auto can be carried as a condition F (cartridge in chamber, hammer cocked, thumb safety off) and as stated before because of the unique grip safety speed is on a par with the best, but safety is adequate. It is noted that many contenders in recent "walk or draw contests" or "combat courses" use a 45 automatic and carry it in this fashion. Certainly the 45 can be carried with a wider range of safety conditions than any other pistol, thus suiting almost any criteria involving the combination of speed and safety; conversely the Luger is especially awkward because its safety is so located as to be difficult of access and moreover no grip safety is available on most models made in the past 40 years or so. It is evident that this awkward safety factor was a principal consideration involved when the Luger was replaced by the Walther P38.

HANDINESS & CARRYING SAFETY
Conditions of Safety of Handguns Tabulated in Order of Speed

CONDI-TION	LUGER PISTOLE '08	COLT 45 M1911	S&W 357 MAGNUM	S&W M39 WALTHER P38
A	No cartridge in chamber, striker not cocked	No cartridge in chamber, hammer down		No cartridge in chamber, hammer down
B		Cartridge in chamber, hammer down		
C	Cartridge in chamber, striker cocked, thumb safety on	Cartridge in chamber, hammer at ½ cock		
D		Cartridge in chamber, hammer cocked, thumb safety on	Cock hammer with thumb	
E			Use double action pull	Cartridge in chamber, hammer not cocked, use double action pull
F	Cartridge in chamber, striker cocked, thumb safety off	Cartridge in chamber, hammer cocked, thumb safety off, grip safety applies	Hammer cocked, no safety applies	Cartridge in chamber, hammer cocked, no safety applies

(Left margin: SLOWEST at top, FASTEST at bottom)

NOTE: All automatics are assumed to have loaded magazines; the revolver a loaded cylinder. After the first shot has been fired (per conditions of the preceding paragraph) I find both automatics superior to the revolver for fast work at short ranges, say hitting a 12 plate at 20 yards; but in getting on to a small target, say a 12 plate at 100 yards, the revolver is again the best. In other words, then:
1. The revolver is fastest and surest for the first aimed shot, starting with gun in hand.
2. For succeeding shots at short ranges the automatics excel in the same areas.
3. For succeeding shots at long ranges the revolver is again the fastest and surest.
In conclusion, it appears that the Luger as we know it is highly over rated — in no class of shooting is it outstanding — and mechanically it leaves a lot to be desired. All comparisons cited were made under conditions as nearly alike as possible, and the loads were: For the revolver — 38 Special (158 gr. at 855 fs).
For the 45 Auto — target type ammo (185 gr. at 775 fs).
For the 9mm Luger — standard military (115 gr. at 1140 fs).

Practical Speed of Shooting

The previous sections dealt mainly with an appraisal of mechanical features of handguns which affect carrying safety and speed of getting into action from the holstered gun. But what about proficiency in catching aim and firing when gun is in hand, at the "ready" but not aimed? How about succeeding aimed shots at various ranges? In order to answer these questions I set up targets at various ranges, a 6" diameter steel plate at 20 yards, a 12" square steel plate at 50 yards and a 12" wide by 24" high steel plate at 100 yards. At various times during the year, with various light conditions, I found in testing the 357 S&W Magnum (regular model with 6" barrel), the 45 automatic and the Lugers (one a 30-cal. 4⅝" barrel American Eagle model, the other a 9mm military model of WW II), that the automatics were about equal but the S&W 6" Magnum was faster for the first aimed shot (the hang and balance of this gun being just about perfect). For this first shot, conditions of safety being ignored, the Luger has an advantage in "pointability" because the barrel is only slightly above the forefinger and is parallel to it, and because the grip is at a proper angle (not like a carpenter's square). Unfortunately, this advantage is offset by the poor sights, skinny barrel, too light forward balance, and long, stiff trigger pull. The net effect is that the Luger is below the revolver and about on a par with the 45 auto for the first aimed shot — remember we are now talking about the gun being in hand ready to shoot and the only problem is to bring it up to aim and shoot. If the Luger were available with a 5" heavy barrel, ⅛" modern micrometer sights and a smooth 4½-lb. trigger pull, it would offer stern competition to even the revolver.

The 38 Special-
New life or last
gasp for police use?

A pipsqueak load, says the author, with — at one and the same time — too much penetration and too little shocking, stopping power. There'll be those who don't agree, but ... ∎ Jan A. Stevenson

THE 38 SPECIAL is America's favorite centerfire handgun cartridge by such a large margin that comparisons become ludicrous. As a police service round, the 38 is the standard and standby of practically every North American police agency, True, a small handful of departments use the 9mm M39 S&W, the M1911 45 ACP, the 41 and 44 Magnum, but these few hardly make a dent in the 40,000-odd police organizations estimated operating in the U.S. most of whom require it to the exclusion of all others.

Additionally, it is the nearly unanimous choice of private police and security agencies, guards, couriers, armored transportation agencies, many branches of the military, householders, storekeepers, and practically everyone else who carries a handgun for defensive purposes.

Thousands of target panners will use nothing but the gilt-edged accurate 38 for centerfire competition. And finally, far more 38 Specials are reloaded annually than all the other pistol and rifle cartridges combined.

With such an enthusiastic following, and such long established acceptance, it would seem that the eternal popularity of the round would be as universally recognized and unchallenged as the 10 Commandments. So it often seems.

Admittedly, the 38 has a lot going for it. If you are shopping for a gun, the weapon you want is chambered for the

38 Special, whether it be a flyweight, snub-nosed belly gun small enough to be concealed in the palm of your hand, or a 3-lb., foot-and-a-half long, scope mounted hunting pistol, or a super-accurate target automatic.

If you buy your ammo over the counter, with no other caliber do you have as wide a choice of loads as with the long-time favorite 38 Special. Approximately 15 different factory loads are available, ranging from blank cartridges to wadcutters, with just enough power to drill a clean hole in a paper target, to high velocity armor-piercing rounds.

The 38 revolver, rejected by the Army in 1904 as too ineffective for combat use, is to be found today on the hip of practically every cop in the country. Police experience over the past 50 years proves the Army was right. 38 Colt Official Police (bottom) compared to the gun it replaced, the 45 Colt New Service. The New Service was the standby of such hell raisers as the Border Patrol. The Canadian Mounties stuck with it for 13 years after it went out of manufacture. Note difference in size of the 38 and 45 cartridges.

All Specials — Far left, the standard 158-gr. round-nose service loading — a notorious pipsqueak. Next, the 200-gr. blunt-nosed "Super Police," an over-rated round. Last three cartridges are attempts to get the 38 on its hind legs. Square-shouldered bullet (center) gives good shocking power, penetration for car bodies. Cup-point bullet expands immediately, minimal penetration. Best for urban use, but generally taboo for publicity reasons. Square-shoulder hollow point (right) is excellent compromise.

If you reload, no other cartridge offers so many convenient possibilities. Brass is always plentiful. The cartridge is a wonderfully flexible one with which to work. It contentedly gobbles up every powder in the book from ultrafast burning Bullseye to slow simmering 2400 rifle powder. Swaged bullets, ready-cast bullets, and dies or molds for making your own are available in endless profusion. The round can be loaded down to be less objectionable than a 22, or upward to equal 357 factory ballistics. Plastic or wax bullet loads are readily gotten.

Police instructors love the 38, because it is superbly accurate, and its mild recoil makes it easy to train recruits with. It has been hailed as "the perfect pistol cartridge." Indeed, the 38 Special is more popular than the Beatles.

With a set of qualifications like this, badmouthing the 38 Special sounds about as level-headed a thing to do as objecting to the institution of motherhood. Yet a lot of level-headed people are doing it these days — the former, not the latter.

Forty yars ago, Elmer Keith was almost alone in proclaiming what knowledgeable police firearms men are now coming to recognize — that as a police cartridge, the 38 Special stinks. Back about the turn of the century, A. C. Gould, writing under the pen name, "Ralph Greenwood," was a voice in the wilderness editorializing against the pipsqueak round. He was in good company with such combat seasoned officers as U.S. Cavalry Lt. Eben Swift, and the British empire-taming army officers, Maj. Gen. H. E. C. Kitchener and Lt. Col. G. W. Fosbery, V.C., of the Bengal Staff Corps. But no one was listening; least of all America's police, who were busy climbing on the 38 Spl. bandwagon.

In a few instances, the adoption of the 38 was a step in the right direction. New York City, for instance, known as one of the world's finest departments, used the 32 before they got in step with the times.

For most agencies, though, the switch to the 38 was a great leap backwards, to borrow a phrase from pseudo-political scientists. The U.S. Border Patrol, as gun savvy an outfit as ever enforced the law, used M1917 45 revolvers until, sometime in the 1930s, they decided to swing with the times. The New York State Police, in the late 40s, abandoned the magnificent New Service 45 Long Colt when they made the changeover.

The last outfit to toe the mark was the renowned Royal Canadian Mounted Police, who reluctantly turned in their old glory-encrusted 455 New Service in 1954 — thirteen years after the weapon went out of manufacture. It was a sad day for the student of police ordnance when the Mounties buckled on the insignificant looking 38s. Compared to the hoary old New Service, the shiny new M&P seemed a slender reed with which to Maintien le Droit.

How did we get stuck with the abomination in the first place? In retrospect, it seems like a prime case of group feeblemindedness — a cruel melange of follow the leader and blind-man's bluff, the results of which unnecessary game has been the death of many a fine officer in the line of duty.

The Army, spurred on by Cavalry Col. Elmer Otis, started the trend to the small bore handgun in April, 1892, when they adopted the 38 Long Colt.

However, the forthcoming Philippine Campaign of 1899–1901 proved in gory and incontrovertible fashion that, as a manstopper, the 38 was a fraction better than hopeless. Posthaste, the Army ungreased a quantity of old single action 45s sitting in stateside storage, and shipped them out to the Philippine field units. After their arrival, there was a marked reduction in the number of headless officers to be crated up after each engagement.

As far as the Army was concerned,

The two up-and-coming rivals to the 38 as a police service arm are S&W's new 41 (top) and Colt's old Government Model 45 automatic (bottom). Colt's 38 Official Police shown center for comparison.

that did it. The famed Thompson-La-Garde Committee was convened to analyze the elements of stopping power in handgun cartridges, and their report, submitted in March of 1904, recommended that no pistol round of less than 45 caliber be considered. The conclusion was a sound one, and the Army has yet to budge from it. The current service automatic, Model of 1911A1, was adopted shortly thereafter in 45 caliber as a result of the Thompson-LaGarde Report.

That the U.S. Air Force issues 38 Specials in some numbers doesn't alter the basic facts. The U.S.A.F. has for long been concerned with ultra lightweight arms — unduly of lives, as witness the debacle with their aluminum-cylinder, small-frame revolver.

Meanwhile, back in the States, Smith & Wesson began diddling around with the discredited 38 Long Colt cartridge.

The bullet weight was increased from 148 to 158 grains; the powder charge was upped from 18 to 21 grains of smokeless powder. This raised velocity from 785 feet per second to 870 fps, and muzzle energy from 205 to 266 foot pounds. The result was christened the "38 S&W Special."

By any logical evaluation, the improvement in performance was negligible, but for some incomprehensible reason, the nation's police decided that the new round was the total answer, and the rush was on.

The current 38 Special load with l58-gr. round nose lead bullet is even less potent, while the 1090 foot second load — using the same weight bullet — is not, I believe, in general police use. In any case, this faster load would produce gross over-penetration, an aspect already in bad odor.

The lessons of the Philippine campaign were forgotten, if they were ever considered, and the findings of the Thompson-LaGarde Committee went unheeded. Most surprising of all, no collection and statistical analysis of evolving data on cartridge performance was undertaken for the next 60 years.

Even the FBI, a sage outfit which commands the respect — or perhaps awe of even its most vehement and intractable critics, the organization which has been responsible for the steady upgrading of police training in this country, and who were first to institute training of officers under combat conditions, a crew always in the lead in availing themselves of the means of physical science in police work, never bothered to organize or study the available data on the combat performance of handgun cartridges. The FBI issues the Colt OP,

4" barrel in 38 Special, perhaps the 38 M&P as well. Their regulations permit the 357 Magnum, and back in the 30s they were a popular arm with the FBI. Nor did the FBI, so far as I can learn, make a formal study of the conditions prevailing in armed encounters between officers and felons. If they did, I couldn't run it down, and I dug extensively.

Because of this strange disinclination to consider or believe the results of the military's experience or tests, because of this disinterest in studying the problem from the viewpoint of statistical analysis, because police combat is a fragmented and widespread affair, and it has taken half a century for the cumulative weight of individual tragedies to force themselves into the general consciousness, the love affair with the 38 Special continued unabated until it was the standard of nearly every department in the country.

Only the unheeded John the Baptists mentioned earlier, together with a few knowledgeable and experienced officers, continue to rock the yacht. In 1959, however, Professor Allen P. Bristow, a former Los Angeles County Sheriff's Deputy, and later of the Department of Police Science at Los Angeles State College, undertook an organized study of cases in which an officer was shot in the line of duty. His report was released in 1961, and appeared in the highly respected Journal of Criminal Law, Criminology, and Police Science. It created an immediate ruckus.

Actually, Bristow hadn't intended to consider cartridge effectiveness at all. He was interested primarily in tactical studies, but the data he assembled forced him to conclude that the police use of the 38 Special cartridge was a primary causative factor in officer fatalities.

Typical of the cases Bristow discovered is the following:

At 1:25 AM, an officer forced the suspect, who was driving a stolen car, to the curb; in the following hoopla, the suspect was shot 4 times with the officer's 38 Special, before escaping down an alley on foot, having wounded the officer in the meantime. The suspect was shot through each arm, solidly through the right side, and sustained a flesh wound at the base of the rib cage.

At 2:10 AM, the same suspect robbed a motorist whom he had just forced from his vehicle, but had to flee from the scene on foot before he could make off with the automobile. He was spotted 20 minutes later in a field two miles from the scene of the original shooting, and was again chased by officers on foot, but eluded them.

At 3:00 AM, the same suspect stole a car and was busily engaged in covering ground when he was spotted an hour later by a state patrolman. There followed a 30-minute high-speed chase which ended when the suspect wrecked the car. The suspect crawled out of the wreckage, and high-tailed it for the woods with the trooper hot behind him. When the suspect whirled to fire on the trooper, he was felled by a single 357 Magnum through the head from the state patrolman's service weapon.

In another case, a suspect who had just killed an officer was shot 5 times in the center of the chest at off-the-muzzle range by a second cop's 38. The suspect fell to the ground, as was seemly and proper under the circumstances, but when the officer turned his back to minister to his partner, the suspect stood back up and started shooting again. Five 38s in the chest killed him eventually, but they didn't stop him when he should have been stopped. And that is the purpose of a police sidearm — stopping a sequence of actions immediately.

Killing is not the job of the police, it is a function of the courts. That police bullets kill is simply a regrettable side effect. Their purpose is to stop whatever action forced the officer to shoot in the first place. If the suspect does not stop what he is doing when shot, the police cartridge has failed its duty, and if that failure costs the life of an innocent person, or of the officer himself, then that failure is doubly a tragedy.

This is the kick with the 38 Special. It's a great cartridge, but depending on it to stop a determined man is rather like trying to turn back a gale wind with a windowfan. You will notice that most of the advantages we listed for the round at the beginning of this article are purely matters of convenience stemming from the 38's widespread and unwarranted popularity. A lot of people buy 38s. Hence there is a wide range of weapons available from which to choose. The same reason holds true for the choice and availability of many types of loads and components.

We've said other good things about the 38 Special, but we can't say it's a man-stopper, at least not the way the factory loads it; and if it's not a man-stopper, it is logically not what the police need.

This then is the problem facing every thinking police firearms specialist in America today. Should the department face up to the facts, scrap the 38, and shoulder the burdens involved in adopting a round with more slap-'em-down spunk?

The problems this courageous course of action would entail (not considering that all important one of finances) present themselves in plentitude. Training officers to handle heavier guns is a problem: it's no use adopting a round if it results in a serious decline in practical accuracy. Usually the recruit is expected to reach minimum proficiency with a big bore on the same amount of training expended on the 38. Thus both training and ballistics are involved. Let's look at the 41 S&W. The low speed 41 load's recoil is only a bit less than the 357 gives, both fired in equal-weight guns.

Handloading is the answer, and no department can provide adequate training in any caliber with factory ammunition.

True, the officer should be able to handle full-charge factory service ammo. Our best departments give 50 hours of intensive firearms instruction, and require every officer to fire at least 500 rounds a year to qualify. Some departments train even more extensively. Professionals like these will turn in a creditable performance with any service sidearm, and need only a cartridge that does its share of the job.

However, many departments train rarely, if at all. A 20-man force was recently found with 4 guns that would not fire, one frozen shut by rust! Such departments, invariably armed with 38s, are a hazard to all. Happily, their number diminishes each year.

Educating officers to lug more iron is a problem that inevitably follows the adoption of a heavier sidearm.

It is a serious step for the department to undertake, this ditching of the inefficient old slingshot. More and more police agencies, though, are taking the plunge. On the west coast, a number of departments have gone so far as to abandon not only the unreliable 38, but the revolver itself, and have adopted that old tried and proven battle-ax of many wars, the 45 Automatic.

This shows a refreshing appreciation of the lessons of long combat experience, and was brought about by the very enlightening reports of a vociferous little group known as the Southwest Combat Pistol League, a coterie of combat-competition hobbyists who number among their members many Golden State lawmen.

League competition over the past decade has proven beyond much doubt that in the hands of a highly trained man, the 45 Auto is without peer as a combat handgun. Whether it is the answer to the needs of the police is still a moot question, and the rest of the profession will be observing with interest the practical experiences of those pioneering departments that have adopted the old warhorse.

Amarillo, Texas, was the first of a number of departments to adopt the new 41, which Smith & Wesson brought out in 1964 in answer to the requirements of the police for a man-stopping cartridge tailored specifically for them. However, Smith's was a somewhat timid venture, and the offering to date is hardly versatile enough to proclaim itself as the final answer. For instance, the lightest weapon Smith offers weighs in at' a rather portly 41 ounces, when compared to the 35-oz. displacement of the average service 38. It's bulky too, being built only on Smith & Wesson's big N-frame.

That "mere" 6-ounce difference doesn't sound like much, but it is notice-

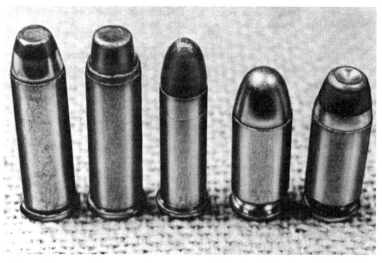

38 Special (center) with contending 41 rounds at left, 45 autos right. 41s and 45s give good knock-down punch without necessitating use of hollow points — also give healthy recoil. 41 Magnum (far left) is a rip roarer (210-gr. bullet at 1400 feet per second — almost twice the 38's velocity. Standard 41 is more sedate. 45 comes in hard ball (4th) and expanding (5th).

able hanging on the belt, loaded as the latter is with department gadgetry.

There is another objection too, as regards the two cartridges offered for this revolver. The Magnum loading is a real rip-roarer — a hot, highly accurate round, and excellent for its purpose. The milder "city" load is also excellent, though a bad bore leader if enough rounds are fired without cleaning.

The hitch is that even the lighter of the loads recoils too much for training purposes, or for general use in an as yet unobtainable lighter weapon, though mass reloading equipment is available for this round. However, if it is brought out on Smith's lighter K-frame in a 5-shot version, and a third and less emphatic cartridge is offered, it will be the hands-down obvious answer to police needs that it was intended to be.

For such a weapon I would favor a 200-gr. or lighter semi-wadcutter bullet as slow as 700 fps even — anything that was comfortable to fire. Such a weapon would be comparable to the 38 only in ease of portability. It wouldn't be much on penetration, but stopping power should be excellent. You'd have, in addition to a heavy bullet of proper nose configuration, all that additional cross-sec-

tional area working for you, transmitting maximum impact energy to the target.

Smith & Wesson offered, until recently, a number of other man-stopping sidearms which, although on the big frame, are light enough not to be objectionable on the hip. These are the 44 Special, and the 45 Auto rim. The fine old 45 Colt is no longer available in a practical double-action weapon, either.

Many departments recognize the deficiency of the 38, but are unwilling to junk the old pipsqueak for one reason or another. Sometimes their reluctance stems from a fear of innovation, an unwillingness to grapple with the problems a change of calibers would entail, or a sheer ignorance of the ballistic behavior of large bore handguns and bullets, and a groundless apprehension of them.

Often the reasons for retaining the 38 are more laudable than these, such as an awareness of the financial, training, and logistical problems involved, and a belief that the 38, in the long run, is still the best gun for the cop.

These departments concede that the 38 Special in its standard service loading, is a farce as a manstopper, ricochets badly, and overpenetrates, with the danger that an innocent person on the other side of the target will be hit. On the other hand, they contend that with proper loads, these faults can be cured, resulting in a weapon-load combination far better suited to police duty than any big-bore.

Some advocate that the 38 be replaced by the 357 Magnum, which offers the advantage of firing 38 ammunition for practice, as well as heaving some excellent armor-piercing projectiles for roadblock or barricade tactics.

The standard 357 Magnum load is a pretty good manstopper. On the other hand, it's a real hollering horror on penetration, which is a disadvantage, and it recoils as fiercely if not more so than a big-bore, so the training problem is no more easily resolved (save by the availability of 38 ammo) than with the large caliber weapons. To top it off the 357 can be a really intolerable bore leader.

Having ruled out the 200-gr. round nose 38 load, and the 357 Magnum option, what then can be done with the 38 Special to make it an adequate round for police use?

Obviously, we have to achieve maximum stopping power with minimum penetration and recoil, and the way to do it is to up the velocity and use light, pure lead, semi-jacketed bullets with wide cavity hollow points, cup points, or hydraulic expansion mechanisms built in, or else depend on extremely high velocity to expand a solid slug without assist from an expansion-inducing nose configuration.

Yet here we tread on tender toes. Super-expanding bullets for police — dum-dums if you will! There is no reason, legal, moral, or tactical not to use them; their employment will save the lives of officers and innocents who might otherwise perish — sacrificed on the cruel altar of bureaucratic timidity. But it cannot be gainsaid that super-expanding bullets are potential dynamite for anti-police propagandists.

Nevertheless, the department which opts to retain the 38 has little choice, if it recognizes its moral obligation to its officers and the public, but to continue the already substantial amount of exper-

imentation with expanding 38s that has been carried out by private parties, and to eventually consider adopting them.

Probably the most impressive formal research into the use of expanding bullets undertaken to date by an enforcement agency is that of the Phoenix, Ariz., Police Department.

Contrary to the norm, the Phoenix program was brought about not by their dissatisfaction with the 38's stopping power, but because of its excessive penetration. An officer was forced to fire on a felon, and did a good job of it, keeping all his shots squarely on target. However, the 38s zipped right through, felling a window-shopper on the next block.

THE PHOENIX PROGRAM WAS BROUGHT ABOUT NOT BY THEIR DISSATISFACTION WITH THE 38's STOPPING POWER, BUT BECAUSE OF ITS EXCESSIVE PENETRATION. AN OFFICER WAS FORCED TO FIRE ON A FELON, AND DID A GOOD JOB OF IT, KEEPING ALL HIS SHOTS SQUARELY ON TARGET. HOWEVER, THE 38s ZIPPED RIGHT THROUGH, FELLING A WINDOW-SHOPPER ON THE NEXT BLOCK

This caused some consternation down at headquarters, and the Phoenix brass-hats determined to load them up a 38 that would stay in the target. This either means dropping velocity still further, making the 38 scarcely more emphatic than a threat, or else, as Phoenix chose to do, upping the velocity to near sonic speed to ensure expansion of soft lead, and adopting a bullet designed to expand in the target, with its concomitant risk of ill publicity.

The chief down there is a cautious man, and in order to build an irrefutable case for the department's new cartridge being the last word in the public's best interest, an impartial, blue-ribbon panel was chosen to conduct the tests. Members were Capt. Gordon Selby of the Phoenix Police, one of America's top combat shooters; a lieutenant, a sergeant, and two crime lab technicians from the Phoenix Police; Ben Avery, outdoor editor of the Arizona Republic,

and Pete Brown, arms editor of Sports Afield magazine.

This illustrious panel of experts, following the extensive tests, suggested that the Phoenix police "adopt a high-velocity cartridge with a bullet designed to mushroom on impact." The department did just that, turning to the Super-Vel Cartridge Corp. (Shelby ville, Ind.), as have 300 other police units.

Super-Vel produces ammunition in four calibers (9mm to 44 Magnum), but most popular are their improved 38 Special loads. The Super-Vel 158-gr. semi-wadcutter is a tremendous improvement over old-school loads, but the one that really breaks with tradition is the 110-gr. ¾-jacketed bullet (solid or HP) at 1370 fps. These disrupt violently when they hit, field and test reports confirming their ample stopping power. These put the final cure on the over-penetration problem.

This then is the painstaking course which must be followed if the department insists on making the 38 perform as it must, and would still protect itself from the specter of unjustified public condemnation.

As an indication that something along these lines must be done if the 38 Special is ultimately to survive as a police cartridge, experimentation similar to the Phoenix program is being carried out all over the country, either formally by department arms units, or informally by individual officers and private experimenters.

An increased knowledge of terminal ballistics, or the action of the bullet within the target, is the result, and this can only be to the good. However the danger is (and it's a very real danger) that through poorly conducted, inapplicable experimentation, a body of misconceptions will be established resulting in the adoption of a cartridge that will not behave in combat as expected.

Usually, the result will be overpenetration, a la 357 Magnum, and the reason is that the medium chosen for terminal ballistics studies does not duplicate human flesh.

Let's face it — cops are human, and in none of them does the scientific zeal for accurate data overcome a very strong, normal, natural, warm, and emphatic human squeamishness. No police unit in the country has the desire to do things as thoroughly and impassionately as the Thompson-La-Garde Committee, and conduct firing tests on live steers in slaughter houses, and on suspended human cadavers. Yet, there is no way to pass the buck and get the Army to test the loads in battle zones, because expanding bullets are militarily taboo since the Hague Accords.

So we're back to the firing range, and the results are ludicrous. One experimenter tests his bullets in "dry, clean playground sand." Another uses moist sand. Why? No one knows. It's meaningless. Other popular mediums for test firing are moist clay, modeling clay, and "wetpack" — compressed, waterlogged phone books and newspaper. Criminals are made of none of these. Nor do criminals resemble steel drums filled with water and tightly capped.

Firing into substances such as these is an interesting game, and good for comparing the conduct of one bullet with another. But to say that the results will predict the action of a bullet in flesh is a farcically naive approach.

The only way to compile predictive terminal ballistic data, other than the long term project of studying the results of ensuing individual police combat affrays over a period of decades, or by hunting light game with test bullets and performing field autopsies after it is felled, is to conduct range tests with a

The old 45 auto is getting a lot of attention from police these days. Plenty of firepower and a slap-em-down cartridge — two virtues the 38 Special lacks.

target medium more closely resembling flesh than those above.

Commercial arms plants usually conduct their bullet expansion tests on blocks of gelatin compound, and if the police intend to precede the adoption of expanding bullets by a body of scientific data that will withstand criticism, it's time they got serious and did likewise.

The next few years will bear watching. That the 38 Special is virtually ineffective and was a bad bill of goods from the start has been well-proven and is no longer a matter for serious discussion among knowledgeable police firearms specialists. What to do about it is.

Foreign ammunition makers such as the Swedish Norma Projektilfabrik and the Canadian CIL are already marketing or are considering introducing high velocity 38s with improved bullet designs, and there is some experimental stirring about in the large American

plants. Custom ammo loaders, and new commercial operations such as the Super-Vel Company, are doing a booming business in expanding bullet, hot-loaded 38s. Cautious but intense experimentation by police agencies across the country is becoming more and more the thing.

The result of all this will and must be that either the 38 Special, that notorious old pipsqueak, now in its second half-century of service, and until now all but unchallenged, will come up with the goods and gain a new lease on life, or else it's breathing its last, unlamented senile gasps, and will soon be buried alongside the image of the Keystone Cop. May they both rest.

Today's Made-in-Spain Pistols

Time was when Spanish auto pistols were — not to put too fine a point on it — junk. Not so now, for Astra, Star and Gabilondo are of good fit and finish, they are accurate and reliable.
▌ Major George C. Nonte, Jr.

THE SPANISH arms industry has a long and illustrious history. Who hasn't heard of Toledo blades? With the coming of modern handguns at the turn of the century, business really began booming in the areas around Eibar and Guernica. Those northern Spain centers gave birth to all manner of small and large companies busily engaged in the manufacture of automatic pistols — not to mention copies of U.S. revolver designs.

The total number of firms involved probably cannot even be determined nor, often, can existing guns even be traced to the original maker. Competition usually improves the breed, but in Spain it had the opposite effect. By the 1920s the quality of Spanish handguns was generally considered about the worst in the world. A few firms made good quality arms, as can readily be ascertained by examining the products of Unceta, Gabilondo, and Echeverria. But there were scores of other makers of guns so crude they've been known to come apart with mild factory loads. Most were poor copies of basic Browning or similar designs, roughly finished and sloppily fitted and assembled.

A great deal of this may be traced to so-called "Cottage Industry" practice. Small shops, often in a home, indifferently filed and finished (?) rough castings and forgings supplied by one maker. Another shop might take barrels from one maker, slides or frames from another, small parts from somewhere else, and assemble guns. Virtually no control existed over tolerances or quality.

Somehow, it seems that the worst of the Spanish autos found their way to the U.S.A. By the mid 1930s, they were so poorly thought of that even a fine Spanish pistol was hard to give away. It is unfortunate that the same attitude still exists to a large degree. The virtually uncontrolled system that produced the bad pistols was not permitted to operate so loosely after the bloody Spanish Civil War. Whatever you might think of Francisco Franco otherwise, he did clean up the Spanish arms industry. Iberian handguns of today are of good quality, and have been for quite a number of years. Only Star, made by Bonifacio Echeverria; Babilondo y Cia. (both of Eibar) and Astra Unceta of Guernica now produce automatic pistols. The latter two also produce revolvers, but we'll not dwell on them here.

All three companies suffered considerably during the Spanish Civil War. Most records were destroyed so it is difficult to determine exactly what went on prior to about 1939–1940. In some instances, specific models exist, but absolutely no information on them is available at the factories.

At least some models of each make are currently distributed in this country and can be bought across the counter — the new law of the land permitting! In addition, the past decade has seen many thousands of surplus military pistols of all three makes sold here at attractive prices. This prompts many questions by shooters who have been told "Spanish pistols are no good." So, let's take a brief look first at the three firms, and later a review of the frequently encountered models.

Astra is the trade name of Unceta y Cia. The firm, founded in 1908, at first produced only pistol parts for other makers. In 1912, it began manufacture of the new Campo-Giro 9mm pistol for the Spanish army. These guns were superbly made, establishing a level of quality adhered to in Astra products from that time onward. I've examined dozens of Astra

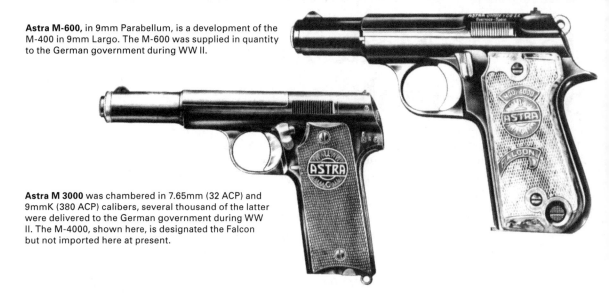

Astra M-600, in 9mm Parabellum, is a development of the M-400 in 9mm Largo. The M-600 was supplied in quantity to the German government during WW II.

Astra M 3000 was chambered in 7.65mm (32 ACP) and 9mmK (380 ACP) calibers, several thousand of the latter were delivered to the German government during WW II. The M-4000, shown here, is designated the Falcon but not imported here at present.

Table 1 Astra Pistols
F.I., importers

Model	Cal.	Mag. Cap.	Wt./ozs.	Lgth./ins.	Bbl./ins.	Price
Cub	22 Short	6	13	4½	2⅛	$39.95
Cub	25 ACP	6	13	4½	2⅛	39.95
3000	32 ACP	7	22	6¾	4	
3000	380 ACP	6	22	6¾	4	
Constable	32/380 ACP	7	23	6⅝	3½	

The 5 models listed are in production, but only the Cub models are available

specimens made in the 1920s, 1930s, and 1940s, and they invariably show very fine workmanship throughout.

Unceta produced many other models over the years, but the name Astra has become virtually synonymous with the tubular-slide Model 400 (also known as 1921 Military Model) developed from the Campo-Giro. Many Browning-type 6.35mm and 7.65mm blowback pocket pistols were also produced — some of them under other names, principally Victoria.

Unceta has prospered and today produces excellent pistols, some models of which are distributed by Firearms International.See our Directory pages for addresses. It also has the distinction of producing the 25 ACP automatic sold as the Colt Junior. This in itself speaks highly of modern Astras.

Gabilondo y Cia is another old-line firm, founded at Eibar in 1904 to produce revolvers. Not until 1914 did it begin making auto pistols, a move which brought it good fortune. The Ruby 7.65mm blowback pocket pistol of basic Colt/Browning design, was the first to be produced. It proved immediately popular, being reliable and well made. The French army ordered great quantities of Ruby pistols for WW I use, demand eventually raeching 30,000 per month. Gabilondo couldn't meet the requirement so they contracted with several other firms to produce the guns under the Ruby name. Eventually, about a dozen companies produced Ruby and Ruby-type pistols. These guns were not always up to Gabilondo standards and account for the derogatory remarks sometimes heard about Ruby pistols.

Following WW I Gabilondo produced well-made copies of the FN/Browning M1910 pistol under the names Ruby, Bufalo, and Danton. Copies of the Browning 6.35mm pistol were also produced, but in 1931, the larger-caliber Colt/Browning locked-breech guns were closely copied and produced under the Llama name. This continues today. These same guns were also produced by Gabilondo under the names Tauler and Ruby. All were well made and samples I've examined performed quite well.

Star Bonifacio Echeverria apparently began producing automatic pistols in 1906 or shortly thereafter. Early records were destroyed during the Spanish Civil War. The first guns were apparently 6.35mm and 7.65mm pocket pistols of conventional design. A 9mm (380) design was added later.

Star importance began to rise when, about 1919, it decided to market an improved version of the Colt/Browning locked-breech M1911 design. The locking system was copied accurately, but the firing mechanism changed entirely. The models 1920, 1921, and 1922 culminated in the Model A, which was widely sold in Latin America in 9mm and 45 caliber. This very good basic design is still produced today in the restyled models S, P and M, and the super S, the current Spanish service pistol. The Star locked-breech pistols all show very fine workmanship, especially the Model B 9mm guns made during and after WW II. The extensive line of Star pistols is distributed here by Firearms International.The 5 models listed are in production, but only the Cub models are available.

Astra Models

Through the wartime destruction of records Astra Unceta y Cia. can't say precisely what models and quantities of pistols were produced before the 1930s. The original firm, Esperanza y Unceta, was formed in July of 1908 by an arms dealer of Eibar, one Perdo Unceta, and Juan Esperanza, a merchant of hardware and other things.

Parts for pistols assembled by other makers were the first products, followed by the Victoria pocket pistol which closely copied post-1900 Browning 25 and 32 models. In 1912, a move was made to a new plant in Guernica — necessary because additional facilities were required to produce the newly-adopted M1913 Campo-Giro 9mm Largo (Long) pistol for the Spanish government. Campo-Giro production solidly established the new firm, and its pocket pistols were widely distributed, also under such other names as Leston, Sat, Museum, etc.

The trade name "ASTRA" was registered in 1914, though probably used before that date. Other, but conventional, pistol designs were produced. During WW I, some 150,000 7.65mm Browning-type pistols were furnished to the French and Italian armies.

In 1921, the Astra M400 replaced the Campo-Giro as the official Spanish service pistol; from then until 1946, some 105,000 units are reported to have been produced. This was an unusual blowback design chambered for the 9mm Largo cartridge and was essentially an improvement of the Campo-Giro developed by Astra. Cartridges of such power are not generally considered suitable for use in blowback designs, but the M400 proved entirely satisfactory.

The basic M400 design was scaled down and modified to form the M300 (300/1,2,3,4) in 7.65mm and 9mm (380) calibers in 1922. In 1944, an improved version was designated M-3000 and continued in production. During this time, several models based on modified Browning designs were produced in large quantities. By the end of WW II, these encompassed the M200, M100 Special, and others of which little record remains.

(Right) **Latest Astra** model is the Constable in 7.65mm. Outwardly it is quite similar to the Walther PP and PPK, but it is much different inside — valuable double-action first shot capability and the hammer can be safely lowered on a chambered cartridge.

(Left) **Astra Cub** is a development of the original external-hammer version of M-200. Currently sold as the Colt Junior, as well as under its own name, it is available in 22 Short and 25 ACP.

During the latter part of WW II, until 1946, approximately 60,000 M600 9mm Parabellum pistols were produced for foreign sales. This was the basic M400 slightly redesigned and made smaller to handle the 9mm Luger cartridge. These guns were very well made. They were followed by limited production in 1958–1960 of an exposed hammer version called the Condor and intended purely for civilian sale. Only 6400 Condors were produced, according to recent correspondence with Astra; they are, however, vague about whether production has permanently ceased.

By the mid-1950s, the old M200 had been superseded by the Astra Cub and Firecat, available in 25 ACP and 22 Short calibers. Both were modfied Browning designs, the former with exposed hammer. Variations within models were produced. The M3000 was available in 32 and 380 ACP.

In 1957, the Firecat was revised slightly and has since been manufactured in Spain for sale by Colt's as the Colt Junior in 25 ACP and 22 Short caliber. It replaces the old Colt 25 Pocket Model discontinued in 1946.

At the present time, a few Astra models are available in this country: the Colt version of the Firecat mentioned above

and the Cub imported by Firearms International. The 32 and 380 M3000 (now designated Falcon) and the new double-action Constable are in production but not generally available here.

All current Astra models are listed in the accompanying table. Workmanship is good in these guns. Personally, I'd like to see the remaining models available in this country.

Gabilondo Models

Perhaps prompted by the apparent success of Star, Gabilondo introduced in 1931 a near-copy of the Colt/Browning M1911 pistol. Initially this gun resembled the Star more than the Colt and had the solid backstrap of the former and a modified firing mechanism. Some such guns were marked RUBY. It apparently became evident that if copying were to be done, it would be best to copy the highly-regarded Colt, and to do it accurately. This was during the time when the reputation of Spanish pistols was gathering speed on the downhill slope. "Just another Spanish gun" wouldn't be enough.

Consequently, the Colt 45 Government Model was copied line for line, measurement for measurement — so well, in fact, that often (not always) Colt

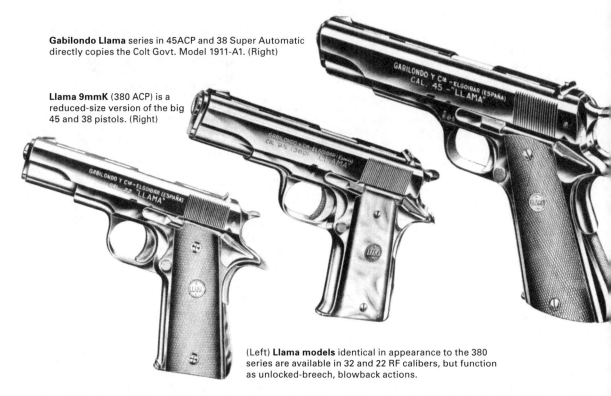

Gabilondo **Llama** series in 45ACP and 38 Super Automatic directly copies the Colt Govt. Model 1911-A1. (Right)

Llama 9mmK (380 ACP) is a reduced-size version of the big 45 and 38 pistols. (Right)

(Left) **Llama models** identical in appearance to the 380 series are available in 32 and 22 RF calibers, but function as unlocked-breech, blowback actions.

parts will interchange. The name Llama was chosen for the new line, which was produced in 9mm Long, 38 ACP, and 45 Auto calibers. Minor variations were produced. For example, the Llama "Extra" barrel was approximately ½" longer, the slide ⅜" longer, than the Colt — leaving the barrel protruding farther from the bushing. Even so, a Colt barrel and slide could be fitted to the Extra. On some variations the grip safety was deleted, and the internal extractor replaced by an external claw let into the slide.

One Senor Tauler, large arms dealer of Madrid, ordered large quantities of Gabilondo/Llama pistols marked with his name. These guns are sometimes thought to be another make, but were identical to Llamas being made on the same assembly lines at the Gabilondo plant. They are usually marked "Tauler Mark P" on the left side of the slide, with "Military & Police" on the right. Usually the manufacturers name appears somewhere on the gun, subordinate to "Tauler." Some identical guns are reported to be marked "Ruby," but I've not examined a sample.

Primarily for export Gabilondo de-

veloped a smaller lighter pistol — the "Llama Especial" — in 9mm Parabellum caliber. It resembled the Star more than the Colt in that the back-strap was solid, deleting the grip safety. The trigger was pivoted, modified lockwork was fitted, an external extractor was used, and the hammer was rounded and pierced a la Colt Commander. I used an Especial extensively in Europe and found it an excellent gun. It was available in the 1950s in this country through Stoeger Arms, but no longer. This model was also made and marked "Mugica" for an Eibar arms dealer, one Jose Mugica.

The basic Colt/Browning copies remain in production today. Following WW II, Gabilondo introduced a 2/3d-scale version of the big autos, chambered for the 380 ACP cartridge. Mechanically identical to the 38 and 45 guns in every way, it is designated here as Model IIIA. The 32 ACP companion Model XA is identical in appearance to the IIIA, but dispenses with the locking system. It functions as a fixed-barrel, blowback design. An identical Model XV in 22 Long Rifle caliber is also made.

Also, since the war, small Browning-

type blowback pistols in 22 Short and 25 ACP have been introduced as the Models XVII and XVIII respectively.

During the early 1960s, ventilated ribs were incorporated into the slides of all Llama models made for U.S. sale. Also, "accurized" versions of the 38 and 45 guns are now made. Called the "Match" model, they incorporate target-type adjustable sights and are carefully hand-fitted for maximum accuracy.

Star Models

Prior to the 1920s, Star pistols were all of elementary blowback design, chambered for the small 6.35mm, 7.65mm and 9mm short cartridges. In 1920 they introduced a large-caliber, locked-breech gun of military style and size. Called the Model 1920, it was offered in 7.63mm (Mauser) and 9mm Long (Bergmann-Bayard).

The M1920 represented the first attempt to this scribe's knowledge to improve upon the Colt/Browning swinging-link, recoil-operated locking system of the M1911 U.S. 45 Automatic. From the chamber forward the design copies faithfully the Browning locking system, as can be seen in the accompanying "exploded" drawing. Rearward of that point, the slide was changed to use a simpler and cheaper spring-loaded claw-type extractor (part No. 66) mounted in an external slot. At the upper rear of the slide was installed a rotating manual safety (see fig. 9). It did not block the sear or hammer, but when engaged rotated a steel block in position to prevent the hammer from striking the firing pin. Engaging this safety also retracted the rear sight into the slide.

The biggest difference from the Browning design was in the firing mechanism. The backstrap was made integral with the frame, doing away with the grip safety and separate mainspring housing. Instead, a simple recess was bored beneath the hammer to house a coil mainspring (part No. 09). This replaced 4 parts with 2, and eliminated several costly machining operations.

The Browning sliding trigger and intricately-shaped disconnector were replaced by a pivoted trigger, a stamped sear bar, and a simple flat interrupter (disconnector) riding in a slot on the right side of the receiver. These innovations reduced costly machining operations and proved to be as durable and reliable as the Browning system. A simple, sturdy pivoted sear was used.

Externally the M1920 greatly resembled the Colt 45 auto, but had a clumsier appearance because of its abrupt stock/barrel angle and straight backstrap.

In this form the Star represented a significant mechanical improvement on the Colt/Browning, not a "cheap copy" as it has frequently been described. It could be produced more quickly at less cost than the Colt, yet possessed the same inherent reliability and durability. It had only one serious shortcoming; the safety did not block the hammer.

The M1921 was essentially the same gun fitted with a long grip safety pivoted near the bottom of the frame. This feature was not considered worth the additional cost by Star customers, and the M1921 was not manufactured in large quantities.

Mechanically, the final form of the

Star high-power design was achieved in the M1922. The slide-mounted safety was discarded and replaced by one pivoted on the left rear of the gun frame. Here again simplicity and low cost were achieved. This safety contains a notch on its shaft. When disengaged, the notch does not interfere with hammer movement, allowing it to fall and strike the firing pin when the trigger is pulled. When engaged, a solid portion of the shaft intercepts and bears down upon a "tail" on the hammer. The hammer cannot move, even though the trigger is pulled. This safety is quite positive and trouble-free in its action, yet is basically simple and easily produced.

The M1922, with only very minor modifications became the Star Model A and was offered in 9mm Long. By April, 1934, approximately 80,000 had been manufactured in 9mm Long, mostly for the Spanish Guardia Civil (Land Police). The Guardia Civil guns were stamped "GC," for the benefit of collectors who like to know who used a gun.

First made in 9mm Long, the Model A was offered in 9mm Parabellum in 1932. The slightly enlarged Model M was offered first in 1924, in 45 Auto and 7.63 Mauser, both as a semi-automatic pistol and as a selective-fire machine pistol with detachable wood holster-stock. In 1925, the M became available in 38 Auto. When the more powerful 38 Super Auto cartridge was introduced, this same gun was used for it without change. By 1934

some 5,000 in 38 Auto (Colt) and 6,000 in 45 Auto had been manufactured. Production of 7.63mm Mauser pistols was apparently quite small.

By WW II the basic Star design had been somewhat restyled, but not changed mechanically. Stock angle and profile were changed, resulting in an appearance almost identical to the Colt 45. In this form the 9mm Long became the Model A; 9mm Parabellum, Model B; 38 Super Automatic, Model M, and the 45, the Model P. Identical otherwise, and with considerable parts interchangeability existing, the A and B are smaller than the P and M. Frames and slides of the latter two are wider and barrels are larger in diameter to accommodate the Colt cartridge. Weight is 1⅝ ounces greater. Dimensional differences are contained in the accompanying tables.

Basic Star design was reduced in size to produce the S series in 7.65mm and 9mmK shown here; later they were further reduced to true pocket size in same calibers.

Table 2   Llama (Gabilondo) Pistols
Stoeger Arms Corp., importers

Model	Cal.	Mag. Cap.	Wt./ozs.	Lgth./ins.	Hgt./ins.	Bbl./ins.	Price
XV	22 LR	9	21	6¼		4¼	$52.50
Exec.	22 Short	6	13½	4¾		2⅜	37.50
XVIII	25 ACP	5	13¾	4¾		2⅜	37.50
XA	32 ACP	8	21	6¼	4⅜	3¹¹⁄₁₆	52.50
IIIA	380 ACP	7	20	6¼	4⅜	3¹¹⁄₁₆	52.50
VIII	38 Super	9	38½	8½	5⅜	5	71.50
IXA	45 ACP	7	38	8½	5⅜	5	71.50
MATCH	38 ACP	9	38½	8½	5⅜	5	131.50
	45 ACP	7	38	8½	5⅜	5	131.50

Engraved, plated, specially finished and special grip models available at extra cost. Cased presentation models available on special order at considerable delay. Models XV, XA, IIIA available as "Airlite" with alloy frames, weighing 4 oz. less, same prices. All models listed are in production and available.

At the present time, all but the Model P are in production. A sample Model AS just received displays excellent workmanship. It functions perfectly with 9mm Long, 38 ACP and 38 Super Automatic factory loads. So long as proper bullets are used, it performs equally well with medium-and full-charge handloads in 38 Super cases. In regard to use of 38 Super Automatic ammunition in Star pistols chambered for the 9mm Long (normally marked "9mm/38") authorities say the guns are intended for use with both cartridges, and that they are proofed with loads developing 150% of 38 Super pressures.

Accuracy with this sample gun and with two 9mm Parabellum Model Bs has been excellent — equal to that of a new Colt 38 Super Automatic pistol with comparable ammunition.

The big-bore Star pistols became quite popular in Latin American countries. As a result, the Brazilian firm Hafdasa produced a nearly identical copy of the Model P in 45 caliber. It differs only in minor dimensions and in the use of the Colt/Browning firing pin and internal extractor design. This gun is known as the Ballester-Molina and was once a standard Brazilian Army service sidearm.

Impressed with the success of the large-caliber locked-breech guns, Star adapted the design to smaller pistols chambered for the 32 and 380 ACP cartridges. Significant among these is the "Starfire" Model DK, the smallest and lightest 380 pistol available today. Only 5¾" long and 4" high, it weighs 14 ounces. More conventional in size are the SI and S in 32 and 380 respectively. They measure 6½" long, 4¾" high, and weigh 22 ounces. Mechanically, these smaller guns are identical to the big military and police models. Star also produces small blowback-design pocket pistols in 22 and 25 caliber. Significant is the "Lancer" Model HK in 22 Long Rifle caliber. Virtually all other pistols this small are chambered only for the 22 Short or 25 ACP — both inferior in striking power to the 22 LR in High Velocity, Hollow Point form.

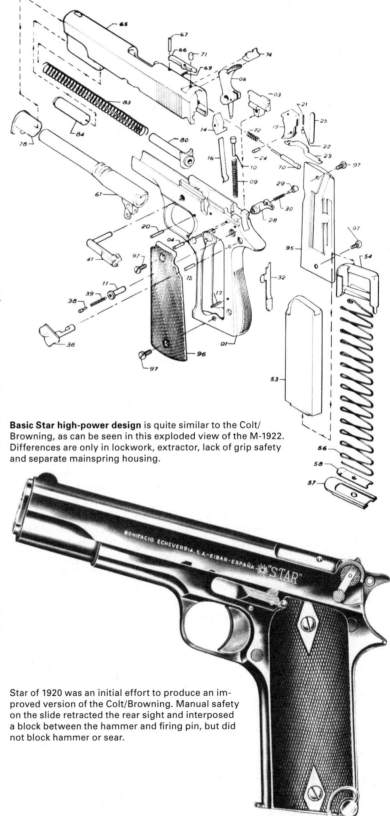

Basic Star high-power design is quite similar to the Colt/Browning, as can be seen in this exploded view of the M-1922. Differences are only in lockwork, extractor, lack of grip safety and separate mainspring housing.

Star of 1920 was an initial effort to produce an improved version of the Colt/Browning. Manual safety on the slide retracted the rear sight and interposed a block between the hammer and firing pin, but did not block hammer or sear.

Table 3   Star (Echeverria) Pistols
F.I., importers

Model	Cal.	Mag. Cap.	Wt./ozs.	Lgth./ins.	Hgt./ins.	Bbl./ins.	Price
F	22 LR	10	27½	7¼	5	4¼	$59.95
FI	32 ACP	9	27½	7¼	5	4¼	
F Sport	22 LR	10	29½	9	5	6	59.95
F Olympic	22 Short	6	28	9	5	6	
HK Lancer	22 LR	8	14½	5½	4	3	
CU	25 ACP	8	10½	4¾	3½	2⅜	59.95
DK	380 ACP	6	14	5¾	4	3⅕	69.95
SI	32 ACP	9	22	6½	4¾	4	69.95
S	380 ACP	8	22	6½	4¾	4	69.95
Super S	380 ACP	8	22	6¾	5	4	
B*	9mm Para.	8	37½	8½	5⅓	5	84.50
M	38 Super	9	39⅛	8½	5⅓	5	84.50
P	45 ACP	7	39⅛	8½	5⅓	5	
Super B	9mm Para.	9	35¼	8¾	5½	5⅕	
Super M	38 Super	9	40	8¾	5½	5⅕	

All guns listed are in production, but only those carrying a retail price are available.
*The Model AS (called in Spain the Model A) is identical to the Model B, but is said to function reliably with 9mm Largo or 38 Super cartridges. It is usually marked "9mm/38."

Present Star configuration is typified by Model M shown here. A and B models are identical but slightly smaller. Super series has an added quick takedown feature.

Star of 1922 embodied all features of later models and became the Model A.

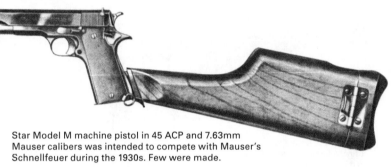

Star Model M machine pistol in 45 ACP and 7.63mm Mauser calibers was intended to compete with Mauser's Schnellfeuer during the 1930s. Few were made.

The current Star line also contains other blowback models in 22, 25 and 32 caliber, most of which are available from F.I. The accompanying chart details the general specifications of all Star models for which we've been able to dig up the information.

The question most likely to be asked concerning any Spanish pistol (and I've received hundreds of letters on the subject) is "How good is it?" Star, Astra, and Gabilondo automatics (actually marked as such, not copies) are of good fit and finish, accurate, durable, and reliable, regardless of model or date of manufacture. Functionally, they are equal to contemporary domestic guns and the better European makes.

In quality of workmanship, the above makes produced before WW II are excellent. Generally speaking, they can be rated (1) Astra, (2) Star, (3) Gabilondo. Fit and finish of Astra M400 and M600 are very fine, only slight deterioration having taken place during WW II.

Star models of the period are virtually equal in quality, with, in my opinion, Model B pistols of the late 1940s, being perhaps slightly nicer than some Astras. These particular guns have barrel and slide fitted with less play than even contemporary domestic models. This is particularly evident in the large lot of guns recently sold by Interarmco.

Gabilondo Llamas of the period are reasonably well finished, but not quite equal to comparable Star and Astra models. This is particularly evident, internally, at points like the ejector, extractor claw, disconnector, etc. Internal parts are rather rough compared to the other two makes.

Regarding current-production guns, I rate them (1) Star, (2) Astra. (3) Llama, with the exception of the Llama "Match" which is carefully hand fitted and priced accordingly (over $130). It ranks at the top of the heap.

In regard to current domestic guns, say the Colt Government Model and

S&W M39, Star very nearly matches them in both fit and finish, while Astra and Llama fall successively farther below.

Functionally, the several dozen specimens I've handled and shot are equal to comparable, current domestic models. As far as any personal preference is concerned, the Star B (9mm P) and AS (9mm/38-38 ACP) currently in use rank second only to my S&W M39. They are very closely fitted, nicely finished, and are both accurate and reliable.

After all this, I can honestly say that current Spanish pistols are good. One need not hesitate for a moment in choosing any of today's Astra, Llama or Star pistols.

Combat Shooting…
A Logical Start

The theory and practice of two-handed combat shooting, intended for adoption by police and other law-enforcement agencies in the British Isles. ▌Colin Greenwood, *photos by Kenneth Marsden*

Part I

THE SUBJECT of combat shooting is of immediate importance to those handgun shooters whose weapons may have to be used under practical conditions. To other shooters it may be a matter of academic interest only, yet even among those the subject frequently arises. Various "experts" are likely to expound at length on the merits or demerits of different combat shooting techniques, and opinions are frequently influenced by experience (often second-hand and exaggerated), by the methods taught in a particular Police or Army unit, by the books and articles on the subject and, unfortunately but not infrequently, by films and TV. This being so, it might be interesting and possibly useful to examine the problems involved in taking the first steps toward combat shooting and to test some of the theories put forward against what the writer fondly thinks is a logical study of the problem.

Combat shooting is usually taken to cover the use of a handgun, offensively or defensively, in situations where the target is shooting back. Such situations arise without forewarning, in difficult locations, frequently in bad light and when the shooter is literally caught on the wrong foot. In short, conditions which are very far removed from the target range. Highly refined target arms will have little place under such circum-

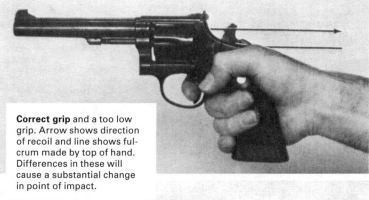

Correct grip and a too low grip. Arrow shows direction of recoil and line shows fulcrum made by top of hand. Differences in these will cause a substantial change in point of impact.

stances, and it is an oft-repeated view that target shooting techniques with all their refinements have no place either. However, this matter should be considered with care.

Combat shooting techniques usually regard the distance from shooter to target as the prime consideration in the choice of method employed. The shorter the range, the faster the method of delivering the shot has to be; conversely, the longer the range, the more precise the method of delivery must be. It is obvious that in some combat situations speed is essential, yet speed always tends to work against accuracy. The larger the target, the less precise the delivery need be, but speed should never be allowed to negate accuracy. There is little point in getting off a fast shot which misses your opponent while he is a fraction of a second slower, but hits. The various schools of thought in combat training almost all start with an instinctive or semi-instinctive technique at short ranges, then move through pointed shots at medium ranges to aimed shots at long ranges. Most fix the maximum range for instinctive shooting at around 20 feet, varying the other styles on a sort of sliding scale toward the longer ranges.

Instinctive styles at ranges of 20 feet or less presuppose a need for speed, with both parties in the open and cover not readily available to the shooter. The distance is short, the target relatively big. Assuming that hits in the torso are the objective, the target will be around 30 inches high by 18 inches wide. It goes without saying that, if a shot is to be a hit, the barrel must be aligned with the target when the bullet leaves it. Accepting that the point of aim is the center of the target, the torso allows for a vertical error of up to 15 inches or a lateral error of up to 9 inches; the latter, therefore, is more critical.

A pointing error can arise in two ways. Firstly, if the pistol is properly aligned, both vertically and horizontally, it can actually be pointing at a spot 8 inches from the center and still be a good hit. However, any misalignment of the muzzle in relation to the grip will be magnified in direct proportion to the distance from muzzle to target. If a 4-inch barrel revolver is used the distance from grip to muzzle will be around 6 inches. If there is an error of alignment of ¼-inch, that is, if the gun is held with the hand pointing towards the target, but the muzzle is ¼-inch off to one side, the error will be multiplied 40 times at a range of 20 feet and the shot will be a miss.

The Perfect Grip

There is only one way to ensure correct alignment of the pistol every time, and that is for the shooter to take up a perfect grip. This has to be taken up quickly and instinctively, but nonethe-

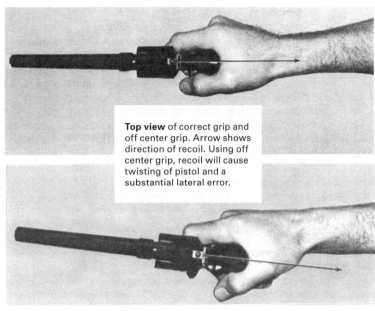

Top view of correct grip and off center grip. Arrow shows direction of recoil. Using off center grip, recoil will cause twisting of pistol and a substantial lateral error.

less perfectly, and the only way to achieve this is first to learn the correct grip and then work at it until the hand is incapable of an incorrect hold. The correct grip for practical or combat shooting is basically the same as the correct grip for target shooting, the only variations being in the tightness of the hold, and possibly the location of the thumb. The center of the backstrap must be located in the center of the V formed by the thumb and forefinger, and the alignment of the barrel from rear sight to front sight must be a continuation of the alignment of the arm from shoulder to wrist, so that if the arm were brought up into the target shooter's stance, there would be one continuous line from shoulder to front sight. No matter how tight the grip for combat shooting, the pressure of the hand must still be predominantly fore and aft on the pistol, and the weight of pressure of the individual fingers should progressively decrease from ring finger to little finger.

The question of grip is also vital in connection with recoil which affects pistol shooting in two ways. Most of the recoil occurs after the bullet has left the barrel, but it can still affect the shooter both physically and psychologically; recoil can quickly make an inexperienced

shot frightened of his gun, causing him to flinch badly in anticipation of the recoil. Flinching is a pretty certain way to ensure missing any target in either combat or target shooting.

The cause of recoil is quite simple. The burning gases under high pressures exert themselves equally in all directions, and only the bullet is free to move. The opposite and equal reaction to this is the backward movement of the gun in recoil; if it were able to recoil freely its movement would be exactly in proportion to the movement of the bullet and the products of combustion. Supposing the total weight of the bullet and the products of combustion to be 200 grains and the weight of the pistol to be 2 pounds (14,000 grains), the velocity and the energy of the recoil will be just one-seventieth of the velocity and energy of the bullet at the muzzle. However, the pistol does not recoil freely when held. If the pistol is properly gripped, the hand firmly in contact with it, part of the weight of the body can be added to the weight of the pistol to represent the mass which is opposing the bullet, thus reducing the actual recoil of the weapon. A perfect grip is therefore essential in controlling recoil and combatting any tendency to flinch.

Recoil Effects

Most recoil movement occurs after the bullet has left, but it starts to operate while the bullet is still travelling along the barrel, which results in a lifting of the muzzle before the bullet leaves. Provided this movement is consistent, it has no significance and can be compensated for by the sights. Any skeptic may test these theories by checking the difference in height above the barrel line of the front sight and the rear sight of a revolver; or he can take a break-open revolver (such as the Webley) and fix the barrel in a vise, bore sighting it at some mark. If the grip is now brought up to close the gun, checking the sights will show them pointing appreciably higher than the mark on which the barrel was bore sighted. This means that the sights are actually directing the shot low at the time of the trigger release so as to allow for the rise of the muzzle caused by recoil. A further test can be made by shooting two different bullet weights from the same pistol, for example the 145-gr. and the 200-gr. bullet in the 38 Smith and Wesson. It will be found that the heavier bullet strikes higher than the lighter — a result of the heavier recoil which the heavier bullet induces.

The recoil acts directly in line with the barrel and, of course, the hand is well below the line of the barrel. Thus the recoil acts as a lever, the fulcrum of which is the top of the hand. If the location of the hand on the pistol is allowed to lift or drop from shot to shot, the leverage asserted changes substantially and the point of impact will be changed in the vertical plane. For all practical purposes, the recoil acts directly to the rear. If the pistol is correctly centered in the hand with the proper alignment from front sight to shoulder, the recoil is transmitted in a straight line to the arm and the body, where much of it can be absorbed, and there will be no lateral disturbance caused by recoil. However, if the grip is not perfect and the pistol is off center in the hand, the recoil will cause the hand to twist before the bullet leaves the barrel. This force can produce a substantial lateral error of alignment.

The force of recoil cannot be overcome by the shooter, but it can be controlled so that it does not adversely affect the shot. This can only be done with a perfect grip.

Another factor likely to cause the fatal ¼-inch of misalignment in instinctive shooting is trigger control. To see just how far bad trigger control can deflect the muzzle of a pistol, get someone inexperienced to try a fast double action shot with an empty revolver, and watch the muzzle swing out much more than ¼-inch, usually high and right. An educated trigger finger is needed to get a shot off quickly from an instinctive position, particularly with a double action revolver. Only excellent trigger control will allow the trigger to be drawn back until the shot breaks without any disturbance of alignment. The term "squeeze," too-frequently used in describing the method of releasing the trigger, is very misleading. The correct method involves pressing the trigger directly backwards without any pressure or deflection sideways and using only the trigger finger without any change of pressure from the other fingers on the grip. This is the type of trigger control required in good target shooting as well as in combat shooting. The problem of trigger control is also closely connected with the problem of grip. If an off-center grip is taken, it will be extremely difficult, if not impossible, to press the trigger straight back, and this will cause a serious lateral error of alignment. Short range, instinctive combat shooting is the form of pistol shooting furthest removed from the target shooter's art, and yet it will be seen that two of the most important factors are common to both.

Instinctive Shooting

Instinctive shooting is limited to the shortest ranges, and most accepted styles indicate that the pistol is held either just outside or just within the fringe of vi-

Typical target stance. To experienced shots, this is more accurate than any combat stance. Its value to combat shooters lies only in the ease with which errors can be diagnosed.

Top view of correct grip and off center grip. Arrow shows direction of recoil. Using off center grip, recoil will cause twisting of pistol and a substantial lateral error.

sion. No attempt is made to align the pistol visually. At ranges beyond 20 feet, most systems use a pointing method of alignment, where the pistol is brought well into the field of vision, but both eyes are kept open and focused on the target. No attempt is made to use the sights, but alignment is visually aided by looking along the barrel. As the range increases, the amount of error which can be tolerated decreases in direct proportion, so that at 40 feet a lateral error of ⅛-inch will cause a miss. Thus the point-shooting method is strictly limited in its effective range, and beyond 40 or 50 feet the sights must be brought into use if accurate shots are to be made. The reduction of permissible error in medium-range point shooting increases the importance of perfect grip and trigger control, and any shooter who is to perform well must first master these elements.

At longer ranges, any combat technique must involve the use of the sights if it is to be effective, and any use of handgun sights immediately raises the problem of where the focus of the eyes should be fixed. No eye is sufficiently flexible to permit both the sights and a target 25 yards away to be clearly in focus. The over-riding importance of correct gun-hand alignment has been explained, and if the terms previously used in connection with alignment are applied to the use of sights at longer ranges, the relationship between a sighting error and the resultant error on the target can be established. Using the same 4-inch barrel revolver the sight base will be about 5 inches, and a range of 25 yards represents 180 sight radii; therefore any error of sighting in these conditions is multiplied 180 times on the target, and a sighting error of a mere .010-inch will cause an error of 1.8 inches on the target, while a lateral error of .050-inch or 1/20-inch will cause a miss at 25 yards.

The combat shooter faced with a target at longer ranges will frequently be required to choose between focusing on the target and accepting the inevitable loss in accuracy which must result, or obtaining fine accuracy by focusing on

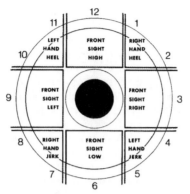

the sights and having a less clear picture of his opponent. In practice, this decision rests on the range involved and the amount of target exposed. At ranges just beyond the maximum for point shooting, the focus remains on the target and the sights are permitted to be somewhat out of focus. This gives a better alignment than the pointing technique. At long range, or where the target is only partially exposed, it will be necessary to fall back on the target shooting technique of focusing on the sights and allowing the target to be blurred. This technique is by no means easy to master and many experienced shots find difficulty in maintaining a concentrated focus on the front sight. Yet this is essential in target shooting and in those combat situations where fine accuracy is needed.

Target Shooting

The essentials of target shooting can be listed as:

1, Correct stance.
2. Perfect grip.
3. Correct sighting techniques.
4. Perfect trigger control.

It will be seen that grip and trigger control figure in all combat shooting, while sighting techniques are vital at all but the shortest ranges. At first glance, it may seem that the target shooter's stance, which has to be so carefully and precisely adopted, has absolutely no relevance to combat shooting and, indeed, it must be conceded that this stance would be quite ludicrous in most combat situations. The stances and positions

adopted in various forms of combat shooting vary considerably, but all are quite different from the target shooter's stance. To be of value, a combat position should offer:

1. Speed of movement in bringing the gun into action and in changing targets.
2. Control to maintain the gun within the limits of the target, and prevent overswing on any change of target.
3. Adaptability to any conditions of terrain and circumstance.
4. Holds which minimize any errors of technique which may arise in the heat of the situation.

This last point provides one of the stumbling blocks in teaching combat shooting. Although a good combat position will reduce any errors of technique, it will not eliminate them and it may well leave them to develop to the point where they are almost impossible to correct. Although errors may be minimized, they will still produce less reliable shots, and will inhibit progress toward proficiency in any type of shooting. No error can be corrected until it has been properly diagnosed, and the use of combat techniques in the first stages of training makes diagnosis virtually impossible.

It is often suggested that errors in technique can be diagnosed by "reading the target," and many shooters will be familiar with a segmented target, with a particular error shown in each segment. Firstly, they cannot explain what error might be present if there are shots scattered all over the target, as is frequently the case with a novice. Secondly, their very simplicity is dangerous and misleading in the extreme. Most of these targets show that shots falling in the 6 o'clock segment are the result of allowing the front sight to fall below alignment with the rear sight. This may be so, but the cause might equally be in a changed height of grip, excess pressure with the little finger, pushing forward the whole hand at the time of releasing the trigger, or indeed, by a combination of various faults. To suggest that the problem is as simple as these charts indicate is nonsense.

The combat shooter must, however, ensure that he has mastered grip, trigger control and sighting techniques, and eliminated any errors which may have arisen, before he can make any real progress in combat techniques. If the combat positions make these first steps difficult to check, and the target does not offer a sufficiently accurate guide to any faults which may develop, the shooter will have to look elsewhere for the most suitable way of learning and checking these basic essentials. The offhand stance adopted by target shooters offers a method in which grip, trigger control and sighting can be taught clearly and in which any errors can be detected and corrected before moving on to combat techniques. An experienced coach, watching the movements of the shooter firing offhand, will be able to spot most errors, and "dry firing" (without ammunition) is frequently useful in tracing faults. However, the inexperienced shooter will be affected by knowing that his pistol is not loaded and, if flinching or trigger snatch were serious problems, he may not show these in dry firing. Possibly the best method of detecting faults in technique is "skip shooting," in which the coach loads a revolver (preferably in 22 caliber) with three live and three fired rounds in an irregular sequence. The shooter does not then know whether a live round or a spent case will be presented and any reaction to recoil or any faults which can be disguised by the effects of recoil can easily be spotted when the spent round is presented. The shooter as well as the coach will then see, not only the error, but the effect which the error has on alignment. If a shooter can see for himself what is going wrong, he is well on the way to correcting it.

A logical study of the problem, therefore, indicates that the first step in learning combat shooting is best taken by following target shooting techniques to the point where the basic elements have been well learned. It is not necessary to go beyond this point in the strict context of basic combat training. However, any organization responsible for training men in combat shooting might

well believe that practical measures taken to encourage target shooting as a sport represent an investment which will be repaid a thousand fold. If a real effort is made to encourage trainees to take up target shooting, even if only a small proportion do so, the organization will benefit from the fact that these men will maintain their mastery of the basic elements of shooting in their own time, probably at their own expense. Further, such interest in handgun shooting generally is likely to increase the amount of interest taken in combat shooting, and lead many of them to devote their time and efforts to improving their efficiency in this field also. In purely economic terms, therefore, such an investment must pay off.

The basic elements of combat shooting are the same as those of target shooting, and the art of pistol shooting can, perhaps, best be thought of as a tree. The trunk consists of the basic elements of grip, trigger control and sighting and, once these have been mastered, the tree forks into the two main branches of combat shooting and target shooting. Each of the main branches has smaller branches which represent the different forms of shooting within each branch. No matter how far he has progressed along the target shooting branch, an experienced target shooter has only reached the fork of the tree when he comes to apply himself to combat shooting. The novice, starting at the foot of the tree, can not reach either branch until he has mastered the main trunk problems. •

Part II

PART ONE of this article demonstrated that skill in any aspect of handgun shooting can only be based on mastery of grip, trigger control and sighting. The second part proposes to take the arguments a stage further; converting the theory into practice, looking at the problems of the individual who wishes to learn combat shooting, and at the organizations which have to teach it.

The teaching of combat shooting should progress through four distinct

stages, each of which provides a logical step forward and each of which is a full, sound base for the next step. The four stages are:

Introductory Dealing with safety; functioning, care and maintenance of arms and ammunition; potential dangers from extreme range, penetration, ricochets, etc.; laws covering carrying and the use of handguns.

Elementary The theory of pistol shooting; grip, trigger control, sighting, position and breath control.

Practical Adapting the basic elements of pistol shooting to positions likely to be of value; different positions from prone to standing; use of rests and support; making rapid changes of target; dealing with moving targets.

Tactical Fitting the practical methods into the tactics likely to be involved; taking cover and making the best use of it; shooting from behind cover; shooting in the dark; fast draw; methods of approaching opponents in widely differing situations.

The introductory stage is not fully covered here, but clearly safe gun usage and a full understanding of the guns and their potential are essential. The standards of safety cannot be anything but the highest, and the handling of a firearm must not cause the slightest danger, nor even the slightest feeling of uneasiness, to anyone whom it is not intended to endanger. A proper understanding of the handgun, how it works and how to care for it, is necessary for safety and for the efficient use of the gun. This must be taught to the stage where everything that happens between picking up the gun and firing the shot is fully understood. The potential of the ammunition in terms of maximum effective range, extreme maximum range, penetrating powers and ricochet dangers affect the safety problem, but they also have a direct bearing on the use of the gun and the later stages of training. The man who knows the penetrating power of a large caliber revolver is not going to take cover behind a thin wooden screen. Similarly, such a man faced with an opponent partly hidden by a thin timber

Two handed grip on revolver when firing single action. The thumb of the left hand is used for cocking and allowed to rest on top of right hand. If revolver is to be used double action, the thumb can rest along the top of the right thumb.

Two handed grip for autos. This grip can also be used with revolvers when firing double action.

screen will know that he can take his opponent out by shooting through the wood instead of trying to hit a small exposed part.

Any agency required to provide men with arms and train them, and any individual who takes it upon himself to use a firearm, must know more than just how to fire it. He must know when to fire it or, more to the point, when not to fire. Time spent covering the law on this subject could save a great deal of trouble later.

Classroom stuff, all this stage one, but it must never be boring lecture material. The rules of safety have to be taught until they are second nature; range, penetration and ricochet problems require talk in terms of yards and miles, of feet per second, and of feet or inches of penetration in a particular material. All this will make more sense and be better retained if the talks and lectures are backed up with visual aids — visual aids which will register. Instead of sim-

ply saying that a 38 Special bullet will penetrate "X" inches of timber at "Y" yards, produce the timber with the bullet still bedded in it or, better still, shoot through the piece of timber and let everyone watch. Shooting at sealed cans of water or at an orange may be pretty old hat, but it does impress. When it comes to impressing people that bullets actually kill and that safety is important, try a color slide of a particularly messy bullet wound — strong stuff, but it impresses.

Theory and Practice

The theory of the elementary stage was the subject of Part I. Now we should see how this theory can best be put into practice. A good coach for each shooter will greatly ease many of the problems, but few shooters will be able to monopolize a good coach, even if they can find one, and no police agency can afford so many instructors. The problem can be eased a little by pairing off the students so that one can carefully watch the other while all are

under the eye of an instructor. This helps in three ways. Firstly, the amount of dead time, when members of a class are simply waiting their turn to shoot, is reduced; secondly, the "coach" can learn a lot from his partner's mistakes; thirdly, the shooter is helped by someone who can watch all his moves at a time when he can only see his handgun.

The pairs of students take their first steps, still in the classroom, by developing grip, sighting and trigger control techniques. Revolvers loaded with empty cases, or preferably with snap caps are used and, of course, both guns and cartridge cases must be checked by each class before starting. The "target" for this stage is a blank, light colored wall — any wall with nothing on or near it to distract the shooter's attention from his sights. When he fully understands the proper sight picture and has, with a little coaching and correcting, got a good grip on the pistol, the shooter takes up the correct offhand stance used by target shooters. Then he concentrates on his sights and keeps concentrating on them while he tries his as-yet-uneducated trigger finger in breaking a single action shot. He must hold his aim, keep looking at the front sight while the shot breaks, then he will see the blade dancing all over the place as all the different pressures tend to wrench it out of alignment. Now he sees the problem; he should stay facing his blank wall until he can take his aim, break a single action shot and still have a near-perfect sight picture a full second afterward. When he can do that he is fit to show his face on a range, but not before.

The first gun to be fired on the range should be a 22 revolver — for a number of reasons. The revolver is the only handgun which can easily be used for skip shooting with alternate live and dummy rounds — there is no better aid to learning the basic principles than this. The revolver is a little simpler than the auto, is less likely to distract the novice at this stage. A novice is always apprehensive about the first few shots and the use of a heavy caliber revolver could make him gun shy, a problem difficult to overcome. There is no real difference between shooting a 22 and shooting a 357 Magnum until the recoil comes, and mastery of recoil follows mastery of the correct grip. Finally, 22 ammunition is cheap and a substantial amount can be allocated to this stage of training without unduly straining the budget. No matter what gun the shooter will eventually use — revolver or auto — and no matter how much centerfire ammunition is available for training, start him off with a 22 revolver.

First Range Shots

The object of the first series of shots is merely to demonstrate to both student and instructor that the lessons against that blank wall have been properly learned, and that grip, sighting and trigger control problems are being overcome. The first few shots will undoubtedly be affected by nervousness, so there should be nothing about the practice which will add new problems or distractions; they should be fired in exactly the same way as the snapping at the blank wall was done. No targets, just a large backstop, but this is not just blasting off half a dozen shots to get the feel of the thing. Each shot must be carefully delivered and then followed through by allowing the pistol to come to rest after recoil and checking the sight picture again. This follow-through sight picture should look pretty much like the sight picture did before the shot was fired.

Prone position. Full two handed grip is used. Gun and body position are kept as low as the terrain will allow.

The next step is to introduce a target, to see whether the early lessons are paying dividends. Arguments about the type of target which should be used for combat training have ranged far and wide; targets currently used vary from the standard round bull competition target to complicated figure targets with odd-shaped scoring zones. These targets all hinder the shooter in attaining his cur-

Kneeling position. By using the type of two handed grip recommended for autos, the pistol shooter is able to fake up the same kneeling position as a rifleman would use. The supporting elbow is positioned just off the knee.

rent object, no matter what value they might have in later stages of training. That round black aiming mark on the competition target draws the shooter's eye like a magnet away from his sights and the scoring rings tend to be very discouraging in the early stages. The same can be said of the silhouette targets in common use. What is needed at this stage is simply a plain rectangle of paper, preferably a matte, off-white color, with no aiming mark to distract the shooter's eye from his sights. Progress at this stage is measured simply by group size; as the shooter's grasp of the basic skills increases, the group size will decrease. A positive method of measuring this progress is needed, so the plain white target should have grouping circles drawn on the back where they will not distract, but will clearly indicate group sizes. Standard competition targets could be used for this provided they are put up with their reverse side toward the shooter, and provided that no account is taken of the score indicated on the back; the scoring rings used only to check the group size. The shooters should start at a range of 30 feet, with a target about 15 inches square. They should be told to shoot for the approximate center of the square, concentrating all their efforts on a good sight picture, a good trigger re-

lease, and following the shot through to check the sight picture.

At regular intervals skip shooting should be introduced into the program, with the "coach" loading the revolver for his partner and checking the follow-through position particularly carefully at each blank round. Until a shooter can regularly group within a 6-inch circle or less at 30 feet, he should stick to this stage of the game. Once this standard has been reached, the shooter should be faced with a round bull target for a few shots to check that an aiming mark will not distract his attention from the sights. Throughout the course the shooter should be returned to the blank wall and target shooting practices at regular intervals to make sure that no errors have arisen. Then, when he has reached the stage of finding man-sized targets pretty easy to hit, to cut him down to size a little.

Combat Stances

The move to the practical stage must start with the adoption of a combat shooting position upon which the variations necessary to meet differing circumstances can be based. The necessary ingredients of a good combat position were stated in Part I to be:

1. Speed of movement in bringing the gun into action and in changing targets.

2. Control to maintain the gun with-

Short Range Shooting

Dealing with fast, short-range targets should be left to the end of the practical stage to give the shooter as much training and experience as possible. The range at which the requirement for speed begins to take precedence over fine accuracy cannot arbitrarily be fixed. It must vary according to the skill of the shooter, the size of the target exposed and the time the opponent will take to get off his shot. At ranges of around 20 feet, when a rapid shot on a fully exposed target is called for, the two-handed grip should

Prone position. Full two handed grip is used. Gun and body position are kept as low as the terrain will allow.

in the limits of the target and prevent overswing on any change of targets.

3. Adaptability to any conditions of terrain and circumstance.

4. Holds which minimize any errors of technique which may arise in the heat of the moment.

No one position will fill all combat needs — these could vary from an ultra-short range shot delivered at lightning speed to a very precise shot at long range, with ample time. However, combat shooters the world over are now turning to the free standing two-handed position as the most useful basic combat method. It fulfills all the requirements listed above and is relatively easy for the novice to master. There are many variations of the two-handed grip, but two are put forward here as being more useful than any others. In both cases the pistol is gripped correctly by the shooting hand, a grip that does not vary in any way from that taught in the elementary stage. If the gun is a revolver, the shooting hand is then gripped by the free hand, with the little finger beneath the grip, the other fingers curled around the shooting hand. If the revolver is to be fired single action, cocking can be done with the thumb of the weak hand; for double action shooting the thumb can lie loosely on top of the thumb of the shooting hand. If the weapon is an auto, this style of grip can result in the loss of a little flesh from the top of the thumb as the slide slams backwards, and it will be far better to cup the weak hand beneath the shooting hand with the fingers around the front of the grip.

In both variations, the shooter faces square to the target. The arms are kept

straight, the shooting arm pushing outwards, and the weak hand pulling inward to form a rigid triangle with the gun at its apex. The pull of the weak hand must be to the rear only, with no sideways pressure. From this position moving targets or changes of target are dealt with by swinging from the hips, keeping the triangular support for the pistol firm and controlled.

Targets well to the side are engaged by moving the feet round to face the target, not by swinging too far out of square. This free standing position should be taught and practiced at a range of about 20 yards, using plain silhouette targets and allowing deliberate fire until the position is mastered. The whole process should then be speeded up until the student can raise his pistol from an angle of about 45 degrees to the ground and fire an accurate shot in less than two seconds. From this point onward the moves through the various positions become much easier. The prone position uses the two-handed grip in exactly the same way as the standing position, the elbows being rested on the ground to give the minimum lift for a clear shot. In the kneeling position, the type of grip recommended for autos can be used in a position similar to that for rifle shooting. When the use of rests and support is taught, the basic two-handed grip will have to be varied except when shooting over the top of cover — a situation to be avoided whenever possible. In all cases, the gun should be kept clear of the cover and support should be obtained by resting the hands or arms against the cover.

be used and both eyes should be kept open, with the focus on the target. If the initial stages of training have been properly carried out, the shooter will still see the sights and produce good alignment without wasting time on the process. Pure instinctive shooting, with the pistol only just within the fringe of vision, must be restricted to the shortest ranges — 10 feet or less, and to fairly large targets. The most experienced pistol shots have to work hard to master this technique, which is only used in those real emergencies when there is nothing else for it. The most common mistake made in combat shooting is in trying to use instinctive shooting at hopelessly long ranges. If the very slight amount of error of alignment needed to produce a miss is recalled, the limits of instinctive shooting are better appreciated. If your man is almost leaning on your gun, instinctive shooting works; beyond that you want to see what your gun is doing before you let off a shot.

Colin Greenwood, 38 years old when this article was written, has been an English police officer since 1954, rising in the years since to sergeant, inspector and, his rank today, Chief Inspector. He has participated in the shooting sports generally, including shotgunning and rifle shooting, but his main interest was, and is, in handgun shooting. He won the British Police Championship twice in ISU centerfire matches, placed several times in those and other handgun events, and was twice a member of the

British Team competing for the European Police Shooting Championships. Mr. Greenwood's articles have been published in the (English) Forensic Science Journal, in several British police journals, in Guns Review, et al. His latest book, Tactics in the Police Use of Firearms, is an excellent work that deals with all phases of the police use of guns and related equipment.

Mr. Greenwood is (if he doesn't mind the term) an enlightened policeman, one who does not believe, ipso facto, that stringent gun controls mean an automatic reduction in firearms crimes. Last year Mr. Greenwood was granted a Fellowship at Cambridge University to reaseach and report on the effectiveness of firearms controls in England. That study has now been completed, and here is what Mr. Greenwood had to say, in part, about his findings: "...firearms controls have done little or nothing to combat armed crime. It can be shown that, when firearms were completely free from control (prior to 1920), there was less criminal use of firearms than there is now!"

Once the first step in the practical stage has been completed, shooting should always be against a time limit except for the periodic return to the blank wall and grouping stages. The difficulty in providing turning or pop-up targets to work to short time limits has led some mathematician of long ago to work out that firing two shots in two seconds is the same as firing 6 shots in 6 seconds. Six seconds is easier to time than two, so pistol training in many parts of the world, not only in America, has been blighted by the "6 shots in 'X' seconds" bugaboo. Six shots in 6 seconds is certainly not the same as two shots in two seconds. Apart from the failure to allow for time to come on target, those responsible for this suggestion seem to have forgotten that no one is going to stand still while 6 shots are fired at him. Combat shooting in this way makes the shooter fire 6 shots each time he draws

Any position will need to be modified to suit the cover or the terrain. The kneeling position is easily modified to take best advantage of the cover afforded by an automobile.

his gun, and there is every chance that such training will take hold when he finds himself in a real live combat situation — he will promptly empty his revolver at the first target to appear, a very dangerous habit. An empty revolver is of little use when the opponent can fire one aimed shot and end the matter. If, under combat conditions, a shooter has not hit his opponent with his first shot, or at worst with his second shot, he might find it more profitable to start on his prayers rather than trouble with the third shot. In training, the maximum number of shots to be fired at each exposure of a single target should be two, and the absolute maximum time allowance should be three seconds.

Final Stages

The final stage of training is beyond the scope of this article, which deals with making a start on combat shooting. In the tactical stage the techniques which have been learned have to be fitted into the conditions likely to be found in combat. This requires a lot of thought and research into the best methods of approaching a particular situation, whether it be taking out a criminal barricaded in a building or defending oneself against a sudden surprise attack. Fast draw falls into this stage of training — almost post-graduate stuff. All too of-

ten half-trained police recruits are asked to master the fine art of delivering an accurate, fast shot from the leather without having had the essential grounding in accurate shooting. The results are frequently tragic. No training system is complete unless it includes some tactical training in its finer forms, such as moving-film targets or a "Hogan's Alley" type of thing, where the shooter is faced with problems requiring quick and correct reaction as well as good shooting.

Combat shooting is not something which can be learned casually by reading a couple of books and watching western or detective movies. It is a science in which the basic lessons have to be well learned before proficiency can be attained. It may well look pretty easy when a practiced combat shot demonstrates his skill, but this is carefully studied ease, the result of training and practice. The novice will need to work hard at this, but if his training follows a logical sequence his progress will be more rapid and certain.

Customizing Contrary Snubs

In spite of its numerous disadvantages and deficiencies, the smaller combat revolver has a place in the current scheme of things. Here are detailed data on how to have a smoother and better snub-nose.

▌Jan A. Stevenson

THE SNUBNOSED revolver is a slender reed on which to prop one's hopes of longevity. Every design aspect of it contributes to ineffective ballistics, hopeless inaccuracy, and a piddling low volume of fire. The pipsqueaks are too light by far to hold steadily on target. The sight radius is so meager that gross errors in sight alingment go all but unnoticed by the shooter. The sights themselves, with rare exceptions, are far too tight and narrow. The snubs have little point or feel for instinctive shooting, and errors in trigger control are magnified manyfold over what they would be with a more substantial sidearm. Trigger reach is too short for all but debutantes, and the grips the factory fits are usually worthless. On discharge the shooter feels an uproar like King Kong unleashed, but the bullet leaves the sawed-off snout at a pace far short of the published ballistics figures, which are based on a 6" barrel. The short barrel means a short ejector rod, which means the empties have to be plucked out by hand, save for a couple of new designs. Whether fired deliberately or instinctively, it's one of the most inconsequential handguns in the book.

But despite its multitudinous disadvantages the much over-rated 38 snub does have its place. It fills a definite need, and in certain circumstances it is the only arm to choose.

For instance, the off-duty cop who must lug his equalizer to the movies, supermarket, beach and church, summer and winter, often finds anything larger than a snub a nuisance to hide. Likewise the undercover operative, the narcotics agent, or the vice squad officer can sometimes get away with a small 38 and have a far more effective firearm than any derringer or watch-fob automatic. The doctor, pharmacist, banker, jeweler, or shopkeeper who works in shirt sleeves, needs a gun that's concealable in a pants pocket holster — so the answer is obvious. Finally, he who insists on concealing his sidearm in a shoulder rig is restricted to the snub because the best of the half-breed harnesses will take nothing else.

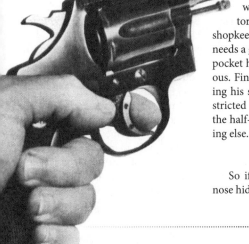

Choice of Snubs

So if you really need a little short-nose hideout gun, what's there to choose

Colt's 1972 Detective Special is a sturdy but small handful, weight just right at 23 ounces. Its improved grips are pretty good combat handles as found.

from? Smith & Wesson has the largest offering: three models in steel frame at about 19 oz. and in airweight at about 14 oz. Their basic model is the Chiefs Special. The Bodyguard is a Chiefs with built up sidewalls shrouding the snag-prone hammer spur. The Centennial model is slicker still, with the hammer completely concealed in the frame; it can be fired double action only and was designed for pocket use. Each of this trio is built on Smith's small "J" frame, is of the same size and heft, and takes 5 rounds. The Chiefs is also available in all stainless steel at 19 oz., if you can find one!

Colt's snubs hold 6 rounds, and are

Snubs, by nature, are the hardest handguns to shoot. The way the factories leave them, though, makes things harder than necessary. Author's battery includes (from left) Colt Agent, S&W Chief's Special (note chopped spur), and Charter Undercover. All have been customized to some extent. Charter wears factory optional Bulldog grips while other two get by with Ace shoes and Tyler adaptors.

consequently somewhat bulkier than the competition. The steel-framed Detective Special hefts 21 oz., and its aluminum alloy look-alike, the Cobra, goes 15 oz. Colt's Agent is simply a Cobra with shorter grip straps.

Colt's 1972 Detective Special, built on the Mark III system, is a big improvement over the older version of the DS. The new ejector rod, now .875-inch long, almost punches the empties out into the clear, but not quite. The ejector is now encased in a housing under the barrel, this adding a couple of ounces to total weight (now 23 oz.), shifting the balance forward, with improved handling and recovery from recoil.

The new grips are a major improvement, too. They're beefier, making for better control, with a second-finger filler built-in. They drop below the straps over a half-inch, another plus.

The Baughman-style ramp front sight, nicely cross-grooved for glare reduction, is ⅛-inch wide.

Otherwise the new Colt DS is much like its predecessor, and the latest mod-

el appears well put together — good finish, good quality control.

The knowledgeable customer usually selects a steel frame, and puts up with the extra weight involved. These guns are small enough to start with, and a few extra ounces are a big help in dampening their vicious recoil. Moreover, besides the extra strength of a steel frame, steel contact surfaces tend to work harden, and the more you fire the gun, the smoother it operates. Aluminum alloys have no such virtues, sometimes deteriorate after long usage.

In addition to such hoary names as Colt and Smith & Wesson, a relative newcomer to the field, the Charter Arms Corp. of Bridgeport, Connecticut, also offers an excellent 38 Special snub, their Undercover model. Externally resembling the Chiefs Special, the Undercover weighs 16 oz., has a

chrome-moly steel frame, high carbon or chrome-moly critical parts, and an aluminum alloy grip strap/ trigger guard unit — clearly a non-stress part. I favor the Charter as perhaps the best compromise since it's the lightest steel-frame 38 made, has the widest sights of the lot, and is offered with a fine pair of combat grips direct from the factory. But take a good look at the 1972 Colt DS as well.

Having now chosen one or the other, how do we go about wrenching the maximum potential accuracy and controllability from the perverse little gun?

This problem wants considerable thought, and then a good bit of work since, as they come from the factory, the little guns are rather barren of virtue and each of the limitations enumerated in the opening paragraphs must be overcome as far as possible.

Sights

Snubs come with non-adjustable milled sights, and in any altercation beyond off-the-muzzle range, your health and welfare are likely to depend on their quality. Ideally they're big, eye catching, and open enough to allow quick alignment even in dim light.

Smith & Wesson is the worst offender. Their front blade, nominally a slender 1/10", often mikes to a mere .073"–.075", and it's combined with a too-narrow rear notch. I've seriously considered having a competent pistol-smith knock the things off entirely and replace them with something usable. If going to this extreme, a 1/10"-⅛" gold or ivory bead in a wide "V" British Express-style rear leaf might prove an interesting combination.

The old Colt, with an .011" wide front post, has considerably more going for it. The rear notch is narrow-ish but can be opened by careful filing. You'll probably have to do this to sight the gun in anyway. The new Colt DS front sight mikes about the same, but the rear notch is a bit wider.

Charter's Undercover is by far the best of the three. Their front blade, nominally ⅛ (.125") actually measures a generous .139" and .141" on my guns. The rear notch is beautifully shadow-boxed into the frame and gives a dead-black picture. It too is a bit on the tight side, and stock removal is best done on the providentially fat front post.

Snubs are usually regulated at the plant to throw 158-gr. factory loads 2"–2½" high at about 15 yards, 6 o'clock hold. It's unlikely that your gun, from your hand, will put the load you want to use to the point of aim. If she shoots low, just file down the front sight a bit at a time till you're on target. If she shoots high, well, that's bad. You have to have a higher front sight. A good gunsmith may be able to lay a welding bead up there, or he may have to braze or dovetail on a complete new ramp and blade. If windage is adrift, the group can be brought to taw by carefully filing a bit of stock from the rear sight notch or from the front sight blade, on the side toward which you want the group to move. As we've noted, this operation has the additional advantage of opening the rear sight, giving more light on each side of the front sight blade — a distinct advantage for defense shooting.

Actions

A small revolver, if it is to deliver any sort of double action accuracy, needs a butter-smooth action. Many hours of careful handwork, which the factories simply can't afford to do, will be required. A few aristocratic gunners obviate this laborious action smoothing by having each moving part gold plated. This slicks the action right up, but us pore boys better do it the hard way.

Besides disassembly tools — screwdrivers, pin drifts, a brass headed hammer, etc., you'll need an India stone, a hard Arkansas stone, and several sheets of crocus cloth. Medium grade emery cloth may be substituted or the stones. A ⅛"power tool with an assortment of rubber abrasive heads is handy but not essential. Felt buffing wheels and Tripoli compound on the same tool will bring things to a mirror finish, but so will worn crocus cloth. A hand-held small parts vice is invaluable, and a pair of spring snips sees good use on a Smith & Wesson. All these items and a wealth of others are available from such good gunsmith's supply house as Brownell's (Main and 3rd, Montezuma, Iowa 50171) or Mittermeier's (3577 E. Tremont Ave., New York, New York 10465).

Colt

Colt actions are the easiest to work with, and usually show the most marked improvement for your efforts. Tool marks are rampant (no pun intended), and the object is to make every contact surface absolutely smooth — to take off all the burrs and bumps and scratches and rough areas the factory left in. Go over everything lightly with the stones (India first, then Arkansas) or emery cloth, then finish up by polishing with the crocus cloth. Be careful to keep the stone and the cloth back-up (a file or a wooden block) absolutely flat on the work; don't change any angles or bevels. Keep corners square but not sharp. Bear in mind that you're removing burrs, not stock.

The rebound lever, which has the lower leg of the V-mainspring bearing on its back, is the heart of the regular Colt mechanism. On the right side of it (inside), about 3/5 of the way up at its widest point, is a triangular shelf (called the "cam" at the factory) which engages the cylinder stop or bolt. Stay clear of this cam like the plague. The cylinder stop itself is another verboten zone — don't touch it under any circumstances; likewise the two teeth on the top of the hand which engage the ratchet.

There's no point wasting labor on areas which aren't abrading. As for which parts do need work, the best approach is to dry snap the gun several dozen times, then take it apart and look for scrape marks. Probably that portion of the trigger adjacent to its axis pin will be grinding against the frame on one side and against the sideplate on the other. Forget the frame since you can't get at it, and polish instead both sides of the trigger and the inside of the sideplate.

The nose of the rebound lever has a long sliding contact with a shelf on the hand. Polish both of these surfaces, but take pains to keep them flat. The outside of the hand tends to grate against its recess in the sideplate, so here's another good place to work; the sideplate recess poses accessibility problems, though. For that matter, polish the entire hand — except for the ratchet engagement teeth — but be careful not to thin it appreciably lest it tip away from the ratchet during cylinder rotation.

The front face of the rebound lever, just ahead of the cam, engages the back of the hammer to rebound it to safety position. Polish both parts (the hammer and the lower angle on the front face of the lever; not the cam). Remove the safety bar and go over it very lightly to remove any really prominent burrs.

The back of the hammer, below the spur, is apt to rub on the frame or the sideplate or both; look for contact marks and polish if need be. The lower part of the hammer, below the axis pin, is quite rough, but generally doesn't touch anything, so don't worry about it.

The most important engagement in a Colt, from the point of view of the D.A.

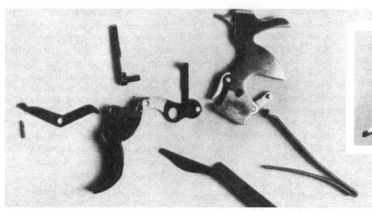

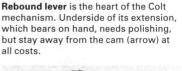

Rebound lever is the heart of the Colt mechanism. Underside of its extension, which bears on hand, needs polishing, but stay away from the cam (arrow) at all costs.

Colt's action, despite its seeming simplicity, is incredibly subtle and complex. Work with caution, never weaken springs in this gun.

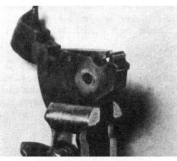

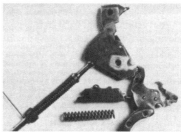

Smith & Wesson action is straightforward and efficient by design, wants only minimal smoothing. Note hammer-trigger engagement — this is where the hammer trips off on double action.

Double action sear surface on Smith hammer can stand a very light stoning — just enough to knock off the tall spots — but stay off the single action notch just a little above it.

Smith's two massive coil springs can both stand pruning — generally up to two coils. Bob the rebound spring first. A dehorned hammer, like this one, has less mass than normal, needs an extra margin of mainspring behind it.

Sides and back of Colt hammer, bearing flats on each side of trigger, can stand polishing, but trigger-strut engagement is the prime governor of the D.A. pull. Don't drift hammer pin all the way out — just far enough to free the strut.

pull, is that between the top of the trigger and the lower inside of the hammer strut. Tool marks run across the trigger from side to side creating a gritty hop-hop-hop sequence as the hammer rocks back. Polish it smooth. Rounding off the top shelf of the trigger at the back helps double action, but plays hob elsewhere, drastically increasing the weight of the single action pull and causing the hammer to fall off early on D.A., thus inducing misfires and perhaps throwing the gun out of time. Best to leave it as flat as the factory did, and tolerate a bit of pressure buildup at the end of the D.A. pull. Again, polish; don't remove stock.

Likewise for the hammer strut. Drift its pin far enough to remove it from the hammer and polish both its underside and outside scrupulously. But don't change its length or profile; don't round it off at the bottom. Polishing the underside of the strut will make for a smooth double action and polishing its front face will

contribute to a snappy trigger return.

Stay away from the single action sear surfaces on both trigger and hammer, and don't monkey with the mainspring. Colt hasn't made a too-stiff spring since the Great Depression, and weakening it will invariably cause misfires and a mushy trigger return.

The Colt, as we said, is a gratifying action to work on. Smoothing it up will not only take the grinds and jerks out of the pull, but will reduce its weight by two pounds or more. Ignition will be improved and trigger return will be speeded up. In

short, the gun will feel like a pre-war Colt.

These instructions apply in no way to the new Mark III, which uses an entirely different mechanism and doesn't lend itself to this procedure.

Smith & Wesson

Smith & Wessons usually show very fine internal machining and come with creditably smooth actions. That's fortunate, since the trigger and hammer are case hardened to an average depth of 6 or 7 thousandths, and there's not a whole lot that can be done with them. The surface is almost glass hard, and while it's deep enough to take a bit of stoning, too vigorous an approach will break through into the softer core and the part is ruined. Just a light stoning to take off upstanding burrs (and there won't be many) is all these parts want or need.

I like to polish the rounded area at the upper back of the trigger where it contacts the hammer strut, but I'm willing to leave a bit of roughness lest I stone too deeply. This is just above the single action sear, with which you do not want to meddle. The strut on the S&W is only in contact during the first portion of the D.A. cycle. It soon rocks clear as a lower shoulder on the trigger picks up the hammer proper. I make a wishful pass with the fine Arkansas stone on both these locations, but I'm careful not to touch the adjacent single action sear notch on the hammer.

The hammer strut need not be removed, and indeed its working surface shouldn't be touched. Wedge it forward and polish its front face lightly to assist trigger return.

The hammer sometimes rubs the frame or sideplate, in which case it's best to polish the frame or sideplate, as the case may be, rather than the hammer. On my Chiefs, the cylinder latch screw protruded through and interfered with the hammer. Check that.

Other S&W components can stand a bit of work. The rebound slide wants smoothing on all sides except on top, and the frame flat on which it rides can do with polishing. Again, no stock removal or you'll foul up clearance between the hammer and the safety bar. The ramp face on the lower body of the cylinder stop and the trigger nose can both be polished for a smooth trigger return. The side of the cylinder stop body sometimes galls the sideplate; if so, polish directly on the stop.

Both the trigger and the hammer ride between bosses on the frame and sideplate respectively; those on the sideplate may be profitably polished, but be careful to stay flat on the work.

And that's about it. Be cautious and tread lightly.

The Colt springs were off limits under pain of certain malfunction. Not so the Smith. The Smith & Wesson snub comes from the factory equipped with the lustiest springs in the business. There are two of them we're interested in, both coil type, and they are so placed as to do their job in the most direct and efficient fashion possible. The rebound spring, or trigger return spring, pushes the trigger forward with such gusto that two coils probably won't be missed. Lopping them off will help take some of the stiffness out of the trigger pull, and won't sap an iota of punch from the hammer. Removing more than two coils may result in a mushy trigger return — a clear liability in fast double action shooting. Bob the spring a half-coil at a time, trying it as you go. Prudence dictates having some spares on hand before we go grinding off springs.

The Smith hammer belts the primer a hearty smack. I've often found that cartridges which repeatedly misfired in other revolvers would dutifully discharge in the Chiefs. This sort of reliability is comforting. It also contributes to the stiff trigger pull, and offers safe margin for improvement. First try polishing the outside of the mainspring swivel, a cup-shaped part which seats in the grip frame and is pierced through the center by the mainspring guide rod. Then, to ease things still further, have at the spring itself, a half-coil at a time; you can cut off two full coils with no great fear.

After any weakening of the mainspring, the revolver should be test-fired double action with at least 50 rounds of each type of ammunition you expect to use. If any misfires occur, go back to a full-strength spring.

The Smith, it should be noted, is 75% impossible to reassemble without a special tool which, fortunately, is easily made. Take a screwdriver and file or grind about ⅛" off either side of the bit, leaving a sufficient nubbin protruding at the center to enter the rebound spring coil. Each side of the spring then will rest on the shoulders of the tool, and the spring and slide may now be shoved handily into place.

Here's the philosophy of it. With the Colt, grittiness, jerkiness, un-evenness of pull was the problem. We smoothed the action for smoothness' own sake, and in order to help the spring put more energy where it was needed. The Smith was smooth enough, but too stiff. Smooth-

ing its action merely gives a bit of safety margin for spring bobbing. For it's the compounded forces of the mainspring on top of the rebound spring that make the S&W stiff on double action.

Charter Arms

The Charter is a bit of a hybrid. The hammer is case hardened like an S&W, whereas the trigger and other action components are full hardened like a Colt, and can well stand working over. There's no sideplate on this gun, and polishing the inside faces of the frame with emery and crocus cloth over a file blade sometimes yields good results. Spring tension in those Charters I've seen is about right, and I don't recommend reducing them.

Grips

As vital as a smooth double action is for combat accuracy with the mini-guns, the improvement brought about will hardly be as monumental as that which can be attained by simply screwing on a set of new grips. This point was painfully reemphasized the other day while I was testfiring a Charter Undercover. It carried the splinter-like standard factory grips and had almost no feel or sense of direction, and consequently squirmed about in the hand. Volley firing or accurate burst shooting was all but impossible, and establishing a good shooting grip from the leather was hopeless. On each shot my middle finger took a bruising blow from the trigger guard, and the right thumb was in danger of laceration by the cylinder latch. Trigger reach was so dismally short that my trigger finger kept ramming other assorted digits, and the muzzle flipped from side to side during trigger pull.

Merely screwing on a pair of well-designed combat grips — in this instance Jay Scott Gunfighters — made the miserable little beast a deadly accurate piece of equipment, and a pleasure to shoot, even with full charge loads. The grip was firm, solid, and substantial, and shifted not a whit in recoil. Recovery time was optimum, and follow up shots were rapped out in rapid succession with very pleasing accuracy.

Smith & Wesson grips are of the same configuration as the Charter's, and should be removed from the weapon and used for kindling fires.

Colt's earlier DS grips were designed upside down, being bulbous at the bottom where compactness is a virtue, and emaciated at the top where a healthy span for the encircling middle finger and the tender, recoil-absorbing web of the hand is needed. However, they are more substantial than the others, and since they ride on a larger-framed gun, they are usable if a grip adaptor and trigger shoe are added. Colt's rasp-like checkering should be sanded down flush along the backstrap for comfort's sake, and the tops of the diamonds smoothed generally to avoid undue wear on clothing. As noted earlier, Colt's new DS grips are much better, being pretty good combat types as is.

One of the most crippling liabilities of an off-the-shelf snub is the rarely mentioned factor of insufficient trigger reach — the distance from the face of the backstrap to the curve of the trigger. For instance, the reach on a Chiefs Special is a scant 2⅜", compared to 2¾" for the larger M&P. The tiny Charter, likewise at 2⅜", is equally as sad a case as the Chiefs. Fingers just don't ordinarily come short enough. I know one gunner whose trigger finger was amputated at the first joint, and the remaining stub fits the Charter reach just right. The Colt, being a larger-framed gun with a more sweeping trigger pull, is much better provided for — it has a full 2½" reach.

The problem can be attacked from both ends. Any of these weapons will benefit from the addition of a trigger shoe. The sharp serrations and edges of the shoe should be ground down smooth prior to installation.

The reasonable, and only really effective, way to lick the problem, though, is by the installation of a set of custom combat grips which increase trigger reach by putting lumber behind the backstrap.

Steve Herrett's popular "Shooting Star" grips unaccountably fail to correct this problem. They're lovely to look on, but stop flush with the back-strap. His more recent "Shooting Ace" is almighty ugly, but puts the wood where you need it. Besides Herrett (in Twin Falls, Idaho 83301), Jay Scott Grips, of 81 Sherman Place, Garfield, N.J. 07026, or the Caray Sales Co. (Enforcer Brand Grips), 1394

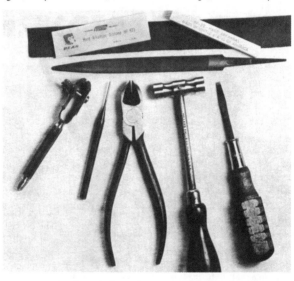

Basic tools for action smoothing include stones and crocus cloth (top) and (from left) small-parts vice, pin drift, spring snips, brass headed hammer, and screwdriver. File is used only to back up the cloth.

15th Street, Palisades, N.J. 07650, also do things right. Charter Arms, with the introduction of their optional equipment "Bulldog" grips, became America's only gunmaker to offer decent combat stocks straight from the factory. They're good, too.

Custom grips usually add bulk by extending below the bottom of the grip straps and giving enough wood to seat the little finger. This makes for better handling, but is awkward if you carry the gun in a pocket. However, the excess timber can be whittled off flush with the straps for a conventional 2-finger grip. If your shooting style demands that the pinky be anchored, the extra bulk has to stay.

Other Alterations

Snubs in the hands of pseudo-savants are often seen with the front of the trigger guard chopped out. This alteration does give more elbow room in the crowded guard, but trigger guards were designed for fingers, not elbows. So, unless you have to shoot with gloved hands, venting the guard is a poor notion, and is inherently unsafe. If the gun is inadvertently dropped or instinctively used as a bludgeon (a remarkably poor application, by the way), a chopped guard can easily bend up to jam the trigger. The function of a trigger guard is to guard the trigger, and if it's not there, it can't do it. However, slimming the leading starboard edge of the obstruction to half of full width is not a bad idea on a steel-framed Smith or Colt.

One desirable alteration is grinding off the hammer spur. This claw-like appendage, constantly snaring itself on pockets, jacket linings, and shirttails, is quite unnecessary on a gun primarily intended for double action use. Witness the justifiable popularity of Colt hammer shrouds and Smith's Bodyguard and Centennial models. A dehorned hammer can readily be cocked for single action shooting if the top edge is serrated, or even if it's not. Cock it part way with the trigger, roll the thumb over the top of the hammer, and finish the job just as if the spur were there.

These modifications will make your snub — most contrary of handguns — accurate and easily handled, a gun to bank on in the worst circumstances. A customized snub, for its purposes, is the best possible choice, and the mark of a knowledgeable shooter.

New SIG-Sauer Pistols

Two of them, in fact, the P-220 and P-230, both designed for utilitarian service. Production samples functioned and shot well in Switzerland.

▌J.B. Wood

FOR THE PAST 25 years the beautiful SIG P-210 has been considered by many to be the most finely made of all automatic pistols. Now the Schweizerische Industrie Gesellschaft of Neuhausen, Switzerland, has developed two new pistols, to establish what will surely become a distinguished series. Both pistols, designated the P-220 and P-230, are so recently produced that it was not possible to obtain test samples before publication time.

We do, however, have extensive information on them, obtained by Editor John T. Amber during a visit to Neuhausen last year. Mr. Amber examined both models, and fired them on the SIG range. He says their performance was flawless. He also noted that neither was as finely finished as the P-210. Two possible good reasons for this: Intended for combat-military and personal-police use respectively, their utilitarian finish and less costly construction may help to keep the price within reason. Their old stable mate, the P-210, is expensive.

The new pistols are to be a cooperative effort, in association with the old and respected firm of J. P. Sauer & Sohn of Eckernförde, West Germany, who will actually manufacture the guns. To reflect this combination of design and production skills, the pistols will be marketed under the name "SIG-Sauer."

SIG P-220

The P-220 is the larger, combat-type pistol. It has an unusual feature, a de-cocking lever, located at the top forward edge of the left grip panel. This is similar to the system used on the Sauer Model 38H pistol but, unlike the Sauer, the P-220 lever is for lowering the hammer only.

The firing pin has an automatic block which is moved only by the last fraction of trigger pull. Thus, when using the de-cocking lever, there is no chance of accidental firing, even if the thumb slips. There is also a wide safety-step on the hammer at normal rest position. Between these two systems, the P-220 will be safe even if dropped on the hammer, say the SIG people. There is no manual safety, and on this point the Swiss engineers are in complete agreement with this writer. On a double action pistol with an external hammer, who needs it?

The P-220 has an aluminum-alloy grip frame and plastic grips. The magazine release is a bottom-of-handle type. The location of the slide stop, at top center of the left grip panel, is perfect. Sights are the Stavenhagen-patent "contrast" type, these said to allow quick alignment, even in low-light conditions. These consist of a white-outlined square-notch rear sight, with a white dot inlaid into the rear surface of the post front sight. The front sight is integral with the slide, and the rear is adjustable laterally by drifting in its dovetail. Vertical adjustment will also be possible by changing rear sight units — 5 sizes will be made.

Left-side view of SIG-Sauer P-220.

The SIG P-220 will be available in 45 ACP, with optional conversion units for 38 Super, 9mm Parabellum, 7.65mm Parabellum, and 22 Long Rifle.

Magazine capacity is listed at only 7 rounds in 45 ACP, 9 rounds in the other centerfires. One wonders why they didn't use a larger capacity magazine, such as the one in their experimental SP 44/16, the forerunner of the P-210.

There is one constructional element of the new P-220 which, like the de-cocking lever, is similar to the old Sauer 38H arrangement. The breechlock is a separate part, secured in the slide shell by a heavy top lug at its forward end, and by a cross-pin. The front strap of the trigger guard is shaped to afford a good rest for a finger of the other hand when using the two-hand hold, a feature which has previously been available

only on custom-made combat alterations. The unique features and cartridge
options of the P-220 should make it a
good competitor with the Walter P-38,
Smith& Wesson M39 and M59, and
Heckler & Koch P9S — the other double
action pistols of comparable size.

SIG P-230

The SIG P-230 will, in the U.S., be
considered a pocket pistol for personal
defense. In Europe, it will have some
consideration as a police pistol. Externally it bears a striking resemblance
to the Beretta Model 90 pistol. Like its
big brother, the P-220, it also has the
de-cocking lever. The slide stop is not
external, however — it is an internal
automatic type, released from last-shot
hold-open by a slight retraction of the
slide.

The double action P-230 also has the
hammer-step and firing-pin-block safety
systems of the larger pistol, an external
hammer, Stavenhagen sights and an alloy frame and plastic grips. Basic chambering will be for a new loading called
the "9mm Police," with optional conversions to 9mm Short (380 ACP), 7.65mm
Browning (32 ACP) and 22 Long Rifle.
We have no dimensional data on the
"9mm Police," but its muzzle velocity is
listed at 1110 feet per second, which is
comparable to the old 9mm Browning
Long. I note, however, that a different
magazine is not required for conversion
to the other centerfire rounds, so perhaps it is only a slightly lengthened 380,
like the Russian 9mm Makarov, which
also has comparable ballistics.

To handle the increased power of the
new special cartridge, the slide used with
that chambering is 2.47 ounces heavier

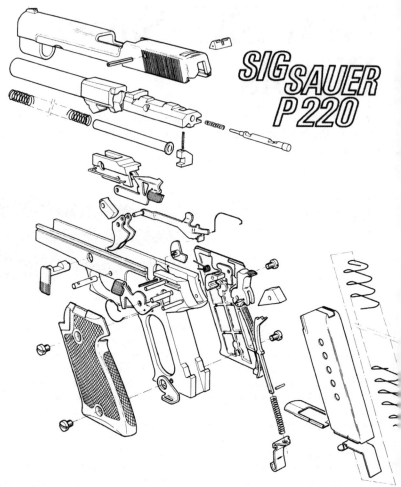

than the one on the standard 380 model.
The P-230 slide is one-piece, with an integral breechblock. In its size and price
range, the pistol will be compared with
the Walther PPK-S, Beretta Model 90,
and Mauser HSc. It should be a strong
sales contender, especially in the "9mm
Police" version.

Though not as costly as the celestial P-

210, the new pistols are relatively expensive. The P-220 lists at 640 Swiss francs,
the smaller P-230 at 580. At early 1974 exchange rates this comes to $192 and $174
respectively. Whether these are European
prices or the cost in the U.S. is not known
at this time. I doubt that they include the
import tax. SIG-Sauer have set the approximate availability dates as follows:
P-230 7.65mm
 (32 ACP) 9mm kurz
 Oct., 1974
 (380 ACP) "9mm Police"
 Nov., 1974
 March, 1975
P-220 9mm Parabellum Aug., 1975
Considering their features, and the
two names they bear, these two should
be worth waiting for! •

Specifications

SIG-Sauer P-230		SIG-Sauer P-220	
Weight:	460 grams - 16.23 oz. (380 ACP)	Weight:	830 grams - 29.29 oz. (9mm Parabellum)
Length:	168mm - 6.61 in.	Length:	198mm - 7.79 in.
Height:	119mm - 4.68 in.	Height:	143mm - 5.62 in.
Width:	31mm - 1.22 in.	Width:	34mm - 1.34 in.
Barrel:	92mm - 3.62 in.	Barrel:	112mm - 4.40 in.

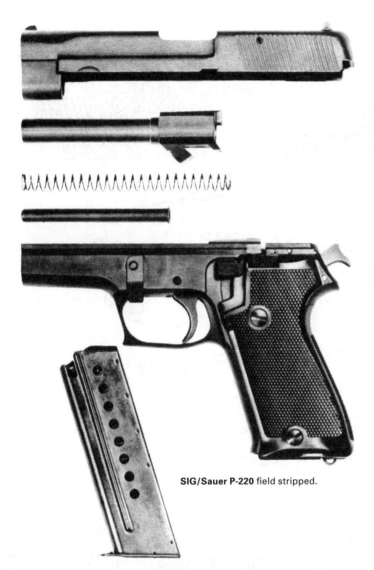

SIG/Sauer P-220 field stripped.

Double-Action Triggering
If the hammer is not cocked, the shot can be fired double-action. The trigger is squeezed, cocking the hammer via the trigger rod, which also presses the safety lever against the lock pin. The sear is moved away from the hammer and the firing pin is released by the lock pin. Completing the trigger pull lifts the hammer out of register and fires the shot.

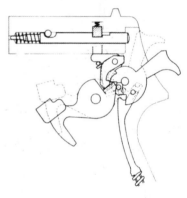

De-cocking Lever and Hammer Safety Catch
The de-cocking lever permits lowering of the hammer into the safety notch so the loaded pistol can be safely carried. The safety notch is the rest position for the hammer. The firing pin is always blocked during and after de-cocking.

Firing Pin Safety Catch
For maximum safety, the firing pin is locked. It is released automatically by trigger action without manipulation of any lever. The catch willfully fired.

Operating Principles to the SIG/Sauer P-220
With the pistol loaded the first shot is fired by pulling the trigger double action. The trigger moves the trigger rod, which lifts the sear out of the hammer notch.

At the same time, the trigger rod moves the safety lever, which takes the lock pin out of engagement with the firing pin, releasing the firing pin just before the shot is fired. The hammer is swung forward by the hammer spring to strike the firing pin, firing the cartridge.

Recoil from the fired cartridge operates the system (comprising the slide and barrel) back against the recoil spring. After recoiling about 3mm, the lock between the barrel and slide is released, the barrel swinging down and being held in place. The slide continues its backward motion, cocks the hammer, extracts and ejects the empty case, and compresses the recoil spring. The slide recoil stroke is limited by a stop on the frame. The recoil spring now forces the slide forward, stripping a cartridge from the magazine into the chamber. Just before reaching battery position, the barrel is again locked to the slide. The trigger rod can now engage the sear and the gun is ready for single action firing (hammer cocked.)

After firing the last shot the slide is caught by the slide stop, actuated by the magazine follower. The slide stop is so-located that it can be used with the thumb of the shooting hand without shifting the gun from the line of fire as a loaded magazine is inserted.

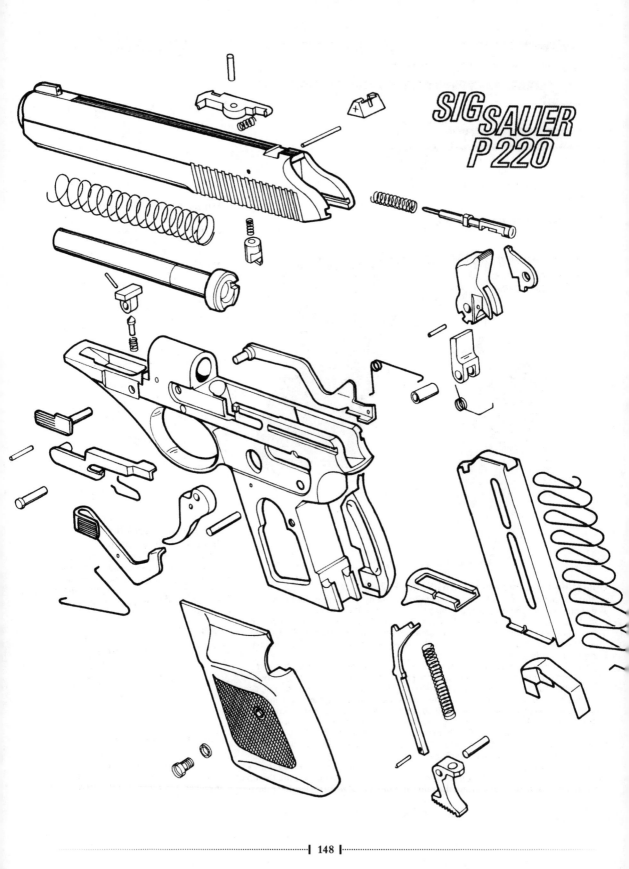

SIG SAUER P 220

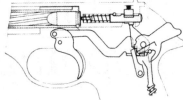

Double-Action Triggering

If the loaded pistol is not cocked, the shot can be fired by way of double-action. The trigger is squeezed, cocking the hammer via the trigger rod, and the safety lever is pressed against the lock pin. The sear is moved away from the hammer and the firing pin released by the lock pin. Further pulling of the trigger lifts the hammer out of register and fires the shot.

Operating Principles of the SIG/Sauer P-230

With the pistol loaded the first shot is fired by squeezing the trigger double action. The trigger moves the trigger rod, lifting the sear out of the hammer notch.

At the same time the trigger rod moves the safety lever, taking the lock pin out of engagement with the firing pin and releasing the firing pin just before the shot is fired. The hammer is swung forward by the hammer spring to strike the firing pin, firing the cartridge.

The forces of recoil push the slide back against the recoil spring, cocking the hammer, extracting and ejecting the spent case. The slide recoil stroke is limited by a stop on the frame. The compressed recoil spring now pushes the slide forward, stripping a cartridge from the magazine into the chamber. With the slide in battery position the trigger rod again engages the sear, readying the gun for firing.

After firing the last round the slide is held open by the slide stop, actuated by the magazine follower.

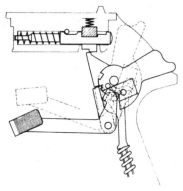

De-cocking Lever and Hammer Safety Notch

The de-cocking lever permits lowering of the hammer into the safety notch so that the loaded gun can be safely carried. The safety notch is the rest position of the hammer. The firing pin is always blocked during and after de-cocking.

SIG/Sauer P-230 right-side view.

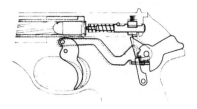

Firing Pin Safety Catch

Because of the automatic firing-pin safety catch, the pin is locked until just before the hammer is released. The safety catch is not released until the shot is intentionally fired. Even if dropped with the hammer cocked, the gun will not fire.

Handgun Stopping Power

The ability of the handgun's bullet to act as an effective deterrent in combat or self-defense has been of intense interest for many years — and never more so than today. Here is a carefully researched exploration of various past stopping power formulas, correlated and critically compared. ▌Kenneth L. Walters

Introduction

THE PROBLEM of calculating handgun stopping power has been of interest to sportsmen and military men for decades. As early as 1927, J.S. Hatcher was proposing an empirical formula for relative stopping power (RSP) based largely on handgun projectile kinetic energy.[1] By 1935 Hatcher had changed his method so that RSP was proportional to projectile momentum.[2] This formula, Hatcher's second, and variations thereof, have been in use to the present day.

Within the past few years several articles have appeared which contain variations of Hatcher's equation[3].5.7 Thus it seems appropriate to reexamine the RSP formula, compare the several implied alterations, and examine their results. Of the three variations discussed, all differ from Hatcher's second formula only in the number of terms sacrificed in the name of computational simplification.

Hatcher's RSP Calculation

For reasons no longer obvious, General Hatcher presented his second RSP calculation in prose only. Thus the first workable formula of which the author is aware appeared in 1972 in the excellent book by M.H. Josser-and and J. A. Stevenson.11 These authors postulated, Equa. (1):

RSP = WVAyH
where W = bullet weight in grains,
  V = initial velocity in feet per second,
  A = cross-sectional area in square inches,
  y = an empirical bullet-shape factor discussed later,
  and H = Hatcher's unit of bullet mass, i.e., Hatcher's Constant.

Hatcher's own work clearly indicates the formula to be that shown above but without the last term, the Hatcher Constant, and using bullet mass, M, instead of bullet grain weight. Unfortunately this equation (Equation 2 below) yields values inconsistent with Hatcher's own published results. To quote Josserand: "those who endeavor to work a given cartridge through the Hatcher formula (Equation (2) and arrive at a figure for RSP which will correspond to those Hatcher gives in his tables are foredoomed to disappointment; the esteemed general used a unit of mass known only to himself, and did not leave the key to posterity."[3] Josserand, however, successfully back calculated and determined the missing constant to be 0.00000221.

Hatcher's Constant

As it seems difficult to believe General Hatcher deliberately obscured his own calculations, the author has examined Hatcher's constant in detail, and found a nearly four-decade old error. Consider the following steps necessary to convert bullet weight in grains to bullet mass as required by Formula 2. First, convert the bullet weight in grains to the corresponding weight in pounds. For a bullet weighing one grain this is: 1 grain = 1 grain/7000 grains per pound = 0.0001428 lbs. Second, convert the bullet weight in pounds to the corresponding bullet mass. Again, for a one-grain bul-

let this is:

Equation (3)
mass = bullet weight in pounds
acceleration of gravity
= 0.0001428 lbs.
  32.16 ft/sec^2
  =0.00000444 lbs-sec ^{2}/ft

This value for the mass of a one-grain bullet is clearly twice Hatcher's constant, and the factor of two comes directly from an error in Hatcher's formula for projectile momentum. Hatcher states: "Note — if the energy and velocity of a bullet are known, the momentum is obtained by dividing the energy by the velocity."[2] The correct expression is obtained, however, by dividing twice the energy by the projectile velocity.

Oddly enough Hatcher's error has been repeated quite recently. Jeff Cooper, in his interesting article "Stopping Power Revisited," states: "General Hatcher's use of mass, measured in pounds divided by twice the constant of gravity... does give us a physically correct measure of momentum in pounds/feet."

As the General may well have known, his error is of no real consequence. Its net effect is to simply halve an arbitrary multiplier used in his bullet shape factors.

Smith & Wesson's Model 66, the Combat Magnum revolver in stainless steel.

Hatcher's formula as presented by Josserand (Equation (1) is essentially correct. Its only, minor fault is the use of a magical multiplier, H, determined by back calculation. To eliminate this difficulty and for ease in comparisons with the other equations to be discussed, Equation (1) can be rewritten as:

Equation (4)

$$RSP = \frac{1}{2(32.16)} \; \frac{WV}{7000} \; A \; y$$

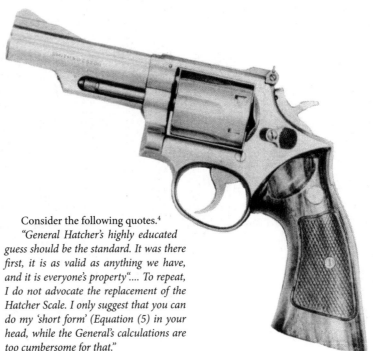

Alternate RSP Equations

Formulas 4 thru 7, as indicated below, represent the variations of Hatcher's equation, intentionally or otherwise, known to the author. Equations 6 and 7 have been obtained from secondary sources since the author's library does not contain the original works.

Hatcher's RSP	$\frac{1}{2(32.16)}$	$\frac{WV}{7000}$	$\frac{A\,y}{}$	Equa. (4)
Cooper's RSP		$\frac{WV}{10000}$	$\frac{A}{0.102}$	Equa. (5)
Taylor's KO		$\frac{WV}{7000}$	$Caliber^5$	Equa. (6)*
Keith's p/ft		$\frac{WV}{7000}$	^{5}	Equa. (7)*

*These equations were probably intended for use with rifle data, where the factors omitted from Hatcher's formula are considerably less critical.

Since it seems generally accepted that stopping efficiency of the normal round-nose jacketed 45ACP bullet is twice that of the standard round-nose lead 38 Special bullet, all 4 indicators of stopping power will be used on these two cartridges. The necessary data used are as indicated in the Table and marked by an asterisk. Considering the 38 Special first, Hatcher's method yields 30.10 vs 61.83 for a ratio of 1:2.05. Similarly Cooper's yields 13.35 vs 30.48 (1:2.28), Taylor's 6.79 vs 12.60 (1:1.86), and Keith's 19.07 vs 27.93 (1:1.46).

Effects of Approximations

The main differences between Formulas 4 thru 7 are the increasing number of terms either dropped or approximated. While the author has insufficient references to decide if this is an intentional approximation in Taylor's and Keith's work, it clearly is in Cooper's equation.

Consider the following quotes.[4]

"General Hatcher's highly educated guess should be the standard. It was there first, it is as valid as anything we have, and it is everyone's property".... To repeat, I do not advocate the replacement of the Hatcher Scale. I only suggest that you can do my 'short form' (Equation (5) in your head, while the General's calculations are too cumbersome for that."

To assist in this mental calculation, Cooper provides the A/0.102 ratio worked out for all real cases of interest. His table, however, lists the wrong A value for the 44-caliber case and the A ratio quoted, using either the value presented or the correct one, is also in error.

If the whole point of the various "short forms" of Hatcher's equation is simplification, there is obviously a way of greatly reducing the work in Hatcher's equation without sacrificing any of its inherent value. This can be done by just dropping all the physical conversion factors.

$$RSP = \frac{WVAy}{1,000,000} \qquad \text{Equation (8)}$$

The factor of 1,000,000 is used to more conveniently place the decimal point. This could be done before actual calculation by dividing the bullet-grain weight, bullet velocity, and y values all by 100 each. With this simple task done the formula becomes:

$$RSP = WVAy \qquad \text{Equation (9)}$$

For the two bullet comparisons previously discussed, this equation (or Equation 8), yields identical values of 13.62 vs 27.98 for a ratio of 1:2.05, exactly that predicted by Hatcher's second equation. Regardless of the formula used, the great

majority, this author included, will need paper and pencil to do the calculations. Thus there seems to be no real reason for using any approximation technique (such as Equations 5 thru 7) since the price paid is a possible severe loss of accuracy. For these calculations, the reader is advised to use either Equations 1, 4 or 8. All yield the same relative RSP values and Equation 8 is particularly nice because no unnecessary conversions are made.

Note that the answer obtained from Equation 9 can be easily converted to those obtained from Equations 1 or 4 by simply multiplying the results by 2.21. Only Equations 1 and 4, however, will directly give RSP results exactly like Hatcher's results.

Expanding Bullets

M.H. Josserand and Jeff Cooper[3,4] have both realized the possible inability of the RSP method in handling expanding bullets. As such handgun projectiles were not even dreamed of in the 1930s, this is more than understandable. It is the author's contention, however, that Hatcher's calculation will work here also. Based largely on the excellent discussion of expanding bullets given by Cooper[4], there seem to be at least two ways to handle this difficulty.

Ballistics Information

Descriptive Ballistics Information[1]				Necessary for Calculations[3]					Handgun Stopping Power[5]				
Cartridge	Barrel Length	Data Source	Bullet (grains)	Velocity (fps)	Area Col. 1	Shape Factor Col. 2	Caliber Col. 3	Product Col. 4[4]	Cooper's RSP	Keith's p/ft	Taylor's KO	Equation 8	Hatcher's RSP
22 LR	2⅛	17	40	860	0.039	1000	0.22	34400	1.32	4.91	1.08	1.34	2.96
	6	3	40	1060	0.039	1000	0.22	42400	1.62	6.06	1.33	1.65	3.65
22 LR H.V.[2]	2⅛	17	37	897	0.039	1350	0.22	33189	1.27	4.74	1.04	1.75	3.86
	6	3	40	1125	0.039	1350	0.22	45000	1.72	6.43	1.41	2.36	5.26
25 ACP	2	3	50	810	0.049	900	0.25	40500	1.95	5.79	1.45	1.79	3.95
32 ACP	4	3	77	900	0.076	900	0.31	69300	5.16	9.90	3.07	4.74	10.48
380 ACP	4⁷⁄₁₆	14	95	925	0.102	900	0.355	87875	8.79	12.55	4.46	8.07	17.83
380 ACP H.V.[2]	4⁷⁄₁₆	14	88	1104	0.102	1350	0.355	97152	9.72	13.88	4.93	13.38	29.57
	3⁷⁄₈ (assumed)	18	88	1040	0.102	1350	0.355	91520	9.15	13.07	4.64	12.60	27.85
38 Super	5	3	130	1280	0.102	900	0.355	166400	16.64	23.77	8.44	15.28	33.76
9mm Luger	4	3	124	1120	0.102	900	0.355	138880	13.89	19.84	7.04	12.75	28.18
9mm Luger H.V.[2]	4 (assumed)	10	108	1280	0.100	1350	0.355	138240	13.55	19.75	7.01	18.66	41.24
38 Special	2	12	200	572	0.102	1000	0.356	114400	11.44	16.34	5.82	11.67	25.79
	4	15	158	845	0.102	1000	0.356	133510	13.35	19.07	6.79	13.62	30.10
	6	13	158	850	0.102	900	0.356	134300	13.43	19.19	6.83	12.33	27.25
38 Special H.V.[2]	2	11	110	1030	0.100	1350	0.3564	113300	11.11	16.19	5.77	15.30	33.80
	3½	11	110	1135	0.100	1350	0.3564	124850	12.24	17.84	6.36	16.85	37.25
	6	11	110	1295	0.100	1350	0.3564	142450	13.97	20.35	7.25	19.23	42.50
357 Magnum	2½	15	158	1128	0.102	900	0.3564	178224	17.82	25.46	9.09	16.36	36.16
	6	15	158	1298	0.102	900	0.3564	205084	20.51	29.30	10.46	18.83	41.61
	8⅜	3	158	1410	0.102	1100	0.3564	222780	22.28	31.83	11.36	25.00	55.24
357 Magnum H.V.[2]	3½	11	110	1300	0.100	1350	0.3564	143000	14.02	20.43	7.28	19.30	42.66
41 Magnum	6	16	210	972	0.132	1100	0.410	204120	26.42	29.16	11.96	29.64	65.50
	6	16	210	1386	0.132	1100	0.410	291060	37.67	41.58	17.05	42.26	93.40
44 Magnum	6½	3	240	1470	0.146	1250	0.429	352800	50.50	50.40	21.62	64.39	142.29
45 ACP	5	15	230	850	0.159	900	0.451	195500	30.48	27.93	12.60	27.98	61.83
44 Special	3	19	246	1000	0.146	900	0.429	246000	35.21	35.14	15.08	157.88	71.44
	3	19	158	1100	0.146	1250	0.429	173800	24.88	24.83	10.65	154.92	70.10
9mm Police	3.6	20	95	1050	0.102	900	0.355	99750	9.98	14.25	5.06	44.72	20.24
380 ACP	3.6	20	95	984	0.102	900	0.355	93480	9.35	13.35	4.74	41.91	18.97
32 ACP	3.6	20	77	984	0.076	900	0.31	75768	5.65	10.82	3.36	25.31	11.45
22 LR	3.6	20	40	968	0.039	1000	0.22	38720	1.48	5.53	1.22	7.38	3.34
45 ACP	4.4	20	230	804	0.159	900	0.451	184920	28.83	26.42	11.91	129.24	58.48
22 LR Conv. Unit	4.4	20	40	968	0.039	1000	0.22	38720	1.48	5.53	1.22	7.38	3.34

1 — Barrel length and velocity measuring devices used affect reported velocity, hence, indirectly, all indices of handgun stopping power indicated.

2 — Values reported for stopping power of high velocity expanding bullets should be considered as an absolute upper limit. It is assumed that these bullets arrive on target with sufficient velocity for proper expansion, and that the bullet expands correctly.

3 — Cross-sectional bullet area in squre inches is represented in equation 1, 2, 4, 5, 8 and 10 by the symbol A and listed in Column 1.

The empirical bullet shape factor is represented in equations 1, 2, 4, 5, 8 and 10 by the symbol y and listed in Column 2. Bullet caliber as used in Equation 6 is listed in Column 3.

4— Bullet weight times bullet velocity is necessary in all the methods for calculating handgun stopping power. This intermediate result is provided in Col. 4.

5 — Cooper's RSP is calculated by multiplying the entry in Column 4 by that in Column land dividing the result by 1020.

Keith's p/ft is calculated by dividing the entry in Column 4 by 7,000. Note the ease in interconverting between Taylor's and Keith's indices.

Taylor's KO is calculated by multiplying the entry in Column 4 by that in Column 3 and dividing the result by 7,000.

Entries in Equation 8 are calculated by multiplying the entry in column 4 by the entries in both Column 1 and Column 2. This result is divided by 1,000,000. Note Equation 8 results are related to Hatcher's values by multiplying the former by 2.21.

Hatcher's RSP is calculated by multiplying the entry in Column 4 by the entries in both Column 1 and Column 2. This result is then divided by 452488.6877 or multiplied by 0.00000221 winchever is considered easier.

High-speed expanding bullets depend on two factors in order to effect their increased stopping power. These are, obviously, their increased velocity upon target impact, and the large wound caused by their expansion. Mr. Cooper's contribution to the RSP calculation rests upon his apparent ability to gather data as to the reliability of these expanding bullets when they encounter a human target.

Given this type of data, which some have called "wound ballistics," the RSP equation, Equation 8, could be altered to include the probability of bullet expansion, p, and the expected area increase after contact, A'. This inclusion would modify the RSP equation to:

$$RSP = 2.21 \, WVAy \, (1+pA') \quad \text{Equa. 10}$$

where $p = \dfrac{\text{number of successful bullet expansions}}{\text{total number of cases examined}}$

$A' = \dfrac{\text{total area after contact minus A}}{6A}$

The factor of 6 in the A' expression is to limit the size the pA' term can multiply a given RSP calculation. For a 100% certain bullet expansion p=1.00, its maximum value. Thus if the total area after contact could be expected to be no larger than 2.5A, the 1 + pA' term would yield:

$$1+pA' = 1+1(2.5A-A)/6A$$
$$= 1+A(2.5-1)/6A$$
$$= 1+1.5/6$$
$$= 1.25$$

This factor of 1.25 coupled with a probably y factor of 1100 produces an Equation 4 type RSP value of 30.11 for the high speed 380 vs 29.57 predicted using y=1350. Thus Equation 10 could predict a RSP value for this cartridge ranging from 24.09 to 30.11, depending solely on the p and A' values used.

The 2.5A value for total area after contact seems reasonable since this yields a value of 0.102(2.5) or 0.255 for a 38-caliber bullet. This implies that the 38 is approximately 0.57 caliber upon contact. Should this value be too conservative, the 6 could be replaced with something more reasonable.

Such p and A values would have to be determined by examination of large amounts of data and would have to be determined separately for each major type of bullet used, i.e., 9mm, 38 Spl., etc.

As an interim method, until accurate p and A' values can be reliably determined, the author suggests that the RSP equation could be used in its current form, Equation 8 or alternately Equation 4, with the modification that y = 1350 for expanding bullets. With this empirical addition, a deliniation of the y values becomes:

y=900 for jacketed bullets with round nose,
1000 for jacketed bullets with flat points or lead bullets with rounded noses,
1050 for lead bullets with blunt rounded points or with small flat on point,
1100 for lead bullets with large flat on point,
1250 for lead bullets with square point or the equivalent, and
1350 for high-velocity, expanding bullets.

Since the use of this new y value is an attempt to expand Equation 8 to allow for high-speed expanding bullets, if p and A' values are later determined, the new y = 1350 must be dropped to avoid duplicate correction.

It should be noted that Equation 10 is completely compatible with Equations 1 and 4 for normal, non-expanding bullets assuming the factor of 1,000,000 has been divided out as was done in Equation 9. In Equation 10 both the probability of bullet expansion, p, and the area increase A' will be very nearly zero, and so the pA' product will be even closer to zero. Thus the 1+pA' term will approach unity, yielding an equation equivalent to Equation 4.

Sample Calculations

Since several different calculations are being compared, a tabular arrangement of the data is helpful. One such arrangement is indicated in the Table, which also provides a simplified calculational technique for all the methods discussed.

Hatcher's RSP is calculated by mul-

tiplying the entry in Column 4 by the entries in both Column 1 and Column 2. This result is then multiplied by 0.00000221 ordivided by 452488.6877, whichever is preferred.

Equation 8 values are calculated by multiplying the entry in Column 4 by the entries in both Column 1 and Column 2. The resulting product is divided by 1,000,000. These values can be converted to Hatcher's RSP numbers by a multiplication by 2.21.

Keith's p/ft results are obtained by dividing the entry in Column 4 by 7,000. Taylor's KO is obtained by multiplying the result of the Keith calculation by the entry in Column 3.

Cooper's RSP is calculated by multiplying the entry in Column 4 by that in Column 1 and dividing the result by 1020.

For the specific case of the 45ACP cartridge discussed earlier and marked with an * in the Table, these computational schemes are worked out below. Note, with the recent revolution in inexpensive electronic calculators, including the Texas Instrument Model TI-3500 used by the author, no real effort is necessary to obtain the results indicated. Since it is not now possible to accurately evaluate the p and A' terms in Equation 10, no such results are included in the Table.

Equation 8 = Col. 4 (Col. 1) (Col. 2)/1,000,000
= 195,500 (0.159) (900)/1,000,000 = 27.98
Hatcher's RSP = Equation 8 Value (2.21)
= 27.98 (2.21) = 61.83
Keith's p/ft = Col. 4/7,000 = 195,500/7,000 = 27.93
Taylor's KO = Keith's Value (Col. 3) = 27.93 (0.451) = 12.60
Cooper's RSP = Col. 4 (Col. 1)/1020 = 195,500 (0.159)/1020 = 30.48

For the Sake of Completeness

In addition to the approaches to calculating RSP based on the Hatcher method, two other articles have appeared in recent years dealing with this problem but from an entirely different approach.[8,9] For those who may have seen these works, they are referenced but as yet do not appear to be workable theories from which RSP type calculations can be made.

Conclusions

The real proof of any theory is its ability to stand the test of time. Hatcher's relative stopping power theory has existed for nearly 40 years without ever being successfully challenged. Indeed, its only minor flaw, the non-inclusion of high speed expanding bullets, may be easily overcome by the methods contained herein.

References

1. Hatcher, J. S., Pistols and Revolvers and Their Use, 1927, Small-Arms Technical Publishing Co., Plantersville, SC.
2. Hatcher, J. S., Textbook of'Pistols and Revolvers, Ch. 12, 1935, Small-Arms Technical Publishing Co. Plantersville, SC.
3. Josserand, M. H., and Stevenson, J. A., Pistols, Revolvers, and Ammunition, Ch. 6, 1972, Crown Publishers, Inc., New York, NY.
4. Cooper, J., "Stopping Power Revisited," 1973 Guns & Ammo Annual, pp. 24–29, 1972, Petersen Publishing Co., Los Angeles, CA.
5. Fowler, T., "Knock-Out Values," 1973 Guns & Ammo Annual, pp. 312–313, 1972, Petersen Publishing Co., Los Angeles, CA.
6. Resnick, R., and Halliday, D., Physics for Students of Science and Engineering, Vol. I, p. 122, Ch. 7, 1962, John Wiley & Sons, Inc., New York, NY.
7. Waters, K., "Ye Compleate Exterior Ballistics," 25th ed. GUN DIGEST, pp. 289–291, 1970, Digest Books, Inc., North-field, IL.
8. Menck, T. W., "Estimating Bullet Punch," p. 88, Guns & Ammo, May 1972, Petersen Publishing Co., Los Angeles, CA.
9. Cooper, J., "Jeff Cooper on Handguns," pp. 56, 78, Guns & Ammo, May 1970, Petersen Publishing Co., Los Angeles, CA.
10. "Super-Vel Loading Manual," Handloader's Digest, 5th ed., p. 68, 1970, Digest Books, Inc., Northfield, IL.
11. Grennell, D. A., and Williams, M., Handgun Digest, p. 41, 1972, Digest Books, Inc., North-field, IL.
12. Ibidem, p. 43.
13. Ibidem, p. 64.
14. Ibidem, p. 188.
15. Ibidem, p. 36.
16. Ibidem, p. 37.
17. Hargrove, Allen, "Rating 'Panic Pistol' Power," Guns & Ammo, November 1972, pp. 48–49, Petersen Publishing Co., Los Angeles, CA.
18. Terrel, Ron, "The .380 Auto Pistols," Guns & Ammo, February 1973, pp. 38–44, Petersen Publishing Co., Los Angeles, CA.
19. Hurwitz, Harvey G., "Charter Arms .44 Special Bulldog — The Not Quite Magnum," pp. 24–6, Gun Sport, March 1974, Pittsburgh, PA.
20. "SIG-Sauer Presents," an extensive factory pamphlet delineating their new line of double action automatics, available from SIG.

A Pair of Autos

The Gun Control Act of 1968 banned importation of numerous small handguns, inviting manufacture of such types. Here are details of two that answered the clamorous call.

▌ George C. Nonte, Jr.

POCKETSIZE auto pistols are the rage these days. The countrywide demand for such arms is probably far greater today than at any time in our history. In spite of — perhaps partly because of — emotional clamor for the prohibition of handguns, especially small ones, more people than ever want or feel they need a small sidearm. It isn't because everyone feels he must carry a pistol — though enough do that as a measure of self preservation — but that nearly every household in the land feels more secure with a gun at hand.

Private citizens aren't the only market. Today we have almost a million armed law-enforcement officers, counting private security and investigative agencies. Nearly all of these people have or want at least one spare gun, and a pocket-size pistol is usually preferred.

At the time certain imports were restricted by the Gun Control Act of 1968 there was not one worthwhile pocket auto pistol produced in this country. Probably a dozen companies have been working ever since to remedy that lack, and over the past few months we've been trying some of their wares.

First received was the Back Up 380, a stainless steel very small handgun designed by Harry Sanford of Auto Mag fame. There was no advance fanfare, PR program or hoopla. When it was truly ready, with production guns coming off the machines, they were advertised and sold. The second gun is the Sterling 380, a larger, plain steel double-action type.

This one was announced and press-released to death two years before production!

The two guns represent completely different design approaches. Their only points of similarity are: both are autoloaders in 380 ACP caliber, and both use advanced metal-fabrication technology.

Comparison

The Back Up gun is very small (3¾"×5"), weighs a mere 17 ounces empty, and is of concealed-hammer, single-action design. Made entirely of stainless steel, it's intended solely as a very basic, simple gun for concealed

Above is the Sterling 380, with slide-removal screwhead forward of trigger pivot. At right is the new Back Up, 380 also, with its grip safety fully rearward, showing that the gun is cocked.

use by law officers. On the other hand, the Sterling measures 4¾"×6½" and weighs 27 ounces. It has an exposed hammer, double-action lockwork, large magazine capacity, and an adjustable rear sight.

Both guns were put through the same tests and examinations. Functionally, both were impressive. The firing of several hundred cartridges, using different makes and types from' every imaginable stance, saw not one legitimate malfunction. The only bobbles were failures to extract, through chamber fouling, which was deliberately allowed to accumulate. We wanted to learn at what point it would cause trouble.

This right-side view of the Back Up reveals a simple, uncluttered design.

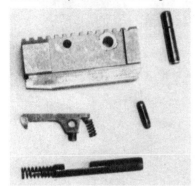

Back Up's breechblock is easily taken down by pressing out the loose extractor pin; round lug on extractor bottom (beneath pinhole) retains firing pin by entering the cutout. Pin at upper rights holds breechblock to slide.

Here the cross-grooved removable breechblock is seen seated in its recess in the slide. Note also integral sights cast into slide.

Back Up slide is removed by pushing it forward slightly, lifting up the rear and easing it forward off barrel.

Seen here are fixed ejector (straddled by the hammer) and the conventional feed ramp.

At close range the guns are equally accurate, though the heft, length, and better sights of the Sterling make it the easier of the two to shoot well. Beyond 25 yards the Sterling has a distinct edge. On the other hand, the Back Up was designed for close-in, point-and-shoot work, with length and sights secondary to compactness and concealability.

There is a distinct handling difference between the two, as would be expected. The short-coupled, short-butted Back Up fits the hand less well, though its magazine finger-rest helps a good deal. Its light weight accentuates recoil, and it's a handful in rapid fire. The weight and bigger butt of the Sterling make it more controllable, and apparent recoil is less.

The Sterling reloads easier and faster, with its behind-the-trigger magazine catch and automatic slide stop, which holds the gun open after the last shot. The Back Up has a butt-mounted catch and no slide stop.

The Sterling is easily dismounted without tools, but the Back Up requires a punch, a hammer and a long, thin screwdriver or similar instrument.

Don't let my comments mislead you into thinking that the Back Up is the less satisfactory pistol of the two. I emphasize again that several otherwise-desirable features were deliberately left out of the Back Up design to achieve compactness and light weight. The Sterling is more of a general-purpose pistol, whereas the Back Up is a highly specialized hideout gun. The Sterling is best for its purposes, but in the job for which it was designed, the Back Up is superior.

The Back Up

Mechanically the Back Up is innovative in several ways. The barrel is welded to the frame; the removable breechblock is within the slide, and the grip safety pops out only when the hammer is cocked, thus serving as a cocking indicator.

Disassembly is unusual. Magazine out, chamber cleared, hammer cocked: observe the blued pin in the slide's left side, above the grasping serrations; with a correct-size drift and a small hammer, rap the pin sharply to unseat it from the internal lock ring, then push it out to the right; invert the slide and shake out the breechblock, using a dowel or pencil inserted through the magazine well if necessary.

Next, with the gun upright, reach in through the breechblock recess with a rod or screwdriver and press the hammer down 1/16" or more and push the slide forward over it; lift up the rear of the slide to clear its guide ribs; ease slide forward, up and off barrel. Shake the recoil spring and guide out of the frame and field-stripping is complete.

See the photo caption for taking the breechblock apart.

Magazine capacity is 5; actually 6 rounds can be placed in it, but the magazine cannot then be seated fully in the gun. To obtain 6-round availability, load 5 in the magazine, seat it, cycle the slide to chamber the top round, then remove the magazine and insert one more round and replace it in the gun. Of course, engage the manual safety immediately after chambering the first round.

Grips on the Back Up are smooth walnut, secured by socket-head screws (the only screws in the gun). Sights are cast integrally with the slide, recessed in a rounded channel running the length of the slide. The sides of the slide and trigger are polished bright, as is the top of the breechblock; the rest is sandblasted, leaving the matte, grey color of uncoated stainless steel.

The Sterling 400

The Sterling M400's lockwork is of conventional double-action type, quite simple, with a single bar, on the right side, connecting the trigger to the hammer and sear. The bar also acts as a disconnector. The magazine catch looks like the Browning design but is not. A long leaf spring rides under the right grip with the catch plunger attached to its front end. The plunger passes through the frame behind the trigger to protrude on the left side.

The slide-mounted manual safety appears like the Walther type but isn't. It does not drop the hammer when engaged, nor does it block the sear. The hammer may still be dropped, manually or by trigger action, but is prevented from striking the firing pin by the safety shaft. The shaft shrouds the head of the pin when engaged, exposes it when disengaged. This simple hammer-blocking type of safety is found on few other guns, notably the French M1935 and M1950 military series. Though not all that popular here, it is the simplest, sturdiest, and most reliable of all systems.

The frame is massive and heavy, the barrel held in an integral lug a la Walther PP. The recoil spring surrounds the barrel. Slide removal is a bit unusual. A slotted screwhead protrudes from the right side of the frame, ahead of and above the trigger. Pressing this screw inward and rotating it 90 degrees clockwise turns a

An automatic internal stop of Walther type locks the Sterling slide open when the last round has been fired.

The Sterling barrel is pin-fixed to an integral boss. Normally concealed by the slide, here the automatic slide stop is readily visible; a means of manually operating the slide stop would be useful, but even the latest Walther PP Super lacks such construction.

The Sterling safety looks much like Walther's, but it does not drop the hammer when rotated. Instead, this is a very simple hammer block, which rotates to prevent the hammer from striking the head of the firing pin, yet does not block sear, hammer, or trigger movement.

slide-stop block from vertical to horizontal. The slide may then be drawn back far enough to be lifted off its guide ribs at the rear and eased forward off the barrel. In its vertical position, the stop block sits between the slide and frame abutments, halting rearward slide travel before it reaches the end of the guide ribs. This is a simple, low cost system but, if it is disassembled, reassembly can give you fits getting the spring back in place correctly. There is really no need for disassembly so this presents no problem. Technical curiosity prompted me into disassembly.

An integral narrow rib is cast into the slide and the front sight is part of it. The rear sight is movable for windage by means of opposed clamp screws.

The Sterling's ultra-simple lockwork is shown here: a single drawbar connects trigger to hammer and sear, as required, and also functions as a disconnector.

Grips are checkered, of brown wood-grain plastic, and metal parts are blued (black) throughout.

The Sterling M400 and the Back Up make extensive use of precision castings — less obvious in the Sterling but easily seen in the Back Up. Stainless is more difficult to cast, which may account for the pinholes or blowholes visible in the Back Up slide and frame. Aside from that, both guns show quite good workmanship, though trigger pulls are not great in either. The Back Up's pull goes 6½ pounds but is reasonably clean; the Sterling goes 12 pounds DA and 4½ pounds SA, with quite a bit of roughness. Both guns do work well, which is what counts most.

The Sterling is about $130, the TDE Back Up about $160.

Double Action Auto Test

Four D.A. auto pistols were fired extensively to check reliability -250 handloads and 50 factory rounds were put through each. There were problems. ∎ Kenneth J. Walters

DOUBLE ACTION big bore auto pistols have been available since the middle 1930s when Walther introduced the P38. Though such large-magazine-capacity single-action 9mms as the Browning were introduced about the same time, it was not until the early 1970s that a gun combining the D.A. mechanism and a high magazine capacity — the S&W M59 — went into production. Since then other multi-shot pistols, the 9mm Beretta and Browning, plus the H&K 45 D.A. have also appeared. It is these two styles of automatics, large magazine capacity double action 9mm Luger and double action 45 ACP's, that are discussed and functionally tested herein.

For many years it was felt that a good single-action auto, say the Colt Commander or the 45 ACP, was all anyone really needed, and that such guns as the S&W M59 were, because of their more complex mechanisms, overly trouble prone. In the S&W case this criticism was valid until very recently, as substantiated in at least one article.1"The S&W Model 59, Boon Or Bust," by J. Hillock, Guns Illustrated, 9th ed., 1976. (S&W recalled all of these M59s). However, my functional testing shows that the D.A. Beretta, the new or repaired S&W M59, the D.A. Browning and H&K 45s not only rival the functioning quality of the older Colts but, indeed, pass them.

To test these 4 pistols I decided, somewhat arbitrarily, to investigate their ability to handle cast bullet reloads, among others. Why? Well, for the average shooter to become proficient with a handgun requires more than casual practice, extensive shooting which few could afford to do with factory ammunition. Also, since the several 45 ACP guns I've owned worked very well with factory ammunition but not at all well with cast bullets, the latter would provide a more severe test. Each gun was tested with 250 rounds of reloads and 50 factory cartridges.

Lyman bullet 356402 (truncated cone) was used for the 9mms and their 452374 (round nose) for the 45s because they're highly popular, at least of Lyman's offerings. New 9mm cases were used because those were all I had, but various old lots of GI brass were used in the Browning and H&K in the belief that they would increase the chances for trouble. Of course both 45s were fed equal quantities of cases of all types. A Star press was used to minimize unintentional variations in assembly.

Magazine Performance

The first test observations concerned magazine functioning in the 9mms. These big-capacity magazines held the rounds almost in direct line with the bore. Thus when the slide comes forward and catches the cartridge it is very easy for the truncated-cone bullet to go straight into the

1978 should see the introduction of Walther's new PP-Super pistol in 9mm Police, 380 and 32 calibers.

chamber. The Walther P38sThe Walther importer, Interarms, when told about this said they only recommend the use of round-nose bullets in their guns. and a Colt Commander, however, showed that these single-column magazines seem to hold the bullet just slightly lower. When the slide in these guns grabs the cartridge, the bullet nose usually drops a little, causing the bullet to hit the ramp too low for reliable feeding. Individual guns will vary, of course, so the functioning of any auto pistol should be repeatedly checked before serious use. Still, the large capacity 9mms do seem well suited to using Lyman's excellent bullet.

Walther's excellent P38 9mm Parabellum (Luger) double action automatic. Introduced in the 1930s and used throughout WW II, this was the first of its kind.

Smith & Wesson's M59 9mm Para, pistol was the first widely produced automatic to incorporate a double action mechanism with a large (14 shot) magazine capacity.

The Beretta 16-shot double action 9mm Para, pistol. No malfunctions occurred in firing 250 reloads and 50 factory cartridges.

The Browning D. A. 45, initially offered in 9mm Para, and 38 Colt Super, is no longer available in those calibers because of cost increases.

The Beretta and Browning took first honors with none and one malfunction respectively. Since the Browning failed to chamber one of the cast bullet loads, its performance wasn't perfect, but certainly one failure in 300 tries is an impressive record. Both of these guns were felt to have passed these tests with no problems whatsoever.

Since the Beretta and Browning tied for first place, or almost so, what rating does the H&K get, which jammed only once but failed to extract the reloads three times? While I'm not capable of explaining how it came about, a statistician friend determined that in spite of the number of H&K failures, it wasn't exhibiting a lower reliability level.

The S&W M59 malfunctioned 12 times in the first 150 rounds, at which time its hammer broke. Clearly we have no problem, statistically or intuitively, calling this performance a failure.

Since the gun wasn't properly chambering cartridges because of what seemed to be a faulty extractor, which dragged on the case to the point where the slide couldn't go fully forward,This opinion was confirmed by two local gunsmiths. and because the hammer notches were sheared off so that it would fire only in double action mode, the factory was called and new parts requested. A new hammer, drawbar, sear, extractor, extractor pin and extractor spring were supplied without charge. These parts clearly eliminated the hammer problem, which I'm sure was an unlikely fluke caused by a bad part, Several local gunsmiths and shooters could remember no other difficulty of this kind occurring.but the failure to chamber remained. The gun was then returned to the factory.

Smith & Wesson Recall

While the gun was being repaired S&W announced "new product improvements to present owners of S&W Model 59 autoloaders." This total, no-cost recall was for alterations of the extractor, magazine follower, and slide-stop lever. Tested after its return showed it to be performing very well; it failed to chamber only twice, once while firing 250 reloads, and once with the 50 factory cartridges. Another M59, run as a control and which did not have the factory rework, also failed twice — once to eject and once to feed, both with reloads. It appears that those M59 troubles have now been overcome.

As an aside, the original S&W magazines supplied with my M59 hold 16 rounds easily. The one sent to the factory and returned with the pistol now holds only 14 cartridges, but both work equally well.

As far as I and some local gun store owners can determine, there is absolutely no way — other than perhaps by magazine capacity — to tell whether a used M59 has been back to the factory for repairs. It seems clearly a case of "buyer beware." The same people told me, incidentally, that S&W is lowering production on the M59 and other guns because of falling sales. Certainly the gunshops in this area face reduced demand for the pistol.

The Heckler & Koch pistol, patterned after their similar 9mm gun, was the first mass-produced D. A. 45 ACP automatic.

The proposed H&K 18-shot capacity D.A.-only VP70Z. Import difficulties make sales of this auto pistol in the U.S. uncertain.

Walther's forthcoming models will consist of the P38 IV, the P5 ond the P38 K (shown here), all having a new D. A. mechanism.

So, if we now consider these 4 guns equally serviceable, though differing in minor mechanical detail, the potential buyer could select any of them without worry.

Other Makes/Models

These 4 pistols, of course, don't represent all possible types offered, but simply all that were available to me at the time. LES, for instance, has been on the verge for some years of producing the Steyr-designed 9mm, and LES had a booth at the NRA meeting, a sample pistol on view. An LES spokesman, during a recent phone talk (mid-April, 1978) said that their gas pistol was being shipped to dealers, but could give no name of any Chicago area outlet which had been sent one, or more, nor was he willing to send us a sample gun for appraisal and testing. J.T.A

Too, it is well known that Colt has developed big bore prototypes. A source in the company told me that the firearms division has approved the design for full production but, alas, no decision has yet been made.

Also, though S&W categorically denies it, friends working there have seen prototypes of an 11-shot D.A. 45 which, they were told, would go into production in early '79. S&W prototypes in this caliber go back many years, so there is room for doubt about series production, but Colt sources confirm that S&W had recently hired several engineers who once worked on Colt's double action.

On a somewhat more promising note, the Thomas 45 D.A. (only) automatic is being produced, though in limited numbers. Dean Grennell has reported "The i-Dotting Thomas 45," Dean Grennell in Gun World, January, 1978. that his test pistol had chambering problems, but Walter Rickell said he had no such difficulties. "The Thomas 45," Walter Rickell in The American Handgunner, January/February, 1977.

Finally, according to Hubert Zink, executive V.P. H&K, that firm will decide in '78 whether to produce their

VP70Z. There are, I'm told, problems in getting it approved for importation, so its future is unclear.

Though many-shot D.A. pistols in 9mm Parabellum caliber were slow in arriving, and D.A. 45s have only recently appeared, I think the years ahead will see rapid growth in both of these areas.

Walther's P5 Pistol

The new generation in police handguns takes new tacks. Or are they? ▮ James P. Cowgill

I MAGINE an autoloading service pistol with no safety lever.

"No way," one might say. "It wouldn't be safe to carry loaded."

But wait. Is your typical service revolver safe to carry loaded?

"Of course," one thinks. "Modern double-action revolvers can be safely carried, hammer down, with all chambers loaded."

Then where is the safety lever on your revolver?

"There is none. A safety lever on a revolver is unnecessary because the firing pin cannot contact a primer unless the trigger is pulled all the way to the rear."

Exactly. But the West German firm of Carl Walther has produced a new autoloading service sidearm, the P 5, with no safety lever. This pistol, however, is safe to carry with hammer down and a round in the chamber.

The P 5 was developed in response to a German government competition to standardize police handguns and ammunition. Federal police and the military use the 9mm Parabellum Walther P 1, the lightweight-alloy framed version of the famous P 38 double-action autoloader. State and local departments use a variety of pistol types with .32 autoloaders probably the most popular. The Polezei are very big on submachineguns, universally issued in 9mm caliber. The different calibers in use cause some logistics problems in ammo interchangeability, procurement, and stockage.

A committee drafted specifications for their concept of the ideal European

Sam Scott didn't find the leftward pitch of the empty brass bothering him as he worked with Walther's newest cop gun in 9mm

law enforcement handgun, including these criteria:

Caliber: 9×19 mm Parabellum (Luger)

Magazine capacity: 8 rounds minimum

Muzzle energy: 369 ft.-lb. minimum

Over-all length: 7 in. maximum

Over-all height: 5⅛ in. maximum

Width: l15/116 in. maximum

Weight: 2 lb., 3 oz. maximum

The specifications also stated that the pistol would be safe to carry with a round in the chamber, ready to fire instantly without the necessity of operating cocking or safety levers. In testing, the pistols were required to fire 10,000 service rounds without major failure.

The surviving three of four candidates were:

• Heckler & Koch's Model PSP (P 7) with its unique gas-delayed blowback action.

• Sig-Sauer's Model P 225, an abbreviated P 220 (BDA).

• Walther's Model P 5, which improves upon the P 38's (P 1's) safety features.

The P 5 bears a strong family resemblance to the P 38. Both have double-action triggers and steel slides. The P 5 shares the P 1's lightweight alloy in its frame. Unlike its predecessors, however, the P 5 has no safety lever.

Obviously, neither its designers nor the German committee felt it needed one. The P 5 has four independent working safety features:

First, the firing pin is, as translated

There are no operating controls on the right side of the P5 and no ejection port either. German police and the Dutch government like the gun.

From this angle, the P-38 ancestry can be seen, although the inside isn't all ancient history. The "safety" is actually an operating lever; see test.

from the German operating manual, "arrested from longitudinal axis motion" at all times, except when the trigger is pulled fully rearward. That is, the firing pin is blocked in a safety rest position until the trigger is pulled. Thus the weapon will not fire if dropped muzzle-down on a hard surface.

Second, there is a cavity cut in the striking surface of the hammer. When the trigger is forward, the firing pin rotates downward so that the base of the pin is aligned with the cavity. Even if the hammer should fall, it would not strike the firing pin.

Third, the hammer, in its uncocked resting position, is held by a hammer latch at a stand-off distance from the firing pin, even if the pin were rotated into the path of the hammer striking surface.

Fourth, a disconnector mechanism prevents firing unless the slide is fully closed in battery.

A unique feature of the P 5 is the operating lever on the left side of the frame. This lever has two functions: to close the open slide, and to uncock the weapon.

To load the pistol, the slide is pulled to the rear and the slide stop engaged either manually or automatically by the follower of an empty magazine. A loaded straight box magazine (8-round capacity) is inserted. The operating le-

Gun closes when operating lever is depressed, chambering round and leaving hammer cocked. To uncock, depress the operating lever a second time.

ver is pushed downward with the thumb of the shooting hand (righthanders), which closes the slide, chambering a round. The weapon is now cocked and ready to fire. Releasing the operating lever and depressing it once more safely lowers the hammer. The pistol is now safe to carry but ready to fire by either pulling the trigger for double-action, or by thumb-cocking the hammer for a single-action first shot.

The recoil of the slide cocks the hammer for subsequent shots, but the operating lever can be used to lower the hammer at any time.

With proper familiarity and training, the P 5 can be as safe to carry as a revolver — and just as ready to fire. The firing pin cannot strike the primer unless the trigger is pulled all the way. But, since the weapon is double-action, the firing pin will be struck by the hammer every time the trigger is pulled.

Nothing mysterious here. P5 breaks easily into the usual slide, frame, barrel and magazine groups. The barrel is a little more complicated, true.

The P 5 has a typical German griph-eel magazine catch. Takedown into four major groups (magazine, slide, frame, barrel) is done simply by rotating a "barrel-stop lever" located on the left front of the frame.

The P 38-type locked breech is of proven reliability and accuracy potential. Locking lugs connect the barrel to the slide in battery. Upon firing, the slide and barrel recoil together for about an eighth of an inch, when a shaft on the bottom of the locking lug assembly hits the frame and cams the locking lugs away from the slide, freeing it to recoil fully rearward. Spent brass is extracted and ejected. Dual slide springs return the slide which picks up a round from the magazine and chambers it.

How big is a service pistol? Here are three: the P1 (P-38), the Colt M1911 and the new P5, which is much the smallest.

Magazines for the P-1 (P'-38) and P5 look alike, but they are not. Each holds eight rounds, though.

(LEFT) **The bright-metal** projection in the center of the frame is the disengagement lever, shown in the raised position it reaches only when the trigger is Fully to the rear. This lever lifts the firing pin into Nring position.

(BELOW) **The base of the firing pin** rests in the safety position. Only pulling the trigger will lift it into line so the striking surface of the hammer can hit it. This is one of four basic safety mechanisms in the new Walther P5.

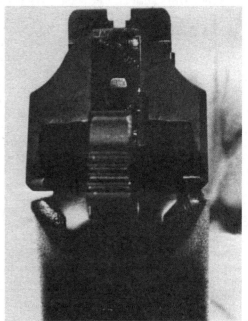

Walther Model P 5 Technical Data

System: Locked-breech, **recoil:**operated, self-loading
Breech: Locking toggle, slide-to-barrel
Caliber: 9mm Parabellum (Luger)
Dimensions: 7" long, 5" high, 1¼" wide. 3½" barrel; 5¼" sight radius.
Frame: Lightweight alloy
Weight: 28 oz. unloaded
Magazine capacity: 8 rounds
Manufacturer: Carl Walther, Ulm (Do), West Germany
Importer: Interarms, Inc., 10 Prince St., Alexandria, VA 22313

Author found the pull smooth though heavy; recoil with Federal 125-gr. loads mild; accuracy good. He must like the gun — he bought one.

Double-action trigger pull is a lot heavier than that of a PPC revolver, but the single-action trigger feels much better than that of other double-action autoloaders. After taking up the slack characteristic in this type of action, there was no mush in the test auto's single-action trigger. Very economical movement fired off each shot.

When the slide is in battery, two things happen at the trigger's rearmost travel — the trigger bar forces a disengagement lever upwards moving the firing pin off its safety rest and into the path of the hammer; and the hammer latch is pulled from the rear notch on the hammer, allowing it to fall and strike the firing pin.

A recess is cut in the slide for the disconnector. The recess is aligned with the disconnector only when the slide is fully closed. If the slide is partially open, the disconnector nose on the trigger bar contacts the slide, forcing the bar downward and out of position to release the hammer latch, preventing firing from an open breech.

When the pistol is uncocked, the hammer latch holds the hammer away from the slide so that it cannot contact the firing pin base even if the firing pin were moved off its blocked position in the slide.

Thus there are multiple, independent, and redundant safety features incorporated into the P 5's design. However, even the safest weapon can be dangerous through improper operation. Training remains the ultimate key to safety for all firearms.

Test firings, using factory-loaded Federal 123-grain full-metal-case bullets and handloads with Sierra 90- and 115-grain jacketed-hollow-point projectiles, had no stoppages at a local range (300 rounds fired). NRA target ten-ring accuracy at 25 yards from bench rest was no problem, surely adequate for a service pistol.

The Patridge sights are highlighted with a white dot on the front post and a white square immediately under the rear notch. This arrangement helps in low-light and dark-background shooting situations (the white surfaces do not glow in the dark). The rear sight is adjustable in windage.

The P 5 has been adopted as the duty sidearm for several German police jurisdictions. The Netherlands government, after extensive competitive tests, has ordered 35,000 P 5's. The U.S. importer is Interarms, 10 Prince Street, Alexandria, VA 22313.

The P 5 is a safe, reliable, and accurate service autoloading pistol. Now the mystery: The ejection port is on the left side of the slide, and ejected brass caroms high over the shooter's left shoulder. Why is the port on the left, when conventional industry practice puts it on the right side? Is this feature designed for left-handers? Or does the port position make inspection of the chamber easier for right-handers? Did a blueprint get reversed in reproduction at the factory? If you know the answer, please tell me!

The Bren Ten: Intended To Be Better

▮ Jeff Cooper

HANDGUNS evolve slowly. Before there were automobiles, radios, or airplanes men carried sidearms that served their purpose just about as well as anything we have today, and while the pistol on my belt is indeed better than that used by Alvin York it is very similar to his, differing only in refinements that make it somewhat easier to shoot but hardly more efficient.

This is remarkable, but may be explained by analysis of the problem a sidearm is meant to solve. As a reactive instrument for decisive short-range action without advance notice, the pistol has had no real need to evolve, since its purpose has not changed and our technology has not come up with anything better able to accomplish that purpose.

Thus it is that significant improvements have been few and widely spaced for more than a century. The self-contained metallic cartridge was probably the single most important forward step, coming into common use just about 100 years ago.

When this was combined with smokeless powder and the development of reliable self-loading mechanisms, we arrived at the modern "automatic pistol," just in time for World War I. Since then we have seen only the addition of the double-action feature in the self-loader; an advance which, while very exciting at the time of its announcement back in the '30s, proved to be essentially illusory — an answer in search of a question. Some very powerful new cartridges have appeared which make the handgun suitable — in highly skilled hands — for taking game up to about 400 pounds in weight, and quite a bit more in special circumstances. This use of the pistol,

however, is a bit esoteric. It is very interesting to those who specialize in it, but not really relevant to the primary mission of the weapon type.

Is there, then, no way to improve upon what we have had for three generations? With the U.S. government now going backward from one antique but highly effective pistol cartridge to another which is even more antique and about half as effective, it would seem that further progress is held to be impossible. But we know that should not be so. Progress is always possible, given the will and the wit.

In the magnificent Browning/Colt 45 auto pistol of 1911 we have a superb balance of stopping power and controllability, augmented by simplicity, durability, reliability, and compactness. Can we do better than that? Yes, we can. Until some entirely different principle is discovered, we cannot build a handgun that departs in any single radical characteristic from what we now have, but we can combine all the best features of the weapons we now have into one design, under the guidance of the people who know the

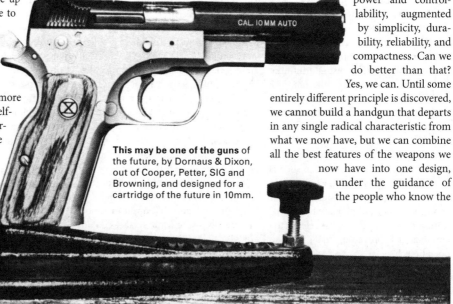

This may be one of the guns of the future, by Dornaus & Dixon, out of Cooper, Petter, SIG and Browning, and designed for a cartridge of the future in 10mm.

most about practical shooting, and produce it by the most modern methods so that it is ready to go "out of the box."

This has been done. We shall have the Bren Ten if present plans mature. Here we have a very powerful, medium-sized, easily controlled, high capacity, selective action pistol utilizing thoroughly proven mechanical systems and enhanced by a number of unique features found in no other piece. Its heart is a new cartridge that offers the stopping power of the illustrious 45 in a more compact package together with increased kinetic energy, range, and (if desired) penetration. Its durability, reliability and accuracy have yet to be put to the test of time, but since the relevant materials and systems have been individually time-tested in antecedent weapons we can safely predict their success in combination.

Any smallarm must be considered as a composition of two elements: weapon and cartridge. The Bren Ten is unusual in that it is the only pistol taking the new 10mm auto pistol cartridge, and that it

will take no other. You can't have the one without the other. If it is indeed a great leap forward, it is because the design doesn't drag any leftovers along.

The action is of the Browning tilt-lock type and derives from Browning through Petter to SIG 210 to Cz 75. The latter piece is admittedly the inspiration for the new gun, as shown in the name. The Czech arsenal at Brno is the parent of both the renowned English Bren gun (Brno plus Enfield came out "Bren") and the Cz 75 9mm pistol. The 75 is the best of the 9's and it seemed to me that if it could be had in 45 caliber it might eventually supersede the 1911. That idea was expanded to include the experimental 10mm cartridge originally pioneered by Whit Collins and Irving Stone, and wound up as a prototype built by Tom Dornaus, late of the Pachmayr organization. This prototype can fire either the 45 or the 10 since a barrel and slide for either cartridge has been made, plus one 45 magazine. This was done to permit us to shoot the weapon, since the 10mm ammunition is not in production and must be made by hand at this time.

The original 10mm cartridge was made by cutting off the 30 Remington rifle case and fitting it with the 180-grain bullet of the 38–40 (which is of 40 caliber). This combination gave astonishing perfor-

mance — well up toward 1200 f/s with fairly modest charges of Unique — in a test barrel. We felt that more mass was in order and settled on a 200-grain JTC bullet which, when loaded to an overall length of 1.3", still leaves enough case volume to break 1100 f/s without excessive pressure or recoil. A 40-caliber, 200-grain, flatpoint starting at 1100 fps gives us a pretty balance of mass, velocity, impact area, and Hatcher "k." It also shows more energy at 100 yards than the 45 does at the muzzle.

Power is easy — look at the big-bore magnums. How about recoil? Well, if we take the momentum of the two loads we find that the 10 is to the 45 as 22 is to 19.5. It kicks a little more, but not quite as much as a really hot 45, such as the old Western Super X load. When we fired the 10 out of the prototype, we found that the advanced butt design borrowed from the Cz 75 made up for the difference, and that the Bren, despite its increased power, was every bit as "soft" as the Colt, easily managed with thumb and forefinger alone by a trained person.

Unlike almost all other handguns, the Bren Ten was designed by shooters for shooters. It incorporates all sorts of nifty features that only serious shooters would think of. It is, for example, dehorned, with no sharp corners or edges rearward to abrade hands or clothing. Its fully adjustable rear sight is reveted in a solid steel cup to protect it from hard knocks. Its front sight, though stronger than those on most autos, is instantly replaceable by field stripping. Its recoil-spring guide doubles as a combination tool. Its magazine release of the Browning type can be set two ways by half-turning a detent screw. The magazine may either fly free as with a Colt or be held half-ejected for those who fear magazine loss or damage. Magazine capacity is 11 rounds.

The trigger-cocking (double-action) mechanism is another system borrowed from the Cz 75, and is the smoothest and lightest of its type. It is offered only to please the unenlightened, however, for the selective action allows the pistol to be properly carried in Condition

Jeff Cooper draws nicknames (Chairman Jeff, Dr. Death) and respect alike in his role and posture as a handgunner for all seasons: His mark is on the Bren Ten.

One on the belt. The thumb safety is positioned forward under the swell of the thumb for comfortable operation. It is reversible, and may be quickly plugged-in on the right side for a lefthander. This feature is unique with the Bren Ten, and far better than ambidextrous safeties seen on modified Colts — stronger, more comfortable, and not to be rubbed off inadvertently in the holster. It is easily operable with the trigger finger of the weak hand in case of strong-hand disability.

The pistol is very similar to the 1911 in size, and weighs two ounces less when unloaded. It is very similar in "feel" to the Cz 75. Barrel, frame, and springs are of stainless steel, but not the slide. Stocks, the only parts that the customer may want to modify to his individual taste, are of maple on the prototype but will be black plastic on the production guns. The Patridge sights are illuminated by the three-dot system as on the H-K P-7, but can easily be filled in by shooters who stick to black-on-black. Any sort of trick front sight can be plugged in in seconds, without tools.

It would be economically unsound to produce an instrument as advanced as the Bren Ten by old-fashioned methods. I was told in Germany that the Cz 75 was marketable at a competitive price only because the commissars can set any price they fancy, and that the piece would have to go for at least $1200 if it were made by conventional methods and free labor. Such is not the intention

Much of its antecedents can be seen in the stripped Bren Ten: CZ75 shape; Browning lock; SIG slide-inside-frame. It's meant to be the complete defensive arm, out of the box.

with the Bren Ten. Tom Dornaus has set up his brain-child to be run off on programmed automatic cutters which dispense with operators and need only directors and trouble-shooters. The machines have been checked out and they work. By this means the pistol can be produced for something like $450 retail, which is a bargain considering that it comes across the counter ready to go with no sights to install, no trigger job, no dehorning.

Ammunition plans have been made, and the manufacturer stands ready to throw the production line switch on the day the cutters are ordered.

The Bren Ten is not just another new pistol design. We have plenty of those. We do not need another big,

cumbersome, expensive 9. Those who can live with that power level are best advised to go to the Heckler & Koch P-7 (PSP), which is the right size and weight for a second-line cartridge. Neither do we need a giant pistol suitable for hunting moose and elk. But we armed citizens do need something with which to replace the grand old 1911 45, not because it won't do but rather because it is due for phase-out. Colt Industries has long indicated that it is not happy in the gun business and would get out if it could do so comfortably. With the Pentagon about to replace a really good pistol with a mediocre one at huge cost to the taxpayers we cannot look to the new service pistol as an adequate replacement for our own use. The Bren Ten, if it works, is the obvious answer.

Will it work? The prototype sure does. Not being a machinist, my reservation is that I do not know whether or not the programmed cutters can mass-produce triggers like the one in the prototype. Tom assures me that they can, and he ought to know, but until I have personally tested a respectable number of production guns I cannot swear to this. I do know that production triggers can be excellent, so where there is a will there is apparently a way.

As I write this the financing of the project is still not ready, though there have been a lot of nibbles and a couple of hard strikes. Quite a lot of money is involved, and if it is to be raised by public subscription the situation will be complicated. At least one foreign government has bid to back the whole show at one stroke, but with governments there are always strings attached. As long as anyone listens to me, for instance, there will not be a "Bren Nine."

In the absence of some evidence to the contrary I am going to go out on a limb and assert that the Bren Ten is indeed the better mousetrap.

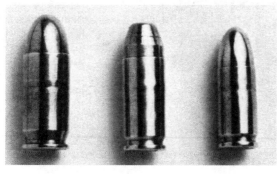

The 10mm cartridge may be thought of as a rimless 38–40, or just something sort of halfway from 9mm to 45, but not like either one.

Rating Handgun Power

This Power Index rating puts all handgun cartridges in their proper places.
■ Edward A. Matunas

FOR A LONG TIME the best possible way to estimate the potential effectiveness of handgun ammunition has been to compare the kinetic energy developed by a given round of ammunition with the kinetic energy of other rounds. As you may know, kinetic energy figures are expressed in foot pounds. This method is a reasonable approach to the problem as it is very objective and it is supported by the laws of physics. It is, however, not without its shortcomings.

For example, the kinetic energy system shows us that a 38 Special using a 158-grain round nose bullet, travelling at 755 ft./s, has 200 foot pounds of energy. It also tells us that a 158-grain semi-wadcutter's bullet travelling at the same speed has the same energy. And while it is true that both bullets possess the identical energy, the semi-wadcutter is a superior performer. This performance superiority can be proven by shooting into gelatin blocks or by examining records based on actual shootings involving police officers.

The vagaries of the kinetic energy system for rating handgun ammunition are numerous. No knowledgeable shooter would expect a full metal jacket 9mm bullet to perform as well as an expanding bullet of the same caliber and weight traveling at the same velocity. The expanding bullet is vastly superior. And despite the similarities in energy, a factory 9mm Luger with a 124-grain full-metal case bullet at 339 foot pounds of energy will not perform as well as a factory 45 Auto with a 230-grain full metal case bullet at 335 pounds of energy.

A number of systems have been devised over the years to express a handgun bullet's ability to get the job done. One of the most publicized expressed the bullet's performance by listing its momentum. The various methods tried have failed because they have ignored or played down the bullet's kinetic energy.

In some circles, extensive testing has been conducted in various media to get the bullet to perform as it would in tissue. These tests, usually conducted by or for a well financed police department, have resulted in some very elaborate charts which graphically depict bullet performance. These charts have been a giant step forward as they indeed show the superiority of expanding bullets over otherwise identical non-expanding bullets, but the drawbacks are very real. First, they are not readily available to most shooters; Second, they are useless when a new round is being considered; Third, they are subject to errors created when test performance is nontypical, caused by a lot of ammunition with velocity above or below nominal velocity or by a firearm that produced nontypical results.

The shooter therefore has been left to choose ammunition using the objective value of the kinetic energy of the round combined with his intuitive and subjective reckoning on the performance of a particular bullet style. As often as not, this has led to a great many misconceptions. For instance, most handgunners feel the 45 Auto will outperform any 38 Special round. This simply is not so. A number of 38 Special high speed rounds which use expanding bullets are far superior to the standard 230-grain full-metal case 45 Auto bullets.

Of course, a shooter can resort to testing each and every interesting round in gelatin blocks. Or if he has great influence he could perhaps examine 5-6,000 case histories from a major police department's records of shootings. Neither approach is very practical.

I have devised a method that fully takes into account the bullet's kinetic energy, its shape, its ability to expand and its basic diameter. I have been working with the basic idea for almost 20 years and I have reworked the idea many more times than I care to admit. Each time I discovered a discrepancy it was back to the drawing board. The system now, in my opinion, is what it was intended to be — a reliable indicator of handgun bullet performance, regardless of the bullet style, caliber, velocity or weight being considered. I call this new system Power Index Rating or PIR. (Note: I call it the Matunas Number. Editor.)

Any system which purports to express the ability to reflect an accurate representation of a bullet's capability to get the job done must somehow incorporate the bullet's kinetic energy. The formula for kinetic energy is, as you may know:

$$K.E. = \frac{V^2 Bg}{450240}$$

In this formula: V = the velocity in feet per second; and Bg = the weight of the bullet in grains.

Here are a **Speer** 158-gr. round nose 38 Special bullet, unfired, and a 158-gr. Speer semi-wadcutter, fired and unfired. The PIR System clearly shows the superiority of the semi-wadcutter over the round nose. Both are non-expanding, carry different energy transfer values.

These are 158-gr. lead hollow point bullets. They were fired from a 2-inch revolver. These were loaded by Winchester as +P ammunition, and expansion was obviously perfect. Such bullet performance gains high ratings in the PIR System.

Classic expansion was obtained in a 3-inch 38 Special with these Sierra 125-gr. hollow points. These newest Sierra bullets feature jacket cuts at the nose. It is these cuts which allow such perfect expansion.

These are Speer 110-gr. 38-caliber hollow points fired from a 2-inch 38 Special revolver, while the nose lead smeared to some extent these bullets do not qualify as expanding bullets when fired from this length barrel at the tested velocity.

Shown are Winchester 85-gr. Silvertips fired from a 380 Auto. The bullets on either side were fired into thoroughly soaked phone book pages. The bullet in the middle was fired into identical material which had not yet become completely soaked. The importance of using 100% saturated phone books is clear.

Even the 140-gr. Sierra hollow points expanded when fired from a 2-inch S&W Chiefs Special. While expansion of this heavy bullet is not tremendous in such a short barrel, it is sufficient to give the bullet a maximum energy transfer value in the PIR System.

This is the Sierra 125-gr. jacketed hollow point unfired. There are notches or cuts in the jacket at the nose end, and it is these notches that make these new Sierra bullets predictably good expanders.

This shows an unfired 125-gr. Sierra soft point 38/357 bullet alongside of a fired bullet of the same make and style. No expansion took place when this bullet was fired in a 4-inch revolver, which is why each style and type of bullet needs to be tested for expansion.

A 9-inch pile of soaked phone books stops all expanding bullets up to 115-gr. 9mm Luger rounds. For heavier calibers substantially greater thickness is required to stop the bullet in the books.

Bullet performance can, of course, be tested in clay blocks. However, such testing is very time-consuming and very costly. The author feels wet phone books are quicker, cheaper, and just as reliable.

By measurement, the weight of the bullet and its actual velocity can be determined. It is then a very simple matter to square the velocity, multiply the resulting figure by the bullet weight and divide all this by the constant 450240. The basis of the above formula has been verified and explained in a great number of places including my book, American Ammunition and Ballistics. Kinetic energy remains an important part of the PIR formula.

Any system to rate bullet performance must also address itself to the bullet's ability to expand because, as stated, an expanding bullet is far more effective than an identical non-expanding bullet at an identical velocity. And flat nosed, non-expanding bullets are better performers than other shapes of non-expanding bullets.

Since expansion is a vital part of bullet performance, I have tested a great number of bullets. As you may have expected, a number of bullets purported to be expanding turned out to be non-expanding. As an example, note the accompanying photo of three factory bullets fired from a 380 Auto PPK/S Walther. One is a Remington 88-grain Hollow Point, one is a Federal 90-grain Hollow Point, and one is a Winchester 85-grain Silvertip Hollow Point. Neither the Remington nor the Federal bullet expanded, while the Winchester bullet expanded in a classic style. Obviously in this case, with three almost identical bullets at nearly identical velocities, the expanding bullet is a far superior performer. All of my bullet tests were 15-round tests, at minimum.

You can easily duplicate my expansion tests. It is not necessary to prepare elaborate blocks of ordnance gelatin. All you need is a good supply of thoroughly soaked telephone books. It will speed up the soaking process if you remove the covers and backing which hold the books together. Before testing flip through the pages to make certain all the pages are completely wet.

WARNING: Bullets will penetrate through a much greater thickness of dry pages than through wet pages. And bullet expansion in dry pages will be extremely poor. Be certain that the book pages are completely soaked.

A 9 to 10-inch stack of wet phone books will stop expanding bullets up to and including the 9mm Luger. For heavier calibers or for non-expanding bullets you will have to increase this thickness notably. Be certain your bullets stop inside the wet paper. Bullets which completely penetrate can be severely expanded against your backstop.

For my testing I dug a hole in the ground about 24 inches deep. I poured a concrete floor some 5 inches thick in the bottom of the hole. The concrete aided in holding water and insured that the book pages would lie flat. At the beginning of my tests I failed to use enough paper and two different bullets hit the concrete and flattened out to about the thickness of a quarter. Expansion looked tremendous. Both bullets however, completely failed to expand when they hit an adequate thickness of wet pages. A bullet in tissue will perform very differently than a bullet hitting a very hard object.

The wet phone books produce a very visual impression of a bullet's performance. The hole from a high velocity expanding bullet will be considerably larger than the bullet's actual expanded diameter. The holes left by non-expanding bullets will be quite small. Good expanding bullets will actually cause an eruption of tiny wet particles out of the bullet hole. The width and depth of the bullet hole will be a good indicator of bullet performance. However, for our purposes you simply need to determine if a bullet will reliably expand shot after shot. Therefore I suggest that you test no less than 5 and preferably as many as 15 bullets.

Establishing expansion is essential, as my formula for determining the bullet's Power Index Rating applies a factor for expanding bullets and a different factor for non-expanding, flat nosed bullets and still a different factor for non-expanding, non-flat nosed bullets. My formula also allows for the increased performance of larger diameter bullets. Be certain that you test for expansion at the range (velocity level) for which you wish to determine performance. Some bullets expand well at 7 yards or from a given barrel length, but fail to expand at longer ranges or from shorter barrels.

The formula for the Power Index Rating of handgun ammunition started out as:

$$PIR = \frac{V^2 ETvBg}{(450240 \times 269)} \times Dv$$

In this formula: V = Velocity in feet per second; ETv = an Energy Transfer value; Bg = the Weight of the Bullet in Grains; Dv = A Bullet Diameter value.

$$\left(\frac{V^2 Bg}{450240} \right)$$

The PIR formula retains all the factors involved in obtaining kinetic energy figures, plus it allows for bullet shape and expansion or lack thereof (ETv) and also for basic caliber size (Dv). Additionally, it allows a factor (269) that will bring a specific level of cartridge performance to a value of 100. Most handgun ammunition performance is geared to defensive use, so I have used a constant that will result in a value of 100 for any cartridge/bullet combination that would prove to be highly effective as a man-stopper at short ranges and neither lighter nor heavier than needed.

This value was assessed equal to a 38-caliber bullet of 158 grains, capable of expansion at a muzzle velocity of 875 feet per second. This level of perfor-

mance is generally accepted by a large number of progressives who have adopted the 38 Special +P 158-grain lead hollow-point load. It is important to realize that if you disagree with this performance level the formula still remains completely accurate. You can simply select a value higher than 100 to represent your minimum acceptable level of cartridge performance.

In the interest of making the formula easier to use, the original values for ETv (Energy Transfer Value) were modified simply by moving the decimal position. This allowed for the constant factor of (450240 × 269) to be reduced to 12111, thus giving a more manageable formula of:

$$PIR = \frac{V^2 ETvBg}{12111} \times Dv$$

As in the earlier formula: V = Velocity in feet per second; ETv = Energy Transfer Value; Bg = Bullet Weight in Grains; Dv = Bullet Diameter Value.

The ETv values were arrived at only after years of research and trial and error applications. These values now used have been proven correct in every conceivable application. They are as follows:

Bullet Type	ETv Value
Bullets that actually expand	.0100
Non-expanding flat-nose bullets	.0085
Other non-expanding bullets	.0075

A bullet qualifies as a non-expanding flat-nosed bullet only if it has a total flat area equal to 60% or more of its diameter. All wadcutter and semiwadcutter bullets that I have examined qualify for the flat nosed ETv. Almost all other non-expanding bullets have an ETv of .0075. To any "expanding" bullet that does not actually expand should be applied one of the non-expanding ETv's. For instance, the 88-grain Remington Hollow Point 380 Auto bullet that failed to expand in our tests received an ETv of .0075. The Federal 90-grain bullet for the 380 Auto also failed to expand. But it had a relatively flat profile and therefore received an ETv of .0085.

It is vital to the application of the formula that you determine whether or not a bullet expands in your use. You can do so from the included data chart or by actual firing into wet phone books. If the barrel length of your gun is shorter than our test firearm then, due to reduced velocity, a bullet that expanded in our test gun may fail to expand in your shorter barrel. You must apply the correct ETv value if the formula is to express the real potential of any particular gun/cartridge combination. For a shorter or longer barrel, an appropriate velocity correction must be made. For my tests and charts I used fourinch barrels for most of the data collection. In some calibers, I have included data for other lengths.

The Dv values for bullet diameters have been proven to be correct in application as follows:

Actual Bullet Diameter	DV Value
.200" to .249"	0.80
.250" to .299"	0.85
.300" to .349"	0.90
.350" to .399"	1.00
.400" to .449"	1.10
.450" to .499"	1.15

Obviously some very fine lines were drawn when establishing the Dv values. However, the values used have been carefully checked against actual performance records. I am unaware of any case where a Power Index Rating derived from the formula did not accurately reflect the performance of a bullet in actual usage.

As an example of the formula's application, let's run through a simple exercise.

Question: How does the 38 Special 95-grain SJHP Remington Factory + P load compare to the 38 Special 158-grain LHP Winchester factory + P load in a three-inch barrel? By measurement, the 95-grain Remington bullet delivers a velocity of 1100 ft/s and the Winchester 158-grain bullet delivers a velocity of 875 ft/s.

To determine our answer we have the following:

$$PIR = \frac{V^2 ETvBg}{12111} \times Dv$$

Remington Bullet
(As specified in a 3" barrel)

$$PIR = \frac{1100^2 \times .0100 \times 95}{12111} \times 1.0$$

$$PIR = \frac{1149500}{12111} \times 1.0$$

Winchester Bullet
(As specified in a 3″ barrel)

$$PIR = \frac{875^2 \times .0100 \times 158}{12111} \times 1.0$$

$$PIR = \frac{1209687.5}{12111} \times 1.0$$

PIR = 99.88337 × 1.0
(Round to nearest whole number.)

Power Index Rating = 100

Therefore, the Winchester load in question will perform at a somewhat (5.3%) higher level than the Remington load. Obviously, in a shorter barrel the results would be somewhat different. In a two-inch barrel, the results would be as follows, given a velocity of 990 ft/s for the Remington bullet, which will still expand, and a velocity of 790 ft/s for the Winchester bullet which also still expands:

Remington Bullet
(As specified in a 2″ barrel)

$$PIR = \frac{990^2 \times .0100 \times 95}{12111} \times 1.0$$

$$PIR = \frac{931095}{12111} \times 1.0$$

PIR = 76.880109 × 1.0

PIR = 76.880109
(Rounded to nearest whole number.)

Power Index Rating = 77

Winchester Bullet
(As specified in a 2″ barrel)

$$PIR = \frac{790^2 \times .0100 \times 158}{12111} \times 1.0$$

$$PIR = \frac{968078}{12111} \times 1.0$$

PIR = 81.42003 × 1.0

PIR = 81.42003
(Rounded to nearest whole number.)

Power Index Rating = 81

Thus a two-inch barrel, in this caliber and with the ammunition being considered, is some 23% less effective than a three-inch barrel.

It can be seen from the above that our formula fully allows for velocity changes, kinetic energy changes, expansion (or lack of expansion) and basic bullet diameters. The formula shows that the heavy lead bullet load was supe-

rior to the other in both barrels.

Earlier we stated that the 124-grain FMC 9mm Luger factory load (velocity of 1110 ft/s) possessed almost identical kinetic energy (339 foot pounds) to a 45 Auto 230-grain FMC factory load (velocity of 810 ft/s) with 335 foot pounds. We said that in actual usage the 45 Auto round would outperform the Luger round. Let's apply the PIR formula to both of these loads to see if it reflects the superiority of the 45 load.

$$PIR = \frac{V^2 ETvBg}{12111} \times Dv$$

9mm Luger Bullet
(As specified)

$$PIR = \frac{1110^2 \times .0075 \times 124}{12111} \times 1.0$$

$$PIR = \frac{1145853}{12111} \times 1.0$$

PIR = 94.612584 × 1.0

PIR = 94.612584
(Round to nearest whole number)

Power Index Rating = 95

Here are a fired and an unfired Speer 100-gr. 9mm bullet, and Winchester 115-gr. Silvertip 9mm's also unfired and fired. Most 9mm Luger expanding bullets perform very well but these two types afford classic expansion every time at all practical ranges.

These three fired Speer 100-gr. 9mm Luger hollow points were recovered from wet phone books at 7 yards. They perform as well or better than most of the bullets the author has tested and so are favorites for hunting varmints with a handgun. They would, of course, attain very high ratings in the PIR System.

PIR

Formula and Values for Power Index Rating of Handgun Ammunition

$$\text{Power Index Rating: } PIR = \frac{V^2 ETvBg}{12111} \times Dv$$

In which: V = Velocity in feet per second
ETv = Energy Transfer Value
Bg = Bullet Weight in Grains
Dv = Diameter Value of Bullet

ETv Values:

For all bullets that actually expand[1]	= .0100
For non-expanding bullets with a flat nose equal to 60% of diameter	= .0085
For all other non-expanding bullets	= .0075

[1]Determined by actual test at range and velocity for which Power Index Rating is desired.

Dv Values

Actual Bullet Diameter	Value
.200″ to .249″	0.80
.250″ to .299″	0.85
.300″ to .349″	0.90
.350″ to .399″	1.00
.400″ to .449″	1.10
.450″ to .499″	1.15

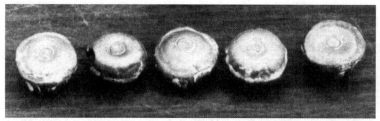

The difference in barrel length with regard to bullet expansion is clearly shown by these photos. The bullets above were fired from a 4-inch revolver and those below from a 3-inch revolver. The loads are identical. The velocity gain in the longer barrel produced classic expansion while the shorter barrel results were almost marginal for expansion, as evidenced by the third bullet.

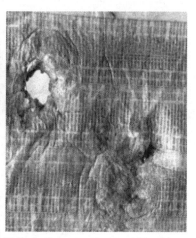

Holes in these pages were made with a 380 Auto. The large hole was made by an 85-gr. Winchester Silvertip which expanded perfectly. The others were made by Federal 90-gr. hollow point and a Remington 88-gr. hollow point. The channel created by the expanding bullet is much larger than its expanded diameter. The PIR System will accurately reflect such differences in bullet performance.

45 Bullet
(As specified)

$$PIR = \frac{810^2 \times .0075 \times 230}{12111} \times 1.15$$

$$PIR = \frac{1131772.5}{12111} \times 1.15$$

$$PIR = 93.449963 \times 1.15$$

$$PIR = 107.46746$$
(Round to nearest whole number.)

$$Power\ Index\ Rating = 107$$

The clear advantage of the 45 Auto in actual usage is indicated by the formula showing it 12.6% more efficient. To further prove our point let's consider a 9mm Luger round loaded with a 115-grain Silvertip Hollow Point to a velocity of 1255 ft/s (a Winchester factory load). This bullet does expand remarkably well.

$$PIR = \frac{V^2 ETvBg}{12111} \times Dv$$

$$PIR = \frac{1255^2 \times .0100 \times 115}{12111} \times 1.0$$

$$PIR = \frac{1811278.7}{12111} \times 1.0$$

$$PIR = 149.5564 \times 1.0$$

$$PIR = 149.5564$$
(Round to nearest whole number.)

$$Power\ Index\ Rating = 150$$

In this example we find the expanding 115-grain bullet load in the 9mm Luger vastly superior to the 124-grain non-expanding bullet load in the same caliber and also greatly superior to the 45 Auto 230-grain non-expanding bullet. And this is a very real reflection of the various loads' effectiveness in actual usage.

Because the PIR formula takes every possible aspect into account, the use of a wrong value or a wrong velocity can cause serious errors. For this reason, if you wish to compare the Power Index Rating of any given load at 25 or 50 yards (or any other range) you must first determine if your chosen load will offer bullet expansion at the range in question and then apply the correct ETv value. You will also need to know the exact velocity of your load at the range in question. Velocities may be obtained by actual measurement with a chronograph or from various data sources. After you have used it, the Power Index Rating system will prove itself to you as an unfaltering, easy-to-use system that will reflect a bullet's actual performance. (Please keep in mind that everything connected with the PIR system is copyrighted. Any one is free to use the system; however no commercial application of the PIR may be made without the written consent of the author.)

The Power Index Rating system has been applied to rifle cartridges wherein a value of 1000 equals an adequate amount of power to kill game of 300 pounds. However, almost all rifle bullets are of the expanding type, so the current kinetic energy levels continue to be fairly accurate appraisals of a load's worth.

I cannot over-stress establishing the actual velocity obtained with your handgun. This is particularly true in guns with three-inch or shorter barrels. In such guns, actual firearm dimensions can cause significant changes in velocities from one handgun to another, even the same brand, model and barrel length.

In testing two two-inch 38 Special revolvers, I found one would give consistent expansion with a 110-grain hollow point load while the other revolver wouldn't expand that or any other tested load. Results in four-inch or longer barrels are far more consistent and one can usually count on similar results from one gun to the next. Velocity averages should be taken from 15-shot strings, at least; 5-shot strings do not reveal average velocities sufficiently.

POWER INDEX RATING CHART

CALIBER	BULLET Wgt./Grs.	Brand	Style	POWDER Type	Wgt./Grs.	Barrel Length (Inches)	Velocity in ft/s	Bullet Expansion	Kinetic Energy in Foot Pounds	Power Index Rating
22 Short SV	29	all	LRN	Factory Load		6	865	No	48	11
22 Short HV	29	all	LRN	Factory Load		6	1010	No	66	15
22 Long HV	29	all	LRN	Factory Load		6	1095	No	77	17
22 Long Rifle SV	40	all	LRN	Factory Load		6	950	No	80	18
22 Long Rifle HV	40	all	LRN	Factory Load		6	1060	No	100	22
22 Long Rifle HV	37	CCI	LHP	Factory Load		6	1080	Yes	96	29
22 MRF	40	all	JHP	Factory Load		6½	1480	Yes	195	58
22 Jet	40	Rem.	JSP	Factory Load		8⅜	2100	Yes	392	117
25 Auto	45	Win.	EP	Factory Load		2	835	Yes	70	22
25 Auto	50	Rem.	FMC	Factory Load		2	810	No	73	17
30 Luger	93	all	FMC	Factory Load		4½	1220	No	307	77
32 Short Colt	80	all	LRN	Factory Load		4	745	No	99	25
32 Auto	71	Win.	FMC	Factory Load		4	905	No	129	32
32 Auto	60	Win.	STHP	Factory Load		4	970	Yes	125	42
32-20 WCF	100	Win.	LFN	Factory Load		6	1030	No	237	67
9mm Luger	95	Win.	JSP	Factory Load		4	1355	Yes	387	144
9mm Luger	115	Win.	FMC	Factory Load		4	1155	No	341	95
9mm Luger	115	Win.	STHP	Factory Load		4	1255	Yes	402	150
9mm Luger	115	Fed.	JHP	Factory Load		4	1165	Yes	347	129
9mm Luger	124	Rem.	FMC	Factory Load		4	1110	No	339	95
9mm Luger	100	Speer	JHP	231	5.8	4	1300	Yes	375	140
9mm Luger	125	Speer	JSP	231	5.6	4	1150	Yes	367	136
38 Special + P	95	Rem.	JHP	Factory Load		2	990	Yes	207	77
38 Special + P	95	Rem.	JHP	Factory Load		3	1100	Yes	255	95
38 Special + P	95	Rem.	JHP	Factory Load		4	1175	Yes	291	108
38 Special + P	95	Win.	STHP	Factory Load		2	945	Yes	188	70
38 Special + P	95	Win.	STHP	Factory Load		3	1050	Yes	233	86
38 Special + P	95	Win.	STHP	Factory Load		4	1100	Yes	255	95
38 Special + P	110	all	JHP	Factory Load		2	880	Yes	189	70
38 Special + P	110	all	JHP	Factory Load		3	975	Yes	232	86
38 Special + P	110	all	JHP	Factory Load		4	1020	Yes	254	94
38 Special + P	110	Sierra/Speer	JHP	231	5.9	6	1090	Yes	290	108
38 Special + P	110	Sierra/Speer	JHP	Bullseye	5.4	6	1090	Yes	290	108
38 Special	110	Sierra	JHP	800-X	7.2	3	950	Yes	220	82
38 Special + P	125	all	JHP	Factory Load		4	945	Yes	248	92
38 Special + P	125	Sierra/Speer	JHP	231	5.6	6	990	Yes	272	101
38 Special	125	Sierra	JHP	800-X	6.9	3	875	Yes	213	79
38 Special + P	140	Sierra/Speer	JHP	231	5.5	6	935	Yes	272	101
38 Special + P	158	Win.	LHP	Factory Load		2	790	Yes	219	81
38 Special + P	158	Win.	LHP	Factory Load		3	875	Yes	269	100
38 Special + P	158	all	LHP	Factory Load		4	915	Yes	294	109
38 Special	148	all	LWC	Factory Load		2	525	No	91	29
38 Special	148	all	LWC	Factory Load		3	575	No	109	34
38 Special	148	all	LWC	Factory Load		4	710	No	166	52
38 Special	148	all	LWC	231	3.0	2	550	No	99	31
38 Special	148	all	LWC	231	3.0	3	600	No	118	37
38 Special	148	all	LWC	231	3.0	6	750	No	185	58
38 Special	158	all	LRN	Factory Load		2	630	No	139	39
38 Special	158	all	LRN	Factory Load		3	700	No	172	48
38 Special	158	all	LRN	Factory Load		4	755	No	200	56
38 Special	158	all	LSWC	Factory Load		2	630	No	139	44
38 Special	158	all	LSWC	Factory Load		3	700	No	172	54
38 Special	158	all	LSWC	Factory Load		4	755	No	200	63
38 Special	158	Speer	LSWC	231	4.3	2	655	No	151	48
38 Special	158	Speer	LSWC	231	4.3	3	725	No	184	58
38 Special	158	Speer	LSWC	231	4.3	6	850	No	254	80
38 Special	158	Rem.	LSWC	800-X	5.9	6	880	No	272	86
38 Special	200	all	LRN	Factory Load		2	545	No	132	37
38 Special	200	all	LRN	Factory Load		3	600	No	160	45
38 Special	200	all	LRN	Factory Load		4	630	No	176	49
38 Special	200	Rem.	LRN	800-X	4.6	6	725	No	233	65
38 S & W	145	all	LRN	Factory Load		4	685	No	151	42
357 Magnum	110	all	JHP	Factory Load		4	1295	Yes	410	152
357 Magnum	110	Speer	JHP	231	8.8	6	1370	Yes	459	170
357 Magnum	125	all	JHP	Factory Load		4	1450	Yes	584	217
357 Magnum	125	Speer	JHP	231	8.6	6	1310	Yes	476	177
357 Magnum	140	Speer	JHP	231	8.0	6	1200	Yes	448	166
357 Magnum	158	all	JHP	Factory Load		4	1235	Yes	535	199
357 Magnum	158	Speer	JHP	Unique	8.2	6	1200	Yes	505	188
38 Super + P	130	all	FMC	Factory Load		5	1245	No	448	125
38 Super + P	125	Win.	JHP	Factory Load		5	1280	Yes	455	169
380 Auto	85	all	STHP	Factory Load		3	1000	Yes	189	70
380 Auto	88	Rem.	JHP	Factory Load		3	990	No	192	53
380 Auto	90	Fed.	JHP	Factory Load		3	1000	No	200	63
380 Auto	95	all	FMC	Factory Load		3	955	No	192	54
41 Magnum	210	all	JSP	Factory Load		4	1300	Yes	778	322
41 Magnum	210	all	LSWC	Factory Load		4	965	No	434	151
44 Special	246	all	LRN	Factory Load		4	755	No	311	96
44 Magnum	240	all	JHP	Factory Load		4	1180	Yes	742	304
44 Magnum	240	all	LSWC	Factory Load		4	1350	Yes	971	397
44 Magnum	200	Speer	JHP	2400	23.0	7½	1475	Yes	966	395
45 Auto	185	Win.	STHP	Factory Load		5	1000	Yes	411	176
45 Auto	230	all	FMC	Factory Load		5	810	No	335	107
45 Auto	185	all	JWC	Factory Load		5	770	No	244	89
45 Auto	200	Speer	JHP	231	6.3	5	950	Yes	401	171
45 Colt	225	Win.	STHP	Factory Load		5½	920	Yes	423	181
45 Colt	225	Fed.	LHP	Factory Load		5½	900	Yes	405	173
45 Colt	255	all	LRN	Factory Load		5½	860	No	419	134

PIR GUIDELINES

Level	PIR Values	Application
1	24 or less	Loads within this value range should never be used for personal protection. They are suitable only for target shooting and plinking.
2	25 to 54	Loads in this value grouping would require very exact bullet placement if used for personal defense. If a killing shot was not made, your antagonist might only be further enraged. Loads in this group could prove satisfactory for small game but must be considered less than satisfactory for personal defense.
3	55 to 94	Loads within this PIR grouping are somewhat popular as personal defense weapons. However, the experience of many people shows these cartridges to be marginal even when good hits are made. Many police departments are armed with cartridges in this group. However, more than one police officer has lost his life when he was unable to stop an assailant with a load from this group. Loads in this category must be considered at best marginal.
4	95 to 150	Loads fitting in this category will meet the requirements of most military applications. They will also prove adequate for police departments that wish to arm personnel with weapons that are likely to prove effective under almost any situation. These are ideal loads for personal protection. Many police departments are now equipping their men with loads from this grouping.
5	151 to 200	Loads in this range will usually take the fight out of any opponent with only fairly placed hits. However, loads of this power level are difficult to control and most shooters have trouble scoring hits due to the recoil and noise levels. With extensive practice they can be mastered and prove useful to a highly skilled shooter.
6	201 or more	Loads in this category are best described as overkill in self-defense. They are hunting loads best used for protection from bears gone crazy rather than against human opponents. Few shooters can develop the necessary skills to handle the very heavy recoil and noise levels of cartridges with PIR values in the 200 plus range.
PLEASE NOTE:		It is impossible to suggest specific values for any specific application unless all the criteria are known. The above table is offered as a general guideline.

Cal. 44 Component Bullets

W-W 240 Gr. LEAD

REMINGTON 240 Gr. LEAD

Bullet expansion does not always occur when one might expect. For example, the new Sierra 125-grain Hollow Point bullets will reliably expand in my three-inch S & W Chiefs Special when pushed by 6.9 grains of DuPont 800-X. The Sierra 125-grain Soft Point bullet will not show the slightest trace of expansion with the same powder charge. In fact, there is no load that will cause expansion of the Soft Point bullet in that gun. The new Sierra 38/357 Hollow Point bullets with notches cut into the jacket nose have proven to be the very best expanding handgun bullets normally available to reloaders.

In two-inch 38 Specials one must stay with 95 to 110-grain bullets if positive expansion is desired. Very few will offer any expansion with heavier bullets and none of those I have tested would offer expansion with bullets over 125 grains unless + P loads are used. In three-inch 38 Specials bullets up to 125 grains can usually be made to expand reliably if you select the proper bullet and powder charge. +P loads will offer expansion regardless of bullet weight. And in four-inch 38 Specials, bullets up to 140 or 158 grains will often expand if good bullets are used with appropriate powder charges.

Other calibers are equally affected by changes in barrel length.

Please keep in mind +P loads must be avoided in any aluminum frame revolver. Many shooters have found the Speer 110-grain Hollow Point 38 Special ammunition loaded to standard pressures, will offer expansion in three-inch or longer 38 Specials when no other standard pressure ammunition will. This load is worth investigating when you want maximum performance from

Only the 44 Magnum was capable of driving lead semi-wadcutters fast enough to insure the positive expansion of this style bullet. The 44 S&W Special won't do it.

an alloy frame revolver.

There are a number of good bullets which offer good expansion in handguns of various calibers, properly used. The accompanying chart lists many popular loads for you. If you want to select maximum performance ammunition for your handgun it is up to you to assure, by testing, that the bullet you use will expand. The Power Index Rating system clearly shows only expanding bullets get the maximum potential from a handgun. If a load that interests you is not in the table, apply the PIR formula after determining if the bullet will expand in your gun.

The Extraordinary Glock

From no idea to radical prototype to selected service pistol in under four years? Where was the bureaucracy? ∎ Raymond Caranta

I N OCTOBER, 1982, a Belgian magazine, over the signature of a German gun writer, reported a certain Austrian Glock 17 pistol, chambered in 9mm Luger, mostly made of plastics and stampings. The Glock 17, it was said, was considered for adoption by the Austrian army.

The gun was displayed nowhere at European shows, and was not taken very seriously until this year, when it was learnt that the Glock 17 had been officially approved as the Austrian Army service pistol. It replaces the German P-1, the light alloy descendant of World War II's P38.

In the gun business, only a few people knew the Glock Company, which was until recently mostly involved in cutlery. Headed by Gaston Glock, an independent engineer specializing in advanced plastics and metal technology for more than a quarter of a century, the firm has only 45 employees. It is located in Deutsches-Wagram in Austria.

The first significant commercial success of the Glock Company occurred in 1978 when its Field Knife 78 was adopted by the Austrian army, which placed orders for 150,000 pieces since then. About the same quantity was sold on the sporting market. Then, Gaston Glock designed, in connection with Dynamit Nobel, the German giant of chemical products, powders and ammunition, an extraordinary hand grenade made of plastics and bursting into 5,000 fragments.

The Glock 17 is very low in the hand contrary to most pistols using this style of barrel mounting.

In 1980, when Gaston Glock learned that the Austrian army contemplated replacing their old service pistols with a double-action model featuring a large magazine capacity, he immediately realized that the Steyr pistol could not be alone. He soon toured the competitors, asking for subcontracts as an industrial compensation, should a foreign product be selected.

Then, back in his facilities, he was amazed at the conventional technology on which most competitors relied and was soon analyzing the patents and consulting German-speaking experts about the requirements for a new design. He was not, himself, a firearms enthusiast, but five months later, still in 1980, he had developed a first prototype of the Glock 17 which was selected, late in 1983, as the service pistol of Austria. The Army's order is 25,000 units, 5,000 of them to be delivered in 1984.

The Glock 17 is a 9mm Luger short recoil-operated pistol on the Browning "High Power" principle as improved by SIG in their P-220, P-225 and P-226 models. Its capacity is 17 rounds. It is, regardless of operating principle, a most unusual gun.

The slide is a square-section extrusion accommodating a welded machined bolt which carries the striker and pivoted Walther-style extractor. The one-piece hammered barrel is of the linkless cam style, but the breech end is square and matches the inner slide square contour, which offers the centering function necessary for ensuring a high level of accuracy. This slide is 7 inches long and guided over an interrupted length of 5.19 inches by rails. The recoil spring unit is conventionally located under the barrel and the slide-barrel-recoil spring assembly weighs 16.8 ounces so as to dampen the recoil.

The receiver is an extremely light high-resistance casting of plastic material weighing only 5 ounces, including the trigger mechanism. The receiver slide guides, insuring the sturdiness of the pistol over an expected 15,000-shot service life with NATO ammunition, are made of sheet-metal imbedded in the plastic.

The steel slide-barrel-recoil spring assembly represents 40 percent of the total weight of the pistol.

Note the slender grip of the Glock 17 in spite of the unusual 17-shot magazine capacity; design allows variation in pitch.

The solid trigger guard is square for two-hand shooting and, as the pistol is striker fired, the trigger mechanism is entirely enclosed in the upper section of the receiver. Therefore, the grip, which only accommodates the magazine, is provided with an important hollow section at the rear and can be pitched as required, according to the customer's wishes.

The two-column staggered magazine is also a new design as it is entirely made of high resistance plastic material, with the exception of the spring and lips which are metalic. Thus it weighs only 1.43 ounces, empty, while accommodating nearly a half-pound load of service ammunition. The magazine catch is fitted at the rear of the lower branch of the trigger guard. The empty magazine lags a little and must sometimes be withdrawn by the weak hand, but this trait disappears when the gun has been broken in.

While not new at all, as its principle was already used in the Austrian cavalry pistol model of 1907 (popularly known as the 8mm Roth-Steyr), the Glock's firing mechanism is the only "pre-cocked" design

made today. Single-action pistols must be hand cocked for the first shot; those shooting only double-action require a long pull each shot; and those fitted with selective lockwork require two trigger-finger positions between the first and following shots. The Glock 17 firing mechanism requires a single trigger-finger position as all the shots are fired in a "semi-double-action" mode; the trigger pull equals that of a good service pistol. The trigger travel, while shorter than that of a typical double-action gun, is longer than that of a single-action pistol.

With the Glock 17, when chambering the first round, the striker is "pre-cocked", i.e. it is retained at about half travel and the firing pin is partially compressed. The effort necessary for firing the chambered round is set at about five pounds instead of ten, as usually required in a genuine double action mechanism. The trigger travel is limited to .40-inch.

This facilitates the basic training, avoids the "breaking the glass" climax of single-action handguns and makes the pistol with a chambered round instantly available for action. In case of misfire, the slide must be withdrawn with the weak hand only .40-inch to get another striker blow.

Beside the "semi-double-action" firing mode for all shots, the Glock 17 pistol is fitted with a very clever automatic trigger safety lever consisting of a spring-loaded thin metal plate fitted along the vertical center line of the .27-inch thick plastic trigger. At rest, the safety lever protrudes in front and behind the trigger, its heel preventing any trigger motion until it is depressed. This is automatic when the finger pulls the trigger. Under this action, the front end of the safety lever swings backwards, retracting the upper rear section which normally bears against the receiver, jamming the trigger. The pressure required is very low and the operation seems highly reliable.

With its low and square slide fitted over its slim plastic receiver, the Glock 17 looks quite strange at first glance. The highly pitched grip is attractive. At first handling, one is astonished at its unusually low weight of 23.2 ounces. However, when the gun is loaded with 17 service rounds, its 31-oz. weight, while still very low, enables an excellent control in practical shooting.

The grip of the Glock 17 is perhaps the best of the market as it is suitable for every size of male or female hand, which is an exception to usual large capacity double-action pistols chambered for such a powerful ammunition. Moreover, the high pitch of this grip, combined with the "semi-double-action" feature, is excellent for instinctive shooting.

This grip is exceptionally flat despite the 17-shot magazine capacity

The trigger mechanism is entirely made of stampings; gun is striker-fired.

(1.18-inch thick) and its sanded temperature-proof plastic surfaces afford a very pleasant contact to the shooting hand and are not slippery. Empty, the Glock is balanced above the front area of the trigger, but this point moves about half an inch backward when loaded with 17 rounds.

The gun has Patridge-type sights and they are just 1.34-inch above the shooting hand. The rear sight notch contour is underlined in white while the ramp front sight features a 1/10-inch white dot. They are better than the average for combat shooting and still good for slow fire.

The **automatic** trigger safety of the Glock 17 is most efficient; it is also very simple.

Thirty rounds offhand at 25 meters under I.S.U. slow fire conditions scored 249 out of 300; the 10-ring is two inches (5cm) wide

A seasoned shooter using the Glock 17 for the first time will need some dry-firing to get used to the peculiar trigger pull. Nevertheless, the shooting technique is very simple; while raising the pistol and controlling your breathing, briskly pull the trigger over the first ⅞-in. until you feel a definitely stronger resistance and, then, carefully aim while pressing the last ⅛-in. of pull. Tyros will find this quite natural, as will double-action revolver shooters, but people used to conventional automatics may suffer at the beginning.

Computation shows a respectable recoil velocity (defining the pressure on the hand) of 10.55 feet per second, but the recoil actually felt seems lower and just a little more than that of a conventional 9mm Luger service pistol such as our old Beretta Brigadier.

In 25-meter slow fire, offhand, our scores were in the 250 out of 300 range at the I.S.U. big bore target featuring a 2-inch ten, which is standard performance for a service pistol, the best scoring slightly above 260 of 300 and the worst under 240 of 300. On a combat shooting course involving a long run over the 17-shot magazine string with stopping, turning and shooting on command, the Glock 17 was rated by this writer as very good, but his two partners, who normally shoot Star and Colt automatics, missed several times and were slower than usual.

Thirty rounds offhand at 25 meters under I.S.U. slow fire conditions scored 249 out of 300; the 10-ring is two inches (5cm) wide.

In our sample, bearing a serial number in the 200's, we shot 364 rounds without cleaning that included 100 rounds of French service ammunition made in 1982; 64 very old French submachine gun rounds with hard primers; 50 new German Geco half-jacketed rounds; 50 commercial full jacketed Geco rounds; 50 commercial full jacketed Remington rounds; 50 reloads with jacketed bullets and French powder. The only malfunction was a misfire with the

Not many problems for Austrian GIs here. Herr Glock knows simple when he sees it.

old submachine gun ammunition and some slide hesitation when chambering the first half-jacketed truncated Geco round from the magazine.

The Glock 17 is an original, inexpensive, compact, accurate and reliable service pistol featuring a clever but controversial construction leading one to think of it as the "Tokarev" of this turn of century.

A Second Look At The Glock 17

▮ Donald M. Simmons

WHEN THE Glock 17, also known as the Plastic Pistol, started arriving on these shores, a rhubarb developed over a "pistol that could pass through our airport security systems." It seems pretty late to remind one and all that the Glock 17 automatic pistol can be spotted by security personnel, that it is not an all plastic pistol, and even if it was it would, if loaded, still be detectable by X-ray, but all those things are true.

Because of the media circus carried on by the anti-gun crowd over the Glock 17, some of its interesting design points and innovations that have nothing to do with airport security have been overlooked. The Glock was designed by Gaston Glock in just 6 months; even more impressive is the fact that Herr Glock had never designed a firearm before and was, in fact, completely unfamiliar with firearms.

The Glock 17 is manufactured in Deutsches-Wagram, Austria, in a small progressive plastic injection moulding company. In 1983; Gaston Glock began with an order from the Austrian Military for 28,000 Glock 17 pistols, which is, as they say in poker games, not bad for openers.

The Glock pistol should not be called a plastic pistol, partly because the bulk of its weight is steel. What is unusual about the Glock is the method used to intermingle steel stamping with a polymer plastic which improves each.

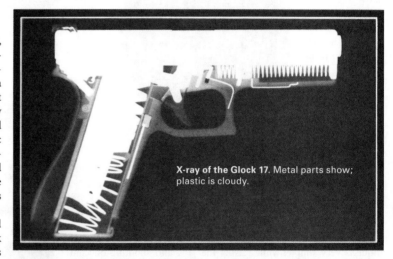

X-ray of the Glock 17. Metal parts show; plastic is cloudy.

The Glock's frame starts life as a mould into which various steel stampings are inserted. This mould is then injected with a thermal setting plastic under exceedingly high pressure and, after curing, there is a complete frame assembly with its necessary strong points reinforced with steel. This strong light frame is impervious to moisture and can stand extremes in temperature. So much for the obvious.

The overlooked innovations are as exciting if not more so than the obvious fact that the frame is mostly plastic.

Barrel

The barrel of the Glock is steel and basically the barrel found in a Browning Hi-Power pistol with two big exceptions. The barrel locks to the slide during initial recoil by a rectangular boss fitting the slide's ejection port, thus eliminating ribs on the barrel and grooves in the slide, found in the Browning. Though the Glock ejects to the right, its ejection port is in the middle of the slide to give a large locking area. This type of ribless locking was found in the French Model 1935-S. The lower lug on the Glock barrel has a 45-degree camming surface which, during recoil, disengages the boss from the ejection port, and that unlocks the slide to continue the full recoil. The mating surface which acts on the barrel's lug is a steel insert pinned into the plastic frame.

The other exception is the rifling, not conventional land and groove, but more like that in some Heckler & Koch barrels. Glock calls their rifling "hexagonal" rather than "polygonal." Instead of engraving a series of grooves in the bullet, you squeeze it into a hexagon which spirals from breech to muzzle one turn in 10 inches. You get bullet stabilizing and a much easier barrel to clean. In cross-section, the Glock's barrel is a series of six flats connected by small arcs. The spherical distance around the inside of the rifling is the same as the circumference of a 9mm projectile. It forms a new shape, but doesn't distort; the bullet retains its original length.

Magazine

Gaston Glock obviously was not too familiar with the normal takedown of a pistol's magazine. The floorplate of most European pistols is removable by pushing up on the dimple on the base plate with a loaded cartridge and sliding the floorplate off forward. Not so with the Glock 17, where you just squeeze the sides of the magazine tube right over the base plate and the plate can be slid off frontwards, which allows the disassembly of the entire magazine for cleaning. The Glock's magazine is plastic with a metal insert. The pistol comes with two magazines and a plastic loading tool that really works.

Safeties

There are four types of safety devices in a Glock 17. The one that is not found is the more or less standard manual safety. Safety number one is a trigger safety, which is reminiscent of the turn of the century Iver Johnson revolvers and the Sauer "Behörden" Model 1930 pocket automatic pistol. This safety, located in the finger pressing area of the trigger, must be depressed to allow the trigger to be pulled and so prevents the gun from being fired when, as one example, it is inserted into a too-tight holster.

The Glock has a striker safety or striker block. This locks the forward movement of the striker, and, is only deactivated when the trigger is pulled to its extreme rearward position, as in

Right side of the Glock 17 pistol. Notice that the slide is serialed, but the frame isn't.

firing the pistol. The purpose is to prevent firing in the event that the pistol is inadvertently dropped or otherwise impacted.

The Glock is unique in the third safety device, which puts the trigger in a semi-cocked position, from which it requires a long pull to fire the pistol. We will be going into this unusual mechanism in detail further on.

The last safety feature is the disconnector which holds the pistol to just one shot for each pull of the trigger. In the Glock, the disconnector is hardened sheet steel and it puts the sear's nose into engagement with the striker with each cycle of the slide, whether the trigger is released or not.

With all those safety features, the Glock could be carried with the trigger in the semi-cocked position and the chamber loaded, but in our liability-minded society the Glock company says, "No way!" I quote directly from their manual: "Always carry your pistol empty, with the trigger rearward except when you intend to shoot, so that your pistol cannot be fired where it is unsafe to do so."

Fire Control

The words double action and two-stage trigger have been applied to the Glock 17. Technically, neither is correct.

The Glock has a trigger cocking action, but it goes much further than mere trigger cocking. The Glock firing pin or striker is spring loaded to move forward, but the sear which engages the striker is spring loaded in the opposite direction. It is a system in which, at rest, two springs' tensions counter-balance each other. When the slide is retracted and returns to the closed position, the striker is partially cocked, and when the trigger is subsequently pulled with a predetermined tension, the striker is pushed to its full-cocked position and then released and the pistol fires. By either increasing the tension on the sear spring or decreasing the tension on the striker spring, the trigger pull can be reduced to whatever tension is wanted. The feel of the Glock pull has been likened to that of a two-stage trigger, but that, too, is not accurate. A typical two-stage trigger has a low tension slack take-up, followed by a heavier sear release stage. In the Glock, the effort required to pull the trigger is nearly constant from initial contact until the striker is released. The Glock's trigger might better be called two-function. First it cocks the striker, and then releases it. The trigger pull on my Glock is a very constant 5 pounds, with little or no over-travel.

The idea has been expressed that Glock might go to a plastic slide. I doubt this very much from an engineering point of view. In the design of a self-loading pistol, the weight of the slide is a predetermined factor after the type of cartridge has been decided on. Just to take the subject of the weight of the slide to the ridiculous, suppose that the slide and the bullet weighed the same amount, then the bullet would leave the muzzle and the slide would recoil at the same high velocity. This just won't work. The slide must travel at a speed that can

The slide with barrel and recoil spring removed. The round button just behind the ejection port is the striker block.

The polymer plastic frame showing the metal inserts, which are emplaced before the plastic is molded.

be stopped at full recoil without damage to itself or other parts. When you are designing for the 9mm cartridge, a slide using a Browning system of locking and unlocking should weigh around 7/10ths of a pound. To get that weight in the same density plastic now used in the Glock, the slide would have to have about seven times the size — IMPOSSIBLE.

The Glock's slide now is made from steel bar stock and is fully machined. The next logical step to reduce cost would be to go to an investment cast slide with little or no machining required. If a plas-

tic slide seemed still to offer a savings, then one which had a steel insert in the breech and ejection port area would be required. There would also have to be a lead insert to get the weight back up to the 7/10ths of a pound.

Do I like the Glock pistol? To this I can give an unqualified, YES. I further think that one unfamiliar with conventional automatic pistols would quickly master the Glock's system. And it is not

so far out of line as to confuse practiced persons. It is a fine pistol.

The author wishes to thank Mr. Karl Walter, U.S. sales manager for Glock, for his assistance in the writing of this article. Also Mr. Fred Pelcen for his invaluable help in X-raying the Glock 17.

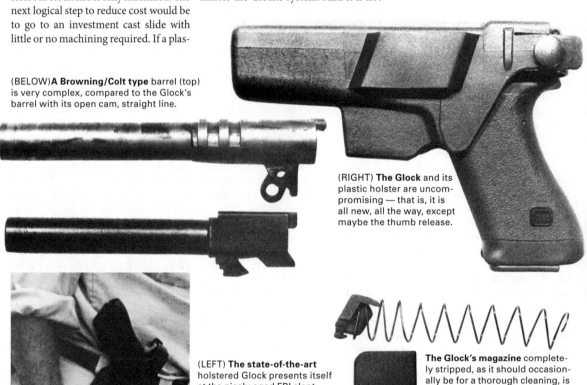

(BELOW) **A Browning/Colt type** barrel (top) is very complex, compared to the Glock's barrel with its open cam, straight line.

(RIGHT) **The Glock** and its plastic holster are uncompromising — that is, it is all new, all the way, except maybe the thumb release.

(LEFT) **The state-of-the-art** holstered Glock presents itself at the nicely aged FBI slant.

The Glock's magazine completely stripped, as it should occasionally be for a thorough cleaning, is surprisingly conventional.

Blowback Nines

Some designs succeed, but most have not. ▌John Malloy

T HE 9MM PARABELLUM (9mm Luger) cartridge was among the early high-pressure pistol cartridges, designed for an extremely strong, locked-breech action. It hardly seems suitable for a straight blowback action, but such pistols have been made and are still being made today.

The cartridge, introduced in 1902, was adopted by the German navy for their Parabellum or Luger pistol of 1904. It became known worldwide following its adoption by the German army for the best-known Luger ever — the famous Pistole 1908 or P08.

The design of the Luger allowed-in fact, required — a high-pressure cartridge. Consider that the entire upper part of the pistol — the barrel, receiver and breechblock, with its toggle lock and contained mechanism — must be moved backward after firing.

At a point, the toggle unlocks, the barrel and receiver stop, and the breechblock continues rearward to eject the fired case. Then, enough residual force must be available from spring compression so that the barreled receiver will return and the breechblock will run forward to chamber the next cartridge.

Obviously, the 9mm Parabellum cartridge had to generate high pressures to make such an action function reliably.

Still, shortly after the introduction of the P08, attempts were made to adapt this cartridge to a blowback design. And real blowback nines arrived on the scene within a few years of 1908. The efforts to make successful blowback pistols chambered for the 9mm Parabellum

round spread to a number of countries throughout the world, spanned the intervening decades and continue today.

The first was the German Dreyse. Niklaus von Dreyse (1787–1867) had been the inventor of the famous Prussian "Needle-Gun." He was already long dead when his company was taken over by Rheinische Metallwaren und Maschinenfabrik (later known as "Rheinmetall") in 1891. In 1907, the company brought out its first pistol, a 32-caliber blowback. Because of name recognition and company tradition, the pistol was offered as the "Dreyse," although it had actually been designed by Louis Schmeisser.

A year after the introduction of the Dreyse 32, the German army adopted the 9mm cartridge. Schmeisser began to modify his design for the new army round. He found that the pressure of the cartridge could be contained with an extremely stiff recoil spring. The 9mm Dreyse pistol probably has the strongest recoil spring ever used in a pistol. Because of the heavy spring, it was almost impossible for any but the strongest of men to operate the first prototype.

The solution was the addition of a connector bar along the top of the pistol. The bar was pivoted at the front.

The Dreyse 9mm pistol was the first attempt to use the 9mm Parabellum cartridge in a blowback design. It used an extremely powerful recoil spring to delay opening of the action. When the rear sight was lifted, the recoil spring was disconnected so that the slide could be easily retracted. (From the 1911 ALFA catalog).

When it was lifted at the rear, the slide and recoil spring were disconnected. The slide could then be pulled back easily, compressing only the striker spring. With a cartridge chambered, the connector was pushed back into place, connecting the recoil spring to the slide again.

Dreyse 9mm pistols were offered for commercial sale about 1910. When the World War began in 1914, the Dreyse military 9mm was reportedly considered as a substitute standard for the German army, but was not adopted. Still, a small number were apparently carried by officers as personal side-arms. Production stopped before the end of the war and the total number manufactured was very small — perhaps not more than a few hundred pieces.

The problem with the Dreyse military pistol centered on the spring dis-

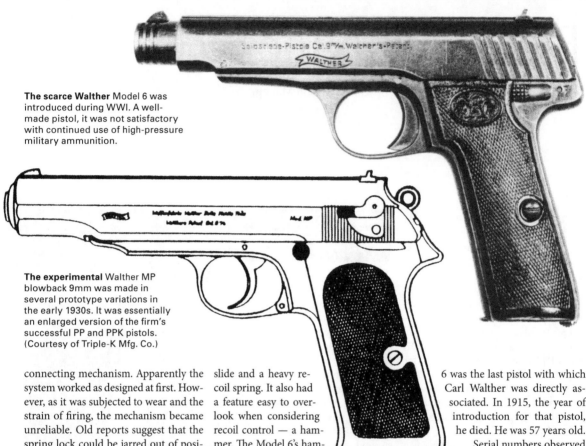

The scarce Walther Model 6 was introduced during WWI. A well-made pistol, it was not satisfactory with continued use of high-pressure military ammunition.

The experimental Walther MP blowback 9mm was made in several prototype variations in the early 1930s. It was essentially an enlarged version of the firm's successful PP and PPK pistols. (Courtesy of Triple-K Mfg. Co.)

connecting mechanism. Apparently the system worked as designed at first. However, as it was subjected to wear and the strain of firing, the mechanism became unreliable. Old reports suggest that the spring lock could be jarred out of position during shooting. The construction of the pistol would keep the slide from being blown off toward the shooter, but recoil without any spring control could put the pistol out of service.

World War I introduced another German 9mm blowback pistol that fared slightly better than the Dreyse — the Walther Model 6.

The Walther firm had been founded in 1886 by Carl Walther and had manufactured sporting rifles and shotguns into the early 1900s. In 1908, the first pistol — the Model 1 — was produced. It was a blowback 25-caliber pocket model. Thereafter followed a successful line of small pistols in 25 and 32 calibers. The Model 5 was introduced in 1913, the year before the war began.

The need for more pistols during the early stages persuaded Carl Walther to enlarge his basic blowback design to use the 9mm service cartridge. The resulting pistol, the Model 6, had a fairly heavy

slide and a heavy recoil spring. It also had a feature easy to overlook when considering recoil control — a hammer. The Model 6's hammer is concealed, but the effect was present. The uncocked hammer was held forward by its spring. Because of the short lever arm presented at the point of contact with the slide, it offered considerable initial resistance to the rearward movement of the slide. Once the hammer began to move, resistance fell off rapidly. At the moment of greatest chamber pressure, though, the hammer gave at least some extra control that the striker-fired Dreyse had not had.

Unfortunately, it was not enough. The Model 6, as were all Walther products of the time, was beautifully made and felt good in the hand. However, neither the weight nor the recoil spring was quite enough, and the pistols could be battered by extensive firing with the service load. They were, however, carried as personal sidearms by some German officers during the war. By early 1917, though, the Model 6 was no longer in production. The blowback 9mm Model

6 was the last pistol with which Carl Walther was directly associated. In 1915, the year of introduction for that pistol, he died. He was 57 years old.

Serial numbers observed or reported range from under 100 to something over 1000. Probably over a thousand, but less than two thousand, specimens of the Model 6 were made. They are scarce pistols today.

At this point, we need to make a side trip, for events were taking place in Italy that require us to be specific about our field of interest.

In 1910, the Italian government had adopted the 9mm Glisenti semi-automatic pistol. The Glisenti was a weak locked-breech design that used a vertical swinging member below the bolt to prop the bolt closed for a short time. The cartridge was dimensionally identical to the 9mm Parabellum, but, because of the weak action, was loaded to a much lower power level. Cartridge collectors today generally refer to it as "9mm Glisenti."

Once the cartridge was adopted, it was inevitable that other Italian designs chambered for it would appear.

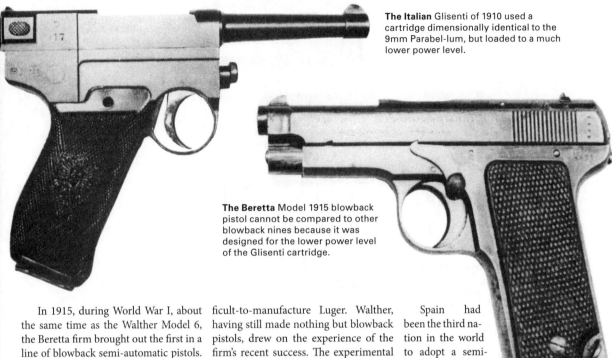

The Italian Glisenti of 1910 used a cartridge dimensionally identical to the 9mm Parabel-lum, but loaded to a much lower power level.

The Beretta Model 1915 blowback pistol cannot be compared to other blowback nines because it was designed for the lower power level of the Glisenti cartridge.

In 1915, during World War I, about the same time as the Walther Model 6, the Beretta firm brought out the first in a line of blowback semi-automatic pistols. They included a chambering for the 9mm Glisenti. These pistols, along with later 1919 and 1923 variants, supplemented the Glisenti as Italian military pistols.

The lower power of the 9mm Glisenti cartridge made it easily adaptable to traditional blowback design. To make the story as complete as possible, the Beretta 9mm blowbacks must be mentioned, but they cannot be compared with the others, as they were never meant to be used with cartridges of the Luger power level.

Following Germany's defeat in World War I, manufacture of military pistols in that country was restricted. Walther introduced the Models 7, 8 and 9 as constantly improving pocket pistols. And in 1929, the firm introduced its famous 32-caliber Model PP (Polizei Pistole). Still a blowback pistol, the PP introduced the double-action trigger mechanism to the Walther line and ended the system of designating pistol models by number. The new PP was immediately popular, and in 1931 a smaller version, the PPK, came out.

By the early 1930s, Germany had begun to rearm in violation of the Versailles Treaty. A standard 9mm military pistol was wanted to replace the dif-

ficult-to-manufacture Luger. Walther, having still made nothing but blowback pistols, drew on the experience of the firm's recent success. The experimental 9mm blowback pistols designed had the appearance of an enlarged PP, with a similar double-action trigger mechanism. Aware of the shortcomings of the Model 6, the company lengthened the barrel from 4¾ to 5 inches, allowing a longer spring and heavier slide. Total weight increased from 33 to 39 ounces.

The pistol — actually several different variations — was designated the Walther Model MP (Militär Pistole). The design still was not able to withstand the continued use of the 9mm Parabellum service ammunition.

Discouraged by the performance of their new blowback 9mm, Walther began development of a locked-breech pistol, retaining the double-action mechanism. This development led to the adoption by the German army, in 1938, of the now-famous Walther P-38. Only a small number of Model MP blowback 9mm pistols were made, and they are very scare today.

While the Germans had produced several unsuccessful pistols in an attempt to field a blowback that would work well with the 9mm Parabellum cartridge, the Spanish did much better with another, slightly more powerful cartridge.

Spain had been the third nation in the world to adopt a semi-automatic pistol. The Bergmann locked-breech pistol of 1903 had been chosen as the official sidearm. Caliber was 9mm Largo (9mm Bergmann-Bayard), a cartridge of the same diameter as the Luger round, but using a case four millimeters longer.

In 1921, a simpler pistol for the same cartridge was adopted. This was the Astra Model 400, designed by the Spanish firm of Esperanza y Unceta. The 400 was a blowback. Its long 6-inch barrel allowed a very long, very strong recoil spring — second only to that of the Dreyse in strength. It also had a slide of substantial weight and a concealed hammer which helped hold the slide forward during the time of highest pressure.

The Astra 400 worked well and was used through the Spanish Civil War. When German forces occupied France in 1940, they purchased about 6000 of the big Astras as substitute standard pistols. However, this gave some soldiers pistols chambered for a nonstandard cartridge.

Now, it has been said that the Astra 400 will function reliably with the shorter 9mm Parabellum cartridge. Without

(Above) **An undetermined** number of Llama 9mm Parabellum pistols were made in blowback configuration.

(Left) **Most parts** for the Llama 9mm blowback are the same as those of the locked-breech version. The barrel has no locking notches and no link.

going into the differing opinions on this subject, it seems sufficient to say that the Germans did not find the practice satisfactory.

About 1942 or 1943, the Germans requested that the Astra design be revised, specifically to use the 9mm Parabellum cartridge. The resulting pistol was called the Astra Model 600, although German records refer to it as the Model 600/43.

The redesigned 9mm Parabellum pistol was slightly smaller and lighter than the original 400. Its barrel length of 5¼ inches still allowed a long, strong recoil spring and a fairly heavy slide. The pistol worked well and was accepted by the German army. An acceptance stamp appears on some pistols; apparently the Germans trusted Astra workmanship and it has been reported that not all pistols accepted were stamped.

There were 10,450 reportedly delivered to German forces by late 1944. Then, after the Allied invasion of Europe, Ger-man occupation of the French-Spanish border area ended and the Germans retreated. An order of appoximately 28,000 pistols was not delivered.

A basically good pistol chambered for an increasingly popular cartridge, the Astra 600 stayed in production through World War II and for a short time beyond. A number were sold to the post-war German government for police use. Total number of pistols made was 59,400.

World War II was also responsible for another blowback 9mm Parabel-lum design. The little-known Tarn pistol was designed by a Polish exile. Development work was carried out at the Swift Rifle Company in London, reportedly by Free Polish engineers eager to provide arms for a possible reoccupation of Poland. The Tarn used a slide of substantial weight and a strong recoil spring around its fairly long barrel to control the 9mm cartridge.

Several specimens were tested by the British in 1945, with negative results. The pistols were found to be poorly made, the recoil was said to be violent, and it was difficult for the test personnel to pull the slide back.

Only nine Tarn pistols were made, all experimental prototypes with varying features. After the war, the pistols were acquired by an American importer and sold to collectors.

The years after the war saw new military interest in lighter firearms. The U.S. Army drew up requirements for new weapons, including a new lightweight pistol. For the first time, the 9mm Parabellum cartridge was seriously considered.

A series of tests was begun in 1948. Evaluated against the standard 45-caliber pistol were four 9mm entries. Colt produced a shortened 9mm Government Model that later became the Commander. Smith & Wesson offered a new 9mm pistol which became their Model

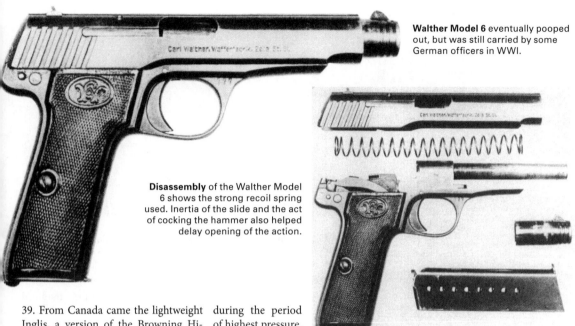

Walther Model 6 eventually pooped out, but was still carried by some German officers in WWI.

Disassembly of the Walther Model 6 shows the strong recoil spring used. Inertia of the slide and the act of cocking the hammer also helped delay opening of the action.

39. From Canada came the lightweight Inglis, a version of the Browning Hi-Power with an aluminum frame. The final 9mm entry was a new concept — the blowback T3.

The T3 was developed by High Standard Manufacturing Company under a contract with the U.S. Army. It was the first attempt to specifically adapt the 9mm Parabellum cartridge to a short, light pistol of blowback design.

The T3 had a heavy spring around the barrel and an external hammer, both of which aided control of the initial pressure of firing. However, results with the light pistol were not promising until a new chamber design was tried.

An annular cut was made around the circumference of the chamber. On firing, the cartridge case expanded into this cut; the force required to reduce the case back to original size retarded the rearward movement of the slide during the period of highest pressure. This novel method of adapting the 9mm Parabellum round to the blowback design showed considerable potential. The T3, however, did not do particularly well in the tests.

About 1955, the decision was made to retain the 1911A1 45-caliber pistol in service. Work on the T3 was stopped.

It is uncertain just how many T3 pistols were made. All the pistols apparently differed somewhat from each other. Some variations that were begun were never completed. Estimates of finished pistols range from less than a dozen to about two dozen.

Although the T3 project was not successful, the American shooter derived benefits from the test program in the forms of the Colt Commander and the Smith & Wesson Model 39. These two American pistols, along with the large numbers of World War II souvenir pistols, introduced American shooters to the 9mm. Thus began the popularity of that caliber in the United States.

During the 1950s and 1960s, with western nations updating their arsenals, other 9mm pistols and huge volumes of surplus ammunition came on the market. Surplus ammunition selling at a few cents per round made it desirable to own a 9mm pistol, even if that caliber were not a shooter's first choice. During this post-war period, there was a demand for newly made pistols as well as for the low-priced but serviceable surplus arms. Three new blowback nines were introduced.

One of the new designs, which never really reached the production stage, was the Bernardelli.

The Bernardelli firm of Gardone, Italy, had been in the firearms business since 1865. Their first semi-automatic pistol was a simple but well-made vest-pocket 25. It appeared at the end of the war, in 1945. By the end of the decade, the company had expanded its line to include larger pistols of 22-, 32- and 380-caliber, all of the same basic blowback design.

Observing the popularity of the 9mm Parabellum cartridge, company

Collectors may cringe, but the writer fired a Walther Model 6 in 1987, with reduced hand-loads.

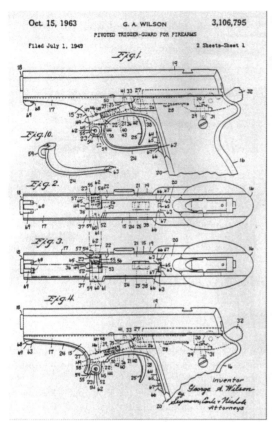

After WWII, the U.S. Army tested a blowback 9mm pistol, the T3. This is an experimental double-column magazine version that was never finished.

officials began a project in the 1950s to see if the Bernardelli design could handle the larger cartridge. The resulting 9mm Parabellum pistols were enlarged versions of the basic blowback mechanism. They featured a strong recoil spring around the 315/16-inch barrel, a moderately heavy (11-ounce) slide and an outside hammer with a noticeably stiff mainspring. Buffers on the frame beneath the barrel cushioned the slide at its rearward travel.

These features were not enough. Performance with the full-power cartridge was not satisfactory. Only a small number of the pistols were made, and they are very rare today. The total number produced (which includes several variations, including striker-fired versions) has been estimated at less than 100.

A second design introduced during the 1950s was the Astra Model 800 "Condor." The Spanish manufacturer, by then doing business as Unceta y Cia., sought to capitalize on the good repu-

tation of the Astra Model 600. The wartime Model 600 was redesigned and the resulting pistol was introduced in 1958.

The Model 800 retained the tubular appearance and stiff springs of the wartime pistol, but featured an exposed hammer and a slide with a shorter rear portion. The redesigned frame did away with the grip safety and positioned the thumb safety at the rear, behind the left grip.

Although it apparently enjoyed some success in Europe, the Condor pistol never appeared in America in any great quantity. It is reported that a total of slightly more than 11,400 were made before production ended about a decade later, in 1968.

A third 9mm Parabellum blowback design of the '50s was the MAB Model R.

The French firm, Manufacture d'Arms Automatique, of Bayonne, had made 32-caliber pocket pistols from 1933 until 1940. After the occupation, many thousands were made for the Germans during World War II.

In the post-war years, the company expanded its line of small- and medium-size pistols. Included were guns of 22, 32 and 380 calibers. During the mid-1950s,

the basic blowback design was modified in an attempt to offer a 9mm Parabellum pistol.

The design was innovative. As might be expected, the overall size was enlarged, and a strong spring and fairly heavy (12-ounce) slide were used. An outside hammer was utilized.

The really novel feature, however, was the barrel mounting. Instead of being fixed to the frame, the barrel was allowed some forward-backward movement. With the slide back, the barrel was pushed to its rearward position by a small coil spring.

With the action closed, the slide, under the influence of the strong recoil spring, pushes the barrel to its forward position. On firing, the barrel (under rearward pressure from its small spring) tends to move back as the slide moves back. MAB engineers apparently hoped this feature would provide at least some of the benefits of a locked-breech system, in which the barrel and slide move back locked together.

The 9mm pistol had a 4¾-inch barrel and weighed about 36 ounces. It was marketed in the United States by Winfield Arms Company of Los Angeles as "Le Militaire." A related company, Western Arms Company, also handled the MAB pistols. To the right-side slide legend of "MADE IN FRANCE" was added an additional stamping, "FOR W.A.C."

MAB Model R, right view, shows addition of "FOR W.A.C." to the original legend. Model R was made in the late '50s to early '60s.

The barrel of the Model R could move rearward under spring pressure for a short distance, as the slide began to move. The design concept seemed to allow the barrel and slide to move back together, thus gaining some of the benefit of a locked-breech system. The actual effect may be different.

In 1943, a redesigned Astra pistol, the Model 600, was produced in caliber 9mm Parabellum for the German army.

The Astra Model 600 has a very heavy recoil spring. The combined 13-ounce slide and muzzle-cap weight and the energy used to cock the hammer also help control opening of the action.

The Model R did not sell well. It was introduced in the late '50s and by the early '60s was no longer offered. The pistol is illustrated only for years 1958 through 1963 in the Gun Digest catalog sections.

The price remained stable at $62 throughout this period. However, during this time a brand-new commercial Browning Hi-Power (in the same caliber) retailed for $74.50. The lower price was not enough to spur sales of the French pistol.

A demonstration of the Model R does not create a positive impression. There is no manual slide release or man-ual slide lock. Both these functions are controlled by the magazine. The strange mechanics of the design thus required a good magazine.

After firing, the slide locks open against the magazine follower. When the magazine is withdrawn (with some difficulty, as it is held by the slide under strong spring pressure) an auxiliary lock moves up to retain the slide open.

Inserting a loaded magazine releas-es this lock, automatically running the slide forward to chamber a round. In-serting an empty magazine will (usual-ly) release the slide a split second before the follower catches it again. Lacking a good magazine, there is virtually no way to release the slide without a partial dis-assembly of the pistol

These factors, along with the awk-ward stretch to the thumb safety and the high, sharp sights, probably were enough to dampen most shooters' en-thusiasm for the pistol.

Serial numbers of observed speci-mens range from those in the 200 series to the 1100 series. Experimental turn-ing-barrel locked-breech designs (also, for some reason, designated as Model R) have been reported in the 1500 series. It would seem that the total production of these blowbacks may be somewhere

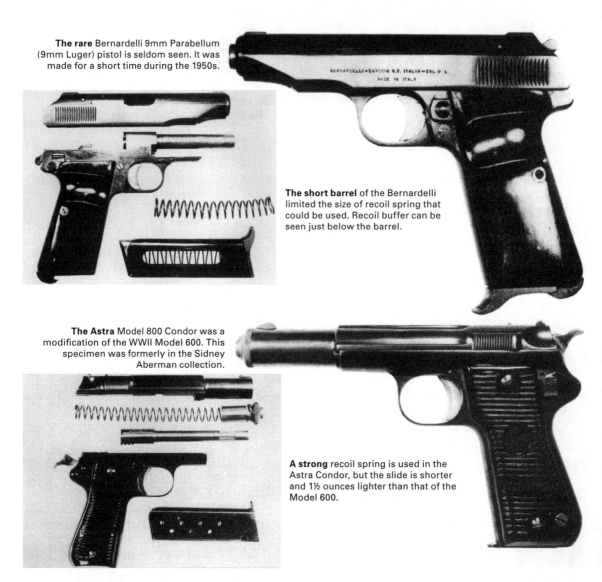

The rare Bernardelli 9mm Parabellum (9mm Luger) pistol is seldom seen. It was made for a short time during the 1950s.

The short barrel of the Bernardelli limited the size of recoil spring that could be used. Recoil buffer can be seen just below the barrel.

The Astra Model 800 Condor was a modification of the WWII Model 600. This specimen was formerly in the Sidney Aberman collection.

A strong recoil spring is used in the Astra Condor, but the slide is shorter and 1½ ounces lighter than that of the Model 600.

around 1200 to 1400 pieces.

The unusual system of having the barrel follow the slide back without a positive lock was not unique to the French pistol. During 1955–1957, the J. Kimball Arms Company of Detroit, Michigan, made a pistol for the U.S. 30 Carbine cartridge. The barrel also moved back with the slide without a mechanical lock.

However, the Kimball had longitudinal grooves or flutes cut into the chamber. The concept seemed to be that the cartridge case would expand into these grooves and be held to the barrel by friction while being held to the slide by the

extractor. The barrel and slide would move rearward together, delaying the blowback action.

It is well known that the Kimball system did not work as planned. A number of guns were damaged by the dangerous recoil, and the company failed within two years.

What is not so well known is that Kimball made a single prototype pistol to test the system in 9mm Para-bellum caliber. The writer examined it a number of years ago, but its location is unknown to me now.

During the late 1960s, the German firm of Heckler & Koch engaged in

development of a military firearm that could function as both a pistol and sub-machine gun. The caliber, naturally, was to be 9mm Parabellum.

Announced about 1970, the VP70 was a large blowback double-action-only pistol. It could be fitted with a shoulder stock. With the stock detached, it was a semi-automatic pistol; with the stock attached, it was capable of three-shot burst fire.

A modified version, the VP70Z, could be used only as a semi-automatic pistol. This version was marketed in the United States, beginning in about 1973 or 1974.

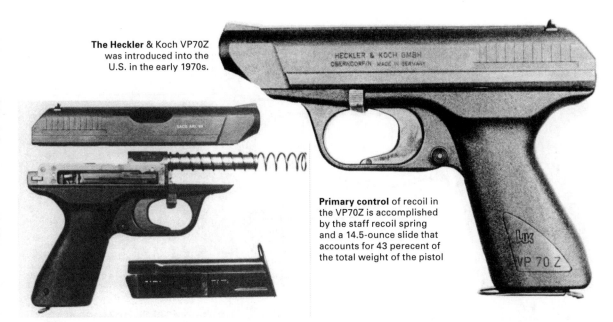

The **Heckler** & Koch VP70Z was introduced into the U.S. in the early 1970s.

HECKLER & KOCH GMBH
OBERNDORF/N · MADE IN GERMANY

Primary control of recoil in the VP70Z is accomplished by the staff recoil spring and a 14.5-ounce slide that accounts for 43 perecent of the total weight of the pistol

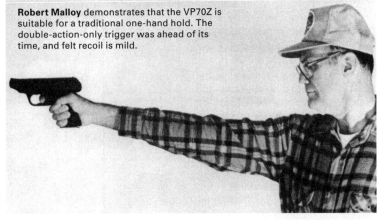

Robert Malloy demonstrates that the VP70Z is suitable for a traditional one-hand hold. The double-action-only trigger was ahead of its time, and felt recoil is mild.

Here we must make another side trip to define the scope of our interest in blowback nines. Other 9mm semiautomatic pistols based on blowback submachine-gun origins have been made and are being made. The Uzi, Wilkinson, Sterling and MAC designs are only a few. They are pistols in the legal sense, but do not lend themselves to natural one-hand use or traditional holster carry. Although they are fun to shoot and useful for special purposes, they will not be considered here.

The VP70Z, however, is a pistol by almost anyone's definition. Although large and bulky, it is suited to traditional one-hand shooting and holster carry.

The total weight is only about 33 ounces, but 43 percent of that weight is in the slide. It has a very heavy 14.5-ounce slide and a strong recoil spring. The final rearward motion of the slide is stopped against an insert in the takedown latch.

The VP70Z was comfortable to shoot and held 18 rounds. Still, it was not particularly popular. It was expensive, and for the money a shooter got a well-built, but ungainly and clumsy-looking, pistol with a long trigger pull for each shot. So the VP70Z was dropped from production about 1984.

The Spanish firm of Gabilondo,

manufacturers of the Llama line, made a 9mm Parabellum blowback pistol during the 1980s.

The reason for this is unclear. Gabilondo had been making locked-breech pistols of the Colt 1911 design under the Llama name since 1931. Llama locked-breech pistols in 9mm Parabellum caliber had been imported into the United States by Stoeger since about 1952.

With the manufacturing experiences and the machinery already in place, there would seem to be little advantage in switching to a blowback design, since most of the parts of the blowback 9mm are essentially the same as those of its locked-breech brethren. The barrel,

however, simply remains stationary in the frame. It does not tip up at the rear to lock into the slide and, indeed, had no locking notches or link. The standard under-barrel recoil spring arrangement of the locked-breech design was used.

While it apparently eliminated some machine work during manufacture, the blowback Llama 9mm was not a success. After a number had been produced, a product advisory was issued, and the blowback pistols were recalled.

Up until the 1980s, all blowback nines reaching the production stage had been full-size military-style pistols. The experimental T3 and the essentially experimental Bernardelli had been unsuc-

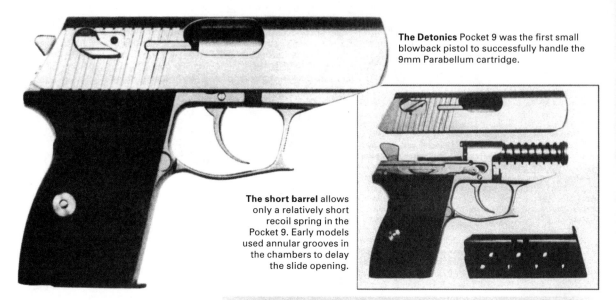

The Detonics Pocket 9 was the first small blowback pistol to successfully handle the 9mm Parabellum cartridge.

The short barrel allows only a relatively short recoil spring in the Pocket 9. Early models used annular grooves in the chambers to delay the slide opening.

cessful attempts to scale down the size.

By the mid-1980s, in spite of cautions from some circles, the 9mm Parabellum cartridge was widely accepted in the United States for police use and personal defense. The niche for a compact 9mm was recognized. Such a pistol would be more easily concealed and could serve as a same-caliber back-up for police officers who carried a nine as a duty pistol.

Two compact blowback designs appeared, the first of which was the Detonics Pocket 9.

Detonics Firearms Industries began in 1976 in Bellevue, Washington. Gradually, the firm became well known for its compact 45-caliber pistol. That pistol was a small locked-breech design based on a modification of the Colt 1911 system.

Detonics had made a few 9mm specimens of its standard compact locked-breech pistol. However, the 9mm was the same size as the 45 and offered few advantages.

A different prototype 9mm Parabellum pistol had been displayed at firearms industry gatherings for several years. In 1985, it was put into production as the Detonics Pocket 9.

A totally new pistol, the Pocket 9 was a blowback. It was made of stainless steel and featured a double-action trigger, ambidextrous safety and recessed sights.

The writer finds that the Pocket 9 works well, but can be a punishing pistol to shoot for an extended period.

Its short 3-inch barrel did not allow a very heavy slide (only 10.5 ounces) or a very long recoil spring. To control the opening of the action, the Detonics "Chamber-Lok" breech system was used.

A 1984 discussion between the writer and a Detonics representative (prior to the marketing of the Pocket 9) revealed that annular grooves were cut into the chamber walls. The case expanded into these grooves. Moving the case out of the chamber required a slight resizing, which delayed the slide opening. This is essentially the same method employed by High Standard during the development work on the T3.

For some reason, Detonics discontinued the "Chamber-Lok" annular grooves during the production of the Pocket 9. A pistol observed in the P2300 serial range has the grooves. One in the P3800 range does not.

Production of the Pocket 9 was short-lived — 1986, its second year of production, was also its last.

It is interesting to look at the 1986 Detonics price list. The standard version of the Pocket 9 is there, but two other versions are also listed. The Power 9 is the same pistol with a polished finish. The Pocket 9 LS is a "long-slide" variant with a 4-inch barrel. I have never seen either.

The **barrel** of this early Pocket 9, in the P2300 serial range, shows annular grooving in the chamber.

The **barrel** of this later Pocket 9, in the P3800 serial range, has a smooth, ungrooved chamber.

About the time the Detonics Pocket 9 went out of production, its niche was filled by an Israeli import.

The Sardius SD 9, originally known as the Sirkis SD 9, was the design of Israeli engineer Nehemiah Sirkis. The new compact blowback was imported in small quantities about 1986. By 1987, the SD 9 was handled in the United States by the Maryland firm Armscorp of America and was advertised nationally.

The Sardius is an interesting design. Made to be produced quickly and cheaply, a number of components are derived from heavy stampings. The grips are wrap-around plastic. Obviously designed for close-range undercover use, the trigger is double-action only. However, a manual safety is provided.

The breechblock is a separate piece, but locks solidly into the slide. The short 3-inch barrel did not allow a long, heavy recoil spring, so a new system was used. Four coil springs of different outside diameters are positioned, one inside the other, to operate on the same axis rod below the barrel. The four springs are held captive on their rod and are easily removed as a unit for disassembly.

This combination of springs, resisting the movement of the 10.5-ounce slide/breechblock assembly, serves to delay the breech opening.

The first SD 9 pistols imported into the

United States had some mechanical problems. Too, the crudely made European-style catch at the base of the magazine did not find favor with American shooters.

By 1989, a modified Sardius pistol had been introduced. The magazine release of the newer design was at the top of the left grip, where it could be operated by the shooter's right thumb. A trade-in policy was established. The owner of an early SD 9 could return it and step up to the later model for a small fee.

By early 1991, import and distribution of the Sardius SD 9 was being handled by the VWM company of Stafford, Virginia. At the time of this writing, VWM is still distributing the pistol, and a company representative reports that it is popular with law enforcement officers as a back-up pistol.

As we have seen, for a long time — almost three-quarters of a century — all blowback nines produced had been full-size military-type pistols. Then, in the mid-1980s, compact pocket-size pistols in blowback form appeared.

By the end of that decade, a new type appeared with the introduction of the Maverick.

Although full-size, it had little in common with previous military pistols. Its intended niche seemed to be for personal use as an inexpensive home defense pistol.

In September 1987, the new Maverick blowback 9mm pistol was quietly introduced to the American market. The concept of Ohioan Ed Stallard, the new pistol combined some of the design features of early pocket pistols with a full-power cartridge and late 20th century manufacturing techniques.

Ignoring current trends, the pistol has a single-action trigger mechanism, single-column magazine and thumb safety on the left only. The simple striker firing mechanism also uses the firing pin as an ejector. The design offers few surprises to those familiar with the blowback pocket automatics of many decades ago.

The construction of the pistol, though, is strictly modern. Plastics, easily cast alloys, steel stampings and unbreakable coil springs are used throughout. Roll pins instead of screws are used for assembly — the only screws are the grip screws. The grips themselves retain parts on the side of the frame.

The resulting pistol was made inexpensively and sold at a low price. It was heavy, with a squared-off, boxy shape and a wrinkle paint finish. By traditional standards, it was not particularly handsome, but it was the cheapest new pistol on the market chambered for the 9mm Parabellum cartridge.

Weight was the primary reason for the Maverick's easy handling of the 9mm cartridge. The original version was listed as 48 ounces (about as much as a Smith & Wesson 44 Magnum) and some specimens even ran a few ounces heavier. The 22-ounce slide is a large 43 percent of the total weight of the pistol. The inertia of the massive slide helps keep the case in the chamber longer, giving pressures a chance to drop.

Strangely, the recoil spring is not particularly heavy. Perhaps to make the pistol workable for women and the elderly, spring strength was kept moderate, and prime emphasis was placed on weight.

However, some other subtle techniques were used to control pressures. The rifling is cut only about .002-inch deep, about half the standard practice. This lowers initial resistance to the bul-

The **Sardius SD 9** was introduced in the late 1980s. It is manufactured in Israel, and heavy stampings are used in its construction.

SD 9 pistols of current manufacture have the magazine release button at the upper part of the left grip.

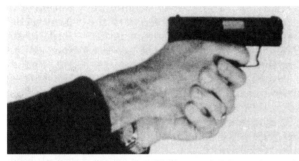

Although the grip of the Sardius SD 9 has a good shape, the recoil is heavy and the pistol is not pleasant to shoot for an extended period of time.

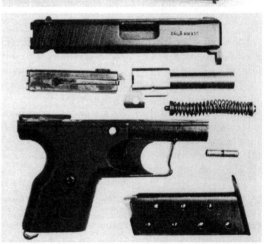

Slide opening of the Sardius SD 9 is delayed by four coil springs of different diameters, which are held captive around a common rod.

let and helps keep chamber pressure down. In addition, the slide in battery is designed for "zero headspace," allowing the cartridge no play between the chamber shoulder and the breech face. Looseness would have the effect, however slight, of letting the case "slam" back against the slide. Zero headspace allows only a "push" against the slide.

As the new pistols began to sell, the "Maverick" name was called into question in 1988. Although it had been registered by Stallard in Ohio, "Maverick" was registered nationally by a Texas shotgun company. A friendly agreement was reached, and the name of the pistol was changed.

Renaming of the pistol was in keeping with the policy of keeping expenses down. The original pistols bore this legend on the slide:

MAVERICK
FIREARMS
MODEL JS-9MM
Mfg. By Stallard
Arms Inc.
Mansfield, Oh.

The same die for the legend was kept, but the top line was simply ground off, getting rid of "MAVERICK FIREARMS." The pistol was known thereafter as the "Stallard."

In early 1991, a new grip frame with a curved rear portion was offered, with contoured grips to match the frame shape. The new frames were made of a lighter alloy. The total weight of the pistol went down to about 39 ounces, close to the weight of a Colt 1911. The weight of the slide, relative to the other parts, thus went up.

The version introduced in mid-1991 does away with the wrinkle finish in favor of smooth black or nickel. With little fanfare, the Stallard seems to be finding a market as an acceptable 9mm pistol at a low price.

In any discussion of blowback nines, the question of recoil naturally arises. How much do they kick? What is the recoil really like?

First, a clarification: Any cartridge has a certain recoil energy potential, and this is independent of what kind of arm fires it.

What we are really concerned with is "felt" recoil — the recoil sensed as shock

The Stallard JS-9MM pistol was originally introduced in the late 1980s as the "Maverick." Its boxy shape and wrinkle finish gave it a distinctive appearance.

Using a relatively light recoil spring, the JS-9MM pistol depends primarily on massive slide weight to delay opening.

to the shooter's hand. This is influenced, for all pistols, by their weight and the shape of the grips. For semiautomatic pistols, we must add the effects of how rapidly the slide moves back and how abruptly it stops at the end of its travel. We have seen that different designs have addressed these effects in different ways.

Second, a consideration: Shooting any firearm should be safe — for both the shooter and the firearm.

A shooter of a gun of historical or mechanical interest is a custodian of a bit of history. He should be certain of the firearm's condition and use only suitable ammunition. For some of the blowback nines, original ammunition is not suitable ammunition.

With these points in mind, let me share a few thoughts:

Your writer has never seen a Dreyse 9mm. In view of the rarity of the pistol and the warnings often repeated in old texts, it would probably be best not to shoot one, even with reduced loads.

The Walther Model 6 is also a scarce item. It is so nicely made, however, that I can well understand a desire to shoot one. Collectors may cringe, but in 1987, my brother, Robert Malloy, and I had the chance to shoot a Model 6. Only light handloads were used. As might be expected, it performed flawlessly. Felt recoil with the reduced loads was moderate. We suspected, though, that full-power 9mm loads might have been hard on both the shooter and the pistol. Parts for these pistols are not available. Think carefully before shooting one.

The Walther MP blowbacks are rare, indeed. I have never seen one, and apparently the few existing specimens are in museums or private collections. One would expect traditional Walther quality and shooting characteristics somewhat better than those of the Model 6. I would love to try one out, but only with reduced loads.

Shooting the Astra 600 is a different story. Due to the heavy spring, heavy slide and hammer-cocking leverage, the rugged Spanish pistols seem to digest any 9mm Parabellum loads without ill effect. The felt recoil is moderate.

A characteristic of the Astra Model 600 seems to be good accuracy. Although the sights are not adjustable, all the 600s I have shot will shoot good groups, close to the aiming point. I have carried mine in the field. For small game and furbearers up to about raccoon or nutria size, it can be very effective.

The same, in general, can be said about the Astra Condor. Accuracy and effectiveness are essentially the same. For field use, the outside hammer can be an advantage. Strangely, though, although it is often considered an improvement of the basic 600 design, the Model 800 Condor is much harder to control during recoil.

A close look at the pistol tells us why. In order to adapt an outside hammer, the rear of the slide was shortened. The slide of the original 600 weighs 13 ounces; that of the 800 only 10.5 ounces. The lighter slide comes back faster and stops harder. In addition, with the hammer and thumb safety moved rearward, the rear frame configuration is different. The web of the hand rides awkwardly low on the grip, making muzzle rise difficult to control.

In 1984, I spent some shooting-range time with a Condor. Accuracy was excellent. However, my notes show recoil as "heavy." Cases were ejected 20–25 feet to the right. Shooting with one hand, the muzzle jump was sometimes bad enough that the thumb tended to push the safety "on" during recoil. Although a good-shooting pistol, the Astra 800 Condor does not offer the control of the 9mm round that its predecessor did.

The Tarn pistol was dropped from consideration by the British due to its "very violent" action. This would indicate that the power level of the military 9mm load was too much for this design to handle. With only nine experimental pieces reported made, the rare Tarn should not be considered a shooter.

The High Standard T3 was made in prototype form only, with almost every specimen slightly different from the others.

Contemporary reports indicated a substantial reduction of felt recoil using the grooved chamber over the plain chamber. Apparently the system was not without problems, however, and final military specifications pointedly required a plain chamber.

About 20 years ago, I had the opportunity of handling what was probably the first working model of the T3. It was then owned by automatic pistol collector Harry F. Klein. It felt good in the hand,

and I wondered what it would be like to shoot. The T3 pistols are all historically significant, and their shooting characteristics have been documented. There is hardly any reason that one should be shot now. Still, it certainly would be interesting.

The 9mm Kimball is a one-of-a-kind prototype. I examined it some time ago when it was also owned by Klein. While it would probably perform better than the 30 Carbine Kimballs, its present owner should cherish it as a collection piece only.

The Bernardelli 9mm Parabellum is a rare pistol, and few would get a chance to shoot one. I was fortunate that one was in the possession of my brother, Robert Malloy in 1987.1 shot the pistol only with light handloads. The large frame offered a good grip, but recoil was heavy, even with the reduced loads. Any positive effect of the recoil buffers must have been slight. I wondered then, since Bernardelli had enlarged the frame beyond pocket pistol size, why they had not made a version with a longer barrel. This would have allowed a heavier slide and stronger spring.

The MAB Model R is a strange pistol. For shooting, the unusual mechanism makes it very difficult to clear a malfunction if one does occur.

Recoil has been described by another shooter as "stiff." I have fired three of these pistols and feel that perhaps that term is not strong enough. Cases go at high speed 20 to 30 feet to the right. My notes indicate that the recoil seems to increase as you shoot; this may just be subjective, though. Certainly, the pistol kicks fiercely with full loads. It is not pleasant to shoot, even with reduced loads.

The Model R's rearward-moving barrel has no positive effect that I could note. Indeed, a suspicion has been growing in my mind that the spring-loaded barrel, contrary to its intended function, may actually give the slide an additional rearward push at the beginning of its cycle.

The Heckler & Koch VP70Z is another strange pistol, but primarily because of its bulk and double-action-only trigger mechanism. As a shooter, it is controllable and actually fun to shoot. The heavy 14.5-ounce slide and strong spring seem to effectively tame the recoil of any standard 9mm loading. A friend of mine described his as a "pussycat."

I have never fired one of the blowback Llama 9mm pistols, but I have examined a specimen. Like the other 1991-styled Llamas, the parts are big and substantial looking. The Louisiana shooter who owns it also has a standard locked-breech Llama 9mm. He could remember little difference between firing the two guns. However, remember that a recall notice was issued on the blowback version. If fired, it should be with mild loads only.

The small Detonics Pocket 9 looks as if it would be brutal to shoot, and most shooters feel it lives up to that appearance. The word most commonly used to describe the recoil is "sharp." Your writer agrees. The pistol I fired (one of the later ungrooved-chamber versions) delivers a hard, sharp blow to the hand with each shot. No one who tried it wanted to shoot it for long. However, the pistol itself does not seem to be affected by the recoil. As a police backup or a personal protection arm, it would be fired very little. For its in tended purpose, the heavy recoil is acceptable.

Late-production Stallard pistols, beginning in 1991, featured a lighter frame with a curved rear strap, contoured grips and other refinements.

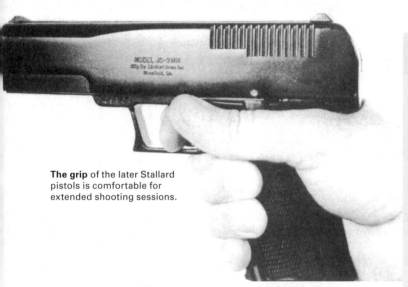

The grip of the later Stallard pistols is comfortable for extended shooting sessions.

Selected Bibliography

Antaris, Leonardo M. Astra Automatic Pistols. Colorado: Firac Publishing Company, 1988.

Cormach, A.J.R. German Small Arms. New York: Exeter Books, 1979.

Ezell, Edward C. Handguns of the World. Harrisburg, PA: Stack-pole, 1981.

Fjestad, S.P Blue Book of Gun Values. Minneapolis, MN: Blue Book Publications, Inc., 1991.

Hatcher, Julian S. "Kimball Pistol." American Rifleman, (October, 1955), p. 74.

Hogg, Ian V, and John Weeks. Pistols of the World. San Rafael, CA: Presidio Press, 1978.

Krasne, J.A., editor. Encyclopedia and Reference Catalog of Auto Loading Guns. San Diego, CA: Triple K Mfg. Co., 1989.

Magee, Darel. "Big Bore Blow-Back Auto Pistols." Gun Collector's Digest, p. 171–177. North-brook, IL: DBI Books, Inc., 1974.

Petty, Charles E. High Standard Automatic Pistols, 1932–1950. Charlotte, NC: American Ordnance Publications, 1976.

Smith, W.H.B. Book of Pistols and Revolvers. Harrisburg, PA: Stackpole, 1968.

Whittington, Robert D., III. "Astra Pistols in the German Army." Guns Magazine, (November, 1968), p. 41.

Wilson, R.K. Textbook of Automatic Pistols. Plantersville, SC: Small Arms Technical Publishing Co., 1943.

It is possible that the earlier grooved-chamber version would be gentler to shoot. Still, its small size and relatively light weight suggest it would not be pleasant.

Although one owner described the recoil of his Sardius SD 9 as "more like a 44 Magnum," I experienced slightly less felt recoil shooting one than when shooting the Pocket 9. Because the total weight and slide weight of both pistols are almost identical, it may be that the four springs of the Sardius really do make a difference. Or it may be that the larger grip, of different shape, allows a better grasp to help keep the pistol under control.

This is not to say that shooting the SD 9 is pleasant. It is decidedly unpleasant to shoot for any length of time. Again, though, designed for undercover use, it would not be fired much, and the recoil would not be noticed in an emergency situation.

If one's only introduction to blowback nines had been the compact ones just described, trying out the Maverick or Stallard pistols would open a new world.

The tremendous weight of the original pistol just soaks up 9mm recoil. With the recent lighter version, the weight has been principally removed from the frame, not the slide. This means that the weight of the slide has actually increased — relatively — to a full 50 percent of the total weight of the pistol.

With either version, felt recoil is moderate. A variety of commercial loads, military ammunition and hand-loads were tried, and all were pleasant to shoot. Cases, depending on load, landed 5 to 10 feet away. My 13-year-old son, Patrick, often assists me in trying things out. He considers the Stallard fun to shoot.

The story of blowback nine pistols is an interesting one. Designed specifically for a strong locked-breech action, the 9mm Parabellum cartridge had held an appeal for manufacturers in many countries who have tried to adapt it to the simpler blowback design.

Heavy recoil springs, multiple springs, hammer-cocking leverage, recoil buffers, grooved chambers, fluted chambers, shallow rifling, zero headspace, spring-loaded barrels and heavy slide weight — all these things have been tried. Various combinations of these factors have been used with different pistols.

Some have worked better than others. Some blowback nines had extremely short production runs. Some were essentially experimental, with only one or a few pieces made. Others achieved relatively large-scale production, with thousands or tens of thousands of pistols made.

Through it all, the unlikely combination of the 9mm Parabellum cartridge and the blowback design has endured for over eight decades. Blowback nines may well be with us for some time to come.

Special thanks to Robert Malloy, Harry F Klein, Robert W Schumacher and the other shooters and collectors who shared their experiences and made their pistols available to the writer.

38 Snubbie or a 9

In defensive guns there's a choice of two! ▮ Ralph Mroz

AN AWFUL LOT of trees die each year to provide paper for the never-ending attempt to educate the buying (emphasis on buying) public about their choices in handguns. This is because there are a lot of handgun manufacturers who each make a lot of guns, so there is a lot of stuff to write about. I do some of that writing myself. It goes: "The new Splatzmatic from the former Soviet Republic of Elbonia is really a nifty piece of defensive gear," and "Here's a new gun made entirely of recycled cardboard from Florida," and "Mary Gunsmith in Rugged, Montana, does things to a gun that you just have to see to believe."

I'm sure you know what I'm talking about.

I used to believe it was imperative for anyone considering a defensive handgun to carefully consider all of the choices available.

"What gun do you recommend for self-defense?" I have been asked many times.

My standard reply was, "That's like asking me what kind of woman (or man) you should marry. It's very individual. You have to consider your lifestyle; the kind of attack you are likely to encounter; your dress habits; the acceptance of guns in the company you keep; your physique; how important absolute concealment is to you; whether you have kids or not; and so on.

"After all," I'd say, "a suburban professional male might reasonably expect that his most likely assault would come in the form of random street violence from one or two perpetrators. He can get by with a low-capacity gun, and if he's average size or larger, then concealment isn't a problem. A petite woman who owns a restaurant, however, might have to be prepared for a planned home invasion by gang members intent on stealing the night's cash receipts. Shell need a high-capacity firearm, and she will have a concealment problem."

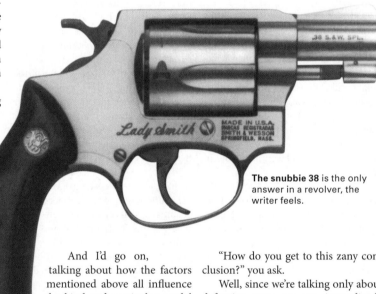

The snubbie 38 is the only answer in a revolver, the writer feels.

And I'd go on, talking about how the factors mentioned above all influence the kind and particular model of gun that you should buy. "Take your time," I'd say. "Evaluate all these factors and make a logical, reasoned decision."

That is good advice, and I still recommend that people do that. It helps them plan for the kind of defensive scenario they may someday encounter. But the problem is that those chains of reasoning all lead to only two handguns: The right gun is always either a J-frame snubnosed 38 Special revolver or a high-capacity 9mm pistol.

Now I'd better do some explaining. First off, I'm talking only about defensive handguns. Not long guns. Not competitive guns. Not hunting guns. Not offensive guns. Not duty guns. And, by corollary, I'm talking about a gun that must be carried concealed.

"How do you get to this zany conclusion?" you ask.

Well, since we're talking only about defensive guns, we can immediately rule out all single-action guns. Bye-bye to the 1911 and all its clones. Yes, I know that the 1911 is the best gun-fighting pistol in the world. I love 'em. If I were a CIA operative in Central America, I'd pack one. But I live in America, and when I shoot someone, I can't just smoke a cigar and burn rubber down the road. I will be responding to threats on my (or my family's) life, not participating in an act of war. I need to have the legal requirements of ability (my assailant had the ability to kill or cripple me), opportunity (he had the opportunity to do so), and jeopardy (he actually placed my life in imminent jeopardy) fulfilled, and I will face the possibility of criminal and civil charges.

As many more accomplished writers have pointed out at length, a defensive gun is a threat management tool, not an offensive weapon. The SA 1911 does indeed deliver the fastest and most accurate first shot, but the extra time needed for a DA first shot is hardly measurable in a real encounter. A criminally negligent accidental discharge from a cocked pistol with a 3-pound trigger, however, is a real possibility in the super-charged atmosphere of a life-or-death encounter. Under those circumstances, you don't want to try holding an aggressor at gunpoint with your trusty Colt. If you have to shoot someone defensively, you want to make damned sure that you shoot him only deliberately, and you want a gun that you can't later be accused of fir-

documented shootings with this round will change that opinion fast. It simply doesn't work very well. Yes, it's a gun, and it goes "Bang," but would you, literally, entrust your spouse's life to it?

If the snubbie doesn't suit, you have to go with a smallish 9mm.

Remember that all handgun rounds are anemic in terms of "stopping power." None of them has anywhere near the kind of record that you would, all else being equal, want to trust with your life. I mean, if you know you're going to be attacked today, you carry a shotgun or leave town, right? The only reason we carry handguns is because we don't know if today is the day we'll be assaulted, but we think it might be, and the considerations of our society disallow the toting of a shotgun ev-

40 (or 40 Smith & Wesson) round is almost a 9mm and less street-proven. There's just no reason (yet) to choose it over a 9mm. That is, the ballistic difference between a 40 and a 9mm is trivial compared to the difference that shot placement makes. If you like it, fine — choose a round that feeds reliably and no harm is done. For defensive purposes, I consider the 40 to be a minor variant of the 9mm.

The 45-caliber is certainly a good round, but all DA 45s are big guns — too big to conceal well (or at least comfortably) for most people. And again, the difference between 45 and 9mm ballistics is irrelevant to the difference that shot placement makes. Get the smaller gun and practice a lot with it — something you should do with any gun, anyway. Besides, if I have the choice of sixteen (pre-ban) 9mm rounds or ten 45-caliber rounds, I'll go for the higher capacity every time. This is not because I'm such an incredibly poor shot I have to "spray and pray." It's because I've role-played scenarios with paintball, and I can assure you that, when you have to defend against multiple opponents or attackers who are partially behind cov-

> IF I HAVE THE CHOICE OF SIXTEEN (PRE-BAN) 9MM ROUNDS OR TEN 45-CALIBER ROUNDS, I'LL GO FOR THE HIGHER CAPACITY EVERY TIME. WHEN YOU HAVE TO DEFEND AGAINST MULTIPLE OPPONENTS OR ATTACKERS WHO ARE PARTIALLY BEHIND COVER, YOU WILL WANT AS MANY ROUNDS AVAILABLE AS POSSIBLE.

ing wrongly because of a reckless "hair trigger." Yes, there are men and women out there so highly trained with an SA pistol that they are probably immune from these caveats. They know (with the humility that comes from competence) who they are. Chances are you aren't one of them.

Moving on to caliber — that's easy, too. No one seriously recommends any caliber under 38 for defensive purposes. Some will make a stretch and include the 380, but a review of the available

erywhere. We carry handguns because they are the most potent weapon we can conveniently carry, not because they're the weapon we really want when harm comes our way.

Within this context, 38s, particularly in +P, have a good reputation for incapacitating aggressors. There are lots of good 38 loads to choose from. The 9mm is an acceptable round, too, if you choose your loads carefully. There are some abysmal rounds in this caliber and some with a good record. The

er, you will want as many rounds available as possible.

Yes, if I can't hit a single assailant who's in the open at 5.3 feet with 2.6 rounds (or whatever this year's averages are), then I do have a marksmanship problem, not a capacity problem. But that's not what I said. So if you really love the 45 and you're able to conceal it in a DA pistol on your (presumably size large) frame, then hey, go for it!

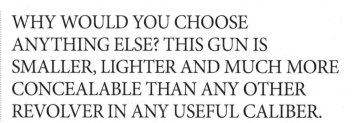

The 38 Special cartridge is about optimum for the carry-every-day defensive round.

So we are now reduced to a DA 38 revolver or a 9mm pistol. This is getting easier. If you go for the 38, you should choose a 2-inch aluminum J-frame revolver — that is, a Smith & Wesson 442. Why would you choose anything else? This gun is smaller, lighter and much more concealable than any other revolver in any useful caliber. It's accurate out to reasonable combat distances (up to 20 yards). It can't take a steady diet of +P loads, true, but there are some very nice standard 38 loads to choose from — Magsafe being perhaps the best choice. It offers only 2-inch ballistics, yes, but if you intelligently choose your ammunition (see my comments about Magsafe ammo), you can compensate.

defensive reason to choose any other revolver.

If you go with the 9mm, then nearly all of the high-capacity 9mm pistols from the major manufacturers are reliable, and most are close to the same size. Simply choose the smallest one that best suits your hand and personality. You old-fashioned guys will want one of the heavy all-steel jobs; you new-age types will go for the plastic; and those of you in between will probably opt for an alloy-frame gun.

So, as promised, here we are: The right gun is always either a J-frame snubnosed revolver or a high-capacity 9mm pistol!

Of course, everyone has their individual preferences in a gun. Some like tritium night sights (I think they're a must), and some don't (go figure.) Some people want their backstraps

The 9mm Luger is the only other choice for defense, the writer believes.

and/or frontstraps stippled (never checkered!), and some can do without. Men and women with small hands will want shorter triggers and smaller

work on 442s and 9mms. These modifications and options are what allow only two guns to compose the entire practical universe of defensive guns.

And OK — other guns are alright, too, once the shooting starts. Larger revolvers are fine, if you want to carry the extra bulk. Larger caliber pistols are OK, too, as explained above. It's just that there are better reasons to make the 38 snubby (in a 442) or the wonder-nine your first choice.

Industry events of the last couple years have added some alternatives. Magsafe rounds, for example, and others have brought new levels of incapacitation potential to the tiny calibers, and they may prove to give the 22, 25, 32 and 380 acceptable effective power. As shootings with them accumulate, the record will tell. Also, the size of major-caliber pistols has come down, with the 45 AMT Back-Up being the most notable example. To the extent that this gun is reliable with your load of choice, it is a good first choice, too.

However, the right first-choice defensive gun is always either a J-frame snubnosed revolver or a high-capacity 9mm pistol. No doubt about it!

WHY WOULD YOU CHOOSE ANYTHING ELSE? THIS GUN IS SMALLER, LIGHTER AND MUCH MORE CONCEALABLE THAN ANY OTHER REVOLVER IN ANY USEFUL CALIBER.

You could go with a steel-frame small revolver, but there's no need to. You could choose another 2-inch revolver from Smith & Wesson or another manufacturer, but you wouldn't want to rely on it firing from within a pocket (whereas the 442 has an enclosed hammer). You could go to a longer barrel length (even J-frames are available with a 3-inch barrel), but you'd give up some concealability and certainly almost all pocket carryability. There's just no

grips. Some damned fools (like me) even like their triggers grooved (even on a revolver!). Some folks want their guns shiny (a liability-deterring asset, I think), and some want them dark (for those clandestine assassinations, I can only assume.)

That's fine. All of those modifications and others are easily accomplished on a Smith & Wesson 442 or any of the high-quality 9mm pistols. Gunsmith Karl Sokol is particularly well known for his

Are 22 Pocket Pistols Practical?

▌ Warren Peters

FLT (Old Model) Auto Nine: left thumb releases safety; fair shooter. John Malloy photo.

Wilkinson Sherry can disappear in your hand — has 138 bulk factor.

More than half of these United States now permit honest citizens to carry concealed weapons. With this privilege — which many of us think is a right — comes a need for discretion. Many people and some police take offense at behavior they perceive to be culturally incorrect. In winter, handguns of all sizes may be easily shielded from nervous eyes, but summer in the south and west challenges concealment. A couple strolling in a city in muscle shirts, walking shorts, and thongs must have pocket pistols if they are to be armed.

In that context, I visualize pocket pistols as barely, marginally, and readily concealable. These classes encompass many current and discontinued handgun models.

Barely concealable are snubnose 38 Special revolvers of the type made by Smith & Wesson, Rossi, and Taurus, and most 380 autoloading pistols.

Marginally concealable are the smaller 380s such as the Grendel and AMT Backup, and 22 autos of similar size. Some marginally concealable 22s are available in larger calibers.

Readily concealable are tiny 25 autos like the Baby Browning and its clones, plus a few 22 autos (some available in 25, even 32) and 22 revolvers of like size.

To compare all these, I have coined the term Bulk Factor, which is the product of a handgun's length, height, and width (to the nearest 1/10") and weight (to the nearest 1/2 oz, fully loaded). Weight is an important concealability element because of sag. The Bulk Factor of a number of pocket pistols appears in the included table. The boundaries between

my concealability classes cannot be fixed rigidly because other factors apply, such as shape of the gun, its carrier's size, and garment fashions.

This report focuses on the marginally and readily concealable 22 autoloaders because of their surging popularity, in spite of their questionable defensive capability and functional reliability. I don't condemn the choice of others merely because I prefer something a little heavier. Practice is an essential factor in defense, and the 22 undeniably is the least expensive route to extensive shooting. All references herein to the 22 are directed to the 22 Long Rifle cartridge, unless otherwise indicated.

To get this going, I acquired one of each gun discussed below, along with assorted brands of 22 ammunition. Velocities spanne hyper, high, standard, some target and subsonic. The shooting was conducted over the course of more than a year. I broke in all new pistols with at least 100 rounds, mostly with

high-velocity ammo. Then, unless otherwise noted, in each gun I fired four full magazines, plus a round in the chamber, of each ammo variety on hand. I stopped after two loadings if a particular ammo variety clearly wasn't working, and I formally tested the subsonic only in the smallest pistols, one load only. Initially I had an elaborate table to show each gun's performance with all loads, but this system broke down from sheer volume.

Few of the pistols worked reliably with hyper or standard ammo, and most expressed preferences among varieties of high-velocity ammo. Hyper velocities are achieved with a light bullet, subsonic 22s did not open slides enough to eject the hulls from any of the small pistols, which have relatively light slides and stiff recoil springs; one must suppose that the fabled assassins' silenced pistols are specifically regulated. Accuracy was not a performance criterion for those belly guns; however, they all did a heavy number on the seven-yard combat target, despite generally miserable sights. No key holing was observed at this short range, but from a few guns it did appear at 25 yards.

Barely Concealable Guns

Barely concealable 22s available to me were the Smith & Wesson Model 2214 (short version of S&W's slabsided 22 auto), Smith & Wesson 61 (ancestor of the 2214), Llama XV (a miniature of Colt's 1911), AMT 22 Backup, and Heckler & Koch HK4.

All performed well with various high-velocity and standard-velocity loads. Because of their size and their availability (except for the Smiths) in 380 (Llama also in 32, and H&K in 32 and 25, as well as in 380), I did not break them in and test them as thoroughly as I did the smaller pistols. The 2214 was the only test pistol in this or any category that functioned well with hyper-velocity ammo. Others tended to smokestack with hyper, although the H&K did this only once. The 2214 ejected subsonic loads, but did not feed them satisfactorily; I did not try those loads in the others. If I had to settle for this size 22, then smooth performance, price and current availability would propel me toward the S&W 2214.

Marginally Concealable

Marginally concealable pistols I tested were the Galesi 9, Walther TPH, Iver Johnson TP22 (some were sold under the "American" label), and the Phoenix HP22. All but Walther come in 25, as well.

The Galesi, no longer imported (a few came in 22 Long), exhibits the best quality, and mine has a good trigger. However, its magazine will not feed if loaded with more than five rounds (the bullets tip downwards), and its weak firing-pin spring occasionally fails to light the fire. All high-velocity rounds and two standard-velocity brands cycled perfectly when they did ignite.

The Walther TPH, basically a scaled-down PPK made in brilliant stainless steel by Interarms in the USA, was a $325 disappointment. In addition to its difficult safety and mushy trigger, my TPH could not be persuaded to perform reliably with any ammo. An assortment of maladies, including feeding, extraction and ejection, defied analysis. This model was discontinued for a while and recently re-introduced; I've not tested a later sample. The European version is made with a duraluminum frame, which might drop it into the readily concealable category. I cannot comment on that version's performance because it doesn't meet BATF's thoughtful import points minimum.

Iver Johnson, also a PPK copy (this one by Erma) has a fair single-action trigger pull, but double-action (first round) is gargantuan. However, my TP22 works well with all high-velocity ammo.

The Phoenix HP22, which like the TP22 sells for a bit over $100, is a racy design with two (count 'em-two!) safeties; one on the slide and one frame-mounted. This belt and suspenders arrangement prevents not only firing, but also slide retraction, cocking, and magazine removal. I had to use my bowscale to weigh its single-action trigger pull: 17 pounds! The Phoenix has a rear sight that is adjustable for windage only. During break-in, hardly any ammo worked, but afterwards my HP22 functioned perfectly even with target loads. Moral: don't give up too quickly.

Readily Concealable

Readily concealable 22 pistols tested were the Lorcin L22, Jennings J-22, Sterling 302, SEDCO SP-22 (all of which

Sterling 302: easiest slide to jack, good shooter — bulk points up to 252.

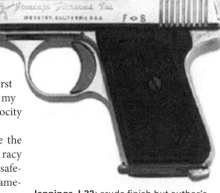

Jennings J-22: crude finish but author's favorite autoloader. Bulk factor: 213

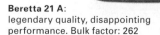

Beretta 21 A: legendary quality, disappointing performance. Bulk factor: 262

Walther TPH: stainless double-action; very expensive, disappointing. Bulk Factor: 270

Galesi Mod. 9: well-made, good performer, no longer imported. Bulk factor: 339

cost less than $100), Beretta 21-A, Norton TP-70, FTL Auto Nine (old model), and Wilkinson Sherry (new model Auto Nine).

Lorcin may offer the cheapest 22 pistol, a totally pot-metal production. Compactness is compromised by a magazine extension I am tempted to grind off. Esthetics aside, the L22 flawlessly digested all high-velocity ammo offered it.

The Jennings has a gritty trigger and the least expensive appearance, with chrome mottling and alloy casting bubbles. It appears fragile, but no parts failed during the test. Despite this, my J-22 welcomed both high-velocity and standard-velocity ammo. It has a thin, serrated sliding safety that is easier to manipulate than it appears to be.

Sterling is the sturdiest looking. Its trigger pull is aggravated by a sear angle that retracts the cocked striker an additional 1/16" before let-off. My 302, representing one-quarter of Sterling's blue/stainless 22/25 family, did well with

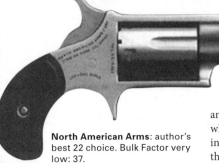

North American Arms: author's best 22 choice. Bulk Factor very low: 37.

most, but not all, high-velocity ammo.

The SEDCO, of neatly painted non-ferrous alloy, is the sleekest of the lot, with smoothly beveled corners and edges. Unfortunately, I couldn't get any ammo to work reliably in my SP-22. Usually a fired case remained in the chamber, indicating a problem.

The American-made double-action Beretta 21-A is the single-action 22 Shot Minx/25 Jetfire on steroids. Available also in 32, it compares very well in apparent quality with its Italian cousins. I did not test an identical model made by Taurus. Trigger action in both double-action and single-action modes is smooth and light, although in double action it is difficult to keep the finger from rubbing on the bottom of the trigger guard. First round must be loaded in the tip-up barrel; attempts to jack a round into the chamber from the magazine resulted in unintentional field stripping. Sharp edges on the slide are guaranteed to lacerate the shooter's hand. My specific 21-A had major feeding problems not cured by a new magazine and feed-ramp recontouring, very disappointing for a $150 gun.

At this point I should say that all gun manufacturers appear anxious to help shooters keep their guns safe and reliable. Invariably, they will do whatever they can to correct a problem in a new gun, never at more expense to the owner than shipping the gun to the

factory. You needn't go through a dealer for this, by the way. The Norton TP-22 is one of the reincarnations of the Budischowsky, all of which now are discontinued $200-plus collectors' items. Several pieces of mine broke during its test, prompting my gunsmith to comment, "It's not what it appears to be." One of the smallest 22s (also made in 25) and possessing all the bells and whistles of the double-action wonder nines, the attractive TP-22 might have been my top choice. Unhappily, mine would not extract some ammo brands at all, had numerous misfires, and was altogether unreliable.

The two Auto Nines are nothing alike, mechanically. The old model (FTL) was inspired by the striker-fired Baby Browning, with fine alloy frame, steel side, and twist-barrel takedown. Trigger pull originally was atrocious. Upon disassembly, the sear protrudes above the frame and the mating striker falls into your hand. A little honing on both surfaces produced an excellent pull. The FTL performed well with only two brands of high-velocity ammo. The new model (Wilkinson Sherry) is of similar quality and materials, but is a concealed hammer design that employs an entirely different pinned breechblock takedown, rather like that of the AMT Backup. With a much better trigger, the Sherry likewise performed well with only two ammo brands, but not the same brands as the FTL. Both guns are in the $150 range.

Alternatives

Double derringers were not considered because of their two-round limitation. Some 38 derringers are as light as their 22 counterparts because of their larger bores. The market offers a couple of relatively cheap four-shot derringers I felt were beyond the scope of this test.

The little five-shot North American Arms and similar Freedom Arms stainless revolvers offer, in my opinion, a reasonable alternative to the 22 pistol. Aside from limited capacity, the main drawback is the single-action-only firing mode. Fumble-cocking and relatively severe recoil through their tiny bird's-head grips hamper target recovery. On my North American Arms revolver, the cocked hammer's firing pin obscures the rudimentary sights. These revolvers also are available in 22 Short (why bother?) and 22 Magnum. The Magnum would appear to be the better choice, but its greater length and fierce recoil disqualify it for me.

The upside is that both derringer and revolvers are essentially 100% reliable with all 22 ammunition.

Conclusions And Recommendations

Even large-caliber, centerfire auto-loading pistols are limited to a relatively narrow range of ammunition for reliable function. The variety of available 22 rimfire ammo is much broader than that. All 22 pistols, even large ones, tend to be ammo-sensitive, being regulated for either high-velocity or target ammo, seldom both. Small pistols are more finicky because of their smaller mass. Limp-wrist shooting may disable the best of them, because the frame is recoiling along with the slide, which then can't open correctly. It should be clear that price has nothing to do with performance. Generally, size is a better indicator of reliability.

A professional trigger job should be contemplated. This might cost half as much as the pistol did, but it could help achieve the multiple 22 hits that may be required, which is the main advantage of the auto-loading pistol. Make sure

Lorcin L22: tiny safety, still easy to release. Author photo.

High Standard DM-101 22 Magnum derringer: double-action only. Very flat.

your pistol works when it is clean, because that's the way you probably will be carrying it. Check the bore occasionally for lint and other obstructions picked up from your pocket.

All owner's manuals recommend carrying the pistol with an empty chamber. However, jacking a round into the chamber is one of the most dependable ways to jam one of these little guns. Some of their safeties are very difficult to work, and even more difficult to trust. For liability reasons, I offer NO carry-mode recommendations.

I cannot recommend any particular brand of gun or ammo, nor did I intend to do that when I undertook this project. Your gun, which may appear identical to mine, almost surely will behave differently. So what is the point of all this? It is to convince you that you must not buy one of these little guns, load it with something off your ammo shelf, drop it into your pocket, and feel protected.

Try out your gun like I did. Find a load that is reliable (hopefully a high-velocity hollow point) and buy a couple of bricks of it to practice with, shoot them a lot, and then trust the gun. Of all the options there are in pocket pistols, this is the only one you must select.

Author's Concealment Specs

Gun	Bulk Factor
North American 22	37
Baby Browning 25	112
FTL Auto-Nine 22	126
Wilkinson Sherry 22	138
Sedco SP-22—22	181
Norton TP70—22	187
Beretta Minx 225	189
Jennings J-22—22	213
Sterling 302—22	252
Beretta 21—22	262
S&W 61—22	263
Walther TPH22—22	270
AMT Backup-380	285
Iver Johnson TP-22—22	316
Galezi 9—22	339
Grevdel P-10-380	443
Lorcin L-22—22	445
Phoenix HP22—22	482
S&W 2214—22	648
Liama XV-22	825
S&W Chief's Special-38	8420

Attention All 1911 Fans!

Robert K. Campbell

If you're a fan of the 1911 (and if you're reading this you probably are!), we invite you to check out *Shooter's Guide to the 1911* from Gun Digest Books. Whether you're a shooter, collector or historian, this entertaining book has everything you need to know about the most famous handgun in the world.

Written by renowned 1911 authority Robert K. Campbell, *Shooter's Guide to the 1911* is the definitive summary of John M. Browning's most famous creation. Of special interest to 1911 enthusiasts is Campbell's chapter on firing tests in which he puts 52 different handguns through their paces. The following excerpt covers several models from Springfield Armory. Enjoy!

To get your copy of Shooter's Guide to the 1911, plus other notable volumes such as Patrick Sweeney's 1911: The First 100 Years and the entire line of Gun Digest brand books, visit www.gundigeststore.com.

Springfield Ultra Compact 9mm

A 9mm 1911 – blasphemy! Just the same, the genre is quite popular and this is a great shooting little pistol. One advantage is that the pistol is capable of digesting great amounts of 9mm +P or +P+ ammunition without complaint. Due to the low bore axis and well designed beavertail grip safety, the pistol is comfortable to fire with practically any loading. The factory supplied Hogue grips are ideal for most uses, but would probably be changed in a dedicated defensive handgun. This is a handgun without issues. The compact size, Novak sights, good trigger compression and light recoil make it a joy to use and fire.

I try to be open to other cultures and maintain a cosmopolitan outlook. The 9mm Luger cartridge is very popular and the 9mm 1911 is a byproduct of commerce. Some favor the 9mm perhaps from a sense of romantic idealism while others look as if they have swallowed a lemon at the sight of a 9mm pistol. I will state the matter rather plainly. I have usually kept a Browning High Power 9mm or two around the house for various reasons. The Springfield 9mm is better suited to personal defense or recreational shooting due to the superior trigger compression and general fit. With Metalform magazines, the pistol offers 10 rounds. The Buffalo Bore loads in 9mm offers a degree of authority in a small bore cartridge. While I prefer a big bore, a 124-grain bullet at 1250 fps (1300 fps from a 5-inch gun) is nothing to sneeze at. Building a relationship with your pistol has much value in survival, and the Springfield 9mm is an easy pistol to get to know and a likeable one at that.

10-yard group
Fiocchi 124-grain XTP.............................. 2.5 inches
25-yard group
Buffalo Bore 124-grain .... 2.65 inches
Combat Course
20 rounds Fiocchi 124-grain XTP
10 rounds Buffalo Bore 124-grain JHP
Rating...10
Malfunctions.................................... 0 (1500+ rounds)

Springfield Long Slide

This is a friendly enough pistol, long, heavy and accurate. The long slide is simply a 1911 with a 6-inch barrel and slide. This extra inch considerably enhances the balance and handling of the 1911 when it comes to long range pursuits. If you have never handled a long slide 1911, you have really missed something. The long slide is not something you will wish to carry concealed but as a hunting pistol or home defense handgun it has much to recommend it. The pistol does not leap into your hands as a Commander pistol will but it

The Springfield Ultra Compact is a fine pistol if a 9mm is your cup of tea.

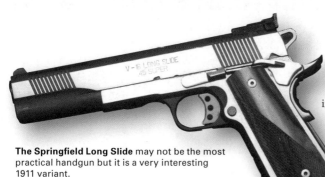

The Springfield Long Slide may not be the most practical handgun but it is a very interesting 1911 variant.

offers a stable firing platform. I thought it odd that the pistol features a very good Springfield adjustable rear sight but the front sight is a simple staked-on post. It worked okay for most shooting chores, but I would have preferred a taller front sight.

The level of accuracy demonstrated by this pistol has been more or less in the high grade 1911 arena, nothing startling. However, on one occasion I fired the single best group I have ever fired in my life at long range with a 1911 pistol. On a lark I took aim at a 100 yard silhouette. I had had the long slide less than a week, and had fired fewer than 200 rounds in the piece. I was sighting in a .308 rifle at the time. I laid the Springfield across the shooting bench, took a solid rest, and fired three rounds. I have never been more relaxed as I was not firing for record. To top it off, the ammunition was Wolf 230-gr. ball. Wolf is reliable ammunition

but not match-grade by any means. When I walked to the target, the three bullets had struck about twelve inches low and three to the right. They were in a pyramid pattern, with one at the top and the others forming almost a perfect base. The bullets measured less than four inches apart. I have never duplicated this group or even come close, but it happened. The Springfield long slide may not be the most practical .45 but it an interesting piece.

10-yard group
    Hornady 230-gr. XTP +P .... 4.1 inches
25-yard group
    Hornady 200-gr. XTP .... 1.75 inches
Combat Course
10 rounds Double Tap 200-grain JHP
10 rounds Wolf 230-gr. FMJ
10 rounds Winchester SXT
Rating 8
Malfunctions..0

Note: There is always interest in the approximate velocity gained with a 6-inch barrel. I carefully recorded the differences in velocity, using the 6-inch-barrel Springfield, a 5-inch-barrel Smith and Wesson SW 1911, and a 4.25-inch-barrel Smith and Wesson 1911PD. The results were interesting. It appears the Springfield long slide gets the last foot per second from a given loading.

Velocity

Load	Springfield 6-Inch	SW1911 5-Inch	SW 1911PD 4.25-Inch
CorBon 165-gr. JHP	1309	1223	1112
Federal 185-gr. HS+P	1140	1101	1058
Double Tap 200-gr. JHP	1100	1054	1004
Wilson Combat 200-gr. JHP	925	–	875
Mastercast 200-gr. JHP	1020	948	908
Black Hills 230 gr. JHP	880	855	815
Winchester SXT +P	960	945	914

Springfield GI Pistols

The Springfield GI was the original "Springer" and the one that changed the 1911 world. This is a no-frills GI pistol in appearance, but do not let its appearance fool you. The pistol has superior manufacturing beneath that plain vanilla exterior. The pistol will feed modern hollowpoint ammunition. The trigger action is often smooth and crisp. The firing pin is a lightweight type with a strong return spring for added safety. The pistol features the original GI slide window in deference to GI .45 fans. We tested both a plain working gun (a parkerized GI pistol) and a rather nice stainless steel

Springfield GI pistol. The stainless GI pistol should be a good working pistol but we ran into a snag. The trigger action was heavier than the parkerized pistol, which we can live with, but the stainless pistol suffered several break-in malfunctions. That is okay, too, but we seldom see break-in malfunctions these days. Just the same, either is a good serviceable pistol well worth the price.

Parkerized Springfield
    Ten round group
    Fiocchi 230-gr. FMJ................................ 4.75 inches
    25-yard group
    CorBon 185-grain JHP .... 4.0 inches

Combat Course
10 rounds Fiocchi 230-gr. JHP
10 rounds CorBon 200 grain JHP
10 rounds CorBon 185 grain JHP
Rating..10
Malfunctions...0

Stainless Steel GI pistol
10-yard group
Black Hills 230-gr. RNL .... 5.1 inches
25-yard group
Hornady 230-gr. XTP+P .... 4.6 inches
Combat Course
Black Hills 230-gr. RNL
Hornady 230-gr. XTP
Hornady 185-grain XTP
Rating..7
Malfunctions...................... 9 break-in malfunctions,
                    all failures to fully close the slide

The Springfield LW .45 has done yeoman service for several years.

Springfield Champion

The Champion is a 4-inch-barrel variant of the 1911, with a full length 7-round grip frame. The barrel features the proven bull barrel lockup common to 1911 pistols with barrels shorter than 5 inches. This variant features Novak sights, a speed safety, and a well-designed beavertail grip safety. While the pistol proved quite reliable and never stuttered, there were a couple of disappointments. I attempted to carry the piece in a favored Sideguard holster in which other 4-inch variants had resided quite well. The over-large speed safety of the Champion tended to rub to the off position in the holster. This is the type of safety used on the long slide but not the same one used with the Loaded Model. A second complaint was that the pistol was not as accurate as we would have liked. Four-inch groups at 25 yards will save your life, but from Springfield a four-inch group is pedestrian. These complaints are as significant as you care to make them. The pistol is fast from the holster, controllable, and lifesavingly reliable.

10-yard group Magnus 200-gr.
SWC/Unique/780 fps................................. 3.5 inches
25-yard group
Federal 230-gr. HST................................. 4.1 inches
Combat Course
10 Federal American Eagle 230-gr. ball
10 Magnus 200-gr. SWC handload
Ten Hornady 185-grain XTP
Rating 7
Malfunctions...0

The author often carries his LW Springfield Loaded Model in this DGL holster. This is a good combination, proofed and tested.

more flash due to the two tone treatment. After a day's work at the range you may be rubbing your wrists as the pistol is lighter than a steel frame pistol but the performance cannot be faulted.

10-yard group
Hornady 185-gr. XTP .... 3.65 inches
25-yard group
Hornady 200-gr. XTP .... 3.5 inches
Combat Course
20 rounds CorBon 185-gr. JHP
10 rounds Horandy 185-gr. XTP
Rating..10
Malfunctions 0

Springfield Lightweight Loaded Model

This is one of my personal carry guns. The pistol features a long sight radius coupled with a lightweight aluminum frame, a startlingly effective combination. This pistol has digested perhaps 8,500 rounds of ammunition and continues to remain completely reliable. That is all we can ask. The pistol has the standard features of the Loaded Model, but has

Springfield Loaded Model

The Springfield Loaded Model was largely an answer to Kimber's introduction of a pistol loaded with features. Some of the first loaded models were fitted with Novak rear sights but not dovetail front sights. They were often GI guns with a few features added. We deserved more, and today the Loaded Model is often recommended as a best buy by sage shooters.

A target grade .45 and Federal ammunition is a dream come true for those who pursue accuracy.

The pistol is fitted a bit tighter than the GI pistol and usually is capable of greater intrinsic accuracy.

When you begin to look to acquire a good 1911 of the better type, the Loaded Model should never be overlooked. The pistol is readily available. It has a good warranty and an excellent service record. Let's look at the Loaded Model's performance. The Loaded Model is well worthy of use as a personal defense handgun. There are many Loaded Models in use and I recommend the type without hesitation.

10-yard group
Federal 230-gr. American Eagle .... 3.5 inches
20-yard group
CorBon 230-gr. Performance Match 3.0
Combat Course
20 rounds Wolf 230-gr. FMJ
10 rounds CorBon 165-grain JHP
Rating 9
Malfunctions 0

Springfield Loaded Model Target

This is simply a target sighted version of the Loaded Model. Our pistol showed remarkable fit and it is also tighter than any previous Loaded Model we have tested. The pistol demanded a modest break-in period, but that is SOP for such a tight pistol. Accuracy was excellent and in the end so was reliability. Does Springfield fit the target sighted pistols more tightly? Perhaps.

10-yard group
Hornady 185-grain XTP .... 2.8 inches
25-yard group
Hornady 200-grain XTP .... 2.15 inches
Combat Course
20 rounds Fiocchi 230-gr. ball
10 rounds Mastercast 230-gr. JHP
Rating 9
Malfunctions .... 11 (all break-in related)

Springfield LW Operator

The LW Operator is simply an Operator type built on the Champion LW aluminum frame. This pistol displayed safety and beavertail grip safety fit equal to that of any handgun tested including the high-end pistols. Trigger compression is a smooth, tight 4.25 pounds. The sights were properly regulated for 230-gr. loads. This pistol proved especially accurate with the Hornady 200-gr. XTP. The XTP breaks 900 fps from the Springfield's 4-inch barrel. Considering the light weight of this .45, a lighter bullet that delivers a good balance of expansion and penetration is ideal. This is a formidable service pistol, especially when compared to polymer frame pistols of the same size and weight.

10-round group
Hornady 230-gr. XTP +P .... 4.5 inches
25-yard group
Hornady 200-grain XTP .... 3.25 inches
Combat Course
10 rounds Winchester 230-gr. FMJ
20 rounds handload using Nosler
185-grain JHP at 900 fps
Rating 10
Malfunctions 0

Springfield Novak Custom 1911

This pistol started life as a Springfield GI pistol and it is still a GI pistol, but it has been improved with high visibility, capable handgun sights. Novak's also tuned the extractor and generally checked out the entire upper unit for function. The end result is a classic that will stand the test of time. The pistol does all a combat pistol is supposed to do.

10-round group
Black Hills 230-gr. FMJ .... 4.0 inches
25-round group
Black Hills 185-gr. JHP .... 2.9 inches
Combat Course
20 rounds Black Hills 230-gr. FMJ
10 rounds Black Hills 185-gr. JHP
Rating 10
Malfunctions 0

This is a rapid fire group with the Novak .45. Good performance from a legendary shop.

The Gun Digest® Book of Combat Handgunnery

6th Edition

How to Defend
- Your Family
- Your Home
- Yourself

Massad Ayoob

JG
PRESS

Published by

World Publications Group, Inc.
140 Laurel Street
East Bridgewater, MA 02333
www.wrldpub.com

ISBN-13: 978-1-4643-0277-0
ISBN-10: 1-4643-0277-4

Designed by Patsy Howell
Edited by Ken Ramage

Printed in China

Introduction

About The Author

Since publishing his first firearms article in 1971 (*GUNsport* magazine) Massad Ayoob has authored thousands of articles in firearms, law enforcement and martial arts journals, and written more than a dozen books including *In the Gravest Extreme*, widely considered the authoritative text on the use of deadly force by private citizens in self-defense. His life achievement awards include Outstanding American Handgunner of the Year, National Tactical Advocate, the Roy Rogers Award for promotion of firearms safety and the James Madison award for authorship promoting the Second Amendment.

Ayoob served twenty years as chair of the firearms committee for the American Society of Law Enforcement Trainers (including several years on ASLET's ethics committee) and four on the advisory board of the International Law Enforcement Educators and Trainers Association. He has taught at regional, national and international seminars for the International Association of Law Enforcement Firearms Instructors, and has taught the investigation of justifiable homicides at venues ranging from the DEA Academy in Quantico to the International Homicide Investigators Seminars. Mas also served two years as co-vice chair of the forensic evidence committee of the National Association of Criminal Defense Lawyers, one of the very few non-attorneys to ever hold such a position with that organization.

For most of his adult life, Mas has worked full time studying violent encounters, teaching how to survive them, and writing about same. He founded Lethal Force Institute (PO Box 122, Concord, NH 03302, (www.ayoob.com) in 1981. Part-time, he has been testifying as an expert witness since 1979, and has spent 33 years as a part-time, fully sworn law enforcement officer, most of that time as a supervisor with command authority over full-time personnel. At this writing he is handgun editor of *Guns* magazine, law enforcement editor of *American Handgunner,* and associate editor of *Combat Handguns* and *Guns & Weapons for Law Enforcement.* The first five-gun Master in IDPA, Ayoob presently holds the New Hampshire State, Florida State, New England Regional and Florida/Georgia Regional Champion titles with the stock service revolver.

Dedication

Live long enough, and you can write enough books to dedicate some to your mom and dad, your spouse, your kids, your colleagues, and your mentors. Been there, done that.

This book is respectfully dedicated to my graduates, from Lethal Force Institute and many other programs, especially those who used what they learned to survive. Some of you were kind enough to credit me with saving your lives.

It was good of you, but I have to say you were wrong. You saved your *own* lives... but, in so doing, you validated mine.

Massad Ayoob
July 2007

Patrolman Massad Ayoob, 1978. Privately owned, department-approved service revolver is his . Moran Custom Colt Python .357 Magnum. Photo credit: Dick Morin, Manchester (NH) Union-Leader newspaper.

Captain Massad Ayoob, 2006. Service pistol is department issue Ruger P345 .45 auto. Photo credit: Grantham (NH) PD.

Contents

CHAPTER ONE

The Defensive Combat Handgun: An Overview

It is an honor to have been asked to write this edition of *The Complete Book of Combat Handgunnery*. Whomever steps into this authorship has several big pairs of shoes to fill.

This topic has been, literally, a life-long study for me. I grew up around guns, in part because my father was an armed citizen who survived a murder attempt because he knew how and when to use a handgun. He had learned that from his father. My grandfather, the first of our family to come to this country, hadn't been on these shores long when he had to shoot an armed robber. I grew up with a gun the way kids today grow up with seat belts and smoke detectors. It was simply one more common-sense safety measure in a sometimes-dangerous world.

The day came when what I had learned from my forebears, in terms of having defensive weapons and learning skill at arms, saved my life, too, and the lives of others I was responsible for protecting. I passed the skill on to my daughters. My eldest got her license to carry concealed when she was 18. A year or so later, the Smith & Wesson 9mm in her waistband saved her from two would-be rapists. She represented the fourth straight generation of my family in the United States to be saved from violent criminals by a lawfully possessed firearm.

Life takes us down unexpected paths. If, during my somewhat rebellious teen years, you had asked me what I was least likely to become, I would probably have answered, "Cop or teacher." Before long, I had become both. Pausing for a 25-month breather in the early 1980s, I've been a police officer since 1972, and have been teaching about guns during that entire time. My first article in a gun magazine was published in 1971.

There have been a lot of books and thousands of articles under the dam since then, and enough training to fill seven single-spaced résumé pages. Competitive shooting has been good to me; I've earned several state championships, a couple of regional wins, two national champion titles, and three national records. Only a couple of state championships still stand today. I've spent 15 years as chair of the firearms committee for the American Society of Law Enforcement Trainers, a few of those also as a member of their ethics committee, and a couple of years as co-vice chair of the forensic evidence committee for the National Association of Criminal Defense Lawyers.

We live in interesting times for armed citizens. On the one hand, our rights to protect our loved ones and ourselves are constantly attacked by people, often rich and powerful and articulate, who just don't have the first clue. On the other, so many states have passed "shall issue" concealed carry laws that more law-abiding citizens can carry hidden handguns in public today than at virtually any time in the last century.

Researching these things, studying how they happen, and how to prevail and survive if they happen to you, has become my life's work. I founded the Lethal Force Institute in 1981, and it has been a labor of love ever since. The on-scene management of violent criminal threat is a life study, and a multi-dimensional one that goes far beyond the gun itself. We cannot cover them all in one book. No one can. The laws that encompass these things and more, are all dynamic and fluid and subject to change.

The purpose of this book is to transmit a working knowledge of the current state-of-the-art of defensive handgun technology and its corollary topics, of how to effectively use them and how to find out how better to use them and more importantly, *when* to use them. Every effort will be made to explain where certain recommendations and trends came from.

Our guns, ammunition, and holsters are better than ever. So are state-of-the-art techniques that have been developed from modern and "post-modern" studies of what happens to the human mind and body under life-threatening stress. Better than ever also is our understanding of courtroom dynamics as they apply today in the often terrifying aftermath of the justified use of deadly force.

These skills are needed today. Since September 11, 2001, many experts believe they will be needed more than ever. The continued ability to choose to develop these skills, and exercise them if we must, is constantly under attack. It will be a long, hard fight, perhaps a never-ending one, but in the last analysis, that is the nature of the human experience.

I hope you find this book useful. If something seems new and radical compared to older "doctrine," try it yourself before you decide. I can promise you that there is nothing recommended in this book that has not been proven where it counts.

Stay safe.

Massad Ayoob
Live Oak, Florida
2007

CHAPTER TWO

Enduring Classics

The Single-Action Autos

The Model 1911

Roald Amundsen reached the South Pole behind a team of 17 Huskies. The most popular song of the year was "Alexander's Ragtime Band," by Irving Berlin. Ty Cobb was the dominant baseball star. Marie Curie won the Nobel Prize for chemistry. Milk was 17 cents a gallon, two bits would get you 10 pounds of potatoes and three pennies change, and 18 cents bought a pound of round steak. Louis Chevrolet and W.C. Durant introduced the former's automobile. Born in that year were Lucille Ball, Mahalia Jackson, Vincent Price, Ronald Reagan, Tennessee Williams, and the Colt Government Model .45 caliber "automatic pistol."

The year, of course, was 1911. The prices (including that of the Colt) have multiplied. The Chevrolet is vastly changed. The people, for the most part, have passed into

Gen. William Keys, USMC (ret.) has revitalized Colt's commitment to the 1911 since he became CEO of the company.

history. Only the 1911 pistol remains with us largely unchanged, and still going strong.

Today, if the covers of gun magazines are any indication, the 1911 is the most popular handgun design of its time. A scan through the catalogue pages of *Gun Digest* shows it is also the most influential. It seems that every year brings at least another 1911 "clone" to the marketplace.

Little has changed in the pistol's core design, but many subtle evolutions have taken place. The first wave came after WWI, when the American military began a study of how small arms had performed in the most recent conflict. The study was rather leisurely, it appears, as the list of complaints wasn't announced until about 1923. About half of the doughboys thought the trigger of the 1911 was too long. Many said the grip tang bit their hands. Most found the front sight post and rear notch so tiny as to be useless. It was also noted that when soldiers missed with it, they generally hit low.

About 1927, answers to these concerns were implemented, creating the 1911-A1 model. The grip tang was lengthened to prevent bite to the web of the hand. The trigger was shortened dramatically, and the frame at the rear of the trigger guard was niched out on both sides to further enhance finger reach. Believing that the low hits were a function of the pistol "pointing low" as opposed to the operators jerking their triggers, the designers gave the A1 an arched mainspring housing that sort of levered the muzzle upward and made the gun "point higher."

The 1911 is a classic that remains in service. This officer wears his Kimber stainless .45 to work today.

The 1911's ergonomics are timeless. The author used this 1991-A1 Colt tuned by Mark Morris to place 2nd Master in the 2001 New England Regional IDPA Championships.

Para-Ordnance pioneered the high capacity 1911. The author used this one frequently at the National Tactical Invitational, where its extra firepower (14 rounds total) came in handy.

Finally, a slightly better and more visible set of fixed sights was mounted to the pistol.

Gun companies and steel foundries were also making advances in metallurgy. It is generally accepted today that early 1911s are made of much softer steel than the 1911-A1 and later commercial Colts. This is why pistolsmiths have historically recommended against tuning early guns for accuracy. They felt the soft steel would not "hold" the fine tolerances required in precision accurizing, a process that became popular among target shooters in the 1930s and has remained a cottage industry within the gunsmithing business ever since.

The 1950s brought the epoch of Jeff Cooper who, writing in *Guns & Ammo* magazine, almost single-handedly re-popularized the 1911. Its one-third firepower advantage over the revolver, eight shots to six, plus its rapid reloading was but one advantage. The short, easy trigger pull – particularly when the gun had been worked on – delivered better hit potential under stress than the long, heavy pull of a double-action revolver. Though it appeared large, the Colt auto was flat in profile and easy to conceal, particularly inside the waistband.

The resurgence of the 1911's popularity had begun. By the 1970s, copycat makers were coming out of the woodwork. Through the 1980s, it at last occurred to makers to furnish the guns at the factory with the accoutrements that were keeping a host of custom pistolsmiths in business. These included wide grip safeties to cushion recoil, with a recurve to guide the hand into position and speed the draw, and a "speed bump" at the bottom edge to guarantee depression of the grip safety even with a sloppy hold. This part was also available "cut high" to allow the hand to get even higher on the grip. A low bore axis had always been one reason the pistol felt so good in the hand and was easily controlled in rapid fire by someone who knew the right techniques. Now, even the folks at the Colt factory began relieving the lower rear of the trigger guard, in hopes that the hand could ride still higher for even better performance. Now too, at last, 1911s were coming out of the factories with heavy-duty fixed sights that offered big, highly visible sight pictures.

There were also high-capacity versions, first with metal frames and then with polymer. Once, it had been

standard procedure to send your Colt to a gunsmith to have it "throated" to feed hollowpoints and semi-wadcutters; now, Colt and Springfield Armory and Kimber and many more were producing the guns "factory throated."

By the dawn of the 21st century, the 1911 still ruled, though Colt did not. Kimber had become the single largest producers of 1911 pistols, offering a variety of sizes and formats. Springfield Armory was close behind in sales and equal in quality. Customized target pistols still ruled the bull's-eye firing lines, as they had for decades, but now competitors were showing up and winning with factory match 1911s from Les Baer and Rock River. Since the International Practical Shooting Confederation was founded at the Columbia Conference in 1976, the 1911 had ruled that arena, but now the

1911s are capable of awesome accuracy. Springfield Armory TRP Tactical Operator pistol, mounting M3 Illuminator flashlight, put five rounds of Winchester .45 Match into this 1-inch group, hand held with bench rest at 25 yards.

Four top-quality manufacturers and styles of modern 1911s, all .45s. From top: Compact Colt Lightweight CCO. Service Kimber Custom II. Hi-Cap Para-Ordnance P14.45. Tactical Springfield TRP with extended dust cover and M3 light.

Colt collectors will spot the WWII-vintage ejection port and sights on "retro" Colt 1911A1, reintroduced in 2001.

winning gun in IPSC was less often the old Colt than a high-capacity variant like the STI or the Para-Ordnance.

Over the years, the 1911 has been produced in a myriad of calibers. The .38 Super 1911s and hot 9mm variants win open class IPSC matches in the third millennium, and fancy inside, ordinary outside 1911s in caliber .40 S&W rule Limited class in that game. The 9mm 1911 is seen as the winning gun in the Enhanced Service Pistol class of the relatively new International Defensive Pistol Association contests, but the .45 caliber 1911 is much more popular, known in IDPA circles as a Custom Defense Pistol. However, in IDPA, even more shooters use Glocks or double-action autos, making the Stock Service Pistol category even more populous than the 1911 categories. The overwhelming majority of 1911s in serious use today are .45 caliber. No one has yet made a more "shootable" pistol in that power range.

Thus, with timeless continuity, the 1911 has outgrown the Colt brand with which it was once synonymous.

The P-35

"Porgy & Bess" opens in New York, and Steinbeck's "Tortilla Flat" is published. The hot dance is the Rhumba. Milk is up to 23 cents for half a gallon (delivered, of course). Boulder Dam, Alcoholics Anonymous, and the Social Security Act all come into being. It is the birth year

for Woody Allen, Elvis Presley, Sandy Coufax, and the Browning Hi-Power pistol. It is 1935.

The P-35 was the last design of John Browning, who also created the Colt 1911. Many would also consider the Hi-Power his best. Known in some quarters as the GP or *grand puissance,* the pistol may owe more of its ingenuity to Didionne Souave than to Browning. In any case, it was the first successful high-capacity 9mm semiautomatic, and for more than a quarter of a century was the definitive one. It remains today the standard-issue service pistol of Great Britain and numerous other countries.

For most of its epoch, the P-35 was distinguished by a tiny, mushy-feeling thumb safety and by sights that were not the right size or shape for fast acquisition. In the 1980s Browning fixed that at last with its Mark II and later Mark III series pistols, which reached their high point in the Practical model. Good, big sights...a gun at last throated at the Browning factory to feed hollowpoints...big, positively operating ambidextrous thumb safety...legions of Browning fans were in heaven. That the guns by now were being manufactured for Browning in Portugal instead of at the Fabrique Nationale plant in Belgium mattered only to the most rigid purists.

Like the Colt 1911, the P-35 is slim, easy to conceal, and comfortable to carry. The 13+1 magazine capacity seemed to be its big selling point. But if people bought it for firepower, they kept it because it had a more endearing quality: It simply felt exquisitely *natural* in the human hand.

Before people used the word "ergonomics," John Browning clearly understood the concept. No pistol is as user-friendly. Col. Cooper, who has been called "The High Priest of the 1911," once wrote that no pistol had ever fit his hand better than the Browning. What a shame, he added, that it was not offered in a caliber of consequence.

Produced for the most part in 9mm Parabellum and occasionally in caliber .30 Luger, the Browning got a boost in popularity stateside during the 1990s when it was introduced in .40 S&W. The bigger caliber feels rather like a 1911 slide on a P-35 frame, but it shoots well. There were early reports of problems, but the factory quickly squared these away. The 9mm Browning has always been a rather fragile gun when shot with heavy loads. I've seen baskets of broken Browning frames in English military stockpiles and in Venezuelan armories. The hammering of NATO ammo, hotter than +P+ as produced by England's Radway Green and

Venezuela's CAVIM arsenals, was the culprit. Fed the hot loads only sparingly, and kept on a practice diet of low-pressure standard American ball ammo, the 9mm Browning will last and last. The massive slide of the .40 caliber version, along with its strong recoil spring, is apparently enough to keep the guns in that caliber from breaking epidemically.

The Browning's mechanism does not lend itself to trigger tuning in the manner of the 1911, that is one reason it has never been popular with target shooters. For most of its history, its magazines would not fall free unless the pistol was deprived of one of its trademark features, the magazine disconnector safety. The latter, when in place, renders a chambered round unshootable if the magazine has been removed. In the 1990s, Browning came up with a magazine with a spring on the back that positively ejected it from the pistol.

The timeless styling of the Browning made it a classic, but make no mistake: Its easy "carryability," and especially its feel in the hand, have made it an enduringly popular defense gun. From petite female to large male, every hand that closes over a Browning Hi-Power seems to feel a perfect fit. One caveat: Though it will hold 13+1, serious users like the SAS discovered that it wasn't very reliable unless the magazine was loaded one round down from full capacity. Just something to think about.

Classic Double-action Autos

Some gun enthusiasts would argue whether the words "classic" and "DA auto" belong in the same sentence. Can there be such a thing as a "classic" Mustang? Only to the young, and to fans of the genre. Ditto the DA auto.

Surely, in terms of firearms design history, there were at least a couple of classics. The Walther designs of the 1920s and 1930s are a case in point. There is no question that the P-38 dramatically influenced duty auto designs of the future, though no serious gun professional ever made that pistol his trademark if he could get something else. European soldiers and police dumped them at the first opportunity for improved designs by HK, SIG-Sauer, and latter-day Walther engineers. South African police, who stuck with the P-38 for decades, told the author they hated them and couldn't wait to swap up to the Z88, the licensed clone of the Beretta 92 made in that country.

The Walther PP and PPK have timeless *popularity* that comes from small size and ease of concealed carry, splendid workmanship in the mechanical sense, and a *cachet* more attributable to the fictional James Bond than to genuine gun experts who shot a lot, though the great Charles "Skeeter" Skelton was a notable exception who actually carried the PP and PPK in .380. By today's standards, the ancient Walther pocket gun is a poor choice. If it is not carried on safe, a round in the chamber can discharge if the gun is dropped. If it is carried on safe, the release lever is extremely awkward and difficult to disengage. The slide tends to slice the hand of most shooters in firing. Walther .380s often won't work with hollow-points, and though inherently accurate thanks to their fixed-barrel design, often require a gunsmith's attention to the sights to make the guns shoot where they are aimed. There are not only better .380s now, but smaller and lighter 9mm Parabellums!

In the historical design and "influence on gun history" sense, one could call the Smith & Wesson Model 39 a classic. But it, too, was a flawed design, and it would take Smith & Wesson almost three decades to really make it work. The S&W autoloader was, by then, a redesigned entity and a part of the new wave, rather than a true classic like the 1911 or the Hi-Power.

S&W Service Revolvers

In 1899, President William McKinley signed the treaty that ended the Spanish-American War, the first of the Hague Accords were drafted, and Jim Jeffries was the heavyweight-boxing champion of the world. Born in that year were Humphrey Bogart, Gloria Swanson, James Cagney, Fred Astaire, and the Smith & Wesson Hand Ejector .38 revolver that would become known as the Military & Police model.

The Smith & Wesson double-action was the "Peacemaker" of the 20th century. As the M&P's name implied, it was the defining police service revolver for most of that century, with many thousands of them still carried on the streets today. S&W revolvers fought with American troops in both world wars, Korea, and Vietnam. There are doubtless still some in armed services inventories to this day.

One of the first of many small modifications to the design was a front locking lug that, many believed, made the Smith & Wesson a stronger double-action revolver than its archrival, the Colt. While the Colt had a better single-action cocking stroke and trigger pull for bull's-eye target shooting, the S&W had a smoother, cleaner double-action trigger stroke for serious fast shooting. It was largely

Here is a circa 1930s production 6-inch S&W M&P with factory lanyard loop and instruction guide.

Markings show that this pre-WWII S&W M&P was worked over by Cogswell & Harrison of England.

S&W's Military & Police Target model .38 Special predated the K-38 Masterpiece series.

At left: Jordan, living legend to handgunners, matter-of-factly completes what men who should know call the fastest draw of any living man.

Inset: Massad Ayoob discusses the .41 Magnum load with Bill Jordan, who helped develop it. Jordan proved as fast with his smile as a gun.

The author at 25 with Bill Jordan. Bill is demonstrating the S&W .41 Magnum he helped bring into existence.

because of this that, by the end of WWII, S&W was the market leader in the revolver field. It remains there to this day, though at this writing Ruger exceeds S&W in total firearms production.

The most popular by far was the .38 frame, now known as the K-frame. One thing that makes a classic handgun is perfect feel. The average adult male hand fits the K-frame perfectly. Larger hands can easily adapt. Smaller hands adapt less easily. In 1954, Border Patrol weapons master Bill Jordan convinced Smith & Wesson to beef up the Military & Police .38 and produce a gun of that size in .357 Magnum. This was done, and another classic was born: S&W's .357 Combat Magnum, a staple of the company's product line to this day.

The same mechanism was adapted to a .44/.45 frame gun, known today as the N-frame. In 1917, S&W engineers created half-moon clips to adapt rimless .45 auto cartridges to revolver cylinders, to fill the Army's need for more handguns during WWI. This concept lives today in S&W's Model 625 .45 ACP revolver, a gun all the more practical since more recent full-moon clips allow the fastest possible six-shot reload. The first of the classic N-frames was the exquisitely crafted .44 Special Triple Lock. 1935 saw the next giant step, the first .357 Magnum revolver. That gun lives today as the practical, eight-shot Model 627 from the Smith & Wesson performance center. The N-frame was also the original home of the mighty .44

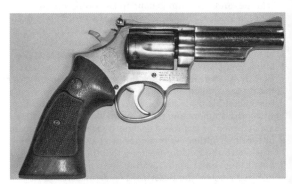

In the 1970s, the S&W Model 66 became a modern classic.

S&W created clips for .45 ACP cartridge, and the 1917 revolver was born. The series reaches its zenith in the Model 625 revolver, this one was tuned by Al Greco and is wearing Hogue grips.

Tapered barrel (upper right) was standard configuration of S&W M&P until the late 1950s. Never discontinued, it was overshadowed by the more popular heavy barrel configuration, below.

America's most popular service revolver before WWII, the Colt Official Police .38 Special was subsequently pushed into second place by the S&W. This Colt wears a Pachmayr grip adapter, a common accessory.

State-of-the-art equipment at the end of the police revolver era: A Colt Python with Hogue grips in Bianchi B-27 holster, with speedloaders in a Safariland quick-release carrier.

Magnum cartridge in the legendary "Dirty Harry" gun, the Model 29.

In the 1970s, it became the habit of police to train extensively with the hot .357 Magnum ammunition they were carrying on duty, with the particularly high-pressure 125-grain/1,450 fps load being their duty cartridge of choice. This was too much for the .38 frame guns, which began exhibiting a variety of jamming and breakdown problems. S&W upscaled to a .41 frame gun, which they dubbed the L-frame. This turned out to be a much sturdier .357 Magnum, the most practical version of which is probably the seven-shot Model 686-Plus.

There were some growing pains, including L-frames that broke or choked. S&W got that fixed. By the time they were done with it, the L-frame was utterly reliable and deadly accurate...but by that time, police departments were trading to auto pistols *en masse,*

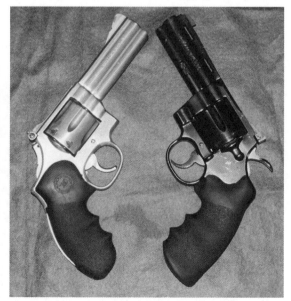

Here are two classic .357 Magnum service revolvers. Left, S&W 686; right, Colt Python. Both of these wear Hogue grips.

sounding the death knell for what many believed was the best police service revolver ever made.

Colt Service Revolvers

Colt's service revolvers, like S&W's, trace their lineage to the 1890s. The Colt was the dominant police gun until the beginning of WWII, with S&W pulling ahead of their archrival in the post-war years and achieving near-total dominance in that market by 1970. Thereafter, Smith service revolvers were challenged more by Ruger than Colt.

The early Army Special and its heirs, the fixed-sight Official Police and the Trooper, were slightly larger and heavier than their K-frame counterparts. While the medium-build S&W was constructed on a true .38 frame, the Colts were actually built on .41 frames. Tests in the 1950s indicated that the Colts were stronger and better suited for hot loads like the .38-44, which S&W only recommended in their .45-frame guns.

Some gunsmiths felt the Colt would stay accurate longer, because its design included a second hand (cylinder hand, that is), which snapped up to lock the cylinder in place as the hammer began to fall. Others said it was less sturdy, because the primary hand seemed to wear sooner than the S&W's. Certainly, there was little argument on trigger pull. Virtually all authorities agreed that the Colt had the crisper trigger pull in single-action and the S&W, the smoother stroke in double-action.

In 1955, Colt introduced what would be their ultimate classic in this vein, the Python. Originally intended to be a heavy barrel .38 Special target revolver, it was chambered for .357 Magnum almost as an afterthought, and that changed everything. The full-length underlug and ventilated rib gave not only a distinctive look, but a solid up-front hang that made the gun seem to kick less with Magnum loads. At the time, the best factory craftsmen assembled the premium-price Python with extra attention lovingly added to the action work. Though he chose to carry a Smith & Wesson as a duty gun, NYPD Inspector Paul B. Weston, an authority of the period, dubbed the Python's action "a friction free

S&W's Centennial Airweight is a classic snub. This original sample from the 1950s has a grip safety, a feature absent on the modern incarnation.

S&W Model 640-1 is the J-frame Centennial rendered in .357 Magnum. These Pachmayr Compac grips help to cushion the substantial recoil.

environment." Few challenged the Python's claim as "the Rolls-Royce of revolvers."

The underpaid cop of the time carried one as a status symbol if he could afford it. Three state police agencies issued them. A few went out to selected members of the Georgia State Patrol, and more than that were issued to the Florida Highway Patrol, while the Colorado State Patrol issued a 4-inch Python to every trooper. Today, no department issues this fine old double-action revolver. All three of the above named SP's have gone to .40 caliber autos: Glocks in Georgia, Berettas in Florida, and S&Ws in Colorado.

The Classic Snubbies

Up through the middle of the Roaring Twenties, if you wanted a snub-nose .38 you were stuck with a short .38 caliber cartridge, too, the anemic little round that one company called .38 Smith & Wesson and the other called

.38 Colt New Police, in their Terrier and Banker's Special revolvers, respectively. (As late as the early 1970s, the Boston Police Department still had a few Banker's Specials issued to detectives. By then, the gun was a true collector's item.)

Then, in 1927, Colt took 2 inches off the barrel of their smaller frame Police Positive Special revolver and called the result the Detective Special. The rest, as they say, is history. A six-shot .38 Special small enough for the trouser or coat pocket, and easy to carry in a shoulder holster, was an instant success. "Detective Special" became a generic term, like "kleenex" or "frigidaire," for any snub-nose .38.

Late in 1949, Smith & Wesson entered the small frame .38 Special market with their Chief Special, so called because it was introduced at an annual conference of the International Association of Chiefs of Police. It only held five shots, but was distinctly smaller than the Colt. Immediately, it became a best seller among both cops and armed citizens.

After *that* little ace trumping, Colt was quick to respond. Both firms had built ultra-light revolvers for the USAF's Aircrewman project, and Colt was first to market with the Cobra, a Detective Special with a lightweight alloy frame. The alloy in question was Duralumin, aluminum laced with titanium, Alcoa #6 or equivalent. The company also came up with a bolt-on device aptly called a "hammer shroud." It covered the hammer on both

The shrouded hammer makes S&W Bodyguard snag-free while retaining single-action capability. This is the stainless version in .357 Magnum.

Colt's .38 Detective Special is absolutely a modern classic. This sample is the popular 1972 style.

Taurus CIA (Carry It Anywhere) effectively copies the established styling of the S&W Centennial series. It's available in .38 Special and .357 Magnum.

sides to keep it from snagging in a pocket or coat lining. Paul Weston had correctly described the Colt hammer spur as being shaped like a fishhook. The Shroud covered the hammer, left the tip exposed to allow single-action thumb-cocking if necessary.

S&W threw a two-fisted *riposte*. Their aluminum-frame snubby, being smaller, was also a tad lighter. A Detective Special weighed 21 ounces, and a Cobra, 15.5 ounces. S&W's Airweight revolver in the Chief Special was listed as a feathery 12.5 ounces compared to 19 ounces in all-steel configuration. Also introduced (first in Airweight, in fact) was their Bodyguard model with built-in hammer shroud. Sleeker than the shrouded Colt, it was also more pleasant to shoot; the rear flange of the screw-on Colt shroud had a tendency to bite the web of the hand. However, the S&W was more difficult to clean in the area of the shrouded hammer, which proved to be a dust-collector with both brands.

Next came a true "once and future" classic, the Centennial. Smith & Wesson took the configuration of the

Shown with his firm's CIA, Taurus CEO Bob Morrison is proud that his firm's snub-nose .38s are among the most popular.

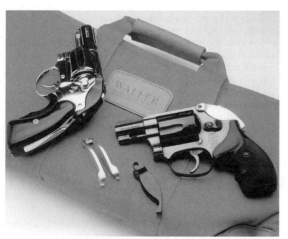

Colt hammer shrouds for D-frame guns (left) and a new variation for J-frame S&W's (right) are available through W.W. Waller & Son.

Bob Schwartz at Waller offers a hammer shroud for the S&W Chief Special that turns it into the Bodyguard configuration.

old New Departure Safety Hammerless top-break and grafted it onto the .38 Special Chief, creating what had to be the sleekest revolver of the genre. It even had the antique gun's signature "lemon squeezer" grip safety, the only solid-frame S&W ever so equipped. Ironically, because few shooters had yet mastered the double-action shooting concept and most felt they needed the crutch of cocking the hammer to hit anything, sales of the Centennial were mediocre and the gun was discontinued. As soon as it became unavailable, the Centennial became a much sought after "in-gun" among the cognoscenti. It was reintroduced, *sans* grip safety, and has been a best-seller ever since.

Classic combat revolvers are far from obsolete. These StressFire Instructor candidates at Lethal Force Institute learn to shoot and teach the wheelgun.

By the end of the 20th Century, the classic .38 snub had evolved further. The Colt had been given a heavy barrel treatment in 1972. Even before then, serious shooters tended to prefer the Colt over the Smith in a small snubby. The sixth shot had been the least of its advantages. Most found that with its bigger sights and longer action throw – the one comparison between Colt and Smith in which the Colt would likely be voted to have the better DA pull – the littlest Colt would outshoot the littlest Smith. Now an ounce and a half heavier, with a lot more weight up front, it kicked even less than the S&W and tended to shoot like a 4-inch service revolver. In the latter 1990s, the action was updated and stainless versions were produced, including a splendid .357 Magnum version called the Magnum Carry. The gun then went out of production, though at this writing, was high on the list of "old favorites" to be reintroduced by Colt under the new management regime of retired Marine Corps General Bill Keys.

The baby S&W, meanwhile, had been in stainless and Airweight, and even lighter AirLite Ti (titanium) and SC (scandium) models. Calibers included .22, .32 Magnum, .38 Special, 9mm, and .357 Magnum. A "LadySmith" version had also been marketed successfully. The firm had made larger versions in .44 Special.

During that period Taurus had come up from a cheap alternative to a genuinely respected player in the quality handgun market. Their Model 85, resembling a Chief Special, was particularly accurate and smooth, dramatically underselling the S&W and becoming the firm's best seller. The new millennium saw the CIA (Carry It Anywhere) hammerless clone of the S&W Centennial. The first to produce a "Total Titanium" snubby, Taurus made their small revolvers primarily in .38 Special and .357, with larger snubbies available in .44 Special, .45 Colt, and even .41 Magnum.

Rossi also sold a lot of snub-nose revolvers. So did Charter Arms in its various incarnations from the 1960s to the 21st Century. Charter's most memorable revolver was the Bulldog, a five-shot .44 Special comparable in frame size to a Detective Special.

Beyond Classic

Each of the combat handguns described above remains in wide use today in many sectors of armed citizenry, and/or security professionals, and/or police and military circles. Some consider them still the best that ever existed; others put them in second rank to the guns of today. Certainly, those classic revolvers remain in the front rank for those who prefer that style, but in autoloaders, there are many more modern choices. Who is right about what's best today? Let's examine "the new wave" of combat autoloaders, and see for ourselves.

Purchasing Used Handguns

Buying a used handgun isn't as fraught with peril as buying a used car. It's a smaller, simpler mechanism. If it has been well cared for, you'll be able to tell.

Buy from people you can trust. It's a sad commentary on human nature that so many people will deal with a lemon product by simply selling it to someone else. Most reputable gun dealers will stand behind the guns in their second-hand showcases. They may not be able to give you free repairs, but if something goes drastically wrong with it, someone who makes his living from the

Though pitted and ugly with its badly worn finish, this S&W Model 15 was clean inside and tight. It would shoot 1-inch groups at 25 yards with match ammo.

goodwill of the gun-buying community will take it back in trade and apply what you paid for it to something else you like better.

Some gun shops have a shooting range attached. With a used gun, you can normally pay a reasonable rental fee, take the gun right out to the range, and give it a try. If you don't like it, you paid a fair price to try a gun. If you do buy it, most such dealers will knock the gun rental off the price, though it's not fair to ask them to knock the range fee off, too.

Checking the bore without bore light. A white card or paper is held at the breechface and a flashlight is shined on the white surface, lighting up the bore so the interior can be easily seen from the muzzle end.

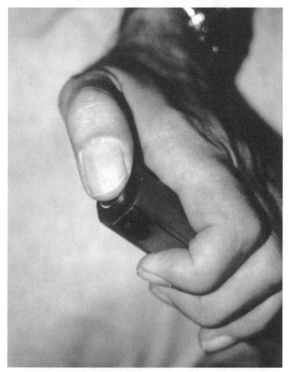

The thumb rotates against the muzzle of an empty 1911 with the slide closed to check for sloppy fit.

Universal Examination Points

As a general rule, a gun in pristine condition outside has *probably* been well cared for internally. This is not written in stone, however. Accompanying this segment are photos of a vintage Smith & Wesson Model 15 Combat Masterpiece .38 Special. It was found for sale among several others in a North Dakota gun shop in 1998, bearing a price tag of $130. Externally, what blue hadn't been worn off had been pitted. It looked as if someone had left it out in a field for the last couple of years. However, when the buyer examined it, he found the bore to be perfect, and the action so smooth and in such perfect tune it felt as if it had just left Smith & Wesson's Performance Center. He cheerfully paid the asking price, took it home, and discovered that it would group a cylinder of Federal Match .38 wadcutters into an inch at 25 yards.

It can go the other way, too. One fellow left the gun shop chuckling that he'd bought a fancy, premium brand .30/06 rifle, without a scratch on it, for at least $300 less than what it was worth. Then he got it to the range, and

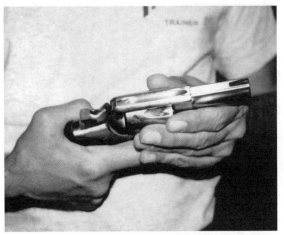

Testing a revolver's timing. With the free hand thumb applying some pressure to cylinder as taking a radial pulse, the trigger finger starts a double-action stroke…

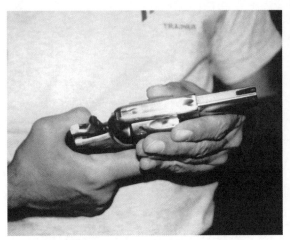

…and the cylinder has locked up tight even before the hammer falls, showing that this Ruger Service-Six is perfectly timed, at least for this particular chamber.

discovered it was less accurate than a Super-Squirter. Only then did he check the bore, to discover it rusted to destruction. The previous owner had apparently burned up some old, corrosive WWII surplus ammo in the expensive rifle and neglected the necessary immediate cleaning chores. The gun needed an expensive re-barreling job.

Before you do anything else, triple check to make sure the handgun is unloaded. I have seen people work a firearm's action at a gun show and freeze in horror as a live round ejected from the chamber. Don't let your natural firearms safety habits grow lax because the environment is a shop or show instead of a range.

Have a small flashlight with you, and perhaps a white business card or 3x5 card. (The Bore-Lite made for the purpose is, of course, ideal.) With the action open, get the card down by the breech and shine the flashlight on it, then look down the barrel; this should give optimum illumination.

If the bore is dirty, see about cleaning it then and there. The carbon could be masking rust or pitting. What you want to see is mirror brightness on the lands, and clean, even grooves in the rifling.

Watch for a dark shadow, particularly one that is doughnut shaped, encircling the entire bore. This tells you there has been a bulge in the barrel. Typical cause: someone fired a bad load that had insufficient powder, and the bullet lodged in the barrel, and the next shot blew it out. The bulge created by that dangerous over-pressure experience will almost certainly ruin the gun's accuracy. Pass on it.

Try the action. If everything doesn't feel reasonably smooth and work properly, something is *very* wrong with the action, and unless home gunsmithing is your hobby, you probably want to pass on it.

Now, let's branch into what you need to know about function and safety checks for revolver versus auto.

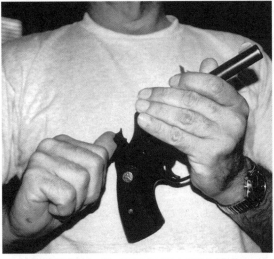

Testing for "push-off" with cocked Colt Official Police. Hammer stayed back, passing test.

Drawing the trigger or hammer back slightly to release the cylinder locking bolt, slowly rotate the cylinder to analyze barrel/cylinder clearance.

Checking the Used Revolver

Double check that the gun is unloaded, and keep the muzzle pointed in a safe direction. Check the bore and action as described above.

If it has both double- and single-action functions, cock the hammer. Keeping fingers away from the trigger, push forward on the cocked hammer with your thumb. If it snaps forward, you've experienced "push-off." This means either that the gun has had a sloppy "action job" done on it, or was poorly assembled at the factory, or has experienced a lot of wear. Since most experts believe a combat revolver should be double-action only anyway, and a good plan is to have the single-action cocking notch removed after you've bought it, this may not matter to you. Keep in mind, however, that it's an early warning sign that something else might be wrong with the gun.

With the cylinder out of the frame, spin it. Watch the ejector rod. If it remains straight, it's in alignment. If it wobbles like the wheels of the Toonerville Trolley, it's not, and there's a fairly expensive repair job in its immediate future.

Close the cylinder. Looking at the gun from the front, push leftward on the cylinder as if you were opening it, but without releasing the cylinder latch. Watch the interface between the crane or yoke, the part on which the cylinder swings out, with the rest of the frame. If it stays tight, the gun is in good shape. If there's a big gap, it tells

The author drops a pencil, eraser-end first, down barrel of cocked and empty S&W 4506. Note hammer is back, and decocking lever up…

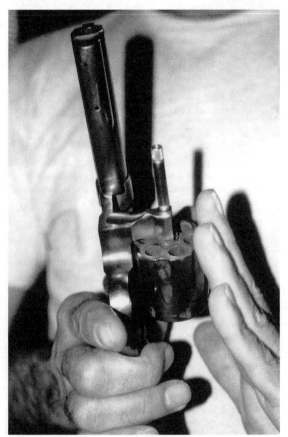

The cylinder of S&W 686 is opened, then spun. Watch the ejector rod. If it wobbles, it's out of line and may need replacement.

…when the decocking lever on the left side is depressed the pencil stays in place. This shows that the decocking mechanism is working properly.

you that some bozo has been abusing the gun by whipping the cylinder out of the frame like Humphrey Bogart. This will have a negative effect on cylinder alignment and will mean another pricey repair job. A big gap in this spot always means, "don't buy it."

With the cylinder still closed and the muzzle still in a safe direction, take a firing grasp with your dominant hand. Cup the gun under the trigger guard with your support hand, and with the thumb of that hand, apply light pressure to the cylinder. Use about the same pressure you'd use to take your pulse at the wrist. This will effectively duplicate the cylinder drag of cartridge case heads against the frame at the rear of the cylinder window if the gun was loaded.

Now, slowly, roll the trigger back until the hammer falls. Hold the trigger back. With the thumb, wiggle the cylinder. If it is locked in place, then at least on that chamber, you have the solid lockup you want. If, however, this movement causes the cylinder to only now "tick" into place, it means that particular chamber would not have been in alignment with the bore when an actual shot was fired. Armorers call this effect a DCU, which stands for "doesn't carry up." You want to repeat this check for every chamber in the gun.

When the revolver's chambers don't lock into line with the bore, the gun is said to be "out of time." The bullets will go into the forcing cone at an angle. This degrades accuracy, and causes lead shavings to spit out to the sides, endangering adjacent shooters on the firing line. As it gets worse, the firing pin will hit the primer so far off center the gun may misfire. With powerful loads, it will quickly lead to a split forcing cone. It definitely needs to be fixed. (When you get an estimate, if the armorer or gunsmith says you need a new ratchet, get a second opinion. Maybe five out of six times, all the gun needs is to have a new cylinder hand stoned to fit. Replacing an extractor is at least four times as expensive.)

Do all that again, and this time, once each chamber locks into place, wiggle the cylinder. If there's a lot of slop and play, there's a good chance that perfect chamber/bore alignment will be a chancy thing, and

In a test that will make you cringe, unloaded pistol begins at slidelock with finger on slide release lever...

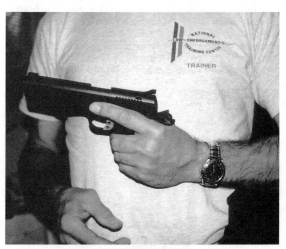

...and the hammer remains cocked as the slide slams forward. This shows Kimber Custom .45's sear mechanism to be in good working order. However...

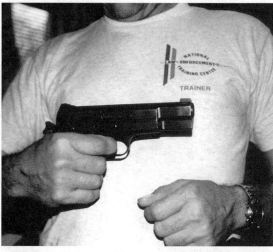

With magazine removed, hammer cocked, and safety off, the trigger is pulled on an empty Browning Hi-Power. Hammer does not move, demonstrating that magazine disconnector safety is functioning as designed.

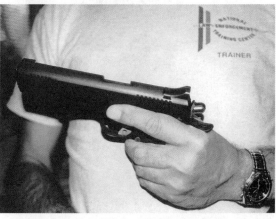

...if the hammer had "followed" slide to the half-cock position as replicated here, gun would need repairs before being worthy of purchase.

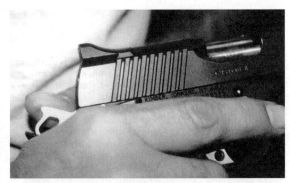

A less abusive test for hammer-follow on an auto is to hold it as shown and repeatedly flick the hammer back with the free hand thumb.

accuracy will suffer. This is generally a sign of bad workmanship in a cheaply made gun, and excessive wear in one of the big-name brands.

Push the cylinder back and forth; front to back and vice versa. A lot of slop means excessive headspace. Particularly with a big-bore or a Magnum, it may be a sign that the gun has been shot so much it's approaching the end of its useful life. A good gunsmith can fix this with some cylinder shims, however.

Check to see if magazines insert and drop out cleanly. This HK USP40 Compact passes the test.

Get some light on the other side of the gun, so you can look through the gap between barrel and cylinder. Hold the hammer back with your thumb until the bolt drops, and then rotate the cylinder, watching the gap. If you examine enough guns, you will find some that actually touch the forcing cone of the barrel. This is unacceptable; the cylinder will bind, the trigger pull will become uneven, hard, and "grating" as your finger works to force the cylinder past the bind point, and eventually the gun will lock up and stop working. On the other end of the spectrum, you may see a barrel/cylinder gap so wide that you could probably spit through it without touching metal. You can expect poor accuracy and nasty side-spit from such a gun. Reject it unless the seller is willing to pay for the repairs to bring it up to spec.

If the cylinder comes closer to the barrel on some chambers than others, the front of the cylinder is probably not machined true. Most experts would pass by such a revolver.

Autoloaders

With any autoloader, double check that it is empty and keep the muzzle in a safe direction. Try the action a few times. When you rack the slide, everything should feel smooth. The slide should go all the way into battery – that is, all the way forward – without any sticking points that require an extra nudge. If the gun binds when it's empty, you *know* it's going to bind when the mechanism has to do the extra work of picking up and chambering cartridges. If the gun is clean and is binding, pass it by.

Make sure magazines go in and out cleanly. Some guns (1911, for example) are designed for the magazines to fall completely away when the release button is pressed. If the test gun won't do this with new magazines that you know are in good shape, there could be some serious warpage in the grip-frame or, more probably, something wrong with the magazine release mechanism.

Some guns (early Glocks, most Browning Hi-Powers, any pistol with a butt-heel magazine release) can't be expected to drop their magazines free. However, the magazine should still run cleanly in and out of the passageway in the grip frame.

You want to check the sear mechanism with a hammer-fired pistol to make sure there won't be "hammer follow." The test itself is abusive, and you want to make sure it's OK with the current owner before you do it. Insert the empty magazine and lock the slide back. Making sure nothing is contacting the trigger, press the slide release lever and let the gun slam closed. Watch the hammer. If the hammer follows to the half-cock position or the at-rest position, the sear isn't working right. Either it has been dropped and knocked out of alignment, or more probably, someone did a kitchen table trigger job on it, and the sear is down to a perilously weak razor's edge. Soon, it will start doing the same with live rounds, which will keep you from firing subsequent shots until you've manually cocked the hammer. Soon after *that*, if the malady goes untreated, you will attempt to fire one shot and this pistol will go "full automatic."

Because the mechanism was designed to be cushioned by the cartridge that the slide strips off the magazine during the firing cycle, it batters the extractor (and, on 1911-type guns, the sear) to perform this test. However, it's the best way to see if the sear is working on a duty type gun. (Most target pistols have finely ground sears and won't pass this test, which is yet another reason you don't want a light-triggered target pistol for combat shooting.) If

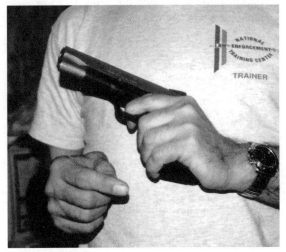

Checking the manual safety/sear engagement on a 1911. First, cock the empty gun, put the manual safety in the "on safe" position, and pull the trigger firmly as shown...

gun, one that would have fired the round in the chamber if you had tried to decock it while loaded.

Now, to test the firing pin, we'll use the Bic Stik or the #2 pencil again. This time, we'll pull the trigger. If the writing implement is launched clear of the barrel, you have a healthy firing pin strike. If it isn't, either the firing pin is broken or the firing pin spring is worn out.

Caution: In both of the last two tests, wear safety glasses and have a clear "line of fire" with no one in the way! That sharp-tipped pen or pencil will come flying out of the barrel with enough force to cause a cut or nasty eye damage! Also in both of these tests, you'll need an empty magazine in place if the pistol has a magazine disconnector safety.

To make sure that the magazine disconnector safety is operating, remove the magazine from the empty pistol, point it in a safe direction, and pull the trigger. If the hammer falls, the disconnector device either is not working or has been disconnected.

A sloppily fitted auto pistol is not likely to deliver much in the way of accuracy. Bring the slide forward on the empty gun, put the tip of a finger in the muzzle, and wiggle it around. If it's tight, it bodes well for accuracy. If it slops around a lot, the opposite can be expected. With the slide still forward, bring a thumb to the back of the barrel where it is exposed at the ejection port, and press downward. If it gives a lot, that tells you that the rear lockup isn't as solid as you'll need for really good accuracy. In either of these measurements, it's hard to explain how much play is too much. Try this test with some guns of known accuracy, and you'll quickly develop a "feel" for what is and is not what you're looking for with that particular make and model.

this test is unacceptable to the gun's owner, try the following. Hold the gun in the firing hand, cock it, and with the thumb of the support hand push the hammer all the way back past full cock and then release. If when it comes forward it slips by the full cock position and keeps going, the gun is going to need some serious repair.

If the pistol has a grip safety, cock the hammer of the empty gun, hold it in such a way that there is no pressure on the grip safety, and press the trigger back. If the hammer falls, the grip safety is not working.

If the gun has a hammer-drop feature (i.e., decocking lever), cock the hammer and drop a #2 pencil or a flat-head Bic Stik pen down the bore, with the tip of the writing instrument pointing toward the muzzle. With the fingers clear of the trigger, activate the decocking lever. If the pencil or pen just quivers when the hammer falls, the decocking mechanism is in good working order. However, if the pen or pencil flies from the barrel, that means it was hit by the firing pin. You're holding a dangerously broken

Summary

Well-selected "pre-owned" handguns are an excellent value. Firearms are the ultimate "durable goods." How many people do you know who drive their grandfather's car or keep the family food supply in their grandmother's ice box? Probably not too many. But if you start asking, you'll be amazed how many people you know still cherish their grandparents' firearms.

It's no trick at all to find a perfectly functional combat handgun, revolver or auto, on the second-hand shelf at half the price of a new one. That leaves you more money for ammo, training, skill-building...and enjoying the life and the people you bought that gun to protect.

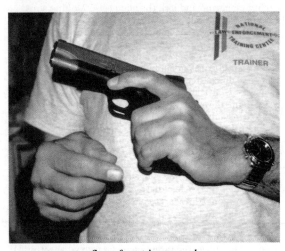

...now, remove finger from trigger guard...

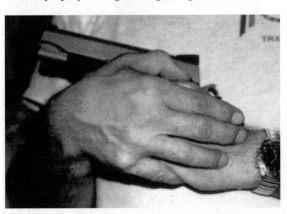

...and release the thumb safety. If hammer stays motionless as shown, that portion of the mechanism is in good working order. If hammer falls at this point, gun is DANGEROUSLY damaged!

CHAPTER THREE

Modern Paradigms

The Glock

Gaston Glock had made a fortune producing assorted polymer items at his factory in Austria. His reputation was such that more than one firearms company soon approached him to make a polymer pistol frame. Being (a) a manufacturer, (b) a businessman, (c) a designer, and (d) smarter than hell, it occurred to him that he could design his own gun to manufacture. He set his design team to work, giving them a clean sheet of paper.

In the early 1980s, there was little new under the sun in the form of handguns. The most high-tech auto pistols were largely refinements of older designs. For example: take the 1950 Beretta service pistol, add on a 1930s vintage Walther-type hammer-drop safety and a 1908 vintage Luger magazine release, and you had the "new" Beretta. But what came off the Glock drawing board was something new indeed.

It looked like something out of Star Trek. It was sleek, with a raked back grip angle that could be compared to a Luger or a Ruger only in the angle, not in the shape. It was square at front and back. It had no hammer, inside or out; the pistol was striker fired. The polymer frame, plus a design created from the ground up for economy of manufacture, ensured under-bidding of the competition. The other makers' guns carried 14 to 16 rounds of 9mm Parabellum, but this one carried 18. The trigger pull was very controllable, and consistent from first shot to last. More importantly, the thing worked with utter reliability and survived torture tests.

It wasn't the first "plastic gun." Heckler and Koch had pioneered that more than a decade before, with plastic framed P9S and VP70Z lines, only to be met with poor sales. No one predicted success, figuring that the Austrian army's adoption of the pistol was merely a sign of chauvenism.

It is doubtful that any greater underestimation was ever made in the world of the handgun.

The Glock's entry into the American handgun marketplace was nothing less than stunning. The American branch of the firm, Glock USA, was established in Smyrna, GA. A couple of guys who knew the marketplace were on board: Bob Gates, late of Smith & Wesson, and Carl Walter.

In the Glock light-weight, compactness, controllability and power come together in the author's favorite of the breed, the .45 caliber Glock 30. This one holds the short 9-round magazine designed for maximum concealment.

Author appreciates "shootability" of Glocks. He used this G17 to win High Senior and 2nd Master at 1999 New England Regional IDPA Championships, placing just behind national champ Tom Yost.

A number of signs in the marketing heavens were in alignment, and this confluence of the stars would make Glock the biggest success story in firearms in the latter half of the 20th century.

American police chiefs still clung tenaciously to their service revolvers. Unique among police equipment, the revolver had not changed materially since the turn of the century. Uniforms were better, the cars had modernized along with the rest of America, communications were state of the art, and even handcuffs had improved and been streamlined. But if you went to a police museum, you would find that only two things had gone basically unchanged since the dawn of the 20th century: the police whistle, and the police service revolver.

Patrolmen's unions and well-versed police instructors were clamoring for autoloaders. For years, the chiefs had put off these requests with stock answers. "Automatics jam." "Our guys won't remember to take the safeties off when they draw to fire in self-defense." "They're too complicated." "Automatics cock themselves and go off too easily after the first shot."

Meanwhile, instructors were chanting the old military mantra, "Keep it simple, stupid." Any auto adopted by most of them would have to be simple, indeed.

Enter the Glock.

It endured torture tests for thousands of rounds. Buried in sand and mud and frozen in ice, it was plucked out, shaken off, and fired. It worked. Sand and mud and ice chips flew along with the spent casings, but the guns worked. One adventuresome police squad deliberately dropped a loaded Glock from a helicopter at an altitude of 300 feet. The gun did not go off. When it was retrieved, though one sight was chipped, it fired perfectly.

Safety? There was no manual safety per se. All safeties were internal and passive. "Point gun, pull trigger," just like the revolver. When BATF declared the Glock pistol to be double-action only in design, the argument about cocked guns being dangerous went out the window, too.

The first pistol was the Glock 17, so called because it was Gaston Glock's 17th specific design. It became the flagship of a fast-expanding fleet. Though Glock would later describe it as "full size," it was actually smaller than a Model 1911 or a Beretta 92, more comparable in overall length to a Colt Lightweight Commander, and it weighed even less.

Next came the even smaller Glock 19 with its 4-inch barrel. The 16-shot 9mm was roughly the overall dimensions and weight of a Colt Detective Special with 2-inch barrel that held only six rounds of .38 Special. At the other end of the size spectrum, Glock introduced a target model in the late 1980s, the 17L with 6-inch barrel. This gun had a light 3.5-pound trigger pull, a pound and a half lighter than the standard gun. Other trigger options were also made available. New York State Police said they'd adopt the gun, but only if Glock made it with a heavier trigger. Thus was born the New York Trigger, which brought the pull weight up to roughly 8 pounds. NYSP adopted the Glock 17 so equipped, and their troopers carry it to this day.

1990 was a pivotal year for Glock. They announced their big-frame model, the Glock 20 in 10mm, the caliber expected to sweep law enforcement after the FBI's recent announcement of adopting the S&W Model 1076 in that caliber. The gun was quickly adapted to .45 ACP. In January of that same year at the SHOT Show in Las Vegas, Smith & Wesson and Winchester jointly announced the development of the .40 S&W cartridge. Gaston Glock returned home with ammo samples and very quickly the standard Glock was reinforced to handle the more powerful cartridge with its faster slide velocity. Within the year, the South Carolina Law Enforcement Division had adopted the full size Glock 22 in that caliber and proven it on the street, and others were ordering the compact Glock 23.

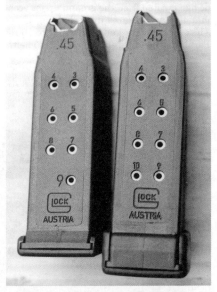

Different magazines add to the Glock's versatility. Left, a short-bottom nine round magazine for maximum concealment; right, 10-round mag with little finger placement support. Both are for the Glock 30 .45 auto.

The Glock 17 holds 18 rounds of 9mm Parabellum in a pre-ban magazine. This specimen has Glock's oversize slide release and Heinie sights.

In 1993, after a gunman with a 9mm murdered a young NYC cop while he was reloading his mandated six-shot revolver, the Patrolman's Benevolent Association at last prevailed over management and NYPD reluctantly went to the auto. All new recruits would have to purchase a 9mm instead of a .38, and in-service officers could buy one if they wanted. NYPD had always required their personnel to buy their own guns. Three double-action-only 16-shooters were authorized: the SIG P226 DAO, the S&W Model 5946, and the Glock 19. The Glock was by far the lightest and most compact for off duty and plainclothes carry, and by far the least expensive; it became first choice by such an overwhelming margin that many observers around the country thought NYPD had standardized on the Glock.

In the mid-1990s, the company found another huge success with their baby Glocks. The size of snubby .38s with twice the firepower and more controllability, the babies shot as well as the big ones. They were dubbed G26 in 9mm and G27 in .40 caliber. Slightly larger compacts were offered in 10mm Auto and .45 Auto, the Glocks 29 and 30 respectively. When a groundswell of popularity emerged in police circles for the powerful and accurate .357 SIG cartridge, Glock offered that chambering through the line as Model 31 (full size), Model 32 (compact) and Model 33 (subcompact).

The company didn't stop there. Integral recoil reduction ports were offered, creating a factory compensated gun in either compact or full size. These kept the same model numbers as the base guns, but with the suffix "C". The firm also introduced the "Tactical/Practical" series. Midway in length between full size and long-slide, they were exactly the length of the old Colt Government Model. This suited the .40 caliber G35 well for the Production class in IPSC shooting (where that caliber barely "made major"), and the 9mm G34 perfectly for Stock Service Pistol class in IDPA, where Dave Sevigny has used one to win repeated national championships. A number of departments from Nashua, NH to Kerrville, TX have made the Glock 35 the

standard issue duty pistol, usually with a retrofit of a New York trigger.

By the turn of the 21st century, the Glock pistol dominated the American law enforcement market to the tune of roughly 65 percent.

Modifying the Glock

The pistol comes from the factory with what the company calls a "standard" trigger, which uses an S-shaped spring to connect the trigger to the unique cruciform sear plate. (The "Tactical/Practical" comes with a 3.5-pound trigger, like the long-slide 9mm 17L and .40 G24 models.) Supposedly delivering 5 pounds of pull, the standard trigger generally weighs out to about 5.5 pounds. Most civilian shooters leave it as is, as do many police departments including Washington, D.C. Metro, the Illinois State Police, and the FBI.

Many, including this writer, have followed the lead of the NYSP and gone with the original weight New York Trigger, now known as the NY-1. The intention of this design was to mitigate accidental discharges caused by human error. There is some three-eighths of an inch of travel from when the Glock trigger is at rest and ready to when it reaches its rearmost point and discharges the pistol. On the standard set-up, it feels like a Mauser military rifle trigger with a long, light take-up and then about a tenth of an inch of firm resistance before the shot is fired. When human beings are in danger, their inborn survival mechanism triggers a number of physiological changes, one of which is vasoconstriction. That is, blood flow is shunted away from the extremities and into the body's core and the major muscle groups. This is why frightened Caucasians are seen to turn ghostly pale, and it is why frightened people become clumsy and lose tactile sensation in their fingers under stress. In such a situation, it is feared that if the finger has erroneously strayed to the trigger prematurely, the shooter won't be able to feel it taking up trigger slack until too late.

The advantage of the NY-1 trigger is that it offers a very firm resistance to the trigger finger from the very beginning of the pull, a resistance so strong it probably *will* be palpable to the shooter even in a vasoconstricted state. This means a lot more than merely 3 pounds additional pull weight. (The NY-1 increases the pull to a nominal 8 pounds, which usually measures out to more like 7.75 pounds.) This, plus excellent training, allows NYSP and other departments to have an excellent safety record with these guns.

New York City Police Department initially put some 600 Glocks in the field among specially assigned personnel, ranging from Homicide detectives to the Missing Persons unit. These first guns had the standard 5-pound triggers, and after a spate of accidental discharges, the Firearms Training Unit

Top, the Glock 27 holds 10 rounds of .40 S&W ammo; bottom, NAA Guardian holds 7 rounds of .380 ACP. Which would you choose?

mandated an even heavier trigger than the State Police had. Thus was born the NY-2 trigger module, also called the New York Plus. This brought the pull up to a stated 12 pounds, which usually measures about 11.5 pounds on a well broken-in Glock.

This writer personally thinks the NY-2 passes the point of diminishing returns by making the trigger harder to control in rapid fire. Like many, I actually shoot better with the NY-1 at 8 pounds than with the standard pull. The reason is that the different design gives a cleaner "trigger break" as the shot goes off, and the heavier spring better resists "backlash."

Finally, I've found as an instructor that the little S-spring on the standard trigger system is the one weak link in an otherwise ingenious and robust mechanism. I see several break a year. The NY module that replaces that spring is much sturdier and I've personally *never* seen one break. For all these reasons, I have the NY-1 in every Glock that I carry, and strongly recommend it for any Glock carried for duty or defense.

Atop some models sits the other weak link: plastic sights. Retrofit steel sights (the Heinie unit is particularly good) or metal night sights with Tritium inserts that can be ordered on the gun from the factory solve this problem. There is the rare breakage of locking blocks, but that is no more common than cracked locking blocks on Berettas or cracked frames on SIGs, Colts, etc. The finest machines can break when they are used hard and long, and it is no reflection on the product. Outfit your Glock with an NY-1 trigger and good steel sights, and there's nothing left on it that's likely to break.

The Appeal of the Glock

This gun is simple. Most armorer's courses (in which you are taught by the factory to repair the guns) take a week. Glock's takes one day. The pistol has only 30- some components. Almost all armorer's operations can be done with a 3/32-inch punch. You do need a screwdriver to remove the magazine release button.

There is no easier pistol to learn to shoot well! No decocking lever to remember; that's done automatically. No manual safety to manipulate; the safeties are all internal and passive. If your gun was made prior to 1990,

call the factory with the serial number and see if it should have the no-charge new-parts update. Then, like every Glock produced for more than a decade, it will be totally impact resistant and "drop-safe."

Insert magazine. Rack slide. That's it. Now shoot it like you would a revolver, taking care to keep your thumb away from the slide and your firing wrist locked, as you would with any semiautomatic pistol.

If you want a manual safety for weapon retention purposes, or because it just gives you peace of mind after a lifetime with some other brand of pistol carried on-safe, an excellent right-hander's thumb safety can be installed at very reasonable cost by Joe Cominolli, PO Box 911, Solvay, NY 13209.

The Glock is an extraordinarily reliable and long-lived pistol. It is light, fast-handling, and very controllable. The polymer frame can be seen to flex in high-speed photography as it fires, and this seems to provide a recoil-cushioning effect that is enhanced by the natural "locked wrist" angle of its grip-frame. The Hybrid Porting conversion, which reduces recoil by sending several gas jets up through the top of what used to be the slide, will vampire as much as 100 feet per second of velocity and create a louder report, but allows amazing shot-to-shot control. While it seems to take a master gunsmith to make Hybrid-porting work reliably on a 1911, the Glock seems to function perfectly with it installed.

The Glock is southpaw-friendly and lends itself to ambidextrous shooting. A growing cottage industry offers useful accessories for it. Laser sights are available from Laser-Max and Crimson Trace. Models made in the last few years, compact size and larger, have an accessory rail that will accommodate a flashlight. The company has always been scrupulously good about customer service in terms of parts and repairs.

Accuracy is adequate at worst and excellent at best. The only Glocks that seemed to be really inaccurate were the very first runs of the Glock 22, and the company squared that away quickly. I have a Glock 22 that, out of the box, will stay in 2.5 inches at 25 yards with good ammunition; this specimen was produced in 2001. The baby Glocks are famous for their accuracy. This is because the barrels and slides are proportionally thicker and more rigid on these short guns, and also because the double captive recoil spring that softens kick so effectively also guarantees that the bullet is out of the barrel before the mechanism begins to unlock. Modifying a Smith & Wesson auto to have that same accuracy-enhancing feature costs big bucks when done by the factory's Performance Center; it comes on the smallest Glocks at no charge.

The .45 caliber Glocks also seem to be particularly accurate. First, the .45 ACP has always been a more inherently accurate cartridge than the 9mm Luger and particularly the .40 S&W. Second, the .45 barrels are made on different machinery than the other calibers at Glock, and seem to be particularly accurate. The "baby .45," the Glock 30, combines both of these worlds and may be the most accurate pistol Glock makes. My Glock 30, factory stock with NY-1 trigger and Trijicon sights, has given me five-shot, 1-inch groups at 25 yards with Federal Hydra-Shok and Remington Match ammunition.

There is a good reason for the Glock pistol's predominance in the American law enforcement sector and, to a slightly lesser extent, the armed citizen sector. Quite simply, the product has earned it.

Contrary to popular belief, Glock was not the first auto pistol with a polymer frame. This Heckler & Koch P9S which pre-dated the Glock considerably with a "plastic frame," was not a huge marketing success.

Today's Double-Action Autos

Walther popularized the double-action auto with a de-cocking feature in the 1930s. It was seen at the time as a "faster" auto, the theory being that with a single-action auto like the Colt or Browning, you had to either move a safety lever, or cock a hammer, or jack a slide before firing. With the DA auto, it was thought, one could just carry it off safe and pull the trigger when needed, like a revolver.

At the time, most of America felt that if they wanted an auto that worked like a revolver, they would just carry one of their fine made-in-USA *revolvers,* thank you very much. In the middle of the 20th century, 1911 flag-bearer Jeff Cooper applied an engineer's phrase that would stick to the double-action auto forever after. The concept was, he said, "an ingenious solution to a non-existent problem."

Whether or not that was true at the time, a problem later came up to fit the solution. America had become, by the latter 20th century, the most litigious country in the world. With more lawyers per capita than any other nation, the United States became famous for tolerating utterly ridiculous lawsuits that, had they been brought in a country that followed the Napoleonic Code, would probably have ended up penalizing the plaintiff for having brought an unmeritorious case. Two elements of this would have impact on handgun selection in both police and private citizen sectors.

Gun control had joined abortion as one of the two most polarized debates in the land. Prosecutors were either elected by the same folks who elected the politicians, or appointed by elected politicians. Some of them found it expedient to "make examples" of politically incorrect shootings of bad guys by good guys. For this, they needed a hook.

Contrary to popular belief, prosecutors don't get big occupation bonus points for winning a conviction for murder instead of manslaughter. If they get a conviction, they get credit, period. If they bring a case and lose, they lose credibility and political capital. This is why a good chance of a win on a lower charge beats a poor chance of conviction on a higher charge. To convince a dozen people

Ruger's P90 beat every other double-action .45 tested and became the issue weapon for author's police department in 1993, along with Safariland SS-III security holster.

with common sense sitting in a jury box that a good cop or a decent citizen has suddenly become a monstrous murderer is a pretty tough sell. But to convince them that a good person could have been careless for one second and made a mistake is an easy job, because every adult has done exactly that at some time. A murder conviction requires proving the element of malice, but a manslaughter conviction requires only proving that someone did something stupid. Thus, it came into vogue to attack politically incorrect justifiable homicide incidents with a charge of manslaughter.

It is common knowledge that a light trigger pull – what a lay person would call a "hair trigger" – is more conducive to the accidental discharge of a firearm than a long, heavy trigger pull that requires a deliberate action. Cocking a gun, or pointing an already cocked gun at a suspect, could therefore be seen as negligence. Now, the key ingredient of a manslaughter conviction was in place.

It reached a point where prosecutors would actually manufacture a "negligent hair trigger argument" even in cases where the gun was never cocked. One such case, *State of Florida v. Officer Luis Alvarez,* is mentioned elsewhere in this book. Alvarez' department responded by rendering all the issue service revolvers double-action-only. Some saw this as a weak concession to political

A relic of the early 20th Century, the slide-mounted safety/de-cock lever of Walther PPK inspired designs of S&W, Beretta, and others much later in the "wondernine" period.

correctness. It must be pointed out, however, that if the double-action-only policy had been in place before the shooting, the prosecution never would have had that false hook on which to hang the case, to begin with.

And that was just in criminal courts. On the civil lawsuit side, something similar was happening. Plaintiffs' lawyers realized that the deep pockets they were after belonged to insurance companies, not individual citizens who got involved in self-defense shootings. Almost everyone who shot an intruder had homeowner liability insurance, but such policies specifically exempt the underwriter from liability for a willful tort, that is, a deliberately inflicted act of harm. The lawyers could only collect if the homeowner shot the burglar by accident. Thus was born the heavy thrust of attacking guns with easy trigger pulls, and of literally fabricating the "cocked gun theory of the case." Private citizens who kept guns for self-protection and were aware of these things began to see the advisability of double-action-only autos as well as revolvers for home defense and personal carry.

A two-pronged concern was now in place. Fear of accidental discharges of weapons with short trigger pulls, and fear of false accusation of the same. Police chiefs who had once authorized cocked and locked Colts and Brownings for officers now banned those guns. Detroit PD and Chicago PD are two examples. Many private citizens who carried guns and followed these matters saw the trend, and decided that a design that was double-action at least for the first shot might have an advantage.

Thus was born the interest in DA pistols. The compactness of the Walther .380 had already made it a popular concealed carry handgun. Smith & Wesson's double-action Model 39, introduced in the mid-50s, had captured the attention of gun buffs. It was a good looking gun, slim and flat to carry in the waistband, with a beautiful feel in the hand, and it was endorsed by such top gun writers of the time as Col. Charles Askins, Jr., George Nonte, and Jan Stevenson.

The 1970s saw the development of high-capacity 9mm double-action designs, and of hollow-point 9mm ammo that got the caliber up off its knees. With expanding bullets, the 9mm Luger's reputation as an impotent man-stopper in two world wars was rehabilitated to a significant degree.

These guns became known as "wondernines," a term that was coined, I believe, by the late Robert Shimek. Known to gun magazine readers as an expert on handgun hunting and classic military-style small arms, Shimek was known only to a few as a career law enforcement officer who wore a 9mm SIG P226 to work every day.

These "wondernines" worked. In the late 70s and early 80s, the manufacturers refined the designs to meet the virtually 100 percent reliability requirements in the JSSAP (Joint Services Small Arms Project) tests that would determine the service pistol that would replace the ancient 1911 as the U.S. military sidearm. As a result, they were thoroughly "de-bugged." The prospect of a giant, lucrative government contract proved to be a powerful incentive to "get the guns right."

They would become the platforms of the .40 S&W cartridge in 1990, and of the subsequent .357 SIG cartridge. They would be enlarged, keeping the same key design features, to handle the .45 ACP and the 10mm Auto.

These were the guns that would change the face of the handgun America carried.

Beretta

Beretta snatched the gold ring when the ride on the JSSAP merry-go-round was over, winning the contract as the new primary service pistol of the U.S. armed forces. There were a few broken locking blocks and separated slides. Though some of these involved over-pressure lots of ammo that would have broken any gun, and others involved sound suppressors whose forward-levering weight didn't allow the locking blocks to work correctly, jealous manufacturers who lost the bid amplified the "problem" to more than it was. Almost without exception, military armorers and trainers who monitor small arms performance in actual conflicts have given the Beretta extremely high marks for its performance in U.S. military service.

It has also stood up nobly in the U.S. police service. For many years now the issue weapon of LAPD (almost 10,000 officers) and Los Angeles County Sheriff's Department (some 7,000 deputies), the Beretta 92, 9mm has given yeoman's service. Thanks to its open-top slide design, it is virtually jam-free, and one of the very few pistols that can equal or exceed the Glock in terms of reliability.

The glass-smooth feel of the action as you hand-cycle the Beretta is the standard by which others are judged. The 92F series, with combination manual safety/decocking lever, may have the single easiest slide-mounted safety to operate. Two large departments, one East Coast and one West, mandate that their personnel carry the Beretta on-safe. Each department has logged numerous cases in which the wearers' lives were saved by this feature when someone got the gun away from an officer, tried to shoot him or her, and couldn't because the safety was engaged.

The Beretta is also a very accurate pistol. Five rounds of 9mm commonly go into 1-1/2 inches at 25 yards from the standard Model 92. The Model 96, chambered for .40 S&W, passed the demanding accuracy tests of the Indiana State Police and was adopted as that agency's standard issue sidearm. The state troopers of Rhode Island, Florida, and Pennsylvania joined Indiana and issue the

A new wave classic, to mix a metaphor, the Beretta 92 proved to be an utterly reliable 16-shot 9mm, winning the U.S. Government contract and arming countless U.S. police agencies. This is a G-model, customized by Ernest Langdon, who won national championships with such guns.

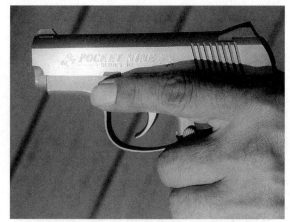

Colt's Pocket Nine, a 9mm Parabellum the size of a Walther PPK but lighter, was the company's high point in double-action auto manufacture. For reasons explained in the text, it is no longer produced at this writing.

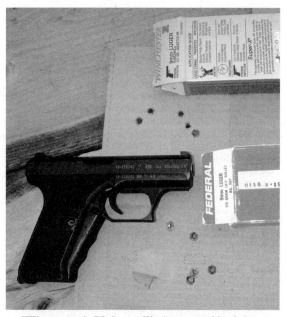

HK's ergonomic P7 shows off its "guaranteed head-shot accuracy" at 25 yards with two of the most accurate 9mm rounds available, 115-grain Federal 9BP and Winchester's Olin Super Match 147-grain, both with JHP projectiles.

96 at this writing. The city police of San Francisco and Providence also issue the 96.

In .40 S&W, my experience has been that the Beretta is a notch below its 9mm cousin in reliability. For this reason, Ohio state troopers dumped the 96 for the SIG equivalent.

Beretta's updated Cougar is a good gun. It is the issue weapon of the North Carolina Highway Patrol (in caliber .357 SIG) among others. The latest version, the polymer-frame 9000 series, is not particularly ergonomic and has not been so well received.

Colt

America's most famous producer of single-action autos has not fared well on the double-action side of that table. Their first, the Double Eagle, misfired constantly in its original incarnation. When I broke the story on that, Colt was gracious enough to recognize the problem and correct it. The pistol, however, still looked like what it was: a Government Model with a double-action mechanism cobbled together in a fragile way to get past the Seecamp Conversion patent. It did not fare well and is no longer in production.

Colt's All-American 2000 was a sad and ugly thing. Jams. Misfires. Pathetic accuracy and a horrible trigger pull. Heralded by the newsstand gun magazines as a great leap forward in technology, it soon died a well-deserved death.

Colt's only good double-actions were their last, both DAOs. The little Pony .380 worked, and the Pocket Nine 9mm *was* a breakthrough: a full power, seven-shot 9mm Luger exactly the size of a Walther PPK .380 but 5 ounces *lighter,* utterly reliable, and capable of 2-inch, five-shot groups at 25 yards. While the triggers were heavy, they were controllable. Alas, only about 7,000 Pocket Nines were produced before a patent infringement suit by Kahr Arms shut down production.

Heckler & Koch

HK's 1970s entries in the double-action auto market, the VP70Z and the P9S, did not succeed. The former

worked well as a machine pistol and poorly as a semiautomatic. The latter, exquisitely accurate, was before its time. It needed its chamber throated to feed hollow-points reliably, and its decocking mechanism, which involved pulling the trigger, was enough to make police firearms instructors wake up in the middle of the night screaming.

The P7 was much more successful. With an ingenious combination of gas operation and a squeeze-cocking fire control system that the company called Continuous Action, it created a cult following among handgunners. The gun was either loved or hated with no middle ground. A fixed barrel made it deadly accurate, with sub-2-inch groups at 25 yards more the rule than the exception. The squeeze-cocking came naturally and the pistol was super-fast to draw and fire. A low bore axis, plus the gas bleed mechanism, made it the lightest-kicking of 9mm combat pistols. Widely adopted in Germany, it became the issue service pistol of the New Jersey State Police in 1984 as the P7M8, with American style mag release and eight-round magazine. The double-stack P7M13 was subsequently adopted by Utah state police.

Its strength was that it was easy to shoot; its weakness was that it was easy to shoot. Many instructors associated the design with a likelihood of accidental discharge. Cost of manufacturing plus the changing balance of dollar and Deutschmark soon rendered it unaffordable for most civilians and almost all police. Still produced in the M8 format, this unique and excellent pistol is fading from the scene, but still cherished by a handful of serious aficionados, all of whom seem able to shoot it extremely well.

HK tried to get back into the police service pistol market with the gun they sold to the German armed forces, the USP. A rugged polymer-framed gun, it is available in several variants: lefty, righty, double-action-only, single-action-only, safety/decock or decock-only lever, and assorted combinations of the same. Available calibers are 9mm, .40, .357 SIG, and .45 ACP. It was the USP that introduced the now widely copied concept of the dust cover portion of the frame being moulded as a rail to accept a flashlight attachment.

I've found the USP conspicuously reliable, except for occasional jams in the 9mm version. It is also extremely accurate. Though competition versions are available, the standard models, particularly in .45, are tight shooters in their own right. Starting with probably the heaviest and "roughest" double-action only trigger option in the industry, they now have one of the best in their LE module, developed in 2000 for a Federal agency and offered to the civilian public in 2002. The HK USP is approved for private purchase by Border Patrol, and is the standard issue service pistol of departments ranging from San Bernardino PD to the Maine State Police.

Kahr

Brilliantly designed by Justin Moon, the Kahr pistol is slim and flat, comparable in size to most .380s, and utterly reliable with factory 9mm or .40 S&W ammo. The double-action-only trigger is smooth and sweet, and the guns have surprising inherent accuracy. My K9 once gave me a 1-3/8-inch group at 25 yards with Federal 9BP ammo.

The only real complaint shooters had about the Kahr was that, being all steel, it seemed heavy for its size. This was answered with the polymer-framed, P-series guns. Whether the polymer-framed P9 and P40 will last as long as the rugged little K9 or K40, or their even smaller MK (Micro Kahr) siblings, is not yet known. NYPD has approved the K9 as an off-duty weapon for their officers, and Kahrs sell quite well in the armed citizen sector.

The Kahr's controls are so close together, given the small size of the pistol, that a big man's fingers can get in the way a little. By the same token, the gun tends to be an excellent fit in petite female hands.

Improving on the Kahr is gilding the lily, but a few gunsmiths can actually make it even better. One such is Al Greco at Al's Custom, 1701 Conway Wallrose Rd., PO Box 205, Freedom, PA 15042.

Kel-Tec

In the early 90s, noted gun designer George Kehlgren pulled off a coup: the Kel-Tec P-11. With heavy use of polymer and a simple but heavy double-action-only, hammer-fired design, he was able to create a pocket-size 9mm that could retail for $300. At 14-1/2 ounces it was the weight, and also roughly the overall size, of an Airweight snubby revolver, but instead of five .38 Specials it held 10 9mm cartridges. One California law enforcement agency hammered more than 10,000 rounds of Winchester 115-grain +P+ through it with very few malfunctions and no breakage during testing.

The magazine is a shortened version of the S&W 59 series. This means that hundreds of thousands of pre-ban, "grandfathered" 14- and 15-round S&W 9mm magazines exist to feed it. This is handy for spare ammo carry and for home defense use where concealment is irrelevant.

Kel-Tec has made the same gun in .40, but not enough are in circulation for the author to have a feel of how they work. Numerous Kel-Tec P-11s have been through our classes, and the only problem with them is that the heavy

trigger pull becomes fatiguing during long days of shooting. However, any competent pistolsmith can give you a better pull for only a small portion of the money you save buying a P-11. Early problems with misfires in the first production runs were quickly squared away.

Perhaps Kehlgren's most fascinating design is his tiny P-32, which will be discussed two chapters subsequent.

ParaOrdnance

When the sharp Canadians who popularized the high-capacity 1911 brought out their double-action-only model, they called in the LDA. The shooting public automatically assumed it stood for Light Double-Action, even though ParaOrdnance never called in that per se. They didn't have to. The assumption was correct. The pull stroke feels so light that your first thought is, "Will this thing even go off?"

It will. There were some minor problems with the very first LDAs, but the company got them squared away in a hurry. The ones we've seen since, in all sizes, have worked great. Factory throated with ramped barrels and fully supported chambers, they have the slimness and quick safety manipulation of the standard 1911, and in the single-stack models take the same magazines. This .45 is an excellent choice for the 1911 devotee who thinks it's time to go to something in a double-action.

Ruger

Ruger's P-series of combat auto pistols, scheduled to debut in 1985, did not hit the marketplace until 1988. Bill Ruger had shown me the blueprints and rough castings of his original design, an affordable 9mm auto, in the early 1980s and had sworn me to secrecy. Early tests showed some jamming problems with some departments, though the ones we tested were perfectly reliable, but accuracy was sloppy with 4-inch to 5-inch groups being common at 25 yards. The P85 was not a success.

Stung by this, one of the few failures in the history of his company, Bill Ruger and his engineers set to work with a vengeance to correct the problems. The P85 Mark II and later the P89 had total reliability and better accuracy. There would be excellent medium- to service-size .40s and more compact 9mms to come. For my money, though, the triumph of the P-series was the P90 in .45 ACP.

Accuracy is a hallmark of the Ruger .45. The author's department-issue P90 has just scored 597 out of 600 points on a PPC course.

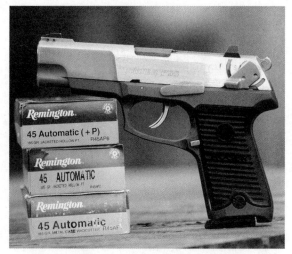

Unlike most 1911s, the "new wave" Ruger P90 feeds reliably with everything from light target loads (bottom) through standard .45 ACP (center) to the hottest +P with 10mm auto power level (top).

Adopted and proven by Huntington Beach (CA) PD, the SIG P220 popularized the double-action .45 auto among America's police and armed citizenry. This is the latest version, all stainless, with 9-round total capacity.

Designed at a time when it looked as if the 10mm would be the best-selling law enforcement round, the P90 was engineered to take a lifetime supply of that powerful ammo. Ironically, it was never chambered for that cartridge commercially, but in .45 the gun was "over-engineered," meaning it could take unlimited amounts of hot +P ammo with impunity. Moreover, thanks to some input from Irv Stone at BarSto, the P90 was the most accurate duty auto Ruger ever produced. One and a half inches for five shots at 25 yards is typical, and with the best ammo, I've seen these guns produce groups under an inch at that distance. There is no more accurate "modern style" .45 auto, though the Glock, SIG, and HK USP may equal, but not exceed, the Ruger in this respect.

The P90 is also extraordinarily reliable. In testing for the 1993 adoption of a duty auto, my department found that the Ruger P90 outperformed two more famous big-name double-action .45s, and adopted the P90. It has been in service ever since and has worked fine. Gun expert Clay Harvey tracked .45 autos of all brands used intensively for rental at shooting ranges, and found the Ruger undisputedly held the top spot in terms of reliability. In the latter half of the 1990s, Ruger introduced the P95 9mm and P97 .45 with polymer frames. These allowed production economy that made these guns super-good buys at retail, and both had superb state of the art ergonomics and fit to the hand.

San Diego PD bought large numbers of Ruger 9mm autos and reported excellent results. Ditto the Wisconsin State Patrol, which issued Ruger 9mm autos exclusively for many years.

SIG-Sauer

Originally imported to the U.S. long ago as the Browning BDA, the SIG P220 .45 was adopted by the Huntington Beach, CA PD. Numerous other agencies followed after learning of HBPD's excellent experience with the gun. And, after decades of ignoring their home-grown 1911 pistol, numerous police departments looked

at swapping .38 revolvers for .45 autos. A trend was emerging. When the P226 16-shot 9mm didn't make it out of the finals for the military contract, the police community welcomed the pistol with open arms.

The SIG fits most hands well, and soon there was a short-reach trigger available for those with smaller fingers. The trigger action was deliciously smooth, and the SIG was easy to shoot well. Straight-line feed meant that it fed hollow-points from the beginning. Texas and Arizona troopers went from revolvers to SIGs early, and though both have changed calibers since, neither has changed brand. One of the first auto pistols approved for wear by rank and file agents, the SIG has been a popular FBI gun ever since. It has long been the weapon of Secret Service and Air Marshals. The troopers of Connecticut, Delaware, Massachusetts, Michigan, Vermont, and Virginia have joined Texas and Aarizona troopers in adopting the SIG. This writer has carried the P226 and P220 on patrol for many a shift and always felt totally confident in the weapons.

With the early P226 and P220, the springs on the side-mounted magazine release tended to be too light,

"New wave" combat handguns deliver accuracy users of some of the classics could only dream about. Here are three five-shot groups at 25 yards with different .45 ACP rounds from SIG P220 stainless double-action.

resulting in an occasional unintended drop of a magazine. This was fixed some time ago. One runs across the occasional cracked frame, but SIG is good about fixing them, and the guns are so well designed they keep running even if the frame is cracked. The most annoying problem is a tendency for the grip screws to work loose.

SIGs tend to be very accurate pistols. I've seen more than one P220 group five shots inside an inch at 25 yards with Federal Match 185-grain .45 JHP, and the P226 will go around 1-1/2 inches with Federal 9BP or Winchester's OSM (Olin Super Match) 147-grain subsonic. The side-mounted decocking lever is easy to manipulate, and the SIG-Sauer design is more southpaw-friendly than a lot of shooters realize. Your experience, if you buy a SIG, is unlikely to be sour.

Smith & Wesson

The company that introduced the American-made "double-action automatic" took a while to get it right. There were a lot of feed failures and breakages in early Model 39, 39-2, and 59 pistols. Moreover, those guns were not drop-safe unless the thumb safety was engaged. Illinois State Police made them work by having their Ordnance Unit throat the feed ramp areas of all 1,700 or so pistols in inventory.

The second generation was drop-safe, and designed to feed hollow-points. These were characterized by three-digit model numbers without hyphens: the 9mm Model 459, for example, the Model 469 compact 9mm that the company called the "Mini-Gun," and the first of the long-awaited S&W .45 autos, the Model 645.

Ergonomics, however, still weren't great. The trigger pull suffered by comparison to the SIG, and the grips felt boxy and square. The introduction in 1988 of the third-generation guns with four-digit model numbers (5906, 4506, etc.) cured those problems. The only remaining source of irritation on S&W's "conventional style" defense autos is the occasional badly placed sharp edge.

From CHP to the Alaska Highway Patrol, S&W's 12-shot .40 caliber Model 4006 is the choice. S&W .40s are also worn by the troopers of Iowa, Michigan and Mississippi, while Idaho has the double-action only S&W .45 and Kentucky State Police issue the 10mm S&W Model 1076. A number of S&W autos are found in the holsters of FBI agents and Chicago and New York coppers, and S&W 9mm and .45 pistols are the only approved brand in addition to the Beretta for LAPD officers. The Royal Canadian Mounted Police use the S&W 9mm auto exclusively, in DAO models.

In concealed carry, two S&W autos stand out above all others. One is the accurate, super-compact, utterly reliable Model 3913 9mm. Endorsed by every leading female firearms instructor from Lyn Bates to Gila Hayes to Paxton Quigley, the 3913 works well in small hands and its safety features, like those of its big brother, make it ideal for those at risk of disarming attempts. Not only does the standard 3913 have a slide-mounted manual safety, but like the Browning Hi-Power and its own traditional siblings, it has a magazine-disconnector safety. This means that if someone is getting the gun away from you, you can press the release button and drop the magazine; this will render the cartridge in the chamber "unshootable" unless pressure was consistently applied to the trigger from before the magazine was dropped. This feature has saved a number of police officers in struggles over service pistols. It makes sense to security-minded private citizens, too.

The double-action-only version of SIG P226 (note absence of de-cocking lever) is in wide use by Chicago PD, NYPD, and numerous other agencies.

The other standout, a genuine "best buy" in the compact .45 auto class, is the Model 457. Compact and light in weight, this 8-shot .45 auto has controllable recoil, delivers every shot into about 2.5 inches at 25 yards, and is a stone bargain because it has S&W's economy-grade flat gray finish. The action is as smooth as that of its pricier big brothers. A whole run of these were made in DAO for the Chicago cops, and they were snapped up immediately. Cops know bargains.

Taurus

In the last two decades of the 20th Century, the Brazilian gunmaker Forjas Taurus doggedly rose from an also-ran maker of cheap guns to establish a well-earned reputation in the upper tiers of reliability and quality. Much of the credit belongs to their PT series of auto pistols. Originally these were simply licensed copies of the early model Beretta 9mm. Over the years, Taurus brought

John Hall, right, then head of the Firearms Training Unit of FBI, shows the author the Bureau's new S&W Model 1076 10mm in Hall's office at the FBI Academy, Quantico. The year is 1990. Photo courtesy Federal Bureau of Investigation.

in some design features of their own, notably a frame-mounted combination safety catch and de-cocking lever similar to the one that would later be employed on the HK USP.

We see a lot of Taurus pistols at Lethal Force Institute. The PT-92 through PT-100 models in 9mm and .40 S&W come in, shoot several hundred rounds, and leave without a malfunction or a breakage. Accuracy is comparable to the Beretta, but cost is hundreds of dollars less. Finish may not be quite so nice, nor double-action pull quite so smooth, but these guns are definitely good values. Some find the frame-mounted safety of the Taurus easier and faster to use than the slide mounted lever of the modern Beretta, particularly shooters who come to the double-

action gun after long experience with Colt/Browning pattern single-action autos whose thumb safeties are mounted at the same point on the frame.

Taurus has also introduced a high-tech polymer series called the Millennium, aimed at the concealed carry market. This gun has not yet established the excellent and enviable reputation for reliability that the Taurus PT series has earned.

There are many other double-action autos on the market. These listed above, however, constitute the great majority of what American citizens carry, and almost the totality of what American police carry. These were the guns that shaped the double-action auto cornerstone of the new combat handgun paradigm.

Super-Light Revolvers

Combat handguns with lightweight aluminum frames have been with us for more than half a century. Smith & Wesson's Airweights immediately followed the introduction, circa 1950, of the Colt Cobra and lightweight Commander. The aluminum frame became standard a few years later on S&W's 9mm. The 1970s would see Beretta and SIG follow S&W's lead with aluminum-framed duty autos, and of course, Glock popularized the polymer frame in the 1980s.

Great leaps were made in the latter 1990s, however, as Smith & Wesson introduced Titanium and then, at the turn of the century, Scandium to create a generation of light and strong revolvers unseen until this time. Taurus followed immediately with their Ultra-Lite and Total Titanium series. Today, we have medium-sized revolvers in easy-to-carry weights that fire .38 Special, .357 Magnum, .44 Special, .45 Colt, and even the mighty .41 Magnum.

For each such gun that finds its way into the field, there are several small-frame "super-lights" that are being carried in .22 Long Rifle, .32 Magnum, .38 Special, and even .357 Mag. The majority of these are .38s.

The reason the little super-lights are so much more popular than the big ones doesn't have much to do with the fact that they've been around just a little bit longer.

It's a convenience thing. There is a huge market among civilians with CCWs and cops already overburdened with equipment. People want small, powerful handguns that don't drag and sag when worn on the body. Let's examine some of the weight standards we're talking about.

Smith & Wesson's Centennial "hammerless" revolver is a case in point. I own them in all four of the different weight configurations. It's interesting to see how they "weigh in," in more ways than one.

Model 640 all-steel

This is one of the first of the re-issued Centennials, produced circa 1990 with the frame stamped +P+. I've always carried mine with the 158-grain +P FBI loads. It shoots exactly where the sight picture looks. It is very accurate, and head-shots at 25 yards are guaranteed if I do my part. Recoil with the +P is stiff; not fun, but not hard to handle either. Shooting a 50-round qualification course with it is no problem. It weighs 19.5 ounces unloaded.

Model 442 Airweight aluminum-frame

As with the 640, this gun's barrel and cylinder are machined entirely from solid ordnance steel. This gun shoots where it is aimed. It is reasonably accurate. A

A seven-shot L-frame snubby is a good "envelope" for the ultra-light .357 concept.

A recoil-absorption glove is a most useful accessory when shooting the lightest, smallest-frame revolvers!

Here are the four S&W Centennials discussed in this chapter. From top: all-steel, Airweight, AirLite Ti, and AirLite Sc.

Top, a factory brushed nickel Model 442 Airweight, and below, an AirLite Ti. Both have Crimson Trace LaserGrips. The lower gun is one third lighter, but feels twice as vicious in recoil. The author prefers the Airweight for his own needs.

perfect score on the 50-round "qual" course may not be fun with the now distinctly sharper recoil, but it is not my idea of torture, either. A perfect score on the qualification isn't that much harder to achieve. The more visible sight configuration on the newest Airweights helps here. Weight is 15.8 ounces unloaded.

Model 342 AirLite Ti

This gun's barrel is a thin steel liner wrapped inside an aluminum shroud, and its cylinder is made of Titanium. Like most such guns I've seen, it hits way low from where its fixed sights are aimed. I cannot shoot +P lead bullets (the "FBI Load") in it because the recoil is so violent it pulls them loose. Jacketed +P is the preferred load. The one qualification I shot with this was with jacketed CCI 158-grain +P. Recoil was so vicious I was glad I had a shooting glove in the car. When it was over, I was down two points. Rather than try again for a perfect score, I took what I had. It was hurting to shoot the thing. This gun is not as accurate as the all-steel or Airweight, putting most .38 Special loads in 3-inch to 7-inch groups at 25 yards. Weight, unloaded, is 11.3 ounces.

Model 340 Sc Scandium

Chambered for .357 Magnum, this gun manages not to tear up the FBI load in the gun's chambers, but doesn't shoot it worth a damn for accuracy. Admittedly, this isn't the most accurate .38 Special cartridge made, but the load gives me about 5 inches at 25 yards in my Airweight, versus 15 inches of what I can only call spray out of this gun, with bullets showing signs of beginning to keyhole. This gun also shot way low. Recoil with Magnum loads was nothing less than savage. The little Scandium beast was somewhat more accurate with other rounds, but not impressively so. After five rounds, the hands were giving off that tingling sensation that says to the brain, "WARNING! POTENTIAL NERVE DAMAGE." When passed among several people who shoot .44 Magnum and .480 Ruger revolvers for fun, the response was invariably, "Those five shots were enough, thanks." I didn't even try to shoot a 50-shot qualification with it. Unloaded weight is 12.0 ounces.

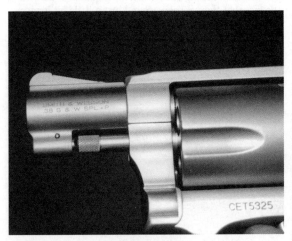

The little notch at the tip of ramped front sight is an improvement on current S&W J-frame snubbies with all-steel barrels. This is the LadySmith Airweight.

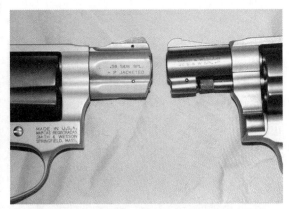

Accuracy is in the barrel assembly. The 342 AirLite Ti, left, has a thin barrel within a shroud, and a too-high sight that makes shots print low. The conventional one-piece steel barrel of Airweight LadySmith, right, delivers better groups and proper sight height puts shots "on the money."

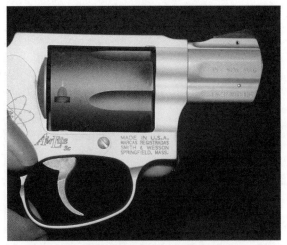

A warning on the barrel shroud of AirLite Sc: it reads, 357 S&W MAG/NO LESS THAN 120 GR BULLET.

The thin steel barrel sleeves of the Ti and Sc guns just don't seem to deliver the accuracy of the all-steel barrels of the Airweight and all steel models. All four guns are DAO, so it wasn't the trigger. The same relatively deteriorating accuracy was seen in the super-lights with mild .38 wadcutter ammo and big Pachmayr grips, so it wasn't the recoil. To what degree this is important to you is a decision only you can make.

Now, let's put all that in perspective. In the 1950s when all this ultra-light gun stuff started, Jeff Cooper defined the genre as meant to be "carried much and shot seldom." Alas, the days when we can do that are over, at least in law enforcement. Any gun we carry on the job is a gun we are required to qualify with repeatedly. As I look at my 340 Sc and 342 AirLite Ti, it occurs to me that if I'm deliberately going to do something that hurts like hell, I should go to Mistress Fifi's House of Pain and at least get an orgasm out of the deal.

This is why, for my own small backup revolver needs, I tend toward either the Model 442 or the Ruger SP-101. While the latter gun is even heavier than the Model 640, it fires the .357 Magnum round with very controllable recoil. A qualification with the SP-101 using full power 125-grain Magnum ammo could be called "exhilarating." The same qualification with the same ammo in the baby Scandium .357 qualifies absolutely as torture, at least in my hands.

Different people have different abilities and needs. My fellow gunwriter Wiley Clapp admits that the 342 Sc kicks like hell, but it's his favorite pocket gun nonetheless, even when stoked with Elmer Keith Memorial Magnum ammo. As you look at our differing preferences, note two things. First, Wiley is a big, strong guy. I, on the other hand, resemble the "before" picture in the Charles Atlas ads. Second, Wiley is retired from law enforcement and no longer required to qualify at regular intervals with

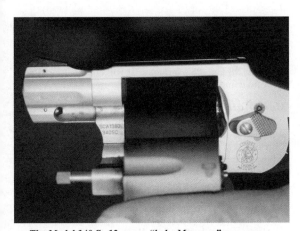

The Model 340 Sc 12-ounce "baby Magnum" was among the first S&Ws to receive integral lock treatment; note keyway above cylinder latch.

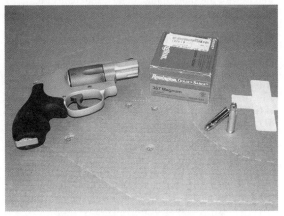

The Scandium J-frame gave 100 percent reliability with Golden Saber medium-velocity .357 Magnum, but uninspiring accuracy.

The grimace on the face of this shooter after firing his first full Magnum round from the Scandium J-frame says it all.

Here's what happens when you use full-power lead bullets in a Ti or Sc S&W. Inertia from the violent recoil pulled the bullet nose of the 158-grain Magnum forward, "prairie-dogging" out of the chamber and preventing rotation.

backup guns and their carry ammo. Those repeated qualifications are something I'm still stuck with.

For me, the balance of the super-light versus the Airweight comes out in favor of the Airweight for two reasons. At least in .38 Special, I can use my favorite load, that +P lead hollow-point that would pull loose in the chambers of the lighter guns. Moreover, in my career as an instructor I've seen a whole lot of people conditioned to flinch and jerk their shots because their gun hurt their hand when it went off. I don't want that situation to develop with me especially when I'm into the last layer of my safety net, the backup gun in my pocket. That's why, since I have to shoot a lot with any gun I carry, I want to carry a gun I'm comfortable shooting a lot.

We have more choices than ever, choices that fit some of us better than others. That's a good thing.

There are a great many people who can benefit from the super-light small-frame revolvers. Before you choose, check out the Taurus line. Some are equipped with integral recoil compensators that make them distinctly easier to shoot than a Smith & Wesson of equivalent weight with the same ammo. In fact, the comps take enough oomph out of the kick that the lead bullet +P rounds *don't* start to disassemble themselves in the chambers of Taurus guns so outfitted.

Another option is caliber change. My colleague Charlie Petty recommends the .32 Magnum in these guns. The recoil is much more controllable and the power level will still be more debilitating to an opponent than a mouse-gun. And, speaking of mouse-guns, a considerable number of the AirLite Ti revolvers have been sold as the Model 317, an eight-shot .22 that weighs only 9.9 ounces unloaded.

Let's think about that last concept. No, I'm not *recommending* a .22 for self-defense. But if the person is only going to carry a 10-ounce .25 auto anyway, they're far better served with a top quality eight-shot, 10-ounce .22 revolver. The Model 317 will go off every time you pull the trigger, which is more than you can say for most .25 autos. Unlike most small auto pistols in .22 Long Rifle, this revolver will work 100 percent with the hot, hypervelocity .22 rimfire ammo typified by CCI's Stinger, the cartridge

The Model 340 Sc jammed after the third shot. Note how the bullets of Remington 158-grain SWC .357 cartridges have pulled forward from recoil inertia. At right is a properly sized round from same box for comparison.

that began that concept long ago. Perhaps because the .22 doesn't generate enough heat to affect the thin steel barrel sleeve, the AirLite .22 will generally group better than the .38 and .357 versions. It will outshoot most any .25 auto going.

More Wattage for the Lite

The super-light revolver comes into a different perspective when you look at the larger models. In the Taurus line, I've found all the Ultra-Lites and Total Titanium models I've fired to be good shooters. The larger frame models come with the company's unique Ribber grips, for which I give great thanks. They soak up recoil better than anything S&W currently offers. Add to that the option of the integral recoil compensator, and you have a much more shootable gun.

Alas, as with the Smiths, all is not perfect with these guns, either. I've run across several Taurus revolvers of this genre whose cylinders were simply too tight and were rubbing against the forcing cone of the barrel, mucking up the trigger pull and binding the action. A quick trip back to the plant to widen the barrel cylinder gap fixes this, however. I've also seen several that didn't shoot to point of aim.

Groups, however, were consistently good. I recall one snubby .41 Magnum Taurus that put five shots into 2-5/16 inches at 25 yards. The ammo was PMC 41A, a full power 170-grain .41 Magnum hollow-point. If the late, great Elmer Keith, the father of the .44 Magnum and co-parent of the .41 Mag, still walked among us, I suspect this little Taurus is what he'd carry for backup.

Both S&W and Taurus have produced L-frame .357 Magnum super-lights. They weigh in the range of 18 ounces, which is about the heft of the old six-shot K-frame Model 12 Airweight .38 snubby. But instead of six .38s, these sleek shooters give you seven rounds of .357 Magnum. Recoil can be snappy, but nothing you can't handle. Use the Ribber grips on the Taurus, and get a pair of K-frame round-butt Pachmayr Decelerator Compac grips for the S&W to take the sting out. These are comfortable holster guns and conceal well under a light jacket, or in a good inside-the-waistband holster under a "tails-out" shirt.

S&W has also sold a number of their Model 396 revolvers, hump-backed L-frames that hold five rounds of .44 Special. The shape of the grip-frame forces you to have your hand low on the gun, and this puts the bore at such a high axis that the gun has a nasty upward muzzle whip. Personally, I can't warm up to this gun. Accuracy is mediocre, in a world where even short-barreled Smith & Wesson .44 Specials have historically shot with noble precision. I tested one next to a Glock 27 on one occasion. The auto pistol was smaller, roughly the same weight, and held 10 rounds compared to the wheelgun's five, in roughly the same power range. The Glock shot tighter groups faster and was actually easier to conceal.

All these guns have a place. The light .357s and the little Taurus .41 make good sense when you're in dangerous animal country and want something very powerful for up-close-and-personal defense, but want to keep the backpack as light as you can.

The big contribution of the super-lights to combat handgunnery is found, nonetheless, in the smallest ones. Easier to conceal on an ankle or snake out of a pocket than a square-backed auto pistol, easy to load and unload

The finger points to where sights were aimed at 25 yards. The 340 Sc hit far below that, with a poor group.

This federal agent experiences the recoil of a .357 Mag round in S&W 340 Sc.

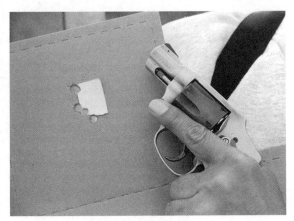

At 7 yards, the J-frame Scandium .357 gave this acceptable head-shot group.

Here is the Taurus CIA (Carry It Anywhere), that firm's answer to the S&W Centennial.

Trainer Michael de Bethancourt shows the aggressive stance required to control "baby Magnums" such as this 340 Sc.

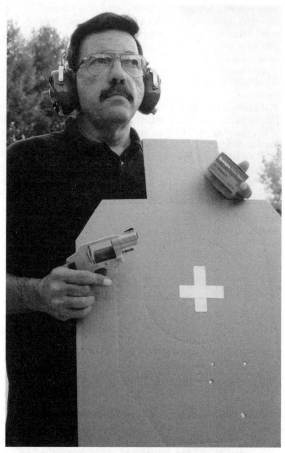

The five gut-shots were aimed at the center of the chest from 25 yards. Ammo was medium-velocity Remington Magnum fired from the 340 Sc. The author is about as pleased as he looks.

and utterly reliable, these little revolvers make up for their vicious recoil with their reassuring presence: being so easy to carry and to access, they're always *there*.

When Bert DuVernay was director of Smith & Wesson Academy, he made the very good point that while revolvers were indeed becoming a thing of the past as mainstream police service weapons, the small-framed revolver with a 2-inch barrel seemed assured a spot in the law enforcement armory as a backup and off-duty weapon. He seems to have called it right.

In states where "shall-issue" concealed carry has only recently been instituted, armed citizens are learning all over again how handy the "snub-nose .38" is as a personal protection sidearm. Many of the permits are going to law-abiding civilians who use these as their primary carry guns. For many of them, the option of the super-light models makes carrying a gun easier. For some, the super-light guns make carrying a gun *possible*. For that reason alone, I am grateful that these good guns exist.

Micro Handguns

First, let's define our terms. How small is small? Smith & Wesson dubbed their 13-shot 9mm pistols of the 1980s, the Model 469 (blue) and 669 (stainless), "Mini-Guns," but they were substantial enough that a number of cops wound up wearing them as uniform holster weapons. Glock's smallest models have been known as the "mini-Glocks" and the "baby Glocks." Kahr Arms dubbed their smallest series with an MK prefix, for "Micro Kahr."

How small is mini, baby, or micro? We can start smaller than that in the world of the combat handgun.

For many years, the tiny .25 auto was considered the quintessential "ladies' gun" and the "gentlemen's vest pocket pistol." There has been the occasional save of a good person with one of these guns because they simply had a gun, and might not have had anything bigger when the attack came. However, we'll never know how many people have been killed or crippled by attackers who weren't stopped in time by the feeble bite of these tiny

sub-caliber guns. As the streetwise martial artist Bill Aguiar put it, "A .25 auto is something you carry when you're not carrying a gun."

Sometimes a .25 is all you can handle. A psycho was beating a single mom in California to death when her little boy, pre-school age, grabbed her Raven .25 auto and screamed, "Get away from my mommy!" When the man did not, the child carefully shot him in the head, killing him instantly and saving his mother's life. I doubt he'll grow up troubled by the act. In Washington, an elderly man with an invalid wife fended off the attackers with the only weapon available, his wife's little .25 auto. As the attackers broke down the door and came at him, he fired once and the men fled. One died a few steps from the back door from a tiny bullet wound in the carotid artery. The other was captured within a few blocks. The grand jury almost instantly exonerated the old gentleman, and probably considered chipping in to buy him a bigger gun.

Comparable in size are the Colt Pony Pocketlite .380 (left), Beretta Tomcat .32 (center) and Seecamp LWS –32, (right). Author picks the .380 for deep concealment.

Both at 14.5 ounces, S&W Airweight .38 Special at left is only slightly larger than Beretta Tomcat .32, right. Author chooses the .38 hands down.

Since the 1970s we've had tiny, single-action, spur-trigger revolvers that harken back to S&W's No. 1 revolver of Civil War vintage, only smaller. They range in caliber from .22 Short through .22 Long Rifle to .22 Magnum. These guns are so tiny they are awkward to manipulate. A fellow on the range recently handed me one to fire. I pointed it downrange too casually, and when I triggered a shot, the gun jumped right out of my hand. I had only been holding it with part of one finger. Embarrassing? Yes, but not nearly so embarrassing as if it had happened in a fight.

Let me be the first to say that there are people who owe their lives to these little guns. In Los Angeles, a woman carrying one was savagely attacked. She pressed the muzzle into her assailant's chest, pulled the trigger, got him just right, and killed him where he stood. The slaying was ruled justifiable. In the south, a police officer was disarmed of his .41 Magnum revolver. The resolute lawman drew his mini-revolver from his pocket and laid into the attacker, who decided that rather than be shot with *anything,* he would give the revolver back. In South Africa, a gang of armed thugs set upon a man outside his suburban house. Rather than let them get in to attack his family, he drew his miniature single-action .22 revolver and opened fire on them. It was rather like sending a Chihuahua to attack a wolf pack, but he pulled it off. He managed to wound one or two of them. Deciding that being shot even with tiny bullets was not nearly as much fun for them as terrorizing helpless people, the attackers fled.

Yes, there are people who have used tiny guns with tiny bullets successfully for self-defense. There are also people who have jumped out of airplanes with non-functional parachutes and survived. It is respectfully submitted that neither is a promising model for the rest of us to follow.

Next up on the handgun ballistics food chain is the humble .32 ACP cartridge. There is no credible authority who will recommend this gun as a primary weapon, but everyone in the business admits that it's a quantum leap beyond .22 or .25 caliber. Evan Marshall's research into actual shootings indicates a significant number of one-shot stops with this cartridge. However, a review of the cases synopsized in his books shows a disproportionate number of these were either gun-against-knife or disparity of force cases. Disparity of force is the legal term for when one or more unarmed men attack someone with

such force that likelihood of death or great bodily harm becomes imminent. The attacker's greater size, strength, skill, or force of numbers is treated as the equivalent of a deadly weapon that warrants the use of a genuine deadly weapon in lawful self-defense.

The Winchester Silvertip, the CCI Gold Dot, and the Federal Hydra-Shok are hollow-point .32 rounds developed in hopes of getting the .32 caliber up off its knees. They get all the power out of the round that is probably possible. The problem is, there isn't that much there to start with. We've tested these in the slaughterhouse on smaller hogs and goats. The bullets usually deform. Sometimes they expand and sometimes they don't and sometimes the hollow cavity just turns into a little fish-mouth shape. However, unlike some .380 rounds, they don't seem prone to ricochet. If they don't get the caliber up off its knees, they at least get it up off its belly and onto its knees, and that's *something.*

Jeff Cooper once said that people buy .45s for the powerful cartridge, and buy 9mms because they like the design features of the guns. It follows that people buy tiny guns so they can have some sort of firearm without being inconvenienced by a significant weight in the pocket or by wearing a concealing garment.

Tomcat with tomcat, Beretta on left and Scottish Fold on right. Some have job descriptions more suitable for "mouse-guns" than others.

The brilliance of the Seecamp design, the pistol that re-popularized the .32 auto in our time, was that Louis Seecamp was able to conceive a pistol the size and shape of a Czech .25 auto that would fire the larger cartridge. The Seecamp is all the more brilliant in that it *works*. Now, this is the gun of Jeff Cooper's nightmares: double-action for *every* shot, no sights, and only a .32. The mission parameter was for a pistol that would be used at arm's length. Famed officer survival instructor and gunfight survivor Terry Campbell used to call these little pistols "nose guns," because the only way you could count on stopping the fight was to screw the muzzle up the attacker's nose and then immediately pull the trigger.

The supply of Seecamp pistols has never caught up with the huge demand in the marketplace. Other companies entered the field with "Seecamp clones": Autauga Arms, and North American Arms with their Guardian pistol. I never did test the former. The latter wasn't quite as reliable as the Seecamp but was easier to hit with because it had at least vestigial gunsights.

Next up was the gun that quickly became the best seller of its *genre,* the Kel-Tec P-32. One of several ingenious designs from the fertile brain of George Kehlgren, the P-32 weighs an incredible *6.6 ounces* unloaded. No bigger than the average .25-auto and almost wafer-thin, it has tiny little sights that you can more or less aim with, and a surprisingly nice double-action-only trigger pull. Polymer construction is what reduces the weight. By contrast, the NAA Guardian 13.5, and the Seecamp, 10.5 ounces. Each of these guns holds six rounds in the magazine, and a seventh in the firing chamber. All are DAO. The Kel-Tec is the lightest, the least expensive, and has the easiest trigger pull.

I have seen the occasional Kel-Tec that malfunctioned, usually when it was dirty or had at least gone a lot of rounds between cleanings. I've also shot some whose owners swore they had never jammed. Kel-Tec takes good care of their customers if they have a problem.

Perspectives

The young lady in Los Angeles who killed the rapist was in a situation where she simply could not afford for it to be known that she was armed. From undercover cops to private citizens with gun permits who work in anti-gun environments, the same holds true for a lot of people. Yeah, I know, I'm the guy who said "Friends don't let friends carry mouse-guns." But for some people it's that or nothing.

Let me tell you about one of my clients. He was a hunter and target shooter who owned some fine rifles and shotguns. The only handgun he owned was a gift from a friend, a Smith & Wesson .22 Kit Gun. He took it on hunting trips. He would while away the slow times plinking at tin cans from the porch of the hunting cabin, and the little .22 also allowed him to quickly dispatch a downed deer without damaging the skull for mounting. The night came when a burglar alarm went off in his home, telling him a flower shop he owned was being broken into for the umpteenth time.

If he had gone intending to kill someone, he would have loaded his .30/06 auto rifle or one of his 12-gauge shotguns. Thinking about protection, he grabbed his only handgun, the little .22, and loaded it on the way to the shop. Given the lateness of past police responses in this community in which the cops were heavily burdened with calls, it was his intent to frighten away the intruders. But

Relative sizes, different power levels. Clockwise from noon, S&W Model 3913 9mm, Kahr K9 9mm, S&W Sigma .380, S&W M/640 .38 Special. In the center is Walther PPK .380.

The NAA Guardian .380, center, is barely larger than FN .25 auto, above, or Beretta Jetfire .25 ACP, below. The .380 would be the definite choice here; the Guardian is among the smallest available.

when he got to the scene he was attacked. He fired two shots and the attacker fled.

It reinforced both sides of the issue. *If the guy ran, he wasn't incapacitated.* Yes. I know. That's why I don't recommend .22s. *That guy ran a mile before he bled to death!* Yes. I know. That's why I don't recommend .22s. *If that guy had gone into fight mode instead of flight mode he could have still killed your client!* Yes. I know. That's why I don't recommend .22s. *Then why are you talking about this as if his having a .22 was a good thing?* Because the circumstances were such that a .22 was the only gun he would have had with him...and it saved his life. End of story.

Perspectives

It's all well and good to say, "If you don't carry a .45 or a Magnum, you're a wimp." But there is idealism, and there is what Richard Nixon called *realpolitik*. We have to face reality. I'm fortunate enough that my job, the place I live, and my dress code allow me to carry a full-size fighting handgun almost all the time. Not everyone is that fortunate.

There's another argument in this vein that goes one tier up. I know a lot of cops who are proud of how they look in their tailored uniforms, and don't want the unsightly bulge of a big gun for backup. Shall I tell them if they don't carry a chopped and channeled .45, they deserve to have no backup at all?

The Guardian .380 is a late-arriving "hide-in-your-hand" pistol barely larger than some .25 autos. A definite "new paradigm" combat handgun.

I know a lot of armed citizens who already realize what a commitment it is to carry a gun all the time, period. If they're going to carry a second gun – a good idea for civilians, too – their wardrobe may not allow the small revolver or baby Glock I favor. For them, the backup weapon might be a Kel-Tec .32, or nothing at all.

When you demand all or nothing, history shows us, you're generally likely to end up with nothing. A tiny, small-caliber handgun is not what you'd want to have in your hand if you knew you were going to get into a fight to the death with an armed felon. But it's at least something. And something is better than nothing.

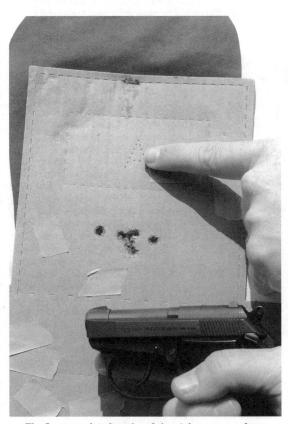

The finger touches the point of aim. A decent group from the Beretta Tomcat .32 went extremely low at only 7 yards.

The Guardian .380, top, is only the tiniest bit larger than the .32 version (below) that preceded it. Nod goes to the .380.

CHAPTER FOUR

A Blueprint For Learning The Combat Handgun

I was reading the deposition of a man who was being sued for shooting a contractor who showed up at his house early. He thought the man was a burglar. When asked why he shot him, he replied he didn't mean to; he intended his shots to warn, he said under oath. Did he aim the gun? No, he just pointed it. Had he been trained with his home defense gun, or even fired it before the day in question? No, he snapped indignantly, it wasn't like hunting where you needed a training course...

That man ended up paying a great deal of money to the man he shot, to that man's attorneys and to his own. Firing guns at human beings is not something you want to be ill prepared for in a moment of crisis. How does that preparation begin?

Some states have made training mandatory before issuance of a concealed carry permit. A few have even put together specific courses that must be taken. Two of the best are found in Arizona and Texas. Neither lasts long enough to give you anything close to all you need, but they give a solid foundation.

There are doubtless people reading this who have been shooting and carrying handguns longer than I, have forgotten more than I know, and could outshoot me on demand. They and I will both, however, be teaching others who are completely new to this discipline, some of whom are going to buy this book for that very reason. Therefore, let's address this progression beginning at new shooter level.

The Basics

Don't leave the gun shop without having a professional show you how the gun works. Loading and unloading, manipulation of safety devices, even field stripping. Make sure you have an owner's manual with it. Once you have it...READ the owner's manual before going any farther.

If you are new to the gun, don't go out shooting by yourself. It's like a new pilot starting solo, or trying to learn to swim all alone. Find someone who knows this stuff.

Focus at first on safety...and keep that focus for as long as you own firearms. We bought a combat handgun to provide safety for ourselves and those we're responsible for. Whether or not we ever have to draw that gun on a dangerous felon, we know that we will spend the rest of our lives with that gun. Putting it on, wearing it, taking it off...loading it, unloading it, checking and cleaning it...sometimes when we're distracted or tired or stressed...*in proximity to the very*

Match sponsors have the wherewithal to set up more complicated scenarios than most of us can on our own. Here a range officer follows a shooter through a complex stage at the S&W Mid-Winter IDPA Championships, 2002.

Police Chief Russ Lary tries his hand with his off-duty compact S&W .45 at the IDPA Mid-Winter National Championships, 2001.

Left to right: Cat Ayoob, Peter Dayton, and Mas Ayoob pause between stages at the National Tactical Invitational, 1996. This event has always been a useful training experience.

Shooting under the eye of experienced shooters is a fast track to improved skill. This is an LFI class in progress at Firearms Academy of Seattle.

The author awaits approval of the range officer (back to camera, wearing body armor) before ascending the stairs in Jeff Cooper's "Playhouse" simulator at Gunsite.

people we bought the gun to protect. The price of gun ownership is like the price of liberty: eternal vigilance.

It's always a good idea to start with a basic handgun safety class. The National Rifle Association has tons of instructors all over the country. Check locally – your gunshop will know where you can get training. This is one reason to buy your gun at a dedicated gunshop instead of a Big Box Monster Mart where today's gun counter clerk is yesterday's video section clerk. Another excellent source of information is your local fish and wildlife department, which generally has a list of basic firearms safety instructors as well as hunter safety instructors.

You may not be ready yet to compete, but you're always ready to learn from the best. Find out from the gunshop what local clubs are running IPSC or IDPA matches. Contact those clubs. See about joining. *Ask about safety classes offered by the IPSC and IDPA shooters!* These will focus on important elements like drawing and holstering that might get short shrift at a basic firearms safety class. Find out when they're having matches, and go a few times to watch. Remember to bring ear and eye protection. Watching skilled practitioners handle their handguns gives you excellent early role models.

Be A Joiner

Definitely join a gun club. You'll like the people, you'll enjoy yourself, but more importantly, you'll now be exposed to a whole group of seasoned shooters who have ingrained good safety habits. Never be afraid to ask questions. These folks enjoy sharing a lifestyle they love, and are always ready to help a new shooter get started.

Another good thing about joining a club is that on practice nights, there's usually an opportunity for people to try one another's guns. Finding out that the Mark II Master Blaster Magnum isn't nearly as controllable as the gun magazine said it would be is much more painless at the gun club trying a friend's, than after you've shelled out a thousand bucks for your own. This factor alone can more than make up the cost of your membership and range fees.

Formal Training Begins

I truly wish that shooting schools like the many available today existed when I was in my formative years. It would have saved me a lot of wasted time learning as I went. Unfortunately, the boom in concealed carry permits has drawn out of the woodwork a swarm of get-rich-quick artists who smelled a fast buck, took a few courses, and declared themselves professional instructors. As Jeff Cooper once commented on the matter, "There are a great many people teaching things they haven't learned yet."

When you inquire for particulars at a shooting school, request a resume of the person who will be the chief instructor at your course. If he gets indignant and refuses, he's told you all you need to know. Keep looking. Once you get the resume, do what you would do with any other prospective employee's resume, and check it out to make sure he's been where he says he's been, and has done what he says he's done. (You're hiring him to perform a service for you, right? Of course, he's a prospective employee.)

This shooter puts his 1911 to work from behind a realistic barricade during an IDPA match at the Smith & Wesson Academy.

Local police officers experience role-playing training set up by Lethal Force Institute students, who are playing the bad guys and bystanders in this scenario.

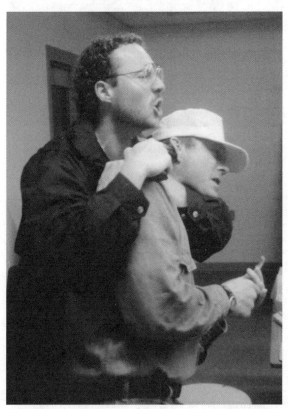

Using a dummy gun, this role-player takes another student hostage in live-action scenario training at LFI.

If in the early stages the prospective instructor is patronizing or condescending, move on. One of the truly great officer survival instructors, Col. Robert Lindsey, makes a profound point to his fellow trainers. "We are not God's gift to our students," Lindsey says. "Our students are God's gift to us."

Nationally known schools may be more expensive, but they are generally worth it. If a cadre of instructors has been in business for 15 or 20 years, it tells you that there aren't too many dissatisfied customers. Particularly in the time of the Internet, word gets around. The various gun chat rooms on the 'Net are also a good source of customer feedback. The best, however, is advice from someone you know and can trust who has already been to the school in question.

Once you get there, *be a student.* Soak up all you can, paying particular attention to the explanation of why the instructor recommends that a certain thing be done a certain way. Litmus test: If he says, "We do it that way because it is The Doctrine," add more than a grain of salt to whatever you're being asked to swallow. Try it the instructor's way; you're there to learn what he or she has to teach. You wouldn't throw karate kicks at a judo dojo; don't shoot from the Isosceles stance if the instructor is asking you to shoot from the Weaver.

Don't be afraid to ask for a personal assessment or a little extra help. Any instructor worth his or her title will take it as a compliment that you asked, not as an imposition.

Journeyman Level

You have progressed. You're into this stuff now. You want to get better. *Yes!*

Remember at this stage that revelatory, life-changing experiences tend to come one to a customer. After you've become a reasonably good shot, further improvement will probably be incremental. In your first few schools in a discipline, you're trying to absorb it all and wondering if you're a bad person because you might have missed some small point. As time progresses and you get more courses under your belt, some of what you hear at successive schools will sound familiar. That's OK. It never hurts to reinforce and validate something positive that you've already learned. You'll be all the more appreciative when you do pick up something new, and all the more insightful when you put that new knowledge to use.

The instructor can't do it all for you. Skill maintenance is the individual practitioner's job. Martial artists and physiologists tell us that it takes 3,000 to 7,000 repetitions to create enough-long term muscle memory that you can perform a complex psycho-motor skill, such as drawing and firing a pistol, in the "automatic pilot" mode that trainers call Unconscious Competence. One intense week a year at the gym, and 51 weeks as a couch potato, won't keep your body in shape. That kind of regimen won't keep your combat handgun skills in shape, either.

By now you should have found at least one gun/holster combination that works well for you. Stay with it for a while. Don't try to buy skill at the gunshop. Buy ammo or

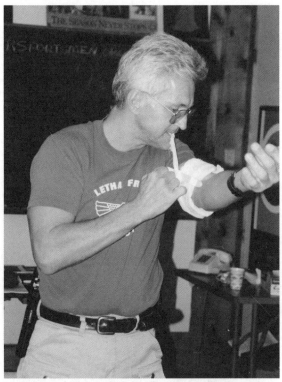

Self-defense training goes beyond shooting. Do you know self-treatment for a gunshot injury if you're alone and wounded? Paramedic and LFI Staff Instructor Bob Smith demonstrates for a class.

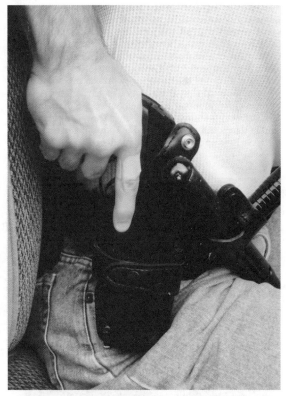

Learn to draw from compromised positions. This officer clears an issue DAO Beretta Model 8040 from a Safariland 070 security holster while seated in vehicle.

Sometimes intense training can hurt. Allan Brummer takes a full power hit of OC pepper foam...

...and proves he can "fight through it," drawing a dummy gun and issuing commands while carrying out tactical movement.

reloading components there instead, to better reinforce and enhance the skills you already have.

This is a good time to be thinking about some sort of practical shooting/action shooting/combat shooting competition. Doing well gives us motivation to get better. Being exposed to others who've been to different schools and shoot with different styles will broaden your horizons and give you new ideas you can put to good use. Sometimes even more importantly, this will introduce you to a new circle of friends and acquaintances who have the same self-defense values as you. Even if the thrill of the competition wears off, the pleasure and value of the friendships you make there will stay with you.

Remember as a journeyman that safety still has to come first. You're shooting enough now to be a high profile potential victim of the "familiarity breeds contempt" syndrome. Avoid that at all costs. The carpenter is more skilled with a hammer than the home craftsman, but he can still hit his thumb. The reason is that he uses it more, and is that much more exposed to that danger. So it is with us. Remember...eternal vigilance.

In The Land Of The Experts

When you get really deep into this, and really good at it, improvement comes even more slowly. When Mike Plaxco was the man to beat in combat competition, he told me, "I get slumps just like everybody else. When I do, I change something in my shooting style. It makes me focus again, makes things fresh again, and makes me work at it again." Good point.

Here the author rinses out his teenage daughter's eyes after she has taken a hit of pepper spray.

Can you draw weak handed if your dominant hand is taken out? Here the author clears a Glock 22 from Uncle Mike's duty rig.

Ambush waiting! The Beamhit system uses guns modified to non-lethal function and vests to carry the sensors which register only stopping hits.

Wearing protective gear and using Code Eagle modifications of S&W revolvers that fire only paint pellets, these students act out a car-jacking scenario.

We're not going to preach here, but there are a great many people in this country who need to know these things, and not all of them can afford to travel to shooting schools to learn them. There comes a time when giving back is almost a moral obligation, like courtesy on the road. Consider teaching. Helping at a course at your local club, or volunteering to help someone who has once trained you, is a good place to start.

When you teach something, it forces you to see the forest for the trees. I can remember taking classes in things I didn't care about, but needed the course credit for. It was as if my mind was a tape recorder that held the information long enough to play it back on the final exam, and then erased the tape once the chore was done. That wasn't "life learning," and I regret it now. There were times when I took a class just for myself, saw something I liked, kept it, but didn't really get into the details of why I did it that way. If we don't understand why we're doing what we're doing, even if it works for us, we don't truly command the skill. I regret those learning experiences now, too.

I learned that I didn't really command a body of knowledge until I had been certified to teach it. "Hey, wait a minute, people are going to be asking me why we do it this way, and why we don't use technique X instead? I have to explain that? Hey, Coach, brief me on that one more time…"

Teaching not only ensures that we have it down, it puts the final imprimatur of understanding on our own performance in that discipline, sharpening us like the double-stamping of a coin. Since the inception of ASLET, the American Society of Law Enforcement Trainers, I've been chair of its firearms committee. ASLET's

Have you learned how to return fire from disadvantaged positions if wounded? Here, LFI-II students go through one of several such drills.

Make sure your self-defense training is not confined to just the gun. OC pepper spray requires training to use to its best advantage.

motis is *qui doscet, disket*. Translated loosely from the Latin: "He who teaches, learns." Thousands of my brethren and I have learned the truth of that through ASLET and similar organizations such as IALEFI, the International Association of Law Enforcement Firearms Instructors.

On qualification day at an LFI-I class, the instructor's target...

You're not comfortable with public speaking or perhaps some other element of formal teaching? That's fine, but if you look around there will be people in your family, your neighborhood, your workplace or somewhere else in your ambit who are interested in acquiring a defensive handgun or have already done so, and desperately need to know these things. Take those people to the range. Be patient. Be supportive. Give them what you wanted to get when you began in this discipline.

If nothing else, you'll make a good deposit in the karma bank and you won't come back as a dung beetle.

Final Thoughts

Read on the topic. Watch the new generation of combat shooting videos. It's one thing to read about it, and another to actually see masterful speed shooting in action. One thing videos can do that even experience cannot is deliver instant replay in slow motion, showing subtleties of technique frame by frame.

Learn from your mistakes. Losing a match or a having bad day at the gun class doesn't mean you're a bad person and you need therapy. Winning gives you warm fuzzy strokes, and it also gives you positive reinforcement, validating that you're doing it right. But losing is where you learn. Think about it: How many of life's lessons did

...has become the traditional award for the most-improved shooter. The staff, whose collective vote determines the recipient, signs it. Here John Strayer waits his turn to sign as Steve Denney pens some words of encouragement to the winning student.

Training should give you fallbacks for worst-case scenarios. Here, author drills on weak-hand-only with his Glock 22.

you learn by messing something up? Sometimes, that's the strongest reinforcement of the learning experience. On days when you win, you can say to yourself, "A day well spent. I'm on the right track." On days when you lose, you can say to yourself, "A day well spent. I've learned a lesson, and I will *not* repeat the mistake I made today." Sometimes, the "instructional days" are a lot more valuable than the "positive reinforcement days."

It has been said that experience is the collected aggregate of our mistakes. But wisdom, said Otto von

Don't assume that statistics are right, and you'll only be in a gunfight at point-blank range. Here bodyguard Lars Lipke deploys his HK P7M13 at 50 yards, from standing position...

Bismarck, is learning from the collected aggregate of the mistakes of others. That's why we read and study and reach out beyond our own experiences.

How do you best practice? This way: Stop practicing! This doesn't mean that you don't shoot or drill in your movement patterns or perform repetitions of tactical skills. It means that if before you practiced, now you *train!*

Practice can easily turn into just hosing bullets downrange. Often, you wind up reinforcing bad habits instead of enforcing good ones. Training, on the other hand, is purpose-oriented. Where practice can easily degenerate into "just going through the motions," training sharpens and fine-tunes every motion. If practice was going to be a couple of hundred rounds downrange, training might be as little as 50 rounds, but all fired with purpose. You, the box of ammo, and the electronic timer (one of the best investments you can make in your own skill development) head to the range. Instead of creating 200 pieces of once-fired brass, your goal is 50 draws to the shot. Each will be done in a frame of time that satisfies you and results in a good hit, or you'll analyze the reason why not and correct what's going wrong.

Shoot in competition. It hones the edge. A gun club that's enthusiastic about IDPA or IPSC (see the chapter on Combat Competition) will be able to set up complicated and challenging scenarios that you or I might not have the time or the money to construct. You'll get to watch top shooters in action and pick up subtle lessons from how they handle various tactical problems.

If there's no competition near you, or not as much as you like, shoot with a buddy or a loved one. Personally, I find I put forth my best effort against someone who shoots about the same as I do. When I shoot against world champions, it's exciting, but I know I'm not really going to beat them. When I shoot against someone who's had a lot less opportunity to develop skill, I'm not challenged. Someone who's at the same level seems to bring out the greatest internal effort.

Go ahead and side-bet with each other. That's a good thing, too. It conditions you to the reality that every time you pull that trigger, something rides on the outcome. You'll pay for a bad shot and be rewarded for a good one. Soon, shooting under pressure becomes the norm.

Your partner is not as good a shot as you are? Pick a course of fire and each of you go through it a couple of times and determine an average score. Subtract the one from the other, and give the difference to the lower scoring shooter as a handicap.

...and from the more effective Chapman Rollover Prone.

Learn to make tactical movement as thoroughly ingrained as stance and trigger press. Here Justine Ayoob, 15, performs a tactical reload while moving behind cover at the New England Regional IDPA championships.

Be able to shoot effectively from non-standard positions. National IDPA champ Ted Yost shows his form with a "cover crouch," which gets him down behind the rear of a car faster than conventional kneeling.

Let's say it's a course of fire with 300 points possible. You average 299 and the partner averages 230. Give the partner 69 bonus points as a handicap. Now he or she is challenged: beating you is within striking distance, where before it seemed hopeless. This will encourage the partner to really focus and put forth his or her best effort. Before, you weren't challenged, but now you know that the newer shooter with the faster learning curve only has to get a little better to beat you. You, in turn, are now motivated to shoot a perfect score, the only thing that will keep you from losing the bet.

At Lethal Force Institute, we have the instructors shoot what we call a pace-setter drill on the last day. Just before the students shoot their final qualification test, the staff will shoot the same course of fire as a demonstration. This does several good things. First, it lets the students see what's expected of them. Second, watching us do it

"Simunitions" has ushered in a new dimension in reality-based training. This Glock has been factory modified to fire only the Simunitions paint pellet rounds.

helps them "set their internal clock" which in turn helps them make the times required for each string of fire. Third, it gives them a mental image of what they are supposed to be doing.

Bob Lindsey, the master police officer survival instructor, noted in the 1980s that a number of cops who were losing fights would suddenly see in their mind's eye an image of an instructor performing a technique. They would act out that image, make it work, and prevail. He called it "modeling." This is the main reason we do the pace-setter drill. Until then, I had followed the advice I'd been given in firearms instructor school. "Don't shoot in front of the students," I had been told. "If you're as good as you're supposed to be, it will make some of them despair of ever reaching your level. And if you blow it, you lose your credibility."

That had made sense. If a student asked me back then, "When do we get to see *you* shoot," my standard answer was, "When you go to Bianchi Cup or Second Chance. You're not here to see how well I can shoot. You're here to see how well *you* can shoot."

Lindsey's research changed my opinion on that. It was after hearing Bob's presentation on modeling that we started the pace-setter drills at LFI. Since we've been doing it, the scores of the students have gone up, and fewer of the students have had problems getting all their shots into the target before the cease-fire signal.

One thing we added was an incentive. Whatever score I shoot, if the student ties me he or she gets an autographed dollar bill with the inscription, "You tied me at my own game." If the student beats me, it's an autographed $5 bill that says, "You beat me at my own game." It's the cheapest investment I can make in their shooting skill, and it pushes them to do their best. It's natural for a student to want to exceed the instructor…and frankly, accomplishing that is the highest compliment a student can pay to a dedicated teacher.

My favorite award to give out is "most improved shooter." This award is the instructor's target, signed by all the staff. Often, the student who has accelerated "from zero to 50" has accomplished more than the already-skilled student who came to class at 100 miles an hour and was only able to get about 5 miles an hour faster.

In the end, it's up to you. Your skill development will be proportional to how much time you're prepared to spend training yourself, and acquiring training from others.

Getting good training is cost-effective, because despite tuition and travel expense, it saves you re-inventing the wheel. Yes, it takes a lot of years to get a Ph.D. in nuclear physics, but it would take you a helluva lot longer to figure out nuclear physics by yourself. Shooting isn't nuclear physics, but you don't need years in the university to learn it either. A few well-chosen weeks, backed up by your own commitment to a training regimen of live fire when you can and dry fire the rest of the time, will be the best investment in skill development you can make.

I do this for a living, as a full-time teacher and part-time cop, part-time writer, and part-time everything else. I'm supposed to have "arrived." But it's never wise to kid oneself. This sort of thing, at its greatest depth, is a life-study. As soon as you think you've "arrived," you stop moving forward. That's why I budget a minimum of a week a year for myself to take training from others. It keeps me sharp, and keeps the mind open. The old saying is true: Minds, like parachutes, work best when they're open.

The Heart Of The Beast: Mastering Trigger Control

Agreed: What kind of bullet we're firing doesn't matter unless the bullet hits the target.

Agreed: The bullet doesn't have to just hit, it has to hit something vital.

Agreed: The bullet doesn't have to just hit something vital, it has to hit something so immediately vital that the person can no longer continue to attack.

Agreed: We'll have a very short time frame in which to accomplish this.

Agreed: As much as we might rather have a rifle, a shotgun, or a submachinegun to deal with this problem, the tool we're most likely to have with us is a handgun.

If we can agree that all these things are predicates to stopping a deadly fight with a combat handgun, then we are agreed that accuracy is extremely important. It's like high school Logic 101: If A is true and B is true, then AB must be true.

A lot of things will impact our ability to deliver accurate shots rapidly while under stress. Will you use a one-hand or two-hand hold on the gun? Two-hand is more accurate, but one-hand is sometimes more expedient. Will you use Weaver or Isosceles stance? There are times when it can matter, but they are relatively rare. Any basic marksmanship instructor will tell you that once you've brought your gun on target, there is one key element to

making the shot fly true: *You must pull the trigger in such a way that the gun is not jerked off target.*

We know that because the bullet flies in a relatively straight path, any deviation of the sight alignment is magnified in direct geometric progression. If your trigger pull jerks the muzzle off target by the tiniest fraction of an inch, the shot may hit in the white of the target, but not the black of the center scoring area at 25 yards. "Hah," say the clueless. "That's a target shooter talking! Those increments don't matter in a close-range gunfight!"

Ya think? Then, consider this.

You and I start the fight at the distance of only *one yard,* 36 inches torso to torso. You have drawn to shoot from the hip so I can't reach your gun. Let's assume further that your pointing skills are perfect today and your gun is dead center on my torso. You now jerk your trigger, moving the gun muzzle a mere inch to your strong-hand side. *Only one yard away, your shot will miss my main body mass.* It might go through the "love handle" and give me a .45 caliber suction lipectomy, or it might even hit my arm if it's hanging to the side, but it won't do anything to effectively stop me from harming you.

That's why, in real world combat shooting and not just match shooting, trigger control is so important. *The trigger is the heart of the beast! If you don't control the*

Trigger control need not sacrifice speed. Here, Marty Hayes is firing four rounds in a fraction of a second from a prototype Spectre pistol. Note two .45 ACP casings in mid-air above the gun, a third below, and the muzzle flash of the fourth round.

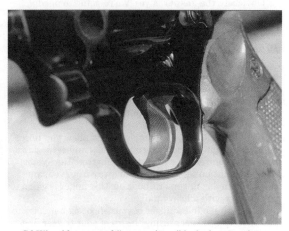

S&W's wide, serrated "target trigger" is the best type for single-action target shooting, but the worst choice for double-action combat shooting.

trigger, you don't control even what should have been the most perfectly aligned shot!

How can we hope to control the trigger under extreme stress? By being trained and conditioned to do it beforehand. Is it easy? No, and that's why we've devoted a whole chapter to the concept.

Understanding The Mission

Too much combat handgun training has been borrowed from the world of target shooting. While some of the concepts survive the translation from range to street, some don't. One that doesn't is the *targeteer's* concept of trigger activation.

We are told that we should contact the trigger with the tip or the pad of the trigger finger. When asked why, we are told that this is the most sensitive portion of the finger and therefore the part most suited to this dextrous task. That makes sense as far as it goes, but let's analyze the target shooter's task versus the defensive shooter's.

In bull's-eye pistol matches, the core event is shot with the .22 caliber. You have, let's say, a High Standard .22 match pistol. It weighs 48 ounces, more if you have it scoped, and it has a crisp 2-pound trigger pull that needs to move only a hair's breadth. The gun is loaded with standard velocity (read: low velocity) .22 Long Rifle, which kicks with about as much force as a mouse burp. In this course of shooting events, "rapid fire" is defined as five shots in 10 seconds. All well and good.

But let's put ourselves somewhere else, perhaps a darkened parking lot. Our 260-pound assailant, Mongo, is coming at us with a tire iron. We are armed with a baby Glock, the G33 model that weighs only about 19 ounces. Its New York trigger gives us a pull weight of almost eight pounds over 3/8 of an inch. The power of its .357 SIG cartridge is that of some .357 Magnum revolver rounds, generating significant recoil. For us, "rapid-fire" has just become five rounds in *one* second, before Mongo reaches us with the tire iron.

Let's see, we have a few things to think about: a 3-pound gun with a 2-pound trigger, versus a 1-1/4-pound gun with an 8-pound trigger. We have 1/10 of an inch of movement versus 3/8 of an inch. We have almost no recoil versus sharply noticeable and palpable recoil. We have five shots in 10 seconds versus five shots in one second. Have the mission parameters changed for the trigger finger?

Obviously, the answer is yes. We're going to need a stronger finger, a finger with more leverage, to achieve the necessary results.

Placement And Fit

You'll find that you have much more control of a longer, heavier combat trigger pull if you contact the trigger with *the palmar surface of the distal joint* of the index finger. It is at this point that the digit has the most leverage to draw the trigger rearward with the most speed and the least effort.

At LFI, we developed a simple test to allow you to see and feel this for yourself. Open this book and set it down where you can read it with your hands free. Take your non-dominant hand, turn its palm away from you, and extend the index finger. Stiffen it up: this finger is going to be a trigger with a heavy pull.

Now, with the index finger of your shooting hand, try to pull that "trigger" back, using the *tip* of your trigger finger. You'll have to use great effort – enough effort to probably distract you from focusing on much else – and when the finger does start to give, it will move in fits and starts.

S&W's "Ranger" trigger has smooth surface so the finger can glide across it during fast double-action work without pulling the muzzle off target.

Now try it again, making contact with the *pad* of your trigger finger. The pad is defined as the center of the digit, where the whorl of the fingerprint would be. You won't feel much difference.

Now, for the third and final portion of the test. With your "finger/trigger" still rigid, place your trigger finger at the same spot. Make contact with the crease where the distal phalange of the finger meets the median phalange, as shown in accompanying photos. Now, just roll the stiffened finger back against its force. Feel a huge difference? This is why the old-time double-action revolver shooters called this portion of the trigger finger the "power crease." It is here that we gain maximum leverage.

Of course, for this to work the gun must fit your hand. In the early 1990s, when gearing up to produce their Sigma pistol, Smith & Wesson paid some six figures for a "human engineering" study of the hands of shooters. It turned out my own hand fit exactly their profile of "average adult male hand." Not surprisingly, I found the Sigma to fit my hand perfectly.

Gaston Glock did much the same. However, he went on the assumption that the shooter of an automatic pistol

In the old days, shooters tried to "stage" double-action revolvers, especially Colts like this snub Python. Today's more knowledgeable shooters use a straight-through trigger pull. Note the distal joint contact on the trigger.

This is the hand of a petite female on a gun that's too big for her, a Model 625 from S&W Performance Center. Note that she has been forced to use the "h-grip," in which the hand and forearm are in the shape of lower case letter h. One can get better trigger reach with this method, but at the expense of weakened recoil control.

Many prefer the short-reach trigger on a 1911, particularly those with small hands or those who use distal joint contact on the trigger as the author does. This is a 10mm Colt Delta Elite customized by Mark Morris.

would be using the pad of the finger. When I grasp the Glock properly in every other respect, my finger comes to the trigger at the pad. To make it land naturally at the distal joint, I need the grip-shape slimmed and re-shaped, as done by Robar (21438 N. 7th Ave, Suite E, Phoenix, AZ 85027) or Dane Burns (700 NW Gilman Blvd, Suite 116, Issaquah, WA 98027). On a K-frame S&W revolver whose rear grip strap has not been covered with grip material, my trigger finger falls into the perfect position. Ditto the double-action-only S&W autos, and ditto also the Browning Hi-Power with standard trigger and the 1911 with a short to medium trigger.

Proper grasp means that the web of the hand is high on the back of the grip-frame, to minimize muzzle jump and stabilize an auto's frame against the recoiling slide. The web should feel as if it is pressing up into the grip tang on the auto, and should be at the very apex of the grip frame of the revolver. The long bones of the forearm should be directly in line with the barrel of the gun. This properly aligns skeleto-muscular support structure not only with the handgun's recoil path, but also with the direction of the trigger pull. The trigger finger, we mustn't forget, is an extension of the arm.

Although the Glock was designed to be shot using the pad of the trigger finger; the author finds he has better control in extreme rapid fire with his finger deeper into the trigger guard.

When the gun doesn't fit and the finger can barely reach the trigger, it will tend to pull the whole gun inboard. That is, a right-handed shooter will tend to pull the shot to the left. If the gun is too small for the hand and the finger goes into the trigger guard past the distal joint, the angle of the finger's flexion during the pull will tend to yank the shot outboard, i.e., to a right-handed shooter's right.

This is why gun fit is critical. The key dimension of determining the fit of the gun to the hand is "trigger reach." On the gun, it is measured from the center of the backstrap where the web of the hand would sit, to the center of the trigger. On the hand, it is measured from the point of trigger contact (distal joint suggested) to the center of the web of the hand in line with the radius and ulna bones of the forearm.

Avoid if possible the expedient hand position called the "h-grip," intended for adapting a too-small hand to a too-large handgun. In it, the hand is turned so that, with the hand at the side, hand and forearm would resemble a lower case letter "h." This brings the backstrap of the gun to the base joint of the thumb and brings the index finger forward far enough for proper placement on the trigger.

While this can work with a .22 or something else with light loads, it's a matter of robbing Peter to pay Paul. What is gained in getting the trigger forward is lost by a weakened hand grasp on the gun. Recoil now goes directly into the proximal joint of the thumb. Doctors tell me that this is a quick short-cut to developing artificially-induced arthritis in that joint. Such a grip was one of the "remedial" techniques employed by FBI instructors in the late 1970s for small-handed female agent recruits firing +P ammunition. It not only failed to work, it beat up their hands. It was one reason that in the landmark case of *Christine Hansen, et. al. v. FBI* we won reinstatement and compensation for a number of female agents who had been fired because they couldn't qualify with the old-fashioned bad techniques. The same court ordered FBI to "revise and update its obsolete and sexist firearms training."

Distal joint contact works well even for single-action autos. Even when the pull weight is relatively light, "leverage equals power, and power controls the pistol."

With DA-to-SA pistol, like this Beretta 92G, placing finger at distal joint will give good control with both types of trigger pull.

Trigger control is all the more important with more difficult tasks like one-handed double-action work with a light gun, such as this Colt Magnum Carry .357 snub.

This placement of the finger eliminates the old shibboleth of double-action first shot pistols that said one had to change finger position between the double-action first round and the single-action follow-up shots. Place the distal joint on the trigger for the first heavy pull, keep it there for subsequent shots, and all will be well.

Rolling Pace

From here on, it's a matter of pace. Learn trigger control as you would develop any other physical skill. Remember what I call "Chapman's Dictum": Smoothness is 5/6 of speed. Crawl before you walk, and walk before you run.

Start slowly. Do lots of dry fire. Watch the sights as they sit silhouetted against a safe backstop. *Do not let the sights move out of alignment at any point in the trigger stroke, particularly when the trigger releases and the "shot breaks."* Then, gradually, accelerate the pace.

Generations of combat shooters can tell you: accuracy first, speed second will develop fast and accurate shooting skills much more quickly than a curriculum of speed first and accuracy second. If you stay with it for several thousand repetitions, you will find that you can roll the trigger back as fast as your finger will go, without jerking your sights off target. Put another way, we can learn to hit as fast as we were missing before.

The key to trigger manipulation under stress is to *distribute the trigger pressure.* A sudden 4-pound jerk will inevitably pull a 2-pound gun off target. Smooth, evenly distributed trigger pressure done at the same speed will fire the gun just as quickly, but without moving the alignment of bore to target. The key words here are *smooth* and *even.*

Generations of shooters and gunfighters have learned to talk themselves through the perfect shot. They chant it to themselves like a mantra. "Front sight! Squeeze the trigger. *Squee-e-eze…*" One instructor says "squeeze," another says "press"; this writer uses "roll." To me, the word "roll" connotes the smooth, even, uninterrupted pressure that I want. The word doesn't matter so much as the concept.

Don't try to "stage" or "trigger-cock" the pistol. This is fine motor intensive, and our fine motor skills go down the drain when we're in danger and our body instinctively reacts. Such skills just won't be with you in a fight. Learn from the beginning to keep the stroke smooth and even, executed in a single stage.

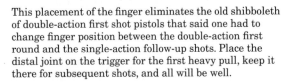

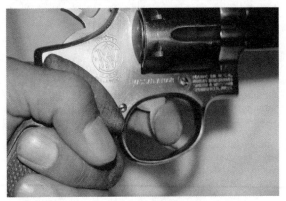

Proper trigger finger placement for DA work with K-frame S&W .357.

A smooth double-action trigger stroke is bringing the next .357 round under the hammer of this S&W Bodyguard.

A workable solution. This Colt Python has a serrated trigger, usually undesirable for double-action work, but the ridges between the serration grooves have been polished glass smooth, solving the problem.

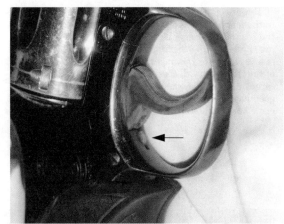

Note S&W's internally adjustable trigger stop, coming down into trigger guard at a point behind the trigger. Because there is a remote chance it can come out of adjustment and block the trigger...

...it is usually removed from a duty gun, as it has been from author's S&W Model 66.

A word on "surprise trigger break." Marksmanship instructors tell us to let the trigger go off by surprise so we don't anticipate the final release and jerk the gun. However, if you say in court that the shot went off by surprise, it sounds to anyone without your training as if you didn't mean for it to go off. That can turn a justifiable, intentional shooting into a negligent act of manslaughter. *We don't begin pressing the trigger back – we don't even **touch** the trigger – until the intent to immediately fire has been justifiably formulated!* The only surprise should be in what fraction of an instant the deliberate shot discharges.

Trigger Mechanicals

A light trigger pull is, more than anything else, a crutch for bad trigger technique. It is also "plaintiff's counsel's guaranteed employment act" in the civil liability sense. On a defense gun, you don't need a *light* trigger pull, you need a *smooth* trigger pull.

The surface of the trigger should be glassy smooth, with rounded edges. Grooves, serrations, or checkering on the trigger will trap the flesh of the finger and translate any lateral finger movement to undesirable lateral gun movement. As the finger moves back, it may change its exact contact point with the trigger very slightly, and if that happens, we want the finger to be moving smoothly and easily across the frontal surface of the trigger. On revolver triggers in particular, it's also a good idea to round off the rear edges of the trigger, to keep the flesh of the finger from being pinched between the trigger and the back of the trigger guard at the end of each firing stroke.

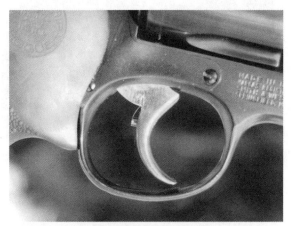

Here's a true combat trigger stop. It is welded in place. It can't move and cause problems, yet it cures aim-disturbing trigger overtravel. Installed on author's S&W Model 25-5, in .45 Colt, by Al Greco.

Beware of "backlash." This is the movement that occurs in the instant between when the sear releases, and when the rear of the trigger comes to a stop. Because spring pressure resisting the finger has just been released, there is a tendency for the finger to snap back against the rear of the trigger guard, possibly jerking the muzzle off target. An "anti-backlash device" or "trigger stop" is a good idea, *if* it is constructed in such a way that it cannot come out of adjustment, move forward, and block the trigger from firing. This problem was known to occur in the old "built-in" trigger stops of Smith & Wesson's target and combat-target revolvers (K-38, Combat Magnum, etc.) and it got to the point where departments ordering such guns would specify that the trigger stop device be left out entirely. A good pistolsmith can weld up a stop on the back of the trigger or the back of the trigger guard, then grind or file it to a point where the trigger will always be operational.

Power stance in action. Dave Sevigny, National IDPA champion, shows winning form with a Glock 34 at the New England Regional Championships.

Smaller people need the power stance more than big bruisers. Justine Ayoob is 15 in this photo as she wins High Novice in the enhanced service pistol class at the New England Regional IDPA championships. Note power stance as she delivers head-shots with a Novak Custom Browning 9mm.

Lost Secrets Of Combat Handgun Shooting

Evolution of doctrine is a strange thing. Sometimes, we do something after we've forgotten why we started doing it. Sometimes, we forget to do things we should be doing.

There are secrets the Old Masters of combat handgunning knew, secrets that have been lost to most because they weren't incorporated into this or that "doctrine." Just because they are lost doesn't mean they don't still work. Let's look at a few of them.

Lost Secret #1: The Power Stance

In true *combat* handgun training, as opposed to recreational shooting, you are preparing for a fight. This means you should be in a fighting stance. Balance and mobility can never be compromised in a fight. Accordingly, your primary shooting stance should be a *fighting* stance.

When the body has to become a fighting machine, the legs and feet become its foundation. You can expect to be receiving impacts: a wound to the shoulder, a bullet slamming to a stop in your body armor, and certainly the recoil of your own powerful, rapidly fired defensive weapon. Any of these can drive you backward and off-balance if you are not stabilized to absorb them and keep fighting.

The feet should be at least shoulder-width apart, and probably wider. Whether you're throwing a punch or extending a firearm, you're creating outboard weight, and your body has to compensate for that by widening its foundation or you'll lose your balance.

We have long known that humans in danger tend to crouch. It's not just a *homo sapiens* thing, it's an erect biped thing. The same behavior is observed in primates, and in bears when they're upright on their hind legs. In his classic book "Shoot to Live," Fairbairn observed how men just on their way to a dangerous raid tended to crouch significantly. Decades before Fairbairn had noticed it, Dr. Walter Cannon at Harvard Medical School had predicted this. Cannon was the first to attempt to medically quantify the phenomenon called "fight or flight response" as it occurs in the human. While we know now that Cannon may have been incorrect on some hypothesized details, such as the exact role that blood sugar plays in the equation, we also know that on the bottom line he was right on all counts.

When threatened with deadly danger, the erect bipedal mammal will turn and face that danger, if only to observe and quantify it before fleeing. Its torso will square with the thing that threatens it. One leg will "quarter" rearward. This is seen today in the boxer's stance, the karate practitioner's front stance, the Weaver stance of

A high-hand grasp is best taken with the gun still in the holster, as shown here pulling a Para-Ordnance .45 from Alessi CQC holster.

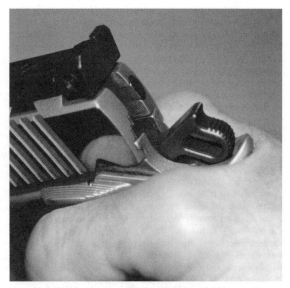

A high-hand grasp on a Kimber Gold Match .45; note the "ripple of flesh" at the web of the hand.

pistol shooters, and the "police interview stance" taught at every law enforcement academy.

The head will come forward and down, and the shoulders will seem to hunch up to protect it. The knees will flex, lowering the center of body gravity, and the hips will come back, coiling the body for sudden and strenuous movement. The feet will be at least shoulder-width apart laterally. The hands or paws will rise to somewhere between waist and face level.

This, and not the exaggerated "squat" of the ancient FBI training films, is the true and instinctive "combat crouch." The body is balanced forward, rearward, left and right, its weight forward to both absorb and deliver impact.

There is no good reason for the combat shooter not to stand like this. Indeed, there is every reason for him or her to do it.

A key element of the power stance as we teach it at Lethal Force Institute is the application of the *drive leg*. In the martial arts, you generate power in a punch by putting your whole body behind it. Whichever leg is to the rear is the drive leg. Beginning with the knee slightly flexed, the practitioner digs either the heel or the ball of the foot into the ground, straightening the leg. This begins a powerful turn of the hips. The hips are the center of body gravity and the point from which body strength can most effectively be generated. The punch and extending arm go forward along with the hip. The forward leg has become the weight-bearing limb; it needs to be more sharply flexed than the rear leg because as force is delivered forward, it will be carrying well over half of the body's weight.

Lost Secret #2: The High-Hand Grasp

It's amazing how many people come out of shooting schools and police academies not knowing the most efficient way to hold a handgun. The primary hand's grasp, which some instructors call "Master Grip," needs to be able to stand by itself. In a shooting match that calls for a two-handed stage, we know we'll always be able to achieve the two-fisted grasp. In the swirling, unpredictable movement that occurs in close-range fights, however, we can never be sure that the second hand will be able to get to its destination and reinforce the first. It might be needed to push someone out of the way, to ward off the opponent's weapon, or simply to keep our balance. That's why the initial grasp of the handgun with the dominant hand must be suitable for strong control of one-handed as well as two-handed fire.

The hand should be all the way up the backstrap of the grip-frame. With the auto, the web of the hand should be so high that it is not only in contact with the underside of the grip tang, but pressed against it so firmly that it seems to shore up a ripple of flesh. On the revolver, the web of the hand should be at the highest point of the grip-frame's backstrap. There is only one, easily fixed potential downside to a high hand grip. If the grip tang has sharp edges, as on the older versions of the 1911, this can dig painfully and even lacerate the hand. Sharp-edged slides on very small autos, like the Walther PPK, can do the same. Simply rounding off sharp edges or installing a beavertail grip safety fixes that.

Now let's count up the many advantages of the high-hand grip. (1) It lowers the bore axis as much as possible, giving the gun less leverage with which to kick its muzzle up when recoil hits. (2) It guarantees that the frame will

A high-hand grasp on a revolver. Note that the top edge of the gripframe is higher on the "hammerless" S&W Centennial (AirLite version shown), affording the shooter more control than a conventionally styled revolver. Note also the white-nailed "crush grip."

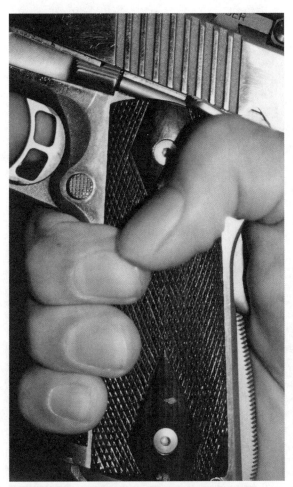

The crush grip in action on a Kimber .45. Note that the fingernails have turned white from max-force gripping pressure.

be held as a rigid abutment for the auto's slide to work against. With too low a hold, the whipsaw recoil that follows moves the frame as well as the slide, dissipating some of the rearward momentum needed to complete the cycle. The result is often a spent casing caught "stovepiped" in the ejection port, or a slide that does not return fully to battery. (3) On most handguns, this grasp allows a straight-back pull of the trigger. If the gun is grasped too low, a rearward pull on the trigger becomes a downward pull on the gun, jerking its muzzle – and the shot – low. Draw is hastened because (4) the grip tang of the auto is the easiest landmark for the web of the hand to find by feel.

Pick up a gun magazine with one or more stories on action shooting championships, and watch how the winners hold their guns. The webs of their hands will be riding high. Now you know why. The champions know what so many other shooters have missed.

Lost Secret #3: The Crush Grip

In target pistol shooting, light holds are in vogue. The bull's-eye shooter is taught to let her pistol just rest in her fingers with no real grasp at all as she gently eases the trigger back. The IPSC shooter is taught to apply 60 percent strength with the support hand and 40 percent with the firing hand (occasionally the reverse, but 50 percent of available hand strength in any case).

Common sense tells us this will not do for a fight. For one thing, it is dexterity intensive, and dexterity is among the first things we lose in a fight-or-flight state. For another, the genuine fight you are training for always entails the risk of an opponent attempting to snatch your gun away. We know that action beats reaction. If you're holding your handgun lightly or with only half your strength and it is forcibly grabbed or struck, it will probably be gone from your grasp before you can react. But if you have conditioned your hand to always hold the gun with maximum strength, you have a better chance to resist the attack long enough to react, counter with a retention move, and keep control of your firearm.

A third tremendous advantage of a hard hold, one that world champion Ray Chapman always told his students, is that it's the ultimate consistency in hold. "40 percent hand strength" is one thing in the relatively calm environment of the training range. It's something else when you're at a big match shooting for all the marbles, and it's something a league beyond that when you're fighting for your life. One effect of fight or flight response is that as dexterity goes down, strength goes up precipitously. Even in target shooting, marksmanship coaches agree that a consistent hold is a key element of consistent shot placement. There are only two possible grasps that can be guaranteed to stay truly consistent: no pressure at all, or maximum pressure.

A fourth big advantage for the crush grip is that it prevents "milking." When one finger moves, the other fingers want to move with it. The phenomenon is called "interlimb response." As the trigger fingers tighten, so do the grasping fingers, as if they were milking a cow's udder, and this jerks the shot off target, usually down and to one side. But if the fingers on the gripframe (NOT the trigger finger!) are already squeezing as hard as they can, they can't squeeze any more when the index finger separately pulls the trigger, and milking is thus made impossible.

Finally, the hard hold better controls recoil. If you had me by the throat and were holding me against a wall, and I was struggling, would you relax your grip or hold harder? The harder you hold me against the wall, the less I can move. Similarly, the more firmly you grasp your gun, the less *it* will move in recoil, in terms of both overall gun movement and the stocks shifting in your hand.

Detractors of the concept call this "gorilla grip," and warn that it interferes with delicate movement of the trigger finger and can cause small tremors. Those of us who advocate crush grip answer, "So what?" Delicate manipulation of the trigger disappears once the fight is on. The hands are going to tremble under stress anyway, and the shooter might as well get used to it up front in training. If the sights are kept in line, the gun's muzzle won't tremble off a target the size of a human heart.

Lost Secret #4: Front Sight

Every marksman who is accomplished with open sights remembers the day he or she experienced "the

The front sight is the key to good hits. In close, even an image like this, well above the rear sight, will put the shot where it needs to go.

The most precise, almost surgical, accuracy comes when the eye focuses on the front sight, with the rear sight in secondary focus and target in tertiary focus.

epiphany of the front sight." The phrase "watch your front sight" doesn't mean just have it in your field of view. It doesn't mean just be aware of it. It means focus on it as hard as possible, making sure it's on target, and that it's not moving off target as you stroke the trigger. Pistol champions and gunfight survivors alike have learned that this is the key to *center* hits at high speed under pressure.

As discussed in the chapter on point shooting, you don't need the perfect sight picture of the marksmanship manual. But remember that the handgun is a remote control drill, and it must be indexed with where we want the hole to appear, or the hole will appear in the wrong place. The sights, at least the front sight in close, will be the most reliable such index.

A smooth roll of the trigger becomes more critical as the shooting problem becomes more difficult. With the 11-ounce .357, double-action, and weak-hand-only, you can be sure the author is focusing on this trigger stroke.

Lost Secret #5: Smooth Roll

A smooth, even, uninterrupted roll of the trigger, as discussed in the last chapter, is critical if the shooter is going to break the shot without jerking it off target.

Note that the last two elements, "front sight" and "smooth trigger roll," are not listed as "to the lines of secrets four and five, prior." This is because it's debatable whether they are really lost secrets, and if so, who lost them. Every competent instructor will teach the students how to use the sights and how to bring the trigger back. The problem is, these things are very easy to forget until the student develops the discipline to first think about doing them, and then finally ingrain the concepts through repetition so they are done automatically.

Power stance. High hand. Crush grip. Front sight. Smooth roll. I try to go through it in my mind like a pre-flight checklist before I even reach for the gun.

You don't even have to think about it all at once. As soon as you know there may be a stimulus to draw the gun, slip into a power stance. It might be a thug giving you the bad eye as you wait for a bus, or it might be that you're on the range awaiting the "commence fire" signal. If you're in the position to start, you don't have to think about it any more.

Condition yourself to always begin the draw by hitting the high hand position. Once it's there, it's done and you don't have to think about it any longer.

Crush grip? I tell my students to think of the eagle's claw. When the eagle sleeps, it does not fall from its perch because its claws automatically clutch it with a death grip. If we condition ourselves to do this whenever we hold the gun, it'll happen on its own when we need it without us having to think about it.

Power stance…high hand…crush grip…front sight…smooth roll. Recover these "lost secrets" and apply them…and watch your combat handgun skill increase.

Power stance, high hand, crush grip, front sight, smooth roll. The author, foreground, brings it all together as he wins a shoot in the Northwest. Note that spent casing is in the air above his STI, but gun is already back on target despite recoil of full power .45 hardball. Photo by Matthew Sachs.

CHAPTER FIVE

"Maxing" Qualification And Competition

The master gunfighters of the 20th century – Bill Jordan and Elmer Hilden of the Border Patrol, Jim Cirillo and Bill Allard of the NYPD Stakeout Squad – all felt that shooting in competition sharpened your ability to shoot under stress in defense of your life. If you haven't tried it, you should.

Just in case you haven't competed, let's see what it's like. Come with me and shoot a match. I can't make it up for you. I don't do fiction. The only way to do it is for you and I to "channel" together, as the Yuppies say. It's June 5, 2001. We're at the Cheshire Fish & Game Club, the host range for the event, sponsored by the Keene, NH Police Department. The occasion is the annual conference of the New Hampshire Police Association, and the combat shoot that accompanies it is the *de facto* state championship in police combat shooting for cops in the Granite State.

You want a gun and ammo that you know will work. With the Glock 22 (NY-1 trigger, Meprolight fixed sights) and Black Hills EXP ammo, you have both.

Getting Ready

Bad news: you're stuck doing it with me, a "geezer cop" in his fifties. Good news: this particular geezer knows this particular beat, and you and I are prepared to compete on a level playing field.

Rules are that you have to compete with the gun you carry on duty. No tricky recoil compensators or optical sights. Holsters must be suitable for police wear, with retaining devices not only present but fastened before each draw. Ammunition must be suitable for law enforcement use.

My department issues a traditional-style double action .45 auto that is justly famous for both its accuracy and its reliability, two things I appreciated when I won this match with my issue weapon last year. For the whole second quarter, I've been in plainclothes – actually allowed to wear a beard, which I can't in uniform – because I'm a captain who handles primarily administrative and training tasks. These include test and evaluation of new equipment, etc. I've been assigned to test two new uniform security holsters that are about to come into the field. Since the Glock pistol is by far the most common in law enforcement today, it is what these new holsters were initially made to fit. My chief has given me permission to carry one on duty for testing purposes. It's the Glock 22, .40 caliber, the single most popular Glock thanks in large part to police sales, and at the same time, the single most popular police service handgun in the U.S. today. It is as it came from the factory: bone-stock, equipped with the 8-pound New York (NY-1) trigger and Meprolight fixed night sights.

The new security holsters haven't come in yet, so my gray whiskers and I have a reprieve for a while yet in plainclothes, but I'm carrying the G22 to get bonded with it beforehand. It's a good little pistol, particularly with the ammo my department issues for off-duty or plainclothes wear with that caliber, the Black Hills EXP. It sends a 165-grain Gold Dot hollow-point out of the barrel at an honest 1,150 feet per second, a .357 Magnum power level, and it is loaded to match-grade quality specifications. When we sighted in this gun/ammo combo for the first time at 50 yards, aiming for the head of a silhouette target, we jerked one shot down into the neck and didn't count it. But the other four shots were in the head in a *one and seven-eighths inch group*. Is *this* gonna be accurate enough for the B-27 target with competition scoring rings, where the tie-breaking center X ring measures 2 inches by 3 inches? *Oh,* yeah!

We're wearing what we wear to work these days. BDU pants (loose, comfortable, lots of pockets, great for

Each shooter finds his own pace. The hands of the shooter in the background are beginning to separate as he prepares to reload his Beretta while transitioning from standing to left-side kneeling; the officer at right is already in a kneeling position and has just fired the first shot from that position with his Glock.

strenuous things like going prone and running, which we'll have to do here.) Polo shirt with the department patch logo on it, one size large to help conceal the bullet-resistant vest. (We wear the vest on duty; we'll wear it here.) Handcuffs in a Galco quick-release plainclothes carrier. The dress gun belt is by Mitch Rosen, as are the first magazine pouch and the holster. The rig fits us perfectly, as it should; it's the one Rosen called the ARG for Ayoob Rear Guard. It rides comfortably inside the waistband behind the strong side hip, secured by a thumb-break safety strap. Backing up the Rosen pouch with its 15-round Glock "law enforcement only" G22 mag are two more pouches, both Kydex, one by Blade-Tech and one by Ky-Tac. This match will have some stages where two reloads are necessary, and then we'll have to reload

Firing prone from 50 yards. Note that each officer has a slightly different technique.

to "hot" condition before refilling magazines, etc. Hence, the need for four magazines on the person, including the one in the gun.

Let's get our head right. We're going for the title of top dog, or in this case, top law-dog. That engenders pressure. There's a little more of that on you and me than on most of the others. One person has to be the defending champion from last year, and that raises the price of the ego investment bet on the table. That person, right now, is us.

We get the briefing on the course of fire. There has been a last-minute change in rules. At the barricades, we cannot touch the wall with either gun or hand to stabilize for the shot. OW!

Particularly at 50 yards, this hurts accuracy: we're firing free-hand instead of with support. The good news is everyone has to do the same. It's fair, a level playing field. We are *awfully* glad, you and I, that we have a lot of experience shooting at long range with a pistol held in unsupported hands from the standing position.

50 Yards

We'll have exactly 60 seconds to go prone, fire six, reload, stand, fire six from one side of the barricade (no support, remember), reload again, and fire six more from behind the wall on the other side without actually touching that wall. We MUST be effectively behind cover or we'll be penalized.

We load the Glock 22, holster, fasten the safety strap, and stand by, hands clear of the holster. On the signal, we draw and drop into the rollover prone technique you and I learned from world champion Ray Chapman so many years ago. AAUUGGHH! There's grass between us and the target, obscuring aim! We scoot to the side, get a clear shot, and begin shooting. The readjustment of position has put us behind the other shooters from the get-go.

We fight the urge to hurry. Front sight is dead in the center of the target. We carefully press the trigger back until the shot breaks. Then again. And again.

Those six are done, and the clock is ticking. We feel the shots went right in where we wanted them. A review of the target in a couple of minutes will prove us right. But now, as we leap to our feet, our right thumb punching the Glock's magazine release as our left hand snatches a fresh mag from behind the left hip and snaps it home, the left thumb pressing down on the slide lock lever to chamber a fresh round, there is a sense that we are behind the others in time. This is a quick stage. Normally in police combat shooting, 24 shots are fired from this 50-yard distance, all of them supported either by the barricade or in the sitting or prone position, and you have two minutes, 45 seconds. That works out to 6.875 seconds per shot. We've just fired the only *six* shots where we'll have support, that of the ground in the prone posture, and we're firing at a rate of 3.33 seconds per shot, faster than double speed.

The first shot from standing feels perfect. But on the second we feel ourselves jerk the trigger, actually *see* the front sight dip in the notch as the shot breaks. The sight hasn't gone down that much, but there's a geometric progression here. The slightest drop of the front sight means a bullet *way* low by the time it reaches its mark half a football field away.

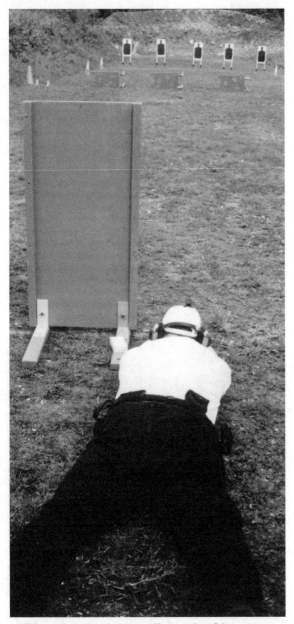

Fifty yards seems a long way off, even when firing prone.

Brain cells front and center! We have to tighten up! Consciously, we harden our hold to better stabilize the gun (since there's nothing but our bare hands to stabilize it at all) and dig our rear leg into the ground to drive our body forward. This will let our body weight help better to snap the gun down out of recoil and back into line with the target, giving us fractions of a second more time per shot to "hold and squeeze."

Those six are done. Speed reload. We're back on target with not a lot of time left, standing just behind the cover on the other side of the barricade. We chant to ourself consciously but silently, "Power stance! High-hand grasp! Crush grip! Front sight! Smooth ro-o-oll of the trigger."

We finish about 10 seconds ahead of that unforgiving clock. We reload and holster, set about refilling our magazines, and then prepare to go forward to score. Jerry St. Pierre of the Keene Police is leading the host team. He knows how easily the whole target can be missed from this far away. He's going to score and mark the 50-yard hits before we go any further.

As we approach the targets, we see something in the pelvis of our silhouette target. Oh, *please,* let that be a staple or something! No such luck. The shot we jerked would have been a take-down hit on a man, and would have been worth three out of five points if the target was scored in the police qualification fashion. But this is the police *competition* scoring system, and that shot is counted as a miss. Ten points gone for one bad shot!

In a regular PPC match, that would ruin you. The master class shooters here get 580 and 590 out of 600 scores routinely with their match guns at standard time, and 10 points gone for one of the 60 shots would tank you out of the match for good. Fortunately, here *everyone* is shooting at double speed and using service guns. The playing field is still level...*but you and I can't afford any more mistakes!*

25 Yards

We start with six shots kneeling. Then fire, six from the left side of the barricade, standing, and six more from the right, the same way, with a mandatory reload between each stage. The latter is done to level the playing field for any shooter who has a revolver or a low-capacity auto. This is the first year I've been here where not a single wheelgun is in evidence. In this state, the transition to the service pistol is virtually complete. You usually have 90 seconds for this stage in a Police Combat match, and can stabilize your support hand on the barricade. Here, we can't use anything to steady on, and time is only 60 seconds. Only two-thirds the time, and at least double the difficulty.

The timer sounds. We draw first, then drop to kneeling – even at speed, we don't cross a bent lower leg with the muzzle of a loaded gun – and lock in our front sight. The gun was sighted to hit dead on at 50 yards and this means we have to hold a tad low in close, taking a 6 o'clock sight picture that balances the "X" on top of the front sight.

We are thinking "front sight, smooth roll...front sight, smooth roll" for each shot. The reloads, practiced so many times, seem to happen on automatic pilot. There is just time enough to "ride the link" of the Glock trigger, to fire each shot, let the trigger come back forward just enough until we feel the click of the mechanism resetting, and then we draw the trigger back again, feeling the smooth subtle movement of the Glock pistol's cruciform sear plate until each subsequent shot is released.

Rather than brace an elbow at the knee, these officers use "speed kneeling" around replicated cover at 25 yards.

Officers fire over the barricade at 25 yards, and also from around both sides. Duty pistols are Glock in the foreground, Beretta 9mm at left.

We make the time. That's no sweat. Under pressure, things go faster than you think. Glance downrange. There are a very few shots out in the 9-point ring, but the rest have gone true to center. Life is good.

Now comes what, for some, is the toughest stage. You stand at 25 paces facing the target, hands at your side. On the signal, you draw and fire six shots…in ten seconds, including reaction time. Getting the shots off is no problem. Making the hits in that tiny center ring is the problem.

You and I breathe deeply as we hear the command sequence begin, holding the air in and letting it hiss slowly out. It's the internalized version of that "breathe into the paper bag" trick we cops always use with people in crisis who are hyperventilating. Ya can't do the bag on the range or in a fight, though. Some call it "crisis breathing." You and I learned it decades ago in a karate dojo where they called it *sanchin* breathing.

The signal comes. We draw, lock in, get the front sight on target, and roll the Glock's trigger back. Our head is forward and down, like a vulture's, the way humans stand when in the grip of "fight or flight" response. This helps us stay focused on the front sight ("target identified, missiles locked on target, launch, maintain target lock for next missile…"). We finish a good second before the cease-fire

On signal, officers sprint forward from 25-yard line…

…to 15 yards, where they draw and fire. Note safety officer moving in behind the firing line.

Note individualized versions of the low ready positions as officers await command on the firing line...

...to react, bring up the gun, and score two hits at 15 yards, all in two seconds.

signal is sounded. We glance downrange as we reload. There aren't any more errant hits outside the 10/X rings than there were before.

15 Yards

Reloaded, we begin standing at the 25-yard line. On the signal, we have to run forward to the 15-yard line, draw, and fire two shots, all in only six seconds. The horn sounds. We lunge forward. Time slows down. As we approach the line we use a trick we learned from World Champion Ray Chapman: a little jump in the air, then land at the finish point on flexed and coiled knees as the gun comes out, as is only now allowed. There isn't much time left. We snap it to line of sight in an Isosceles hold, and instead of using the usual post in notch sight picture, we just align the three big dots of the Meprolight fixed night sights that came on our service Glock, and roll the trigger back, fighting the urge to hasten the shot. Bang, bang, *beep!*

We've made the time. Not everyone else has been so fortunate.

Now we go to a low ready stance. Three more times, the signal will come to shoot, and each time we'll have only two seconds to raise our service weapon, align it, and get two shots into that heart-sized center ring. We must start with our finger outside the trigger guard. Most are holding it straight on the frame: safe, but slower than it needs to be. Not all of them make the time. Many are starting with their fingertip on the front of the trigger guard. Fast, but tricky: under stress, this position holds the trigger finger taut, and when it snaps into the trigger it hits with impact, often breaking the shot prematurely. That's tragedy on the street, and it's a bad hit here on the line. Some others learn that today the hard way.

You and I start with our trigger finger flexed, the tip of the finger touching the takedown niche on the side of the Glock frame. Now, on the signal, as we raise the gun we can thrust the finger swiftly into the trigger guard *across* the trigger, until we find that sweet spot where the distal joint of the finger feels virtually centered on the trigger so we have maximum leverage for a fast, straight-back pull that won't move the muzzle off the target. BAM-BAM! We're in! And again, BAM-BAM. We're doin' OK.

The officer at left is down on his right knee behind left side cover; the officer on right has chosen the left knee for better balance with slight leftward lean.

One-hand-only stages at 7 yards are the cruncher for time.

With the six-round magazines that are demanded (to level the playing field between the different service guns styles), we're at slidelock, and we quickly reload. Some of our brother and sister officers have come to grief at this point, and they're out of the running. Their guns jammed. When you have only two shots left, and two must be fired, and your pistol locks up in the middle of that, two seconds simply isn't time enough to recognize the malfunction, clear it, reload, and fire another round. Fortunately, you and I have a Glock with Black Hills ammunition, two exemplars of reliability, and that disaster does not befall us.

7 Yards

This is the final stage. The cruncher. The one where cops are most likely to fail to get their shots off in time. In PPC, it's 12 shots in 25 seconds, including the reload, in a two-hand stance. But here in New Hampshire, you draw strong-hand-*only,* fire five shots, reload, then shift the gun to your other hand and fire five more shots weak-hand-*only,* all in only 15 seconds.

We're ready. We've practiced this. We start in a fighter's stance, not a target shooter's stance, and on the start signal we draw and bring the gun into the target like a Shotokan karate fighter throwing a punch. The body weight behind the Glock keeps it on target with the stout recoil of the hot Black Hills load, the three dots already back at center in the time it takes to re-set the trigger. The gun goes to slidelock. Speed-reload, hand change. We sense the clock ticking and, losing our sense of time we fire faster than we should, finishing the whole thing in about 10 seconds. But all ten of those last shots are inside the 10 and 10-X rings, and our job is done.

It Ain't Over

Now you stand by your target and await the official scorer. Smoke 'em if you got 'em and cope with the stress. It's like waiting for the biopsy to come back from the lab. The stress isn't *nearly* over yet.

We check the target along with the scorer. We don't like it, but he has it right. It's not the best we have ever done. On the other hand, it *is* the best score on the first relay, and we're in the lead.

The match sponsors have announced that each shooter can get one second chance over the course. However, *as soon as they fire the first shot of their second try, their first score becomes null and void.* You and I immediately go over to the registrar, pay an entry fee, and book a slot to shoot again if we have to.

Now comes a war of nerves and ego. You and I don't like that score, particularly the 10 points down shot from 50 yards. We want to try again, strut our stuff, shoot better than we did before. That's understandable. However, ego must come second to The Job. I represent my police department here. My chief wants our department to keep the title from last year. If I get beaten,

This state trooper is at 7 yards as he draws and fires five shots strong-hand-only with his issue S&W .45 auto...

...he ducks down to reload (good survival training in action!) and then...

...fires the last five shots weak-hand-only.

All draws begin with the safety devices fastened.

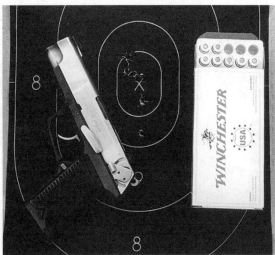

This is the combination that won the year before: Ruger P90 with fixed IWI night sights and Winchester USA 230-grain .45 hardball.

I'm ready to shoot again…but if my chief of police ever finds out that I had victory solidly in my hand, then shot again to feed my ego *and lost what I already had locked up,* he is going to start wondering whether I should really keep command authority after making such a stupid decision. Soon I will be walking foot patrol in the sanitary landfill or something.

So we must wait these tension-filled moments, you and I who are shooting together, until the scores are in and "last relay" is called.

Several have tried twice. None have beaten the top score on the board. That score is ours.

The end of the match feels almost anti-climactic. It is announced that you and I have won. We shake hands with the match director, Officer Jerry St. Pierre, and some kind person takes a photo.

You and I have won the state shoot. Our prize is a Glock 27 pistol, donated by Riley's Sport Shop in Hooksett, NH. It's identical to the one that has been strapped to our left leg the whole time in an Alessi ankle holster, a fallback in case something goes wrong with the Glock 22 and we quickly need a gun to finish the match. The Glock 27 will take the Glock 22's magazines that are already on our belt.

But we'll leave with some lessons even more valuable than that excellent Glock pistol.

Focus on the task, not the goal. The task was to shoot perfect shots, 60 of them. We dropped our focus on one and blew the shot. Our 59 decent hits turned out to be enough to get us through the "trial." If we focus on the goal, we'll neglect the tasks necessary to achieve it, but if we focus on the tasks, the goal will achieve itself.

You need a damn good gun with damn good ammo for something like this. With the Glock 22 and the Black Hills EXP .40 ammo, we had both. Others who might have beaten us failed when their equipment failed. Ours didn't.

The trigger is the heart of the beast. When you control the trigger, you control the shot. You and I just experienced living proof that a heavy trigger isn't

Match director Jerry St. Pierre, right, congratulates the author on winning the title.

uncontrollable. Those 8 pounds of pressure were manageable enough. In my experience, the New York trigger gives a cleaner trigger break and less trigger backlash. It's a win-win thing, and that's why I have a New York trigger on every Glock I ever carry for anything serious, like this one, which is, for now, my police service pistol.

One in the hand really is worth two in the bush. Right brain warring with left brain, I desperately wanted to shoot the course again to get a better score. But logic won out over ego, as it always should. You don't throw away a locked-in victory for a mere *chance* at a more spectacular victory. This is just one example of many of how competition teaches us how to make life decisions.

Self-coaching works. Often times, you'll be coaching a friend and watching him miss the plates. You yell, "Front sight!" and then comes, BANG-CLANG, and the hit is achieved. You don't need a separate coach if you're constantly reminding yourself of what to do. Works in a match, works in a fight, works in any life crisis.

Combat competition isn't gunfighting. You know you won't die if you fail. But it's as close to a microcosm of a gunfight as you can come in training as far as pressure is concerned. I've done my share of Simunitions and similar realistic role playing, and I can tell you the stress is more in a big match.

Anything that conditions you to shooting under pressure can help you stay alive with a gun in your hand. Combat competition is the most cost-effective, most readily available avenue to getting used to the pressure.

Combat Competition

There are those of us who can remember when we shot bull's-eye pistol matches because, in part, we wanted to stay sharp with the guns we carried for self-defense. Why? Because it was the only game in town! Today, things are a lot better.

Let's take a look at the combat shooting competition that is currently available to the law-abiding private citizen in the United States. It's not that any one has it all over the other. Each element will have a piece of the puzzle.

IDPA

Bill Wilson and some others who felt that available defensive handgun competition had become more of a game than a training tool founded the International Defensive Pistol Association in the mid-1990s. It has been the fastest-growing shooting discipline of its kind since. For the author's money, it's the "best game in town," but it still doesn't have everything.

You need a "street gun" in a "street holster," which in most stages will be concealed when the start signal comes. The holster must ride behind the hip, and hide under the concealing garment. The ubiquitous 1911 .45 auto and its 10mm sister compete in CDP (Custom Defense Pistol) class. A Browning Hi-Power or other cocked-and-locked 9mm, .38 Super or .40 pistol will be used in ESP (Enhanced Service Pistol). A double action auto or a Glock

would enter the single most popular category, SSP (Stock Service Pistol). For wheelgunners, there is SSR (Stock Service Revolver). Even with high capacity guns, the shooter is limited to 10-round magazines in the interest of a level playing field.

A shooter who does not use available cover will be penalized. Just like in a gunfight, only in a match, the penalties aren't nearly as harsh. Often, the shooter is required to move while shooting, and will be penalized if he comes to a stop to fire.

A stage may begin with the practitioner seated in a car, lying in bed, even sitting on a toilet. Don't worry; they'll let you keep your pants up. Failure to neutralize a bad guy target gains a penalty. Hitting a no shoot target is a BIG penalty. In these things, again, IDPA is reflecting real world values.

There will be a penalty for leaving live ammo behind or making a reload on the run. As in real life, IDPA figures it's healthier to stay behind cover and only move if you have a fully reloaded gun already in hand. While I think the emphasis on tactical reloads over speed reloads is a bit excessive, that's just one participant's opinion.

The target is reasonably realistic, a cardboard silhouette with an 8-inch maximum point "A-zone" in the center of the chest. Some targets will be steel knock-downs. I've seen events where the targets were on their sides, simulating a pack of wolves or wild dogs. Protecting yourself from vicious animals is legitimate self-defense too, one too often neglected in the other shooting disciplines.

If you've been to a lot of matches, you've seen chronic whiners and "gamesmen" who aren't there to learn, just there to win, and sometimes they are there to take their insecurities out on others. IDPA has an answer for that. Anything that smacks of cheating or bad sportsmanship earns a "failure to do right" penalty that is so massive it blows the offender out of the match. It has served to keep egos well in line.

To see what it's all about, to find a club offering IDPA events within reach of you, or to see about starting up such matches yourself, check out the website at www.idpa.com

IPSC

The International Practical Shooting Confederation was founded in the mid-1970s under the direction of Jeff Cooper, who had created "replicated gunfight" matches as early as the 1950s with his "Leatherslaps" and the founding of the Southwest Combat Pistol League in California. Until then, the efforts of Cooper and company were exotica that we read about, but couldn't share unless we moved to the West Coast; now, it was available to all.

Four flavors of Glock .40. From top, G35, G22, G23, and G27. The author has seen them all used in matches by people who actually carried them on the street.

When he carried the S&W 4506 on duty (top), the author had Wayne Novak make him up a custom single-action version for matches (center), and later had another crafted in .45 Super by Ace Custom (below). However, as time wore on...

...experience taught him to just shoot the duty gun in matches. He did OK.

These officers shot the Washington State Championships with the .45s they carried on duty. Left, Bill Burris with street-tuned Para-Ordnance; right, the author with his issue Ruger P90.

The early days of IPSC were much like IDPA today. "Real" guns. "Real" scenarios. I had the privilege of running the first IPSC Sectional Championship in the United States, with Col. Jeff Cooper and section coordinator Jim Cirillo present, in 1976. The event was weighted toward larger caliber guns with "Major/Minor" scoring. A hit in the center ring was worth five points with either a 9mm or a .45, but outside that ring, you lost twice as many points if you were shooting 9mm instead of .45. The Colonel said that this appropriately rewarded the more competent gun handler, who was dealing with more recoil and wielding a "more serious" weapon.

That made sense a quarter century ago, when high efficiency ammunition for medium calibers such as 9mm and .38 Special was just coming in. Today, however, a 115-grain 9mm at 1,300 feet per second will kill a criminal just as dead as a 230-grain .45 ACP at 850, and might actually cause more tissue damage. This is why IDPA chose to avoid major/minor, instead instituting a "power

Bill Fish shoots an IDPA match with his Glock 34. The skills transfer…

floor" in each caliber and having like guns shoot against like guns.

I was there over the years when IPSC seemed to change course. The first big switch to the "race guns and space guns" came when John Shaw had pistolsmith Jim Clark build him a Colt .45 auto with forward muzzle weight. The gun was originally for the Second Chance bowling pin shoot, which is why that genre became known as "pin guns," but John quickly found it advantageous in IPSC and promptly won the national championship with it. The race was on: Mike Plaxco, Bill Wilson, and other master shooters with gunsmithing skills soon built expansion chamber recoil compensators to further tame the recoil.

Then Rob Leatham discovered that he could hot-load the .38 Super to make major, and the intense pressure of the red-line-loaded cartridge created more expanding gas for a recoil compensator to work with. Muzzle jump was now nil. Then Jerry Barnhart proved that with an Aimpoint red dot sight, one could see the aiming index and the target on the same visual plane and hit faster. Next thing you knew, every gun had a big "can" on top for the shooter to aim through. Holsters for these guns evolved into super-fast skeletons carried at the front of the belt, with such a precarious hold on the pistol that Barnhart was successful selling a device he called a "walk-through strap." This was a strap that would keep the gun from falling out of the holster while the range officer walked the

…to the Glock 19 and Glock 26 he carries. In fact, he is known to compete with all three. Note the identical "Glock socks" on each.

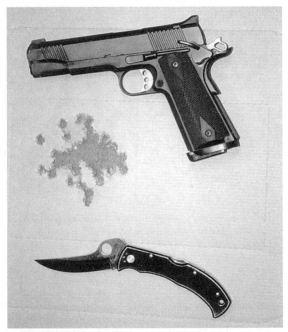

Many combat handguns are accurate enough for competition yet reliable enough for carry. This out-of-the-box Kimber Custom II has shot a perfect score on a 60-round qualification, in a 4-inch group as measured by the Ayoob Spyderco knife. Ammo was full power .45 hardball.

competitor through the course! Clearly, the "Practical" element of IPSC was coming into grave question.

Next, pioneered by Para Ordnance, came the wide-body "fat guns" that held huge magazines. I saw .38 Super pistols with extended fat mags that could fire more than 25 shots without reloading. By now shooters were using triggers with as little as 28 ounces of pull – an accident waiting to happen in a real-world stress situation, but a winner's edge in IPSC. Competing against a pistol that didn't need to be reloaded and had a trick sight and no recoil and a telekinetic trigger left a cop with a department issue nine-shot double-action .45 asking himself, "Why bother?"

The sport began to stagnate. People broke off and formed things like IDPA. Gun expert Andy Stanford wrote in *American Handgunner* magazine of what he called "The Lost Tribe of IPSC," people like Bill Wilson and Ken Hackathorn and Walt Rauch and myself who had been in at the beginning, but had become disenchanted with IPSC.

The typical IPSC course is a "search and destroy" assault in which the shooter runs through a maze of targets and shoots the ones who are supposed to be bad guys, suffering only a 10-point penalty for shooting an innocent bystander. It is little wonder that the cops started to back away. That was a shame, because the realism of the early IPSC days had done wonders when grafted into the training of forward thinking police departments like that of Orlando, Florida.

This is not to say that one might not *need* a dollop of "run and gun" as they prepare their training recipe for real-world defensive handgunning. In January 2002, a Palestinian terrorist whipped an M-16 out from under a long coat and opened fire at a bus stop in Jerusalem,

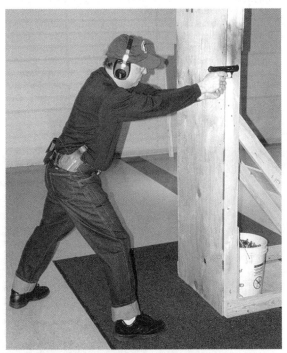

This shooter fires from behind cover at 20 yards in the IDPA National Mid-Winter Championships at the S&W Academy. The pistol, drawn from thumb-break concealment holster, is his daily carry gun, HK P7 9mm,...

...which he reloads tactically behind cover, a hallmark of IDPA, before he continues shooting from opposite side of the barricade.

Bill Wilson, founder of IDPA (center) explains the target's scoring system to the author and an unidentified IDPA member.

The owner of this target grade HK P9S 9mm has carried it on police patrol, worn it concealed, and shot it at the Bianchi Cup.

killing two innocent women and wounding at least 14 more people. Nearby, a plainclothes Israeli police sergeant named Hanan Ben Naim, dressed in jeans and tennis shoes, drew his Jericho and gave chase. At the end of the foot pursuit Naim faced the terrorist at a range of 20 feet and fired with the Jericho, a 9mm pistol that resembles the Czechoslovakian CZ75, as the terrorist opened up on him with the M-16. The assassin missed. The brave young sergeant didn't, and his pistol fire killed the machinegun-armed terrorist where he stood.

Today, IPSC is trying to return to its roots with a Revolver class, a Production Class, and a class called Limited-10. The latter is an iron-sight pistol with no compensator and a magazine that can hold no more than 10 rounds. Production Class is geared to Glocks and double action semiautomatics. At this writing, it has not taken off like IDPA, but perhaps it needs more time for the word to get out.

IPSC in the United States is governed by USPSA, the United States Practical Shooting Association. For information contact their website www.uspsa.com.

PPC

Get a bunch of police pistol team types together in a bar after a match, and it's about a two-beer argument whether "PPC" stands for "Practical Police Course," "Practical Pistol Course," or "Police Pistol/Combat." Some of the run-and-gun types suspect it stands for "pretty pathetic crap" because the shooting goes slower than they like.

Going back half a century, this course of fire began with police officers using revolvers and ammo loaded one cartridge at a time out of belt loops or pouches. With speedloaders for revolvers, let alone magazines for semiautomatic pistols, there's no question that the times in PPC may be overly generous. 25 seconds to draw, fire six, reload, and fire six more, two-handed, from 7 yards? Come on. NRA, the governing body of PPC shooting, has brought that down to 20 seconds, which is a start.

NRA has never let civilians shoot this match under their auspices; for reasons of political correctness, they don't want the negative publicity of citizens shooting at "pictures of human beings," as reporters like to call the B-27 silhouette target. Nonetheless, many gun clubs offer PPC shooting matches to civilians.

I started shooting bull's-eye. I went to PPC, known locally as "Police Combat," as soon as I could because it was faster, more relevant, and frankly more fun. I jumped from there to IPSC when it became available. By comparison, PPC was old and slow. Many years later, I came back to it. For one thing, *I* was now old and slow.

It's obsolete in terms of shooting speed, but PPC offers some good things. It puts more emphasis on use of cover than any other kind of combat shooting competition. Consider the microcosm of PPC, Match Five, also known as the National Match Course. You'll fire 12 shots from 7 yards, 18 from 25, 24 from 50 yards, and the last 6 at 25 again, this time standing without cover and support. The

This shooter runs a PPC match from standing right-hand barricade position.

The Para-Ordnance pistol, top, will kick harder with the same .45 ammo than match Colt Government with D.R. Middlebrooks JetComp compensator, below, but manipulation will be similar.

The center rings are too low, focusing on the solar plexus area instead of the heart. However, the 10-ring is almost exactly the size of a human heart. The IDPA target with its 8-inch center circle and the IPSC Brussels target with its 6-inch wide by 11-inch high center rectangle are altogether too generous. In either, what in the real world would be a "lung shot" has the same match scoring value as a "heart into spine" shot. That's simply not practical.

Even before IPSC, PPC evolved into an equipment race with "space guns." In open class, the weapons you need to win are "PPC revolvers" with massive barrels and sight ribs, or long-slide autos with similar sights. Both would be impractical to carry. Fortunately, NRA has been emphasizing stock gun classes for revolver, auto, and "off-duty guns," and I think these will be the salvation of the sport. Last year's National Championship in the stock service pistol event, I'm told, was won by a Richmond (VA) cop with the *SigPro* pistol he was issued by the department, and department-issue 125-grain CCI Gold Dot ammo, caliber .357 SIG. This is a good sign.

If you're a full or part-time police officer or security professional or in the military with an MOS in law enforcement, you're eligible for PPC shooting under NRA's auspices. Contact the National Rifle Association and direct your inquiry to the Police Competitions division. If you're a private citizen, you'll have to check around with the gun shops and gun clubs to see who in your area offers PPC shooting to the public.

18 at 25 are all from behind a vertical wall called a barricade: six kneeling strong hand, six standing weak hand, six standing strong hand. At 50 yards, it's six each from sitting, prone, left barricade and right barricade. The low positions replicate taking cover behind something like an automobile. This means that of 60 shots, all but 18 – more than two-thirds – train you for shooting from behind cover.

The cover rules are strict. You'll be penalized if your foot steps past the barricade's edge, because that would have put some of your main body mass out into the field of fire. By contrast, IDPA allows up to 50 percent of your body to be exposed before you're penalized for failure to use appropriate cover. In the real world, the single tactical failure that gets most good guys killed is failure to use cover that was available before the fight started.

Don't write off the 50-yard shooting as irrelevant; the distances at which the cops engaged the gunmen exceeded that in both the North Hollywood bank robbery shootout and the Columbine incident, two infamous case studies in the need for intensive marksmanship training on the part of the good guys. Another good point for PPC is the B-27 target they use.

It's not my favorite target. Originally known as the Prehle target, it came about many years ago when a smart trainer named Prehle superimposed the scoring rings of the Olympic Rapid Fire target over the old Colt silhouette.

Using guns modified for non-lethality, Chris Edwards and the author shoot each other as the latter opens a closet door during a force-on-force stage at National Tactical Invitational. Ayoob recommends the NTI as a learning experience for any who haven't tried it.

In this stage, officer Jerry Lashway rushes forward to snatch a "baby" from high chair and pull her to "cover"...

...as he returns fire weak-hand-only with his Les Baer .45 auto. The scene was part of the 2002 Smith & Wesson MidWinter Championships.

Tactical Shooting

My fellow LFI instructor Peter Dayton and I were the only two men to compete in all six of the first National Tactical Invitational shooting events. It was a concept developed by three well-qualified men, Chuck Davis, Skip Gochenauer and Walt Rauch, to truly test tactical skills in not only shooting but building search and related disciplines. We loved it. Alas, in the mid-90s, it took a different direction. Rauch and Davis were no longer really in the picture. It ceased to be a competitive skill test and became more a learning experience, in which the sponsors were teaching the lessons. That is certainly useful for some people. It was simply no longer what Dayton and I and some others were looking for, so we went elsewhere.

I've been told that the NTI has gotten better since then. It is certainly a good learning experience. Follow *Combat Handguns* magazine for information on how to apply for the next NTI; the group that runs it usually makes their announcements there.

Pin Shooting

In the late 1960s, armed citizen Richard Davis won a gunfight with three armed robbers. He was hit twice himself during the fracas. As he recovered from his wounds, it occurred to him that there had to be something better to stop bullets with than one's own body. He invented the concealable soft body armor he called Second Chance. By January of 2001, more than 2,500 identified good guys and gals had been saved by the concept, more than 800 by Richard's Second Chance brand alone.

In the early days, he had to overcome the myth that the blunt trauma of a bullet striking the soft armor would render the officer helpless. He needed a visually dramatic target that would show the truth. He set up a table on a dirt firing range in Walled Lake, Michigan, on which he placed a couple of blocks of Roma Plastilena modeling clay (then used to demonstrate bullet effect before the

coming of improved ballistic gelatin). He also set up a few bowling pins.

What happened next, as a home movie camera whirred erratically, was law enforcement history. Davis loaded a Colt .357 Magnum with hot Smith & Wesson brand .38 Special ammo that was the forerunner of today's +P, and he blew up the clay blocks with a couple of rounds.

Then he turned the gun on himself ... and shot himself in the midriff.

Immediately, to show that the impact of the slug had not impaired his ability to fight, he spun back toward the table and with the three rounds left, shot the three bowling pins.

Practical matches replicate practical situations. This IDPA stage begins with pistol lying on "toilet tank" in "restaurant rest room." Shooter will begin seated on replicated toilet. In the interest of dignity, pants won't be dropped.

Match gun? Street gun? Two guns in one! The author used this S&W Model 625 in .45 ACP to shoot a personal best at Second Chance (faster than he'd ever shot a comp gun) and to make Master at the IDPA Mid-Winter National Championships in 1999…and it is the gun he would carry on duty if he was required to switch back to a service revolver tomorrow.

A few years later, already a millionaire from his invention, Rich wanted to give something back to the cops who had made him successful. He decided to create the Second Chance Street Combat Shoot, in the mid-1970s. He invited a few friends to the first one for a "test drive," and then opened it up to all cops in 1976.

I was there. I found it a lot tougher than it looked. If you think about it, a bowling pin is a very anatomic target. The neck/head area of the pin roughly duplicates the human cervical spine. The pin widens at the same place and to about the same width as the human heart, and truncates at about where the xiphoid process would be on a human sternum. A powerful bullet that hits the pin anywhere would pretty much do the job on a human antagonist.

Richard's Second Chance match became a regular stop on the "professional tour" of handgunning…and more. If the big shooting matches were rock concerts, Second

So inexpensive it's a best buy, the reliable Ruger P90 is accurate enough to win combat matches.

Chance was Woodstock. It was a "happening." Free food and barbecues, parties, fireworks, and a smorgasbord of shooting that was sort of like a carnival midway, except that the games weren't cheating you and if you performed well, you won guns. There were people who went to the eight-day festivities who didn't even compete anymore, and just came to be with other like-minded shooters. A few years into the experience, Richard had remembered his roots as an armed citizen and opened it to civilians.

Second Chance, sadly, was discontinued in 1998, a victim of fear of civil liability on the part of the corporate board. But it had left a legacy. There are hundreds and hundreds of "pin matches" held now at local clubs around the country. Check at your gun shop or gun club and find out where they're happening near you.

The range is close, 25 feet. However, just as in real life, only center hits count. The object is to blow each bowling pin all the way back off its 3-foot-deep table. Whoever gets all the pins off fastest, wins. If you hit more than an inch off center with a powerful bullet, the pin will spin sideways instead of falling back, and you'll have to shoot it again. It will roll in unpredictable directions and you'll have to track it carefully to shoot it once more and finally blow it away. But if you hit it dead center, it's "out of the fight."

Richard and I got together some years ago and wrote a book on how to do this, called "Hit the White Part." The joke went around that it was my combat shooting book for black guys. In fact, the title came from the single most common question/answer sequence Richard had to go through with new shooters. They would ask arcane questions like, "Where on the bowling pin should I aim?" Richard would reply, "Don't overcomplicate it. Just hit the white part." The book is available for $11.95 +$4.90 shipping from Police Bookshelf, PO Box 122, Concord, NH 03301, or you can order from the website, www.ayoob.com.

Advice in General

I went through the whole thing with the race guns and space guns and PPC guns. They're still in my gun safe. They hold pleasant memories, and they're good investments, but I never seem to shoot them anymore. I retired from the "pro tour" in 1981, and have since shot matches just to keep my hand in. The matches are my personal "pressure laboratory," to see how well a given technique works under stress, and to constantly keep testing myself for self-defense ability.

How deeply you get into it is up to you. Even when I was into it deeply, I made a point of shooting a gun that was analogous to what I carried. When my department issued the K-frame S&W Combat Magnum, I shot a K-frame S&W PPC gun that had been tuned by Ron Power. I won my share of matches and trophies and guns with it, and every stroke of the trigger in competition was pretty much the same as what I had with the revolver I carried on police patrol.

When my match gun was a Plaxco or Middlebrooks Custom .45 tricked out with a recoil compensator, my carry gun on duty and off, and the gun I kept by the bed, was a Colt Government Model or Commander .45. The same feel, the same trigger, the same manual of arms.

In a time when I could carry my Colt Python on duty, I had Austin Behlert put a heavy match barrel and sight rib on a Colt that I shot in open PPC matches. I used the

4-inch duty gun in NRA Service Revolver, a 6-inch Python in the NRA's Distinguished event, and a 2-1/2-inch Python tuned by Reeves Jungkind (who also did my PPC gun's action) for the snubby events. I won the state championship in police combat two or three times with the 4-inch Python, which had been slicked by Jerry Moran, and once with the snub-nosed Jungkind gun shooting against the 4-inch revolvers. I never felt handicapped when I didn't have the crutches of the heavy barrel and the massive sight rib.

When my department issued the S&W 4506, I dedicated myself to that gun. Bob Houzenga slicked up my personal duty pistol, and I bought another 4506 and sent it to Wayne Novak, who made it single action and put in a Model 52 match trigger for competition. I shot that for a year or two, and then realized the trigger wasn't the same and I was kidding myself, so I just competed with the 4506. One year at Second Chance I shot the target version in the Pin Gun event and the duty gun in the Stock Gun class, won a gun with each, and discovered to my surprise that I had shot a faster time with the gun I carried on duty than with the target pistol. Not long after that, my team won the four-man state championship in a bowling pin event called "Rolling Thunder." One contestant shot a rifle, one a pistol, one a pump shotgun, and one an auto-loading scattergun. I anchored on pistol with my duty 4506, double-action first shot and all, and we took home the big one.

The lesson is this: *compete as much as possible with the gun you actually carry.* This way, you'll maximize the effect of "shooting the match as training." If you think about it, one definition of "training" is the LFI definition: "authentically replicated experience." The more you shoot matches with the gun you're likely to actually have in your hand if you have to fight for your life, the more each of those matches becomes a true, relevant training experience.

A lot of times, I'll shoot a match with whatever gun I'm testing for a gun magazine at the time. Testing guns is part of my job. How it works in human hands under stress is one of the things I test for, and that's why when the scheduling permits I'll shoot a match with whatever handgun I'm writing up. I don't do that for myself. I do it for the readers of the test.

There are also times when I'm shooting a match to win, and I know I'm up against stiff competition who are all equipped with the best guns, and I'd be a damn fool not to have the best gun myself. In those events, I might indeed use a high tech, state-of-the-art custom match pistol if one is allowed.

But the ones I like most are the matches where you *have* to use the gun you carry. Our state championship for cops is like that where we live. I've found that whether you carry a K-frame or a Python, a Ruger .45 auto or a Glock, doesn't make that much of a difference. If you've bonded to the gun, as you should with the weapon you carry to defend your life and the lives of the innocent, you'll do OK with it.

Competition with the defensive handgun is one of the strongest avenues to developing the skills that will save your life. It has been my experience that the only people who say otherwise are those that haven't tried it, and therefore don't have a right to the opinion, or those who shot so badly in competition that they're desperately trying to deny the future they saw when they failed on the range that day.

These two S&W target-grade .38s complement one another. Top, Combat Masterpiece Model 15 for carry; below, 6-inch Model 14 with BoMar sight rib, for PPC shooting. Identical frames, actions and Hogue grips allow strong skill translation from match gun to duty gun.

This shooter tests his skill with his Glock carry gun against the ringing targets of the Steel Challenge.

CHAPTER SIX

Combat Handgun Controversies

Revolver Versus Auto

They've never stopped arguing about this one…and they've rarely made the most cogent points for either side!

In days of yore, gun magazine editors who ran out of fresh ideas could always get another few pages out of the "revolver versus auto" thing. The auto guy would write about "wave of the future" and "firepower!" The revolver guy would warn about the hazards of untrustworthy jam-amatics compared to "our trusted friend, the six-shooter" and point out that since most gunfights were supposed to be over in 2.3 rounds, if you couldn't do it with six you couldn't do it at all.

What happened? Basically, things changed. In those days, about the only reliable autos were the Colt .45 and the Browning 9mm, and then only if you fed them ball ammo. Round-nose, full-metal-jacket was an adequate stopper in .45, though it didn't optimize the cartridge's inherent potency, but it was woefully inadequate in 9mm. When loaded with hollow-points, most of the autoloaders of the mid-20th century *did* jam, if not epidemically then at least enough to worry about.

In the 1970s, when police departments and armed citizens started switching to 9mm high-capacity pistols, someone coined the term "wondernine" for this new hardware. There was nothing wondrous about a 9mm auto with a double-stack magazine; the classic Browning

Hi-Power had been around since 1935. What was wondrous was that this new breed – Beretta, Heckler & Koch, SIG-Sauer, second-generation Smith & Wessons – actually *worked* with JHPs. In 1985 came the Glock, just as reliable and even simpler to operate, and the dominance of the modern auto became a *fait accompli*.

The revolver remains the choice of handgun hunters, who but rarely go after game with their .44 and .50 Magnum Desert Eagle and .45 Magnum Grizzly autos, but that's a topic for a different book. The wheelgun is by no means dead in the combat handgun world. Bert DuVernay, the master instructor who once ran the Smith & Wesson Academy, said that the revolver would remain strong as a backup and off-duty gun among police. The years have proven him correct on that.

The cylinder gun also remains the choice of most experts when outfitting novices who won't necessarily be getting the structured training and in-service refresher time that a cop will get with his duty automatic. That's a good place to start when listing the real-world attributes of each design concept.

Better hit potential under stress seems to be a cardinal advantage of the self-cocking auto pistol with its short, light trigger stroke, such as this Beretta 9mm.

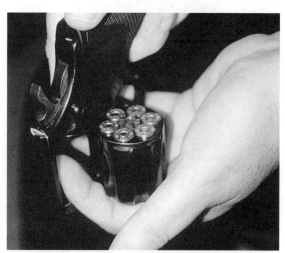

It's easy for a new shooter or someone with weak hands to open the cylinder of a double-action revolver like this Colt Detective Special and check to see if it's loaded or not.

Revolver Advantages

Ease Of Administrative Handling. The routine loading, unloading, checking, and cleaning that a combat handgun demands is more easily accomplished with the revolver. That's particularly true if the user is debilitated or injured, or lacking in strength in the hands and upper body. There's no tough recoil spring to muscle a slide against, and no hidden firing chamber where a live cartridge can secrete itself while an amateur thinks the removal of the magazine has unloaded the gun. Even a little old lady with osteoporosis can activate a cylinder release latch, push a cylinder out of a frame, and check to see if the revolver is loaded or not.

Simplicity Of Function. No magazines to worry about. Nothing that you need to run a revolver can get separated from it except for the ammunition. Load gun, point gun, pull trigger. If cartridge misfires, pull trigger again. That simple.

Reliability. Yes, revolvers can jam, and yes, some of our modern autos are splendidly reliable. That notwithstanding, if you take *all* auto pistols currently in defensive use and compare them to *all* modern revolvers, the autos are at least slightly more likely to malfunction. The auto requires maintenance, particularly lubrication. The auto's magazine springs can take a set after being kept loaded for too long. A Smith & Wesson hand ejector model of 1899, if kept in a cool dry place for more than a century and then loaded with fresh ammunition, would undoubtedly fire. Few of us would want to stake our lives on the functionality of a 1911 pistol whose magazine spring had been fully compressed since before WWI.

A wide mouth guarantees these Federal 125-grain Magnum loads will expand when fired from this S&W 686 revolver, but few auto pistols would feed such ammo reliably.

Ammo Versatility. Your revolver will run blanks, snake-shot or rat-shot, light target loads, standard service rounds, or Monster Magnum cartridges. No alteration is required when you change ammo. Your auto, however, was designed with a slide mass/spring compression rate geared for a certain range of duty ammunition. Too light a load won't run the gun. Too hot a load may actually cycle the slide so fast it closes again on an empty chamber because the magazine spring didn't raise the next cartridge fast enough to be picked up. A bullet profile with

Street cop and six-time national champion Bob Houzenga carries a department issue Glock .40 as primary duty gun...

...but prefers a revolver, specifically this S&W Model 642, for backup for reasons explained in the text.

Most autos are easier to shoot well under stress than most revolvers. In this qualification shoot, Tracy Wright (left), the author, and Bob Smith (right) have all shot perfect scores with 1911 Tactical .45s tuned by Mark Morris, standing at rear.

No guarantees, but if something even *might* work to your advantage, it's worth considering.

Barricade Advantage. When you have to fire from behind cover, you want to maximize that cover. With an auto pistol, the gun has to be out away from the wall or its slide can jam from friction. This means your head has to come out that much more from behind cover to aim, and where your head goes, your body follows. With the revolver, you can lay the barrel right against the barricade. This also steadies your aim somewhat (though it also increases felt recoil), but mainly, it brings you in deeper behind protective cover.

Low Maintenance. Unless you've rusted it shut or crapped it up so much there's a layer of carbon binding the cylinder's rotation past the forcing cone of the barrel, or debris built up under the ejector star, your revolver will probably do OK without a cleaning. An auto, even if pristinely cleaned after its last firing, should be lubricated regularly. The long bearing surfaces of slide and frame require lubrication for reliability. When the gun is carried in a holster, the liquid lubricant drains out. It can also evaporate. This can lead to a jammed-up pistol. The revolver, in my opinion and that of many experts, actually shouldn't be lubricated inside. Doesn't need it. That means a person who doesn't clean and lube his revolver regularly is not susceptible to gun lock-up when they need their handgun most, but the auto shooter most certainly is in danger of that.

Deep Concealment Access. When you carry in a real hideout location – ankle rig, pocket, belly band, or Thunderwear – the gun is pressed tightly against your body. The flat sides of the small auto's grip frame will be so close to your flesh that, in a fast-draw emergency, your fingers almost have to claw to gain a solid drawing grasp. But the rounded profile of a small revolver's grip-frame guides the firing hand right into drawing position. Deep concealment is slow to draw from anyway; using a revolver there minimizes that problem.

For those who wear ankle holsters, there's something else to consider. The gun is inches above the ground, with dirt and grit being kicked up around it with every step. This is why an "ankle gun" is generally covered with a fine film of grit after you've been out and about wearing it for a few days. The finely-fitted moving parts of most small auto pistols won't take that. We've had cases from California to Florida where the good guy drew a small auto from an ankle holster, got off a couple of shots, and suffered a malfunction at the worst possible time. A quality revolver, by contrast, will shoot even if it has dust bunnies in it.

Cost/Value. Look in the catalogs of companies that produce both revolvers and

too flat a nose or too short an overall cartridge length may compromise your auto's feed reliability, too. None of that compromises the turning cartridge wheel from which the revolver draws its nickname.

Intimidation Value. When a homeowner points an automatic pistol at an arrogant intruder, he may believe it's a toy. He might convince himself it's your grandfather's war souvenir with cobwebs instead of cartridges in the chamber. If that makes him go for his gun, or for yours, he might get lucky. But if you're pointing a revolver at him, he will almost certainly see something else: the heads of live cartridges pointing right at him. The sight of these missiles poised for launch may make the difference in convincing him that you're not running a bluff, and result in his deciding not to attack.

Shooting from right to left, John Lazzaro smokes a table of pins with his modified S&W 1917 .45 revolver. With only five pins, a shooter this good won't need more than six shots.

Even the finest auto pistols can jam. This is a failure to eject with the Kahr P9.

Though complicated for a novice to handle, the HK P7 pistol is extremely easy for most people to shoot fast and straight once they are familiar with it.

semiautomatic pistols. Taurus and Smith & Wesson are good examples. You'll generally find, grade for grade, that the revolvers are significantly less expensive.

Accuracy. As noted elsewhere in this book, accuracy can be more important in a combat handgun than many traditionalists believe. We can get by with the accuracy of any of the auto pistols recommended in this book, but more never hurts. The revolver, by and large, is more accurate than an auto pistol of similar quality grade.

In 1988, the department I then served became the fourth in the nation to adopt Smith & Wesson's third-generation .45 automatic, the Model 4506. It was a splendid gun. Ours averaged about 2.5-inch groups from the bench at 25 yards. However, the S&W Model 13 .357 Magnum revolvers we traded in for them were capable of holding the same size group at twice the distance.

Autoloader Advantages

High Hit Potential Under Stress. When the Illinois State Police adopted the Smith & Wesson Model 39 semiautomatic in 1967, they were ahead of their time. They and other cops with revolvers of the period were hitting bad guys with about 25 percent of the bullets they fired in action. With the adoption of the 9mm auto, hit ratio skyrocketed to somewhere around 65 percent.

The auto pistol is more ergonomic. Most revolver users who knew their stuff put after-market grips on their wheelguns as soon as they bought them. In the 1990s, S&W and Colt wised up and put the after-market grips (Uncle Mike's and Pachmayr, respectively) on their own guns at the factory. "If you can't beat 'em, join 'em."

The auto's lower bore axis reduced recoil. Most autos have a shorter trigger pull, at least after the first double-action shot, which means that shooter panic is less likely to muscle the gun barrel off target as the defender jerks at the trigger. It is significant that ISP noted a lot of those 35 percent misses were the first double-action shot.

It should also be noted that the best hit potentials in the field have been with *single-stack* (8- or 9-shot) pistols. With high-capacity guns – especially when the cops were told the new pistols had been bought for "firepower" – the firepower seemed to become a *raison d'etre* that led to a "spray and pray" mentality. Significantly, ISP troopers' hit percentages in the field reportedly went down when they went from single-stack Model 39s to higher capacity guns.

Proprietary Nature To The User. We have case after case on record of suspects getting the gun away, trying to shoot the officer, and failing because the snatched weapon was a semiautomatic pistol carried "on safe." Most tests on this over the last 20 years (the first was published circa 1981 in

There's that firepower thing. An auto will still be shooting when revolver is reloading and, with both starting empty, the auto will be shooting sooner than the revolver, all other things being equal.

Not every .45 auto will handle this broad range of ammo without a malfunction, though this SIG P220 stainless passed the test.

Police Chief magazine, the journal of the International Association of Chiefs of Police) have resulted in the unfamiliar person taking an average of 17 seconds to figure out which little lever "turned on" the pistol.

Many auto pistols don't have this feature. Many double-action models are in the hands of people who don't choose to use this feature. This feature *can* be retrofitted to some revolvers: the Murabito safety catch conversion, and the "smart gun" conversion called MagnaTrigger. That said, the ability to serve as proprietary to the user is primarily a function of the semiautomatic pistol.

Firepower. Purists will tell you that you can't call it "firepower" until you get into belt-fed weapons. Realists know that since the first two cavemen started throwing rocks at each other, whoever threw the most rocks the fastest and straightest had an advantage.

The degree of advantage varies from gun to gun. If you go from a five-shot .38 revolver to a seven-shot Micro Kahr 9mm, it's a 40 percent increase. When California Highway Patrol went from six-shot .38 service revolvers to 12-shot S&W Model 4006 autos, they doubled their firepower. When any department went from six-shooters to the 18-shot Glock 17 in 9mm, they had 300 percent the firepower they had before. And that's just the in-gun reservoir of ammo. The auto pistol is also faster to load (in case a gun is kept unloaded for home defense), and faster to reload, especially under stress.

You can get awfully fast at refilling a wheelgun with speedloaders. You may get to where you can reload a revolver faster than I can reload an auto pistol. But you'll never get to where *you* can reload a revolver faster than

you can reload an auto pistol, assuming the same amount of practice with each gun.

Times have changed. We're seeing more multiple offender assaults, more and more perpetrators involved in professional armed robberies. In the horror of September 11, 2001, we saw hijack teams of up to six terrorists. If hit potential might be as low as one out of four shots in the stress of combat, and multiple opponents are increasing, you don't need to be a math major to see the advantage of a defensive weapon with more firepower.

Add to that the fact that the bad guys are using small-unit guerrilla tactics (fast movement, and cover) and are more likely than ever to be wearing body armor. Both of these factors mean you're likely to have to fire more shots before one takes effect. Firepower is more important today than when revolvers ruled.

Relative Compactness. A semiautomatic is flatter than a revolver of equal power. That makes it easier and more comfortable to conceal discreetly. That goes double for spare ammo: speedloaders for revolvers have as much bulge as another whole revolver's cylinder, but flat spare magazines for autos "carry easier."

Relevant Training. That "takes any ammo that fits its chamber" thing is sometimes an advantage for the revolver, but it became a disadvantage under the old paradigm of cops training with .38 wadcutters that kicked like mouse farts, yet actually carrying Elmer Keith Memorial Magnum rounds for serious business. Revolvers are gone from the police scene now for the most part, and toward the end of their reign police instructors made officers qualify with the same rounds they loaded for work, but you still see that "practice with light loads, carry with heavy loads" thing with armed citizens.

Ya can't do that with an auto pistol, gang. Go below the threshold of what the gun was designed for, and your auto pistol won't work. That means the auto forces you to use ammo that's at least reasonably close to the power of what you'd carry on the street. That means its design enforces more relevant training.

Lower Muzzle Flash. Large-bore auto pistols generally have less muzzle flash than large-bore revolvers. The .357 SIG auto round doesn't flash as much as the .357 Magnum revolver round, and most 9mm auto

This Colt 1911A1 .45 auto is locking open after the last shot. A shooter can reload it faster than a revolver.

ammo flares less at the muzzle than does equivalent .38 Special revolver ammo. We are in the time of low flash powders for premium ammo for both types of gun, so this is not as huge a difference as it was in the old days...but the difference is still there, and it favors the auto pistol. A gun whose muzzle flash blinds you when you fire it at night is not conducive to your being able to see the sun rise the next morning.

Conclusions

There are still very real revolver advantages versus auto advantages. As Bruce Lee said, each practitioner of the given martial art must assess her own strengths and weaknesses, and choose what she will fight with accordingly.

When in doubt, carry one of each. For most of my adult life, I've carried two guns. The primary was usually (but not always) a service-size semiautomatic pistol. The backup was usually (but not always) a small frame snub-nosed revolver. The main fighting weapon gave me improved hit potential and all the other factors when it was an auto. The backup revolver gave me fast access and certain function from deep concealment, and also allowed me to arm a compatriot with a gun whose manual of arms I wouldn't have to explain when there wasn't time.

I always figured if I carried a revolver *and* an auto, when I got to the Pearly Gates I'd be covered, whether Saint Peter turned out to be a Jeff Cooper fan *or* a Bill Jordan fan.

DAO Versus DA/SA

The double-action auto pistol in its conventional style – i.e., self-cocking itself after the first DA shot and becoming single-action for each shot thereafter until de-cocked – at first seemed hugely logical for police and armed citizens. Many think it still does.

The DAO SIG E26 fired the top group at 25 yards. An older DAO P226 fired the second group down. A DA first shot with four SA follow-up rounds from a conventional P226 delivered the third group, followed by the bottom group, the same gun fired single-action for all five shots.

Later came DAO, or double-action-only. This, in effect, was a mechanism that allowed the gun to "de-cock" itself after every shot. Some, especially in the higher echelons of law enforcement, believed this was safer for the rank and file. It has become hugely popular in policing, somewhat less so among the private citizenry.

Jeff Cooper said that *any* double-action auto was "an ingenious solution to a non-existent problem." He considered double-action-*only* autos to be anathema to good shooting as he knew it, and at one point forbade such guns from his famous shooting school, Gunsite. A gunwriter once remarked, "Double-action-only is so stupid, they're making jokes about it in Poland." Meanwhile, three of our six largest law enforcement agencies mandate DAO auto pistols: NYPD, Chicago PD, and the Border Patrol.

Who's right? Let's hash out the arguments and decide.

In 1990 I found myself teaching a class for the DEA Academy at Quantico. DEA shares the same facility as the FBI Academy. They call each other "the guys down the street." I took some extra time to spend with John Hall, then the chief of the FBI's Firearms Training Unit. They

If you've already fired a shot under stress, and aren't deeply familiarized with your weapon, you may not remember to de-cock. In such circumstances, this lady is well served with DAO Kahr K9 as she covers the threat zone from behind cover while calling 9-1-1.

Don't tell a seasoned shooter that a good DAO auto isn't controllable. The author shot this 60-round qualification group with Beretta 96D Centurion and full power .40 S&W ammo. The "D" suffix after a Beretta model number means double-action for every shot.

Bill Laughridge lines up the DAO auto that may be the easiest of all to shoot well, the Para-Ordnance LDA.

were in the news big time because they were then in the process of implementing the adoption of a gun they had designed with Smith & Wesson, the Model 1076 10mm. 10mm Auto was the hot ticket during that period.

Some departments were already going over to the DAO concept. I asked John why he and his agency didn't buy into that. The reply was clear and succinct. The rationale of the double-action trigger with its long, heavy pull, John explained, was to reduce the likelihood of accidental discharges under stress. He and the Bureau accepted that. This was why it was only DA first shot autos that were approved for the Bureau's then approximately 7,000 agents. Only the *crème de la crème,* the elite Hostage Rescue Unit, was allowed to carry single-action autos. At the time the HRU had Browning Hi-Power 9mms customized by Wayne Novak, and local-office FBI SWAT teams had the DA/SA SIG P226 9mm.

Hall continued his explanation. "Almost all accidental discharges are one-shot events," he said. "After the first shot, if he needs to continue shooting, the agent is in a gunfight." Hall and company wanted that agent to have the easiest possible job of making those subsequent shots count under stress. The self-cocking trigger was deemed the best way to achieve that obviously worthwhile goal.

This made sense to me. I had always been an advocate of a broad weapons policy that let officers pick, within reason, the guns that worked best for them. As the motorcyclists say, "Let those who ride, decide." I still believe that. But, two years before, my new chief had decided that we would all carry the same gun, and all I had left to say about it was what gun it would be. I had been instrumental, in 1988, in selecting an issue gun very much like what Hall came up with: the Smith & Wesson 4506.

The reasons Hall had cited were there. So was the fact that our people had to patrol in some nasty winters, and for a third or more of the year would have to manipulate guns with hands impaired by either numbing cold or feel-blunting gloves. With the gloves, a lot of double-action-only guns – including the S&W .357 Magnum revolvers we issued up until then – could have their trigger return blocked by the thick glove material on the trigger finger. This could turn the six-shot .357 into a single-shot. With the DA/SA Smith auto, once they fired the first shot, the trigger would stay in a rearward position until all further necessary shooting was done. Then, with the trigger finger removed from the guard, the officer's thumb could easily manipulate the slide-mounted de-cocking lever. It seemed the safest and most practical method.

Frankly, it still does. Well over a decade later, I now serve another department. We've had similar guns, the Ruger P-series .45 autos, as standard issue since 1993. The previous department, last I knew, still had their conventional style S&W autos. I note a point: *neither department, in all those years, had an accidental discharge with those "traditional style" DA/SA semiautomatic pistols!*

Genesis of DAO

In the early 1980s, police chiefs became increasingly aware of accidental discharges caused by the "hair trigger" effect created when officers cocked their service revolvers. LAPD started what became a trend, an alteration of the revolver's mechanism (the simple removal of the cocking notch of the hammer) that rendered the gun double-action only. Sure enough, when no one could cock the gun, cocked gun "accidentals" disappeared. Miami PD, NYPD, and Montreal PD soon followed suit.

I can tell you the inside story on two of those last three. Miami made their S&W Model 64 .38 revolvers DAO after the controversial killing of Nevell "Snake" Johnson in an inner-city video arcade by Officer Luis Alvarez. It was a cross-racial shooting that triggered the second largest race riot in the city's history. Janet Reno was then the State's Attorney (the chief prosecutor) for Dade County, which encompasses Miami. The city needed a scapegoat. Alvarez was offered up. He was charged with manslaughter. The prosecution's theory was that Alvarez had cocked the hammer of his gun to show off as he arrested Johnson for possession of an illegal weapon, and that the resultant hair-trigger effect had caused the gun to accidentally discharge because Johnson, while turning to surrender, unexpectedly startled Alvarez. Since it was against regulations to cock the gun for a routine arrest, this theory created the element of negligence, a necessary ingredient to the state's formula for manslaughter conviction.

There was one small problem. The story was all BS. Alvarez never cocked the gun. His defense lawyers, Roy Black and Mark Seiden, retained me as an expert witness. We were able to *prove* that he had never cocked the gun. The jury learned that Johnson had spun toward Alvarez and his rookie partner and had reached for the stolen RG .22 revolver in his waistband, with the obvious intention of killing both cops. At that moment, Luis Alvarez had instantly and intentionally done the right thing: he shot and killed the gunman.

The trial lasted eight weeks, the longest criminal trial in Florida history. It ended with an acquittal after only two hours of jury deliberation, including dinner. The acquittal triggered the *third* largest race riot in Miami history, but that's another story. This trial comprises one fourth of famed defense lawyer Roy Black's superb book, *Black's Law*, if you want to read more about it.

"New" doesn't always mean "progress." The author found in testing of these two Berettas that the newest Model 9000-D, below, didn't hold a candle to older Model 96D, above. Both are DAO in caliber .40 S&W.

The point is, the city had all their revolvers rendered DAO between the shooting and the trial. The local cops called them "Alvarized" guns. Though it was nothing more than a concession to political correctness, it's entirely possible that later, down the road, this alteration did have some positive safety benefits. I can't say either way. If nothing else, it kept unscrupulous prosecutors from throwing any more innocent cops to the wolves with the bogus "cocked gun" theory.

The Montreal decision to go DAO came after the case of *Crown v. Allan Gossett*. Canadian firearms training of the period was at least 20 years behind that of the U.S., and Gossett had become a constable of the Montreal Police when they were still taught to shoot a revolver by cocking the hammer and squeezing off single-action shots at bull's-eye targets. The night came when he was in pursuit of a felony suspect, and had to draw his issue S&W Model 10 .38 caliber service revolver. As the suspect spun toward Gossett, the constable was seen to jerk as if startled, and his gun fired. The violent jump of the gun with mild .38 recoil, and the look of shock on Gossett's face as it discharged, were noted by witnesses and tended to confirm the fact that it was an unintentional discharge.

It was believed that the gun was cocked. Gossett didn't remember cocking it. I believed him and so, in the end, did those who tried the facts, the only ones whose beliefs counted. The Crown, as the prosecution is known up there, charged him with manslaughter on the same grounds as Reno had charged Alvarez. It was their theory that negligence (intentional cocking of the gun), plus death (which obviously took place) equals manslaughter.

I testified for Gossett, too. Like Alvarez, he was ultimately acquitted. We believe that one of two things happened: he went back to his original training reflexively and in those high-stress moments cocked the gun without realizing it, or the hammer had become cocked by accident. We'll never know which. At the time, Montreal issued a crappy holster that appeared to be living proof that you could tan the hide of a chicken and make gunleather out of it. The safety strap went over the back of the trigger guard instead of over the hammer. The unprotected hammer could thus snag on seat belts, coat sleeves, or just about anything else and become cocked while still in the holster, unnoticed by the constable wearing it.

After Gossett's ordeal, Montreal got some decent gunleather and ordered the Model 10s made DAO.

What does all this have to do with auto-loading pistols? Glad you asked. It *is* a long story.

Shortly after the Alvarez trial, the Miami street cops and their union went to the chief in Miami and asked for high capacity 9mm autos to replace their .38 six-shooters. They were confiscating an increasing number of high-cap autos from dopers – their city was then the illegal drug capitol of the nation – and they sought parity. Sure, the chief said, you can have hi-cap autos...*if* you can find one that's double-action for every shot!

The union (and the city firearms instructors) pleaded with Beretta, SIG, and S&W to make a 9mm auto that was double-action for every shot. The companies thought the idea was stupid and blew them off. At about that time, the Bureau of Alcohol, Tobacco, and Firearms declared the Glock pistol's mechanism, which its inventor designated Safe-action, to be "double-action only."

It was delicious. The chief who hadn't wanted autos for his troops was "hoisted by his own petard." In desperation, seemingly impossible torture tests were ordered for durability. The Glock passed them. To cut to the chase: Miami became the first really big, high-crime city to adopt the Glock. They were the flagship of the fleet, and soon Glock was outselling all the rest combined. Beretta, SIG, and S&W *now* felt the impetus to come out with DAO guns…but they were too late to stop the huge momentum Glock had developed in the police market.

Today, Miami PD still issues the Glock, having upgraded from the 9mm to the .40 S&W caliber. Montreal, when they went to autos, went DAO too, as did virtually all of Canadian law enforcement. While most provincial and municipal agencies in Canada chose the .40 caliber, the Royal Canadian Mounted Police and the Montreal PD went with DAO Smith & Wesson pistols in 9mm.

The Decision Today

There are shooters who prefer DAO because having only one trigger pull to work with for every shot is easier for them. I won't argue the point. I've seen too many shooters for whom that was true. If you anticipate the shot and jerk the trigger when you're working with a gun that has a short, light pull, the DAO is something you should try.

There are departments that can't devote as much time and money as their instructors would like to train the rank and file with handguns. NYPD (40,000 officers) and Chicago PD (13,000 cops) are well known for being in that situation. Both of them require that all personnel, except for older officers who are "grandfathered" with permission to carry double-action revolvers, carry DAO auto pistols on duty.

I've seen people under stress "lose it" to the degree that after they had fired one or more shots, they forgot to de-cock their conventional DA autos before holstering. In one case in California, an officer did this with his Beretta 92F 9mm after shooting an attacking pit bull. He had not only forgotten to de-cock, he had forgotten to take his finger off the trigger. As he put the gun back in his holster, his finger caught the edge of the leather that was designed to cover the trigger guard, and came to a stop. However, the gun kept going, driving the trigger against the finger. BANG! He shot himself in the leg. Now even more stressed than before, he tried to shove the gun into the holster again. BANG! He shot himself a second time in

the space of only a few seconds. The unique "partially open front" design of his department's trademark holster had allowed the Beretta to cycle while partially holstered.

Some believe this is a training issue. For the most part, it is, but the fact remains that the harder it is to pull the trigger, the harder it is to pull the trigger *accidentally*. When you have a light, easy, single-action trigger, there is good news and bad news. The good news is it's easy to shoot. The bad news is it's easy to shoot. It's the situation that will determine whether a certain type of trigger pull is a good thing or a bad thing.

Design Features

All DAO handguns are not created equal. The ParaOrdnance LDA (an acronym its users have determined stands for "Light Double-action"; the manufacturer never actually spelled it out) has a deliciously easy trigger pull. Some police departments (such as North Attleboro, Massachusetts) have already adopted it for standard issue. Some others (such as the San Bernardino Sheriff's Department) have approved it for duty if deputies wish to buy their own.

Next up on the "ease of manipulation" ladder are the DAO guns of Kahr Arms and Smith & Wesson. Both are extremely smooth and easy to shoot well. The Kahrs are small, reliable hideout guns; the S&W line encompasses small to large and includes duty-size service pistols.

The DAO Berettas tend to be lighter than the regular Berettas in the big 92 and 96 series guns, but heavier than LDAs, Smiths, or Kahrs. The absence of a single-action sear removes a friction point, and I believe the springs are a bit lighter. On the other hand, Beretta's little Model 9000 polymer gun has a nasty double-action pull.

The theory is that transitioning to DAO gives you one less manipulation to worry about, that is, de-cocking after the shooting is over. That's true as far as it goes. On the other hand, a great many people find a shorter, lighter trigger pull is less likely to jerk shots off target, particularly when firing under great stress and at great speed.

Beretta's 96D in double-action only (short barrel Centurion model shown) has earned a good reputation in the field.

Don't say DAO autos aren't accurate. Illinois State Rifle Association president Rich Pearson, right, holds a cutout group he watched the author shoot at 25 yards with hot Triton 115-grain/1,325 fps 9mm ammo from this SIG P226 DAO.

Personally, I can live with either style. I've explained why I'm partial to the "conventional" style, the DA/SA. That's not a habituation thing, that's an "I've looked at everything I and my people need where we are" thing. But my people and I aren't you and yours, and we may be in two different places in more ways than one, with two distinct sets of needs.

I serve a small police department where we can train intensively. Whether or not we're all likeable, we're all demonstrably competent. What if I had to take responsibility for training 40,000 personnel, most of whom were not interested in spending a minute to develop confidence and competence with the gun if they weren't being paid for it? What if I could only pay for a couple of days a year of that training? In that case, the double-action-only concept would look very good, indeed.

When the police instructors and supervisors pick a gun for their officers, two commandments must be kept in mind. *Know thy specific needs,* and *Know thy personnel.*

When a law-abiding citizen makes that decision between these two common types of semiautomatic pistol, a similar process makes sense. Before you decide whether you want a DAO pistol, or a "conventional" DA pistol, or perhaps something else, there are again two commandments: ***Know thy specific needs*** and, perhaps more important, ***know thyself.***

On-Safe Versus Off-Safe

Pick up a standard model S&W, Beretta, or Ruger auto pistol. Manipulate that little lever at the rear of its slide. If two typical firearms instructors are standing one on each side of you, ask them, "What *is* that lever?"

On a typical day, one might answer, "It's the safety." The other would be likely to scream, "That's not a safety, it's a de-cocking lever!"

And if a firearms engineer was there, he'd probably sound like the Doublemint Twins. "It's two levers – *two* levers! – two levers *in one!*"

Who's right? In a greater or lesser way, all three.

Popularized on Walther pistols developed in the 1920s and coming to prominence in the 1930s, refined by Smith & Wesson on their first 9mm pistols in the mid-1950s, this dual-purpose lever may be the single most misunderstood piece of equipment that you'll find on any combat handgun. If you look at the patents, Smith & Wesson's for example, you'll find it listed as a "safety/de-cock" lever.

I was very much a part of things when autoloaders began pushing revolvers out of the law enforcement handgun picture in the mid-1980s. I saw some scary things, some of which still exist. A few others and I had been voices in the wilderness crying out in the early and mid-1970s that these "automatics" had some advantages that might make them worthy of replacing our ancient "service revolvers."

Most of the police chiefs back then didn't know from guns. They relied on their firearms instructors for input on that. The problem was most of their firearms instructors only knew the revolver. Such an instructor had a set of pat answers when cops came to him asking why they couldn't carry autoloaders.

"Those autos will jam on you," the instructors would say. "Besides, the revolver is loaded and ready to go when you're in danger! Just draw and shoot! With an automatic, you'd have to slow down and take the safety off – if you remembered!"

Then, in what must have seemed to some of them like a cataclysmic change of worlds, the union guys had won, and the chiefs were giving them the autos they had asked for. Groping desperately to catch up with technology they had spent their firearms training careers trying to pretend didn't exist, a lot of these instructors had no *clue* how to manipulate the slide-mounted safety on firearms coming into service. Some examples included the Ruger auto the Wisconsin state troopers had adopted, the Beretta that had been chosen by LAPD, and the Smith & Wesson chosen by the Illinois State Police before any of the rest.

Rather than teach its manipulation, it was easier to pretend that it didn't exist. "It's not a safety catch, it's a de-cocking lever" became the mantra. Now, had this gone to court, I can say as both a police prosecutor and an expert witness that the argument would probably have been destroyed in less than a minute of cross-examination.

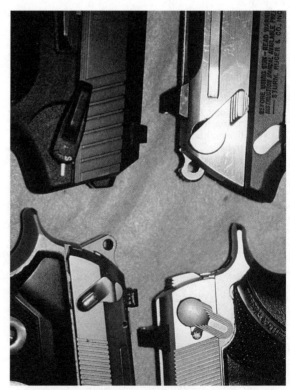

Four popular combat handguns with safety/de-cock levers. Clockwise from noon, those of Ruger, S&W, and Beretta are slide-mounted, while that of HK USP is mounted on the frame.

"Sir, you are the department's designated firearms expert, correct?"

"Yes."

"And you say this part is not a safety, it's strictly a de-cocking lever?"

"Yes."

"Sir, I show you these two documents. Exhibit A is the patent for the gun you issue your department. Exhibit B is the nomenclature sheet produced by the factory that manufactured the gun you issue to your officers. Can you tell the jury what the part in question is called by these authoritative sources in these documents?"

"Um, it says 'safety/de-cocking lever'..."

"Nothing further."

You can't say something isn't what it obviously is, just because you want it to be so. That's Stalinist revisionism. It didn't even work for Stalin.

It is possible for departments to lose their own sense of institutional history. When you forget where you came from, it's always a bad thing. Case in point: the Illinois State Police, who in 1967 became the first major police department in the USA to issue autoloading pistols.

Here's the real story. ISP at the time let the troopers buy their own Colt or S&W, .38 or .357 revolvers. They were required to be armed off duty, and virtually all carried small-frame snub-nose .38s. The department wanted them all to qualify with the off-duty guns as well as the duty weapons. The scores with the snubbies were pathetic. Let's face it, guns like that were tough to shoot on courses of fire that emphasized 25-yard shooting at the time. The superintendent tasked Louis Seman, then head of Ordnance for the department, with finding a solution.

The solution was the Smith & Wesson Model 39. Weighing only 26.5 ounces, it was midway in heft between a 19-ounce off-duty Chief Special and a 34-ounce K-frame service revolver. It was flat in silhouette, easy to conceal in plain clothes. It reloaded more quickly – *way* more quickly – than loose revolver shells from the dump pouches of the time. While it lacked the inherent accuracy of the guns it replaced (you were doing well to get a 4-inch group at 25 yards), its beautiful hand-fitting ergonomics made the Model 39 9mm autoloader easy to shoot. Maybe it wouldn't equal the revolvers in a machine rest, but you could *put* all its shots into that 4-inch group at 25 yards, and that meant a perfect qualification score.

A decade or so later, I came to Illinois under the auspices of the Troopers' Lodge 41 of the Fraternal Order

of Police, the entity that represented the troopers in bargaining. I did the first poll of the troopers on this gun. Some 87 percent of them wanted to go to something else. These 1,700 or so people resented having an alien concept foisted upon them by what they perceived to be one Ordnance Corporal and one desk-bound superintendent.

But, an interesting thing showed up in all that research. Those troopers had been in a bunch of deadly encounters, and I was given *carte blanche* by the administration to study them. Even though the majority of the troopers at that time wanted to go back to the revolver, there was overpowering evidence that Seman had made the right choice.

I was able to identify **13** troopers who were alive because they'd had the S&W automatic, and would have probably been killed if they'd been armed with six-shot revolvers. I could find **no** case where a trooper armed with the 9mm was shot by a criminal and would not have been shot if the trooper had been armed with a revolver instead.

Everyone thinks firepower is the *raison d'etre* for an auto instead of a revolver. It certainly is a factor, but not the main factor. I found two officers who survived because either the seventh or eighth shot put down the attacker. Trooper Ken Kaas was facing a charging attacker who had a 20-gauge auto shotgun, and a man who had already shot people and was wielding a 12-gauge pump was charging Trooper Les Davis. Both fired their last couple of shots and dropped their would-be murderers. Troopers Lloyd Burchette and Bob Kolowski both ran dry and needed quick reloads to keep up the pace of fire that finally saved their lives in a sustained firefight.

That was four. Of the remaining nine, a few, who were in struggles for their guns were able to hit the magazine release button, and thus activate the magazine disconnector safety. This is the feature seen on the standard S&W auto, the Browning Hi-Power, and some other guns that renders weapon unable to fire, even with a cartridge in the chamber, if the magazine has dropped out of place. In each of those cases, when the suspect finally got the gun away from the trooper, the attempt to shoot the officer failed.

However, the overwhelming majority of those "auto pistol saves" were cases in which the suspect got the gun away from the trooper, pointed it at him, and pulled the trigger...*and the gun did not go off because the trooper had been carrying it on safe.*

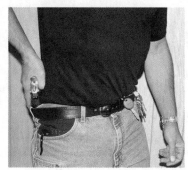

The draw begins. The S&W 4506 is carried on-safe in an LFI Concealment Rig...

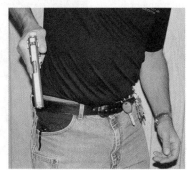

...At about the time the gun clears the body, the thumb has pushed the lever into "fire" position...

...Since the action was accomplished during the draw, there has been no significant time loss in getting a ready-to-fire .45 up on target. Note that the lever is in the "fire" position with the red warning dot exposed.

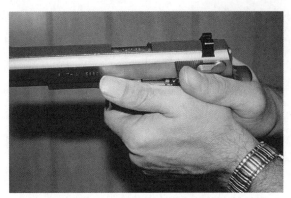

This ergonomic grasp, widely used by combat champions, is perfectly compatible with disengaging a slide-mounted manual safety.

From 1967 until well into the 1980s, Illinois troopers were given the option of carrying their gun "on safe" or "off safe." They were shown how to flip off the safety as they drew. The decision was then left up to them.

Then, in the 1980s, some personnel changes took place in the Ordnance Section. Seman was long since retired. Now it was time for the wise senior men who had replaced him, Bob Cappelli and Sebastian "Bash" Ulrich, to take their well-earned retirements too. As transfers, promotions, and retirements would have it, some new people soon flooded into ISP Ordnance. The department thought it best to send them to an outside instructor school.

The school they went to was a famous one that will remain nameless. The instructors were told at that school, "It's not a safety catch, it's a de-cock lever. The gun should be carried off-safe at all times, because it's too awkward to move the lever under stress."

Never mind that in the history of the department, no Illinois State Trooper had ever been hurt because he couldn't get his gun off-safe in time. "The Word From Afar" now became "The Doctrine." Troopers were now *mandated* to carry their S&W autos off-safe. This situation continued until the late 1990s, when the department switched from the S&W 9mms they carried – 16-shot third-generation models by that point – to the Glock 22 pistol, which has no manual safety at all, and requires no decocking lever.

I suppose that's one way to deal with the problem…

The Lessons of Engineering…

Certain auto pistols *must* be on-safe to shield the user from unintended discharges. No logical, sane, and experienced firearms instructor would argue that a single-action auto pistol should be carried off-safe. There is simply too much danger of its easy, short-movement trigger being unintentionally activated.

The Colt .45 and all the many clones of that 1911 design, the Browning Hi-Power, the Star FireStar, and other such designs, are all carried cocked and *locked* by any professional worthy of the name.

When such guns are drawn, the safety is flicked down into the "fire" position as the gun muzzle comes up into the target, after the intention to immediately fire has already been formulated.

There are also certain double-action autos that are not "drop-safe" if the manual safety is not engaged. These include all Walther PP and PPK series guns, and all first-generation Smith & Wesson double-action autos. Two-digit primary model numbers distinguish the latter. The Model 39, 39-2, 59, etc., do not have internal firing pin locks. This makes them and the previously mentioned Walther designs subject to "inertia firing" if dropped or struck on the muzzle or the rear of slide. The firing pins on these guns are only "locked and/or blocked" if the manual safety is engaged.

An officer with an off-safe Model 59 in his holster was carrying a large box of evidence out of the police department. His hands being full, he tried to activate the bar that opened the front door by hitting it with his hip. His pistol's hammer was the contact point, and – BANG! The pistol fired in the holster.

A couple tried to carry a loaded, off-safe Walther .380 into the house along with several bags from a shopping trip. The gun slipped and fell, landing on the floor on its hammer. BANG! The pistol discharged and struck one of the spouses, producing a grave gunshot wound.

…and the Lessons of History

Gun retention is the big advantage of on-safe carry. Gun retention is the corollary science to gun disarming. It is the defeating of the disarming attempt.

Washington: The suspect jumps a cop, gets his cocked and locked 1911 .45 away from him, tries to shoot him. Nothing. Suspect, still with gun, runs. Cop

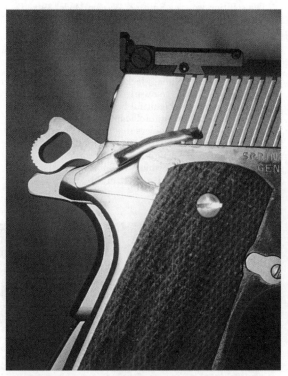

The many 1911 fans think having to carry their gun on-safe is a tactical advantage. The author thinks they're right. Here's the easily manipulated ambidextrous safety of Ayoob's cocked and locked Springfield Trophy Match .45.

Practice plus proper technique equals fast, sure draws to the shot with a double-action pistol carried on safe.

commandeers passing car, takes suspect at gunpoint with 2-inch .38 revolver, and suspect surrenders. A cop-killing was prevented.

Indiana: Armed robbers take a gun shop owner at gunpoint, relieve him of his HK P7 pistol, take him into back room to murder him. The suspect with the P7 tries to shoot: no effect. He has not fully squeeze-cocked what might be called the "safety lever" at the front of the gun. The gun shop owner grabs a secreted .357 revolver, shoots down two robbers and survives.

Alabama: A suspect being arrested grabs an officer's S&W 9mm from the holster, aims at him, pulls trigger. Nothing happens; gun is "on-safe." The officer draws a back-up Taurus .38 from his ankle holster. The terrified suspect drops the gun and surrenders. No blood is shed.

Illinois: Two suspects attack, disarm, and beat a state trooper. One suspect takes his gun and tries to shoot him. He can't because the S&W Model 39 is on-safe. At this point a second trooper arrives, orders men to stop; suspect points gun at this trooper and pulls trigger. The S&W still won't fire. Second trooper shoots and kills gunman, saving both troopers' lives.

Utah: Many witnesses watch as an officer is sucker punched and knocked unconscious. The attacker pulls the gun from the uniform holster, points it at the officer, and pulls the trigger. Nothing. The S&W 9mm was being carried on safe. The suspect jacked the slide, ejecting a live round, aimed and attempted to shoot again. Nothing. The suspect then fiddled with the slide release lever trying to find the safety, aimed at the officer, and pulled trigger. Nothing. The suspect pressed the button behind the trigger guard and the magazine dropped under a car where it was found later. The suspect again tried to shoot the cop. Nothing. Finally finding the safety lever, the suspect tried again to shoot the cop. Nothing. The magazine disconnector safety had been activated, preventing the firing of the round in the chamber. The suspect then threw the gun at the prostrate officer and fled. The officer survived.

Florida: A suspect has stolen a Smith & Wesson 9mm auto that is fully loaded with round in chamber, but has been left on-safe. As he robs and attempts to murder cab driver, the gun does not fire. When the cab driver sees the suspect pulling the trigger, he goes for his own gun, a cocked and locked Colt .45 automatic. Since he owns the gun, the cab driver knows where *his* safety is. He shoots and kills the robber, saving his own life.

The list goes on…

Know Thy Weapon

The choice is yours. But be sure it is an informed choice. Look at all sides, weigh all the risks, then decide what works for your balance of need versus risk.

It pains me to see cops and law-abiding citizens giving up a life-saving tactical advantage because their instructors don't know how to operate their tools. More than a decade ago, I was at a seminar where one of the instructors who told those Illinois State Police instructors to give up their safety catches was teaching. He chanted the mantra: "It isn't a safety, it's a de-cocking lever."

I just said the truth to him. "On my department, the chief has mandated that we carry our S&W .45 autos on-safe. Show us what you think is the best way to do that."

He stood there for a moment fumbling with an S&W, wiggling the last digit of his thumb off its median joint as if he was trying to shoot marbles. He said, "You can't. See?"

I didn't want to attack him in public, but he was wrong. You *can*, and I *can* see, and so can you.

With the slide-mounted safety, where the lever has to be pushed up, certain guns are awkward. The little Walther is a case in point. Its lever is at the wrong angle for mechanical advantage. It's one of many reasons I don't carry that tiny .380.

But with the S&W, the Beretta, or the modern Ruger, it's a piece of cake. Simply *thrust the firing hand's thumb up, at a 45-degree angle, as if you were trying to reach the ejection port. Unless your thumb is very short or bends outward to an unusual degree, this will pop the safety catch into the fire position.*

With some holsters, the thumb strap or strap paddle may get in the way. While it would be dangerous to off-safe a single-action auto in the holster, I'm comfortable doing that with a double-action; hell, everybody else is telling you to carry it off-safe to begin with! Videos and high-speed photos of me when I'm drawing showed me that I disengage the safety lever at about 45 degrees of muzzle angle as I'm coming out of the holster. I win my

This 45-degree straight angle thrust of the thumb of the firing hand is the most efficient way to disengage a slide-mounted manual safety.

share of matches, and have outdrawn my share of scumbags, and all I can say is, "It works for me."

I'm prepared to test this under pressure. I've done it already. Smith & Wesson owns videotape of me in police uniform doing it, in a film made but never released after my old department adopted the 4506 and Tom Campbell, then an S&W staffer, brought me down to do the flick. S&W Academy's great instructors Bert DuVernay, Brent Purucker, and Tom Aveni were all present when I went to an advanced instructor school there and beat everybody else on the draw to accurate shot, using a 4506 carried on-safe. There were lots of witnesses when I won the 2000 New Hampshire state shoot for cops, on a fast 7- to 50-yard combat course using an on-safe Ruger P90 .45 drawn from a fully secured Safariland 070/SSIII holster.

The techniques are there. The safety catch factor in weapon retention is there. If you find the techniques don't fit your hands, so be it, but make your decision of "off-safe" instead of "on-safe" an informed decision, not just a blind acceptance of something you were told by someone who might not have known how to do it.

The life on the line is your own.

Point Shooting Versus Aimed Fire

For more than a decade, this is a topic that has been guaranteed to not only sell gun magazines, but to generate a flurry of angry letters to the editors. Gun expert Dave Arnold was the first to make a key point about it. "A lot of this argument," Dave said, "is simply a matter of terminology."

As one who has been in or around the center of that debate since 1990, I'll certainly buy *that!* Let's see if we can't quantify our terms at the very beginning so we're all working off the same sheet of music.

Two concepts need to be understood first: *index* and *coordinates*. Index is what lines up the gun with that which is to be shot. Coordinates are the things we have to accomplish to achieve index.

There are perhaps three possible indices by which we can line up our gun with the target or the threat:

Body Position Index. This would be the situation where you can't see where the gun is aimed, so you're using a certain body position to align the gun with the target. In the obsolete FBI crouch, the coordinates are backside low, upper body forward, gun punched forward to keep it from going too low. In the speed rock, discussed elsewhere in this book, the coordinates include leaning the upper torso all the way back to bring the forearm lateral as the gun is fired immediately upon levering upward away from the holster. In pure hip-shooting, you are relying on either long-term muscle memory developed through exhaustive practice, or by a degree of talent few of us could ever hope to possess. I would define any type of body position index as "point shooting."

Visual Index. This is where you are indexing by seeing the gun or the gunsights superimposed on the target. If you can see the gun is on target, I consider this aimed fire. Whether you are superimposing the silhouette of the whole gun over the target, or looking over the top of it, *or* taking a classic sight picture, the only question remaining is whether it's coarsely aimed fire or precisely aimed fire.

Firearms instructor Andy Stanford explains the cone of shot dispersal and the importance of indexing the gun on target. In his hand is a Ring brand dummy gun with Ashley Express high-speed sights.

Here's a situation where hip-shooting will work. The target is at the height of the driver in an average-size car. If the driver pulled a gun during a traffic stop, the officer's hand already on a backup gun in his pocket could give him a fighting chance with this technique.

This is a StressPoint Index. It is almost as accurate at close range, and much faster than a conventional sight picture, especially if eye focus is on the threat instead of on the defense gun.

Artificial Index. This would be something like a laser sight. Let's say you have a ballistic raid shield in one hand, and a gun in the other. It will be awkward and difficult to bend the arm into a position where you can

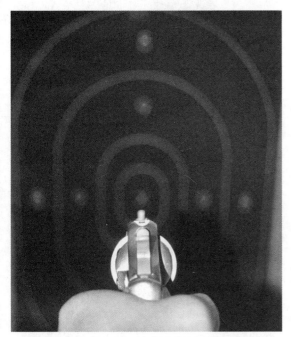

The front sight doesn't have to be in focus to index the shot when it is sitting up out of the rear notch. The revolver is S&W Model 64.

aim through the Lexan view port using the regular sights. If you reach your gun around the side of the shield and see your red dot on target, the artificial mechanism of the projected laser dot has indexed the weapon for you, rather than you visually aligning the gun or aligning it by body position index.

Since the laser sight is by no means universal, this argument of point shooting versus aimed fire really comes down to an issue of body position index versus visual index.

A gun must "point" for you if you're going to hit with true "point shooting." If the natural hold is center for you with this customized Glock 23...

...then you'll probably shoot high with this slim-gripped S&W Model 60 revolver...

...and way low with this Beretta Model 21 pocket pistol.

The middle road position is, "practice both." That saves controversy, but if you're teaching cops or others with limited time who can't waste even minutes on useless stuff because you don't have as much time as you need to give them key life-saving skills, you can't afford to save controversy any more. A great many police departments have either gotten away from point shooting entirely, or given it very short shrift. The reason is that their cops get into a lot of shootings, and they can quickly find out what works and what doesn't. Departments that have learned to re-emphasize sighted combat fire include LAPD and NYPD, to name but a few. Both saw a significant jump in hit percentages in actual gunfights after renewing their emphasis on visually indexing the duty sidearms.

A book could be written on this topic – some have been, and more will be – but let's cut to the chase. The bottom line is this; a lifetime of studying real-world gunfight dynamics has taught this author that true point shooting simply doesn't work, except for a handful of extremely skilled and highly practiced shooters.

Perhaps the easiest way to proceed directly to the bottom line is to debunk the myths that have developed, particularly in the past 15 years or so, about point shooting.

Myths of Point Shooting

"Point shooting worked for Capt. William Fairbairn of the Shanghai Police, who survived over 600 gunfights shooting this way." **WRONG.** If you read Fairbairn's classic book "Shoot to Live," you'll see that the *entire 1,000 man Shanghai Police force* was involved in some 660 gunfights during the 10-year period in question. While it's entirely possible that in a violent city Fairbairn might have had his gun out of the holster 600 times on the street, he was not in 600 gunfights and never claimed he was. If you think about it, Fairbain would have killed more opponents than were accounted for by Sgt. Alvin York, Audie Murphy, and Carlos Hathcock combined.

"The great Col. Rex Applegate taught point shooting and quantified statistics showing that it worked for the OSS!" **MISINTERPRETED.** Col. Applegate was indeed a great man. I knew him. I was there to congratulate him

when he won his long overdue Outstanding American Handgunner of the Year award, and he was there to congratulate me when I won mine a few years later. We both spoke before the Joint Services Small Arms Project on the Personal Defense Weapon project, at Oak Ridge.

Unlike many who quote him, I had the privilege of him showing me his technique. A photo of that experience accompanies this article. You can see that he has brought my Beretta pistol up to arm's length, and you can draw a line from the pupil of his eye to the front sight to the target.

Rex *called* it point shooting to distinguish it from the precise, focus-on-the-front sight concept taught in the traditional marksmanship manuals. But, make no mistake, Rex had the gun up where the eye couldn't miss it, even in the tunnel vision state of fight or flight reflex. That's why his technique worked, and that's why shooting that way still works, as Sgt. Lou Chiodo and the California Highway Patrol have proven. It's just not really "point shooting." Again, we're back to Dave Arnold's point: a lot of this is semantic quibbling.

"Point shooting can be learned in 50 shots live-fire, or even just by dry firing in the mirror!" **UNTRUE.** This has been set forth in print by two separate point-shooting advocates, neither of whom to my knowledge has actually ever run a live-fire shooting class. Both have repeatedly turned down invitations to demonstrate their skills in public. One has produced a video in which, if you look carefully, he can be seen to be scattering his shots all over

Ed Lovette demonstrates the Applegate-based point shooting he learned from Lou Chiodo. This style will work, because the gun and its sights intrude into the cone of tunnel vision and the weapon can be visually indexed.

End of argument. Rex Applegate demonstrates his point shooting technique for Ayoob's camera with Ayoob's Beretta 92. Note that you could draw a line from the pupil of his eye to the front sight to the target. This, the author submits, is coarsely aimed fire, not point-shooting.

a huge target at close range with his point shooting techniques. The other caused to be published a photo of himself dry-firing at a mirror. If you look carefully at the picture and lay a ruler over the gun barrel, you can see that he is performing the almost impossible feat of missing himself in his own mirror. The shot would have gone over the reflected image's shoulder. Shooting at a mirror is a false approach to learning body-position index shooting anyway, since the eye can see where the mirror image is pointing and automatically correct, which would never happen in real life.

"Aimed fire was proven useless when NYPD had only 11 percent hits with it." **WRONG.** That low hit potential figure attributed to aimed NYPD fire is taken from the single worst year in more than 30 years of the department's SOP-9 study. Standard Operating Procedure Number Nine is the intensive debriefing of all officers on that PD who fire a shot with their duty or off-duty weapons other than on the range. The low hit percentage years turned out to be due primarily to officers *not* seeing their sights when they fired. This led John Cerar to institute a "back to basics" training program when he took over NYPD's Firearms and Tactics Unit, which emphasized the use of the front sight. Soon, progressively, hit percentages crept upward and with more officers using their sights when they fired "for real," actual hits in street gunfights tripled over the previously quoted figure. The people who incorrectly applied that statistic obviously never contacted the NYPD. I did. The facts are there, documented with excruciating thoroughness, for anyone who wants to seek the truth.

"The effects of epinephrine dumping into your body under stress will make it impossible for your eyes to focus on your sights, so you **have** *to point shoot!* **UNTRUE, and proven so.** In experiments conducted by the Olympic Training Center and the U.S. Army Marksmanship Training Unit (1981) and at Lethal Force Institute (1998), shooters were injected with doses of epinephrine calibrated to equal the "fight or flight state." In all cases, the shooters were able to see their gun sights with crystal clarity, and to hit what they shot at aiming that way.

"I've read of people who fired and hit and don't remember seeing their sights." **UNFOUNDED ARGUMENT.** You've also read about people who didn't remember firing, but they did. A large percentage of gunfight survivors didn't hear their shots, but that doesn't mean their guns were silent. Some remember seeing their sights, and some don't. That doesn't mean they didn't see their sights, any more than not remembering consciously pulling the trigger means they didn't pull it.

Problems With Point Shooting

Dennis Martin, the martial arts and small arms expert who for some time was Great Britain's coordinator for the International Association of Law Enforcement Firearms Instructors, has little use for point shooting. He told me, "When the SAS had as their primary mission the eradication of enemy soldiers in combat, they taught point shooting with a high volume of gunfire. But as soon as their mission was changed to include hostage rescue, they switched from point shooting to Col. Cooper's concept of the 'flash sight picture.' Now they had to shoot through narrow channels between innocent people, and it would have been irresponsible to do that without aiming their weapons."

This is as clear an explanation of the problems with point shooting as I've ever seen. As an expert witness for the courts in weapons and shooting cases for more than 20 years, I realized early on that again and again, point shooting was culpable when the wrong people were hit by the good guy's fire. One case is mentioned elsewhere in this book. The man "pointed" his .38 for a warning shot and hit, crippling for life, a man he said he was trying to miss. More common are people hitting those other than the ones they're trying to hit. I was retained on behalf of one police officer who "point-shot" at the tire of a car that

A shooter attempts point shooting. Note the widely scattered hits even at very close range.

was going toward a brother officer and instead hit in the head and killed a person inside the vehicle. I was retained on behalf of another who, at little more than arm's length from a murderer trying to shoot him, resorted to the point shooting he had been taught and missed with all but one shot. The one hit, almost miraculously, nailed the bad guy in the arm and cut the radial nerve, preventing his attacker from pulling the trigger. But one of his misses struck, and horribly crippled for life, an innocent bystander – one of the potential victims the officer was trying to protect.

You don't need too many cases like that to understand why true point shooting, firing without being able to see where the gun is oriented, can quickly pass the point of diminishing returns. Law school students are taught that the exemplar of recklessness is a "blind man with a gun." A person who is firing a gun when they can't see whether or not it's on target is, in effect, a blind man with a gun. It could be eloquently argued in court that, *ipso facto,* firing without being able to see where the gun is aimed creates recklessness. In turn, recklessness is the key ingredient in the crime of Manslaughter and in a civil court lawsuit based on Wrongful Death or Wrongful Injury.

Enough said?

Point Shooting Alternatives

If there isn't time for a precise, perfect marksman's sight picture, at the closer distances it will suffice to simply be able to see the gun superimposed over the target. As noted earlier, if you can see the gun, it's aimed fire. Now it's just a matter of how precise the visual index is. Let's analyze the precision, from the most precise on down.

A classic marksman's sight picture, with that 1/8-inch-wide front sight visible in the rear sight's notch, level on top and with an equal amount of light on either side, is absolutely "do-able" in combat. Countless gunfight and military battle survivors have proven it. In Jim Cirillo's most famous gun battle, his strongest memory was seeing the front sight of his S&W Model 10 in such stark clarity that he was aware of every imperfection in the tiny grooves machined across its surface. In that gunfight, he shot three men in three seconds, and he shot one of them out from behind a hostage. Bill Allard was the one guy on the NYPD Stakeout Squad who shot more armed criminals in the line of duty than Jim, and he told me he always saw his sights. His strongest memory of *his* most famous gunfight, a pistolero and a rifleman that he took out in a hail of bullets, was seeing the front sight of his handgun so sharply that he could have counted the grooves in it. Ed Mireles, the hero of the infamous 1986 FBI shootout in Miami, told me that among his most vivid memories were the giant white ball that was the front sight of his Remington 870 12-gauge shotgun, and the giant orange front sight of his S&W Model 686 revolver, as he fired the shots that blew away the two cop-killers in question.

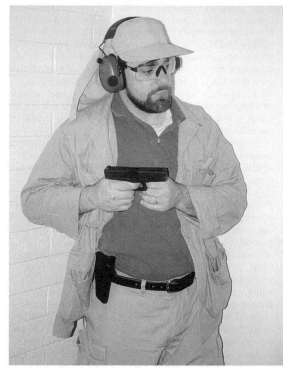

An instructor demonstrates the protected gun position at National Tactical Invitational at Gunsite.

Next down the list of precision is the "flash sight picture" popularized by Jeff Cooper. The sights are more or less in line, but you're not trying for a perfect image. You just quickly verify that they're on target and break the shot. It can be done at surprisingly high speed.

Ratchet down one more notch on the coarseness level to the StressPoint Index, a concept I developed in the 1970s and published in the 1980s. You're focused on the target – something you always have to be prepared for

Firearms instructor and combat pistol champ Andy Cannon has just shown an entire class of students that their guns are sighted in close enough...

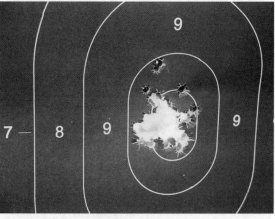

...by putting six shots from each into this heart-size group. Try that with point shooting!

because nature makes us look at what threatens us – and over the spot on the threat you want to hit, you see superimposed the image of a front sight sitting on top of a rear sight. Break the shot, and if you're inside 7 yards or so, that spot you're focused on is exactly where you'll see the bullet strike. Todd Jarrett rediscovered this concept later, calling it "shooting out of the notch" to describe the front sight's orientation with the rear, and he won national and world championships with it at super-speed.

One more notch down and you have what master gunfighter Jim Cirillo calls the "silhouette" technique. You see just the silhouette of your gun superimposed over the target. If you know your gun, you can tell instantly from the shape if it's "on." The rear of the cylinder will be round instead of oblong, and the "safety wings" of a Smith & Wesson or Beretta standard model auto will be silhouetted. Don't hesitate, break the shot. You're there.

The better shooting technique systems that have been called "point shooting," the ones that actually work such as Applegate's, all bring the gun up to the line of sight so high that it will intrude into the cone of tunnel vision. As Cirillo has said, you'll see it subliminally even if you don't see it consciously. That will let you hit at close range. That will give you a good chance of getting through the fight.

Bottom Line

If the gun is where you can see it at close range, you can hit. You're visually indexing your gunfire. You're aiming. Perhaps you're aiming crudely instead of precisely, but you're aiming. If the gun is where you cannot see it, it can be argued that you are not really in control of it. You're relying on a body position index. There are problems with that.

The body position index only works on a static range. You can get yourself set up exactly with the target, then go through the motions and repeat the alignment. But this is false to reality. On the street, the opponent may be above or below you. As soon as he moves laterally, as he undoubtedly will unless he has a death wish or is

terminally stupid, all the coordinates will break and you'll be back to being a "blind man with a gun."

The ultimate boast of shooters is, "If I can see it, I can hit it." This is admittedly a bit over the top. You and I can both see the moon and the sun, but neither of us can hit them with a bullet. But there is a corollary here: *if we can't see the gun in relation to its target, we probably can't hit the target.*

We live in a world where if we fire for real and don't hit the target dead center, it can remain hostile long enough to murder us or those we love. We live in a world where if we launch a deadly bullet when we can't see the predictable course it will take, we can not only expect to perpetrate a tragedy, but expect to pay dearly for it in both criminal and civil court.

That's the problem with point shooting. If you are truly convinced that your main plan of action should be to fire in self-defense without being able to see where your gun is pointing, do yourself a favor and at least equip the weapon with a laser sight.

One rationale the author can see for hip shooting: you've been manacled behind your back with your own cuffs and have sneaked out your backup gun. This is a great argument for a laser sight! Note that one shot has gone low right out of the vital zone.

Author can point shoot when he has to, as in this required stage on three targets in tight time frames at first National Tactical Invitational. He finished in the top 10. The pistol is a Colt Government Model stainless by D.R. Middlebrooks.

CHAPTER SEVEN

Defensive Handgun Ammunition Selection

Morgue Monsters And Jello Junkies

Handgun "stopping power" has been a topic of heated debate for more than half a century. The debate shows little sign of fading away.

On one side are those concerned primarily with field results. In their forefront are Evan Marshall, a retired homicide detective and SWAT instructor from the Detroit PD, and his colleague Edwin Sanow, a trained engineer who has been accepted by the courts as an expert on the topic. Marshall's research of several thousand shootings has been compiled in books from Paladin Press including *Handgun Stopping Power* and *Street Stoppers*, co-authored by Sanow. Their research indicates that in certain calibers, medium- or slightly lighter than medium-weight bullets at high velocities have the most immediate effect on felons who are shot. Those calibers include 9mm Luger (115-grain JHP at +/- 1,300 fps) and .357 Magnum (125-grain SJHP at +/- 1,400 fps). They have also found that in some calibers, the heaviest projectiles normally encountered, moving at moderate velocities, did the best job. These include .38 Special (158-grain LHP at +/- 850 fps) and .45 Auto (230-grain JHP at +/- 850 fps).

On the other side of the fence are those led by Dr. Martin Fackler and an organization he created called International Wound Ballistics Association (IWBA). Fackler's theory, based largely on measurement of wound paths in a specific 10 percent formula of ballistic gelatin that he created, is that penetration of at least 12-inches in the human body is essential to hit vital organs. This favors the heaviest available bullet, traveling at moderate velocity. In .45 Auto and .38 Special, both sides are in agreement. In 9mm Luger, they are not, with Fackler and his colleagues recommending the subsonic 147-grain JHP at +/- 970 fps.

Those who follow the street research believe that if lab research isn't proven by what happens in the field, the lab research, by definition, must be flawed. Those who believe in the lab research cite its repeatability, noting that every shooting is at least subtly different from every other.

Who is right? Each side has a piece of the puzzle. The laboratory research can explain to us why certain rounds may work better than others. It can predict a round that will dangerously over-penetrate, or which will break up so soon it won't reach vital organs in time to stop a murder attempt. But field results assembled over time do, quite definitely, point to certain trends. When we ignore what happens in the real world, we do so at our peril.

Vern Geberth, who wrote the authoritative text on homicide investigation, felt that all 9mm rounds were highly lethal. Shown is SIG P226 with 115-grain hollow-points.

Before the bullet matters, it must hit the target. A stock Ruger P90 .45 has just put five rounds of inexpensive Remington-UMC training hardball into about 1-1/4 inches, center to center, at 25 yards.

The Scope of the Task

How a gunshot wound causes a violent human being to cease hostilities is a much more complicated question than it sounds. IWBA feels that only three such mechanisms exist, and only two can be reliably counted upon. Disruption of the central nervous system can do it. So can the effect of hemorrhage when it reaches the point that there is insufficient flow of oxygenated blood to sustain consciousness. IWBA indicates that any "stop" not attributable to one or the other of these two mechanisms must be attributable to psychological surrender; basically, the opponent wimped out after he was shot.

Central nervous system (CNS) impairment will certainly work. So, obviously, will massive hemorrhage, though the latter will take time. Most physicians agree that if the brain is fully oxygenated at the moment of the shot, the patient can maintain consciousness and perform physical action for up to about 14 seconds *even if the heart stops completely at the shot.* Thus, the great many instant one-shot incapacitations that we have on record in which the bullet's path never touched brain or spinal cord cannot be explained away by blood loss. Many of these individuals were hard fighters, impervious to fear, and it is most unlikely that a psychological dread of being shot caused them to faint.

Dr. Dennis Tobin, a neurologist, has hypothesized that a mechanism called "neural shock" can cause collapse from a gunshot wound even when vital organs are not permanently damaged. Others believe that the temporary cavitation around the wound track, which becomes larger as velocity increases, has the effect of stunning organs that sustain no permanent, quantifiable damage. This flies in the face of the IWBA theory that only tissue actually destroyed by the bullet's passing will materially contribute to incapacitation. Yet it has happened too many times to ignore.

Chuck Karwan, who wrote *The Complete Book of Combat Handgunnery* two editions ago, did an absolutely excellent essay on this concept in those pages. A military combat veteran and advanced martial artist, he noted that blows to many parts of the body could cause instant incapacitation, yet leave no permanent wound cavity per se. Since many of the men so incapacitated were

Bullet designer and multiple gunfight survivor Jim Cirillo believes bullet design is critical. Here he shows the importance of a sharp-shouldered bullet when a projectile strikes hard bone on an oblique angle.

hardened, trained fighters willingly in the ring, it is hard to imagine that they fainted or otherwise experienced a "psychological stop" because someone punched them.

Those who disagree with Sanow and Marshall attack their statistics and their interpretation of them. Statistics can be argued. Reality cannot. During the period the Indianapolis Police Department issued the 125-grain .357 Magnum hollow-points at about 1,400 feet per second, some 220 violent felony suspects were shot with that round by IPD officers. City officials told me there was never an effective return of fire from a felon hit with one of these bullets in the torso. The Kentucky State Police had essentially the same experience with the same load. The Illinois State Police for almost 20 years carried the 115-grain +P+ hollow-points at 1,300 fps velocity. It worked so well in their troopers' many gunfights that it became known as the Illinois State Police load among the nation's cops and gun enthusiasts.

Yet because both rounds are designed to penetrate 9 to 11 inches and stop, after having created a massively wide wound path, both are seen as inadequate by the IWBA because they do not meet IDPA's mandatory 12 inches of penetration in the gelatin used to simulate muscle tissue. One memorable gelatin test of the early 1990s gave the 9mm 115-grain/1,300 fps load a wound value of zero, even though it had caused the wound cavities with the largest volume, because by design none of the projectiles reached the foot-deep penetration mark! The bullets instead averaged between 9 inches and 10 inches of bullet penetration. This is about the depth of the average adult male chest, front to back. That interpretation would have been laughable enough, had it not been for the fact that the same report listed a .380 hollow-point as having a "minus" wound value. Presumably, if you were shot with it you would feel better than had you not been shot at all. Such interpretations destroy any value of the underlying work that went into the testing, which is a shame.

Dr. Bruce Ragsdale at the Armed Forces Institute of Pathology embedded pig aortas in Fackler gelatin. He noted that when a round like the ISP load passed close to the vessel without actually striking it, the stretch cavity was still sufficient to transect the aorta – that is, to tear it

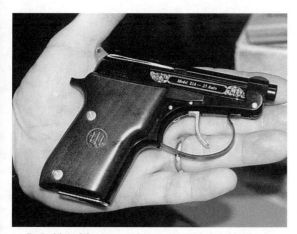

Both sides of the ammo controversy agree that .25 autos like this Beretta Model 21A are insufficiently powerful for self-defense.

Most would agree that the .480 Ruger, a powerful, deep-penetrating cartridge intended for hunting large game, is probably too hard to control and penetrates too deeply for most to consider for self-defense against humans.

More than a decade ago I sat down in an outdoor café with a physician who is an apostle for the "deep-penetrating bullet" theory. I gave him the names of personnel at the Indianapolis Police Department and the Kentucky State Police who would confirm the real-world performance of the 125-grain Magnum ammunition he said was over-rated and ineffective. He replied that there was no need to do so, because the gelatin told the whole story.

It was this attitude that caused Evan Marshall to coin the term "Jello Junkies" for those who would not venture beyond the laboratory environment to correlate their theories with real-world findings. It was a gun magazine editor who coined the term "Morgue Monsters" for those who felt that only the results of actual shootings would tell the tale. The two sides have remained at odds with one another ever since, with some very acrimonious comments being issued. Interestingly, most of the personal attacks have been by followers of the IWBA dogma attacking Marshall and Sanow. Make of that what you will.

The problem with this dichotomy is that both sides have authoritative backgrounds. When two experts disagree, who is the layman to believe? The person who carries a gun for serious self-defense is now in the position of a juror assessing conflicting expert testimony in a court case. It becomes necessary to compare the arguments and weigh them in light of logic, common sense, and life experience.

That's what we'll attempt to do in the following pages.

apart. He presented those findings at a bona fide wound trauma conference. A senior IWBA official, who was present, never uttered a peep…but continued to write that, at handgun velocities, only tissue actually touched by the bullet and damaged by it would contribute to incapacitation. Hmmm…

Recommended Loads

There are so many different calibers and loads that we can't cover them all here. That would take a separate book. In fact, Marshall and Sanow have written more than one book on the topic and they still haven't covered all the load combinations! Therefore, let's stick with the most popular and most effective of the self-defense calibers.

We won't be working with .480 Ruger, .454 Casull, or .50 Desert Eagle. These big boomers are hunting rounds and generally too powerful for personal defense. Nor will we work with cartridges so tiny and notoriously impotent that most police departments forbid their officers to carry them even as backup. The .22 and the .25 auto can certainly kill, but they can't always *stop,* which is a different thing altogether. Such small rounds require literally surgical bullet placement, with the primary point of aim being deep brain. However, both are notorious for ricocheting off human skulls, so where does that leave you?

.32 Auto. It is a little known fact that NYPD became the first police department to issue semiautomatics early in the 20th century, with a quantity of Colt .32s. They got away from them in part because they were too feeble, and the department standardized on the .38 Special revolvers instead, many of which remain in service. European police departments issued .32s for decades because the sidearm was seen as a badge of office, and these small autos were convenient and had a low-key look. Then terrorism and violent crime struck Europe, and the cops needed real guns; they switched en masse to .38 Special revolvers and 9mm autos.

Today, thanks to the defining Seecamp LWS-32, pistols the size of .25s are now available in this caliber, and it has become an in-thing to carry them. Various hollow-points are available. All open sometimes. None open all the time. The Winchester Silvertip was the .32 cartridge the Seecamp was built around, and has the best track record. The Marshall Study shows a surprisingly high one-shot stop rate, but also includes a disproportionate number of strong-arm robbers and rapists or attackers with clubs

The Seecamp .32 auto was made to work with Silvertip ammo, which is as good an ammo choice as any in that caliber.

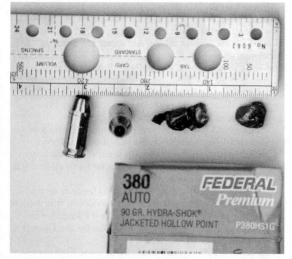

This is what a .380 Hydra-Shok looks like after being fired into living tissue.

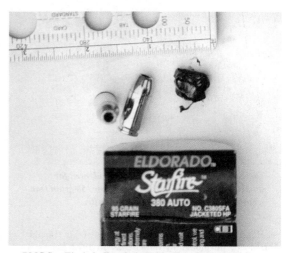

PMC StarFire's bullet, designed by Tom Burczynski, is as dynamic an expander as you will find in .380 caliber. This one was retrieved from a slaughterhouse test.

and knives instead of guns, who may have simply given up after realizing they were up against a gun and had already been shot once. Still, the Silvertip has the most established track record, and when I carry my own Seecamp .32, it's the round I choose.

.380 Auto. Known in Europe as the "9mm Short," this round seems to constitute the acceptable minimum dividing line in defensive handgun potency. Some experts will say it's barely adequate, and the others will say it's barely inadequate. The ball rounds penetrate too deeply and can ricochet, creating narrow, puckered wounds in the meantime. The hollow-points, when they open, may not go deep enough.

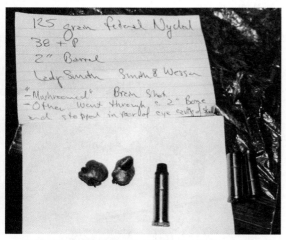

Federal Nyclad Chief Special load, a standard pressure, nylon-jacketed 125-grain hollow-point, gives the most dynamic bullet performance the author has seen in a low-recoil .38 Special cartridge. Note the significant expansion even when fired from 2-inch barrel into living flesh and bone.

In some of our advanced classes, we have the student kill a large animal with their carry gun and load, then dissect the wound to see what it did. Seven times now I've seen .380 JHPs either stop in the frontal wall of the skull or ricochet around the skull to the ear. Not impressive. These days, for students with the smaller gun, we use very small swine to prevent torturing the animal. All animals used in this way were destined to be slaughtered for meat on the given day anyway, but a clean and painless death is ethically required here. The .380 doesn't seem to deliver that reliably.

I haven't run across an actual shooting yet with the Remington Golden Saber, which at 102 grains is the heaviest bullet available for the .380. I did shoot a hog with it on one occasion. The bullet just got through the frontal wall of the skull and barely touched the brain. Most JHPs weigh 85 to 90 grains. Winchester Silvertip and Federal Hydra-Shok seem to lead the pack and perform about the same.

.38 Special. This is the universally accepted minimum or above-minimum load for self-defense. With certain loads, it's far below minimum. The classic example is the old 158-grain lead round nose. It provides too much penetration and too little stopping power. For most of the 20th century, this round was the police standard, and only the commanders who issued it had anything good to say about it. Street cops called it "the widow-maker" because so many times, an officer would empty it into his attacker, and the assailant would live long enough to still make the cop's wife a widow.

Hollow-points work better, but not all hollow-points are created equal. Where low recoil is imperative – a very light revolver, or a .38 in a very frail hand – the best of the standard pressure, mild-kicking loads seems to be the Federal NyClad Chief Special. As the name implies, it was expressly designed for small, light revolvers. The soft lead bullet begins to deform as soon as it hits. We've never seen it fail on large animals in the slaughterhouse, and it showed up well in the Marshall study. The nylon-jacketed bullet weighs 125 grains.

There is no more proven .38 Special load, even for snubbies like this Taurus Model 85, than 158-grain lead semi-wadcutter hollow-point at +P velocity.

Head and shoulders, the best .38 Special is the old "FBI load," developed by Winchester in 1972. It is comprised of an all-lead semi-wadcutter bullet with a hollow point at +P velocity. FBI, RCMP, Metro-Dade Police in Miami, St. Louis, Chicago PD, and a great many others used this round in countless gunfights, out of snubbies and service revolvers alike. They all had excellent results with it. Because there is no copper jacket that has to peel back, a design feature that seems to require considerable velocity to work, the soft lead slug seems to open even when fired at lowered velocity from short barrels and even when fired through heavy clothing.

Recoil is snappy in the small, light guns, but very easy to handle in a service revolver. The "FBI load" is a legendary man-stopper. It delivers the performance ammo makers were hoping for with the 147-grain subsonic 9mm at 970 fps. Alas, the copper jacket of the 9mm round didn't always open up the way the lead slug of the .38 FBI load did.

Most brands give reasonably similar performance, though over the years the Winchester has used the hardest lead and the Remington the softest, with the Federal brand in the middle. Evan Marshall's observation that the .38 Special FBI load hit about like GI .45 hardball seems to have been proven out in 30 years of extensive field testing.

9mm Luger. Illinois State Police were not the only ones to prove that the +P+ 115-grain JHP at 1,300 feet per second was the best man-stopper in this caliber. U.S. Border Patrol and Secret Service found the same in extensive study of real-world experience. ISP used mostly the Winchester brand, Border Patrol the Federal, and Secret Service the Remington. There was little difference between the brands, which had one other thing in common: all were sold to police only, and not to the general public.

However, CCI Speer has recently released this load to the law-abiding public with the Gold Dot bullet. An identical cartridge produced with top quality has been available for some time as the Pro-Load Tactical, and the Triton Hi-Vel is very similar.

124-grain "hot loads" at about 1,250 feet per second also have a good track record. The Gold Dot in this format has worked splendidly for NYPD since its adoption in 1999, and is also the 9mm load of choice for the Denver Police Department.

Many older guns won't stand up to these high pressure loads in constant shooting, and some people don't like the little extra jolt of recoil they give. In the same size gun, a +P or +P+ 9mm kicks about the same as a standard pressure .40 S&W load. In a modest recoil 9mm, history has shown us that you can't beat the Federal Classic 9BP, a 115-grain JHP at about 1,150 feet per second. It is standard issue for Philadelphia PD and New Jersey State Police at this time; both have had many shootings with it, and been satisfied with the results.

Most law enforcement agencies that adopted the 147-grain JHP subsonic, as noted above, have gotten away from it after disappointing results in the field. Expansion failures and overpenetrations occurred too often. While some departments, such as Las Vegas Metro and Jacksonville simply went to faster-moving 115-grain JHPs, others simply bought more powerful guns that fired the .40 Smith & Wesson, the .357 SIG, or the .45 ACP. LAPD, LA County and Chicago PD got around the 147-grain subsonic's perceived weaknesses by authorizing privately-owned .45 autos for those who didn't trust the slow-bullet 9mm ammo.

Federal's 9BP 115-grain load is the most effective standard-pressure 9mm cartridge the author has found. It worked very well for many years for the New Jersey State Police in their HK P7M8 pistols such as the one shown.

The Remington 115-grain JHP 9mm proved accurate in this STI Trojan pistol, but higher-velocity versions of the same round have been more dynamic "on the street."

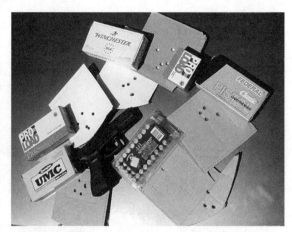

Accuracy of given load in given gun is a definite factor. These are assorted .40 S&W cartridges, fired from Glock 22 at 25 yards.

With 135-grain/1,300 fps ammo for personal defense needs and 165-grain/1,150 fps for police service use, the 16-shot (with pre-ban magazines) .40 caliber Glock 22 is a potent sidearm indeed.

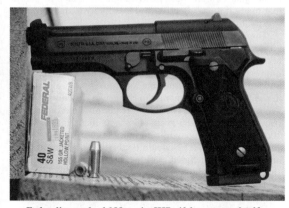

Federal's standard 155-grain JHP .40 has proven itself well in the field in pistols like this Beretta 96D Centurion.

.40 S&W. Conceptualized by Paul Liebenberg and Tom Campbell at Smith & Wesson and created by them and Winchester, the .40 Smith & Wesson was simply a 10mm Short. Indeed, the sarcastic called it the .40 Short and Weak when it was introduced in 1990. Intended to be a bridge between the 16-shot 9mm and the 8-shot .45, the 12-shot .40 proved to be a viable compromise. Within a few years it was the most popular law enforcement cartridge as measured by new gun orders.

With its original load of a 180-grain subsonic bullet at 980 fps, it was indeed a viable compromise, and it worked out better than many of us feared it would, though it still had some tendency to overpenetrate. As new loads were developed that performed better, many saw the .40 as upscaling from compromise to optimization.

The 165-grain bullets at 1,150 fps and 155-grain slugs at 1,200 or better, dubbed "cruiserweights" by gun expert Dean Spier, passed all the FBI barricade and gelatin tests and still expanded and created significant wounds. Border Patrol reports excellent results with the 155-grain Remington and Federal JHPs, Nashville has experienced extraordinary performance with the Winchester taloned hollow-point weighting 165 grains The 165-grain Gold Dot bullet as loaded by Speer delivers similar performance, and when the same projectile is loaded as the hot EXP by Black Hills, performance plus match-grade accuracy is achieved.

Dick Kelton conceptualized the 135-grain .40 caliber hollow-point at 1,300 fps in the early 1990s, and I convinced a small ammunition company to manufacture the load after extremely impressive slaughterhouse testing results. When the first field shooting report came in, it was from a coroner's office asking what sort of explosive had been put in the bullet! Striking in the abdomen a man who was attempting to stab a police officer, the 135-grain JHP had flung him back and to the ground. He was clinically dead within 10 seconds, a result not explainable by an abdominal wound, however massive this one was.

The 135-grain/1,300 fps combination is now available with excellent quality control in the Pro-Load Tactical and Triton Hi-Vel lines, using the same well-proven Nosler projectile. Its 10-inch wound depth, however wide the wound, does not excite police who want their ammo to pass FBI 12-inch penetration/barrier protocols, but is ideal for armed citizen self-defense scenarios as they generally unfold.

.357 SIG. What is, in essence a .40 S&W cartridge necked down to take a 9mm bullet, the .357 SIG was an attempt to gain .357 Magnum power level in a moderately sized auto pistol. It clearly succeeded. The cartridge is now in use by the state troopers of Delaware, New Mexico, North Carolina, Texas, and Virginia. It replaced the +P+ 9mm ammunition of the Secret Service and the Air Marshals. Simply put, the latter two agencies liked what they got out of a 115-grain 9mm bullet at 1,300 fps, and figured they'd get more of it with a 125-grain 9mm bullet at 50 to 100 feet per second greater velocity.

They were right. With the cartridge in use for several years, uniformly excellent results have been reported. Richmond, VA has had seven shootings at this writing, all very fast stops. In only one was the suspect shot several times, probably because he was attempting to murder a downed officer and brother officers hosed him as fast as they could pull the triggers of their *Sig Pro* pistols. In a Texas shootout, a veteran trooper shot at the gunman ensconced in a semi-tractor trailer, but the bullets from his .45 did not go through. His rookie partner's SIG P-226 spat a .357 SIG Gold Dot through the cab and through the gunman's brain, killing him. Richmond noted that despite 16-inches of penetration in gelatin, all the 125-grain .357 SIG Gold Dots they've fired into men have stayed in the bodies, or in the clothing on the opposite side.

One Virginia trooper told me that what impressed him the most about the .357 SIG was that it dropped offenders instantly even when hit in non-vital areas like the abdomen. Numerous officers noted that it delivered instant one-shot stops on pit bulls, when in the past they'd had to pump round after round of 147-grain 9mm subsonic into similar animals. While 115-grain through 150-grain loads exist, virtually all shootings on record have been made with the 125-grain round. The Gold Dot is the most proven.

The .357 SIG has drawn the wrath of at least one critic, who insisted that it was no better than 9mm subsonic and that its massive temporary wound cavity surrounding the bullet's path was irrelevant. The cops just rolled their eyes, reviewed their dynamic real-world results, and kept carrying their .357 SIGs.

.357 Magnum: Amply represented in police gunfights since its inception in 1935, the original 158-grain flat-nose bullet load immediately earned a reputation for excessive penetration that continued when hollow-point bullets of the same weight were introduced. Not until Super Vel introduced a high velocity 110-grain hollow-point did law enforcement have a .357 round that would stay in a felon's body and use its energy effectively. When Remington introduced the 125-grain hollow-point at 1,450 fps, the round hit its stride. With a wound channel 9 inches to 11 inches deep and massively wide, it set the all-time standard for one-shot stops in actual field shootings. The price, however, was a nasty kick, an ear-splitting blast, and a blinding muzzle flash. Nonetheless, the full power 125-grain remains the clear winner of the .357 Magnum defense load sweepstakes.

10mm Auto. Touted in the mid-1980s as the long-sought "ultimate man-stopper," the 10mm's popularity got a shot in the arm when the FBI adopted the caliber in the late 1980s. Unfortunately, to make recoil more

Speer Gold Dot 125-grain .357 SIG has given dynamic street performance in many shootings. The pistol is full-size P226.

Winchester Ranger 165-grain high-velocity .40 load has been spectacularly successful for Nashville (TN) Metro Police. Greg Lee of that department demonstrates with an issue Glock 22 service pistol.

controllable they watered down the power to the level of a .40 subsonic. The FBI load for 10mm was jokingly called a "minus-P". Prior to that, most of the ammo available for the 10mm was hard-jacketed, deep-penetrating stuff better suited to hunting hogs than anti-personnel work. When people were shot with it, it tended to go all the way through without having much immediate visible effect. Interest had waned in the caliber before the really promising anti-personnel ammo, 155 grains at 1,300 fps or 135 grains at 1,450 fps, had a chance to be represented in actual gunfights.

Flat-shooting and accurate, the 10mm like the .41 Magnum never had a chance to prove itself. The author carries one frequently as a personal weapon, generally loaded with 155-grain JHP at 1,300.

.45 Auto. All those 20th century gunwriters weren't exaggerating when they called the .45 ACP (Automatic Colt Pistol) round a "legendary man-stopper" even before hollow-point bullets became available for it. Hollow-points just made it more effective and less likely to dangerously overpenetrate.

There are 165-grain JHPs available for it at a screaming 1,250 fps, but to my knowledge no one has ever been shot with one and its real-world ability remains unproven. However, Remington's 185-grain +P at 1,140 fps and similar loads by other makers have been well proven in the field, and are among top choices in the caliber. What you're losing in extra recoil, you're gaining in a flatter trajectory. The +P 185-grain .45 shoots like a full-power 10mm and allows easy hits on man-size targets out to 100 yards and beyond. This would be the load of choice if the mission profile included likelihood of long shots. Because short-barrel .45s lose velocity dramatically, some feel the +P load is a logical compensation when loaded in a "snubby" auto of that caliber.

For typical pistol distances, jacketed hollow-points with the same ballistics as the GI ball round proven for more than nine decades (230-grain bullet at 830 to 850 fps from a 5-inch barrel) have earned undisputed top dog status. With the high-tech hollow-points, more shootings have occurred with the Federal Hydra-Shok than any of the others, but we also get excellent reports on the Winchester SXT, the Remington Golden Saber, and CCI Gold Dot. In one slaughterhouse test, the PMC StarFire outperformed all of them by a slight margin. There are many good loads to pick from here. The high-tech modern bullets mentioned in the last couple of lines were all expressly designed to open even at reduced velocity when fired from short-barreled guns.

Another advantage of the 230-grain standard-velocity round is that once you know the full-price hollow-points will feed in your weapon, practice with relatively inexpensive "generic hardball" gives you the exact same recoil and point of aim/point of impact as the duty load.

These are the rounds this writer would personally recommend. Some go more toward the Fackler side of the house, and some more toward the Marshall/Sanow side. What do you do when you're advising someone who is torn between those two authoritative sources? Why, you find something both sides agree on, and we'll look at that next.

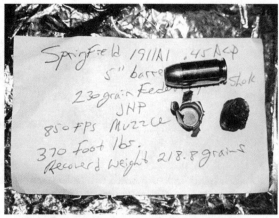

Federal's 230-grain Hydra-Shok is seen by many as the "gold standard" for .45 auto rounds at regular pressures. This is what one looks like after impacting living flesh and bone. The pistol used was a Springfield Armory, with a 5-inch barrel.

Compromise Ammo

When life just isn't black and white, a shade of gray is often the real-world middle ground. Sometimes we just have to compromise.

Let's say it's the early 1990s, and you are the head of firearms training for a 100-officer department. The chief wants to go to one standard pistol for all armed personnel. Half your guys and gals like the firepower of the typical 16-shot 9mm. The other half are more concerned about per-shot power, and want eight-shot .45s. The solution, of course, is the 12 shot .40 S&W. Each side gives a little, gets a little, and can claim to have won the argument. Now everyone is free of the controversy and can focus on what really wins gunfights: mindset and preparedness, proper tactics, and shooting skill.

But what if the caliber has already been selected, and the argument is what load to select? If the troops have been reading the gun magazines or are on the net, and you have 50 of them in the Marshall/Sanow camp and 50 on the Fackler side, a decision for one side will tick off the other. Far worse, it will leave half your troops with a lack of confidence, and confidence is always one of the cornerstones of competence.

The trick is to find rounds that both sides agree on. Believe it or not, they exist. Let's look at the serious calibers only.

.38 Special: The old FBI Load. Previously, we discussed the .38 Special lead semi-wadcutter hollow-point at +P velocity. This is the round recommended for the .38 Special by the group Dr. Fackler founded and leads, the IWBA. It has also been at the top of the Marshall/Sanow list in the caliber more times than not.

The author's department issues Black Hills 230-grain .45 ACP for their Ruger P-90 duty weapons...

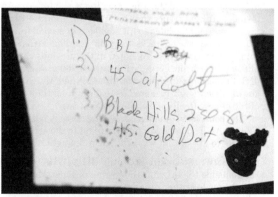

...and this is one reason why. Massive expansion of the Gold Dot bullet has caused a large wound at the proper depth in living tissue. Both sides of the stopping power argument agree on a 230-grain JHP at 850 fps.

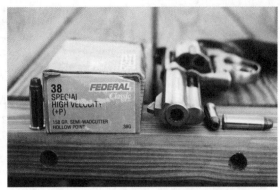

For a .357 Magnum revolver like this S&W Model 686, the only defense load both sides agree on is the old FBI .38 Special round, a +P all-lead semi-wadcutter hollow-point.

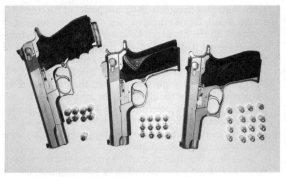

Caliber is one of the compromise options. You could choose (from the left) a nine-shot .45, a 12-shot .40 or a 16-shot 9mm. The .40 splits the difference. These are all S&W pistols; the 4506, 4006 and 5906.

There has been the occasional year where lighter, faster bullets seemed to be working better in recently compiled shootings, but over all the years Marshall's work has been published, it has led the pack in .38 Special. This has been true with snub-nose revolvers as well as service-size guns with longer barrels.

When *these* two warring factions agree on something, it's got to be good. The consensus is almost universal among serious professionals. The lead SWCHP +P is street-proven *and* lab-proven as the best .38 Special self-defense load there is.

.45 ACP: 230-grain JHP. Both sides find this type of cartridge the top choice in the caliber. They seem to differ only on the brand choice. The Marshall Study has consistently put the Federal Hydra-Shok ahead of other rounds of its type, though not by much. Fackler has stated that he considered the old Winchester Black Talon (which in .45 ACP was a 230-grain at standard velocity) to be the greatest advance in handgun ammo since the hollow-point bullet.

Personally, I've found the Hydra to open a little more consistently than some others, and to be truly match-grade in accuracy, for whatever that's worth in combat ammo selection. But the FBI uses the Remington Golden Saber in 230-grain. I've seen 230-grain Gold Dots dug out of human flesh, and the mushrooming was impressive. My own department issues that bullet in the accurate Black Hills duty round, loaded to hit 850 feet per second from the 4-1/4-inch barrels on our issue guns, and I'm extremely comfortable carrying it. As noted in the previous chapter, one test I performed comparing hi-tech 230-grain .45 ACP JHP in the slaughterhouse resulted in the PMC StarFire showing very slightly more tissue disruption than in any of the others. Really, it's almost a coin toss.

The point is, both sides agree. The issue is resolved. The .45 Auto shooter can now move on to those things mentioned above that will *really* win the fight.

.40 S&W: 180-grain subsonic JHP. IWBA recommends the original 180-grain subsonic. Marshall and Sanow list other rounds, notably the full-power 135-grain and 155/165-grain loads, as having slightly more stopping power. However, the Federal Hydra-Shok 180-grain subsonic is very close to the top of their .40 charts, and certainly on the list of recommended loads.

Again, the only difference is in the details. Where Evan and Ed rate the Hydra-Shok tops among the subsonic .40s, Marty seems to clearly prefer the Winchester. While I have to side with Sanow and Marshall on the best 9mm and .357 loads simply because my field research comes out yielding the same top rounds as theirs, I have to go to Fackler's side of the line in brand selection among 180-grain subsonic .40 S&W offerings. I've run across several shootings with Winchester's talon-style Ranger load. All but one stayed in the body. All have opened up exactly like a Winchester publicity photo. All have stopped hostilities immediately. The one that exited the offender involved a slender female who was trying to murder an officer. The bullet that punched through her left a massive exit wound and instantly stopped her attempted cop-killing.

Unfortunately, the Ranger load is currently offered only to law enforcement. Fortunately, there is not all *that* much difference. The California Highway Patrol has

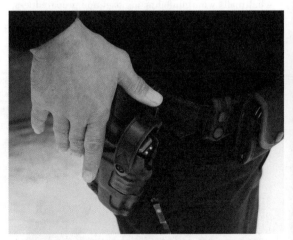

When you can't decide on a 9mm load you like, reach for a .40 caliber of the same make and model! Both sides of the argument are satisfied with the 180-grain .40 subsonic JHP, though the author loads hotter ammo into his Glock 22, carried here in a Safariland Raptor snatch-resistant duty holster.

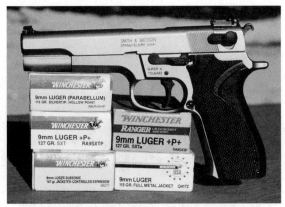

Which of these 9mm loads is the best? The debate continues. Of those shown, the author would take the 127-grain +P+. The pistol is the S&W Super 9, made for the European market and seldom seen in the U.S.

issued the ordinary Remington 180-grain subsonic (not the hi-tech Golden Saber version) for most of the time since their 1990 adoption of the .40 S&W cartridge. CHP's thousands of highway patrolmen collectively log a great many shootings. The agency has pronounced itself quite pleased with the performance of that ammunition as well as the performance of their chosen sidearm, the Smith & Wesson Model 4006.

In other calibers, there seems to be no such common ground between the two camps. This is not to say that compromise is not possible.

Let's say your choice of handgun is the .357 Magnum revolver. There is simply no Magnum round on which both sides agree. But any .357 Magnum revolver will fire .38 Special +P ammunition. A logical choice presents itself: Load with the FBI .38 Special formula, and you're good to go.

The 9mm Luger remains one of our most popular caliber choices. There is no 9mm round on which both sides agree; indeed, this caliber has probably been the focus of more argument between the two camps than any other. So, the logical compromise in a 9mm is ... the 180-grain subsonic .40 S&W.

Think about it. Almost any modern handgun you want to buy in 9mm is also available in .40 caliber, sacrificing

only one to four rounds of magazine capacity. Beretta, Glock, Kahr, SIG, Smith & Wesson, Taurus ... even if you prefer the 1911 or the Browning Hi-Power; if the company makes that gun in 9mm they make one identical or almost identical to it in .40 caliber.

Sometimes compromise isn't possible. Sometimes, though, it's a necessity. And sometimes it's a good thing, because it gets us past the small arguments so we can focus on more important matters.

The placement of the shot will be more important than the "wound profile" of the bullet we launch. Tactics that put us where we can shoot the offender more quickly and easily than the offender can shoot us, may be even more important than shot placement. And being alert enough to see danger signs in time to avoid being shot at all might be more important still.

That said, the ammunition in our gun is one of the few variables in a violent encounter that we can control before the fight starts, and we'd be fools not to load the most effective ammunition for the purpose. One thing that is not examined enough is tailoring the ammunition to its "mission profile."

You wouldn't hunt small antelope and moose with the same ammunition. Different jobs require different tools. If you were a police officer on rolling stakeout, tracking armed offenders and pulling them over at opportune times, it would be reasonable to expect that you would often have to fire through auto bodies and auto glass, and you would want ammo with deep tactical penetration. If you were the court security officer in a crowded Hall of Justice designed by an architect who thought marble was the key to structure, you have much greater concerns about over-penetration and ricochet, and this could and should alter your approach to ammunition selection.

Pick something suitable for the task, something that has already been proven on the street as well as tested in the laboratory. Don't be "the first on your block" to get the cool new ammo that is the subject of full page ads in gun magazines, but has never been used for its intended purpose and thus, in real world terms, remains untried. Let someone else be the guinea pig. In this discipline, the price of failure is simply too great.

Getting bogged down in one corner of a multi-dimensional discipline will not serve you well. There is a legal maxim that is on point to this: *De minimus non curat lex.*

The law does not bother with trifles.

Since The Last Edition

Between the Fifth Edition of this book and this Sixth, forests have possibly been denuded for gun magazine articles and bandwidth sacrificed on the Internet for the discussion of stopping power, but in reality remarkably little has changed.

The fast, medium-weight bullets have further proven their value on the street in 9mm, specifically the Winchester Ranger 127-grain +P+ and the Speer Gold Dot 124-grain +P. The latter was adopted by the Chicago PD after numerous dismal failures with assorted 147-grain subsonic JHPs, and no complaints have arisen since the ammo change. The NYPD, many more shootings later, is reportedly delighted with the performance of the +P 124-grain Gold Dot.

Ironically, the 147-grain subsonic has finally grown into its promise with current iterations of Speer Gold Dot, Winchester Ranger, and Federal's new HST ammunition, but in the last half-decade still more departments have just dumped the 9mm and gone to something bigger, or optionalized something bigger, or gone to faster 9mm rounds as Chicago did. Today's 147-grain high-tech subsonic is the best ever, but still not quite up to the 127-grain +P+, the 115-grain +P+, or the 124-grain +P.

The .357 SIG continues its triumphant march, with a few more state police agencies adopting it after the splendid success it has enjoyed in street shootings in Texas, Virginia and elsewhere. Most are using SIGs in either the full-size P226 or the more compact P229 format

A 230-grain .45 GAP bullet, from a 5-inch Springfield XDLE, has slightly outpenetrated its .45 ACP equivalent from a 5-inch Springfield 1911A1, above. Both are Winchester Ranger 230-grain JHPs.

The 5.7mm FN pistol has generated much controversy, but not yet any substantial confidence. Author does not yet consider it "a player" in the combat handgun world.

(the latter is also the choice of Secret Service and Air Marshals), but the state troopers of New Mexico and Tennessee and the conservation officers of Pennsylvania tell me they are delighted with their Glock 31 pistols in the .357 SIG chambering. Other manufacturers have offered this caliber as well.

The big cartridge story of the five years between editions of this book has been, I think, the .45 GAP. As noted in more detail in the chapter on the latest handguns, this .45 **G**lock **A**uto **P**istol cartridge is a .45 **A**utomatic **C**olt **P**istol casing shortened and made stronger with scientific sophistication, thanks to a design team led by Ernest Durham. The shorter round equals, and often exceeds, the one that's been around since shortly after the turn of the 20ᵗʰ century, so long as you compare the .45 GAP to standard pressure .45 ACP. +P .45 ACP will outrun the .45 GAP by as much as it outperforms the standard .45 ACP with the same projectile. However, standard-pressure .45 ACP ballistics

have become something of a gold standard for stopping power, so that puts the .45 GAP in good company.

The *raison d'etre* of the .45 GAP is that it puts .45 ACP performance into a 9mm envelope by using a cartridge the same overall length as the 9x19. In 1990, the .40 S&W became the ultimate compromise cartridge because it delivered *close* to .45 ACP ballistics in the 9mm-size pistol envelope; the .45 GAP goes all the way and delivers *true* .45 ACP performance in that envelope, albeit with somewhat fewer rounds.

The .45 GAP has proven to be an accurate cartridge. Author shot this group at 25 yards with Winchester USA 230-grain ball, out of XD45 pistol. Note that 4 of 5 bullet holes are touching.

The .357 SIG is solidly ensconced and rising in popularity. Here are but a few of the ammo selections that have been offered in this caliber.

Here are just seven of the assorted loads currently available in .45 GAP.

The new .50 GI cartridge for the 1911 pistol is still a novelty at this time, but may prove to be a player if it becomes a sufficient presence "on the street" to prove itself.

The world of the gun is a conservative planet, and the .45 GAP was not an immediate bestseller. Fans of the .45 ACP predicted its doom and called it a vanity cartridge because it had the Glock name on it. A few years into its epoch, however, the .45 GAP was adopted by the Georgia State Patrol (eleven-shot G37 model for uniform wear, and a G29 seven-shot subcompact to every trooper for backup and off-duty use). Shortly thereafter New York State Police, disappointed with the effects over many years of 9mm 147-grain subsonic and, toward the end, 124-grain standard pressure JHP, also adopted the Glock in .45 GAP. It is said at this writing that the state police agencies of South Carolina, Pennsylvania, and Kansas may follow. We are probably looking at the beginning of a domino effect, and we don't know yet how far the dominoes will fall.

Ammo for the .45 GAP is now produced by virtually all the big makers and many of the smaller ammunition companies. I've shot guns Springfield Armory has made for it – their short-stroke subcompact 1911 and their standard-size XD, which proved to be deliciously accurate

These 230-grain Ranger SXT bullets exhibit near-identical deformation and penetration depth in gelatin. Without the labels, could you tell the recovered projectiles apart? (Photo courtesy Olin)

in the 5-inch Tactical model – and am told that ParaOrdnance is also now making pistols in .45 GAP. Glock, meanwhile, has the standard size G37, the compact G38, and the subcompact G39, all of which seem to work just fine.

To understand why the GAP appeals to law enforcement and some others, listen to the words of a police sergeant in New York State, who wrote me, "I just read your article about the .45 GAP in *Tactical Response*. I chose the G37, G38, and G39 for our department this past spring. You hit the nail on the head when you wrote about the grip frame being a consideration. Our officers favored the G37 frame 10:1 over the G21 frame. The GAP fills our needs: I wanted to keep the .45 ballistics and go to a simpler gun. I just read another article of yours about the problems with the decocking of a pistol. I found this to be true during many Q (qualification) courses. I saw good officers failing to decock or failing to recognize that the decocker/safety had been activated. This was a problem I did not like to see occurring on the range because I know the consequences that could happen on the streets. We went through 85 officers transitioning to the GAP and had no problems attributed to the gun. The guns performed well and were very accurate. We did have some problems with a batch of ammo but Winchester fixed that without any hesitation. All our officers said good things about the Glock and almost everyone shot better than on previous Q courses. Keep up the good work, it is appreciated by the officers." – *Sgt. Dave Iacovissi, Rome, NY Police Department.*

No, this new cartridge won't change the world, and it probably won't outsell Glock's other pistols in more popular and time-proven chamberings. But the .45 GAP has proven itself a real answer to a real problem, and a useful new tool to have on board. I suspect you'll be hearing much more about it several years from now in the next edition of the GUN DIGEST BOOK OF COMBAT HANDGUNNERY. There will be many more investigated shootings with the .45 GAP on file by then. I'm predicting that they'll show just what we're seeing now. In the several gelatin tests I've observed, and in two actual fatal shootings (one with FMJ ball, one with Winchester 230-grain Ranger), the results were instant stop, instant death and penetration and expansion exactly consistent with the same projectiles out of a standard pressure .45 ACP.

CHAPTER EIGHT

Defensive Gunleather Today

Concealment Holsters

Thanks to the enlightened and widespread adoption of "shall-issue" concealed carry legislation, more ordinary American citizens are carrying guns in the 21st century than at any time in the 20th. As determined by Professor John Lott, and others, to a point that can no longer be realistically questioned, this seems to have improved the public safety.

We have more good concealment guns and concealment holsters than ever before. The term "gunleather," once the catch-all for belt, holster, ammo carrier and related accoutrements, must now be expanded to include leather-look synthetics like Uncle Mike's lightweight Mirage, Kydex holsters by countless makers, other related "plastic" technology as exemplified by Fobus, and fabric units ranging from ballistic nylon to Cordura.

Before looking at where the holster goes, let's look at what it's made of.

Leather has among its good points tradition, style, and pride of ownership. With the potential for perfect fit, it remains for many the preferred choice. Downsides: requires a modicum of care, may be tight when new and loose when very old, and may squeak if not properly cared for.

Plastics, whether Kydex or polymer or whatever, require no break-in. They generally fit perfectly from the start. They are *very* fast, so much so that synthetic holsters now rule all the combat shooting events that include quick-draw. Downsides: they can break, particularly in a struggle for the holstered gun. With rare exceptions like the suede-lined Hellweg, they make a distinctive grating sound when the gun is drawn, which can hamper a surreptitious draw in certain danger situations. They are dramatically cheaper than leather as a rule, quality level for quality level.

Fabric "gunleather" is generally the cheapest of all. It rarely offers a perfect fit, but does generally allow silent draw.

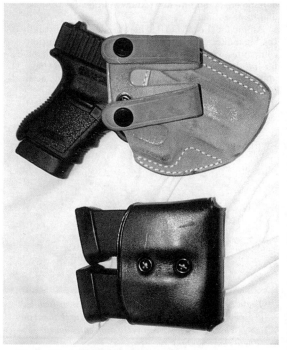

Carrying a handgun loose in the waistband is never the best idea. This HK P7M8 has shifted position and accidentally released its magazine.

Here a Glock 30 rests in a leather IWB holster, with a double spare magazine pouch, all by Galco.

Dave Elderton, founder of Ky-Tac, left, discusses his super-fast and super-concealable Kydex holsters with a satisfied customer and national champ, Bob Houzenga.

Now, let's look at the most street-proven holster styles for lawfully concealed handguns.

Strong-Side Hip Holsters

For plainclothes police and armed citizens alike, particularly males, this is overwhelmingly the most popular concealment holster site. On the male body, a

Uncle Mike's holsters drove the market price downward in Kydex rigs, and work fine. This one holds a Kimber target grade .45 auto with Pachmayr grips.

pistol just behind the hip bone tends to ride very comfortably, and is naturally hidden by the drape of the concealing garment in the hollow of the kidney area. Just behind the ileac crest of the hip is the best location. At the point of the hip, the holstered gun will protrude obviously on one side, and dig at the hip bone on the other. The dominant hand is very close, being on the same side, which is conducive to a tactically sound fast and efficient draw. The dominant-side forearm is in a position to naturally protect the holster.

The higher, more flaring hip of the typical female, plus her proportionally shorter torso, makes the strong-side hip holster work against her. A disproportionate number of females choose to carry their guns in other locations.

Crossdraw Belt Holsters

Whether you see it spelled crossdraw, cross-draw, or cross draw, it's all the same. We're talking about a belt-mounted holster mounted butt-forward and requiring the dominant hand to reach, to at least some degree across the abdomen for access. Hence, the terminology "crossdraw."

NRA director and firearms instructor Mike Baker examines the first "tuckable" holster, designed by Dave Workman. The deep area between the belt loop flap and the holster body allows the shirt to be tucked in around a holstered gun. A key chain on the belt loop makes it look harmless. Draw is done with a Hackathorn Rip. This may be the most widely copied of the new concealment holster designs.

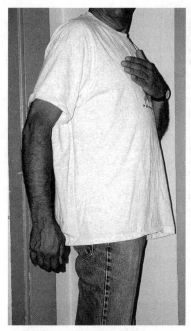

Untucked T-shirt, one size large, completely conceals…

…a 4-inch square butt, Hogue-gripped S&W .357 Combat Magnum in Bianchi #3 Pistol Pocket holstered inside the waistband.

forward of the hip, which causes concealment problems. In a face-to-face struggle, the butt of the gun in a crossdraw holster is presented to the opponent and may be actually more accessible to him than to you.

Shoulder Holsters

The gun is suspended under the weak-side armpit by a harness that goes around the shoulders, hence the name of this rig. A shoulder holster draw is a form of crossdraw. Broad-chested, broad-shouldered men may have difficulty reaching the gun, though buxom women don't seem to have the same problem. For a number of reasons, shoulder holsters tend to be more readily

Good news: This is very fast for a seated person, particularly if the gun is forward of the off-side hip. It is particularly well suited to males who have rotator cuff problems or other conditions that limit the mobility of the strong-side shoulder. For reasons discussed above, it also works better for females than for males as a rule. The typical female's arm will be proportionally longer and more limber vis-à-vis her more narrow torso. The crossdraw tends to conceal better for women than for their brothers, and to be more accessible. Bad news: For most males to be able to reach the gun they must have it

Many female shooters are more comfortable with crossdraw holsters. This one has done well with hers.

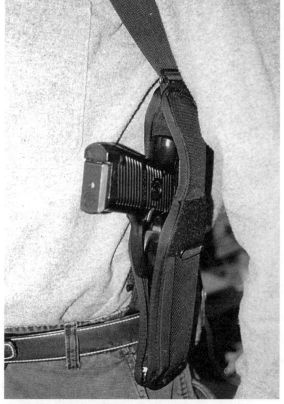

The upright shoulder holster works particularly well with large guns under heavy winter coats. This is author's Bianchi Ranger, holding a Ruger P97 .45 auto.

Unusual, but useful, is this security shoulder system by Strong Holster. From their Piece-Keeper series, it has a unique two-way safety strap release that's easy for the legitimate user to operate, but tough for a snatcher. This one holds the author's department-issue Ruger P90 .45 auto with IWI night sights. In the belt pouches are spare magazines and OC pepper spray.

A particularly useful variation of the shoulder holster is the type of rig that attaches a small handgun to the opposite armpit area of a "bulletproof vest." Noted Officer Survival authority Jim Horan designed the very first of these.

Women seem partial to shoulder holsters. They solve the problem of having to wear a heavy-duty belt that is incongruous with the typical professional woman's wardrobe.

Bad news: Many find shoulder holsters uncomfortable, and as noted, they are not the easiest to keep discreetly concealed. A jacket or some similar garment must be kept on at all times. If the harness is not secured to the belt, the holstered gun and magazines will bounce around and hammer the rib cage mercilessly if you have to run.

Small of Back Holster

Often called SOB for short, this holster carry is thought by some to earn that nickname in more ways than one. The pistol is carried at or near the center of the lumbar spine. The theory is that even if the concealing garment blows open, it will not be visible from the front. It is reasonably fast with a conventional draw and particularly easy to access with the weak hand, an attribute shared by the crossdraw and the shoulder holster.

Good news: Excellent concealment from the front and fast access when standing. Bad news: Almost impossible to reach from a seated position, especially with seat belts in place. A gun in this position is extremely difficult to defend against a gun snatch attempt. The gun tends to catch the rear hem of the concealing garment and lift it up in such a way that the wearer can't see or feel it, but everyone behind him or her sees the exposed gun. Finally, any rearward fall guarantees the equivalent of landing on a rock with your lumbar spine.

detectable under a supposedly concealing garment than many other types.

Good news: Cops in particular like "shoulder systems," a concept developed by Richard Gallagher, founder of the old Jackass Holster Company and today's gunleather giant Galco. If you are right-handed, the handgun rides under your left arm and pouches containing spare ammunition and handcuffs ride under the right. This provides balance and comfort despite the added weight. More to the point, it allows you to put on all your gear at once as quickly as putting on a jacket, and taking it all off just as easily.

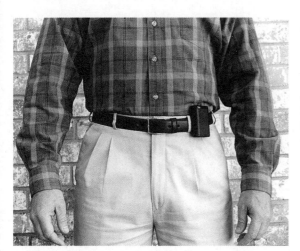

This individual doesn't appear to be carrying a gun...

...until he pulls up his Pager Pal holster with AMT .380 auto. With this draw, be careful the muzzle doesn't cross the support hand. Photos by Pager Pal.

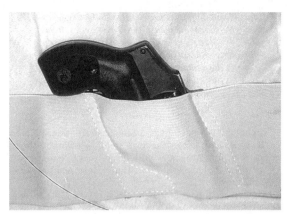

The belly band is often the most practical concealed carry system in a business environment. This one, by Guardian, holds a Model 442 Airweight S&W .38 Special with Crimson Trace LaserGrips.

Belly Band Holster

This is a 4-inch-wide elastic strip with one or more holster pouches sewn in. It is ideal for wear with a tucked-in shirt or blouse and no jacket. The belly band is worn "over the underwear and under the overwear."

Most advertisements for such products show them being worn inefficiently. For the male, these rigs work best at belt level, with the handgun just to the side of the navel, butt forward in what has been called "front crossdraw" carry. To speed the draw, the second button above the belt may be left undone. A necktie will cover this minor lapse of fashion protocol.

Many women prefer to wear the belly band just below the breast line. Natural fabric drape hides it well.

Good news: Unbeatable for discreet carry under business clothing. This holster is faster than it seems and can be combined with a money belt.

Bad news: Some find this carry uncomfortable. The wearer is, practically speaking, limited to a fairly small gun. A small-frame, short-barrelled revolver with rounded edges is particularly suitable for belly band carry.

Pocket Holster

At this writing, loose-fitting pants of the Dockers and BDU persuasion are in style, and literally cover the wearer in situations from "tie and jacket" to "tailgate party informal." All are well suited for small handguns in the pockets. The larger cuts will allow pistols up to the size of baby Glock autoloaders. Tight jeans, on the other hand, may limit you to the tiniest "pocket autos."

This is not to say that the wearing of a pocket gun is entirely "fashion dependent." Fortunately, certain "timeless" styles lend themselves to pocket carry. These include police and security uniform pants, military style BDUs, and the seemingly eternal men's "sack suit."

Just dropping the gun in the pocket is not enough. It will shift position, often winding up with its grip-frame down and the muzzle pointed straight up, a nightmare if you need a reasonably fast draw. In the pocket, "the naked gun" will also print its shape obviously to the least discerning eye, and will tend to wear holes in the pocket lining.

A pocket gun needs a pocket holster. This product serves to break up the outline, protect pocket lining and thigh alike from chafing, and to assure that the handgun is always oriented in the same, appropriate position. The front side trouser pocket is almost universally deemed the pocket of choice for "pistol-packing."

Good news: The hand can be casually in the pocket and already holding the gun. The draw can be surprisingly fast. A jacket can be removed with impunity if the gun is carried in the pants.

Bad news: The gun can be lost from all but the best pocket holsters when rolling and/or fighting on the ground. It is difficult for the weak hand to reach if necessary and limits the user to a fairly small handgun.

Ankle Holsters

Since the first horseman stuck a pistol in his boot-top, this method of carry has been with us. It is somewhat fashion-dependent. Peg-bottom jeans or Toreador pants just weren't made for ankle rigs. On the other hand, "boot-cut" jeans, "flares," and the old bell-bottoms were perfect for ankle holsters. Standard cut men's suits and uniform pants adapt to this carry well.

The ankle rig is the holster people are most likely to find uncomfortable. Very few of them fit well. The holster

A pocket holster is essential for pocket carry. This one, by Alessi, holds a S&W Centennial Airweight with Uncle Mike's affordable version of Spegel Boot Grips.

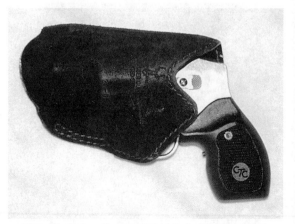

The author's favorite pocket holster is the Safariland, here holding a S&W Model 640 Centennial with LaserGrips.

Fobus ankle holster can conceal this baby Glock .40 if the pant legs are loose enough.

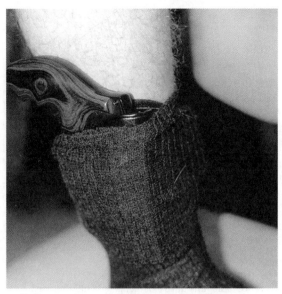

Pulling a sock up over the ankle holster distinctly enhances concealment.

body wants to be firm and well-fitted, but the part of the rig that touches the leg needs to be soft and supple. All-wool felt lining seems to be the best interior surface option; even those allergic to wool can cure the problem with hypoallergenic white all-cotton socks under the holster. Some ankle rigs are available with sheepskin lining.

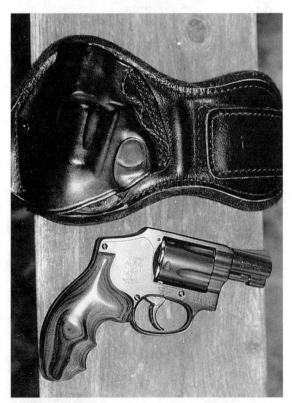

Alessi is the author's choice in an ankle holster for all-day wear. This one holds a Gunsite Custom S&W Model 442 Airweight with Hogue grips.

It takes about a week of constant wear to become accustomed to the new weight and constriction at the ankle. Hint: It conceals better if the sock is pulled up over the body of the holster, leaving the butt exposed for a quick draw. Also, because running through brush or simply crossing your ankles can release a safety strap, it is imperative that an ankle holster's scabbard portion fit the gun tightly enough to keep it in place during strenuous activity.

Good news: Ankle rigs are among the fastest holsters to access while sitting and are perhaps *the* fastest to access when you're down on your back. Since the legs no longer bear the body's weight, you can simply snap the ankle up to the reaching hand. Most users find that wearing it on the ankle opposite the dominant hand, butt to the rear, works best.

Bad news: These are among the slowest to draw from when standing and can be uncomfortable. Weight and particularly constriction around the lower leg can aggravate phlebitis and any number of medical conditions where impaired circulation to extremities is a concern.

Fanny Pack

From the defining DeSantis "Gunny Sack" to the Second Chance "Police Pouch" that opens up into a bullet-resistant shield, belt packs designed to contain firearms have become ubiquitous, particularly in hot climates. Some in the world of the gun believe the fanny pack is the ultimate tip-off to an armed person. If so, they'll get awfully paranoid at the beach or Disney World, where every second person seems to be wearing one.

Good news: These are very convenient. When you have to leave your gun in the car to comply with the law, simply locking the fanny pack in the trunk draws no attention.

Bad news: Fanny packs offer a very slow draw. Weight can cause problems with lumbar spine for some wearers. The fanny pack is seen as the location of a wallet and folding money and may thus become the very focus of a criminal attack.

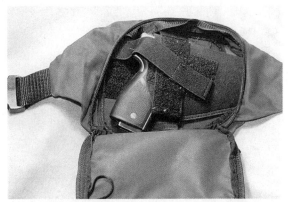

Fanny packs aren't the fastest way to get to a gun, but are often the most convenient way to carry one. This one is home to a Kahr K9 compact 9mm.

Off-Body Carry

Since handguns have existed, people have carried them in saddlebags and purses, suitcases and briefcases, mounted on saddles or in the glove boxes of automobiles. Today we have all manner of purses, attaché cases and day planners designed to contain hidden handguns. Particularly useful is the Guardian Leather "legal portfolio," which contains a panel of body armor along with the hidden sidearm.

Good news: These options are very convenient and are not fashion-dependent, meaning the gun might be along when it would otherwise have been left at home.

Bad news: When you've set it down, security has disappeared. People in other countries where loss of a firearm is considered presumptive evidence of criminal negligence have gone to jail for leaving their gun-bearing purse or case behind in a restaurant. Leave the room where you're visiting, and ask yourself if the host's child might wander in and pick through the purse you left beside your chair. Once again drawing from almost all these devices is painfully slow. Besides, the attack on you might revolve around a mugger or purse-snatcher grabbing the very object that contains your firearm.

Common Questions

"Should my holster be inside or outside the waistband?" Inside the waistband is certainly more concealable. The drape of the pants breaks up the outline of the holster,

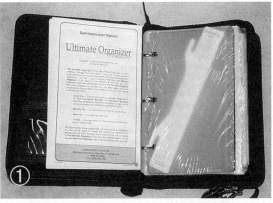

Designed to work (and function) as a personal organizer, this handy little unit...

...helps organize survival by also concealing a Micro Kahr pistol.

❶ *Here is one of several variations of a briefcase...*

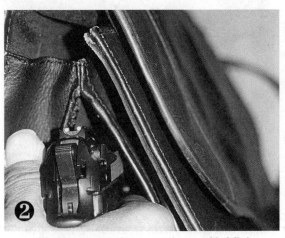

❷ *...with hidden pockets that can easily carry this full-size Beretta service pistol.*

❶

This Kydex holster by Sidearmor holds a Glock 30 compact .45 comfortably inside the waistband...

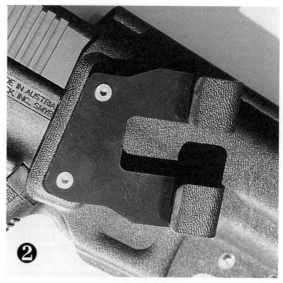

❷

...and securing to the belt with J-hooks.

❸

...protecting its finish against sweat thoroughly, thanks to the built-up inside surface...

A safety strap is always a good idea on a defensive holster. This scabbard with a thumb-break is by Galco and holds an HK USP.

and the concealing garment can come all the way up to the belt without revealing the holstered gun. For comfort, however, the pants should be about 2 inches larger in the waist than what one would normally wear. If you have tried inside the waistband (IWB) carry and found it uncomfortable, try it again for a week, but this time leave the top button of the lower garment undone. If it's now comfortable, you can buy new clothes with wider waistbands or let out the ones you have. (We could also lose weight, but hey, let's be realistic here.)

"Should my concealment holster have a safety strap or other security device?" It is a myth to believe that you'll never have anyone try to snatch your gun because it's concealed and they don't know you have it. The gun might momentarily become visible. The attacker might be a disgruntled employee you've fired, who not only knows that you carry a gun, but knows where you carry it. And any physical fight is likely to reach a point where the opponent grabs you around the waist to throw you, at which time he'll feel your gun and grab at it. Therefore, at least one "level" of retention, such as a simple

The author has become particularly partial to these Toters™ jeans designed by Blackie Collins especially for gun carriers. All pockets are reinforced for small handguns, cuffs are cut for ankle rigs, and the "mature cut" waistband works well with belly bands and IWB holsters.

---

thumb-break safety strap, is desirable. More snatch-resistant holsters than that are available in concealable styles, such as the Safariland 0701 or the Piece-Keeper from Strong Holsters.

"Is quick access really important?" Frankly, yes. When the general public sees a uniformed police officer with a gun in his hand, they're not afraid of him, they're afraid of the situation that made him draw his gun and they get out of the way. When the general public sees an ordinary person with a gun in his hand, panic often ensues and someone may try to be a hero and disarm him. There will be some situations where responding police officers might also mistake an unidentifed armed citizen for "the bad guy," setting the stage for a mistaken-identity shooting. Thus, the armed citizen is often wise to wait 'til the last possible moment to draw, meaning that speed of presentation is all the more important.

Police Uniform Holsters

Through the late 19th century, most police officers bought their own handguns and their own means of carrying them. Many Eastern officers simply put their revolvers in a coat or trouser pocket. The Western lawman generally carried a heavier six-gun, normally in whatever scabbard was available at the gunsmith's shop or the saddle-maker's place of business.

The mid-1890s purchase of the Colt New Police .32 revolvers by the police departments of New York City and Boston began the trend of departments issuing guns and, inevitably, holsters in which to carry them. The earliest police holsters were simply gun pouches with something to hold the gun in place. Some departments opted for a simple safety strap to perform the latter function, while others preferred a military style flap. The rationale for the latter was three-fold. First, the flap holster had a military look that went well with the whole concept of uniformed police as a paramilitary structure during the early part of

the 20th century. Second, it gave the department-owned gun some protection from rain and snow when the cop was out there walking the beat. Third, some saw the flap as more impediment than the strap to a suspect gaining control of the officer's sidearm.

As the years rolled along, advocates of the "strap" won out over advocates of the "flap." S.D. Myres' holster company was one of the early pioneers in designing sparsely cut, fast-draw scabbards that need only have a strap over the hammer added to placate the security demands of police chiefs. Berns-Martin's radical break-front holster of the 1930s was the first effort in really

Dating to the first third of the 20 century, this duty holster was made for a 5-inch Colt service revolver by...

...the legendary S.D. Myres company.

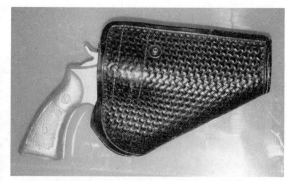

High-tech, in the 1930s, was embodied by the Berns-Martin holster. Shown here with a K-frame Odin Press dummy gun…

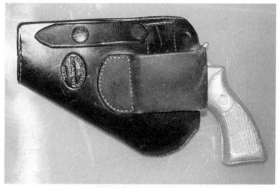

…the Berns-Martin was generally carried with its frontal strap fastened thus out of the way for a quick draw.

giving a cop a fast duty rig that was also secure. The gun came out the front, in keeping with the theory of the time that a draw should be a forward swing that ended with the revolver being fired from below line of sight.

Time went on. By the 1970s, three significant developments had taken shape. Bill Jordan's rigid steel reinforcement of the Myres type scabbard had become hugely popular. Jordan, the Border Patrol's most famous gunslinger, had redefined the paradigm. He had designed the holster to be worn unfastened, with the strap out of the way and fastened only when a cop was going into a bar fight or about to undertake a vigorous foot pursuit.

The thumb-break holster, pioneered at about the same time by the Bucheimer Company in Maryland and brilliant gunleather designer Chic Gaylord in New York, made so much sense that it took cops by storm. Don Hume, the sole licensed producer of the Jordan holster (though everyone seemed to make copies) offered the classic with a thumb-break attachment. This allowed the strap to be kept fastened with virtually no sacrifice in drawing speed.

The 1970s also saw the return of the Berns-Martin concept in John Bianchi's updated break-front holsters, the first of which was the Model 27. The first design had a

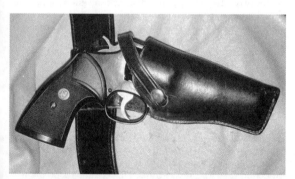

By the 1970s, this was the paradigm: A S&W Model 10 (or Combat Magnum for the lucky ones) in a simple Jordan-style holster.

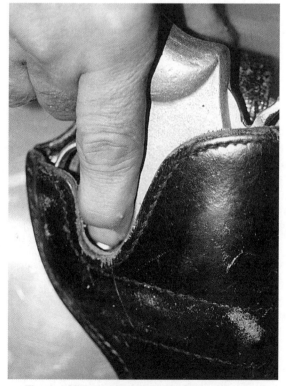

The trigger finger had to be pressed into the trigger guard to release the revolver from the Audley holster.

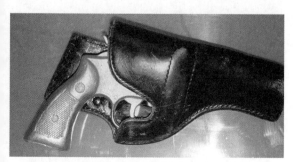

The Audley duty holster never gained much popularity except on the East Coast.

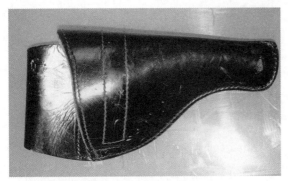

Though ugly, cheap, and made of less than premium materials, the Jay-Pee NYPD holster was credited with saving multiple lives.

Smith & Wesson's Security Plus holster was extremely popular during the last days of the police revolver era, and defined the "split-front" as opposed to "break-front" design.

major in "fast" and a minor in "secure." The Bianchi break-front reversed the priorities. It had a major in "secure" and a minor in "fast." It quickly earned a reputation for saving lives, and the holster industry geared up for "security rigs" to attack Bianchi's dominance in the lucrative police gunleather market.

Along the way, several "gimmick" holsters came and went. Appearing primarily on the West Coast, especially popular with the LAPD, was the clamshell holster. A button was "hidden" in front of the trigger in the exposed trigger guard. When pressed, the spring-loaded holster flipped open like the shell of a clam. It was very fast, but since the trigger finger had to be working at the trigger area just to get the gun out of the holster, it lent itself to unintentional discharges under stress. Legend has it that smart-aleck kids learned to run up behind a cop, press the release button, and run away laughing when the service revolver clattered to the ground. Most episodes of the old TV cop series "Adam-12," still shown on some "oldies" channels, show the clamshell in use.

On the opposite coast, the Audley holster was regionally popular for decades. Like the clamshell, the trigger and guard were exposed, and the shooter had to reach past the trigger to release the gun. The Audley lock was a simple spring tongue that pressed against the inside front of the trigger guard. Like the clamshell, it was implicated in numerous accidental discharges.

If the Audley was an Eastern Seaboard phenomenon, the Jay-Pee holster developed for the NYPD had few fans beyond that city. Selling at one time for $12 per holster, it had an inner welt of leather that secured at the rear of the revolver's cylinder. A twist of the revolver in a certain direction released it for draw. At least, it had a covered trigger guard. All three of these holsters normally left the hammer spur unsecured, where it could be accidentally caught and drawn back, becoming cocked in the holster and setting the stage for unintentional discharges. This is one reason LAPD, and later NYPD, eventually ordered service revolvers altered department-wide so they could not operate in single action.

Enter the Autos

As the competition rushed at the Bianchi break-front, new designs emerged such as the "split-front." Typified by the Security Plus from Smith & Wesson's then-popular leather division and also by Bianchi's own Hurricane, this was seen as a less radical alternative to the

break-front with similar security function. Instead of sweeping the whole gun out the front of the holster, the officer would release the thumb-break, rock the gun forward to clear the rear trigger guard shield, and then draw straight up and out. Truth to tell, this could also be done with the breakfront.

By the 1980s, more and more departments were going to auto pistols. Bianchi spent a then-unprecedented $100,000 in research to design the snatch-resistant Auto-Draw holster. It was difficult to draw from, but extremely retentive, against a disarming attempt. Meanwhile, an FBI veteran named Bill Rogers had designed a holster he called the SS-III. The officer had to break two safety straps and then rock the gun in a certain direction to release it for draw. The good news was it was so ergonomically designed that any committed officer could learn to make the draw quickly. The SS-III was to become the most successful security holster ever. By the year 2001, some 20 years after its inception, over a million had been sold. Early on, Safariland had bought out Rogers, kept him as a consultant, and renamed the SS-III holster the Model 070.

Rogers gilded the lily in 2001 when he came out with a higher-tech version called the Raptor. It effectively addressed what many police tacticians saw as the one weakness in the 070 design. While an officer could learn to quickly draw from the 070, it took a few seconds to re-fasten the two safety straps. This could be a problem when the officer had to holster and secure his weapon for

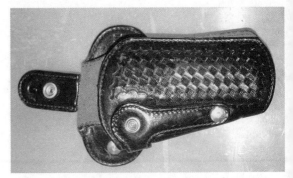

This was the Bianchi Auto-Draw. The author carried one on duty with a Colt .45 for years.

A cutaway of the new Raptor security holster shows its state-of-the-art mix of modern features. The gun is a dummy Glock by Ring's.

a foot chase or to handcuff a temporarily compliant suspect. With the Raptor, the securing device at the rear locked automatically as the gun was inserted into the holster, and the forward device locked back in place with a flick of the finger. This had been borrowed directly from a popular mid-1990s Rogers/Safariland development, the SLS (Self Locking System).

The Safariland SS-III/070 is the "gold standard" in police security holsters. This one carries a Ruger P90 .45 auto.

The Safariland 070 is standard-issue for officers on the author's department. Old vets and newer officers appreciate its balance of high security with good speed of draw.

Duty Belts

The first police gunbelts were simple, soft strips of leather. After WWI, the military Sam Browne belt became almost universal issue among American police. More than 2 inches wide, it much better distributed the weight of the officer's equipment. The Sam Browne concept included an over-the-shoulder strap, which helped to bear the weight of the service revolver and other gear. To this day, some departments still use the diagonal Sam Browne shoulder strap. Officers also learned to wear belt keepers, simple loops of leather that snapped over both the "underbelt" – the officer's regular pants belt, usually a Garrison style – and the heavy belt that went over it. This held them together and prevented the duty belt from shifting during strenuous activity.

In the last 30 years of the 20th century, new refinements became popular. "Buckle-less" belts, using Velcro or sometimes hooks, were seen by some agencies as more streamlined and less evocative of Santa Claus (who also was usually depicted with a Sam Browne style belt, albeit without the shoulder strap). Some officers felt that removing the polished belt buckle also removed a "bull's-eye" that an opponent could aim at in a dark alley.

Safariland pioneered Velcro-lined belts that mated with under-belts with an outward Velcro surface. This did away with belt keepers. The result was a more streamlined belt, and several seconds taken off the time it took a cop to dress for work and remove the belt at the end of the shift.

Meanwhile, the police belt was beginning to resemble Batman's "utility belt." Photos of American police (and depictions of them in old movies) in the first half of the

Despite triple-level security, the draw is quick from the author's department-issue 070 holster. On-safe carry adds one more level of retention capability.

20th century show them wearing a revolver, perhaps 12 spare cartridges, and a handcuff pouch. By the 1960s and 1970s, it came into vogue to wear a baton on the belt. Portable radios had become standard issue, and these, too, were belt-mounted for the most part. Streetwise officers learned to carry a second pair of handcuffs. In the 1980s and 1990s, awareness of the dangers of blood-borne pathogens made latex and nitrile gloves standard issue. While these didn't weigh much, their pouch took up more of the decreasing space on the duty belt. First Mace and then pepper spray became standard issue, and another pouch had to be added to the belt.

Police unionization was growing, and with it came more concern for occupational hazards. Studies finally quantified what had long been suspected: One of the occupational hazards of police work is lower back problems, much of it traceable to the massive equipment belt worn around the waist for eight to 10 hours a day. An officer with a heavy radio and a heavy police flashlight at his waist might have a belt that weighed 18 to 20 pounds.

There was a strong demand to lighten the load. With it came another concern, that blood-borne pathogen thing. Leather is organic and can absorb blood. It is very difficult to clean after it has been bloodstained. Enter the fabric duty rigs!

These were lighter. That was more comfortable. They were softer and more supple. That was more comfortable too. If they were splashed with blood, they could simply be machine-washed. But some departments didn't feel anything less than leather was professional-looking, so Uncle Mike's set the pace with their synthetic, leather-look "Mirage" line.

Female officers were particularly hard-hit by belt comfort and weight problems. The 1970s saw the development of an orthopedic curved belt that was instantly dubbed the "Sally Browne" style. It flared at the hip to better distribute the weight of the equipment load. Shortly after the turn of the century, Bill Rogers made another leap forward with his Levitation belt. As light as the lightest synthetic, it incorporated soft, rubbery tubes on the top and bottom edges to cushion the weight and pressure of the belt. It was determined that the belt shank of attached equipment pouches in general and of holsters in particular, tended to cause nerve damage after pressing into the body for a long period of time. Bill Rogers developed an ingenious new locking mechanism that secured the holster and accessories to the top and bottom edges of the belt. This left only a soft, smooth surface facing the officer's body. This writer has worn the Levitation belt system on uniformed duty and believes it may be the wave of the future in police duty equipment.

Another concept to emerge in the late 1990s was "duty suspenders." Pioneered by Magnum Software under their Orca brand and popularized by Uncle Mike's, these distributed the weight of the duty belt across the shoulders. They have become regionally popular, particularly in the Pacific Northwest. There is the possibility that they give a physical attacker something else to grab hold of to throw the cop around; that was always a concern with the Sam Browne shoulder strap as well. On the other hand, they make good "drag handles" for pulling a wounded brother officer out of the line of fire.

Some trends developed in combat shooting matches, proved themselves there, and were then gradually accepted into day-to-day police work. Revolver speedloaders and semiautomatic pistols are two cases in

State-of-the-art today is the Levitation duty rig system from Safariland. Velcro lining mates with a Velcro underbelt...

...and a unique Bill Rogers attachment design prevents inner edges of the attachment loops from digging against wearer's body, yet...

...the system is strong enough that this NYPD officer can hang from his gun butt without pulling the holster loose from the Levitation belt.

Many consider the Rogers-designed Raptor holster to be the police duty rig of the future. The author tests this one on patrol with Glock 22.

The thigh holster is a concept borrowed from the military that has found favor with police tactical units. This one is a Safariland SLS style, shown with a Glock 17.

point. However, some concepts that were successful in matches and even in real-world concealed carry just didn't make the jump into law enforcement. The Kydex holster is a case in point. Its anchoring on the belt has proven too weak to stand up to a determined gun snatch attempt, in most models. While certain plastics, like Safariland's "Safari-Laminate," have stood the test of time on patrol, most others have not.

If the first borrowing from the military was the flap holster and the second was the Sam Browne belt, the third – much later – was the tactical thigh holster. Popularized by the British SAS, it carried the holstered handgun down out of the way of heavy, hardshell body armor and load-bearing vests worn by SWAT officers. Thigh holsters do not give the officer good leverage to defend against a gun-grab. However, a lunge for the holstered police pistol is not likely to happen when a SWAT cop and at least four of his colleagues blow open a door with explosive entry, throw in a "flash-bang" concussion grenade, and then charge in wielding MP5 sub-machineguns or M4 assault rifles.

Police duty "leather" has come a long way in the last century. Indeed, the term itself is becoming archaic. By many informed industry estimates, less than 50 percent of police duty belt gear is now actually made of leather.

Ammo Carriers

A gun without spare ammunition is a temporary gun. This is why combat competition puts significant emphasis on the ability to quickly and efficiently reload. But you can't reload if you don't have ammo, and if you don't have a comfortable, convenient way of carrying it, you *won't* have it when you need it. Once you have it, you need to be able to access it quickly and get it into the gun. Because revolvers and semi-automatic pistols reload in completely different manners, they'll be treated separately.

Revolvers

Belt Loops. Belt loops go back almost to the dawn of the self-contained cartridge. It their time, they were awesomely efficient. Even today they're not too shabby.

In cowboy days, the loops were sewn directly to the belt. Today, whether for concealed carry or for uniformed personnel equipped with revolvers, the loops are on a slide that attaches to the belt. The first thing a professional looks for is to see that the loops are at the very top edge. This will allow the rounds to be plucked out much more quickly. Only amateurs (or those issued the cheapest equipment bought on bid) use carry loops that are sewn to the middle of the belt slide. You practically need tweezers or forceps to get the cartridges out of the latter.

It is no trick to load two cartridges at a time. Use your dominant hand: This is a dexterity-intensive function, and

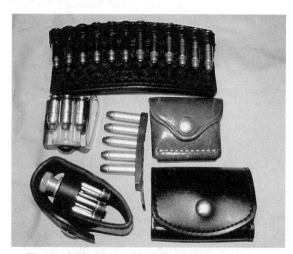

There are half a dozen options for spare revolver ammo. Clockwise from noon: shell loop slide (Don Hume), dump pouch (Bianchi), 2X2X2 carrier (DeSantis), Rogers-style speedloader carrier w/HKS speedloader (Safariland), .45 full-moon clip in Shoot-the-Moon carrier. Center: Bianchi Speed Strip downloaded by one round as the author suggests.

Loading with belt loops. The revolver is a Ruger SP-101 with Bob Cogan recoil reduction venting. The belt slide is by Don Hume…

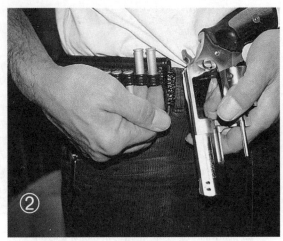

…the Hume loops sit out from the slide, making it easy for two fingers to pop up two rounds…

…that are now easily plucked up by the first two fingers and the thumb…

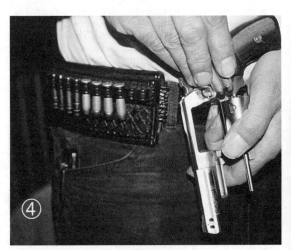

…and, inserted on this slight angle for greater speed…

Mother Nature demands that you use your dexterous hand if you want to accomplish it under stress. Carry the loops on your strong-hand side. As your hand comes down, palm toward you, use the tips of your index and middle fingers to push up the bullet noses of two rounds. This will bring the bases of the cartridges up clear from the loops. Now, grab them at the base with those two fingers and the thumb. Angle them slightly as you feed them into adjacent revolver chambers, and you can load two-by-two. I've seen very practiced people who could load three cartridges at a time this way.

Cartridge Pouches. Slim, flat, and streamlined, these looked good on police duty belts. Stamped with a single die and then sewn together, they were cheap to make and always won low bid. This is why they were almost standard by the 1960s. Pouches as a rule are the slowest method of reloading. Some "dump pouches" were designed to flip down and spill the rounds into the officer's palm; as a result, they were also known as "spill pouches." Trouble was, leather can shrink over time. Many of us can remember seeing officers claw desperately to get their

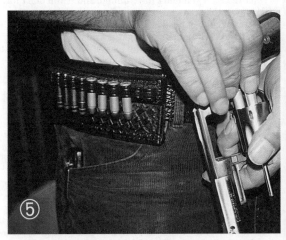

…snap them into the chambers. The thumb then rotates the cylinder to receive the next "ammo delivery" while the dominant hand is returning to the belt loops.

rounds out of these pouches, or jumping up and down trying to shake them loose. That wouldn't work if you were down on your knees behind cover. Some resourceful cops learned to take tin shears to a license plate and cut liner strips for the inside of their spill pouches so the cartridges would actually spill.

John Bianchi was a young policeman during the years when the cartridge pouch was the dominant spare ammo system for cops. He later became a master holster designer, and he also designed the brilliant Bianchi Speed Strip, a little rubber thing that would hold six .38 or .357 cartridges in line inside the pouch. Once you got your Speed Strip out of the pouch and learned how to use it, you could reload about as fast as with belt loops, which was reasonably fast.

The best of the stand-alone pouches were the "2X2X2" style. These became standard issue for FBI in their last years with revolvers. The pouch would tilt out to about a 45-degree angle when its flap was opened. The cartridges were held in three pouches of two each. This could be about as fast as using Speed Strips or loops, but the added leather required by the design made for a bulkier unit that was harder to conceal, though less obvious if it became exposed.

Bianchi Speed Strip. Developed to augment the belt pouch, the Speed Strip was also a stand-alone device. It was exactly the right size to fit in the watch pocket of a pair of jeans, or that little business card pocket you often find inside the right outside suitcoat pocket. This made spare ammo convenient to carry, especially for concealed revolvers.

This writer discovered over the years that the fastest way to use a Speed Strip was to load it one round down from capacity, leaving the sixth hole near the handling strip empty. Instead of six rounds flopping on the end of a soft tab, you had five rounds that you could quickly stabilize for a positive, fast reload. The middle finger would curl around the space left by the removed cartridge, and the index finger lined up along the spine of the Speed Strip. This is the way most surgeons hold their scalpels,

with the index finger along the back, and in both cases it gives tremendous accuracy. Feeding of the five remaining cartridges into the chambers is faster and more positive.

In the old days when auto pistols weren't as reliable as current ones are today, law enforcement justified its reliance on the revolver with the principle, "six for sure beats 14 maybe." This method with the Speed Strip gave you five for sure, positive and fast, instead of six with fumbling. Today, a huge number of revolvers carried for

The Bianchi dump pouch is small and unobtrusive, but not the fastest of reloading devices...

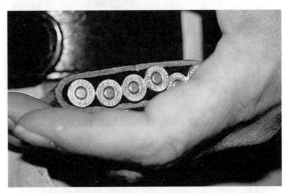

...available. The author uses it by spilling the contents into the palm of the non-dominant hand ...

...and using the palm as a "loading tray" as the dominant hand inserts the cartridges into the cylinder.

Here is a DeSantis 2X2X2 pouch in action, loading two at a time. The revolver is a .38 Colt Detective Special with Pachmayr Compac grips.

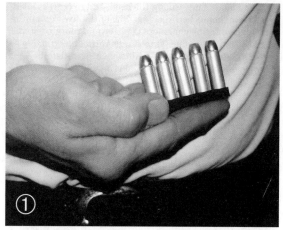

The author developed this grasp of the Bianchi Speed Strip shortly after it came out. The round near tab is removed beforehand, allowing the middle finger to lock there securely while the index finger takes a scalpel position on the back of the strip...

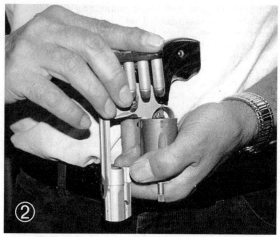

...the top two rounds will enter the S&W AirLite's cylinder first...

...with the index finger snapping them into the chambers...

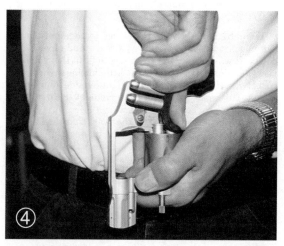

...and the Strip is peeled off the cartridge rims as shown...

self defense are small-frame five-shot guns anyway, so the concept comes together better than ever.

Speedloaders. There were six-shot charging units for the first Colt revolvers with swing-out cylinders in the 1890s. The concept did not catch on with combat shooters until the 1960s. Even then, because each loader was the width of a revolver's cylinder, the pouches in which they were carried bulged on the belt and were seen as "unsightly" and "unprofessional."

Then, in 1970, came the Newhall Massacre. Two heavily armed robbers in the course of a felony car-stop in Newhall, California, killed four young California Highway Patrolmen. The last survivor was down on his knees, wounded through the chest and both legs, desperately trying to reload his revolver. He had to take one cartridge at a time out of his pouches, access to which was partially impaired by his kneeling position. He had been taught to fire six, reload six, fire six more, and had reverted to training under enormous stress. He was just closing the cylinder on the fresh load when one of the killers completed his stealthy approach, screamed "Got you now,

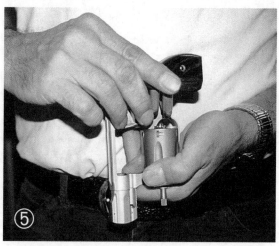

...with the process repeated until all five rounds are in the gun.

Here is how to speed-reload the revolver. Once the empties have been punched out, the weak hand holds the gun thus as the dominant hand goes for speedloader pouch...

...the fingertips are extended past the bullet noses to help guide the loader into the cylinder of this Sile-gripped Ruger .357...

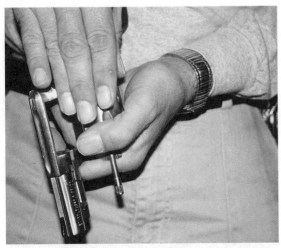

...and insertion is accomplished thus. Release the payload, let the empty loader fall away, close the cylinder, and go back to business.

(expletive deleted)," and shot him in the head. In the wake of this tragedy, the CHP became the first major department in the nation to authorize, and later issue as standard, speedloaders for duty wear. Not until 20 years later would CHP adopt a semiautomatic pistol, the .40 Smith & Wesson Model 4006, which carried 12 rounds and offered a fast reload.

Numerous speedloader designs have come and gone. Two have remained: the HKS and the Safariland. The latter is faster, being a one-stroke unit. It releases as the center hub of the unit hits the center of the revolver's ejector star. The HKS is a two-step device; after insertion, it requires the second step of turning a release knob.

Does a second step make it second rate? Not at all. The HKS is by far the most rugged speedloader ever put on the market. Years ago, this writer loaded some up with .357 Magnum hollow-points and put them in an empty paint can, and then put the can in a Red Devil paint mixer and flipped the switch. (And, admittedly, took cover.) When the cycle was over, the paint can had been torn apart, and all the bullets had expanded back to their case mouths. However, the HKS speedloaders still worked. Other brands turned into plastic dust under the tremendously powerful vibrations.

Safariland makes three variations of speedloaders. Their smallest and oldest, the old JFS design, is called the Comp I. It is very compact and very fast, but John Farnam has noted that after about 500 reloads, it will break. I also found it breakage prone. Since no one counts their reloads, and no one throws away equipment that still seems to be functioning, this unit is an accident waiting to happen. The Comp II is proportionally larger and proportionally sturdier, and just as fast. The Comp III is huge. Modeled after the old Austrian Jetloader, it is shaped like an old German "potato masher" hand grenade. Duty pouches for it are disproportionately large. However, it is extremely fast and does not seem to break. The trick is concealing it. This writer did find that the shape is such that when it is tucked into the right side of a right hip pocket, with a handkerchief in the same pocket to keep it in position, it tucks into the natural hollow of the gluteus maximus. Carried thus, the Comp III is reasonably concealable and comfortable, and very accessible.

Lining up six or so cartridges with as many same-size holes is a dexterity task, and once again Mother Nature demands that we use the dexterous hand to perform it. Keep the speedloaders on the dominant hand side. After ejecting the spent cartridges, I like to grab the revolver around the front of the frame with my left hand, using the left thumb to hold the cylinder out, and bring the gun butt in to touch the center of my abdomen. This creates a felt index that keeps the gun in the same spot all the time, and also orients the muzzle downward so I can take maximum advantage of gravity to help insure that the fresh cartridges fall all the way in and don't tie up the cylinder.

Years ago, a speedloader designer named Kubik came up with the most effective grasp of such a device. Hold it with the fingertips ahead of the bullet noses. This shapes the fingers to the shape of the cylinder. Even in the dark, as your fingertips feel the cylinder, all you have to do is give the loader a light jiggle and all the rounds should slide into place.

When the cartridges release, let the loader fall away. Close the cylinder before you bring the gun up, so centrifugal force doesn't throw a round backward as the cylinder is closing and jam things up. Once the cylinder is closed, return to firing position.

A full-moon clip goes right into the gun with the ammo.

Reloading with a moon clip. The spent "moon" has been ejected from this S&W Model 625, and the dominant hand goes for the loaded moon...

Moon Clips. Half-moon clips were developed by Smith & Wesson to adapt rimless .45 auto cartridges to revolvers, for their 1917 Model, in WWI. It would be more than 50 years before someone would figure out that a single "full-moon clip" of six cartridges would be far more practical than two "half-moon clips" of three cartridges each.

The full-moon clip is, without question, the fastest way to reload a revolver. There is nothing to release, and no empty loader to cast aside. You simply shove the whole thing in and close the cylinder. With a .45 ACP sixgun and a moon clip of round nose jacketed ball, you can literally throw the loader into the cylinder!

How fast is fast? Jerry Miculek holds the record for firing six, reloading, and firing six more from a double-action revolver (and hitting the target with every shot). He used a Smith & Wesson Model 625 and full-moon clips. The time? 2.99 seconds!

The only down side of moon clips is that they can become bent, which renders them inoperable in the gun. This means that they must be carried in a rigid, protective pouch of some kind. On a duty belt, a pouch that will hold one N-frame .357 or .44 Magnum revolver speedloader will hold *two* short, efficiently sized moon clips of .45 ACP. A compact, protective unit suitable for concealment that holds the moon clip with the bullet noses toward the wearer's body is available from leathermaker Chris Cunningham at 1709 5th Ave., West Linn, OR 97068.

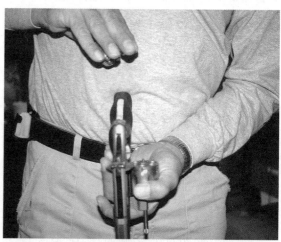

...with the fingertips ahead of the bullet noses to interface with the cylinder, the fresh charge is on the way...

Autoloaders

Many see firepower as the auto's cardinal advantage over the revolver and this certainly holds true in reloading. You can easily get so fast with a speedloader that you'll refill your sixgun faster than a criminal can recharge his stolen autoloader. You can even get so fast that you can reload your revolver faster than the average trained cop can reload his service pistol. But you'll never get so fast with the revolver that you can reload it faster than *you* can reload a semi-automatic pistol with the same amount of practice.

Reloading the revolver is a fine motor skill that requires dexterous manipulation by the dominant hand. Shoving a large magazine into a large receptacle and thumbing a lever or jacking a slide are simple gross motor skills, much more easily learned and more easily applied under stress.

...and the whole kit and kaboodle goes into the gun, making it the fastest of all revolver reloads.

A combination magazine pouch and flashlight carrier (Glock and SureFire, respectively) was first conceptualized by gunwriter Dean Spier. This one is produced by Blad-Tech.

Unlike a revolver, the auto doesn't need to be brought down to the ammo supply at the belt. It's faster to do as the author does with this Colt Government in this multiple exposure, and keep the auto in your line of sight as you reload.

The spare magazines should be on the weak-hand side of the body. The frame of the pistol should be held in the dominant hand, using the support hand to perform most or all of the reloading function. Most fabric magazine pouches are floppy and slow, hard to conceal because they lean out from the belt, and require an action-slowing flap to hold them in place. Leather pouches can be too tight when they're new, and stretch to become too loose after extended wear. Kydex pouches, properly made, are "just right." They hold the magazines friction tight when you run or even somersault, yet give you maximum speed of access.

Police, soldiers, and outdoorsmen have traditionally used flapped pouches to protect the equipment, which is worn exposed, from rain and snow, and from mud when the wearer goes prone out there in the elements. The concealed pouch is protected by the garments over it, and is normally worn behind the hip for concealment, eliminating concerns of mucking it up if one dives to one's belly. Thus, most concealment pouches, like most competition magazine pouches, are open-top.

Worn vertically on the weak-hand side with bullet noses forward is the orientation that the overwhelming majority of experts and shooting champions prefer. This allows the support hand to drop down to the magazine, with the palm touching the floorplate. Thumb and middle finger, the two strongest digits on the hand, grasp the inside and outside surfaces of the magazine respectively, while the index finger takes a position outside the pouch and pointing down. Now, the hand pulls the magazine out and rotates to a palm up position. The magazine is correctly oriented toward the magazine well in the butt of the gun, and the tip of the index finger is under the nose of the topmost cartridge.

Left hand magazine ejection: The trigger finger of a southpaw can probably reach the magazine release button faster than the thumb of most right-handed shooters.

Magazine pouches are available in leather (Bianchi, top right), "plastic" (Safariland, bottom right), and fabric (Bianchi, left).

This allows the index finger to do its job and *index,* literally pointing the fresh magazine into the gun. The reason for the bullet noses being forward in the pouch now becomes apparent: At the moment of insertion, the entire line of the forearm's skeletal support structure is directly aligned with the magazine, virtually guaranteeing a positive, full insertion. A tip: With most pistols and magazines, it will be smoother and faster if you allow the flat back of the magazine to make contact with the flat back of magazine well as the insertion begins.

If the pistol has been shot completely dry, its slide will probably have locked back, and the speed reload or emergency reload must be completed by bringing it back into battery. Instructors seem to split down the middle on this. One camp holds that thumbing the slide lock release lever is the preferred method, since it is much faster and can be done as the support hand is returning to the two-hand firing grasp. This also guarantees that the support hand doesn't "ride" the slide, which could cause a failure of the first round to chamber. The other school of thought

Here is a speed reload of an auto pistol. The support hand goes for the spare magazine as the thumb of firing hand moves to the magazine release button...

...as soon as the hand is on the fresh mag, the depleted one in the gun is ejected...

...and the palm rotates upward as the fresh magazine approaches the butt...

...with the index finger guiding it in as the shooter watches the threat zone...

...the palm drives the magazine firmly home, and the support hand prepares to return to its two-hand grasp position...

...thumbing down the slide stop and chambering a round on the way. The S&W .45 is now reloaded, cocked, and ready to continue firing.

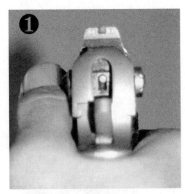

Tactical reload, seen from shooter's eye view. There are some unfired rounds in the gun that you want to save; the double-action S&W is cocked and off safe...

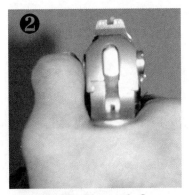

...the first move is to get the finger out of the trigger guard and decock. Note that the lever is down and the hammer is forward. Immediately push the lever back up so you can fire if necessary...

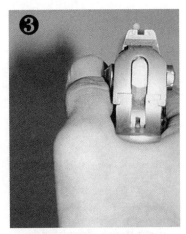

...the spare magazine is brought up to the gun as if for the speed reload...

...but now the fresh magazine goes between the index finger and the middle finger as the hand maneuvers into position...

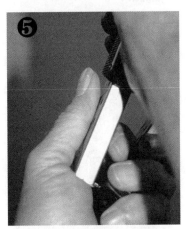

...to catch the spent magazine's floorplate at the base of the thumb, with the thumb and index finger grasping it...

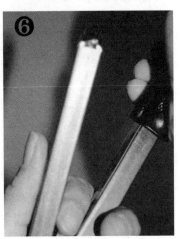

...the spent mag is pulled free and the hand rotates slightly to insert the fresh magazine...

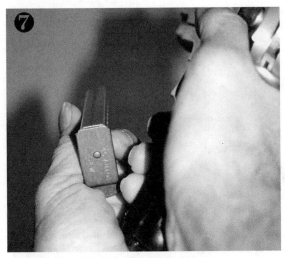

...the palm slaps the fresh magazine home...

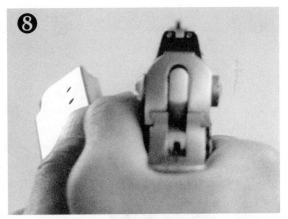

...and, still holding the depleted magazine, the support hand takes a firing hold in case the sound of the reload has brought on a second attack. When all is secure, the free hand will put the spare magazine away.

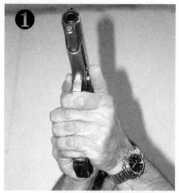

Here's another tactical reload technique the author is fond of. As always, the index finger leaves the trigger guard before anything else. A single-action is put on safe and a double-action is decocked...

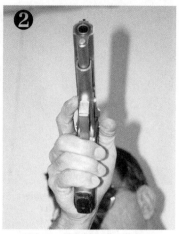

...the support hand drops to grab a fresh mag in the normal fashion...

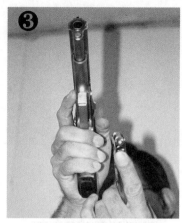

...as the support hand comes up as if to do the speed reload, the hand rotates under the butt as shown...

...the ejected magazine is caught at the heel of the palm. The little finger splays out...

...and the little finger and ring finger are now in position to wrap around the ejecting magazine...

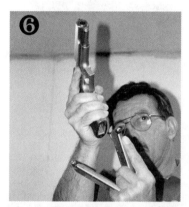

...and pluck it out, holding it in place as the hand rotates the fresh magazine (with ball ammo) up to insert it the same way as in the speed reload...

...slapping the fresh mag into place...

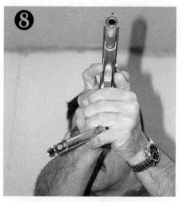

...and the hands resume a very strong firing hold. The magazine held as shown is not in the way. Once it is determined that there is still no further need to fire...

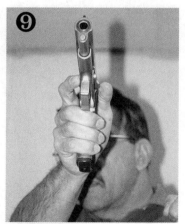

...the S&W 4506 is held on target as the free hand puts the partial magazine away.

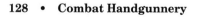

holds that vigorously jerking the slide back and letting it slam forward is more positive and more "do-able" under pressure. Lethal Force Institute injected volunteers with enough epinephrine to equal a "fight or flight" state and then ran them through a double speed combat course in 1998. We saw that simply thumbing the slide release lever was much faster and less fumble prone in the shaking hands of the volunteers.

As noted, the above protocol was the "speed reload," sometimes called an "emergency reload." It is the logical technique to employ when the gun has emptied and there is still immediate shooting to be done. A useful but less necessary, technique is known as the "tactical reload." This maneuver is done when the practitioner believes the shooting is over, or that there is at least the proverbial "lull in the action." It makes sense to use this time to fully reload the pistol in case a need to fire resurfaces, but the shooter does not want to throw away the partial magazine of live ammo still in the pistol.

Every instructor seems to have his own signature method of the tactical reload. Some are dangerously overcomplicated. Let's look at just a couple of techniques that are easy to learn.

International Defensive Pistol Association encourages a technique it calls "reload with retention." This is the simplest to learn. The shooter pulls the partial magazine out of the pistol and places it in a pocket or some other location where it can be quickly recovered on demand. Then the shooter inserts a fresh magazine as outlined above. This is the simplest such technique, and the easiest to learn and teach. However, many tacticians feel the "down-time" is too great. That is, there is too much time in which the pistol can fire only one shot or, if it has a magazine disconnector safety, cannot fire at all.

A method attributed to Clint Smith is almost as easy to learn and results in a fully reloaded pistol much more quickly. Smith reportedly developed it while chief instructor at Gunsite before moving to his own school, Thunder Ranch, and it is still taught at both facilities. It goes like this.

First, remove your finger from the trigger guard. I suggest you also decock or on-safe the pistol, since a tactical reload can be a fumble-prone procedure. Draw the fresh magazine as if you were going to perform a speed reload. As the support hand comes up to the gun, move the full magazine over "one finger." That is, where the index finger was under the bullet nose, the magazine should now be between index and middle fingers. With the now-free index finger and the thumb, pull the partial magazine out of the gun and keep it between those two digits. Rotate the support hand and shove the fresh mag into the pistol, taking care to roll the fingers forward so

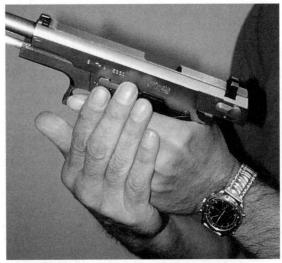

Slide release for southpaws. After the supporting right hand has slapped in the magazine, it is positioned to "spear-hand" up with the fingertips and quickly release the slide stop before sliding back into firing position.

they don't block insertion. You now finish in a good approximation of a two-hand hold, with the partial magazine between the thumb and forefinger of the support hand. Scan your area, put the partial magazine away, and carry on.

Let's discuss a few points on tactical reloads. 1. As noted above, they are difficult to accomplish. 2. In an actual fight, a tactical reload sounds like some poor SOB trying to reload an empty gun. You have just given a wounded rabbit call to the coyotes! This is a high-risk time for a secondary attack, which is why minimized downtime is so important. 3. Be sure the partial magazine is someplace where you'll reach for it under stress if you *do* need it later. If you put the partial in your pocket, spend some practice time retrieving it from the pocket and reloading. Conversely, if you carry only one spare magazine, you can simply put the depleted one in the now-empty pouch. It's where you're used to reaching, and with the one fresh magazine now in the gun, there's nothing for it to get mixed up with.

Fast reloading isn't always needed in actual defensive shootings, but it happens often enough that being able to quickly and positively reload is an important skill. Make sure you've practiced it sufficiently that you can do it in the dark.

Tips For Faster, Smoother Draw

Defensive handgunning isn't all about quick-draw, but that's a definite component. We've all heard the bad joke about the guy who brought a knife to a gunfight. More than one good guy has died because he didn't get his gun to the knife fight in time. The person not readily identifiable to all in sight as a good guy (off duty cop, or armed citizen with carry permit) may not be able to draw his or her weapon in public as soon as a uniformed officer

when the danger is not yet clarified. Thus, drawing quickly is important.

A draw breaks down into two steps: access and presentation. *Access* is actually the hard part. This is where the hand makes its way to the sidearm, takes a firm firing grasp with everything but the trigger finger and, perhaps, the safety-manipulating thumb, and releases all security devices that keep the gun in the

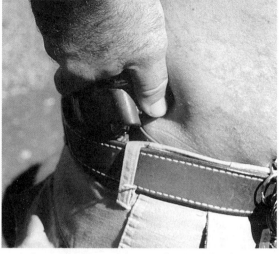

Dennis Luosey demonstrates the Hackathorn Rip, the most effective technique for drawing from a hip holster that is worn under a closed bottom garment. As better seen in close-up...

...the gun hand is executing a perfect thumb-break movement with the safety strap version of the classic Bianchi #3 Pistol Pocket inside-the-waistband holster designed by Richard Nichols. The revolver is a 3-inch S&W Model 65.

holster. *Presentation,* by contrast, is a simple gross motor skill. This is where the already-grasping hand pulls the gun from the holster and brings it into line with the target or the threat.

Ray Chapman, the first world champion of the combat pistol, was an engineer in his first career and a master small arms instructor in his second. He brought his engineering mindset to both careers, and his ability to analyze things was what made him such a great teacher. Chapman said, *"Smoothness is five-sixths of speed."* I first heard him say that in 1979, and nothing I've seen since has caused me to question the validity of his advice. Go for smoothness, and the speed will take care of itself. Go for speed, and all you're likely to get is a faster foul-up.

Let's go through each type of draw, step by step.

Strong-side Hip

Access. You always want to be prepared to make the draw from concealment. Assuming that the concealing garment is an open-front jacket, begin by letting all four fingertips of the dominant hand touch your abdomen at midline. Now immediately sweep the hand back to the gun. The fingers will automatically brush the coat back without you having to think about a separate movement.

The hand immediately falls to the gun in a firing grasp with all but the trigger finger, which should be kept clear of the trigger guard area. The web of the hand should be pressing firmly into the grip tang of an auto pistol, or located high on the backstrap of the revolver's frame. The thumb now presses straight in toward the body to release the safety strap if one is present.

When the gun is under a closed-bottom garment, you may not have both hands to do a Hackathorn Rip. In that case, the author recommends...

...this one-handed draw. The author's thumb is pointed inward, tracking up the peroneal nerve and lifting the shirt hem to allow the left-handed draw of a baby Glock .40.

A straight draw from the hip with an open-front concealment garment...

...begins as four fingertips of the drawing hand touch the centerline of the body. As the hand tracks to the gun, the coat will automatically clear. Meanwhile, with fingers pointed forward for better self-defense ability, the heel of support hand also touches the centerline of the body...

...the firing hand takes a high grip, with the thumb breaking the safety strap, and all fingers but the index taking a firm hold on the handgun...

...the pistol is cleared with this "rock and lock" motion...

...and the support hand comes in from the side and behind the muzzle to meet the firing hand. Note that the trigger finger has at no point entered the trigger guard...

...and the shooter flows into the preferred firing stance. If the need to fire is present, it is now that trigger the finger enters the guard, as shown.

Access is the tough part. Six-time national champ Bob Houzenga has achieved that and is halfway through presentation when he pauses at low ready, awaiting the signal of the author's PACT timer...

...and when it comes, completion of the presentation and the first shot with a Glock 23 are almost instantaneous.

During this, the support hand has been brought in to the centerline of the body at about solar plexus level. If the inside of the wrist touches the body and the fingertips point straight ahead of you, you're in the strongest and safest possible position. 1.) That hand is poised to fight off a close-range physical assault or a felon's grab for the gun. 2.) That hand now will not be crossed by the gun as it is drawn. 3.) The support hand is in place to most efficiently join its mate in a two-hand hold as the draw continues.

Presentation. Lever back on the gun butt and bring the muzzle up level with the downrange target or threat as soon as it clears leather. This movement, called a "rock and lock," allows you to most quickly engage a fast-closing threat if necessary. Thrust the pistol straight forward to the target, letting it come up to line of sight naturally. *After the muzzle has safely passed the support hand,* it (the support hand) thrusts forward and takes its position to complete the two-hand hold.

As you draw, *be sure to keep your elbow straight back!* This creates the strongest alignment of the arm's skeleto-muscular support structure, giving you more leverage and thus more speed, strength, and efficiency. It is doubly essential with "directional draw" security holsters.

If the concealing garment has a closed bottom, like a sweatshirt or pullover sweater, an alteration is needed. Ken Hackathorn developed the most efficient draw for use with this garment. For what is called a "Hackathorn Rip," the right-handed shooter uses the left hand to grab the bottom edge of the garment at about appendix level, and jerk it upward to the shoulder. This pulls it clear and allows the gun hand to draw as above. The garment may not have enough stretch to reach the shoulder, but if you try for the shoulder you should at least get it up high enough to allow the gun to clear. It's kind of like, "If you aim for the stars, you at least hit the moon."

In case the support hand is needed to fend off a contact-distance assault, you also want to practice a one-handed version. Let the thumb of the gun hand point toward your body and track upward, on a line level with the trouser seam or the common peroneal nerve of the leg.

This will catch the hem of the waist-length closed-bottom garment and lift it enough to let the hand reach the gun. Throw your hips straight to the side away from the gun; that is, to the left if you are right-handed. This will give you more range of movement to complete the draw.

Crossdraw

The across-the-body-draw is not efficient if done facing the threat squarely. Crossdraw holsters are banned from most ranges and many police departments because of their tendency to cause the muzzle of the loaded gun to cross a shooter standing beside the practitioner on the firing range. A crossdraw can also be very easily blocked

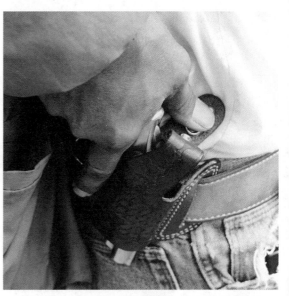

A thumb break holster is useful for gun retention, and takes almost no additional time to release if done properly. Here the author draws a short-barrel Ruger .357 from a Bianchi Black Widow belt holster.

A crossdraw from a belt holster begins...

at contact distance. Finally, with the butt forward, if you stand square to the opponent it is easier for him to reach and draw from your holster than it is for you.

So, before the draw begins, turn your body edgeways so the holstered gun is toward the threat. Make sure your arm on the holster side is up out of the way where the gun muzzle won't cross it.

Access. Point all fingers straight, like a martial artist's "spear hand," and keeping the palm close to your torso, knife the hand in to the gun. This will help you reach through partially closed coat fronts, a situation where a crossdraw can be advantageous to the wearer. Take a firm grip and release the safety strap as with the hip draw, above.

...with a step-back of the gun side leg to blade the holster side of the body. Simultaneously, the free arm rises in a blocking position, for protection against close-range assault and to clear it from the path of the muzzle, as the firing hand knifes through the opening in the garment to grasp the holstered gun...

...the draw path is straight back instead of a crossways sweep, putting the muzzle on target almost immediately...

...as the pistol is thrust forward toward the threat (note that the finger is still away from the trigger) and the support hand moves in from above and behind muzzle...

...and the two-hand hold is achieved and the shot can be fired at this point, as indicated by the finger on the trigger of this S&W 4506. The classic Weaver stance shown lends itself to crossdraw work.

Presentation. Again rock the butt back and the muzzle up as it clears the holster; if you are standing edgeways, the gun is now immediately pointed at the threat and can be fired from here if necessary. Now thrust the gun forward toward the target, letting the gun rise to eye level if possible. After the muzzle has passed it, the support hand takes its position for a two-hand hold. This gets the gun on target much faster than a swing across, which would have been necessary, had you not bladed your body.

Shoulder Holster

Drawing from a shoulder holster is much like executing a crossdraw, but with a slight variation. Because the gun is higher in relation to the arm, and literally located under the armpit, it is important to take extra measures to make sure you don't cross your own support arm with the gun muzzle.

Access: As with the crossdraw, blade the body with the holster side toward the threat. *Raise the support arm sharply until the elbow is shoulder high and pointed toward the threat.* It also creates a simple and extremely effective block to a punch or bludgeon attack, developed decades ago by police martial artist Kerry Najiola. Let the drawing hand "knife" in to the gun's gripframe through the garments as with a crossdraw. Take a firm grasp and release the safety strap, as above.

Presentation: As with the crossdraw, bring the gun out and back across your chest so it is immediately pointed at the threat. Now thrust it forward toward the threat, bringing the gun to the line of sight if possible. The support hand comes to the firing hand from above and behind to safely take a two-hand hold. Note: With the crossdraw hip holster or the shoulder holster, it will

generally be fastest to draw to a Weaver or Modified Weaver/Chapman stance, since the body is already pre-bladed for that position.

Safety point: When reholstering, you may have to turn your body with your back to the target to keep the gun downrange, particularly if the shoulder holster is the horizontal or upside-down type.

Small of the Back Holster

In essence, this is same as strong-side hip. Be aware of the following, however.

Many SOB holsters rake so sharply that a draw crosses a practitioner standing next to you on your weak hand side at the firing line. It may also cross a range officer behind you. The same can happen upon reholstering. This, and reasons cited in the chapter discussing that holster, explains why so few professionals choose this mode of carry.

Belly Band Holster

In the usual front crossdraw position, draw as if with a crossdraw holster at the same point on the belt. If the gun is carried on the strong hand side, use strong-side hip draw techniques as above, with Hackathorn Rip.

Pocket Holster

Use a "spear hand" to get into the pocket. Since locking the thumb in a firm firing grasp creates a fist that can snag coming back out of the pocket, place your thumb on the back of the hammer or slide. This narrows the profile of the hand, and causes the thumb to act as a "human hammer shroud," thus minimizing snag potential in two ways. Otherwise, this is the same as strong side hip holster draw.

You play like you practice. Bill Fish demonstrates his practiced draw of the Glock 19 he usually carries. Note the support hand coming in from behind the muzzle of the gun...

...and he does it the same way under pressure at an IDPA match with his Glock 34, showing the value of getting the core movements down!

1 A shoulder holster lends itself to use with heavy winter clothing. The shoulder draw begins…

2 …with backward step of the strong-side leg to quarter properly. The free hand rises in a blocking position as the gun hand "spears" through the opening in the coat to the grip-frame of the holstered weapon…

3 …as the gun hand draws the pistol straight across the chest, the support arm has already risen to the "Najiola block" position. This not only protects the head from close-range assault, but clears the upper arm from the path of the muzzle during the draw…

4 …ote that the muzzle is pointed toward the threat even before the heavy coat is cleared…

5 …once cleared, the gun thrusts forward toward the threat as the support hand begins to drop down…

6 …and the firing hold is achieved. The classic Weaver stance as depicted works particularly well with a shoulder holster draw.

The ankle holster is particularly easy to draw from when supine...in a relaxed position like this, or knocked down on your back in a fight.

Ankle Holster

There have been many techniques taught for this the most difficult to reach of holsters. Some look like the strange mating dances of demented storks. The following technique was developed at Lethal Force Institute and is the fastest we've seen.

Access. Plant the leg to which the handgun is strapped. Use the support hand to grab a fistful of trouser material above the knee, and pull it sharply upward. Step

widely outward with the free leg, and perhaps also back. (The gun-side leg is stationary; you don't want to move the gun away from the reaching hand.)

Rather than bending at the waist, bend sharply at the knees so you can watch what is going on in front of you. With the dominant hand, grab the gun's grip-frame in a proper firing grasp as above and release the holding strap if necessary.

The author demonstrates the high-speed/high-mobility ankle holster draw he developed at LFI. The first move is for the weak hand to grab the weak-side trouser leg and pull up. The non-holster leg takes a deep step back, and the pelvis drops as the gun hand begins the reach...

...which allows a fast draw as the S&W Model 442 clears the Alessi ankle rig. The support hand is now free to move to a two-hand hold...

...and the shooter can either fire from a low cover crouch as shown, or rise to a preferred firing stance if time allows.

The author begins the draw of a backup gun with his weak hand. Note that the index finger is straight and clear of the trigger guard, and the thumb is over the hammer area to lower the profile of the hand for a more snag-free draw...

...and the shooter can finish with a one-handed or two-handed firing posture.

Presentation. Rock the muzzle forward as soon as it clears and thrust the gun toward the target. Support hand can come in for a two-hand hold at this point. You may fire immediately from this deep crouch, or if time permits, rise to your preferred stance.

Option: If you are down on your back, orient yourself so the sole of your holster-side foot is toward the target or opponent. Snap the ankle up toward the reaching gun hand and take firing hold, releasing the strap if necessary. As the gun is pulled, stomp the foot forward and *down* to clear it from your line of fire as you prepare to shoot from the supine position, one- or two-handed.

Fanny Pack

If the fanny pack is worn toward the strong-side hip, use a strong-side draw. If the pack is worn at the front of the torso or toward the opposite hip, use a crossdraw. The support hand may be needed to open the fanny pack. If so, practice intensively ripping it open and then getting that hand immediately out of the way so you won't cross it with your own gun. Spend half your practice time with the support hand in a position to fend off the attack, using the gun hand to both open the pouch and make the draw.

Off Body Carry

Carry the purse, briefcase or whatever in the non-dominant hand or slung from the weak-side shoulder. When the time comes, swing the whole thing to body center, blading your body so that your weak side is toward the threat. Now draw as if from a crossdraw holster, keeping the muzzle downrange. With some guns, this will allow you to fire through the container if necessary, and with all handguns should allow you to get one shot off. Hold the container with the hand high to minimize crossing that hand with the gun muzzle. You can now drop the container and go to your preferred two-hand hold. If the container includes a panel that can stop bullets, press it flat to your torso with the weak hand and pivot at the hips so that it is squarely between you and the incoming fire as you prepare to shoot back one-handed.

Final Advice

A combat *match* shooter may spend 100 percent of drawing practice time on the draw to the shot, automatically finishing each presentation with a pull of the trigger. The real world defensive gun carrier can't do that. It conditions you to fire every time you draw, and history shows that "we play like we practice." Most of the time, police and armed citizens alike do not have to fire the guns they draw to ward off a criminal threat.

If it turns out that you do need to immediately fire as soon as you draw, you'll know it. There should be no perceptible loss of speed. As a general rule, those who carry guns "for real" probably should make at least 90 percent of their drawing practice a draw to "gunpoint," not a draw to the shot.

As in all dry fire practice, make sure the gun is always oriented toward something that can safely stop the most potent round the gun is capable of discharging. A "dummy gun" of similar weight to the real one is an excellent practice tool for this.

In regular dry fire, our watching of the sights will tell us if we had the trigger press down pat or not. A draw is more complicated. If you can't do it with a friend to critique each other, take a video camera to the practice session and set it up on a tripod, and critically review your performance on tape later. Finally, while practicing in front of a mirror is over-rated in terms of most types of firearms training, it is an excellent way to learn smoothness and economy of movement as you drill on access and presentation.

Since The Last Edition...

Holsters have been around for a long time, and are largely mature technology. Thus, we don't see great leaps in five-year increments.

In the intervening half-decade since the last GUN DIGEST BOOK OF COMBAT HANDGUNNERY, holster makers were reminded that safety straps needed to be wider than trigger guards. Otherwise, the strap gets caught inside the guard during holstering and snags on the trigger. Trigger now stops, gun keeps going, and wearer shoots self. It happened several times, precipitating callbacks on two well-known brands.

In one highly publicized case that could have happened with *any* holster that had a covered trigger guard, a peace officer got the drawstring of his windbreaker lodged inside the trigger guard of his Glock 40 S&W as he holstered. When he went to take things off, the pistol discharged, wounding him. Nature may be telling us all to remove the drawstrings from windbreakers, sweatshirts and other such gun-concealing garments.

Kydex continues to rule, but it's not the only useful synthetic holster material out there. Using its own blend, Blackhawk products created their CQC holster line with a "carbon fiber" motif. These quickly proved popular among IDPA shooters and concealed carriers. The big hit was Blackhawk's revolutionary SERPA holster. Concealable, with every model sold with both belt slot attachments and a removable paddle device, these rigs have a low-profile paddle on the *outside* of the holster, which is hit by a straight trigger finger during the draw, and which – with a little practice – releases the pistol effortlessly. Without the paddle being depressed, the gun is locked in place by a hidden component that secures on the inside front edge of the trigger guard.

The SERPA became a huge success, particularly among plainclothes cops, though I've seen quite a few of them among armed citizens, too … proof that there are folks out there who realize it's not just uniformed cops in Sam

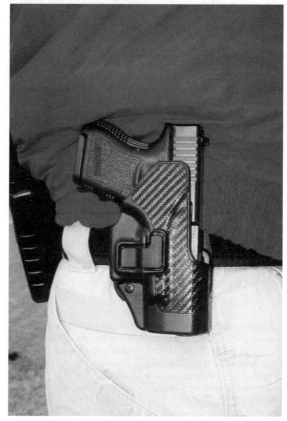

SERPA holster is big news in last few years. This one holds a Glock 39 on the belt of a Georgia State Patrol sergeant in plainclothes.

This Kydex holster from Blade-Tech is concealable, and carries author's Glock with heavy duty InSight M3X tactical light already mounted.

Springfield Armory's plastic XD Gear holster has quick release rail attached for carrying tactical light unit, in this case a Streamlight TLR-2 combined white light and laser. It will attach to the rail on the frame, visible on this Springfield Armory XD45ACP Compact.

Bianchi Carry-Lok, shown here (with full-size Glock) *in the variation that snaps onto belt, gives automatic locking upon holstering, has a hidden weapon retention feature that is easy for the user to manipulate — and is still made in traditional high-quality leather. Photo courtesy Bianchi.*

Not a security holster, but very fast and adequately concealable, Blackhawk CQC is becoming quite popular in IDPA circles. Pistol is Springfield Armory XD45ACP Service model.

Browne belts with guns hanging out who have to worry about weapon snatches. This is particularly important with renewed private citizen interest in open carry of handguns in public. Meanwhile, the SERPA has morphed into a popular thigh holster for military and tactical officers, and a new Level II police uniform scabbard.

Bianchi's Carry-Lok series is also proving popular as a fast-draw, concealable holster with a hidden retention device, for those who prefer leather. Another advantage in both the Bianchi and the Blackhawk approaches is that these holsters secure the gun automatically; self-locking when the handgun is inserted, without requiring a separate movement to fasten a safety strap.

Another trend has developed in the past five years: carrying pistols with flashlight units already attached. First the province of SWAT cops and K9 officers, this quickly spread to police patrol units, and even to concealable holsters for guns so equipped. Blade-Tech is one maker that produces concealed-carry holsters for flashlight-mounted guns in both outside and inside-the-waistband variations.

CHAPTER NINE

Close Quarters Battle

Conventional CQB Techniques

Most gunfights don't occur in the middle of Main Street at high noon. Most gunfights take place with the participants within 7 yards of each other, and the majority of *those* are at more like 7 feet. The conventional response has always been to shoot from the hip or some other position below line of sight that hopefully keeps your weapon out of the close-range attacker's reach. There is good news and bad news with this. Good news: for a brief moment, at least, you've kept your firearm beyond the attacker's grasp. Bad news: if you can't see to aim, you probably won't hit what you want to hit.

Close quarters combat shooting is often taught like this. However, there is a possibility that at this angle, the heavy winter coat could block the auto pistol's slide.

Consider this real-world case in point, from the book "A Cold Case" in which author Philip Gourevitch shares the recollection of a New York City beat cop who had to kill a criminal named Sudia. For our purposes we'll call this brave lawman "Officer 1."

"Officer 1" told Gourevitch, "They were heroin addicts, and deserters from the Marine Corps, and they'd got in a shooting in the Hotel Whitehall on 100th Street and Broadway. I didn't know it. I was standing down on Riverside drive, a new cop, on what they call a fixer. That's a fixed post. You have to stand there. This was December, a cold December night, and for some reason they decided to run toward me. I could hear them running down the street. There was no one else around from West End Avenue to the Drive, just a lot of doctors' cars. I figured they'd broke into a car, no big deal. So when they got abreast of me, I stepped out and had my arms out with my nightstick. Sudia put a pistol to my head and said, 'You c---sucker, hand me your gun, or I'll kill you.' So – I'm not sure of this exchange, but I'm pretty sure – I said, 'OK, OK.' And I went into my coat. We had big heavy coats that you're too young to have seen. They wrapped around you. Terrible heavy coats. If you could stand up in them all night, you were lucky to walk home. Anyway, when I cleared the holster, I fired through my coat. I shot at him six times. You know how many times I hit him? Twice. Once in the heart – he had a tattoo of a heart on his heart – and once in the knee. The others passed through his clothing, and our noses were touching, so I guess I was frightened. He was dead by the time his head was by my knees."[1]

This account is worth some time to digest for all its learning points. First, we are dealing with one *very* lucky police officer. Even being so close to his attacker "our noses were touching," only two out of six shots actually took flesh, striking 3 feet apart on the offender's body. Only one of those hits was really dynamic, the heart shot, unless the knee hit came first and buckled the would-be cop-killer's body down into the path of the gun to allow for the cardiac shot.

Let's contrast that with a shooting some years later involving another NYPD officer. We'll call him "Officer 2." He was off duty in a subway car, also in the winter, with his 4-inch Model 10 .38 under his suit coat and overcoat and his 2-inch Colt Detective Special .38 in his right hand coat pocket. Suddenly, two men sat down on either side of

---

[1]·Gourevitch, Philip, "A Cold Case," New York: Farrar, Straus and Giroux, 2001, pp. 16-17.

him. The one on the right pulled a knife, and the one on the left drew a Sterling semiautomatic pistol and placed the loaded gun to the officer's head, demanding his wallet.

Like Officer 1, Officer 2 feigned compliance, reaching with his right hand into the coat pocket as if for a billfold. Then, in a single fast move, he brought up his left hand and slapped the gun away from his head, his palm staying in contact with the attacker's wrist and the back of his gun hand to keep the weapon diverted. At the same time, he swung the snub-nose .38 up with his right hand until he could see it in peripheral vision and fired one shot into the gunman's brain, killing him instantly. He spun to engage the armed felon on his right, who leaped away. The pair had timed the robbery just before a stop to facilitate escape, and the second offender was able to run through the opening door and escape into the crowd. He was subsequently captured and sent to prison.

In both cases, the officers had loaded guns held to their heads. Both exhibited great valor and tenacity, and both prevailed and emerged unhurt. Clearly, though, if we are going to emulate one or the other, the second is the role model. The first officer fired six shots with one immediately stopping hit and one wounding hit, a 33 percent hit delivery and 16.7 percent delivery of "stopping hits." The second officer delivered 100 percent on both counts.

He did two things differently than the first officer. For one thing, *Officer 2 waited the tiniest fraction of an instant until he could see his gun in peripheral vision, to target*

the shot, before he fired. Investigators were impressed to note that the single .38 Special bullet had struck the gunman squarely between the eyes. Perhaps more importantly, *he diverted the suspect's weapon before he did anything else.*

We need to remember our priorities. Shooting the attacker is not the object of the exercise. Not getting shot is the object of the exercise. Shooting the attacker is certainly one legitimate way of accomplishing it, but if we get the goals confused, we do so at our peril. With the assailant's weapon unrestrained in the first case, the officer had to fire blindly and desperately, and was lucky to score the hit that saved his life. With the weapon at least momentarily diverted from him, the second officer was able to take the tiny extra fraction of a second to put the first shot where it would immediately end the deadly threat to him.

Analyzing Conventional Techniques

We are taught that all we have to do to hit something with a gun is point it as we would point our finger. The problem is, the gun does not always point in the direction of your finger. When the gun is pulled back, away from the attacker, our gun naturally points low.

This is a critical problem with "hip-shooting," either Bill Jordan-style or with the technique called the "speed-rock." Bill Jordan was my friend and one of my mentors. I witnessed his awesome display of point shooting skill in which, from the hip, he shot aspirin tablets at a range of

With the gun hand rotated out 45 degrees the slide will be clear of body and clothing, and Kimber .45's muzzle will be angled in more to the center of your opponent's body.

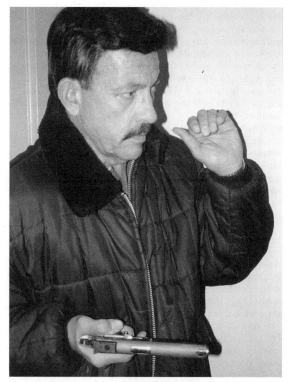

This sometimes-taught technique angles shots inward to the opponent's center, but takes shooter's wrist to the end of its range of movement and leaves him vulnerable to being disarmed.

10 feet with wax bullets! Interestingly, the targets were mounted somewhat low.

Look at pictures of Bill shooting. You'll find them in his classic, must-read 1966 book "No Second Place Winner," now published by Police Bookshelf, PO Box 122, Concord, NH 03302. You'll see that his revolver barrel appears to be angling downward. In the book, he also makes reference to the effectiveness of "a bullet judiciously applied to the region of the belt buckle." He later confirmed to me that this was his point of aim for gunfighting. "Seems to hit a man like a solar plexus punch," he drawled. Now, you have to remember that Bill Jordan was a long drink of water who stood about 6 feet, 7 inches tall.

Put that all together. Bill is taller than his opponent. His gun arm is pointing downward enough to strike the shorter opponent at waist level. You and I are the same height as our assailant, or perhaps our attacker is taller. Our gun is angling in the same downward direction. We're likely to deliver a leg shot, not a fight-stopping hit.

The fast draw artists of the 1950s, who learned to compensate for it by rocking their upper bodies backward at the hips to bring the gun more level, noted this tendency to shoot low. The problem is, rocking back hyper-extends the back and takes the shooter completely off balance. If there is still aggressive forward movement by the opponent – even if he falls into us – he's going to plow right into our off-balance bodies and take us to the ground with him. And he'll be on top, pinning us under his weight. Not good.

Does this mean you shouldn't get some practice shooting from the hip or using the speed rock technique? No. If the attacker has you backed up against a wall with his forearm across your throat, hip-shooting may be the only option you have left. If he has you bent back over the hood of an automobile, he has already put you into a speed rock. Either of these techniques will work well for a cop making a traffic stop on a typical passenger sedan, because the seated driver is now right in line with the cop's duty gun belt and the hip shot or the speed rock will be most effective.

When practicing either technique, get up close and personal with a cardboard silhouette target in a soft wooden frame. Don't use a steel target frame. Until you have it down pat, you can wind up like that first New York cop and put some of the shots wide even at the closest range. If the lead bullet strikes the steel frame it's going to send some vicious particles your way, enough to cause penetrating gunshot-like injury.

Here's a tip for handgunners in general and auto pistol shooters in particular: you might want to rotate your gun hand about 45 degrees to the outside when doing this. We tend to practice on sunny days in T-shirts, but may have to fire on a cold, rainy night when we're wearing a billowing raincoat. If the auto pistol is oriented straight up, the slide may foul on the garment and jam the pistol. A very overweight male or large-busted female can stop the slide's mechanism against his or her own body. The outward rotation of the pistol prevents these mishaps, because the slide now clears both body and loose garments.

The outward rotation has another advantage. If you are face-to-face, squared off with one another, and you're right-handed, a shot from the hip with the gun straight up will strike the far left side of your opponent's torso. You don't want to hit the love handles; you want to put the

The gun is angled the wrong way here, and highly likely to jam when the slide is fouled in a coat or blocked by the body after first shot.

bullet in the boiler room. The outboard rotation angles the muzzle proportionally inward, and within arm's length is more likely to put your shot in the middle of his torso, at least in terms of windage if not elevation.

Don't go overboard with the angle. I have to disagree with those who teach rotating the gun all the way over on its side, i.e., so the right side of the slide is toward the ground in a right-handed man's grasp. This brings the gun hand's wrist to the very end of its range of movement, and weakens the joint against upward pressure. If the opponent tries to shove your gun up away from him, it will point right up into your face. With the wrist at a 45-degree angle, you'll have a much stronger lock and a better chance of resisting that ploy.

The Step-Back

It is widely taught that you should step back, possibly striking your opponent first, then draw your gun and come up to an extended-arms stance and shoot. This works much better on still targets than on moving attackers. Another school of thought holds that you should back-pedal, firing as you go.

The problem here is that in the real world, dealing with a living, thinking, reacting, and homicidal human aggressor, *you can't back up faster than the aggressor can move forward.* The human body isn't built to move rearward as effectively as it moves forward.

Excellent videotape exists graphically proving this point. Offered by Paladin Press, it was put together by a friend and graduate of mine who is an accomplished police trainer, named Ralph Mroz. In live action sequences using non-lethal guns, Ralph vividly shows how quickly you can be overrun by an aggressive man with knife or club when you try hip-shots, speed-rocks, step-backs, and shooting while backing up.

Ralph found only one technique that worked, the same CQB principle that we've taught for years at Lethal Force Institute. It's a parrying movement off mid-line that "changes the structure of the game." We'll look at that principle next.

Advanced Techniques

In the early 1990s, I met Reynaldo Jaylo at an American Society of Law Enforcement Trainers seminar. Rey has been involved in more than two dozen shootings. The Manila newspaper at the time credited him with killing some 23 criminals in gunfights, most of them at point-blank range. Working in the Philippines for their equivalent of FBI, he was a very senior commander who "led from the front." Many of his

The LFI circling parry is demonstrated. Snow falls as the officer, at 6 o'clock, confronts a suspect at 12 o'clock, who suddenly produces a weapon. With the gun side hip back, the suspect is out of reach of a smothering disarm...

...and the officer's right hand goes to rear of shoulder joint on the non-gun side. The suspect is simultaneously spun toward the gun side as the officer takes a deep step behind him. The object of the combined movements is to get the good guy behind bad guy so the bad guy, at least for a moment, will have to shoot through his own body to hit the good guy...

...The officer's left hand now takes control of the shoulder, "monitoring" movement and helping to keep himself behind bad guy, as the officer's right hand draws the service pistol...

...and parity has now been restored. If the suspect does not immediately drop the gun, officer is justifiable in firing because in a fraction of a second, suspect's gun can again be pointed at the officer.

Note how the bladed hand strikes exactly at the point where the arm meets body, from the rear. This seems to be a high-leverage "pivot point" for moving a resistive adult's torso.

shootings had occurred at arm's length distances during drug buys.

I asked him what technique he used. "Point shooting," he replied. I asked him to demonstrate. I used a Spyderco Police knife as Rey demonstrated with my carefully unloaded Colt .45 auto. As I moved toward him, he parried to my weak hand side, brought his weapon to eye level at arm's length, and instantly "fired" directly into my chest. I observed that he lowered his head in line with the gunsights as if to verify a sight picture.

Rey Jaylo confirmed that this was exactly what he was doing, and this was what he meant by point shooting. He explained that this close, if you didn't get the other man

dead center immediately and shut him off, he was certain to kill you.

This is unarguable logic, and Reynaldo Jaylo is living proof that it works. It was absolute validation of what many others and I had been teaching along that line.

At close range, it's not a shooting contest; it's a fight. Specifically, it is a gunfight at knife-fighting range. This means it's not so much a shooting thing as a martial arts thing, and the martial arts are where you have to look to find the answer.

No practitioner of any martial art will tell you to lean back off balance to escape your attacker, nor to try to back-pedal from him. As the opponent is seen to commit to a line of force – whether he's projecting it with his fist or the muzzle of a gun – the only proven counter is *lateral movement away from the midline of the attack.* If you are on the antagonist's weapon-hand side, as with Officer 2 in the previous chapter, logic says that you should strike the weapon hand aside. If his weapon hand is out of reach, as mine was when Rey Jaylo demonstrated, then you should move in a circular pattern around his non-weapon side, toward his rear. In a fistfight, this would put you beyond the range of that fist. In a knife fight, it would put you for a moment beyond the blade's effective field of action, a knife fighter's term for what a boxer calls reach. If the opponent has a gun, you have for this instant made him unable to shoot into the center of your body without hitting the edge of his own. This is what buys you time to draw, index your weapon, and make the hit that stops the fight.

Action/Reaction Paradigms

Keys to understanding the reality of such encounters are the action/reaction principles. Principle I: **Action**

When you and your opponent have opposite hand dominance, the circling parry is done thus. Mark Maynard (right, in attacker role) uses his left hand to draw first on defender Mike Briggs...

Briggs uses his left hand at the rear joint of Maynard's non-gun-side shoulder to turn him as he simultaneously steps to the "safe side" and draws...

...and is able to perform a head shot barely ahead of opponent's ability to stay on target. Rationale of the shot to the head is the instant cessation of action, and best guarantee that the defender doesn't shoot his hand in the real-world swirl of violent movement. Note that the control hand remains at shoulder.

beats reaction. If the two of you are very close together and he moves first, he will complete his move before you can react to evade what he's sending your way. This works even if he is less skilled than you, less swift than you, and armed with a less suitable weapon. This is why master combat firearms instructor Clint Smith makes the point we'll call, for the moment, Principle II: **Proximity negates skill.**

If proximity negates our superior skill, we need to negate the proximity to restore dominance. We need to create **reactionary gap.** Space buys time, and time allows us to react and stop the threat. Thus, Principle III: **Time and distance favor the trained defender.**

Plan A for applying this, of course, is never allowing the belly-to-belly confrontation in the first place. A police officer has to get close to a suspect; how else can he handcuff and search him? The alert citizen can more easily see danger signs and evade such close-quarters traps, in most cases.

That alertness is the key. The mightiest air armada is useless if it has no radar to alert it to the approach of enemy bombers that can destroy it on the ground. The radar is useless if no one monitors it for warning signals. The warning signals are useless if no one on the ground responds to the alert of impending danger. So it is in individual conflict. This is why most training programs in this discipline follow Jeff Cooper's "color code" principles. Cooper used four different color codes; some of us use five.

Condition White is unprepared. If you are caught off guard, you are likely to be too far behind the power curve to ever catch up in time.

Condition Yellow means relaxed alertness. You're not checking around corners with a periscope, but you make a point of knowing where you are and who's around you. At any given time, you could close your eyes and point out lanes of access or egress, and objects nearby that could be used for cover. You don't have to be armed to be in "yellow," but if you are armed that should certainly be your mental status.

Condition Orange means an unspecified alert. Something is wrong, but all the details aren't confirmed yet. You now focus acutely on sensory input and other intelligence that will help you determine what is going on.

Condition Red is, in essence, an armed encounter. The threat is identified, and dangerous enough for you to draw your weapon and take the suspect(s) at gunpoint.

Condition Black means the presence of maximum danger, as on the pigment color scale black is the presence of all colors. This means that you are under lethal assault. At this point, your response is to unleash the deadly force you held at bay in the gunpoint situation, and return fire.

Alas, not every human being can maintain a perfect and continuous alertness scan. If the Plan A of seeing the danger in time to avoid or outflank it doesn't work, and we're trapped in that unforgiving arm's length range of deadly danger that instructors have come to call "the hole," we need a Plan B. The studies of Ralph Mroz mentioned in the previous chapter, centuries of martial arts experience, and simple common sense tell us that Plan B is to move quickly off the line of attack, if possible parrying or controlling the opponent's weapon, as we counterattack with an encircling motion.

Training Problems

Why are these principles not taught more? They take some time, they don't lend themselves to mass practice like square range shooting drills, and they are not particularly fun.

Shooting is fun. Even shooting while moving backward can be fun, if it is done safely under careful supervision. The circling parry movement and similar drills require you and a practice partner to be grabbing arms and slapping shoulders, and that starts to hurt. If you're not into martial arts, this action soon ceases to be fun.

Shooting from the hip or while moving backward or whatever can be done en masse. A circling parry, which can be as much as 180 degrees of movement, is all but impossible to arrange on a firing line with more than one shooter and one coach. It is not time and cost effective for large training groups. It should only be done with people who already have a very strong grounding in firearms safety, quick presentation of the firearm, and decisive confidence in their shooting skills. At our school, we don't get into circling parries and similar CQB drills until the second level of training.

This training should be done primarily with dummy guns and live partners, in a gym or dojo environment. It can be done that way 100 percent. On the range, some of these techniques will end up with muzzle contact shots, which quickly tear apart paper or cardboard targets, and muzzle contact shooting will swiftly ruin expensive three-dimensional targets.

Nonetheless, these techniques are your most certain route to survival of an aggressive, real-world lethal force assault that begins at arm's length.

We must heed the warning of Abraham Maslow: when the only tool we have is a hammer, every problem begins to look like a nail. We are conditioned that if the opponent has a deadly weapon, we must respond with a deadly weapon. That is often the case. It is the case more often than not when some significant distance separates the parties at the moment of truth. But there are times at very close range when, even if you are armed with the best fighting handgun and are extremely skilled with it, there might be a better option for you than to draw and fire. We'll examine that option in the next chapter.

Always use dummy guns in this type of training! *Left, an actual Smith & Wesson .40 caliber Sigma SW40F. Right, an identical copy rendered in "dead metal" by Odin Press.*

Close Quarters Battle

Disarming

One more time, is the object to shoot the other guy, or is it to not get shot? Correct, it is the latter! With that in mind, continuing at the distance my friend Cliff Stewart, the master bodyguard and martial artist calls WAR (Within Arm's Reach), let's look at a non-shooting option.

You are facing the other person a yard away. He goes for his gun. You go for yours. You are good at this: you can react, draw from concealment, and get off a shot in 1.5 seconds. Hell, let's say you're *extremely* good at this and can do it in a second, flat.

You're still behind the curve. The best you can hope to do, realistically, is shoot him just before he shoots you, or shoot each other simultaneously. Only if your bullet has hit upper spinal cord or brain will you be certain of interdicting the message his brain has already sent to his trigger finger, and then only if you fired first.

He is already past the apex of the power curve by the time you can react. His hand is already on his gun, completing the tough part of the draw, the access. Now all he has left to do is the simple gross motor skill part, the ripping the gun up, shoving it toward you, and jerking the trigger. Even if he's a bozo with a stolen gun he has never fired before, he can do this in half to three-quarters of a second. You are so close you have to assume you'll take a hit. Remember what Clint Smith said in the last section: "proximity negates skill."

Even with your one-second draw and lightning reflexes, there is an excellent chance that his shot will go off a quarter-second ahead of yours. Have there been men who could "beat the drop," and outdraw even a drawn gun? It has happened in the field. Post-fight analysis usually indicates that the man who started with the drawn gun didn't think his opponent would be crazy enough to resist, and when he did, was so surprised that

he had a long reactionary gap. The person who outdrew that drawn gun got inside that gap.

However, this is not an overconfident schmuck holding you at gunpoint and making demands. He's an angry homicidal criminal, trying to draw a gun and shoot you as fast as he can, and his attempt to do so is already underway. That's why you're behind the curve.

A handful of human beings have been fast enough to react and shoot first even in this situation. The late Bill Jordan is on film reacting to a visual start signal and

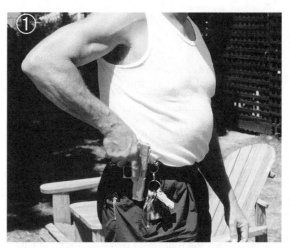

Bad guy at left begins his draw. Good guy at right is behind the curve. However, human instinct is for the hands to attempt to smother the threat…

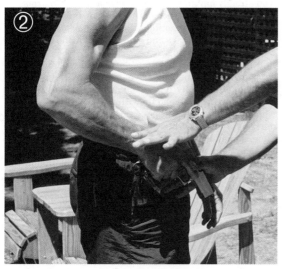

…and the good guy's forward-thrusting hands block the gun as it is coming up. The lower hand seizes the barrel/slide of the pistol as the upper hand seizes the opponent's wrist…

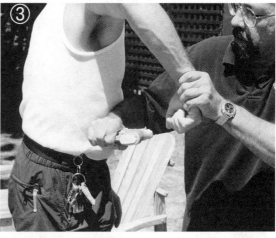

…and as the wrist is pulled out to the side, the gun muzzle is levered toward opponent's body and almost effortlessly stripped from his hand. In this close, disarming works faster than a reactive draw, if you know how to do it. Note: such techniques should always be practiced with dummy guns. This is an Odin Press model of S&W 5946.

accomplishing a draw/fire/hit sequence with a K-frame Smith & Wesson double-action revolver in 0.27 of one second, including the reaction time. My friend and holster-designing colleague Ted Blocker established the world fast draw speed record with a single-action revolver out of a speed rig of his own making at 0.25 of one second.

But I know I'm not nearly that fast, and you may not be either, and that's why in this situation the best we can hope for, realistically, is that we shoot the bad guy an instant after he shoots us.

Dying together in the same ambulance is not victory. This won't work.

Why couldn't you catch up? Remember what we discussed earlier: the drawing and firing of a pistol is a complex psychomotor skill, a chain of events in which each link must be accomplished with something close to perfection if we're going to make that 1.0 to 1.5 second time. Our reaction time to an anticipated stimulus, based on Lethal Force Institute's extensive research, will be about a quarter second, on the average. Perhaps as little as 0.17 second in the athletic young adult, maybe even faster than that in people like Bill Jordan with uncanny reaction speed. A quarter second into things, we begin a chain of dexterity-intensive events against a man who only has to perform the easier, faster, gross motor skill of "present and fire."

Suppose we had the option of responding with a simple gross motor skill ourselves. Suppose further that ours was easier to accomplish than the opponent's. Would we now have a fighting chance to beat the draw he has already begun? Yes, absolutely.

And, oddly enough, that option exists.

If you are an arm's length apart and facing one another, as he goes for his gun, *you go for **his** gun too!* It is instinctive for humans to use their hands to ward off danger coming toward them at close range. Let your hands do what is instinctive. Depending on how fast your opponent is your hands should interdict his gun and gun hand as the weapon is coming out of the holster or just after it has cleared leather.

This movement will "stall the draw" or "smother the draw." It will keep his gun muzzle pointed down away from you for an instant. You have just bought yourself time. You have just created reactionary gap. You have just kept him from shooting you, at least for the moment.

Now, finish what you began. With your lower hand, firmly seize his gun and with your higher hand, grab his wrist. Ideally, against a right-handed opponent, you'll have more leverage if your left hand is topmost to grab the wrist, and your right hand is just below it to grab the gun, but this hand placement is not absolutely essential.

There is a principle of human body movement that comes into play here. "If he's moving north and south, he has no resistance east or west." That is, once an opponent has committed himself to move in a certain direction, he cannot immediately resist lateral force delivered from a 90-degree angle.

The "north and south" line of force here is his bringing the gun up toward you. The "east and west" movement is what you need to do now. Your left hand, holding his wrist, pulls to your left as your right hand, holding his gun, pulls to your right. You will feel an almost effortless release as his hand separates from his gun.

Where you go from here is up to you. Run away with his gun. Shift his gun to your other hand as you create distance between the two of you and draw your own gun. Options are wonderful. But the point is, you have stalled his draw and disarmed him faster than you could have drawn your own gun and shot him...*and you haven't been shot!*

Controversial New Techniques

The search for a better mousetrap never stops. Sometimes the quest is for a hardware fix that will make a dangerous task less so. Sometimes a software fix is a better approach to reducing long-recognized dangers, or new dangers that have emerged with changing patterns of encounter.

Some new approaches work. Some just plain don't. Some are so new that field testing and training analysis are still underway, and the jury simply isn't in yet.

Let's review some current "hot-button topics."

Finger On Or Off The Trigger?

All the way through the early 1990s, FBI agents were taught to place their fingers on the trigger as a part of the draw process. Countless TV programs and movies showed everyone from cowboys to cops with their fingers on their triggers as they went into danger.

In the last few years, properly trained police and the best-trained armed citizens have learned to keep their fingers off the trigger until the actual moment to fire has arrived. The reason is, we know a lot more than we used to about sudden, convulsive movements as they relate to unintended discharges of firearms with potentially fatal results. In the 1990s, the work of a brilliant physiologist named Roger Enoka was widely circulated through the professional firearms training community. Dr. Enoka's study of accidental shootings had shown that the startle response, postural disturbance, and interlimb response were the primary culprits. When we are startled, our muscles react, and at least in the human hand (if not in the anti-gravity muscles of the legs), flexor muscles are stronger than extensor muscles. This is why if you're startled with a gun in your hand, you are far less likely to drop the weapon than you are to fire it unintentionally. When we lose balance or fall (postural disturbance) similar reactions can occur, triggering an unwanted shot. When the support hand closes (as when grabbing a suspect or applying handcuffs) the primary hand sympathetically wants to close with it. BANG! Another accidental discharge tragedy.

A strange and atavistic article appeared a few years ago in a privately published newsletter that sometimes resembles a medical journal and sometimes resembles a parody of one. A leader of the organization in question co-authored an article on a "study" that purported to show significant difference in lag time if the officer did not already have his finger on the trigger if a suspect held at gunpoint chose to attack. Ironically, though this organization attacks others for not performing studies to sufficiently scientific standards, this "study" they did

Sometimes derided as the "Sabrina Position," named after the character on the old "Charlie's Angels" TV show, the tactical high ready position seen here can actually be the best choice in some scenarios. The operator can easily scan a dangerous scene looking past the pistol, but with the muzzle in line with the eye, and can come on target faster. If the gun is grabbed, this is the most defensible start position for such a struggle. The pistol is an STI.

themselves did not quantify the experience or training of the officers involved, the types of handguns used, nor the technique of holding the finger off that was used in the testing. The writer in question issued a strong editorial urging police to have their fingers on their triggers when making gunpoint arrests or performing dangerous searches.

The professional community reacted with predictable anger and strong criticism. The people who published the deeply flawed "study" backpedaled quickly, but their credibility with professionals had taken a severe hit.

Real professionals, such as Manny Kapelsohn, had done more scientific studies that showed you would probably lose no more than a tenth of a second of reaction time by having your finger outside the trigger guard instead of on the trigger. There is an undeniable history of

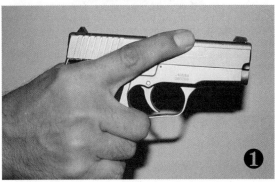

Different takes on how to keep the finger off trigger in a "ready" grasp. The finger at the ejection port, recommended by some, is awkward for many hands and can weaken primary grasp of pistol...

...the finger straight along the frame is most commonly taught, and is acceptable...

...the finger straight at the front of the trigger guard is dangerous. The author believes the finger can be held taut and can snap back to the trigger and fire an unintentional shot...

...for reasons described in the text, Ayoob prefers this technique, with finger flexed and indexed on the frame. The demo pistol is a Kahr K40.

many cases of tragic accidental discharges in which a finger prematurely on the trigger was a culpable factor. There is also the unassailable logic of Dr. Enoka's research. This is why any credible instructor today will tell you to keep your finger off the trigger until you have actually decided to fire.

That old bugbear, combat semantics, enters the scene again. It became common to teach "on target, on trigger; off target, off trigger." This was good enough for the range but not sufficient for the dynamic realities of the street. When the suspect was taken at gunpoint, the good guy subconsciously considered himself "on target," and therefore went "on trigger," bringing us back to square one and re-setting the stage for tragedy.

The principle needs to be, "keep the finger outside the trigger guard *until the intent to fire immediately has been formulated.*"

Where To Place The Finger

Any good concept can be carried too far. Some have advocated keeping the fingertip so high that it touches the flat of the slide or even the barrel of the auto pistol. The problem with this is that in many if not most combinations of hand and gun, this can bring the finger up so high that it breaks or at least weakens the grasp, and lowers the muzzle to an extreme degree. This may be going too far.

The finger on the front edge of the trigger guard *is not safe!* The problem is that with a long guard and a short finger, the fingertip may not be in firm contact. The extended finger is "held taut" in this position, and when there is a startle response, a postural disturbance, or an interlimb reaction, the finger can snap back toward the trigger with so much force that there is a high likelihood of unintended discharge.

The most commonly taught technique is to keep the index finger straight along the frame above the trigger guard. This is better, but still not perfect. There are four problems identified with this grasp. 1) If there is a lateral strike to the gun, the most common opening gambit of an expert disarming attempt, the extended index finger is now hyperextended. It has to let go or break, and the other three fingers sympathetically release as well. 2) If the hand-to-gun interface involves a long finger and a short trigger guard (i.e., a big hand on a 1911 pistol), the frontal portion of the trigger guard may get in the way and slow the finger's access when it does become necessary to fire immediately. 3) If the finger does somehow get into the guard, it has again been held taut, and therefore is again likely to strike the trigger with rearward impact. 4) With some guns (1911, P-35, some S&W autos, and many other guns) a right-handed shooter will inadvertently be applying leftward pressure to the exposed stud of the slide stop, which might also be called the takedown button. If this part is moved to the side by this pressure, the gun can lock up after the first shot has been fired.

All four of these problems are remedied by the StressFire (TM) technique that goes back to the 1970s. Here, the trigger finger is flexed, and the tip of that finger is placed at an index point on the side of the frame. On a revolver, the index point would be the sideplate screw. On a P7 pistol, it would be the forward edge of the grip panel. On a Glock, it would be the niche of the takedown lever, which due to the Glock's design cannot inadvertently begin takedown. On a 1911, Browning, or

Smith, the fingernail is placed behind the slide stop stud, where it can now exert pressure in any direction without doing harm.

Fingerpoint Technique

One fellow on the Internet and some of his friends are responsible for a rather aggressive campaign pushing a radical technique. The shooter points the usual trigger finger, the index finger, at the target, and uses the middle finger to actuate the trigger. The primary advocate of this technique admits that he has little handgun experience, and that when he shot better than he thought he would firing this way he had the epiphany that he had discovered the ultimate shooting technique. He recommends and all but requires a finger shelf attachment that affixes to the pistol's frame to facilitate this technique.

This group is not the first to suggest this shooting style. The famous photos of Jack Ruby murdering Lee Harvey Oswald in Dallas in 1963 show Ruby using his middle finger to trigger the single fatal shot from his hammer-shrouded Colt Cobra .38 Special revolver. Some assassination buffs decided that this was a secret technique of master gunfighters that showed that Ruby must have been a professionally trained hit man. Actually, the reason Ruby fired his gun this way probably had more to do with the fact that the distal portion of his index finger had been bitten off in a fight years before.

The theory is that the handgun will automatically point at the target and enhance "instinctive" hit potential. Unfortunately, the theory does not translate well to reality. Ace law enforcement weapons trainer Tom Aveni published a calm, reasoned analysis of this technique in *The Firearms Instructor*, the respected journal of the International Association of Law Enforcement Firearms Instructors. He pointed out that when firing right handed, the index finger can bind the slide or block the ejection port of many auto pistols, and that the officer now has a very feeble two-fingered hold on the gun when the middle finger leaves the trigger. Since modern handguns are designed to point naturally with the index finger at the trigger, using the middle finger drops the muzzle so far

Problems with the radical "fingerpoint" shooting technique include: only two fingers around grip-frame to secure the gun in case of snatch attempt; the index finger can block ejection port; and the muzzle of gun is radically lowered, impairing "pointing" characteristics. This pistol is an SW99, cal. .40.

Fingerpoint shooting technique can be dangerous with small pocket pistols like this Seecamp LWS-32. The tip of the finger is exposed to muzzle blast at the very least.

Tactical high ready comes into its own when the searcher is moving upward, as shown. The pistol is a Ruger P90 .45.

that a shot "pointed" at the opponent's torso is more likely to hit at the opponent's feet. The technique is obviously too weak to allow effective weapon retention, and the "finger flange" device that is all but required would cause serious holstering problems.

All things considered, it's safe to say that the "point with the index finger, shoot with the middle finger" is impractical for the serious combat handgunner.

Position Sul

As the use of special tactical teams grew in domestic American law enforcement, it became increasingly apparent that when personnel were "stacked" one behind the other while making entry through narrow areas like doorways or preparing to do so, Officer A's gun muzzle could end up pointing at Officer B. Accidental discharges occurred with tragic results.

Respected tactician Max Joseph's answer was a technique he called "Position Sul." In Portuguese, "sul" means "south," and the technique draws its name from the fact that the handgun's muzzle was pointed south, that is, straight down. This entailed drawing the gun in close to the front of the torso and bending the wrist of the shooting hand, while releasing the two-hand grasp.

This technique is also one answer to the question, "How do you do a 360-degree danger scan after firing without pointing your loaded gun at victims, innocent bystanders, and brother officers who might be present?"

I know of tactical teams that have adopted this technique. Though it has some obvious good points, it also brings some concerns with it. The gun is now low enough that it is out of the field of peripheral vision, particularly if tunnel vision has kicked in. This means that if the gun muzzle points at one's own lower extremities, the operator may not notice. The bent wrist also forces the gun arm

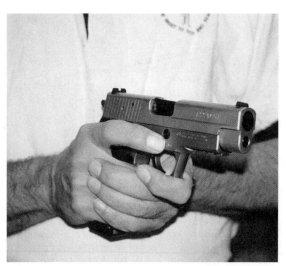

In lieu of this more commonly taught tactical ready position, some instructors and operators prefer...

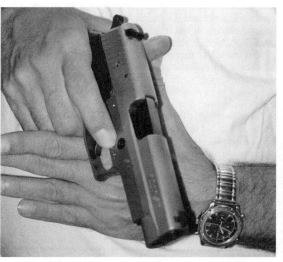

..."position sul," demonstrated here with a SIG P220 all-stainless .45.

Respected defensive shooting instructor Andy Stanford demonstrates Position Sul, a concept he likes.

into something approximating a "chicken wing" arm-lock that could severely impair the operator's ability to protect the gun from a snatch attempt.

"Position Sul" is still a fairly new concept. The jury of real-world users has not yet come in with a definitive verdict on its usefulness. Time in the field will tell us how well it works.

The Scan

The wise shooting survivor, recognizing the internal danger of tunnel vision and the external danger of vicious criminals who travel in packs, wants to immediately scan his or her environment for additional danger once the first identified threat has been neutralized. This has led the more advanced instructors to teach lowering the gun after firing and scanning the area.

All good, so far. Unfortunately, there are smart ways to do it and stupid ways to do it. Sometimes, the easiest way to make a good thing into a bad thing is to overdo the good thing.

DO NOT SWING THE GUN ALONG WITH THE HEAD AS YOU SCAN! The statistics are sketchy on this, but the best information we have is that about 40 percent of gunfights involve multiple bad guys. Conversely, this means that *60 percent of gunfights involve only a single opponent.* Just because he's down doesn't mean he's out. He could be playing possum and waiting for an opportune moment in which your attention is diverted so he can pick up his gun and attempt to murder you a second time. An opportune moment like, oh, your swinging your gun off him to look for someone who isn't there.

Suppose you have turned to look 90 degrees to one side to scan for criminal accomplices when, out of the corner of your eye, you see the first downed felon reach for his fallen weapon. You must now swing the gun back toward him. You'll have to slow down as it comes onto him or you'll swing past. Or, you'll have to pull the gun into your chest, pivot, and then punch your gun out at him. Either of these things will take time…perhaps enough time for him to shoot you.

But suppose instead that you have been smart enough to *keep the gun trained on the downed suspect while you turned only your head to scan for accomplices.* Now all you have to do is get your finger back into the trigger guard and fire immediately. Try it on a safe, 180-degree firing range with an electronic timer and see for yourself. By keeping the gun trained on the identified threat, de-cocked if double action or on-safe if single-action, and of course with your finger removed from the trigger guard, you will be *much* faster if you have to engage the identified threat a second time.

But what if as you scan, you *do* see a second lethal threat? How much will it slow you down if the gun is pointed at the first bad guy 90 degrees away instead of at the new one you just spotted? The answer is, not much. You need to identify the threat, determine that deadly force is justifiable, and make the decision to shoot. While you're doing that, there will be time to bring the gun around 90 degrees and get it indexed.

DO NOT SCAN 180 DEGREES AND ASSUME THAT THE AREA HAS BEEN CLEARED. Ninety degrees left and 90 degrees right only clears half the circle. You still have to clear the most potentially lethal area, that which is 180 degrees behind you at 6 o'clock. Remember, the smartest predators will ambush you from behind.

Bring it all together and you get the following recommendation for performing the scan. When the initial threat goes down, analyze it for a moment and determine if it seems neutralized. Remove your trigger finger from the trigger guard, and de-cock or on-safe the gun, depending on its design. Take a quick look to your most exposed side. Now look back to the threat and make sure it's still neutral. Now you can check to 6 o'clock on the same side or to 3 or 9 o'clock on the side you haven't scanned yet. Now back to the initial threat to check it again. Finally, check whatever the last quadrant is that you have not visually scanned. During this procedure, it would be wise to be moving toward cover. You'll also find that as you scan toward your 6 o'clock in the last portions of the scan, the gun will stray less if you pull it closer to your body, as illustrated in the accompanying photos.

There is another reason not to perform the scan with the gun tracking along with the head and eyes. What you have trained yourself to do is what you most certainly WILL do when deadly danger has you in its grip. There is an excellent chance that the shooting scene will contain, or even be filled with, innocent bystanders. If you have performed the scan with your gun held on the downed, identified threat, those witnesses will perceive that "the person with the gun shot the suspect and then looked around to make sure we were all OK." However, if your gun has tracked with your eyes, they will perceive that "the person with the gun shot the suspect and then pointed the gun at all the rest of us, too!"

The scan is a life-saving technique. Armed conflict expert John Farnam reported the case of a South African police officer that shot and killed a terrorist. He was seen to scan left and right, and then lower his gun, apparently thinking himself safe at last. He was then shot in the back of the head and killed instantly by a second terrorist with an AK-47, who had been directly behind him and had gone unseen in the "half a circle scan" the brave officer had performed.

Yes, the scan is a good thing and you should practice it. But you should practice it *correctly,* because there is very definitely a right and a wrong way to do it.

Ayoob demonstrates the post-shooting tactical scan. With the shooting over, gun de-cocked and finger removed from trigger guard, the gun stays on the identified threat, presumably downed in the snow, ...

...as the officer quickly checks to his right, with gun still on the identified threat...

...and glances back to make sure the downed suspect is not playing possum...

...followed by a quick check to officer's left...

...and back. The pistol is drawn slightly more into the shooter's body to make it less likely to turn off target as...

...the officer re-scans to the right, this time looking behind him to his 6 o'clock...

...and back...

...the scan is completed with final sweep to the left to six o'clock...

...and in a very short time, a 360-degree scan is completed and focus returns to downed identified threat, who has been monitored throughout the scan.

Chapter Ten

Better Technique = Better Performance

Enhancing Grasp

Ethicists say that their discipline exists on two levels. There is simply "ethics," which can be a sterile and philosophical debate that often takes place in the proverbial ivory towers. Then there is "applied ethics." The latter, says Professor Preston Covey, head of the Center for Advancement of Applied Ethics at Carnegie-Mellon University, "is where the rubber meets the road."

In handgun shooting, particularly the kind that is done rapidly under stress, we have to do something similar. We need to make the transition from "shooting" to "applied shooting." Many long-standing rules of marksmanship go out the window when the adrenaline dump hits and the "fight or flight" response sends dexterity down the toilet and strength up through the roof.

As noted elsewhere in this book, the grasp of the firearm is where operator meets machine, and a key point where "the rubber meets the road." Let's review necessities for *combat* handgunning that might not be required for sport or recreational shooting.

The grasp **needs to work with one hand only,** in case the other hand is performing a critical survival task and "can't make it to the appointment" for the two-hand hold that might have been the original plan.

The grasp also **needs to work two-handed,** for maximum life-saving efficiency, in case the circumstances evolving from the surprise that has called the combat handgun into play allow this to happen.

The grasp **needs to be strong enough to maintain control of the firearm even if the gun or hand are grasped or struck,** both predictable occurrences in the sort of situation that is the combat handgun's *raison d'etre.*

Master Grip Concept

Called the "master grip" by many instructors, a grasp of the gun that fulfills the above parameters is essential. Ideally, if the gun fits the user's hand, the following coordinates will all be achieved.

The trigger finger will have good leverage on the trigger. The web of the hand will be high up into the grip tang of the auto, or at the highest possible point on the backstrap of the revolver's grip-frame. The barrel of the gun will be in line with the long bones of the forearm.

With most handguns the author prefers the "wedge hold." The index finger of the support hand is wedged under the front of the trigger guard, camming the muzzle up and driving the grip tang more forcibly into the web of the hand. The V-shaped wedge of flesh and bone under the front of the guard also helps prevent lateral deviation of the gun muzzle due to a frisky trigger finger. Here, he demonstrates with a Glock 22.

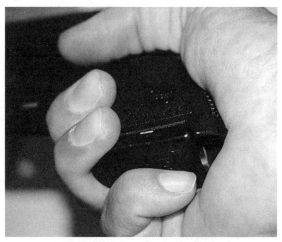

The rear of the butt of a baby Glock is ideally shaped to pull into the hollow of the palm. With the little finger tucked under the butt, if you don't use a Pearce grip extender, this grasp gives a surprisingly strong hold. Note the white fingernails, indicating desirable crush grip.

Thumb-lock grip. The thumb of the support hand presses down on the median joint of the bent thumb of the firing hand, bonding both hands together. This grasp works particularly well with handguns producing jackhammer recoil, like this S&W J-frame Bodyguard in .357 Magnum.

Note "ripple of flesh" effect at the web of the hand with a high hold, reinforced by the wedge grasp of the support hand's index finger under the front of trigger guard. With a crush grip applied with both hands and the trigger finger at the distal joint contact, the shooter has maximum control of this GlockWorks custom Glock 17.

The hand should have firm enough a contact that the gun does not slip or move in the hand during recoil. No part of the hand(s) should be blocking essential functions of the handgun. No part of the hand(s) should be blocking the function of other parts of the hand(s).

While most of the last paragraph is self-explanatory, some of the last points need explanation for newer shooters. With a small gun and a large hand, if the grasping hand takes a natural "fist grasp" with the thumb curled down, the thumb may block the trigger finger's completion of the trigger pull. In larger hands, this can occur with the small J-frame revolvers or with the small Kahr pistols. The solution on the revolver is custom grips that extend backward from the grip-frame, which move the web of the shooter's hand back, lengthening the reach to the trigger and preventing "overtravel" of the trigger finger through the trigger guard. With the Kahr, the easiest solution is to go to a "high thumbs" grasp.

Obviously, we don't want to use the old-fashioned two-hand hold still seen on TV in which the thumb of the support hand crosses over the back of the firing hand. The hyperextension of the thumb in this direction weakens the grasp of the support hand, but this is the least of our concerns. With most auto pistols, this grasp puts the weak hand thumb directly behind the slide. This tends to result in a nasty laceration, could cause even worse physical damage than that, and also is likely to jam the gun at the worst possible moment. Even with a conventional revolver, this grip when taken hastily, or by someone with big thumbs and a smaller revolver than they are accustomed to, can block the hammer's rearward travel and prevent the gun from firing.

As we shall see momentarily, sometimes compromises must be made. Let's say that you are a right-handed shooter who uses a Beretta 92F, a Smith & Wesson Model 4006, or a Ruger P90 or something similar. Each of these guns has a slide-mounted de-cocking lever that also

serves as a safety catch. The lever will need to be in its "up" position, the length of the lever parallel with the length of the bore, for the pistol to fire when you need it to. Carrying the gun off-safe is not enough to guarantee that this will happen. We have documented cases where such a safety "went on" without the user's knowledge. This is not something the gun does by itself. It usually occurs if there is some sort of struggle for the gun, or the user accidentally hits the de-cocking lever while operating the slide, or the user has left the lever down while chambering a round and forgotten to raise it.

There are also those of us who intentionally carry such guns "lever down," on-safe, for handgun retention reasons. In either case, whether you carry off-safe or on, you want to either get that lever up as you draw or *verify* that it's up even if that's where you left it. This means a grasp in which the thumb of the firing hand is about 45 degrees upward, pointed straight toward the ejection port. The support hand thumb goes directly underneath it in a two-hand grasp. However, this hold often causes one thumb to ride on the slide stop and may prevent the pistol from locking its slide open when the magazine runs empty. This will vary from shooter to shooter and from gun to gun, depending on the size and shape of pistol and of the hand. The author, for example, does not have this problem when shooting the S&W or Ruger, but invariably deactivates his own slide stop when taking this grasp on the Beretta pistol. Sometimes, the balance of competing harms and needs requires us to violate a lesser rule to more strictly enforce a more important one. In this case, it is less important to me to have the fastest of all possible reloads after I've fired 16 rounds of 9mm from my Beretta 92F, than it is for me to be certain that the first shot from that gun will be delivered as expeditiously as possible if needed in self-defense. The first shot is usually the most important, and the 17th is rarely the deciding factor.

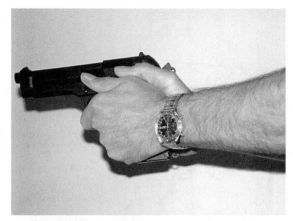

A "Straight thumbs" hold guarantees proper manipulation of the slide-mounted safety on this Beretta 92F, but one thumb will ride the slide stop and keep gun from locking open when empty.

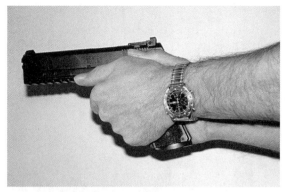

The Leatham-Enos hold is demonstrated on a Springfield Tactical Operator .45 auto. The support hand cants downward from the wrist, creating a strong lock. The thumb of the gun hand rides the safety as that of the support hand points downrange, aligning the hand with the radius bone of the forearm.

This is one of three chapters in this book in which grasp is discussed, the others being "lost secrets of combat shooting" and "handgun fit." In those we explain in greater detail the importance of the barrel being in line with the forearm and the web of the hand high, and in the former we explain in detail the rationale of "crush grip" versus other concepts of strength of grasp.

A key element to finding a comfortable, effective hold for the individual combination of handgun and shooter is the placement of the thumbs. This is a good point at which to examine that issue in detail.

Thumb Position

Handgun coaches and marksmanship manuals often simply say or demonstrate, "hold your thumb(s) like this." It is disturbing that they often don't explain why. For the shooter to determine if a technique is right for the gun, the job, and the moment, he or she needs to understand the reasons for use of the technique: what its purpose is, whom it was developed for, and why it was developed. Let's apply this to thumb positions. We'll be focusing here on the "master grip," that is, on the primary hand's interface with the combat handgun.

Thumb Down. This is the way most people instinctively hold a gun, and there is much to be said for it. We're talking about a grasp in which the thumb is bent at the median joint and the tip of the thumb is pointed toward the ground. It resembles a tightly curled fist. Most top revolver shooters use this grasp on their double-action wheelguns.

There is no stronger hold. The human hand evolved to work off its unique opposing thumb, and hyper-flexion of the thumb strengthens the hold. You can perform this simple test with one hand, without even putting this book down: Take your free hand, raise the thumb, and close the four fingers as tightly as you can. Mentally measure the

The author does his best 1911 shooting with both thumbs curled down in this "thumbprint over thumbnail" grasp that engenders maximum hand strength. The 1911 trigger guard is too short for him to take the wedge hold he prefers.

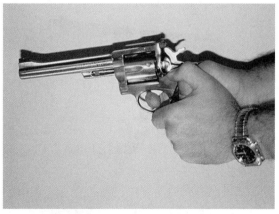

A thumb-lock grasp works perfectly with powerful sixguns like this Ruger .357 Magnum. If the thumb of the support hand crossed over the back of firing hand it would weaken the grasp, possibly block the revolver's hammer, and be in the way of an auto pistol's slide.

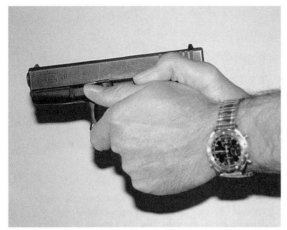

What feels most comfortable is not necessarily what you'll shoot best with. The author's hands are more comfortable with this Leatham-Enos type grasp, augmented with wedge hold on his 9mm Glock 19...

...but he shoots faster and straighter with his thumbs curled down, as shown here. The wedge hold works regardless of thumb position.

strength you are applying. Now, still exerting maximum gripping force and still mentally measuring, *slowly close the thumb until its tip is pointed down.* You just felt a significant increase in strength as the hand closed.

An advantage to the thumb-down grip is that it puts a bar of flesh and bone, the thumb, in position to close what is otherwise an open channel on the side opposite the palm of the hand. If an opponent, one who knows what he's doing, attempts to disarm you, he will begin with a lateral strike to the gun to move it off his midline. If that strike is directed toward the open side of the hand, your gun could be knocked or torn loose from your grasp before you could react. With the thumb locked down, you have at least a fighting chance of keeping the gun in your grasp

long enough to react and perform a handgun retention technique.

When the support hand comes in to assist, that hand's thumb has three options. It can simply hang out in space, a technique used by some to ensure that it doesn't block a part of their gun like the slide stop. While it's true that a thumb held in this fashion isn't getting in the way of anything, it is also true that it isn't doing anything positive to help you shoot faster and straighter. A second option is to lock the support hand's thumb at or behind the flexed joint of the primary hand's thumb. This works particularly well with revolvers, and frankly, it also works with most auto pistols. It is probably the single best "universal grasp" that is "friendly" to all manner of

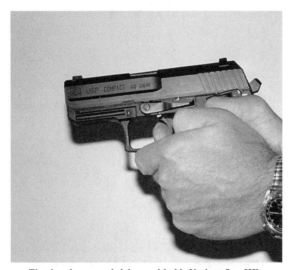

The thumbs are curled down with this Variant One HK USP pistol. If the thumb rides the USP's frame-mounted de-cocking lever, it can accidentally drive the lever down into de-cock position during a string of fire.

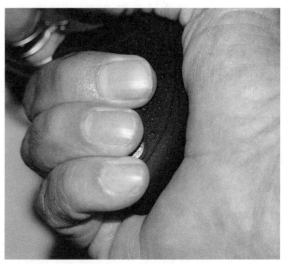

The pinky finger curls under the grip of a concealable, short-butt Taurus CIA. Though it can't help hold the gun directly, this finger's hyper-flexion adds strength to the other fingers that are wrapped around the stocks.

handguns. I call it the "thumb-lock grip" because when the support hand's thumb presses down on the median joint of the flexed thumb on the shooting hand, it bonds the support hand to the firing hand. This prevents the hands from separating when there is really powerful recoil, as with a super-light .38 or with a .44 Magnum. Finally, the thumb of the support hand can come in with its thumbprint placed on the thumbnail of the firing hand. Now both hands are flexed and exerting maximum gripping strength.

Note that with some hands on some guns, the downward-pointing thumb can hit the magazine release button inadvertently. We have seen this on occasion with really huge hands on the 1911 pistol, and with average size male hands on the scaled down Colt .380 Government-style pistols.

Thumb Straight. This is the preferred technique of the target shooter. With the thumb pointing parallel to the barrel, the trigger finger will have its straightest and smoothest track to the rear. The difference is very subtle and very small, but master competitors take every edge they can get. It is also a fairly strong position, as it aligns the extended thumb with the long bones of the forearm. Japanese archers learned centuries ago to hold their bows with a similar grasp.

With a two-hand hold, the support hand's thumb is also straight. It tends to be forward of the firing hand's thumb, and parallel to it, perhaps a little below it. In the version of this grasp popularized years ago by combat match champions Rob Leatham and Brian Enos, the thumb of the firing hand thumb has little, if any contact, with the gun and rides atop the base joint of the support hand's thumb. Many shooters using 1911 pistols will leave the thumb of the shooting hand placed atop the manual safety lever.

Though not as strong a primary hold against a disarming attempt as the thumb downward master grip, this hold is much stronger in that regard than any of the high thumb positions. It is also very conducive to a grasp

that evolved in IPSC shooting in which the support hand is canted slightly down from the wrist, so that the thumb is directly in line with the radius, the upper bone of the forearm. Some physiologists who have applied their skills to analysis of combat handgun technique insist that this gives the forward arm more strength with which to work.

Thumb 45 Degrees Upward. This is the grasp explained earlier in the chapter, and recommended for pistols with slide-mounted manual safety levers.

High Thumb. Characterized by a thumb that is in a high position with the median joint flexed and pointed upward, this hold is widely taught with the 1911 and similar pistols with frame-mounted safeties. While it does

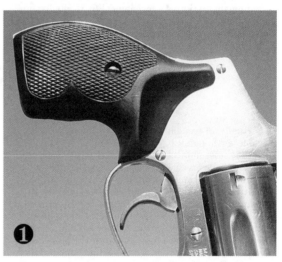

The master grip is important on small-frame revolvers like this S&W Centennial with Uncle Mike's Boot Grips...

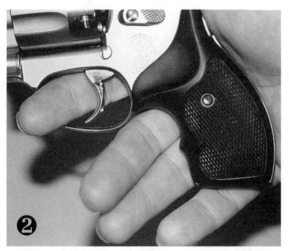

...as the web of hand goes all the way up to the top edge of the rear gripframe the curve of the backstrap will be pulled tight into the hollow of hand. Note that only two fingers will be able to grasp the stocks, and that there is "too much trigger finger" for the short trigger reach. So...

...the little finger is locked under and the index finger is cocked out slightly to the right so distal joint makes contact with the trigger. The thumb is curled down for strength, and is barely clear of the tip of the trigger finger in the rearward position. If the hand was any bigger, the thumb might have to be moved upward out of the way. Note that on "hammerless" style guns, the web of hand can ride higher than with conventional revolvers, proportionally lowering bore axis and giving the shooter more control.

indeed depress the thumb safety, it tends to pull the web of the hand away from the 1911 pistol's grip safety. This can render the gun unable to fire at the worst possible time. Those who have taught this grasp have traditionally, for obvious reasons, also recommended that the grip safety be deactivated. However, as explained elsewhere in the book, it is a Herculean task to try to convince a jury that someone who would intentionally deactivate a safety mechanism on a deadly weapon is anything but reckless. This grasp also tends to apply thumb pressure to the slide, particularly when gloves are worn or when strength goes out of control in a fight-or-flight state, jamming the pistol. The prevalence of this grasp caused Pachmayr and others to develop a device called a slide shield that keeps the high thumb from binding the slide. Common sense tells us that any technique that requires a mechanical fix to shield your gun is probably a technique that could present problems in a life-threatening emergency. This writer cannot in good conscience, recommend this grasp.

Vertical Thumbs. This is a stylized technique that is a signature of certain schools. The thumbs are pointed straight up. We have seen slides retarded in this fashion, causing jams. As the earlier experiment with your open hand showed, this thumb position minimizes your hand's overall grasping strength. Try as we might, we have not been able to elicit a logical, bio-mechanical explanation of any advantage offered by this technique. All we hear is "high thumbs equal high scores." That's a slogan, not an explanation, and frankly it's a slogan not borne out in major competitions where speed and accuracy of fire are directly and fairly tested.

Summary

Fingerprints and palm prints are unique to the individual. Hand sizes and shapes as they interface with gun sizes and shapes are almost as much so. The shooter wants to spend lots of time experimenting with different grasps to see what works for *that* combination of user and hardware.

Two-Handed Stances

Virtually all credible experts agree that when it is possible, a two-handed grasp of the handgun will give the combat shooter more control, and thus more speed and accuracy. If one accepts that defensive shooting is a martial art, it is similar to other such arts in that practitioners love to argue over subtleties of style. In Korean martial arts, the debate might revolve around the circular blocks of *Tang Soo Do* versus the more linear blocks of *Tae Kwon Do*. Among combat handgunners, when the topic of stance comes up after the guns are locked away, it's more than a two-beer argument. Lay in at least a case before the discussion even opens.

Countless hours have been whiled away discussing the Isosceles stance versus the Weaver, with modified forms of each (usually the latter) often thrown in to spice up the discussion. This is rather like boxing fans debating the merits of the left jab versus the right cross versus the uppercut. The difference is, no knowledgeable boxing fan would recommend his favorite punch to the exclusion of all others, but an amazing number of shooters insist that their preferred shooting stance is so superior to every other stance in every respect, it is the *only* way to shoot.

The fact is, each stance became popular among knowledgeable people because it had significant strengths. By the same token, each stance has become less than first choice for some other knowledgeable people because it may have had significant weaknesses. A more sensible approach might be the one taken by boxers: an understanding that while every fighter will have a best punch, a one-punch fighter will not last long in the ring. There is a time and a place where each stance may come into its own and be the technique of choice, even if it is not the given shooter's particular favorite.

Is the shooter long-limbed or not? Does the shooter have limited range of movement? Does he or she wear body armor, or perhaps clothing that could restrict body mobility? Is the shooter muscular or slim? Are the shooter's dominant eye and dominant hand on the same side, or does "cross-dominance" exist? Any of these factors and more could determine the best stance for each individual shooter at a certain time in their lives.

The proper Isosceles stance: With the chest squared to the target, both arms are locked straight out, the upper body is very aggressively forward with the feet still farther apart, front-to-back as well as left-to-right.

Grandmaster Mark Mazzotta has won countless matches with the Isosceles stance.

Let's examine the three primary stances, warts and all, listing strengths and weaknesses.

Isosceles

This is perhaps the oldest two-handed pistol stance; this one involves thrusting both arms all the way forward until they are straight, forming an Isosceles triangle with the chest, which faces the target. Capt. William Fairbairn depicted it in the early 20th Century in his classic gunfight survival text "Shoot To Live," and Jeff Cooper at one time referred to the stance as the Fairbairn Isosceles.

Over the decades, this stance has gone through all manner of permutations. Done correctly, it is extremely powerful and has been used to win many championships shooting at high speed with powerful handguns. Done improperly, it may be the weakest of all shooting stances.

In the old days, when cops qualified with mild .38 Special wadcutters with insignificant recoil, they were taught to face the target squarely, standing straight up. If one Isosceles triangle (the arms) was good, coaches of the time seemed to be thinking, then two must be better: the officer was taught to spread the legs wide apart and often

...and quickly extend...

The Isosceles stance is the near unanimous choice of today's top professional shooters, such as Doug Koenig, shown here at the Mid-Winter National IDPA championships at S&W in 2001.

...to the Modern Isosceles stance, firing the whole way, if needed, with good accuracy.

to lock them as well. Since there was now only precarious front-to-back balance, the legs being parallel, the outboard weight of the gun at the end of two fully extended arms tended to pull the shooter forward. To correct, shooters were taught to lean their shoulders back.

Balance was now completely gone. Even the .38 wadcutter would cause the gun's muzzle to rise significantly upon recoil. A more powerful gun could rock the shooter back on his heels with a single shot, and by the second or third round from a rapidly fired .44 Magnum, the officer might be tottering backwards. This sort of stance was to a proper Isosceles stance as Frankenstein's Monster was to humanity: a grotesque parody of the real thing.

A proper Isosceles stance, as taught in the StressFire (TM) shooting system, will see the chest squared to the target (as Dr. Walter Cannon, the first in-depth researcher of the fight or flight response, said the human body would do naturally in such a state), and the arms locked straight out to the target. However, the feet will be wide apart, not only side-to-side *but front to back,* and the head will come aggressively forward. Knees will be flexed; with the front leg's more so than the rear, but not to the exaggerated extent of the old, obsolete "FBI

Various upper body shooting postures may be needed to adapt to certain positions when shooting from behind cover. Here, author finds the Isosceles works well from kneeling barricade position.

The Isosceles stance, in squaring torso with an identified threat, maximizes the portions of the body protected by armor...

...while the more bladed Classic Weaver stance opens the armpit and some of the side to incoming fire. The Weaver stance predated the development of soft, wearable body armor.

crouch." The head will be forward of the shoulders, and the shoulders forward of the hips.

Isosceles Advantages: 1) This is a very simple posture. We take the fight or flight stance defined by Dr. Cannon and simply put a handgun at the end of two arms that extend fully toward the target. Physiologists who have looked at Isosceles shooting describe it as a simple gross motor skill, the kind easily accomplished under stress. 2) From Col. Rex Applegate to today's Bruce Siddle, trainers who look at these things scientifically find the Isosceles the most natural and logical two-hand hold for use under stress. 3) If the shooter is wearing body armor, this stance maximizes the armor's protective value as it squares the torso with the identified threat. 4) With the gun the maximum distance from head, the Isosceles minimizes ear damage if hearing protection cannot be worn. 5) It is ideal for night shooting. The Isosceles lines up the gun with the center of the shooter's head and body, and the head and body will align themselves instinctively in the direction of a suddenly perceived threat. 6) The Isosceles is ideally suited to pivoting toward the body's dominant hand side when feet are trapped in position and stepping is not possible.

Isosceles Disadvantages: 1) It works poorly if the shooter is off balance. 2) The stance may be impossible for those with elbow injuries, and difficult or impossible for those with inflamed elbow joints. 3) The gun bounces more than in a Weaver stance if the shooter fires when moving. 4) It is not compatible with tight, restrictive upper body garments such as tailored business suits, fastened motorcycle jackets, or some types of cold weather gear. 5) It provides a limited range of pivot toward the non-dominant side of the body when the feet are trapped in position.

Cross-Dominant Correction: None. Since this stance brings the gun to the centerline of both the head and body, the left eye and the right eye align themselves naturally with equal ease no matter which is dominant. This is the easiest technique, by far, for the cross-dominant shooter.

Master shooter and instructor, and gunfight survivor, John Berletich prefers the Isosceles stance for all two-fisted handgunning. The pistol is Para-Ordnance LDA .45 auto.

Weaver Stance

In the 1950s in California, Col. Jeff Cooper began gunfight simulation contests originally called "Leatherslaps" as a research tool to determine the fastest, most accurate ways to return fire with handguns. It was thought originally that unsighted fire and one-handed

Look what's on Phil Goddard's gun arm. Tendonitis or other arm problems can make Classic Weaver the technique of choice...

...as it is for Phil.

shooting, being fastest, would rule. In the late 1950s a figure emerged to change that assumption forever. Jack Weaver was a deputy with the Los Angeles County Sheriff's Office. He brought his duty gun, a 6-inch Smith & Wesson K-38 revolver, to eye level for aiming and fired from a two-handed stance. He did both no matter what the distance...and he almost invariably got the center hits faster than the competition. Soon, his competitors realized that it wasn't just talent but superior technique that was at work.

The late John Plahn, an associate of Col. Cooper, was the one who really quantified Weaver's technique as more than just two-handed, eye-level shooting. He noticed that Weaver stood in a somewhat bladed stance, the strong side leg back to about 45 degrees, and that Jack bent both his arms sharply at the elbows. Weaver pulled back with his forward hand and pushed forward with his firing hand, with equal and opposite pressure.

The classic Weaver Stance: Forward elbow down, both elbows bent, gun hand pushing, support hand pulling back.

Decades earlier, J.H. "Fitz" FitzGerald of Colt's had written a book on combat handgun shooting in which, as an alternate technique for use when one had time, he demonstrated the exact same technique, nuance for nuance. There is no reason to believe that Weaver copied him. Rather, Weaver appears to have re-invented the stance independently, and used it to great advantage. It was Col. Cooper who named the stance after Weaver and was almost single-handedly responsible for promulgating it. During the 1980s, it was probably taught as the technique of choice by more police departments than any other, though by the 90s departments were tending to return to the Isosceles stance for a number of reasons.

Like the Isosceles, the Weaver is often interpreted incorrectly. If the body is too bladed, i.e., completely edgeways to the target, balance is lost. Great emphasis must be placed on a firm forward push of the gun hand and an equal and opposite rearward pull with the support hand. Without this dynamic, the bent arms lose force and not only is the gun's recoil exaggerated, but the frame can move so much that the slide "runs out of steam" and a cycling failure occurs, jamming the autoloader.

To avoid confusion with the many variations of "modified Weaver" stance, we'll refer here to the stance of Weaver and Cooper as the "Classic Weaver."

Classic Weaver Advantages: 1)Because the bent arms are foreshortened and do not extend as far, this Classic Weaver stance offers the shortest and therefore fastest path from holster to line of sight. 2) Because the gun is closer to the shooter's main body mass, it has less distance to move when the shooter must track multiple targets or moving targets, and is thus slightly faster in that regard. This is simple geometry based on the ARC principle (Axis, Radius, Circumference). 3) Because recoil is absorbed by the taut, bent arms acting as shock absorbers, this is the only two-handed stance that will survive an off-balance position in which the shooter's shoulders are leaning backward over the hips. 4) Because the gun is closer to the body and the elbows are tautly bent, that same shock absorption effect works from the ground up as well, making the Classic Weaver the most stable upper body position to use when firing while moving. 5) The Weaver's bent arms posture is much more comfortable for those with elbow injuries or ailments. 6) It is ideal for engaging to non-dominant side flank if the feet are not where they can quickly move. 7) Bringing the gun sights closer to the eyes, the Classic Weaver stance may work better for myopic shooters or with guns with small sights.

Classic Weaver Disadvantages: 1) The Classic Weaver is not at its best with shooters who are light on muscle mass and tone in the arms. 2) With body armor, the somewhat bladed torso posture of the typical Weaver practitioner turns the vulnerable open portions of the vest toward the threat. 3) This stance is poorly suited for engaging to dominant-side flank if the feet cannot quickly step to a new position. 4) The gun is held closer to head than with other two-hand stances, increasing potential for ear damage from gunshot report when used in the field without hearing protection. 5) It is generally considered a complex psycho-motor skill by physiologists, and is more difficult to learn than the Isosceles.

Cross-Dominant Correction: Drop the head toward strong side, i.e., right cheek to right shoulder to align left eye with gun in the right master hand. The original Weaver stance usually proves to be the most difficult two-handed technique for the cross-dominant shooter.

Seasoned competitor and daily gun carrier Bill Fish finds Chapman's stance works best for him. The pistol is a Glock.

"Modified Weaver": The Chapman Stance

Ray Chapman, a contemporary of Jeff Cooper, understood the advantages of the Weaver stance over the old-fashioned version of the Isosceles. A fan of strong shooting platforms, he did not like what he perceived to be the weakened firing mount that occurred when the elbow of the firing arm was bent, sometimes bent to the point where the wrist also unlocked. Chapman shot his way to the top of the heap with his own technique. The gun arm was locked at every joint, rigid behind the gun, and the forward arm was bent at the elbow and pulling the whole locked gun arm into the shoulder, as if pulling in tightly on a rifle stock.

Because the gun arm is locked, it can become a lever that jerks upward with accentuated recoil if the shoulders are at body center or tilting backward, the same dynamic that made the old-fashioned Isosceles a poor choice. Unfortunately, some who teach this stance did not get it direct from its developer and teach a rearward lean, which limits the level of speed their students can achieve with it. Chapman himself always emphasized that the body should be in a forward lean, with the shoulders forward of the hips at least slightly, to get maximum benefit from his shooting stance.

Chapman called his technique simply a modified Weaver stance. In the last quarter of the 20th Century, it had come into vogue to call almost every two-handed stance a "modified Weaver," and this became imprecise and confusing. Those who knew Chapman and saw and copied specifically what he was doing, called the posture "the Chapman stance." Some schools, ranging from Lethal Force Institute to Firearms Academy of Seattle, still use this term to distinguish the stance developed by Chapman from the myriad other "modified Weavers" that abound in the shooting field.

The Chapman stance can be seen in many ways as a bridge between the two more famous-name stances, the Classic Weaver and the Isosceles. On the dominant hand side we have the locked skeleto-muscular support structure of the Isosceles stance, and on the support hand

The Chapman stance, AKA Modified Weaver. The gun arm is locked with the shoulder forward; the bent forward arm pulls back tightly against gun arm. Note that feet are slightly farther apart and stance is slightly more aggressive.

Veteran street cop, combat shooting champion, and LFI instructor Denny Reichard uses the Chapman stance by choice with his preferred weapon, the Smith & Wesson .44 Magnum loaded with full-power ammo.

side, we have dynamic tension, if not the truly isometric tension of the push/pull Classic Weaver. Thus, for many shooters this stance combines the best of both worlds without accepting the worst of either.

Chapman Stance Advantages: 1) This stance provides excellent commonality with long guns, as the gun arm functions like a rifle stock. 2) This posture is not particularly dependent on body shape or muscle tone/mass. 3.) It is better than the Weaver for those who wear body armor, since as the gun arm locks and the shoulder comes forward, the chest squares somewhat with the target.

Chapman Stance Disadvantages: 1) It does not give so much range of movement in pivot to the weak side as Weaver, nor to strong side as Isosceles. 2) The stance requires that shoulders be forward to work effectively, like Isosceles. 3) Not so effective for body armor wearers as

SWAT cop and LFI instructor Larry Hickman demonstrates the correction for cross-dominance with a Classic Weaver stance...

...and with the Chapman stance...

...and with the Isosceles. The pistol is Beretta 92FS 9mm.

Isosceles. Chapman himself taught police officers to shoot from Isosceles for this reason.

Cross-Dominant Correction: Keep the head erect, bringing the jaw or chin to the shoulder or bicep. While the tilted-head position necessary to make this correction with the Classic Weaver is awkward and "buries" most of the weak eye's viewing scan, the Chapman correction keeps the full danger scan and merely moves it a few degrees to one side. Though easier than with Weaver, the cross-dominant correction with Chapman is still not so easy as with the Isosceles stance.

The author feels a competent defensive shooter should be conversant with all three of the primary two-hand stances. Here, at right, Ayoob leads a class through an empty-hand refresher on the Chapman stance just before they fire for qualification.

Notes On Terminology

Terminology in the world of the gun can be confusing, and once again "combat semantics" rears its ugly head.

Shooting champion and master pistolsmith D.R. Middlebrooks has developed a stance in which the

As Ayoob fires a "double tap" from an aggressive StressFire Isosceles stance on the way to winning an IDPA match, Penny Maurer's high-speed camera clicks. Look carefully at the area around the STI Trojan 9mm pistol...

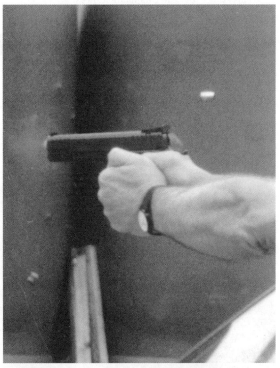

...and you can see the blur of the hammer falling and the bloom of flame at the muzzle from the second shot while the spent casing from the first shot is still only inches from the ejection port. The Isosceles stance gives many people the best control. Photos by Penny Maurer.

support arm is locked but the firing arm is bent, pushing against the locked gun arm. Some have called this a "reverse Chapman stance." The semantic correctness of this is debatable; it may appear that arms have swapped posture, but the dynamics are completely different.

A stance variously called "modern Isosceles" and "strong Isosceles" has become popular in IPSC circles. Both elbows are bent and a relaxed 40/60 percent pressure grasp is applied to the pistol. With elbows bent, the Isoscles triangle is broken into an uneven pentagonal shape. While this dexterity-intensive stance works in competition, and can certainly work in combat for someone who has practiced with it sufficiently to make it second nature, it may not be appropriate to call it any kind of an Isosceles stance.

Perhaps the most important point is this. Champions and gunfight survivors have used each of these stances alike. Each comes with a strong pedigree. Like the jab and the cross and the uppercut, there is a time and a place for each, and the competent fighter wants to know how to execute each of these techniques to perfection.

In the end, all those arguments over shooting stance may have been meaningless. For serious fighting, the ability to traverse from far weak side (favoring Weaver) to far strong side (favoring Isosceles) when you are caught on stairs or in tight spaces where you can't step into your favorite position has to be addressed. It really never should have been "Weaver versus Isosceles (versus Chapman stance)" at all. For the thinking practitioner of the combat handgun, it should be seen as knowing and being able to perform the true Weaver stance *and* the Isosceles stance *and* the Chapman stance.

The author demonstrates an aggressive StressFire version of the Isosceles with a Kimber .45 auto while doing a Bill Drill (6 shots, 2 seconds, 7 yards, from the holster) at the IDPA New England Regional Championships, 2000.

One-Handed Stances

We all know that two-handed shooting is the most effective way to deliver fire with a combat handgun. Unfortunately, we also know that we won't always be able to use that method to return fire, so we have to have a Plan B in place. Plan B is a strong one-handed stance that gives you maximum delivery of accurate, rapid handgun fire under pressure.

Why can't we always do it from our strongest stance? It's one of those places where the rules of the range collide with the realities of the street. On the range, we normally

Firearms instructor Sam Young shows one reason one-handed shooting skills are important: you may have to use one hand to communicate while the other covers the danger zone. His home defense pistol...

...is this .40 caliber Glock 22, mounted with an M3 Illuminator. Note that with the trigger finger manipulating the flashlight switch, it is kept safely off the trigger.

know when we're going to fire and (we hope!) in what direction. Thus, we "address the target." That is, we get ourselves set to fire in a certain direction from a certain preferred stance, sometimes without even realizing we are doing it.

Unfortunately, attacks often come from unpredicted directions. A smart opponent will attack from the rear or the flank. As you spin to engage, one arm may reflexively go outward for balance as the other raises the gun. The subconscious, knowing that the support hand isn't going to reach its intended destination, sends its message to the trigger finger: "Open fire, *now!*"

Problems might arise because other situations besides the angle of attack. One hand could be pushing a victim out of the line of fire, or dragging a wounded partner, or clutching a communication device or a flashlight that's your only source of illumination in the darkness. There is also the possibility that the opponent has seized you by one arm, or has already wounded you there. Even those trained and practiced with two-handed shooting to the point where it constitutes 95 percent of their experience firing a handgun, may have to shoot one-handed when trouble strikes in the real world.

How often does that happen? Back in the 70s, I spent some time in New York City with the legendary Lt. Francis McGee, then head of NYPD's Firearms and Tactics Unit. I studied under him at the outdoor range facility at Rodman's Neck during the day, and picked his brains far into the night at his home, where I was staying. The SOP-9 study had by then been in place for several years. Standard Operating Procedure Number Nine, the intensive debriefing of every member of the service who fired his or her weapon anywhere but on the range, included the question, "Did you fire with one hand or with two?" The results thus far indicated that approximately half the shootings had caught the officers in such a position that they'd had to return fire one-handed.

Strong Stances

With half as many hands as we had to control the gun before, we have to get every ounce of hand strength out of the one we have left to fight with. If you don't care to shoot with the thumb curled down in two-handed

A locked-down thumb and a strong Shotokan Punch stance let the author easily control this powerful .357 SIG, Model P229.

postures, you might want to consider going to it now for added strength. Years ago, I hosted then-world champion Rob Leatham to teach an advanced combat competition course. Though Rob was a pioneer in shooting with the thumbs pointing toward the target in his own version of an Isosceles hold, he made a point of telling the advanced shooters to curl their thumbs down for added strength when they had to fire one-handed.

What to do with the other arm? It needs to be out of the way where its mass, roughly 9 percent of body mass, won't pull the body to one side and take the gun off target. We teach that it be curled up tight to the side, palm up in a fist, the way the non-striking hand would be for a karate practitioner executing a reverse punch. This puts the hand about where it would be if it was holding a cell phone or police radio, or dragging a wounded partner. Turning the palm upwards and clenching the fist tightly creates a sympathetic tightening throughout the entire upper body's voluntary muscle structure, helping to tighten the firing hand still

The locked down thumb is important for one-handed shooting, and the author will sacrifice it only for something more important – in this case, disengaging the safety of this Ruger P90 .45...

...or making sure the thumb doesn't block the trigger finger with this small-handled Kahr K40 Covert pistol.

In the StressFire (TM) shooting system, if the opposite leg is forward you're in a reverse punch position...

...with feet parallel, you flex your knees and drop your butt back in a mild version of a karate "horse stance"...

...the single strongest stance is probably a forward punch posture, shown here...

...and all three can be combined with the McMillan/Chapman rotation of the pistol, which is especially suitable for cross dominant shooting. Note that in all cases the fist is drawn up to the pectoral muscle for added strength. A dummy Glock 19 is being used for photographer's safety.

A lightweight, polymer-framed Ruger P97 is at the height of its recoil as Ayoob fires from 4 yards with .45 ball ammo.

LFI assistant instructor Cliff Ziegler demonstrates for students, keeping all hits in a tight chest group rapid-fire with his HK USP40 Compact.

more. In fact, because human hands can manifest a phenomenon called interlimb response, the one hand won't reach full strength in grasp until the fingers of the opposite hand are sympathetically contracting.

It is interesting to look through a few decades of gun magazines and shooting manuals to see how the one-handed stance has evolved. In the old days, the shooter would stand erect, gun arm straight out, and free hand either hooked on the waist, tucked into a pocket, or on the

Note that the rear leg is digging into ground, driving the upper body forward into the Colt 10mm during one-hand rapid fire. The recoil compensator on this Mark Morris gun helps, too!

hip or behind the back. Some would just let the arm hang free. And, if the camera captured the moment of the shot, the gun muzzle could be seen to be kicking skyward.

The institutionalization of IPSC in the mid-1970s brought some conformity to technique as the top shooters, known as the "super squad," generously shared their shooting tips with others. A hand flat on the belly got it out of the way and eliminated the "pendulum effect" of the loose arm swinging, but did nothing to actually enhance the firing hand's ability to do its job. The simultaneous development of the StressFire (TM) martial arts-based "punch" techniques, with the free hand now a fist, palm up, under the pectoral muscle, also emerged. These were widely copied.

With the upper body aggressively forward, and the head also forward (because "where the head goes, the body follows") shooters achieved much more powerful one-handed stances than those of the past. With one hand recoil was now controllable to the degree of the early version two-handed Weaver stance, and actually stronger than the old-fashioned version of the Isosceles. It was not, however, possible to make the one-handed posture stronger than the strongest, most efficient two-handed stances, and in all probability that will never prove possible.

Foot Position

The International Shooting Union (ISU) and practitioners of America's "Conventional Pistol" (i.e., bull's-eye) are taught to stand with their right foot forward if the pistol is in their right hand. This is because it applies no torque to the spine, it balances the shooter well, and it extends the outboard weight of the upper limb directly over the weight-bearing lower limb.

Unfortunately, we can't always jump into our favorite position when attacked. The shooter needs to know how to fire effectively whether his strong foot is forward, or his weak-side foot is forward, or his feet are parallel. In the latter case, flexing at the knees and dropping the hips back will give a stable posture if the head and shoulders are forward. If the weak side foot is forward, one can shoot from a well-balanced stance as if throwing what a karate stylist would call a reverse punch and a boxer, a right cross. The single strongest one-handed posture,

In one-handed shooting, it is all the more important that the gun fits the hand. A Pearce grip extender for the little finger to grasp, and a locked down thumb help this shooter control the baby Glock.

Phil Goddard uses slight McMillan rotation when firing with the non-dominant hand only. The big .45 slugs from his Colt Combat Commander are staying in the "A" zone of the target.

however, will still be dominant hand forward/same side leg forward. This is the position a boxer would call a jab and a karate practitioner, a forward punch.

Turning the Gun

It has come into vogue in recent years to tilt the gun over to one side. Does this come under cinematic BS, or true secrets of the handgun ninja? Well, the answer is yes to both, depending how it's performed...

The technique goes back to the late 1950s. A young Marine pistol ace named Bill McMillan was shooting for the gold, but had one small problem: He was cross-dominant. He figured out that by adjusting the sights of his pistol, a cant of about 45 degrees inward aligned the sights dead on with the eye opposite his gun hand and still put the shots dead center. Soon he had moved to the head of the pack, winning the Gold Medal for the United States in the Pan-American Games circa 1960.

Ray Chapman picked up on this trick and made it his technique of choice for one-handed work in practical handgun competition. With less precise accuracy

required, the sights didn't need to be adjusted for the typical close range work. Chapman discovered that whichever side the shooter's dominant eye happened to be on, that slight turning of the wrist created a more propitious alignment of the skeleto-muscular support structure of the arm, resulting in a stronger hold. Chapman, it should be noted, always taught accuracy ahead of speed and always emphasized very strong shooting positions. Clint Smith, who later became head of the famous shooting school Thunder Ranch, has also taught the "McMillan rotation" for several years as the preferred one-handed technique.

Some find it works better for one hand than the other. At our school, we tell the students to feel free to "mix and match." Many end up preferring to shoot with the gun straight up on their dominant eye side, and in the McMillan/Chapman rotation when firing with their other hand. (Some shooters find that the rotation works in two-hand shooting as well. Larry Nichols, the nationally famous rangemaster and master police trainer from the Burbank (Cal.) PD, teaches this as technique of choice.

Tilting of the gun may happen naturally when emergencies require you to fire at awkward angles like this...

...or like this, as one California StressFire graduate had to when he came under fire from an ambusher with a rifle. The graduate won, killing his assailant.

LFI student Joyce Fowler keeps them all in the A-zone with her .45 auto, while firing weak-hand-only using McMillan Tilt and StressFire Punch techniques. She went on to become multiple-time IDPA National Champion in the women's division.

Gila Hayes, another nationally known instructor, teaches it as a two-handed option for the cross-dominant shooter.)

The proper rotation is between 15 and 45 degrees. Less than that doesn't do much; more than that, and the arm is past the point of maximum strength. However, several years ago films exploiting urban violence began showing gang-bangers shooting with a strange hold in which the pistol was turned over 90 degrees. "Life imitates art," and soon this technique was being observed on the street, generally in the hands of the bad guys.

Where did it come from? We may never know for sure. One theory is that a director or a technical advisor saw a security camera film of a felonious shooting in which the armed robber held his gun this way to reach over a counter and shoot a clerk who was trying to hide from him, and apparently decided that this was the new signature technique of the "gangstas." Another theory is that directors figured out that turning the pistol over

Despite an injured elbow, Phil Goddard keeps every shot in a heart-size group with a straight-up hold and StressFire Punch technique, strong-hand-only.

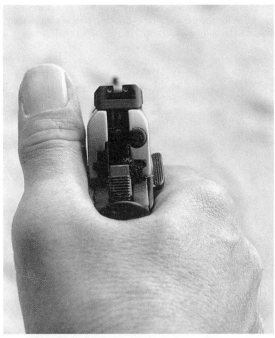

A shooter's eye view as the thumb prepares to "wipe" a 1911's safety catch. One should always use the gun hand thumb to manipulate the safety, since often that's the only thumb that will be available to perform the task.

Firing from this awkward downed position, a shooter can't get body weight into the gun; the triceps muscle of the arm should be practiced in pulling this Glock 22 down from recoil.

allowed the menacing gun, and all of the actor's facial features, to be seen in the same frame by the camera. Who knows?

In any case, it is demonstrably a stupid way to shoot. The wrist has by this point run out of range of movement, and a person holding a handgun in this fashion can be disarmed with minimal effort. The recoil tracks the gun violently toward the weak hand side. This limits the ability to put multiple shots into the same stubborn aggressor, and it also probably accounts for some of the innocent bystanders hit by gang members who fire at one another this way.

The only time we've seen anything like this prove useful is for the person who is ducking to one side as they fire. As the body goes forward to the side, it will prove

awkward to keep the sights upright, and it will be almost impossible to align them. In one California shooting, an officer trained in StressFire (TM) shooting came under fire from a suspect with an autoloading rifle as he bailed out the door of his patrol car. Raising his SIG P220, he saw the service pistol was turned over 90 degrees, but also that the sights were on the suspect. Remembering his instructor's admonition that if the sights were on target the shot would go true, he fired...and center-punched his attacker through the chest with a 230-grain .45 hollow-point, saving his own life.

Numerous "downed officer" positions, such as down laterally on the weak hand side, may make this position natural. However, vis-a-vis the body position, it *is* natural from here, since the shooter's arm is in its usual alignment with the torso.

Bottom Line

You want to practice with the one-handed techniques just as with the two-handed, to see which work best for you. Your brother may be a straight-up shooter and you may do your best with the McMillan tilt, or vice-versa. You won't know until you try them all and analyze your performance.

Be sure to spend lots of time practicing *weak-hand-only* shooting. This is a good reason to have an ambidextrous safety and/or decocking lever. History shows that because humans look at what threatens them, and what threatens the armed criminal is the gun in the good person's hand, the good person's gun arm is disproportionately likely to draw fire and take a bullet. While a wound to the gun arm or hand may not leave you incapable of firing with that hand, there are no guarantees.

We also need to think ahead. We may not be disabled in a fight. We might simply break our dominant arm or wrist in a routine accident. This will be a lousy time to start learning how to defend ourselves and our families with a weak-hand-only option. It makes sense to start thinking right now about having an ambidextrous gun in a weak side holster from which we are familiar with drawing and firing using the non-dominant hand.

None of us seems to practice enough on one-handed shooting. When street results indicate that a good half of the time, that's exactly what we'll have to do, logic may be telling us to restructure our training priorities and schedule a whole lot more one-handed combat pistolcraft drills.

Using techniques recommended in this chapter, Ayoob is on his way to winning the revolver class at an IDPA match, sweeping an array of targets weak-hand-only with a Bob Lloyd-tuned S&W 4-inch Model 686.

CHAPTER ELEVEN

Avoiding Mistakes

Gun Accidents

In the term "defensive weapon," the emphasis is normally on the first word. But as far as safety, the emphasis has to shift to the second. A weapon, by definition, can become a vehicle of unintended harm if handled or stored carelessly. We do not leave a can of lye open on the floor where the baby can reach it. We do not leave our car parked on a hill with the transmission set in Neutral. The firearm demands similar rules of common sense.

In the early 1990s, I was teaching a class being filmed by a crew doing a documentary on private ownership of firearms in the U.S. The topic had come around to home safety, and when I was done speaking, we opened it up for questions and answers. The person in charge of the documentary had noticed that my 9-year-old daughter was in the room, and he asked pointedly if I had taught her the safety rules I was propounding. I just said, "Why don't you ask her?"

They stuck the camera a few inches from my little girl's face and asked her about gun safety. With a perfect poise that approached nonchalance, Justine sweetly replied, "Treat every gun as if it is loaded. Never let it point at anything you aren't prepared to destroy. Never touch the trigger until you are going to fire, and always be sure of your target and what is behind it."

The film crew was dumbstruck. The father, on the other hand, had an ear-to-ear grin of pride. Justine had just recited the four primary rules of firearms safety as promulgated by one of the great leaders in the field, Col. Jeff Cooper.

Justine, like her older sister Cat, had grown up among firearms. Both her parents were licensed to carry, and one was required to at work. When they were tiny, guns were stored in such a way that they could not reach or activate them. Each began helping me clean guns at the age of 5. This de-mystified an object that the entertainment media had glorified as an instrument of power, and also de-glamorized it. They understood quickly how guns worked. An important benefit of this was that if they were ever in a playmate's house and the other child took his parents' gun out of the closet or nightstand, I wanted my kids to know how to "de-fang the snake" – how to unload the gun and/or lock up its firing mechanism.

Both began shooting at the age of 6 with .22s. Both had progressed to more powerful weapons by the age of 10 or 11. Neither ever gave their mother or me a minute's worry about firearms safety.

Loaded guns should not be left unsecured. They are vulnerable to burglars (who might turn them on innocent people sooner than you think, perhaps even on you or a family member who comes home unexpectedly and interrupts the burglary). They are vulnerable to certain members of the family, friends, and acquaintances who drop by unexpectedly and rummage about in other people's homes without permission. We always think of securing guns from children, but irresponsibility knows no age limit: the guns should be kept from *all* unauthorized hands. As the responsible owner, you are the one who determines who is authorized to touch the firearm.

Routine Handling

Every now and then you get something like a cartridge stuck in the chamber of an auto pistol. It will require you to forcibly manipulate the slide, maybe whack it with something, and you suddenly realize there's a live round that is stuck in there that can be fired from the gun. At such a moment, you'll want a safe direction in which to point the pistol. Accidental discharges have occurred during loading and particularly unloading. For all these reasons, think about something like a big bucket of sand in a corner of a kitchen. If a curious guest asks what it's doing there, you can honestly answer, "Fire safety."

All expert shooters can tell you that dry fire – going through the motions pulling the trigger of an unloaded gun – is an important route to shooting mastery. But we can all tell you stories of the day a live round somehow migrated

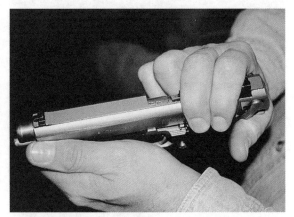

This "armorer's grip" is sometimes used to check the chamber of double-action autos. It gives more control when pulling slide back against a hammer that is being held down by a powerful mainspring.

into an empty firing chamber. This is why you should rigidly discipline yourself to dry fire only at something that could safely stop the most powerful bullet that might possibly emerge from that particular gun's muzzle.

This is one reason why basements have become favorite locations for shooting hobbyists' "gun rooms." I think it's a good idea for any armed citizen to own a bullet-resistant vest. I keep mine stored under the bed so I can throw it on any time the alarm goes off. Remember, the first definition of "alarm" is "a call to arms." Any situation for which I need a defensive firearm is a situation where a quickly donned vest would be comforting. And, more to the point at the moment, the bullet-resistant vest can always be set against a wall and used as the backstop for dry fire practice. It can always be set against the wall or on the floor when dealing with that pistol that had a round stuck in the chamber. It is simply one more safety net. How many things do we have in our homes that are designed to stop bullets? This is one.

Safe Manipulation

When you check the chamber of an auto pistol, don't do it from the front. If the hands slip, the strong recoil spring will slam forward hard enough to leave the muzzle of the loaded gun pointing at one or more of your fingers.

It's not just "on target, on trigger; off target, off trigger." That creates a subconscious mindset of putting the finger on the trigger as soon as you're taking a suspect at gunpoint, since the subconscious may believe that you are indeed on target. The rule is, *do not let the finger enter the trigger guard until the immediate intention to fire has been formulated and confirmed.*

Safety devices can fool you. They're just one more net in a layer of safety nets, and you never rely on just one. In the Midwest, a police officer wanted to show someone how the round in the chamber of his S&W 9mm would not fire if the magazine was removed. However, he maintained pressure on the trigger as he removed the magazine. This action bypassed the disconnector safety. He then put the palm of his hand in front of what he knew to be a still-loaded gun, and pulled the trigger. He shot the hell out of his own hand. Oddly enough, his response was to sue Smith & Wesson...sigh.

Do not lower the slide of a 1911 pistol while holding the trigger back. It is an archaic practice that will eventually lead to a slip and an accidental discharge. In the immortal words of John Dean, who was admittedly talking about something else at the time, "That information is no longer operative."

Do not carry the 1911 pistol with the hammer down, or at half cock, with a live round in the chamber. No matter what generation or style of manufacture, there is likely to be an unintended discharge if the hammer is struck, and there is a high likelihood of an accidental firing when cocking or lowering the hammer because of the awkwardness of the procedure. If you are not comfortable carrying it cocked and locked as it was designed to be, go to a double-action pistol or leave the 1911's chamber empty.

It is always safer to retract an auto pistol's slide with the "slingshot" rather than the "overhand" technique (see photos). With an overhand grasp, the arm wants to align itself in the direction in which it is applying force and, if your concentration slips for an instant, you can find the muzzle pointing at the elbow or at someone next to you. Similarly, avoid pulling the gun into your body for leverage as you work the slide. If it is too hard to pull

back, use the heel of the free hand to cock the hammer. This will relieve mainspring pressure that is being exerted against the slide through the hammer, and allow the slide to be more easily retracted.

If the gun goes "poof" instead of "bang," *stop shooting!* An underloaded round has probably lodged a bullet in the barrel. Another shot behind it will lead to catastrophic pressures that can blow up the gun and cause serious injury.

Never assume that someone else has cleared a gun of ammunition, even if he appears to do so. If I or any other professional hands you a gun we have just cleared, we

This old method of chamber-checking a 1911 is dangerous since, at various points in the procedure, finger gets too close to loaded gun's muzzle and thumb gets too close to trigger...

...this method is better, but still brings hand uncomfortably close to business end...

...and this, the slingshot technique, is the safest way of all.

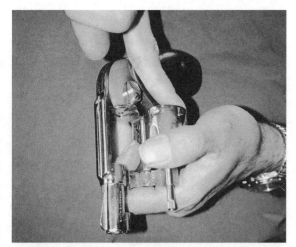

When checking to make sure the handgun is empty, get into the habit of checking by feel as well as sight. With a revolver, like this S&W Model 38 Bodyguard, press the index finger of the dominant hand into every empty chamber...

...with an auto pistol, use the little finger of the non-dominant hand to probe the magazine well...

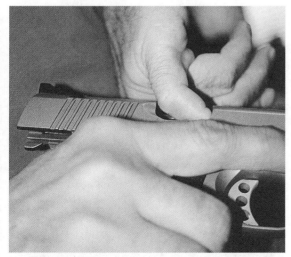

...and the firing chamber. This habit will fail-safe you when checking handguns in the dark or when there are distractions.

expect you to double check it to confirm that it is unloaded. We may even be testing you. If you check what we just checked, no professional will be insulted; if you *don't,* we'll think you're an amateur.

When determining that a gun is unloaded, check by sight and feel. With the revolver, get into the habit of probing each empty chamber with the tip of your dominant hand index finger (usually the most sensitive of the 10 digits) until you feel the sharp-edged recess. With an auto pistol, lock it open and probe the magazine well and the firing chamber with the little finger of your non-dominant hand (usually the narrowest of the 10 digits). You may feel stupid doing this in clear light where you can plainly see that it is unloaded, but you are programming yourself for some high-stress dark and stormy night when you have to check a gun and can't see what's in it.

When you have set down an unloaded gun and left the room, or even turned your back on it, *check it again.* When an unloaded gun has left your line of sight, consider it contaminated.

When you remove a live cartridge from a semiautomatic pistol's firing chamber, don't eject it into your palm. This practice is a holdover from the old days of early military pistol designs with short ejectors. A long ejector, as found on today's 1911 pistols, most double action autos, and the Glock, can every now and then get into alignment with the primer, and if the primer is driven against it hard, it can fire the cartridge. This "open chamber detonation" will turn the shell casing into a hand grenade that spews brass fragments at high pressure into the palm of your hand, lacerating vulnerable nerves. We have seen cases of this that resulted in a reported 70 percent nerve damage to the afflicted area. Let the cartridge fall clear, keeping your face away from it. Always be wearing some sort of eye protection.

When dry firing, make sure there is no live ammunition anywhere in the same room. Never practice speed reloading and trigger-pulling on the same night. When practicing reloading, use dummy ammunition or, better yet with an auto, weighted dummy magazines available from Dillon.

When cleaning the gun, make sure you're in a well-ventilated space, preferably outdoors. The carbon tetrachloride in some gun cleaning compounds can be toxic in cumulative doses. It is a good idea to wear latex or

A thickly packed stand-up pile of books or magazines makes a safe backstop for dry fire. Mark Maynard demonstrates with an S&W Model 686 revolver.

nitrile gloves while cleaning guns. This keeps lead and other toxins from getting into microscopic cuts on the hand. Wear an inexpensive gauze mask when cleaning. Remember, each time you pull that brush out of the barrel, you're putting tiny bits of lead into the same cubic yard of air you're about to inhale. Finally, always wear eye protection. In my experience, Gun Scrubber in the eyes is worse than pepper spray, and we know of one pistol champion who lost partial sight in one eye when the recoil spring cap of his pistol snapped free and hit his unprotected eye when he was taking the gun apart.

Gun Abuse/Substance Abuse

Common sense tells us that if we're going to get smashed at the New Year's Eve party, we should leave the gun at home. We also need to be certain about prescription medication. Any prescription with a warning label that says, "Do not operate dangerous equipment" can also be read as "don't go shooting while taking this medication." It is telling us that our concentration will be sufficiently impaired that we won't be at our best in maintaining our usual rigid care in firearms handling.

Similarly, if you are fatigued or distracted or angry, it is not a good time to be handling potentially lethal weapons. Anything that gets in the way of your concentration will get in the way of safe gun handling.

Things People Don't Think About

One reason shooting is such a great hobby is that it's a tremendously good stress-reliever. A lot of people don't understand how this works. They think that we go to the range, imagine our boss's face on the picture downrange, and act out some homicidal rage by shooting it again and again. That's not how it works at all.

A "bullet-proof vest" has more safety uses than the obvious, as pointed out in this chapter.

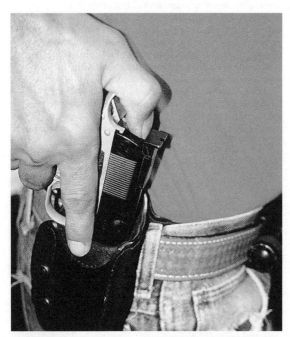

When holstering, keep the trigger finger extended so it can't foul the trigger, and the thumb on hammer. The thumb can catch a hammer that starts to move forward before a shot is fired, as with this Colt 10mm auto...

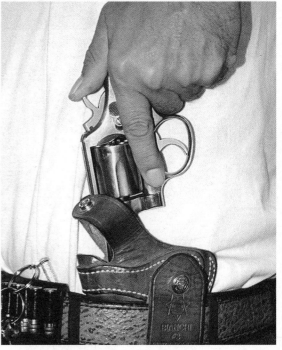

...or feel a double-action hammer rise in time to stop things before that hammer can fall and cause a discharge.

The reason shooting is such a good stress reliever is that, like sky-diving or rock climbing or SCUBA diving, *you have to concentrate on what you're doing to the point where all other BS is excluded from your mind. You must concentrate or you can get killed!* Our focus on safe shooting banishes our thoughts of job stress, family problems, or whether our team won the Super Bowl. If at

The home defense gun should be only one of several layers of protection. Consider getting a good, properly trained dog…

…a good alarm system…

…and some kind of safe. Even the better hotel rooms, as shown here, have safes available for guests.

any time we find ourselves on the line preoccupied with other, more compelling thoughts, it's time to pack up and stop shooting for awhile, perhaps for the rest of the day. Not because we're going to have a psychotic break, but because we can't concentrate sufficiently on something that demands our complete attention. We do it this way for the same reason that we tell our teenage children not to drive when they're upset.

In defensive shooting, as in martial arts, the practitioner seeks to become so skillful that the techniques may be employed automatically without thinking about them when the proper stimulus comes. This is all to the good. However, we must walk a fine line when it comes to firearms safety. Automatic pilot is a fine thing, but it cannot be trusted exclusively. We must always strive for a "conscious competence" level when we're performing firearms safety tasks. We must think about what we are doing. If we have achieved the ideal Zen state of unconscious competence in firearms handling and do everything correctly without thinking about it, that's wonderful, but we need to double check once more at the conscious competence level to confirm the good job that we hope our unconscious competence carried out.

We need to be ruthlessly and honestly critical of ourselves. If we have what are currently called "anger management problems," we won't be ready to have immediate access to loaded firearms until those things are under control. If we sleepwalk, it may not be a good idea having guns available in the bedroom.

A good friend of mine is a world-class competitive shooter with a strong background in law enforcement. He is one of the most well adjusted human beings and family men I know. He also happens to be a very deep sleeper, and tends to be a bit groggy and disoriented for several seconds when suddenly awakened. Recognizing that, he has made a point of keeping his home defense pistol, a Browning 9mm semiautomatic, in a secured drawer across the bedroom. It is stored with the chamber empty. He knows that by the time he has gotten up, crossed the room, retrieved the gun, and chambered a round, he will be awake and clear-headed. This is the kind of self-analysis we all need to go through.

Layered Defense

The police officer on the street has layers of physical defenses. He is taught Verbal Judo (™), a crisis intervention skill. He is taught "soft" come-along holds and "hard" strikes with fist and forearm, with knee and foot. He carries pepper spray, and can resort, next, to his baton. He will have a handgun on the duty belt, and hopefully a shotgun and/or rifle in the patrol car if things get worse yet.

The citizen should have layered defenses in the home. Good locks in solid doors, secure windows, alarms, perhaps an intercom or even a closed-circuit TV at the door, perhaps professionally-trained protection dogs and, of course, firearms.

Gun safety also demands a layered series of defenses. We secure the guns from unauthorized hands. We are constantly aware of where any lethal weapon is and what its condition is. We check by sight and feel. Redundancy is the key. We want to create net after net after carefully deployed net to keep accidents from happening.

Let's close with a very insightful statement by an NRA Director and firearms instructor named Mike Baker. Says Mike, "Seemingly obsessive concern with firearms safety is the mark of the firearms professional."

The Concealed Carry Faux Pas

"Sex and Violence: You can't enjoy the one if you don't survive the other."

> Richard C. Davis, inventor of soft body armor, armed citizen, and gunfight survivor.

"I don't mind where people make love, so long as they don't do it in the street and frighten the horses."

> Beatrice Tanner Campbell, arbiter of etiquette in days past.

Richard Davis and Beatrice Tanner Campbell aren't usually discussed in the same paragraph, but it's appropriate here. We lawfully carry guns because we want to stay alive to enjoy the good things in life. Because we are licensed to wear them in public, we do indeed "do it in the street," and therefore we must take all the more care not to "frighten the horses."

In most jurisdictions, concealment is not only authorized by the license, but also tacitly required. Rookie cops are known for the need to "flash," to just show someone that for the first time in their life, "they've got the power." Armed citizens are well advised to avoid that temptation. The mark of the professional is that few people know that they go about armed. Discretion is critical.

A spiritual descendant of Mrs. Campbell is Judith Martin, who writes the popular "Miss Manners" etiquette column for the newspapers. Some years ago she had a column that read something like this:

"Dear Miss Manners:

"My job requires me to carry a gun. Recently at a party, I sat down awkwardly on a couch and my gun fell to the floor in plain sight. Everyone stared and I was quite shaken. It was most embarrassing. What does one do in such a situation?"

 (signed) "Armed and Confused"

The columnist's reply was similar to this:

"Dear Armed and Confused:

"You should have immediately picked up your firearm and secured it. You should have then self-effacingly stated, 'I'm terribly sorry. My job requires me to carry a gun. Don't worry, no one is in danger.' Then you should have made a graceful exit. And *then* you should have gone out immediately and purchased a holster that would not let your gun fall out. – Miss Manners"

Clearly, Judith Martin is one of us!

You want to avoid "flashing" the gun or allowing it to "print," that is, to become visible in outline under the concealing garments. If you carry in a pocket, use a pocket holster designed to break up the gun's distinctive outline. Another option is to fold up a road map or pamphlet lengthwise, and put it in the pocket between the outer fabric and the gun. If you have a shallow pocket, this will

WRONG! A high reach with the hand on the holster side pulls up the jacket and flashes the gun, in this case an S&W .45 auto.

RIGHT! Discreetly holding down the hem of the jacket on the gun side, the pistol-packer makes the high reach with the opposite hand.

The jacket covers the pistol, but let's say it's just too warm...

...however, leaving the gun exposed like this could "frighten the horses"...

...so instead you shrug off the jacket while seated, like this...

...and sort of puff it out around the holstered gun. You're comfortable. The gun is accessible but out of sight. Remember, however, to put your arms back into your sleeves before you stand up again!

also prevent someone standing in a waiting line behind you from glancing down and seeing the backstrap of the pistol peeking out of the opening of the pocket.

If you wear a shoulder holster, make sure the concealing garment is made of substantial fabric that the lines of the harness do not print. When you bend forward, use one hand or forearm to hold the garment closed on the holster side. Otherwise, a shoulder holster that is not secured to the belt may swing forward and become visible to someone on the side opposite the gun.

If you bend down to pick something up, do it like a back patient. Keep the spine and torso vertical, and bend at the knees. Bending at the waist causes a gun in a hip holster to print starkly.

Avoid middle of the back holsters. Anywhere else on your waistband, if the gun catches the hem of the garment and pulls it up revealingly, you'll quickly either feel it or notice it in peripheral vision. Neither will be true if the gun is in the small of your back. It may be completely exposed, and you'll be the only person within 300 yards who *doesn't* know that your gun is hanging out.

It will be apparent in this book that the author is a believer in safety straps. That's partly so the gun won't be lost in a fall or foot pursuit or other strenuous activity. It's partly because if you're grappling with someone and his hands go around your waist, feel the gun, and begin tugging, you want to buy some "reactionary gap" time. It is also partly to avoid something as simple as sitting in a lattice-back chair and having your gun suddenly leave the holster.

I was once vacationing in Florida, legal to carry a gun, with a 1911 .45 auto, in an open-top, inside-the-waistband holster, under a loose sport shirt. I sat down in a beach chair next to a pool, adjusted the back of the chair up and settled myself. I heard a "clunk." I thought, *"Clunk? Vas ist das Clunk?"* I glanced down and saw a remarkably familiar combat custom .45 auto lying at poolside. So did a couple of other rather wide-eyed people. I scooped up the pistol and tucked it away, remarking to one concerned onlooker, "Sorry, I'm a cop, they make me carry this damn thing." Then, like the poor soul who wrote to Miss Manners, I beat a hasty retreat.

What had happened was that as I shifted my weight upward to settle in the chair, the butt of the pistol had become caught in the open latticework at the back of the

chair. When I lowered myself, the movement in essence pulled the holster down and out from around the gun, which then toppled to the pavement.

This is also a good reason to carry a pistol that is "drop safe." It isn't enough to smugly say, "I don't intend to drop my gun." I didn't intend to, either. But if things we didn't intend to do never happened, we wouldn't have to carry guns in the first place. Out West, a lady with a cute little derringer in her purse dropped the bag accidentally. The pistol inside received the impact as the purse hit the floor and discharged, sending a bullet up out of the handbag and into the chest of a man standing nearby.

When you are reaching upward, particularly with a short jacket on, take care that the garment does not lift so much that it exposes the gun or even part of the holster. If the pistol is on your right hip, you might want to discreetly hold the hem of the jacket in place with your right hand as you reach with your left. If that will flash my spare magazine pouch, which some might find just as unsettling, this writer is of such an age that he can commandeer some passing youngster and say, "Excuse me, son, could you reach an item on that top shelf for an old man?"

If you have an ankle holster on, before you leave the house, sit down and see how much the pant's cuff rides up when you're seated. If the bottom of the holster becomes exposed, nature is telling you to pull your sock up on the *outside* of the holster, taking care that it does not come up over the edge of the holster mouth where it could snag a draw. Now, if the cuff lifts while you're sitting in a restaurant, it just looks like you have a baggy sock. You may get a summons from the Fashion Police, but the Gun Police will leave you alone.

When in restaurants, try to sit with your gun/holster side toward the wall. This will minimize chances of the gun being spotted as you get up.

A good insurance policy against the gun coming out of the holster is a safety strap design. Here, an S&W Model 10 rides in a Strong Piece-Keeper...

...which uses a unique two-stage thumb-break that won't release by accident and is also likely to thwart an intentional gun-grab by unauthorized hands.

If you are wearing a jacket and find yourself seated someplace unbearably hot, you can take off the jacket without flashing the gun. Simply sit down with the garment on, then shrug out of the sleeves and let the jacket sort of fluff up around your waist. Done with care, this will hide the gun. Now you'll be comfortable, and you won't become conspicuous by being the only person in the place wearing a jacket.

If you carry your firearm off-body in a purse or fake Daytimer (™) or whatever, *for Heaven's sake, don't get in the habit of setting it where you might get up and leave it unattended.* There are other countries where people have gone to jail for that, convicted of criminal negligence, if the abandoned weapon is stolen or found by a child. If the container is small enough, put it in your lap. If it's too big for your lap, put it on the seat *against* your hip. If you must, put it on the floor *against* your leg. Have it on the exiting side or between your feet. Yes, the exiting side is more accessible to the purse-snatcher, but ask yourself one question. How many times in your life has a thug snatched your purse or briefcase, compared to how many times in your life have you had to go back into a house or restaurant for a carry bag you inadvertently left behind? Between the feet is better, but on the exit side is acceptable too, because it's always where you can feel it and you can't slide out or get up without noticing it and reminding yourself to keep it with you.

Bending at the waist causes a hip-holstered gun to "print." Keeping the torso vertical and squatting, "like a back patient," would be much less revealing.

Securing Guns In Vehicles

Do the neighbors and passers-by need to see you carrying guns out to your car for a day at the range? Dedicated gun bags, like the excellent Waller unit, look more like high quality gym bags or travel bags, and don't attract attention. The new generation fully enclosed golf club cases designed for air travel are ideal for transporting rifles and shotguns. If the case of ammo you put in the trunk looks like a plain cardboard box, no one is going to look twice.

We have a generation of "gun-free workplaces" where an armed citizen can be arrested for trespass after warning if they enter the office armed. Federal buildings such as post offices are normally considered to be off limits for gun carrying, even if you have a license to do so in public, and in many jurisdictions the same is true for courthouses, schools, and even places that sell alcohol. This means that if you're an armed citizen on a day off doing errands that include mailing a package, picking up a copy of a deed at the courthouse, and purchasing wine for a dinner party, you'll have to take your gun on and off at least three times during the trip.

You don't want to do it conspicuously. A frightened citizen who sees someone "doing something with a gun in a parked car" violates Mrs. Campbell's edict, "Don't frighten the horses." A thug who sees you put a pistol in the console knows that he can smash out a window with a rock and steal a pistol as soon as you're out of sight.

If you regularly carry a gun, it makes sense to get a small lock-box that easily opens by feel with combination push buttons, and bolt it to the floor or the transmission hump of your car, within reach of the driver's seat. This allows you to secure the gun as you approach your parking space, and carefully slip it back out and put it back on as you drive away. Why do this while you're in motion? Because most people won't be able to see you. (Take care about being observed by people in high-seated trucks, however.) You're much more likely to be noticed by a pedestrian who is walking by your parked car, since his natural visual angle is downward into your vehicle.

You might also want to slip the gun into a sturdy cloth shopper's bag (a fanny pack might become a target for a thief because it looks like it might contain a wallet) and lock it in your trunk when you go into the post office, then retrieve it into the passenger compartment when you return to your car.

While we're talking about guns and cars, it's not sound tactics to have gun-related decals or bumper stickers on your vehicle. Did you ever make a political decision and change your vote because you saw something on someone's bumper sticker? Probably not, and no one will vote for your gun rights because they saw your bumper sticker, either. However, those things put some cops on hyper-alert when they pull you over for having a taillight out. Your NRA bumper sticker may give some road-raging bozo the idea to call the police and say you threatened him with a gun. When the cops pull you over and find out you do indeed have a gun, you "fit the profile."

You also have to consider that the criminal element isn't entirely stupid. When they see a gun-related sign on your car, it tells them that you feel strongly about guns. That tells them you probably own several guns. They love to steal guns because firearms and prescription drugs are the only things they can steal from you that they can fence on the black market for more than their intrinsic value, instead of maybe a nickel on the dollar. Now they know that if they follow this car to its home, they can watch the house until people are gone, and then break in and steal guns. This is why the bumper sticker thing is just not wise. Show where your heart is on your rights to own firearms by working and contributing to gun owners' rights groups, instead. It'll do everyone, and the cause, and particularly you, a lot more good.

The Routine Traffic Stop

It can happen to any of us. We're driving along and suddenly the red, or blue, or red and blue lights start flashing in the rearview mirror. We're being pulled over! *And we're carrying a concealed gun!* What do we do?

Well, since we are law-abiding citizens and carrying legally, we pull over. Smoothly, steadily, turning on the signal as soon as we see those lights. At roadside, we park and turn off the ignition and engage the emergency flashers. At night, turn on the interior lights. Stay behind the wheel. If you get out and approach the officer unbidden, you not only indicate to him that there might be something inside the car that you don't want him to see, but your actions mimic the single most common pattern of ambush murder of police during traffic stops. Just stay in the car. Leave your hands relaxed in a high position on the steering wheel. Do not reach for license and registration in glove box or console or under the seat, either now or before coming to a stop. From a vehicle behind you, these movements mimic going for a weapon.

Remember Mrs. Campbell's advice. No cop gets through a police academy without horror stories of brother and sister officers murdered in traffic stops. The officer is carrying a gun and this is the *last* of Mrs. Campbell's horses that you want to frighten.

The officer will ask for license and registration. Make sure that when you open the glove box for the latter, there isn't a gun sitting there. If you have indeed left *la pistola* in the glove box, tell the officer, "I'm licensed to carry, and I have one in the glove box with my registration. How should we handle this?" It would be much better for the gun not to be in that location at all.

In some jurisdictions, when a permit is issued, there is a requirement that you identify yourself as armed any time you make contact with a police officer and are carrying. The easiest thing to do is carry the concealed handgun license next to the driver's license, and hand both to the officer together. Don't blurt something like, "I've got a gun!" It sounds like a threatening statement.

If you try to explain about the pistol and passing traffic obscures some of your words and the only thing the officer hears is "gun," your traffic stop can go downhill. Just hand over the CCW permit with the DL.

You'll want to do the same in jurisdictions where such identification may not be required by law, but where the Department of Motor Vehicles cross-references with issuing authorities on carry permits. In those jurisdictions – Washington state, for example, and many, if not most, parts of California at this writing – the officer will have been told by dispatch or will have seen on his mobile data terminal that you're someone who carries a gun. If you don't bring it up first, such action can seem to the officer as if you're hiding something from him. Again, hand over the CCW with the DL.

In jurisdictions where neither is the case, it's up to you. If I pull you over for a traffic stop in my community, and you are a law-abiding citizen who has been investigated, vetted, and licensed to carry a gun, it's none of my business. If I'm worried about it, I'll ask you if you have one, and will expect an honest answer at that time.

If at any point the officer asks you to please step out of the vehicle, things have changed. Either someone with a description similar to yours did a bad thing (which means you're going to be field interviewed and patted down until it's clear that "you ain't him"), or your operation was careless enough to give the officer probable cause to believe you're driving under the influence. This means there will be a roadside field sobriety test. In the typical Rohmberg test, arms will be going straight out to your sides, coats will be coming open, and this would be a very bad time to "flash."

So, if the officer asks you to step out, I would suggest you reply with exactly these words, if you haven't already handed over the CCW: "Certainly, Officer. However, I'm licensed to carry. I do have it on. Tell me what you want me to do." The cop will take it from there.

Now you're seeing why those of us who've been carrying for a long time understand a principle the courts call the "higher standard of care." It holds that we, of all people, should be smart enough not to make stupid mistakes with guns. This is why, among many other things, those of us who carry guns tend to rely more on the cruise control than the radar detector, and actually make an effort to drive at the speed limit, so we won't get pulled over in the first place.

Securing The Combat Handgun

Shooter A is a professional instructor in combat arms. He's on the road about half the time, usually alone. He keeps a pair of handcuffs in his suitcase and travels with a primary handgun and a backup weapon. When he goes to bed at night in a hotel room, one loaded pistol is in one of the shoes he plans to wear the next day, at bedside. The other is in the other shoe on the opposite side of the bed. He untucks the sheets and blankets at the bottom of the bed before turning in.

Rationale? He can reach the gun immediately if there's an intrusion. If he has to roll to the other side of the bed, he can reach a gun there too. If, like some of the victims he has met over the years, he wakes up with

the attacker on top of him in bed, there will be no tucked-in bedclothes to bind him like a straitjacket and he can roll the attacker off. If he has to leave the guns behind for any reason, he can lock them in the hard-shell case he keeps inside his regular suitcase, then use the handcuffs to secure the case to pipes under the bathroom sink.

The latter tactic is because research has taught him that many hotel burglars have suborned hotel staff and use their keys to enter rooms while guests are out. It's unlikely that these punks will have handcuff keys with them. If they break the pipes to get at the case, it will call immediate attention to their activities. Hotel

The latest S&W revolvers come with both external (shown) and internal trigger locks. On this one, the case is lockable to boot.

management will alert to what's going on, change locks and keys, and kill the golden goose.

Shooter B is a police officer with young children not yet at the age of responsibility. He is subject to call-out from off-duty status at any time. He has arrested and sent to jail some people who aren't too happy about it, and he feels that nothing less than an instantly accessible loaded handgun will keep him and his young family safe enough for his peace of mind.

The solution is a lock-box secured in his closet. When he comes home from work he is carrying his duty sidearm, a .45 auto, as an off-duty weapon. He simply leaves it on his person until he goes to bed. When that time comes, he goes to the lock box. The .45 goes in, and out of the box comes another gun that has reposed safely there all day. It is a Smith & Wesson .357 Combat Magnum revolver, loaded with 125-grain hollow-points and customized with a device called MagnaTrigger, which is not externally visible. When he turns in, he slips this gun under the bed where it's out of sight but he can reach it immediately.

From his night-table drawer come two simple looking stainless steel rings. He puts one on the middle finger of each hand, and goes to sleep.

The rings have magnets attached to the palm side. There's one for each hand because he learned in police training that the dominant hand could become disabled in a fight and he might have to resort to his support hand. He is now the only one who can fire the MagnaTrigger gun, whose retrofitted mechanism blocks the internal rebound slide. At the bottom of the block is a piece of powerful cobalt samarium magnet. Only when a hand wearing a magnetic ring closes over the gun in a firing grasp will reverse polarity move the block out of the way and make the gun instantly "live." This device has been available and working well since 1975, and is currently available from Tarnhelm Supply, 431 High St., Boscawen, NH 03303. On the Web at www.tarnhelm.com. It can be applied only to a Smith & Wesson double-action revolver, K-frame or larger at this time.

Two very different people, and two very different approaches. Neither is likely to have a gun stolen. Neither is likely to have an unauthorized person handling their guns without their knowledge. Yet each is ready to instantaneously access a defensive handgun if there is a sudden, swift invasion of their domicile.

This writer has been a big fan of the MagnaTrigger concept since it came out in 1980. I no longer need it much, as my children are grown and have guns of their own. But with one child married already, I suspect it won't be long before the pitter-patter of grandchildren's feet calls the old Magna-Trigger gun out of mothballs. It is also useful for any time I want to have a gun in off-body carry instead of on my person. The gun is in the bag, but the rings are on me, and if anyone grabs the bag and runs, there's nothing they can do with the gun inside.

Why have you not heard about the MagnaTrigger from the mass media, in all their articles about gun control advocates calling for "smart guns"? Well, simply because those gun control advocates don't really want smart guns. They want no guns at all. Their strategy is to pass legislation requiring something that does not yet exist on

Here's how to use handcuffs to lock up a 1911 single-action auto. The hammer cannot come forward even if the trigger is pulled and the sear is tripped.

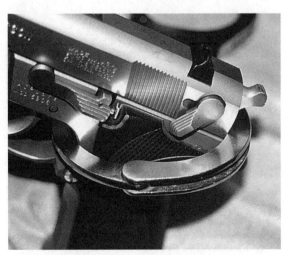

The latest S&W revolvers come with both external (shown) and internal trigger locks. On this one, the case is lockable to boot.

the market: electronically controlled pistols. This will give them an avenue to ban "stupid guns" as dangerous, and then leave gun owners with nothing because the "smart guns" promised to replace them don't come through. If the public found out there actually was a smart gun that worked, the anti-gunners fear that people who don't buy guns now would buy these, and that would thwart their plans. The smart gun that works now is indeed the MagnaTrigger, hampered only by the fact that the technology has not yet been successfully translated to semiautomatic pistols.

Lock Boxes

The lock box, a small, rapid-access gun safe, has been a boon to armed citizens and off-duty police and security personnel. It leaves the gun as secure as if it was in a gun safe if the lock box is bolted to a floor or otherwise made so that it can't be just picked up and walked away with. I've personally had good luck with the Gun Vault brand, but there are several good units out there.

More lock boxes come out every year. Do yourself a favor and visit a gun shop with a wide selection, and try several demonstrator models. A combination dial will be difficult in dim light with shaking hands. You want push buttons, set well apart in ergonomic fashion, and one reason to try it in the shop is to make sure the unit you like fits your particular hands. Be sure to practice with it frequently. Remember that anything battery operated needs to have its batteries changed regularly. Get into the habit of changing the batteries in such a lock box when you change the batteries in your emergency flashlights and your smoke alarms: twice a year, when you change the clocks for Daylight Savings Time.

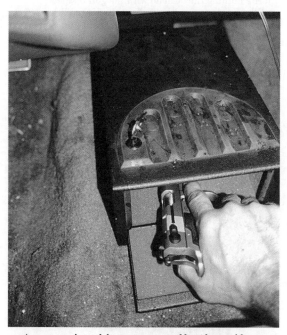

An ergonomic push button pattern and keyed over-ride are good features of the Gun Vault unit. This one is bolted to the transmission hump of an automobile. It is an ideal set-up for people who cannot bring their carry guns into certain buildings.

This old S&W Model 39 9mm auto is kept in a cut-out book. Note the warnings the owner has surrounded it with.

One Safe Place

No matter where your gun is stored, it is possible that a violent intrusion will happen so rapidly that you can't get to it in time. The one way to always be certain you can reach your gun is to always wear it. This doesn't mean you have to walk around the house with a Sam Browne belt, a high-capacity 9mm, and 45 rounds of ammo in pre-ban magazines. A snub-nose .38 in a side pocket will do nicely.

With the gun on your person, it is at once readily accessible to you and inaccessible to unauthorized hands. I wrote that more than 30 years ago in one of my first magazine articles. It was true then, and it is just as true now. Perhaps more so: armed home invasions seem to have become more frequent in certain areas.

There's another advantage to simply always being armed. You don't forget and leave your gun at home. I'll never forget one cop, the hero of one fatal gunfight a few years before, who told me, "I was on my own time, downtown, shopping. I heard the first gunshot go off, and my hand went to my hip, and there was nothing there because I had forgotten to put my gun on…" That particular event turned out all right, but I doubt that he ever made that mistake again. Educators call it "a reinforcement of the learning experience."

Gun Locks and Trigger Locks

For decades in police work, it has been common practice to keep gun lockers at the entryways to each booking area or fingerprinting setup. We learned to slip our service weapon into the small locker, secure it, and pocket the key. Law enforcement quickly learned to put the guns in loaded, leave them loaded, take them out loaded, and re-holster them loaded.

Each time you load and unload, you're handling a live weapon, and that always creates an opening for an accidental discharge. There was always the possibility of an officer forgetting to reload and going back on patrol with an empty gun. This collective experience has proven that a loaded handgun in a lock box is as safe as safe can be.

I do not like the idea of trigger locks. If someone puts one on a loaded gun, the lock can jiggle against the trigger and cause an unintended discharge. There is no trigger lock that will keep the gun itself from being loaded. I simply don't trust that technology, and a lot of other long-time firearms professionals share that opinion.

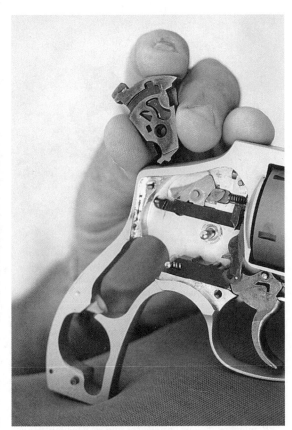

These are the operating parts of Smith & Wesson's internal gun lock, introduced in 2001.

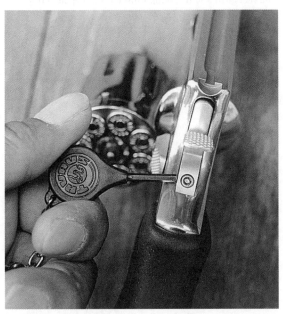

An easily manipulated key operates the hammer lock on standard model Taurus revolvers. Note the keyway between hammer spur and frame.

If I have to lock up the gun without putting it in a container in which the firearm cannot be touched, I prefer something that locks the firing mechanism. First Taurus, and now Smith & Wesson, have begun producing their revolvers with integral locks. While some people oppose this concept on principle, I've so far seen nothing wrong with it mechanically. Neither the hammer-mounted lock of the Taurus nor the side plate-mounted integral flush lock on the S&W seem capable of "locking up" by themselves when you need them to fire, and I've hammered the heck out of these guns with hard-kicking ammo. We're talking full-power .454 Casull in the Taurus Raging Bull revolver and full-power .357 Magnum in the Smith & Wesson 340 PD, which weighs only 12 ounces. Similar technology exists now in some auto pistols.

One of my colleagues has speculated that if some of these guns are dropped into sand, the keyways will be blocked and the owners won't be able to make the lock work to "turn the gun on." Unless one is camping out of doors, I don't see too much problem with that. There's no reason for a locked gun to be exposed anyway; it should be in a container if you're someplace where the gun must be secured.

The Handcuff Trick

Since long before this old guy pinned on a badge, cops have been securing their guns at home with their handcuffs. With the conventional double-action revolver, the bracelet goes between the rear of the trigger and the back of the trigger guard, and over the hammer. This at once blocks the rearward travel of the trigger and the rearward travel of the hammer, positively preventing firing. On a "hammerless" style revolver, the trigger is still blocked.

On a single-action such as the 1911 or the Hi-Power, the handcuff's bracelet is applied differently. On the 1911, which has a sliding trigger, it goes under the outside of the trigger guard at the juncture of the grip-frame, and over the back of the slide in a way that holds the hammer down if the chamber is empty, or back if the gun is cocked and locked and loaded. With the Browning, which has a freestanding trigger, it can be done just as on a revolver or

This is a double-action revolver secured with handcuffs. The hammer can't rise (and therefore can't fall), and the trigger can't be pulled far enough for discharge, because a handcuff bracelet blocks those parts on the S&W 686.

A wise police instructor, Peter Tarley, came up with the concept of unloading the Glock and then field stripping it. A practiced shooter familiar with the gun can quickly reassemble and then load it.

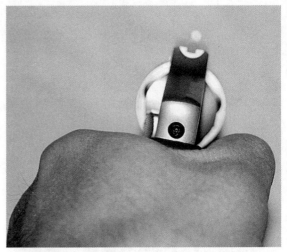

On Taurus' "hammerless" CIA revolver, the integral key lock is high on the backstrap of the grip-frame, just above the web of this shooter's hand.

if the gun is cocked and locked, the bracelet can be between the hammer and the slide while also blocking the trigger's travel toward the rear of the guard. A double-action auto would be secured the same way, holding the hammer in the down position.

I don't see any way to effectively lock up the Glock pistol with handcuffs. What the Glock does lend itself to better than most other guns, is a home safety concept I first heard suggested by Peter Tarley, the world-class instructor who used to work for Glock. Simply unload the pistol, and field strip it. The Glock's barrel/slide assembly comes off *en bloc* as with many other guns, but unlike most others, there is no takedown lever that has to be manipulated a certain way during reassembly. When

danger threatens, grab the barrel/slide assembly with your non-dominant hand, your frame assembly with your dominant hand, and put the two back together. Then holding the gun in the dominant hand, seize the loaded magazine, insert it, rack the slide, and you're holding a loaded Glock pistol. It's surprising how quickly this can be done. The old HK P9S, no longer produced, was one of the few other guns with which this trick works as well.

Remember, it's our gun. Power and responsibility must always be commensurate. When we need the power, we must accept – and live up to – the responsibility. In the end, most of the time, you never needed the power, but you feel good about having fulfilled the responsibility.

CHAPTER TWELVE

Accessorizing

Responsible Customizing

Man has enhanced his weapons since he first stood erect and picked them up. Perhaps one caveman realized that a club with a wider end would have more momentum and hit harder then the untapered club used by the leader of tribe in the next valley. Sometimes the personalizing was just in the form of decoration to mark the weapon as this warrior's own and helped prevent theft. It also gave him more ego investment in the tool that might one day save his life.

A couple of men I respect enormously, who've both "been there and done it", are known to possess what they call "barbecue guns." These are fancy, nay, *ornate* pistols that certainly work just fine, but most of the attention lavished upon them has been cosmetic rather than utilitarian. For one shooter it's an engraved and gold inlaid Colt .45 automatic with ivory grips. For the other, it's an engraved Smith & Wesson .44 Magnum with stag handles. My friends wear these guns to commemorate special occasions.

Pride of ownership is a good thing. Having your name or initials engraved on your gun makes it less desirable to a thief and easier to recover if stolen, though it impairs resale value. Today, most custom work done on handguns is more utilitarian than cosmetic.

That includes refinishing. While a gun with a new hard-chrome finish may look better than before, it's also more impervious to the elements. Some finishes, like

Robar's NP3, add an element of lubricity that make the gun work better.

Action Jobs

In many cases, the most useful modification will be an "action job" that allows the trigger to be pulled more smoothly and cleanly. Remember, you don't need "light" so much as you need "smooth." That said, some guns that come with very heavy triggers – Colt DAO autos, the Kel-Tech P-11, and some others – can afford to lose a few pounds of pull weight.

What you don't want on any handgun that might actually be used to hold a human being at gunpoint is what a layman might call a "hair trigger." Most gunsmiths and forensic evidence technicians would define 4 pounds as an absolute minimum pull weight. Some go a little higher.

It never hurts to have the trigger's surface smoothed off, at the front and on the edges. Some may need the back edge of the trigger and the rear edge of the trigger guard smoothed as well. Certain shooters may benefit from having the inside bottom surface of a Glock's trigger guard

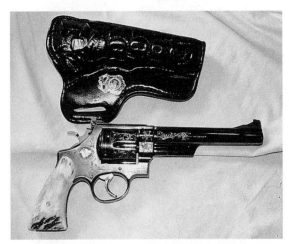

The author's Glock 17 has all "working mods," most from GlockWorks. Sights are Heinie Straight Eight with tritium. Pre-ban +2 magazine brings the fully loaded capacity to 20 rounds of 9mm Parabellum. InSights M3 light installs quickly on the frame and comes off almost as fast.

A "Barbecue Gun." This engraved, gold-inlaid S&W Model 629 also sports an action job by its owner, Detective Denny Reichard, and MeproLight night sights. Yes, he can control .44 Magnum recoil with those slim bone grips. You have to know Denny. The hand-tooled holster, with a miniature of the owner's shield, completes the ensemble.

White spots on an anodized blue S&W Model 3944 show where Rick Devoid has taken the sharp edges off. Such a job is cheap and the "user-friendliness" is huge. Devoid usually blends finish back as it was...

Garrey Hindman at Ace Custom did the superb trigger work on this S&W 4506. The rear of the trigger guard and the trigger have been polished glass-smooth to match the internal action hone. The jewelling on the trigger and barrel are cosmetic, but nice touches.

taken down a little as well, if the size and shape of their fingers are such that the trigger finger drags on the inside of the guard. Smooth triggers are also an important amenity for those who train seriously. We've found that after two or three days of intensive shooting on the range, a serrated trigger will often have produced a weeping blister.

It is always a good idea for any revolver that is going to be kept or carried for self-defense to be rendered double-action-only. This eliminates the danger of both a hair trigger discharge if the gun is cocked, and the false allegation that such a thing happened when in fact it didn't. Grinding off the hammer spur isn't enough. The

You want smooth, not light. This Gunsite Custom S&W Airweight by Ted Yost is just as slick, and even more reliable, with a long mainspring (top) instead of the shorter, slightly lighter aftermarket replacement spring, below.

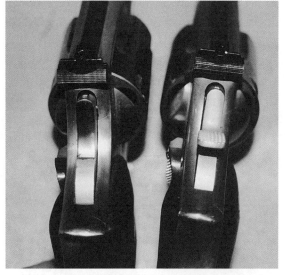

Right, a stock S&W Model 686; left, the same gun rendered double-action-only with the hammer spur removed. Reshaped and lighter, the hammer falls faster — better reliability in double-action shooting and slightly faster "lock time," i.e., a shorter interval between when the hammer begins to fall and when the shot goes off.

In addition to double-action-only action slick and spurless hammer, Al Greco has installed a permanent trigger stop on the author's S&W Model 625 to reduce backlash.

single-action cocking notch on the hammer (internal) needs to be removed by a competent and qualified gunsmith or armorer, or a new DAO hammer needs to be fitted.

This seems less necessary on semiautomatic pistols. The more rearward placement of the hammer spur on an auto makes it more awkward to thumb-cock and, thus, less believable that someone would do so. A cocked auto pistol will also usually have a heavier trigger pull than a cocked double-action revolver. That said, fear of both accidents and false accusations of accidents have led a great many police departments, and more than a few citizens, to go with the double-action-only trigger concept on semiautomatic pistols as well as revolvers.

Safety Devices

A 1911 grip safety can dig and even lacerate the hand if it is not wide, edge-free, and smoothly polished. The thumb safeties of 1911 and P-35 type pistols are often too small, and rarely ambidextrous. An enlarged thumb safety lever makes that part more positive in use for many shooters, while the ambidextrous safety is desirable for any serious potential combatant and is of course a necessity for southpaws using such guns.

Excellent aftermarket parts of this type are available from Cylinder & Slide Shop, 800-448-1713; Ed Brown Products, 573-565-3261; and Wilson Custom, 870-545-3618, among many others. These three sources can usually retrofit the parts to your gun for you.

A thumb safety can be added to some guns that don't normally come that way. Joe Cominolli, at www.cominollio.com, can install one for your Glock, though at this writing he makes the unit for right-handed use only. Do you have a DAO S&W auto with a "slickslide" design? Rick Devoid, at www.tarnhelm.com, can install a dedicated, ambidextrous thumb safety on its slide for you. He's also the source for the one functional "smart gun" available at this writing, the MagnaTrigger-modified S&W revolver, and finally, he can install a Murabito safety on any frame size S&W wheelgun to make the cylinder latch perform double duty as a thumb safety that works with a downward stroke like a 1911.

Removing or deactivating a safety device can get you into a world of trouble if you're ever accused of

Most oversize magazine releases cause problems, but this useful one from GlockWorks is the exception. Author's Glock 17 also sports a Cominolli thumb safety.

wrongdoing with a gun. A good lawyer won't have much trouble convincing a dozen laypersons that anyone who would deactivate the safety device on a lethal weapon had to be reckless. However, when you pay out of your pocket to enhance the safety devices on a firearm – to literally make it safer than it was when it left the factory – you can easily be shown to possess an unusually high degree of responsibility.

As a rule, any after-market "safety" that makes the gun go to the "fire" position faster and more positively when needed, will also make it go to the "on-safe" position faster and more positively, and it's hard to argue with that.

Reliability Packages

Some guns need an internal work-over before they achieve optimum function. For many years, this was true of the 1911 and the Browning P-35. For most of their history, they were military-specification pistols designed to work with mil-spec ammo. That is, full-metal-jacket round nose. Out of the box, they would feed hardball ammo, or Remington hollow-points that were jacketed up and over the tip to the same ogive as hardball, and that

A thumb safety the size of a gas pedal is too big for carry, but some like it for competition. Adjustable sights can be argued either way. Springfield Armory, however, has already replaced the too narrow grip safety with a beavertail on current versions of this gun, their Trophy Match .45.

You want your defense gun work done by a master. Bill Laughridge, shown in the middle of his busy Cylinder & Slide Shop, fills the bill.

Shown are two of the author's favorite "combat custom" Colt .45 autos. Top, is the LFI Special by Dave Lauck; below, is a "Workhorse" by D.R. Middlebrooks.

was about it. If you wanted them to run with more efficient, wider-mouth JHP bullets, you had to pay a gunsmith to "throat them out."

Both types of guns are now produced by a number of sources. Some companies still make "mil-spec" versions of

The author is partial to this Glock 23 for certain competitions. Modifications include…

the Colt and the Browning, of which the above remains true. But there are many versions that now come from the box "factory throated" and ready to feed most anything you stuff in it. These include currently produced Colt and Browning brands, and also the Kimber, the Para-Ordnance, and the upper lines of Springfield Armory production.

Your Beretta, Glock, HK, Kahr, Kel-Tec, Ruger, SIG, S&W, or Taurus auto as currently produced should not need a "reliability package." However, like some of the other models mentioned, they might benefit to a greater or lesser degree from having some of the sharp edges beveled at hand contact points. This is particularly true of the standard-line Smith & Wesson pistols. Any of them might also benefit from a good action hone, too.

Recoil Reduction Devices

The general consensus among defense-oriented combat shooters is that most recoil reduction devices pass the point of diminishing returns because they vent hot gases upward in a way that could strike the shooter in the face or eyes when shooting from a "speed rock" or "protected gun" position. That said, they also tame muzzle jump very effectively. Some people who carry guns simply don't have those close-to-the-body shooting positions in their repertoires and don't feel a loss in carrying a "compensated" gun.

For concealed carry, you don't want one of those humongous comps that hangs off the end of the gun and looks like a cross between a TV spy's "silencer" and Buck Rogers' ray gun. A good "Carry-Comp", as executed by Mark Morris in Washington State (www.morriscustom.com), will end up the same size as a Colt Government Model, but will feel almost recoil free. I have one in 10mm on which the comp works so efficiently, the gun all but recoils downward. When they're properly installed, you won't lose accuracy; my Morris 10mm CarryComp has won first place open-sight, big-bore awards for me at 100-yard NRA Hunter Pistol matches, shooting against Thompson/Center single shots and long-barreled Magnum hunting revolvers. It will just let you

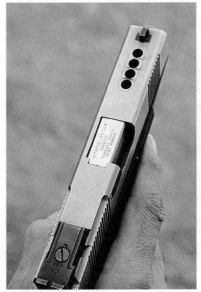

…Schuemann Hybrid-Porting, which radically reduces recoil, and BoMar sights, which enhance the capability of precision hits. Note the warning stamped on the chamber area of barrel, however.

shoot a whole lot faster. This is the gun I was shooting when my daughter, Justine, and I won the speed-oriented match that made us National Champion Parent/Child team in sub-junior (child age 13 and down) class at the first National Junior Handgun Championships. The ammunition was Triton's powerful Hi-Vel, spitting a 155-grain bullet at an honest 1,300 feet per second. With the CarryComp, the gun just sort of quivered as it went off.

With the exception of the brilliant Mag-na-Port concept pioneered by my old friend Larry Kelly, most recoil reduction jobs will magnify the blast of each shot, often to unpleasant levels. Mag-na-Port, I've found, works best on revolvers and long guns, and on autos with open-top slides like the Beretta, Glock Tactical/Practical, and Taurus. The factory-compensated Glocks work on a similar principle.

Seen in profile, Hybrid-Ported Glocks look like ordinary full-size (top) and compact .40s. The stainless Caspian slide on the bottom gun is easier to mill for adjustable sight installation than the super-hard Glock slide.

Combat pistol champ Marty Hayes has won awards with this Hybrid-ported Glock 22 in .40 S&W. He prefers...

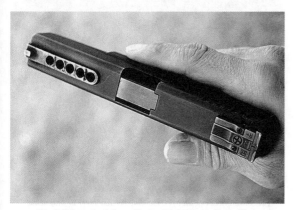

...this full-length sight radius, with Millett adjustable sights.

Hybrid-porting, developed by the brilliant Will Schuemann, gives dramatic recoil reduction with a series of big ports that go down the top of the barrel. The upside is great recoil reduction; downside is bright flash in front of the eyes in night shooting and significant velocity loss. This system seems to be at its best on the revolver and the Glock pistol, though the best gunsmiths can carefully balance a 1911's action to make it work with the reduced recoil that comes with the concept.

Beveled and Funneled Magazine Wells

When the 1911 single-stack pistol was *the* gun for serious combat shooters, a popular modification was beveling out the magazine well so a magazine would slip in more easily during loading or reloading. This worked, and has become a standard feature, on top-line 1911's by Colt, Kimber, Springfield Armory, etc. The guns with wider, double-stack magazines benefit less from this feature, since the tapered top of the magazine combines with the already large magazine well to create a funnel effect.

The cottage industry developed the concept into magazine chutes, which could either bolt onto the gun (requiring padded-bottom magazines, since the edges of the chutes extended below the pistol frames) or be swaged or welded into the gun butt by a good pistolsmith without lengthening the grip frame. For a single-stack magazine pistol in particular, this is an excellent idea. There is a distinct improvement in reloading speed even for experts, and those new to the gun will benefit even more.

Magazine chutes are now even made for the Glock, which probably doesn't need it. The bottom line of any

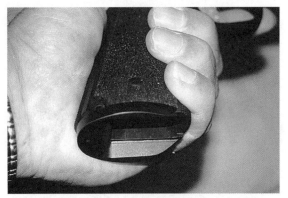

Variations on a theme. The extended, oversize magazine well on this Springfield TRP enhances reloading speed, but makes gun slightly less concealable and demands padded-bottom magazines for positive seating.

Merely beveling the frame without add-ons works quite well, as on this Springfield Trophy Match.

modification is, if it doesn't hurt anything and it helps something, it's probably a good idea. Properly installed magazine chutes and beveled magazines fit that description. If they don't extend the length of the grip-frame, they have no disadvantages except cost. They definitely do make magazine changes easier all the way around.

Extended Slide Releases

As a rule, these are not a great idea. The slide releases of most standard pistols are adequate in size. Enlarging them can cause holster fit problems. There are also reliability issues. Oversize slide lock levers put extended weight on the part that levers it out of position and either keeps it from doing its job when the magazine runs dry, or more commonly, causes it to bounce up and lock the slide open prematurely while the pistol is cycling.

The single exception is probably the Glock pistol. Glock intentionally made the slide release a low-profile part, assuming that most shooters would jack the slide to reload the gun instead of the faster method of thumbing the lever. A slightly extended slide stop lever is available

from Glock, originally developed for the target model guns, that will fit the concealed carry and duty models. The FBI has reportedly ordered it on all its duty Glocks. If you have trouble operating the standard lever, definitely retrofit with this one. It is a Glock part, so it doesn't void the warranty, and it works fine and has no disadvantages.

Checkered/Squared Trigger Guards

Some of the earlier practical shooting masters, such as Ray Chapman and Ross Seyfried, shot with the index fingers of their support hands wrapped around the front of the trigger guards of their Colt .45 autos. They had large hands and short guards and could get away with it. To make it work better, they checkered the front of the trigger guard and sometimes changed the guard to a more square shape.

For the overwhelming majority of shooters, having the support hand's index finger under the trigger guard will work better. If, however, the shooter insists on securing the weak hand finger on the guard, checkering will help reduce its natural tendency to slip off.

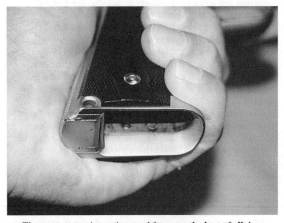

The most expensive option, and for some the best of all, is a swaged out magazine well, this one by Dave Lauck on a Colt.

You shouldn't need an oversize slide release lever or magazine release button on most pistols; standard 1911 size parts do fine, as seen on this top-grade Springfield Armory pistol.

Well thought out "factory customizing" is seen on this Springfield Armory top-grade TRP (Tactical Response Pistol). Rugged adjustable night sights, easily manipulated ambidextrous thumb safety, "just right" street trigger, Barnhart Burner grips, checkered front-strap for a non-slip hold, and ergonomic beavertail grip safety with "speed bump" to allow activation in any reasonable firing grasp.

Flashlight Attachments

The HK USP began the trend of a dust cover (the front portion of the frame) molded or milled to accept a quickly attaching and detaching flashlight. HK had its own, called the UTL (Universal Tactical Light). Other companies quickly followed suit.

Glock, Springfield Armory, and a broad array of other brands have this option. The M-3 Illuminator by Insights Technologies works particularly well in this function.

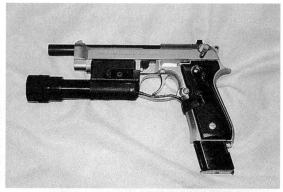

Looks spacey, works great. The author's bedside Beretta, a 92FS tuned by Bill Jarvis. A 6-inch Bar-Sto barrel gives pupil-of-the-eye accuracy at home defense distances, and added velocity that brings hot 9mm ammo up to otherwise unattainable ballistics. The extended barrel is Mag-na-Ported to reduce muzzle jump. Trijicon night sights allow precise shooting if the user chooses not to activate the powerful SureFire flashlight. The extended magazine creates a 21-shot pistol. The result is a high-capacity handgun with surgical accuracy that combines the recoil of a .380 with the power of a .357 Magnum and gives the user command of various light situations.

The trigger finger can operate the M3 light one-handed on this Springfield TRP Tactical Operator pistol. Adjustable night sights give a back-up option in dim light.

If your pistol does not have an integral attachment rail, do not despair. SureFire makes a pistol-mounted flashlight that attaches to a standard 1911, Beretta, or other auto, with a part that replaces the slide stop. This is my personal favorite "gun flashlight"; it is naturally ergonomic, extremely bright, and ruggedly durable. I keep one on the pistol that I usually have at my bedside when at home. It is intended to be a dedicated unit, not a quickly attaching and detaching accessory.

The flashlight can be a lifesaver in more ways than one. We'll never know how many people who were shot when they reached in the dark for "something that looked like a gun" would be alive today if the person who shot them had been able to see that they were holding a harmless object. It wasn't the shooter's fault, but this technology would have saved those shooters much suffering, internal self-doubt, and lawsuits.

The powerful flashlight can also blind and intimidate an opponent. I've seen it happen in the field. However, remember that using your flashlight to search is like using the telescopic sight of your rifle to scan for game: you're pointing a loaded gun at anything you look at. I want a heavy trigger pull and/or an engaged safety on the

There's nothing wrong with personalizing. This Seecamp .32 was special ordered with the author's initials as the serial number.

weapon to which my light is attached. This will minimize the chance of a "startle response" causing an unintended discharge when the user sees something that startles him but doesn't warrant a deadly force response. Obviously, the finger should be clear of the trigger guard when searching with such a unit, but the heavy trigger and/or manual safety is one more redundant safety net to prevent tragedy.

Liability points

Few creatures can be more desperate than an attorney who has no case. Many people involved in law enforcement have seen attorneys try to find negligence in after-market grips, colored or glow-in-the-dark gun sights, even the name of the gun. "Persuader" sounds more sinister than "Model 500," and "Cobra" sounds more violent and deadly than "Agent," even though in both

cases it is essentially the same shotgun and revolver, respectively, under discussion.

Does this mean you shouldn't modify your gun, as some have suggested? This writer personally thinks that is going too far. Certainly, it would be a good idea to avoid a gun with a controversial name like "Pit Bull" or "Bonnie and Clyde," both of which have actually been used by American gunmakers. More important, however, is to avoid a "hair trigger" (lighter than 4 pounds) or a deactivated safety. Either can create the impression of a reckless gun owner.

We've covered the innards and what might be called the superstructure of the handgun, but have not yet touched upon two critical points, the sights and the type and fit of the grips or stocks. That's because each is so important that they're worth their own chapters. We'll get to that immediately.

Combat Handgun Sights

The sights are your weapon's primary aiming tools. When a defense gun has to be employed, the sequence is something like this: Enemy fighter sighted, need to shoot confirmed…missiles locked on target…missiles launched…track target, prepare to launch more missiles if necessary.

The "missiles locked on target" part is accomplished by indexing the handgun, and that is best accomplished with the sights. But we must be able to see the sight under adverse conditions such as dim light, tunnel vision, and animal instinct screaming at us to focus on the threat when knowledge tells us to focus on the sights.

Sights on a combat handgun should be big, blocky, and easy to see under assorted light conditions. They should be rugged enough that they won't fall off the gun or be knocked out of alignment if the wearer falls on the holstered gun in a fight, or the gun bangs against a wall as the user ducks for cover, or if the gun is dropped on a hard surface in the course of a struggle.

The general rule of thumb is that fixed sights are more durable than adjustable sights. There are exceptions to

that rule, however. We've seen fixed rear sights held in place in their dovetail by an Allen screw come loose and drift sideways or even fall off a pistol. The plastic fixed sights that come on some modern guns may be more likely to break than the most rugged steel adjustable sights. The latter include such time-proven units as the BoMar or the MMC adjustable night sight, which has large, shielding "ears" on either side, similar to the current S&W service auto adjustable sight design.

Night Sights

Tritium night sights go back to the Bar-Dot developed by Julio Santiago back in the 1970s. They have come a long way. Available in a multitude of shapes and colors, they not only aid in sighting on an identified target in the dark, but can help an officer find a gun that was dropped in the dark after he has won the struggle with the offender trying to take it. For those of us who travel a lot, waking up in the middle of the night in a dark, strange room is not conducive to finding your pistol. The glowing dots of the night sights, if the gun has been positioned

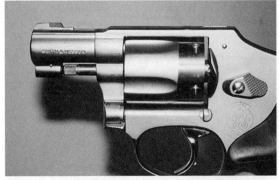

Master revolversmith Andy Cannon built up the front sight of this Model 940 S&W 9mm revolver for the author, and widened the rear sight proportionally. The improvement in "shootability" is dramatic.

Because of the precise adjustments many consider these BoMar adjustable sights target equipment; but, they are extremely rugged and suitable for heavy duty.

The big rear notch of standard Beretta fixed sights...

...coupled with its proportionally large front sight, makes an easy combination for old or myopic eyes to see.

with the sights toward the sleeping owner, are like airstrip landing lights that guide the legitimate user's eye and hand to the defensive weapon.

You can get three dots all the same color that line up horizontally, the type that works best for this writer. You can get one dot on top of the other; the configuration master pistolsmith and designer Dick Heinie dubbed the "Straight Eight" because it resembles a figure-8 in the dark. IWI pioneered an option now available from most other makers: one color front dot, a different color for the rear dots. If the front dot is the brighter color, the eye goes to it instinctively, and this concept also keeps the new shooter, or the one whose gun doesn't fit, from aligning the dots incorrectly and shooting way off to one side. Some, like officer survival expert Jim Horan, prefer just

the single tritium dot on the front sight with no corresponding rear reference.

Eyesight varies hugely between different people. Any of these concepts can work. The best bet is to try them all and see which works best for you. This writer has found the three-dot system to be most visible to his particular eyes. It also works with the StressPoint Index concept mentioned in the point-shooting chapter. When the shooter sees an equilateral triangle of dots, the top one will be on the front sight, and the StressPoint Index is in place.

There are many brands. At one time, it was a choice of Trijicon and a few also-rans. Today, the quality has gone up across the night sight industry, though I don't think anyone has yet exceeded Trijicon. I've been happy with the IWI night sights on my department-issue Ruger .45, with green up front and amber at the rear. I have no problem with the Meprolight sights on a pet Glock 22 that I carry often. Trijicons adorn my bedside Beretta, and a couple of my Glocks and SIGs. I have Heinie Straight Eight sights on a Morris Custom Colt .45 and a Glock 17. They all work fine.

It has been said that you shouldn't need night sights, because if it's too dark to see your sights it's too dark to see your target. That's untrue for two reasons. First, the vagaries of artificial illumination and natural light and shadow are such that you might indeed be able to identify your opponent but not get a clear sight picture. Moreover,

The big rear notch of standard Beretta fixed sights...

...and which is seen here in its multiple variations on Ring's brand dummy guns.

if the shape in the dark yells at you, "Die, infidel American!" and you see a muzzle flash, I think your target is identified and I for one would like for you to have the option of night sights.

Express Sights

Pioneered by my friend and student Ashley Emerson, whose company Ashley Outdoors is now in other hands and making these excellent sights under the title AO, the express sight with Ashley's copyrighted Big Dot makes a lot of sense for a lot of situations. The far-sighted person who can see to identify the threat just fine but can't see anything but a fuzzball at gun-sight distance is an ideal candidate for these. The rear is a shallow "v" with a white line down the middle, and the front sight is a humongous white (or glowing Tritium) circle. Put together, it looks like a big lollipop. Easy to see, fast to hit with in close. The express sight got its name because it has been used for well over a century on the powerful Express rifles hunters used for the biggest, most dangerous game at close range.

As noted earlier, it's subjective. This writer can't shoot worth a damn with express sights on a pistol at 25 yards. At very close range, though, they are slightly faster for me and tremendously faster and more accurate for those who can't see a regular sight picture. Definitely worth looking at, no pun intended.

Full- And Half-Ghost Rings

"Ghost ring" was Jeff Cooper's term for the 19th century deer hunter's trick of removing the sight disk from an aperture ("peep") sight and just looking through the big circle that held it to get a faster, coarser sight picture with his rifle. On a rifle or shotgun it turns out to be remarkably accurate, and Jeff did us all a favor in revitalizing the concept.

It has been tried on pistols with less success. Because the aperture is so much farther from the eye than it would be on a long gun, you don't get the same effect. It can be fast in close, and does give a big sight picture for those who can't focus on conventional sights, but there don't seem to be a lot of people who are terribly accurate with them. Some are, mind you, but not many. There are various brands available; for current options, check the advertising pages of *American Handgunner* magazine.

More useful to more people is a concept developed by gun expert Gary Paul Johnston and made a reality by Wayne Novak, master combat pistolsmith and designer of the famous, streamlined Novak fixed rear sight. The ghost ring is simply cut in half. A big, rectangular post front sight is now seen through a huge rear "u" notch. It is easy to line up even for myopic people with their corrective lenses off. I shot the one on Gary Paul's Novak Custom Browning when we were at a Winchester ammunition seminar together at Gunsite Ranch in Arizona, and was very favorably impressed with the combination of speed and accuracy it delivered. *Definitely* better than full ghost ring sights in this writer's opinion, but an apparently well-kept secret and, to my knowledge, available only through Novak's .45 Shop, 304-485-9525.

I once told William McMoore, designer of a fascinating work in progress called the Sceptre pistol that blends elements of the Glock and the 1911, that I thought the best "geezer sights" would be simply a square notch rear and a post front, but both absolutely huge. He tells me he has Ashley Emerson working on that very concept. Stay tuned.

Police gun expert Gary Paul Johnston displays the "half ghost ring" sight he designed for Wayne Novak. The author feels this brilliant concept has not achieved the popularity it deserves.

Optical Sights

Conventional telescopic sights for handguns are too big for all-day-carry holstering, and because of their long eye relief generally too slow to aim with under combat conditions at combat distances. World champion Jerry Barnhart proved in the 1980s that the internal red dot sight was faster than any conventional iron sight. He proceeded to kick butt with it in matches until, in open class, red dot sights were all you saw.

They are so fast and accurate because the unit's big screen gives a "head's up display" that is much more easily seen than the image in any telescopic sight when you're moving and shooting fast. The aiming dot and the target appear to be on the same visual plane, so the old problem of good focus on opponent or good focus on sights but not good focus on both is eliminated. U.S. military elite teams have gone to these in a big way. In Somalia in 1993, and much more so in the Afghanistan reprisal of 2001 and beyond, international news cameras caught countless images of these high-tech sights on American M-4 assault rifles.

"Geezer sights" Gunsmith/cop Denny Reichard "hogged out" the rear sight of this N-frame S&W for an aging shooter, and created a sight picture even fuzzy eyes can see.

The author's friend John Pride, gunfight survivor and many times National Police Handgun champion and Bianchi Cup winner, has a Tasco Pro-Point on the match gun he's wearing on his hip. But in his hand is a compact S&W auto with what may be the only practical concealed carry red dot optical sight at this writing...

...the extremely compact Tasco Optima...

...which fits on a pistol thus.

The state of the art has improved enormously since the early days, but there are two problems. One is that they run on batteries, and anything that is battery-dependant can fail you at the worst possible time. The other is that most of them are too bulky to carry in a holster, particularly concealed.

There have been numerous attempts to make a small, practical, concealed carry internal dot sight. Only one, in my opinion, is worth looking at: the Optima 2000 from Tasco. Resembling a high, circular rear sight, it sits behind the ejection port on the slide of a semi-auto pistol, clear of the holster. It may not hide under a T-shirt well, but it can conceal under a sport jacket. To conserve battery life, it turns itself off in the dark and turns itself on when exposed to light. (Hmmm...could this be a problem in a very dark room?)

The concept isn't perfect, but Tasco sets it up so you can use the pistol's regular sights right through the lens of the Optima 2000, whether you can see the red dot or not. This protects against battery failure. If you have vision problems and are ready to try a high-tech solution, this is worth looking at. Unfortunately, Tasco has recently closed its doors. While Tasco products will remain available on the secondary market, there won't be anything new rolling off the production line. At this time no one can tell what this will do to prices.

Laser Sights

Because I didn't embrace the laser sight as the wave of the future I've been described in letters to gun magazine editors as an old Luddite who can't understand new technology. *Au contraire.* I merely pointed out that while the laser sometimes has intimidation effect, it sometimes doesn't, and may even provoke a homicidal response. I speak from experience.

This doesn't mean the laser has no tactical place in the defensive handgun world, it just means it has to be seen and used rationally. Says famous police combat instructor Marty Hayes, "Maybe the laser will intimidate the bad guy, and maybe it won't. But if there's even a chance it will, I want the laser on my side and my officers' side."

Personally, I don't think "intimidation factor" is anywhere near the top of the list of the laser sight's attributes. In a tactical setting, I think a laser-sighted pistol is the tool of choice for anyone working with a "body bunker," the bullet-resistant barrier that is carried like a shield. To aim through its Lexan viewing port with conventional sights, you have to bend your arm to an angle so weak that you risk gun malfunctions, and accentuated recoil slows down your rate of accurate fire. Keeping the wrist locked (and most of the arm behind the shield, another advantage), aiming with the projected laser dot, simply makes more sense and is safer for the officer. (Or the civilian: I also think the ballistic raid shield would be an extremely useful thing for an armed citizen to have in the bedroom closet in case of a home invasion.)

If both your arms are injured and you can't raise the gun, the laser dot gives you options. If you insist on using point-shooting techniques, the laser sight may indeed be the only thing that saves you. Marty Hayes' tests with students indicate that they handle night shooting problems distinctly better with laser sights than with regular night sights.

Certainly, there are downsides. The laser beam can track right back to you visually, giving your position away

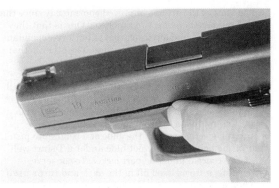

While they don't do much in the dark, these fiber-optic sights...

...can be a Godsend for aging or myopic eyes when there is any reasonable amount of ambient light for them to gather.

in the dark. This is made worse in fog or smoke, including gun smoke. A laser beam aimed through a window can be refracted, and the dot is no longer truly indicating where the gun is really pointed. If more than one of the good guys have lasers, it can be hard to tell whose dot is whose. If the bad guy is holding a hostage, you and your partner raise your guns, and one dot appears on the hostage's head and another on the criminal's, which one of you pulls the trigger?

In the end, all these problems can be solved by simply turning off the laser in dim light and fog, and trusting your regular gun sights when multiple dots are on multiple people or you have to shoot through glass. However, many instructors worry about shooters becoming "laser-dependent" and losing core skills. That, really, will depend on the students more than the instructors.

I feel the laser sight absolutely comes into its own as a firearms instructional aid. I use mine often to show students how easily a shot can be jerked off target by bad trigger control, or how accurately the students can shoot with their hands shaking violently. The demonstration can be done dry-fire in a classroom with a neutralized gun. In the students' own hands, the laser gives proof when they're jerking the trigger, and gives them instant positive feedback when they make a smooth stroke. In live fire in the dark, students can follow the laser dot's track and see graphically which techniques are working better for them in terms of recoil control.

Of the many laser sight options available, the most practical seem to be the modular ones that don't change the profile of the gun. At this writing, you're talking about two companies: Lasermax and Crimson Trace. Crimson Trace LaserGrips work particularly well in this regard. If you don't like them or don't need them, you can take them off. They are easily adjustable. On some models, the "finger in register on the frame" position can block the laser dot if you are shooting right-handed. The firm offers

a pair on a dummy gun that is practical and economical for classroom training purposes.

The Lasermax unit replaces the recoil spring guide rod on Glock, SIG, Beretta, S&W, and 1911 pistols of that design, among others. This puts the light directly under the bore, an advantage. However, being at the "working end" of the pistol, the unit is also subjected to more heat and battering during firing than grip-mounted units. The Lasermax projects a pulsing dot, the Crimson Trace a solid one. The Crimson Trace best serves my own needs, but the Lasermax has also earned staunch supporters.

Fiber Optic

A fiber optic cylinder that gathers and focuses light and replaces your front sight can be a great aid in a fast, close pistol match done outdoors or in fading light. In the dark, it's useless – you want night sights for that – but for something like a bowling pin match, these things are ideal. There are also a number of people whose guns are likely to be used in lit conditions – shopkeepers, for example, given the fact that most store robberies take place during business hours or just before or after closing, when the lights are still on – for whom such sights might be ideal. Accuracy is not so precise as the conventional post-in-notch sight picture, but speed can be awesome.

See the Proof

To determine what sights will be best for you for self-defense work, there is no substitute for getting out there and shooting under different conditions. You have to find out for yourself what works best. Eyes are too individual for another person's suggestions to necessarily be the best for any one shooter. Once you've found something that works for you, check the other systems every few years. As we age, our eyes change, and a sighting system that just didn't work for you five years ago might be absolutely perfect for you now, and vice versa.

Making The Handgun Fit

Suppose you had to run a marathon, but they issued you the wrong running shoes. Three sizes too small, or three sizes too large. It's safe to say you won't perform

your best, and if the mismatch in size is too grotesque, you may not be able to run at all. You might even get an injury trying.

A K-frame S&W is a perfect fit in the average adult male hand with (Hogue) grips that expose the backstrap. Note that the trigger finger is perfectly centered at the distal joint.

The author won this Ruger Security Six more than a score of years ago at a regional championship. It has a Douglas barrel and action by Lou Ciamillo. Pachmayr Professional grips, cut only to the backstrap, give a perfect fit.

Different race: the stock car championships. You've got the most powerful, most maneuverable car on the track. Unfortunately, the driver's seat has been locked into position for someone a foot different from you in height. If you're too close to the wheel, you're hunched over it with a profoundly slowed ability to steer, and you can't reach the pedals without banging your knees on the steering column. If you're too far back, you have poor leverage for steering and cannot operate the accelerator, clutch, or brake pedals efficiently.

It's safe to say you're not going to win the race. In fact, the driver behind you in a less capable machine, but one that fits him perfectly, will soon leave you behind. And, if

things get hairy and you can't manipulate the controls quickly and positively enough, you might go into the wall and be hurt or killed.

The police department doesn't issue every officer size 14 uniform shoes, nor does it lock the seat of every patrol car into position for a 6-foot, 7-inch lawman like Bill Jordan. Yet an amazing number of police departments issue the same size gun, often one that fits only larger hands, to all officers including the smallest. Then they seem surprised when many officers don't perform up to their potential.

As my teenager would say, "Well, *duh…*"

Fit of the equipment is critical to performance with the equipment. One advantage the private citizen has is that he or she doesn't have to trust his or her life to an issue firearm that's the wrong size. The "civilian" can go to the gun shop and buy something that fits properly. Now he or she is on the way to a maximum personal performance level.

As noted elsewhere in this book, the key dimension to fit is trigger reach. The index finger of the firing hand should be able to contact the trigger at the proper point

Show and Go can go together. Hogue stocks on the author's Langdon Custom Beretta 92 fill the palm and feel great, while also looking great.

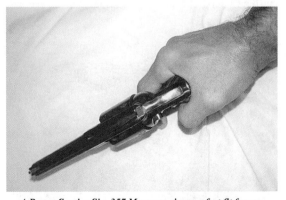

A Ruger Service Six .357 Magnum gives perfect fit for an average male hand with these Craig Spegel grips cut only to the backstrap of the grip-frame. Note that the barrel is in line with forearm, and the distal joint of the index finger is centered on the trigger.

Here is a Beretta double-action 9mm in the hand of a 5-foot, 10-inch man...

...and 5-foot woman. Note that she can barely reach the trigger.

while the barrel of the gun is in line with the long bones of the forearm. This will give the strongest combination of firm grip to control recoil in rapid fire, and maximum finger leverage for good trigger control at high speed.

Let's look at some examples of adapting guns to fit hands. The hands of the aforementioned Bill Jordan were huge, at least a digit longer in the fingers than those of the average man. Bill had to have his gloves custom made. Accordingly, the famous Jordan grips he designed for Steve Herrett had a big portion of wood added to the backstrap area, to push the web of his hand backward and give him "reaching room" to get his finger right to the joint on the trigger. The first time I picked up one of Bill's personal service revolvers, I felt like a little kid holding Daddy's gun. Bill, in turn, would have felt cramped using the smaller grips of my revolver.

The design factors are such that the revolver is much easier to adapt to different size hands than is the auto. This is particularly true of larger hands. Note how many big-handed men have put custom grips on tiny J-frame revolvers, grips that come rearward from the backstrap to increase their trigger reach. A petite female, conversely, will find that the J-frame fits her exactly when the web of her hand meets the backstrap. A female 5 feet 5 inches or shorter, with proportional hands, will usually lack about one digit's worth of finger length compared to the average adult male.

The more research-oriented gun manufacturers have recognized this. Beretta figured out early on that their full-size Models 92 and 96 were big guns with long trigger reaches. They have offered their customers at least four hardware fixes for this. First came a shorter-reach trigger, which could be retrofitted at the factory or by a factory-trained police armorer. Next came a special frame done for the Los Angeles County Sheriff's Department, which issues the Beretta 92 to deputies of all sizes. It had some material taken out of the frame at the upper backstrap area to get the web of the hand more "into" the gun and give the trigger finger greater reach.

Next came their Cougar series. Engineer types were most taken with the gun's rotary breech, but shooters and firearms instructors had far more appreciation for the altered frame dimension. The upper backstrap area was "niched out" to bring the hand more forward. Available in 9mm, .40 S&W, .357 SIG, and even .45 ACP, the Cougar was and is a much better fit for the small hand. Most recently, a redesigned 92/96 series pistol called the VerTek was introduced by Beretta. Essentially, it's the same gun with a light attachment rail up front and, much more importantly, a grip frame distinctly thinner in

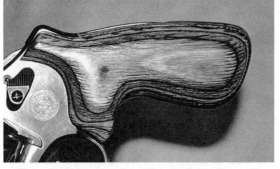

These slim N-frame revolver grips were designed by world record holder Jerry Miculek to give maximum reach to the trigger. They come standard on this S&W Performance Center Model 625 in .45 ACP.

Today's manufacturers pay more attention to "human engineering." This 9mm Ruger P95 is an extremely good fit in the average male hand.

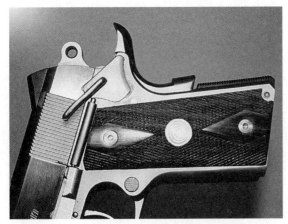

This compact .45 caliber ParaOrdnance LDA Companion comes from the factory...

...with these slim-line grips. A slight enhancement for concealment, they can deliver huge enhancement of feel and control.

circumference. The shooter can not only get the trigger finger more forward, but can also get a stronger shooting hold with proportionally more of the grasping fingers in contact with the more svelte "handle."

Certain guns have had the almost mystical ability to feel good in hands of all sizes. The D-frame Colt revolver, typified by the Detective Special, is big enough for big hands yet small enough for small hands. In auto pistols, the classic examples are the Browning Hi-Power and the slim-grip M8 version of the HK P7.

Walther pioneered the concept of an auto pistol with grip inserts that could adjust the size and circumference of the grasping circle. It was kept in the SW99 pistol, the collaboration between Smith & Wesson and Walther. This is a step forward.

Case In Point

The gun fit issue can be seen in microcosm by studying the history of the famous pistol that Colt introduced in 1911. In the early 20s, a study of how small arms had performed in the Great War determined that many

soldiers felt the trigger of this pistol was too long to reach well. By the end of the decade, the military had created specifications for the 1911-A1. Among other changes, it had a much shorter trigger and a frame that was niched out just behind the trigger on each side. The intent was to enhance trigger reach, and that intent was dramatically fulfilled.

Before long, target shooters (who preferred to use the pad of their trigger finger, instead of the joint, for precise shooting) were having their personal guns retrofitted with longer triggers. Time went on. By the 1960s, the manufacturers' standard in place was that the "carry" Colt .45 auto, the Government Model or one of the Commander series, would have the short 1911-A1 trigger. In contrast, the Gold Cup target model would have a long, broad-surfaced trigger in what is known as the National

With the short 1911-A1 trigger on this Springfield Micro .45, the average adult male hand has perfect leverage with distal joint trigger finger placement...

...while a petite woman has a proper grasp with the pad of the trigger finger in contact on the same gun.

The Browning Hi-Power, this one tuned by Novak, has the "magical" ability to fit well in the hand of the average man...

...or a petite woman.

Match configuration. This actually worked out pretty well for all concerned. Tastes changed as time wore on, and by the turn of the 21st century, most guns sold for carry had long triggers again. Progress is sometimes circular.

Let's say you have someone with truly huge hands. One of the regular competitors at the old Second Chance shoots was about 6 feet, 9 inches tall with proportional hands. He had a custom gunsmith build him a 1911 .45 auto with an incredibly long trigger, almost out to where the trigger guard is on a factory gun. The 'smith welded up a new trigger guard farther forward on the frame. This in turn, of course, demanded custom holsters, but the good-natured (and good-shooting) giant handgunner now had a 1911 that was literally made for his hand.

On the other end of the spectrum, the smartest female shooters and their coaches analyzed the situation too. In WWI, nutrition and prenatal care not being what they are today, the average adult male stood about 5 feet, 6 inches. The 1911-A1 trigger had in essence been engineered for hands proportional to that height, or smaller. The average adult female of today in this country stands about 5 feet, 5 inches. This means that the 1911-A1 pistol is *exactly the right size to fit most petite female hands* in terms of trigger reach. If the grip-frame is too long, the shorter Officer's size is readily available from Colt and other manufacturers. Thus, incongruous as it may sound, the big .45 auto – the gun of Mike Hammer and Sergeant Rock – is actually an excellent choice for the petite female hand. Privy to the 1920s study and 1911/1911-A1 metamorphosis and the reasons behind it, John Browning and Didionne Souave kept essentially the same trigger reach dimension as the 1911-A1 when they carefully crafted the Browning Hi-Power of 1935.

This is why the Hi-Power fits so well in so many different hands, and why it is particularly appreciated by those with shorter fingers. Now, fast-forward again, to a modern pistol first produced in the 1990s, the Kahr. This gun is also particularly well configured for the small hand. It also points well. If you lay a Kahr over a Browning Hi-Power, you will see a remarkable similarity in shape. One of two things is clearly proven here: either Kahr designer Justin Moon did his homework and adapted the best of the Browning/Souave design to his own brainchild, or it is indeed true that great minds work in similar directions.

After-market Revolver Grips

In the occasional moment when there's nothing else to argue about, bored gun experts are known to debate whether those "handle thingies" are properly called "grips" or "stocks." For our purposes here, let's use the terms interchangeably.

Wooden grips, or synthetic grips that duplicate wood, tend to be smooth and unlikely to snag clothing. They conceal well. They also look good; there's a definite "pride of ownership" thing there. Custom grips with finger grooves and palm swells put you in mind of that hoary saying, "It feels like the handshake of an old friend." However, wooden grips do relatively little to absorb recoil. Smooth ones, especially without finger grooves, tend to shift in the hand when the gun kicks. The old, tiny grips that used to come with small revolvers, known to shooters as "splinter grips," made controlled shooting notoriously difficult. Checkering to secure the stocks to the palm helped some, but not much.

Composition stocks, known colloquially as "rubber grips," have long been a favorite of serious revolver shooters. The ones that cover the backstrap cushion recoil into the web of the hand like a recoil pad soaking up kick

These big Trausch grips give maximum recoil control with the author's hard-kicking S&W lightweight Mountain Gun in .44 Magnum, but note that they also restrict trigger reach for double-action work.

Standard J-frame S&W grips give adequate trigger reach to the very short fingers of 5-foot-tall woman...

...but allow too much finger to get in the guard when the average adult male hand is applied...

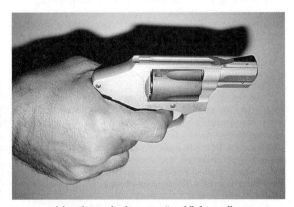

...requiring that male shooter to "cock" the median knuckle of the trigger finger slightly outward to adjust.

on a shotgun. Pachmayr led the market with their Decelerator brand by actually using, in the backstraps of the grip, the same shock-absorbing materials found in state-of-the-art recoil pads. Hogue offers a similar model.

This sort of stock tends to give the most comfortable shooting. Especially in the Hogue finger-grooved version, they allow much less slippage even when firing Magnum

loads. The main revolver-makers have picked up on this, and so accoutered many of their double-action models at the factory. Smith & Wesson has used mostly Uncle Mike's and lately Hogue; Colt has used Hogue and Pachmayr; and Ruger has come up with its own in-house version made of what they call "live-feel" composite for their SP-101 hideout gun, their GP-100 service revolver, and some of their larger double-action Magnums. Taurus also uses in-house grips; particularly useful are the Ribber ™ style found on the .454 and .480 big boomers, and some of their "baby Magnums."

From a practical standpoint, the only downside is that the tacky surface of some "rubber" grips adheres to jacket or shirt linings and causes the fabric to lift, revealing the guns. This doesn't happen with all such grips nor with all clothing.

Try before you buy, if possible. Finger-grooved grips don't fit all fingers. Women's police combat champion Sally Van Valzah of Georgia came up with a neat idea that was rediscovered a few years later by Lyn Bates, long time president of Armed Women Against Rape and Endangerment (AWARE). This is to simply remove the top flange, the one between the top two finger grooves. In that "average adult male hand" the industry always talks about, this leaves the middle finger and the ring finger with nothing in between, which is really no big deal. However, for a typical woman with slender fingers, all three of the grasping digits now wrap securely and fit well in the space of two male fingers. Most women who've tried this report improved feel and control.

Auto Pistol Grips

The auto pistol shooter seems less likely to need aftermarket grips than the revolver stalwart. Most semiautomatic designs, being more recent, have taken more account of human engineering factors. This makes them more likely to fit the shooter's hand as they come from the factory.

That's the good news. The bad news is if the gun doesn't fit to start, there's less you can do with it. A revolver's grip frame needs only hold the mainspring, and it lends itself to being reshaped, sometimes radically. The auto pistol's grip frame has to house the magazine *and* the mainspring, and the dimensions required for this limit your options as to reshaping.

If a gun feels a little thin in your hand, Pachmayr or Hogue auto grips will fill the palm, and also give you a non-skid surface. However, a lot of us have found that the "rubber" grips slow the draw ever so slightly, because they're a little less forgiving of last-instant hand adjustment as the gun hand slides into position.

Sharply checkered wood or Micarta™ grip panels are more commonly seen. These come in a variety of styles. Many years ago, ace shooter and pistolsmith Mike Plaxco created the first slimline 1911 (for combat shooter John Sayle's lovely wife, Sally). Part of the job was taking metal off the front and back of the grip frame and tang, and part of it was creating the thinnest possible grip panels. This gives a dramatically improved reach to the trigger. Jeff Cooper pronounced it desirable not only for women but for most male shooters. Having that "average adult male hand," I can attest that a "slimline" job seems to give me a greater sense of control, and certainly more trigger reach. The last I heard, Plaxco is no longer doing gunsmithing, but the Gunsite custom shop does grip-slimming of the 1911 as a regular procedure. So does pistolsmith Dane

The very short trigger reach of this SIG P239 is one reason such a small gun seems so controllable in so many hands, even when chambered for the powerful .357 SIG cartridge like this specimen.

Slim-line grips are factory standard on the STI Trojan pistol, and allow the average length adult male finger to reach relatively long trigger with the distal joint.

Burns. For many shooters, just the slimmer grip panels will be enough, and these are advertised in the gun magazines from a variety of sources. Some makers offer slim-line .45 autos right off the gun factory production line. These include the Springfield Armory Micro .45 in a small hideout gun, the Para-Ordnance LDA Companion

Jerry Barnhart's "Burner" grips, seen here on the Beretta Elite of multiple IDPA national champion Ernie Langdon.

in a carry-size piece, and the STI Trojan in a full size Government Model.

On the other hand, some like a more substantial grip on a 1911, but may want something a little less tacky (in surface, and sometimes in looks) than neoprene. Makers such as Kim Ahrends (Custom Firearms, Box 203, Clarion, IA 50525) offers thicker 1911 panels that fill the palm with an exquisite feel, and pride of ownership is enhanced by finely finished exotic wood and superbly executed checkering.

Custom checkering has historically been part and parcel of handgun grip customizing. On a revolver, it's usually on the backstrap. Make sure, however, that you're comfortable with the grips you have now. If you go later to a grip design that covers the backstrap, hiding that fine workmanship you paid for will be like putting a drape over a Vermeer painting.

Auto pistols are more commonly checkered, usually on the front strap of the grip-frame and often on the back. We've found in training that the finer checkering gives all the slippage reduction you need, and doesn't chew your hands up during day after day of rapid-fire training with full power ammunition. Note that if you have checkering on both the frame and the grip panels, there can be so much traction that you wind up in the same situation as with wraparound neoprene grips and have difficulty making last-instant adjustments. For this writer, the combination that has always worked best on an auto has been either checkered stocks and smooth front and backstraps, or checkered frame front and back and smooth grip panels. Remember, though, our hands are not all the same.

Another option is the Burner grip sold by Jerry Barnhart. The world champ crafted grip panels for 1911s, Berettas, and a few other guns with surfaces that feel like sandpaper. They give a rock-solid hold in the hand. I've worn them on a carry gun briefly and experienced no problems, but a friend who competes with the Beretta he carries says the Barnhart grips tend to eventually chew up coat linings. The surface is, after all, abrasive.

Reshaping The Glock

The Glock pistol exhibits excellent human engineering and fits many hands perfectly as it comes out of its box.

If a factory produced "Glock sock" seems too expensive, you can make one like this out of bicycle inner tube.

Some, however, want something bigger in their hand. They are customers for what have become known as "Glock Socks," rubber sleeves that fit on the grip rather like a piece of inner tube but with checkering, sometimes finger grooves, and always more class. Hogue, Pachmayr, and Uncle Mike's all offer suitable units. Some with smaller hands agree with the great architect Mies van der Rohe that "less is more." For them, Robbie Barrkman pioneered the concept of filling the hollow back of the Glock grip frame with epoxy, then grinding the whole thing down. The Robar frame trim brings the web of the hand and the trigger finger forward. If you are among the one in 100 or fewer with hands so large the slide of the Glock contacts your hand as the pistol fires, he can also craft on an extended grip tang that will solve the problem. Dane Burns is another who has mastered the grip slimming and reshaping on the Glock. The addresses for Burns and Barrkman appear elsewhere in these pages.

The grip area of the handgun is the interface between the operator and the machine. A gun that fits is critical to good performance. You can get to where you can shoot very well with a gun that doesn't fit your hand. Hit with it, qualify with it, even win matches with it. But you will never achieve the personal best that you are capable of with a gun that does not fit you. The pinnacle of your ability to shoot fast and straight with a combat handgun will not be reached until you and that firearm fit together at the interface point as if you were made for one another.

CHAPTER THIRTEEN

Beyond the Stereotypes

Women And Combat Handguns

The public stereotype is that the gun is an icon of violence, that men are inherently violent, and that therefore women should be anti-gun. Like most stereotypes, this is flat-out wrong.

Why did a cluster of left-of-center political activists call that joke they started "the Million Mom March"? Probably because they knew from the start that they couldn't get a million *dads* to march in favor of banning guns. Guess what? It turned out they couldn't find a million moms, either. It wasn't even close. The Million Mom thing petered out as soon as it stopped being trendy. Perhaps the fact that at the end, the Misguided Moms were outnumbered at rallies by their opposite number, the Second Amendment Sisters, had something to do with it.

A society that expects women to be anti-gun is a society still mired in sexist stereotypes. It is a cruel irony that some of the strongest opponents of gun owners' rights consider themselves part of the women's liberation movement. It is as if these speakers were saying, "You can have your own career, you can support yourself, you can become politically active. You can be financially and politically and emotionally independent...but you must always have a man around for protection, because you can't protect yourself to the extent a man could." What kind of enfranchisement is that? One book written by a noted feminist said that women should not own guns because the gun was the very icon of male violence, and each time a woman acquired one marked a symbolic triumph of male domination.

What a crock.

Terri Strayer, left, and Lieschen Gunter lecture an LFI class on concealed carry options for females.

How many men do you know who can do this? LFI instructor Debbie Morris fires five 12-gauge Magnum rounds into a target in one second, flat, with her Benelli Super-90 shotgun. Those flying cigar-shaped objects are a trio of 3-inch Magnum spent shells simultaneously airborne.

This is a Second Amendment Sisters Mothers' Day rally. It outdrew "Million Mom March" in same state in terms of attendance.

206 • Combat Handgunnery

Dexterity in action. Shooting southpaw, right-handed Gila May-Hayes pumps out a perfect qualification score with her 9mm Glock.

Natural flexibility gives women better balance when firing from awkward cover positions. Jana-Pilar Gabarro demonstrates with her carry gun, a 9mm S&W Model 3913, during an IDPA match.

If you look at it, the history of women's successful entry into male-dominated job markets was a history of using mechanical devices to make up for lack of upper body strength. Women didn't start off in construction as hod carriers, but at the hydraulically operated controls of tractors and backhoes. Similarly, women were able to function very well on police patrol because their batons and guns served as mechanical equalizers of strength…"force multipliers," as the current military terminology goes.

Women's Strengths

It is true that most handguns and holsters were designed by men, for men. It is true that the average woman has less upper body strength than the average man. Yet it is the almost universal observation of handgun instructors that females learn the handgun faster than males.

We can postulate several reasons for this. It is certainly true that firearms are dexterity intensive tools, and women tend to have greater fine motor dexterity than men. This is why women perform almost all the hand-assembly of the finest watches in Switzerland, and most of the precise hand checkering on expensive gunstocks like those of Ruger's top-line rifles and shotguns. Activities like knitting are considered so exclusively the domain of the delicate female hand that when a football player like Roosevelt Grier takes up knitting, it becomes national news.

There is also evidence that, given the same training and understanding of the situation, women can handle crisis better than men. In the past we have hooked up LFI students to sophisticated telemetry, and sometimes just

Attorney Rebecca Rutter shows masterful control of full-power Colt .45 automatic.

Gila Hayes at instructor school with a perfect target fired during the revolver phase with a J-frame S&W .38. She outshot all the male instructors on the firing line.

taken their blood pressure and pulse, then sent them into a high-stress role-playing scenario. At the end of the exercises, we found that the women's vital signs did not increase so rapidly as the men's with what some would call "anxiety factors," and they would plateau sooner and at a lower level.

If a woman hasn't been brought up with the cultural predispositioning that tells her to faint when spoken to sharply or to jump onto a chair and scream when she sees a mouse, she has the internal wherewithal to handle stress and quite possibly, to do so better than her brothers.

Being more flexible (on the order of 30 percent more flexibility in the pelvic girdle alone), women can adapt better to awkward, expedient shooting positions or cramped zones of protective cover. The same factors that allow so many women to bend at the waist with their legs straight and put their palms to the floor, when so few of their brothers can do the same thing, allow this adaptation. Even standing the same height and weighing exactly the same, the female will have a lower center of gravity and, pound for pound, proportionally stronger legs.

Many experts believe that women have greater powers of concentration than men, and longer attention spans. They are able to stay focused on a task longer. In a discipline that requires concentration, such as shooting, this is a distinct advantage.

Female shooters tend to learn the handgun quicker than males; this student has already exhibited perfect stance on first day of training.

The author congratulates Sally Bartoo, who led her LFI-I class with a perfect 300 qualification score, beating all the males including the SWAT cops.

Perhaps the most important factor is that women do not have a gender-based ego investment in gun handling. The motorcycle instructor, the karate sensei, and the firearms coach can all tell you the same thing: many males instinctively resist being taught something with macho overtones by another man. The psychological process seems to be, "The teacher is the parent and the student is the child. But this thing is a manly thing. For me to accept that the teacher knows more than me about this is for me to accept that he is more of a man than I am. This I cannot do, so I must resist what I am being taught."

Female students are not burdened with this testosterone-filled baggage. Their attitude is generally more like, "I paid good money to learn how to do this, and it better work. What did he say to do? OK, I'll do it. Hey, it worked. OK, what's next?" There seems to be a much faster learning curve.

As the great female instructors have noted, women learn things differently than men. When women are asked to do something, they want to know why. Let's say that on two different sides of the city, a man and a woman, total strangers, are each about to buy their first firearm. I can about give you odds that when they go to the gun shop, the woman will spend more time asking the gun dealer how each specimen works. She will spend more time looking at lock-boxes and other safety devices. She will ask more questions in general, and she is more likely to seek formal training with her new gun. She tends to build at the foundation.

These are all good things.

Resources

In this book, we've taken care to address female needs in each chapter, including holster and gun selection, and gun fit. The stereotype that women should have cute, tiny little guns has been behind us for a long time. When I re-read the chapter on female shooters in one of my own early books, I am reminded of how far we have come.

The gun and other force multipliers were what allowed women to function effectively as police officers.

SECOND AMENDMENT SISTERS
Guardians
Of the RIGHT to Defend
Ourselves ★ Our Families

Penni Bachelor of the Pennsylvania chapter of Second Amendment Sisters addresses a rally for gun owners' civil rights.

Because of the pervasive cultural predispositioning that says guns are for boys and not for girls, a female often requires more soul-searching than a male before she arms herself. It is helpful for her to have access to positive female role models. Back in the 1980s, Lethal Force Institute was the first of the major training academies to offer special all-women's classes. We recognized that some of the students would likely be survivors of male violence, and that the presence of alpha males could detract from their learning experience. We tried as much as possible to have all-female training staffs.

In our regular "co-ed" classes for private citizens, which tend to average around 15 percent female enrollment, we find the women often outshoot most of the men. The big difference I noted in the all-women's classes was that the students were more enthusiastic, as if they felt free to be themselves and discuss their personal concerns.

It is always good to start with reading. Two books I recommend so strongly that I keep them in stock are Paxton Quigley's *Armed and Female*, and *Effective Defense: the Woman, the Plan, and the Gun* by Gila Hayes. Each of the authors is a woman who at one time had little use for firearms; indeed, Quigley began as an anti-gun activist. But, in each of their lives, they lost loved ones to hideous criminal violence that could only have been prevented by armed force. Each came on her own to the logical conclusion: when you are the smaller type of the species, when society itself calls you "the weaker sex," some sort of an equalizer is needed. Against the sort of force that produces death or great bodily harm, the only effective such equalizer is the firearm. Gila and Paxton make that more clear than I ever could.

The books do not duplicate themselves. *Armed and Female* is a manifesto for the empowered woman. It is a major in why a woman should be armed, and a strong minor in how to go about doing it responsibly. *Effective Defense* is better on the details of how to shoot, what hardware to select, and where to get training, and a strong minor in the philosophy and rationale of the armed woman. The two books thoroughly complement one another. They are available from Police Bookshelf at 800-624-9049.

Paxton is a moving and powerful speaker. Gila is one of the finest combat small arms instructors of either gender that I've had the pleasure to work with. Lyn Bates, former president of AWARE, is another powerful and inspirational spokesperson for the concept of the armed woman.

Consider treating a lady you care about to an excellent magazine called *Women and Guns*. Produced by the publishers of *Gun Week*, *W&G* has always been edited by women who carry guns. Gila, Lyn, and many other knowledgeable authors appear in every edition. Like the aforementioned books, this magazine reminds the public in general and women in particular that men have no hegemony over strength, and that no woman need sacrifice her femininity in any way when she seeks to not only own, but master, the defensive firearm. To order a subscription to *Women and Guns* call Second Amendment Foundation at their *Gun Week* publishing headquarters, 716-885-6408.

The Second Amendment Sisters, mentioned above, has state and local chapters. A visit to one of their meetings or rallies will do wonders to inform a woman who is thinking about picking up a gun. This group has also been extremely effective in neutralizing the bogus statistics that the now almost defunct "Million Mom March" group has been able to over-publicize and promulgate, and they've been extremely effective testifying at state legislatures against poorly conceived anti-gun and anti-self-protection legislation. For more information, including a referral to your nearest state chapter, contact Second Amendment Sisters, Inc., 900 RR 620 S., Suite C101, PMB 228, Lakeway, TX 78734, toll free phone 877-271 6216.

Empowerment

It's not about "I can do your 'guy thing.' " It's about empowerment. Responsibility and power are commensurate. Responsibility without power is doomed to become helplessness, and power without responsibility can easily become tyranny. One responsibility of every adult is the ability to manage life-threatening crisis at a first responder level. That crisis might take the form of a fire, a car crash, someone choking on a piece of meat, or a violent assault. If we are going to be responsible for holding the line against these threats to life until the designated professionals get there to deal with it, we need wherewithal. This is why we have smoke alarms and fire extinguishers in our homes. This is why we learn first-aid. This is also why defensive firearms exist.

The arming of America's women is slowly breaking down the last bastion of the "Susie Housewife" mentality. It is nothing less than empowerment. It is the fulfillment of a final step to achieving full enfranchisement.

Minorities And Combat Handguns

The defensive handgun is a tool possessed primarily to protect oneself and others lawfully from violent criminal assault. Violent criminal assault is more likely to occur in high-crime neighborhoods. High-crime neighborhoods also tend to be low-income neighborhoods. Low-income neighborhoods tend to be peopled largely by minorities. Most crime victims share ethnicity with their assailants.

Therefore, one doesn't need a Masters Degree in socio-economics or criminology to figure out that the decent people who constitute the overwhelming majority of residents of minority neighborhoods are more likely than anyone else to be victimized by violent criminals. This means that these are the people who most need firearms to protect themselves and their loved ones.

The stereotypes fed to the public by the media strike again. While a great many people from the rainbow of ethnic backgrounds in high-risk areas do indeed acquire a firearm for self-defense, and are more likely than the average Joe Sixpack to need it for its intended purpose, they are less likely to seek training and skill with the gun.

Society has painted the gun as a symbol of the "white right," and the "gun culture" as a "whites-only" club. It has been a long time since any of us have seen a mainstream newspaper publish a political cartoon that caricatured an African-American as Sambo or Stepin Fetchit, or a Jew as a hook-nosed Shylock, though there are many alive in this country who can remember when both images were commonly seen in such places. Even in the emotional turmoil that followed the atrocities of Sept. 11, 2001, we don't see cartoons that depict Arabs as snaggle-toothed vultures anymore. Yet, constantly,

Attempts to ban inexpensive small-caliber pistols such as this perfectly functional Raven .25 auto have had a strong negative impact on law-abiding citizens in lower income communities and disparate impact on minority citizens.

An African-American officer tests his combat handgun skills at the Smith & Wesson Championships of 2002. Pistol is SIG P229 in 9mm.

Ken Blanchard, ex-lawman and author of Black Man With a Gun, *is one of our most persuasive voices for the black community's need to preserve their civil rights as gun owners. Here he addresses the annual Gun Rights Policy Conference hosted by Second Amendment Foundation and the Citizen's Committee for Right to Keep and Bear Arms.*

and female competing in the same arena. You'll see millionaires hanging out with laborers.

Perhaps a small part of it is the gun's history as an equalizer. A far more significant reason is that the combat handgun range is a meeting place of people with similar values...people who have looked at life, seen the same responsibilities, and come to the same conclusions. This is why the world of the combat handgun is perhaps the most egalitarian sphere in the galaxy of sports-related activities.

Kenneth V. Blanchard has written an excellent book titled *Black Man With A Gun*, available from the Second Amendment Foundation (425-454-7012). In it he

mainstream newspapers caricature American gun owners and NRA members as drooling troglodytes with Cro-Magnon foreheads. The depiction is invariably that of a white male.

This sort of prejudice has left a lot of the public believing that the gun world is racist. Ironically, the exact opposite is true, particularly in defensive handgun shooting sports such as IDPA and others. You don't see a lot of poor people or blue-collar workers at the golf club or at tennis matches. But if you go to a combat shoot (or a Second Amendment rally) you'll see a rainbow of ethnic backgrounds and religious backgrounds. You'll see male

details the single best philosophical argument I've seen for why every responsible, law-abiding member of the African-American community should not only own a gun, but join the NRA. He points out how members of the National Rifle Association welcomed him and other black people of his acquaintance with open arms, while a number of supposedly more liberal organizations were neither so forthcoming nor so honest.

Ken makes the point as well that the Dred Scott decision had to do with firearms. In the most shameful chapter in the history of the United States Supreme Court, that body ruled that the slave Dred Scott had no rights as a citizen, in part because if such a precedent were established, people of his race would be able to go armed.

The Dred Scott decision was not the last evidence that "gun control" in this country has been aimed largely at the black population. Prior to the Civil War, no citizen needed a permit to carry a loaded and concealed weapon in public. It was done as a matter of course, absolutely legal, and left to the citizen's discretion. The law merely forbade the practice to convicted felons and the mentally incapable. But in the post-bellum years of Reconstruction, fearing the wrath of freed slaves no longer forbidden to own

The Klan won't be riding in any time soon on this African-American citizen, testing his skills with his Colt .45 auto at an IDPA match in New Hampshire. Many laws restricting firearms ownership have been proven to be based in postbellum racism.

Minority citizens, often at the greatest risk of becoming victims of violent crime, have a proportionally great need to own, and become skillful with, defensive firearms.

history of gun control, beginning in the early part of the 20th century and escalating until, before the millennium, auto-loading rifles and all handguns had been confiscated by the British government.

Flash back to the present in the U.S.A. The same "divide and conquer" strategy is in play when anti-Second Amendment forces prey on the fears of minorities by painting gun owners as white racist. The gun club or pistol match as a "Caucasian only entity" has suffered from a self-fulfilling prophecy effect. We will never know how many people of color who wanted to get into organized combat pistol shooting decided not to, because they had been falsely led to believe that they would not be welcome.

Other sociological factors were at work as well. Poverty not only breeds crime, it leads to broken families. The matriarchal family is a strong tradition in lower income African-American communities. Mothers there know that criminal violence is the greatest danger their sons face. Strongly influential in their sons' lives, they aggressively warn their male progeny against drugs, gangs, and guns. Thus, the gun itself becomes psychologically demonized along with the true causes of crime and danger. It is a big obstacle to hurdle when a law-abiding young black man comes to realize that he needs more than phrases like "just say no" to keep his loved ones safe in a dangerous place.

A number of African-American police recruits have had to overcome this deeply-instilled prejudice against firearms to qualify with their service guns when they became law enforcement officers.

Improving The Situation

Because there was an image in the black community that police were hostile to African-Americans, that group rarely applied to become law enforcement officers. The police community was able to improve that situation by aggressively recruiting for officers in the black community. It is time for the "gun culture" to do the same.

Ditto the Asian community, ditto the Latin community, ditto every "hyphenated-American" community. The egalitarianism of the "gun culture" is a well-kept secret that needs to be told. Gun clubs, shooting associations, and gun owners' civil rights groups need to be more active in recruiting minority members. We need to be arranging firearms safety training programs, affordably or at no charge, in the inner city and in other ethnic enclaves.

It is here that decent citizens are most at risk. It is here we find the people who need to exercise this freedom the most…and a huge, untapped resource to help us defend that freedom, for the sake of us all. Not only our generation, but also those to come…a topic we'll go to next.

weapons, an ethnocentric white majority passed laws that would require a license to carry a gun in public. The plan was to make the sheriffs the issuing authority, and then be sure to elect only white males who would be sure to issue the permits only to other white males.

The strategy worked, with such frightening efficiency that it remains in force in many jurisdictions today. While more than 30 states have "shall-issue" laws that give equal rights in this respect to rich and poor, white and black, and male and female alike, there remain several states where the issue of the permits is discretionary. There are jurisdictions where "discretionary" is a code word that means, "We'll give you the permit if you're white, male, rich, and politically connected."

The motivation lay in economics as well as race. Industry and management had the clout to elect politicians, and they didn't want to empower labor to be able to shoot back at strikebreakers. The wish to "declaw" the working public is more clearly seen in Great Britain's

Young People And Combat Handguns

In February of 2002 in South Bend, Indiana, a man held a box-cutter to a widow's throat and demanded her valuables, including her late husband's weapons collection. A convicted armed robber and self-confessed drug dealer, the 27-year-old intruder meant business. The woman, Mrs. Sue Gay, thought she was going to be killed.

But Mrs. Gay's grandson ran upstairs and obtained a loaded .45 caliber pistol. He rushed back down and confronted the man, who tried to use the grandmother as a human shield. However, the petite hostage proved to be too small to hide behind. Seeing an opening and fearing for his grandmother's life, the grandson fired one shot.

The criminal turned and ran out the door. Mrs. Gay rushed forward and slammed it shut behind him and called 911. When police arrived, they found the career criminal outside, bleeding from a .45 caliber gunshot wound of the chest. He died in the emergency room.

Mrs. Gay told South Bend Tribune reporter Owen O'Brien of her rescue by her grandson. "He hit the bottom of the stairs with the .45 and stood (in a) ready stance with the gun...one shot and he got him. He's my little hero."

The boy who fired the rescue shot was 11 years old.

The youngster had lost his father to a heart attack three years before. Prior to his death, however, the conscientious father had taught the boy shooting skills and gun safety. "Before his dad died, they'd go target shooting. He knows they're not toys and not something to mess with," the grandmother confirmed.

St. Joseph County prosecutor Chris Toth almost immediately ruled the shooting justifiable. "The young man reasonably believed his mother and himself to be in danger of dying. It was clear to us this was a justifiable homicide," the prosecutor told reporters.

The killing of a human being was "an unfortunate burden for an 11-year-old to have on him," the prosecutor said, and surely all of us can agree with that. At the same time, there is no question that having his grandmother murdered before his eyes as he stood helpless would have been much more traumatic.

As we look over the lists of righteous armed citizen shootings that have been compiled for decades by the National Rifle Association, we see things like this cropping up, albeit infrequently. We mention elsewhere in this book the case of a much younger boy who saved his mother, who was being beaten to death by an adult male psycho. A .25 caliber bullet fired by the child from an inexpensive Raven pistol into the attacker's brain preserved his mom's life. In another incident, a boy only slightly older than the one in South Bend was home in bed when a stalker broke into the family home. Obsessed with the woman the boy's father had brought into the home, the stalker had come to commit murder, and did. He killed the woman and the boy's older brother, and shot and gravely wounded the father, leaving him for dead. As the mass murderer entered the young man's room to complete what he thought was the extermination of the family, there was one thing he didn't know.

The dad had trusted the youngster to have a handgun of his own in his room. By the time the stalker entered, the kid had been able to arm himself with his Ruger Single-Six .22 sporting revolver. A moment later the rampage ended as the murderer fell to the floor with one of the boy's small caliber bullets in his brain. The youth and his father survived.

We don't like to think of it, but any of our children could be caught alone in a terrible situation. We tell

This little one is learning that parents Heidi and Jeff Williams will reward her for her responsible behavior in adult-oriented theaters.

This little guy is still in elementary school, but he turned in a strong performance with a Smith & Wesson K-22 at the National Junior Handgun Championships.

them what to do (drop and roll) if their clothing catches fire. We put them through "drown-proofing" programs when they're little. This is simply another emergency that could befall a child for whom we are responsible when we aren't there to physically protect them.

It doesn't always involve an adult human predator. Some years ago, a pack of vicious dogs attacked a little girl playing in her yard. Her older brother, an early adolescent, grabbed a .22 rifle and used it to excellent effect, saving his sister's life.

A few years ago in California, a girl in her early teens was in charge of her younger siblings when an adult male, who could be described as a homicidal maniac, burst

The parents of this little boy don't know that his shooting coach is a psychologist and an accomplished combat handgunner; as they watch from beyond camera range, they only know that their son is in safe hands.

into the home, armed with a pitchfork. She ran for her father's guns, which she knew how to use, but they were locked up and inaccessible to her. She managed to escape to a neighbor's house, begging for a gun; the adult neighbor refused the weapon and kept her with him, but called the police. When officers arrived the maniac attacked them, and they shot him dead. They entered the home to discover that he had already murdered the other children. Their grandmother has since publicly stated her conviction that, had the older child been able to access a gun, she could have saved the lives of the little ones.

Perspectives

When the U.S. was more rural than urban, children were taught firearms safety and marksmanship as a matter of course. When they were little boys, Alvin York and Audie Murphy were sent into the woods, alone, with a .22 rifle and a few cartridges, and expected to bring home meat for the family table. They lived up to these responsibilities, and the skills they learned served them well when they had to defend their country, in WWI and WWII respectively. Each earned

the Congressional Medal of Honor. Each was preserved, thanks to his shooting skills, to return home to his family.

This book is not suggesting that young children be taught "gunfighting." What is suggested is that children be taught firearms safety, and safety protocols for every other potentially dangerous "adults-only" object in the adult-oriented world that surrounds them.

We know that the Eddie Eagle firearms safety program for younger children has been a huge success.

The author watches as Samantha Kemp coolly and precisely perforates a target with her dad's Glock 19.

Few people realize that it evolved from a program developed by Florida firefighters to prevent injury to children who came upon blasting caps or other explosives that had been left unattended. A Spokane firefighter who was also a firearms instructor, Robert Smith, learned of the program and suggested to the NRA that they develop something similar for children who find themselves in the presence of a firearm not supervised by an adult.

The program teaches children to memorize a four-step protocol. "Stop! Don't touch! Leave the area! Tell an adult!"

The entertainment media has made the gun in general and the handgun in particular an emblem of heroism and power. Child psychologists tell us that because children are little and weak and dependent, they crave strength and freedom. They seek responsibility and power, the cornerstones of adulthood, and the gun becomes an embodiment of both. Bill Watterson for many years wrote a fabulously successful comic strip called "Calvin and Hobbes," about a 6-year-old boy with an active fantasy life that revolved around his stuffed tiger. Watterson's work, like Mark Twain's, was multi-dimensional, simple humor on one level but biting social satire on another. In one telling cartoon, Calvin describes to Hobbes what adulthood should be: "Women should all wear tight clothing," he tells his toy tiger, "and men should all carry powerful handguns."

Satire is a reflection of social values, and here, Bill Watterson had it nailed. Calvin constantly imagined himself a private eye with a .38 or a .45, or "Spaceman Spiff," armed with a deadly ray gun. This is precisely the effect that TV and movie depictions have on our nation's youth. It makes a real gun almost irresistible to touch.

What is a parent or guardian to do? The father of the little boy in South Bend had it right. Outdoor sportsmen say, "When you take your child hunting, you won't have to go hunting for your child." When a parent or other trusted adult takes a child to the range and teaches her or him to shoot, the curiosity about guns aroused by the media is satisfied, and channeled safely and appropriately.

Your state's department of Fish and Game or Wildlife has responsibility for Hunter Safety Programs. You can phone them for a list of courses and instructors near you. This in turn will lead you to a list of gun clubs in your area. Your local gun shop (though probably not the clerk at the firearms counter of the Big Box discount store) can also guide you to gun clubs and firearms learning opportunities near you.

At this writing, the Boy Scouts of America still endorse optional firearms safety programs and offer merit badges for riflery, though there is no provision within the current BSA for handgun shooting. Your local 4-H Club may also have youth shooting opportunities available.

The National Rifle Association has Junior Rifle training and competition programs available nationwide. Contact them to learn about local programs at 11350 Waples Mills Road, Fairfax, VA 22030. Some of the hosting clubs also have junior shooter programs available that involve handguns.

The National Junior Handgun Championship was created at the famous Second Chance Shoot in 1997. John Maxwell, already coaching his son Cody successfully toward a spot in Olympic shooting, led the study team. Tom Sheppardson of Michigan, a middle school administrator, and this writer joined him. Sheppardson, with access to extensive research in physical education for young people, determined that the best breaking point between child and young adult would be age 13. Because

Gun expert Andy Kemp bought this combination – a Walther TP-22 pistol and Ky-Tac holster – to teach his little girls safe gun handling. Gun and holster were proportional. His oldest was winning IDPA awards with a Glock 19 in 9mm by age 11.

An LFI-III graduate supervises a youngster with an adult-size Beretta 92 9mm. Note that the coach's folded hands show body language of confidence, but this responsible adult is in position to reach instantly and correct things should there be a lapse of safety.

the Second Chance format of bowling pin shooting requires powerful guns, we wanted to make sure that youngsters with growing and forming bones didn't damage themselves by absorbing too much recoil from powerful sidearms. Age 14-17 was set for Junior class, and age 13 and down for Sub-Junior. The kids in the Junior class shot the same target array with the same type of handguns as the adults, while the younger ones had a "five-pin tipover" event with the pins set at the back of the tables so they could shoot lighter-kicking .38s, 9mms, and even .22s.

Firearms instructor Jeff Williams coaches a youngster with a full-size SIG P226 9mm. In a few minutes, the boy will "fly solo" under watchful guidance.

The first National Junior Handgun Championships, sponsored by Richard Davis at Second Chance in 1998, was resoundingly successful. Unfortunately, after that year the Second Chance Shoot went on hiatus and another venue was sought. Steve and Clare Dixon hosted it the following year in Iowa, using the same format. That venue was suspended also, and the event went into hibernation until the Pioneer Sportsmen Club, Inc. in Dunbarton, NH, took it over and, with the support of the Second Amendment Foundation, scheduled a match for the summer of 2002. The format was changed to all .22 caliber handguns, and the course of fire was made a mix of bull's-eye shooting, a Steel Challenge event, and an NRA Hunter Pistol stage of fire. Sub-Juniors could shoot two-handed throughout, while Juniors would have to shoot the bull's-eye stage in the traditional one-handed fashion. Information is available through Pioneer Sportsmen, Inc., P.O. Box 403, Concord, NH 03302.

Tool Of Parenting

This writer can honestly say that he has found the gun to be nothing less than a tool of parenting. My kids started shooting at 6. My older daughter won her first pistol match against adult males at 11, and she was 19 when she won High Woman at the National

Tactical Invitational at Gunsite. She beat not only a very strong field of highly accomplished adult female *pistoleras,* but most of the male SWAT cops, etc., as well. My younger daughter was 11 when she shot her first match, a side event at a national tournament, and at 13 carried her dad to National Champion Parent/Child Handgun Team in Sub-Junior class in 1998.

The awards were the least of it. Throughout the years of their growing up, their handgun owning and shooting

Taking your kids shooting exposes them to wonderful people. Justine Ayoob was 13 in this photo when she listened carefully to the advice of famed grandmaster shooter Ken Tapp.

privileges gave their mother and I one more way to show them the path to adulthood. As young women in a world dominated by adult men, they learned that if they developed their skills and understood the rules, they could beat grown-up men at their own game on a level playing field. They learned that when they were given power, commensurate responsibility would be expected of them, and when they lived up to that responsibility, they would be given more power, and so on…a microcosm of adult life path.

Each grew up comfortable in adult company, not intimidated by those who for the moment had more power than they, and learning how to give respect without obeisance. Each earned academic honors that both parents were proud of, but more importantly, each grew up to be a natural protector, someone to whom their peers would come when in trouble.

Understanding of when to use force was something else they absorbed. When the younger was about 10, she switched from karate to aikido because she had learned that in the latter art, she could spar against adults instead of children. When she had been a *karate-ka,* her father had watched from the back of the dojo with heart in mouth as she sparred against young men three years older than she and head and shoulders taller. She never lost. In one such encounter, she evaded a vicious punch to the head and countered with a roundhouse kick delivered so hard that it emptied the air from the boy's lungs temporarily and dropped him, heavy protective gear notwithstanding. A few years later, attacked for real by a mentally ill young man much stronger than she, who was trying to smash her in the head with a bottle, she coolly performed the exact same maneuver, saving herself and dropping her attacker in a gasping heap.

The older daughter had taken comfortably to the gun, and was issued a concealed carry permit at the unusually early age of 18. A little over a year later, she was targeted by two adult males as she came from the sidewalk up the steps of her house. Realizing that she could not get her key in the door before the first fast-running attacker would be upon her, she spun to face them and went for the Smith & Wesson Model 3913 9mm she carried in her waistband. The would-be rapists turned and fled. I suspect they were less intimidated by the small, silver-colored pistol than by the body language and facial expression of the resolute young woman who so swiftly and expertly drew it.

Parent As Teacher

Just as the teacher is a surrogate parent for much of a child's day, the parent is also a teacher for much of the rest of the time. Before the baby bird leaves the nest, it must be taught to take care of itself.

Whether or not a given parent wants their child to possess firearms even when they grow up, the fact remains that some 40 percent to 50 percent of American homes contain guns. Unless we keep our children from ever visiting a friend's home, we cannot guarantee that they won't be exposed to guns. But knowledge is power, and there is no safety in ignorance.

A child who knows how to make a firearm safe is a child who is not endangered by the mere presence of one. There is no set age at which to introduce a child to firearms; only the parent can gauge the development of the necessary responsibility. I have been hunting in the field with little kids whom I trusted behind me holding loaded guns, and I have been in the presence of adults who are still not ready for the responsibility. One good barometer is watching how the child handles pets. If they keep feeding and brushing the puppy even when the newness has worn off, it's a positive sign.

The "gun culture" is an aging one. Opponents of the civil right of firearms ownership have used the same techniques of "manufactured social undesirability" that worked to reduce cigarette smoking, to demonize interest in legitimate firearms ownership among the young. It is working. We of this generation need to remain tirelessly politically active if we are to pass on to our successors the right to own weapons to protect oneself and one's family. Concomitantly, we must work to educate the young to appreciate this right, and to protect and cherish it as we do, or it will be lost forever.

John Maxwell said it best, simply and starkly: "The children are the future."

CHAPTER FOURTEEN

The Latest And Best Combat Handguns

In the five years since I wrote the Fifth Edition of the GUN DIGEST BOOK OF COMBAT HANDGUNNERY, there have been some interesting and useful advances in combat handgun design. During this period I was writing for several gun magazines and law enforcement publications. One was *On Target*, edited by Ben Battles. My title on that particular masthead is "Defensive Handgun Editor," and my job each issue is to wring out one of the "latest and greatest." Ben has given me permission to reprint and/or adapt and update those reviews for the Sixth Edition of COMBAT HANDGUNNERY. Some of what follows appeared there first, and it has been updated and edited by yours truly to allow for things we've learned about each particular handgun since, in the field. We'll run them in alphabetical order.

Beretta Px4 And Cougar

Beretta has done a number of good things since the last edition of COMBAT HANDGUNNERY. They've invested a huge amount of money in their US production facility in Accokeek, Maryland, which I recently toured. The result has been an even better level of accuracy for the already famously accurate Model 92 pistol.

Beretta appears to have finally dumped its first excursion into polymer pistol production, the egregious Model 9000. Sleek external styling by the House of Giugiaro was, in this case, a classic example of trying to

make a silk purse from a sow's ear. As I wrote in the GUN DIGEST BOOK OF BERETTA in 2005, I suppose they'll have to put an example of the 9000 in the Beretta museum in Italy to keep the collection complete, but they should drape that particular exhibit in black crepe. It would be appropriate to mourn the poor human engineering, mediocre accuracy and substandard reliability – all grotesquely uncharacteristic of Beretta – that were embodied in this fortunately short-lived gun.

Better were the upgrades to the superb 92 series, well-proven by time and battle. The M9 pistol saw heavy use in Iraq and Afghanistan, and the only problems reported by the troops were poor stopping power with the 9mm NATO ball *(predictable, and certainly not the gun's fault)*, and malfunctions with cheap Checkmate magazines bought on bid. Beretta and MecGar magazines *(the same thing, really)* became *the* gifts to send to American soldiers and Marines fighting in those hotspots, and with those, the M9 service pistols became reliable again.

In 2002, at about the time the Fifth Edition of GUN DIGEST BOOK OF COMBAT HANDGUNNERY was coming out, Beretta introduced the Vertec. This was the 9mm Model 92 and/or .40 S&W Model 96 with a straighter grip angle, and a slimmer one that brought the hand deeper into the gun and the finger deeper into the trigger, significantly improving handling for many shooters. National Champion Ernest Langdon, who shot his way to fame with the Beretta 92, switched to the Vertec and told me he considered it the best pistol Beretta had ever made. High praise indeed from the master of that particular gun, who abandoned it when he went to work for Smith & Wesson.

The Beretta Px4. This is the slickslide "C" model, with revolver-like DA pull.

Ninety-two is latest incarnation of the Beretta 92.

New grip shape is a cornerstone of the Beretta Ninety-Two redesign.

The latest iteration of this modern classic is the Ninety-Two. Jack up the barrel/slide assembly of an original Model 92, run a polymer chassis under it, and you have Beretta's answer to trendy plastic frames with, of course, the obligatory flashlight rail. I haven't put one through its accuracy paces yet, but those who have tell me they see no difference in that regard between it and the original, which is a good thing. Trigger reach is good. Feel is decent. Hopefully, the Ninety-Two update will keep this good gun in the running among those for whom modernity is the watchword. *(But, I have to ask, why that name? How does one, with the spoken instead of written word, distinguish between Model 92 and Model Ninety-Two? In my circles, folks describe it as the "Ninety-dash-Two." Some more thought should have gone into that moniker...)*

I think the big design news from Beretta in the last five years, as far as combat handguns anyway, is the Px4.

I was one of several gun writers flown to Maryland by Beretta USA for the gun's debut in the summer of 2005, and we all liked what we saw, for the most part. The interchangeable grip panels were well thought out, and very easy to install or change out. Takedown was simple, and designed to thwart the mythical "they'll field-strip the gun in your hand" disarm. *(Talk about ingenious solutions to non-existent problems. My feelers have been out for a long time, and the best I can determine, a "rip the slide off your Beretta disarm" has never occurred in the field.)*

I liked the grip angle and the pointability of the Px4. Accuracy was good, and recoil was soft. We were all shooting CCI's 180-grain Gold Dot .40 S&W ammo, perhaps the hottest of the subsonic hollowpoints in that caliber, and the kick was no problem at all even in rapid-fire hosing. None of us could make it jam even with intentional limp-wristing, and we were shooting the Gold Dot by the case. Accuracy was decent, too. I would have liked a grip that was a little rougher on the surface for a bit more traction, but that's subjective.

The Px4 designation stands for "pistol times four," since four calibers were planned: 9mm, .40 S&W, .357 SIG and .45 ACP. I've seen only the first two thus far. Of particular interest was the police-only option called the Type C fire control mechanism, a new take on double-action-only. The "C" stands for "constant action." It's a true DAO, and one of the few which, in an auto pistol, really feels revolver-like. The first ones in the U.S.A. went to the Chicago Police Academy, since Chicago requires DAO pistols and the Beretta is one of the most popular brands on their approved list. I tried the Type C in Chicago, and discovered why the coppers who test-drove it said they liked it so much. Some dealers are telling me today that the Px4 is their best-selling Beretta, though it's certainly not their best-selling *pistol*. My one big gripe about it was that the safety and/or decock levers on the F and G series were unpleasantly sharp, and did not operate as smoothly and naturally for the thumb as the Models 92 and 96, or even the Cougar.

Now, the Cougar is a particularly interesting story. Utilizing a rotary breech design that does indeed suck up recoil, this gun proved itself adequately reliable over the years but never developed the *cachet* of its older brother. My personal favorites were the big blasters. These were

Ayoob testfires the Beretta Px4 in .40 in Maryland. He was impressed with the new gun's features.

Px4 F works well for southpaws. Safety lever was intended to be improved in shape over that of the 92 series.

the Cougar 8357, made especially for the North Carolina Highway Patrol, which adopted it as standard in the F style and in the .357 SIG. Carried on safe, like the Beretta 92 and Beretta 96 pistols the Patrol had carried since the early '80s, it continued to save lives when bad guys got the guns away from troopers. The 8045, at least one run of which in a special barrel length was produced exclusively for the LAPD, was an excellent service .45 auto. Unfortunately, Beretta Cougars stopped coming into the United States in 2005. Only a few Beretta .45s remain in service in L.A.; the popular approved .45s there *(always bought out of the officer's own funds unless they're on SWAT or the Special Investigations Section)* are the S&W stainless and the Glock 21.

There's an interesting story behind that sudden disappearance of the Cougar. Beretta had moved its Cougar production line to Turkey, in part hoping to take advantage of cheap labor, and in part because they had supposedly gathered up a huge contract for service pistols in that country. All seemed well, rumor has it, until

someone in Turkey cited a law there that forbade shipping weapons to countries that were at war. The United States, of course, was actively engaged in the War on Terror.

In late 2006, the Cougar resurfaced stateside. My old friend Dick Metcalf got the scoop and broke the story in the pages of *Guns & Ammo* in its January, 2007 edition. He reported that Stoeger had been acquired by the Beretta Holdings Group in 2002, and was in charge of the Beretta effort in Turkey…and that the guns would be coming into the U.S.A. after all.

The most important element of his scoop, Dick reported, was that the plan to make the guns more economically had worked. He wrote, "Best part? The recommended retail price for a new Stoeger Cougar is a mere $349. Ten, count 'em, 10 years ago, the recommended retail price for an identical Beretta-label Cougar was $697."

Now known as the Stoeger Cougar but otherwise identical to its predecessor, this gun at that price is *big* combat handgun news. It will literally undersell the Ruger P95, now perhaps the "best buy" economy 9mm on the U.S. market. Good news, indeed. Quality self-defense should not be limited to those who can spend four figures per gun.

COLT

Still struggling to stay alive, and keeping its doors open mainly through large military contracts for its splendidly-produced M-16 and M-4 series, the firm can still make a fine 1911 pistol when it gets around to it. After all, this is the company that created the 1911. The .45 and .38 Super autos they're producing today are, in my opinion, distinctly better guns than the Series '70 pistols that have engendered such cultish lust among shooting enthusiasts.

Indeed, Colt has brought back the "pre-Series '80" guns due to popular demand. The best of these by far is the GSP, Colt's iteration of the Gunsite Service Pistol as envisioned by Jeff Cooper. It feeds superbly, has a good trigger and it delivers surprisingly good accuracy – all commensurate with its price. Less successful were the "retro" 1911 and 1911A1, which as a friend of mine says, "coupled a premium price with all the worst features that we all worked so hard for decades to get past." Apparently, most of the rest of the gun-buying public felt the same.

The 1911 .45 has never been more popular than today. **Top to bottom:** *Kimber Custom II, Colt 1991A1 (modified by Mark Morris), SW1911, Springfield Armory TRP Operator, and ParaOrdnance single-stack.*

Colt still produces a fine .45 auto. Here, author wins an IDPA match with an out-of-the-box Commander-length Colt and .45 hardball.

Colt's double-action revolvers appear to be gone for good now, more's the pity, though rumors persist of modernized versions that wait on the drawing boards in the bowels of the Connecticut plant. In the meantime, the many of us who have learned to appreciate the subtle advantages of double-action Colt revolvers continue to haunt the gun shops and gun shows looking for good samples, and wincing at the constantly rising prices of used Colt six-guns.

CZ75 Tactical Sports

The CZ75! Discovered at its ComBloc roots some three decades ago by Jeff Cooper and pronounced by him a superb design, this Czech 9mm service pistol soon became an iconic gun the world over. One of the most avidly copied of modern handgun designs, renditions of the Czech 75 have been produced in England, Italy, Switzerland, Turkey and the U.S.A., and I may have missed some. Of course, the one firm with the most experience making it continues apace, Ceska Zbrojovka in the city of Brod in what is now the Czech Republic. Their latest offering is a sophisticated match target variation of the CZ75, called the Tactical Sports model. Our test sample bears serial number A121834, and was shipped to us by CZ-USA in Kansas City, Kansas.

The barrel is a full five inches in length, with slide and frame lengthened correspondingly. (Standard length is 4.72 inches.) Like the SIG P210 and other European pistols before it, this gun uses the Petter principle of the slide running *inside* the frame rails instead of outside them.

Workmanship was impressive. I've seen sweet CZs over the years and rough ones, and this one is *nice*. The silvery matte finish of the frame has almost a "crackle" look, and the slide and barrel are nicely polished and blued.

The Patridge front sight is big, square and blocky, just as it should be to give a fast and clear sight picture in an action-shooting match. The rear sight is *huge,* and serrated horizontally to break up glare. The rear notch is wide enough and deep enough for fast "flash sight pictures" without compromising precision accuracy potential.

One thing I've never liked about the CZ75 design is that the slide is buried so deep inside the frame rails, there's little for the hand to grasp. That big sight is actually the easiest grasping point for working the slide!

CZ75 Tactical Sports is an impressive handful of target pistol.

Test sample CZ75 gave occasional extraction failures with Winchester ammo.

This variation of the 75 has forward cut grasping grooves in the slide, but they are well back from the front, almost at midpoint of the slide. This solves my pet peeve with front grasping grooves, which is that they bring the support hand too close to the "business end" of a pistol. Not on this one.

No serious competitor much cares how a match gun *looks*. We care about how it *feels*.

Looks and feel are both subjective, but all of our several testers liked the feel of this one. Coarse machine checkering on the front and back straps of the grip frame combined with the checkered hardwood grip panels and the natural "shape" of the CZ frame to allow a secure and hand-filling grasp. Fit is perfect in the average adult male hand, if you want the barrel in line with the long bones of the forearm and the pad or tip of the index finger in contact with the trigger.

While the standard CZ75 is DA/SA optional, meaning it can be fired double action or single action for the first shot, the Tactical Sports is single action only and must be carried cocked and locked. The thumb safety is ambidextrous and, in the CZ75 tradition, is mounted fairly high on the frame. One good thing about that is that even with a big hand, the knuckle of the trigger finger won't accidentally knock the ambi-lever up into the "safe" position in the middle of a string of fire, as can happen with some iterations of the ambidextrous safety on 1911 pistols. The only sharp edges on the test gun that irritated shooters were on the bottom edges of the safety levers, which dug into the thumb when pushing the lever up to *safe* the pistol.

Trigger reach is long, again a traditional element of CZ75 design. Colonel Cooper always taught high thumb placement and the use of the far end of the finger on the trigger; the CZ75's dimensions virtually require this, which may be one reason the good Colonel liked it so much. These same dimensions, however, can require a bit of a stretch for those with shorter digits.

The magazine release button extends almost 1/2-inch from the forward part of the frame, making it easy to reach for quick mag changes without breaking your primary grasp. Reloads won't be that frequent, though, since this pistol comes with three *20-round* magazines. We found 19 rounds went in easy; getting the 20th into the mag just wasn't worth the effort. Empty mags dropped out cleanly at a touch of the release button, and a flower

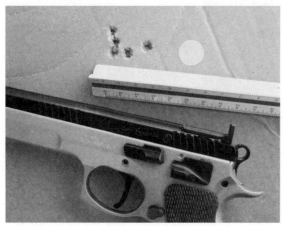

Tactical Sports CZ put five shots in a little over an inch at 25 yards.

pot-size mag well (1.3 inches wide side-to-side, 1.8 inches wide front to back!) allowed super-fast reloads. The mags fit a standard Glock-size magazine pouch.

The trigger pull immediately gets attention. Adjustable, this one came from the factory with a feathery let-off. Pull-weight averaged 2 pounds, 10 ounces at the center, and 1 pound, 14 ounces when the pressure was applied at the toe, or tip, of the pivoting trigger.

The Tactical Sports was taken to the 25-yard bench with five high-quality 9x19 loads, encompassing three manufacturers, three bullet weights and velocities from subsonic up through standard, +P and +P+. The clear, crisp sight picture and the light, sweet trigger pull made good groups come easy.

Winchester brand comprised three of those loads, and the two most accurate. Amazingly, the cheapest ammo shot the tightest. Winchester USA white box, generic 115-grain ball with full copper jacket, plunked five shots into a group that measured 1.20 inches center-to-center. The best three of those were exactly a half-inch apart. Often available for around thirteen dollars per hundred, the "WWB" (Winchester white box) gave champagne accuracy at a beer price.

The same company's 147-grain 9mm subsonic jacketed hollowpoint, originally developed as the OSM (Olin Super Match) load to give SEAL Team Six brain-hitting

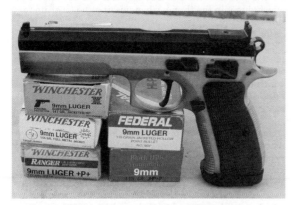

Current CZ75 is built to take the hottest 9mm.

accuracy at 50 yards with their sound-suppressed HK MP5 9mm sub-machineguns set on semiautomatic, has proven to be one of our most accurate pistol loads in this caliber. It lived up to that reputation with the long-nosed CZ pistol. The Winchester subsonic punched a quintet of holes that measured 1.25 inches center-to-center. The best three shots in the group constituted a cluster of merely 0.65-inch.

Another famously accurate 9mm jacketed hollowpoint is the Federal Classic 115-grain, factory code 9BP. Often the most accurate cartridge in 9mm handgun tests, the 9BP didn't take those honors this time, but still produced a satisfying group of 2.30 inches, with the best three hits in 1 inch even.

Coming up out of standard-pressure 9mm Luger ammo into hotter loads, the test gun wasn't quite as accurate. It wasn't a handling thing. This is a big, heavy, all-steel pistol and even with the hottest loads, its recoil is remarkably mild. It just didn't spin the faster bullets into such tight groups. Black Hills 115-grain +P JHP was only a little more open in grouping than the Federal standard pressure, delivering a 2.80-inch group for five shots and 1.5 inches for the best three. Velocity out of the five-inch barrel would have been a bit over 1300 fps. Winchester's 127-grain +P+ Ranger, factory-rated at 1250 fps, produced a 3.65-inch group, though the best three were in 1.45 inches.

Let's put that in perspective. CZ's website, www.czub.cz, says the Tactical Sports model was developed for IPSC, the International Practical Shooting Confederation. IPSC has large targets, for which any load we tested in this gun would deliver ample accuracy. NRA Action Pistol, which reaches its apotheosis at the Bianchi Cup, is built around a target whose 10-ring is eight inches in diameter and whose tie-breaking center X-ring measures four inches. Keep in mind that the "best three" measurement is intended to factor out unnoticed human error and give a prediction of the gun's inherent mechanical accuracy, and you realize that the CZ75 Tactical Sports is a pistol that could win the Bianchi Cup's stock gun iron sight class.

All groups were slightly left of the aiming point. If I were going to keep this gun, it would be the work of moments to drift the big "fixed" rear sight a tad right and tighten it down with the set-screw. No problem there.

In the hands of a half-dozen or more shooters, the CZ75 digested assorted reloads and several brands of factory ammo – hundreds and hundreds of rounds – without cleaning. There were three malfunctions; all extraction failures leading to "double feeds," and all with Winchester white box ball. That's one of the most reliable 9mm rounds in existence, and I'm at a loss to explain it. The CZ75 has a robust outside-mounted extractor, and this gun worked fine with everything else.

If I still shot Bianchi Cup every year, I would strongly consider the CZ75 Tactical Sports for the next stock gun event there. At $1152 suggested retail, the price is not at all bad for the accuracy, capacity, and features this 9mm target pistol delivers.

Glock 37: Promise Fulfilled

By the late 1990s, Gaston Glock's G22, a 16-shot pistol chambered for the .40 S&W cartridge, was the single most popular law enforcement handgun in the United States. But Gaston hadn't gotten to where he was by sitting back smugly and resting on his laurels. He knew that there were still a lot of police departments – and individual purchasers – who preferred a .45 caliber. The problem was, in his guns, the .45 ACP cartridge required a frame large enough to be awkward for those with small hands.

We're talking about a guy who made it big by looking at problems and sitting down to solve them on a fresh sheet of paper instead of looking to old solutions. Big-frame performance in a medium-frame gun required a proprietary cartridge. The result is the .45 GAP: **G**lock **A**uto **P**istol.

At CCI Speer, Ernest Durham led the team that designed the new round. It was, essentially, a shortened .45 ACP, though in the technical details it's much more than that. Speer thought at first that to keep pressures safe within the short overall length, a bullet no heavier than 200 grains would be the ticket, and their first loads offered 200 and 185-grain heads. However, Winchester had learned a few things about putting heavy bullets in short cartridges without exceeding safe pressures while developing their successful WSM (Winchester Short Magnum) line of high-power rifle cartridges, and they were able to make the GAP work with a traditional 230-grain bullet. Glock was now ready to introduce their medium-frame .45 automatic.

They said the frame would be identical in dimension to the standard size service pistols: the Glock 17 in 9mm, the G22 in .40 S&W, and the G31 in .357 SIG. They succeeded.

They said it would take the same size magazine, fitting the magazine pouches you might already have for your standard size Glock. They succeeded.

They said their new short cartridge, the .45 GAP, would equal the power of the tried and true .45 ACP. With a little help from their friends in the ammo industry, they succeeded there, too.

They said the gun would fit your regular-size Glock holster. Well, they *almost* succeeded…

The Glock folks discovered that modern metallurgy notwithstanding, a slide originally dimensioned for the 9mm Luger cartridge simply wasn't right for the powerful buffeting it would receive from the equivalent of a .45 ACP. The slide had to be widened, to approximate the .45 ACP slide of the big-frame Glock 21. However, all other dimensions of the slide appear the same.

This means that the gun is too thick to fit a Glock 17 holster, unless the holster in question was a pretty sloppy fit to begin with. However, we found that holsters made for the Glock 21 .45 or the dimensionally identical Glock 20 10mm seemed to fit the Glock 37 very well. There may be some very specifically fitted holsters out there that were made for the big Glock and might be a little loose around the trigger guard with this smaller one, but we haven't seen one. I've been wearing the test gun in a Glock 21 rig by Aker and have tried it in several others, and it works just fine therein.

All other promises were kept to the letter. The Glock 37 magazine fits a Glock 17 magazine pouch. If you stuff it all the way full, it holds ten rounds, the maximum allowed under the old Crime Law before the sunset clause mercifully killed it. The last two or three cartridges, particularly the very last, are a bear to force into the magazine. We found that people with weak hands, injured hands, or just very cold hands couldn't always get that last round in without help. When the magazine is finally full, it needs a sharp rap to get it into the pistol frame if the slide is forward. This is because there is literally no flexion left in the magazine spring, and it's a very tight fit. If you don't slap it in firmly, you run the risk of failing to seat it. We see the same thing in many other magazines where capacity has been maxed out. A lot of the ten-

rounders for guns originally designed to be high-caps, for instance, and eight-round magazines for 1911 .45s. Once the magazine is inserted, the compacted spring is pushing cartridges upward, which means the magazine is being pushed downward against the internal latch. This in turn requires a very firm press on the magazine release button to dump a full magazine when you're unloading.

My solution was simple. I load my G37 all the way up, since it's always calm when you do "administrative loading," and make sure the magazine with ten rounds is fully seated, giving me eleven rounds to start, counting the cartridge in the chamber. I then carry the spare magazine(s) downloaded to nine rounds to better guarantee full insertion in a fast, stressed-out speed reload or tactical reload.

The .45 GAP cartridge was originally introduced by CCI Speer in 185 and 200-grain bullet weights. In the latter, we found that it exceeded the standard-pressure .45 ACP in velocity. The 200-grain Gold Dot .45 ACP from a Glock 21 averaged 956 fps, while the same weight Gold Dot .45 GAP from the Glock 37 ran an average of 971 fps. Some said, "It won't be a *real* .45 until it shoots a 230-grain bullet!" Winchester has answered that, introducing a half-dozen loads for the .45 GAP, of which at least four feature 230-grain bullets. Ranger SXT 230-grain .45 GAP spat its high-tech hollowpoints at an average 862 fps, with the 230-grain ball rounds averaging 805 fps (conventional full metal jacket) and 803 fps (brass enclosed base). The new round is necessarily short in length to fit a "9mm pistol envelope," but it is by no means short of power.

There were few unexpected surprises shooting the Glock in .45 GAP. The slide of a standard Glock is slightly thinner than its frame; that of the Glock 37 is not. So that shooters could reach the slide lock lever, Glock installed the slightly extended one they make for the G34 and G35 Tactical/Practical models. This makes the lever easier to manipulate. It also means that if you shoot right-handed with your thumbs pointed straight to the target, one or the other thumb may override the slide stop and interfere with its functioning.

In the hand, the G37 feels like a heavier G17 due to the slightly more massive slide. It's a little like switching from a Browning Hi-Power in 9mm to the same gun in .40 S&W, since the Browning's manufacturers also had to increase slide mass when they went to a more powerful cartridge.

Big news from Glock is their .45 GAP series. This is the smallest, the 7-shot Glock 39.

As is true any time you go to a .45 from a 9mm, the G37 kicks more than the G17. It's a little snappier than the .40-caliber G22, and not much different from a .357 G31. We shot it for comparison with a .45 ACP Glock 21, and reviewers were mixed as to which kicked more, with some saying they couldn't tell the difference. Personally, I thought the smaller gun had a tiny bit more recoil, but not enough to worry about.

Accuracy was typical "standard-size Glock service pistol," not quite up to the spectacular standard set by the .45 ACP G21 and G30. We shot 200-grain Speer Gold Dot and flat-nose Lawman, Winchester 230-grain SXT and hardball, and Federal's new 185-grain Personal Defense series Hydra-Shok. All delivered about the same accuracy, in the 2-1/2 to 4-inch group range for five shots at 25 yards, hand-held from a benchrest.

Reliability was top-notch, which is also up to expectation with the Glock service pistols. We experienced no extraction failures, ejection failures, feed failures or cycling failures. Our test pistol was one of the first G37s, and had the early magazines with followers that extended a little too high. The slide would occasionally catch on the rear edge of the follower instead of locking open on the slide stop. This required the shooter to pull the empty mag out manually, at which time the slide would snap closed on an empty chamber. Glock took a few thousandths off the follower while retaining the same shape, and with the new magazines, the pistols work perfectly.

The big question seems to be, "Why a new .45 auto cartridge?" The answer is so the legendary ballistics of the .45 ACP, which historically required a large-frame pistol, can be transferred into a smaller-frame gun. The reach to the trigger is certainly easier with the smaller-frame G37 than with its big brother, and the shooter can wrap proportionally more stabilizing flesh and bone around the grip-frame, resulting in the perception – and perhaps the reality – of a more solid hold. We found the trigger reach about identical to that of a 14-shot Glock 21 .45 ACP whose frame had been "slimmed" by Robar, Inc. Purchasing the G37 means you're sacrificing three rounds to save the money it would cost to customize a G21 to better fit your hand. The only additional "cost" is having to buy .45 GAP ammo instead of using stores of .45 ACP you might already have on hand.

Some Glock fans will stay with their big-frame .45 ACPs, grips slimmed or not. Some will opt for the seven-shot Glock 36 subcompact .45 ACP, to get the advantage of its even slimmer grip profile and shorter trigger reach. But, for many, the Glock 37 in .45 GAP will prove to be the ideal compromise of size, power and cartridge capacity.

Glock predictably followed the "service size" G37 with the compact Glock 38 (analogous to the Glocks 19, 23, and 32 in 9mm, .40, and .357 SIG respectively), and with the subcompact Glock 39, a "baby Glock" comparable to the G26 9mm, G27 .40, and G33 .357. I tested them for *Tactical Response,* a controlled circulation professional journal for SWAT personnel. Both turned out to be remarkably controllable for their size and power. The G38 carries eight rounds in the magazine and a ninth in the chamber, exceeding the firepower of a single-stack GI-issue 1911 by one round, and equaling what you'd get in a modern commercial 1911 with today's eight-round magazines, or in a full size double-action .45 "service automatic" by Smith & Wesson or SIG. The G39 baby Glock carries six-plus-one rounds of .45 GAP.

Both proved accurate. The G38 put five rounds of Federal American Eagle 185-grain full metal jacket training ammo into 2.15 inches, with the best three clustered in a group exactly an inch smaller than that. Speer Gold Dot 200-grain hollowpoint put five shots into 1-3/4 inches, the best three under an inch. All this was at 25 yards.

The G39 did the "4+1" thing, with the first hand-chambered round going to a slightly different point of aim/point of impact than the next four automatically cycled cartridges. Thus, the Gold Dot had a measurement of just over 4 inches for all five rounds, but four of them were in 1.65 inches and the best three measured 1.05 inches. Winchester 230-grain .45 GAP hardball from the baby Glock delivered a 5-shot group that went 3.90 inches counting the first shot, with the last four in 1.90 inches and the best three in 0.95-inch.

Reliability? In all three sizes, the Glocks in .45 GAP live up to the company motto: "Glock Perfection."

HK 2000SK 9mm Compact

It was a dark and stormy night.

Well, it *was,* dammit!

The dark and stormy night in question was December 23, 2004. It was stormy enough to shut down the Philadelphia airport, stranding thousands of people including me. Frigid rain swept Philly in torrents, a blizzard was smothering the Midwest, and planes weren't coming in *or* getting out. It became national news: thousands of us stranded there, and tens of thousands of suitcases lost. People were sleeping in the airport because hotels were full and there was "no room at the inn."

Fortunately, a buddy of mine lives in Philadelphia, and when I called him, Dr. Tony Semone was there for me. In my circle of friends, certain protocols are observed, and when you pick up a stranded friend at the airport, you have more in the car for him than a cool CD on the Boze. Tony knows I'm legal to carry in Pennsylvania, and knew that my weapons were locked in my lost checked baggage, so when I got into the car a couple of things were already waiting for me. One was a neat little Elishowitz folding knife.

The other was Heckler and Koch's new subcompact pistol, loaded with hot 9mm hollowpoints: the Model 2000SK.

That, I'm here to tell you, is a comforting thing to have on a dark and stormy night. I liberated it from its fanny

Approved in the ICE tests for Homeland Security, the HK pistols of today are robust and reliable.

pack, slipped the spare 10-round magazine into a side pocket of my Royal Robbins 5.11 BDUs, and tucked the loaded pistol inside my waistband at the spot where I'm used to reaching for it.

So, you might say, I was predisposed to feeling a bit warm and fuzzy toward the HK 2000SK when editor Ben Battles told me it was my next assignment for *On Target* magazine.

Heckler and Koch has earned the reputation as one of the most respected armsmakers over the latter half of the 20th century and thus far into the 21st, and it's no surprise that the 2000SK carries an impressive pedigree. HK introduced the very first of the polymer-framed semiautomatic pistols, the P9 and P9S series, going back to 1977. It was a gun ahead of its time, and production ceased in 1984. Next came the excellent USP (Universal Service Pistol) of 1993. This was the first successful marriage of the polymer frame with traditional double-action, outside-hammer design, and it remains popular among law enforcement and armed citizens alike. Third came the P2000, introduced in 2003, initially for the European market but quickly winning fans in the U.S. Similar in size to the USP Compact, it was more streamlined. It also came with molded frame rails of the Picatinny style for the InSight and SureFire attachable flashlights, a concept that had superseded the UTL (universal tactical light) and its roll-on side grooves which, in the original USP, had gotten that whole "light attached to service pistol for quick on and off" thing going a decade before. The P2000 was the first successful service pistol to be designed with an ambidextrous slide lock lever, making it truly southpaw-friendly. It also featured the interchangeable backstrap pioneered by Walther in their P99 series.

Now comes the 2000SK, an even more compact version of the P2000. With a magazine capacity of 10 rounds in 9mm Luger and nine in .40 S&W, plus one more in the firing chamber of each, this pistol has a shorter barrel that brings overall length down to 6.4 inches. It is comparable in size and weight to a baby Glock, such as the G26 or G27, or an all-steel, small-frame snub-nose 38 revolver.

At the heart of our test gun is the LEM concept, the Law Enforcement Module. I was present at the introduction of the USP at the SHOT Show in the early 1990s, and a double-action-only trigger was one of the seven fire control options HK offered for it. Let's just say that it was not the best option. Long, heavy, and a little bit gritty, the original DAO pull on the USP lacked the controllability of a traditional double action such as the Variant One, which proved by far to be the most popular HK USP format, and the one in which I chose to buy every one of my own USPs.

However, the law enforcement market was calling for double-action-only trigger systems in the name of simplicity of training and civil liability insulation against accidental discharges. HK responded with the LEM trigger, first seen in the U.S.A. by the Border Patrol. The trigger pull was much lighter. Moreover, if the shooter had the subtlety of technique, and the presence of mind under stress, to maintain finger contact with the trigger as he fired, the trigger would reset itself with only a partial forward return after the first shot, making subsequent rounds still easier to squeeze off. There had been complaints about DAO trigger systems by companies like Glock, Kahr, Para-Ordnance and Smith & Wesson which did not allow a second pull of the trigger if the first did not

cause the shot to go off and the slide to cycle. The LEM system had built in a fallback mechanism, which would allow another crack at the recalcitrant cartridge in the chamber, albeit at the price of a heavier trigger pull.

Thus, the search for a good double-action-only pull had ended with, not a single uniform pull for every shot, but two different kinds of trigger pull depending on how the trigger was manipulated, and a third kind of trigger pull as insurance against misfires. The good news is that the first-shot pull is very nice indeed, even if your finger doesn't "ride the link" and get the even nicer pull for follow-up shots. It's similar to the sweet and easy pull you get with the Para-Ordnance LDA: one of the lightest, easiest and most controllable DAO trigger pulls that the industry offers. This LEM trigger group was part and parcel of our test HK 2000SK.

The test gun arrived the day I was leaving for the SHOT Show, so I left it with my crew at home base and they put several hundred rounds through it before I got home and took my turn. They had no malfunctions. Neither did I. We all found the recoil mild.

Accuracy testing was done off an MTM rest on a concrete bench at 25 yards. Each 5-shot group was measured once overall for "practical accuracy," and once again for the best 3 shots to factor out human error and get a better idea of potential "inherent accuracy." Three good brands of JHP carry ammo, in as many bullet weights, went downrange.

The 147-grain 9mm subsonic JHP was developed for accuracy, and the Winchester Silvertip in this formula continued that tradition, putting all 5 into 1-3/8 inches, the best 3 in 1 inch even. If they had centered on a 50-cent piece, all 5 bullets would have nicked the coin. Federal's famously accurate 9BP Classic, a 115-grain conventional JHP, went 2 inches even for all 5 and snugged its best 3 hits into 1-1/4 inches. Black Hills +P, with the street-proven combination of a 124-grain +P Gold Dot loaded to 1250 fps, delivered 2-1/8 inches for 5 shots, and the best of the "best 3" measurements, with a trio of bullet holes only 15/16ths of an inch apart, center-to-center. This is outstanding accuracy for a pocket-size 9mm pistol.

The big, blocky sights helped. They were easy to see quickly. The gun shot a little bit left, but the rear sight is movable in its dovetail and that would be easily corrected.

The only sharp spot is at the toe of the trigger. Carried inside the waistband without a holster in PA, I found nothing that dug into me or caught the clothing. At home, this light, small pistol was exquisitely comfortable in its high-ride hip holster and mag pouch from Galco's well-made Concealable series, this set bearing HK logos.

My only complaints were about that sharp toe on the trigger, and the fact that the accessory grooves on the frame were too short to lock in the InSight M3 and M6X, and SureFire X200 flashlights I tried to attach. I would have liked to try it with one of the mini-lights Springfield Armory offers for its similarly-sized XD subcompact, but didn't have one available. Overall, the HK 2000SK 9mm is a handy, ergonomic, remarkably accurate and utterly reliable concealed-carry gun, true to its HK pedigree.

And I can tell you from personal experience that it is a comforting thing to have with you on a dark and stormy night.

HK USP Tactical .45

As noted above, many years ago I was at the SHOT Show writers' seminar where Heckler and Koch introduced their USP. The designation stands for "Universal Service Pistol," and that about sums it up. HK had priced itself out of the service pistol market with its P7 squeeze-cocker, a BMW of pistols; the unpretentious, conventionally styled polymer-frame USP was more of a Ford 150 pickup truck. It wasn't pretty, but it got the job done with reliability, precision and user-friendliness. As the line expanded, there would even be an F-350 version, as it were, the giant Mark 23 SOCOM pistol.

The USP has earned its good reputation. Only it and the SIG-Sauer passed the demanding tests for the Homeland Security contract. It has been adopted by police literally coast-to-coast, with the Washington State Patrol carrying USP.40 pistols and the Maine State Police issuing the USP.45.

The latest variation is the USP Tactical with high-profile adjustable sights and an extended barrel threaded for a sound suppressor. (I didn't test it with a "silencer" because I couldn't find one that would fit the HK's unusual threads. It's set up for the $1000 Reed Knight suppressor, and I understand GemTech now has one out to fit it.) Amenities include an adjustable trigger stop, and a frame in the currently trendy desert tan.

All small arms will shoot a little better with some types of ammo than others. On occasion, you find a gun that just seems to shoot well with everything. The HK Tactical fits the latter category. Three of the 6 loads tested grouped within 0.05-inch of each other.

The high-profile adjustable sights were spot on, right out of the box. This shows excellent attention to detail and bottom line performance at the factory. I can't say I've seen this on every Heckler and Koch pistol I've ever tested, but I've seen it so often I've come to think of it as something of an HK hallmark.

Despite its relatively light weight, this is a big, robust pistol that was built to handle heavy loads. It's in the family of HK's big SOCOM gun, for which the Special Operations Command acquired a large lot of 185-grain, 11.40 fps +P hollowpoints on a special contract from Olin. Olin does not offer that load to the public, but Remington, which pioneered it, still does. From the USP Tactical, the Remington 185-grain JHP +P delivered 2.85 inches for a five-shot group, with the best three of those hits 1.20 inches apart. All accuracy shooting was done hand-held from an impromptu benchrest at 25 yards, with "all five"

HK USP Tactical .45 is a handful, but has many good features.

and "best three" measurements done to the nearest 0.05-inch. Hornady's famously accurate, deep-penetrating XTP 230-grain +P left the muzzle at 950 fps and punched five holes through the target in a 2.30-inch group, with the best three in a cluster measuring 0.70-inch.

That 230-grain bullet weight is the one most associated with the .45 ACP, and a good plan is to load "for the street" with a high-tech hollowpoint in that weight and then practice with inexpensive 230-grain FMJ hardball, both at standard velocity (830-880 fps). This gives you identical recoil and trajectory, carry round to training round. The representative pair in this test was CCI Gold Dot for the HP, and remanufactured "blue box" Black Hills for the FMJ. The Gold Dot gave the best 5-shot group of the test. This group measured 1.60 inches, with the best three shots in 0.70-inch, tying the Hornady round.

Testing also included that famous old "manstopper," the copper-jacketed Speer 200-grain JHP with a mouth so wide that the late, great Dean Grennell dubbed it "the flying ashtray." This particular load was from the economy Blazer line, with the aluminum Berdan-primed casing. The 5-shot group measured 2.25 inches, with the best three nestled into 1.40 inches. Finally, this sweet-shooting pistol would be suitable for some types of competition that don't require the full .45 ACP power levels, such as Steel Challenge shooting, PPC, the Bianchi Cup stock gun division, IDPA Enhanced Service Pistol, etc. A good light load for that kind of work is Winchester's 185-grain mid-range Match, with a 185-grain full jacketed semiwadcutter bullet. In the USP Tactical, this load gave us 3.0 inches exactly for all five shots, with the best three in 0.65-inch, the best 3-shot group of the test.

Let's take a moment to analyze that. The six loads tested pretty much covered the range of available .45 ACP power levels. The 5-shot groups measured 1.60, 2.25 (2x), 2.30, 2.85 and 3.00 inches. The average was 2.375 inches. This shows user-friendliness, a gun amenable to letting the shooter "keep 'em all in the X-ring."

Perhaps the most significant figure comes from the "best three" groups, which are measured in hopes of factoring out human error sufficiently to serve as a "poor man's test of inherent accuracy" when you don't have a machine rest available. With this pistol, those measurements were 0.65, 0.70 (2x), 0.80, 1.20 and 1..40

Uber-tacti-cool *protruding muzzle threaded for silencer is a distinguishing feature of the USP Tactical .45.*

USP Tactical, upper right, compared to author's 9mm HK P9S Sport Target, below. The P9 series inaugurated plastic-frame pistols, before even Glock.

The unit that started the detachable gun-light craze, HK's UTL (Universal Tactical Light) is geared to HK's proprietary rail system.

inches. *All* were under 1-1/2 inches at 75 feet, for an average of 0.908-inch.

That, my friends, is remarkably good accuracy potential. It also demonstrates extraordinary consistency, which tells you that we're shooting a finely made machine here.

Accuracy is almost meaningless without reliability, but reliability is another HK hallmark. In the entire test, I experienced only a single malfunction. This was a failure to go into battery with the 200-grain Blazer. That flying ashtray bullet is a notorious gun jammer, partly because of its very wide mouth and partly because of its short overall length. That single stoppage was cleared by a quick rack of the slide that ejected the round from the large ejection port, and swiftly chambered another. The Gold Dot 230-grain has a similarly aggressive wide mouth, but it is longer overall with a more "hardball-like" ogive, and it never presented any sort of feeding or cycling problem with the test pistol. There were no other malfunctions of any kind.

This is a big pistol, and won't feel at home in a very small hand. In single action mode, it feels about like a full-size Glock in .45 ACP or 10mm, and with the trigger forward in double-action mode, the reach for the index finger is even longer.

The double-action pull was fairly smooth, but nothing to write home about. If you want a truly sweet DA pull in an HK service pistol, you want the LEM (law enforcement module) trigger group, which was not installed on the test gun. The DA stroke averaged right at 11 pounds even, measured on a Lyman digital trigger scale.

The single-action pull *was* something to write home about. It averaged 4 pounds, 7 ounces on the Lyman device, and it felt lighter. This comes from the pivoting trigger design: get your finger down low on the trigger, and you have more leverage. When the trigger is pressed, the hammer falls with a soft "tick" in dry fire. In live fire, you feel only a gentle bump as the pistol recoils. I think the polymer frame is definitely absorbing some of the recoil shock, and a lot of the rearward momentum is also dissipated in cycling the big slide against its recoil spring. Thus, while the gun has a high bore axis, it doesn't jump all over the place. It's very controllable and very comfortable to shoot, even with the potent +P loads it digests so enthusiastically.

The adjustable sights not only give a sight picture above an attached "can," but a sight picture that's easy to see. For true "tactical" work, though, we'd favor night sights over the plain black target shooter's image these afford the user. The flashlight rail molded into the frame is for HK's proprietary UTL (Universal Tactical Light). This is a good unit, but I'd rather see a generic rail that allowed the shooter to attach a more powerful, more modern InSight or SureFire white light unit.

I wish the combination safety/decock lever were ambidextrous. It can be reversed for left-hand use, but HK recommends armorers for that, and there's no time for an armorer when you're searching dangerous premises and need to change hands as you approach a weak-side corner. The options of off-safe double action, on-safe double action, and cocked and locked carry are good for the shooter in my opinion. Because of trigger reach considerations, I found myself using it single action, on-safe.

All in all, though, the USP Tactical .45 was a very pleasing package. The tan color option will appeal to many. Everyone who handled it during the test period liked it. Costlier than a regular HK USP, the Tactical is worth the higher sticker price for features that some end-users genuinely need. Overall, it's an excellent service/target pistol.

Head shots at 25 yards proved easy with the USP Tactical .45.

Kahr PM9

With a bumper crop of wild and exotic new handguns these days, why did I put a plain-looking subcompact 9mm up for an Editor's Choice award in the pages of *On Target* magazine? Because for every shooter who buys a huge, thousand dollar 500 Magnum for stalking the elusive wooly mammoth, there will be hundreds who have need for a small, reliable, accurate handgun powerful enough to protect them from human predators. The PM9 fills the bill.

The latest evolution of the Kahr pistol, which has become remarkably popular in the relatively short time it has been with us, has a polymer frame that brings weight down to under a pound unloaded. Slimmer than a Glock, it hides easily in pocket or waistband – or even ankle holster. It is one of the few small autos that can withstand the grit that accrues with ankle carry and still work.

We've achieved surprising accuracy with Kahr pistols in the past. When you're hosting an accurate pistol, you want to serve accurate ammo, so we put four of the most

straight-shooting 9mm rounds on the PM9's table. Accuracy testing was done from the 25-yard benchrest with a two-hand hold.

Most ammo exhibited the common auto pistol phenomenon called "4+1," with the first hand-cycled round printing its bullet a little away from the cluster formed by subsequent, automatically cycled rounds. Winchester's once-trendy 147-grain subsonic put five shots in 3-1/8 inches, with the best three measuring 1-5/8 inches. Federal's 9BP 115-grain at standard velocity stretched to 3-3/4 inches, its best three in 2-1/4 inches, while Pro-Load's hotter Tactical 115-grain at +P velocity went 4-7/8 inches for everything including the errant 4+1 shot, with its best three in 2-1/4 inches. Best accuracy came with the cheapest ammo: Black Hills blue box 115-grain remanufactured. The 5-shot group measured a pleasing 2-1/4 inches for five shots, the best three in 1-5/16 inches.

All the above loads were hollowpoints. They fed fine. The only malfunction of the test was one failure of a spent casing to clear the ejection port when firing the low-momentum Winchester subsonic. Kahr guns thrive on hot loads. Feeding was excellent.

Recoil was surprisingly soft for such a light gun. All testers commented on the mild kick, even with the Pro-Load +P ammo.

These little guns compete with the Airweight 5-shot 38s. They are slimmer and flatter, shorter overall and hold two more shots. The "carry" magazine holds six rounds, not counting the seventh in the chamber, and leaves the grip-frame so short you have to tuck your pinky finger under it to fire. Each comes with a second, longer magazine that holds one more round and, when inserted, allows you wrap the last finger of the firing hand around something solid.

The trigger mechanism, double-action-only, is butter-smooth and surprisingly light. Kahr has one of the best actions of this type in the industry... quite possibly *the* best. Sights are generous and easy to see. Workmanship is good, and fit is snug, as you'll be reminded every time you take one apart for cleaning.

If the accuracy of the tiny PM9 doesn't sound up to Kahr's usual standards, consider that some precision is generally lost when you make a gun smaller. For perspective, the center zone on an IDPA silhouette target is 8 inches in diameter, and this .380-size pistol would never have missed it. Buy a larger all-steel Kahr 9mm as a companion gun for training, recreational shooting and

Available Kahr sizes. From top, target-size T9; standard-size P-.40; Covert model with standard barrel/slide and shortened butt; and subcompact, PM9 shown.

Tiny polymer-framed Kahr will take today's hottest (and most desirable) 9mm self-defense and police duty loads.

Hiding in the hand, small size and low price of the Kel-Tec .380 have made it extremely popular.

home defense; they function identically. The PM9 is an excellent deep concealment protection sidearm, and well worth its price of $625 suggested retail, $719 with Tritium night sights.

I'm not the only one who thinks highly of the PM9. In late 2005, Andy Stanford at Options for Personal Security (OPS) inaugurated his annual series of training summits with the Snubby Summit. I had the honor of doing the kick-off talk on the history and role of the snub-nose defense revolver, and a hands-on bloc on shooting it through concealment: through a coat pocket, etc. Andy had assembled an all-star cast of instructors that my colleagues and I immensely enjoyed training with. One was Tom Givens, who took the role of the loyal opposition in explaining why he felt a powerful subcompact auto

pistol made the small-frame short-barrel revolver obsolete. He made a compelling argument; his recommended gun? The Kahr PM9.

Over the years this neat little pistol has been available, I've known a great many people who owned and carried them. Only two had any problem. Both found malfunctions, and in both cases the pistols were made good with a single trip back to the factory. My one problem with this pistol is that when I carry it in a pocket, because I wear my backup guns on my weak side, it's in the *left* trouser pocket. The magazine release button on all Kahrs is on the left hand side of the frame behind the trigger, and it is not reversible. This caused the button to be depressed enough if I bumped my left side into something that it would release the magazine in the pocket. I experienced no such problems carrying the little Kahr in a right-side pocket, or in any belt holster.

Finally, I have to address the PM40, the same little gun chambered for the .40 S&W and with one round less capacity than the 9mm PM9. To make a long story short, I don't like it. While recoil isn't bad at all in the ultra-light 9mm, it's downright nasty and right at the edge of controllability with the .40 round, especially with the hotter loads. I've also seen the magazine release break, and the recoil spring lose its tension and stop working properly, on too many PM40s to trust it. I believe a gun this small and light just isn't going to stand up to the high slide velocity and nasty buffeting to internal parts that

Ruger SP101 .357 Magnum, top, was designed for concealment but appears huge in comparison to Kel-Tec .380.

Size comparison: Top, Ruger SP101 5-shot .357 Magnum; center, 7-shot Kahr PM9 9mm; below, 6-shot Colt SFVI .38 Special.

P3AT was tested with three brands of ammo.

the relatively high-intensity .40 S&W cartridge delivers. George Kehlgren found the same thing with the little Kel-Tec polymer-frame pocket autos he has manufactured in the same weight range in .40, and he discontinued that caliber but kept the 9mm in the series. There is, I humbly submit, something to be learned from that.

Kimber

Until recently, Kimber was selling more 1911 pistols than any of the many other manufacturers. Dealer feedback tells me that Springfield Armory is now neck-and-neck with Kimber and may even be surpassing them. This is due to two good reasons. One is that Springfield came out with a very good, very reasonably priced, bare-bones 1911A1 pistol that caught the fancy of the market. Another is that Kimber made the ill-advised decision to go with an external extractor on most of their models, and reliability suffered greatly and notoriously. When the U.S. Marine Recon troops sought a 1911 with conventional *internal* extractor, Kimber built them one the old-fashioned way and won the contract. This told them something. LAPD SWAT, by the way, ordered two Kimber .45s apiece for their famed SWAT team – one with and one without dedicated flashlight, per officer – and I'm told they also specified internal extractors.

The market voted with its wallet, and Kimber now seems to be in the process of phasing out the external extractors. I applaud their decision. The history of external extractors in 1911 pistols goes back a long way, and has never been a distinguished one. Even the excellent SIG GSR conceptualized by Matt McLearn has had the occasional problem with its external extractor, traced to a single production run as near as I can figure. Only Smith & Wesson seems to have made it work, and their SW1911 is indeed one of the best available today. But Smith & Wesson has been making service-caliber auto pistols with external extractors for more than half a century, and has the arcane subtleties of the process nailed down.

Kimber still makes a great pistol. Just get it with the internal extractor. And always remember: it's not nice to fool Mother Nature *or* John Browning.

Ruger's New P345 .45 Auto

Sturm, Ruger & Co. has of late put most of its emphasis on sporting as opposed to defensive handguns, but its products in the latter vein all seem to be well thought out. Consider their latest .45 auto, the P345. All "lawyered up" with safety devices, this best-buy big-bore

is also "gunned up" with accuracy, reliability and controllability.

Right after the P345 was announced, *On Target* editor Ben Battles called me on my cell phone and asked me how soon I could get my hands on the new .45 ACP from Ruger. "Oh," I answered, "as soon as I can find a spot to pull over and get it out of the trunk." I had one in the car because I

Author has traveled thousands of miles around the country with this Kimber Custom II .45...

...and been to many a barbecue with this stainless Kimber Classic, dressed with engraved pewter grips from Colt Collectors' Association. He likes his Kimbers...

...but insists they have original internal extractors, to which Kimber is returning after ill-fated flirtation with external extractor design.

was testing it for my police department, having already written it up for one of the other gun magazines.

Ruger's first .45 auto, the P90, came out in the early '90s. This gun has earned a reputation for reliability that would do Mikhail Kalashnikov proud if he had designed it, instead of his friend William B. Ruger, Sr. The P90 was as accurate as a target pistol. However, it had a blocky frame and looked and felt clunky to some shooters, even though it had a good trigger pull in both double and single action. Fed up with complaints about the "clunkiness factor," Ruger followed with their next .45 autoloader. The P97 had a polymer frame instead of aluminum, the same sweet trigger pull, and much better fit in the hand. However, in my experience it didn't have quite the Camp Perry-like accuracy of its predecessor.

Enter the third Ruger semiautomatic in this caliber, which is probably why the company designated it the P345. The reach to the trigger is the shortest yet. The grip shape of its polymer frame fills the palm nicely, and pointing characteristics are excellent. The P97 was made in only decocker or double-action-only styles, and was never commercially available with a manual safety option like its budget-priced polymer stablemate, the 9mm P95, or its predecessor, the P90. The manual safety was important from my perspective because about half of the cops in my department carried their issue P90s on-safe, in case the bad guy got the .45 out of their duty holster.

Under strict new "safety legislation" in California and some other states, new pistols have to be sold with loaded chamber indicators, integral gun locks, and even magazine disconnector safeties. The P345 has all of that, and is the first Ruger to have the latter.

When I first put the P345 on the bench at 25 yards, it stunned me with a group measuring less than an inch. Five rounds of 230-grain Federal Hydra-Shok plunked into a cluster measuring 0.95-inch. Rather than repeat a test with the same ammo as in another publication, I pulled into the range with the half-dozen different .45 ACP ammo types I had in the car. They encompassed a couple of match loads, two brands of inexpensive generic "hardball" training ammo, and a couple of jacketed

Author considers the P345 to be the epitome of Ruger service autos.

hollowpoint duty loads. Each 5-shot group was fired two-handed from a benchrest at 25 yards, and measured once for the whole group and once again for the best three hits.

Nothing equaled that magnificent group with the Hydra-Shok, but the accuracy was certainly adequate with virtually everything we shot. The three-best-shot measurements were especially promising, particularly with the match loads by Triton and Winchester. Each printed 3-shot clusters in under an inch.

The good human engineering, the slight flex inherent in the polymer frame, and a cam block design that intercepts the slide before it smashes into the frame, all help to make this a particularly soft-shooting .45. Testers ranged from cops to kids, from slender-wristed people to hairy-armed weightlifters, and all the men and women who shot it commented on how comfortable it was in recoil. That combined with its excellent pointing characteristics to bring it back on target very quickly in rapid fire. It was no trick to keep every shot in a ragged hole at 7 yards.

The most important thing about its feel is that when you pull the trigger on a live round, you get a "bang." The P345 will not blacken the Ruger .45 autos' hard-won reputation for total reliability. In almost a thousand rounds fired, the test pistol did not malfunction in any way. It was not cleaned or lubricated during this period. We want to see how long that sort of abuse will take to make it malfunction. It hasn't happened yet.

I didn't have a uniform duty rig for this gun at that time, but I wore it in plainclothes quite a bit. It fit a concealment holster I had for an HK USP. Concealment is better than with the square-edged old P90. There are no sharp edges to bite the hand. Even the crisply knurled thumb safety lever does not chew flesh. The officers of my department who test-fired it found the P345's safety very easy to release during the draw, easier than the safety on their familiar P90 pistols.

Those with short fingers were delighted with the easy reach to the P345's trigger. In fact, those with longer fingers actually found it awkward: their fingertip was sometimes bumping on the frame before the sear released. A light touch of the Dremel tool should fix this problem. A senior Ruger executive I discussed that with said he saw no problem in taking a little bit of material off the frame behind the trigger guard.

Brand	Bullet Type	5-Shot Group	Best 3 Shots
Black Hills	230-grain JHP	3 1/8"	1 3/4"
Hornady +P XTP	230-grain JHP	2 5/8"	1 3/8"
MagTech	230-grain FMJ	3 7/8"	3.00"
Triton Competitor	165-grain FP	1 5/8"	5/8"
Winchester Match	185-grain JSCW	2 1/4"	7/8"
Wolf	230-grain FMJ	4 1/2"	1 13/16"

JHP: Jacketed Hollow Point.
FMJ: Full Metal Jacket.
FP: Flat Point.
JSCW: Jacketed Semi-Wadcutter.

The P345 will accept 7- and 8-round magazines furnished by the factory for the P90 and P97, and the 8-round Millett aftermarket magazine for the P90. The magazine release button, though not reversible, is easy to reach and magazines dropped cleanly. The slide always locked back when the gun was empty, even if shooters were slightly riding the slide stop with a forward thumbs hold.

The test pistol shot distinctly high with 230-grain ammo, and more to point of aim with lighter bullets. I think it needs a higher front sight. Ruger was all over that when the initial complaints came in, and I no longer run across that problem with P345 pistols.

Since the brand's inception, Ruger has been synonymous with quality firearms at a bargain price. That has been true of the P90 and the P97 and is now true of the P345. The gun has it all: promising accuracy, carrying comfort and excellent "shootability."

And it has more. There are some who act as if new safety devices on firearms are somehow un-American, but the fact is, a lot of consumers will find good use for them. This is the first Ruger pistol to come with a magazine disconnector safety. The gun will not fire a live round in the chamber if the magazine has been removed. This is useful as a weapon retention tactic. If you believe the man who is trying to disarm you is gaining the upper hand, you can punch the mag release button and "kill the gun." It's also one less tragedy that can occur if someone less familiar with it than you gains control of it when you are not present. The pistol's manual safety is a proven lifesaver in gun snatch attempts, too.

The integral lock works off the right side of the ambidextrous safety/decocking lever. Thumb the lever down into the "on-safe" position. Now, insert one of the two keys provided by Ruger into the hole in the manual safety and into the slide. You've now entered the keyway. Turn the key, and the firing mechanism is all locked up. The pistol also comes with something resembling a bicycle lock, which is designed to be run down through an open magazine well through the slide's ejection port, locking the unloaded pistol securely.

Some appreciate these features. Some see them as creeping big-brotherism. If we like them, we can use them. If we don't, we can simply not activate them.

In 2005, my department's P90s were twelve years old. They had given noble service, but the night sights had died out from age and we didn't want to wait for wear-out

and breakage to replace the guns. After testing several .45 autos, including some that weren't in production when we did the exhaustive testing that had resulted in the 1993 adoption of the P90, we adopted the P345. To a man (and woman) the troops like these guns better than the P90, because of their ergonomics. More are carrying them on-safe and thus gaining a weapon retention advantage than did so with the P90, because on the P345 they can reach the safety lever more quickly and easily.

The new pistols have proven totally trouble-free. We consider ourselves well-armed with the Ruger P345.

RUGER P95: The Best Economy 9mm?

In 20 years of building 9mms, Ruger has brought all it has learned into the currently-produced P95.

Well over twenty years ago, I sat with Bill Ruger, Sr. in the executive office at his Newport, N.H. plant as he swore me to secrecy and showed me the blueprints for the new pistol he planned. It was a high-capacity 9mm semiautomatic, engineered to give high quality at a low price. A hi-cap 9mm for Everyman. It would debut as the P85, and over the years was to go through several upgrades. After a score of years, during which a huge number of Ruger 9mm autoloaders have been sold to police departments, military units and particularly the ordinary armed citizens Bill Ruger loved, we have the latest refinement of the concept: the P95 pistol as currently produced.

Announced a decade ago as Ruger's bid to catch up with Glock, the market leader in this type of handgun, the P95 has the cost-effective, lightweight polymer frame the market has come to love. Its grip frame is more ergonomic than the earlier, all-metal P85 and P89.

Recent tweaks have made it even more desirable. The grip area has been stippled for a more secure hold. An attachment rail has been added, with flashlight mounting working very well on this gun. With a SureFire X200 snapped on, it was no trick to hit the steel silhouette in the dark at 50 yards with the test pistol. Law enforcement is definitely going in this direction – for rank-and-file patrol in many departments, as well as the traditional light-mounted gun bastions of K9 and SWAT – and an attached light can make enormous sense for home defense pistols.

Best of all, the current P95 is the high value, economy-priced pistol Bill originally envisioned. Suggested retail price is $425. By comparison, a Glock 17 in the same caliber lists at $624. The Ruger will often be found discounted to well under $400.

This pistol comes out of the box comfortably light in weight, though a bit large for most people's idea of a concealed carry gun. Ours was finished blue on the slide; the stainless version is slightly more expensive.

The P95 is available with three fire control options. One is DAO, or double action only. This has not caught on well with the private gun buying public, but has an enormous following among institutional purchasers. In Chicago's police department, where officers purchase their own DAO autoloaders from an approved list, the Ruger is hugely popular because of its great value. TACOM, the U.S. Army's tank command, recently purchased several thousand Ruger P95 DAO 9mm pistols.

The P95 is available in two versions of what is called TDA, or traditional double action. This means that only the first shot requires a long, heavy double-action pull, and thereafter the pistol cocks itself to single action

Ayoob finds the safety easy to manipulate on his department-issue Ruger P345, and likes the loaded chamber indicator feature. PD guns have these Trijicon fixed night sights.

during the firing cycle, necessitating decocking if the string of fire is interrupted before the gun runs dry. One option is the P95 DC, which stands for DeCock (only). If you want the easy pull on shots after the first, but don't want to mess about with a manual safety catch, this is the P95 you want.

Finally, there is the standard model, which is what I got to test. It's TDA, and the decocking lever doubles as a safety catch. On this gun, it's an ambidextrous lever, larger on the left than on the right on the assumption that it will be a right-hander's thumb doing the manipulation. This variation would have been my choice. I like a pistol I can carry on safe in case the wrong hands get on it in a struggle. But each of us decides based on our needs, and the point is, Ruger gives us the choice.

This pistol sits well in the hand. Trigger reach was good for average size adult male hands. In the right hand, the safety was perfectly easy to manipulate. The flatter lever on the southpaw's side was a bit more difficult to operate.

There were some sharp edges. For a $425 MSRP, there isn't much in the manufacturer's budget to allow a "melt job" that rounds all the surfaces. The front edge of the pistol is smoothly rounded, though, and the slide tapers slightly, which speeds holstering significantly and, some think, accelerates the draw slightly as well. The sharp edges that proved irritating were on the front of the safety decock levers, and became palpable when working the slide.

The double-action trigger is on the heavy side and stacks slightly; that is, when you draw the trigger back slowly, the resistance seems to increase. That sensation disappears in rapid double-action work, however.

The single-action pull is roughly five pounds, with a clean release. As with the long pull, the short one feels different in slow fire than in rapid. With a leisurely squeeze, you can feel a tiny bit of movement in the sear. This makes it feel almost like a two-stage pull. In rapid fire, however, all you feel is a clean release that doesn't have objectionable backlash.

But the proof is in the shooting. It was time to take the P95 to the range.

On the 25-yard line, we shot NRA timed- and rapid-fire bullseye centers with the P95, using a two-hand hold from the bench. It shot a bit high, so a six o'clock hold made sense. Black Hills +P with the 115-grain Gold Dot bullet punched five holes in 3.30 inches center-to-center, the best three measuring exactly 1.00 inch. Federal 9BP standard pressure 115-grain JHP plunked five 9mm holes in 3.25 inches, with the best three in a 1.80-inch cluster. Winchester 147-grain subsonic JHP did a five-shot group measuring 3.40 inches, its best three shots 0.95-inch apart. Groups in the three-inch range were about what I'd expected from a Ruger 9mm, though the consistency – 3.25, 3.30 and 3.40 inches – clearly showed this pistol wasn't finicky about its ammo.

But then, Jon Strayer loaded the Ruger with one of the very best 9mm carry loads out there, the 127-grain +P+ Ranger police round from Winchester, and put five of those high tech hollowpoints into a group that measured only 2.40 inches, exactly an inch tighter than the Winchester 9mm loading most famous for its accuracy, the 147-grain subsonic. Go figure.

The "best three" cluster with the 127-grain Winchester measured 1.45 inches. If one accepts the hypothesis that the best three hits of a hand-held five-shot group that had

no called flyers will closely predict a five-shot group from the same gun and ammo with a machine rest, this means the test P95 could be a one-inch pistol at 25 yards. All were under two inches in this measurement; three out of four were under an inch and a half; and two were an inch or better.

The tightest three shots give you an idea how accurate a certain handgun can be. The total of five shots give you an idea of how accurate *you* can be. To find out how accurate you can be with the same gun and ammo under pressure, you have to test the gun with some pressure on. I shot one of my state's approved off-duty gun courses with this pistol. The course of fire entailed one-hand-only shooting with each hand, assorted standing and low cover positions, and several speed reloads, all under time.

The pistol pointed well, the sights going directly to the center of the target without last-instant adjustment of hand or wrist. The second shot fired, from a weak hand only stance, went a little low right because I had forgotten just how sweet this gun's single-action pull is once you're past the double action, but the bullet stayed in the center zone. The trigger was predictable after that, nicer than the trigger of a gun this inexpensive has a right to be in this day and age. Reloads were smooth and uncomplicated, using a mix of new magazines and old ones, going all the way back to the original P85. All full-length Ruger 9mm mags seem to work in this latest model.

When it was over, 50 shots had resulted in as many center zone hits and a perfect score of 250 out of 250 possible on the challenging IPSC target. Forty-nine of those bullet holes were in a group that measured just under four and a half inches, but that darned second shot had opened the total to over six inches. That was my fault, not the Ruger's, and I was very happy with the pistol's performance.

In keeping with the economy theme, I used an Uncle Mike's duty holster for the qualification and a Bianchi Cobra for when the flashlight was attached. I used a SureFire X200, which fit perfectly, went on and came off easily and smoothly, and absolutely centered the sight picture in its brilliant LED beam.

My only real complaint was that this particular P95 shot high. A taller front sight, not hard to install since the front post is securely but removably pinned, would fix that. Throughout the test, in the hands of several shooters, the P95 never malfunctioned despite hundreds and hundreds of assorted rounds.

Reliable. Remarkably shootable. Surprisingly accurate. Low in price. The Ruger P95 may well be the best value in an economy-grade 9mm auto today. Bill Ruger, Sr. would be proud.

Smith & Wesson Model 327TRR8

Herb Belin, the head of revolver production at S&W, first showed me the new TRR8 at the 2006 SHOT Show. My first reaction was, "You've GOT to be kidding." He wasn't.

At first, it looks almost like a parody of *uber*-cool tactical ninja automatics. Picture a revolver with a Picatinny rail under its barrel, mounting a white light and laser unit, and with a red dot optical sight atop its frame on another Pic rail. My first reaction was to laugh.

I shot one for several weeks. And I'm not laughing anymore.

But I'm still smiling.

The Model 327 TRR8 (**T**actical **R**evolver with **R**ail, **eight**-shot) is the latest descendant of the original .357 Magnum. The timeline goes like this. **1935:** After consulting with period experts Phil Sharpe and Elmer Keith, Smith & Wesson and Winchester create the first .357 Magnum revolver/cartridge combo. The cartridge is based on a .38 Special, lengthened so it can take more gunpowder and so it won't fit an older .38 and blow it up, and it's capable of running a 158-grain bullet in the 1500 fps velocity range. The very first goes to J. Edgar Hoover, head of the FBI. **1948:** When production resumes after WWII, the design is updated with more efficient adjustable sight, and short action. **1954:** An economy version, the Highway Patrolman, is introduced. **1957:** When S&W goes to numeric model designations, this one becomes the Model 27 and the Highway Patrolman, Model 28. Subsequent dash-suffix designations will indicate changes such as doing away with pinned barrels and recessed chambers. **1989:** A short-lived stainless version is introduced with unfluted six-shot cylinder and heavy, underlugged barrel, called the Model 627. **1994:** The Model 27 is discontinued. **1997:** The 627 designation is resurrected for a series of special-run Performance Center N-frame .357s with eight-shot cylinders. **2005:** The Model 327 with lightweight scandium frame and eight-shot cylinder makes its appearance. **2006:** The TRR8 is introduced at the SHOT Show in Las Vegas.

The more experience you gain with the TRR8, the less funny-looking it becomes. The barrel is 5 inches, the length Skeeter Skelton and some other experts always felt gave the best balance – in both the visual sense, and the tactile sense – with these large-frame revolvers. Milled flat on the side and using S&W's recently developed two-piece barrel construction, it consists of a rifled steel tube within an outer sleeve. This keeps it from being muzzle-heavy, and gives it a "lively" feel, yet still allows it to hang steady on target.

An interchangeable front sight offers numerous options: Ours came with the gold bead that master wheelgunners from Ed McGivern to Jerry Miculek have favored for speed shooting. The tactical light rail was perfectly formed, and an InSight M6X heavy-duty combination white light and laser unit fit perfectly, and slid on and off easily. The rear sight is the same one that's been on the 27 series for 58 years, and still works just fine. The topmost Pic rail of the test sample carries a Tru-Glo red dot sight.

The eight-shot cylinder is made of stainless steel, machined on the breechface side to allow the use of moon clips with standard rimmed .38 Special and .357 Magnum cartridges. Three clips are included with the revolver. Each chamber has been laboriously chambered to allow faster insertion of cartridges.

The frame is scandium. This brings the weight down from the typical mid-forty-ounce range to 35.3 ounces…slightly less than a Model 19 Combat Magnum, the classic "carry weight" .357. This definitely contributes to the "lively" feel of the gun when tracking quickly between multiple targets such as steel plates or bowling pins.

Grips are soft Hogues, shaped with finger grooves and cut to expose the backstrap of the grip frame. The trigger is semi-narrow, smooth in front and rounded at the edges, clearly designed with double-action work in mind, and comes with a trigger stop perfectly fitted. The hammer spur is a triangular spade shape, easier to thumb-cock quickly than the conventional service style, but not likely to get in the way like the old beaver-tailed Target hammer.

More than half a century ago, gun expert Bob Nichols wrote that the heavy all-steel S&W .357 had more recoil with magnum ammo than most men could handle. What's it like with ten or so ounces of recoil-absorbing weight taken off?

The answer is: *sweet.* This gun has no recoil reduction devices *per se*, but the Hogue grips soften the bite to the web of the hand. The barrel configuration, including the forward-mounted accessory rail, holds the muzzle down. The test shooters included a couple of petite females, and none experienced discomfort even with full-power magnum loads.

From the first, the Model 27 series has been accurate, and this revolver certainly lives up to the tradition. We tried it off the bench with target .38 wadcutters, an all-around .357 load, and a hollow-point magnum round suitable for hunting. All grouped well, hand-held from the 25-yard bench on an MTM pistol rest and fired single action.

Federal's Gold Medal Match 148-grain mid-range wadcutter .38 Special is famous for accuracy. It delivered a five-shot group that measured 1.65 inches center-to-center and, allowing for human error by measuring the best three shots, we got 1.20 inches.

Winchester's 145-grain Silvertip .357 hollowpoint out-shot the target load. It punched a five-shot group of 1.15 inches, with the best three in 0.50-inch. The latter measurement would extrapolate to a 2-inch group at a hundred yards!

Most accurate of all was the 158-grain semi-jacketed HP from Black Hills. This excellent ammunition punched a quintet of holes that measured 0.80-inch, with the best three hits in the same half-inch cluster as the best three Silvertips. The .357 is suitable for game such as javelina and small deer, and in the TRR8 delivers accuracy in keeping with the history of its predecessors. Col. Douglas Wesson traveled the world killing big game,

Joe Bergeron, head of auto pistol production for S&W, gives a briefing on the company's products. Joe was the lead designer of the M&P auto pistol.

The scandium frame allowed S&W1911PD to achieve light Commander weight without the perceived weaknesses of an aluminum frame. LaserGrips from Crimson Trace were installed by S&W as a package option.

such as moose and brown bear, with one of the very first .357 Magnums.

The double action was very smooth, if not necessarily the smoothest we've seen come out of the Performance Center, nor the lightest. I looked in vain for a suitable match in which to shoot it, and couldn't find one whose scheduling coincided with mine. Making do, I put my Bianchi Barricade on the 25-yard line and shot that stage from the Bianchi Cup with the TRR8. That involves six shots from either side, in eight seconds per run. The result: all shots (158-grain .38 Special semi-wadcutter reloads) were inside the ten-ring, and most of them inside the tie-breaking center X-ring within it. It was better than I ever shot the *actual* Bianchi Cup the eleven times I competed there. But as my old friend Tom Campbell used to say, "practice ain't race day." Tom having shot more Bianchi Cups than anyone else I know, I find his comments comforting.

This would be a choice revolver for ICORE (International Congress of Revolver Enthusiasts) matches. It would be great for bowling pin shooting in Open class, giving the six-gunner parity with the .45 autos and a three-shot fudge factor on five-pin competition tables. (Jerry Miculek, pin-shooter *extraordinaire*, had a lot to do with the development of the eight-shot S&W .357 and switched to it for pin shooting as soon as he could get one in hand). If I were to shoot a revolver at Bianchi Cup again, I think this one would be my choice. It's only six-shot sequences there, but the two rounds in reserve can salvage a misfire or similar catastrophe. Along about 1986 at the Cup, I watched a front-runner from the LAPD Pistol Team lose the title because he short-stroked the trigger of his S&W .38, cycling past the chamber. He couldn't pull the trigger six more times to make that shot before the moving target disappeared. With the TRR8, one more stroke of the trigger would have kept him on track for the National Champion title.

Home defense? Bulky as the TRR8 looks, house guns aren't holster guns necessarily. I'd have iron Trijicon sights on top. I'm sold on white light attachments for home defense pistols, but on this revolver, the unit is too far forward for my thumb to reach the toggle switch from a two-hand hold, and if it was long enough, it would be exposed to barrel/cylinder gap gas blast. Still, eight rounds of .357 Magnum are more comforting than six when a potentially armed burglar is climbing through the window.

The flashlight attachment on this particular gun, for me, would only make sense if I was legally shooting at night (raccoon hunting, for example) and could leave the beam locked on. Still, I remember Skeeter Skelton and his favorite 5-inch Model 27 revolver that he carried on duty down near the Border. If we could send him this one back in time – super accurate, with two more shots, and as light as a Combat Magnum – I have no doubt at all that it might find its way into his duty holster.

At $1260 suggested retail, the Smith & Wesson Model 327 TRR8 is priced commensurately with its quality and its fascinating mix of features. It is more useful than it looks at first glance, and will write an interesting chapter in the more than 70-year history of the fabled Smith & Wesson .357 Magnum revolver.

Awesome Eight-Shooter: S&W Performance Center Model 327

Smith & Wesson started the scandium/titanium revolution in construction of defensive carry handguns. One of their latest works in this *milieu* is the Model 327 snubby from the company's elite Performance Center.

"They sent you an empty gun case," said Gail Pepin, tricked by the revolver's feathery heft. Upon opening the container, another observer remarked, "It's freakish. The barrel looks...*vestigial.*" My own reaction was, "It looks and feels like a toy." When I was a child, I owned a plastic toy revolver of the same coloration: gray cylinder, glossy black frame, and if memory serves, about the same weight, too. As my youngest used to say when she was little, "It's ugly, and its mother dressed it funny."

Well, to paraphrase Forrest Gump, "Ugly is as ugly does." The S&W PC327 went into the testing cycle with my southern crew, for a mix of practical shooting and concealed carry. When it was over, the 327 didn't seem so ugly anymore.

Herb Belin, S&W's head of revolver production, explains the metallurgical bouillabaisse that comprises the Model 327. "The frame is scandium," Herb told me. "The cylinder is titanium, and its yoke is steel. The two-piece barrel is comprised of a stainless steel barrel tube and an aluminum shroud. The internal mechanism is carbon steel." The handsome hardwood stocks look like Ahrends, and lack the traditional inset S&W logo medallion.

Like all current S&W revolvers, this one has the internal lock, its keyway located directly above the cylinder release latch. The locking piece rises slightly up and out of the frame on the test sample, but showed no problems in actual shooting or carry.

This is an N-frame gun, and its fat .44-size cylinder is bored with eight chambers for .357 Magnum or .38 Special cartridges. With a typical Performance Center touch, the edges of the chamber mouths have been very lightly chamfered to speed the reloading process, which is done with proprietary S&W full-moon clips. This gun's all-steel big brother, the Model 627, has given awesome accounts of itself in bowling pin matches, ICORE events, and other speed-shooting arenas where a powerful eight-shot revolver comes into its own.

That startlingly incongruous snub-nose barrel, only 1-7/8 inches from forcing cone to muzzle, combines with the exotic high strength/light weight metallurgy to make this revolver amazingly light for its frame size. On a calibrated postal scale, it registered one and three-eighths pounds, or 22 ounces. This is about the weight of a .32-size J-frame S&W Model 60 .38, and two or three ounces less than the all-steel five-shot Chief Special in .357 Magnum. In the hand, it felt exactly like my old S&W Military & Police Airweight, a K-frame .38 snubby, perhaps because it had an identical K-size round butt grip frame. Trigger reach was a good fit for my average size male hand.

The express-style V-notch of the 625-10, basically the same gun rendered as a six-shot .45 ACP, has been abandoned on the 327 in favor of a conventional square notch rear sight milled out of the topstrap. A bright orange front sight, though fixed, is dovetailed and therefore replaceable and presumably crudely adjustable for windage, and for elevation by changing its height.

The double-action trigger was quite good, in the nine-pound range and smoother than most scandium and titanium guns I've shot. The single-action pull was particularly sweet, breaking at between two and three pounds.

The first thing we all noticed in shooting it was that recoil was much milder than expected. I've shot scandium Smiths from the vicious little 11-ounce 340 PD .357 to the torturous Model 329 PD 26-ounce .44 Magnum, and I can tell you they all hurt like hell when they go off, particularly with wooden stocks like these.

The 327 kicked less than the equivalent .45 from the Performance Center, even with hot Winchester 125-grain .357 Magnum loads. That's counter-intuitive, I know. Hell, it's contrary to the laws of physics. I just report the perception, folks; I can't always explain it. It might be that the grips on the 327, being distinctly larger than the shaved-down Eagle "secret service" stocks on the snub .45, were distributing recoil more efficiently to the hand.

With that tiny barrel and only a 3 Ω-inch sight radius, we didn't expect much for accuracy at the standard handgun testing distance of 25 yards, but the Model 327 surprised us. We started with Federal's Gold Medal Match 148-grain mid-range wadcutter in .38 Special. This is the lightest target load in its caliber that you can buy from a major manufacturer. It was fun to shoot, and rewarding: the five shots were in an inch and seven-eighths, and the best three of those – always a good indicator of pure mechanical accuracy potential since it helps factor out human error – were only 5/8-inch apart.

Many seasoned shooters prefer to load .38 Special +P in these super-light .357 Magnums to avoid recoil punishment. Hornady's high-quality XTP 125-grain JHP +P .38s shot softly enough, and delivered a 2 1/2-inch 25-yard group with all five shots, and 1-5/8 inches for the best three.

But the 125-grain .357 Magnum round, even out of a short barrel, has earned a reputation as one of the best "manstoppers" on the street. It was with Winchester 125-grain Magnum semi-jacketed hollowpoints that we discovered how controllable this gun's recoil is. Five of those Winchester screamers hit the target two and a quarter inches apart, with the best three an inch tighter than that. With all ammo, the gun shot distinctly low. This specimen needs a shorter front sight to bring the

muzzle up, which with the dovetail arrangement shouldn't be too hard to achieve.

Testing it for its primary mission, I carried the 327 loaded with Winchester Magnum for three consecutive days. Day One: in the left side pocket of a Tropical vest, the lightest that Concealed Carry Clothiers makes. Day Two: The deep left-side pocket of Royal Robbins 5.11 BDU pants was capacious enough to swallow this large-frame snubby, which rode in a size large pocket holster by Bob Mika. Day Three: the 327 dwelt just behind my right hip in a leather belt slide holster by Mitch Rosen. Conclusions: carrying this 22-ounce lightweight, even with eight rounds of live ammo, felt about the same as carrying an all-steel small-frame .38 snub loaded with five rounds. This 22-ounce gun feels like a 22-ounce gun. Duh...

S&W Performance Center guns aren't cheap, but they deliver what they advertise and become lifetime heirlooms and conversation pieces, like Rolex watches. This particular one fills a definite niche. It can also be had with a 5-inch barrel, adjustable rear sight, and gold bead or fiber optic front sight.

The snub-nose version of the Performance Center 327 is a pleasing handgun. For the many who prefer a revolver to an auto for personal defense, it delivers fast, accurate shots smoothly and gives you eight rounds of .357 Magnum with which to protect your family, while carrying at the same weight as older technology that gave you five rounds of .38 Special. Some handgunners, once they've fired one and discover how "shootable" it is, will consider this revolver an answer to a prayer.

Smith & Wesson's New Military & Police Autoloader

There has been a lot of excitement about Smith & Wesson's latest design, the new Military & Police autoloader. If my memory serves, it's the first S&W handgun since 1957 to have a model *name* instead of a model *number*. And the name is one that S&W fans conjure with.

"Military & Police"

Introduced in 1899, Smith & Wesson's Military & Police model became the paradigm of the modern double-action revolver. It remains in production, more

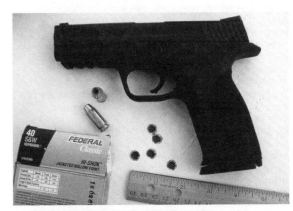

Federal Classic 155-grain JHP .40, which earned an excellent reputation on the street, proved most accurate in Ayoob's first test sample S&W M&P.

than a century later, as the Model 10. Over the years, the M&P sobriquet graced revolvers in calibers .22 Long Rifle, .32-20, .38 S&W, .357 Magnum, .41 Magnum, and the favorite by far, .38 Special.

This year, S&W introduces two new guns with the M&P stamp. One is a 223/5.56 rifle in the AR15 format. And the other has been proclaimed by many to be the strongest challenge to the Glock pistol to yet come down the pike.

Passed around to gun writers in the latter half of 2005, the M&P pistol didn't start reaching customers in quantity until 2006. So far, reviews have been mostly positive. That's understandable.

First, this pistol is *sleek*. Finished in Melonite, S&W's answer to Glock's much loved Tenifer finish, the slide sits on a polymer frame with steel insert. The popular interchangeable backstrap grip option, popularized by Walther and copied since by countless others, reaches its highest evolution in the Military & Police. That may be one reason why the first thing most people comment on when they try an M&P is the good feel of the new pistol.

Three inserts are offered. The small one gives tremendously good reach to the trigger. I can very easily get in to where my index finger contacts the trigger at the distal joint, the hold we old double-action revolver shooters learned gave most of us the best control of the trigger pull. It won't be hard for short-fingered people to reach. The medium size still has good trigger reach, and a bit more girth. Most hand-filling of all is the large size, with pronounced palm swells that fit a lot of people's hands better than anything else. I've run across folks with medium-size hands who love the size large M&P insert, and some with truly huge hands who wish there was something still bigger. For most, however, the grip size that will fit them comes in the box with the new M&P.

The grip frame arches back over the web of the hand, resembling a Robar conversion of the Glock pistol. Bore axis is very low in the hand. That feature is one reason why muzzle rise is not bad for the .40 S&W (the M&P's first available chambering), and testers were unanimous that this was a soft-shooting gun, even in extended runs of rapid fire with the high-pressure .40 round.

The magazines are steel. They drop free at a touch, as designed. They even have "positive release." That is, if you turn the pistol upside down and press the release button, the magazine will pop up about half an inch. These steel mags are thinner than plastic mags of similar capacity. In .40 S&W, the M&P's payload is the same as a Glock 22's: 15 in the magazine, one more in the chamber. However, the slimmer S&W magazine rattles around inside a Glock mag pouch. Magazine exchanges are particularly smooth, clean, and fast with the new Smith.

The trigger will be loved or hated, depending upon pre-existing taste. The trigger is hinged, in a fashion similar to the Glock but lacking the latter gun's centrally-located trigger safety lever. This means that the M&P's trigger can be brought back to fire by rearward pressure on the outside edge of the trigger.

The pull itself is…different. There is a short, early take up that seems to grate a little, even after hundreds and hundreds of pulls. Then the finger meets firm resistance, and the grating goes away. There is now a short distance farther to pull, and the "soft-feeling" trigger suddenly releases the shot. At this point, the trigger slaps to the rear of the guard with significant "backlash." S&W seems to have molded vestigial, nubbin-like trigger stops into the rear of the trigger guard, but they don't reach forward far enough to stop the annoying extra rearward movement.

An accessory rail is molded into the front dust cover, as on all polymer duty pistols these days and even some of the .22 "fun guns." An InSight 6X heavy-duty white light/laser unit worked perfectly on the test sample M&P. The test gun had a magazine disconnector safety, and visible loaded-chamber indicator.

Some attributes of this gun did not meet with the universal approval of the test team, all experienced handgunners. The ambidextrous slide release seems a good idea, but on the first M&Ps produced was so flush-fitted and sits so deep inside the little niches built into the frame, that it was literally protected from the digits trying to operate it. "Impossible," some testers snapped in exasperation. When reloading from slidelock, we all had to release the slide forward with a rearward tug.

Now, some say that this is the way it should be done anyway, on the theory that under stress hitting a lever with a thumb is too much of a fine motor skill to count on. I don't entirely buy that, but we could debate it for an hour. One thing you and I probably won't debate is this: you and I, not the designer, should determine how we can most efficiently fire our guns. I discussed this with former National IDPA Champ Ernie Langdon, now head of governmental sales for S&W, and Joe Bergeron, head of auto pistol production for the company. Both assured

Steve Sager sends brass and lead flying in rapid fire with .40 M&P, but muzzle remains on target. Human engineering is, by and large, excellent.

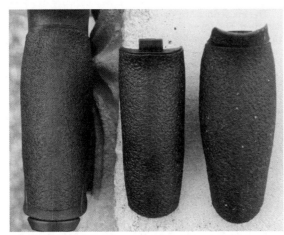

In Ayoob's opinion, these three M&P grip inserts, packed with every gun, set a new standard for adjustability of grip fit to hand.

me they were on top of it, and optional oversize ambi slide releases were already in production.

Once those came out, the problem was solved. Who knows but that in fifty years, gun collectors will be seeking rare, unconverted "first run" M&P pistols with the too-small release? Fortunately, today's shooters no longer have to worry about it.

I experienced some problems with the sights. The white insert in the front fell out when the fifth shot was fired from the new-in-the-box pistol. About halfway through the second hundred rounds, we noticed hits drifting to the right. Sure enough, the rear sight had come loose and was sliding to starboard in its dovetail. The gentle kiss of the proper wrench solved that particular problem.

Joe Bergeron had told me the guns were built to deliver 3-inch groups at 25 yards. We put M&P serial number MPA5274 on the bench to see. With Black Hills EXP 165-grain JHP, 3.45 inches was the measurement of the first 5-shot group, with the best three in 1.55 inches. (We later got a group with the same ammo measuring 2.30 inches for all five, and 0.75-inch for the best three, with four of the shots in 0.95-inch. That was more like it for this unusually accurate .40 S&W load!)

Remington's Golden Saber is a high tech evolution of the original .40 S&W duty load, the 180-grain subsonic. Five of the brass jacketed hollowpoint bullets went into 2.45 inches, with the best three clustered in only 1.85 inches. Winchester's street-proven Ranger police round with a 165-grain JHP punched a 2.75-inch cluster at the same 25-yard distance, with the best three snuggled in 0.95-inch.

The single most accurate five-shot group came from Federal Classic 155-grain JHP, a load that has earned its chops with cops on the street. The quintet of bullets formed a wedge-shaped group that measured 1.50 inches on the nose, with the best three in 0.85-inch! All groups were measured center-to-center, to the nearest 0.05-inch, with the "best three" measurement included to help factor out human error.

To shorten the story, the Smith & Wesson Military & Police .40 is even more accurate than its manufacturer says it is. My compliments to the chef! I wonder what sort

of accuracy we'll see when people start doing trigger jobs on them to reduce the backlash.

The 9mm followed the .40 in the M&P. Julie Goloski promptly started winning IDPA championships with it, along with Team S&W stablemate Ernest Langdon and others. Todd Kennedy, of the Federal Law Enforcement Training Center, reportedly captured First Expert honors at the prestigious Carolina Cup (IDPA) with a Smith M&P auto. The 9mm and particularly the .357 SIG have, historically, been inherently more accurate cartridges than the .40 S&W. The .357 SIG version of the M&P should be available by the time you read this, having worked very well in testing according to factory insiders, but I haven't been able to get my hands on one yet. And a compact version is to be announced at the SHOT Show of 2007, as this edition of the GUN DIGEST BOOK OF COMBAT HANDGUNNERY makes its way to Krause Publications in manuscript form.

The 9mm, like the .40, is very soft shooting, and the .357 SIG version should be as well.

A bunch of us shot the M&P .40 and later the 9mm when we got our hands on them. Everyone had heard about it and wanted to try it out. It was fired by the big and the small, the short and the tall. So long as we kept our wrists firmly locked, strong hand or weak hand or both hands, it went *bang* and never failed to cycle. We also never experienced a misfire in several hundred rounds.

However, we discovered that the .40 was prone to stoppages with a "limp-wrist" hold. The pattern was always the same: a 6 o'clock misfeed at the bottom edge of the chamber. Invariably, a light backward tug on the slide instantly cleared the stoppage. Now, it is well known that *any* auto pistol can theoretically jam from "limp-wristing." The pistols are designed for the slide to run against the firm abutment of a solidly-held frame. A weak grasp lets the frame recoil with the slide, dissipating rearward slide energy to the point where it runs out before the cycle can be completed. Some guns are less susceptible than others: the Beretta 92 in 9mm and Px4 in .40, for example. Our test sample M&P .40 did seem susceptible. However, when the gun was held the way it was supposed to be held, it ran 100 percent.

Apparently, Bergeron and company were on top of that, too. Subsequent to my early sample, I've not heard of any M&Ps exhibiting problems when fired limp-wristed. My fellow Gun Digest book author Pat Sweeney tested his subsequent sample exactly for that, and reported that it ran without a bobble.

Joe Bergeron led the design team on this gun, and the M&P auto pistol is really pretty much his baby. He has been extremely responsive to constructive criticism. Sergeant Ken Paradise of the Iowa State Patrol, which has adopted the M&P .40, told me, "Of our first three test guns, we had one that would occasionally fail to fire, with light striker hits on our CCI primers. Smith & Wesson redesigned the striker after we reported this to them, and the problem disappeared." Today, says Sgt. Paradise, "They are working out very well so far. We've found that the medium-size grip insert seems to be the favorite among our troopers."

Other departments have also reported satisfaction with the M&P. The North Carolina Department of Corrections bought 5,700 M&P .40s, and their firearms training director, Max Mathews, told me that they're working out very well. The interchangeable grip feature has been beneficial to those NCDOC personnel permanently issued their own weapons (transport officers, dog handlers, escort personnel, and some 1,400 probation officers). They appreciate being able to tailor their new service pistol to fit their hands. The remaining guns are "pool weapons" that will be issued to authorized personnel as needed, and these are all fitted with the size medium insert, in hopes of fitting the most hands adequately.

The Columbus, Ohio police department purchased two thousand of the same .40 S&W M&Ps. "The simple design of the M&P, with no decocker or manual safety, was a plus in its selection, said Officer Ron Barker of the CPD firearms training unit, who also told me, "The ambidextrous slide lever is friendly to our many left-handed officers, and the interchangeable grip units are extremely user-friendly for our wide range of hand sizes, particularly our smaller female officers."

Cincinnati, Ohio has also ordered M&Ps for all their sworn police officers. All 1,500 pistols will be chambered for 9mm, however.

With pricing in the Glock range, the Smith & Wesson Military & Police will give the other polymer pistols a run for their money. "Feel" is a subjective thing, but in this writer's admittedly subjective opinion, the M&P is now the frontrunner in the "Ergonomics Sweepstakes."

The M&P is already evolving. By the time you read this, in addition to the compact models and the .357 SIG version, there should be two .45 ACP versions available, according to Paul Pluff in S&W's marketing division. One will be just like the 9mm and .40 in conception. The other will have a polymer frame of suitable GI hue, and a manual safety, to fit the specs put forth by the government for the next military trials of .45 service pistol candidates.

It is significant to notice that, in a world where lawyers seem to demand integral locks and magazine disconnector safety devices, and enthusiasts almost reflexively rail against them, S&W did a "Burger King" on the M&P pistol and in essence said, "Have it your way." Government agency or gun dealer, policeman or law-abiding armed citizen, you can have the M&P pistol with or without the integral lock and the device that keeps a chambered round from firing if the magazine is out of the gun. Bergeron tells me that the way orders are running right now, 30 percent of M&Ps are going out the shipping room door with the integral lock and mag disconnector in place, and 70 percent are being shipped without them.

Joe Bergeron is a young "wonder child" in the industry, having first earned his reputation at Colt's, a ways downstream from S&W in Gun Valley. His work on this design has impressed me. But what impresses me more is the willingness with which he and Smith & Wesson have solicited constructive criticism, listened to it, and immediately fixed each and every concern the end users have expressed regarding the new pistol.

That is a most refreshing attitude in the gun industry, where the attitude has traditionally been, "We *made* the damn gun, and we know more about it than you, so don't you dare be telling us how to make our product better!" I hope this attitude continues at Smith & Wesson. I hope it spreads across their entire product line. Indeed, I hope it spreads across the entire *industry*.

The Smith & Wesson Military & Police semiautomatic pistol is new, different and worthwhile. It's worth your time to check it out.

Single-Action SIG-Sauer .45: The P220 SAO

SIGARMS dropped a bomb on all of us in the gun press when they quietly displayed their new single-action-only P220 .45 at the 2006 SHOT Show in Las Vegas. Yes, you read that correctly: single action only, or SAO as they call it in their sales literature, though the pistol itself is simply marked "SIG Sauer P220."

Now, the traditional double-action SIG-Sauer P220 pistol, double action for the first shot and self-cocked to single action thereafter until the operator activates the decocking lever, has been around for 30 or so years. For the last several years, we've had the DAO (double-action-only) model, popular in the Chicago Police Department and elsewhere. More recently we've had the DAK, which stands for Double Action/Kellerman. Named after its designer in Europe, this is a sophisticated double-action-only trigger mechanism – self-decocking, if you will – that gives an excellent, manageable pull that has found great favor with the Border Patrol and other Homeland Security-related law

No matter what the bullet weight, S&W M&P .40 proved very soft-kicking.

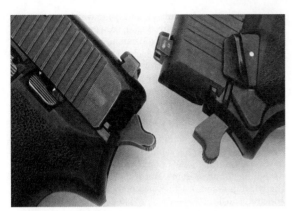

Left, conventional SIG P220, decocked with hammer at rest. Right, SAO version of same gun, cocked and locked. Note ambi thumb safety.

enforcement organizations. A number of private citizens have picked up on its advantages, too.

But single action only? We have to ask ourselves why.

It won't be a fruitless quest, because there are indeed some solid answers.

To understand "the tao of the SAO," we have to face certain facts. Some folks just don't like pulling a long, heavy trigger for their first shot. Some even thumb-cock their double action autos for that first round. That's a slow and awkward procedure when done with both hands, and can be a *fatally* slow and awkward procedure when attempted one hand only.

Tradition has it that a cocked pistol should be a *locked* pistol when it's being carried as opposed to being actually fired. In other words, it has a manual safety engaged. The one SIG has fitted to the P220 SAO is comfortable – not too narrow to hit, and not so broad that it conflicts with safety straps or alters your grasp of the pistol – and it's more or less ambidextrous. I say "more or less" for a reason. When firing right-handed, all our testers were

able to off-safe and on-safe easily with their firing hand thumb. They were able to off-safe just as easily when shooting southpaw… but that extra lever on the right side of the frame just didn't want to go back up into the "safe" position. I found that I could turn my left hand on the gun and get the ball of the thumb's median joint on the lever with enough force to on-safe it left hand only, but most of us just used our right hand to perform that function. I submit that a defensive pistol should be able to run using one hand only, with either hand, because that's a distinct real life possibility in a defensive handgun's mission statement.

I thought the lever on the right might just be stiff on our sample, but apparently not. A southpaw friend at SIG told me he's seen the same. "I don't have any trouble with it, but right-handed people seem to, when they work one of these left-handed. My left is my dominant hand, so maybe it's a strength issue," he observed.

Like all late production P-220s, the magazine release button on this one is convertible to right side placement for southpaw shooters, or for those righties who prefer to dump the magazine with their trigger finger instead of their right thumb. Most of the shooters on the test team were right-handed, so we just left the test gun as it was.

Why a cocked and locked SIG? For one thing, it's not a 1911. The classic 1911 pistol set records for military weapon reliability when it was left with its original recoil spring system and loaded with 230-grain full metal jacket round-nose military ammo. For generations, however, American enthusiasts, gunsmiths, and gun designers have messed with it hoping to improve it. They change the springs, they tighten the tolerances, they change the feedway, they load it with gap-mouthed hollowpoints or sharp-edged semi-wadcutters, and guess what? It's not always so reliable any more.

The P220 .45 was built from the ground up for reliability with hollowpoint ammo of the Western world. It has more of a straight-line feed angle than does the 1911. All things considered, many people believe the P220 is a more reliable platform. For those who feel that way, a cocked and locked P220 is a blessing from Heaven and not just from SIGARMS.

At an Amarillo class, Ayoob shot this virtually one-hole 60-shot group during timed qualification. Pistol is SIG P220 SAO in short 3.9-inch barrel Carry format, drawn from LFI Concealment rig and loaded with Rem-UMC .45 hardball. Target is Texas DPS.

Starting with flush bottom (for concealment) older generation 7-round mag, author put eight rounds into this satisfying group from 25 yards, right-hand barricade, with SIG P220 Match with 5-inch barrel.

Another thing the P220 delivers more readily than most 1911s is accuracy. You're generally looking at spending $2500 with a pistolsmith, minimum, to get a 1911 that will shoot much under two inches at 25 yards and not jam all the time because its tolerances have been choked up too tight. That's just about the level of accuracy that comes out of the box with a SIG P220 .45 ACP. I've shot two of them that put five shots in 7/8-inch at that distance, both pistols in out-of-the-box condition, and both using Federal's fabulously accurate 185-grain Classic hollowpoint. It's not guaranteed, but the accuracy potential is certainly there. This one broke the 2-inch group mark with half of the ammo tested. However, it should be borne in mind that this particular pistol was the Carry model, with a sub-four inch barrel and proportionally shorter sight radius.

As noted, the P220 SAO is not a 1911, and that means some other things. It means that you can leave the manual safety engaged when operating the slide. It means you have the fabulously easy takedown of the SIG-Sauer system.

It means that this is one cocked and locked pistol that *won't* discharge if you *first* pull the trigger and then, while holding it back, release the safety. You'll feel a strong resistance when you try to do this, and will discover that only when you ease up on the trigger and let it move a little forward will you be able to start rearward pressure again, and *then* pull the trigger of the now-off-safe pistol.

Also unlike the 1911, the P220 SAO offers a convertibility factor. Merely by sending your P220 SAO to the SIGARMS plant in Exeter, N.H., you can have it converted to traditional double-action first shot, or double-action-only (DAO), or DAK, SIG's light pull, high-tech DAO system. This is only possible with P220 frames manufactured in the last few years. They are easily distinguished by the size of the window cut in the frame for the trigger. If your pistol has a 10mm wide trigger window in the frame, says SIGARMS engineer Joe Kiesel, you're good to go on the conversion. If you have the older frame, where that window is only 8mm wide, your only

options are traditional DA/SA, or the older style of DAO with the heavier pull. The SAO and DAK require the current production frames.

The P220 SAO won't take 1911 magazines, either, but there are so many bad magazines of that type floating around that this fact is probably a blessing. Stick with SIG magazines, and those made by MecGar of Italy, who have produced a huge number of SIG-Sauer's own magazines anyway. A third that I would trust is the Novak, though mine hold only seven rounds. The test pistol worked fine with early generation P220 American magazines, 7-round with a flat bottom that helps concealment in most types of holster. It worked fine with a second-generation 8-shot "DPS" magazine, created by SIG for Texas cops with P220 .45s. And of course, it worked fine with the two 8-round stainless magazines of the type SIG is now supplying with these guns, complete with a bumper pad for positive insertion and my favorite of the pack. About all it *won't* work with are aftermarket junk, or early P220 European and Browning BDA magazines, which were designed for butt-heel release and don't have the proper cutouts for a current SIG.

SIGARMS offers the SAO P220 in three barrel/slide configurations. One is the short 3.9-inch barrel Carry version, like the SAO itself a recently introduced option; another is the standard 4.4-inch barrel length; and a third is a 5-inch target model. SIGARMS sent a Carry configuration SAO to *On Target,* the first of the DAO SIGs I was able to test in depth.

The test pistol's barrel measures 3.9 inches in length. The traditional P220 is listed in the specs as having a 4.4-inch barrel. The .45 ACP cartridge has, over the years,

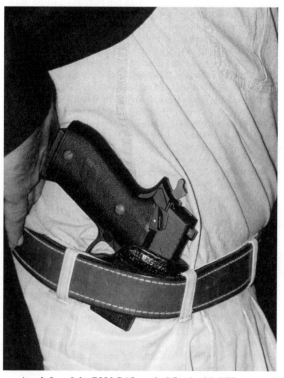

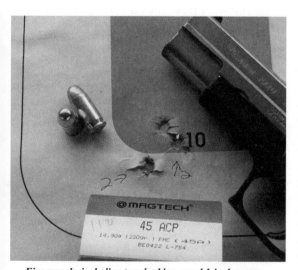

Five rounds, including two doubles, equal 1-inch group with inexpensive MagTech .45 hardball and SIG SAO P220 match. Distance was 25 yards.

Ayoob found the P220 SAO worked fine in this LFI Concealment Rig by Ted Blocker, cut for standard P220.

been notorious for its sensitive "velocity floor" insofar as conventionally designed hollow-point bullets opening. I did one test with a trio of Colt .45 autos back in the '80s, using 185-grain Federal hollowpoint fired into slaughterhouse animals under humane conditions. The bullet from the 5-inch Colt Government Model mushroomed perfectly and dramatically. The one from the 4.25-inch Lightweight Commander deformed into a distinctly smaller mushroom shape. The one from the 3.5-inch barrel of an Officer's ACP did not deform at all, and probably could have been reloaded into a fresh cartridge if I'd wiped off the blood and flesh.

Today's high-tech hollowpoints are expressly engineered to open at the lower velocities predictable from shorter barrels. These include CCI/Speer's Gold Dot, Federal's Hydra-Shok and particularly their HST series, PMC's Eldorado Starfire, Remington's Golden Saber, and Winchester's SXT and Ranger lines.

We compared the P220 SAO with a regular P220 on a Chrony, using Speer's popular Lawman 230-grain full metal jacket .45 ACP practice load. The standard P220 averaged 786.64 fps. The shorter P220 SAO averaged 769.94 fps. The difference? A mere 16.7 fps. Not anything to worry about. You'll often see more difference than that between two supposedly identical cartridges out of the same lot of ammunition, fired from the same .45 pistol.

We noticed something else: this short, light pistol kicked less than its big brothers. It kicked less than the standard aluminum-frame P220. It kicked a little less than even the heavy, all-steel P220 ST. Not believing our hands, three of us shot those three guns side by side and the verdict was unanimous: less jump, distinctly, in the P220 Carry than either of the others, including the all-steel gun.

This is counter-intuitive. A 16 fps reduction in muzzle velocity does not reduce corresponding recoil enough to notice. Joe Kiesel opines it's the lighter mass of the shorter slide going back and forth that is reducing both the muzzle jump and the rearward kick. Live and learn.

The SIG-Sauer P220 has always been one of my favorite double action .45 autos, and the only thing I would have added to it if I could, would have been a thumb safety. Those things can be life-savers when you're in a struggle for your pistol with the bad guy. Now, I *have* a SIG-Sauer P220 with a thumb safety. Thank you very much, SIGARMS of America and Sauer of Germany! *(My sources tell me the P220 SAO project was 50/50 between the two entities.)*

That P220 SAO Carry wound up with Editor Ben Battles at *On Target.* We might have fought over which one of us was going to send a check to SIGARMS and keep it, but I was holding out until I tried the longer guns. After all, Paul Erhard in SIG marketing was promising 1-inch groups with the 5-inch target model, and I hadn't tried that one yet.

I subsequently got a 5-inch, the configuration they call the Match, and damned if it *didn't* shoot into an inch! Even more impressive, the ammo was cheap Brazilian Mag-Tech hardball, and the "bench rest" was the top of a 55-gallon drum on one of the tactical ranges at Marty and Gila Hayes' excellent training facility, the Firearms Academy of Seattle. This gun, too, shot soft in terms of recoil. The only thing I didn't like about it was the sharp edges on its adjustable sights. After I wrote it up for the cover story in *Guns* magazine (February, 2006 issue), I sent it back. *Almost* bought it, but had a feeling that the standard length gun might be the one for me. I already

SIG P220 SAO in standard size configuration with 4.4-inch barrel.

had plenty of leather for the standard size, and as mentioned above, I had been able to achieve that magic one inch at 25 yards twice before with standard size P220s in the double-action configuration.

Then, lo and behold, *American Handgunner* editor Roy Huntington decided he wanted an article on the whole kit and kaboodle, so he sent along one in each length! The 3.9-inch Carry proved functionally identical in every respect to the one tested for *On Target,* including the same accuracy, the same soft recoil and the same high order of reliability. My only beef with it was that the sights weren't spot on. The long-barrel Match model shot direct to point of aim/point of impact right out of the box, though, and proved that it could hit the magic inch with that equally magic Federal 185-grain JHP, which used to be called Match Hollow Point on the box for good reason.

But, at long last, I had a 4.4-inch standard size P220 single action! I was a bit disappointed to discover that it shot distinctly to the left, but I knew that was nothing I couldn't fix with a Brownell's fixed sight moving tool, or the equivalent available through SIGARMS Academy for us armorer's school graduates. And, by golly, the elusive inch didn't prove that elusive at all. You guessed it: Federal Classic 185-grain hollow point was the ticket, though this pistol shot everything else pretty well, too.

I've spent weeks at a time carrying one or another of these guns concealed. Only one, the first P220 Carry, ever accidentally wiped its cocked and locked safety to the down position, doubtless from brushing the outermost of its ambidextrous levers with my forearm while carrying it in an open-top holster. The safety lever works very positively on all these guns. Indeed, the standard model was fitted so tightly I couldn't thumb it back on-safe with the firing hand, and had to do so with a separate movement of the support hand.

I've worn them in the heat of a Texas summer (Amarillo, Carry model, LFI Concealment Rig inside the waistband by Ted Blocker, July '06) and in the chill of a Minnesota winter (Minneapolis, 5-inch Match model, Ted Blocker thumb-break belt-slide, December '06). It worked fine with gloves and cold hands. The thumb-break of the Blocker holster shielded body and clothing alike from the sharp upper corners of the adjustable rear sight.

I've also finally had time to shoot all three of them in IDPA matches. Each time I was shooting against 1911s, in the Custom Defense Pistol category created for cocked and locked .45 autos. Summer, Oak Park, Illinois: Second Master. Illinois State and Midwest CDP Champion Rich DeMondo beat me with his custom 1911, though not by much. I shouldn't complain. He's a hell of a shot, and to salve my ego, he's one of my LFI graduates. I had been shooting my first test Carry model in that event, with Speer Lawman .45 hardball. Autumn, Orlando, Florida: shooting my second test sample Match SAO and Winchester USA .45 hardball, I took First Master. Winter, Jacksonville, Florida: shooting the 4.4-inch configuration SAO with 230-grain match loads developed expressly for CDP-class IDPA shooting by Atlanta Arms and Ammo, I managed to win First Master and CDP category overall.

The matches tell you less about inherent accuracy than they do about handling under stress. What they told me was that this new SIG will, as Bill Jordan used to say, "Do to ride the river with."

If you like the idea of a cocked and locked .45 but for this or that reason are put off by the 1911 design, this is the gun for you. The most expensive, the Match variation, can be had for just under a thousand dollars with fixed night sights, and just over that with the adjustables. If that sounds steep, consider that a 1911 that will give the same 100 percent reliability and one-inch-at-25-yards accuracy would cost between $2500 and $5000, and would probably entail a waiting period of up to five years before the master gunsmith got through his backlog to work his magic on your gun.

I call that a helluva deal, and I call the SIG P220 SAO one of the most noteworthy pistols to make its debut in the last five years.

SIG P226 DAK .357

SIGARMS' P226 pistol was once the most popular police service auto in this country. Of late, the SIG brand has been Number Two in law enforcement sales, behind the Glock, but the company is surging forward again. SIGARMS and Heckler & Koch share a huge Homeland Security purchasing contract. The SIG pistols approved by Homeland Security include the full size P226, the compact P229, and the subcompact P239, all in calibers 9mm Luger and .40 Smith & Wesson. All are in double-action-only formats, the first two with a relatively new trigger group called the DAK.

The acronym stands for Double Action, Kellerman, named after its European designer. An improved double action only concept, it actually embodies three potential trigger pull modes. It competes directly with HK's LEM (Law Enforcement Module) trigger group, which is slightly different mechanically and in that subjective quality of "feel." For purposes of an article *On Target* provided me with a P226 DAK, serial number UU 605295. I also attended the SIG Armorer's Course for the DAK pistol (specifically, for the functionally identical P229 DAK) in Arlington Heights, IL.

Our test pistol was chambered for the .357 SIG round. Going back a dozen years, this cartridge resembles a .40 S&W casing necked down to 9mm, though engineering-wise, it's much more than that. Ted Rowe, then a prime mover at SIGARMS, wanted to put the lightning-strike power of the most popular .357 Magnum revolver round among police, the 125-grain hollowpoint at 1.450 fps, into

SIG P226 DAK in .357 SIG.

the ergonomic SIG pistol. SIG and Federal Cartridge pretty much succeeded, and the .357 SIG round was born.

So, we have here a proven pistol, an excellent and promising fire control system, and a cartridge that has worked out extremely well on the street. Let's look at each of those elements separately, to better see how they come together in the test pistol.

The P226 Pistol is essentially a P220 design with its grip frame widened to take a double-stack magazine, and built "American style." The P226 was created more than twenty years ago by the Swiss/German collaboration of SIG and Sauer to compete in the JSSAP trials for selection of the new American 9mm military service pistol. Though it tied and, by some accounts, beat the Beretta 92, the U.S. armed services contract went to the Italian-designed pistol. A more compact version, the SIG P228, was adopted by Army CID, however, and the Navy's SEALs have insisted on the P226 9mm as their sidearm for many years. Over the decades, the P226 was redesigned for greater strength, an upgrade that made the powerful .357 SIG and .40 Smith & Wesson rounds practical in that envelope, and the design has received other timely "tweaks." Among them is the Picatinny rail on the dust cover of the frame of the P226R variation, which encompasses our test sample.

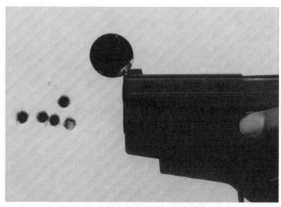

SIG's manageable "double-action Kellerman" trigger gave this excellent group at 25 yards.

The DAK Fire Control Mechanism is an important breakthrough. Some police departments feel that a trigger pull that works with a long, deliberate stroke for every shot, plus a mechanism that "decocks itself," is safer, more stress-resistant, and less prone to civil liability. SIG's standard DAO pull was adopted in the P226 by Ohio State Patrol (caliber .40) and as an option for NYPD (9mm), among others. However, many officers and instructors wanted something with an easier pull.

It was with this in mind that Kellerman designed the new system, which I first tested in prototype at the SIGARMS facility in Exeter, N.H. in 2003. The initial trigger pull is long, but light and very controllable. The shooter may use this pull for every shot by simply returning the trigger all the way forward each time. However, there is also the option for the skilled user of allowing the trigger to go forward just until it catches its first "link." It is now past the disconnector mechanism and has engaged the sear, and second and subsequent shots can be fired from this position. It requires a shorter stroke of the trigger, but since a shorter pull gives less mechanical advantage, the pull weight increases by a pound and a half or so. Finally, as a fallback, if the hammer goes all the way forward (something it can only do if the trigger has been pulled) but the chambered round doesn't fire, the shooter can take another whack at it by simply pulling the trigger again, though with the longer trigger now moving the hammer farther, the pull weight increases to over three pounds more than the first trigger stroke.

The .357 SIG Cartridge, while available in a fairly wide variety of bullet weights, is most widely adopted as a 125-grain JHP at 1325 to 1425 fps. The SIG in .357 has been adopted by a number of agencies, including the Texas Department of Public Safety (P226), and the state troopers of Delaware, Rhode Island, and Virginia, all of whom use the more compact P229. The P229 .357 SIG is

Ayoob rolls a double-action shot from weak-hand barricade at 25 yards with the SIG SAS P239 .40. He prefers to allow the DAK trigger to reset all the way forward for each shot.

standard issue for the U.S. Secret Service, and the Sky Marshals. In close to fifteen years on the street, the 125-grain .357 SIG round has earned the same reputation for fast man stopping as its six-gun predecessor.

If you've shot the ubiquitous P226 9mm, picture it honked up with a heavier recoil spring (making the slide somewhat stiffer to manually retract, and the slide stop lever a bit harder to push down when the pistol is at slide-lock). Imagine it a bit snappier in recoil, and distinctly louder. That's what it's like to shoot a P226 in .357. No big deal as far as controllability. Unlike most .357 revolvers with Magnum loads, it won't hurt to shoot unless you have a hand or arm injury.

The DAK is easy to get used to, and easy to like. That first pull, spec'd at just under 7 pounds in the literature, averaged slightly over 7 pounds on a Lyman digital trigger weight scale. "Catching the link" after each cycling of the slide, we experienced a trigger stroke with a shorter throw but an average pull weight of 8 pounds, 15 ounces while 9 pounds, 5.5 ounces was the average weight of the

*Accuracy Test: SIG P226 DAK .357

Brand	Load	Nominal FPS	5-Shot Group	Best 3 Shots
Black Hills Red	125-gr BHP**	1325 fps	1-1/4"	9/16"
CCI Speer Gold Dot	125-gr BHP	1350 fps	2-1/4"	1.00"
Federal Premium	125-gr JHP	1350 fps	3-1/4"	1-1/16"
Wolf	230-gr	FMJ	4-1/2"	1-13/16"
Winchester USA	125-gr JHP	1350 fps	2-7/8"	13/16"

* Hand-held on MTM rest @ 25 yards.
** Bonded (jacketed) Hollow Point

"To the barricades." Author finds SIG SAS compact accurate enough and shootable enough for NRA Service Automatic class of PPC shooting.

SIG P239 SAS with DAK trigger.

default trigger pull designed for misfires. *(We were never able to actually fire it in default mode, since that would require a misfired cartridge, and as with every DAK I've shot since 2003, this gun never misfired.)*

It seems counterintuitive, but I shot a tad better with the long "first shot" pull, and soon learned to let the trigger return all the way forward for each shot. Testing with Winchester USA economy 125-grain JHP, I got a 25-yard group of 3 and 3/8 inches while "riding the link" for each shot, and a tighter 2 7/8-inch cluster (5 shots each) while using the longer "first pull," as a true DAO. The lightness of the longer "first pull" helps.

The SIG P226 is an accurate pistol, and the .357 SIG is an accurate cartridge. Firing single action from a rest at the same 25-yard distance at the Manchester Indoor Firing Line in Manchester, NH, a standard format P226 gave me a one-inch 5-shot group with CCI Speer 125-grain Gold Dots. That was one of the Firing Line's rental SIGs, at that! The DAK gun was almost as tight with its favorite load, delivering five Black Hills rounds (loaded with the 125-grain Gold Dot bullet) into 1-1/4 inches. The Gold Dot group was only an inch bigger with the DAK. The best three-shot clusters (often your best indicator of inherent accuracy when firing hand-held from a rest) went into an inch with the Gold Dot, and an extraordinary 9/16-inch with the Black Hills, which unfortunately is no longer produced in .357 SIG. Federal and Winchester ammo also proved suitably accurate.

There were no malfunctions of any kind. The SIG P226 has earned a reputation for extremely high reliability over more than a score of years in 9mm, and the same seems to be true in .40 S&W and .357 SIG. The latter round, being bottlenecked, feeds into the chamber with a smooth wedge effect that only enhances its feed reliability. Early incidents of case neck separation with some brands of .357 SIG ammo seem to be history.

Extraordinarily reliable, extremely accurate, adaptable to quick-detaching flashlights and laser sights thanks to the front Pic rail and now fitted with the Kellerman trigger for better, safer performance under extreme stress, the P226 DAK seems to have it all. The price is commensurate with its high quality and reflects good value. According to scuttlebutt from SIG, the state of Texas is going with the DAK mechanism while keeping their P226 and the .357 SIG round, both of which have worked extraordinarily well for them on the street.

Springfield Armory XD In 45 ACP

You can't go on an Internet gun forum anymore – even one dedicated to other brands, such as GlockTalk – without seeing someone singing the praises of Springfield Armory's new XD.45 pistol in .45 ACP.

First, "XD.45 pistol in .45 ACP" is not a redundancy. The XD stands for "X-treme Duty," the Croatian pistol that used to be known as the HS2000 before Springfield Armory cornered the market on its U.S. importation. "XD9" is the 9mm version, "XD.40" is chambered in .40 S&W, and "XD.357" is the same polymer-frame pistol in .357 SIG. However, the first "XD.45," which was introduced in late 2004, was actually chambered for the .45 GAP (**G**lock **A**utomatic **P**istol) cartridge.

I liked the heck out of that gun. Mine, a 5-inch "LE Tactical" version, was the most accurate pistol I had ever fired with the new cartridge, giving phenomenally tight clusters at 25 yards with Winchester's humble USA brand "white box" generic 230-grain hardball load. It fit the hand exactly like one of its 9mm Luger, .40 S&W, or .357 SIG stable-mates... which is to say, it fit the hand superbly.

However, the decision was made in 2005 to tool up to answer the demand for this pistol in caliber .45 ACP. Like Glock, they decided they needed a bigger frame for the longer .45 ACP round. The result is the new XD.45ACP. If you review almost any electronic gun forum on the Internet, you'll see this gun's praises being sung by a variety of end-users, with scant complaints from those who've actually fired the pistol. Is it really that good?

XD .45ACPs in, top to bottom, Tactical size, Service size, and Compact. First two hold 14 rounds, latter, 11.

In a word, yes.

We tested two XD.45ACPs, a standard size (4-inch barrel) serial number US605996, and a Tactical version with 5-inch barrel and proportionally lengthened slide, serial number US608092. Each had the standard array of modern XD features. Molded-in frame rail for attaching a tactical light. Ambidextrous magazine release buttons, which are extremely handy for right-handed shooters as well as lefties, as we shall see. Grip safety, which must be depressed to fire the pistol or to operate its slide, ensuring a firm firing grasp during handling. Trigger safety, a la' Glock, intended to require a properly located finger to apply intentional pressure before the pistol can discharge. Fixed Patridge sights with three white dots. Loaded chamber indicator, clearly visible and palpable, rising like a shark fin at the rear of the firing chamber. Melonite finish, to quell complaints of rust on earlier XDs.

The first thing most experienced shooters noticed with these guns was the impressively narrow girth of the grip-frame. By using a steel-bodied magazine instead of one with thicker polymer – and adapting the design to the existing shape of the standard XD, which has been superbly ergonomic from the beginning – the engineers ended up with a very "grasp-able" double-column .45 ACP. There is a user-friendly short trigger reach, which lets the average size adult male get a lot of finger on the trigger, and allows anyone with short fingers to reach the trigger with the pad or tip of the index finger while still keeping a firm hold on the pistol, with its barrel in line with the long bones of the forearm.

The grip safety works as intended. With any sort of firing grasp, it releases itself. It is almost a passive safety in that, so long as the shooter is taking a good hold, no deliberate movement is required to release the safety and allow the pistol to fire.

With a release button low behind the trigger guard – *and one on each side* – the pistol is extremely easy to reload quickly. A shooter can use the index finger instead of the thumb to dump the depleted magazine. This has the safety advantage of guaranteeing the finger is out of the trigger guard at this point. It is also generally faster because the shooter need not shift his or her grip to get the thumb to the release button, as is often the case with many other pistols in many shooters' hands. With the XD, the right-handed shooter works the right button with the trigger finger, and the southpaw shooter, the left button. On each side, the buttons are hidden into recesses in the frame that very effectively shield them from being inadvertently depressed during carry or firing.

Adding to the reloading speed is a wide-mouth magazine well, which combines with an upwardly tapering magazine for a very slick and generally fumble-free insertion. Of course, you get this with most any pistol magazine that is double-stack in design. However, combined with the handy ambi mag release, the XD is particularly fast. For those who prefer the speed method of pressing down on the slide stop to close the slide at the end of a slide-lock reload, the XD presents only one problem: the slide stop lever is a little bit sharp at its upper left corner, and can start chewing on the thumb in a long practice session. Those who prefer the slower but more traditional method of closing the slide by tugging it to the rear and letting it snap forward will avoid that minor discomfort, but at some cost in speed.

The slide stop lever and the takedown lever are the only two parts of this pistol that present undesirable

Ayoob found the Compact Springfield Armory XD to be uniformly accurate with all bullet weights of .45 ACP.

sharp contact points to the shooter's hands in routine manipulation and firing. Using the straight thumbs position that has become popular in IDPA and IPSC, a right-hander's thumbs took a definite chewing from these parts, particularly the forward thumb. Being an old revolver shooter, I just curled the thumbs down double-action style and got them out of the way. A southpaw shouldn't have a problem with it, since the offending parts are on the left side of the pistol. Still, I'd like to see Springfield Armory get these parts rounded on the edges.

Recoil was pleasantly mild for a .45 ACP. We passed these guns around to a lot of friends who were .45 fans eager to fire this new iteration. Comments were unanimously positive. One shooter promptly went out and ordered one in each barrel length from his favorite dealer.

There has been a lot of discussion as to how this pistol compares to the gun it appears to be designed to compete with directly, the full-size Glock 21 in the same caliber. Most of the discussion centers around recoil. This is a highly subjective comparison. Personally, I can't see much difference in either rearward "kick" or muzzle rise between the G21 and the XD.45. Several county deputies who were qualifying on my range with their issue Glock 21s took advantage of my offer to try the XD.45ACP. Most

Springfield Armory XD-.45 LE in .45 GAP with InSight light/laser unit. Five-inch barrel allows muzzle to be parallel with lamp.

said they felt it kicked less than their department service pistol, and one reportedly went right out and ordered a 4-inch version for off-duty carry. I think it may be that the smaller circumference of the XD.45ACP's grip frame gets proportionally more hand around the gun, giving the shooter more control, or at least a sensation of more control. On the other hand, the bore axis of the Glock in .45 ACP is slightly lower, giving the muzzle less leverage to climb. In my own hands, I think those two factors amount to a wash. Proportionally more hand around the "handle" gives me more leverage on that end, but less muzzle rise from the Glock's lower-axis bore cancels that out on the other end. It's probably why I personally can't find a real difference between the two, but as noted above, that's highly subjective.

We tested these guns with a variety of loads. Surprisingly, the longer-barrel gun did not exceed the shorter in accuracy, despite its greater sight radius. The Tactical felt better balanced with more weight out front, but I couldn't detect any real difference in muzzle climb or rearward recoil between the two. The 4-inch came out of the box shooting spot on, while the 5-inch left the factory shooting a tad high and left.

Off the bench at 25 yards, none of the several loads we tested failed to make the old and generous standard of 4-inch groups. Most did better. The tightest group with the Tactical measured 2.05 inches for all five shots, and a stunning 0.80-inch for the best three. That was with Remington 185-grain +P jacketed hollowpoint, fired by IDPA Five-Gun Master Jon Strayer. With that same ammo, the 4-inch pistol did 2.30 inches (five shots) and 1.35 inches (best three shots).

A handload put together by Steve Sager, consisting of a 230-grain Precision polymer-coated round-nose bullet over 5.5 grains of Universal Clays gunpowder and Winchester Large pistol primers started out to be 1.40 inches, but a single flyer expanded the five-shot group to 2-3/4 inches. It is to factor out such human error that I like to measure the best three shots as well. With this gun and the Sager load, that measurement was an incredible 0.55-inch, which included two bullets in one barely-enlarged hole. Needless to say, the XD.45ACP shows promise of being a very accurate pistol.

Tactical (top) and Compact Springfield Armory XD .45ACPs.

I've carried the 4-inch XD.45 considerably. It comes with a plastic double magazine pouch and plastic holster, both made overseas. I found both to lean out a bit from the body. As this gun becomes more popular, more companies are making leather for it. I ordered a carbon fiber CQC and a leather Avenger holster for it from Blackhawk, and was rewarded with better concealment and a more comfortable ride on the hip. When I carried it loaded and concealed, no sharp edges attacked my body or clothing. I later acquired a Blackhawk SERPA, the concealable security holster in the CQC line discussed elsewhere in this book. (And, yes, I liked the XD.45 so much that I bought both test samples from Springfield Armory.)

When testing a hunting gun, it's best to go on a hunt with it, to test its attributes in its intended environment. With a defensive handgun, the closest you can come to that is to shoot a combat match with it, and see how it performs when fast handling and straight shooting are demanded under stress. With this in mind, I took the 4-inch gun with me in the holster it came with to an IDPA match in Orlando, Florida on the first Sunday of March, 2006. I brought some of Sager's handloads.

The provided holster and mag pouch, from the line Springfield Armory calls "XD Gear," proved amply fast. The sights were easy to see against gray or white steel knockdowns, and against buff-colored cardboard silhouettes. Reloads, as testing had predicted, were lightning fast. The gun always came right back on target, and hit point of aim.

IDPA, the International Defensive Pistol Association, allows Glocks to be fired in the Stock Service Pistol category against conventional double-action autos, but requires the XD to vie against the cocked and locked 1911-type autos. This is because, mechanically, the XD is defined as a single-action pistol, even though its smooth, even trigger pull (between six and seven pounds in both test samples) feels more like shooting a Glock than anything else. I entered in the Enhanced Service Pistol (ESP) category, and to make a long story short, nailed First Master there, won the ESP category, and posted the high overall score of the well-attended shoot.

The XD.45 had proven its shootability. With over a thousand rounds through each, there had been a single ejection failure (with the 4-inch gun during its early break-in period, and never repeated). It's not hard to see why the XD.45ACP won NRA's Golden Bullseye award. If you're looking for a high quality, high-tech, high-capacity .45 ACP that doesn't demand a huge hand *or* a huge bank account, check out the Springfield Armory XD.45ACP.

Springfield Armory X-Treme Duty Tactical .40

With lightweight polymer frame and extreme simplicity of operation, the Glock pistol has become America's most popular. Several imitators have sprung up, but none has caught on quite as well as the Croatian HS 2000, currently imported and advertised as the Springfield Armory XD ("X-treme Duty"). The line has expanded rapidly. There is the XDV10, with integral recoil compensation ports; there are subcompacts to compete with the baby Glock; and now there is a slightly extended-length Tactical version. For the Editor's Choice edition of *On Target* magazine, I tested the latter in caliber .40 S&W. The XD series is also available in 9mm Luger and .357 SIG.

The trigger pull is a smooth, soft press. This helps to achieve the surprise break marksmen appreciate. Sights on the test gun were fixed, with a fiber optic red front that stood out well against any background. Unlike many fiber optic units, this one sits in the center of a solid, square-edged Patridge front sight, giving the shooter the option of raw speed or precise aim.

Distinctively, the Tactical has molding on the front of the polymer frame for snap-on flashlights like the InSight M3 or M6, and at the back, is extended out over the web of the shooter's hand in the manner of a RoBar reshaping of a Glock. As with all XDs, there is ample reach to the trigger. This allows an average size hand to make trigger contact at the distal joint, which many combat shooters feel gives more leverage, and it allows those with the shortest fingers to still get the pad of the index finger solidly onto the trigger without compromising grasp.

At the 25-yard bench, we tested the XD.40 Tactical with all three generations of .40 S&W ammo. Winchester full metal jacket with the first generation formula of a 180-grain bullet at subsonic velocity delivered a 5-shot group that measured three inches even, its best three in a tiny cluster measuring only 1-3/8 inches. Typical of the second generation in ballistics was Black Hills' red box EXP load, comprised of a 165-grain CCI Gold Dot at 1150 fps. It gave a cluster measuring just over three inches for 5 shots, with the best three in 1-14 inches. Third generation is typified by a 135-grain hollowpoint at a roaring 1300 fps, such as Pro-Load's Tactical. The Tactical ammo in the Tactical gun gave us a 5-shot group of just over 4 inches, with its best three in less than 1-1/2 inches.

As a rule, the "best three" measurement factors out human error and gives a good approximation of what the gun would do for five shots in a machine rest. This one indicates high accuracy potential. The forgiving trigger, the good sights, and the overall excellent ergonomics of the XD make this a shooter's gun. Recoil was mild with all loads fired, and we simply couldn't make it malfunction even once.

Functioning in essence like a squared-off Glock with a grip safety, and markedly underselling the Austrian pistol, the Springfield Armory XD is making rapid inroads with American gun owners. The Tactical version is particularly nice. Expect to see more of these guns. It would definitely be worth your while to pick one up and see what all the fuss is about.

Steyr-Mannlicher M9A1 Pistol

In June of 1999, Willi Bubits visited me in New Hampshire with a pistol he said I would be the first in the United States to fire. I was kind of proud of that… and I thought a lot of the gun. A former Glock engineer, Willi had come up with a "steel inside, polymer outside" pistol that Glock didn't want, but Steyr-Mannlicher did. It was a very promising pistol with some radical design features.

It was out-of-print for a while when Steyr-Mannlicher and its continued imports to the U.S. were both in doubt, and there was a period when remaining stocks of the M-series pistol were sold dirt-cheap. That's over now. Steyr-Mannlicher is back from the dead and ready to party, and they're sending us a new "A1" modification of this controversial sidearm, available in .40 S&W as the M.40A1 and in 9mm Parabellum as the M9A1. We got one of the latter in for testing.

The new series retains the best of the old, and has answered the few complaints with design updates that

Steyr's sweet-handling new updated design, the M9A1, shot this tight group in rapid fire at seven yards.

solve the previous concerns, real or imagined. Let's examine it feature by feature.

Grip. The grip-frame has been subtly re-shaped, retaining the steep grip angle of approximately 111 degrees. All our wide range of testers liked the feel. Whether the shooter's hands were elfin or elephantine, we kept hearing "It fits perfectly." This specimen doesn't have the currently popular grip inserts to alter size. It doesn't appear to need them. The reach to the trigger is very short. Those with small fingers can easily get the pad of the trigger finger onto the "bang switch" without having to weaken their grasp of the grip-frame itself. Those with medium to long fingers can easily attain the "distal joint of the index finger on the trigger face" placement that double-action revolver shooters have long found gives them the best leverage.

The key to this is a backstrap deeply niched out to bring the web of the hand in closer to the trigger. Bubits called this grip shape a "camel-back" grip. It works.

Trigger. Reminiscent of the Glock's trigger in appearance, the A1's is different in feel. There's a short take-up, and a relatively short overall movement. Original M-series pistols had five-pound pulls with a seven-pound option for police departments and other conservative types. Armorer Rick Devoid tested the sample's trigger on an official NRA Referee's pull weight

Unique Steyr sights will be liked or hated. Author likes them.

After a rapid-fire magazine from 10 yards, young Courtland Smith is pleased with the performance of the 9mm Steyr.

I never heard of one firing from impact or inertia. However, many police departments (and some cautious shooters) insist on an internal firing pin lock, so the A1 is outfitted with one.

Light rail. Heckler and Koch pioneered the molded-in attachment rail with their USP series more than a decade ago, and it has become a "must-have" option on modern autos. The A1 comes so equipped. For home defense or police work, I like the idea of a quick-on, quick-off powerful white light unit like the InSight or the SureFire. It can solve target identification problems and prevent tragedies. It can blind opponents at opportune moments. It's *A Good Thing.* Just make sure you use it as a target confirmation and target-blinding device, not a searchlight: anything the gun-mounted light illuminates, will be dead in line with your loaded Steyr pistol and its easy trigger. Keep a conventional flashlight handy for the search function, even if you have a lamp attached to your firearm.

Trigger finger niche. Another pioneering feature came from Taurus with their 24/7 series: niches molded into the frame to help the trigger finger stay there "in register," and out of the trigger guard at inappropriate times. I don't see any reason for every new pistol not to have this useful feature, and I'm glad to see it on the Steyr M-A1.

Trapezoidal sights. Perhaps the most novel and controversial feature on the original Steyr M, these remain on the new iteration. The rear sight rises up in two matching angles as if to form a bridge that is cut away in the center. What goes in the center instead is the tip of a point-up white triangle that is the front sight. For those accustomed to the conventional post-in-notch sight picture, or three dots in a horizontal row, or the dot-the-"i" von Stavenhagen sighting image, this is a radical departure.

It's worth trying, though. It is *very* fast for a "flash sight picture," and keys in very well with the excellent pointing characteristics afforded by the Steyr's Luger-like grip angle. Once you get the hang of it, the pointy top of the front sight can index very precise shots. The concept is reminiscent of the old silver or gold bead atop the front sight, which led to the phrase, "drawing a fine bead on the target."

Internal gun-lock. Continued from the first iteration is an internal lock located on the right side of the frame behind the takedown lever. (Takedown, by the way, is simple and uncomplicated.) The lock is activated by a quarter-turn with the two-pronged key provided in duplicate on "civilian" models, or a handcuff key on "police" models. I think the latter is a brilliant idea, since

device, and found that it broke at seven and a half pounds. Most who fired it guessed the pull weight at four to four and a half pounds. Those who like to "ride the sear" or "ride the link" when manipulating an auto pistol's trigger will find it easy to do on the Steyr M-A1.

Manual Safety. I've always been a proponent of a manual safety on a handgun, but only if it's user-friendly. The one on the original Steyr M wasn't. It was awkward to both engage and take off. They've simply removed it from the M-A1, and that may be for the best. If they want a gun that competes with the Glock, they want a gun that is operated like a Glock.

Passive firing pin safety. The original did not have an internal firing pin lock. Bubits had designed the pistol not to need one, and was convinced that it was "drop-safe."

Ayoob found the Nighthawk consistently accurate at 25 yards.

Nighthawk is among the most promising new brands of 1911. This is the Predator version in .45 ACP.

most of the cops I know carry a handcuff key with them at all times, on or off duty. While internal gun-locks provoke the same visceral debates as motorcycle helmet laws, I have no problem with them so long as they don't activate by themselves. I've never heard of that happening on a Steyr pistol.

The first thing every single person on our test team noted once the shooting started was that, even for a 9mm, this was a very soft-shooting gun. Ammo included Federal's hot, police-only 9BPLE load, which spits a 115-grain JHP at 1300 fps, and Remington's public market Golden Saber +P with a 124-grain brass jacket hollowpoint at 1250 fps. Part of the easy recoil can be traced to kick-absorbing flexion in the polymer frame, and part to the very low bore axis of this pistol. Those funny looking sights were back on target *immediately* after the prior shot.

Reloading was fast and smooth. The magazines, which appear to be manufactured by MecGar, have polished

metal bodies. They insert cleanly, and drop cleanly when the non-ambidextrous mag release button is pressed. The slide release lever is shaped for easy manipulation, and the frame has thumb-niches to help keep that digit from over-riding the lever and preventing it from doing its job of locking the slide open on an empty magazine. Two magazines come with each pistol.

Accuracy testing was done on a range where 25-yard benches were not readily available, so I shot from the rollover prone position developed by Ray Chapman. Our test M9A1 showed itself to be afflicted with "four plus one" syndrome, commonly seen in popular-price semiautomatic pistols. The first hand-chambered shot always seemed to go to a slightly different point of impact than the subsequent mechanically-cycled shots.

I saw something with this gun that is uncommon: mediocre accuracy with three out of four tested loads, and phenomenally good accuracy with one. Remington 124-grain Golden Saber HP had a 4.70-inch group in the center ring of the IDPA target, due largely to that first shot. Rounds #2 through #5 grouped in 3.60 inches. The best three shots, which help factor out human error – present here to a larger degree, since I was shooting without a bench rest – formed a 2.70-inch group. All measurements were to the nearest 0.05-inch, center-to-center between the bullet holes.

Winchester's 147-grain subsonic JHP, famous for accuracy, put five shots in a disappointing 5.50 inches; without the first shot, that group would have measured only 3-1/2 inches. The best three hits were in 2-1/4 inches. Another famously accurate load is Federal's 9BP, a standard pressure 115-grain JHP. This one gave a 5-shot group that measured a sub-standard 5 inches even, but without the first errant shot would have been 2.85 inches. The best three were in an even tighter 1.70-inch cluster.

However, the star of the show was a surprise. The humble, inexpensive, steel-case Wolf 115-grain FMJ practice load gave awesome accuracy, even though it shot low and right from point of aim. All five shots were in 1.10 inches. That included the slightly errant first shot. Rounds #2 through #5 punched a single, connected hole measuring only 0.45-inch! The best three of those were in about a quarter inch! Every shot could have been covered with a 25-cent piece.

I don't usually use that many exclamation points in one paragraph. But I don't usually see a group like that, either.

Suffice it to say that the M9A1 has awesome accuracy potential. It's also safe to say that one will have to grow accustomed to the unusual sight picture to extract that accuracy. It might be well worth the effort. A small coterie of IDPA shooters have

Taurus continues to be a major player in the combat handgun market. This is the excellent five-shot Tracker, which uses .45 ACP ammo with proprietary full moon clips.

become dedicated fans of the M-series Steyr-Mannlicher because they've found it *very* fast to achieve hits with in "combat shooting," thanks to its combination of excellent pointing characteristics, those quick-to-the-eye trapezoidal sights, and the user-friendly trigger pull and reset.

Willi Bubits' original design had a great deal to recommend it. The A1 modifications are all good, and a definite overall improvement. Light and comfortable to carry, packing fifteen 9mm Parabellum rounds in its double-stack magazine, and offering very low recoil and muzzle jump for quick shot-to-shot recovery, the Steyr-Mannlicher M-A1 series is full of potential for the serious *pistolero* or *pistolera*.

I for one am looking forward to shooting the M9A1 in an IDPA match.

Taurus

The last five years have seen a quantum leap in improving the quality of polymer frame Taurus defensive autoloaders. The egregious Millennium has been upgraded into the Millennium Pro, which actually *works*. Better is the slightly larger, but still concealed carry size, Model 24/7. An excellent amalgam of features – striker fired, double action only, ergonomic manual safety – it has a feature I'd like to see on all pistols. This is a well-thought-out fingertip niche on each side of the frame, above the trigger, in which to "register" the trigger finger by feel and help keep it off the trigger when it shouldn't be there. I've had good luck with the 24/7 in all three of its calibers: 9mm, .40 S&W and .45 ACP.

Put on the market shortly before this Sixth Edition went to press, the PT1911 is a well-conceived 1911 with many expensive pistol features, but a sub-$500 retail price. Only complaints I've heard so far are sharp edges, and a rather fragile finish on the blue guns. You might want to hold out for the stainless.

In Summation

It has been an interesting half-decade between the fifth and the sixth edition of this book. The hardware, certainly, has kept pace. What does the next half-decade hold? I would expect to be seeing a lot more .45 GAPs, and more .357 SIG pistols. These guns have found their respective niches, and are proving themselves.

I think we've got the small revolvers as light and high-powered as they're going to go, but there may be a little room to go farther in the same direction with small autos. We'll see. The 1911 is in more police holsters by far than when the fifth edition was written, and I think that's going to continue. The notoriously conservative Boston Police Department has ordered SIG GSR 1911s for their tactical teams, and the San Diego Police Department approved cocked-and-locked 1911s and saw the troops

Seen at Bill's Gun Shop outside Minneapolis in late '06, the Taurus 1911 combines high-priced features with extremely low suggested retail, and could become a best-seller among 1911s. They're working well in the field so far, though Ayoob has had reports of blue wearing off quickly, and suggests the stainless variation.

flock to buy them. Coast to coast, I'm seeing more 1911s *On The Job*.

The military? It's been up and down, but don't be surprised to see a large caliber pistol back in the hands of our troops by the time the seventh edition of *Gun Digest Book of Combat Handgunnery* rolls around.

Armed citizens? When the very first edition came out, there were seven states where there was no provision to carry, and now we're down to two. One of those, Wisconsin, has come achingly close to achieving *Shall Issue*, losing only by a vote or two in the over-ride attempt on the anti-gun governor's veto after passing by a clear majority in the state house in Madison. The Wisconsin stalwarts for gun owners' civil rights will stay in the fight, and I think they'll ultimately prevail. Illinois will be the last anti-self-defense bastion to fall, but a national concealed-carry option that would over-ride their home rule as the Law Enforcement Officer Safety Act did for cops nationwide is less of a pipe dream than ever. In extremely restrictive shall-issue states, the best option may be test cases selectively brought before the states' Supreme Courts. In Hawaii, where for years police chiefs by mutual agreement chose not to issue as state law allowed them to, we are now seeing permits issued for security personnel. The right lawyer with the right clients bringing the right class action suit might just fold that arbitrary and capricious ban on issuing self-protection permits like the fragile house of cards it is.

It's been an interesting five years since the last edition.

But not, I suspect, as interesting as the next five years may be.

CHAPTER FIFTEEN

Parting Words

As I was putting the foregoing chapters together, I leafed through the first edition of *Combat Handgunnery* written by Jack Lewis and Jack Mitchell in 1983. I remembered how much I had enjoyed reading it when it came out. Their incisive commentary has stood the test of time.

There were a few pictures of me in it. It's good to be reminded that there was a time when I didn't have a potbelly and only had one chin and nothing had gone gray yet. But that sort of thing reminds us all of how much can happen in 20 years.

The input of physiologists and kinesiologists into both the shooting sports and scientific firearms training has brought things forward in quantum leaps. Technology has evolved, but technique has evolved more. It's not about more high-tech "space guns." The shooters of today, using stock guns of a kind available a score of years ago, are shooting faster and straighter than the champions of two decades ago did with tricked-out specialty target guns.

It's not about the gun so much as it is about the shooter. It's not even about the shooter so much as it's about consistent application of proven tactics and techniques.

There's simply too much to put into any one book. Things have to be prioritized. Some of the topics of previous editions – malfunction clearing, for example,

Make it a plan to get behind cover before the shooting starts.

and night shooting – had to be left on the cutting room floor when we ran out of space in this edition. It was more important to nail down advances in shooting technique, how to pick the most suitable tools for the task, and how to avoid doing the wrong thing in an increasingly complex tactical environment. In any case, malfunction clearing and night shooting have been covered very well in past editions.

In the very short space that remains, let's talk about priorities. Training is always a better investment than equipment. Software in your brain is always with you, and there's only so much hardware you can carry. And there are places where you can't carry this kind of

Get experience beforehand in shooting from awkward, "downed" positions.

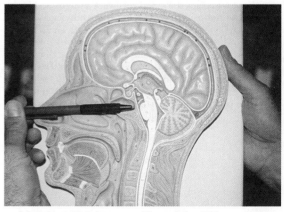

Marksmanship is important. The pen of an LFI consulting physician shows how small the target is for a hit in the part of the brain that will collapse an opponent without him pulling his trigger even reflexively.

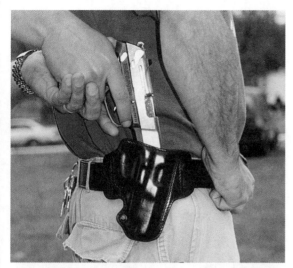

Think about handgun retention. An open-top holster does nothing to protect this Ruger .45, which is fortunately on safe...

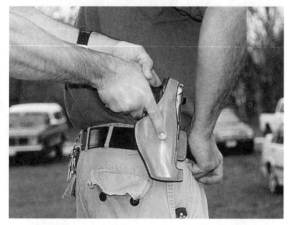

A thumb-break holster buys you more time...

...and this concealable Piece-Keeper security holster is even more snatch-resistant, and only slightly slower on the draw.

Underlying all this hi-tech kit is a Second Chance Ultima ballistic vest. Any situation where you want a defense gun is a situation where you want body armor.

hardware at all. I take at least a week of training a year for myself, and would recommend the same regimen to you. I can recommend without reservation schools like Chuck Taylor's ASAA, Chapman Academy, the Critical Reaction Training Center near Milwaukee, John Farnam's DTI, Firearms Academy of Seattle, Front Sight, Gunsite, the Midwest Training Group, Clint Smith's Thunder Ranch, and more. You're also welcome to inquire about my own school, Lethal Force Institute, at PO Box 122, Concord, NH 03302 or on the Web at www.ayoob.com.

Remember that awareness and alertness are more important than combat tactics, because they can keep you out of combat to begin with. Tactics are more important than marksmanship, because they can often keep you out of danger without you having to fire a shot. Skill with your safety equipment, including your weapons, is more important than what type of weapon you have. With all those things accomplished, your choice of equipment is one of the few things you can work out before the fight, so it makes sense to have the best quality gear of a kind ideally suited for your predictable threat situation.

Don't just drill on drawing and firing. Drill on movement. Make the use of cover a high priority. Take a

The author seconds the advice about awareness on this "tombstone."

"If you need a gun," said street-wise commentator Phil Engeldrum, "you probably need two." NAA Guardian .380, left, and Kahr MK40 are both popular backup pistols.

Your plans should include what your partners are going to do. These Lake County, Mont., deputies prepare for the day they may have to drag a wounded brother to safety under fire.

class in handgun retention, the art and science of defeating a disarming attempt. Learn to shoot from downed positions and with either hand. Learn from the cops: More than 2,500 officers at this writing have been saved by the concealed body armor that armed citizen Rich Davis invented in the early 1970s. As Kevlar Survivors' Club member #1946 and Second Chance Save #682, I can tell you that the stuff works. If your local dealers won't sell it to law-abiding private citizens, look up the LFI Web site, but be prepared to show proof of a clean criminal record.

If you need to carry a gun, you probably need to carry two. Invest in a backup gun if you're licensed to carry. Backups have saved countless police officers, and could have saved countless more if those slain officers had had recourse to a second weapon.

Make sure your loved ones and your regular companions know what the plan is going to be if this particular kind of danger strikes. That "fight or flight" thing is really "fight, flight, or freeze." The ones who freeze are the ones who don't have a plan. If you have something in your mind that says, "Given stimulus A, I *will* carry out response A," you've made the best possible investment in survival. You want to share the same concept with people you care about, who might be with you when a crisis strikes.

Thanks for taking the time to read this book. The plan is to update this book on a fairly regular basis. I don't know who's going to write the next one...but I'm going to do everything I can to make sure I'm around to read it.

Good luck. Stay safe.

Massad Ayoob
Live Oak, FL
2007

GunDigest® Book of

CLASSIC AMERICAN
COMBAT
RIFLES

edited by Terry Wieland

JG PRESS

Published by

World Publications Group, Inc.
140 Laurel Street
East Bridgewater, MA 02333
www.wrldpub.com

Cover photography courtesy Chip Morton Photography, morton.chip@gmail.com,
www.chipmortonphoto.com, 951-699-7873

ISBN-13: 978-1-4643-0277-0
ISBN-10: 1-4643-0277-4

Cover Design by Tom Nelsen
Designed by Dave Hauser
Edited by Corrina Peterson and Terry Wieland

Printed in China

Contents

Introduction

Welcome to the *Gun Digest Book of Classic American Combat Rifles*

No country in the world owes as much to the rifle as the United States. The rifle brought victory in the War of Independence, held the country together through a devastating Civil War, won the West, and made America a great power through the 20th century.

In many ways, America's combat rifles — firearms purchased by the government, and issued to our troops — tell the story of the country itself. At any given time, the rifles used by the U.S. Army, Navy, and Marines reflect America's progress toward technological and industrial might.

Today, there is more interest than ever before in the rifles Americans have used in combat throughout our 235-year history. We have rifles in use in historical reenactments of Revolutionary and Civil War battles, period rifles used in cowboy-action competitions, the current interest in the AR-15 platform as

a hunting, defense, and target-shooting rifle for civilians, and, of course, the continued activity of arms collectors at all levels.

Since its first issue in 1944, the study of America's combat rifles has been a major part of *Gun Digest*. We have published articles on the romance, design, performance, historical and technical significance, and — of course — the shortcomings of the many rifles which have been used by American troops in battle.

Most shooters recognize names like Springfield, Garand, ArmaLite, Sharps, and Spencer. But those are only the rifles that made it to the top and stayed there. Many other rifle designs were tested and adopted by the U.S. military, only to see limited use in action before sliding into historical oblivion. Other patterns bridged gaps between major technological advances.

One thing all of these rifles have in common is that, at their time, they were tre-

mendously important to the men who used them, and they are all part of the history of the American combat rifle.

In this volume, we have gathered the best articles on American combat rifles published by *Gun Digest* during the last 66 years. Like GD itself, they are quite varied; some are historical accounts by academics in the field; others are first-hand looks by soldiers who used the rifles in combat. To us, one of the most interesting aspects of compiling a book like this is not only the many different points of view, but the chronological view points — for example, looking at the rifles of World War II just as that war was ending and without the benefit of historical perspective and distant hindsight.

The history of *Gun Digest* extends back to a time when men living, shooting, and writing about it were personally acquainted with soldiers who lived through everything from the Civil War to the two World Wars, and could recount their experiences first hand. This gives the *Gun Digest Book of Classic American Combat Rifles* a different flavor than we would find in even the most comprehensive history written by one author.

Here, we have articles by some of the best-known and respected writers working in the field during the second half of the 20th century. On the Springfield rifle, we have Col. Townsend Whelen and Lt. Col. William S. Brophy, Jr.; on the rifles of World War II, Charles T. Haven, the noted Colt historian and technician at Johnson Automatics; on the M14, John Lachuk, one of the acknowledged fathers of the .44 Magnum.

From 1946, when he became editor, until 1984, when he retired, John T. Amber guided the editorial fortunes of *Gun Digest* with the enthusiasm of a shooter, the intense interest of an historian, and the editorial rigor of the best editor ever to work in the firearms field. Amber was interested in every aspect of firearms, but he loved rifles the best; he was escpecially interested in those little-explored nooks and crannies of rifle history.

When a writer came to Amber with an idea, he was given a forum and as much space as he needed to tell the story — provided the story was worth

telling. When the manuscript was submitted, Amber then applied standards of accuracy worthy of a college thesis. As a result, much of the material that appeared during his tenure could be reproduced, without apology, in a professional technical journal.

Even after John Amber's retirement, having an article published in *Gun Digest* remained a goal that writers, both professional and amateur, regarded as a mark of having arrived as a gun writer. Both Amber's demanding ways, and the professional commitment of his writers, is reflected in the articles published here.

Almost as interesting as what we have included is what was not covered in the pages of *Gun Digest*. By and large, Amber did not assign topics to writers; writers came to him with ideas, and Amber either approved them or not. This left his subject matter at the mercy of the interests of his writers, and this in turn was dictated by their own experience and the attractions of the rifles themselves.

The short-lived M14, for example, warrants only one article. For years, it was viewed in military terms as a stop-gap between the Garand and the AR-15; today, the virtues of the M14 are more widely recognized (as witness the success of Ruger's Mini-14, a small rifle modeled on its action.) Similarly, there is little on the trapdoor Springfield, which is now enjoying renewed interest on several different levels.

One reason for this is that Amber was dealing with an annual publication. He was not — and did not want to be — in competition with more frequent periodicals such as the NRA magazines. He preferred to devote his editorial space to subjects that were not being covered elsewhere, including arcane and under-appreciated designs such as the Hall rifle, the Whitworth, or the rifles of James Paris Lee.

If a writer wanted to deal with a more main-stream topic that was already widely covered elsewhere, he needed to come up with a unique angle in order to interest John Amber. The result is a substantial body of firearms literature that concentrates on the obscure corners of firearms history, or gives radical views of more familiar topics.

For example, James Paris Lee is regarded by some as a second-tier rifle designer, none of whose designs made it to the big time as an American combat rifle. Amber's view (and that of writers Larry Sterrett and John Wallace) is that Lee was far ahead of his time, and both he and his designs deserve more recognition than they receive.

Lee qualified for this book (barely) by the fact that the U.S. Navy adopted his rifle and 6mm cartridge, albeit briefly, and we have reprinted three articles that both give Lee his due and are excellent examples of the scope and quality of *Gun Digest* articles over the past 66 years. It is this willingness to look beyond the obvious that made *Gun Digest* what it is, and gives this collection of articles a unique historical perspective on that subject of endless fascination, the American combat rifle.

Terry Wieland, Editor

Muskets, Powder and Patriots

The firearms used in the Revolution were of many types and of highly mixed ancestry, yet they served the patriots adequately, if not well, in their struggle to victory.

▌M. L. Brown

The fabled "long rifle" was a novelty in the eastern colonies. In July, 1775, amazed patriots at Cambridge, Mass., watched in awe as one company of frontier riflemen placed all its shots in a 7-inch target at 250 yards — or so the story goesl Credit: Department of the Army.

GRIM-VISAGED Massachusetts Militia from Acton, Carlisle, Chelmsford, Concord and Lincoln nervously fingered loaded muskets on the muster field beyond Concord town. A dark column of smoke suddenly smudged the clear morning sky above the tiny Middlesex village and, as if on signal, determined patriots marched in double file toward the ominous beacon. Leading the van was taciturn Acton gunsmith Capt. Isaac Davis, and when his small band of citizen-soldiers approached "… the rude bridge that arched the flood …," they were met by a thunderous volley of musketry from three companies of British light infantry. Davis was killed instantly, the first patriot officer to fall in battle. It was April 19, 1775, and an infant nation saw birth in the bloody throes of revolution.

Gen. George Washington faced many difficulties throughout the Revolution, among them critical shortages of artillery, small arms and gunpowder. He triumpted, accepting Lord Corn-wallis' surrender at Yorktown, 19 October 1781. Credit: Library of Congress.

Craftsmen, farmers, frontiersmen; mariners, merchants, statesmen and scholars rallied to that clarion call of freedom and they would desperately need vast quantities of arms and munitions to meet the insatiable demands of the arduous struggle ahead. As early as 1750 Parliament attempted to curtail colonial iron production and discouraged other American enterprise, yet despite severe restrictions iron production flourished clandestinely. An adequate supply of iron was available throughout the war, although the vagaries of combat often made procurement difficult while inflation escalated prices.

In 1774, as relations between stern Mother England and her recalcitrant child rapidly deteriorated, Parliament placed an embargo on all firearms exported to the colonies and, on 1 September, Gen. Thomas Gage, Royal Governor of Massachusetts, confiscated the gunpowder stored in the public magazine at Charlestown and brought from Cambridge two fieldpieces to strengthen defenses at Boston. Aggrieved patriots retaliated when on 13 December they seized British gunpowder at Fort William and Mary.

Two months before Longfellow's immortal farmers "… fired the shot heard round the world …," Massachusetts organized Committees of Safety, which were soon emulated elsewhere. The committees were empowered to mobilize the militia, confiscate military stores, encourage the expansion of domestic arms-making and procure arms and munitions from domestic and foreign sources either by contract or purchase from available supplies.

It has been estimated that at the outset of the Revolution only a third of the firearms in the colonies were of domestic origin while lead, essential for casting projectiles, was almost exclusively imported, as were prime gunflints; each was discovered to be in short supply after hostilities commenced. The shortage of gunpowder was even more acute, and a usually optimistic George Washington was forced to admit that "Our situation in the article of powder is much more alarming than I had the most distinct idea of."

Under British rule militia service was compulsory for all able males between 16 and 65. Although most colonists were prosperous enough to own firearms, and

were required by Crown regulations to possess a musket and accouterments suitable for military use, they were poorly trained and equipped in comparison to British regulars. Familiarity with firearms doubtlessly sustained patriot efforts early in the conflict and, when integrated with the iron discipline hammered out by Baron von Steuben at Valley Forge in the harsh winter of 1777-78, welded the battered rebels into a more formidable foe.

Variety of Arms

Throughout the war Pvt. Yankee Doodle, of necessity, embraced virtually anything that would shoot. This was early indicated by a Pennsylvania Council of Safety report that in several units up to seven types of ammunition was required for the variety of arms in use, while at Valley Forge a perturbed Von Steuben complained that "muskets, carbines, fowling pieces, and rifles were found in the same company." American, British, Dutch, French, Hessian, Prussian and Scottish arms all found their way into patriot hands by various means, quantity generally prevailing over quality, though early in the Revolution British arms predominated; many of these were seized by patriot forces at the outset. To these were added a number of French arms, captured relics of the French and Indian War (1754-63).

The large caliber, single-shot, muzzle-loading, smoothbore flintlock musket was the mainstay of the 18th century weapons system, and in the colonies it was often used for hunting as well as military service. Its combat effectiveness was enhanced by the bayonet, and it was frequently loaded with ball or shot or a combination there-of.

The average musket had an effective range of 80 to 90 yards and, in the hands of seasoned troops using paper cartridges containing both powder and ball, could be loaded, primed and fired four to five times a minute, while the heavy lead ball inflicted a devastating wound. Excavations of various Revolutionary War encampments and battlegrounds have uncovered musket balls of both British and patriot origin bearing obvious mutilations — some with nails driven through them—doubtlessly calculated to inflict more horrible wounds.

Lack of ranging power and low accuracy had little bearing on the effectiveness of the musket, for military tactics of that era were based on a massed volume of fire delivered at close quarters. Troops were trained to point rather than aim, firing in unison on command, and speed in loading was the essential factor. Theoretically 500 men could in 20 to 25 seconds, deliver 1,000 rounds into enemy ranks at less than 100 yards and, on the heels of the final volley, came the spirited dash with the bayonet executing even more carnage. That mortal men faced such murderous fire and the cold steel that followed is difficult to comprehend in this Nuclear Age; that they did it so regularly is astonishing.

The gradually emerging American rifle performed a minor role in the Revolution despite popular concepts to the contrary. Until the conflict began the rifle was virtually unknown to colonists in the coastal settlements and few American victories can be exclusively attributed to patriot riflemen. The rifle was primarily the weapon of the sniper, forager, picket and skirmisher, having little success except on the frontier. There it was used advantageously in the sanguinary Indian-fighting campaigns by skilled woodsmen accustomed to that deceitful type of warfare.

Highly accurate up to 200 yards, as many British officers and artillerymen belatedly discovered, the American rifle nevertheless had two distinct disadvantages when used as orthodox tactics demanded. The tight-fitting, patched ball, requisite for range and accuracy, made it more difficult and slower to load than the musket — riflemen delivering about three shots a minute — and the absence of a bayonet dictated by its less rugged design and construction often proved disastrous. That was the case at Princeton, 3 January 1777, when Hugh Mercer's Virginia riflemen were shredded by the 17th Leicesters and 55th Borderers.

Pistols were used extensively in the Revolution. Basically cavalry and naval weapons, these single-shot, muzzle-loading arms were used at short range. Generally carried by officers, they were issued to enlisted men in some units of the British Army. Many were fitted with left-side hook, attached to the sideplate, to prevent slipping when thrust into the sash or belt. Horsemen generally carried a pair of pistols in specially designed cloth or leather holsters with a brass muzzle cap. The holsters were joined by a wide leather band and slung across the saddle pommel. Some were ornately decorated.

Martial pistols were rather cumbrous, having massive butts serving as bludgeons after the initial shot. John Paul Jones, spirited captain of the *Bonhomme Richard*, used his pistols in a somewhat unorthodox fashion during the epic struggle with the *Serapis* on 23 September 1779. Angered by a gunner's cowardice, Jones threw both of his pistols at him, one of them fracturing his skull!

In addition to the various types of muskets, rifles and pistols in patriot ranks there were carbines, commonly called musketoons, wall guns and special-purpose weapons such as signal pistols and grenade-launching muskets. Carbines served both cavalry and artillery, those of the former having a sidebar and ring for attachment to a shoulder belt. Most were 10 to 12 inches shorter than the average musket, many of them made by shortening damaged musket barrels. Contemporary authors often used the word "musketoon" as a synonym for carbine or to denote a martial blunderbuss. The latter was widely used on both land and at sea to repel boarders and to defend narrow passages such as bridges, fords, doorways, barricades and staircases. The *amusette*, known variously as the wall or swivel gun, also saw sea and land service. Considerably larger than the common musket, weighing up to 50 pounds and firing up to a 2-inch ball or shot, the amusette incorporated a swivel attached to the forestock which was mounted on the walls of forts and other embrasures. Despite its weight it was a portable weapon and often substi-

Washington's Chief of Artillery, Maj. Gen. Henry Knox (1750–1806), reached patriots surrounding Boston in January, 1776, with a vital cargo of heavy ordnance, gunflints and lead from Fort Ticonderoga, subsequently forcing the British to evacuate the port. Credit: Library of Congress.

tuted for light artillery, especially on the frontier where rough terrain often made it difficult to transport heavy ordnance. Some specimens were rifled.

Until the beginning of the War of Independence Massachusetts was the hub of colonial arms-making, producing more firearms than the remaining colonies combined. Rifle-making, however, centered in southeastern Pennsylvania and, because of the variety of arms made by Pennsylvania riflesmiths during the conflict, the Lancaster area became famous as the "Arsenal of America." When war began arms-making facilities were expanded and new installations built in most of the colonies; however, the southern colonies made fewer firearms due to shortages of skilled labor and the minimal development of natural resources, yet this was offset by the vast quantities of arms and munitions entering southern ports from abroad.

Unfortunately there is no complete record of the hundreds of gunsmiths actively engaged in fabricating arms for the various Committees of Safety, the Continental Congress or the infant states, and space limitations preclude listing all known makers in the text. The gunsmiths were an integral part of the socio-economic life of the colonies; most were respected community members and many were sedulous civic and military leaders. Whatever his ability and experience, the gunsmith was a skilled craftsman, either learning the trade through an exacting apprenticeship-often a maximum of seven years' duration-or under the tutelage of his father or a relative, for gunsmithing was not only a trade, but an art passed on from one generation to the next.

Gunsmiths of the Revolution

Many 18th century American gunsmiths could trace their ancestry to English arms-makers of the early colonial era. Such was Gen. Seth Pomeroy, gunsmith and French and Indian War veteran, who fought as a private at Bunker (Breed's) Hill. Pomeroy died, age 71, at Peekskill, N.Y., 19 February 1777, on his way to join Washington in New Jersey. He was the grandson of gunsmith Eltweed Pomeroy who in 1630 came to the Bay Colony from Devonshire, England, siring a family of arms-makers active until 1849.

It was a patriot gunsmith who first learned of British intentions to march on Lexington and Concord to confiscate public arms and munitions stored there. Known simply as "Jasper," his shop located in Hatter's Square, Boston, he warned

the Committee of Safety which promptly sent post riders William Dawes and Paul Revere to arouse the militia on the eve of that fateful day in American history.

Innumerable gunsmiths served as armorers in the militia and Continental Army; so many in fact that Congress requested they be exempt from military service because their technical skills were vital to the war effort. Richard Falley of West-field was the first official armorer for the Massachusetts Bay Colony and John Fitch, who in 1769 established a gunsmithery on King Street in Trenton, New Jersey Colony, served as an armorer and lieutenant in the Continental Army. Fitch made muskets for the N.J. Militia until burned out by the Redcoats in 1776. One of history's tragic figures, he is now best remembered for his pioneering efforts in the application of steam power to sailing vessels.

One of the most prominent Massachusetts gunsmiths active during the Revolution was Hugh Orr. Born in Scotland, 2 January 1715, Orr immigrated in 1737, settling at Easton, Pa. He moved, a year later, to Bridgwater, Mass. An experienced gun-and — locksmith, he established a scythe and axe works featuring the first trip-hammer forge in New England. In 1748 he made 500 muskets for the Massachusetts Militia, most of these taken from Castle William by the British when on 17 March 1776 they evacuated Boston. Shortly after the war began Orr erected a foundry, casting both brass and iron cannon while also making large quantities of ammunition. He died at Bridgewater, 6 Dec. 1798.

Another active and eminent maker of firearms for the patriot cause was William Henry. Born in West Caln Township, Pennsylvania Colony, 19 May 1729, Henry was apprenticed to Lancaster rifle-maker Mathew Roeser and from 1755 to 1760 was chief armorer to the Pennsylvania forces in the French and Indian

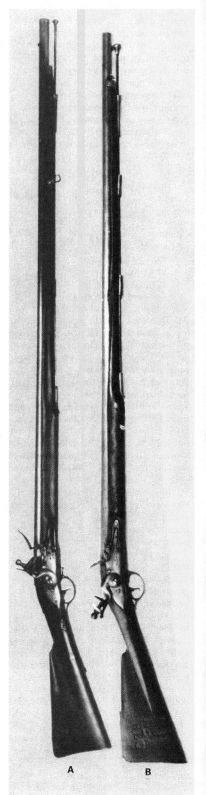

(A) John Churchill, Duke of Marlborough, introduced the 1st pattern "Brown Bess" infantry musket ca. 1714. This specimen, made by Jordan of London in 1747, probably served in the French and Indian War. "US" mark is visible on the lockplate. Credit: West Point Museum.

(B) Committee of Safety musket made by Henry Watkeys, New Windsor, Ulster Co., N.Y. (fl. 1770–80). Watkeys and Robert Boyd contracted for 1,000 muskets at £ 3–15s each for the N.Y. Colony on 13 June 1775. Stock is branded "N-Y REG." Credit: Smithsonian Institution.

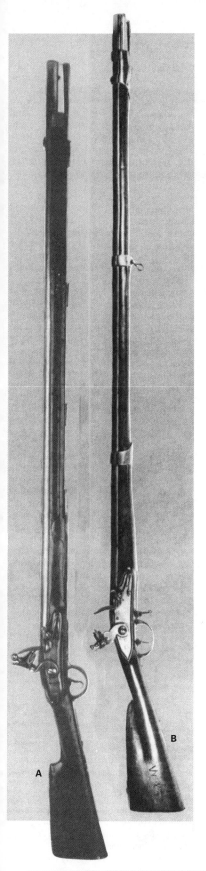

War. During the war he was a member of Congress and the Pennsylvania Council of Safety, and served as assistant commissary general for the Lancaster district. There he supervised the manufacture of clothing and ordnance for the Continental Army. His reputation as a quality riflesmith was well known, and shortly after the war began he expanded his Lancaster rifle works to include repair work and musket and bayonet manufacture. After his death on 15 December 1786 his two sons continued in the trade, and the last family member active in gunsmithing, Granville Henry, died in 1912.

As gunmaking was primarily an individual household enterprise during this era, most shops were rather small; some no more than an addition to the man's home. There were a few larger shops and these were, from a contemporary description, "expected to contain 3 or 4 barrel forges, a grinding mill for grinding and polishing barrels, a lock shop with 7 forges, and benches for 40 filers, 10 benches for gunstock makers, a brass foundry for mountings with several finishing benches, a couple of forges for bayonets and ramrods, together with a mill for grinding and polishing them, another forge for fittings, and an assembly shop."

Committee of Safety Arms

In the tense months immediately preceding the conflict few colonies acted to secure adequate supplies of arms and munitions or to ensure future procurement; however, a few musket contracts were awarded by various colonies to independent makers. As far as it can be determined, the numerous Committees of Safety (COS) did not authorize any contracts prior to the events at Lexington and Concord, while by the end of 1778 the functions of the committees had been absorbed by other agencies within the newly formed state governments.

Such arms as were produced under COS direction can be presumed to have been made between late April, 1775, and

(A) Many foreign arms served patriot forces. This Prussian musket is one of two specimens believed to have been captured at Bennington, Vt., from the Brunswick Grenadiers. Credit: West Point Museum.

(B) One of the most popular imported arms serving Continental forces was the MI1768 French infantry musket. This specimen, made at Charleville, has a "US" property stamp on the lock. The initials "WK" may have been those of its user. Credit: West Point Museum.

the latter part of 1778. Firearms made prior to or after those rather ambiguous and arbitrary dates are not considered authentic COS specimens by discerning arms students and collectors. Although most COS arms were muskets it is possible that pistols were also contracted, but, no concrete data have been found to substantiate this, nor have any handguns appeared which can be definitely identified as a COS product.

Muskets produced for the various COS generally followed the pattern of the then standard British infantry musket, that is, the 2nd model "Brown Bess" although extant evidence indicates that distinctly different patterns may have been used by a few colonies. John Churchill, Duke of Marlborough, is thought to have introduced the original "Brown Bess" design between 1710-20, and it saw several minor modifications. Most COS muskets produced in early 1775 closely followed the specifications outlined by the Continental Congress in November of that year:

"*Resolved* That it be recommended to the several Assemblies or conventions of the colonies respectively, to set and keep their gunsmiths at work, to manufacture good fire locks, with bayonets; each firelock to be made with a good bridle lock, ¾ of an inch bore, and of good substance at the breech, the barrel to be 3 feet 8 inches in length, the bayonet to be 18 inches in the blade, with a steel ramrod, the upper loop thereof to be trumpet mouthed: that the price to be given be fixed by the Assembly or convention, or committee of safety of each colony...."

As all firearms during this period were hand-forged and subject to the idiosyncracies of the gunsmith, and because the 'smith frequently had difficulty obtaining adequate materials, innumerable variations can be detected in the character of domestic arms produced throughout the conflict. Muskets made for the Massachusetts COS generally conformed to Congressional standards although barrels were an inch longer. Connecticut musket barrels were two inches longer and the bayonet blade was shortened to 14 inches. Barrels of Maryland COS muskets were two inches shorter, while the bayonet had a 17-inch blade.

Of whatever origin, COS muskets generally had 42-to 46-inch barrels of 75 caliber pin-fastened to walnut and, occasionally, maple stocks. Furniture was usually iron, but brass was also used. Locks were predominantly pre-war English or of European make although some were

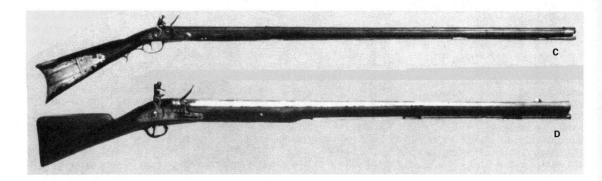

(C) A prime example of the American rifle-smith's craft is this "Kentucky" rifle made by Henry Albright of Lancaster, Pa., ca. 1770. Contrary to popular concepts, rifles performed a minor role in the Revolution. Credit: The Metropolitan Museum of Art. Gift of Winfrid Wood, 1956.

(D) This full-stocked British Tower-marked wall gun with belled muzzle weighed nearly 25 lbs., with an overall length of 72¾ . Bore was nearly an inch in diameter. Credit: Smithsonian Institute.

of domestic origin. Double-bridle types were ordinarily specified, but, single-bridle types were substituted when necessity dictated. Sling swivels were common on army muskets although conspicuously absent on naval models which were usually kept in racks aboard ship, and the barrels of navy models were up to 10 inches shorter; this made it easier for marines and sailors to load when in the rigging or atop masts. The musket in the famed Minuteman statue at Lexington, Mass., is a typical navy specimen.

Massachusetts COS arms-makers were paid £ 3 each for muskets complete with iron ramrod and bayonet, that is, a stand, shortly after the war began. During this early period the average cost of a stand was $12.50, although inflation escalated prices as the war continued. A letter from a group of Lancaster riflesmiths to the Pennsylvania COS on 16 March 1776 commented that "… We are apprehensive of meeting with many obstacles in making … a new contract. Our workmen universally complain that the sums already fixed are inadequate to their Labours; that the Sacrifice they made in *quitting their rifle business** is greater than they can well bear without some equivalent. … they cannot in Justice to their families, provide the muskets and bayonets at a less

sum than £ 4 10s or £ 4 15s. We are very sensible that their observations … are not without foundation …." Fiscal as well as labor and material procurement problems would plague patriot gunsmiths throughout the war.

Marks and Stamps

The often repeated assertion that patriot gunsmiths refused to mark their products, fearing British reprisals, is not substantiated by fact. Most COS muskets were signed by the maker and displayed in various forms the mark of the colony as well. Connecticut required that muskets be "… marked with the name or initial letters of the maker's name." The letters "CR" and the Rhode Island coat of arms appears on all arms purchased by that colony, while Massachusetts ordered that its muskets be stamped with the letters "MB" (Massachusetts Bay). Other markings are also found on arms used or produced by the various colonies, including captured and imported specimens.

In Pennsylvania alone COS contracts accounted for 4,500 muskets, most of these produced by gunsmiths in 11 countries between October, 1775, and April, 1776. While COS arms were generally contracted from independent gunsmiths, many colonies established and operated their own arms-making facilities. Peter DeHaven supervised musket production at the State Gun Factory in Philadelphia and, to prevent capture the works was moved to French Creek near Valley Forge in December, 1776; thence for the same reason to Hummels Town in September, 1777. The factory was dismantled and sold in 1778. The Pennsylvania State Gun Repair Shop was founded at Allentown on 26 September 1777 with James Walsh as superintendent. On 11 May 1778 Walsh reported that 800 complete muskets were available and 150 more were in the assembly stage.

In neighboring Maryland the State

Gun Lock Factory was established at Frederick in 1777 with Charles Beatty, James Johnson and John Hanson named commissioners. Samuel Boone, nephew or brother to the famed Daniel, managed the works and on 17 June was directed to deliver 110 gunlocks to musket-maker Nicholas White. This installation was sold in November,1778.

The Hunter Iron Works, operated by James Hunter on the Rappahannock near Falmouth, Va., was purchased by the colony in June, 1775. Known thereafter as Rappahannock Forge, the works produced muskets, pistols and wall guns for the Virginia Militia and may have made pistols for sale elsewhere as indicated by one specimen marked "CP" (Commonwealth of Pennsylvania) on the lockplate. Operations ceased in 1781. Located at nearby Fredericksburg was the Virginia State Gun Factory established by an act of the assembly on 4 July 1775 and supervised by Col. Fielding Lewis and Maj. Charles Dick. Producing muskets and bayonets, the works closed late in 1783.

Ordnance facilities were also established by the North Carolina Colony early in the war. The Charlottesville Rifle Works produced rifles, muskets and pistols for the militia in 1775-76, while at Halifax the North Carolina Gun Works, founded in 1776, made muskets under the supervision of James Ransom who served as Master Armorer there until 1778.

The Continental Congress also evinced interest in arms manufacture, and on 23 February 1776 appointed a committee to "contract for the making of muskets and bayonets for the use of the United Colonies …." On 8 March a $10,000 appropriation was authorized, while on 23 May the committee directed the manager of the "continental factory of firearms at Lancaster, and the manager of the gunlock factory at Trenton to deliver … all muskets and gunlocks … for the more expeditious arming of the continental battalion …."

---

*Italics supplied. MLB.

Muskets and rifles and perhaps pistols were contracted under Congressional auspices, but because of a large inventory of serviceable weapons few Continental arms contracts were made after 1778. Also noteworthy is that many state installations halted production in that year. However, thousands of arms were refurbished at the Congressional arms repair shop at Carlisle, Pa., and at Springfield, Mass.; the latter facility was established at Gen. Washington's behest in 1777 as an arsenal and powder magazine, but was subsequently expanded to include repair work and the manufacture of cartridges and gun carriages.

Musket Patterns

Continental muskets were apparently not patterned after the 2nd model "Brown Bess," for Congress furnished contractors with pattern pieces, which would otherwise have been unnecessary since most gunsmiths were familiar with the British musket. What patterns were used is not indicated by any extant documentation. The arms produced for the Continental Army were stamped with the maker's name or initials only, but, it was determined that a more distinctive mark of public ownership was necessary because such arms were frequently stolen and later sold. After repeated and generally unsuccessful attempts to halt this nefarious trade Congress, adopting the recommendation of the Commissary General of Military Stores, declared on 24 February 1777 that:

"… the several States … take the most effectual steps for collecting from the inhabitants, not in actual service, all Continental arms, and give notice of the number … to General Washington.

"That all arms or accoutrements, belonging to the United States shall be stamped or marked with the words 'UNITED STATES:' all arms already made to be stamped upon such parts as will receive the impression, and those hereafter to be manufactured, to be stamped with the said words on every part comprising the stand; and all arms and accoutrements so stamped or marked shall be taken wherever found for the use of the States, excepting they shall be in the hands of those actually in Continental service.

"That it be recommended to the legislatures of the several States to enact proper laws for the punishment of those who shall unlawfully take, secrete, refuse or neglect to deliver, any Continental arms or accoutrements which they may have in their possession."

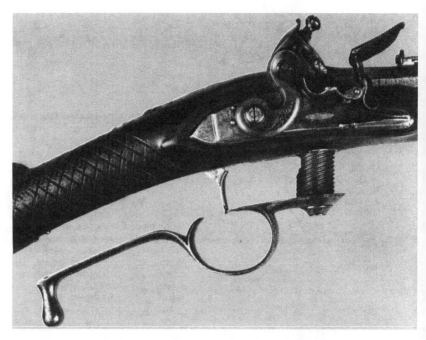

To this was added a suggestion by Brig. Gen. Alexander McDou-gall, writing to Gen. Washington on 12 April 1777, that all barrels and locks be stamped and all stocks branded with the words "UNITED STATES." That this was found acceptable can be seen on many Revolutionary War arms with "U. STATES" burned into the stock. Noteworthy is that such markings were also abbreviated to "US," while state and COS arms were also branded on the stock with appropriate letters.

As most COS muskets were made early in the war, few survived the vicissitudes of battle, while time and cannibalization contributed to the scarcity of the remainder. Continental and imported arms fared little better. When hostilities terminated, Congress, in a rare spate of gratitude, voted the patriots their arms as a farewell gift. While some were doubtlessly kept by those weary, intrepid veterans, many were sold to defray travel expenses home, for the magnanimous Congress that presented them their weapons had frequently neglected to feed, clothe, shelter and pay them during the war.

Colonial Rifles

The American rifle, termed variously the "Kentucky" or "Pennsylvania-Kentucky" rifle, slowly evolved from the shorter, more massive Jager rifle brought to the colonies around 1710 by German and Swiss immigrants setting in the Lancaster region of southeastern Pennsyl-

Rotating the trigger guard a full-turn opened the breech of the Ferguson rifle. The ball, followed by the powder, was inserted into the opening atop the breech. The rotating breech plug provided an excellent gas seal and also sheared the excess powder. Credit: West Point Museum.

vania. Just prior to the Revolution the American rifle entered its second phase of development and at this point had nearly attained the pinnacle of perfection.

Congress, by the Act of June 14, 1775, authorized 10 companies of riflemen, two each from Maryland and Virginia and 6 from Pennsylvania, and while the war stimulated the demand for rifles and production increased it was often at the expense of quality. Although many riflesmiths were engaged in producing muskets, others continued to make rifles either on a contract or individual basis. There were about three to five hundred riflesmiths in the colonies when hostilities commenced, the majority in Pennsylvania; others were located in Maryland, Virginia and the Carolinas. A few of the most prominent artisans were Henry Albright, Peter Angstadt, John Beck and Peter Humberger, Sr., all from Lancaster, Pa.; William Graeff of Reading, Pa., and Abraham Morrow of Philadelphia, who had a U.S. contract for flintlock rifles.

While there is no such thing as a typical American rifle, for no two were made

This rifled wall gun was made at Rappa-hannock Forge in 1776 and is one of four surviving the ravages of time. It fired a 6-oz. ball of about 1.25 caliber and had an effective range of 1,000 yards. Note sliding wood cover on patchbox. Credit: West Point Museum.

exactly alike, the rifles of this period illustrated similar characteristics, and were atypical of those produced after the war. The average specimen displayed a generally unmarked, hand-forged lock somewhat inferior to English or French flintlock mechanisms, and a rather straight, heavy stock with a slight drop. A patchbox was located on the right side of the stock, usually fitted with a hinged brass cover and sideplates although sliding wood covers are noted. Barrels were fully octagonal, about 42 to 48 inches long and of 45 to 50 caliber. The barrel was held to the stock by round pins and a screw passing through the barrel tang. Both front and rear sights were laterally adjustable, and an iron ramrod was provided; most furniture was brass. Innumerable variations in design and ornamentation are the rule.

Despite continuous but at times sporadic domestic production, the bulk of the shoulder and hand arms in patriot ranks during the latter part of the war were of European origin. Of these the regulation French infantry musket was commonly encountered, and it has been estimated that at least 102,-000 French long arms were imported between 1776 and 1781. These ranged in character from the obsolete M1718 to the M1768, although the M1763 infantry musket predominated.

The Blockade Guns

Benjamin Franklin, serving as one of the American commissioners to France, reported in April, 1777, that "… We have purchased 80,-000 fusils, a number of pistols, etc., of which the enclosed is on account, for 220,000 livres. They were King's arms and second-hand, but so many … are unused and exceptionally good that we esteem it a great bargain if only half of them should arrive."

Franklin's enthusiasm was matched by his proverbial thrift, for the purchase of French muskets at an average of $5.00 each was a boon when compared to domestic prices. In June, 1777, Continental forces received an unexpected gift of 250 M1763 muskets from the Marquis de Lafayette who joined the patriot cause.

Numerous modifications marked the evolution of the French infantry musket. The popular M1768 later served as the

pattern for the first (M1795) U.S. martial musket.* It was considered superior to the "Brown Bess" due to its slender profile, excellent balance, reinforced cock, banded barrel and greater range. Over-all length was 59⅞ inches with a round, 69 caliber barrel of 44¾ inches. The walnut stock was fixed to the barrel by three spring-held iron bands; the upper band fitted with a brass blade front sight and the center band with a sling swivel. Excepting the sight, all metal parts were iron, finished bright. The flashpan was detachable from the lockplate and the lower sling swivel was attached to the trigger guard.

Like other French arms the M1768 carried such armory markings as *CHARLEVILLE* in script, surmounted by a *D* topped with a star; *MANUF ROYAL de ST. ETIENNE* with a crowned *HB*; and *MAUBEUGE* with a crowned *H* above, all appearing on the lock. Variations of the *US* stamp is often seen on the lock, barrel tang or barrel, while stocks were frequently branded *U. STATES*. In many instances these *US* markings were crudely executed, indicating that the responsible facilities had not received official dies.

Available records show that French arms shipments began in early February, 1776, when Connecticut received 3,000 assorted muskets, and continued until August, 1781, when the *Resolute* delivered 16,800 long arms to Boston. Through the efforts of Silas Deane, another American agent in France, and the support of Pierre Garon de Beaumarchais, a dummy corporation known as Roderique Hortalez et Cie was organized in May, 1776, to channel arms, munitions and other war materials to the beleaguered patriots. Hortalez was active until late 1778 when France, declaring war on England, obviated the necessity for subterfuge.

Ten ships were dispatched by Hortalez either directly to the colonies or the French West Indies ports, where vital cargoes were transferred to American vessels, mainly privateers. Only one of the 10 ships was intercepted by the British. First to arrive was the brig *Mercury* out of Nantes. In April, 1777, she made Portsmouth, N.H., unloading 364 cases of arms (11,987 muskets), 1,000 barrels of gunpowder, 11,000 gunflints, large supplies of shoes and clothing, and reported that no less than 34 other ships were clearing French ports for the colonies. Another vessel, the *Flamand*, docked at

*Many arms historians have confused the M1768 with the M1763; the latter was equipped with a long ramrod spring between the two upper bands, a larger lock and different bands. See The American Rifleman, Vol. 115, No. 7., p. 19.

Portsmouth on 1 December with 3,000 muskets and 1,100 carbines.

Pliarne, Penet et Cie, also a French subsidized firm, sent arms and munitions to the colonies in concert with a subsidiary, James Gruel & Co. Muskets purchased from these firms were of poor quality, made at Liege. The industrious Dutch were also active in the brisk, profitable arms trade, shipping large numbers of quality muskets either directly to Massachusetts or via St. Eustatius in the Dutch West Indies. These arms are believed to have been contracted from reliable makers by Franklin, representing Massachusetts, and extant examples are marked THONE, AMSTERDAM on the lock-plate and bear Amsterdam proof marks on the barrels of 65 caliber secured by three brass bands; the upper band distinguished by its 8-inch length.

Captured Hessian muskets were also employed by patriot forces, their characteristics varying considerably because of the different types supplied to the Hessian auxiliaries supporting the British Army. Extant specimens have brass furniture whether barrels are banded or pin-fastened, and all have elliptical brass front sights either attached to the barrel or upper band. The round barrel is 41 to 44 inches long and of 75 to 80 caliber. Lockplates are blunt at the rear and the frizzen is identified by its square top. Stocks are heavy with a massive butt and high comb. Raised carvings around the mountings are characteristic. Most were inferior to the English, Dutch, French and American muskets.

Hessian rifles also appeared in the colonies. Limited in number, they were short, heavy arms with octagonal barrels of 28 to 30 inches. Caliber ranged from 60 to 70. The stock was rather cumbrous

with a massive butt incorporating a patch box with sliding wood cover and the forearm extended to the muzzle. Furniture was usually brass. Hessian rifles compared favorably to American in range and accuracy.

English rifles also served in the Revolution. These unique arms, invented by Maj. Patrick Ferguson, were the first flintlock breechloaders adopted for military use by any nation. In all probability less than 300 saw service, mostly by Loyalist riflemen recruited by the inventor. Aware of prior developments in breechloading systems, Ferguson produced a more practical version scaled to the dimensions of the standard Brown Bess. Both officer's and enlisted men's models were made. The rifle weighed 7.5 pounds and the enlisted model was of 58 caliber. Barrels ranged from 34 to 36 inches long, rifled with 8 grooves. It could be loaded and fired five to six times a minute and was accurate up to 300 yards. Traditional military resistance to new concepts dimmed Ferguson's hopes for the future of his invention, and his death at King's Mountain sealed the fate of his rifle. If the British had adopted the accurate, fast-firing rifle on a large scale the American colonies might never have won their independence. (See the Gun Digest, 1959, p. 53.)

The Patriots' Pistols

As a rule American martial pistols followed the British pattern. Those produced at Rappahannock Forge bore an exact resemblance to the new model British martial pistols appearing in 1760. They were marked RAPa FORGE on the lock-plate and had heavier brass furniture than most domestically made pistols. Both old and new model British martial pistols served in patriot ranks, many of them captured

at the outset of hostilities.

Adopted about 1714, old model British martial pistols were relics of King George's War (1744-48) and the French and Indian conflict. They had round, 12-inch barrels of about 60 caliber, pin-fastened to the walnut stock, with additional support provided by the breech-plug tang screw. The convex iron sideplate, lockplate and brass furniture resembled that of the 1st model Brown Bess musket. The bulbous butt was capped with brass as was the wooden ramrod. Most were engraved with the letters GR (George Rex), in script, surmounted by a crown in the center of the lock-plate, while behind the cock the word TOWER appeared in a vertical arc. The broad arrow ordnance stamp, denoting Crown ownership, also appeared on the lock, while barrels displayed either London or Birmingham proofmarks. Some specimens have only the maker's name and date on the lockplate.

The new model British martial pistol was somewhat shorter and stronger, having a 9-inch round barrel of 69 caliber. Some of the brass furniture was eliminated or redesigned. The sideplate and lockplate were flat with stamped rather than engraved markings. Navy models incorporated a belt hook and retained the longer barrel of the old model. Both types were profusely copied by patriot gunsmiths.

The various Highland regiments serving the British in America were the only units in which all enlisted men were issued pistols. These unusual arms were of all-metal construction. Officer's models were primarily holster pistols, made exclusively of iron and highly ornamented, often heavily chiseled and inlaid with precious metals, while enlisted men's models were of iron with a brass stock. Ramrods of both were iron, and the soldier's type was equipped with a belt hook. Those made before 1758 were marked HR (Highland Regiment), those thereafter RHR (Royal Highland Regiment). Most were made in Scotland prior to 1762 when Birmingham and London emerged as production centers.

Highland pistols had no trigger guards or sights and all displayed button-type triggers. The lock internally resembled the so-called English dog lock, popular a century earlier, as there was no half-cock position and the sear acted laterally, protruding through the lockplate. Barrels were round of between seven and eight inches while caliber fluctuated from 55 to 57. Both types illustrated kidney-shaped, heart-shaped or fish-tailed butts, with officer's models often terminating in a ramshorn design. A removable knob, located in the center of the butt, served as a combination oiler/vent pick.

John Waters of London and Birmingham produced many plain Highland pistols, some with London proofmarks on the barrel. Another maker, Isaac Bissel of Birmingham, made officer's models characterized by a ramshorn butt with an oval petal grip design and channeled cock pin, oiler/vent pick and button trigger. Highland pistols display a wide range of ornamentation, and variations in design are common.

France, largest European supplier of muskets to patriot forces, also provided a large number of pistols. However, no accurate or complete record exists which can verify the precise number or type. Most were martial specimens. Both army and navy patterns of 1763 were popular, featuring round, 9-inch barrels of 67 caliber, held in a walnut stock by a tang screw and long, double band at the muzzle held by a retaining spring. The lock resembled that of the M1763 infantry musket with a reinforced cock and iron pan. The furniture of the army model was iron and that of the navy model brass. Each had a button-head iron ramrod, and most were produced at St. Etienne.

In 1776 France adopted a new pattern martial pistol which differed radically from the M1763. The M1776 first appeared in 1777 in both army and navy models. Each was of 69 caliber with a 7.5-inch barrel, tapering toward the muzzle. Navy models were provided with a belt hook. Frames were brass and the brass pan was integral. The cock, frizzen and ramrod were iron. There was no forestock or sights. The butt curved sharply, supported by an iron backstrap and terminated with a brass cap. Arsenal marks appeared in an arc under the cock and the stock was stamped with an inspector's mark and date. The M1777 French martial pistol served as a pattern for the first U.S. martial pistol (M1799).

The few German pistols used in the Revolution varied considerably in character and were generally inferior to other imported and domestic pistols. They commonly had brass furniture and pin-fastened, round iron barrels of 75 caliber.

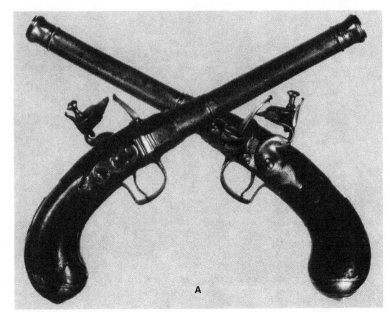

A

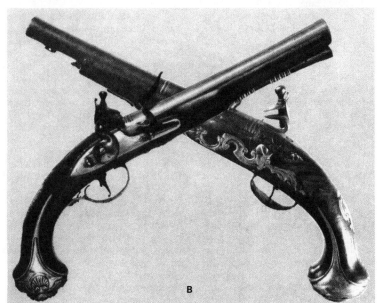

B

On some models the iron ramrod was attached to the barrel by a swivel. These pistols, normally fitted with a brass front sight, had a reinforced, convex cock and were bought by American agents in the various German states and Holland.

An undetermined number of Prussian pistols, mostly old and unserviceable, found their way into patriot hands. Many were bought by representatives of the Virginia Colony. Barrels were round, 11¾ inches long and pin-fastened to

(A) These somewhat battered pistols, made at Rappahannock Forge, were patterned after the British martial pistol of 1760. Rappahannock Forge pistols were generally of better quality than most domestic handguns. Credit: Smithsonian Institution.

(B) Early type Queen Anne "turn-off" screw-barreled pistols by Cornforth of London (Il. 1760-90). Cannon-shaped barrels distinguish these popular pistols and many appeared in the colonies, serving as the pattern for the "Kentucky" pistols emerging ca. 1740. Credit: Smithsonian Institution.

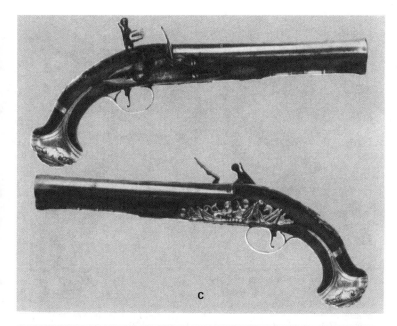

C

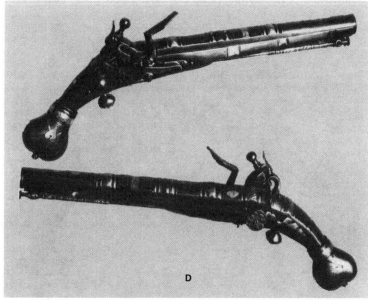

D

Of better quality than German or Prussian pistols were those provided by the Dutch. Most are stamped *THONE, AMSTERDAM* in two lines on the lockplate. Both army and navy models were bought, the latter displaying a belt hook. Each had a 10-inch, round, pin-fastened barrel of about 69 caliber, iron ramrod, brass blade front sight and notch-type rear sight. The cock was convex and the pan brass. There was no sideplate. The stock had a bulbous butt minus a cap, while the fore-end was capped with brass.

In addition to the various types of martial pistols used in the Revolution there were numerous non-martial types of domestic and foreign origin. Most were of British make, and highly popular was the Queen Anne screw-barrel or so-called "turn-off" pistol. Early models (c. 1740) had the cock situated on the right side of the gun, but after about 1760 the cock was centrally hung. Over-all length was about 11.5 inches, and the round, cannon-shaped barrel was of about 60 caliber. Loading was accomplished by unscrewing the barrel, pouring the powder into the chamber, placing the ball atop the charge and replacing the barrel. Those made for cavalry use often had a short chain attached to the barrel and breech to prevent loss when loading. Range and accuracy were superior to the average pistol as there was virtually no gas leakage around the ball, and in rifled specimens accuracy was extremely good. Many of these and other personal pistols were exquisitely ornamented.

Colonial riflesmiths produced pistols similar in character to the Queen Anne type while retaining features common to the American rifle. These so-called "Kentucky" pistols, made prior to and during the Revolution, differed in many respects from later specimens. The earliest known type dates from about 1740. Most reflected the Queen Anne barrel style although all were loaded at the muzzle and the majority were smoothbores. Caliber varied from 36 to 50, and barrel length ranged between 7.5 and 9.5 inches. Both brass and iron pin-fastened barrels are encountered, while brass and coin silver were generally used for furniture and or-namentation. Stocks normally extended the full length of the barrel although some were half-stocked and most had birds-head grips. Figured maple was favored for stocking, but cherry and walnut were also used, while ramrods were often made of hickory tipped with brass or silver. Specimens are found with and without sights; the sights patterned after the rifle type.

(C) All-metal pistols such as this ornate pair were carried by officers of the Scots Highland regiments. Knob in center of heart-shaped butt is attached to combination vent pick/oiler. Credit: The Metropolitan Museum of Art. Gift of Mrs. Elizabeth Cameron Blanchard, in memory of her husband, J. Osgood Blanchard, 1916.

(D) George Washington's silver-mounted, brass-barreled pistols were made by Hawkins of London (fl. 1750-75). Over-all length 13½", 8" barrels of 66 caliber. Washington is said to have owned at least 50 firearms. Credit: West Point Museum.

the stock. All had brass front sights, and some displayed a rudimentary rear sight consisting of a shallow notch filed into the breech plug tang. Furniture was of brass, and the stock was characterized by a heavy buttcap and fore-end cap. The lock and sideplate were flat, and there was no ramrod. Proofmarks were found on the trigger guard and barrel while the royal cipher appeared on the buttcap. Some are marked *POTZDAMMAGAZIN* (Potsdam Arsenal) on the lockplate.

Imported locks were generally used, and markings varied considerably; some specimens have different names or initials on the lock and barrel, for even during this early period specialization in arms-making was apparent. The craftsmanship displayed on these often elegant pistols was decidedly superior to that found on most domestic specimens of the period.

The Gunpowder Shortage

With the commencement of hostilities gunpowder was everywhere lacking. Restrictions by Parliament, difficulty in procuring the ingredients in sufficient quantity, and the superiority of English gunpowder all contributed to the decline of domestic powder making. While charcoal was abundant, sulfur was exclusively imported and saltpeter production disturbingly irregular. The powder seized at Fort William and Mary in 1774 had served the patriots at Bunker Hill, but one reason for the American withdrawal was a dire powder shortage.

In July, 1775, patriot forces ringed Boston, outnumbering the Redcoats two to one, yet Washington had neither enough artillery nor powder to oust the British. Young Henry Knox, affable and brilliant Boston bookseller who became Washington's chief of artillery, proposed a wild scheme whereby captured ordnance at Fort Ticonderoga could be transported to Dorchester Heights above Boston. Despite protests Knox left in November and found at the fort 78 serviceable pieces of ordnance and 30,000 gunflints in addition to 2,300 pounds of lead. By boat, sledge, wagon, determination and pure guts he shepherded the vital cargo across frozen rivers, snow-capped mountains and frigid wilderness in the dead of winter to Boston, 300 miles distant. Arriving with 55 assorted cannon, mortars and howitzers in January, 1776, he was delighted to discover that the capture of the British supply ship *Nancy* had provided the powder for his guns.

Shortly after the war began most of the colonies took steps to rectify the powder shortage, and mills sprang up on various locations. Oswell Eve ran a powder mill at Frankford, Pa., and it was probably there that Paul Revere studied the manufacture of powder, erecting a mill near Boston after the war. Two other mills were situated near Eve's works and another was located in Dauphin County.

Numerous complaints concerning the quality of Eve's gunpowder reached Congress and, on 7 June 1776, a committee was appointed to investigate. On 28 August the committee suggested that inspectors be assigned to the various mills with orders to mark every acceptable keg of powder with the letters *USA*. This was the first use of the marking subsequently applied to all U.S. arms and other ordnance material.

In 1780 a powder mill was constructed near Washington's winter headquarters at Morristown, N.J., concealed in the deep woods. Saltpeter for this facility was provided by the local populace, probably from natural deposits although possibly from artificial niter beds produced by soaking the earth with human urine rich in nitrate.

The estimable victory of patriot riflemen at King's Mountain on 7 October 1780 was substantially assisted by 500 pounds of gunpowder donated to the cause by Mary Patton who, in the absence of her husband serving in the army, operated a powder mill in Tennessee. It was an expensive gift, for at that time powder was selling for a dollar per pound.

The scarcity of gunpowder on the

French Cavalry M1777 pistol differed radically from most handguns of the Revolutionary War era. The 7.5" round barrel was cased in a brass housing supporting the lock and iron ramrod. The pistol served as a pattern for the first U.S. martial pistol, the North & Cheney of 1799. Credit: West Point Museum

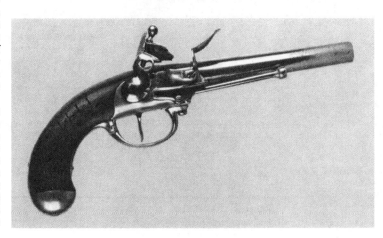

frontier was even more crucial, for it was there that a thin, buckskin-clad line valiantly withstood the savagery of Indian attacks promoted by the British, who supplied their numerous Indian allies with arms and munitions throughout the war. A frontier settlement obliged to defend itself expended more powder in an hour than would have been used in a year of hunting. Despite the powder shortage the generally outnumbered frontiersmen miraculously prevented British-led Indian marauders from penetrating the populous coastal settlements and harassing Washington's weary Continentals.

Patriot frontiersmen went to great lengths and took considerable risks in procuring adequate supplies of gunpowder. In 1775 George Rogers Clark persuaded Virginia authorities to part with 500 pounds of powder for the defense of Kentucky. Second Lieutenant William Linn and 15 volunteers left Fort Pitt in July, 1776, for New Orleans, where the officially neutral Spanish covertly sold powder to American agents. Linn procured 98 barrels—nearly five tons—and began the hazardous 2,000-mile return trip, eluding both British and Indians to arrive at Wheeling on 2 May 1777, just in time to meet the summer threat of Indian attacks. His party had been gone 11 months. Clark also took advantage of Spanish co-operation, and gunpowder from New Orleans bolstered his chance for victory when, in the summer of 1778, he invaded Illinois, capturing Kaskaskia and Vincennes.

Although domestic powder-making increased as the war progressed, American powder was never made in sufficient quantity to supply patriot forces, nor was it comparable to English, French or Spanish powder in quality. Due primarily to the advancements in chemistry achieved by Antoine Laurent Lavoisier (1743-94), French gunpowder was superior to any produced in the world at the time of the Revolution, and it has been estimated that French gunpowder fulfilled 80 percent of patriot requirements. Much of it reached the colonies through the efforts of Hortalez et Cie.

The road from

Lexington to Yorktown was a long and bloody road. The American War of Independence was won not only by the inordinate courage displayed on the grim field of combat, but by the simple determination and singular purpose of a united people working toward a common goal. The contribution to victory generated by the many who left bloody footprints in the snow and survived by gnawing the bark from frozen trees was no more vital than what was given by the many who toiled long hours in the blazing heat of the barrel forge or sat hunched over a filer's bench.

Bibliography

Primary Sources

Carey, A. Merwyn. *American Firearms Makers*. New York: Thomas Y. Crowell, 1953.

Chapel, Charles Edward. *Guns of the Old West*. New York: Coward-McCann, Inc., 1961.

Gardner, Robert. *Small Arms Makers*. New York: Bonanza Books, 1962.

Gluckman, Arcadi. *United States Martial Pistols and Revolvers*. Harrisburg, Pa.: The Stackpole Co., 1956. __.*United States Muskets, Rifles and Carbines*. Buffalo, N.Y.: Otto Ulbrich Co., Inc., 1948.

Kauffman, Henry J. *Early American Gunsmiths*. New York: Bramhall House, 1952.

__*The Pennsylvania-Kentucky Rifle*. Harrisburg, Pa.: The Stackpole Co., 1960.

Peterson, Harold L. *Arms and Armor in Colonial America*. New York: Bramhall House, 1956.

Russell, Carl P. *Guns on the Early Frontiers*. New York: Bonanza Books, 1957.

Secondary Sources

Lancaster, Bruce and Plumb, J. H. *The American Heritage Book of the Revolution*. New York: The American Heritage Publishing Co., 1958.

Martin, Joseph Plumb (Scheer, George F., ed.). *Private Yankee Doodle*. New York: Little, Brown & Co., 1962.

Miller, John C. *The First Frontier: Life in Colonial America*. New York: Dell Publ. Co., Inc., 1966.

Perry, Clay. "Big Guns for Washington," *The American Heritage Reader*. New York: Dell Publ. Co., Inc., 1956.

Peterson, Harold L., ed. *Encyclopedia of Firearms*. New York: E. P. Dutton & Co., 1964.

Scheer, George F. and Rankin, Hugh. *Rebels and Redcoats*. New York: World Publ. Co., 1957.

Van Every, Dale. *A Company of Heroes*. New York: Wm. Morrow & Co., 1962.

Woodward, Wm. *The Way Our People Lived*. New York: Liveright Publ. Corp, 1944.

Periodicals

The American Rifleman, The National Rifle Assn., of America, Washington, D.C.

Gun Digest, Digest Books, Inc., Northfield, Ill.

Guns & Ammo, Petersen Publ. Co., Los Angeles, Cal.

Patriot victory at Trenton, 26 December 1776, succeeded in reviving American morale and prompted French, Spanish and Dutch assistance in procuring additional troops and arms. Credit: Department of the Army.

Breechloaders in the Revolution

Ferguson's rifle – and his rifling – were years ahead of their day.
▌ Jac Weller

Patrick Ferguson, a wax bust now owned by Keith Neal, noted arms expert, and the author of *Spanish Guns*.

P AT FERGUSON'S rifle was capable of delivering aimed fire at 220 yards. The usual smoothbore musket of that era couldn't hit a man-sized target at 50 yards more than once in three shots. The Ferguson rifle was a breechloader and could be fired seven times in 60 seconds, even while the filer was prone. These things were a century ahead of their time. Although Ferguson's rifles were used successfully in the American Revolution, they were never adopted either in the British or American armies. Few regular infantry soldiers were armed with rifles before 1850; breechloaders weren't introduced successfully until almost a hundred years after Ferguson's death.

The story of the Ferguson rifle begins with the young British officer's service on the European continent in the early 1760's. He saw a good deal of fighting; a few of the German allies were armed with ponderous rifles. Ferguson was wounded and came home to his native Scottish highlands to recuperate; he had a passion for deer stalking and accurate fire. He experimented with all rifles then known.

In 1768, Ferguson, a captain at 24, went out to join his new regiment, the 70th Foot, then stationed in the West Indies. The British position in these islands at that time was anything but secure. Both Spain and France had larger areas, populations, and garrisons. Even on the individual Carribean islands held by Britain, there was frequently opposition from the natives.

reinforcements if you find you need them. Take a few days to get your bearings, and then let me hear what you propose."

Ferguson, accompanied by a sergeant and his own servant with a second rifle, made his first reconnaissance that very evening. Tobago was not unlike the Scottish highlands, save for the tropical vegetation. A single excursion gave the young captain an idea.

With the aid of his company sergeant, he picked eight men and rearmed them for the job at hand.

Ferguson had brought with him eleven cased sporting rifles, no two of which were exactly alike. With these, he made his selected squad into marksmen in less than ten days, firing up some 40 pounds of powder and 250 pounds of lead. The sergeant and the new men couldn't shoot

Three views of the Ferguson rifle in sporting version, made by D. Egg of London. Note sliding bayonet, and that multi-thread breech-plug is without vertical slots to help carry off powder fouling.

Ferguson was assigned to the hal fof the 70th stationed on Tobago Island. His servant hadn't even unpacked his clothing and small arsenal of sporting arms when the major in command gave his latest replacement officer a tough assignment. This island, like several others, was inhabited by Black Caribs, descendants from the original Caribs living on the islands at the time of European discovery and black slaves who had escaped from the plantations. These people had given the British garrison on Tobago a great deal of trouble. They were fierce and utterly hostile; there was some reason to believe that occasionally they reverted to cannibalism. Because of their knowledge of the island and their agility and swiftness of foot over the mountainous terrain, they were extremely hard to catch. Further, they had firearms and ammunition supplied by the French. Chasing these men with a company of infantry in full uniform and armed with smoothbore, muzzleloading muskets was futile, and costly in British lives.

"Your first assignment, Captain Ferguson, will be to bring these Black Caribs under control," the major said. "There aren't more than 200 men and boys, but regular tactics have been of little use against them. According to your record, you have skill and experience in stalking. I warn you, however, that this game shoots back."

"What force will I have at my disposal, Major?

"Your own company and

as well as Ferguson, or his old Highland body servant, but they were incomparably better with their new rifles than any soldiers armed with smoothbore muskets.

Once his squad could shoot, Ferguson went to work on their equipment. Heavy packs, sometimes carried even in combat in those days, were discarded. Red coats, white leather belts, white breeches, and all polished articles were left behind. Ferguson took his squad out into the mountainous country in the drab clothing of the hunting field. He taught them tactics based in part on his deer stalking experience. They soon became active and resourceful.

The very first morning of active operations, the Black Caribs, accustomed to the range of the Brown Bess muskets, gave Ferguson's men nine shots at from 150 to 200 yards. They scored two certain kills. The next day they did even better.

Within a week, Ferguson was penetrating into the very heart of the mountainous island. The enemy, which had been so formidable against formal, slow-moving British Redcoats armed with smoothbore muskets, proved less numerous than was supposed. Even though they far outnumbered Ferguson's squad, they lacked the discipline to press home an attack against his deadly aimed fire. The British commander managed to avoid hand-to-hand fighting by keeping, where possible, to the very crags and rocks where the natives had formerly performed to their best advantage.

Within a month of the young captain's arrival, the Black Caribs were disarmed and peaceful, all at a cost of two men wounded by the enemy and one killed when he fell off a cliff. Even the Caribs lost only a dozen or so; their confidence in themselves was broken by being suddenly out-climbed, out-stalked, and out-shot by the same men they had come to despise.

For almost six years, Ferguson continued in the West Indies, save for a short assignment in Nova Scotia and a rather extended visit to New England. He became an expert at fighting in the West Indies, even on islands where the Black Caribs were far more numerous than on Tobago. His knowledge and his ability to train light infantry for such warfare were used frequently. On Saint Vincent Island, in 1773 and 1774, there was a full scale small war against several thousand of these Caribs who had been supplied with arms and military advisers by the French.

Ferguson, and a special light infantry corps he commanded, performed brilliantly. The British forces were completely victorious and at relatively small cost to themselves.

Development of the Ferguson Rifle

When Ferguson returned to Britain in 1774, he had very definite ideas about the rifle that now bears his name. While in the West Indies, he had ordered certain special rifles made according to his developing experience. Of these early rifles used against the Black Caribs, an English breechloader was the best. By means of a wrench, a plug could be unscrewed from out the top of the barrel, exposing the chamber for loading. It shot extremely well, since its oversize ball completely sealed the bore and fitted the grooves of the rifling completely. However, it was slow and complicated to load.

The London gunmaker, Durs Egg, had made several rifles for Ferguson in 1770 with a breechplug unscrewing towards the bottom. In these the plug was attached rigidly to the trigger guard, which served instead of a separate wrench. This rifle was a tremendous improvement, but twelve turns of the trigger guard were required to completely uncover the chamber. Further, the threads of the long plug fouled badly; only half a dozen shots were possible before cleaning of the breech was necessary.

Ferguson had ideas to remedy both these defects. He planned to use a multiple-thread breech and plug. Instead of turning a single-pitch threaded plug

twelve times, he was going to turn a ten- or twelve-pitch threaded plug once. The only catch was the possibility that the gun-makers of that era could not make a tight multi-pitch thread.

A refinement of Ferguson's design was an arrangement for interrupting the threads on the breechplug in such a way that fouling which collected on the threads would be forced into these interruptions and dropped out of the bottom of the gun after each opening.

Trials in the Highlands

So confident was Ferguson of the practicality of his new weapon that he ordered a dozen of a military type stocked to within a few inches of the muzzle and equipped with special bayonets. Somehow, the gunmakers solved the problem of producing tight multi-pitch threads. When the rifles were ready, Ferguson went personally to London and brought them back to Aberdeenshire. He and his original servant, now more of an assistant, tested these in all sorts of ways.

Mere stalking excellence was now not enough. These rifles were shorter and lighter than the Brown Bess. They balanced superbly and were easily carried in difficult country. They were hard-hitting and probably the most accurate weapons made until that time. But the two problems Ferguson was most anxious to solve were ease and speed of loading.

Tests proved these new rifles to shoot faster by far than any other rifles ever made; soon both men could get off more aimed shots than even the best drilled soldiers could fire from smoothbore muskets with undersize bullets. They were so easy to load, for at least a score of rounds after a complete cleaning, that *any* man could do it while lying flat on the ground, a feat approached by only a very few skillful men with muzzleloaders.

Ferguson now recruited ten militiamen, mostly his father's employees, and trained them in the handling of the rifles. Since there were no Black Caribs at hand, he took his small force out to shoot game. A casual witness would have thought Britain invaded. Ferguson's men would advance in open order and then suddenly let go with a volume of fire worthy of a whole company. The enemy, however, was usually only a mass of driven rabbits, extremely plentiful in parts of the Highlands. The twelve-man squad could fire better than 70 shots in a minute. Ferguson's last doubts as to his rifles and their usefulness in war were now at rest.

Trial in Combat

Ferguson demonstrated his rifle before the King and his senior officers. A squad of men from one of the Guards regiments was trained quickly to handle these weapons. The results were truly remarkable both as to accuracy and ease and speed of loading.

The top British brass were sold on the Ferguson rifle idea. They had seen with their own eyes what could be done; they knew Captain Ferguson's record against the Black Caribs. An order for 300 rifles was placed with Durs Egg and William Hunt in the summer of 1776. A corps organization, to consist of both infantry and dragoons, was tentatively set up for use in the war in America. However, the manufacturing of these arms delayed Ferguson's departure; he arrived in New York with his orders for the special corps and the weapons to arm them in the spring of 1777.

The select corps, consisting of a few men from many British regular regiments, was trained carefully by Ferguson. This was the first group of native Britons ever trained as riflemen, although units of American colonial riflemen and the German Jagers had been used in the British Army for some time.

Ferguson's Corps led one of the two British columns in the actions that culminated in the Battle of Brandywine. So well did they do their job in the final stages of the approach that the British line troops moved through broken country already cleared of all opposition right up to the American position. In this advance guard fighting, the easy loading of the Ferguson rifle, even from a prone position, was of great value.

Just before the battle, in the woods south of Brandy-wine Creek, George Washington and a single aide appeared less than 60 yards from Ferguson and some of his men. Even though Ferguson obviously believed in aimed fire, he refused to allow his men to shoot the two unidentified officers or fire himself. He even refused to allow a sergeant to kill Washington's horse. He felt it unsporting to take advantage of the ill luck of the two, then, unidentified officers. Apparently, there was an interval of about thirty seconds before Washington put spurs to his horse.

Ferguson's corps accomplished its mission and probably inflicted a fair number of casualties on the Americans, while losing only two men wounded themselves. Unfortunately, one of these was Ferguson.

During Ferguson's time in the hospital, Sir William Howe broke up the Rifle Corps and returned the men to their old regiments. He ordered the Ferguson rifles to be returned to "store" and had the men re-issued Brown Bess muskets. Howe was never favorably disposed toward Ferguson's rifle, probably because they had been approved on "orders from home."

Ferguson's American Corps

When Ferguson came out of the hospital with a permanently stiff right elbow, he found his command gone, his special rifles either lost or in storage and his own regiment at Halifax in Nova Scotia. However, with characteristic ability, ambition and cheerfulness, he set about making himself useful. His elbow, healed but forever set at an angle of about 90°, allowed him sufficient use

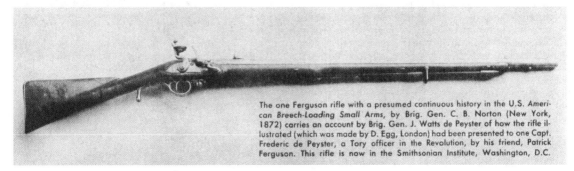

The one Ferguson rifle with a presumed continuous history in the U.S. *American Breech-Loading Small Arms*, by Brig. Gen. C. B. Norton (New York, 1872) carries an account by Brig. Gen. J. Watts de Peyster of how the rifle illustrated (which was made by D. Egg, London) had been presented to one Capt. Frederic de Peyster, a Tory officer in the Revolution, by his friend, Patrick Ferguson. This rifle is now in the Smithsonian Institute, Washington, D.C.

of the arm to handle a rifle tolerably with practice. He learned to handle both a sword and pistol with his left hand. He served at the Battle of Monmouth as an aide.

Once the British Army was back in New York, Howe had no intention of wasting the obvious talents of the young Scots captain. He called Ferguson in and offered him command of a corps of American Loyalists who were to be enlisted, paid, and trained as regulars rather than militia. Ferguson was to have charge of the recruiting and arming of these; some were to be dragoons.

Ferguson accepted immediately and soon found himself back training new men in his way of fighting. These men from New York, New Jersey, and Connecticut learned quickly to handle his rifles, of which, perhaps, 200 remained — possibly, far fewer than that. He soon had his men ready for active duty.

In the eighteen months that followed the Battle of Monmouth, Ferguson built himself a reputation for sagacity, daring and strategic ability. He commanded the army portion of a successful amphibious attack on a privateer base. He surprised and defeated Pulaski's Legion. He held the fortifications at Verplanck's Point even after the sister fortress across the river at Stony Point fell to Wayne's Light Infantry. He reoccupied, refortified, and held Stony Point.

Southern Campaign

Early in 1780 Major Ferguson and his Corps of Provincial Regulars were ordered south to take part in the British southern campaign, now about to start in earnest. It was thought that the abundant Loyalist sentiment, particularly in Georgia and the Carolinas, would aid in swinging the tide towards the British Government. Ferguson landed at Savannah and marched inland to Augusta. A portion of the Corps was now mounted. Their service around Augusta was short; they were ordered to join the main British army, which was advancing on Charleston, still in American hands.

The Corps performed with credit in the fighting that led up to the fall of Charleston. Ferguson was again wounded this time in the left arm, but recovered. After Charleston fell, the stage was set for Ferguson's last and greatest performance; the part he was called on to play required every bit of his military and political ability.

Ferguson, now with the rank of lieutenant colonel, was dispatched on 22 June, 1780, with his Corps (numbering about 200) to the back country of South Carolina. He made the village of Ninety-Six his headquarters. For three and a half months he did one of the outstanding jobs in the Revolution for the British side. He showed a considerable grasp of conditions in this country and a flair for appealing to people on a personal basis. He could sit down and talk to Americans in a way unique among British officers. Much of this hill country had been settled only a few years before by Scottish highlanders — from regiments disbanded at the end of the Seven Years War — on land given to them by the Crown. As a Highlander himself, he was instantly popular with these men.

Command in the Hill Country

However, he was almost equally popular with the other sections of the hill country population. He was modest and seemed younger than his 36 years. Not imposing in looks or actions, he was strikingly handsome with a courteous, unostentatious manner. He signed some of his proclamations simply, "Pat Ferguson." Somehow, all recognized his keen logical mind and, what was far rarer, his fairness and kindness even to the families of those in arms against him. The people found him a first-rate soldier, a superb shot and a regular guy. He was clean in mind and language. He tried to prevent thievery and the like, which had become almost universal with both sides in the South late in the Revolution. On several occasions, he paid damages from his own pocket to people injured by his soldiers. Ferguson was so infuriated in one instance by the behavior of some of Tarleton's Tory dragoons that he was with difficulty restrained from hanging them on the spot, even though he was not their commander.

Ferguson enlisted, organized and trained an army of some 2,500 Tory militia, although it wasn't practical to have them all under arms at one time. He restored the King's authority over large stretches of back country. However, his very success roused the patriots against him. Ferguson's oral messages to the "overmountain" men were twisted into insults. American riflemen from western North Carolina, Virginia, and what is now Tennessee, rose as never before. They hemmed-in Ferguson and a portion of his army at King's Mountain.

Final Defeat

Ferguson's position on 7 October, 1780, was on top of a small wooded hill about 600 yards long by less than 50 yards wide in most places. His forces were utterly defeated and he himself killed by American backwoods riflemen in one of the strangest actions ever fought. Ferguson, with about 1,000 of his Tory militia and some 130 provincial regulars, was overwhelmed by a slightly smaller number of hunter-backwoodsmen who surrounded his men and shot them down Indian fashion. These mountain men, commanded by nine different independent officers, volunteered for the sole and specific purpose of "catching and killing" Ferguson. Their movements were determined by a council of their officers. Somehow, this council managed to accomplish its purpose exactly. After winning the battle, they divided the spoils, and went back to their homes.

There was no battle ever fought in warfare where aimed fire was of more importance. The mountain riflemen had no semblance of drill or order. They had no intention of awaiting a charge by Ferguson's bayonet-wielding infantry. They took shelter as best they could. They pressed in from all sides, up the difficult slopes. When attacked in one sector, they gave ground there, but pressed in everywhere else. They held Ferguson inside this fluid line and exposed themselves little as they fired from behind trees and boulders. They riddled the British formations with their accurate fire.

Ferguson's forces could make no effective defense against this form of attack. His provincial regulars were in part armed with his superb rifles; however, he needed these very men to spearhead each of his bayonet charges. He couldn't order his riflemen to take cover and fight as he had taught them without leaving the Tory militia with no stiffening for their formations. Ferguson gambled that solidarity and the bayonet would be victorious. He lost.

The backwoods riflemen shot dead 157 loyalists and wounded as many more, while suffering only 90 casualties, both killed and wounded. Ferguson, who during the entire action exposed himself recklessly, seemed to bear a charmed life; he rode from one Tory command to another, everywhere heartening his men for the fight. Suddenly, his luck ran out. In the space of a few seconds, while leading one last charge, he was hit by seven bullets. After Ferguson fell, the remaining British forces surrendered.

The Whigs in this section were near complete defeat before the battle; this victory restored the situation. The Tories of the South never really dared to assert themselves again. Cornwallis abandoned his invasion of North Carolina temporarily. The next time he moved north, it was but to surrender finally at Yorktown. King's Mountain was the Saratoga of the South.

These now famous weapons were praised by all who saw them. Too far ahead of their time, perhaps, both in design and mechanical details of construction, the Ferguson rifle probably wasn't practical mechanically when invented, or for years later. Even in Britain, which then led the world in gunmaking skill, there wasn't enough capacity to turn out the multi-pitch threads required in the breech mechanism with sufficient nicety for sealing off the powder gases. At least 100,000 weapons would have been required to arm the British forces. The entire capacity of the gun-makers in England to produce these intricate threads was probably less than one per cent of this.

We shouldn't compare the Ferguson to the NATO rifle. But when seen alongside its contemporaries, which were both muzzleloading and smoothbore, they are truly remarkable. They were the first standard military weapons to be capable of delivering aimed fire. For accuracy, they were at least the equal of the far

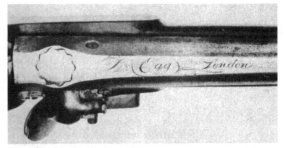

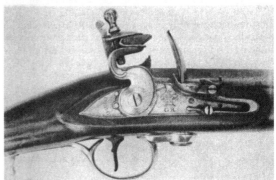

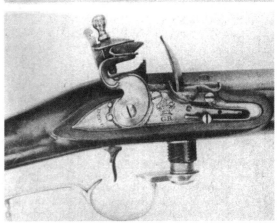

Above — Ferguson rifle made by Durs Egg of London, one of England's best gun craftsmen. The ten-thread breechplug is slotted to help carry powder fouling away. One turn up or down closed and opened the breech for loading. Now owned by the author, this specimen was bought in North Carolina around 1900, carried to England and returned here recently.

Above — Ferguson rifle, also with a ten-thread breechplug, made by Wm. Hunt of London about 1776. In W. Keith Neal's collection.

more delicate, less powerful, American or "Kentucky" rifle which was privately produced and completely nonstandard. The Ferguson rifle could deliver aimed fire in larger volume than the finest trained men with smoothbore muskets could shoot at random. Ferguson's rifle could deliver at least three shots for every shot fired by any other rifle; it would probably deliver at least six times as many rounds as the usual American rifle of the Revolution.

Ferguson the Man

In one of his last letters Ferguson said, "One cannot control the length of his life, but he can decide how it shall be spent." He seems to have lived by this; he was a scholar, a gentleman, and a soldier. He eternally refuted the statement sometimes heard that a soldier cannot also be a sensitive, humane individual.

Ferguson was an enemy and defended a way of life that we in America didn't want; however, he understood us better than any other British officer. He also understood the theory and practice of fighting with a rifle as well as any man who ever lived. We can admire now his skill, his ability, and his courage. After all, we beat him at his own game.

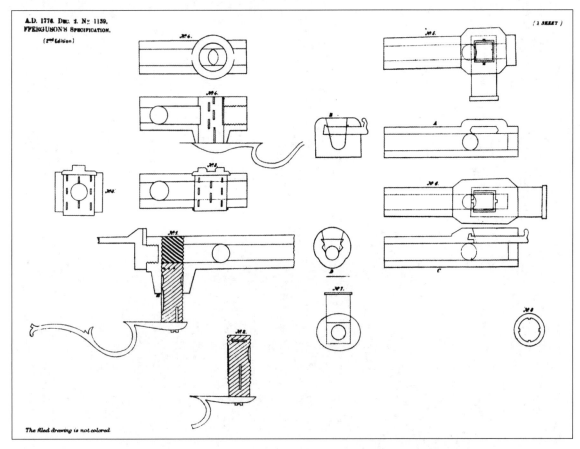

Ferguson's 1776 English Patent. Figs. 1 and 2 show the design found in Ferguson rifles, but the inventor also included other breechloading plug forms, such as the sliding and rotating types seen in Figs. 3 through 7. Note Fig. 8, showing a 4-groove barrel in section. Could anything be mors like modern rifling? His patent specification reads, in part: "...the projections formed in the ball by the cut of the rifle being twice as large as they commonly are, will not be liable to strip." Ferguson's rifling was not to see general use until some 80 years later, when W. E. Metford, great English engineer and rifleman, developed the groove form we know as Enfield rifling today — indistinguishable from Ferguson's!

The Mississippi Rifle

A watershed design in military history. ▌Edward R. Crews

Many a Confederate carried a U.S. Rifle Model of 1841 to his big war — it was a very serious weapon. (Virginia Historical Society photo)

THE MEN OF the 1st Mississippi Regiment watched the Mexican cavalry advance toward them. The enemy horse soldiers looked like an overwhelming force, but they had to be stopped. If not, Gen. Zachary Taylor's tiny American Army deep in Mexico near a hacienda named Buena Vista would be crushed.

The task of holding the American line at the Battle of Buena Vista rested mainly with Col. Jefferson Davis, his Mississippi troops and their rifles.

It was the second time that day — February 23, 1847 — that the Army's fate lay with this unit. Earlier, a 4500-man Mexican assault force broke another American unit and threatened to flank Taylor's Army. Davis recognized the danger immediately. He ordered his 370 volunteers to attack. His men stopped the Mexicans and then pushed them back.

Now, the American Army again was in danger. And, again, Davis and his soldiers stood at the key point on the battle line. That so much depended on these men and their weapons was a bit ironic.

Months earlier, when Davis was outfitting his regiment for service in the Mexican War, top Army brass opposed his idea to arm an entire regiment with rifles. Senior officers believed that the U.S. Army of 1846 would get the mass firepower it needed from standard-issue smoothbore flintlock muskets. Davis disagreed. He probably would have conceded that the flintlocks offered comparatively high rates of fire. However, they were cumbersome and finicky (particularly in wet weather), and their range and accuracy were exceedingly poor.

Even freshly minted West Point lieutenants knew the flintlock's shortcomings. Ulysses S. Grant, who served in the Mexican War as a twenty-three-year-old junior officer with the 4th Infantry Regiment, said of the smoothbores: "At the distance of a few hundred yards, a man might fire at you all day without your finding it out."

Unlike some officers, Davis recognized that a major revolution had occurred in small arms technology. And he wanted to take advantage of it. Thanks to a major breakthrough in musket ignition

systems, the rifle was becoming a practical infantry arm, offering outstanding range, power and battlefield reliability.

Davis' decision to arm the 1st Mississippi with rifles would receive a severe test at Buena Vista. Failure could mean defeat and death; success could change warfare forever.

Prior to the Mexican War, smoothbore advocates could argue that the flintlock had served the Republic well in the Revolutionary War, the War of 1812 and on the frontier. To fire this musket, a soldier loaded his weapon with blackpowder and a round ball. The two were seated at the breech using a ramrod. The musket's external hammer held a piece of flint. When the trigger was pulled, the hammer fell from its fully cocked position. The flint struck an upright piece of metal, called a frizzen. This striking action created sparks, which fell into a small pan containing a priming charge. That charge burned through a hole in the barrel to ignite the main charge, thus firing the musket.

Military flintlocks typically were smoothbores. Range accordingly was limited. A soldier might hit an individual at 80 yards and a tightly packed military unit at 100 yards. Infantry tactics dictated by this weapon's technology were simple. Commanders massed large bodies of troops. These units were marched within range of the enemy. Once there, the troops would fire as rapidly as possible. The idea was to smother the enemy with a high volume of fire. When they were weakened and demoralized, an attack was made with the bayonet. Battered forces usually either stood and fought to the death or ran. If they took the latter course, they faced the possibility of being pursued by saber-wielding cavalry.

Like all military weapons from all periods, the smoothbore flintlock offered a mix of advantages, disadvantages and compromises. On the plus side, it could be loaded and fired rapidly. The British army during the American Revolution expected troops to fire fifteen rounds in 3.75 minutes. Recruits could master the weapon in a comparatively short time. The weapon also was proven in battle,

and its tactical deployment was understood perfectly by officers. On the minus side, the flintlock ignition system often failed to work properly. Some historians estimate that even under ideal conditions it misfired 20 percent of the time. Rain, sleet and snow could prevent any use of this long arm.

Interest in developing a better ignition system became widespread near the close of the 18th century. Various inventors began to experiment with different explosive compounds, searching for something that would be both reliable and easy to use.

The ignition problem largely was solved about 1816 by Joshua Shaw with the creation of a reliable percussion cap. Some historians identify Shaw as a British painter or an American sailing captain. But whatever his true vocation, he built on the work of earlier inventors to create an ignition system that is the great-grandfather of that used for weapons today. Shaw took a small metal cap and filled it with fulminate of mercury, a highly explosive substance. The cap was placed over a nipple that led directly into a musket's breech, where the main charge sat. When the hammer fell on the cap, the resulting small explosion fired the main charge. The cap and nipple arrangement thus replaced the flintlock's flint, priming pan, frizzen and priming charge. Not only was the percussion cap easy to use, it also allowed for quicker loading and proved much more reliable in bad weather.

Army Ordnance (but not all commanders) embraced the percussion cap and the rifled musket in 1841 when it accepted the U.S. Rifle, Model 1841, caliber 54. To load it, soldiers were issued a paper cartridge, which they bit open. They then poured the powder down the barrel and seated a patched round ball atop the powder with a ramrod. A good shot could hit a man-sized target at 300 to 400 yards with this weapon.

The rifle was about 49 inches long, had a 33-inch barrel and weighed almost 10 pounds. The firearm featured a patch box in the stock. Fit and finish were superb. The rifle's lines were pleasing, and one can look at this musket today and arguably call it the most handsome weapon ever issued to American troops. Its only shortcoming was the absence of a bayonet lug.

Although designated the Model 1841, the rifle preferred by Jeff Davis would not get a significant combat trial until the Mexican War began in 1846. This conflict largely was about territory. The United States wanted to expand westward into large land tracts claimed by Mexico. The American government had offered to purchase a great deal of property. Mexico, however, said no. Tensions heightened in the 1840s until March, 1846, when U.S. President James K. Polk sent Zachary Taylor with a 3000-man force toward an area near the Rio Grande claimed by both nations.

Southern sentiment was strongly in favor of the conflict. Accordingly, the call for volunteers to fight was enthusiastically greeted in Mississippi. The state was authorized to raise one infantry regiment. Competition to enlist was keen. Davis, a West Pointer turned civilian, was chosen to serve as colonel of the unit, which was formed officially on June 16. As mentioned earlier, Davis demanded his men carry rifles and got these weapons after a fight with Army commanders.

The road to Buena Vista was long for Davis and his men. They arrived in the theater of operations in July and fought in the Battle of Monterey in September. The 1st Mississippi was serving with Taylor when he took Saltillo in November and Victoria in December.

Along with the rest of Taylor's command, Davis and his men found themselves in a dangerous position in January.

Through captured documents, Mexican General Antonio Lopez de Santa Anna learned that the U.S. Army was stripping Taylor of troops and sending them to another force commanded by Winfield Scott. Santa Anna decided to attack Taylor in his weakened state and then move to crush Scott.

Taylor and Santa Anna met at the Battle of Buena Vista. Santa Anna's plan was simple but sound: Turn the American left flank and destroy Taylor's Army.

The Mexican commander opened the fight with a diversionary strike at the well-emplaced American right flank. Then, he sent the main assault force to strike the left and head for the Saltillo Road. The main force smashed an American infantry regiment, forced another into disorganized retreat and scattered yet another cavalry unit.

It was at this point that Davis reached the battlefield and sent the 1st Mississippi into the attack. After halting the Mexican advance and silencing enemy cavalry firing on his rear, Davis waited for reinforcements. They arrived in the form of one cannon and the 3rd Indiana Infantry Regiment.

Davis' force didn't have to wait long for an enemy response. Santa Anna sent another cavalry force to try and punch through to the American rear. The conventional means for infantry to repel a cavalry attack was to form a square and use a bristling fence of bayonets on rifles to keep the horses at bay. Tested and proven, this formation was useless to the 1st Mississippi because their rifles had no bayonet attachments. Davis would need to do something else.

He quickly formed the two regiments into a V. The Mississippians formed the northern wing; the Indianians formed the southern one. The field gun was placed with Davis' regiment.

The Mexican cavalry began its advance. Davis ordered all the men to hold fire until he gave the command. The battlefield became quiet. When the enemy was within about 100 yards, the Americans opened fire. The result was devastating.

Possibly the most handsome shoulder arm ever issued in the U.S.A., the Model 1841 earned its name, the Mississippi Rifle, in Mexico. (Virginia Historical Society photo)

Men and horses fell. A retreat ensued. The Mississippi sharpshooters again had played a key role in saving the day. Davis' men would be called on again later in the day to fight the determined Mexicans. Though badly battered, Taylor's force was safe when night fell.

Santa Anna eventually retreated, having failed to crush Taylor, who would contribute little more to the conflict, but would use his reputation established there to run for president and make it.

The 1st Mississippi's performance at the Battle of Buena Vista vindicated Davis' belief in the percussion rifled musket, establishing it firmly in the Army as a reliable weapon. It also gave the weapon a new name — the Mississippi Rifle — in honor of the regiment that saved the American Army.

Buena Vista was the last pitched battle that Davis' unit fought. During the next few weeks, the regiment would serve as an anti-guerrilla force charged with keeping American supply lines open. In May, Davis and his men headed home. They reached Vicksburg in June and received an enthusiastic heroes' welcome before being mustered out of service. Mississippi's legislature gave them their now-famous rifles as a token of honor and respect.

His Mexican War service made Davis a national figure. He became a U.S. senator from Mississippi shortly after returning home. During his service in Washington, D.C., Davis naturally carved out a niche as an expert on military matters. He served on the Senate's Military Affairs Committee and as President Franklin Pierce's secretary of war. Some historians believe that Davis was the most able administrator ever to hold that post.

Secretary of War Davis naturally

A believer in the new tactics of the rifle, Jefferson Davis covered himself and the rifle he chose for his regiment with enough glory to take him to high office in two nations — the U.S.A. and the C.S.A. (Virginia Historical Society photo)

The flintlock musket had been the Queen of Battles before the rifle, none more royal than the Brown Bess of England. (Colonial Williamsburg Foundation photo)

showed a strong interest in weapons. He pushed for the widespread use of percussion rifles, supported adoption of the Minié ball (a rifle bullet that did not need a patch and was the primary infantry projectile of the Civil War) and directed the conversion of smoothbore flintlocks to rifled percussion arms. He also followed closely the developments in breech-loading rifles.

Through the years from 1847 to 1860, Davis also acted as a spokesman for the South as regional relations worsened in the United States. This, plus his military reputation and knowledge, made him a logical choice to serve as president of the Confederacy when the Southern states seceded.

During the Civil War, Davis sent thousands of Southern troops into battle with percussion rifles firing Minié balls. The Civil War was the first time in history that this sort of accurate firepower was widely in the hands of ordinary foot soldiers.

Both Union and Confederate soldiers would carry the Mississippi Rifle into battle. It would have a special place in the hearts of Southern soldiers. Many of these weapons had been rebored to 58-caliber in 1855 and could use the Minié ball.

The U.S. Army gradually shifted to breechloaders in the post-war years. The Mississippi Rifle and other muzzleloaders disappeared from the Army's inventory. However, many Civil War veterans knew the value of a reliable firearm and carried surplus Model 1841s with them to tame the American West.

The Mississippi Rifle was an important transitional weapon in American military history. Well-made and reliable, it signaled the arrival of a new technology and a profound change in combat that still can be felt to this day.

The Guns of John Brown

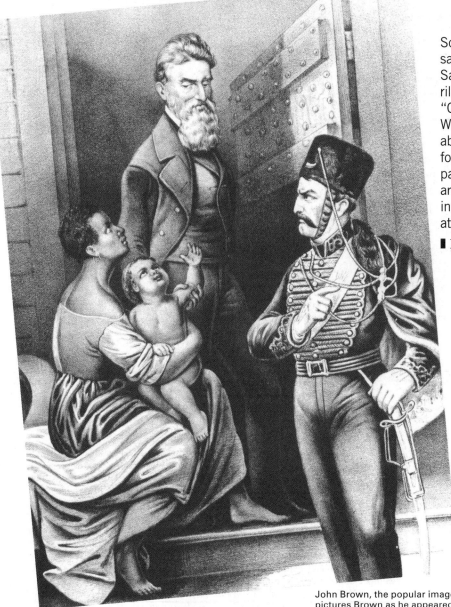

Some believed him a saint, others said he was Satan, this fierce guerrilla leader they called "Osawatomie" Brown. Whichever, he fought to abolish slavery years before the Civil War — and paid with his life. These are the weapons he used in "bleeding Kansas" and at Harpers Ferry.

▌Louis W. Steinwedel

John Brown, the popular image. This old Currier & Ives pictures Brown as he appeared to the Northern public — the popular martyr, a near saint against a background of almost classic symbolism.

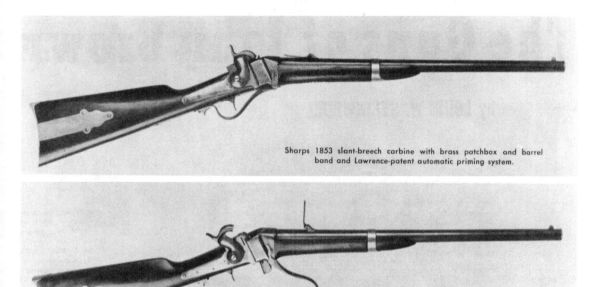

Sharps 1853 slant-breech carbine with brass patchbox and barrel band and Lawrence-patent automatic priming system.

Sharps 1853 slant-breech carbine with action and patchbox open.

RONY AND contradiction are often the warp and woof of history, but there are enough unnatural measures of the unknown in the lurid story of John Brown to spin many a tale weird enough even for modern television. Most of these are best left to the historian, psychologist or armchair thinker to ponder, but at least one of the curious circumstances of Brown's bloody career is of interest to gun collectors — how Brown came to defy Virginia, the Union and the world with 200 of the best rifles money could buy and an equal number of probably the worst revolvers.

The so-called "John Brown Sharps rifle" is fairly well known to collectors, the slant-breech model of 1853 with brass patchbox in the buttstock and brass barrel band and buttplate. The raiders' guns were not, as some people apparently still believe, the similar but more modern vertical breech model 1859 Sharps which appeared the same year as the storied seizure of the Federal armory at Harpers Ferry. Less well known to collectors are two other facets of the fanatic's armament: his long standing personal association and preference for Christian Sharps' advanced rifles and his extremely unlikely supply of sidearms.

John Brown bought his first Sharps rifle in 1848, the first year of the gun's introduction, and became — in his own way — one of the first boosters of this re-

markable breechloader. For some reason known only to Brown, he wanted this personal gun unmarked, and that was the way he got this potent, accurate arm that served him well through the years of border war in "bleeding Kansas." The Sharps was the ideal weapon for the early day guerrilla warfare that he and his free-soilers waged and perfected in Kansas. Settlers backed by fiery New England abolitionists and opposed by equally determined Southerners anxious to replant slavery to fresh Western soil bled along with Kansas through the 1850s on a miniature Civil War battleground.

Determined that the advocates of slavery in the West would do the bulk of the bleeding, Henry Ward Beecher and other less vitriolic New Englanders sent the best guns they could buy to be sure that their version of right was backed by a sufficient supply of might. Crates of sparkling blue, brass, and casehardened Sharps breechloaders sallied forth secretly from their native New England with the incongruous deception "Bibles" neatly blackened on their white pine sides. Beecher (along with his sister Harriet Beecher Stowe, authoress of *Uncle Tom's Cabin*), shouldered probably more personal liability for the Civil War than any other one man, possibly even more than Brown himself. He got a little extra claim to fame when his Sharps rifles blazed their way across the Kansas prairie nicknamed "Beecher's Bi-

bles." It was altogether fitting.

Brown's Personal Revolver

John Brown's personal sidearm through much of the Kansas bloodletting was the perfect complement to the advanced rifle he carried — an 1851 Colt Navy 36, recognized from the Barbary Coast to Balaclava as the best friend a man could have in his holster. Of graceful lines, beautifully balanced and comparatively light for its day, the Navy was patently impressive, either coming out of leather at full speed or simply lying at rest on the green felt of a gaming table. How Brown got his Navy Colt, the fifty-one thousand and tenth to be made, and how he parted with it is another ironic twist to the Brown legend.

William F. Amy, a canny Kansas politician and abolitionist, eyeing the bearded fanatic's devotion to the cause with appreciation, strategically chose to overlook the more disagreeable facets of Brown's quixotic personality. Amy believed that this ardent fighter in Kansas' "holy war" should be materially rewarded with a token and, fittingly, gave him a gun. Amy chose the best, the long barreled Colt Navy 36, plain finished except for the usual naval battle scene rolled onto the cylinder. Brown accepted it and conscientiously carried it in Kansas. For two years it became a witness to the most Inquisition-like page in American history.

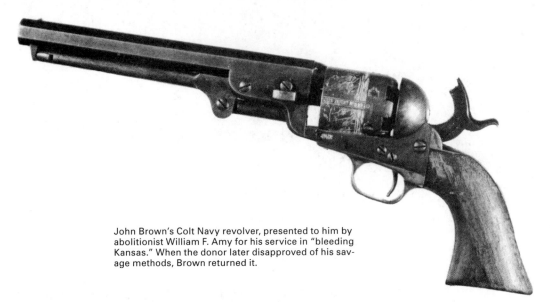

John Brown's Colt Navy revolver, presented to him by abolitionist William F. Amy for his service in "bleeding Kansas." When the donor later disapproved of his savage methods, Brown returned it.

"Osawatomie" Brown, as he liked to be called, after the best known site of the Kansas conflicts, was a psychologically fascinating man. He was burdened with precious few scruples over murder on the coldest terms when it furthered his cause, or even over feeding his sons to his hopeless ambitions at Harpers Ferry, yet he was meticulously honest. Eventually Brown's bloody Biblical-like vengeance mercilessly visited upon the "offenders" sickened even the devoutly abolitionist Arny. When Brown learned that he had fallen from favor in the mind of the donor of his revolver, he reasoned that the gift was conditional and that he no longer had any right to it. Accordingly, W.F. Amy promptly received from Brown one Colt's Navy 36, serial number 51010. However, the slim Colt had apparently been to Brown's liking since he soon acquired another one, with his own cash no doubt. Such a gun, or at least the remains of one, was found in the aftermath of the Harpers Ferry debacle in 1859, though not used there. Its barrel was sent to Hartford as a souvenir for Samuel Colt.

By the middle of 1856 a shaky peace had descended upon Kansas. At this time, however, a shipment of 200 more Sharps 1853 carbines was on the way from Massachusetts, creating a situation not far removed from the Russian missiles-in-Cuba crisis of about a century hence. The New England financiers of the "Kansas Crisis" began to fear that Federal military authorities in Kansas might take a dim view of the presence of this many rifles considerably superior to their own. Also, with the usual ingrained Yankee regard for hard cash, there was an investment of some $5500 to protect.

Brown Gets Rifles

So, the Sharps shipment was secretly diverted to a depot at Tabor, Iowa. The attempt at secrecy did not of course include so trusted a warrior as John Brown. That, as history shows was a mistake, because the power inherent in 200 superb rifles was simply too much for the Kansas guerrilla, who saw bigger things in the wind to resist. It did not take much persuasion for Brown to get possession of the guns with the stipulation that he sell them privately and distribute the proceeds as relief funds. Brown did nothing so charitable, and the Sharps carbine showed up three years later on the rented Kennedy farm a few miles from the U.S. Armory at Harpers Ferry. Osawatomie Brown was apparently willing to compromise even his lofty principles about rightful possession when the "cause" stood to profit by an abuse of the Eighth Commandment.

The fast, accurate, easy handling Sharps served Brown astonishingly well in his otherwise botched raid at Harpers Ferry, permitting seventeen men to, as Henry Ward Beecher phrased it in a sarcastic sermon, "overawe a town of two thousand brave Virginians and hold them captive until the sun had gone laughing twice around the globe."

The Sharps was a splendid weapon, but the revolvers which Brown carried East stood in stark contrast to it. These were tiny 31-caliber revolvers made by the Massachusetts Arms Co. for the firm of Wesson & Leavitt. Some 200 of these handguns, complete with such accouterments as flasks, nipple wrenches and bullet moulds, had originally been sold to Boston abolitionist George L. Stearns. Through some espionage they ended up in the hands of John Brown in Iowa in 1857, and they too made it to the Kennedy farm in Maryland two years later.

This Massachusetts Arms Co. revolv-er was about as far as you could get from John Brown's hefty Navy Colt, and a highly unlikely nominee for the quasi — military foray on the banks of the Potomac. It was chosen, apparently for financial reasons; these 31-caliber jobs cost only $6.50 complete with accessories while a Navy Colt cost roughly double that — and was worth more.

The Massachusetts revolvers were unusual in concept and appearance, not unlike some of the very early attempts at revolving repeaters. With the exception of a topstrap over the cylinder which served to hold the cylinder pin and barrel to the rest of the parts, the gun appeared almost frame — less, like a dueling or target pistol

John Brown, the private image. This rare, unbearded view of Brown was regarded as his best picture by the family. He appears less ferocious than usual here, but the cold and expressionless eyes are the perfect symbol of his character.

with a cylinder added as an after-thought. The revolver's only touch with the times was its Maynard automatictape primer which was intended to eliminate the necessity of a separate percussion cap for each shot. The system had been invented in 1845 by a Washington dentist named Edward Maynard and enjoyed a measure of popularity by the 1850s, particularly when adapted to the muzzle-loading military musket.

The Maynard system was simple. When the hammer of the gun was cocked a small arm pushed up the end of a coil of waterproofed paper containing small fulminate charges, almost exactly the same as toy caps for children's cap pistols. On musket conversions the original percussion nipple was retained, so ordinary copper caps could be used in a pinch. However, the Maynard adaptation to the revolvers which Brown's men used completely did away with the usual nipples at the rear of the cylinder. Instead, the roll of caps was fed to a single nipple mounted in the frame which communicated the flash of the cap explosion through a tiny vent in the rear of each chamber in the cylinder. This was one of those ideas which look great on paper but which have a way of turning out to be unmitigated disasters.

It is understatement to say that the Maynard system was not noted for its reliability. Despite its claim to waterproof caps, a Maynard equipped gun often would not fire during damp weather. During such conditions, the militiaman could slip an old-fashioned copper cap on the nipple of his musket and be sure of a kick when he pulled the trigger, but the Maynard priming system was exclusively and forever married to the Massachusetts Arms revolver. Having the ignition system reach the powder chambers by a small vent hole was a throwback to the flintlock, and had the same problem of black powder residue fouling the vent after the first or second firing. These two factors combined made the Massachusetts Arms revolver dependable for little more than casual Sunday afternoon shooting, yet fate capriciously sent it along on one of history's boldest expeditions.

By another quirk, fate chose a U.S. colonel named Robert E. Lee to yank Brown from his makeshift fortress with the gracefully arched windows and the top-heavy looking cupola. The breaching of the armory firehouse took only three sweeps of the minute hand of Colonel Lee's big gold watch, but it quickly became popular history that is still providing fodder for movie and television screens.

The whole thing was a holiday in the

1853 Sharps and stocked Colt Navy carried by John Brown, Jr. The Collins cavalry officer's saber was presented to Brown, Jr., by his Civil War regiment. Wooden canteen was the senior Brown's.

picturesque Virginia hills and it did not take the revelers long to locate the bulk of Brown's private arsenal at the rented Kennedy farm a few miles away in Maryland. One of the regiments at the farm, the "Baltimore Greys," did not consider it unprofessional to re-appropriate some of the expensive abolitionist carbines as spoils of war.

Collector's Sharps

Fortunately for history, one of the shiny brass-bound Sharps carbines found its way into the hands of Colonel A. P. Shutt, commander of the 6th Regiment of Maryland Volunteers. In civilian life Shutt worked for the Baltimore & Ohio Railroad and was in Harpers Ferry mainly to protect company property from the gun-toting mobs that had swarmed in for the carnival and free whisky. The colonel was one of the few recipients of Brown's guns that sensed a bit of drama about it rather than a simple windfall of a good gun. He gave the unused carbine to his son and the lid of the inlaid brass patchbox was later engraved: "Captured from insurgents at Harpers Ferry, Va. October 18, 1859 by Col. A. P. Shutt and presented to his son Augustus J.C.L. Shutt." Today, the gun belongs to the Maryland Historical Society. It is the most authentic of the extremely few Brown guns and relics that survived the years after the raid. Its serial number is 15864.

Officially, 102 Sharps carbines and an equal number of Massachusetts Arms revolvers were removed from Brown's rented base of operations, so apparently the better part of a hundred of each were carried off by enterprising souvenir seekers. Some

of the other remnants of Brown's shattered dream of a slave rebellion included 23,000 percussion caps and 100,000 percussion pistol caps, ten kegs of powder, plus spears, pikes, and assorted martial hardware with which Brown had planned to arm the slaves which never rose to follow him. The guns were removed to the Federal arsenal, where they were appropriated once again when the town later was captured by the Confederacy and — the greatest irony of al l— the guns for John Brown's "holy war" vanished into the ranks of the rebel cavalry.

The scene of the raid seemed to suffer a fate under Brown's curse which no other piece of American territory has ever had to endure. Like some little European border town, with spectacular Rhineland-like scenery to complete the comparison, Harpers Ferry was alternately shelled by armies as they advanced, pillaged of its machinery while they were there and burned as they retreated, until by the end of the war it literally ceased to exist. Years later the ghost of Osawatomie Brown seemed to still haunt the spot with a vengeance as the usually placid Potomac swallowed it.

• • •

John Brown was a saint or a satan, generally depending on which side of the Mason-Dixon line the opinion originated, but there is no argument that he was an enigma, a strange blend of idealism and savagery, something mysteriously apart from the ordinary mould of men — and that the exotic about him extended even down unto his armament.

"The Minié Rifle"

■ E. F. Donnelly

JUST OUTSIDE the little town of Gettysburg on a hot July afternoon in 1863, some 15,000 crack Confederate infantrymen of General Lee's command moved out from their positions on Seminary Ridge. Forming into three main attack groups or divisions, the men started off across the open fields towards the gentle slopes of Cemetery Hill. Their objective was to take that hill and the jumping-off hour had arrived. In a day before dog tags were issued to soldiers, many of these men had scribbled their names and home towns on scraps of paper and thrust them into pockets. There was a nervous checking of cartridge boxes and other equipment as they surveyed the distance they'd have to traverse before closing with the enemy. 1100 to 1400 yards separated the three divisions from the quiet Federal lines on Cemetery Hill, and no one was more aware of the distance involved than these waiting men, many of whom were about to die. Already a few ranging shells from the Federal batteries had burst in and about the gray lines, when at last the word was given to move forward. With heads bent as though walking in a strong gale, they weathered an ever increasing barrage of shot and shell flung at them from batteries already thought silenced until a moment before. Torrents of grape and canister tore through the ordered ranks, but then, closing with their objective, they hurled themselves on the waiting lines of Yankees dug in along the ridge.

Ironically, hung on the cemetery gate about which a portion of the Yankee lines were formed, was a sign which read, "All persons found using firearms on these grounds will be prosecuted to the full extent of the law." With utter disregard for the law, however, the blue-clad troopers poured such a storm of musketry into the oncoming Rebels that, within an hour, the

massive assault was stopped. Crushed and beaten, the survivors of that great action known as "Pickett's Charge" sullenly fell back to the shelter of their own lines. With a gallantry unsurpassed in the history of warfare, the Rebels had marked the trail of their three pronged attack with some ten thousand casualties.

What type of weapons had caused the valiant South to sustain such a horrific loss in one hour of attack? A loss which is shocking, even when compared to the great battles of the world's two most recent wars.

This awful carnage was not accomplished with the aid of machine gun, atomic cannon or fighter-bomber, for such items were yet to be developed. No, the weapons in the hands of the Blue and Gray on that hot afternoon so long ago were such simple little arms as the Springfield and Enfield rifle-muskets, rifled and smoothbore artillery pieces, Colt's and Remington revolvers, and the inevitable bayonet. Antiquated weapons to be sure. Yet with such outmoded weapons, Americans of more than than ninety years ago managed to inflict almost one million casualties on each other in a war which still stands as the most costly to American lives. The military experts list many reasons for the terrible death rate between 1861 and 1865, but the fact remains that the war was primarily an infantry affair. Despite grape, canister, shot and shell; disease, improper camp sanitation and lack of medical skill; the greatest single killer in that war was the Springfield rifle-musket. This weapon, sometimes known as the "Minié" rifle, was the principal shoulder arm used by the Civil War soldier. Without becoming either too technical or involved in explanation, this article will describe some of the characteristics of that weapon.

The great bellow of Civil War cannon is mostly stilled these days, except for those rare occasions when Hollywood calls for its services, but the bark of the muzzle-loading Springfield rifle can still be heard in many parts of the country. Gun collectors and shooters are now finding the old Springfields both enjoyable and economical to fire, and as a result, gun stores, collectors' meetings and old attics are being scoured in an effort to locate more of the old charcoal burners. Public interest even extends to the Camp Perry National Rifle Matches, where one of the non-scoring events consists of an exhibition of shooting with the service muzzle loader of the 1860's. A couple of years ago, to the surprise of many of the spectators present, the muskets shot exceptionally well. This,

U.S. Model 1842 Percussion Musket, 69 caliber smoothbore. Barrel, 42", total length without bayonet 57.8". Weight with bayonet 9.8 lbs. Walnut stock. Front sight is a brass knife blade attached to top barrel band. Spread eagle on lockplate looks back toward hammer. Arsenal name and year of manufacture is stamped on lockplate just to rear of hammer. Breech end of barrel is marked with a V.P., an eagle's head and the year. This musket, manufactured at both the Springfield and Harper's Ferry Arsenals, was the first issue musket ever made on the completely interchangeable plan. Discontinued in 1855, it was the last of the government's smoothbores, while also the first of the percussion muskets. Many of this model were rifled just prior to the Civil War. (This musket property of Rock Island Arsenal Museum.)

U.S. Model 1855 Rifle-Musket, 58 caliber. Barrel length 39¾", total length without bayonet 58½". Weight with bayonet 9.75 lbs. Walnut stock. Markings: a spread eagle on the Maynard tapebox cover; "U.S. Springfield" or "Harper's Ferry" and the year of manufacture on the lockplate; a V.P. with an eagle head on the breech of barrel. The most noticeable feature is the Maynard Patent Priming Device of the lockplate. Barrel retaining bands are flat and held in place with band springs. The cone seat has a clean-out screw, used in cleaning out the barrel vent. This model may be found with an adjustable slide-type rear sight or with the typical two-leaf rear sight so common to Civil War muskets. (This musket property of R.I.A. Museum.)

U.S. Model 1864 Rifle-Musket, 58 caliber. Barrel, 40", total length without bayonet 56". Weight without bayonet 8.6 lbs. In this model there is a change in the cone seat, which had been accomplished in the 1863 model. However, the most obvious change in the '63 and '64 models is in the shape of the hammer. (Musket shown is property of the writer.)

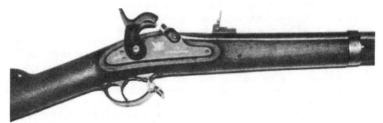

Special Model 1861 Rifle-Musket, 58 caliber. Sometimes referred to as the Colt Pattern or Special Model 1861 Musket, this weapon was manufactured for the government by the Colt's Patent Fire Arms Mfg. Co., Inc., the Lamson, Goodnow & Yale Co. of Windsor, Vt., and the Amoskeag Mfg. Co., of Manchester, N.H. Barrel length and twist of rifling same as the 1855 and 1861 models. Except for the trigger guard assembly and rear sight, parts made for this model will not interchange with the other issue muskets of the period. The hammer shape is noticeably different than the 1861 model. (This musket is the property of the writer.)

of itself, is an indication as to how short-lived is the human memory. A generation ago, our grandfathers could have told many a story testifying as to the deadly effectiveness of their old Minié rifles.

By a strange quirk of fate, it is interesting to note, the Springfield 58 caliber Rifle-Musket, Model of 1855, was approved for the general use of the Army by the then Secretary of War, one Jefferson Davis. In a letter to the Chief of Ordnance in the summer of '55, Davis approved and recommended changes proposed for the service musket by the Army Ordnance Board. The musket preceding the new 1855 model had been the regulation shoulder weapon of the Army from 1842, and held the rather unusual position of having been the first percussion arm to be adopted for the service and at the same time being the last of the smooth-bore muskets. This big weapon fired a 69 caliber lead ball in a manner hardly to be described as accurate; but in spite of its erring ways, the services clung to the old musket with that affection borne of long familiarity.

To equip the entire Army with a rifled arm stirred up quite a controversy in the War Department of the 1850's. Actually, small units of the U.S. Army had been equipped with flintlock and percussion rifles from the very beginning of our history, but the principal arm of the infantry had always been the smoothbore musket. There was no doubt as to which was the most accurate, but with the black powder then in use, the smoothbore musket was much easier to load and fire than the rifle. The latter, requiring a tightly fitted patched ball which was difficult to ram down a fouled and dirty bore, took roughly twice as long to load as the inaccurate smoothbore. The proposed reduction in bore size created an additional furor.

Many of the veteran officers and enlisted men, schooled in the use of the 69 caliber smoothbore, felt that to reduce the caliber to 58 would leave the soldier with such a "small bored" weapon that he would no longer be able to, make "good Indians out of bad ones." Those of us who have been in the service in recent years know that the 50 caliber machine gun bullet is a slug to be reckoned with, yet our gentle ancestors were afraid that a 58 caliber bullet would fail to stop an Indian. In spite of the objections raised by the diehards, however, the proposed changes were made, the caliber reduced to 58. The length of the infantry musket's barrel was set at forty inches, and it was to be rifled. It was decided, in fact, that all future mus-

BALLS FOR NEW RIFLE-MUSKET AND PISTOL-CARBINE.

No. 1.   No. 2.

Weight of No. 1, 500 grains.   Weight of No. 2, 450 grains.
Weight of powder, 60 grains.   Weight of powder, 40 grains.
No. 1, section of musket ball.
No. 2, section of pistol-carbine ball.
Both balls have the same exterior.

kets would be rifled to make use of the newly developed Minié ball, a recent hollow-based importation from France.

This Minié ball or bullet, an adaptation of the original bullet developed by Captain Minié of the French Army, was as much an outstanding innovation to the military of the 1850's as is the guided missile and atomic weapon of today. For the first time since the invention of black gunpowder, the Minié ball's accuracy placed the infantrymen more on an even footing when facing artillery fire. By the same token, the artilleryman found that he must either move back out of range of the enemy's aimed rifle fire, or else die fighting his guns. Prior to this, when facing the smoothbore musket or even such rifled arms that used a patched round ball, the enemy soldier or artilleryman hit by deliberate aim at much over one hundred yards was an unlucky individual indeed. However, with the adoption of the Minié ball, conventional warfare underwent some drastic changes. Aimed effective rifle fire was increased by two hundred yards, but what was probably of greater importance, the soldier at last been given an arm which inspired him with confidence. If he took good aim, he could score a hit.

The military muzzle loader had just about reached perfection in the late '50's and early '60's, but its full development could not have been attained without the Minié ball. This fact was quickly realized by the Army's Ordnance Board, after it had experimented with the French projectile. Adapting the original projectile to its own needs, the Ordnance Board reached the following conclusions: first, by using the elongated, undersized ball, the muzzle loading rifle could be loaded and fired almost continuously, without stopping to

clean out a barrel fouled and caked with burnt powder residue. Expanded upon firing, the self cleaning Minié would push the residue from preceding shots out the barrel ahead of itself. Secondly, the expansion of its hollow base, forming nearly a perfect bore seal, resulted in a better utilization of the propelling gases and also gave greatly increased accuracy. This in contrast to the loose fitting round balls of former times, which had lost much of their range and accuracy by permitting the propellant gases to escape up the bore.

With the addition of Dr. Maynard's patent primer tape device, which speeded up the process of loading, the U.S. Rifle-Musket of 1855 was certainly the fastest loading, if not one of the world's best muzzle loading weapons. Jefferson Davis played his small part in approving the weapon that would help destroy the Confederacy, yet to be born.

During the first ten years after its adoption, the new 58 caliber weapon was modified and again remodified to meet those various needs of the services, needs that only active field use can discover and develop in any type of Army equipment. Basically and ballistically, it was the same weapon, although the government identified it by the year such changes were made, e.g., the Model 1855, the Special Model 1861, the models of 1863 and 1864. The rifle-musket was manufactured both with and without Maynard's patent priming device. It was put out with barrel lengths from 33 inches to 40; sometimes as a carbine, other times as a rifle. During the war years, the North found that its government arsenals could not even begin to supply enough rifles to meet the needs of an ever increasing armed force; to meet this demand, contracts were

CARTRIDGE FOR EXPANDING BALLS

FULLSIZE FOR NEW MUSKET

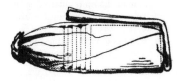

OUTER WRAPPER

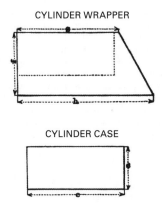

CYLINDER WRAPPER

CYLINDER CASE

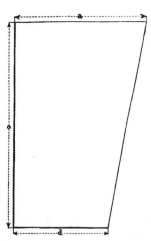

given to private arms manufacturers. As a result, arms collectors will find Civil War period muskets made not only at the Springfield Arsenal but also by Colt's, Remington, Whitney, Savage, Norwich Arms Company, and a host of others too numerous to mention here. (See C. Fuller's The Rifled Musket, described fully in the book review pages.) Without attempting to discuss the various modifications of the original weapon, let us select one item, an 1863 Springfield.

The '63 model rifle-musket had a long slim barrel some 39¾ inches long, rifled with three shallow grooves, the twist having a uniform pitch of one complete turn in six feet. It was bound to its walnut stock with three iron barrel bands. Its lock, trigger guard, bands, and in fact the barrel itself, were all finished bright. The "bright" finish of the weapon shows what complete disregard our Ordnance then had for what is now known as good camouflage discipline. A column of infantry marching along on a clear day could usually be seen for miles, the sun reflecting merrily off the bright and shiny barrels of scores of muskets. Mounted atop this gay and gleaming barrel was a two-leaf rear sight, quite common to the Civil War musket. With both leaves down the piece was sighted in for one hundred yards; one raised leaf gave a 300-yard sighting, the other 500. Could they hit anything with those three-and five-hundred yard sights? They could indeed, but more about that later.

It had been found from experience that the 1855 model, when fitted with the Maynard device, a mechanism quite similar to a toy repeating cap pistol, was not as reliable as was first anticipated. After receiving many complaints from soldiers in the field, the Models 1861, 1862 and all the later versions were again fitted with the older, simpler type lock, one similar

to that used on the 1842 musket. If that seems like progress in reverse, possibly it was. However, reliability of functioning was a compelling requirement, not always to be had with the Maynard mechanism. Under ideal conditions Maynard's device functioned quite well; as the hammer was pulled back a capsule of mercury fulminate automatically appeared over the nipple. Unfortunately, conditions and field use developed unexpected quirks in the mechanism and it was dropped from further use. Once again the soldier was required to place each percussion cap in position with his fingers. Naturally this method was slower but, on the other hand, it was a more reliable way to insure the rifle going off when desired.

That "going off or ignition system of a percussion musket is simplicity itself. The percussion cap bears the same relationship to the loaded rifle as the spark plug does to the automobile cylinder loaded with gasoline vapor. Screwed into the breech end of the barrel at the right side is a "cone" or "nipple," whose axis is pointed upward and rearward. Drilled through the center of this nipple is a channel leading directly into the barrel, while the upper opening of the nipple is positioned just beneath the descending hammer. To fire such a piece, one rammed powder and ball down the barrel, then slipped a percussion cap over the nipple. Pulling the trigger caused the hammer to strike the cap, which, exploding, flashed its fire into the main charge.

In spite of its length (58½ inches), the weight of the rifle with bayonet attached came to just 9¾ pounds. Compared with the familiar Garand Ml of today's Army, the tip of the muzzleloader's bayonet was about on a par with a tall man's head. Ballisti-cally the rifle-musket was a short range weapon, and on paper its velocity

and stopping power are almost laughable. Laughable, that is, if one considers the terrible losses at Antietam, Cold Harbor and Spotsylvania a subject for merriment. To understand the lethal potentialities of the musket, one must again consider the Minié ball used in it.

A charge of sixty grains of black powder drove the 500-gr. hollow-based Minié out of the muzzle at a velocity of 950 feet per second; extremely slow when compared to the Ml rifle's 2800 feet per second. In spite of its slow speed, however, the lumbering Minié ball was a mean killer. Wounds made by it were particularly destructive because the bullet was given to tumbling end over end in its passage through the body. Joints and bone tissue struck by it were almost always shattered beyond any hope of healing, and unless the poor unfortunate so wounded died at once, he was usually subjected to the added misery of a battlefield amputation. If his wounds didn't kill him, the amputation or resulting infection usually did.

The ability of the rifle-musket to deliver this deadly missile to a given target was quite acceptable for the day and age. While not comparable to some of the contemporary sporting or target rifles, its accuracy was sufficient to enable the shooter to hit a target the size of a man on horseback at a full six hundred yards. Old Ordnance records list the musket's capabilities as follows: Its heavy bullet could penetrate four inches of soft pine at 1000 yards. When fired from machine rest, the musket was expected to place all of its bullets in a four-inch circle at 100 yards, in an eleven-inch bull at 333 yards, and into a 27-inch bull at 500 yards. Altogether the combination of rifle and bullet gave quite respectable accuracy. As for accuracy, possibly the reader may recall how proficient he became with the smoothbored air gun of his boyhood, assuming, of course, that he was lucky enough to own one. Remembering that, one can readily see how deadly proficient Billy Yank and Johnny Reb became in the use of this long slim rifle-musket. As contemporary Ordnance reports indicate, however, not all of the soldiers used their muskets with either proficiency or as the regulations prescribed. For example, in the excitement of battle an inexperienced soldier might insert his paper-wrapped cartridge into the barrel upside down, the powder on top! He might fail to tear the cartridge open before ramming it home. He might load his musket properly, then forget to prime it with a percussion cap. He might think that he had fired the piece and then ram another load down atop the first load. He might correctly load, but then forget to remove his ramrod. The latter mistake often resulted in the interesting phenomenon of a ramrod flashing through the air like a silver arrow. The soldier might just finish loading his piece and then before getting a chance to fire it, become a casualty himself. As often happened, another soldier might come along, pick up the same gun and ram one more charge down the long bore. In any of these events the musket so treated either failed to fire or fired so poorly as to be worthless.

Old Ordnance records again provide an interesting commentary on the ease with which even the best of military muzzleloaders could be temporarily put out of action. Reports tell us that of the 37,574 stand of muskets listed as battlefield pickups after Gettysburg, some 24,000 were loaded. Of this number 6,000 had one load each; 12,000 had two loads each; 5,999 had from three to ten loads each; and one barrel contained twenty-three loads. After these figures were released even the most stanch adherents of the muzzleloader agreed that it just had to go. We couldn't effect the change while actively engaged in a war, however, and so the adoption of an efficient breechloader was delayed until after the war.

To give the modern infantryman a notion of how well off he is with his semi-automatic rifle, just consider all the motions that Billy Yank or Johnny Reb had to go through before he was ready to deliver that fatal Minié ball. These will be the typical motions of the soldier as he loaded and fired at will — as opposed to the methodical motions employed when firing by volleys at a given command. Let's assume that the soldier has just fired his piece. As the considerable puff of white smoke drifts away, the soldier brings the

rifle down from his shoulder and pulls the big hammer back to its half cock position. (Some veteran soldiers maintained that the hammer should not be pulled back, but should be left closed, as is the damper on a stove.) He reaches back into his leather cartridge box and brings out a paper wrapped cartridge; a unit containing both powder and Minié ball. The soldier brings the cartridge up to his mouth and tears it open with his teeth. He then pours the powder down the barrel, squeezes the bullet out of the paper tube and inserts it into the muzzle. He next draws the ramrod from its groove underneath the barrel, and in two or three strokes, rams the ball down on top of the powder. Sometimes he uses the cartridge paper as wadding and rams it down on the powder, too, at other times he throws it away. If he's pressed for time, as during an attack, he just bites the cartridge so that it's at least partly open, rams it down the bore, and trusts to luck that it will go off. Crouched behind that fence or tree, our soldier doesn't even bother returning his ramrod to its place beneath the barrel. For the sake of speed, he thrusts it into the ground at his feet, where it will be handy for the next shot. As the last act of loading his piece, the soldier reaches into the cap box attached to his belt, pulls out one percussion cap, places it on the nipple of his musket, then draws the big hammer back to full cock. He's now cocked, primed, and ready for another target.

Reports tell us that some veteran infantrymen became so expert at reloading that two or three shots a minute were not considered exceptional for the times. Reports also mention that after a few volleys on the battlefield the smoke from the thousands of muskets would become so dense that the troops would be unable to see each other until the wind had cleared the smoke away. This is pure conjecture, of course, but possibly the casualty rates in a typical Civil War fire fight can be

tied in with the difficulty the soldiers had in reloading their muskets. After going through the entire wearisome process of loading they were going to try to make every shot count, if at all possible.

No discussion of the rifle-musket would be complete without pointing out some of the more interesting uses to which the weapon was put. For example, the weapon was often used as a fairly effective shotgun. With its slow twist rifling, the musket did not disperse a load of shot

Dimensions.	Rifle muskets.			Rifles.		Pist carbi
	1822.	1840.	1855.	1841.	1855.	185
	Inches.	Inches.	Inches.	Inches.	Inches.	Inch
Barrel.. { Diameter of bore	0.69	0.69	0.58	0.58	0.58	0.5
Variation allowed, more	0.015	0.015	0.0025	0.0025	0.0025	0.0
Diameter at muzzle	0.82	0.85	0.78	0.90	0.90	0.8
Diam'r at breech between flats.	1.25	1.25	1.14	1.15	1.14	1.
Length without breech screw.	42.	42.	40.	33.	33.	12.
Bayonet.—Length of blade	16.	18.	18.	21.7	21.7	....
Ramrod.—Length	41.96	41.70	39.60	33.00	33.00	12.
Arm comp'te. { Length without bayonet	57.64	57.80	55.85	48.8	49.3	17.6
With bayonet fixed	73.64	75.80	73.85	71.3	71.8	....
With butt-piece	......	......	......	......	......	28.9
Grooves { Number	3	3	3	3	3	3
Twist	6.	6.	6.	6.	6.	
Width	0.36	0.36	0.30	0.30	0.30	0.3
Depth at muzzle	.005	.005	.005	.005	.005	.0
Depth at breech	.015	.015	.015	.013	.013	.0
WEIGHTS.	Lbs.	Lbs.	Lbs.	Lbs.	Lbs.	Lb
Barrel, without breech screw	4.	4.19	4.98	4.8	4.8	1.4
Lock, with side screws	* 95	.95	.81	.55	.81	.0
Bayonet	0.73	0.64	.72	3.05	3 05	....
Arm comp'te. { Without bayonet	9.06	9.51	9.18	9.68	9.93	3.5
With bayonet	9.82	10.15	9.90	12.72	12.98	....
With butt-piece	......	......	......	......	......	5.0

PRINCIPAL DIMENSIONS, WEIGHTS, ETC., OF SMALL ARMS.

* Maynard primer.

as readily as a modern rifle's rapid twist will do; shot loads were frequently substituted for the service round. If so used, with a little luck, Johnny or Billy might then proceed to toast a duck or a rabbit on the end of that old reliable all-purpose ramrod.

Another specialized load for the old gun consisted of a lighter 300-gr. bullet which, backed up by 100 grains of black powder, attained a speed close to 1800 feet per second. A fairly hot load indeed, and supposedly used by sharpshooters only. Another special bullet was issued on occasion and this one might truly be termed an explosive bullet. Something akin to the Minié ball, this nasty little number contained a three-second time fuse and a small portion of fulminate. Developed by a chap named Gardiner, this bullet was supposed to be fired into the enemy's artillery caissons. Judging from the number of blown up caissons in any given battle of the Civil War, it is fairly safe to assume that not all of them were blown up by counter battery fire. Possibly the little explosive bullets did their intended work after all.

There were other muzzleloading shoulder weapons in considerable use throughout the war, but the majority of them were roughly in the same category as the Springfield when it came to celerity of fire, accuracy, and range. Possibly the best known of these weapons was the English 577-caliber Enfield rifle-musket. These were brought into the South by means of fast Confederate blockade runners, and were greatly in demand by the Confederate who was probably still toting his Grandpap's War-of-1812 flintlock. The Whitworth sharpshooters rifle, another English import, was never brought into the conflict in any great numbers, but was one of the most highly prized because of its exceptional accuracy. The 54 and 58 caliber Harpers Ferry rifles, a product of the U.S. government arsenal of the same name, were also found in considerable quantities on both sides of the lines. The U.S. 1842 models were also brought out of retirement and issued for use, along with thousands of other muskets (both foreign and domestic) that should have long before been relegated to the scrap heap. For example, the Federal government purchased thousands of Austrian muskets; a fair percentage of these were of such poor and antiquated quality that, in at least one instance, Federal soldiers staged a minor mutiny rather than accept them. In the Confederate Army, the constant shortage of weapons caused the use of any and all

weapons that could be scraped from the arsenals and attics of the South. They used flintlocks, converted flintlocks, shotguns, sporting rifles, and what-ever arms could be captured from the Yankees; many were captured, never doubt it. They even turned to the manufacture of weapons, and the few made were good. Only the lack of raw materials stopped production in quantity. At times Johnny captured new breechloaders from the Yanks, but because he could not make the special ammunition they required, or else lacked the parts to repair the weapons, he deliberately remade them into muzzleloaders. Johnny was resourceful when it came to weapons, and in his capable hands they all performed quite well.

There are many of the old rifle-muskets still about, and if found to be in good condition, there is no reason why they shouldn't be fired. Bullet moulds, powder and percussion caps are available from many sources in this country, and one can fire these old timers today about as inexpensively as a 22 rifle. When using the rifle-musket, as well as any other muzzle-loader, always remember that the old weapons were built to handle black powder only. Black powder is safe to use in any of them, but modern smokeless powder will almost invariably blow them apart. In addition to the danger of using the wrong powder, there are also such factors as metal fatigue and rust. Before firing any muzzleloader, if you have even the slightest doubt about the strength of the barrel, have the weapon checked by a competent gunsmith.

It's been nearly a hundred years since the days of our last muzzle loading rifle. It was rugged, sufficiently accurate, and easily mass produced. It served its purpose well when the chips were down. Nothing better can be said of any weapon.

The Whitworth Rifle a great milestone in rifle history

The first comprehensive and critical review of a famous rifle, the result of the author's deep and diligent research. Fully illustrated.

▌ DeWitt Bailey II

Fig. 1. Military Match Rifle, cased in oak and complete. The first commercially available Whitworth, which appeared in 1859, this is the pattern given as prizes by the National Rifle Association of Great Britain in 1860, 1861 and 1862. This type was also given as a prize by many Volunteer units and civic organizations during those years. Note that the case is unlined. The round capbox, the lock and breech design, the smooth-headed ramrod and stock design are characteristic of this model. Courtesy E. J. Burton.

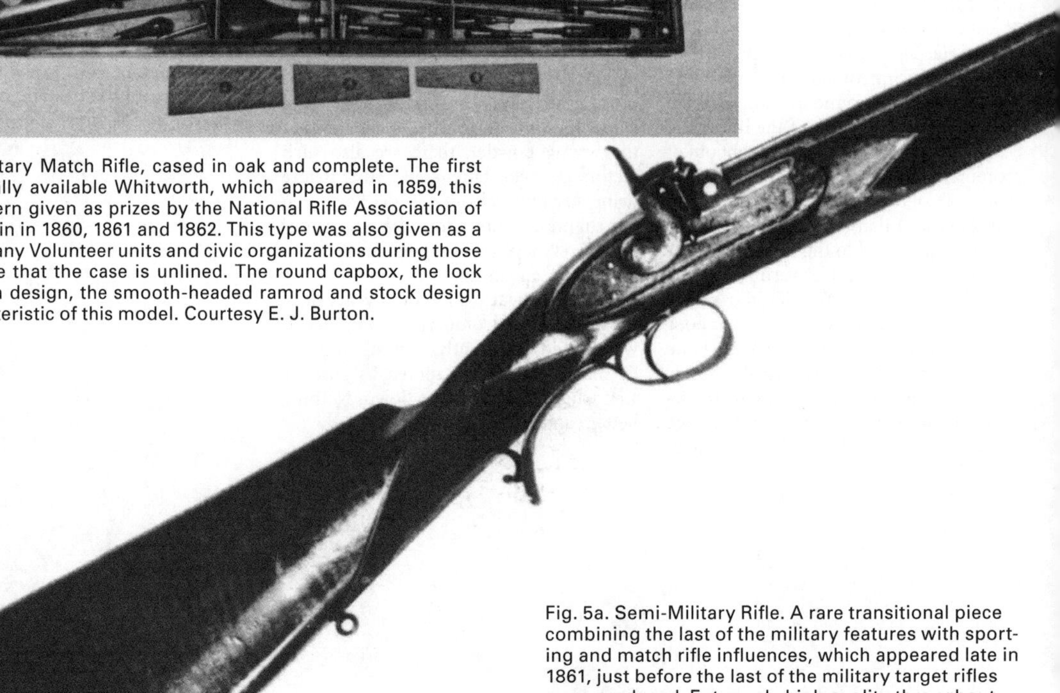

Fig. 5a. Semi-Military Rifle. A rare transitional piece combining the last of the military features with sporting and match rifle influences, which appeared late in 1861, just before the last of the military target rifles were produced. Extremely high quality throughout. Thirty-six inch barrel, Baddeley bands, break-off patent breech with three flats. Scroll engraved mounts and breech, military pattern steel ramrod. Sights were removed as on match rifles, and consist of wind-gauge front and rack and pinion rear sight, there being no provision for a tang sight on this example.

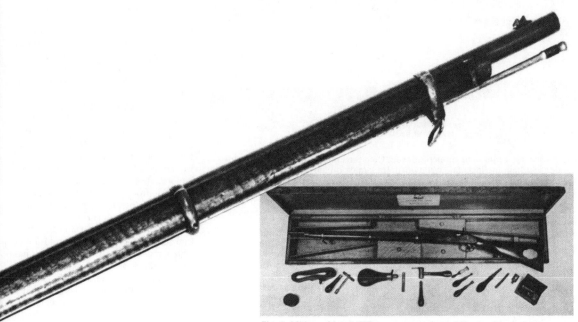

Fig. 2. Military Match Rifle, a reverse view of fig. 1, with contents displayed. Implements are, from left – cap tin, sling, punch for pushing bullet from mould, combination tool, German-silver topped leather covered flask, WHitworth patent cartridge, conical mould and base plug, lock brush, hammer face cleaner, nipple cleaner, screwdriver, torque bar, oil bottle, japanned tin for holding wads and other small pieces. Courtesy F. J. Burton.

JOSEPH WHITWORTH began his career as a toolmaker in Manchester in 1833. He died in January, 1887, with a world-wide reputation as the most eminent producer and designer of precision machine tools. The standards set by his machines are still current today. His standardization of screw threads, dating from the 1840s, still stands.

Problems with the production and performance of the Pattern 1853 Enfield rifle musket, the absence of standardization of tools and gauges, the problem of supply in the face of the Crimean War and its extraordinary demands, led the British government to call upon Whitworth in 1854 to suggest remedies to existing difficulties. Whitworth's exhibits at the Great Exhibition of 1851 had won his international acclaim, and as the nation's most outstanding engineer and machine tool manufacturer it was natural that he should be selected to investigate the standardization and mass-production possibilites of the Enfield works.

In 1854 Joseph Whitworth was not well acquainted with the manufacture of small arms, and in order to familiarize himself with the processes and practices involved he visited most of England's leading gunmakers. His basic conclusion from these visits was that gunmakers proceeded upon little if any actual proven theories, but rather from hit-and-miss experiments and methods learned during their apprenticeships. From this it followed that there was no rational explanation for the irregularities in the performance of the Pattern 1853 Enfield; before Whitworth would undertake to criticize this particular weapon he felt it necessary to establish in his own mind just what the perfect form of rifled small arm should be. From the experiments he conducted to find the answer to this question came the Whitworth rifle and the heavy ordnance so well known, at least in name, to arms collectors today.

It appeared to Whitworth that both the caliber and barrel dimensions of the Pattern 1953 Enfield had been chosen by arbitrary and unscientific methods. It was obvious to him as well that the problems encountered in its performance were due to inaccuracies in the interior of the barrels, possibly even in their basic construction. Whitworth explained his views to the government and offered, if the government would pay his expenses, to conduct a series of tests to determine the best form of small arm for military service. He refused to accept any salary for his work.

In the early stages of his work, Whitworth experimented with a wide variety of rifling twists, calibers, barrel lengths and metals, reaching such extremes as a 20-inch barrel with a twist of one turn in one inch. Whitworth had apparently not examined any other than the standard Enfield 577-caliber barrels, but had seen a polygonally-rifled barrel designed by Isabard Brunel and constructed by Westley Richards. Richards and Whitworth worked closely together during the early stages of Whitworth's work, and much of Whitworth's knowledge of the firearms trade must have been gained from Westley Richards. It was not until the end of 1856 that Whitworth appears to have settled on a design for his rifle; its first official tests came in April, 1857. From

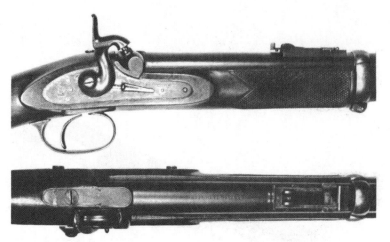

Fig. 3. Military Target Rifle, breech closeup. Note the Enfield style snail, with underside overhanging lockplate, Whitworth trademark on tail of plate, sliding safety bolt and typical WHITWORTH marking above bolt. The rear sight is an early pattern before the rack-and-pinion type was adopted; many of this model are found refitted with a rack-and-pinion sight of an early type. Hammer, trigger guard and trigger, checkering pattern and form of breech (note patent breech but absence of hook breech) are typical of this model. Courtesy E.J. Burton.

this time onwards, the now-familiar hexagonal bore, with a twist of one turn in 20 inches, seems to have been the standard in Whitworth rifles. The tests of 1857 and 1858 proved the far superior accuracy of Whitworth's system against that of the 577 Enfield (which were rifled with three lands and grooves having a twist of one turn in 78 inches, with the depth of rifling gradually decreasing from the breech to the muzzle), but as accuracy was but one of the criteria to be considered in the acceptance of any system for military use, the basic issues were far from solved. Such questions as fouling, tendency to miss-fire, ease of handling, manufacture of ammunition suitable for military conditions, costs of manufacturing — all seemed to create some doubts in the minds of the investigating committee members. In addition, a small-bore Enfield had performed very nearly as well as the Whitworth rifle, and there was some question whether Whitworth's system might be the only answer.

The Crimean War had been weathered, the national emergency were over, and thoughts of economy were again uppermost in the minds of the government. By 1859 the whole project had been narrowed down to two basic problems. First, would other manufacturers be able to produce the standard of precision required to manufacture Whitworth rifles in some future emergency, if they were to be produced on a large scale? Secondly, Whitworth still asked £10 per rifle for 1,000 or 1,200 rifles, while the Pattern 1853 rifle musket cost £3.5.1 from contractors or £1.19.8 from Enfield ($48.00 for the Whitworth as against $15.44 and $8.48 for the

Pattern 1853 Enfield). Economy won the day and the question of Whitworth vs. Enfield was dropped. It was at this point that Whitworth turned his energies to heavy ordnance rifled upon his hexagonal principle. During the next 5 years a nationwide controversy developed as to the comparative merits of the Whitworth and Armstrong systems. During the Civil War the Confederacy purchased a number of Whitworth field guns and naval cannons in breech-loading and muzzle-loading styles; the Confederate ironclad ram *Stonewall* was armed with two of Whitworth's heavy naval guns.

Concurrently with the military experiments being conducted on behalf of the government, an increased interest in rifle shooting was developing among civilians, culminating in what was termed the "Volunteer Movement." The political friction between England and France present in the 1850s had increased after the conclusion of the Crimean War (in which the two countries had been allied) largely because of the expansionist tendencies of Napoleon III, and the discovery that the Orsini bomb plot against Napoleon had been planned and developed in England. The always invasion-conscious British public, egged on by a ubiquitous and inflammatory press, increasingly clamored for protective measures against possible French invasion.

In 1859 the parliamentary act authorizing the raising and equipping of volunteer corps to fight on English soil, in case of invasion — which had been passed in the Napoleonic Wars period — was regenerated. A rapid rise in the number of rifle companies throughout England resulted.

As of January 1st, 1860, one hundred per cent of such troops would be equipped at government expense if the necessary conditions were met. It soon became obvious that a national organization devoted to the development of accurate rifle shooting was highly desirable, and the National Rifle Association of Great Britain came into being in November, 1859. The first meeting was held at the beginning of July, 1860.

First Whitworths

At this meeting Queen Victoria fired the opening shot with a Whitworth rifle mounted on a rest. For the next 8 years the Whitworth rifle, in various models, was always among the top contenders for honors at British rifle matches.

Aside from the rifles themselves, the initiative of Joseph Whitworth in creating a superbly accurate rifle (for its time) spurred other gunmakers and inventors into action. The result was a profusion of rifling systems, mostly based on the basic Whitworth principles of a 451-caliber bore with a twist of one turn in 20 inches, firing a 530-gr. bullet. The fact that a number of these systems ultimately succeeded in out-shooting the Whitworth in competition does not detract from the significance of Whitworth's contribution in establishing the basic knowledge, and in taking the first positive steps towards a formerly un-thought of degree of both range and accuracy in military and civilian marksmanship.

In the spring of 1860 experimental rifles were again ordered from Whitworth, but the trials were not actually held until mid-1861. Further trials were held in 1862, and both proved beyond any doubt the superiority of "small bore" (.451" as opposed to .577") weapons so far as accuracy was concerned. Other small bore rifles were tested during these trials, but Whitworth's proved the best of the lot. The Ordnance Select Committee, in charge of the trials, had stressed the importance of putting the rifles into the hands of troops to determine their performance under field conditions. It was with this factor in mind that 1,000 rifles were ordered in May, 1862. As these rifles gave no initial indications of the problems which later developed, a further 8,000 rifles of a slightly different pattern were ordered in 1863. These were issued on a trial basis to a number of British Army units in England and on foreign duty. Despite the official adoption of the Snider breech-loading system in 1865, many of these Whitworth muzzleloaders were still in the hands of troops as late as 1867. Whitworth rifles continued to be used in the firing for the Queen's Prize at Wimbledon through 1870.

To bring his rifling system to the broader attention of the general shooting public, Whitworth entered the commercial market in mid-1859, hoping that success among sportsmen and Volunteers would induce the government to take up the matter of his rifles again. The advent of the National Rifle Association was a Godsend to Whitworth insofar as his civilian market was concerned, for the majority of the prize rifles awarded at N.R.A. meetings for the remainder of the muzzle-loading era were Whitworths.

In 1860 a retailing company known as the Whitworth Rifle Company set up offices at 51, Sackville Street, Manchester. Shortly after receiving the order for 1,000 rifles in May, 1862 (it turned out that only a part of these rifles were produced by Whitworth, aside from the barrels), the firm name was changed to the Manchester Ordnance & Rifle Company, an obvious indication that Whitworth was now actively engaged in the production of cannon. By 1865 the addresses of the Manchester Ordnance & Rifle Company and Joseph Whitworth & Company are combined, indicating that the market in both rifles and heavy ordnance was sufficiently diminished that the operation could be combined under one roof. There is, in fact, considerable doubt that the small arms made with Whitworth's rifling were actually fabricated at any Whitworth works. The barrels were probably the only part of the rifles actually made by the Whitworth firm. In the case of the Pattern 1863 Short Rifles Whitworth made but 1,803 of the 8,203 barrels supplied.

The Various Models

The rapid rise of the Volunteer movement and Whitworth's desire to keep his rifling system before the eyes of military men brought about the introduction of what was to become the most common of non-military Whitworths — the *military target rifle*. The earliest form of this rifle made its appearance in the summer of 1859, but it would seem that by the time of the formation of the National Rifle Association, and its first meeting in July of 1860, certain modifications and improvements had taken place to produce the rifle in its best-known form (figs. 1, 2 and 3). This is the rifle used in most small bore competitions at Wimbledon, and the rifle which was presented to Queen's Prize winners and numerous runners-up, as well as for other competitions. Many were presented by various organizations, both

civil and military, to members of Volunteer units who had won local or regional competitions. Whitworth thus received a large measure of "free" advertising through the Kingdom.

In basic outline the military target rifle resembles the Pattern 1853 Enfield, but the refinements are legion and the contours more elegant. Some early examples have 33-inch barrels, presumably to conform more closely to the Pattern 1860 Short Rifle, then the standard issue for rifle companies and for sergeants of line regiments. Three barrel bands of normal Enfield clamping pattern hold the barrel to the full length forearm. The steel ram-road is similar to the Enfield, having a slotted head but lacking the concentric rings of the Enfield. Most rifles have a patent breech, but there is no false breech; the tang screw must be removed to take the barrel from the stock. The patent breech is recessed on the left in the manner of contemporary sporting arms, but the tang and snail closely resemble the Enfield; the snail slightly overhangs the lockplate, and generally has borderline engraving (fig.

3). The lock-plate is of Enfield pattern but smaller, and the hammer is a compromise between the heavy military and lighter sporting patterns, generally having Enfield-pattern border engraving. There is a sliding safety bolt forward of the hammer, and two lock screws hold the lock to the stock; Enfield pattern screw cups support the screws on the left of the stock.

The stock is of dark walnut, some examples having fine contrasting colors. It is fitted with steel furniture throughout, consisting of a forearm cap of Enfield pattern, trigger guard similar to the Enfield, round capbox, and Enfield-pattern buttplate. Sling swivels are mounted on the upper barrel band and through the rear of the trigger guard strap. The wrist and forearm are checkered, the diamonds large and coarse compared to later models, but quite typical of contemporary Volunteer rifles. The furniture, excepting the color case-hardened cap-box, is heat-blued.

The sights of the military target rifle present something of a confusing study to the arms collector. As they went from the works the sights were relatively plain,

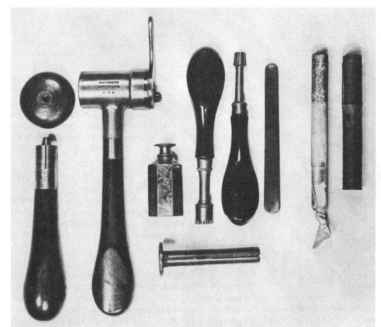

Fig. 4. Typical Whitworth accessories found with military target rifles. Left to right — wooden knob (above) screws onto steel ramrod to aid in loading; base plug for conical bronze one-piece bullet mould; bullet mould with typical Whitworth markings; octagonal steel oil bottle; nipple cleaner; hammer face cleaner; torque bar which fits through slot in head of rod to give a better grip when cleaning or extracting a ball; military Whitworth cartridge; Whitworth's Patent "trap door" cartridge, with military load of 70 grains of black powder and a 530-gr. bullet. Horizontal item at bottom center is hollow bore protector, used when loading and cleaning. Courtesy E.J. Burton.

but because they were the "first of the breed" they later underwent, in many cases, considerable alteration at the hands of not only gunsmith and individual owners, but from the Whitworth firm itself. The original rear sight consisted of a long leaf with platinum-lined notch and slide, graduated to 4° on the left side and 1,000 yards on the right side, both on the bottom of the leaf. There were a number of minor variations in the sight bed; some were virtually flat, or with very slight elevators on either side, while others have one or two distinct steps to the elevators. The front sight was a windage-adjustable blade, a small screw in the center of the front face of the sight base allowing for adjustment.

The great popularity of the Whit-worth rifle and its extensive use at N.R.A. meetings led shortly to a refinement of the sighting equipment, and a hooded front sight with pin-ball post replacing the earlier blade. The famous "rack & pinion" rear sight so often seen on Whitworth rifles was patented by Whitworth and Hulse on August 2, 1861, along with a hooded front sight and a combination tool. Whether the sights were actually being produced before the patent was taken out is questionable, but by 1862 the Whit-worth Rifle Company was notifying dealers that they would re-equip any of their rifles with the new "Patent Sights," re-finish the barrel, and shoot the barrel with the new sights, for £3,10.0 ($16.80 in 1860 dollars). A large number of the military target rifles are found with this new set of sights, which were fitted at the Whitworth works (or at the works of some gunmakers hired

by Whitworth to do the work) in 1862. The first form of hooded windgauge front sight did not have interchangeable discs, but was fitted with the pin-ball post only. The rack & pinion rear sight went through a number of variations in construction, all rather minor and of purely technical interest, but the military target rifles were fitted with the first type, which is slightly more square in appearance and wider than the suceeding types.

The third variation in the sighting equipment of the military target rifle was the fitting of a tang sight. Originally this did not form a part of the sighting equipment, but with the introduction of finer sights on Whitworth rifles, there apparently arose a desire on the part of owners of earlier rifles to have this refinement. In view of the complete lack of uniformity

Fig. 5. Early Sporting Rifle with spur guard and 30 barrel. "Cape" rear sight, windage-adjustable "Express" front sights are typical, as are stock, lock and breech design. First appearing in 1860, these rifles were offered in light- and heavyweight (one pound difference) models, and were made in limited numbers through the muzzle-loading period. They retailed for £35 cased complete with accessories. Courtesy K. T. Brown.

Fig. 6. Whitworth Match Rifle, caliber 451, 36 barrel with "Rigby flats" at breech. Patent breech, hook breech. Whitworth's patent wind gauge front sight, rack-and-pinion rear barrel sight and Vernier tang sight. Completely typical of this model, and the forerunner of the familiar "Creedmoor" match rifles of the 1870s. This type of rifle (which came cased and complete) represents the zenith of Whitworth rifle production as regards precision shooting in all its particulars, although by the time this model appeared in 1862 Whitworth's rifling system was already being seriously challenged by those of Alexander Henry, William Metford and the Rigbys. Courtesy H. Taylor.

in the sight bases which were used to accomplish this end, it is believed that the rifles were taken to various gun-makers who ordered the sight stems from Whitworth and fitted them with their own base design (or that of the owner if he were technically inclined). These variously took the form of extended flat planes made of wood; of extensions of the tang strap which were dovetailed to receive the small base and stem, and windage adjustable by means of a drift and mallet; and various designs of bases being let into the wood directly.

As with most English tang sights, the Whitworth sight base had no tension spring; the stem was held upright by a small stud on its bottom and by increasing the tension of the pivot screw.

Many of this model were furnished cased (figs. 1, 2 and 4). Some of these exhibit a wide variety of implements of which only a certain number can be considered standard. Such standard equipment would include a leather-covered, German-silver topped powder flask, bronze bullet mould for a cylindro-conoidal 530-gr. paper-patched bullet, powder charger for 70 or 85 grains, hammer-face and nipple cleaners, combination tool, octagonal steel oil bottle, leather sling, a tin of caps, a wooden handled rod for pushing bullets out of the mould, instructions for loading and cleaning the rifle, jags and mops for barrel cleaning, grease wads (generally hexagonal in form), and a wooden knob with threaded brass center which screwed onto the end of the ramrod to aid in loading, spare platinum-lined nipples and a screwdriver. Items which may be considered as optional in Whitworth cased sets of this and other models would include a bullet swage, a lock brush, packets of hexagonal bullets, a brass muzzle protector for use in loading; a torque bar which fitted through the slotted head of the ramrod to aid in cleaning the barrel, removing bullets when they had been seated without powder, "bad" loads, and so forth; powder chargers which screw on the end of the ramrod to place the entire charge in the breech, patch paper, patent cartridges, mainspring vise, a ball puller and a tompion or muzzle stopper. Sporting and purely target models also included loading rods and short starters, and a double-ended rod having at one end a Whit-worth hexagonal scraper and at the other a brass charger to breech-position the entire powder charge.

The military target rifle sold for £20 ($96 in 1860 dollars) or £25 ($120 in 1860 dollars) cased complete. The cases were of oak, with varnished finish in natural color, and were unlined (figs. 1 and 2).

Concurrently with the introduction of the military target rifle, Withworth made his bid for the deer-stalking market with the introduction of a Sporting Rifle in the summer of 1859. They appear to have enjoyed but limited sale right through to 1866, judging from a study of serial numbers and markings. Despite the relatively long period of production — so far as Whitworth rifles are concerned — these sporting rifles are among the rarest of Whitworths (aside from the experimental models), since Whitworth production seems to have been very largely taken up with military and semi-military style rifles. This emphasis is, of course, quite nat-ural, since it was the military authorities that Whitworth was primarily interested in impressing.

Whitworth's sporting rifles were very similar to the usual British sporting rifles of the mid-19th century except that they were made only with full round barrels rather than the normal octagon type. They are fitted with a hook or break-off breech, a patent breech design internally, and the snail has a platinum plug. The barrels are blued, the patent breech color case-hardened. The early sporters have 30" barrels, while later rifles have varying lengths down to 28½ inches; 30 inches appears to have been the standard. Another feature typical of the early sporting rifles is the use of a spur trigger guard (fig. 5) rather than a pistol grip stock; the latter feature is found on a few of the later sporting rifles. The furniture, of blued steel, is of typical shotgun pattern, and finally engraved with scroll work and animals. The round capbox is typical. Stocks were of highly polished fine-grained walnut often showing beautiful color contrasts.

The sights of the sporting rifle as they left the works consisted of a long bead "express" front sight which was windage adjustable, and a "Cape" style leaf rear sight having separate leaves folding into the base for 100 and 200 yards, plus a long leaf, with a slide hinged forward of the short leaves, for 300, 400 and 500 yards.

Sporting rifles appear to have been sold only as complete cased sets, as there is no provision for a ramrod on the pro-duction model. This item was included in the set and carried by the gentle-man-sportsman's keeper or bearer. The rifles were offered in "heavy" and "light" weights, 7½ and 6½ pounds respectively. A complete cased outfit consisting of the rifle, "mahogany case, with leather covering … bullet mould, powder flask, 300 rounds of ammunition and a full set of apparatus," sold for £35 ($168 in 1860 U.S. dollars) in either weight.

The continuing growth in popularity of rifle shooting, and the expanding program of the National Rifle Association encouraged Whitworth to further refine and upgrade the appearance of his military target rifles, and the result was the semi-military rifle (fig. 5a), combination of military and sporting features, designed for long range target shooting.

These were first marketed in the late fall of 1861; they appear from the first to have been but a transitional piece. In terms of serial numbers these rifles occur for a brief period just prior to the appearance of the military target rifles with 36" barrels and Baddeley bands. They ceased to be produced about the time the Match Rifle was introduced in the spring of 1862. In point of sales, however, it appears that the supply of military target rifles continued to be sold concurrently with the semi-military rifle. All of the latter type thus far noted are highly finished arms, all having at least some scroll and floral engraving on the locks and mounts, and very fine checkering. Although obviously

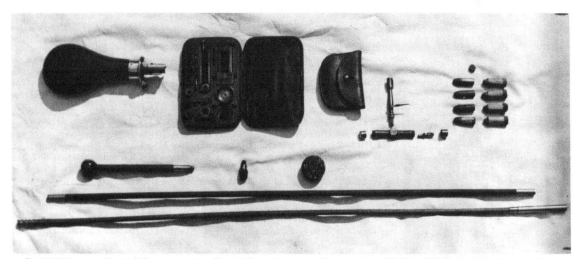

Fig. 7. Whitworth Match Rifle accessories. From left — Patent-top leather covered flask calibrated for two brands of powder; sight case holding wind gauge front, rack-and-pinion rear, and Vernier tang sights, with 8 interchangeable front sight discs, sight-adjusting key, two peep cups (one missing); wallet for small spare parts; combination tool, disassembled; Whitworth hexagonal bullets in various stages from naked to fully cased with wads attached; short starter; hexagonal bore mop; cap tin; loading-cleaning rod; double-ended rod with Whitworth hexagonal scraper on left and charger for placing powder in breech of barrel on right. Courtesy H. Taylor.

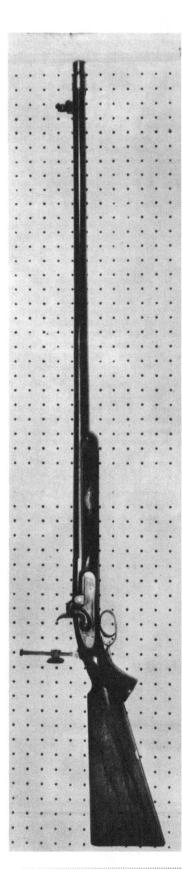

intended as presentation-grade weapons, only a very few of them carry inscriptions or plaques.

The barrel of the semi-military rifle, 36 inches long rather than the 33 inches of the earlier model, is fitted with a sporting pattern breech having three "Rigby" flats and a hook breech. The side of the snail has a platinum plug, and the left side of the patent breech is recessed deeply as on other high-grade sporting arms of the period. The barrel is held to the full length stock with three barrel bands of the type patented by Major J.F.L. Baddeley, R.A., on May 10th, 1861. These bands have smooth outer contours with the screw heads recessed into the band to avoid catching on clothing. The military form of steel ramrod is retained, but of the usual Enfield pattern having both a slotted head and concentric rings, reduced in size to fit 45 caliber. The stock tip remains of the Enfield pattern, but here the military features of the rifle end; the remainder are of a sporting design.

The lock of the semi-military rifle is of the same pattern as the sporting rifle (fig. 5a), but the engraving is not quite as lavish on most examples known. The sliding safety bolt is forward of the hammer, and there is only one lock screw, having a plain circular cup supporting it on the left side of the stock. The tumbler is detented, and rifle rather than musket nipples are used. Those examples known bear the mark WITHWORTH RIFLE CO MANCHESTER on the lower edge of the plate.

The stock is of fine-grained walnut with a lighter color and better contrast than previous models, with a highly polished oil-varnish finish. The checkering is of fine quality and execution. The fore-end is longer between the lock and lover barrel band and displays a greater expanse

of checkering. The furniture is heat-blued throughout and, excepting the stock tip, is of the type found on sporting rifles of the period. The trigger guard has a long checkered spur which acts as a pistol grip, the forward finial being in the form of a round pineapple. The buttplate has a short ornamental top tang, but the two screws securing it to the stock are both on the face of the plate. The capbox is omitted on this model, as on the majority of 36-inch barreled military target rifles.

The sights of this model are virtually identical with those of the match rifle which succeeded it, except that not all semi-military rifles are fitted for tang sights. The front sight, of the Whitworth patent variety, was furnished with at least 8 interchangeable discs of varying types. It was adjustable for windage, a thumb screw entering from the right side. One variation has the discs removable by the use of another thumb screw, while the other makes use of a square key fitting into a flush screw. The windage adjustment screw is also found in these two styles. The rear sight is of rack and pinion style. When a tang sight is present it is of the standard type found on the match rifle (fig. 6).

Judging from the serial numbers there were probably less than 100 of the semi-military rifles produced before Whitworth, in the spring of 1862, abandoned the military style with the introduction of his match rifle. The style of this rifle is what is generally known in the United States as a "Creed-moor" rifle, as it is identical in profile to the Rigby rifles used by the Irish teams at the International Matches held at Creedmoor, New York, beginning in 1874.

The match rifle has a 36-inch full round barrel, with the same patent breech

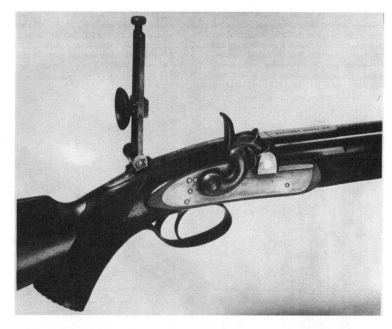

Fig. 8. Probably made in the mid- or late 1860s, the 36" round barrel having the three barrel flats usually found on Rigby target rifles. The center or top flat is engraved METFORD'S PATENT 948. GEORGE GIBBS, 29, CORN STREET, BRISTOL, is engraved ahead of the Metford markings, on the top center of the barrel. The case-colored lockplate is marked GEORGE GIBBS. The nipple boss carries a platinum plug. • The Gibbs serial number, 9764, appears on the trigger guard rear tang. • The Vernier tang sight is calibrated to 4 degrees, in increments of 10 minutes, with **Rad. 37.8** (for the distance between this sight and the front sight) hand engraved on a strip of platinum inlaid into one side of the staff. The front sight is adjustable for windage, takes various discs. • The hard rubber grip cap is fluted in a sunburst design, the hard rubber buttplate grooved crosswise. The fore-end tip is of buffalo horn. • The muzzle has a small pin at its top to take the bayonet-locking slot of the 1¾ long false muzzle. The false muzzle, not common on British match rifles, is rifled with 5 lands, these about the width of the grooves, right hand twist of about one in 30 . This is not Metford's celebrated segmental rifling, but rather his first patented system. It looks much like modern rifling — aside from land width. • The rifle weighs an even 9 lbs. without false muzzle. John Amber's coll.

design and lock as on the semi-military rifle (fig. 6). There is no provision for a ramrod, and the barrel is held to the half-stock by a single wedge or key surrounded by oval steel escutcheons on both sides of the stock. The stock tip is of black horn, as is the grip cap. There is no capbox. The stock is of full pistol grip type, with finely checkered wrist and fore-end. There is an initial plate set into the stock to the rear of the pistol grip. The wood used on match rifles is dark and straight-grained, as was typical on target arms to avoid possible warping.

The sights (fig. 7) consist of the Whitworth patent windgauge front sight, on many rifles the rack and pinion rear barrel sight, and the Whitworth Vernier tang sight. A rear barrel sight is not present on all rifles of this model.

Match rifles were furnished fully cased with loading and cleaning accessories and ammunition. Figs. 6 and 7 show an unusually complete outfit in superb condition. It should be noted that such articles as powder flasks and combination tools and, in fact, all accessories save the bullet moulds (which were not included in target outfits since extruded bullets were considered necessary to first-class accuracy at long range), were not made by Whitworths but were purchased from various contractors in such implements. The great majority are very similar to one another and it is obvious that these tools

were purchased in quantity batches, and that the same contractors were patronized for succeeding purchases; it is not correct, however, to expect one set of implements to be identical to those in another similar cased set. Target Rifles are the only sets in which packets of patched hexagonal bullets should be considered standard rather than optional equipment.

Fig. 8 shows a fine match rifle made by one of Whitworth's chief rivals in the later period. The Gibbs-Metford rifle pictured is described in detail in the caption accompanying it.

At this point in the chronological examination of the various Whitworth models we turn from the best quality target rifle and revert to an issue military rifle: the Pattern 1862 Whitworth Rifle. It was for this rifle that an order of 1,000 stand was placed in May, 1862, but from existing examples it is clear that Whitworth did not manufacture anything close to the total numbers, he may not even have supplied all of the barrels. This rifle is, in fact, correctly termed an *En-field-Whitworth*, as they were set up at the Royal Small Arms Factory at Enfield Lock. There are, however, a number of examples known with commercial markings, (fig. 9) which differ from the issue piece in minor aspects.

The *Pattern 1862 Whitworth* has a 36-inch iron barrel of the usual 451-caliber and rifling characteristics, the barrel being secured by three Bad-deley-pattern barrel bands. As it was made at Enfield, all parts are interchangeable, and in addition all parts excepting the ramrod, stock tip and two forward barrel bands will interchange with the *Pattern 1860 Short*

Rifle (so far as lock and furniture are concerned). The Pattern 1862 was intended to conform as closely as possible to the issue *Pattern 1853 Rifle Musket*, and the barrel takes the same bayonet. The front sight is of similar design, while the rear sight is basically similar but adapted for the use of either cylindrical or hexagonal bullets, the latter graduations extending for another 100 yards.

These rifles apparently met with considerable approval upon being issued to various regiments, and it was decided to equip a larger number of troops with the small bore rifle for extensive trials. The result was the *Pattern 1863 Whitworth Short Rifle*. It was decided to use steel rather than iron for the barrels of this model, and in order to keep the weight within limits the barrel length was reduced to 33 inches, thus making it officially a "Short Rifle" even though it was fitted with three barrel bands rather than the normal two. The sword bayonet fastens to the upper barrel band rather than to a standard on the barrel, as it was considered too difficult to weld a sword bar to a steel barrel. This same welding problem caused the snail to be made integral with the barrel, rather than separately as was the normal practice when using iron barrels.

The *Pattern 1863 Whitworth Short Rifle* (fig. 10) is again an "Enfield-Whitworth" even though Whitworth actually finished up 100 of these rifles at Manchester. The steel barrels were obtained from four different contractors, including Whitworth, who supplied 1,497 barrels which bore normal Whitworth serial numbers beneath the barrel as well as the date of setting up.

Fig. 9. Pattern 1862 Whitworth military rifle, a prototype made at Manchester with commercial markings and non-standard trigger guard. The issue model, of which 1,000 were made at Enfield, has normal Enfield trigger guard and lock markings. Standard Enfield pattern ramrod. 36" barrel with three Baddeley barrel bands. Tower of London collection, British Crown copyright.

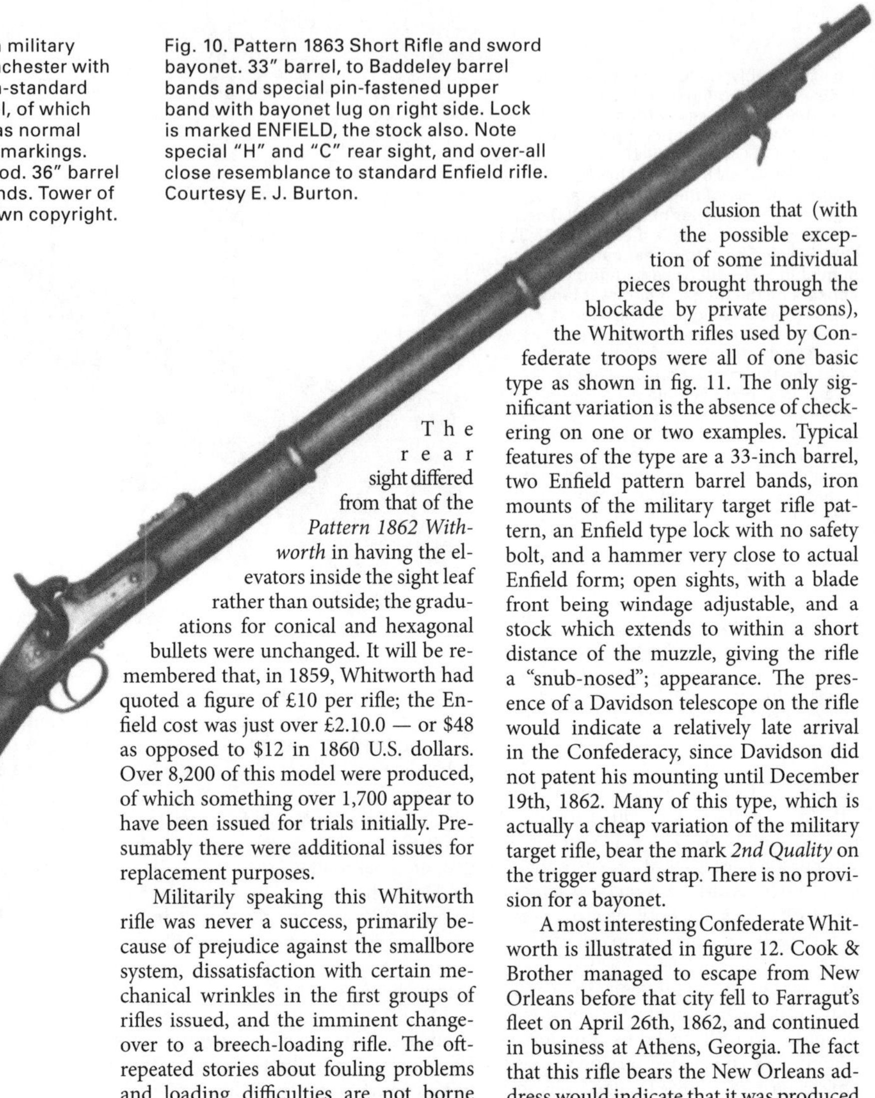

Fig. 10. Pattern 1863 Short Rifle and sword bayonet. 33" barrel, to Baddeley barrel bands and special pin-fastened upper band with bayonet lug on right side. Lock is marked ENFIELD, the stock also. Note special "H" and "C" rear sight, and over-all close resemblance to standard Enfield rifle. Courtesy E. J. Burton.

The rear sight differed from that of the *Pattern 1862 Whitworth* in having the elevators inside the sight leaf rather than outside; the graduations for conical and hexagonal bullets were unchanged. It will be remembered that, in 1859, Whitworth had quoted a figure of £10 per rifle; the Enfield cost was just over £2.10.0 — or $48 as opposed to $12 in 1860 U.S. dollars. Over 8,200 of this model were produced, of which something over 1,700 appear to have been issued for trials initially. Presumably there were additional issues for replacement purposes.

Militarily speaking this Whitworth rifle was never a success, primarily because of prejudice against the smallbore system, dissatisfaction with certain mechanical wrinkles in the first groups of rifles issued, and the imminent changeover to a breech-loading rifle. The oft-repeated stories about fouling problems and loading difficulties are not borne out by the official reports on the trials of these rifles. Aside from obviously prejudiced exceptions the rifles were highly praised on these points from such unlikely areas as India and South Africa. It does not appear that hexagonal ammunition was ever issued in quantity with the military rifles, and in general the troops got on well with them. However, their marksmanship does not appear to have markedly improved over that obtaining with the 577 En-fields, which is rather surprising.

The Confederate Whitworth

The actual *extent* to which Whitworth rifles were used by Confederate troops during the Civil War is still conjectural, but examination of those rifles known to have been used or at least owned by Confederate personnel, and consideration of their serial numbers, has led to the con-clusion that (with the possible exception of some individual pieces brought through the blockade by private persons), the Whitworth rifles used by Confederate troops were all of one basic type as shown in fig. 11. The only significant variation is the absence of checkering on one or two examples. Typical features of the type are a 33-inch barrel, two Enfield pattern barrel bands, iron mounts of the military target rifle pattern, an Enfield type lock with no safety bolt, and a hammer very close to actual Enfield form; open sights, with a blade front being windage adjustable, and a stock which extends to within a short distance of the muzzle, giving the rifle a "snub-nosed"; appearance. The presence of a Davidson telescope on the rifle would indicate a relatively late arrival in the Confederacy, since Davidson did not patent his mounting until December 19th, 1862. Many of this type, which is actually a cheap variation of the military target rifle, bear the mark *2nd Quality* on the trigger guard strap. There is no provision for a bayonet.

A most interesting Confederate Whitworth is illustrated in figure 12. Cook & Brother managed to escape from New Orleans before that city fell to Farragut's fleet on April 26th, 1862, and continued in business at Athens, Georgia. The fact that this rifle bears the New Orleans address would indicate that it was produced and purchased prior to the fall of New Orleans to Federal forces; this, coupled with the high serial number for the Confederate type (C575) indicates that most of the Whitworth rifles used by the Confederates were manufactured prior to the spring of 1862 — wwhich coincides neatly with already established serial ranges and dates. The rifle itself is typical of the type, but it lacks the checkering found on the majority of this pattern.

Later Production

Taken as a whole, civilian Whitworth rifle production tapered off sharply after 1862; while a steady trickle of match rifles and sporting rifles appears to have been turned out during the period 1862–1865, the major part of Whitworth's efforts during this period seems to have been devoted to the production of heavy ordnance, government trials of his rifling system in both ordnance and small arms, and his machine-tool business. Small arms production as such seems to have been secondary to those other considerations. It is, however, during this later period that some of the most interesting of Whitworth's rifles, including the 30-caliber sporting rifle, 568-caliber semi-military rifle, and double-barreled sporting rifle were made, all on a very limited basis which might reasonably be called — with the possible exception of the double barreled rifles — experimental production.

The single barreled sporting rifles produced in this later period generally have full pistol grip stocks, as opposed to the earlier rifles with spur trigger guards, and some of the later rifles lack capboxes.

The double-barreled sporting rifles generally have barrels varying from 24 inches to 28 inches, the majority being about 26 inches long. The barrel group is one piece of steel, into which both bores have been drilled, a feature which Whitworth patented in June, 1857. The half-length stocks have a full pistol grip, two pipes for the ramrod, no capbox, and a black horn cap on the pistol grip. The low bead express front sights have windage adjustment, while the rear sights use a series of flip-up leaves for 100 to 500 yards. The locks have sliding safety bolts forward of the hammers.

Whitworth Production and Serial Numbers

If it is accepted that there are no significant gaps in the indicated serial number ranges of Whitworth rifles, the total number produced with commercial markings would be about 5,000 of all styles, including the early rifles and BSA-marked rifles with Whit-worth-serialed barrels, but excluding the greater part of 1,000 *Pattern 1862 Military Rifles* and all but 1,600 of the 8,200 *Pattern 1863 Short Rifles*; both of these were assembled at Enfield and bear Enfield marks. If these last are included, a grand total of approximately 13,400 Whitworth muzzle loading rifles were

produced from all sources. Those rifles produced under license from Whitworth by such makers as Bissell, Beasley Brothers, and McCririck — which did purport to be honest imitations of Whitworth's rifling — are not included, and would increase the total somewhat.

From a study of existing rifles and fragmentary records, it appears that the serial numbering of Whitworth rifles from their first production in 1857 through the end of the muzzle-loading era and into the breech-loading period proceeded on a regular chronological basis. Having commenced with the number 1, the initial series continued through to 1,000, and then re-commenced with a letter prefix and proceeded through a series of these prefixes as follows:

1 — 1000: first production, 1857 through mid-1860.

B1 — B999: mid-1860 through late 1861.

C1 — C999: late 1861 through mid-1862. If gaps exist it will be in this series.

D1 — D999: spring 1862 to early 1863.

E1 — E999: early 1863 into mid-1864, primarily Pattern 1863 Military Rifles.

F1 — F700: mid-1864 through 1865; after F700 some breechloaders appear in regular numerical order. BSA-marked rifles also occur in this series.

Although there are still some unanswered questions regarding the connections between the Whitworth firm and the Birmingham Small Arms Company, it is clear that Whitworth offered to supply the gun trade with their barrels, in either finished or semifinished state, the latter being rifled only. In 1866 B.S.A. had used Whitworth barrels on their rifles for the N.R.A. and other standard Short Rifle patterns are known with B.S.A. markings and Whitworth serial-numbered barrels; in addition several match rifles of Whitworth profile and rifling have been reported with B.S.A. markings. It is obvious that B.S.A. purchased a batch of barrels from Whitworth in various states of com-

pletion and applied them to a small group of rifles of the several popular styles, in the 1865–66 period.

Whitworth Markings

With the conspicuous exception of those experimental rifles made throughout the entire production period of Whitworth muzzle-loading rifles, a study of the markings on the rifles relates directly to the serial numbers, and makes the assignment of a production date relatively easy. The early Whitworth rifles, made prior to 1860, bear a variety of non-standard marks, but as most of these include a date on the lockplate, the problem is greatly simplified. There are some individual instances, however, where the date is misleadingly late for the rest of the rifle. Lockplates on these early rifles generally bear the mark WHITWORTH PATENT, plus the serial number and Birmingham proof marks. The lockplate is marked, forward of the hammer and above the safety bolt WITHWORTH 1860 in two lines, or simply WHITWORTH. To the rear of the hammer appears the Whitworth crest (a crowned wheatsheaf), a W sometimes appearing beneath the wheatsheaf. The great majority of locks used on Whitworth rifles, even some of the plain military rifles, were made by Joseph Brazier of Wolverhampton; this is shown in some form generally on the inside of the lockplate. This may be his initials — JB or IB — to the most elaborate form noted so far: JOSEPH BRAZIER ASHES, the latter word being the name of Brazier's works.

At the very end of the production period for military target rifles (during which time the "Second Quality" rifles of this type were being made), the lock markings change to WHITWORTH RIFLE Co. MANCHESTER, with the Whitworth crest behind the hammer. This mark continues in use, along with the WHITWORTH PATENT marking on the breech of the barrel, through the period of the semi-military rifle and the early production of the match rifle.

Fig. 11. A Confederate Whitworth with 33 barrel. Except for the Davidson telescope, in typical side mount, the rifle seems a standard Confederate Whitworth in all features. Some are without checkering. Note snub-nosed appearance, two Enfield barrel bands, and early-pattern adjustable open sights. Enfield-pattern lock. Courtesy Tennessee State Museum.

The long Vernier-system folding tang sight is engraved on the rear of the staff, T. MURCOTT GUNMAKER (on one side), with 68 HAYMARKET LONDON N° 509 on the other.

The picture of the muzzle area shows the deep chamfering of the hexagonal rifling and the form of the slotted steel ramrod.

The 33″ barrel is full round, shows double Birmingham proof marks, the serial number 937, and is marked WHIT-WORTH PATENT at the top rear.

The walnut stock shows good figure, and is coarsely checkered at wrist and ahead of the lockplate. Weight of the Whit-worth rifle shown is 9½ pounds. John Amber's collection.

This 451 caliber Whitworth rifle was probably made in mid-1860 in view of the style of markings on the lockplate — WHIT-WORTH RIFLE C° MANCHESTER — and the serial number 937, without letter prefix, on the barrel. The rear barrel sight is of the Vernier type (double pinions and pinion bar are missing); the front sight dove-tail base once held a globe or hooded sight container with windage control knob, these also gone. These sights were added later, perhaps, by Whitworth, using the style patented by Whitworth and Hulse in late 1861. The right side of the rear barrel sight base is marked WHIT-WORTH/RIFLE Co. PATENT, while the top of the folding leaf is graduated on the right side 1 through 12 for 100 to 1200 yards; the left side is marked 10, 20, 30 and 40 for minutes of angle.

Shortly before the conclusion of the C-prefix serial number range, the lock marks change to MANCHESTER ORDNANCE & RIFLE Co.; and this marking continues through the D- and E- or F-prefix serial ranges, being found almost entirely on Pattern 1862 and 1863 military rifles, and on match rifles. The WHITWORTH PATENT mark on the breech of the barrel is retained, as is the Whitworth crest to the rear of the hammer, with and without the W beneath.

The Pattern 1862 Rifle and the Pattern 1863 Short Rifles made at Enfield bear standard Enfield markings for the period; the date is stamped over ENFIELD forward of the hammer, and a crowned *VR* on the tail of the lockplate. The barrel breeches of both military models bear the mark WHITWORTH PATENT. Where the barrels were supplied by the Whitworth firm a normal D-, E- or F- prefix serial number will appear on the underside of the barrel, generally accompanied by a figure such as 6/63, indicating that the rifle was set up in June, 1863.

In the later production period there was considerable mixing of markings, particularly on sights and sight parts. It is not uncommon that a rifle bearing MANCHESTER ORDNANCE & RIFLE CO. markings on the lock will have WHITWORTH RIFLE Co. on the sight base of the rear barrel sight and the stem of the Vernier tang sight. Similarly, a few rifles bearing THE WHITWORTH COMPANY LIMITED on the lockplate will have MANCHESTER ORDNANCE & RIFLE CO. on the above-mentioned sight parts.

In the final production period of Whitworth muzzle-loading rifles, the lock and barrel markings change almost entirely. The Whitworth crest is the only hold-over from previous patterns. The lock markings in the very high E-prefix serial range and throughout the F-prefix range read THE WHITWORTH COMPANY LIMITED, while the markings on the barrel are changed to WHITWORTH MANCHESTER in a circle or oval form. Some of the very last Whitworth muzzleloaders have J. WHITWORTH & Co. Manchester on the lockplate. As this was the firm name of Whitworth's machine tool business, this would seem to indicate nearly the end of Whitworth's production of firearms. An early breech-loading double rifle by Whitworth is marked in a similar manner, with the trade label of the case reading "JOSEPH WHITWORTH & COMPANY Patentees and Manufacturers of WHITWORTH RIFLED ORDNANCE, SMALL ARMS & SPORT-ING GUNS. General Machine and Tool Manufacturers. Works, Chorlton Street, Manchester, London Office, 28, Pall Mall, S.W." This rifle follows closely upon the serial number of the last muzzleloaders, and there is no evidence at present known to prove that production of breechloaders was long continued.

Whitworth's essay into the field of small arms seems never to have gone beyond the scientific and theoretical stage in his own mind. Commercially speaking very little was done by Whitworth to advance the sales of his rifles. Contemporary literature on the topic is noticeable by its scarcity, advertising nil. The success of this rifling system and the presentation of so many of his earlier rifles as prizes went far towards advertising, but quite clearly the rifles themselves were only a vehicle for his system, and a bid for government work. It is curious that while Whitworth's reputation for the introduction of standardization in mechanical and industrial processes is so great, his rifles were no better in construction than any other eminent gunmaker of the time: the parts will not interchange in any respect. Some sights will, by pure luck, fit more than one rifle, but lock parts and furniture all exhibit minor variations to a degree precluding interchangeability. Those military rifles made at Enfield upon Whitworth's system will, of course, interchange to conform to government standard, as will other Enfield rifles made after 1858. All major parts appear to have been obtained through the gun trade, Whitworth manufacturing the barrels only (even this point remains controversial), and the rifles were set up at one point following the normal procedures of the time. Although Whitworth took out several patents dealing with small arms and their appurtenances between 1854 and 1865, very few of the items covered appear to have been produced or used. Even implements peculiar to Whitworth rifles (such as the patent combination tool and hexagonal wad punches appear to have been made in lots by more than one contractor, and there are consequently very few accessories which can positively be labelled as "Whitworth tools," as will be noted in the illustrations.

The place of the Whitworth rifle in the history of rifled longarms and ballistic history is of paramount importance. Sir Joseph Whitworth (he was made a baronet in 1869), through analytical study which had never before been applied to the science of firearms design, demonstrated what could be done with elongated projectiles and precision machining; so well did he succeed in his efforts that he spurred the entire British gun trade into a period of experimental production

Fig. 12. Confederate-marked Whitworth, possibly unique. Made for Cook & Brother before they evacuated New Orleans in April, 1862. The crowned wheatsheaf on the lockplate's tail is a Whitworth trademark. Courtesy Weller & Duffy Ltd.

the likes of which had not been previously witnessed. As a result of the standards for accuracy set by Whitworth's rifles, other gunmakers tried system after system — there were at least two dozen, all primarily variations of the basic Whitworth system of 45-caliber barrels with a twist of one turn in 20 inches and polygonal rifling — to equal or excel the Whitworth. This led to the ultimate development of such systems as those of William Metford and Alexander Henry, which led the world not only in civilian shooting but in military marksmanship and long range accuracy well into the 20th century.

The writer wishes to express his sincere gratitude to Dr. C. H. Roads for permission to use certain facts and figures concerning the experimental and military Whitworth rifles, contained in his superb volume, *The British Soldier's Firearm, 1850–1864*, and to those gentlemen who kindly furnished photographs of rifles in their collections.

Spencer's Great 7-Shooter

■ Norman B. Wiltsey

REDSTROM

TWENTY-one-year-old Christopher Spencer was working at Colt's in Hartford, Connecticut, when the idea of his repeating rifle occurred to his fertile brain. The year was 1854. While several repeating rifles were already on the market, including Colt's revolving - cylinder percussion rifle, Spencer envisioned a repeating rifle of a daringly different type, one that used metallic cartridges. As there was no such rifle in existence at the time, he had nothing to work with but his keen imagination and the gunsmithing that was in his blood. His grandfather, Josiah Hollister, had been an armorer with the Continental Army in the Revolution and, over the years, had imbued young Chris with an enthusiasm for firearms — his skills, too, he had passed on to his eager grandson.

"Don't be afeared to take a chance on somethin' new," the ancient craftsman had told Chris. So, in 1855, Spencer followed his grandfather's advice, quitting Colt's and going to work at the Cheney Silk Mills in Manchester. Here he was invited to work out his "somethin' new" in the plant machine shop — on his own time, of course.

The going was painfully slow. Spencer's spare time for the next several years was spent in making drawings, then various parts of the projected rifle in wood. Finally he was ready to construct his model — Josiah Hollister would have been proud of it. It was so smoothly assembled that Chris and his employers were sure it would work; sure Chris had developed a weapon that would be invaluable to the nation as it moved inevitably toward the holocaust of approaching war.

Spencer's Patent

On March 6, 1860, U. S. Patent 27,393 was granted to C. M. Spencer. The exact wording of the application read as follows:

"My invention consists of an improved mode of locking the movable breech of a breech-loading firearm whereby it is easily opened and closed and very firmly

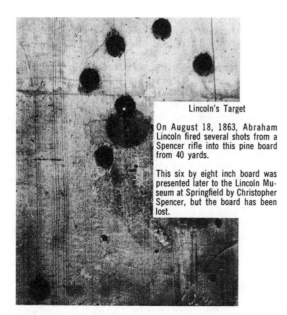

Lincoln's Target

On August 18, 1863, Abraham Lincoln fired several shots from a Spencer rifle into this pine board from 40 yards.

This six by eight inch board was presented later to the Lincoln Museum at Springfield by Christopher Spencer, but the board has been lost.

secured in place during the explosion of the charge. It also consists of certain contrivances for operating in combination with a movable breech for the purpose of withdrawing the cases of the exploded cartridges from the chamber of the barrel and for conducting new cartridges thereinto from a magazine located in the stock."

Briefly, Spencer's revolutionary new repeater was a 7-shot lever action arm; the tubular magazine with in the stock loaded from a trap in the buttplate. J. O. Buckeridge, author of the documentary story of the Spencer, *Lincoln's Choice* [1], describes the action in these words: "… The breech-block, a quarter-circle of steel with a groove on top, was hinged to the box-like frame by a screw at its lower front corner. Whenever the block was lowered by the lever attached to it, a heavy coil spring in the magazine pushed a cartridge onto the groove. The groove served as a cartridge carrier or track. The single motion of raising the lever eased the cartridge into the rear of the barrel and closed the breech. All that remained was to cock the hammer and pull the trigger. A flick of the lever opened the breech, ejected the empty, and lined up a fresh cartridge."

The Spencer's magazine, being within the stock, could not be damaged if the weapon was dropped or accidentally struck against a rock or tree — most important, neither could the copper-cased cartridges. The finger lever served also as a trigger guard; in the patent drawings, a spring-catch locked the lever against accidental opening, but Civil War Spencers do not have this feature. The early Hartford-made smaller Spencers, however, do have a spring that keeps the lever closed, though the patent drawing catch was not fitted. Aside from its unorthodox appearance, the main disadvantage of the new rifle was the awkward fact that it was slow to load — one cartridge at a time. This serious drawback was later corrected with the introduction of Blakeslee's patent cartridge box. This handy device carried ten tubes of cartridges, each tube holding seven cartridges and each tube loadable as a unit.

While Spencer's rifle-design was

ready for the Union forces at the outbreak of the Civil War in April of 1861, it still required refining and revision for mass production.* The problem was to convince the top brass of its practical value. Any inventor who has ever tried to convince high government officials of the value of anything really new can readily appreciate how great was Spencer's problem. Yet, insurmountable as it seemed, it had to be faced. Backed by his friend and partner Charles Cheney, Chris screwed his courage up to invade official Washington.

Gideon Welles, Secretary of the Navy, was a friend and neighbor of Cheney's. This fact helped set up an interview with the busy Secretary. The result was a test of Spencer's repeater at the Washington Navy Yard in June, 1861.

Spencer, as per the rigid conditions of the test, fired his rifle 250 times without cleaning the barrel, on two successive days. The weapon's calculated rate of fire was 15 shots per minute, but Chris exceeded his own estimate by getting off 21 rounds per minute. The Navy officers present were vastly impressed. Commander (later Rear Admiral) John A. Dahlgren, inventor of the famous Dahlgren naval cannon, was so enthusiastic over the Spencer that Capt. Andrew A. Harwood, then Chief of Navy Ordnance, ordered 700 Spencers.

Lincoln visited the Navy Yard the following day, but whether he saw the Spencer then or a short time later is not clear. Bruce (*Lincoln and the Tools of War*) says that Lincoln fired the Spencer carbine some short time later, emptying two magazines-ful into a piece of paper at a "few score feet." Lincoln had whittled a front sight out of wood, one he felt to be an improvement, and used this carved foresight on the Spencer that late evening in

---

[1] Harrisburg, Pa., 1956.

*Spencer had considerable difficulty in living up to his later contracts because of production problems; some of them, certainly, because Spencer himself pressed for numerous changes and modifications in his design.

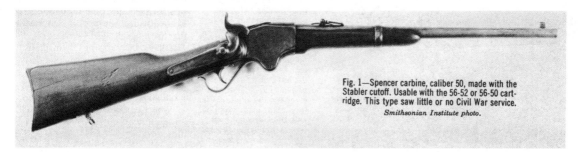

Fig. 1—Spencer carbine, caliber 50, made with the Stabler cutoff. Usable with the 56-52 or 56-50 cartridge. This type saw little or no Civil War service.
Smithsonian Institute photo.

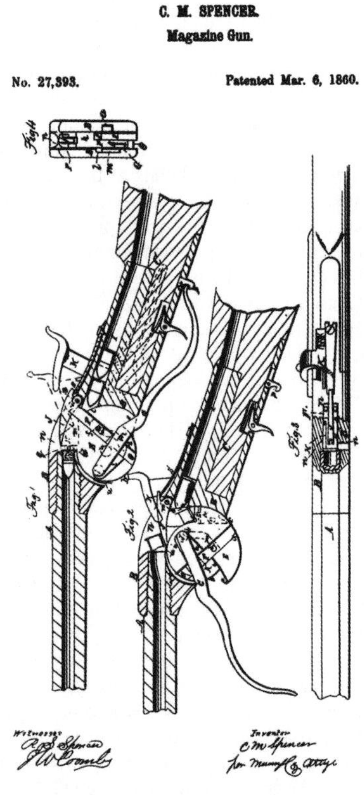

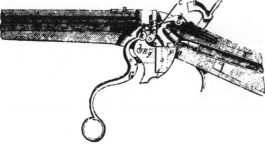

Fig. 2 — Spencer's original patent, No. 27,393, issued March 6, 1860. Note "M", sawblade cartridge extractor and "p", lever lock, neither of which is found on Civil War Spencers. The saw-edge extractor, however, is used on the early Hartford-made smaller Spencers.

Washington.

(It has not been possible to document this alleged earlier meeting of Lincoln and Spencer, or of Lincoln's shooting the Spencer in 1861. Spencer left no record of such a meeting, whereas he did, as we shall see, record in detail his later meeting with the President in 1863.)

Captain A. B. Dyer, of Army Ordnance (later Brig. Gen. Dyer and Chief of Ordnance), tested the new rifle further at

Fortress Monroe, Virginia, in August of 1861.

"I fired in all some 80 times," he reported. "The loaded piece was laid on the ground and covered well with sand to see what would be the effect of getting sand into the joints. No clogging or other injurious effects appeared to have been produced. The lock and lower part of the barrel were then covered with salt water and left exposed for 24 hours. The rifle was then loaded and fired without difficulty … I regard it as one of the very best breech-loading arms that I have ever seen."

The Small Spencers

Nowhere, however, in his report did Captain Dyer designate the caliber of this original Spencer. There is no doubt that it was handmade.

This rifle used in the Navy trials may well have been, in fact, *a 36 caliber rimfire*. Spencer's early rifles, made prior to his contract-arms production in Boston, were *smaller* (about three-fourths the scale of the Civil War weapon) and of 36 rimfire caliber. Three of these smaller Spencers are in the Winchester collection and another, serial number 13, is illustrated in fig. 5.

The small Spencers are marked C. M. SPENCER/HARTFORD, CT./PATd MAR. 6, 1860, in a style suggesting hand-stamping. Spencer lived in nearby South Manchester. The stamping on production Spencers of Boston manufacture is: SPENCER REPEATING-/RIFLE CO. BOSTON, MASS./PATd. MAR. 6, 1860.

These smaller 7-shooters are also distinguished by their cartridge extractor; on these models this is a saw-toothed segment riding in a slot in the bottom of the chamber.

As the lever is dropped, the rounded edge of the breechblock carries this saw-edge back, thus catching the rim of the cartridge and pulling it from the chamber.

Further evidence that these smaller 7-shooters were indeed the type used in early (1861) tests is given

Fig. 3 — This drawing of the Spencer 7-shooter, published in the "Scientific American" for January 25, 1862, shows modifications over Spencer's original patent design — note extractor (c) pivoted at the left side, the absence of a locking catch for the lever and the single-finger loop of the lever, identical with the loop on the 38 rimfire smaller Spencers.

by Capt. Dyer. He wrote, following his severe tests of the Spencer, that the only improvement he "could suggest was to make the extracting *ratchet* of tempered steel to reduce wear."*

Spencer Calibers

Most writers have designated the Spencer arms and ammunition used in the Civil *War* as caliber 56-52, but no less an authority than Col. B. R. Lewis (U.S.A., Ret'd.), author of *Small Arms and Ammunition in the United States Service*, had this to say in a letter to the editor dated January 4, 1961:

"Those dimensions (bullet size, bore diameter and chamber size) for the 56-56 Spencer were: .55", .52" and .564". The cartridge measured .56" and was nearly a straight case. Spencer used cal. 52 barrels because Sharps made them for him … There were other Sharps parts used in the early Spencers also."

"The 56-56 was *the* cartridge used in the Civil War Spencers. The 56-50 was the "ideal" cartridge worked up at Springfield but adopted too late to make much difference in the War, though a lot of that size was bought (and became surplus right after). About 1866-67 Spencer improved the 56-50 a bit by removing the excessive crimp and giving it a slight bottleneck. This was called the 56-52, and was interchangeable in 56-52 and 56-50 rifles, both of which had a .50" barrel diameter. Spencer never promoted the 56-50 commercially, and the Army never used the 56-52 cartridge. So — the CW Spencers were 56-56, the tail-end of the War M1865 Spencers the 56-50, and that size continuing in the postwar years with cal. 50 Spencers. The 56-52 was strictly a sporting cartridge but usable in the 56-50 arms."

Buckeridge mentions also that the Sharps Rifle Company "gave Spencer a barrel and a few common parts," to help out in the construction of his first model, but does not name the caliber. Philip B. Sharpe, in *The Rifle in America*, states that the original Spencer "was turned out in caliber .52 using the standard No. 56 rimfire cartridge which by 1867 was called the .56-56" and goes on to say: "This particular rifle in the hands of collectors (sic) is fitted with a Sharps rear sight bearing the markings R. F. Lawrence Pat. Feb. 15, 1859, and was probably made in the Sharps factory from Sharps rifle parts. It may have been one of his (Spencer's) experimental jobs before he got into actual production.

Mrs. Charles F. Taylor, daughter of the

*Bruce, op cit.

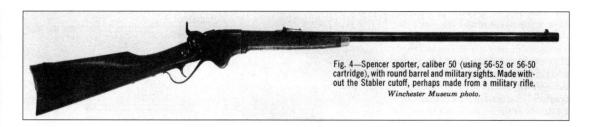

Fig. 4—Spencer sporter, caliber 50 (using 56-52 or 56-50 cartridge), with round barrel and military sights. Made without the Stabler cutoff, perhaps made from a military rifle.
Winchester Museum photo.

inventor, has no idea of the whereabouts of the original model and doubts that it exists. If it is indeed "in the hands of collectors," firearms historians would be grateful if the owner or owners of it would make public a detailed description of it, including the caliber.

Winston Churchill called the Civil War "the last gentleman's war." That it may have been, but it was also the first modern war. The camera, the telegraph, and — most important of all to the ruthless concept of total destruction of enemy manpower — the repeating rifle; all made their debut in this most costly in numbers of casualties of all American wars. Three repeating rifles were used in varying numbers by the Northern troops; the Colt, the Henry, and Chris Spencer's 7-shooter. Of the three, the Spencer was finally judged to be the best by both field and staff officers. But it did not win the confidence it merited from the top military brass until the war was half-over. The Navy accepted the 7-shooter at once, following the rigid tests given the weapon by Captain Dyer, but the great contract with the Army that Spencer had hoped for since he assembled his first successful model took two years to accomplish.

Ripley Rejects the Spencer

Just why this was so is clouded in mystery, but it is known that Brigadier General James W. Ripley, Chief of Army Ordnance until after Gettysburg, rejected the odd-looking repeater without giving it a second look. Ripley was "old Army" in every reactionary sense of the word, favoring muzzle-loaders for Federal troops and even advocating the use of smoothbores over the rifled musket. To Ripley's scornful refusal to see any merit in a weapon he scathingly termed a "newfangled jimcrack" may be credited the fact that Spencers did not get into the hands of Northern soldiers in large quantity until after his replacement as Chief of Army Ordnance.

Despite Ripley, Spencer sought the President's help, and on December 26,1861, Lincoln instructed General Ri-

 pley to order 10,000 Spencer rifles. The Spencer-Cheney group accepted this first sizable order on the last day of 1861.

Had the 7-shooter been adopted for general Army use earlier in 1861 — and furnished in really large numbers — there can be no doubt that the war would have been measurably shortened and many thousands of lives saved.

This bitter fact is even harder to to understand when one realizes that the Federal troops were outgunned by the small arms of the Confederacy all through the first two years of the war. Old flintlock muskets converted to percussion comprised the arms of whole Northern regiments. Many cavalry regiments were armed with nothing but sabers and huge smoothbore horse pistols. Conversely, the largely rural South sent troops into the field armed with rifles they had used since boyhood. These men, crack shots for the most part, represent one reason for the disproportionately large casualties suffered by the North in the early battles of the war. The other reason was the sheer timidity and inefficiency of Union generals. Disgusted with their leaders, doubly disgusted with muzzle-loading muskets that required nine separate, distinct and dangerously time-consuming operations to load and fire, it is a marvel that Northern troops did not desert in droves instead of driblets.

Gradually, armament conditions improved as the appalling Federal casualty lists soared. The Government bought 90,000 Sharps breechloaders, nearly 2000 Henry 16-shot repeaters, and a few thousand Colt's revolving percussion rifles and Berdan telescopic rifles. Bedeviled buyers from Army Ordnance went abroad to purchase 500,000 British Enfield muzzle-loaders, similar in effectiveness to the hopelessly outdated Springfields; picked up another half-million inferior Belgian and Austrian muskets. Small wonder that the angry Colonel of a New York regiment called his poorly trained city boys "poor, damned, doomed devils!" upon receipt of such wretched arms.

All this time, Chris Spencer and his

associates were frantically trying to get Army Ordnance experts to at least try his seven-shooter — to no avail! There was, however, one ray of hope to the young inventor. While the pompous "Colonel Blimps" of the War Department followed General Ripley's lead and professed to see no merit in the new repeater, the officers in the field exhibited keen interest. Colonel C. P. Kingsbury demonstrated the rifle to General-in-Chief McClellan in the fall of 1861, and subsequent tests by a special Army board appointed by McClellan — which included an officer from the Ordnance Department — brought a recommendation that the light Spencer carbine be issued "in limited numbers" to mounted troops in the field for trial. There is no evidence to indicate that the report got beyond the waste-basket in General Ripley's office.

But Spencer was not one to give up in face of repeated rebuffs. Working through his friend Cheney, Chris again enlisted the aid of the Secretary of the Navy, Gideon Welles. The Secretary, in turn, deftly tossed the ball to James G. Blaine, Speak-

Christopher Miner Spencer (June 20, 1833 - January 14, 1922) when he was 30 years old. Photo courtesy Mrs. C. F. Taylor (Vesta Spencer), daughter of the great inventor.

er of the House of Representatives and a New Englander himself. The result of the maneuvering was a meeting between Spencer, Blaine and Welles late in 1861, and an order by the Secretary of the Navy for 10,000 7-shooters *for the Army!* Obviously Secretary Welles took a calculated risk of official censure in placing the order for a branch of the Service other than the Navy, but he cagily minimized the risk by prevailing upon the Assistant Secretary of War Thomas A. Scott to share the responsibility by counter-signing the paper. As we have seen above, Lincoln insisted that Ripley confirm this order.

The 6th Michigan Cavalry, Col. James H. Kidd commanding, was one of the first Federal units to be armed with the 7-shooter out of this lot of 10,000 manufactured at the Boston factory in 1862. None were delivered until the close of 1862.

"… If the entire army had been supplied with it the war would not have lasted 90 days," was Col. Kidd's glowing estimate of the effectivness of the Spencer.

The first skirmish in Chris Spencer's frustrating battle to get his rifle recognized and accepted by the Army had been won. Yet Army Ordnance remained adamant, blocking his efforts to see President Lincoln and to demonstrate the new repeater to him personally. Not until after Gettysburg, in which three Spencer-armed regiments provided the winning edge for the hard-pressed Northern forces, was the inventor able to arrange a meeting with Lincoln.

Blakeslee's patent loading tubes for the Spencer repeater. Ten tubes, each holding seven cartridges, were carried in this tin-wood-leather box.

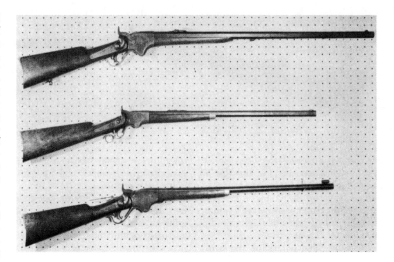

Fig. 5 — Three Spencer sporters. Top — full octagon bbl. is 32" long, cal. 56-46, 5-groove rifling makes one turn in 26", right twist. Length overall, 48¾", serial no. 34198. Wt., 12 lbs. Because of the 5-groove bbl., and the existence of the sling-ring base on this rifle, it is doubtful that the Spencer Co. made it.

Middle — Spencer sporting rifle in the early small-action form, doubtless made prior to any production arms. The octagon-top receiver is marked C. M. SPENCER/HARTFORD, CT./PATd. MAR. 6, 1860, in three lines. The full octagon bbl. is 24" long, and is without marks. Caliber is 36 (approx. groove dimension); five-land rifling, lands about half the groove width, rate of twist one turn in 44 inches, right hand. The action of this early specimen, numbered 13, is 27/16" deep compared to the production Spencer's depth of 33/16". The central saw-edge extractor, part of Spencer's original patent, is found in this sporter. Length over-all, 40 5/8"; wt., 8 lbs.

Lower-Full round bbl. is 25 7/8" long, rifled with 6 grooves making one turn in 30", right twist. A simple (non-graduated) folding tang sight, and a globe front sight are fitted. Serial no. 8386 appears on the top tang and underneath the bbl. Number 7 also is seen underneath the bbl., and in several places on the action parts. An unusual feature is a push-forward set-trigger, seemingly original. Length over-all, 42½";wt., 9½ lbs.

Spencers in Action

It is, of course, impossible here to cover every Civil War engagement in which the Spencer played an important role; highlights only may be noted. The bloody battle of Antietam was the grim theater for the initial appearance of the 7-shooter in American land warfare. Sergeant Lombard, 1st Massachusetts Cavalry, fired the first shots from a Spencer on the day of the great battle, September 17, 1862. This weapon, handmade by Chris Spencer, had been presented to Sergeant Lombard by the inventor early in the same month, when the 1st Massachusetts had been camped near Washington.

Both the Blue and the Gray lost heavily in the indecisive battle of Antietam, but the Federal troops stopped Lee's first attempt to invade the North. General Lee would not try again until the climactic battle of Gettysburg marked the high tide of Southern military fortunes the following summer.

In the winter of 1862–1863, Spencer roamed the Western front of the war, doggedly trying to sell his improved repeater* to individual commanders. At Murfreesboro, Tennessee, the inventor demonstrated his repeater to General Rosecrans and his staff. Impressed, Rosecrans regretfully

---

*Incorporating extractor changes (see U. S. Patent 36062, issued to C. M. Spencer July 29, 1862).

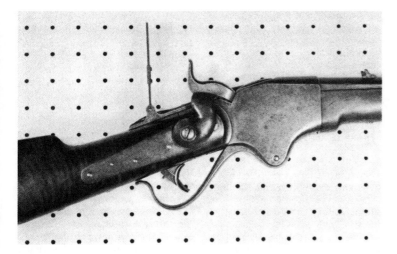

Fig. 6 — Close up of Spencer sporter number 8386 (pictured on these pages elsewhere), showing set trigger. Set-screw in rear of trigger adjusts weight of let-off pull.

informed Spencer that he could not obtain the approval of the War Department to arm his men with the new weapon. But Colonel John T. Wilder ordered 4000 of the 7-shooters for his own brigade.

Army Ordnance flatly refused to honor Colonel Wilder's order. Furious, Wilder asked his men if they would pay for the Spencers with their own money. The brigade voted "Yes" to a man. The Colonel endorsed their notes and made good on all losses incurred. Each rifle cost $35 and most of the men paid off their notes in full — if they lived through the heavy fighting that followed. The 4000 Spencers shipped to Wilder's men from the Boston factory upped the total to almost 10,000 7-shooters in action in the Western campaign in that memorable summer of 1863. On June 24, Wilder's cavalry won their immortal title of "The Lightning Brigade" when the flashing volleys of their deadly Spencers routed the Rebs from Hoover's Gap in the Cumberland Mountains, opening the way for the smashing Federal victory at Chickamauga a few weeks later.

The battle of Gettysburg found 3500 Spencers in the hands of Federal cavalrymen. Jeb Stuart's famous cavalry, 10,000 strong, clashed with the four regiments of the Michigan Brigade led by General Kilpatrick on June 30, 1863, at Hanover, 14 miles southeast of Gettysburg, to start the action. Flamboyant George Armstrong Custer, recently promoted to Brigadier General, was in the forefront of the fighting that historic day at Hanover. His Spencer-armed 5th and 6th Michigan

regiments, aided by the 1st West Virginia Cavalry, poured out such a volume of fire that Stuart's gray-clad legions were forced to swing wide of Lee's main army to Carlisle, 35 miles to the north.

Thus, on the eve of the crucial battle of the war, Lee was deprived of "the eyes of my army," dashing Stuart and his hard-riding, fanatically dedicated troopers. Stuart did not reach Gettysburg until the evening of July 2nd, too late for his weary cavalrymen to perhaps turn the tide for Lee and the Confederacy.

On July 3, the third and last day of the titanic struggle, the deadly Spencer played its usual role of "stopper," checking and finally shattering the stubborn Gray advance. The gallant Confederate soldier, with his archaic muzzle-loader, was now outclassed.

The crushing defeat at Gettysburg signalled the beginning of the end for the Confederacy. Yet there was much bitter fighting to come, and in most of it the Spencer-armed Northern regiments saw heavy and decisive action.

Lincoln Shoots the Spencer

President Lincoln, through direct reports from the front, became keenly aware of Chris Spencer and his repeater after Gettysburg. Lincoln invited the inventor to bring his rifle to the White House for a personal demonstration.

The long overdue meeting took place on August 17,1863. "I arrived at Washington on the morning of August 17th and went direct to the White House," wrote

Spencer in his carefully detailed account. "Presenting my credentials, the guard at the door showed me into the President's office. He was alone when I entered and appeared to be expecting me, as without a moment's delay he took the gun out of my hands, as soon as I removed it from its cloth covering. He examined it carefully and handled it like one familiar with firearms. He requested me to take it apart and show the 'inwardness of the thing' and was greatly impressed that all I needed was a screwdriver …"

"President Lincoln then invited me to return at 2 p.m. the next day, saying, 'we will go out and see the thing shoot.' When I returned at the time designated I found the President standing, with his son, Robert, and an officer from the Navy, named Middleton, on the steps of the White House. As we walked toward the War Department, the President asked his son to go in and invite Secretary of War, Stanton, to join us and see the shooting.

"While we were waiting for him to return and during a lull in the conversation between Middleton and the President, I mustered up enough courage to ask Mr. Lincoln if it were not a great responsibility to govern such a vast country during the war. Turning toward me with a smile he said: 'It is a big chore with the kind of help I have…'"

"The four of us walked over to what is now Potomac Park, near where the Washington monument stands. The naval officer had picked up a smooth pine board, six inches wide and three feet long, for a target, and after making a small smudge at one end for a bullseye, it was set up against a tree. I slipped seven cartridges into the rifle and handed it to the President. Pacing off 40 yards he took his position "… President Lincoln fired his first shot. It was about six inches low. A second one struck the bullseye and the other five were close to it.

"'Now we will see the inventor try his luck!' remarked the President as he handed me the rifle. When the Naval officer reversed the target, I fired, beating him by a small margin. 'Well,' said President Lincoln, 'you are much younger than I am, have a better eye and steadier nerve.'"

"After we returned to the White House the Naval officer sawed off the end of the board which the President had used as a target, and handed it to me as a souvenir. Then I presented the rifle to President Lincoln, and he marched into the White House with it over his shoulder; I walked out of the gate with the target under my arm. In 1883, the target was sent to Springfield, Illinois (home town of Lincoln), to be placed in the collection of war relics there."

Spencer returned to the White House for another test of his rifle the next day. When he left, it was with the thrilling conviction that his long, frustrating ordeal was over — that President Lincoln himself liked his gun well enough to recommend it highly to Army Ordnance. The young inventor's intuition was correct. "After that," he wrote jubilantly, "we had more orders than we could fill, from the War Department as well as the Navy, for the rest of the war."

The deal was swiftly and efficiently expedited by Brigadier General George D. Ramsay, Lincoln's replacement of General Ripley as Chief of Army Ordnance. Ramsay warmly endorsed the rugged, long-range Spencer over the Colt and the Henry, calling the 7-shooter "the cheapest, most durable and efficient of any of these arms."

The first of the new shipments from the Spencer factory went to the Cavalry, and with the welcome receipt of these additional repeaters the Federal horsemen increased their newly won superiority over their Confederate counterparts. Acquisition of the new weapons by picked regiments of Northern infantry accelerated the Southern military decline. The staccato barking of the 7-shooters from the opposing Blue ranks quickly became a sinister symbol of destruction to the harried Confederates, still armed with muzzle-loaders.

After Gettysburg

The Spencer thereby became a valuable weapon in psychological warfare, even though the fancy phrase had not yet been coined. Post-war statements by Confederate commanders disclosed that often the sound of rapid firing from the Union repeaters led them to the erroneous conclusion that brigades instead of regiments of the enemy were moving against them, causing them to discard carefully laid battle plans and resort to hurried and often rash maneuvers. General Bragg, for example, at Chickamauga misinterpreted the tremendous volume of fire coming from five Indiana and Illinois Spencer-armed regiments as the steady volley-firing of an entire corps attacking his left flank. The error caused him to delay a planned wide-scale attack and undoubtedly cost him the battle.

What the unfortunate Federal soldier still lacking the 7-shooter thought of the weapon is revealed in a brief, poignant letter now reposing in the National Archives in Washington. Date-lined Chattanooga, Tenn., September 19, 1863, the first day of the battle of Chickamauga, it shows eloquently and a bit pathetically the hope of survival the new repeater meant to men facing the blazing hell of battle armed only with muzzle-loaders. The letter follows:

Chattanooga, Tenn., Sept. 19, 1863
Spencer Repeating Rifle Company:

Gentlemen: — I take liberty in writing and inquiring about your rifle as to the manufacturing prices, the number to be had, and the time they could be sent to us at Chattanooga. The whole regiment is willing to buy them and pay for them the next payday, as they will have four months pay coming to them, or the Colonel commanding the regiment would secure your pay; and I believe the whole of the 3rd Brigade of Sheridan's division would buy them if we could get them.

Yours respectfully,
John E. Ekstrand
Regt. Ord. Sgt., 51st Illinois Volunteer Infantry, 3d Brigade, 3d Div., 20 A.C.

At Gettysburg, three Spencer-armed regiments had provided the winning punch for General Meade's Army of the Potomac; at Chickamauga, five Spencer-armed regiments did the same for the Blue.

In the bloody three-day melee of the Battle of the Wilderness, in early May of 1864, Grant's army boasted eleven regiments equipped with the deadly repeater. Without the 7-shooters it is extremely doubtful if the surrounded Federal troops could have burst out of the trap so expertly laid for them by Lee and Stuart. Advancing behind a lethal screen of fire from their Spencers, the Union horsemen drove Stuart back to the Po River, permitting the beleaguered Army of the Potomac to move out of the death trap of the Wilderness and on to Spottsylvania. There, on May 8th, the Federals, headed by the Spencer-armed cavalry, defeated Lee in another furious battle.

General Sheridan's great raid, clear around Lee's befuddled army, was the next move on Grant's relentless program of ceaseless hammering away at the enemy. 10,000 Northern cavalry, half of them armed with Spencers, met and defeated Stuart's forces in four major engagements during the hectic 16-day campaign. At Yellow Tavern, on May 11th, Jeb Stuart was mortally wounded, probably by Spencer-toting expert marksman John A. Huff, of Company E of the 5th Michigan Cavalry. Stuart's death, like that of General Jackson's the year before at Chancellorsville, was a stunning personal blow to

Fig. 7 — (Top) post-Civil War Spencer military rifle, caliber 50 (using the 56-52 or 56-50 cartridge), with the Stabler cut-off. Lower, Spencer carbine, chambered for the 56-56 cartridge. Below it lies the Spencer magazine tube. Photo courtesy the West Point Museum.

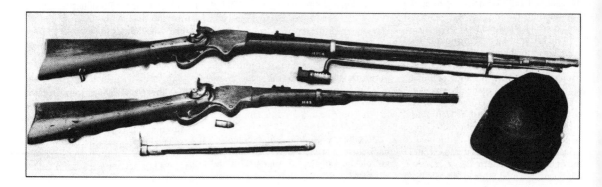

SPENCER
RIFLES AND CARBINES

Spencer models are difficult to classify, as L. D. Satterlee noted in his 2-part article in *The American Rifleman* for May 1 and 15, 1926. The list that follows leans heavily on that invaluable study, as well as on the same author's *A Catalog of Firearms For The Collector* (Detroit, 1927).

Rifles of 30" bbl. length and carbines with 22" bbls., both cal. 52 (bore 519"-20", grooves 537"- 38" taking the 56-56 Spencer cartridge of .885" length, using 42-grs. of powder (black) and a 362-gr. bullet of .540" diameter. These were all 6-grooved barrels, and all were made at Boston in the Chickering Piano Works at Tremont and Camden Streets. Early specimens had no serial num bers. Despite the order for 10,000 rifles given to Spencer on Dec. 26, 1861, none was delivered until Dec. 31,1862, nor were any of the 700 rifles ordered by the Navy earlier in 1861. Part of the delay was because of a design change, presumably the change over to the side position ex tractor (U.S. Patent 36062 of July 29, 1862, assigned to F. Cheney). During the period of non-delivery, Spencer's contract for 10,000 Army rifles was reduced to 7500. Deliveries by the Spencer Company continued up to June 20, 1863.

Following tests in May, 1863, Massachusetts ordered 2000 Spencer rifles, but the federal government was so anxious to have these that they were turned over to the U.S. on Oct. 2, 1863. Spencer then made 1868 rifles and 1176 carbines for Massachusetts, and again these were turned in to the U.S. on May 4 and May 9, 1864.

Meanwhile the U.S. had contracted for 11,000 carbines on July 13, 1863. 7000 only were delivered, from Oct. 3 to Dec. 31,1863, the rest cancelled. On Dec. 24,1863, another contract was given Spencer for 34,500 carbines. 7000 were delivered, from Jan. 20, 1864 to May 17, 1864, the balance cancelled.

On May 24, 1864, Spencer contracted to deliver as many carbines as he could up to Sept. 1, 1865. Between June 4, 1864 and August 31, 1865, 45,500 carbines were delivered.

Post-War carbines of 56-50 caliber. These were fitted with Stabler's cutoff (Edw. Stabler's U.S. Patent 46828 of May 14, 1865), and carried, generally, 20" bbls. 34,496 of this style, all with 3-groove bbls. (to conform to Army practices), and made by the Burnside Rifle Co., of Providence, R.I., were delivered to the U.S. between April 15, 1865 and October 31, 1865. This was in con formance with a contract given to Burnside on June 27, 1864. These are usually stamped "Model 1865."

The Spencer Co. delivered another 3000 of the 56-50 carbines between Dec. 13, 1865 and Jan. 1, 1866, these the same as the 56-50 carbines just described except that some had 22" bbls., and this lot of 3000 were made at the Boston works and so-stamped. Some are stamped "New Model" or "NM" on the barrel.

From about Nov. 1866 to Oct. 1867, Spencer con tinued to furnish 3-groove 50 cal. carbines and rifles (using the 52 cartridge or, as it was soon called, the 56-52. This dates the 56-52 load from about Nov. 1866. Military rifles of 3-groove

form were also sold in this brief period (also using the 52 or 56-52 cartridge — Spencer never advertised the Army's 50 cal. cartridge), as were sporting rifles in 46 or 56-46 caliber. Spencer felt that the Army's 50 cal. cartridge had an excessive crimp, and the 56-52 was his re-design using a bottleneck form. L.D.S. wrote that "Serial numbers start from one (1) up to perhaps about 20,000."

From about October, 1867 to the last days of the Spencer Co. in Sept., 1869, Spencers were made with 6-groove bbls. These barrels were stamped "M-1865", "M-1867" and "N.M.," according to L.D.S. He also notes that the Spencer Co.'s Oct. 1867 catalog "mentions the 'Old Model,' 'Model 1865' and 'Model 1867'" and that serial numbers started over again.

Spencers above serial number 100,000 (states L.D.S.) are sometimes found with a cutoff that Spencer designed and patented (U.S. Patents 58737 and 58738 on Oct. 9, 1866), but that one could have this or the Stabler cutoff or none at all. Generally, Spencers with either cutoff are late specimens. The Spencer type cutoff attaches to the cartridge guide atop the action.

L.D.S. thought that a final Spencer Co. catalog may have been issued in Oct., 1868, and comments that advertising of Spencers in the *Army & Navy Journal* ceased with the Oct. 31, 1868 issue.

The *Boston Post* for Sept. 29, 1869, reported on the sale of Spencer's machinery the day before. $138,000 was realized, this in addition to whatever Winchester may have paid for the patent rights and stocks of firearms on hand. (See *Winchester*, pp. 58 and 398, by C. F. Williamson, Wash., D.C., 1952). C. M. Spencer, at the close of the Civil War, had left the Spencer Repeating Rifle Co., joining Sylvester Roper in the unsuccessful Roper revolving shotgun venture. In 1868 Spencer formed the Billings & Spencer Mfg. Co., with C. E. Billings.

On Dec. 11, 1869, the *Scientific American* advertised the sale by Winchester of 2000 Spencer military rifles, 30,000 Spencer carbines and 500 Spencer sporting rifles.

It is difficult to determine whether a given Spencer sporting rifle was actually made by the Spencer Co. or not — most such types do not carry any barrel stampings to indicate company manufacture. The years that followed the Spencer firm's dissolution saw many jobbers and dealers in firearms offering Spencer arms of all types, among them sporting rifles in various styles, treatments, barrel lengths, etc., and it is a fair assumption that some such "Spencer" sporters were made up by altering Spencer Civil War rifles and carbines.

Delving into Spencer's patents brought out a peculiar thing — U.S. Patent 45952, dated Jan. 17, 1865, covers the loading tube system used in the Spencers from his first handmade models on. The specifications describe the inner and outer tubes, the right-angled locking piece that pivots into position at the buttplate, etc., all features of Spencer arms from their inception, as far as we know.

Fig. 8 — Spencer carbines illustrated in the 1866 Spencer catalog. Note that the Stabler cutoff is not shown. Spencer offered three basic models in this catalog — the Army and Navy rifles, with 30-inch barrels, a Cavalry carbine with 20-inch barrel, these in 56-50 caliber and with 3-groove bbls., and a basic sporting rifle with 26-inch octagon barrel in 56-46 caliber. Longer sporting barrels could be had, and other calibers.

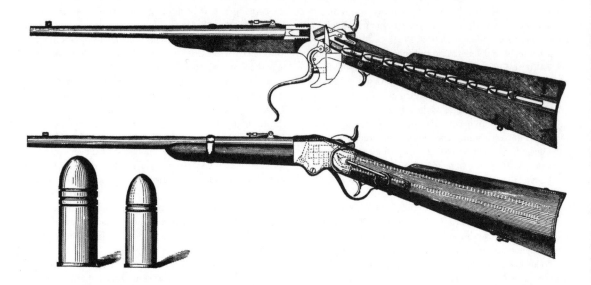

General Lee and a disaster to the crumbling Confederacy.

Sheridan's cavalry sweep through the Shenandoah Valley of Virginia resulted in brilliant victories over the fading enemy at Winchester, Fisher's Hill and Cedar Creek in the month from September 19th to October 19th of 1864. 17 regiments armed with the Spencer provided overwhelming firepower against the opposing troops of Jubal Early.

Brigadier General Garrard's cavalry division, composed mostly of Spencer-armed regiments, spearheaded the 1864 Georgia campaign of Generals Sherman and Hooker. In the ruthless drive to Atlanta, the 7-shooter equipped units blasted a corridor through stubborn enemy resistance. Before the fall of Atlanta, Grant recalled nearly all of the Spencer-armed cavalry and turned it over to General Wilson for a swift move against the Confederate army under Hood.

The end came for the doomed Confederacy early in the spring of 1865. Sheridan, flushed with victory after victory over the hungry, exhausted, outgunned Southerners, led his 10,000 troopers — now almost entirely armed with Spencers — successfully against Lee in the battle of Five Forks, Virginia.

Richmond fell to Grant the next day, and the stolid victor moved at once to join forces with Sheridan. The juncture was effected on April 5.

The battle of Sailor's Creek, last major battle of the war, began April 6. Sergeant William O. Lee, Company M, 7th Cavalry of the Michigan Brigade, wrote of the end of hostilities in these graphic words:

"After standing 'to horse' all night in open order of column by squadrons, about four o'clock on the morning of the 9th, in the gray of dawn, a line of the enemy skirmishers was discovered advancing. The 7th was at once deployed and was soon hotly engaged. Under the steady stream of lead poured out by Spencer carbines, the advance of the enemy was checked, held for a time, and then forced slowly back."

"... As we emerged from the woods, Lee's whole army, deployed for action, came into view and our bugles were sounding the charge. Just at this juncture several horsemen emerged from the woods of the enemy's lines, the leader waving a white flag of truce."

The War Ends

The guns fell silent; there remained but for Generals Grant and Lee to meet at the McLean house near the battlefield and sign the historic terms of surrender. Suddenly, stunningly, after four years of carnage and destruction, the Civil War was over.

Over 106,000 Spencers were contracted for by the war's end — 94,196 carbines and 12,471 rifles. Thousands more saw service, of course, counting the large number purchased by battle groups and individuals, and those that armed several volunteer and militia organizations.

The murder of President Lincoln by the crazed actor, John Wilkes Booth, on April 14th, 1865, not only robbed the nation of its great leader and the stricken South of its best friend, but also deprived the Spencer of its most influential backer. With Lincoln dead and Andrew Johnson in the White House, Army Ordnance quickly reverted to the single-shot Sharps and Springfield.

The bankrupt Spencer firm was sold at auction on September 28, 1869, to the Winchester Repeating Arms Co. 30,000 Spencers remaining in stock were bought by the Turkish Government; all other properties and assets went to Winchester.

By this one keen stroke of business, the Winchester Company eliminated its strongest competition. Even the name "Spencer" was dropped from all future firearms manufactured by the Winchester plant; yet the unique loading system of the Spencer was retained and utilized by Winchester when they produced the first self-loading rifle — the 1903 Model 22 caliber made famous by the great Texas marksman, Ad Topperwein.

After the loss of his rifle company, Christopher Spencer began manufacturing drop forgings and sewing machine shuttles. His invention of the world's first automatic screw machine stemmed directly from his work on the repeating rifle that so briefly bore his name. This ingenious machine — essential in the mass production of practically all metal items — ironically forms the only enduring monument to the inventive genius of Christopher Miner Spencer, who died in 1922 at the age of 89.

Ironic also is the fact that Custer, who won fame in the Civil War with his Spencer-armed cavalry, was an indirect casualty of the failure of the Army to continue using the Spencer.

Armed with the unreliable 45–70 Springfield carbine, more than 200 of Custer's 7th Cavalry, along with their yellow-haired leader, died battling 2000 Sioux warriors at the Little Bighorn, June 25,1876. Custer himself, openly scornful of the Springfield, went into his last battle armed with his 50–70 Remington Rolling Block Sporting Rifle. None knew better than weapons-expert Custer that the Springfield had a fatal weakness in the ejecting mechanism; the heads of the cartridges were apt to be pulled off by the extractors after the guns had been fired steadily for any length of firing time exceeding a few rounds. After the battle, some dead soldiers were found with jammed Springfields clutched in their hands.

The Spencer with the longest service appears to have been, from scanty available records, the Model 1867 Sporting Rifle, caliber 56-46. This weapon was in active service among hunters, especially in the West, many years after the other models were but fond memories or collectors' items.

Buffalo hunter Jim "Rawhide" Wilson, who cherished his 50-caliber Spencer sporter for nearly 40 years, was still killing bear, elk and muledeer with it in 1900.

Yet this was the same sturdy repeating rifle discarded by U. S. Army Ordnance in favor of the unreliable Springfield — a single-shot arm.

No wonder Chris Spencer complained of the density of "those Generals in Washington!"

Fig. 9—Spencer military rifle with 28½-inch barrel, first production type, caliber 52, and using the 56-56 cartridge.
Winchester Museum photo.

The Gettysburg Sharps

■ Paul A. Matthews

I T IS A MATTER OF HISTORY that the battle of Gettysburg stemmed the tide of the Confederate advance during the Civil War, but it is a matter of opinion as to what action turned the tide at Gettysburg. Some historians, and General Lee himself, claimed that Pickett's charge was a blunder. Others give full credit to Meade, who took command of the Federal troops on the eve of the battle, while soldiers in the ranks of the Confederacy said that "the damyankees have finally learned how to fight, ride, and shoot." Rifle-minded historians give credit to the accuracy, operation and fire power of the Sharps percussion breech-loading rifle.

Such credit is not unfounded. Lee was on an offensive action with 75,000 troops as opposed to Meade's 80,000. He had out-maneuvered Meade in the first two days of the fighting, and on the third day had him bottled up on ridges, ravines, and hills south of the town. Admittedly, he under-estimated the Federal artillery on Cemetery Ridge, but even so, Pickett's 15,000 men nearly carried the hill. Had General Longstreet, who was making a flanking movement around the Two Round Tops, not been

the same estimable position as our M1 Garand did in World War II. It was the first efficient, successful breech loader, and was the rifle for the infantry, being especially adapted for skirmish work and a high rapidity of fire when needed. It was far more accurate than the muskets carried by most of the troops, though not a target rifle capable of fine sniping work. Its breech-loading system allowed the infantryman to fire ten shots a minute from the prone position, whereas the musket users had to stand upright or nearly so when reloading — most undesirable and dangerous for the soldier anxious to be as small a target as possible.

The weight of the New Model 1863, eight and three-quarter pounds, was much less than that of the long smooth-bores, and its short overall length, even with a thirty inch barrel, gave the infantryman a light, handy weapon.

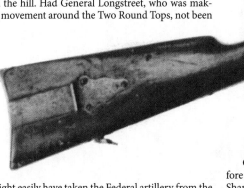

Sharps New Model 1863 percussion rifle.

delayed, he might easily have taken the Federal artillery from the rear and the history of Gettysburg and the Union would have been entirely different. General Longstreet and his 30,000 troops were held back forty minutes by a mere three hundred men, one hundred of which were from Col. Berdan's Sharpshooting Regiment and the others from the 3rd Maine Regiment. Berdan's men, armed with the Sharps rifle, fired about 9500 shots in a twenty minute barrage, at the same time sending word back to Meade to redeploy the troops defending the Round Tops.

Somewhere in that bloody three-day melee — possibly with Berdan on the reconnaissance, maybe with the 2nd U. S. Sharpshooters in the ravine between the Round Tops, or maybe farther north on Cemetery Ridge — was Samuel H. Williams of Company C, 171st Pennsylvania Volunteers. He was armed with a 52 caliber Sharps, New Model 1863, serial C,30303, a hundred paper or skin cartridges, and a bayonet.

The Sharps percussion rifle and carbine used in that war held

One of the principal defects of the early breechloaders, before the advent of brass cartridges, was gas escapage. In the 1863 Sharps, this is cut to a minimum by a deep counterbore in the face of the breechblock, into which is fitted a tapered, sliding faceplate, with a circular opening for the flash tube. On firing the rifle, the explosion exerts a thrust on the inside edge of the plate, driving it forward against the rear face of the barrel, thus sealing the chamber. Even so there is some leakage, and anyone attempting to fire an old Sharps should keep his arms covered and wear gloves. The first time I fired Pvt. William's rifle from the bench, I used a sling and kept my left hand well up on the fore-end, but my sister-in-law, who kept her hand back under the breech when she shot it, suffered blistering burns. Some gas also escapes around the top edge of the block, and on this particular rifle the lower face of the barrel is badly eroded, allowing most of the gas to go in that direction.

Coupled with the gas escapage is the sooty fouling common to all "charcoal" burners. When I first fired the Sharps, the breechblock refused to move when f started to reload. After tap-

Col. Berdan and "California Joe" from Berdan's United States Sharpshooters ... 1861–1865 by C. A. Stevens (St. Paul, Minn., 1892.)

ping lightly on the top of the block with a piece of brass and exerting pressure on the finger lever at the same time, the breech finally opened. As a preventive measure, I first tried greasing the face plate and rear barrel face with tallow. This helped to some degree. Then I tried water pump grease, and finally, after mixing powdered graphite with it, I had a suit able concoction. I also discovered that a small gob of grease on the inside edge of the chamber worked better yet as it blew out with the escaping gas, keeping the residue very soft. When the rifle was in new condition, and the moving parts highly polished, it was doubtless unnecessary to take these precautions each time the gun was fired.

Another advantage of the 1863 breech-loading percussion Sharps, especially from the infantryman's point of view, is the ease with which the breechblock can be removed for cleaning. On the right side of the receiver, just forward of the block mortice, is a spring loaded plunger that keeps the lever-pin from turning when the lever is operated. A small flange on the "arm" of the pin fits into a slot in the receiver, keeping the pin from falling out. When the infantryman wished to remove the breechblock, he depressed the plunger, swung the arm downward, and pulled out the pin. The breech-block then fell out and was easily cleaned. On the right side of the block is a lever-toggle-screw, and on the left side is the vent-cleaning screw.

As a safety measure, Mister Sharps put an "ear" on the upper right hand corner of the lock plate. This fits into the small curve of the hammer, keeping the latter from striking a cap when the breech is partially closed. A lever-spring snaps the lever to a closed position when the shooter brings it up within an inch of

the stock. Once closed, no amount of pressure on the breech-block will open it.

Coming close to making the Sharps a "repeater" is the pellet primer magazine in the lock plate. This could be charged with a tube of fifty of the Sharps pellet primers and then held in reserve for furious action (by Lawrence's patent cut-off) when the ordinary musket cap would be too slow to use. When necessary, such as it must have been at Cemetery Ridge, the cut-off plate was pulled back. This allowed a sliding plate, actuated by a cam on the inside face of the hammer, to push out a pellet synchronized with the hammer; the hammer hits the pellet as it flies over the nipple. (A quite nice job of timing). The pellets, actually thin wafers, were held in a vertical tube with a spring plunger forcing them upward where the plate could pick them up.

The bore diameter of Pvt. Williams' rifle measures .518 inches while the groove diameter is .529 inches, so I purchased the regular Lyman mould #533476, casting a hollow-base Minié-ball weighing 410 grains. I did not size any of the bullets, but merely dipped them in bullet lubricant and scraped off the excess. At first I made a number of paper cartridges using hard tracing paper as a wrapper and water-glass as glue along the sides. This combination worked very well. The water-glass hardens almost as fast as applied, and when the gun was fired there were no burning embers left in the chamber. For a powder charge I used 55 grains of duPont FG Black.

In order to make the paper cartridges, I first had a piece of steel four inches long turned to the .533 diameter of the bullet. Then, taking a piece of paper four inches long and wide enough

Preparing a Paper Cartridge

Fig. 1 — The first step in rolling a paper cartridge around a steel dowel and a lubricated Minié ball.

Fig. 2 — Gluing the top edge of the paper cartridge and along the side seam with water-glass.

Fig. 3 — Charging the cartridge with a scoop of FG black powder. The scoop has been filed off so as to hold 55 grains of powder.

Fig. 4 — Pinching the tube just behind the powder charge. The tail is then clipped to length and glued to the side of the cartridge.

Fig. 5 — The completed cartridge ready for use.

Use nothing but black powder in the old percussion Sharps, and for your eyes' sake, wear a pair of shooting glasses — those escaping gasses are hot!

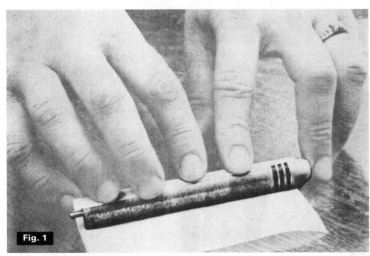

Fig. 1

Silver medal awarded to the Sharps Rifle Mfg. Co. in 1853 by the Massachusetts Charitable Mechanic Association.

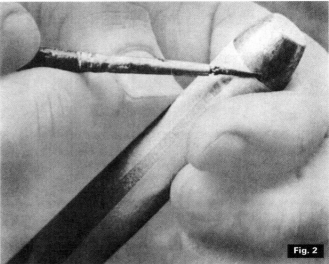

Fig. 2

A closeup shot of the lock plate showing the 'ear' that keeps the hammer from striking the nipple on a partially closed breech, and the vertical, spring-loaded plunger hole of the Sharps' primer pellet magazine.

to wrap around the steel twice, I laid it on the table, the long edge toward me. With the left hand, lay a bullet on the paper, just covering the grease grooves, and then place one end of the steel roller against the base of the bullet. Roll both tightly as a unit, then with a pointed brush run a small amount of water-glass around the top edge of the paper where the bullet protrudes, and down the side of the tube on the edge of the paper. It takes only a few seconds for the water-glass to harden and then the steel roller can be dropped out and the tube charged with powder. This leaves two or three inches of paper tube to be pinched flat, the outer edges folded inward, and then the flat tail folded across the base of the cartridge and up the side. Here again, I used water-glass to seal the tail and stick it to the side of the cartridge tube.

In loading the rifle with paper cartridges, I pulled the tail loose, pushed the cartridge into the chamber, and as the breech was closed, the face plate sheared off the excess paper, leaving the powder exposed to the flame of the cap. The Italian Fiocchi musket caps distributed by the Alcan Company gave plenty of hot flame and never once misfired.

Considering the sighting equipment of the old rifle — a low, narrow-bladed steel front sight and a V leaf rear sight — and the pitted breech end of the barrel, plus a trigger pull upwards wards of

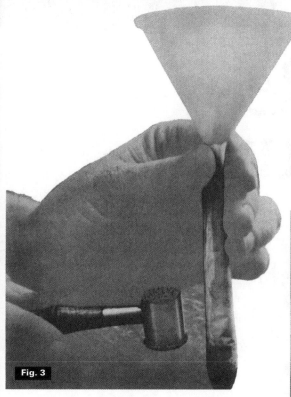

Fig. 3

demise of the company, the falling block design was picked up by other companies and is used to some extent today, as in the five inch anti-aircraft Naval rifles that so many of us became familiar with during World War II.

†W. O. Smith in *The Sharps Rifle* (New York, 1943) writes, "The standard military bullet for the Sharps .54 caliber (sometimes designated .52 caliber) weighed about 475 grains ..." Later, "In 1860 the standard powder charge for the ... carbine was 50 grains, but some of the later cartridges were found to contain as much as 65 grains ..."

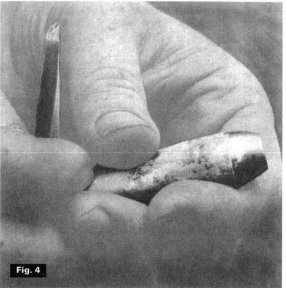

Fig. 4

six pounds, accuracy was not too bad. A ten shot group at 100 yards measured 7 inches vertically and 5½ inches horizontally, with the center of the group about ten inches below the point of aim. Six of the shots went into less than 3 inches. I also detected a slight tendency to tipping with the hollow-base bullet. Possibly I could have used a heavier charge, bringing the group closer to the point of aim, but dealing with an arm over ninety years old, I thought it better to be conservative.†

The success of the New Model 1863 was an outgrowth of several patents and changing designs. Christian Sharps' original patent granted in 1848 covered the sliding breechblock which in models 1851 through 1855 was of the slanting type. In the attempt to prevent gas escapage, these blocks were closely fitted in the receiver mortice, and some carried a fixed platinum ring more erosion resistant that the steel block.

Escaping gas was still a problem, however, and one H. Conant designed a sliding ring closely fitted into a counterbore. The explosion forced the ring forward, sealing the breech. In the 1859 model, R. S. Lawrence improved this by the addition of the sliding face plate described earlier, and this system was used in all subsequent percussion models.

All models following the 1855 model were also equipped with the Sharps automatic pellet primer magazine using the cut-off feature designed by Lawrence. Previous to this, the Maynard tape primer was used, while the models of 1852 and 1853 had the Sharps primer magazine without the cut-off.

It is interesting to note that the Confederacy made several versions of the Sharps carbine, some with parts that had been "borrowed" from the Federal Cavalry.

Though the Sharps was with us for all too brief a time (1848–1881), the company having been plagued with law suits, mortgages, and penalties for late deliveries, it helped bring to an end a muzzle-loading army and heralded the beginning of a new era in the history of firearms. In the years following the

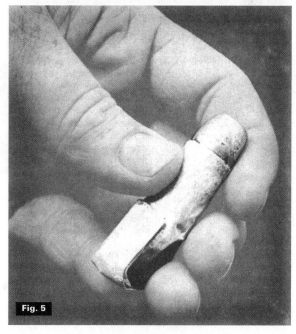

Fig. 5

Johnny Reb and His Guns

■ Edward R. Crews

NO JOHNNY REB manning the Confederate line at Mayre's Heights could be unimpressed at the spectacle before him. On an open plain between this high ground and the nearby town of Fredericksburg, Virginia, thousands of Federal troops were massing for an attack.

William M. Owen, a Confederate artillery officer, watched on December 13, 1862, as the enemy soldiers ran toward him behind unfurled battle-flags, chanting a deep-throated refrain — Hi! Hi! Hi! "How beautifully they came on," he wrote years later. "Their bright bayonets glistening in the sunlight made the line look like a huge serpent of blue and steel."

Union Major General Ambrose E. Burnside was hurling his Army of the Potomac against the Southern defenses. He wanted to rout General Robert E. Lee and his Army of Northern Virginia, and then march into Richmond about 50 miles south and end the war. Burnside had massed 27,000 men for the attack on Mayre's Heights; Lee had only 6000 defending it. Although Federal assaults earlier that day had failed elsewhere along Lee's line, Burnside hoped this attack would work.

The Union attack, however, was doomed to fail. Lee held a superb defensive position. Mayre's Heights commanded nearby terrain and was studded with artillery. At its base, a breast-high stone wall provided shelter for the Georgia infantrymen of Cobb's Brigade. Also, many of Lee's men had rifled muskets, the war's most common infantry weapon. A properly trained soldier could hit targets at 300 yards, firing three rounds a minute.

That so many of these weapons would be in Southern hands was a miracle. When the various states that comprised the Confederacy left the Union in 1860 and 1861, they had few modern military rifles. U.S. arsenals seized by the South held older, less-desirable guns. Plus, the South had virtually no rifle-making facilities. Perceptive Southern

Stonewall Jackson reviews his troops during his famous Valley Campaign of 1862. So much enemy equipment was captured that the Confederates found themselves well-armed when the fighting ended. This mural is in the gallery with the Southern gun collection. (Richard Cheek photo.)

◀ This unmarked Confederate rifle in the Springfield pattern is proof the South had an ordnance system. (Virgina Historical Society photo.

leaders knew that a Union naval blockade eventually could slow, and probably halt, imports. All these factors produced an ill-armed military.

"At the commencement of the war, the Southern army was as poorly armed as any body of men ever had been," wrote John H. Worsham of the 21st Virginia Infantry Regiment. "Using my own regiment as an example, one company of infantry had Springfield muskets, one had Enfields, one had Mississippi rifles, and the remainder had the old smoothbore flintlock musket that had been altered to a

percussion gun. The cavalry was so badly equipped that hardly a company was uniform. Some men had sabers and nothing more, some had double-barreled guns. Some had nothing but lances, and others had something of all. One man would have a saber, another a pistol, another a musket, and another a shotgun. Not half a dozen men in the company were armed alike."

That situation had changed dramatically by late 1862, as Burnside and his men learned at Fredericksburg.

Federal commanders initiated the attack around noon. Their men had to cross about 600 yards of open ground to reach the Confederate position. Union troops began taking casualties as soon as the advance started. When they were within 125 yards of the stone wall, Cobb's infantrymen shouldered their muskets.

"A few more paces onward and the Georgians in the road below us rose up, and, glancing an instant along their rifle barrels, let loose a storm of lead into the faces of the advanced brigade," Owen wrote. "This was too much; the column hesitated, and then, turning, took refuge behind the (nearby earthen) bank."

Burnside repeatedly sent assault waves against the enemy lines all day. Only the arrival of night ended the fighting. No Billy Yank came closer than fifty yards to the stone wall. Federal losses were 8000 compared to 1600 for the South.

Fredericksburg was a testament to the Army of the Potomac's courage. It also showed that the rifled musket was ending the sweeping, grand Napoleonic charge. This weapon represented a significant technological gain in warfare. It was powerful enough, accurate enough and had enough range to pound apart the most determined attack a foe could mount. The industrialized North could supply hundreds of thousands of these arms to its soldiers with comparative ease.

The agrarian South, however, faced staggering supply problems. Against all odds, the Confederacy did get sufficient modern arms to its troops. That required hard work, organization, improvisation and the talents of a remarkable man — Josiah Gorgas. Nobody in the Confederacy would do more to get rifles for Johnny Reb.

A Pennsylvanian, West Pointer and pre-war professional soldier, Gorgas became chief of Confederate ordnance early in the war. Before it ended, he would run thousands of guns through the Yankee blockade and build a Southern weapons industry from scratch. Southerners in 1861 might have gone to war with fowling pieces and old smoothbores, but by mid-1863, thanks to Gorgas, they generally had equipment that matched their Federal foes'. One Southern leader succinctly and accurately described his wartime achievements: "He created the ordnance department out of nothing."

Gorgas knew early on that the rifled musket would play a key role in the con-

flict, and the Confederacy would need large quantities of them. He also understood its capabilities. Compared to today's military rifles, the typical Civil War musket was heavy, big, cumbersome and fired a huge bullet, often more than half-an-inch in diameter. Such muskets required twenty steps to load. A soldier typically did this standing upright and holding his weapon in front of him with its butt on the ground. Ammunition came in paper cartridges that contained a bullet and a standard charge of blackpowder. Johnny Reb would bite off a cartridge end, pour the powder down the barrel, discard the paper, place the bullet in the muzzle and ram it to the breech using a ramrod carried in a channel beneath the barrel. The Civil War musket's ignition system relied on the percussion cap, a metal cap filled with fulminate of mercury. The system was reliable and could function in all weather conditions.

The same could not be said of the previous generation of military shoulder arms. The flintlock muzzleloader depended on a piece of flint striking a piece of metal to create a spark. Much could go wrong with this process, and damp powder doomed it. Knowing the flintlock's limitations, both Civil War armies eagerly embraced the percussion system.

Average Johnny Rebs and Billy Yanks in the infantry used the same weapons and used them the same way, both as individuals and as members of military units.

For much of the conflict, officers in blue and gray deployed troops in large, concentrated units that shot in volleys. This allowed commanders to mass fire and to control fire rates. The only way to move men into these combat formations was through standardized maneuvers, which explains why the 19th century American soldier spent much time drilling.

Although presented with a powerful, comparatively long-range weapon in the rifled musket, generals stuck with those formations and tactics appropriate to the short ranges and inaccuracy of the smoothbore era. Surprisingly enough, leading commanders on both sides failed to immediately grasp the rifle's destructive power. Not only did Burnside embrace the frontal assault at Fredericksburg, but so did Lee at Gettysburg, Ulysses S. Grant at Cold Harbor, and Confederate Lt. Gen. John B. Hood at Franklin, Tennessee. At all these places, the results were disastrous.

As the war progressed, however, the average soldier realized the value of entrenching. Southern infantrymen became adept at creating trenches and rifle pits whenever they stopped, using tin cups and plates as well as shovels to put a few inches of dirt between them and the enemy. The 1864–65 Petersburg campaign, in fact, was largely a fight between entrenched armies that knew a direct attack against such works was tantamount to suicide.

For the average Confederate soldier, combat was a terrifying experience. It also was hard work. To begin, loading the rifle was difficult. Even veteran soldiers could easily forget what they were doing in the heat of battle. Sometimes they loaded a bullet first, powder second, or jammed load after load down the barrel without capping the nipple. Blackpowder also quickly clogged musket barrels and wrapped the battlefield in clouds of dense smoke that made seeing targets difficult, if not impossible.

Johnny Reb also endured his rifle's hefty recoil. Sam Watkins, a Southern soldier, reported firing 120 rounds during the Battle of Kenesaw Mountain. Afterwards, his arm was battered and bruised. "My gun became so hot that frequently the powder would flash before I could ram home the ball," he wrote, "and I had frequently to exchange my gun for that of a dead colleague."

How good a shot was Johnny Reb? We'll probably never know. While the rifled musket could perform outstandingly, and many Southerners lived in a society that prized good guns and marksmanship, battle imposed great demands on the best of shots. The danger, excitement, loading process and smoke-covered battlefields made accurate shooting extraordinarily difficult. One historian has estimated that for every casualty produced, 200 rounds were fired. Others believe the figure to be much higher.

If the tactical implications of the rifled musket were sometimes imperfectly understood, its value as an improved shoulder arm was easily grasped. So Confederate officials knew that getting these weapons into Johnny Reb's hands was vital, and Confederate ordnance chief Gorgas energetically set to work on the problem from the war's start. He knew only three sources of supply existed: capture, import and Southern manufacture.

The Confederacy turned to capture first. As each Southern state left the Union, it seized any Federal arms held at arsenals or armories within its borders. The pickings were lean. These establishments did not have many modern arms. They mainly held older government models of little value. Among these was the U.S. Model 1822 musket, a 69-caliber smoothbore. Many were converted from flintlock to percussion, but the improved ignition system did not compensate for their unrifled barrels. Their range and accuracy was limited. Hitting a specific target more than 100 yards away relied on luck as much as skill.

Once the fighting began in earnest, the Confederacy wasted little time in seizing modern Union weapons whenever they became available. Federal prisoners, battlefield gleanings and captured warehouses yielded first-class arms for the Cause.

As veteran Southern infantryman Worsham noted: "When Jackson's troops marched from the Valley (of Virginia) for Richmond (in 1862) to join Lee in his attack on McClellan, they had captured enough arms from the enemy to replace all that was inferior; and after the battles around Richmond, all departments of Lee's army were as well armed."

Probably the most preferred capture from the Yankees was the 58-caliber Springfield, which came in several models. This rifled musket was superior and typical of its type. The weapon weighed roughly 9 pounds, was 58 inches long, and saw more service with the U.S. Army than any other rifle. Government and private armories produced hundreds of thousands during the war.

Also especially desired by Johnny Reb

Anthony Sydnor Barksdale (1841–1923) of Charlotte County posed with his rifle for this ambrotype (ambrotypes are reversed photos), taken in 1861 when Barksdale was twenty. He served as a private in the 14th Virginia Infantry Regiment and later transferred to Edward R. Young's battery in Mosely's Battalion. Captured in Petersburg in 1865, he was a prisoner of war at Point Lookout for several months. (Virginia Historical Society photo.)

was the U.S. Model 1841. It was first issued in 54-caliber, but many were altered to 58-caliber, and a fair number came into Confederate hands through Federal arsenals in Southern states. This weapon was commonly known as the "Mississippi rifle," from its Mexican War service with Mississippi volunteers commanded by Jefferson Davis.

Confederates also were delighted to get their hands on Federal breechloaders like the Sharps and Spencer. Both represented significant gains in rates of fire and ease of loading.

To load the Sharps, a 52-caliber breechloader, the soldier pulled down the trigger guard. This caused the breechblock to drop and opened the chamber into which was inserted a linen or paper cartridge filled with powder and a bullet. The Sharp's rate of fire was three times that of a musket.

The Spencer fired metallic cartridges. Its tubular magazine in the buttstock held seven rounds. A skilled operator could fire twenty-one rounds per minute. Unfortunately for the South, captured Spencers suffered from an ammunition shortage as the Confederate industry frequently was incapable of meeting cartridge needs created by the weapon's firepower abilities.

Though infantrymen seldom carried revolvers, the Confederate cavalry loved them, especially captured Colts. These were Northern-made, but saw widespread use in both armies. Six-shooters in 36- and 44-calibers, their cylinders could be loaded with paper, foil or sheepskin cartridges, or loose powder and ball. Ignition

required a percussion cap on each nipple at each chamber.

Imports were another vital source of armaments. Europe eagerly provided guns to both sides. Southern weapons had to come through the Federal blockade, and a surprisingly large volume made the trip.

Europe offered some superlative weapons and some junk. Particularly despised by Johnny Reb were rifles made in Austria and Belgium. Unwieldy, inaccurate and unreliable, they were dead last on his wish list.

The most desired import was the 577-caliber Enfield. A British-made musket, the Enfield was rugged and accurate. The Enfields came in several styles, including a carbine. Southern cavalry was particularly attached to the latter, even though as a muzzleloader it lacked the rapid-fire quality of Union repeaters. Another popular and well-crafted British import was the 44-caliber Kerr revolver.

Great Britain also supplied some of the war's best sharpshooter rifles: the 44-caliber Kerr and 45-caliber Whitworth. Southern marksmen treasured these guns, which enabled them to hit targets at 1000 yards. The most famous long-range shooting incident of the war occurred on May 9, 1864, during the Battle of Spotsylvania.

Several Southern marksmen are given credit for what happened, but it is impossible to know who did the shooting. One version of the incident comes from Captain William C. Dunlop who commanded the sharpshooters of McGowan's Brigade. This Confederate unit was ordered to

move ahead of the main body of Southern troops to scout for Federals that day. Dunlop concealed his men in position along a ridge where they could see the Union VI Corps deploying on a distant hill. Immediately, Dunlop's men began firing with telling effect.

Among Dunlop's troops was a Private Benjamin Powell of South Carolina, who carried a Whitworth that day and was looking for important targets. One soon presented itself. Powell could see a Yank officer moving along the enemy firing line, giving commands and viewing the field through binoculars. His behavior and the staff trailing behind him suggested this was an important man.

Powell decided to shoot him. The round traveled 800 yards and struck General John Sedgwick, the corp commander, in the left cheek, killing him. Only moments earlier, the general had tried to calm his troops who were agitated by the sniper fire. They "couldn't hit an elephant at this distance," he said seconds before he died.

One of the most intriguing weapons that made it through the Union's naval blockade was the Le Mat revolver, which could fire nine 41-caliber rounds from its main barrel plus buckshot from a shorter one. (Oddly enough, its main barrel's caliber is variously reported as ranging from 40- to 42-caliber.) The idea for this monster came from Jean Alexander Francois Le Mat, a New Orleans doctor. Once the Confederacy accepted his pistol, the doctor headed for France where it was produced. A carbine model also was developed.

Confederate "Sharps" carbine by S.C. Robinson, a direct copy of the U.S. Sharps model. Lockplate and top of barrel read "S.C. Robinson, Arms Manufactory, Richmond, VA 1862." (Virginia Historical Society photo.)

Whitney "Mississippi" rifle made by Eli Whitney in 1851, U.S. Model 1841, U.S. percussion rifle in unaltered, original configuration. (Virginia Historical Society photo.)

The last source of weapons was from within the Confederacy. Given the virtually non-existent manufacturing base there, Gorgas achieved astonishing results, creating government armories as well as inspiring various private firms to enter the armaments field.

The best Southern-made weapons came from government operations in Richmond and Fayetteville, North Carolina. Early in the war, the Confederacy captured Federal gun-making equipment at Harper's Ferry. This was used at both Confederate plants to produce 58-caliber muskets, known as Richmond and Fayetteville rifles.

These two factories were not the only source of "home-grown" weapons. Other production facilities sprang up in Georgia, Louisiana, South Carolina, Mississippi, Texas and Alabama. Quality and volume varied greatly from factory to factory, as the case of the Confederate "Sharps" proved. These were versions of the Sharps carbine Model 1855, made by the Richmond firm of S.C. Robinson Arms Manufacturing Company. Forty were sent for field-testing to the 4th Virginia Cavalry Regiment in the spring of 1863. The gun was not a success. Reportedly seven of nine burst during firing. Furious, an officer of the regiment, Lieutenant N.D. Morris, fired off a letter to a newspaper, *The Richmond Whig*, which ran a story on the weapons under the headline "An Outrage."

"The lieutenant suggests," ran the article, "that the manufacturers of these arms be sent to the field where they can be furnished with Yankee sabres, while the iron they are wasting can be used for farming implements!"

Ordnance officials rushed to defend the producers and the carbines, suggesting the soldiers using the weapons had not been trained properly, but the bad reputation stuck. Captain W.S. Downer, superintendent of the Richmond armory, also reported to Gorgas that somebody should remind the letter-writing lieutenant about army procedures. "I would also suggest that Lieut. N.D. Morris, of Capt. McKinney's Co., 4th Va. Cavalry, be notified to communicate with the Department through his proper officers, rather than through the columns of a newspaper."

Besides government plants, private firms got involved in weapons production. For example, Davis and Bozeman of Coosa County, Alabama, made 58-caliber rifles. J.&F. Garrett Co. of Greensboro, North Carolina, produced the 52-caliber Tarpley carbine, the only breech-loading

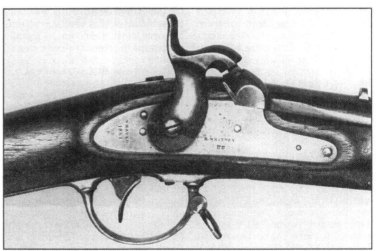

Whether marked "U.S.," like this Whitney Mississippi Rifle (above) or "RICHMOND, VA," as it says on the Robinson Sharpe (below), the Rebs used them all. (Virginia Historical Society photos)

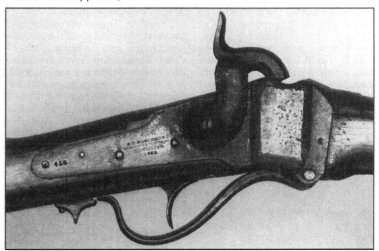

gun patented, manufactured and offered for general sale in the Confederacy.

Private industry made its biggest contribution to weapons production by making pistols. When the war began, the Confederacy had no revolver manufacturers within its borders. But wartime entrepreneurs appeared like Spiller and Burr, Griswold and Gunnison, and Leech & Rigdon.

Many entrepreneurs found that making weapons for the South was a difficult business indeed. Consider the story of Charles Rigdon, for example, a Southern sympathizer who lived in St. Louis. He moved to Memphis when the war started and formed a partnership with Thomas Leech to make swords. Advancing Union armies forced the pair to move

to Columbus, Mississippi, and then to Greensboro, Georgia, where they made 36-caliber revolvers, which were copies of Colt's pistols. The partnership eventually collapsed. Leech kept making revolvers in Greensboro. Rigdon opened a new pistol firm in Augusta, Georgia — Rigdon, Ansley & Co. — that operated until the war's end. Interestingly enough, Samuel Colt sued the company for illegal use of his revolver patents.

One non-issue weapon that came from private manufacturers was the shotgun. Often brought from home, shotguns were popular among certain Confederate cavalry units, particularly in the Western Theater. Shotguns had limited range, limited tactical value and took a long time to load. But at close quarters they were

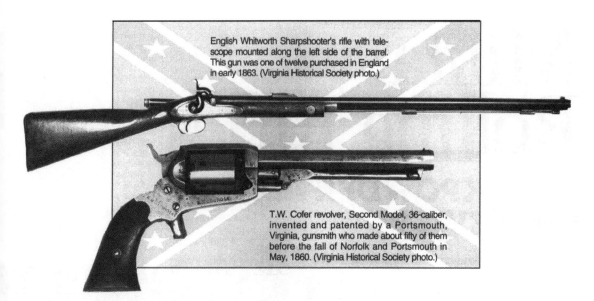

English Whitworth Sharpshooter's rifle with telescope mounted along the left side of the barrel. This gun was one of twelve purchased in England in early 1863. (Virginia Historical Society photo.)

T.W. Cofer revolver, Second Model, 36-caliber, invented and patented by a Portsmouth, Virginia, gunsmith who made about fifty of them before the fall of Norfolk and Portsmouth in May, 1860. (Virginia Historical Society photo.)

devastating. The 8th Texas Cavalry, better known as Terry's Texas Rangers, were particularly fond of scatterguns. During the Southern retreat from the Battle of Shiloh, this unit used these weapons effectively. Ordered to charge Union infantry pursuing the Southern army, the Texans swept forward, halted about twenty steps from the Federal line and fired their shotguns. Each barrel was loaded with fifteen to twenty buckshot. The Federal pursuit fell apart and a retreat ensued. The Texans then put their shotguns aside and pursued the enemy on horseback, firing their revolvers.

Much of the success of Southern weapon production came from the use of slave labor. African-Americans worked in armories and played a key role in the armament industry's labor force. For instance, the Georgia pistol firm of Columbus Fire Arms Manufacturing Co. hired forty-three blacks in 1862 and aggressively tried to find more during the rest of the war.

For blacks, working in weapons production was a mixed bag. It often meant separation from loved ones, hard work, long hours and daily rations of bacon and cornmeal. However, the work gave them valuable skills and provided an unprecedented degree of freedom.

Although the Confederacy ultimately lost the war, it did not do so due to a lack of weapons and ammunition. Granted, the Southern ordnance system had flaws. Armies in the East tended to be better supplied than those in the West. Units in either theater, even late in the war, might carry a hodgepodge of weapons, mostly rifled muskets but sometimes smoothbores, and this variety made ammunition re-supply a headache. Some of the Southern-made rifles and pistols did not meet the standards of Northern or British factories, but on balance Gorgas did a remarkable job.

One anecdote makes the point. When Lee surrendered at Appomattox in 1865, his army was small, sick, ill-clad and poorly fed. However, most men were armed and, on average, each carried seventy-five rounds of ammunition.

Today, Confederate guns are scarce and costly. But the interested student of Civil War firearms can see one of the world's best collections of Southern weapons at the Virginia Historical Society in Richmond. The society owns an extraordinary collection of rifles, pistols, swords, belt-plates and buttons given to it in 1948 by Richard D. Steuart, a Baltimore newspaperman who had two grandfathers and nine uncles who served the Confederate cause. For many years, the collection was displayed to feature the weapons themselves as artifacts and objects of interest.

In 1993, the Virginia Historical Society decided to display its collection in an innovative way. The weapons were moved into a gallery decorated with life-sized murals of Civil War battle scenes. The new display uses the guns to tell the story of how the South armed itself. For the neophyte or life-long scholar of the conflict, the new display is entertaining and informative — you can *see* Johnny Reb and his guns.

For more information on the society and its collections, write: Virginia Historical Society, P.O. Box 7311, Richmond, VA 23221-0311 or call 804-358-4901.

Military Rolling Rifles
of the Rarest Kind

■ George J. Layman

This close-up of the Edward Paget-manufactured military rolling block for the Austrian government with the hammer cocked, shows the spring-charged safety stopper in the frontal position.

The Remington Rolling Block Rifle became an immediate favorite with many of the world's armies and was manufactured under license and modified by a variety of countries.

The story of the Remington rolling block is well known to arms students throughout the world. However, several variations produced in limited numbers are relatively unknown. Herewith, a short overview on the development of the world's greatest single-shot military rifle.

In 1864–65 chief engineer Joseph Rider of the E. Remington and Sons Arms Co. was tasked to redesign and improve the Leonard Geiger breech-loading design. Geiger, a native of Hudson, NY, received his first patent (#37,501) on January 27, 1863; it was reissued in April 17, 1866, whereupon Rider refined the action even further. The complete redesign strengthened the earlier Remington "split breech" action purchased by the government at the end of the Civil War. The split-breech action was based upon the earlier 1864 patent, having its hammer fit between a weaker, slotted, breechblock that was compatible only with low pressure copper-cased cartridges such as the 46 or 56 Spencer rimfire. The new 1866 patent allowed Rider to improve the breechblock by forming it from a solid billet of steel drilled for a firing pin channel. The breechblock's solid crescent contour rolled beneath the hammer's crescent cut for loading and extracting a spent case. It was the strongest system known that could handle the largest blackpowder cartridges to arrive in the coming decades. The term "rolling block" became the action's sobriquet for eternity. Because the government's budget was strained by the war, and because there was a surplus

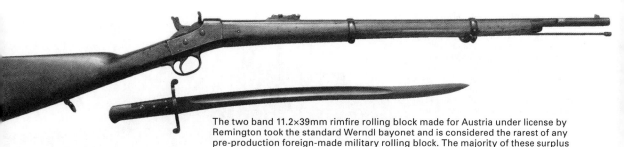

The two band 11.2×39mm rimfire rolling block made for Austria under license by Remington took the standard Werndl bayonet and is considered the rarest of any pre-production foreign-made military rolling block. The majority of these surplus rifles went to China.

of ordnance of all categories, many previously active arms suppliers to the War Department went out of business.

Remington saw this coming and was certain that, unless they quickly found some new business, they would be bankrupt like so many of the other wartime arms manufacturers. Seeking a market for the new rolling block rifle, in the summer of 1866 brother Samuel departed for Europe to demonstrate the qualities of the improved Remington rolling block Rifle. It proved a worthwhile journey; ordnance inspectors from Europe and the Middle East were present for Sam Remington's many hands-on demonstrations of the strength, reliability and rapidity of fire of the new Remington breechloader. Spain, Denmark, Sweden, Egypt, Austria — and a host of other countries — were immediately sold on the remarkable design of the new American breechloader. Once it was awarded a gold medal at the Paris Exposition of 1867, success was at hand.

The Austro-Hungarian Model Of 1866

The Austro-Hungarian delegation became the first nation to obtain licensing rights to produce the rolling block in Vienna. The reason behind such a hasty arrangement was that Austria knew it would soon be at war with Prussia. Upon the particulars being worked out, the Austrian Emperor called on an English firearms engineer, Edward Paget, to come

to Vienna to oversee production. After Archduke Wilhelm's special commission concurred the rolling block would be an ideal breechloading arm for his military and police forces, Austria paid Remington the license fees to produce the rifle, and Paget began work immediately. According to an article in a British publication, *The Engineer*, dated 27 July 1866, the Emperor of Austria was said to contract with Paget to produce 6,000 rolling-block breechloaders; a later published source stated the number was 15,000.

In any event, Paget cleverly incorporated a number of changes on the Austrian 11.2 × 39.7Rmm rimfire rolling-block Rifle not found on the American-made versions. First, hammer and breechblock pins were retained by individual screws in lieu of the standard Remington "button" plate. Second, a spring-charged, hammer-shaped, "safety stopper" mechanism was cut into the center of the hammer. Unless both the stopper and hammer were simultaneously thumbed to the rear, the hammer could not be cocked. This modification prevented the hammer from automatically opening if a faulty cartridge exploded — which could possibly cock the hammer, slamming the breech block open and sending gases into the shooter's face. The chance of this occurring was very remote when using solid-head centerfire cases but, using the earlier thin copper rimfire cartridge it was a possibility. Single-shot author James J. Grant once credited the Swedes and Norwegians with the safety stopper device; later disproved when I finally obtained one of these rare military rolling-block Rifles.

All the Austrian rolling blocks were marked ED.A PAGET WIEN 3. Serial numbers were located on the bayonet lug. Note the breech block and hammer pins are screw-retained, something the Swedes later copied.

The Austrian Model of 1866, produced in Europe, should be acknowledged as the first (albeit small) foreign contract obtained by Sam Remington before he departed from the continent. My specimen (s/n #1952) displays other unusual features such as a non-Remington oval-shaped trigger guard, a unique stock comb contour and a three-screw buttplate. Overall quality is quite acceptable, and the Rifle is marked on the left frame ED. A. PAGET, WIEN J. Only 2000 pieces are said to have been completed by Paget when production was halted following the 1866–67 Austrian debacle with the Prussians at Koniggratz.

The Austrian 4th Battalion and the 21st Jager Battalion were selected to conduct the field trials of the new rolling block. The snag that derailed this rolling block design was the issue of nationalism, as the Austrian press hammered the government for considering a foreign design. Between this and the Prussian troubles, the rolling block lost out to Joseph Werndl's system, which Austria finally chose as the national military arm.

Today, the Austrian Edward Paget-made rolling block is indeed the rarest of any Remington-sanctioned foreign prototype/limited production in existence. For years, many rolling-block students were left wondering about the disposition of the remaining 2000 arms. I discovered the majority of remaining surplus Paget-made Austrian rolling blocks ended up in Korea and China; surviving examples have been uncovered with Chinese/ Korean character cartouches on the buttstock. It is believed they were disposed of through a European version of an American Hartley and Graham military-surplus operation.

Evidence indicates they could have been used by Korean hostiles and their Chinese allies, who repelled the U.S. landing expeditions from the USS Colorado in 1871 during the battles at Kanghwa Island, Korea.

The left frame of the 1868/74 Norwegian rolling-block rifle made at Konigsberg is one of the most well-inspected Scandinavian military rolling blocks to be found. The markings include the manufactured ate, serial number and inspectors' markings — even the screws are numbered. The production precision clearly shows it was made for a special purpose, perhaps for rifle competition.

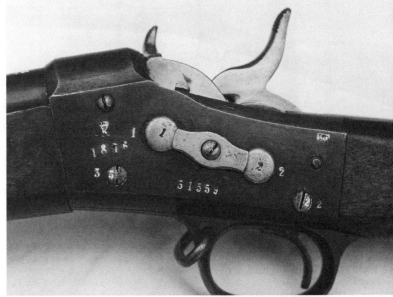

The Danish Model 1867/ 96/ 05 Carbine

In 1867, Denmark became the first quantity purchaser of the Remington rolling-block action, making it their official service arm. Contracting with Remington for 42,000 Rifles and 1800 carbines, the Danes received permission to begin domestic production in 1869. When, decades later, Denmark began to upgrade their older equipment, one of the most radically modified rolling blocks is unquestionably the Danish Model 1867/96/05 *Rytterkarabin* (cavalry carbine). This ultra-rare carbine is chambered for the 11.35×45Rmm Danish Remington carbine centerfire cartridge, which replaced the 11.7×42R rimfire version (for carbines) some years earlier. Beyond seeing one of these in the Copenhagen Arsenal display in 1968, I hadn't seen one in the United States until 1996. A Danish-American acquaintance brought one to this country in the 1950s and eventually sold it to me after several years of pestering. It is the first — and only — one I have seen in the Lower 48.

For years the Danes had experimented with manufacturing special-purpose rifles and carbines based on the rolling-block action. The 67/96/05 carbines were shortened to an overall length of 35.5 inches and were simply modified from the older 1867 Danish Bagladeriffels (infantry rifles) with worn barrels and other defects.

My Model 1867/96/05 was discovered with tang markings of E. Remington and Son indicating its action was from one the original rifles purchased

The rear sight, calibrated in "Alens," is itself serial-numbered to the rifle.

back in 1867. The 67/96/05's designation is derived from the official nomenclature being the Model 1867; '1896' indicated its sling swivels were repositioned, and the regraduation of the rear sight changed from the earlier Danish "Alen" to meters.

The modification of 1905, however, gave the carbine its most radical physical modification. The comb of the buttstock was laterally cut from the thumb rest on back and drilled to hold ten cartridges, thus increasing the soldier's basic ammunition load. Further, a hinged spring-tensioned aluminum cover and base plate kept the cartridges in place. A leather liner pinned inside the cover kept the cartridges silent when they hit against the cover.

Another interesting feature was the rounded, protruding knob installed on the left side of the frame, which served in place of a saddle ring.

With its "mushroom"-style head that fit into a clip spring on the saddle, it somewhat resembled the swiveling concept of the "Bridgeport Device" experimented with on Colt single-action revolvers for the U.S. Army.

The 67/96/05 cavalry carbine was fitted with conventional sling swivels with the rear swivel being angled on the right wrist, and had lightly-rounded finger grooves on the forend. All in all, it made

Having the entire comb of the stock stripped flat and drilled to hold ten cartridges beneath a spring-charged aluminum cover is indeed a radical addition.

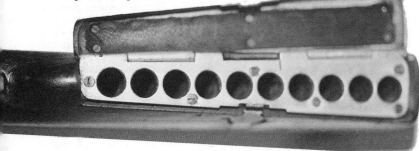

The hands-down rarest of all Belgian-made military rolling blocks is the Nagant-made Dutch contract carbine of 1873. So few of these have been seen worldwide that it is likely the scarcest foreign-made production rolling block.

for a very slick-looking carbine that appears about as far as one could go in modernizing the rolling block. The one feature it lacked was a buttplate.

The total number of 1867/96/05 modified carbines is estimated at 3000. Regarding Danish carbine production as a whole, 2500 Engineer carbines of the Model 1867 were delivered to the army, of which 1950 were altered to centerfire.

With substantial quantities of earlier rimfire ammunition in reserve stocks, a fair number of rimfire rolling-block carbines were left. Thus, breechblocks on some carbines were drilled with two firing pin channels — rim- or centerfire — allowing the firing pin to be moved to either position, depending on the ammunition issued.

Between 1872 and 1883, some 3078 carbines identical to the Engineer Model (with sling swivels on forend and lower buttstock) were received by the Danish navy (Marinen). The only distinguishing feature of service affiliation was the army or navy brass regimental or service disc in the buttstock. One of the reasons for the Danish military carbine upgrade of 1905 was to cover the shortage of 8mm Danish Model 1889 Krag bolt-action rifles. Interestingly, the Model 67/96/05 11.7mm centerfire carbines remained in active service with the regular army until 1914.

The Norwegian 1868/74 Konigsberg Rolling Block Rifle

Another very rare Scandinavian copy of the rolling block made under license was the 1868/74 infantry rifle manufactured at Konigsberg, Norway in 12.11mm Norway/Sweden rimfire. This particular example differs from the typical Swedish-made versions as it has a 38 ½-inch barrel. This Rifle shows the highest quality of workmanship and attention to detail in every single part: the frame, barrel, rear sight, the three barrel bands and all other

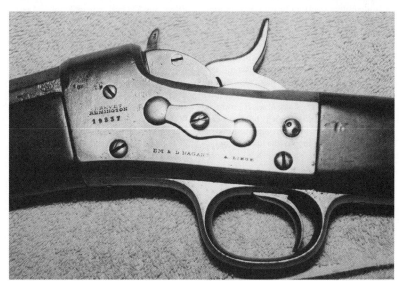

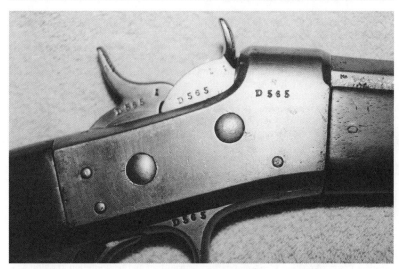

These right and left close-ups of the Nagant Dutch carbine show well-defined markings that identify it. The left frame side (top) has BREVETTE REMINGTON (Remington copy) over the company's master rolling block serial number. The pentagonal barrel flat shows still more inspectors' stampings.

A full-length view of my Chinese rimfire carbinehas nowhere near the graceful lines of the Nagant-made Dutch contract carbine and seems to have been produced in the shortest amount of time possible.

components were serial-numbered. My specimen is s/n 31559 and is marked 1876 indicating continuous serial numbers on all Konigsberg-made rolling blocks regardless of special or standard issue; otherwise, many more of these unique M1868/74 rifles would be in circulation. I believe it was specially-made as a military match rifle due to the overabundance of inspectors' cartouches and overall precise fit. The Konigsberg arsenal produced thousands of rolling blocks for the Swedish crown, but this high quality example does not compare to the usual Konigsberg-produced rolling-block infantry Rifles with dates from 1875 to 1878 that I have observed. Whatever the case, this configuration is truly one to watch for.

The Belgian Nagant Model 1873 Dutch Carbine

Two of Europe's most prolific arms manufacturers from Belgium were Emil & L. Nagant and August Francotte, both of whom had amicable relations with the Remington company in Ilion, New York. By the early 1870s, Remington found it had to work 24-hour shifts to keep up with orders from Spain, Latin America, Egypt and beyond. To meet production deadlines, the system of granting manufacturing rights to reliable, high-quality foreign arms manufacturing companies proved a profitable venture. Remington, though not receiving a full price for each Rifle, would receive a healthy royalty for each unit manufactured under license.

Francotte produced rolling-block Rifles and carbines to help fill the large Egyptian order, and independently took orders for Uruguay and El Salvador for a two-band musketoon in 43 Spanish. Nagant also produced an order of two-band musketoons for Tunisia that had a crescent moon inlaid into the stock, with fleur-de-lis designs in the body of the crescent.

The aforementioned Francotte and Nagant rolling blocks are genuine scarcities, but the real prize among Belgian-made rolling blocks are those of the 1873 Dutch carbine contract made by Nagant. These are so difficult to uncover that ten years ago they could bring $1000 in Europe alone. Holland, though adopting the Beaumont Rifle in 1870, issued its Snider conversions to the home guard and some colonial troops, then in 1873 decided to also adopt a Remington rolling-block carbine to be made under license by Nagant. It would be chambered for the 11.3×45R or 11mm Dutch Remington centerfire cartridge. The Nagant-made rolling-block carbines served three purposes: to arm the cavalry, engineers, and gendarmerie (national police or gendarmes).

The variation shown is part of the collection of Tom Jackson of Kingman, Arizona. I have never owned a Nagant Dutch rolling-block carbine and have heard rumors from Europe that, during the Nazi occupation of Holland, even antiquated Dutch firearms were destroyed or dumped at sea by the Germans to keep them from the resistance groups. If true,

With the action open one can see the early grooved channeled breech block was utilized. The million dollar question which evades explanation up to now is who was the Belgian company involved in setting up this operation in China to build these carbines? Also, did the Chinese build these independently upon their departure?

this could explain the worldwide rarity of these carbines. The thoroughness of the inspectors' markings on Jackson's Dutch carbine are indicative of the quality Nagant demanded on production that directly represented the Remington company. The left frame is marked Brevette Remington, or "Remington copy," with the number 19337 beneath. This is a "tracking serial number," indicating the total of rolling-block rifle actions the Nagant firm produced for royalty accounting purposes for Remington. Em. & L. Nagant markings are also present with the Liege ELG definitive proof on the barrel. The 1873 on the rear of barrel is the model year number and the 1877 on the buttplate is the year of manufacture. The D 565 appears to be the Nagant in-house serial number of how many carbines were produced on the contract so far. The circular Nagant cartouche on the right butt is very clear and it is obvious this carbine is in near excellent condition and obviously did not live a hard life. It can only be estimated that possibly 2000 to 4000 carbines were produced, conjecture based on military and police population size of the day. I have viewed rare photographs of the capitulation of the Dutch East Indies to the Japanese in World War II that show Dutch colonial police throwing what appeared to be rolling block-type carbines into an arms cache of all varieties of captured weapons. Thus it may be that numerous obsolete Dutch weapons, including Nagant-made carbines, were lost as a result of hostilities with Japan.

A Mysterious Chinese Rolling Block Carbine

Rolling block usage in Asia has traditionally been confined to China and Korea. Partial records indicate that, in 1874, Remington received a rather dubious order for 144,000 rolling-block rifles. I have examined Chinese copies of the rolling block, none of which had any Remington or U.S. markings. Some of these were the surplus Austrian rolling blocks made by Edward Paget as discussed previously, and were strictly a surplus purchase without any connection to Remington.

The second copies I examined were a rifle and a carbine, the latter of which I now own. The carbine is a mysterious piece, without markings aside from the number 21 and two Chinese characters — all other major components have the Chinese character of the number ten "+" which is shaped like a cross. Chambered for an unknown 11mm rimfire cartridge, the carbine appears to be of Belgian design with a Springfield-style muzzleloading rear sight (possibly U.S. surplus or replicated production). Other features include a brass buttplate and a circular channel drilled horizontally through the center of the stock evidently intended for some sort of sling attachment device. The barrel has an octagonal chamber and an offset witness mark to line up with the frame. I purchased this carbine from a WWII veteran who brought it back from Manchuria after his assignment involving releasing U.S. soldiers from Japanese captivity. He mentioned he saw many carbines and Rifles of this design at the Mukden, Manchuria arsenal.

Who assisted the Chinese in manufacturing these? If the tooling came from Belgium, it is odd that no Nagant or Francotte markings are present. Both these firms were known for their strict quality control, and the absence of even a token showing of inspector markings

is very odd. Another peculiar note: of all of the surplus military arms coming out of China in the last 20 years or more, not one Remington-marked rolling block has ever been imported. What became of the so-called order of 144,000 rolling blocks? I feel there was a secret (at least at present) arrangement wherein China made an agreement with Remington to produce the arms either in China proper, or in Belgium for subsequent export to the Chinese mainland — or perhaps vice-versa. From a professional viewpoint, after having examined over a thousand foreign- and domestic-made Remington military rolling blocks, the theory of tooling and machinery being shipped to China and the arms subsequently manufactured there, under Belgian supervision, seems the most feasible scenario. Given the warlord system of the day, foreign inspector or manufacturers markings may have been purposely omitted since countless warring factions may have had their arms produced on the identical Belgian equipment overseen by

the same inspectors!

There have been at least two known sales of Chinese-made rolling-block rifles having this carbine's characteristics (excepting the drilled stock channel). They were sold by Kristopher Gasior, a dealer of rare and unusual military rolling blocks (www.Collectiblefirearms.com). The Chinese-made rolling-block rifles were definitely produced under trained Belgian supervision and — so far — have been two-band military rifles with a cleaning rod and a unique elevated rear sight almost eight inches from the receiver ring! Indeed a peculiar arrangement. Caliber of these Rifles appears very similar to that of a 50–70 rimfire cartridge. Regarding the carbine, I know of only one other example — it is in a Massachusetts collection and an exact clone of my carbine. Parts are completely interchangeable, but are marked with the Chinese character number of 216. Perhaps in the future, a long-forgotten arsenal — akin to the recent find of thousands of arms in Nepal's Lag-

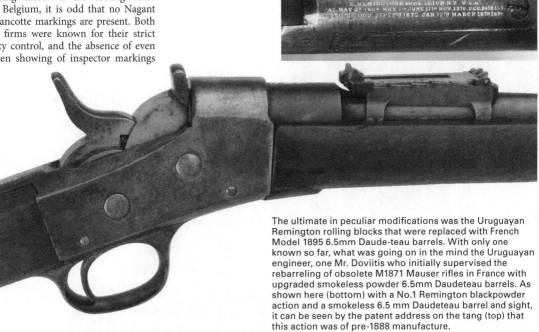

The ultimate in peculiar modifications was the Uruguayan Remington rolling blocks that were replaced with French Model 1895 6.5mm Daude-teau barrels. With only one known so far, what was going on in the mind the Uruguayan engineer, one Mr. Doviitis who initially supervised the rebarreling of obsolete M1871 Mauser rifles in France with upgraded smokeless powder 6.5mm Daudeteau barrels. As shown here (bottom) with a No.1 Remington blackpowder action and a smokeless 6.5 mm Daudeteau barrel and sight, it can be seen by the patent address on the tang (top) that this action was of pre-1888 manufacture.

an Silekhana palace — will be revealed on the Chinese mainland. For now, the so-called Chinese contract of Remington's mysterious "144,000" is a rolling-block version of lost treasure.

The Uruguayan 6.5 Daudeteau/ Doviitis Rolling Block Rifle

One nation that earnestly favored the rolling block system was the South American Republic of Uruguay. Whether made by Remington, Francotte or Nagant, they were probably the most prolific customers for this single-shot Rifle of any country south of the border. The Uruguayan military first purchased several thousand Remington rolling-block Rifles and carbines in 1880 in 43 Spanish, which was the standard chambering of nearly all Latin American countries that were rolling block-equipped. About that same year, Uruguay contracted with August Francotte of Belgium for approximately 2500–3000 two-band artillery musketoons, which are usually found marked "Republica Oriental," the early name for Uruguay.

Since Uruguay was populated by many German, Italian and other European immigrants, there was an ample population of educated machinists on hand, to include former European arms craftsmen. There is a great deal of evidence that they were conducting experiments on rolling block and other existing weapon systems.

Several years ago I obtained a particularly unusual and so far one-of-a-kind specimen, once owned by the late author Jerry Janzen, was obtained by the author several years ago. This Remington rolling-block action was fitted with what is known as the 6.5mm Mauser-Doviitis barrel, one of the great enigmas of foreign converted rolling-block actions. In the 1890s, a mysterious Uruguayan engineer named Doviitis was tasked by his government to take an unknown number of surplus German Mauser Infanterie Gewehr Model 1871 bolt-action rifles and have them reworked by the French Societe Francaise des Armes Portatives of St. Denis in Paris (abbreviated S.F.A.P / St. Denis). Doviitis is said to have supervised the installation of new French-made barrels chambered for the 6.5 × 53mm Daudeteau No.12 caliber to replace the old German 11mm (43 Mauser) tubes on the 71 Mauser actions (these barrels came from the now very rare Model 1895 Daudeteau Rifle sold to Uruguay, El Salvador and Portugal). No one ever seemed to find a record for this order, though many felt it was an interim purchase by the Uruguayan government to supplement its army's M1893 or M1895 Mauser rifles. Another rumor is they were intended to arm rebel factions in one of the Uruguayan states in the outback.

In any case, the arms were shipped from Antwerp, Belgium to Montevideo, Uruguay. A later rumor circulated that quantities of rolling-block actions were soon after being rebarreled in Montevideo arsenal, also with Doviitis in charge of the operation. Whether intended to serve as government training arms or to supply the army (or rebels?) is unknown.

Up to this point, only a single specimen of the 6.5mm Daudeteau-chambered military rolling block is known to me. The late Mr. Janzen may have obtained this rifle on a trip to Uruguay, but no such record exists. If quantities were reworked and clandestinely issued to rebels, or other factions, perhaps none ever returned to be imported through legal means and could likely have been discarded by insurgents in the jungle outback after the ammunition became obsolete. My specimen is in superb condition.

The barrel is clearly marked with the SFAP ST. DENIS scroll behind the original banded ramp rear sight for the 6.5 mm Daudeteau rifle cartridge. The two-band forend has the French 1895 bayonet lug beneath the front sight band, along with the peculiar cleaning rod mounted offset to the right side. I have requested information regarding this Rifle and the Doviitis connection but to this day however, the Uruguayan government is still secretive of disclosing even 19th century military information because of their past troubles with the 1970s Tupamaro rebels, off-shoots of another era. It would indeed be nice to see another specimen offered not only for sale but to simply compare and examine.

The U.S. Model 1870 Uruguayan-Honduran Carbine Conversion

The Uruguayan-Honduran carbine conversion is a true 19th century multi-national rolling-block carbine that started life as the U.S. Navy Model 1870 rifle, purchased by the Navy and made under contract at the Springfield Armory. Almost 10,000 of these two-band rifles with Remington-marked actions, several thousand had the rear sight installed closer to the receiver ring than specified, and were subsequently rejected by government inspectors. Though another 10,000 were assembled properly for the Navy,

Unknown until the 1960s, the Canadian purchase of 60 Whitney carbines to arm the Montreal police department was exposed in a 1965 article in a Canadian arms journal. For years American collectors believed it was merely a rumor.

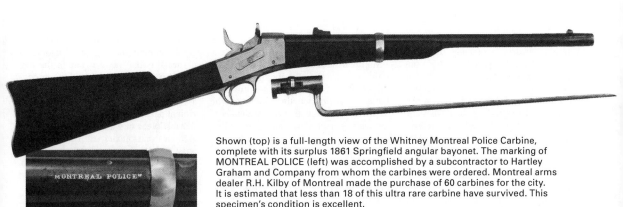

Shown (top) is a full-length view of the Whitney Montreal Police Carbine, complete with its surplus 1861 Springfield angular bayonet. The marking of MONTREAL POLICE (left) was accomplished by a subcontractor to Hartley Graham and Company from whom the carbines were ordered. Montreal arms dealer R.H. Kilby of Montreal made the purchase of 60 carbines for the city. It is estimated that less than 18 of this ultra rare carbine have survived. This specimen's condition is excellent.

many believe this first batch was purposely assembled incorrectly and was nothing more than a ploy to allow American surplus arms dealers to buy them and re-sell them to the French, who were clamoring for military Rifles during the Franco-Prussian War.

This clandestine act of "back-door" diplomacy actually succeeded, but the French ultimately lost the war in 1870.

The Hartley and Graham Company is believed to have bought them from the U.S. government at a bargain price, subsequently reselling them to France. Then, after buying the Rifles back from France, advertised them as "Franco-Prussian War Surplus," selling them for a profit yet again! Prime markets for such sales were Central and South America, where a ready market existed for rolling-block rifles. Many times, a country's numerous rival political groups would buy their ordnance from the same dealer — such as Hartley & Graham — who could care less which side was right. It was all about money. Uruguay, in 1873–75, again ordered some 2500 rolling blocks from Hartley & Graham, advertised as surplus 1870 Navy rolling blocks in 50–70 Govt. that had been repurchased from the French. The Uruguayans requested the Rifles to be re-barreled to 43 Spanish and shortened to carbine length, and fitted with a saddle ring and staple and carbine forend. These modifications would slightly raise the cost per cost of gun, but the contract with Hartley & Graham was nevertheless completed, and Uruguay received the delivery without a hitch. Upon receipt, all were inspected and stamped with the standard Uruguayan circular military cartouche on the left side of the stock with the date and EJERCITO URUGUAYO (Uruguayan Army). Interestingly, the button plate which held the breechblock and hammer pin in place was reversed to the right side

of the frame. The reversal button plate partially obscured the "giveaway origin" of the markings on the carbine actions — the U.S. Springfield 1870 marking and the American eagle motif.

Sometime in the mid-1880s, Uruguay sold a thousand or more of these carbines to Honduras as that rather poor nation could not afford to purchase new rifles from the United States. Over time, some of these carbines were captured by both Honduran rebel factions as well as El Salvadoran troops, and few have survived after years of hard service. My carbine was not terribly abused and its original Uruguayan cartouche is still noticeable. There is also a serial or rack number of "33" on the lower tang, which may be a Honduran addition since I once examined an identical specimen, imported from Uruguay, which lacked any numeration in this area. A "43 Span." stamping over the chamber is also present. Also, an E.H. is found stamped on the comb of the stock which appears to translate to Ejercito Honduras (Honduran Army). Very few of these have surfaced on the U.S. antique firearms market. But one thing is certain; they truly made money for their original American owners at least five times in their heyday!

Right up to the early 1910s, the M. Hartley Company of New York City (formerly Hartley and Graham) remained an agent for the Remington Arms Company, being redesignated as such after the Remington company was reorganized in 1888. As late as the 1900s, the Hartley Co. maintained an extensive inventory of out-of-production blackpowder-era rolling blocks and fulfilled countless orders for the poorer nations of Latin America who could not afford to arm all their soldiers with expensive Mauser bolt-action repeaters. Hartley and Co. produced hundreds of different unique military rolling blocks for numerous countries, which have often

been mistaken as genuine factory-correct Remington-made arms. This specimen of the Hartley & Graham-modified Model 1870 Navy rolling block sold to Uruguay, and then to Honduras, is a good example of how specially reworked rolling blocks confuse rolling block students as to being some sort of special-order contract made at the Remington factory. There are literally dozens of Hartley-converted rolling blocks:carbines with bayonet lugs or two-band full-stock carbines with a shortened cleaning rod, all going to Central or South American countries to arm both governments and rebel factions.

The 1870 Navy conversion sold to Uruguay should be considered among the most difficult to uncover, including those indigenously manufactured in a foreign arsenal under Remington license. Rest assured, many variations never before seen are waiting somewhere in the dark jungles of Latin America.

Whitney Rolling Block Rarities

Along with E. Remington & Sons, the firm of the Whitney Arms Co. of New Haven, Conn. competed in manufacturing a rolling block-action rifle which resulted in two different types of actions offered at different periods of time. The earliest was the Whitney-Laidley patent breech-loading system; peculiar in that the breech-block and hammer components consisted of a five-piece assembly comprised of hammer, locking cam, thumb piece plate and breechblock. Its last patent was registered on July 16 1872. In production from 1871 to 1881, the first model action was eventually redesigned and "Remingtonized" to a less complicated system once the Remington patent expired. This allowed Whitney to closely copy its simpler competitor, resulting in an action more economical to manufacture.

The second model action was produced from 1881 until 1888 when the Whitney Firearms Company closed its doors, and was acquired by the Winchester Repeating Arms Co. Not having come close to the quantities of rolling-block Rifles Remington had churned out, Whitney military rolling-block rifles and carbines nevertheless had their following and, in their entirety, were exported outside the United States to countries primarily in Latin America. In nearly every case, those that returned to the U.S. surplus arms market in scanty numbers have been in conditions ranging from good to poor, indicating hard usage. To find any standard or special order Whitney military rolling-block rifle or carbine in excellent condition is truly sensational. Special production Whitney military rolling blocks for foreign customers have been almost non-existent in the past, but it is accurate to say that arms exporters Hartley and Graham made up at least some specially-modified Whitney rolling blocks for overseas buyers.

There is, however, at least one that was revealed by author Gordon Howard in a Canadian arms journal dated 1965. No one in the United States, including antique firearms expert Norm Flayderman, had ever seen the special Whitney Montreal Police Carbine until it was featured in the third edition of my book, The Military Remington Rolling Block Rifle (1998 Pioneer Press, Union City TN). Years ago, I heard from several Canadians that this arm existed, but had never owned an example until I purchased a single specimen from a Maine dealer/collector who began going on buying trips to Canada in the 1990s when our northern neighbor's government imposed draconian gun legislation. Many rarities were coming out of the woodwork as average Canadian citizens were frantically selling off their firearms, many of which were highly collectible.

The Whitney Montreal Police Carbine was a standard, first model Whitney military saddle ring carbine chambered in 433 Spanish Remington Carbine, a lighter-recoiling number than the full-blown 78-grain load of FFg of the standard 43 Spanish cartridge. The carbine was procured specifically for the city of Montreal in December of 1875 after the city police committee decided to pick out 50 men in the department and arm them with carbines in lieu of revolvers.

At the meeting on September 1, the police council stated…."the men shall be armed with carbines, as they are more useful than revolvers and that the num-ber so armed be limited to sixty…." After $1330 was appropriated for the purchase, a Montreal arms agent named R.H. Kilby residing at Saint Catherine St. was to be the contact man for the procurement. Little is known whether Kilby or the Montreal city council specified details of the carbine regarding caliber, including the angular socket-type bayonets that accompanied all sixty pieces, which appear to have been surplus U.S. Springfield-style bayonets. It is generally felt that Kilby ordered the arms and had them stamped "Montreal Police" by Hartley and Graham Co. in New York City. In Gordon Johnson's article, he notes a former police lieutenant he interviewed believes the carbines were never fired except for brief training practice and were used as reserve weapons. In addition, the lieutenant stated that they were mostly used for escorting prisoners from the courthouse to Bordeaux Jail in the north end of Montreal city. All carbines had rack markings on the buttplate, with mine being #7. As with all Whitney rolling blocks, serial numbers are on the lower tang and, from all indications, they were not consecutively numbered.

In the early 1960s, a very small number of these carbines began to appear in Canada and were in from good to very good condition. The highest rack number known is #59, reported by Gordon Johnson. He also noted (in 1965) that no more than 18 to 20 carbines were said to exist. When they were withdrawn from service during World War I, they were stored in wooden cases in the basement of the Montreal Police School. Around 1923, a substantial number were destroyed or disassembled, and ammunition for the carbines was disposed of as late as 1961. The arms were supplied with a two-position carbine open and peep sight for 200 and 500 yards, and were finished in the white, aside from a blued barrel. Fortunately my specimen appears to have had little to no use — which explains its excellent condition. Only slight wear adjacent to the muzzle stems from bayonet installation and removal. For many years rumors circulated that rolling block firearms were being used in official military or police capacities in Canada, but no proof of this surfaced until the 1960s. The importance of the discovery of the Whitney Montreal Carbine caused it to be included as a special category of its own in the latest edition of FLAYDERMAN'S GUIDE TO ANTIQUE AMERICAN FIREARMS… AND THEIR VALUES.

Another extremely rare Whitney roll-ing block is a second model garden-variety three-band military rifle. What makes it special is that (a) it is one of the rare Mexican contract models and (b), its condition is almost at 90 percent, aside from a bullet hole in its stock indicating its violent past. Though the bullet took out a sizeable piece of walnut, especially at the exit, clear cartouches still remain on the wrist and other places. Whitney Rifles in 43 Spanish were ordered twice by Mexico, both orders being of the first and second models.

The rifle's fifth-generation owner, whose ancestors lived in California near the Mexican border, told me the Rifle was a participant — in the hands of Mexican bandits — in the second famous raid (the first being in 1875) on the "Old Stone" Trading Post in Campo, California in 1881. The trading-post workers won the shoot-outs and captured the Mexicans guns, a dozen or more Whitney rolling blocks recently stolen from a *Federale* arsenal in Mexico. This attests to the like-new condition with brilliant case colors, and the Mexican Sunburst and R.M. (Republic of Mexico) translating to *Republica Mexicana*.

Whitney Rifles in 43 Spanish were ordered twice by Mexico; both orders being of the first and second models.

Remington-Made Rarities of both Black and Smokeless Powder Eras

Genuine Remington factory-made rolling-block military Rifles have their share of scarce models. One of the most elusive rolling blocks catalogued in 1870s and 1880s Remington factory literature is the Spanish Civil Guard Model, simply a two-band military rifle with a shorter 30-inch barrel. I've owned a meager total of four different Civil Guard models in the past 35 years: three from the Philippines and one from Costa Rica.

A most peculiar example I uncovered was found in Belize (the former British Honduras). I speculate it was part of a small lot ordered for Her Majesty's colonial militia in the late 1880s. The profusely British proof-marked Civil Guard Model is in 43 Spanish and has a tinned rear sight, a very peculiar addition. It is the second one from Belize that I have seen in "Del Norte" in about 20 years.

Well identified with numerous British proof marks, the Rifle has scattered pitting typical of the humid region; the bore however is surprisingly clean.

Why England ordered these in lieu of

issuing the standard British service arm, the Martini-Henry, is unknown. The only practical reason is that all British Honduras' neighboring countries used the 43 Spanish Remington rolling block. Thus perhaps the British reasoned from a logistical standpoint that if ammunition ran low during a skirmish with rebel or other forces from nearby Mexico or Guatemala, the interchangeable captured stocks of 43 Spanish cartridges could be utilized if required. Remember, no countries in that region used British Martini-Henry Rifles chambered for the 577/450 cartridge. Definitely a rare interesting rifle!

Another seldom-encountered military rolling-block rifle from that area of Central America, is from the post-1888 order from Guatemala. This period can be verified since the tangs on all these Rifles were marked REMINGTON ARMS COMPANY, indicating their manufacture followed the reorganization of E. Remington and Sons after that year. Fragmented records show that fewer than 2500 were exported to Guatemala between 1890 and 1894. Physical proof they were used to the extreme in that humid and politically violent country is obvious in that their condition ranged from fair to (barely) good. Their primary identifier was behind the rear sight, having the stamped metal displaying "EJERCITO GUATEMALA" (Guatemalan Army) which was often barely visible. The Guatemalan 43s usually ended up in the rebarreling vise to be converted, reblued, etc. into sporters at a time when military rolling blocks in less than new condition regardless of unusual markings, were looked upon as one step above scrap iron. I have found one intact,

with markings, and in very good condition to boot. The Guatemalan army issue model is definitely one to watch for, but look closely for the markings as they are normally very faint.

On the opposite end of the beauty scale, Remington rolling blocks that were made as presentation pieces are in a one-of-a-kind category. One of the most beautiful blackpowder-era examples I had the chance to inspect was a fully engraved three-band rifle in 43 Spanish with a fancy silver inlay on the left side of the buttstock that was presented to a Spanish army general for the capture of Cuban insurrectionist D. Pedro Figueredo on August 10, 1870. The rifle was sold at auction in 2000 by J.C. Devine Auctioneers for well over $7500.

After 1896, the Remington rolling block entered the smokeless era. Examples considered antique scarcities, manufactured during this time frame (1896–1917), are primarily categorized by caliber and the presence of national crests. Since 7mm Mauser was the most widespread smokeless powder chambering in the Remington Model 1902, to discover one in 236 (6mm) Navy, 30–40 Krag and 7.65mm Mauser is so rare that they currently bring as much as $2500 to $3000 in good to excellent condition. The Remington Model 1897 rifles and carbines of the 1899–1900 Mexican contract, with the national crest stamped on the receiver ring, totaled 14,010 Rifles and carbines. Those that returned to the U.S. arms market in the 1960s were, for the most, in very sad shape. The majority of these hardened smokeless steel guns were rebarreled to modern calibers and given

complete makeovers. A Mexican-marked Model 1897 Rifle or, especially, a carbine in very decent condition today is quite desirable and, price-wise, is a well above the 1962 price of $8.28! The condition of the crest is often the primary factor in determining desirability and price.

Aside from the Mexican contract model, the other crested military rolling block of the smokeless era are those of the El Salvador contract of 1902. These are even more difficult to discover because fewer were manufactured. Those that have been found are, on average, in rough and pitted condition. I've seen only one in very good condition in a private collection. The Salvadoran Model differs from the Mexican contract model not because it is a Model 1902, but because of an oversize upper handguard with a pronounced groove. Find one of these 7mm Rifles that worked the humid, wet jungles of El Salvador in excellent condition with a clean national crest, and you have one of the great prizes of the post-1900 era Remington military rolling block Rifles.

The very last Remington military rolling block of substantial number that closed out a 50-year era of steady production were those of the French contract of 1915–1916. It was basically a supplementary order to provide France with a single-shot Rifle in their national caliber of 8mm Lebel. This interim order gave Remington time to tool up for the standard Mannlicher-Berthier repeating bolt-action Rifle. The French purchased 100,291 rolling blocks in World War I, with most going to arm colonial forces from Morocco, Algeria and other colonies. The majority of these rifles saw very hard usage and, after

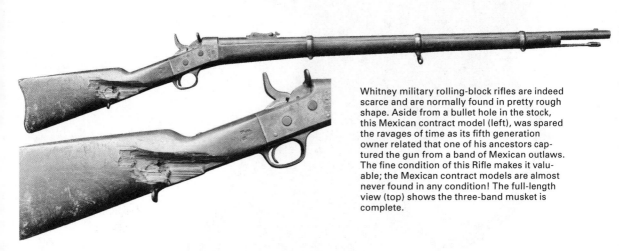

Whitney military rolling-block rifles are indeed scarce and are normally found in pretty rough shape. Aside from a bullet hole in the stock, this Mexican contract model (left), was spared the ravages of time as its fifth generation owner related that one of his ancestors captured the gun from a band of Mexican outlaws. The fine condition of this Rifle makes it valuable; the Mexican contract models are almost never found in any condition! The full-length view (top) shows the three-band musket is complete.

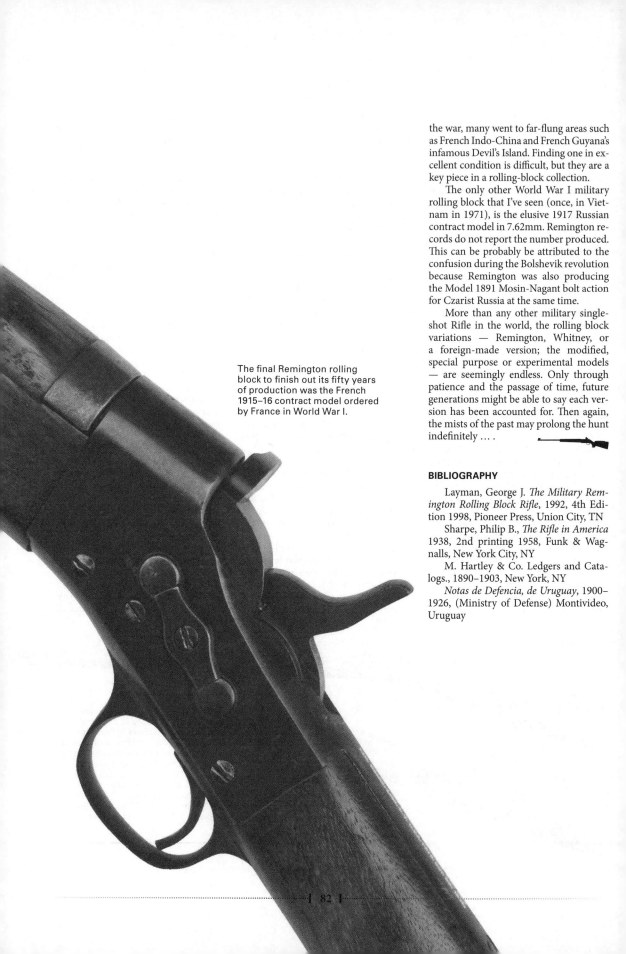

The final Remington rolling block to finish out its fifty years of production was the French 1915–16 contract model ordered by France in World War I.

the war, many went to far-flung areas such as French Indo-China and French Guyana's infamous Devil's Island. Finding one in excellent condition is difficult, but they are a key piece in a rolling-block collection.

The only other World War I military rolling block that I've seen (once, in Vietnam in 1971), is the elusive 1917 Russian contract model in 7.62mm. Remington records do not report the number produced. This can be probably be attributed to the confusion during the Bolshevik revolution because Remington was also producing the Model 1891 Mosin-Nagant bolt action for Czarist Russia at the same time.

More than any other military single-shot Rifle in the world, the rolling block variations — Remington, Whitney, or a foreign-made version; the modified, special purpose or experimental models — are seemingly endless. Only through patience and the passage of time, future generations might be able to say each version has been accounted for. Then again, the mists of the past may prolong the hunt indefinitely … .

BIBLIOGRAPHY

Layman, George J. *The Military Remington Rolling Block Rifle*, 1992, 4th Edition 1998, Pioneer Press, Union City, TN

Sharpe, Philip B., *The Rifle in America* 1938, 2nd printing 1958, Funk & Wagnalls, New York City, NY

M. Hartley & Co. Ledgers and Catalogs., 1890–1903, New York, NY

Notas de Defencia, de Uruguay, 1900–1926, (Ministry of Defense) Montivideo, Uruguay

Days of the Springfield

■ Col. Townsend Whelen

U.S. Springfield, Model 1903, with type "C" stock.

I N THE Spanish American War, 1898, our officers became rather dissatisfied with the Krag rifle performance compared with that of the 7mm Spanish Mauser. The Krag had a muzzle velocity of 2,000 feet per second and the cartridges had to be fed one at a time into the magazine. The Mauser shot a cartridge that had a muzzle velocity of 2,300 fps and thus a much flatter, hence longer danger space, and the magazine could be filled in one quick motion by means of a clip of five cartridges, thus giving much greater sustained fire; both very important features from a military point of view. The Ordnance Department of the Army therefore proceeded to a study of the matter, including an examination of the rifles and cartridges used by other nations.

In late September, 1903, when I returned to my post at Monterey, California, after having spent the summer shooting in army competitions and the National Matches as a member of the U.S. Army Infantry Team, my commanding officer handed me a letter he had received from the Chief of Ordnance, asking him to detail me to make an extensive test of a pilot model of a new rifle that had been developed at Springfield Armory. I was also to express an opinion as to its desirability for issue to the Army to replace the current rifle, the Krag. The rifle and a case of ammunition had also arrived.

This rifle was very similar to the 30-06 Springfield military rifle as we now know it. Its breech action, in fact, was identical. It had a 24-inch barrel, a rod bayonet, an open rear sight operated for elevation by a ramp, adjustable to even hundreds of yards only, but with a peep plate pivoted at the back of the open sight which could be raised for use. The breech action was almost identical with that of the Model 1898 Mauser, except for a combined bolt stop and magazine cut-off on the left side of the receiver, and a two-piece firing pin arranged so that the striker point, the one part most apt to break, could be economically replaced. The 5-shot magazine could be loaded with five cartridges at once by means of an expendable clip similar to the Mauser's. The rifle was numbered J8½T.

The cartridge had a rimless case, very similar to the 30-06 cartridge as we now know it, but loaded with a 220-grain round nose, jacketed bullet identical to the Krag bullet. The powder charge was Laflin and Rand WA smokeless powder sufficient in quantity to give a muzzle velocity of 2,350 fps.

I fired this rifle twice through the Regular Army Qualification Course-slow fire at 200 to .600 yards, rapid fire at 200 and 300 yards, and a skirmish run — and obtained as good scores as I would have had I shot the Krag rifle that I'd used all summer. The rifle, I thought, was a little more accurate than the Krag, and I would have obtained higher scores were it not for the rear sight that could be adjusted to only even hundreds of yards for elevation. I had to hold off a little for elevation at all distances. The recoil was noticeably heavier than that of the Krag, but not particularly disturbing to me. It was intended that this rifle, with its 24-inch barrel, be issued to both infantry and cavalry. In my report I criticized only the rear sight, and stated that otherwise I thought it entirely suitable for our service. Thus I think I was the first officer and rifleman ever to shoot the Springfield rifle on the rifle range.

This rifle was subsequently adopted for service, to replace the Krag, and issuance to troops of the Regular Army started in 1905. But in the meantime it had been found that the quantity of powder giving a muzzle velocity of 2,350 fps was too erosive for the barrel, affording an accuracy life of only about 800 rounds, and accordingly the powder charge was reduced sufficiently to give a muzzle velocity of 2,200 fps. The rifle was now officially called the "U.S. Rifle, caliber 30, Model 1903," and the cartridge the "Ball Cartridge, caliber 30, Model 1903." Popularly the rifle was termed the "New Springfield," but pretty soon the "New" was omitted. A new rear sight was also adopted for it, rather like the sight that had been on the Krag rifle. This rifle was issued to my regiment, the 30th Infantry, in time for the regular target practice season of 1906. The chief difference we found with it, compared with the Krag we had formerly used, was that much more careful and extended practice was needed to accustom some of the men to its heavier recoil. The bore was also more difficult to clean, particularly to *keep* clean, than the Krag bore had been.

After this early season's shooting with my company I was ordered to Fort Sheridan as a member of the U.S. Army Infantry Team, and then to the National

First issues of the 1903 Springfield had a full 24″ barrel, with ramrod-bayonet underneath. Note also forward band position and unusual front sight.

Matches. Here the shooting was with the Krag, the Springfield not yet having been issued to the National Guard. Upon completion of the National Matches I rejoined my regiment which, meantime, had been ordered to Fort William McKinley in the Philippine Islands. Here I found that the regiment had been issued a slightly different type of Springfield rifle, but still called the Model 1903. It was fitted with a knife bayonet to replace the former rod bayonet, and had a slightly different walnut hand-guard above the barrel. It also used a slightly different cartridge. The story of the conversion is an interesting one.

Prior to about 1901 the German army had been equipped with the Model 1898 Mauser rifle using an 8mm (7.9×57mm) cartridge loaded with a 236-grain round nose bullet to a muzzle velocity of 2,200

fps. Groove diameter of barrel was .318". Then after considerable experimentation they changed the bullet to one weighing 154 grains with a very sharp point, called a "Spitzer" point, and increased the muzzle velocity to 2,800 fps. New barrels to take this cartridge were fitted to their rifles, and the groove diameter was increased to .323". The increased velocity and the pointed bullet gave a much flatter trajectory and a greatly increased danger

space, a very considerable military advantage. Our Ordnance Department was not slow to investigate this improvement, and as a consequence our cartridge for our Springfield rifle was changed to take a 150-grain sharp point bullet loaded to a muzzle velocity of 2,700 fps. To convert existing Springfield rifles to take this new cartridge the barrels had to be rethroated. To do this one thread was cut off the breech of the barrel, the barrel set back, decreasing its length from 24 inches to 23.79 inches, and rechambered. The neck of the Model 1903 cartridge case was also slightly shortened, and the new cartridge was called the Model 1906. This is why we now have a Model 1903 rifle taking a Model 1906 cartridge, and why the barrel is 23.79 inches long instead of 24 inches. The new cartridge soon became popularly known as the "30-06."

When my regiment started its target practice shortly after my arrival in the Philippines it at once became apparent to us that the new rifle and the new cartridge were slightly more accurate than the older ones, that the recoil was slightly less, and the allowances that had to be made for wind were considerably smaller, all considerable advantages. But we also noticed another difference which was not so good. After firing for a few days the bore of the rifle, particularly on top of the lands near the muzzle, became coated with a substance that looked something like the lead that we occasionally saw in our older black powder rifles. This was a metal fouling from the cupronickel jackets of the bullets fired at such great velocity. As it accumulated in the bore it gradually interfered with the accuracy of the rifle to a small extent. It was almost impossible to remove this fouling and the only thing we could do, at that time, was to keep it down by cleaning the bore with a brass wire bristle brush. From then on, until we found the solution for this troublesome fouling, I was always distressed with the appearance of the bores of the rifles in my command. I shall refer to this matter of metal fouling later, and show how we gradually solved the trouble.

Meantime an incident occurred which deserves notice. Private Manuel of my company was firing on the range at Fort McKinley when his rifle "blew up." The whole top of the receiver was blown off, and the bolt was blown twenty feet to the rear. Fortunately Manuel received only a few small cuts on the face. There was no question about there *not* having been an obstruction in the bore because he had previously fired two loads from his clip, and those shots had been marked on his target. I was on the firing point only twenty feet away at the time. I immediately took the rifle into the Ordnance office in Manila and we investigated it as carefully as we could there. The only conclusion we could come to was that it had been caused by a defective and very much overloaded cartridge. Of course, as we now know, this was caused by a brittle receiver that occurred in exceedingly rare instances due to the steel used and the method of heat treatment. This trouble was completely cured after World War I by the adoption of a new method of heat treatment, and then by a new steel, and finally all rifles numbered under 800,000 (those having the old steel and old heat treatment) were condemned. The matter is discussed in detail elsewhere.*

In the spring of 1909 I was ordered from the Philippines to the United States as a member of the Army Infantry Rifle Team. Before going to the National Matches we held our initial team practice at Fort Sheridan, Illinois, and two days a week at Camp Logan on the Illinois National Guard range, where we could get experience in shooting in high winds, the Fort Sheridan range being a very sheltered one. This was the first competition season I took part in where the Springfield rifle was used. The rifles shot splendidly with the specially selected ammunition issued to us for the matches. We were still having trouble with metal fouling. Some of us were keeping this at a minimum by rubbing a thin coating of powdered graphite on our bullets before loading them, and others used a light coat of a heavy grease called Mobilubricant, similarly rubbed on the bullets.

Then, through my correspondence with Dr. Walter G. Hudson, I learned that British gunmakers had developed a strong ammonia solution which completely dissolved and removed all traces of metal fouling. Dr. Hudson gave me the formula for it. The bore of the rifle, clean and cold, was plugged at the chamber with a rubber cork, and a short section of rubber tube was slipped over the muzzle. The solution was then poured into the bore until it rose in the tube, let remain in the bore for 30 minutes, then poured out, the bore flushed with water, and dried. Every trace of the fouling was dissolved and the bore was like new. If certain precautions were observed its action was perfect and safe. I tried it on my rifle and it worked perfectly. Then the whole team tried it with similar fine results. After that we cleaned our rifles in this manner each noon and

night. I shot particularly well that year. My average at 600 yards for the entire year's shooting was 49.5 out of a possible 50 points.

That year the Union Metallic Cartridge Company offered special match ammunition. Several of my friends who had tried it said that it was splendidly accurate. It was loaded with a 172-grain bullet having a very sharp pencil or "spire" point. I bought some of it, and used it in

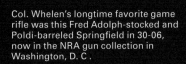

Col. Whelen's longtime favorite game rifle was this Fred Adolph-stocked and Poldi-barreled Springfield in 30-06, now in the NRA gun collection in Washington, D. C .

the Adjutant Generals Match, calling for twenty shots at 1,000 yards, and won that match with it with a score of 99 points, which was said to be the highest score ever fired at 1,000 yards with the service rifle. The following day I also used this ammunition in the Wimbledon Cup Match, also 20 shots at 1,000 yards, and came in second in that match with a score of 97. Thus I ended my competitive military rifle shooting in a burst of glory.

After these competitions I rejoined my regiment, which meantime had been ordered from the Philippines to Fort Jay, New York, and shortly after that I was detailed as Inspector-Instructor with the Connecticut National Guard, and then ordered to Washington to the Division of Militia Affairs. On completion of that detail I again joined my regiment, the 29th Infantry, in the Panama Canal Zone, and served there until the outbreak of World War I when I was promoted to major and assigned as Ordnance Officer of the 79th Division. Later I was placed on the general staff in charge of infantry training in the United States. After the war was over, not having had any battle experience, I thought I would be handicapped in the infantry so I transferred to the Ordnance

Department. My first assignment was to Frankford Arsenal, where all the small arms ammunition for the Army was manufactured. After I had been there ten days the commanding officer fell sick, and I became the commanding officer, and remained there for the next three years.

I at once started out to try to improve the quality and the accuracy of the service ammunition. It was suggested to us that, under the heat and friction generated in the rifle barrel, tin was a good lubricant. Accordingly we made up some of the 150-grain cupronickel jacketed bullets slightly smaller in diameter than normal and

*Hatcher's Notebook by Maj. Gen. Julian S. Hatcher. The Stackpole Company, Harrisburg, Pa., 1947.

tin-plated them with a coating .002-inch thick. It worked. No more metal fouling and much better accuracy. The National Match ammunition for 1921 was loaded with this tin-plated bullet, which the shooters immediately termed "tin can" ammunition, and it shot with splendid accuracy, better than ever before. Then a serious defect developed with its use. The tin alloyed with the steel of the bore, the resultant alloy had a low melting point, and the bore washed out or eroded very quickly — entirely too short an accuracy life. So this experiment failed.

As most of you well know, I have always been an avid experimenter with sporting rifles. The modern ammunition for such rifles employed bullets jacketed with gilding metal — 90% copper, 10% zinc — and apparently these gave no trouble with metal fouling. So next we tried

that an effective range of over 5,000 yards could be obtained with the new projectiles. The most promising bullet tried was one of about 172 grains, sharply pointed, and with a 9-degree boat-tail, but we did not seem to be able to make it shoot with satisfactory accuracy. While we were working with this bullet I was ordered to Camp Perry as Ordnance Officer of the National Matches. While I was there I tried my hand at a little shooting again, this time with the small bore, as I had no time from my duties for 30 caliber shooting. Among other matches I shot in, I was on our International Team in the Dewar Match, but about this time I developed an exceedingly sore boil on my backside. On the day of the Dewar Match I was so sore they had to take me to the firing point in a car and lower me down. Despite so much pain I could hardly move, the sec-

United States. In the meantime, long range barrage fire had gone out of favor in military circles due to great improvement in artillery fire, so we again reverted to our 150-grain flat base, pointed bullet for our standard rifle ammunition, but now jacketing it with gilding metal instead of cupronickel. But that 172-grain boat-tail bullet won't die. It has proved one of the best bullets ever made for 300-meter International Match shooting, and is today again being manufactured at Frankford Arsenal for that use.

Late in 1922 I was relieved from duty at Frankford Arsenal and went to Washington for duty in the office of the Assistant Secretary of War, and after that as Ordnance Member on the Infantry Board, at Fort Benning, Georgia. Then as Executive Officer of the Manufacturing Service in the office of the Chief of Ordnance,

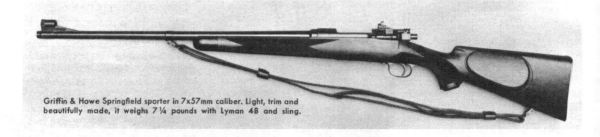

Griffin & Howe Springfield sporter in 7x57mm caliber. Light, trim and beautifully made, it weighs 7¼ pounds with Lyman 48 and sling.

a 170-grain pointed bullet jacketed with gilding metal. There was no longer any metal fouling and the accuracy was very good indeed, better than anything tried before except the "tin can" ammunition.

In World War I combat long-range barrage firing with machine guns had been employed very considerably at ranges up to 4,000 and 5,000 yards. We used in our machine guns the normal rifle cartridge loaded with 150-grain bullet. Its extreme range was only about 3,800 yards, and we were completely outranged by the machine guns of most of the other powers, including the enemy. Their machine gun ammunition employed much heavier bullets, that is, bullets with greater sectional density and a much longer controlled range. After the war we started experiments in an effort to increase the effective range of our rifle ammunition. We started making bullets weighing 170 to 180 grains, and with "boat-tails" and sharper points. These were fired experimentally at Daytona Beach, Florida, by Majors Hatcher and Wilhelm of the Ordnance Department, and it was apparent

ond highest score of the match was mine, being beaten only by Virgil Richards.

When I returned to Frankford Arsenal from these matches I went straight to bed to get over that damned boil. Soon Mr. Matthews, the foreman of the bullet shop, came over to see me. He was very much excited. He showed me group after group he had fired at 600 yards with this 172-grain boat-tail bullet, all within 6 inches. He shouted "I've got it, I've got it." He told me he had managed to make this bullet shoot with such fine accuracy by making the core very hard, and then employing as a final die what he called a "rectifying die," one made very perfectly indeed and changed about every 20,000 bullets, or when it began to show the slightest wear. This was the last die used, and the bullet was driven into it with a heavy blow thus making its form most perfect and hard. This became, eventually, the famous 1925 National Match bullet, the most accurate bullet ever used in the Springfield. The only trouble was it had an awfully long range — 5,500 yds. — and it was unsafe to use on many of our rifle ranges in the

and when that duty was over I went to Springfield Armory as officer in charge of research and development. It was exceedingly interesting here to change from the manufacture of the ammunition to the manufacture of the rifle. Springfield had been manufacturing rifles, the best rifles in the world, for over a hundred years. There was nothing that I, of course, a greenhorn at that art, could tell them, but it was most interesting to watch the meticulous care that was used at every step in the manufacture. I was particularly interested in the bedding of the rifles in their stocks, for I'd never realized how much depended on it. One in every ten service rifles, and every National Match, sporting, and target rifle was finally tested for accuracy by firing from a Wood-worth cradle rest at 200 meters. If it did not come up to the standard prescribed for that type of rifle it was sent back to the manufacturing department for correction and almost invariably the trouble would be in the bedding of the rifle in its stock. So far as I was able to determine by questioning the older employees at the Armory, the technique of this bedding was developed, practically as we now do it,* by Freeman R. Bull, who was Master Armorer at Springfield during the 1880–1890 period. In this 200-meter testing service rifles were tested with service ammunition, and averaged about 3½ inches for five-shot groups. National Match and sporting rifles were fired with National Match ammunition, and averaged about 2¾-inch groups, while the heavy barrel target rifles were tested with Palma Match ammunition, and averaged close to 2-inch 5-shot groups.

Besides the regular issue to the services, Springfield rifles were sold to members of the National Rifle Association. In the course of accuracy testing at 200 meters, every once in a while a rifle would deliver an extremely small five-shot group, almost all shots in one hole. We called these "Bumblebee groups." The group fired was attached to all rifles except the service type. When a man bought one of these rifles, accompanied by one of these Bumblebee groups, he was naturally elated. However, while I was on duty at the Armory I had every rifle that made one of these very small groups retested, and invariably it shot a group of about average accuracy, as above.

At Frankford Arsenal all routine and special testing of ammunition for accuracy was done in heavy Mann barrels held in the Mann V-rest, and these barrels were all star gauged to have a groove diameter of from .3080" to .3082". At the time I left Frankford Arsenal they were making their 172-grain boat-tail bullets also with a diameter of .308". However, when I arrived at Springfield in 1929 I noticed that all these bullets measured .3085". We had frequent conferences with the technical men at Frankford, and one time I asked Mr. Linwood Lewis, the leading ballistic engineer there, why they were now making their bullets so large. He told me that they had determined conclusively that boat-tail bullets of this diameter gave decidedly better accuracy in bores of .308" groove diameter or larger.

I have mentioned "star gauged" barrels above. All National Match, sporting, and target barrels were selected by this method. The star gauge is an instrument that measures the bore and groove diameter of a barrel at every inch of its length from chamber to muzzle. To pass the star gauge test a barrel had to have a groove diameter

of .308" to not larger than .3085", and at no spot could it vary from that range of diameters by more than .0002". As a matter of fact, during the period from 1929 to 1933 when I was on duty there, three-fourths of the barrel production would pass this star gauge test. Note that in Krag rifles of about 1900, also made at Springfield Armory, the barrels varied in groove diameter from .3075" to .311" and larger. The closer tolerances, of course, were due to the great improvement in machine tools and manufacturing techniques which took place in the United States over the intervening period.

The superb record that the Springfield rifle has made in our service for dependability and durability is well-known, as is its remarkable record for accuracy at the National Matches and other competitions where it was used. At the National Matches in the last two years the MI (Garand) rifles, also manufactured at Springfield Armory, are said to have shot as accurately and scored as high as the Springfield 1903 rifle ever did. Our Army has won two World Wars with Springfield rifles.

Hunting

About 1910 Louis Wundhammer, a Los Angeles gunsmith, remodeled four Springfield 1903 service rifles into sporting type, two of these for Mr. Stewart Edward White and Captain Edward Crossman, the others for gentlemen named Rogers and Colby. He fitted these rifles with excellent, light sporting stocks with pistol grip and shotgun type buttplate, and fitted early style Lyman 48 sights to them, removing the military rear sight (though leaving the sight base intact on these first

rifles), and poüishing and blueing the barrels. These were the first commercial Springfield sporters ever made (though Theodore Roosevelt had had Springfield Armory remodel a 1903 rifle earlier), and no more attractive bolt action sporting rifles have ever been built.† Captain Crossman used his rifle (and also later Wundhammer Spring-fields) very extensively for hunting the deer of California and wrote many articles for the sporting press of those days on it. Mr. White used his on three long extended trips into Africa and killed all the game of that country successfully with it except elephant and rhino, I think. He relates its fine performance in detail many times in his several books. He also had a 405 Winchester Model 1895 rifle with him. He tried many different bullets and loads in the Springfield, and in his last book he stated that if he could have the 220-grain Western boat-tail bullet with tip of lead exposed, loaded to a muzzle velocity of 2,300 fps, he would leave his 405 rifle at home, for that bullet in the Springfield killed better, shot more accurately, and was pleasanter to shoot.

My old friend, the late Ralph G. Packard, used a Springfield 30 caliber rifle on two long trips in Africa. He took a great many buffalo with it, an animal acknowledged to be one of the most difficult to kill. For buffalo, he told me, he used the Remington cartridge loaded with their 220-grain "Delayed Mushroom" bullet.

I imagine that there are no two men who, between them, have killed so many Alaskan brown bear as Jay Williams and Hosea Sarber, both now gone to the "happy hunting grounds." After about

Military target shooting near the turn of the century.

---

*The Ultimate in Rifle Precision, 1958. The Stackpole Co., Harrisburg, Pa.

†Book of the Springfield, by E.C. Crossman (Georgetown, S.C., 1951).

1911 Jay used a 30-06 sporting Springfield exclusively for these bear. His rifle was another of those remodeled by Louis Wundhammer. He used the 220-grain soft point bullet almost exclusively for bear, preferring the same Western bullet that White had found superior in Africa. In 1931 while I was at Springfield Armory I rebarreled this old rifle for Jay. He had completely worn out the original barrel. In correspondence with Hosea Sarber shortly before his death he told me that for all game he used the 170-grain open point bullet, made by the Western Tool and Copper Works, practically exclusively in his rifle. Jay Williams relates his experiences in detail in his book *Alaskan Adventure*,* and also described some of Sarber's bear shooting, as he and Sarber were close companions.

For many years Harold Lokken, an old Alaskan sourdough, used to supply all the poor families along the upper Yukon River with meat. Ralph Packard, who had three long hunts with him, told me that he thought it was conservative to say that Lokken had killed a thousand head of Alaskan big game. Lokken told me, when I met him at Packard's home, that in recent years he had hunted with only two rifles, a 270 Winchester and a 30-06 Springfield; and that while the 270 was an excellent rifle for all Alaskan game he rather preferred the Springfield because once he had to shoot five times at a grizzly to kill it with the 270, something that had never happened to him with the Springfield.

I think that each of these six men took more big game all over the world, with smokeless powder high velocity loads, than any men who have ever lived.

When Crossman had Wundhammer remodel those first Springfield rifles for himself and White he wrote me about them, and I had an eastern gunsmith remodel one for me. I did not particularly like it, and I then had another gunsmith do one over. I shot both these rifles very extensively on the rifle range, with excellent results with the latter. Then Fred Adolph, a German gun-maker who had started to work in this country, sent me a German 30 caliber barrel made of Poldi "Anti-Corro" steel, a non-rusting type. It was 26 inches long, and had a raised matted rib, and its groove diameter was .309" with a 10-inch twist. I sent this barrel to Springfield Armory and had them fit it to a Springfield action and chamber it for the 30-06 cartridge. Then Adolph stocked it with a handsome sporting pistol grip stock for me, and I had Lyman fit a windgauge rear sight to the cocking piece and a gold bead front sight. This was in 1912. Modern Guns, a catalog, by Fred Adolph (Genoa, N.Y., no date) shows this rifle. I thereafter used this rifle for many years for hunting North American game. It replaced the 30–40 Winchester single shot rifle that I had previously used. I shot more big game with this particular rifle than with any other rifle that I have used. In almost every case it killed the animal with one shot. I can remember firing three shots at a moose with it, but the last two were really not necessary. I was simply firing as long as it stood on its feet.

My longest and most successful hunt with this rifle was in the Smoky River country in Alberta north of Jasper Park in 1922. In those days that was a glorious wilderness and full of game. I shot grizzly bear, moose, caribou, sheep, and goat with it, and it never failed to kill on the first shot. On that trip I was using a new 30-06 cartridge that the Western Cartridge Company had recently produced, loaded with their 180-grain open point, boat-tail bullet to a muzzle velocity of 2,725 fps. (probably 2,775 in my 26-inch barrel). That bullet, unfortunately, is no longer made. I thought it was a rattling good killer, and it was accurate too — good for 2-inch groups any day with iron sights.

I also used this rifle practically exclusively in Panama from 1915 to 1917, when I was hunting, exploring and mapping there. The only big game there consisted of a small subspecies of white-tailed deer, tapir, peccary and crocodile, so my rifle was used mainly on small game for needed meat, with my favorite and time

*The Stackpole Co., Harrisburg, Pa., 1952.

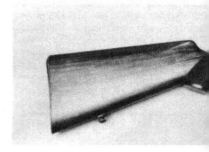

tried small game load, the 150-grain service, pointed, full jacketed bullet and 17 grains of du Pont No. 75 powder (now 18 grains du Pont 4759). Ideal for the purpose, it will shoot through the breast of a grouse and hardly spoil any meat. I had the stem of the Lyman sight plugged so when screwed all the way down it was just right for the full charged cartridge at 200 yards, and when elevated to the first graduation it was just right for this reduced load at 50 yards, a most convenient arrangement. With this reduced load I shot many coati, sloths, agouti, conejo, monkeys, iguana lizards, and many kinds of game birds including creasted guan, which are about the size of wild turkeys. Of all these the best eating by far were the sloths and the iguana lizards. This small game load turns the 30-06 into a real all around rifle for wilderness hunting. I have subsequently shot many grouse, rabbits, and two beavers and one otter with this load. The skins of the last three were not damaged at all. The meat of the beaver, including the fat tail, is the most delicious meat of any wild animal in the United States and Canada. Otters are uneatable.

I also shot four other moose, and quite a large number of mule and white-tailed deer with this old rifle on other hunts. Now, retired after its long and successful shooting history, it rests comfortably in the NRA Museum at Washington.

I think that for all American big game the 30-06 rifle is at its best with one of the 180-grain pointed expanding bullets, choosing the one that shoots most accurately in the individual rifle, and at a muzzle velocity of about 2,700 foot seconds. If the rifle be sighted with a scope mounted 1.5 inches above the bore and zeroed for 200 yards, the bullets will group about 2¼ inches above aim at 100 yards and drop 9½ inches at 300 yards. No one can estimate range exactly, but most hunters with a little experience can tell if the game is beyond 200 yards, and if it is too far away to be hit with any certainty. Between these two distances it will be somewhere between 250 and 350 yards. Then if the hunter aims for the backbone of the animal above the chest area the bullet will drop enough to penetrate the chest or it will strike the backbone, both absolutely fatal shots on all our big game. If the animal does not drop to the shot immediately it certainly will after a mad rush of 25 to 100 yards.

The recoil of the 30-06/180-grain cartridge in an 8-pound rifle is not too severe for ninety per cent of our sportsmen. They will not hesitate to use it on the range, to become accustomed to it, and to get it zeroed precisely. When this is done a 30-06 rifle is as good as any, and in fact I think better than most any other for American big game.

Roaming around big game country in the West this past year I found my objections to those rifles using ultra high velocity magnum cartridges of heavy recoil (so often selected by modern sportsmen) more and more confirmed. If they shoot accurately they are fine for the expert rifleman, yet anything but suitable for the sportsman who takes his rifle in hand only for a couple of short weeks in the hunting season. The recoil is so unpleasant that our weekend sportsmen never practice with such rifles. They never learn to handle their rifles or their zeroes, they flinch horribly when shooting them, and they cannot hit the proverbial barn with them. They kill no surer than the 30-06 except perhaps for a paunch shot, and every real hunter abhors such a shot — it's cruel and the meat is ruined. In the majority of such cases that I have investigated it is the guide who has shot the trophy, not the sportsman. No, for all American big game the 30-06 Springfield rifle, or a good 30-06 of another brand, is never a mistake.

First commercial Springfield sporter, probably, was this Louis Wundhammer stocked 30-06, made in 1912 and used by Stewart Edward White in Africa. One of four such rifles ordered by Capt. E.C. Crossman (see Crossman's *Book of the Springfield* for another view), the rifle shown carries Rock Island Arsenal serial number 166,436, and barrel date of February, 1910.

The Rifles of James Paris Lee

Part One. A thoroughly researched and detailed account of Lee's numerous contributions to firearms technology and advancement. New information and a long-lost model are offered here for the first time. ▮ Larry S. Sterett

J AMES PARIS LEE was one of the most brilliant of all the inventors who contributed to the art of gunmaking. Born at Harwich, Roxborough-shire, Scotland, on August 9th, 1831, to George and Margaret (Paris) Lee, he migrated with his parents to Shades Mills (Gait), Ontario, Canada, in 1836. His education began at the old Gouinlock School in Gait, but was completed at Dickie's Settlement, Dumfries, under a Mr. William Telfer.

James' father, George Lee, was a skilful watchmaker and jeweler. When James was nearly 17, he entered his father's shop to learn the trade. His interest in firearms began to blossom about the same time, for one of his first experiments was to make a rough stock and fit it to the barrel and lock of an old horse pistol he'd been given. When everything was complete the pistol had to be tested and, in his own words, "I got my brother Jack to touch the gun off with a spunk, the immediate effect of which was to blacken my face with powder and hurl the barrel about 20 yards in an opposite direction."

On October 15, 1847, George Lee recorded in his diary: "Jimmie has shot himself and will go limping through the world during life!" James had been hunting in Dickson's woods near Gat and was returning in the evening, cold and wearied, with his shotgun over his shoulder when it fell to the ground and discharged. The charge passed completely through the heel of his right foot from the left side, taking with it a piece of his leather boot and searing the flesh to the degree that profuse bleeding did not occur. Dragging himself on his hands and knees through nearly 200 yards of brush to reach a road, he was found by a passing farmer and taken home. After nine months in bed, James Lee was again up and about, but it was nearly a year and a half before he was able to move about freely.

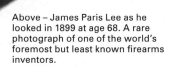

Above – James Paris Lee as he looked in 1899 at age 68. A rare photograph of one of the world's foremost but least known firearms inventors.

Having finished his work with his father, James traveled to Toronto to learn the practical side of the trade. After spending 6 months with a manufacturing jeweler named Jackson, on King Street, he decided to go into business for himself, and to open a shop in Chatham.

Boarding the Gait-London-Chatham stage one day in 1850, James Paris Lee set out on a journey that was to affect his life in more ways than one. Hardly had he settled in Chatham and put out his sign, when he met 16-year-old Caroline Chrysler, the second daughter of one of Chatham's most respected families. It was apparently love at first sight for both, but the marriage was delayed for two and one-half years because of her age. Said to have resembled Empress Eugenie, the famous French beauty of the period, Mrs. Lee was an amiable woman who accompanied her husband on nearly all his later journeys to Europe and in America, until her sudden death in London, England, in 1888, due to heart failure. The union produced two

was being left to rot. Its transportation was so costly that bulk shipments of the bark were unprofitable. Lee conceived the idea of extracting the tannic acid from the bark and shipping it out of the woods in condensed liquid form. In a letter dated July 27, 1898, to a friend, the Honorable James Young, Lee described this ill-fated experience.

"… It looks rather queer to sell tan-bark at $40 per barrel. That experiment took me into the hemlock forests in their original beauty. Great hunting here! I wondered at the great wealth of hemlock bark, and why it could not be transferred to market in a more profitable form. Result was I got a small portable engine through a blazed way (there were no roads at that time), stationed it on the banks of a beautiful lake, erected a mill to grind the bark, and a long copper pan 4 feet wide and 50 feet long, to evaporate the leechings into a thick syrup, getting the tanning strength of eight cords into a 40-gallon cask. The first test of it succeeded in burning up the

ber of magazines, the cartridges in which were placed one above the other. After firing, and ejection of the empty case, a rod pushed a loaded cartridge into the chamber, and at the same time transferred a cartridge from one magazine to another nearest the chamber. Unfortunately metal cartridge cases were not readily available at this time and the mechanism would not operate properly with those available. As a result this rifle never was commercially manufactured, and whether one survives today is not known to the author. It did, however, embody a principle that was to appear later in the rifles of many nations.

While the 40-shot repeater was hanging fire (perhaps literally), Lee developed a successful method of converting the Springfield muzzle-loading rifle into a breechloader, followed by a single-shot cavalry carbine. On July 22, 1862, U.S. Patent No. 35,941, was issued to him for an "Improvement in Breech-Loading Fire Arms." While the patent drawing is for a pistol — only one model of which is

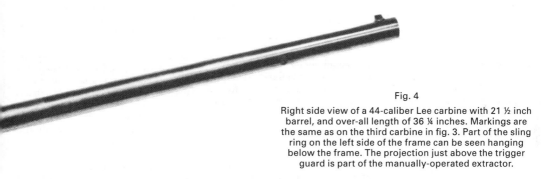

Fig. 4
Right side view of a 44-caliber Lee carbine with 21 ½ inch barrel, and over-all length of 36 ¼ inches. Markings are the same as on the third carbine in fig. 3. Part of the sling ring on the left side of the frame can be seen hanging below the frame. The projection just above the trigger guard is part of the manually-operated extractor.

sons, both of whom later assisted their father in his work.

Remaining in Chatham for nearly 5 years, the Lees moved to Owen Sound for a brief period and then on to Janesville, Wisconsin. Shortly before the Civil War, James Lee was induced to move from Janesville to Stevens Point, Wisconsin, on the Wisconsin River, and to set up as a watchmaker and jeweler. (The 1860 Federal Census lists Lee as a resident of this town of 1533 inhabitants, his occupation, watchmaker.)

Early Venture

The Stevens Point newspaper, The Wisconsin Lumberman, credits Lee with being the "inventor and pioneer in the manufacture of…extract of hemlock." In the area the valuable bark of the hemlock

leather. They didn't dilute enough."

In any case, the end result was to seal the fate of the enterprise, proving unfortunate for everyone concerned.

The extensive lumbering operations indicated a very successful future for the area, but James Lee admitted that the abundance of game and the grandeur of the forests helped to attract him. Deer, bear and wolves were to be found around Stevens Point, and nearly all of his spare time was devoted to hunting or to the production of a repeating rifle to replace the old muzzle-loading models. Not content with three or four shots, Lee wanted to produce a 40-shot repeater and, after numerous attempts, he was successful. The well-made model, which showed much promise, consisted of a rifle with a hollow sheet metal buttstock containing a num-

known to exist today — mention is made in the specifications of "… a rifle or piece with a long barrel," and this was the type later manufactured by the Lee's Fire Arms Co. of Milwaukee, Wis.

Lee's First Contract

In March of 1863, Lee submitted one of his breech-loading alterations of the Springfield rifle to the U.S. Ordnance Department for trial. The rifle was not satisfactory, and in November a second type was submitted. This second model, and a later third model, were acceptable, but a contract for their manufacture was not forthcoming. However, a request for a breech-loading carbine for testing was made, and by April, 1864, Lee had produced one, based on his 1862 patent. This carbine was also acceptable, but some ex-

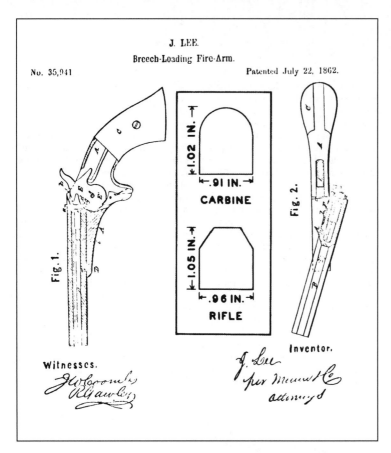

J. LEE.
Breech-Loading Fire-Arm.

No. 35,941

Patented July 22, 1862.

1.02 IN.

.91 IN.
CARBINE

1.05 IN.

.96 IN.
RIFLE

Fig. 1.

Fig. 2.

Inventor.
J. Lee
per Manuel C.
attorneys

Witnesses.

Figs. 1 & 2
The patent drawing on which the Wisconsin-made tee arms were based. Standing-breech profiles (inset) of the single shot Lee carbine and rifle made in Milwaukee, Wis.

traction difficulties were experienced. No doubt expecting a contract, Lee offered to provide 1000 of the carbine model for testing, with delivery to be within 6 months of the date of the order. The offer was approved, as indicated by the following communication:

James Lee Esq.
Washington D. C.
Ordnance Office
May 7th 1864
Sir,
Your letter of April 19th to the Secretary of War offering to furnish 1000 of your breechloading carbines at $18 has been referred to this office with authority to enter into such contract with you. Should you therefore present to this Department a carbine free from the defects mentioned in Captain Benton's report the contract will then be given you. The defect was "The cartridge case ejector frequently failed to start the case, the projection next to the case (on the ejector) appears to be too short to take a firm hold on the rim of the case." The carbine must be presented this or next month.
Respectfully
Your obt Svt
George D. Ramsay
Brig. Gen. Chf of Ord

Lee improved the extractor design without difficulty, and his request for permission to manufacture the gun frames of malleable cast iron instead of wrought iron was accepted. But he had no facilities for manufacturing the carbines in quantity, and his request for an increase in the contract price was rejected.

As for Lee's original plans for manufacturing the carbines, it is a matter for conjecture. He may have intended to have the carbines made elsewhere, under his name, or he may have intended to subcontract the parts and to assemble the carbines himself, with workmen hired for his purpose. In any event, since the letter from Gen. Ramsay did not specify a time of delivery, Lee decided to form a company and make the carbines.

The Honorable W.D. McIndoe, a Congressman and a friend of Lee, apparently saw some potential in the carbine. He helped Lee gain financial backing for the new firm, which was organized in Milwaukee on October 13, 1864[1]. Various sources list this firm as Lee Arms Company, Lee Fire Arms Company, Lee Fire-arms Company, Lee's Firearms Company and Lee's Fire Arms Company. However, the last form is the one appearing on the Articles of Association filed with the Secretary of State in Madison, Wisconsin, on

November 2, 1864.

The Articles stated the objectives of the new firm to be "manufacturing in the City of Milwaukee Fire Arms of the pattern and form specified in Letters Patent and the Schedule accompanying the same, issued by the Government of the United States to James Lee, and also of other patterns if deemed advisable." Incorporation was approved on March 8, 1865. Capitol stock was valued at $100,000, in shares of $100 each. Of this amount only $10,000 was actually paid in. The firm was to be managed by 7 directors, elected on the first Monday of each year. The original 7 included:[2]Charles F. Ilsley, James Kneeland, James Lee, Thomas L. Ogden, Lester Sexton, Solomon Taintor and Daniel Wells Jr. Kneeland was elected president of the Board, with H.F. Pelton, Secretary. James P. Lee was appointed Superintendent of the Works. The Honorable W.D. McIndoe was not listed as being on the Board, possibly because a conflict of interest charge might be leveled in connection with a military contract.

The armory was established at 454 Canal Street in October, 1864, and the job of procuring materials and equipment began. (Canal Street is now Commerce Street in Milwaukee, and the 454 area is a part of the Joseph Schlitz Brewery complex.) A number of parts were presumably bought elsewhere in the finished stage, ready for assembly. These included sling bars and rings, buttplates, and front and rear sights, which appear identical to those made by the Burnside Rifle Co. of Rhode Island, and which are referred to as "Burn-sides" by Col. McAllister in one report.

Barrels were supplied by E. Remington & Sons of Ilion, New York. A total of 1136 barrels were shipped to Milwaukee for rifling and chambering, and to be fitted with sights and extractors. This arrangement was ideal since the Remington firm was equipped to produce barrels, and government inspection and proof was taken care of by the Ordnance Department inspectors before the barrels were shipped to Milwaukee.

Contract Troubles

In April, 1865, the official order for the delivery of the carbines was issued by the Ordnance Department as follows below.[3] Note that caliber 44 is shown in this letter; caliber was not given in the letter of May 7th, 1864:

Fig. 3

Breech details of three tee carbines, showing rear sight locations, trigger guard variations and markings. The crudely-marked top carbine is considered the first specimen made (No. 1). The middle carbine is unmarked, while the third carbine has the standard markings found on commercial production pieces. The two frame holes in the lower carbine are for attaching the sling bar. Note the higher standing-breech on the first two carbines, compared to that of the third. (No. 2183).

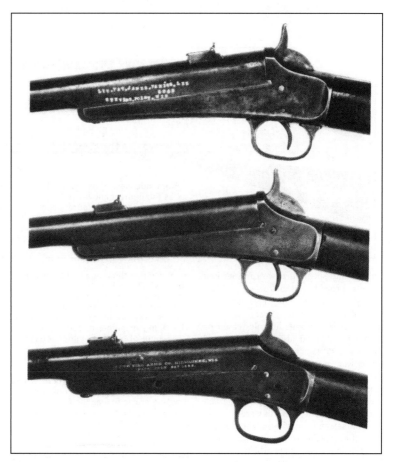

Mr. James Lee
Milwaukee, Wis
Ordnance Office
April 18, 1865
Sir,
You will please deliver to the Inspector of Small Arms, the one thousand breech loading carbines Cal. 44 and appendages the order to furnish which was given to you on the 7th day of May, 1864 for which eighteen dollars ($18) will be paid for each carbine including appendages that is approved by the Inspector. Please forward to this office as soon as possible two (2) carbines to be used as standards in the inspection and reception of the above. These one thousand carbines will be packed in suitable boxes, for which a fair price, to be fixed by the Inspector will be paid.
Respectfully
Your obt Svt
A. B. Dyer
Brig Gen. Chf of Ord

Although the order called for two carbines to be used as standards, a single carbine was shipped to Ordnance for inspection on August 31, 1865. It was rejected. In so doing the following reasons were advanced by the inspector, Gen. W. A. Thornton:

The barrel, indicates rough rifling and to remedy which it has been leaded to such an extent that the edges of the lands are quite round. It is badly ringbored at the muzzle and the breech-chamber is roughly reamed. Front sight ... can be readily pushed out by the fingers. The hammer has a corner broken from the middle notch. Notches roughly filed ... The mainspring is apparently too weak ... The breech piece is ... very doubtful in strength through screw holes at points of junction to the barrel and in tang joining it to the stock. The stock is very roughly cut in bedding the main spring and too deeply cut for the tang of the breech piece ... It is therefore liable to be easily broken. The butt plate has a seam in the material ... The sear spring is broken ...

In January, 1866, the two models originally called for in the order of April,

1865, as inspection standards, were finally furnished. After inspection they were reported on as follows:

Office of Inspector of Contract Arms
No 240 Broadway
New York, January 26, 1866
Maj. Gen 'l A.B. Dyer
Chief of Ordnance
General,
I have the honor to inform you, that I have inspected two model Carbines, furnished by James Lee Esq. of Milwaukee and respecting which I have to report that I find,

Carbine No. 1.
Frame — of Malleable Cast Iron and thin at front end where the screw connects it to the barrel.
Stock — Split at top butt screw hole.
Barrel — Chamber torn in rifling.
Connection Screw — Thread torn.
Butt Plate — Seams in material out side.
— Top Screw hole countersunk too deep.

Carbine No. 2.
Frame — of Malleable Cast Iron.
Barrel — Torn in rifling.
Mainspring — Crooked at Set Screw.
In all other conditions I consider these

arms are well gotten up, and I respectfully recommend their acceptance as Models with the understanding that like Carbines furnished to the United States shall be equally as good in workmanship and free from defects.

Respectfully, I am sir,
Your obedient servant
W. A. Thornton

Even with the recommendation the Ordnance Department refused to accept the two carbines as inspection standards on the grounds of incorrect caliber. According to a letter to Gen. Thornton "... they (the carbines) gauge only .42 calibre while my order of April 13th 1865 calls for .44 calibre. Please see if the carbines will take the cartridge for Spencer carbine cal. .44; if so these may be returned for stamp as model carbines for the inspection."

Thornton apparently informed Lee that the carbines were unacceptable, due to an error in caliber, although Thornton had informed the Chief of Ordnance "... I did not verify them as to the size of their bore when I made their inspection." Lee immediately went to Washington to try and clarify the matter, but was unsuccess-

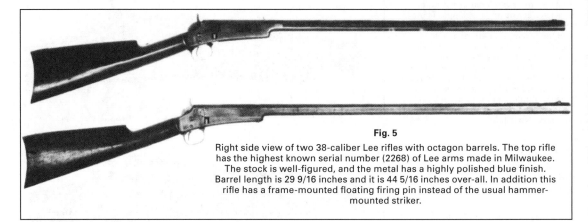

Fig. 5

Right side view of two 38-caliber Lee rifles with octagon barrels. The top rifle has the highest known serial number (2268) of Lee arms made in Milwaukee. The stock is well-figured, and the metal has a highly polished blue finish. Barrel length is 29 9/16 inches and it is 44 5/16 inches over-all. In addition this rifle has a frame-mounted floating firing pin instead of the usual hammer-mounted striker.

ful. By mid-spring the two carbines had been returned to Milwaukee.

By this time Lee may have been convinced that the military were not going to accept his carbine, for one reason or another. It should also be remembered that the Civil War was now over, and the arms were not needed; the caliber may have been only an excuse to hedge on a contract. To recover some of the losses, Lee began to explore the civilian market. Unfortunately surplus arms were flooding the market, and could be bought at a fraction of the cost of the new Lee carbines.

Possibly in an attempt to help a local industry the *Milwaukee Daily Sentinal* published an article entitled: "HOW BREECH LOADING GUNS ARE MADE — A Visit To Lee's Arms Manufactory" on page 1 of the March 23, 1866, edition. (Note that the name of the firm shows still another form attributed to the Milwaukee enterprise.) The article appeared as follows:

We recently paid a visit to Lee's Arms Manufactory, situated on the Canal, in the sixth ward of the city, and were conducted through the various departments by the gentlemanly President, James Kneeland, esq. and the Superintendant and inventor of the arms, James Lee, esq.

Comparatively few of our readers are acquainted with the manner of making guns, and we venture to give a brief account of our tour of observation.

The barrels of the gun are purchased in the rough state and brought to the manufactory here. They are made of the best decarbonized steel. The first process is to mill the barrel down to its proper size and form. During this process it has to pass through 19 different operations. It is then taken to the rifling machine. In order to insure greater accuracy in firing the gun, the barrel has to be grooved or rifled, so as to give the ball, on issuing from the gun, a rotary motion, which like the motion of a top, keeps it unerringly on its course. It has been found by experiment that the shorter the twist in the bar-

rel, the longer the range and the accuracy obtained. The twist in the Whitworth gun, which is acknowledged the best now to be known, has one turn in 20 inches. The twist of Lee's gun is one turn in 23 inches. The rifling machine, at each revolution, takes a cut of but one eighty-thousandth part of an inch. This apparently incredibly small cut is necessary from the fact that a larger one would be liable to tear the barrel and such an accident would render it useless. The shavings from the machine are as fine as the finest of wool. After rifling, the barrel is taken to the polishing room and a fine finish put upon it. It is then taken to the blueing furnace and beautifully colored. It is now ready for use. The barrel passes through 43 different operations from the forging to the blueing process.

The breech is then taken in hand. It is made from the best de-carbonized iron, requiring to be kept at a red heat for 16 days. It is first put through a milling machine, then filed, drilled, polished, and blued, passing through no less than 60 different processes from the forging to the blueing.

The lock is perhaps the simplest part of the gun, having only four pieces — a hammer, trigger, mainspring and trigger-spring. It is so simple that the most inexperienced could take it apart or put it together. Yet the hammer passes through 20 different and separate processes, the trigger through ten, the mainspring through six.

The stocks are made from Wisconsin black walnut, which from its hardness has been found to be the best material for the purpose. As the lock is situated in the breech of the gun, there is comparatively little work about the stock. It is made wholly by machinery; first grooved for the mountings, then formed into the proper shape, then sweated and polished, and lastly mounted.

Every portion of this gun is made by machinery and each part of every gun is the same. The advantage of this is in the fact that when a part of the gun is either lost or broken it can be replaced by another from the manufactory at but little cost. Every gun is subjected to a rigid test, and

any imperfection, no matter how small, condemns it. All the machinery and tools used have been made expressly for the manufacture of the arm, and the company have been at an enormous outlay for the requisite machinery. The manufactory is now in excellent working order, and will soon be able to turn out a large number of guns daily, and will furnish employment to quite a number of men. None but the best of mechanisms are employed, however, as the variation of even so much as a thousandth part of an inch in any of the parts of the gun would spoil it for use.

The arm deserves a minute description, but with our imperfect knowledge of its mechanism, we cannot hope to do it justice. It has many advantages over the ordinary rifle. There are only 8 pieces in the whole gun — less than half the number in either Burnside, Henry or Spencer rifles — and they are so simple that anyone can put them together with ease. It can be loaded and fired 20 times a minute by an expert sportsman, and can be used with one hand when occasion requires; it being light and almost self-working. Its penetration is truly wonderful. With but 23 grains of powder a ball was driven through an inch board, 6 inches of cotton, tightly compressed, and a body of water 6 feet in extent. The force required to accomplish this fact connoisseurs will appreciate. The arm is very light — the heaviest now manufactured being only eight pounds and six ounces. The effective range of the gun is about three-quarters of a mile and its accuracy at that distance is as great as that of any other arm in the United States.

The company is now manufacturing four different sizes of guns, an army carbine, weighing 5 pounds, 6 ounces, a light sporting rifle, weighing 6½ pounds, a heavy sporting rifle, weighing 8 pounds, 5 ounces, and one an ounce heavier.

The manufactory is now busy on a government contract for carbines. The demand for sporting rifles is greater than the supply, and the manufactory will have to be enlarged to enable it to furnish enough for the trade.

This arm has been commended highly by the chief of ordnance bureau and

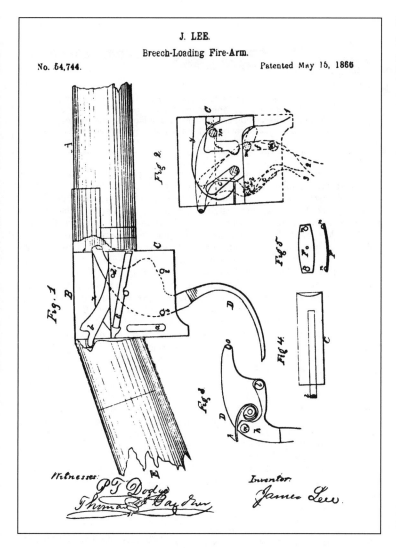

Fig. 6
James Lee's patent 54,744 of May 15, 1866, was the basis for the actions shown in figs. 7 and 8. See text for details.

or from 10 to 12 times per minute with one hand. It has a greater Accuracy, Force and Penetration, with the same quantity of powder, than any other breech-loading rifle, and more than double the force and penetration of any muzzle-loading gun ever made. With 23 grains of powder (only about one-quarter the quantity the Berdan gun requires), it will throw a half-ounce ball of 44–100 of an inch calibre through 10 inches of green, or 12 inches of seasoned pine timber.

In November, 1866, one Lt. Col. J. McAllister visited the "… armory of Mr. Lee …" in order to "… examine into the progress that has been made, the expenditures incurred and the materials on hand for filling the contract, and report the same with such remarks and recommendations respecting a settlement of the case …" On December 20, 1866, after completing the visit, Col. McAllister filed his report.

Lee's Claim Settled

In January, 1867, James Lee wrote to the Secretary of War, E.M. Stanton, requesting compensation for the expenses incurred while attempting to fulfill the contract for the carbines. In due course the request found its way to the then Chief of Ordnance, Bvt. Major General A.B. Dyer. In his reply to Stanton, dated February 18, 1867, Gen. Dyer stated that Mr. Lee had acted in good faith, and should be compensated. But instead of requesting that the contract be fulfilled for 1000 carbines at $18 each, he recommended a compromise. Assuming that Lee's total expenses at the date of McAllister's report were $20,350. 15, the tools and equipment were worth $6,000, and that rifles and parts on hand could be sold for $6,175, the net loss would only be $8,175.15, which the government should be willing to share to the extent of $4,087.57. This method of settlement, according to Dyer, would thus save the government a minimum of at least $6,000.

A year later, the matter still not settled, Lee wrote to Washington protesting the unfairness of the suggested settlement. In turn Dyer stated that Lee had no claim other than the "one of damage which … could only be … properly acted on by legislative authority." This was in accordance with the Congressional act of March 3, 1863, and in December, 1868, "General Jurisdiction Case No. 3263: James Lee vs. the United States" was decided.

by many prominent sportsment and soldiers. As a sporting rifle it possesses great advantages over others and is fast superseding all rivals. Wisconsin inventors have introduced many useful improvements in every department of science, but none is more important than the invention of this breech-loading arm. Mr. Lee has made the construction of firearms a life study, and has succeeded in bringing perfection in this gun. We feel a pride in the success of the invention as should every resident of Wisconsin.

After reading this article, one begins to wonder whether it was written by a reporter for the newspaper or by an advertising agency. The facts do not bear out some of the statements made in the article.

Under the heading "Fire Arms and Ammunition" the same issue carried an advertisement that appeared periodically

into November, 1866. It read:

Lee's Fire Arms Company on the Canal water power, Milwaukee, are manufacturing Lee's Patent Breech-Loading Rifle which the company now offer to the public.

The company own the patent and are the exclusive manufacturers of the Arm in the United States.

In offering to the public this Gun the company claim that it is more complete and perfect in every particular, and cheaper than any other arm in use. The superiority of **LEE'S PATENT BREECH-LOADING RIFLE**, consists in its simplicity of mechanism — it having only about one-half the number of pieces that other breech-loading guns have. Its Superior workmanship, the Barrels of the finest Decarbonized Cast Steel. Rifled in the most approved manner in 6 grooves of equal width to the lands, sharp Whitworth twist, once round in 23 inches — its rapidity in firing over all others. It can be fired 20 times per minute,

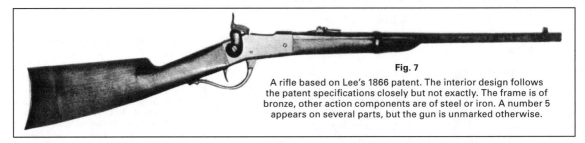

Fig. 7

A rifle based on Lee's 1866 patent. The interior design follows the patent specifications closely but not exactly. The frame is of bronze, other action components are of steel or iron. A number 5 appears on several parts, but the gun is unmarked otherwise.

The verdict depended on whether the carbine was to have been 42 caliber or 44 caliber, which in turn depended on when the contract originated. Lee maintained that the letter of May 7, 1864, accepting the carbine evaluated the month before, constituted the contract, and the carbines submitted later followed this accepted pattern. The Government maintained the order dated April 18, 1865, calling for "… one thousand breech-loading carbines Cal. 44 …" was the actual contract.

Lee had asked $12,000 for expenses and $3,000 for damages. The Court awarded him $6,175 for damages only, since he "… still maintains his machinery and a large amount of material …" Interestingly, the Court held the letter of May 7, 1864, to be the valid contract and advanced the opinion, "When the carbines were needed the calibre was not a matter of serious importance; when they were not needed,5 the calibre became the controlling element "

It is almost certain that by this time Lee's Fire Arms Company was no longer in business. The attempt to sell the civilian market had failed and only 102 carbines had been sold by December of 1866, and these at a loss of $4.50 each. The rifles and carbines were not advertised after November, 1866, and the firm is not listed in the Milwaukee city directories after 1867.

There are many unanswered questions connected with James Paris Lee and his activities, not the least of which are the dates of his residence in various cities. When the Lee family left Stevens Point for Milwaukee is not exactly known. James Lee is not listed in the Milwaukee city directory until 1866, nor in Stevens Point after the autumn of 1864. It is probable, therefore, that the move took place at about the same time of the formation of Lee's Fire Arms Company. Lee doubtless had been in Milwaukee numerous times previously and would have made several contacts. The Lee residence is listed as 130 Prospect in the 1866 to 1873/74 city directories, although Lee is listed with Lee's Fire Arms Company only in 1866 and 1867. In 1900 a boyhood friend of Lee wrote that

Lee had gone to Ilion, N.Y., to work at the Remington factory following the failure of the Milwaukee business. Lee had become acquainted with the Remingtons previously, having used their barrels for his Milwaukee-made carbines and rifles, and it was a tradition of the Remington firm at this time to invite inventors to use the facilities at the Remington Armory. Thus the Lee family apparently stayed in Milwaukee while James Lee worked in Ilion, at least until after May, 1874, when the *Milwaukee Daily Sentinal* noted that Lee had gone east to renew tests of his gun at Springfield (Armory).

The type of arm made at the Milwaukee factory was based on U.S. Patent No. 35, 941. As previously mentioned, the patent model was for a single shot pistol having a spur trigger and a barrel which pivoted horizontally to the left. A tongue on the barrel breech prevented vertical play. The centrally positioned outside hammer was designed so that when it was in the half-cock position the barrel could be swung out for loading. But when the hammer was fully cocked the barrel could not be moved. Extraction of the fired case was done by a manual movement of an extractor sliding in a groove on the right side of the barrel. The rim of the case was acted upon in much the same manner as in double barrel shotguns.

The frame provided for a separate steel breech plate, indicating the frame was to be produced from a softer metal, and at least one brass frame pistol of this same basic design is known to exist. It is said to have a single 6 stamped on the breech of the 44-caliber barrel, which is 8⅝ inches long. Over-all length is reported to be 13 inches.

The Pilot Rifle

Of the long arms based on this patent — 32 are reported to exist — none have spur triggers and the barrels all pivot to the right instead of to the left. Two different standing breech shapes exist, as shown in fig. 1. with the rifles having one shape and the carbines another; carbine breeches also vary slightly in height. The arms were apparently available chambered for

three different rimfire calibers, although only two — 44 and 38 — were advertised, but for exactly which cartridges is a matter for debate. Herbert Uphoff has said that the 44 Henry and 44 Ballard Long cartridges will chamber in some of the 44 caliber arms, but the possibilities of others cannot be overlooked.

The 38 caliber cartridge may have been the 38 Extra Long, but the first mention of a 38 caliber appears in the 1866 advertisments, or about when the 44-caliber carbine was rejected for military use. Yet a recent Norm Flayderman catalog listed a Lee rifle with 1864 markings chambered for a 38 rimfire cartridge.

Several arms were no doubt made prior to the formation of Lee's Fire Arms Company, but only one specimen — a carbine — is known to exist today, unless the just-mentioned 38 caliber rifle is one, which is doubtful. Crudely made, this early carbine resembles the later models but has a differently shaped stock and front sight, and a slightly longer barrel, plus other minor differences. The barrel is very unevenly stamped, on the left side, near the breech, in three lines. The double S in "Pariss" is so stamped:

LEE. PAT. JAMES. PARISS. LEE
1862
STEVENS. POINT. WIS

The greatest difference between this carbine, stamped with a number 1 under the barrel, and the later models is the degree to which the barrel may be swung aside for loading — about 170 degrees to the right, compared to some 8 degrees for the later models based on the same patent. The patent provided for a barrel stop, but this particular carbine does not have one.

Uphoff thinks this carbine is possibly the sample submitted for testing as a standard in June, 1864, since it has the improved extractor on the bottom of the barrel, instead of the side-mounted type mentioned in the patent.

The sights on the carbines are of Burn-side type — dovetailed front blade, and an L-shaped rear, secured to the barrel by a single screw, and having notches for 100 and 500 yards, with a notched aperture for 300 yards. The rifle has a dovetailed front sight, similar to those on the carbines, and an L-shaped rear sight, with a reversible slide having different notches, dovetailed into the barrel.

The carbines made in the Milwaukee factory, if marked, are neatly stamped in about the same barrel position as on the Stevens Point carbine, but in two lines, as follows:

LEE'S FIRE ARMS CO. MILWAUKEE, WIS PAT- JULY 22- 1862.

Rifles were stamped the same way, but in a single line on the top of the barrel.

Carbines and rifle barrel lengths vary from those advertised, apparently because of very liberal manufacturing tolerances. Reported barrel lengths of known carbines range from 21 to 21½ inches, except for No. 1, which has a barrel of 21 15/16 inches long and all barrels are 44 caliber. Rifle barrels vary from 25¼ to 30¾ inches; the average 44-caliber barrel runs 29 inches, the 38-caliber barrels averaging 28¾ inches. This would tend to indicate that the two extremes may not have been standard rifles, but possibly special orders. The barrels were rifled as noted in the advertisment, except for the original sample, which has been reported to have five grooves and a gain twist.

Many of the carbines have sling bars and rings on the left side of the frame. Apparently all of the contract models were so intended, but only two of the known rifle specimens have sling swivels. Of these two rifles only No. 1659 is considered authentic; the front swivel is mounted on a base dovetailed into the barrel about 18 inches ahead of the breech, while the rear swivel is on a plate inletted into the stock 7 inches from the toe.

Here are many unanswered questions concerning the Milwaukee firm and the Lee carbines and rifles based on the 1862 patent. Why are no low number models known? The lowest number located — after the Stevens Point model — is 1247, a rifle. What happened to the rest of the 255 finished carbines, of which 102 had been sold, as reported on December 20, 1866? Were they numbered consecutively? Were the parts for the rest of the contract carbines destroyed, or were they used to produce civilian carbines and rifles to order? This suggests the reason for the apparent random numbering arrangement of the known rifles and carbines. Whatever the answers, Lee carbines and rifles do exist, but obviously Lee's Fire Arms Company of Milwaukee did not fare well.

Rare Lee Design

James Lee continued to work on a better rifle design, even while attempting to sell the 1862 design and attending to his work on Canal Street. On May 15, 1866, shortly after work had been suspended on the military carbines, U.S. Patent No. 54, 744 was issued to "James Lee, of Milwaukee, Wisconsin." The specifications list the patent as an "Improvement in Breech-Loading Fire-Arms," but the drawing is for a "Breech-Loading Fire-Arm." The action of this arm comprised a rectangular breechblock of "iron," moving vertically in the receiver well, and operated by an under lever with an extractor at its forward end. The front of the breechblock was beveled on the upper edge to help force the cartridge into the chamber. A small metal bar was recessed into the top of the breechblock in such a way that when the lever was operated to lower the block "… the rear end of (the bar) is held up, while its front end is carried down with the block, thereby forming an inclined way extending from the lower side of the bore up to the top of the frame … up which the cartridge-shell slides when thrown out by the ejector." The whole affair resembled a merging of the Peabody design of 1862 and the Sharps design of 1848.*

Lee had mentioned to his friend James Young that while at the Remington plant

---

*The only specimen of this Lee patent design to appear so far is owned by John T. Amber, editor of the Gun Digest. A Short rifle or carbine, it has a military style barrel of about 52 caliber, rifled with three broad grooves. The "small metal bar" mentioned above is pivoted in the top of the breechblock, near the middle. Its rear end is hooked to catch on the top rear of the receiver mortise, which is not as it appears in the patent drawing. Besides acting as an inclined plane for the ejection of fired cases, the slender steel bar also served as a loading tray or platform. The receiver is of brass, but all other action components are of iron or steel. As the illustrations show, there is a locking arrangement for the lever. The number 5 appears on several action parts, but the gun is unmarked otherwise. The exact cartridge called for is not certain, but one of the Spencer bottleneck types appears likely.

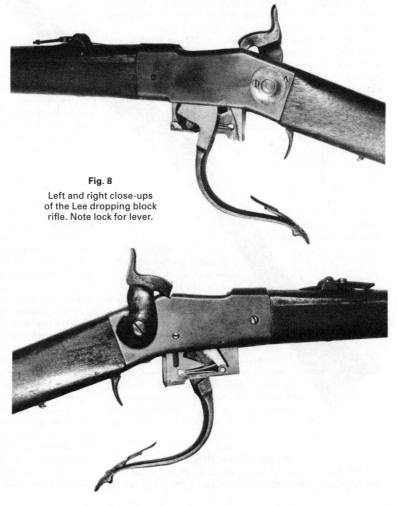

Fig. 8
Left and right close-ups of the Lee dropping block rifle. Note lock for lever.

he tried not only all kinds of experiments, but that his thoughts, both day and night, became so absorbed with them that sleep often became impossible. Sleep may have been impossible, but ideas were not, for the 1870s were the most productive of Lee's inventive years.

On May 16, 1871, U.S. Patent No. 114, 951 was issued to "James Lee, of Milwaukee, Wisconsin, Assignor to Philo Remington, of Ilion, New York." This patent was also listed as an "Improvement ..." and consisted of a Martini-type action, with the breechblock hinged at the rear and tilted downward by the movement of a lever which served as the trigger guard. A centrally mounted outside hammer was used, the mainspring fastened to the lower tang. Although the breechblock was lowered by the use of the lever, the design was such that"... the hammer can be used for operating said block — as, for instance, in closing it as the hammer is drawn back to the full-cock."

Initial movement of the lever lowered the breechblock, with its concave top surface, to guide the cartridge into the chamber, and continued movement activated an extractor to withdraw the empty case. At the same time the lever movement forced the hammer to the halfcock position and retracted the firing pin. Chambering a fresh cartridge caused the breechblock to rise enough to hold the cartridge in place, after which the closing could be finished by the use of the lever or the hammer. This 1871 version apparently did not progress beyond the prototype stage, but it was the basis for some later Lee designs.

On June 20, 1871, U.S. Patent No. 116, 068, for another "Improvement ..." was issued to James Lee as before and assigned to Philo Remington. Again the design was for a Martini-type action, with a centrally located outside hammer, but the under lever had disappeared and the breechblock was operated by the hammer alone. Examination of the patent drawings indicates that this was probably one of the rifles entered in the Army trials the next year, possibly rifle No. 54, having a solid frame and a two-piece stock.

Pulling the hammer back to the halfcock notch caused a hook to retract the firing pin, and lowered the breechblock to the loading position. In the lowest position the breechblock would strike the tail of the extractor, causing it to pivot and throw out the empty case. The extractor then continued on around to catch on the front or free end of the breechblock, holding it in the lowered position. Chambering a fresh cartridge would shove the extractor forward, releasing the breechblock and allowing it to spring up into the closed position under tension from the mainspring. After this, "... the hammer may then be brought to the full-cock, and the arm fired."

Unique Mainspring

This June, 1871, design used a unique U-shaped mainspring, the only other spring in the arm being a short, flat, trigger spring.

The mainspring "... is attached to and moves with the hammer, and has no fixed position ... yet performs all the duties of an expansile and contractile spring ... to raise the breechblock and to attach and detach a hook ... to and from the breechblock."

"The advantage of a ... mainspring so hung is this: being supported at the two ends on and moving with the hammer, and having no sliding bearings, there is no power lost in friction. It avoids the use of a swivel or other intermediate or extra piece to fasten to or with, as now used. It avoids the necessity of extending the guard-strap back to afford a point of attachment."

Excluding pins and a single screw the total number of parts in this 1871 design came to 10, and the action was very compact. Even so, the design was not acceptable when later tested by the government. The reason for the non-acceptance is not known, but the hook mechanism may have been susceptible to breakage.

On January 2, 1872, U.S. Patent No. 122, 470 for an "Improvement ..." was issued to Lee, this one also assigned to E. Remington & Sons. This improvement covered a cartridge extractor, trigger lock, and barrel band without swivel for a rolling block action. Apparently this patent covered no more than it said, indicating that Lee was working for the Remingtons at this time, at least to the extent of improving the Remington rolling block design. These were being manufactured in considerable quantities at this time.

January 16, 1872, saw the issuance of U.S. Patent No. 122,772 for yet another "Improvement ..." to "James Lee, of Milwaukee, Wisconsin." Curiously this patent was not assigned to anyone or to any firm, and might indicate that Lee had returned to Wisconsin to work on his own designs, with the idea still of interesting the government in one of them. Like two previous arms, the 1872 design was for a Martini-type action, the breechblock hinged at the rear and free at the front. The mechanism was also hammer operated, but unlike the 1871 design.

The U-shaped mainspring of the 1871 model had been located below the hammer, and below and behind the breechblock. The 1872 design used a V-shaped spring ahead of the hammer and directly below the breechblock. This spring "... in addition to its duty as a mainspring, also serves to keep the hammer and breechblock in their relative working positions, and to keep the firing-pin in the breechblock." The operation was now based on a "... two-part hammer with an articulated joint between them, ... so that one part may have a slight movement independent of the other part, and so that the first movement of the upper part shall impart a backward movement to the under part to remove the hammer from the firing-pin." The first movement with the 1871 design had been to pull the hammer back to the halfcock position to lower the breechblock; with the 1872 design the first step was to press the thumb-piece of the hammer forward to relieve

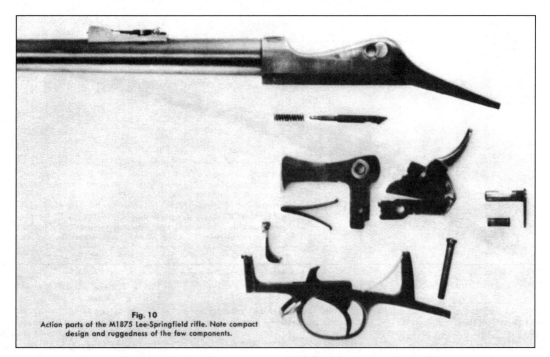

Fig. 10
Action parts of the M1875 Lee-Springfield rifle. Note compact
design and ruggedness of the few components.

the pressure on the firing pin, with continued pressure lowering the breechblock. After a fresh cartridge was chambered, the breechblock was raised by pulling back on the thumb-piece "… as in the act of cocking, which will first raise the breech to a closed position, and by continuing that motion will cock the arm."

One other noteworthy feature of the 1872 design was its take-down. "The breechblock, hammer, and mainspring can all be removed together without disturbing their relative positions by taking out the pin that the breechblock swings on, which, for cleaning or repairs, is quite important."

The 1872 design, coupled with the extractor of the 1871 design, was tested during the government trials of 1872 as entry No. 61. Like the previous 1871 design, it used a solid receiver and a two-piece stock; the buttstock was secured by a throughbolt screwing into the base of the frame, in the same manner as the Peabody-Martini.

On June 6, 1872, Congress approved the appointment by the Secretary of War of a "Board for the Selecting of a Breech-System for Muskets and Carbines" to consist of one general officer, one ordnance officer, and one line officer each from the cavalry, infantry, and artillery. $150,000 were appropriated for manufacturing the arm selected.

1872 Trials

The Board met on September 3, 1872, and continued in session until May 5, 1873. During this time a total of 95 arms or models were examined and/or tested, including 9 arms of foreign manufacture and three designs by James Paris Lee.* The Lee arms were entries No. 53, 54, and 61, and all were listed as "Muskets, calibre .50." The Board stated that "… the service .50 calibre musket-cartridge was employed whenever possible …"

Firing tests were conducted at Springfield Armory and, after nearly 25,000 rounds had been fired, the tests were concluded. A total of 21 arms were then selected for more severe tests. Of Lee's designs, only No. 61 was among the semifinalists; it was not selected when this group was later narrowed to the 6 arms that ultimately resulted in the selection of the Springfield "trapdoor" design — later to become the famous Model 1873.

The author has been unable to locate either the arm or the patent relating to entry No. 53 in the 1872 trials. This gun apparently used a sliding bolt in somewhat the same manner as the straight-pull design of 1895. However, a cam-lever at the upper rear of the bolt was used to lock and unlock the bolt by camming a lug on the underside of the bolt down into and up out of a recess in the receiver. This arm also had a one-piece stock and ejection of the empty cartridge cases was upward.

While the Springfield conversion design had been adopted by the Army, the search for a better one went on, and apparently the 1872 Lee model (No. 61 above) had made an impression, for in 1874 Congress approved the expenditure

of $10,000 for further development of the Lee design.

On March 16, 1875, James Lee was issued U.S. Patent No. 160,919 for another "Improvement …" The application had been filed on May 9, 1874, the last time Lee is mentioned in the Milwaukee papers as being in Milwaukee, he having gone east to renew tests of his gun at Springfield.6

The 1875 model used a one-piece stock following the contours of the 1873 Springfield stock, with the barrel, bands, band springs, swivels, sights, buttplate and ramrod also following the 1873 pattern. It was only logical to use the Springfield parts, since the Lee and Springfield models were both being manufactured at the Armory, with the Lee rifle on a trial basis for testing.

The V-shaped mainspring of the 1872 model was retained in the 1875 model, and pushing forward on the thumbpiece of the hammer lowered the breechblock, causing its bottom edge to strike the extractor, thus ejecting the empty case and locking the breechblock in the loading position. (According to the patent specifications the mainspring, not the breechblock, struck the extractor to eject the case, but in the manufactured rifle it is the breechblock.) Shoving a fresh cartridge into the chamber moved the extractor out

---

*Based on Lee patents and descriptions given in the Ordnance Board reports, entry No. 54 was constructed on Lee's patent No. 116,068 of June 20, 1871, and entry No. 61 is covered by Lee's patent No. 122,722 of Jan. 16, 1872

Fig. 12
The 1879 Lee rifle, as adopted by the U.S. Navy. Note the plain, ungrooved magazine and the straight bolt handle projecting ahead of the receiver bridge. Many writers have called all Lee turnbolt rifles the M1879, but that's like saying every Ford car is a Model T. The M1879 was only the first of several Lee turnbolt models. This particular rifle is marked on the receiver as noted in the text, while the barrel, just ahead of the receiver, is marked: "P." over "W.M.F." with an anchor below.

of the way, unlocking the breechblock and allowing it to rise automatically, via the compressed mainspring. The gun could then be cocked and fired as usual. The entire loading and ejecting process could be done so rapidly that Lee said: "... I have fired 30 cartridges in about three-fourths of a minute, taking each cartridge by hand separately from the cartridge-box."

If the Lee was not to be fired immediately after loading the hammer could be moved back until a "click" was heard, which indicated that the breechblock was fully locked and the firing pin had been retracted. The rifle was "safe" in this position. When the rifle was to be fired immediately after loading the final locking of the breechblock was accomplished during the cocking of the hammer, not as a separate movement.

With a barrel length of 32½ inches and a length over-all of 49¼ inches, the M1875 Lee was still more than 2½ inches shorter than the issue Springfield with the same barrel length. This was due to its compact receiver, which also permitted it to be in-letted into the stock with a simple mortise.

Another feature of this Lee design was its unique take-down. A lip on the front edge of the trigger guard assembly, with attached trigger and trigger spring, slipped into a notch in the lower part of the receiver ring below the barrel, and a single bolt through the rear tang held everything together — simplicity itself.

Only 143 of the M1875 Lee-Springfield rifles were manufactured, according to the Ordnance Report for June 30, 1875, the appropriation having been expended. The design failed to dislodge the Springfield as the issue rifle of the Army; in fact the single-shot Springfield reigned supreme as the choice (?) of the U.S. Army until 1892, many years after other nations

had adopted breech-loading magazine rifles. Stored at Rock Island Arsenal after their trial, the M1875 Lee rifles were finally sold at one of the government auctions for $36 each.

1875 Design Fails

The March, 1896, issue of the now long-defunct English Arms & Explosives magazine reported that in 1875 Mr. James Lee had offered the British authorities a Martini-Henry rifle with the block operated by the hammer, instead of by the lever, and in various trials it had given some wonderful results in the rapidity of firing. Spare cartridges were carried in a single column type magazine, but not fixed to the rifle, which was a single shot. Instead, the magazine, which would hold 30 rounds, was hung from the left shoulder. Upward of 28 shots per minute were fired with the rifle, but it still did not satisfy the requirements of the British for a new rifle. The model offered the British was no doubt the solid-frame Martini-type based on the 1872 patent, rather than the model which was produced at the Springfield Armory about this time.

A vertical (Martini-type) action Remington-Lee rifle, which resembles the Springfield model but which would not chamber a 45-70 cartridge, was listed in Flayderman's catalog No. 70. It had a two-piece stock with full military fore-end and two bands. The barrel length was given as 32½ inches, with Remington markings on top. Minor manufacturing differences, such as frame contours, top of the breechblock, etc., indicate that this may have been an 1872 model of the type offered to the British.

On April 27, 1875, U.S. Patent No. 162, 481 was issued to Lee for a magazine box, but the specifications have not been located. It is therefore not known whether this is the magazine referred to in the British trials above.

Following his failure to interest the British in a rifle, Lee apparently returned to the U.S. to work for the Winchester Repeating Arms Co., for whom he is reported to have developed a refinement of their lever action Model 73. This was in 1877, and he was still attempting to perfect a rifle the U.S. government would accept.

On August 7, 1877, U.S. Patent No. 193, 831 was issued to Lee, "of Milwaukee ..." also covering an "Improvement ..." The application was dated October 9, 1876. (Lee is not listed as being in Milwaukee after 1874, but three years later this address still appears on patent papers.)

The 1877 design was also based on a hammer-operated Martini action. The breechblock was lowered by shoving forward on the thumbpiece of the hammer, but the hammer was a one-piece type instead of the two-piece as previously. The new hammer was a rebounding model, only in contact with the firing pin during the firing cycle. The V-shaped mainspring, with spurs added, was the only spring in the entire action, performing all necessary acts required of a spring. Other improvements were in the shape of the firing pin, the pivot pin for the breechblock, and the sear, plus a slightly reshaped receiver and trigger guard assembly. Altogether there were only 15 parts in the 1877 design, including 7 pins. The design was simple, easy to operate, and apparently reliable, but the fact remained that it was a single shot at a time when repeaters were becoming the vogue.

In accordance with an act of Congress dated November 21, 1877, another Ordnance Board was convened for the purpose of selecting a magazine rifle. This time a total of 29 arms were examined, and No. 25 was one entered by James Lee

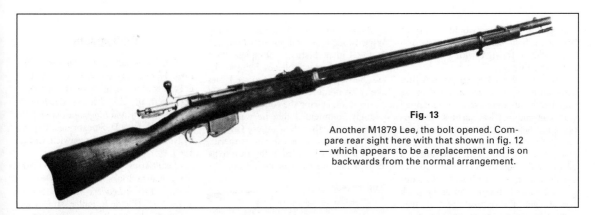

Fig. 13

Another M1879 Lee, the bolt opened. Compare rear sight here with that shown in fig. 12 — which appears to be a replacement and is on backwards from the normal arrangement.

of Hartford, Conn. (As noted above, the 1877 patent was issued to Lee at Milwaukee, but the rifle entered in the trials a few months later places Lee in Hartford, Conn. Later patents will include Ilion, N.Y., and again Hartford.) Which Lee model this was is not known to the author, but it is assumed that it is the 1877 design, possibly with the magazine mentioned previously. This opinion is based on Lee's statement that the 1877 design "… can be loaded and fired at the rate of 37 times per minute, …" Regardless, it was beaten out when the Board selected the Winchester-manufactured Hotchkiss, and recommended that $20,000 be spent toward obtaining a trial lot for field testing.

1879 Bolt Action

Returning to the Remington Armory in Ilion, Lee was provided a workshop by Philo Remington, and such assistance as he needed. His perseverance at last paid off, for in 1878 the Lee bolt action rifle, capable of firing 30 rounds a minute, became a reality. On September 6, 1878, application was filed for a patent, and on November 4, 1879, U.S. Patent No. 221, 328 was granted to "James Lee, of Ilion, New York," for a design that was to become the most famous of all Lee rifles.

Alden Hatch in his book *Remington Arms in American History* relates a curious tale about Lee. During 1878 and 1879, while Lee was working on his bolt action rifle, he was living in a room at the Osgood Hotel in Ilion. He frequently took his drawings and models back to his room to work on them at night. The room directly above his was rented by an enterprising German, who also worked for Remington. It has been said that the German bored a hole in the floor of his room and lay on his stomach for hours, his eye glued to the hole to watch what went on below. The name of the German? Franz Mauser, a brother of the inventors of the Mauser repeating rifle — Peter Paul and

Wilhelm Mauser. Whether the watching was profitable or not is debatable, as the Mauser rifles were not equipped with box magazines until 1886. However, the fact remains that Lee later sued the Mauser brothers for patent infringement.

Lee apparently wanted to manufacture his rifle on his own, so the Lee Arms Company of Bridgeport, Conn. was formed sometime in 1879 in order to do so.7 The address of the firm, at the foot of Clinton Avenue, next to the New Haven Railroad, was the same as that of the Sharps Rifle Company, which was listed in the Bridgeport city directories until 1886. Apparently Lee's financial backers were also of the same group, for E.G. Westcott, president of the Sharps Rifle Company in 1879, was later listed as treasurer of the Lee Arms Company. Previous to 1878, Westcott was listed as president and treasurer of the Sharps firm, but in a rare Sharps folder dated 1878, and apparently intended for British trade, Westcott is listed as vice-president and treasurer, and A.W. Winchester is president. In 1881-82, after the Sharps firm had ceased operations, Winchester is listed as the Sharps treasurer. The backers apparently lost interest in the rifle manufacturing business shortly after the new Lee firm was formed. The last Sharps catalog consisted of an 1879 edition with a blue 1880 price list attached, and operations were suspended in October, 1880, after only a few of the Lee rifles had been manufactured.8

The Lee patents were taken over by Remington, a natural move since the rifle had been developed at the Remington Armory, and the manufacture transferred to Ilion under license. The rifles were produced by Remington for the Lee Arms Company, which continued to act as selling agent, commercially advertising the rifle in the Army & Navy Journal from April 13 to November 27, 1880.

The 1879 patent was very simple and direct. It provided for a "… bolt-gun hav-

ing an opening through the bottom of its shoe or receiver, a detachable magazine … with rear and of different lengths … to allow the cartridges to lie therein in an inclined position, and with their flanges (rims) overlapping one another …" It also provided for two other magazine modifications, including one that circled the gun stock, a firing pin with a knob on the end to allow the pin to be drawn back by hand or to the halfcock position, an extractor and a "…. curved sliding plate (cut-off) … to allow the rifle … to be used as a single-loader …" The actual arm followed the patent specifications closely.

The first rifles were marked on the upper left side of the receiver:

The Lee Arms Co. Bridgeport Conn.
U.S.A.
Patented Nov. 4th 1879

This was followed by a serial number and an inspector's initials, such as W.W.K., W.M.F., and P. Rifles purchased by the U.S. Navy were also stamped with U.S. above an anchor.

The straight bolt handle projected to the right, just forward of the receiver bridge. The one-piece bolt cocked on closing. There were two locking lugs, consisting of the root of the bolt handle with its integral guide rib, and a small lug directly opposite which locked into the left side of the receiver. The cocking piece knob was small, flat, and smooth. The rotating extractor slipped into the front of the bolt and was retained by a hooked piece which fitted into the guide rib. The degree of rotation of the extractor was established by a groove in the bolt body just ahead of the guide rib.

The barrels, 29½ inches long, were rifled with 5 wide grooves. Over-all length was 48½ inches, weight about 8½ pounds.

A gas escape port was located in the left side of the receiver ring ¾-inch back of the forward edge, in the event of case failure. The firing pin could be drawn back to the halfcock position to serve as a safety when carrying it with a live round in the chamber.

The M1879 stock extended to within three inches of the muzzle and had a nose cap. Two bands were used, both retained with conventional leaf springs. The upper band held a sling swivel; the lower swivel was retained by a front trigger-guard screw. A cleaning rod fitted into a groove in the bottom of the fore-end and extended to the muzzle. There was no upper hand-guard and the grip of the stock was straight. The buttplate was of steel, curved, in the same basic shape as on the Springfield M1873.

Two different rear sights have been observed on the M1879. The more common one is a folding tangent, graduated on the notched elevation slide to 500 yards, and on the leaf to 1200 yards. It is adjustable for windage by sliding the crossbar, which has "buckhorn" side elements.

The M1879 was chambered for the 43 Spanish, 44-77 (bottleneck), 45-70 Gov't. and 45-90 Winchester cartridges. The magazine held 5 cartridges and was plain, without grooves or corrugations.

Both sporting and military versions of the M1879 were apparently produced. However, the bulk of the production was the military model.

In 1876 the Navy Bureau of Ordnance had recommended that "… we should adopt a magazine gun, which for naval purposes is in every respect preferable." By 1879 a total of 2500 of the 45-caliber Hotchkiss rifles had been bought for testing. A year later, in the Annual Report of the Secretary of the Navy, mention was made that the Hotchkiss guns, along with 250 each of the Remington Keene and Lee guns — chambered for the 45–70 Gov't, cartridge — were enough to arm the 75 ships then in commission with repeating rifles, and to test the relative value of the three systems — magazine in butt, beneath the barrel, and detachable.

In 1881 it was reported that the "… 300 Lee breech-loading rifles are being manufactured at the Remington Armory." By 1882 the 300 "Lee Arms Co." rifles had been delivered and introduced into the service.

Other countries buying the Model 1879 included Spain, Argentina, and China. The Chinese purchase was the basis for a humorous comment attributed to the inventor some years later. The Chinese were well pleased with the Model 1879, and had used the rifles to defeat some French troops. Afterward an eminent Chinese gentleman named Yung Wing brought several young Chinamen to the United States to complete their education at eastern colleges. Being in the area he stopped by Hartford to see James Lee at his home, and to compliment him on his rifles. During the conversation Lee jokingly commented that he was never quite sure whether the Chinese Government had selected his rifle on its merits, or because they believed its inventor to be a Chinaman, his name being Jim Lee.

References

1. "Lee Firearms Company in Milwaukee," Harry Wandrus. Hobbies — The Magazine for Collectors, December, 1949.

2. H.L. Uphoff lists 6 of the same individuals as shareholders. The exception is an Alexander Mitchell, instead of Thomas L. Ogden. He also lists the president of the Board as Charles F. Ilsley, with James Kneeland, Daniel Wells, Jr., Lester Sexton, and James Lee as directors.

3. This was the only Ordnance Department contract granted to a mid-western arms company.

4. Col. McAllister reported that Lee had on hand 202 carbines in various stages of completion, and that 255 had been finished, 102 of these last sold at $22.50. A full list of the parts Lee had on hand was furnished, their cost, etc., and Col. McAllister noted that Lee stood to lose some $6500 if he finished his contract. A compromise settlement was suggested by Col. McAllister.

5. The Civil War was over.

6. Mention has been made in one source that James Lee enjoyed the distinction among private inventors of being moved by the government from his home at Stevens Point, Wis., to Springfield Armory in Massachusetts to supervise the manufacturing of his rifle. This is doubtful, since only the 1862 patent carried the Stevens Point address, and succeeding patents up to this time carried the Milwaukee address, plus the fact that Lee is listed as residing at 130 Prospect Street in the Milwaukee city directories during the 1866-1874 period. Possibly the government agreed to move his family from Milwaukee to Springfield so that they could be with him.

7. During this period another Lee Arms Co. came into being. Whether it was connected with James Paris Lee is moot. Gluckman and Gardner both list the Lee Arms Co. of Wilkes-Barre, Pa., as makers of "Red Jacket" rimfire revolvers around 1877-80, and Gardner indicates "… possibly before and after" this date, and tacked on "James Paris Lee." Sharpe says that Lee moved to Wilkes-Barre after he had sold his rifle rights to Remington, and there formed a new Lee Arms Co. to make a variety of rimfire revolvers. Only Sharpe and Gardner mention James Paris Lee as connected with the Wilkes-Barre firm, and only Sharpe actually states Lee formed the company. Apparently very little is known about this firm and its organization, but if James Paris Lee was connected with it, it represents his sole departure into the handgun field — other than his 1862 patent for a single shot handgun. This time factor is about correct, as many Lee designs originated during the 1870s. The author's opinion is that James Paris Lee was not connected with the "Red Jacket" revolvers; the main flaw is the apparent term of existence for the firm — 1877-80. Gardner says Roland L. Brewer of Pittston, Pa., (1878–84) was granted U.S. Patent No. 239,914 on April 5, 1881, for a revolving firearm, the patent assigned to J.F. Lee, of Wilkes-Barre. The last name and the location are right for the Lee Arms Co. making revolvers. The same Brewer was later issued three firearms patents — assigned to the Colt. This would seem to indicate the maker of "Red Jacket" revolvers was J.F. Lee, not J.P. Lee. Possibly some reader has better information.

8. What may have been one of the first M1879 Lee rifles apparently produced at the Sharps factory used parts identical to those on the M1879 Sharps-Borchardt military rifle. The rear sight is the same as the Borchardt, the two bands are Borchardt-type (secured with wood screws through the bottom instead of with springs as on the later production) and the buttplate is of flat checkered steel — Borchardt design. The 43 caliber barrel, 32½ inches long is rifled with 6 grooves. Total length is 51⅛ inches. No markings appear on the wood or metal. The magazine holds 5 cartridges. The bolt is one-piece but the handle is behind the bridge instead of in front as on the standard 1879 rifles. Only one such rifle is known.

Bibliography

The Fuller Collection of American Fire-arms, Harold L. Peterson, Eastern National Park & Monument Association, 1967.

Digest of U.S. Patents Relating to Breech Loading and Magazine Small Arms 1836–1873, by V.D. Stockbridge. Reprint by Norm Flayderman, Greenwich, Conn., 1963.

Small Arms Makers, Col. Robert Gardner, Bonanza Books, New York, 1963.

The Breech-Loader In The Service 1816–1917, Claude E. Fuller, N. Flayderman & Co. New Milford, Conn., 1965.

Guns Through the Ages, Geoffrey Booth-royd, Bonanza Books, New York, 1961. "Lee's Firearms Co.," Herbert L. Uphoff, *The Gun Report*, June and July, 1967.

The Lee-Enfield Rifle, Major E.G.B. Reynolds, Herbert Jenkins, London, 1960.

Suicide Specials, Donald B. Webster, Jr., The Stackpole Company, Harrisburg, Pa., 1958.

The Book of Rifles, W.H.B. Smith and Jos. E. Smith, The Stackpole Company, Harrisburg, Pa., 1963.

"Model 1875 Lee-Springfield," Gordon F. Baxter, Jr., *The Gun Report*, November, 1960.

"Remington-Lee Rifle," Ludwig Olson, *The American Rifleman*, April, 1966.

"The Rifles of James Paris Lee," Robt. H. Rankin, *Guns & Ammo*, March, 1964.

Remington Arms in American History, Alden Hatch, Rinehart & Co., New York, 1956.

American Gun Makers, A. Gluckman and L.D. Satterlee, The Stackpole Company, Harrisburg, Pa., 1953.

The Rifle in America, Philip B. Sharpe, Funk & Wagnalls, New York, 1947.

The Gun and its Development, 9th ed., W.W. Greener, Reprint by Bonanza Books, New York, 1967.

"James Paris Lee," James Young, *The Saturday Globe*, Toronto, Can., June 9, 1900.

The United States Navy Rifle, Calibre 6 Millimeters, Model 1895, Description and Nomenclature, P.R. Alger and N.C. Twining, Lockwood & Brainard, Hartford, Conn., 1896.

"The Lee Straight-Pull Magazine Rifle," E.G. Parkhurst, *American Machinist*, November 22, 1900.

Winchester, The Gun That Won The West, H.F. Williamson, The Sportsman's Press, 1952.

The Rifles of James Paris Lee

Part Two. Born in Scotland in 1831, Lee was brought to Canada in 1836, moving eventually to Stevens Point, Wisconsin, sometime before 1860. His first military contract, made in 1864, was hardly successful. A rare dropping block design based on Lee's 1866 patent is pictured and described, as are Lee's M1875 rifle, the various trials of his rifle designs, and his 1879 system — the first one of his great magazine design, and the rifle which would prove to be the forerunner of the British S.M.L.E.

▌ Larry S. Sterett

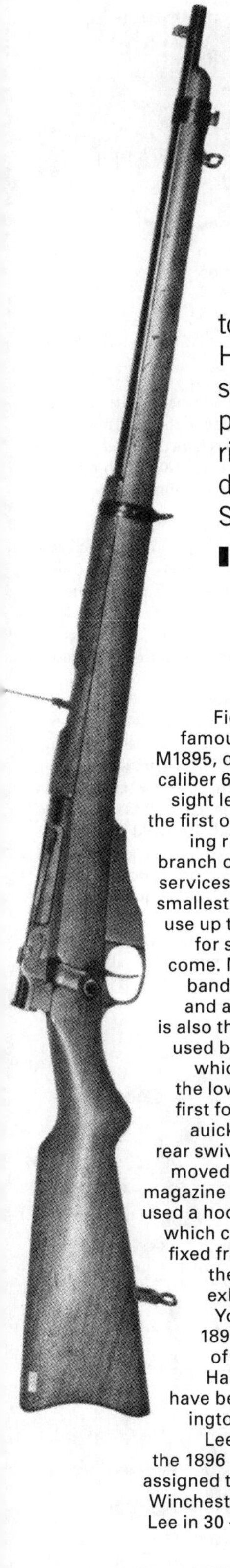

Fig. 14 — This is the famous U.S. Navy Rifle, M1895, or the Lee — Navy, caliber 6mm, with the rear sight leaf erect. This was the first official clip — loading rifle ever used by a branch of the U.S. military services, and was also the smallest caliber in military use up to that time — and for several decades to come. Note that the front band has both a swivel and a bayonet lug. This is also the only Lee design used by the U.S. military which had a swivel on the lower band. Another first for this rifle was the auick — detach — able rear swivel which could be moved to the front of the magazine housing; the sling used a hook — arrangement which could snap into the fixed front swivel. One of the M1895 rifles was exhibited at the New York Militia Trials of 1896, as was an entry of the Lee Arms Co., Hartford. (This could have been a M1885 Remington — Lee, the 1888 Lee design, or one of the 1896 Parkhurst designs assigned to Lee), and later a Winchester — made M1895 Lee in 30 — 40 Krag caliber.

REALIZING THE NEED and, possibly sensing the handwriting on the wall, the Ordnance Department convened the Board of 1882 to pick a suitable magazine rifle. By late September 1882 the Board had tested and examined a total of 53 rifles submitted by 20 inventors, including the M1879 and M1882 versions of the Lee rifle in 45–70 Gov't, caliber. Rifle No. 10 was a M1879 entry of the Lee Arms Co., and No. 36 was a Remington — Lee M1882 with an improved bolt. Rifles No. 24, 31, and 35, were Spencer — Lee rifles entered by J. W. Frazier of New York City.9 The early trials narrowed the field to three basic designs — the M1882 Lee, the Hotchkiss, the Chaffee — Reece — and additional testing was recommended.

Ordnance Office,
War Department
Washington, October 9, 1882

Respectfully returned to the Secretary of War:
A careful examination of the report … convinces me that … while the Lee gun is entitled to the first place, the comparative merits of the three guns put them nearly on a par in point of excellence.
… I respectfully recommend that the $50,000 available … be expended in providing the Lee, the Chaffee — Reece, and the Hotchkiss magazine guns for trial in the hands of troops.
S. V. Benet,
Brigadier — General,
Chief of Ordnance.

The recommendation was approved by Robert T. Lincoln, Secretary of War and Benet was asked to learn the prices of each type of gun:

Ordnance Office,
War Department
Washington, January 10, 1883.
Respectfully returned to the
Secretary of War…

The Remingtons make the Lee gun, and will supply them at $16.66 each in about three months. The prices given for the Lee and Hotch — kiss are fair. I respectfully recommend that 750 guns each of Lee and Hotchkiss may be procured by contract …
In this connection I have to state that as the Lee and Hotchkiss are patented articles and can only be procured from parties owning the patents, the question arises whether or not contracts can be made with them without previous advertisement. If not contrary to law I respectfully recommended it.
S. V. Benet,
Brigadier — General,
Chief of Ordnance.

Respectfully returned to the Chief of Ordnance.

…the making of a contract with the proprietors of the Lee and Hotchkiss guns without advertisement is authorized for the reason that such advertisement would be a useless expense, as… definite articles are wanted, for which there can be no competition.

John Tweedale
Chief Clerk
War Department, January 10, 1883.

Ordnance Office,
War Department
Washington, D.C.,
December 15, 1885.

Fig. 15 — Right side of the Lee M1895 action. What appears to be a small number 7, near the rear of the breech opening, is supposed to be the number 1. Fig. 16 — Left side view of the Lee M1895 action, showing the bolt stop, bolt release and firing-pin lock. The inscription on the receiver reads, in two lines: MANUFACTURED BY THE WINCHESTER REPEATING ARMS CO./NEW HAVEN, CONN. U. S. A. PAT OCT 10, 93, JAN 30, 94, OCT 5, 95.

The Secretary of War.

Sir: I have the honor to transmit herewith a tabular statement of the results reached in the trial of a number of each of the magazine rifles issued to the troops. (Author's note: 713 rifles each of the Lee, Hotchkiss, and Chaffee — Reece [designs] were issued to the troops, and Springfield Armory had produced 3,937 spare magazines for the Lee.) These guns were recommended for trial, in the order named, by a board of officers convened in 1881, under authority of law ...

The reports from 149 companies have been received ... as follows:

Comparing the three magazine guns with each other the reports are:

For the Lee, 55; Chaffee — Reece, 14; Hotchkiss, 26.

As magazine guns, therefore, the reports are largely in favor of the Lee.

Comparing the magazine guns with each other and with the Springfield service rifle as single loaders, the preference is for the Springfield, as follows: For the Lee, 5; Chaffee — Reece, 0; Hotchkiss, 1; Springfield, 21.

Comparing the magazine guns and the Springfield for all uses, the preference is for the Lee, 10; Chaffee — Reece, 3; Hotchkiss, 4; and the Springfield, 46; being largely in favor of the Springfield.

...I am satisfied that neither of these magazine guns should be adopted and substituted for the Springfield rifle as the arm for the Service.

...The Springfield rifle gives such general satisfaction to the Army that we can safely wait a reasonable time for further developments of magazine systems.

Very respectfully,
your obedient servant,
S. V. Benet,
Brigadier — General,
Chief of Ordnance.

Thus, the Springfield single shot rifle was to remain the mainstay of the U. S. Army for another 7 years.

The original arrangement between Lee and Remington called for Remington to manufacture the rifles for the Lee Arms Co. This arrangement did not work out and, in 1884, Lee had entered into an agreement with Remington to manufacture and sell the rifle on a royalty basis. As a result, rifles manufactured after this time were marked:

E. REMINGTON & SONS, ILION, N.Y. U.S.A. SOLE MANUFACTURERS AND AGENTS

On March 25, 1884, "James P. Lee and Louis P. Diss, of Ilion, New York Assignors to E. Remington & Sons, of Same Place" were issued U. S. Patent No. 295,-563 for a "Magazine for Fire-Arms." The basic design was for an improvement of the 1879 model and consisted of a very light sheet-iron magazine with "... spring or detent which holds the cartridges

in the box when not attached to the arm, and in corrugating the body of the box (magazine) ..." This same Diss was issued 8 other firearms patents between 1884 and 1888, with most assigned to E. Remington & Sons.

Sales to the Navy

The 1884 Annual Report of the Secretary of the Navy stated that 700 Lee magazine guns had been purchased on advantageous terms for armament on new cruisers. The model is unknown to the author: that "advantageous" might refer to a closing out of the 1879 model, but this is only an opinion.

In 1885 an improved Lee rifle appeared. This is sometimes called the 1884/85 Lee, but it is usually listed as the Model 1885 Remington-Lee. The rear locking system, with cocking on closing, was retained, but a separate bolt head was used. The extractor was attached to the bolt head, and both were held in place by a hooked piece that fitted into the guide rib and slid rearward to lock. The cocking piece was changed slightly, the flange almost doubled in size.

The barrel was 32'/2 inches long, and rifled the same as the 1882 model. Over-all length of the 1885 model was 52 inches, and the weight was about 8½ pounds.

Fig. 17 — Essential parts of the Lee MI 895. Parts common to all small arms are omitted in this Figure and in Fig. 20. The parts in both Figures are numbered the same, so that they may be compared. No. 1, receiver; 2, bolt; 3, firing pin; 4, mainspring; 5, firing-pin collar; 6, cam lever; 7, trigger guard and magazine; 8, cartridge elevator; 9A, bolt-stop thumb-piece; 9B, bolt-stop; 10, extractor; 11, extractor spring; 12, sear; 13, sear fly; 14, trigger; 15A, trigger spring; 15B, fly spring; 16, elevator spring; 17, elevator-spring shaft; 18, lock pin; 19, firing-pin lock; 20, bolt release; 21, trigger-spring stop-pin; 22, trigger-spring screw.

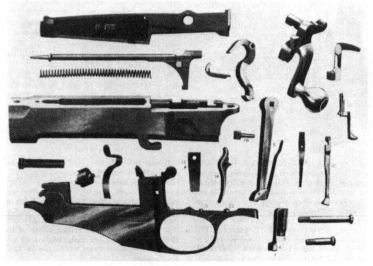

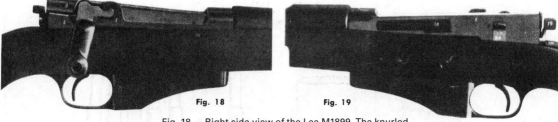

Fig. 18 — Right side view of the Lee M1899. The knurled piece at the rear of the receiver is the safety. Forward of the trigger guard is the magazine cut-off, which the M1895 did not have. Fig. 19 — Left side view of the Lee M1899, showing the bolt-stop and safety lock.

There was no upper handguard, but the two bands, the nose cap, the two sling swivels and their location, the sights, and the 5-round magazine with two vertical grooves were the same as on the Model 1882.

The Model 1885 was Remington marked, per the 1884 agreement, except that after 1888 E. Remington & Sons became the Remington Arms Company. These markings were on the upper left side of the receiver, and the serial number usually followed the second line of the marking. Rifles bought by the U. S. Navy were marked on top of the receiver ring with U.S.N. over an anchor: these markings sometimes had two lines below them consisting of an identification number and an inspector's initials, making a total of 4 lines on the receiver ring.

E. Remington & Sons went into receivership in 1886. (Lee recovered the rights to his designs in accordance with his contract with Remington, and apparently left for England to try to interest the British Government in his magazine rifle.) Of the Remington brothers, Sam was the businessman, so when he died in 1882 the firm started to slip slowly toward bankruptcy. Philo and Eliphalet III tried to keep the huge Armory in operation, and if a sizeable foreign or U. S. contract for the Lee rifle had been obtained they might have been able to do so. Turning out a quality product for which the demand is limited is expensive. For two years the receivers finished the work in process and took what small orders were obtained. Then in March, 1888, Marcellus Hartley, founder of the Union Metallic Cartridge Company, and Thomas G. Bennett, son-in-law of Governor Oliver Winchester (Remington's main competitor), bought E. Remington & Sons, with all of its physical properties and its reputation, for two million dollars. The name was changed to the Remington Arms Company, but the quality products for which the firm was known remained the same.

On May 22, 1888, U. S. Patent 383,363 for a "Magazine Fire-Arm" was issued to "James P. Lee, of New York, N. Y." In the patent introduction Lee lists himself as an engineer and a resident of New York (City), although he is not so-listed in any of the other patents with which the author is familiar.

The patent relates to the 1879 patent and was "… chiefly designed to improve the construction and increase the efficiency of such fire-arms." The arm had been previously patented in England on August 18,1887, and examination of the drawings indicates that this is the basic design for the famous Lee-Enfield rifle used throughout the British Empire for over 60 years.

The wide cup extending below the receiver breech for the attachment of the separate buttstock, so familiar a sight on later Lee-Enfield rifles, is illustrated for the first time. The removable bolt head, which could also be used as a tool for unscrewing the firing pin from the cocking piece, is covered in this 1888 patent, as is the entire striker assembly so much a part of the Lee-Enfield rifles.

Two magazine modifications, which make use of U-shaped follower springs instead of the common zig-zag type, are covered by the patent. Surprisingly, the cartridges illustrated in the magazine are rimless instead of the rimmed or flanged type then in use. The magazine catch is a transverse type, such as became popular later on autoloading pistols, instead of the previous lever type in the upper part of the trigger guard directly ahead of the trigger.

The Annual Report of the Secretary of the Navy for 1888 mentioned that 1500 Lee rifles "… of the latest construction …" had been bought from the Lee Arms Co. for immediate use on ships nearing completion. These would have been the M1885 design, and were no doubt manufactured by the newly formed Remington Arms Company, probably under license from Lee. So far as the author can learn the Lee Arms Company did not have manufacturing facilities, although it apparently continued to exist as a sales agency. Mention was further made by the Secretary that arms being purchased were "… as few as we can pending caliber reductions …," and that Lee had been selected as the builder of reduced-caliber Navy weapon(s), and a contract signed. Apparently the Navy, regardless of what the Army was doing, was planning to reduce the caliber from .45-inch to something much smaller, in keeping with the trend in Europe and England at this time.

In the 1889 Report the Secretary of the Navy mentioned that the 1500 stand of Lee magazine rifles mentioned in the previous report had been completed by the Lee Arms Co. and the work on them very favorably spoken of by the inspector.

Trials of 1891

The U. S. Army was still without a magazine rifle. On November 24,1890, the Adjutant General's office issued a general order for a board of officers to select a magazine gun to replace the single-shot Springfield. The Board convened at New York on December 16,1890, and remained in session until July 1, 1892. A total of 53 guns were examined and tests were made at Governors Island, New York, during July, 1891. Four of the rifles entered in these trials were connected directly or indirectly with

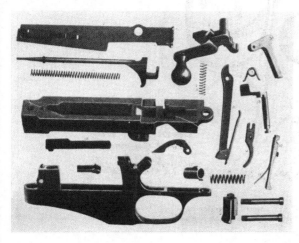

Fig. 20 — Essential parts of the Lee M1899. No. 1, receiver; 2, bolt; 3, firing pin; 4, mainspring; 5, firing-pin collar; 6, cam lever; 7, trigger guard and magazine; 8, cartridge elevator; 9A, bolt-stop; 9B, bolt-stop spring; 10, extractor; 11, extractor spring; 12, sear; 13, bolt retainer (new); 14, trigger; 15, trigger spring; 16, elevator spring; 17, elevator-spring sleeve; 18, extractor-spring stop (new); 19, safety lock (new).

J. P. LEE.
MAGAZINE BOLT GUN.

No. 547,583.   Patented Oct. 8, 1895.

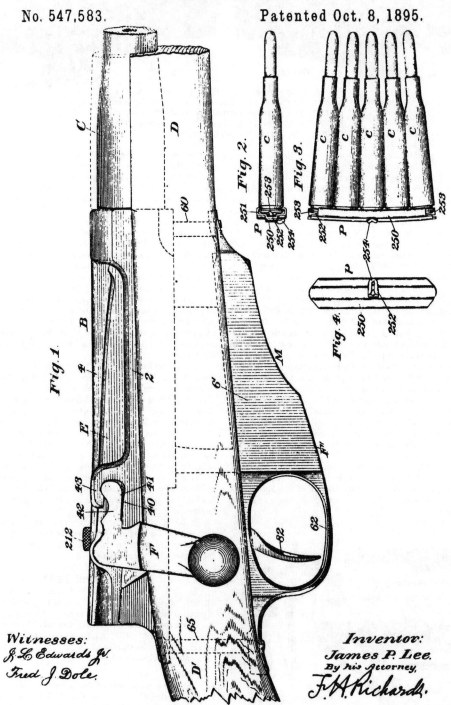

Witnesses:
J. L. Edwards Jr.
Fred J. Dole.

Inventor:
James P. Lee.
By his Attorney,
F. H. Richards

Lee's 1895 U.S. Patent, No. 547,583, covered his design for a
straight pull bolt action rifle. This became the Lee Navy 6mm.

James Paris Lee, as follows:

Rifle No. 1, entered by the U. S. Army Chief of Ordnance, Washington, D. C, was apparently the Lee-Metford or Magazine Rifle Mark I, adopted by England on December 22, 1888. The first models were sometimes referred to as the Lee-Speed. This was not the official name, but Greener and several other authors of this period did not always differentiate between the Lee-Speed, Lee-Metford and Lee-Enfield. The Lee-Speed rifle shown in *The Gun...** is identical to the Lee-Metford and resembles the drawing in Lee's 1888 patent closely. Speed was the name of an employee at the Royal Small Arms Factory at Enfield Lock, possibly that of the Superintendent.

Rifle No. 39, entered by the Lee Arms Co., South Windham, Conn, was probably the M1885. This address in Connecticut is not that of the 1879 firm, but the author has no other information relating to it. By whom rifles No. 25 and 26 were entered is not known to the author, but perhaps these were Remington Arms Company entries.

Again the Lee lost out, this time to the Krag-Jorgensen (No. 5) entered by a Capt. Ole Krag from Norway. The U. S. Army never adopted a Lee design as an official arm, but the U. S. Navy used Lee rifles for nearly 20 years.

Lee had apparently been busy on the new rifle the Navy had requested, for the Secretary of the Navy reported in 1892 that specifications had been given to Lee for a 236 caliber arm. In 1893 it was further reported that while the Army Krag and several European designs had been examined and compared, work was continuing with Lee on the 236.

The year 1893 was a big one for Lee. Beginning on August 19, 1892, Lee had filed patent applications for a series of " ... new and useful Improvements in Magazine-Guns ...," and on October 10, 1893, the U. S. Patent Office granted patents to "James P. Lee, of Ilion, New York" in profusion. Patent Nos. 506,319; 506,320; 506,321; 506,322 and 506,323 were issued for a "Straight-Pull Bolt-Gun" (first three patents), a "Magazine-Gun" and a "Fire-Arm Magazine Case" respectively. On the same date U. S. Patent No. 506,339 was issued to "Francis H. Richards, of Hartford, Conn., Assignor to James Paris Lee, of same place." Richards' patent was for a "Straight-Pull Bolt-Gun" and the application had been filed on September 26,1892, the same date on which Lee had filed the application that became Patent No. 506,321. (Note that patents issued the same day list Lee as at Ilion, N. Y. and Hartford, Conn.) Francis H. Richards is listed on the patent drawings as being Lee's attorney, but on the specifications as a witness; the second witness on the drawings does not appear on the specifications of the first three patents. On the patent for the "Magazine-Gun" a W. G. Richards is listed on both the drawings and the specifications, and again on the specifications for the Richards patent as a witness; Francis H. Richards is listed as the inventor on this last patent (No. 506,339.) The witness whose name appears on

---

*W. W. Greener, London, var. eds., 1881 — 1910.

	Magazine Capacity	Weight	Caliber
No. 1 Lee Speed, England	8 rds.	9 3/8 lbs.	303
No. 25 Lee No. 1, American	10 rds.	8 1/4 lbs.	303
No. 26 Lee No. 2, American	5 rds.	8 1/4	300
No. 39 Lee No. 3, American	10 rds.	8 1/4 lbs.	300

the drawings of all the patents listed above appears to be H. Mallner.

Lee Straight Pull Rifles

The patents all relate to the straight-pull rifle that the U. S. Navy would later adopt as the M1895. The arms are designed for use with detachable 10-round magazines (staggered column) with their release in the trigger guard. The cartridges shown are rimmed, and about 30 caliber-very similar to the 30–40 Krag. Provision was made for loading the magazine with 15-round clips while the magazine was still attached to the rifle. The receiver walls are solid on this design and the ejection is upward, instead of to the right. Other than the firing-pin spring and magazine spring the only spring in this particular design was a U-shaped type that served as sear and trigger spring. There was no safety. The Lee Patent No. 506,321 and the Richards patent are for a model not quite the same as on the other patents, and many of these particular two patent drawings appear to be the same. Basic operation of the rifles covered in the 1893 patents is much the same, as will be covered later in connection with the M1895 Lee-Navy rifle.

The 1894 annual Navy report mentioned that the Navy had designed the barrel, stock, and cartridge, and tested all. Apparently the reference is to the 236-caliber Lee rifle and cartridge, on which work had been underway to some degree for nearly 6 years.

On October 2,1894, at the United States Torpedo Station, Newport, Rhode Island, the Navy tested 12 rifles, including the Lee straight-pull model. Two of the rifles tested were straight-pull designs, including the Lee, one was a slide-action, and the rest were turn-bolt designs, 5 of these last entered by Remington. On November 19, 1894, another trial was held with three additional rifles, including a Luger 6mm rimless caliber design. One of the tests involved penetration (pine?) as related to caliber; the 236 Navy penetrated 23 inches as opposed to 10 inches for the 45–70 Gov't. cartridge, and 18 inches for the 8mm Austrian Mannlicher cartridge.

In May, 1895, a Navy Board, convened at Newport, officially adopted the Lee Straight-Pull, with the shape of the stock, fittings, sling strap, and bayonet determined by the Board. The 1895 report of the Secretary of the Navy mentioned that the 1894 Board had adopted the Lee Straight-Pull, although it may have been unofficial at that time. Bids for 10,000 rifles of the Lee design were requested, and Winchester got the contract. (Lee had sold the rights to manufacture the rifle to the Winchester firm.) However, Williamson in *Winchester ...* says that the contract was for 15,000 of these Lee patent rifles, while factory records indicate 20,000 were made, of which 1,700 were sporting models. The factory records show that all

Fig. 21 — The M1882 Remington-Lee rifle as used by the U.S. Navy. Note the position and type of bolt handle; the head of the cocking piece, and the two vertical grooves in the magazine. The upper band still has two swivels. This model is often mistakenly called the M1879; it definitely is not, but it's a much better design than the original. This particular rifle is marked as indicated in the text, and the left side of the receiver has PATENTED NOV. 4th, 1879. One MI 882 rifle is the Royal Military College Museum of Canada is marked on the receiver: E. REMINGTON & SONS, ILION, N. Y., U. S. A./SOLE MANUFACTURER AND AGENTS/PATENTED NOV. 4th, 1879. The rifle is chambered for the 45–70 Gov't, cartridge, and has the 5-round magazine with two vertical grooves. The bolt handle, cocking piece, and guide rib are polished bright and the rear sight lies immediately in front of the receiver ring; the rear sight is of the type shown in Fig. 12 (See Part One of this article, pp. 48–60, 26th ed. GUN DIGEST.) except it is reversed and in the correct position. Another M1882 rifle in the same collection is completely nickel-plated, except for the highly polished blued magazine, which is without grooves. The stock on this particular rifle is checkered on the fore-end and grip, and the rifle is unmarked. This rifle was in the collection of Porfirio Diaz, once President of Mexico.

Fig. 22 — The M1885 Remington-Lee, caliber 45–70 Gov't. The only noticeable differences from the M1882 are the size of the cocking-piece head, the method of fitting the extractor to the bolt, and the smaller cut-out of the receiver ring on the right side. Markings on this rifle are as indicated in the text. Note there are still two swivels on the upper band. Barrel length of this rifle is 32⅝ inches, giving an overall length of 52 inches. Serial number is 53142.

of them were manufactured in the three years of 1896–1898, as follows:

There were no receivers numbered from 11,719 to 12,002, 13,701 to 13,733 or 14,980 to 15,000, which cuts the 20,000 total by nearly 400 rifles.

Serial Numbers	Year
1 – 1917	1896
1,918 – 10,512	1897
10,513 – 20,000	1898

First Official Clip Loader

The 1897 Navy Report mentions that 10,000 Lee (236 caliber) rifles had been delivered and issued to vessels in commission. Thus the Lee-Navy design became the first clip-loading rifle ever officially used by armed forces of the United States, and the smallest official caliber-disregarding the 22 rimfire-until the introduction of the 5.56mm (223) over 60 years later.

The straight-pull design was not new by any means. Austria had used at least 7 different models of straight-pull rifles by the time the U. S. Navy adopted the Lee. Switzerland had also been using a straight-pull rifle. Most of these designs had used a system of revolving or rotating locking lugs. Lee's design, patented in 1893, used a wedge-type locking lug integral with the bottom of the bolt. Although correct-

ed in later models, once the bolt was locked down in the M1895 it could not be unlocked without pulling the trigger or pushing down on the "dead-lock actuator" on the left side of the receiver.

On October 8, 1895, U. S. Patent No. 547,583 was granted to "James P. Lee, of Hartford, Conn.," for a "Magazine Bolt-Gun." The 16 pages of drawings show clearly that this is the rifle manufactured for the U. S. Navy, even to the extent of illustrating the 6mm rimless cartridge in the 5-round clip.

The M1895 Lee-Navy uses a wedge-type locking lug integral with the bottom of the bolt. By slamming the bolt handle forward the wedge is cammed down into contact with a recoil shoulder in the receiver. Since the wedge is below the line of recoil, discharge tends to lock the breech mechanism securely. After firing a straight-back pull on the bolt handle cams the wedge up out of its recess; a continuation of the movement draws the bolt to the rear until it is stopped by the bolt-stop, which also controls the ejection.

The extractor on the 1895 design is a peculiar floating type-entirely different from that employed in the turnbolt system-on the left side of the bolt. It has three functions-extraction, ejection, and as a stop for retaining the cartridges in the magazine. The extractor remains stationary until the bolt has moved rearward about 1¾ inches. A lug on the bolt

then strikes a lug on the extractor, imparting a violent jerk to the cartridge, pulling it from the chamber and literally throwing it out to the right. An unusual method to say the least.

The 1895 design had no safety, as such, but it did have a "firing-pin locker." This device located on the left side of the receiver wall at the breech, moved in a vertical plane only: when pushed upward it retracted and locked the firing-pin out of engagement with the sear arm. When the rifle was to be fired the "locker" could easily be pushed down out of engagement, allowing the firing pin to re-engage the sear. Two other devices appeared that were not often seen on other designs; The movable bolt stop and the "dead-lock actuator" for the sliding bolt. Located on the left side of the receiver, they locked the bolt closed, but permitted it to be unlocked to remove the chambered cartridge, and the bolt to be removed from the rifle entirely when necessary. Pressing the lock actuator downward would unlock the bolt, causing the rear portion to spring upward, after which it could be drawn back to extract the cartridge.

The 1895 design was essentially a repeating rifle. When a clip of 5 cartridges, with a confining hook at each end of the clip, was inserted into the magazine, either end up, a fixed cam released all the cartridges for feeding. There was no magazine cut-off on this model.

Williamson says that in November, 1897, after the Navy contract had been completed, Winchester introduced a sporting version of the M1895 Lee-Navy to list at $32. It was described thus:

"This gun is known as the Lee Straight-Pull Rifle, and has been adopted as the small arm for use in the United States Navy. The caliber of the gun is .236 in. (6mm) and it shoots a smokeless powder cartridge with a hardened lead bullet, having a copper jacket plated with tin, and giving an initial velocity of 2,550 feet (777.24 meters) per second. The magazine holds 5 cartridges, which may be inserted separately or at one time, in which latter case they are placed in the magazine in a pack, held together by a steel clip. The superiority of this rifle over all other types of bolt guns lies in the fact that the operation of opening and closing is by a 'straight pull' instead of the customary 'up turn' and 'pull back.'"

The sporter, sometimes known as the Winchester-Lee model, was available in 6mm caliber only, with a 24-inch nickel-steel barrel. It weighed 7.5 pounds with the sporting halfstock. The quality was good, but the price was high, and sportsmen were just not ready for a bolt action arm that cost more than the popular lever action so The Lee Straight-Pull sporter hardly got off the ground, although it was listed in Winchester catalogs until 1902.

The 1895 patent mentions a previous patent,-No. 513,647, issued January 30, 1894, to James Lee for a "Bolt-Gun." While this patent incorporates some of the features later used in the M1895 rifle it is mainly for a straight-pull design with a 10-round cartridge packet with an outside-mounted cartridge lifter. (Patent No. 547,-582 was for a 5-round "cartridge

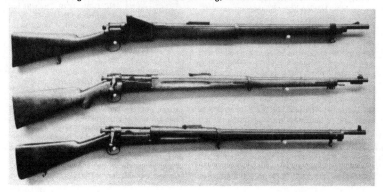

Fig. 23-Top: This is one of the improved Lee rifles with Bethel Burton magazine, of the type entered in the British trials of 1882-87. Note that barrel, fore-end, and bands are identical to those on the older Martini-Henry rifles, indicating that this may be one of the first of the Lee-Burton models. The later Lee-Burton types, which were tested extensively, had a very slim fore-end and only one band, not two • Middle: A Norwegian 6.5×55 Krag-Jorgensen, which served as the basis for our own M1892 Krag rifle • Bottom: M1896 U.S. Krag, caliber 30–40.

packet" as used in the 1895 rifle, and was issued to Lee on the same day as the rifle patent.) The right hand side of the action, as illustrated in this patent, is numbered so that the lifter arm indicates the number of cartridges in the magazine. The basic idea was good, and 16 pages of drawings are devoted mainly to the packet and the cartridge lifter, but apparently it did not reach commercial production.

Last Lee Patent

The 1895 patent was apparently the last one issued to James Paris Lee, although several later ones were assigned to the Lee Arms Company. In 1896, because of his own poor health, Lee had sent one of his two sons-George-to England with the M1895 Straight-Pull Rifle to effect its sale to the British. After examining the rifle the Commander-in-Chief, the Duke of Cambridge, is reported to have asked young Lee: "Why did you not show us this rifle before?"

On March 16, 1897, U. S. Patent No. 579,096, was issued to "William P. Lara-way, of Hartford, Conn. Assignor to the Lee Arms Company, of Connecticut." The application had been filed on April 20, 1896, and the patent was for a "Combined Bolt-Stop and Cartridge-Ejector for Bolt-Guns" to be embodied on a gun similar to that shown on an application of the same date made by one Edward G. Parkhurst. However, the Parkhurst patent was not issued until almost a year later. The Lara-way patent, and the later Parkhurst patents, had previously been patented in England, France, Belgium, Italy, and Austria.

The Laraway invention was a very simple leaf arrangement which slid into a groove on the left side of the receiver to act as a bolt stop and to eject the extracted case out the right side of the receiver. Provision was made for the bolt stop to be depressed to allow removal of the breech-bolt.

The M1895 Straight-Pull Rifle had proved to be easily operated, quick to load and accurate, but a few years of usage revealed some weaknesses not so apparent on adoption. The extractor (not attached to the bolt) had a rather brief life; the bolt-stop was not self-closing; the sear-fly was slightly dangerous and the loading clips were of uneven tension.

To eliminate these weaknesses some new parts were added and a few were done away with completely, the result being a net reduction of 10 parts. This new rifle, the M1899 Straight-Pull, retained the best features of the M1895 and was, according to all reports, safe, sure, and reliable. However, U. S. Navy records show that the only Lee Straight-Pull rifle tested by them ended with the adoption of the M1895 design. No trials were ever held for any later models.

The 1899 Straight Pull

The M1899 Straight-Pull Rifle is covered in U. S. Patent No. 599,287, issued on February 15, 1898, to "Edward G. Parkhurst, of Hartford, Connecticut, Assignor to the Lee Arms Company, of Connecticut." The patent was for a "Magazine Bolt-Gun," but it is basically for

Fig. 24 — This particular rifle — listed as the South American Model and available only in 43 Spanish caliber — apparently falls somewhere between the M1882 and M1885. The front band has only one swivel; the receiver ring resembles that of the M1885; the head of the cocking piece is too large for the M1882 and too small for the M1885. The rear sight is immediately in front of the receiver ring, and is identical to the sights on the two M1882 rifles in the Royal Military College Museum (Canada). Barrel length, over — all length and weight are about the same as for the M1885. The reproduction is from the J 903-04 *Price List of Military Arms, Equipments and Ordnance Stores*, published by M. Hartley Co., of New York, listed as "Agents: Remington Arms Co." This is the same Hartley who bought E. Remington & Sons in 1888, and formed the Remington Arms Company. Hartley also owned at least three other firms, including the Union Metallic Cartridge Company, and operated all of them separately. Note that this South American Model, with 4 magazines and a bayonet, sold for only $18.

Fig. 25 — An advertisement for the Model 1899 Remington — Lee rifle from the 1903 — 04 Hartley Price List. Note that only 3 calibers are listed as being available — two rimless and one rimmed. Bolt construction, locking lug recesses, and sear details are plainly visible in the cutaway view.

improvements on certain features of Lee's patent No. 547,583. Details in the patent follow the M1899 rifle closely, and it is worth noting that the cartridges shown in the Parkhurst patent appear to be of about 7mm caliber, rimless and bottlenecked. It had apparently been Lee's intention to make the caliber of his rifles 7mm, since this caliber had been adopted and found effective by several foreign powers. Just how effective was proved to us a few years later in Cuba, when we ran into the 7mm Spanish Mausers. However, this was the era of high-velocity and small calibers-the Army even experimented with a new rimmed 22 caliber centerfire cartridge-and the Navy apparently decided a 6mm cartridge would not only provide a flatter trajectory and deeper penetration but lighter ammunition.

The M1899 had a magazine cut-off, allow-

ing its use as a single-shot with 5 cartridges in reserve. A bolt retainer (13)-see Straight-Pull Fig. 20-performed the same job as the sear fly in the M1895 and did away with this delicate part and its spring. The bolt release or dead-lock actuator (20) of the M1895 was done away with, allowing the bolt to be unlocked by simply pulling rearward on the bolt handle. The safety lock (19) did away with the firing-pin locker (19) and performed the functions of locking down the bolt to the receiver and camming back the firing-pin, positively securing both. It performed the same function as the safeties of the Krag, Mauser, and later Springfield.

The extractor spring stop (18) of the M1899 provided a stop for the extractor and its spring during the forward movement of the bolt. This lengthened the life of the spring,

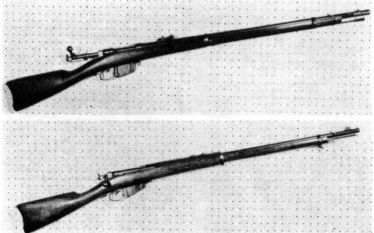

Fig. 26 — M1885 Remington-Lee rifle with the bolt in retracted position. Markings are as on the previous M1885, except top of the receiver ring is marked, in 4 lines: U.S.N.//N°.../A.CD. (There is no number above the dots.) Serial number is 53222, and the barrel length, other details, etc., are the same as on the previous MI885. The upper band on this rifle does not have swivels or provisions for them; it may be a misplaced lower band. From the Remington Arms Company collection.

Fig. 27 — The M1899 Remington-Lee rifle, caliber 30–40 Krag. The rifle is cocked, as indicated by the position of the cocking-piece. Note that this model has a hand-guard, while the M1879, M1882, M1885 and the South American Model do not. Note also that swivels are on the upper band and at the forward trigger guard screw. From the Remington Arms Company collection.

since it was no longer forced out of a niche (twice as deep as it was thick) when under its greatest tension.

To remove the bolt from the M1895 the bolt stop was pressed down, where it remained after the bolt was replaced, unless it was pushed back up. If the shooter forgot to push the bolt back into place, the next rearward movement of the bolt would remove it completely from the receiver, along with the extractor and its spring: the latter two items usually fell to the ground. The M1899 Straight-Pull design had a spiral spring which automatically forced the bolt stop back into position after it was depressed.

In the M1899 design the extractor and spring were held together with a rivet, the flanged head of which slid into a cut in the bolt. This eliminated the annoyance created by these parts in the M1895, where they could easily become lost when the bolt was removed from the receiver.

The clip for the M1899 was redesigned to facilitate loading, provide uniform tension, and retain the cartridges in place when the magazine cut-off was in use. In both the M1895 and M1899 Straight-Pull rifles the clip remained in the magazine, even though the cartridges had been released, falling out the bottom of the magazine after the first or second shot.

The M1895 had a 28-inch barrel, was 47 inches over-all and weighed 8.5 pounds with sling and bayonet. The barrel length of the M1899 was also 28 inches, with an over-all length of 47.6 inches. Other data on this model is indefinite, and just how many of the M1899 rifles were made is not known. Since the Navy was apparently not interested, perhaps only one or two experimental specimens were produced. The rear sight on both models was graduated to 2000 yards in 100-yard increments from 800 yards on the leaf. The battle sight was set for 300 yards and could be moved to 600 yards before raising the leaf. These settings were for the regular service ammunition having a velocity at 60 feet of 2460 fps. No adjustment for windage was provided, as the drift at battle settings was considered negligible.

Before leaving the M1895 Straight-Pull series one note of historical interest should be mentioned. When the U.S.S. Maine was sunk in the harbor at Havana, Cuba, during the Spanish-American troubles, the rifles aboard were M1895 Lee-Navies. These rifles were later recovered by divers and sold at Government auction to Francis Bannerman Sons of New York City. A list of their serial numbers appeared in the Bannerman catalog, which could identify rifles recovered from the *Maine*.

On May 31, 1898, U. S. Patent 604,904, was issued, as before, to "Edward G. Parkhurst ... for a "Magazine Bolt-Gun." But this time the patent was not for a straight-pull design. Instead this patent covered a "turn-bolt" gun, and "... its general object being to provide certain improvements whereby these weapons may be rendered more durable and efficient in service and whereby their constructive features are simplified and improved, reducing the cost of manufacture ..." One unusual feature of this design for a Lee firearm was the Mauser-type extractor, which extended two-thirds the length of the bolt. The bolt head was removable and instead of rear locking lugs there were now two front locking lugs on the bolt head. The bolt rotated 90° to unlock, and cocking was still on closing.

The firing pin was inserted into the hollow bolt body from the front, as in the previous models, and a large flange was provided to prevent the gas from a pierced primer escaping rearward. The rear of the firing pin had interrupted threads so the cocking piece could be slipped on longitudinally and locked in place with a one-eighth turn. The cocking piece now had a knurled section for easier manual cocking.

New Turn-Bolt Rifle

A main feature of this design was a clip for loading the non-detachable magazine. The magazine, an integral part of the trigger guard, assembly, projected slightly below the stock line. It held 5 rounds in a single column, and the cartridges illustrated in the patent drawings were rimmed, of about 6mm caliber. Located on the left side of the magazine was a vertically-sliding cut-off, which allowed the rifle to be used as a single shot while keeping a full magazine in reserve. The magazine lips could be contracted or expanded slightly by means of a cam operated by a vertical-sliding mechanism on the right side of the magazine. With the lips apart the magazine could be loaded by stripping the cartridges down out of the clip. Releasing the lips prevented the cartridges from moving upward, except when being chambered in the normal manner.

The trigger and sear of this design were almost identical to the corresponding parts of the previous Lee turnbolt rifles. However, a coil sear spring was used in place of the U-shaped leaf spring of the Lee designs. Whether any rifles based on this design were actually produced is not known to the author.

The last Lee turnbolt design was the Model 1899, for smokeless cartridges. The bolt head had dual-opposed locking lugs, in addition to the rear locking lug and guide rib, and was exceptionally strong. Offered in both sporting and military versions, the receiver was marked on the upper left side:

Remington Arms Co. Ilion, NY.

and on the left side:

Patented Aug. 26th 1884.
March 17th 1885. Jan. 18th 1887.

In the military version the caliber was stamped on top of the barrel, ahead of the middle band. Several calibers were available, including the 236 Lee, 6mm Navy, 7mm Mauser, 30–40 Krag (30 U.S. Gov't.) and 303 British. The Michigan State Militia adopted and bought 2000 of this model, chambered for the 30–40 Krag cartridge, in 1900. Cuba is reported to have bought 30,000 of them chambered for the 7mm Mauser cartridge.

The military Model 1899 weighed about 8⅝ pounds, the barrel was 29 inches long and over — all length was 49½ inches. Unlike previous models the M1899 had an upper hand-guard extending to the middle band. A short, straight, tangent rear sight, located about three inches behind the middle band, was graduated to 700 yards: the leaf was graduated to 1900 yards, but there was no provision for windage adjustment. The front sight was a detachable blade, its rear face angled some 45 degrees.

The stock of the military Model 1899 was much the same as that on previous models, except for the nose cap, which was designed to support the handle of a knife bayonet. As

Fig. 28 — Top to bottom: The Remington-Beals revolving rifle. M1858; double-barrel Remington- Whittmore shotgun; Remington No. 3 Improved Creedmoor Hepburn Rifle; and the M1899 Remington-Lee Sporting Rifle, a design which is still modern nearly 75 years later.

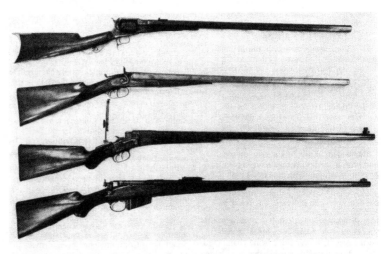

previously, the sling swivels were on the upper band and the front of the trigger guard, and a cleaning rod was held in the fore-end beneath the barrel.

One distinguishing aspect of the Model 1899 was the extremely large knurled head on the cocking piece. This, coupled with the upper handguard and a 5-round magazine with three grooves instead of two, makes the M1899 easy to identify.

The 1899 extractor, a small leaf with a hook on the end slides into a recess on the side of the detachable bolt head; it resembles some of the latest modern designsWith the extractor in place the bolt head, which has a hole bored vertically crosswise near the rear end, is inserted into the bolt body until it lines up with a matching hole in the guide rib of the body. A locking bar, with pin to fit these two holes, is then positioned at approximately 90° to the bolt body, and rotated to line up with the guide rib, of which it will become a part; just before line-up occurs the rear end is lifted slightly to provide clearance for a positioning lug and then let down to engage a matching slot in the guide rib.

The Model 1899 cocked on closing the bolt, as did the previous models. When locked the front lugs were in a vertical plane, and the rear lug and guide rib in a horizontal plane; the left lug was slotted for-and-aft for an ejector in the left receiver wall.

The military M1899 rifle reportedly sold for $30 in 1905, with 4 extra magazines; the knife bayonet, with scabbard, was available for $5 more.

Phil Sharpe mentions that a carbine model with 20-inch barrel, weight some 7 pounds, was available in the same calibers as the rifle. It was not equipped for a bayonet, as the fore-end ended about three inches in front of the middle band. Over-all length was 39½ inches. The author has never seen one of these carbines, which reportedly listed for $28 in 1905.

Model 1899 Sporters

The sporting 10 version of the M1899 was offered in the same calibers as the military model, and a number of other available calibers have been reported by various sources. These last included the 30–30 Winchester, 32 Winchester Special, 32 Remington (rimless), 32–40 Winchester, 35 Winchester, 35 Remington (rimless), 38–55 Winchester, 38–72 Winchester, 405 Winchester, 43 Mauser, 44–77 Sharps, 45–70 Gov't. and 45–90 Winchester.

The walnut stock had a shotgun-type butt with a hard-rubber plate and a pistol grip, with cap. The grip area and the slim fore-end were well checkered, the latter with a small black hard-rubber cap. Sling swivels were not standard, but could be had on special order.

Barrels were round, lengths of 24-or 26 inches were standard. A heavier 28-inch barrel could be had on special order, as could Lyman sights and stock variations. Standard sights consisted of a rear sight adjustable for windage and elevation, and a front bead mounted on a heavier base dovetailed into the barrel.

These sporters varied from 8½ to 9 pounds, and were priced at $25 in 1905. Discontinued in 1906, they no doubt remained in stock for several years.

A limited number of "special" deluxe sporting rifles were also available. These had select English walnut stocks with full pistol grips and fancy grip caps. The butt was finished English-style with separate heel and toe plates. Checkering on the grip and fore-end was of the finest, and special attention was given to the finish on all metal parts.

Barrel length of the "Special" was 26 inches-half-octagon and half-round. Sling swivels were standard, the front unit attached to the underside of the barrel midway between muzzle and the fore-end tip, the rear swivel attached to the underside of the buttstock.

The sights comprised a Lyman bead front, and a Lyman folding leaf rear on the barrel. In addition, there was a Lyman "wind-gauge" cocking-piece sight designed especially for the M1899 action.

The low-volume "special" sporter sold for $60 in 1905.

Although James Paris Lee's old heel wound began to trouble him shortly after the U. S. Navy had adopted the Lee Straight-Pull rifle, it was not until 1897-98 that his general health forced his confinement to bed for many months at his home in Hartford. The extent of his illness can be glimpsed from the remarks Lee made in a letter to his friend, James Young, dated July 1, 1898.

"… I am simply a wreck in human form. This disease is surely gaining on whatever intellect I possessed. Little as it was, it is less today. I sit for hours without uttering a word, and I cannot even walk, as my old shot heel bothers me. I had to give up all business two years ago … I live entirely in the past … In the mornings (lie abed till noon) I think of Galt … and would like to end my days there …"

In April, 1899, on the advice of a Vermont

doctor-a brother-in-law of his son George-Lee traveled to the Post Graduate Hospital in New York City. His troubled heel was cut open and a small portion of the bone removed. In it were found 5 lead pellets embedded there for nearly 52 years. The operation was a success. Lee's health began to improve at once and, although slightly lame, he was able to visit Galt in August of that year. He also was apparently able to return to business, at least to some extent, as indicated by the Improved Lee Model 1901 (straight-pull). However, it is also possible that his two sons were actively engaged in the business at this time.

Described as being above average height, strongly built, with dark hair and dark gray eyes, Lee's warm-hearted, easygoing manner gained him many friends. His inventions reportedly brought him several fortunes, and if he had been as successful in managing his patents and finances as he was in inventing, he might have been a millionaire. However, the expenses of his kind of an inventor were necessarily large, and the last few years were not highly productive; the 1899 models were probably the last ones to reach the manufacturing stage. Even so, Lee continued to work on his designs until his death on February 24, 1904, at South Beach, Conn.

No account of the Lee firearms would be complete without including the British portion of the Lee history. For it was in England that the Lee designs became famous, so much so that the name Lee became almost a household word.

English Beginnings

In England a Small Arms Committee was formed in 1879 to deal with several small arms problems, including the Martini-Henry rifle and the "… the desirability or otherwise of introducing a magazine rifle for naval or military use, or both." Over the next few years a number of American and European designs were examined and tested. The trials were carried out at the Proof Butts at Woolwich Arsenal by a sergeant and three picked marksmen of the Royal Welch Fusiliers. The tests performed included:

(1) Rapidity of fire without aiming.

(2) Rapidity of fire with aiming, at both stationary and moving targets.

(3) Exposure to the weather for three days without cleaning after firing; exposure to a sand blast and firing without cleaning; rough usage; safety tests.

Following the tests all weapons were forwarded to the Royal Small Arms Factory for examination.

Included in the trials held during May and June of 1880, were the arms of Hotch-kiss, Kropatschek, Lee (rifle and carbine), Winchester M1876, Gardner, Green, and Vetterli rifles. The Lee arms were based on his patent of November 4, 1879, in which the mainspring was compressed as the bolt was closed. This was considered a disadvantage, as it prevented the feel of the cartridge being chambered. It was thus thought possible that a cartridge could stick or jam, yet be driven on into the chamber, causing a premature explosion with an unlocked bolt.

The extraction was not considered satisfactory, but the chamber was partly at fault; The rifle and carbine barrels, of the 45-caliber Martini-Henry pattern, were made at the Royal Small Arms Factory, Enfield Lock; these were chambered to take solid-drawn brass-case Gatling service ammunition loaded with 85 grains of black powder behind a 480-gr. bullet. The extractor appeared to have sufficient camming action to start case withdrawal, but its form was considered poor. The guns were returned to Enfield Lock for investigation and repair.

The magazine position was well liked, since it did not alter the balance of the rifle when full or empty, and it was easily loaded. In general the Lee rifle made a good impression, and it was deemed easy to manufacture.

Specifications of the two Lee rifles tested at this time follow:

LEE RIFLE:

Caliber 45

Grooves:

    Number... 7

    Form .... Henry Rifling

    Depth .... 0075"

    Rate of twist .... 1 turn in 22"

Mechanism:

    Closing .... By bolt

    Opening .. Spiral spring and firing pin

Length Over — all........................... 53"

Weight .... 9 lbs. 5 ozs.

Magazine Cap.......................... 5 rounds

Sights............................ To 1,400 yards

The Lee Carbine weight was 6½ lbs. and over all length was 43.5 inches. Sights on the Carbine were graduated to 800 yards.

A month after the trials were over the Lee rifle was returned from Enfield with an improved extractor. It was then used to fire 45 rounds of the Gatling cartridges, which were easily extracted, with an average rate of fire of 20 rounds in 52 seconds. Things were looking up for the Lee design.

The Royal Navy wanted a magazine rifle, but two years later nothing had been decided. The best rifles from the previous trials were to be tested again, plus any other new designs that might be authorized; all were to be capable of firing the Gatling cartridge, the machine gun cartridge then in use.

Further English Trials

In November, 1882, the following rifles were submitted for trial: Schulhof (3), Improved Lee, Spencer-Lee, Chaftee-Reece, Gardner, and Mannlicher. On 3rd May, 1883, the Committee reported that all rifles submitted had been tried and compared to the Martini-Henry, but that all had failed on some point, and were now being altered or repaired. A new Small Arms Committee had been formed, and this time the inventors or their agents were allowed to demonstrate and fire the rifles on the range. More than half of the rifles were quickly rejected, and the inventors of several others were told that their rifles would be rejected unless they could be altered to take the Gatling cartridge. With all rifles taking the same cartridge, the trials continued until 31st October, 1883. At this time it was reported that two Lee designs — the Improved Lee modified at Enfield Lock and the Lee with the Bethel Burton magazine made at Enfield Lock — were promising, but three rifles — a new magazine rifle designed by Owen Jones, employed at Enfield Lock, the Spencer-Lee, and the Mannlicher — were still to be tested.

While waiting for the Spencer-Lee and the Mannlicher rifles to arrive, 6 additional rifles were received for testing, including a Remington-Lee model. Of the 6 new rifles submitted, only the Remington-Lee warranted much interest, but it was not chambered for the Gatling cartridge and was therefore not tested. The other 5 rifles were either too heavy, too complicated, or not chambered for the Gatling cartridge.

By August, 1885, the Small Arms Committee had examined or tried nearly 50 magazine rifles and quick-loading systems. Of these all but three had broken down during testing, or had been rejected for other reasons. The three left were the Improved Lee Magazine Rifle, the Improved Lee with Bethel Burton magazine, and the Owen Jones Magazine Rifle. All three had been improved or manufactured at the Royal Small Arms Factory at Enfield Lock, and the Lee Magazine Rifle was the only survivor of the original testing started 5 years before.

These three rifles had fore-ends of like shape, with a single barrel band a few inches behind the muzzle. A front sling swivel was attached to this band, another to the underside of the buttstock. All had a short upper handguard extending from the receiver ring to the rear sight. From this approximate location the fore-end was reduced in depth. All three rifles carried cleaning rods in a groove in the bottom of the fore-end. The Lee rifle had a one-piece stock, the others separate butt-stocks. All had straight grip stocks; the two Lee models had conventional combs, while the Owen Jones was similar to the latter Enfield models with-

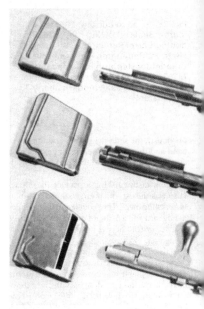

Fig. 29 — Row 1: Breech-bolt of the Ml 889 Remington-Lee with the 3-groove magazine • Row 2: Breech-bolt of the Ml 885 Remington-Lee with the 2-groove magazine • Row 3: Breech-bolt of the M1879 Lee with the M1879 magazine. The wide slot in the magazine was apparently added later by an owner to show the number of rounds remaining in the magazine; it is not considered to be an original feature. Fig. 30 — Top to bottom: Breech-bolts of the Models 1879, 1885 and 1899 Lee and Remington-Lee rifles, with the bolt heads removed to show the methods of attaching the extractors.

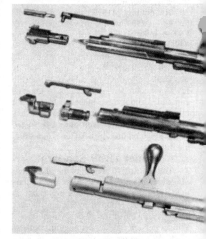

out a pronounced comb.

The Lee-Burton receiver had a very long upper tang, extending almost to the comb; the rear tang of the trigger guard was as long. Both were fastened together by two bolts passing through the grip of the stock from the underside. The Burton magazine fastened to the right side of the action; in use it projected upward above the barrel about 1½ inches. When not in

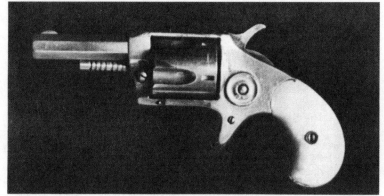

Fig. 31 — The small rimfire revolver which may or may not have been a product of James Paris Lee. The octagon barrel is 2¼ inches long and the top flat is marked: RED JACKET No. 3. The 5 — shot cylinder is 1 3/16 inches long and 5 chambered for the 32 rimfire cartridge. Weighing 10 ozs., over — all length is about 6 inches. It is nickel — plated and the grips are natural pearl. The revolver functions single action only, and the spur trigger has a terrible pull; the hammer does have a half — cock notch. The topstrap is marked: THE LEE ARMS CO./WILKESBARRE, PA. in two lines, with a narrow groove passing between the two lines to serve as a sighting groove. The front sight is a narrow brass blade. Over — all construction and finish are fair, but the steel appears to be rather soft.

use it could be lowered alongside the receiver. It could be loaded with up to 5 cartridges while in the firing position, a point in its favor.

The Improved Lee trigger guard and receiver had short tangs; the guard was attached to the receiver by two bolts from below, one at the rear and one at the front, ahead of the magazine well. The magazine — a plain, ungrooved model — was readily detachable, but it could not be loaded while attached to the rifle (in this early model) and this was felt to be a disadvantage. The cocking piece differed from those on the U. S. Lee rifles.

Setback and Success

The Owen Jones rifle operated by a slide under the buttstock, and was extremely rapid but it was not as cheap to manufacture as the Lee. Still, the Committee apparently thought it superior to the two Lee models and recommended it for trial by the Army and Navy.

While the Committee had been testing magazine rifles the Enfield factory had been developing a barrel of smaller caliber for the single shot Martini-Henry rifle; they'd decided on a 402 caliber with 7-groove Metford segmental rifling, developed over two decades before. These consisted of shallow grooves shaped to the segment of a circle. It was felt that the Owen Jones and the two Lee designs should be tested with the new 402 caliber Metford barrels before a final decision was made. Steps were taken to fit the new barrels, when suddenly the Owen Jones rifle was dropped from further tests because of manufacturing difficulties. The bottom magazine was considered to be the better position, so the Improved Lee Magazine Rifle emerged the victor.

Still smaller calibers were being developed in Europe. After some study 303 caliber barrels with Metford rifling were fitted to the Improved Lee actions and about 350 of the resulting Lee-Metford rifles were issued to the British Army for trials. The results were satisfactory and, on December 22,1888, the Magazine Rifle, Mark I, was approved for manufacture.

British Army Orders, dated 1st December, 1889, contained the following description of the new rifle:

MAGAZINE RIFLE, MARK I

Weight..................................... 9 lb. 8 oz.
Weight of Magazine (empty)....... 4¾ oz.
Weight of Magazine (filled ....13 oz.
Length .... 49 in.
Barrel and Rifling:
Length..................................... 30.2 in.
Calibre...................................... 303 in.
Rifling .... Metford segmental
Grooves .... Seven
Grooves, depth .... 004 in.
Lands, width............................. 023 in.
Spiral, left — handed .... 1 turn in
10 in., or 33 calibres

The rifle embodies the Lee bolt action, with rear locking. The cocking-piece is so arranged that the action can be set at half — cock, in which position the rifle can be carried in safety. Covers are fitted to the bolt and the bolt-head to protect the action in sand and mud. A safety-catch is fitted on the left side of the body, the pulling back of which, when the rifle is at full-cock, prevents any effect being caused by pressing the trigger. When springs are "eased," and the cocking-piece is in the forward position, it locks the action and prevents the bolt from becoming accidently opened.

The magazine consists of a sheet-steel box, inserted in the body through an opening underneath, and directly in front of the trigger guard. It is held in position by a spring in the body engaging in a notch on the magazine. It holds 8 cartridges and can be filled when in position on the rifle, or when detached … they are fed into the chamber by the forward movement of the bolt. A cut-off is fitted to the right side of the body which, when pressed inwards, stops the supply of cartridges from the magazine, thus enabling the weapon to be used as a single-loader. When the cut-off is pulled out, the lower edge of the face of the bolt-head, on the bolt being driven forwards, engages the top edge of the uppermost cartridge in the magazine and forces it into the chamber. The magazine can be removed from the rifle by pressing a small lever inside the trigger-guard. One magazine is attached, by means of a chain link, to each rifle: a spare magazine is also issued with each arm.

The stock, like that of the Martini-Henry rifle, is in two pieces, the fore-end and the butt. …

The butt is secured to the body of the rifle by a stock bolt. The buttplate … is fitted with a trap … to house an oil bottle and a jag …

The nose-cap is fitted with a bar on top for the attachment of the sword bayonet, which is positioned underneath the barrel …

A wooden hand-guard is fixed over the breech end of the barrel to protect the hand when the barrel becomes hot. It is held place by two steel springs, which clip round the barrel.

The rifle is provided with two sets of sights. The foresight and the backsight are fixed in the usual positions on the barrel.

The foresight is a square block, with a vertical cut through it …. The lowest, or "fixed" sight, is that for 300 yards …. The highest graduation is for 1,900 yards. The rifle is also fitted with extreme range sights. The front sight, which is called the dial sight, is graduated from 1,800 yards up to 3,500 yards. It consists of a bead fixed to a revolving index hand. The index is set to the correct distance, which is marked on the edge of the dial plate, and aim is taken by aligning the bead on the object aimed at through a circular hole in the aperture sight … Both these sights are on the left side of the rifle …".

Changes, Changes

On August 8, 1891, the name was changed to the Lee-Metford Magazine Rifle, Mark I, and 5 months later on J anuary 19, 1892, it became the Lee-Metford Magazine Rifle Mark I*, through some sight modifications.

Eleven days later, acting on recommendations to increase the magazine capacity from 8 rounds to 10, to lighten the barrel, modify the bolt head, and some dozen other minor modifications, the War Office officially approved the Lee-Metford Magazine Rifle, Mark II. The new rifle weighed 9 lbs. 4 oz., four ounces lighter than the Mark I.

Three years later a safety catch was added to replace the one which had been omitted since the Mark I*, and the rifle became the Lee-Metford Magazine Rifle. Mark II*. Other minor modifications necessary to the operation of the safety were also made at this time.

On September 29, 1895, in answer to demands from the British Cavalry, the Lee-Metford Magazine Carbine, Mark I, was approved for manufacture. Magazine capacity was 6 rounds, the barrel was 20¾ inches long, overall length 39 15/16 inches, weight 7 lb. 7 oz. Other modifications to the sights, stock, handguard, bands, nose-cap, etc., were made at this time.

In an attempt to overcome the destructive effect of Cordite powder erosion on the shallow Metford rifling, new barrels with Enfield rifling, as developed at the Royal Small Arms Factory, were fitted.† The Lee-Metford rifles with the new barrels became the Lee-Enfield Magazine Rifle, Mark I, on November 11, 1895, the Start of a long line of Lee-Enfield Rifles. On August 17, 1896, modification of the Cavalry carbine to include the new Enfield rifling was approved, with other necessary changes, and the Lee-Enfield Magazine Carbine, Mark I, came into being.

On 19th May, 1899, the clearing rod and clearing rod hole, etc., in the fore-end of the rifle and carbine were omitted, and the designation became Mark I*. The omission of the clearing rod was extended to all 303 caliber arms then in service, including the various Martini patterns.

The next L-E to be introduced was another carbine. It appeared on August 1, 1900, and was intended for the British Land Services. It had a special barrel, fore-end and handguard, weighed 7½ pounds, and was 40% inches long.

In January, 1900, the Small Arms Committee was completely re-organized to include representatives concerned with manufacture, inspection, requirements, and experience with service arms and ammunition. A representative of the National Rifle Association also became a member of the Committee. The Boer War was in progress and in June of 1900 the Small Arms Committee recommended that the Lee-Enfield

---

†Henry Metford had, in fact, patented the so-called Enfield rifling in 1860, even prior to his segmental rifling.

rifle be replaced with a new one. To strengthen their position they listed 7 defects of the Lee-Enfield, and questioned whether an automatic rifle might not be desirable. They went so far as to test an Italian model.

The S.M.L.E.

In late 1900, the Superintendent of the Royal Small Arms Factory let the Small Arms Committee know that he had been able to alter the Lee-Enfield to overcome the defects they had mentioned, and could manufacture the new rifle at once at little or no increase in price. In the memorandum the Superintendent listed 12 alterations which would be made.

The altered rifle was tested at Hythe in December, 1900, and on January 12, 1901, the Secretary of State approved the manufacture of 1,000 Shortened Modified Enfield Rifles in lots of 500 each of Pattern A and B, for troop trials.

The 1,000 rifles were tested by units of the Royal Navy, Royal Marines, Cavalry and Infantry, following a program of 8 parts. The rifle was well received and, on November 10, 1902, the Committee recommended it for adoption with some modifications in the sights and magazine. On December 15, 1902, the R.S.A.F. Superintendent submitted a Short Rifle with 12 minor modifications. The rifle was approved by the Committee and introduced on December 23, 1902, as the Short Magazine Lee-Enfield Rifle, Mark I, for the Infantry and Cavalry. It weighed 20 ounces less than the Enfield it replaced. The first of the S.M.L.E. rifles was a reality.

The new rifle was 41 9/16 inches long, its barrel 25 3/16 in. The bolt cover was omitted, the cocking-piece was shorter, the magazine

was ⅛-inch deeper, and the Navy version was equipped with a cut-off. Buttstocks were issued in three lengths, a safety was located on the left side of the receiver, and changes were made in the fore-end, hand-guard, bands, nose-cap, swivels, and several other components. A few months later some additional changes were made and the rifle was re-introduced on 14th September, 1903.

On January 13, 1902, Lee-Metford Carbines fitted with Enfield barrels and extended nose-cap wings were re-named Lee-Enfield Mark I Carbines. Later, on September 6, 1902, Lee-Metford Mark II* rifles fitted with Enfield barrels became Lee-Enfield Mark I Rifles, if they had the old fore-end nose-cap; if they had the newer, more solid fore-end and nose-cap they became Lee-Enfield Mark I* Rifles.

The year 1903 was to be a busy one. The Lee-Enfield Mark I and I*, and the Lee-Metford Mark II and II* rifles were given new barrels, sights, and other minor modifications and re-introduced on January 16, 1903, as the Short Magazine Lee-Enfield (Converted) Mark II. On August 12, a new cut-off for the S.M.L.E. Mark I was approved for British Naval Service only. November 2nd, the Lee-Metford Mark I* became the Short Magazine Lee-Enfield (Converted) Mark I, a conversion which was declared "obsolete" before it was ever manufactured.

During March, April and May, 1905, as a result of a questionnaire to the British Forces in India, trials were held at Hythe between the Long and Short rifles to compare velocity, accuracy, systems of sighting and speed of loading. The trials indicated that the Long rifles were more accurate, but the Short rifles were handier and better adapted to snapshooting. A

Fig. 32—The Lee-Metford Mark II. Adopted on January 30, 1892, the new rifle weighed 9 lb. 4 oz and had a magazine capacity of 10 rounds instead of the previous 8. Note the short handguard, extending only from the receiver ring to the rear sight; the rear sight leaf is erect.

Fig. 33—The Lee-Enfield Mark I*, advanced from the Mark I by omission of the clearing rod. This rifle is very similar to the previous Lee-Metford Mark II*, except for the new barrel. Note the safety catch on the cocking piece.

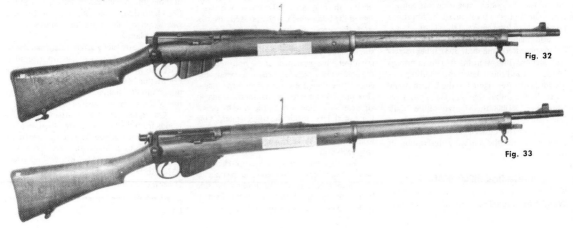

Fig. 32

Fig. 33

new pattern was sealed and, on 2nd July, 1906, the Short Magazine Lee-Enfield Rifle, Mark I*, was introduced. It weighed 4½ ounces more than the Mark I, and differed slightly in the magazine, buttstock and plate, swivels and screws, striker, sights, and hand-guards. On the same day a new conversion was also introduced. The Long Lee-Enfield rifles, Mark I and I*, and the Lee-Metford rifles, Mark II and II*, were converted to become the Short Magazine Lee-Enfield Rifle Converted, Mark II*, which differed from the Converted Mark II, but slightly, in the butt-stock, magazine, and swivel and keeper screws. Six weeks later, on 17th August, 1906, a coin-slotted striker keeper-screw was approved for all Marks of the S.M.L.E., and on 25th October, the cut-off was returned and fitted to all S.M.L.E. rifles in the British Army — the Royal Navy already had them.

Hythe and Enfield Tests

Trials were held at Hythe and Enfield periodically in an attempt to improve the S.M.L.E. A reliable charger-loading feature was in particular demand by the troops, and several other modifications had been recommended. On 31st October, 1906, 6 rifles, which had been sent to Aldershot for testing, were reported as satisfactory. On 26th January, 1906, the modifications were completed and the Short Magazine Lee-Enfield Rifle, Mark III, was approved. The new rifle weighed 8 lb. 10½ oz., and differed from the Mark I and I* slightly in the sights, fore-end, hand-guards, cut-off, bands, buttplate, nose-cap, locking-bolt and bolt-head, and the receiver body had a bridge charger-guide.

On June 17, 1907, a number of conversions

were approved to bring the Lee-Enfield Mark I and I* and Lee-Metford Mark II and II* rifles in line with the new Mark III. The converted rifles weighed 8 lb. 14 ½ oz., and were listed as the Short Magazine Lee-Enfield Converted Mark IV.

On July 1, 1907, another lot of Mark I and I* Lee-Enfield, and Lee-Metford Mark II and II* rifles were converted by adding a bridge-type charger-guide, new magazine, and modified sighting system. The new conversions became the Charger-Loading Lee-Enfield , Mark I*, and Charger-Loading Lee-Metford, Mark II. Each weighed about 9 lb. 5 oz.

On January 4, 1908, a number fo the British Navy's S.M.L.E. Mark I rifles were converted to the S.M.L.E., Mark I** models. Later the same year the S.M.L.E. Converted Mark II rifles became the S.M.L.E., Mark II**, and the S.M.L.E. Converted, Mark II* became the S.M.L.E, Mark II***, with the conversions being made at the Royal Naval Ordnance Depots at Chatham, Portsmouth, and Plymouth. Most of the changes were convered with the trigger guard, magazine, and installation of a charger-guide, with minor changes in the receiver and bolt, stocks, and various screws.

On 1st February, 1909, the Mark II Lee-Metford Charger-Loading conversions were discontinued and the already converted rifles became the Charger-Loading Lee-Enfield Rifles, Mark I*. On November 3, 1910, a new service cartridge—303 S.A. Ball Cartridge Mark VII—was introduced, necessitating an alteration in the sights of all the rifles then in service, plus some minor alterations to the magazines of certain Marks.

As war in Europe approached haste was

made to see that as many rifles as possible were available to handle the Mark VII cartridge. On 22nd April, 1914, the S.M.L.E. Mark I* became the S.M.L.E. Mark I***, and later the same year two other conversions were made, without any apparent change in pattern, other than a C.L. (Charger-Loading) on the sights. On 18th August, 1915, Mark I** rifles in the Royal Navy which had not been altered for charger-loading were so altered to handle the Mark VII cartridge and re-named S.M.L.E. Mark I***.

On January 2, 1916, six minor modifications were made to the Mark III, including the removal of the long range dial and aperture sight, and the rifle became the Short Magazine Lee-Enfield, Mark III*.

Prior to World War I some consideration was given to adopting an entirely new design with forward locking lugs and of smaller caliber. A Mauser-type rifle for a 276 caliber rimless cartridge was made in prototype form and became the Pattern 1913. When the war started it was decided to retain the 303 caliber and the new rifle was modified to handle it, thus becoming the Pattern 1914. The rifle was a limited standard and was not widely used, except in sniping versions.

Advent of the Rifle No. 1

Following the war the search to find an improved bolt action went on. In 1922 a modified pattern was sealed for the Short Magazine Lee-Enfield Rifle, Mark V, which differed from the Mark III in 10 features. The Mark V was tested, but not officially adopted; it was eventually abandoned for a new design which became the Mark VI. The Mark VI was recommended on December 14, 1923, by the Rifle Subcommittee and it was to retain the best features of

(continued on page 118)

Fig. 34—The Short Magazine Lee-Enfield Mark I. Introduced on December 23, 1902, it weighed 1¼ lbs. less than the Lee-Enfie'd it replaced, and became the first of the long line of S.M.L.E. rifles.

Fig. 35—The old official stand-by—the S.M.L.E. Mark III*—for over two decades, and still serving in some areas after half a century. It looks rugged, too.

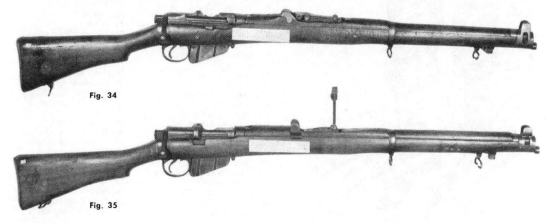

Fig. 34

Fig. 35

Lee-Enfield Rifle No. 4, Mark I*

Historical Notes

The No. 4, Mark 1 Lee-Enfield marks the last of an illustrious line of British Lee rifles that began in 1888 and passed through a bewildering maze of Marks and Numbers, models and revisions. After World War I, British ordnance began looking for ways to improve the old and famous Mk. III series and by 1931 developed the prototype S.M.L.E. (Short Magazine Lee-Enfield) Mk. VI. When the British revised their nomenclature system, this rifle became the Rifle No. 4, Mk I. The major improvements were an aperture rear sight, a simplified bolt-retaining system and bolt release, and a socket type spike bayonet. As is the custom in the British service, the new rifle was harshly criticized, especially the spike bayonet. (It is interesting to note that British ordnance defended the bayonet as being specifically designed to penetrate German overcoats). In 1939, the rifle was redesigned for mass production, but the early World War II years were fought with the Mark III*.

The No. 4, Mk. I* was the North American version. Almost one million were made at Long Branch Arsenal in Canada,

and over a million by Savage Arms Corporation. The Savage made rifles are curiously stamped "U.S. Property," even though they were never intended for our use; perhaps this was prompted by political subterfuge. The major difference between the Mk. I and Mk. I* is the bolt release (see illus.).

As a military rifle, the Lee-Enfields are excellent, but they are not in the same design class as Mausers and Mannlichers. They do not lend themselves to sporterizing. British ordnance does not consider the bolts to be interchangeable. These rifles fire one type of cartridge, the 303 Enfield (British). The 303 Savage cartridge is **not** the same.

Disassembly

Raise the rear sight (3). See illustration on opposite page. Rifle Mk. I: depress bolt release and withdraw bolt all the way to the rear; release bolt release and raise bolt head (28) Rifle Mk. I*: withdraw bolt until bolt head (28) aligns with cutout on guide groove, which allows the bolt head to be pushed up and out of its channel. With bolt head raised in line with the bolt rib, the entire bolt may be withdrawn. Press magazine catch (21) and remove magazine (18). Unscrew band screws (43 & 44) up over the stock. Unscrew guard screws (15 & 16) and remove the trigger guard (14) with trigger (12). Work forestock (35) down and off. Buttstock (32) can be removed by unscrewing the stock bolt (33). The stock bolt is frequently packed with felt and this should be removed first. (If the buttstock is sound and tight, its removal is not recommended.) Unscrew safety screw (8) and extract safety assembly. (Reassembly can be tricky. Be sure the safety bolt and catch are in position shown in illustration before reseating). Sear (9) and magazine catch (21) can be removed by driving out their respective pins (11 & 22).

To disassemble the bolt, first unscrew the bolt head (28), then the firing pin screw (27). The firing pin (25) can be unscrewed only from the front of the bolt. This requires a special wrench. Do not try it with ordinary tools. The firing pin (25) and firing-pin spring (26) will come out the front of the bolt.

Unscrew extractor screw (31), insert end of screwdriver behind lip of extractor (29) and force extractor forward, then out of front of bolt head. Insert a small screwdriver between top of extractor spring (30) and upper wall of bolt head until nipple on spring clears its receptacle. From rear, push spring forward and out.

Remove magazine follower (19) by depressing the rear, allowing the front of the follower to clear the two protruding lips on front of magazine.

Parts List

1.	Barrel	25.	Firing Pin
2.	Receiver	26.	Firing-Pin Spring
3.	Rear Sight	27.	Firing-Pin Screw
4.	Ejector Screw	28.	Bolt Head
5.	Safety Bolt	29.	Extractor
6.	Safety Catch	30.	Extractor Spring
7.	Safety Bolt Spring	31.	Extractor Screw
8.	Safety Bolt Spring Screw	32.	Buttstock
9.	Sear	33.	Stock Bolt
10.	Sear Spring	34.	Stock-Bolt Lock Washer
11.	Sear Pin	35.	Forestock
12.	Trigger	36.	Rear Hand Guard
13.	Trigger Pin	37.	Front Hand Guard
14.	Trigger Guard	38.	Buttplate
15.	Rear Guard Screw	39.	Rear Sling Swivel
16.	Front Guard Screw	40.	Rear Stock Band
17.	Front Guard Screw Bearing	41.	Middle Stock Band
18.	Magazine	42.	Front Sling Swivel
19.	Magazine Follower	43.	Sling Swivel Screw
20.	Magazine-Follower Spring	44.	Front Stock Band
21.	Magazine Catch	45.	Stacking Swivel
22.	Magazine-Catch Pin	46.	Stacing Swivel Screw
23.	Bolt	47.	Front Sight Guard
24.	Cocking Piece	48.	Oiler (in buttstock)

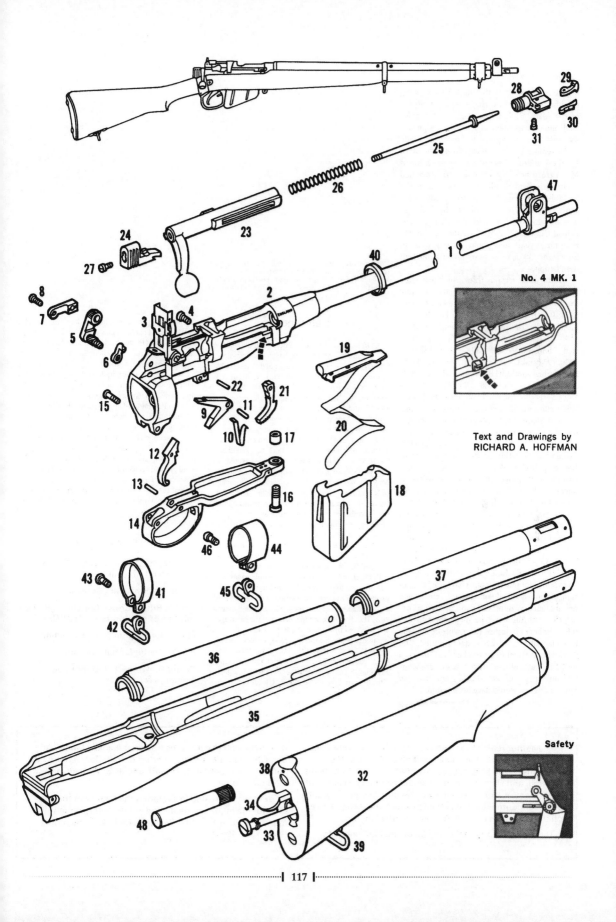

No. 4 MK. 1

Text and Drawings by
RICHARD A. HOFFMAN

Safety

(continued from page 115)

the Mark III. By 1924 the Mark VI was being modified for trial. By early 1926 six prototypes of the Mark VI had been manufactured for trial, and over the next 13 years the design was modified and re-modifed to emerge officially on November 15, 1939, as the No. 4 Rifle, Mark I†. The Lee-Enfield name was no more, for in May 1926, a new system of nomenclature had been introduced. Under the new system the S.M.L.E. Rifle Mark III—the old standby—became the Rifle No. 1, Mark III. Basic design was the same, only the name had changed. The British had used Lee-Metford and Lee-Enfield rifles for 38 years, and would continue to do so for another 38 or more years under a different designation.

Some other famous rifles which also used the Lee centrally-located box magazine include the Swiss Schmidt-Rubin 1889, 1893, 1911 and 1931; Italian Vetterli-Vitali 1887; Dutch Beaumont-Vitali 71/88 and 1888; French Berthier 1890, 07/15, 1916 and 194; Czech ZH29; Russian Mouzin (Mosin) 1891, 1910, 1891/30, 1930, 1938 and 1944; Canadian Ross 1910 Mark III; Remington Model 8, German Mauser 1888; and Austrian 1886, 1888, 1888/90, 1890 and 1895. Several of the rifles listed use the Mannlicher clip in a fixed single-column magazine. Lee and Mannlicher were contemporaries and the Mannlicher version may or may not have been influenced by the Lee design. The 1895 Lee and 1898 Parkhurst designs (assigned to Lee) employ clip-loaded magazines very similar to those employed by Mannlicher. Who influenced whom? Both inventors may have developed by the same designs independently.

Today, 90-odd years after Lee's original 1879 invention, the basic Lee magazine design is used on almost all military auto-loading rifles, such as our M16, M14, and AR-18, the Soviet AK-47, the German G-3, and the British FN L1A1. Machine rifles, such as the BAR, and various submachine guns have used the design, plus most auto-loading pistols, and even a few shotguns. A number of commercial sporting rifles use the Lee-type magazine and untold numbers of rimfire rifles with detachable box magazines have been manufactured. The original Lee patent of November 4, 1879, was a dwarf in material size—two pages of drawings and three pages of text—but a giant in scope. James Paris Lee would have been proud.

†The Short Magazine Lee-Enfield, Mark II, and Mark III rifles were manufactured in Australia, and the later No. 4 Rifle, Mark I* was manufactured in Canada and the United States, but these were not considered to be part of the Lee-Enfield history.

References

9. On March 6, 1883 Hugo Borchardt obtained U.S. Patent No. 273,448 for a detachable magazine for magazine guns, which he assigned to Joseph W. Frazier of New York City. (Borchardt had designed the M1878 Sharps-Borchardt rifle for the Sharps Rifle Co., to which he had assigned Patents No. 185,721 and 206,217, on December 26, 1876, and July 23, 1878, respectively. This would place him in Bridgeport at about the same time as James Lee.) Frazier had filed his patent application on January 4, 1883, and on December 18, 1883, U.S. Patent No. 290,636 for a "Magazine Fire-Arm" was granted to "Joseph W. Frazier, of New York, N.Y., Assignor, by Mesne Assignments to the Spencer Arms Company, of Same Place." This patent covered the adapting of the Lee detachable box magazine—patented by Lee on November 4, 1879—to the slide action rifle patented by Christopher M. Spencer and Sylvester H. Roper on April 4, 1882, in U.S. Patent No. 255,894. The Frazier design consisted of the Spencer-type slide action rifle, with its breechblock pivoted at the rear and free at the front to swing above and in line with the chamber of the barrel. The box magazine was attached to the breechlock and moved up and down with it in normal operation, but was still readily detachable for replacement with a loaded magazine. The chambering and ejection of the cartridges were covered by the Spencer-Roper patent. This then became the basis for the Spencer-Lee rifles entered in the U.S. and British rifles trials of the 1880s.

10. Alden Hatch relates an incident involving a Remington-Lee Sporting Rifle that shook Bridgeport almost to its very foundations. A local lad, return- ing home empty-handed from a deer hunt, decided to take a short cut through a field loosely fenced with barbed wire. On the field were a number of half-sunken stone structures resembling beehives. Deciding that one of these would provide a safe backstop for some rifle practice, he fastened a piece of paper onto the wooden door of one and paced of a hundred yards. Adjusting his sights, he took careful aim with his Remington-Lee and pulled the trigger. With a blinding flash of light the sky vanished and the earth split open with a thunderous roar. Three days later, when the lad came to in a hospital, he learned his "safe" backstop had been on e of the U.M.C. powder-storage magazines. Bridgeport had shivered and windows had been broken as far away as Long Island. That the lad had survived was a wonder. Shortly thereafter the present Powder Park—now a part of the Remington Arms Company complex—was obtained. The new Park is tightly fenced, closely guarded, and the powder magazines are bullet-proof.

Photo Credits

Figs. 16, 19, 22, 23, 24, 26. U.S. Army Rock Island Arsenal.

Fig 36. National Park Service.

Fig. 37. British Crown Copyright. By Permission of the Controller, HMSO.

Fig. 17. Remington Arms Collection.

Fig. 21. Globe & Mail, Toronto.

Patent Drawing—E. I. Dupont de Nemours & Co., Inc.

The author realizes that many questions concerning the activities of James Paris Lee may still be unanswered. There may even be other Lee designs which have not been covered, and such information would be most welcome. In particular the author would welcome data and photographs on the experimental and limited productions designs, even on the variations of the known commercial models.

The author is indebted to the following individuals for their help, and to each goes a special thanks: John T. Amber, Gordon F. Baxter, Jr., Thomas E. Hall, Daniel R. Kuehn, Judith Topaz, Herbert L. Uphoff, James S. Watson, and Eldon G. Wolff.

For those interested in exploring the history of the Lee-Enfield rifle in greater detail, the author highly recommends The Lee-Enfield Rifle, by Major E. G. B. Reynolds (New York, 1968).

The 1903 Springfield

An interesting and detailed account of the most famous military rifle in United States history – including the numerous variations made since its birth. ■ Al Miller

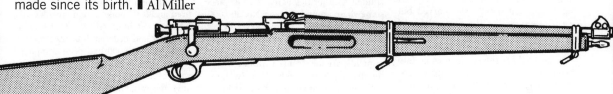

WHETHER OR NOT the Springfield 03 was the best military rifle of its time is still open to argument; Mausers, Lee-Enfields — each has its protagonists. Regardless of their respective virtues though, there can be little doubt that the 03 was the best prepared and finished. No service arm, before or since, ever enjoyed so much painstaking care during its manufacture.

Stocks were made out of good, solid walnut, superior to many found on commercial sporters today. Although machine-inletted, the marriage of wood to metal was unbelievably close, especially on those rifles fashioned between the wars when quality, not time, was the watchword. Metal fittings, all machined from forgings, were carefully polished before bluing. Bolt heads were knurled, triggers serrated. For a while, even buttplates were machine-checkered. Tool marks were rare. Each rifle was a "finished" product when it left the armory.

They were accurate, too. National Match Springfields ruled the target ranges both here and abroad for many years and the service model was no slouch in that department, either.

Every 03 in my racks, including the World War II versions, will keep five shots inside 2½" at 100 yards. This, of course, from a rest and using match ammo, but with issue sights. Perhaps I've been lucky but I've never owned or fired an inaccurate Springfield; nor one which could be described as "just so-so."

The oft-repeated charge that the 03 made a better sporter than a military arm may have some justification. Many of its design features — the excellent finish, the close tolerances — hint of a conception by riflemen, target shots and hunters, rather than by soldiers.

The inherent sporting qualities of the Springfield were noticed shortly after its birth. Teddy Roosevelt had one armory-altered in late 1903, a special stock fitted (serial number 0009), which he took to Africa in 1909. He characterized it as "the lightest and handiest of all my rifles," and he managed to kill an impressive number of animals with it, including both hippo and rhino, using the original 150-gr., full-patch bullet at 2700 fps.

Stewart Edward White, the sportsman-novelist, was another of the early Springfield users. He collected upwards of 400 African trophies using one or another of his 03 sporters, among others, and judged the new rifle-cartridge combination ideal medicine for lions.

White's first Springfield sporter was made up by Louis Wundhammer about 1910, this first rifle one of four that had been ordered by Capt. E. C. Crossman.* Later, Owen, Griffin & Howe, Hoffman, Linden and several others made them.

*The first Stewart. Edward White rifle, serial number 166,346, has a Hock Island arsenal barrel dated February, 1910. Made by Louis Wundhammer of Los Angeles, it is one of four such Springfield 1903 sporters ordered by Capt. E. C. (Ned) Crossman. One was for Capt. Cross-man, the other two for Robert C Rogers and John Colby. See Grossman's *Book of the Springfield* (Georgetown, S. C, 19511 or the *Gun Digest*, 15th edition.

These were handsome rifles, a bit heavy by modern standards but each a thing of beauty: choice wood, tasteful engraving and checkering — and if they were not too well used, still capable today of formidable accuracy. Until the middle 'thirties, when Winchester brought out their Model 70, Springfield sporters set the standards by which other hunting and target rifles were judged.

For years, the 03 was this nation's official service rifle. It lost that title to the Garand in 1935, but with the advent of World War II the 03 and its descendants, the A3 and A4, saw active duty as late as the 1950s. The Springfield's battle honors include campaigns in the Phillipines, Central America, the Caribbean, Mexico, the Western Front during World War I, every theater in World War II and, finally, Korea.

Turned out to pasture, the Springfield's career is far from over. During the past two decades, thousands have found their way into the hands and gunracks of American sportsmen. The NRA offered them, via the Director of Civilian Marksmanship, to its members at bargain rates over the years; surplus stores sold them; every sporting goods store of any stature at all tallied some in its inventory. Today these veterans, most civilianized by fancy stocks, scopes and professional blue jobs, can be seen by the score each fall when the redcoated hordes invade mountain and forest. The 03 isn't dead yet.

But they're getting scarce, at least, the "as issued" specimens are — and the gun collecting fraternity is becoming aware of it. During the past year, Springfield prices have soared. If a man has any ambition to collect them, the time to start is now.

The Early Models

"Sired by Mauser, out of Krag" is the way one wag described the Springfield. Its official birthday was June 18, 1903 when the Chief of Ordnance accepted it, the official designation: *U.S. Magazine Rifle, Model of 1903, Caliber .30*. It came with a 24" barrel, rod bayonet, ramp type rear sight and an odd looking blade with two large holes drilled through it for a front sight. The bolt handle was curved but wasn't swept back. The forward barrel band was located right at the nose of the stock.

The 1903 cartridge, which came into being at the same time, was slightly longer than the current '06 round and fired a 220-gr., full-jacketed round nose bullet at 2200 fps.

In 1905, the rod bayonet was shunted aside in favor of the knife type and, about the same time, an improved leaf rear sight, resembling that used on the Krag, was mounted in place of the unsatisfactory ramp.

Meanwhile, the ever-busy Germans had opened their bag of tricks again, surprising the shooting world by introducing a radical pointed bullet they called spitzges-choss. This new pointed shape enabled them to send the 154-gr. bullet from their 8mm service round at the then astonishing speed of 2800 fps. Quick to see the advantages of the new design, our ordnance people got busy in their ballistics labs and whipped up the now famous 30-06 cartridge.

Pushing a 150-gr. pointed bullet out of the muzzle at 2700 fps, the 06 case was reduced to 2.49" long, necessitated by the 03 case having been too long for the new spitzer bullet by .070". Several thousand 1903 rifles had been produced by this time but, rather than re-barrel them, it was decided, in the interests of economy, to shorten and re-chamber the existing barrels. Two-tenths inch (.200") was shaved off the breech, the chambers altered for the new cartridge, and the threads cut two turns deeper. This operation left the barrels 23.79" long (chamber and bore) and all Springfield 03 barrels made since then have measured the same. Over-all barrel length became 24.006".

The next major change took place in 1918 when the steel used to make receivers and bolts was strengthened. Those critical parts were double heat treated, a process which made the surface metal extremely hard while allowing the core steel to remain relatively soft. Actions fabricated in this manner have weathered test rounds developing pressures of 125,000 psi without a whimper. The tough surface not only wears well but with a little use, cams and runways smooth to a mirror-like glaze, making those particular actions the slickest Springfield ever built.

Despite the time, effort and expense which must have been spent creating the new process, nobody bothered to record the exact point when the change was instituted. Authorities agree it took place somewhere around receiver No. 800,000, but nobody's really sure. Nevertheless, 800,000 is the magic number, it being generally accepted that actions made subsequently are the stronger. Although "low numbered" Springfields, that is, those with serial numbers under 800,000, are regarded as weaker and less desirable, it should be remembered that each was subjected to 70,000 pound test loads, and that these were the same rifles which created the Springfield's reputation in the wars and on the game fields. Nevertheless, it is true that the shattering of several of the earlier case-hardened actions brought on the change in heat treatment in early 1918.

Rock Island 03s received the improved double heat treatment starting with receiver No. 285,507. From No. 319,921 on some R.I. receivers were made of a nickel steel similar to that used later in producing the wartime A3s and A4s. Springfield Armory didn't adopt nickel steel until 1928 but again, no one there in Massachusetts noticed the exact time of the changeover. In all probability rifles produced after No. 1,290,266 boasted nickel steel actions.

Variations in the quality of steel are primarily of interest only to purists. It goes without saying that any high-numbered 03 — always assuming good condition — will accomodate modern loads with perfect safety.

The Pedersen Device

To back up slightly: Shortly after the U.S. declared war on Germany in 1917, a well known arms designer of the day, one J. D. Pedersen, approached the War Department with an intriguing invention. The Pedersen Device, as historians call it, was essentially an automatic pistol mechanism with a stubby, integral barrel which could be slipped into the 03's receiver in place of the regular bolt. Once locked in place — this was accomplished by a flip of the magazine cutoff to "Off" — a long box magazine containing 40 cartridges resembling the 32 ACP was inserted into the right side of the bolt and presto! The Springfield was converted into an instant semiautomatic rifle!

Only three alterations to the rifle were necessary: an ejection port had to be cut into the left side of the receiver; the magazine cutoff had two grooves milled in it, and a small "kicker" was added to the sear. None of these modifications prevented the rifle from using the regular service round when the original bolt was in place.

Although the pistol-sized cartridge fired an 80-gr. bullet at a mere 1300 fps, General Pershing recognized its lethal potential and ordered 100,000 Pedersen units. Some 65,000 had been completed when Armistice Day arrived but none were ever issued to troops. A few years after the war, most of the devices were destroyed. A few, as usual, managed to escape the crushers and are now eagerly sought after by collectors.

It's easy to recognize the 03s modified for the Pedersen unit. There is a small, lozenge-shaped ejection port on the left side of the receiver, and to quell any further doubts the legend, *U.S Springfield Armory Model 1903 Mark I* is inscribed on the receiver. Records concerning this variation are sketchy but it's believed that one rifle, appropriately modified, was produced for each of the Pedersen devices manufactured.

When World War I ended, the Battle Reports and recommendations concerning the various weapons used were reviewed. The 03 came through with flying colors. Complaints were few and suggested changes even fewer. One, that was accepted, concerned the bolt handle. It was angled backwards slightly to bring it more in line with the trigger.

The Marine Corps, always marksmanship oriented, altered the sights of their rifles: the width of the front blade was increased to .10" and undercut, while the diameter of the rear peep was doubled. In addition, the triangular-shaped open sight in the rear leaf was dispensed with. 03s with Marine Corps sights are very much in demand by collectors.

Type C Stocks

After a considerable amount of experimentation, a new service stock, the Type C was chosen in 1928. The original Type S stock had been criticized for its abrupt drop at the heel and because many felt it was too short. The new stock was straighter, its buttstock contour reminis-

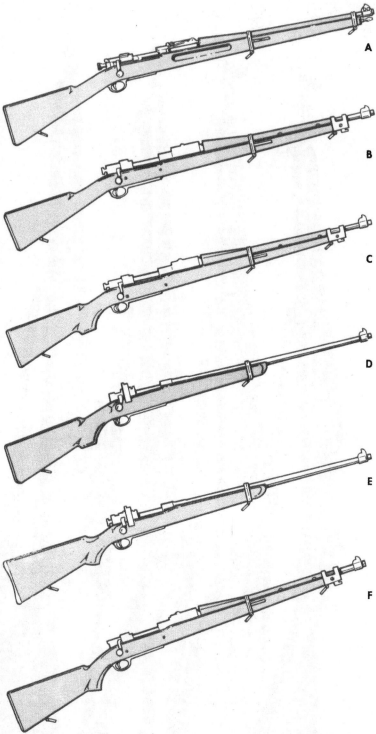

A — Original Model 1903. When it was accepted by the Army in 1903, the Springfield was equipped with a ramp-type rear sight and a rod bayonet. Note that the bolt handle turns straight down. B — The Type S stock was supplied with the service model 03 until it was supplanted by the Type C in 1929. C — The Model 1922 MI stock was supplied on National Match 03s issued to Service Teams. D — The Model 1922 MI issue stock (caliber 22). Note how this oversized pistol grip stock differs from NRA stock on the same action-barrel. E — The Model 1922 MI stock (caliber 30). This was commonly called the NRA or Sporter slock. F — The Type C stock was adopted in 1929. Rifles so equipped were designated Model 1903A1.

cent of those found on good shotguns. A hand-filling integral pistol grip had been added and the finger grooves, so pronounced on the old S stock, were deleted. Rifles with the new stock were designated Model 1903Als.

Although the semi-automatic Ml was chosen to succeed the 03 in 1935, almost a year passed before the last bolt action rolled off the production line at Springfield Armory. A few more were assembled in 1937 and another handful, the last, were produced in 1939. With receiver No. 1,532,878, the 03 became just another obsolete military rifle — or so everyone believed at the time.

Just before production ceased, a second gas escape port was drilled through the forward receiver ring. Up to this point, only one port, about ⅛" diameter, had pierced the ring on the right. Why an additional hole was put on the left is anyone's guess. I've only noticed a handful of 03s so made, all with serial numbers above 1,500,000. When the wartime A3s and A4s appeared, only one port was evident, this time on the left side.

Late in 1941, sensing the hot breath of war and unable to supply our rapidly expanding military forces sufficiently with the new Ml, the War Department issued a contract to the Remington Arms Company to begin production of the 03. Except for the name Remington and the serial numbers, which started with No. 3,000,000, this version of the 03 was a faithful replica of the Armory model in every respect.

With an eye toward increasing production, Remington's engineers took a critical look at the old design. After a few months of fiddling with slide rules and handmade prototypes, they came up with the *U.S. Rifle. Caliber .30. Model of 1903A3.*

Why not A2? Because a Model A2 had already been approved and was in service. Not really a rifle, it was simply a modified barreled action, altered to fit inside the breech of a tank cannon and used for practice to reduce training expenses.

Old-timers howled in anguish when the first A3 appeared. Barrel bands, floorplate and trigger guard were made of stamped metal. To add insult to injury, the barrels, most still bearing lathe scars, had only two grooves instead of the traditional four. Critics admitted that the rear-mounted receiver sight might offer some advantages but most insisted that the rifle would never stand up under battle conditions.

Despite the outraged cries and dire

predictions, the A3 performed creditably throughout World War II, seeing service in every theater and adding new luster to the name Springfield. It was sturdy, as dependable as its famed forefather, and just about as accurate.

This last surprised everyone. The ability of a 4-grooved barrel to group better than a two-groover, if any, must be slight. From a rest, my 03s and A3s deliver the same accuracy: 2" to 2½" at 100 yards with match ammo. The life of a 2-grooved tube is reputedly shorter than the four if AP ammunition is used, but evidently the Army felt the difference in longevity was more than offset by lower manufacturing costs and greater production.

Two Million A3s

Remington turned out most of the two million A3s but Smith-Corona also added another 200,000 or so to the total. A number of the latter will be found with 4-groove and, occasionally, 6-groove barrels which were supplied by High Standard, Savage and several other subcontractors.

The A4, the sniper's model, made its bow in 1943. It was simply an A3 equipped with a Weaver 330C telescopic sight (the Army called it the M73B1 carried in a Redfield Jr. mount. The bolt handle was altered to clear the scope and no iron sights were fitted.

To the best of my knowledge, Remington took no special pains with bedding or action but the A4 sniper standing in my rack is blessed with what must surely be one of the smoothest actions ever made. Its condition indicated that it had never been issued yet the trigger is crisp and light — almost too light — and the rifle will consistently group all shots within 1¼".

The number of A4s produced was very small, something on the order of 28,000 all told. Few were issued before 1944 but many were still in action as late as the early 1950s. The Marines used them in Korea, mounting 8- and 12-power target scopes on them.

There's no way of knowing how many survived but the number must be small. The rarest of all have serial numbers beginning with a "Z" prefix; fewer than 2900 were made.

Of all the Springfields produced, the cream were the target and sporter rifles which trickled out of the Armory during

1903 Service. Left to right: 1903 with S stock; 1903A1 with WW II semi-pistol-grip stock; 1903A3; 1903A4, the sniper's model with a modified Type C stock.

A

B

C

D

E

the quiet years between wars. Less than 2,000 ever saw the light of day in any given year but each was a handcrafted marvel.

Assembled from carefully selected parts, with cocking cams, bolts, sight leaves, extractors and runways polished, stocks fashioned from first-class, straight-grained black walnut, equipped with star gauged barrels and target sights, the National Match Springfields, NRA Sporters and the other limited edition models represented the Armory's finest achievements. Little wonder they dominated the target ranges for so many years.

When I was a boy, the word "star gauged" had a magic ring. This interesting device was a feeler gauge used at the Armory to measure the uniformity of a barrel's bore. If land and groove measurements were within one ten-thousandths of an inch (.0001") from chamber to muzzle the barrel was judged match grade, and a small "star mark" was stamped on the lower edge of the muzzle crown. In U.S. shooting circles a star gauged barrel was regarded as the ultimate.

Target-Sporter Models

More than a dozen different match, target and sporting models were created by Springfield Armory between 1921 and 1940. (Some 1,000 or fewer National Match versions of the A3 rifle, purportedly equipped with Redfield micrometer rear sights, were produced from about 1953 through 1956, but I haven't been able to find a photograph of one of these or a specimen.) Some were designed exclusively for service teams; most were made available to NRA members. In addition, a series of full-fledged 30-caliber target rifles was issued. They were characterized by long, heavy barrels, micrometer sights on the receiver, globe sights at the muzzle, mounting blocks for telescopic sights — some were even decorated with adjustable buttplates and other match-rifle equipment. These remarkable rifles, weighing from 12 to 13 pounds, were just about unbeatable on the range.

During one period, the Armory even made up a few "free rifles" for the International Teams. These had longer, heavier barrels, set triggers, long hook buttplates and palm rests. They were about as good as anything Europe had to offer, and they tipped the scales at a hefty 14 pounds.

Some of those old rifles are still floating around, most of them pretty worn now. I'd never pay extra money for one myself unless it is accompanied by the original Ordnance Dept. bill of sale and its star gauging record.

A — The 1903 Springfield in early standard-issue forms. It has the original S stock with grasping grooves and greater drop, at heel. B — The 1903A1 was simply the standard 03 mounted in a Type C stock. C — 1903A1 in a wartime C stock. Notice the blunted pistol grip, the general absence of clean stock lines. D — The 1903A3. The World War II version of the 03 has a receiver peep sight and is characterized by the use of stamped parts and a two-groove barrel. E — The 1903A4. The sniper's model is equipped with a Weaver 2y2X scope in Redfield Jr. mounts and the Type C stock. No iron sights were fitted.

Needless to say, a clever gunsmith can counterfeit a National Match model without too much trouble. A bit of judicious polishing, a close fitting stock, a home-made star mark on the muzzle, the rifle's serial number engraved on the bolt — as always, it pays to be prudent when purchasing a used firearm.

Chances are, if you do run across one of those old specials, it will be an NRA Sporter. Several thousand were made and quite a few, relatively speaking, seem to have survived.

The Sporter, like the other specials, was put together from near-perfect parts and given the same care as a National Match rifle during production. The barrel — star gauged, of course — was slightly tapered; a Lyman 48 receiver sight was mounted on the bridge but the standard service blade was retained up forward; the stock contour was distinctly different from the service style, resembling those on commercial rifles.

While on the subject, it should be noted that the Armory developed several different stocks. The S and C stocks, which have already been mentioned, were relegated to the service rifles, including the N.M. models, but there were various other supplied for the specials.

The Model 1922 or NRA Model as it was popularly known, featured a shotgun-style butt, a well-turned pistol grip and short, sport-er style fore-end. This was used on the 22 rimfire Springfields and on the 30-06 Sporters when these (and other later versions) were sold for civilian use through the DCM.

This same M1922 NRA stock — except for having finger grooves — was used on the 1922 "Match Springfield," a 30-cal. rifle introduced that year. This rifle was a fore-runner of the "Style T" Match 03 rifle first offered in late 1929 and made in limited numbers for a few years.

The M1922 Ml stock, in its NRA form, differed little from the M1922 stock, but the "issue only" version was considerably different — while a half- or sporter stock, the fore-end had finger grooves, the pistol grip profile showed a flatter angle, and the rear of the buttstock looked like the service rifle or S stock in drops, dimension and form.*

---

*There were numerous other stock styles over the years, some experimental, others of limited production. For full and complete information on all of these, and for the finest account of Springfield rifles extant, see *The '03 Springfield*, by Clark S. Campbell, published by Ray Riling Arms Books Co., 6844 Gorsten St., Philadelphia, Pa. 19119.

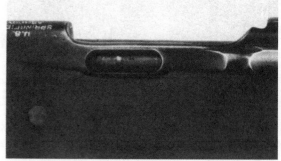

An ejection port on the Mark I Springfield allowed the small Pedersen-designed cartridge cases to escape the semi-automatic bolt. Note the slight stock cutaway beneath the port.

Those Mark I 03s modified to accept the Pedersen device were plainly marked as such on the receiver ring.

Mark I parts. Top, sear and cutoff from a standard 03; bottom, sear and cutoff from a Mark I Springfield modified to accept the Pedersen device.

The Springfield Sporter

To get back to the Sporters: They're heavy by today's standards, scaling pretty close to 9 pounds. Weighty though they may be, those I've fired were very accurate with actions as smooth as silk.

A great number served as the basis for some of the classics turned out by such people as Niedner, Shelhamer, Griffin & Howe and Stoeger during the 1920s and the early '30s.

The first 22 practice rifle based on the 03 action was a single shot. It was fitted with a 24-inch barrel bored off-center at the breech so that the regular firing pin would hit the rim of the small case. The cartridge, by the way, was a special 22 Long Rifle featuring a Pope-designed bullet. It was manufactured by Peters for a limited time and called the "22 Stevens-Pope Armory." Only a few of these arms were produced. Except for the bores, their appearance was indistinguishable from the service rifle.

Another chip off the old block was the Gallery Practice Rifle, Model 1903. Except for chamber and barrel, it too was a duplicate of the issue rifle. Although some

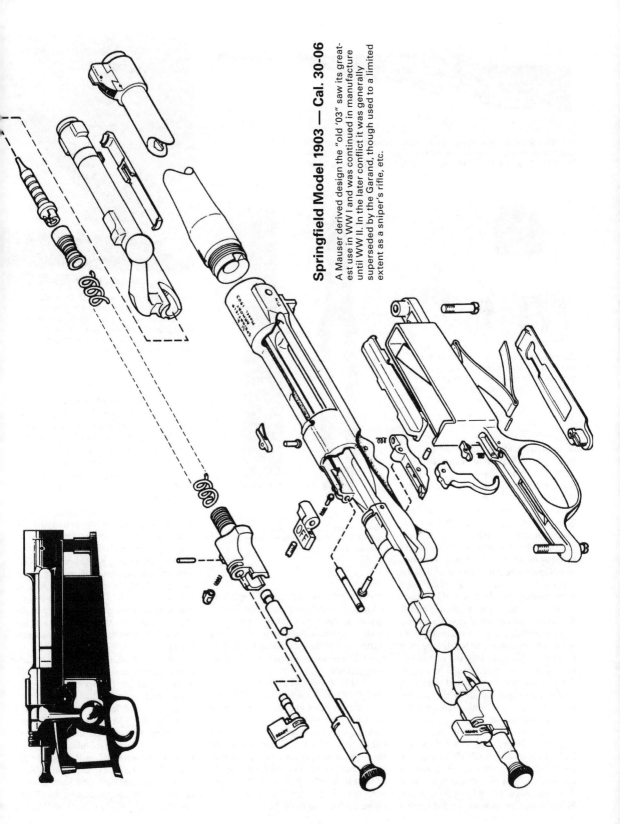

Springfield Model 1903 — Cal. 30-06

A Mauser derived design the "old '03" saw its greatest use in WW I and was continued in manufacture until WW II. In the later conflict it was generally superseded by the Garand, though used to a limited extent as a sniper's rifle, etc.

The NRA Sporter. Assembled from carefully selected parts, fitted with star-gauged barrels and stocked with dense-grained walnut, these rifles sold for $41.50 forty years ago. They were heavy but superbly accurate.

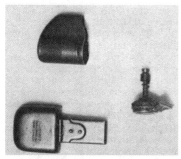

Curiosa. Relics of the days when the 03 ruled the target range. Top, front sight protector; lower left, rear sight protector; right, rear sight micrometer adjuster.

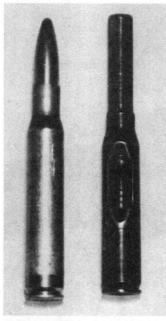

22 Short cartridge adaptor (right), used in the Gallery Practice Rifle of 1907. A 30-06 Military round is shown for comparison.

Micrometer sight adjustor. One of the accessories offered the serious competitor of the early 1920s when the 03 dominated the ranges. These tools permitted accurately controlled small changes in elevation.

of its design features smacked of genius, its accuracy left much to be desired.

Rather than fashion a new bolt or firing pin assembly, Springfield engineers (Majors J. E. Hoffer and J. T. Thompson) created an adaptor cartridge. Made entirely of steel, they were deliberately made shorter than the standard 06 round to prevent one of the latter from being chambered by mistake. Each adaptor contained an integral firing pin and a tiny slot in the side which permitted a 22 Short cartridge to be inserted. The devices could be loaded into the magazine, worked through the action and extracted exactly like the service cartridge. From a training standpoint, the approach was ideal, especially for those ROTC and National Guard units located far from regular outdoor ranges. It meant that the troops could train with a rifle of standard size and weight, shoot from all positions and even practice rapid-fire on indoor ranges.

Clever as the idea was, the adaptors proved impractical. When fired, the bullet enjoyed about half an inch of free travel before it struck the rifling. After a few rounds, lead and grease built up at this point. Accuracy suffered accordingly. In addition, the adaptors tended to rust

in short order, requiring an exasperating amount of maintenance to keep them in operating condition. Most aggravating of all — as far as the shooters were concerned — was the fact that unloading the spent 22 cases was a miserable and frustrating chore.

Despite these shortcomings, it wasn't until 1919 that plans for a new 22 trainer were started. More like the target rifles we know today, its bolt was two-piece and a 5-shot magazine jutted below the floorplate. It still looked in 1920 like the issue rifle except for a Lyman 48 micrometer sight mounted on the receiver. Chambered for the regular 22 Long Rifle cartridge, these prototype versions were the first really accurate 22s that Ordnance had ever developed.

The Model 1922

Two years later (in June of 1922) a refined version, called the *U.S. Rifle. Caliber .22. Model 1922*, was issued. It was the first Springfield to have the half-stock style that was soon to become famous as the "Sporter" stock. By mid-1924 some 2000 M1922 rifles had been made, their price just over $39.

The improved-mechanism Model 1922 M1 which followed also had in its "as issued" form, a half-stock with an oversize flat-angle pistol grip. These had an excessive amount of drop at the heel. The NRA version had the graceful Sporter stock, as before. Bolt travel was still as long as that of the standard 03, a full 3.3 inches, but chamber dimensions were better, the 5-shot magazine was now flush, and the Lyman 48 C receiver sight had ½-minute clicks.

The 1922 M2s, introduced in late 1932, wore a new stock. While a half-stock, it was not the Sporter NRA style used earlier; instead, it had finger-grooves in the fore-end and a buttstock profile about like the N.M. stock. These M2s had a short bolt throw, speed lock ignition and provision for headspace adjustment. That last was incorporated in the locking lug assembly on the final production models.

M2s can still be found hard at work on small bore ranges around the country. Many carry the letters "A" or "B" after

A "long-slide" Lyman 48 micrometer sight, here seen on a Sedgeley sporter.

The reversed safety on the above rifle (arrow) must have been taken from a match rifle, for the serial number on the bolt doesn't match that on the receiver. It pays to be cautious when shopping for collectors items.

This 1903A4 Sniper rifle has a 2½X Weaver telescopic sight in a Redfield Jr. mount, and saw active duty as late as the Korean conflict. Note the altered bolt handle.

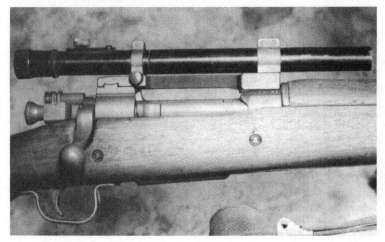

their serial numbers. Those markings signify that the rifles were originally issued as M1922s or M1922s M1s and later arsenal modified to M2 specifications.

"Star Gaging Record" card used to indicate bore and groove dimensions of selected 03 barrels.

Sighting tube. A small number of "sighting tubes" made at Springfield Armory and issued to service rifle teams. The minimum sight setting was 600 yards.

The International Match Rifle, Caliber 30, Model 1924, carried a checkered pistol grip stock, a hooked buttplate, a ball-type palm rest, a Lyman 48 receiver sight and a heavy 30" barrel. These also had double-set triggers of one type or another (see Campbell's book). An identical rifle was made in 22 Long Rifle, using the Model 1922 Ml action, for our successful U.S. International teams, but with the action considerably re-designed. Twelve of the 1924 match Springfields in 22 caliber were made in 15 days, the result of a last-minute order for them!

The old 03 wasn't perfect. Its sights were too delicate for battle conditions; the two-piece firing pin, which failed on occasion, affected lock time adversely; the high bridge made for an overly tall sighting plane and the Springfield action could never cope with escaping gas as well as the Mauser. Nonetheless, it was the best rifle that ever came out of the Armory — and it could shoot. The average 03 was more accurate than any of its contemporaries. Regardless of its shortcomings it looms high on the list of the world's great rifles.

The 03 helped make a lot of history

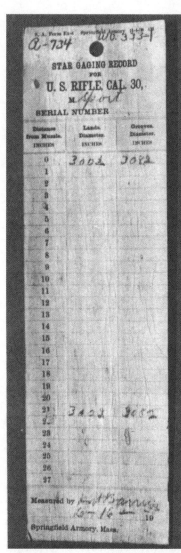

during the first half of this century; on target ranges, battle ground and game fields. More than four million were produced but age, wear and tear, combat, lend-lease and sporterizing have taken their toll. The 03, in military dress, is rapidly disappearing from the scene.

But not entirely. A handful are still on active duty. While watching General Eisenhower's funeral, I noticed the familiar silhouettes when the Presidential color guard hove into view. Sure enough, they were armed with the old bolt actions. Some months ago I saw the Army Drill Team in action. They too were equipped with 03s. I've no idea why they carried them but it was a nostalgic sight to a guy who learned to shoot and run through the Manual of Arms with one.

I remember crossing the English Channel one gray day in June of '44. The ship rolled sluggishly as the helmsman threw the wheel hard over to avoid a floating mine. Several of the troopers broke out their M1s and emptied them at the shiny, dark globe without result. A lanky, tobacco-chewing sergeant muttered an apology as he elbowed up to the rail, cradling a weather-beaten 03 tenderly in his arms. Balancing easily against the ship's gentle heave, he slid into the leather sling and sighted carefully for what seemed to be an eternity. The Springfield's bark was lost in the dull boom of the exploding mine and, as the echoes lost themselves over the tortured water, the marksman cast a scornful glance at the M1s. "Firepower, hell! I'll stick to my 03!"

If the 03 ever needs an epitaph, that should do as well as any.

The Action that Served Two Armies

◼ Wilfrid W. Ward

The 1917 Enfield (a cutaway) action. (Photo courtesy the Smithsonian Institution, Washington)

BRITAIN OFTEN HAS been inadequately prepared for her wars, but not always. This article tells how her preparations to build a new super rifle prior to World War I served not only her own purposes, but later those of her ally, the United States. Ironically, the preparations flowed from British troubles during the Boer War, where the Boers, using Mausers, had usually outshot the British. The press called for a Mauser-actioned service rifle. More realistically, Lord Roberts advocated better rifle training.

Plans for a new rifle began in 1910. On August 26th, the Small Arms Committee was requested by the Director of Artillery to "consider a new mechanism for a new magazine rifle, also any other points, *exclusive of ballistics*, which you may think necessary." This Committee was a typical British institution, which had been founded some years earlier to advise in such matters. It was not universally admired; indeed, the February, 1905, issue of *Arms and Explosives* was acid in its criticism of the Committee to which it referred as "nothing more than a chance assembly of officeholders." This was overly harsh, and Skennerton is probably right in saying that the Committee's advice was a "good cross section of professional opinion and experience."[1]

The Committee met on September 2nd and advised a rifle which was to be used by cavalry and infantry, of approximately the same size as the existing 303 rifle, but with a one-piece stock. It should retain the butt trap, as well as the principles for attaching the bayonet and supporting the barrel, but the nosecap would be lightened in as far as this was compatible with the proper support of the bayonet. The handguard would run the

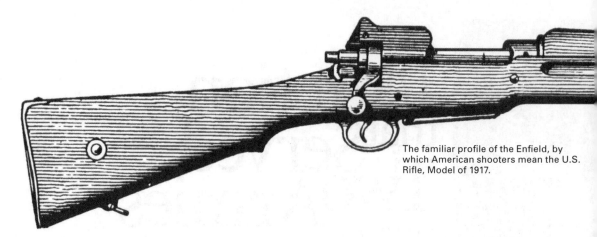

The familiar profile of the Enfield, by which American shooters mean the U.S. Rifle, Model of 1917.

full length of the barrel, and a barrel of 2 pounds 14 ounces was advised.

Furthermore, the recoil was to be about the same as that of the existing rifle. The magazine, which was not to have a cut-off, would carry ten rounds and be charger-loaded with a rimless cartridge. The action, which was one of the fundamental alterations to be incorporated, was to be a Mauser type, giving strength, reliability and symmetry. Forward locking lugs would be used together with a secondary safety shoulder to the bolt. The bolt head should be either detachable or solid with the bolt. A rotary bolt movement would produce primary extraction, and the extractor would not rotate with the bolt. The trigger was to be connect-

ed to the body of the action and not the trigger guard. The safety catch could be locked in both cocked and fired positions. Finally, the striker would be controlled by the cocking piece.

The sights — which eventually turned out to be one of the most advanced and praised aspects of the whole development — were, if possible, to incorporate an aperture backsight calibrated up to 1600 yards and a battle sight (also aperture) for use up to 700 yards. The long-range sight from the Lee-Enfield was to be retained for greater distances.

Further reflection on September 12th led to the recommendations being confirmed, save that the bolt head was to be revolving and detachable. The action

would cock on opening by the rotation of the bolt, the handle of which was to be as near the trigger as possible. By November 3rd the Royal Small Arms Factory at Enfield Lock was instructed to produce a design for such a rifle, and also a rifle for experimental purposes. The design for the rifle and the aperture sight (from Hythe) was ready by December 13th, when the assistant superinten-dant attended upon the Small Arms committee, and by April 3rd he again came bringing an experimental 276-caliber rifle. It was suggested that a different nosecap be fitted and that a bead fore-sight be provided for use with the aperture sight. In addition, a battle sight (not so far included) would be added. The stock in front of the

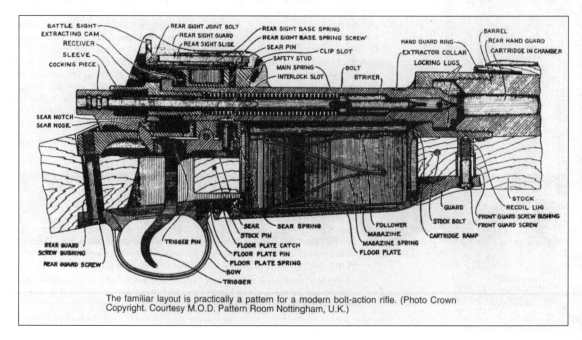

The familiar layout is practically a pattern for a modern bolt-action rifle. (Photo Crown Copyright. Courtesy M.O.D. Pattern Room Nottingham, U.K.)

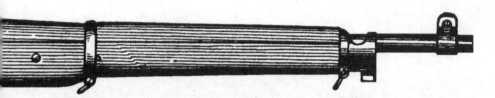

body was also considered too thick. The rifle then underwent rapid-fire trials leading to various minor alterations. Troubles were encountered with the ejection and the sight.

At this stage, the caliber of the new weapon had not yet been decided. The choice was between .276-inch and .256-inch. A series of trials were held in which the 276 caliber was very much more successful, resulting in a report, Minute 1197A, that considered the 276 caliber to have achieved a result which was "very fair for an experimental rifle with experimental ammunition."

The smaller caliber was abandoned quite soon thereafter.

We need not pursue the detailed history of the new rifle through its experimental stages, save to say that the chief source of its difficulties was enabling it to cope with the 276-caliber cartridge. This extremely powerful round generated high pressures, which in turn caused excess heat, extraction difficulties and bulged barrels, even in the two specially designed experimental rifles produced at Enfield for the purpose of the trials. Designated the Experimental Pattern Rifles 1911 Models A and B, they were followed in 1912 by two further models: the Experimental Pattern Rifle 1912, Models 1 and 2. More tests took place in June, 1912, and December 1912, at Hythe, the latter sighting trials. It was also at this stage that the difficulties encountered with the ten-shot magazine led the next experimental rifles to be fitted with five-round magazines; a modification of design which was not only incorporated into the Pattern 1913, but its successor the Pattern 1914. The use was licensed by Mauser and, almost incredibly, full royalty payments were made after the end of hostilities on the whole production. By this stage, the experiments on the design were finished, and a trial order for a nominal 1,000 weapons was put in hand at the Enfield manufactory. The new weapon was designated the "Rifle, Magazine, Enfield, .276-inch" and was officially so described by the War Office on March 15, 1913. These arms were distributed to troops in the British Isles, Egypt and South Africa, in order that they

might undergo the most thorough tests.

A variety of advantages were claimed over the 303. Greater power in the cartridge gave flatter trajectory and higher muzzle velocity, while greater strength (which was needed for this cartridge) was provided. Yet this was achieved with simplification and reduction of components. In particular, the front-locking bolt gave the hoped-for advantage of greater rigidity to both body and bolt. The action and bolt could be stripped without tools. The one-piece stocking allowed a lighter nosecap to be used. This improved the balance, and was not only cheaper to produce, but less likely to break. The aperture backsight was particularly successful, giving the rifle an increased sightbase. In addition, there was a fixed aperture battle sight. Other advantages were the heavier barrel, made possible by other weight savings. The magazine, being entirely within the stock, was less susceptible to accidental damage; moreover it remained open when empty. Overall, it was claimed the rifle showed a general improvement in ease of handling.

While these qualities were justifiably claimed for the rifle itself, the combination with the new cartridge was far less successful. Had it not been for the outbreak of war, the problems (largely oc-

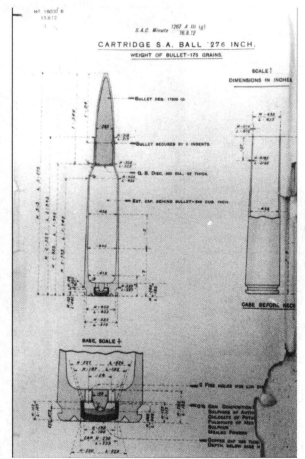

Small Arms Committee Minute setting out detail of 276 cartridge for P13 rifle. (Photo Crown Copyright. Courtesy of M.O.D. Pattern Room Nottingham, U.K.)

(above) Camouflaged sniper using P14. Though the picture is clearly posed, it was almost only in this way that the rifle saw active service. It was very successful. (Photo courtesy Imperial War Museum)

(right) Home Guard Corporal Batcherlor's expression of happy anticipation seemed too good to miss. He was a veteran and probably had experience bayonet fighting during the 1914 war. (Photo courtesy Imperial War Museum)

casioned by the power of the 276 round) would probably have been overcome. The problem was being considered during the summer of 1914. Eventually, the authorities decided to use the new rifle, but with the well-tried, though less powerful, 303 cartridge.

This was not quite the end of the P13, because in late 1915 some of the original thousand P13s, by then returned to store, were converted to 470 caliber for use against snipers' plates — armored firing port covers — and at least one was tried in France. Similar use had been made of heavy-caliber big game rifles, and the latter turned out to be more efficient. These were superseded by the introduction of armor-piercing 303 rifle ammunition. The P13 again was retired, and re-emerged only briefly as an idea in similar context in the 1930s (see below). Its positively final appearance was during the 1939-45 war, when a number were rebuilt and re-issued as sniper rifles. (I am indebted to Mr. David Penn for calling my attention to these.)

The specifications for the substitute rifle, designated "Rifle, Magazine, .303-inch, Pattern 1914," were approved in

October, 1914, and six examples made from the improved version of the 1913 trials rifle were ready in April, 1915. The new pattern was simpler to make than the Lee-Enfield, nonetheless production did not go smoothly, or indeed at all, in Britain. B.S.A., one of Britain's principal arms manufacturers, declined the contract. An order was placed with Vickers for 200,000 rifles to be delivered at a rate of 2000 per week from July 31, 1915, and rise to 3000 a week from November 27. For a variety of reasons, the Vickers rifles were at first delayed, and later the project was abandoned with only a few prototypes to show for it.

In the United States, the arms industry was more accommodating, and contracts were entered into by Winchester

smooth, and a renegotiation of the contracts was deemed necessary. This was completed on December 31, 1916. The new grand total for rifles was 1,811,764. Difficulties had also arisen over the actual cost of the work done. These were sorted out by the British representatives. Britain had agreed to pay all expenses and to buy the plant on completion of the orders.

Before this could happen, however, the United States entered the war as Britain's ally. By the spring of 1917, it was apparent the Enfield S.M.L.E. 303 rifle had served satisfactorily in the trenches, and the 303 Pattern 14 was needed only in a specialized role for snipers and reserve troops. (This policy continued after the 1939–1945 war, and can be vouched for by the author, aged 13, who met his first

(403,126) came out at $28.38 each. Soon after this, the whole enterprise was sold by Britain to the American government at a price of $9,000,000. This was a big loss, but by this stage it was clear that Britain's needs would be covered by 303 Lee-Enfields. The expanding U.S. Army, on the other hand, was shorter of weapons than it had been at any time since the earlier part of the Civil War. The solution was a statesmanlike one, and a success.

Pausing to ask oneself how great a success the new rifle had been up to this point, the answer is only a limited one. Blame must go in many different directions, and a high proportion be laid to bad luck. Nonetheless, there were those who behaved irresponsibly. Perhaps this was occasioned by the fact that the companies concerned were being offered contracts of almost undreamed of size, and as good businessmen they felt compelled to accept first and work out later. Also, in fairness to those involved, one must remember that in the end American industry did find a way. The combination of unpreparedness, tight inspection procedures, lack of enough expert labor (particularly toolmakers) and pressure for fast production was just too much for success. Had the British government insisted on its contractual rights, the likely outcome would have been the ruin of two if not all of the contracting manufacturers. As it was, a substantial sum was saved from the ruins ($9,000,000) by the sale of the whole plant and apparatus to the United States. The balance of the British contract arms were to be completed whilst at the same time work began on the new U.S. rifles. This way Britain's new ally was armed with a first-class rifle (now accepted as the best used in the 1914-1918 war), her small military arms industry preserved, and an acceptable compromise reached.

Strengthened M17 with grenade throwing device used by British Home Guard. (Photo courtesy Imperial War Museum)

Repeating Arms Company of New Haven, Connecticut; Remington Arms Company of Delaware; and Remington Arms Company of Ilion, New York, to make 2,000, 6,000, and 3,000, rifles a day to a total of 3,400,000 in all, for a staggering total of $102,500,000. Tools and gauges were dispatched from Britain, and a British military inspectorate was established in the United States. Again, progress was not

P14, aged about 30, in 1945 in his school cadet force.) Accordingly, production was brought to an end, with an approximate total of 1,233,000, Pattern 14s being produced. The 604,901 rifles made at Eddystone by Remington Arms Company were the most expensive, and together with bayonet and scabbard cost $43.75 each; those from Winchester (225,008) $36.82; while those from Remington Arms UMC

This was not quite the end of the P13/P14 concept in the British service. Apart from the use of the existing 303 rifles for sniping and in lesser theatres, and the later use by the Home Guard of Model 1917s (see below), there was one final flirtation with the action in 1936. That year,

This is the 276 experimental rifle made in 1912. (Photo Crown Copyright. Courtesy M.O.D. Pattern Room Nottingham, U.K.)

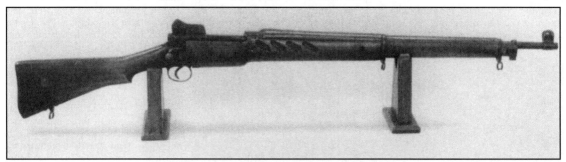

Finally, the 276 Pattern 1913 Rifle looked like this. (Photo Crown Copyright. Courtesy M.O.D. Pattern Room Nottingham, U.K.)

This is the sealed Pattern 1914 Sniper rifle with offset telescopic sight. Mounting the sight directly over the line of the bore obstructed charger loading. (Photo Crown Copyright. Courtesy M.O.D. Pattern Room Nottingham, U.K.)

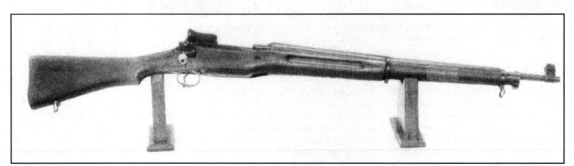

Here is a Winchester-made Model 1917 exported to Britain and used by Home Guard. Note painted band distinguishing from 303 P14.

the Small Arms Committee decided that a rifle with armor-piercing capability was desirable. The result was the "Rifle, Magazine, Experimental, .276 High Velocity." It fired a rimless magnum 276 round and was shaped in the style of a sporting rifle. There were also mounts for a telescopic sight. In 1939, B.S.A. made two prototypes with Mauser-type bolt systems and a built-in five-round magazine. History, however, repeated itself and the same problems of overheating and bullet stripping were encountered, as with the P13. Eventually the war led to a final repetition — the scheme was scrapped. The rifle was called after Captain J.R. Ainley who led the design team.[2]

After the sale by Britain, the first necessity was a complete evaluation of the rifle from an American viewpoint. This led to the abandonment of the 303 caliber in favor of the 30-06 rimless round. Next, and in some ways even more important, inter-changeability of parts was introduced. These decisions, like the British one to replace the experimental 276 with the well-tried 303, turned out well for America both militarily and commercially. Inter-changeability of parts cut production times greatly, and whilst the P14 had only been turned out at about fifty a day, in one day a record 250 Model 1917s were produced. Setting the caliber at 30-06 was clearly a wise decision. As well as the obvious convenience of keeping to one caliber, the performance of the rimmed cartridge had left a lot to be desired, particularly in terms of feeding from the magazine. When the new model arrived in American military hands, *Arms and Explosives* (Sept. 1,1917) tells us that the new rifle received a sympathetic welcome, a reaction not always accorded to new weapons by soldiers. Though doubts had been expressed in advance, the action showed itself quite strong enough to cope with the Springfield round, which had a chamber pressure of some 10,000 pounds more than the 303.

By the time the United States troops got to France, the pattern of trench warfare was well established. That most warlike of Americans, Captain Herbert W. McBride (author of *A Rifleman Went to War* and one of the most famous snipers of the era) had missed the South African War because he was not British. Not to be caught a second time by such a technicality, in 1914 he enlisted in the Canadian forces and was in France from 1915 to 1917. He did his sniping with the Canadian Ross rifle, but formed a favorable im-

Model 1917 closeup of backsight. The aperture battle sight, horizontal when the main sight is raised, can be seen at the base of the backsight. (Photo Crown Copyright. Courtesy M.O.D. Pattern Room Nottingham, U.K.)

pression of the Model 1917 when he had returned to the U.S. as an instructor. (The rifle is also said by the Editor and Wiley Clapp to have been used by Sergeant York in his famous exploit. Doubts are cast on this by Dr. Ezell and an anonymous 1969 *American Rifleman* writer, who both attribute a Springfield to him. The latter article includes York holding a Springfield pictured with his son. In light of such a conflict of authorities, one can only say that if he had had one, it would probably have done him very well! Silencing 35 machine guns, killing 25 and capturing 132 Germans, all with a rifle and a Government 45, doesn't just depend on the make of the rifle.)

There is no doubt that the American version of the Enfield rifle was a great improvement upon its 303 relation. It was simplified, incorporating most of the good points of the P14 and the Springfield. At the same time, there is no reason to doubt that, had the original development at Enfield not been interrupted by war, a first-class rifle would have emerged.

The post-sale development was on strictly American lines. Thus, when one examines the ultra-rare trench-firing device (which I illustrate by courtesy of the Springfield Armory Museum and the Museums and Parks Service), one finds the designer has departed from the British system of raising the whole rifle in a frame containing a separate trigger mechanism, and has hinged the butt, thus permitting the rifle's own trigger and optical sight to be used. The development of the equally rare Pedersen Device, which converted the 1917 — only a few made — into a semi-automatic rifle, was brought to an end with the arrival of peace. In 1934, though not acting for the U.S. government, Remington produced a "Model 1934" as an export to Honduras. Argentina, too, is reputed to have received rifles.

Rumors of the new version of the Enfield had crossed the Atlantic to *Arms and Explosives* by April, 1917, together with justifiable comment on the superiority of the British aperture sight. Final details of the various changes were not published

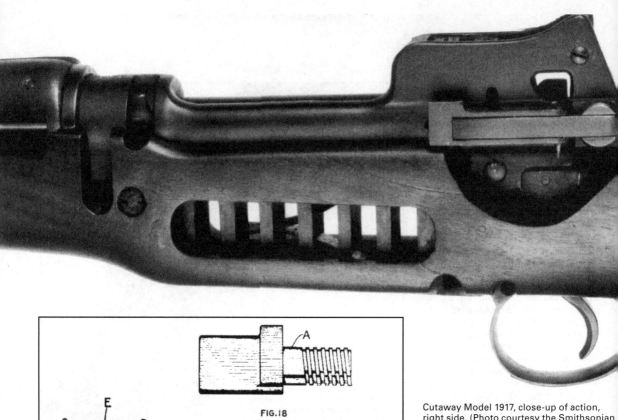

Cutaway Model 1917, close-up of action, right side. (Photo courtesy the Smithsonian Institution Washington)

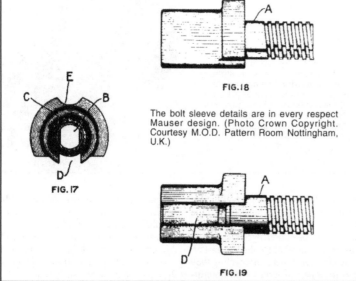

FIG. 18

The bolt sleeve details are in every respect Mauser design. (Photo Crown Copyright. Courtesy M.O.D. Pattern Room Nottingham, U.K.)

FIG. 17

FIG. 19

Seen from below, the 1917 bolt is clearly a Mauser layout. (Photo Crown Copyright. Courtesy M.O.D. Pattern Room Nottingham, U.K.)

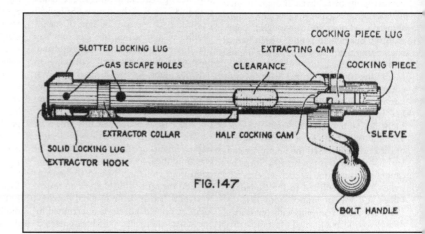

COCKING PIECE LUG

SLOTTED LOCKING LUG   EXTRACTING CAM   COCKING PIECE

GAS ESCAPE HOLES   CLEARANCE

EXTRACTOR COLLAR   HALF COCKING CAM   SLEEVE

SOLID LOCKING LUG
EXTRACTOR HOOK

FIG. 147

BOLT HANDLE

until August, 1917. In the September 1st issue, despite the very strict British censorship, the same paper reported more. The U.S. press, forgetting that the action had been originally designed for the powerful 276 round, expressed fears that the 52,000 pounds of pressure generated by the 30-06 cartridge would prove too much for an action which had only handled the 42,000 pounds of the 303 round. In fact, the 30-06 and the original 276 produced roughly the same pressures. The reaction of the American users was almost universally favorable, although this must have been hard in some instances, bearing in mind that a great deal of the design was still foreign, and that it largely displaced a popular American rifle. The American decision had been to embody chosen changes, but only if they would not occasion delay in production of the new weapon.

Arms and the Man welcomed the new arrival, praising the heavy barrel and the rimless cartridge. (In fairness we must not lose sight of the fact that the P13 was designed for such a cartridge.) The writer, however, hit on the greatest merit, namely the aperture backsight. This, he considered, would make the rifle "stand apart from all others." It was a true prophecy. His other comment that the new naming of the rifle the "U.S. Rifle Model 1917" was "an extraordinary fate for a weapon designed by the British Small Arms Committee" had a ring of jingoism about it, which might have seemed more appropriate from Enfield rather than Washington D.C. Even the proudest Briton could not but agree with one comment that its most striking feature was its "entire lack of beauty."[3]

It would have been too much to hope for that everyone would get it right, though they probably tried harder then in matters of weapons than they do today. The *New York Sun* attacked the change with the headline "Why Our Forces in France Must Use Inferior Rifle," and continued to say that the U.S. Expeditionary Force was to use British Lee-Enfield rifles, rechambered to use the U.S. Springfield cartridge. To make matters worse, the illustration was of the 1895 Lee-Enfield rifle. Furthermore, the writer had gone on to deduce that such a combination would produce an inaccurate weapon, in which he was almost certainly right. To cap it all, he lamented the lack of a telescopic sight for shooting at extremely long ranges.

Such errors at such a time could not go uncorrected, and the NRA's former president, General George W. Wingate, joined Captain Mattice, the officer in charge of the U.S. Enfield project, to correct the record in Arms and the Man. Mr. Skerrett (the author) was said to have shown that he had done considerable research, but "that he was not a practical rifleman." The General's conclusion was that "to enable the soldier to shoot with greatest accuracy and rapidity, the modified Enfield is to my mind superior to the Springfield as the latter is now sighted."

One could continue to quote contemporary sources, but suffice it to say that the near-unanimous view on both sides of the Atlantic was that the "Modified Enfield" was the finest rifle yet developed. Like every other manufacturing process, it had its problems. The Model 1917's were the difficulties encountered in heat-treating the rifle, both at Eddystone and Springfield. It was not absolutely without fault, but it was infinitely ahead of its competitors on both sides of the conflict.

By 1939, the U.S. was re-equipping itself with the semi-automatic Garand, thus the Model 1917 no longer occupied as high a place as it had at the end of hostilities in 1918. Though downgraded to "limited standard" in 1943, it was by no means finished, and appropriately many thousands were exported to Britain under the Lend-Lease agreement. At the beginning of the 1939 war in Britain, home defense was in the hands of the Local Defense Volunteers, who were armed with anything from shotguns, bored out to fire solid ball, to pitchforks. This force was soon reconstituted as the Home Guard. After the regular army had time to reorganize itself and replenish its supplies after the vast losses suffered in the retreat from France in 1940, official attention was turned to the Home Guard. From the status of peasant skirmishers, it became a well-armed, if elderly, force, officered and manned largely by seasoned soldiers who had been service in the 1914 war. In such hands, the Model 1917 was a potent and valued weapon. To distinguish them from the 303 caliber P14, the 3006 Model 1917 rifles were marked with a red band. Though the cartridges of the two rifles were not interchangeable, considerable logistic problems must have arisen from the presence of both rifles in the same units. The P14, too, had not been battle-tested apart from sniping and was restricted to reserve units and a variety of non-standard formations.

Thus, this great and under-used action returned to the country of its origin. By the accidents of timing, it was too late for effective and prolonged service with European users other than for snipers

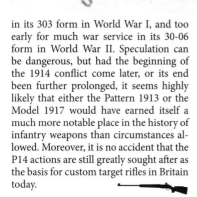

The U.S. idea of a trench rifle involved a hinged stock and a periscope, all hand-held. (Photo courtesy Springfield Armory Museum, Museums and Parks Service)

in its 303 form in World War I, and too early for much war service in its 30-06 form in World War II. Speculation can be dangerous, but had the beginning of the 1914 conflict come later, or its end been further prolonged, it seems highly likely that either the Pattern 1913 or the Model 1917 would have earned itself a much more notable place in the history of infantry weapons than circumstances allowed. Moreover, it is no accident that the P14 actions are still greatly sought after as the basis for custom target rifles in Britain today.

Acknowledgements

I am particularly indebted to Mr. Herbert Woodend of the M O D Pattern Room, Nottingham; to Mr. David Penn, keeper of firearms at the Imperial War Museum; and its trustees for their help and guidance in the preparation of this article and for the opportunity to photograph their exhibits. In addition, I owe thanks to Dr. Ed Ezell and the Smithsonian Institution for photographs of the cutaway Model 1917, and to The Springfield Armory Museum and the National Parks Service for the opportunity to photograph the trench-firing Model 1917 device. Mr. Pete Dickey of the NRA of America provided me with relevant extracts from *Arms and The Man*, and Dr. DeWitt Bailey and Mr. W.S. Curtis those from *Arms and Explosives*. Finally, I refer those readers who seek further information on this very interesting subject to Mr. Skennerton's invaluable work *The U.S. Enfield*, where once again he has almost certainly produced the metaphorical, if not the actual, last word on the subject.

Wilfrid Ward

Footnotes

[1] Ian Skennerton, *The U.S. Enfield* (Margate, Australia: Ian Skennerton, 1983) p.2.

[2] Herbert Woodend, *British Rifles: A Catalogue of the Enfield Pattern Room* (No HMSO, 1981).

[3] "A Causerie About Rifles," Arms and the Man (Washington DC: NRA, June, 1918).

Military Small Arms of World War II

▌ Charles T. Haven

WITH THE victorious completion of World War II, and the return of millions of GI's from world battle areas, military small arms have become of vital, instead of merely academic, interest to most civilians, for in some cases they will prove as much life and death items to the civilian at home as they were to the soldier in the field.

This is brought about by the tremendous influx of "souvenir" weapons and ammunition into the country. Thus, while the first Military Small Arms article in the 1944 Edition of "The Gun Digest" was written so that its readers might recognize weapons seen in news reels or referred to in the papers, the present purpose is to provide information, and in some cases warning, concerning the weapons themselves as they will be seen and handled.

In general, from a safety point of view, the first thing to do with any weapon is to make sure that ammunition to be used is the *correct* ammunition for that gun. The second rule is to make sure that the weapon is safe to fire even though the ammunition to be used with it is suitable for its general type. This applies to American as well as European arms; an obsolete Damascus barrel shotgun loaded with super-duper, nitro express loads is just as dangerous to its user as a worn out Mauser rifle loaded with 8 mm. Mannlicher cartridges.

There have been plenty of excellent weapons made in Europe in the past and plenty of fine arms have been, and will be, sent over to this country; but owing to slave labor conditions, poor material towards the end of the war and a general abuse of weapons in war, many of these arms are unsafe, even with the ammunition originally intended for them.

It is a very good form of life insurance to take any foreign weapon, and the ammunition you intend to use in it,

to a competent authority on firearms for examination before you put your face or hands next to a potential 50,000 pounds or so of breech pressure and pull the trigger. Even United States military weapons may be unsafe if the wrong ammunition is used in them.

Cartridge Characteristics

In the first place, it is advisable to steer clear of any ammunition whose bullets are *not* of normal color, which is either copper or nickel. Specially marked bullets indicate special loads which may get the civilian shooter into trouble in one way or another. In general, the United States marking for special loads in both rifle and pistol cartridges has been adopted by most of the European countries and is as follows:

A red tip bullet indicates tracer ammunition which will set fire to dry brush and should never be fired for target or hunting purposes.

A blue tip bullet is incendiary and is even more likely to set fires than tracer ammunition.

A black tip bullet is for armor piercing, apt to be of higher velocity than normal and may give added strain to rifle actions using it.

.45 and .38 caliber pistol ammunition and also shotgun shells were made for government use in tracer loads and will be recognized by a red tipped bullet, or *tracer* marked on the shell.

Standard British bullet markings duplicate United States markings as to black, red and blue, but have two additional color markings. Armor piercing is marked with a *green* bullet tip as well as a black one; then there are two types of tracer ammunition, a tracer Mark II which burns a thousand yards and carries the standard *red* insignia, and a tracer Mark VI which burns for only six hundred yards, designated by a *white* tip on the bullet.

One of the greatest potential sources of trouble through error and misunderstanding, in connection with foreign guns and ammunition, is the German so-called "8 mm. military cartridge." Actually, there are a number of different 8 mm. cartridges and a number of different rifles for them.

The first and most common is the model of 1898 Mauser and the so-called 8 mm. Mauser cartridge, although to be exact, it is 7.92 mm. This is listed in Germany as the "8" or 7.92×57 mm. rimless cartridge. The 57 mm. stands for length of the cartridge case, 7.92 or .315 being the actual diameter of the bullet. This, in its latest loadings, was the standard German military cartridge and was designed to be used in the 1898 Mauser, in its various models and modifications, and the four different versions of a semi-automatic rifle in use by the German army in the latter stages of World War II: the Gewehr '41, Gewehr '41M, Gewehr '41W and Gewehr '43. It was also used in the standard German rifle caliber machine gun for both ground and aircraft mountings. The rifles chambered for it use it from a Mauser type charger, which does not enter the action, and out of which the cartridges are stripped into the magazine. It is a rimless cartridge with a pointed bullet, very similar in appearance, though slightly shorter and stouter, to our .30-'06. The military type loads have the usual variations of standard ball, tracer and armor piercing, indicated by red and black nosed bullets.

A high velocity load and also an explosive load for machine guns are sometimes encountered. This ammunition is extremely dangerous in a rifle and should not be fired under normal range or hunting conditions. The high velocity load is indicated by a green band around the bullet and the explosive bullet, which is composed of a phosphorous pellet and a lead azite exploding charge, with an inertia firing pin, is indicated by a bullet that is black two thirds of the way up from the neck of the cartridge case and either bright copper or bright silver at the point. This ammunition is even dangerous to disassemble as it may explode in handling. In general, it is advisable to keep away from any military rifle caliber ammunition with unusually marked bullets, and here is a very good example of it:

The modern pointed bullet load, while the case is the same as an earlier load, listed as the model 1888, which uses a round nose, 230 grain bullet, is too high powered for weapons designed for the '88 cartridge, such as the model of 1888 military Mauser and some of the earlier sporting Mauser and Haenel-Mannlieher rifles. Military loads should be used only in modern weapons.

The "8 mm." cartridge, as loaded in this country by the ammunition companies, has a round nosed, hunting bullet with pressures suitable for use in any of the following weapons: The 1888 and 1898 Mauser military rifles, the Sauer-Mauser sporting rifle, the Schilling-Mauser sporting rifle Model 1888 and the Haenel-Mannlieher, model of 1888. No cartridge of the 8×57 dimensions should be used in any other repeating rifle except these and no other cartridge should be used in any of them.

Numerous double barreled and over and under combination rifle and shotgun weapons have been made in Germany, chambered for an 8×57 mm. Mauser cartridge, but in this case it is a *rimmed* cartridge, instead of a *rimless*, to aid in extraction from a break open type weapon. The case dimensions of the 8 × 57 rimmed and rimless are identical and 8×57 rimless ammunition will fire successfully in some of the rifles made for the 8×57 rimmed cartridge. Extraction difficulties can be overcome with an alteration of the extractor. It is, however, advisable to check sporting rifles carefully and, if possible, fire them under proof conditions with this ammunition before shooting such weapons from the shoulder, as there may be variations in pressure between American or military loads and the load in the rimmed case for which the rifle was intended. There are also several other lengths of 8 mm. German sporting cartridges and any sporting weapon, even if it is marked "8 mm.", may be chambered for one of these.

The next most common "8 mm." cartridge found in European weapons imported before World War II, and one that is loaded commercially here, is the 8×56 mm. rimless Mannlicher-Schoenauer, Model of 1903. This uses a round nosed bullet and is a typical rimless bolt action rifle sporting cartridge designed for the Mannlicher-Schoenauer rifle, model of 1903. This should under no circumstances be used in any other weapon as it is shorter in case length than the 8 × 57 mm. Mauser cartridge and will cause headspace trouble and blown cartridges and actions if it gets into a gun chambered for the longer cartridge. Guns chambered for this will, of course, not accept 8 mm. Mauser ammunition without deforming the case and it should never be forced into their chambers.

Another, and entirely different, "8 mm." cartridge is the 8 mm. Austrian-Mannlichcr, designed for the model of 1895 Austrian-Mannlicher military rifle of the straight pull bolt type. This is a rimmed cartridge, very much heavier in the body than other 8 mm. cartridges, which cannot be used in any other weapon except the model of 1895 Austrian military rifle. It uses a round nosed, steel jacketed bullet of 210 grains weight and a muzzle velocity of about 2000 feet per second.

Another "8 mm." European cartridge is the French 8 mm. Lebel cartridge, originally the model of 1886, modified to a pointed, boat tailed bullet at a later period. This in its modern loadings is characterized by a pointed, boat tailed, solid bronze bullet, a rimmed very short, fat case and a muzzle velocity of a little over 2000 feet per second. It is used only in the Lebel military rifle in various models, in three or five shot clips. It was loaded in this country in a sporting load prior to the war, but no standard sporting rifles are made for it. It has become at least semi-obsolete in France by the adoption of the 7.5 mm. rimless cartridge, model 1924-29.

These cartridges are all commonly and loosely called 8 mm. military rifle cartridges, although most of them are available under normal peacetime conditions in sporting type loads. With the exception, under certain conditions, of the 8×57 rimmed and rimless, none of these cartridges are interchangeable and some of them will cause blown weapons if they are wrongly used.

Another cartridge that will be met with extensively in captured trophy weapons, and one which exists in a number of variations, is the "9 mm." pistol cartridge, or to be more exact, the "9 mm." pistol *cartridges*, as there are several that are very easily mixed up.

Taken in the order of their size and power, the smallest is the 9 mm. Browning short. This is identical to our American .380 automatic Colt pistol cartridge which has been manufactured in this country since about 1908. While we do not consider it of military power, it has been used in Europe for a number of standard military pistols, including the Italian Beretta model of 1934, the Hungarian Model of 1937, Czechoslovakian models of 1924 and 1938 and other pocket type pistols issued for military purposes. It is a good medium power cartridge and pistols chambered for it are usually straight blowback actions of medium size and weight.

The next European cartridge in size is the 9 mm. Browning Long. This is a potential trouble maker and should be watched very carefully as it is interchangeable as far as case size is concerned with a Colt .38 ACP, which is a much more powerful cartridge. There are only three pistols made in Europe which are intended for the 9 mm. Browning Long. These are the F. N. Browning Model 1903, the French Le Francais, Model 1928, and the 9 mm. Webley & Scott automatic pistol, Model of 1913, used by the South African mounted police. But since the 9 mm. Browning Long is not at present manufactured in this country, owners of such pistols may try to use the available .38 ACP. *Leave this one alone* as it might cause unfortunate results. Nothing made here will work in them properly.

The next cartridge in size is the commonest of all European cartridges, known in this country as the 9 mm. Luger and in Germany as the pistol cartridge Model 1908, or 9 mm. Parabellum. This was originally designed for the Luger pistol of that year, called in Europe the Parabellum or Pistole '08. The bulk of the heavier European military pistols in use during World War II were chambered for this load. The list includes the F. N. Browning 9 mm. High Power M1935, the Polish Radom, M1935, the Spanish military Astra, the German Walther HP or Pistole 1938, and the Luger.

The earlier Italian service pistol, the Glisenti M1910, is chambered for the same size case but the Italian loadings are very much less powerful than the German and no ammunition that is not beyond all doubt the standard Italian load should ever be used in the Italian Clisenti pistol.

The 9 mm. Luger was also the popular submachine gun cartridge of most of the European nations; unfortunately for the user of captured material, the submachine gun loadings are much higher pressure than normal pistol loadings and will wreck some of the pistols designed for standard loads.

In general, it may be said that during the war all German pistol loading of 9 mm. Luger ammunition is distinguishable by a narrow black band on the bullet just in front of the mouth of the case. All other war time ammunition of this caliber may be high speed loads and should be treated with care. Common distinguishing features that are known to represent high speed loads are: an entirely black bullet in either a brass or steel case, a copper jacketed bullet in a steel case and a gray bullet in a steel case.

Pre-war European loadings with standard brass cases and nickel or copper type bullets are usually of pistol pressure. Italian ammunition, even for Italian submachine guns, is usually loaded to lower pressure than German. American loadings of the 9 mm. Luger ammunition will work satisfactorily in any European pistol that is otherwise in good shape, except the Gli-senti, which has a relatively weak breech action.

There are three other 9 mm. cartridges, all longer than the Luger, which have been in limited use in Europe. These are the 9 mm. Bayard for the Bergmann-Bayard pistol M1908, the 9 mm. Steyr, for the Austrian-Steyr pistol M1911, and the biggest one of all, the 9 mm. Mauser for Mauser pistols chambered for that size. None of these will chamber in weapons designed for the 9 mm. Luger cartridge and they are all somewhat more powerful than the normal loadings of this cartridge. Guns chambered for them should be used only with their own ammunition, which in most cases is not obtainable in this country. Such guns should be considered as souvenirs unless a little of the proper ammunition turns up.

The other common pistol cartridges in Europe are identical with their American versions, notably the .32 automatic Colt, known in Europe as the 7.65 mm. Browning, and the .25 automatic Colt, known in Europe as the 6.35 mm. Browning. These cartridges and their loadings are interchangeable with their American equivalent and in well made weapons are as safe as cartridges manufactured in the same country as the guns.

There is one peculiar cartridge in limited use in France which is not obtainable here; this is the 7.65 mm. long M1935, used in the French M1935 automatic pistol marked MAS. It is about half again as long as our standard .32 automatic Colt pistol cartridge and uses the same type of straight rimless case. Neither this pistol nor its ammunition have any duplicates in this country.

U.S. Weapons

United States small arms of rifle caliber, which include several rifles as well as light and medium weight machine guns, use a cartridge which has always been the subject of some misunderstanding even by a great many soldiers. This is the U. S. cartridge ball, caliber .30 Model 1906 in one of several loads. Originally, the Model of 1906 used a flat based, 150 grain bullet at 2650 feet per second with a breech pressure of about 50,000 pounds. This was the cartridge with which the First World War was fought. Since then, it has been modified to the Ml load brought out in the middle 1920s, which used a 172 grain bullet of boat tailed type at about 2700 feet per second. A further modification just prior to World War II was listed as the M2 load, which returned to the original 150 grain flat based bullet, but increased the muzzle velocity to 28-2900 feet per second. This was the standard load used during World War II. The cartridge is commonly called the .30-'06 from its original designation of caliber .30 Model 1906.

Hunting loads for use in military or sporting rifles chambered for this cartridge have varied from a 110 grain bullet at over 3000 feet per second to a 220 grain bullet at about 2500, but the cartridge is always the standard rimless case of our military weapons.

Two cartridges which are frequently confused with the .30-'06 are the .30-30 Winchester, which is a rimmed hunting cartridge designed for lever action hunting rifles in the middle 1890's and never used for military purposes, and the .30 Model of 1892 or .30 Army, which was standard for the Krag rifle used by the United States Army between 1892 and 1903. It is also commonly called the .30-40. This is a rimmed cartridge with a 220 grain bullet, at about 2000 feet per second, which bears little resemblance to our present army cartridge. None of these cartridges will interchange between different weapons.

We have also used during World War II another .30 caliber cartridge, listed as the .30 carbine Ml, which is a straight cased cartridge using a .30 caliber round nosed 110 grain bullet at about 2000 feet per second and which has been used in the Carbine Ml and M2. This will not interchange with the standard rifle cartridge.

The standard United States Infantry rifle of World War II has been the United States rifle, caliber .30 Ml, popularly known as the Garand, from John C. Garand its inventor. It was adopted as standard by the United States Army in 1936. This is a gas operated semi-automatic rifle, taking its gas from a port near the muzzle. It loads with an eight shot clip which is thrown out when all the cartridges have been fired. It gives to our soldiers nearly three times the fire power of men armed with the bolt action rifle.

Other rifles used by our forces during World War II include the Model 1903 Springfield, which was originally adapted from the basic Mauser turning bolt design of 1898. This is a five shot rifle which has been the standby of the army for many years. It fought through the First World War and proved itself, by the results of many international military rifle matches, to be the most accurate military rifle in the world at the time of its adoption.

Another U. S. Army rifle is the Model 1917, popularly known as the Enfield, as it was a First World War adaptation of the Pattern 1914 British Enfield which was being built for the British government in this country. These were extensively used in World War II as a great many reserve stocks of this rifle were available at the time we entered the war. This is also a turning-bolt Mauser type rifle with a five-shot magazine.

Another semi-automatic of recent development, the Johnson short recoil semi-automatic rifle, with a ten-shot rotary magazine capacity, loading from standard Springfield clips, was used in limited numbers by several United States forces, including the Marine Parachute and Raider Divisions, the Army First Special Service Force and some organizations equipped by the Office of Strategic Services.

As mentioned in the article on "Our Small Arms and Their Makers," a modification of the standard Springfield rifle, Model 1903, streamlined for modern production, was also used by our forces. This was listed as Model 1903A3.

As World War II was essentially a war of movement, emphasis was placed on lightness and mobility, so the light machine gun, exemplified by weapons weighing not much over twenty pounds but giving great fire power to the advanced units, was an important part of Infantry equipment of all nations. Our best known example of this weapon was the BAR, or Browning Automatic rifle, one of the contributions of the great John Browning to United States armament in the First World War. This is a gas-operated, bipod-mounted gun fired from a prone position with a shoulder stock and weighing about twenty pounds.

While the war was in progress an adaptation was made of one of Browning's heavier guns, the light tripod model of the 1917 Browning, to bipod use with a shoulder stock. This was listed as the 1919A6, retained the belt feed and weighed about 35 pounds total.

The Lewis gun of the First World War was also used in limited quantities, especially in the Navy and Coast Guard. This is a gas-operated, air-cooled light machine gun, weighing about 26 pounds and fed from a pan or drum type magazine with a capacity of 47 or 94 rounds placed horizontally on top of the breech.

The Johnson light machine gun, a twelve and a half pound weapon, capable of full and semi-automatic fire, loaded from the left hand side with a 20-shot box magazine and fired either from the shoulder or a light bipod, was also used by some of our Armed Forces, particularly the United States Marine Paratroopers and the Army First Special Service Force.

All these weapons used the standard .30-'06 cartridge in one of its modern loadings; toward the latter part of the war, standard issue was M2 loading in ball, tracer, armor piercing and incendiary varieties, which were designated by the colored tips of the bullets.

A late development of World War I, the submachine gun, which is distinguished from the light machine gun by its use of pistol ammunition rather than rifle ammunition, was also extensively used during World War II. The first weapon of this type to be developed in this country, the Thompson submachine gun, or Tommy gun, was used in a number of models by the Armed Forces of the United States since its first employment by the Marine Corps during the Nicaragua campaign in the 1920's. The Tommy gun weighs about ten pounds and shoots the hard hitting .45 automatic pistol ammunition from several types of magazines, including the earlier 50-shot drum and 20 and 30 shot box magazines. It has been issued in several models, the later ones simplified for more rapid production. The bolt is cocked open and the gun will fire either full or semi-automatic depending on the position of the fire control switch. It provided rapid fire at relatively close range and was especially useful to paratroops, jungle fighters, raiders, commandos, etc.

Another gun using the same ammunition is the Reising submachine gun, manufactured by the Harrington & Richardson Arms Company in several models. This was used by the United States Marines in the early part of the war. It is peculiar among submachine guns in that it fires both full and semi-automatic from a closed bolt, whereas most of these weapons fire from the open bolt position.

Two other submachine guns were developed by the Ordnance Department during the war. These are the M2 and the M3. The M2 is a simplified Thompson gun type weapon, which was never issued in any quantity as before it was in production the M3 was developed. The M3 is an American answer to the cheap live and ten cent store European type submachine gun made extensively from metal stampings. It weighs about nine pounds and can be folded in a bundle less than a foot long by sliding in its extension stock and removing the barrel. It fires only full automatic and is designed to place great fire power in the hands of a great many troops. It was issued extensively to all of our Armed Forces and also considerable quantities were dropped via parachute into occupied areas for use by underground patriot movements, etc.

All United States submachine guns have been chambered for the .45 automatic pistol cartridge except the M3, which was also chambered for the 9 mm. Luger cartridge for dropping into countries where that load is more common than our .45 ACP.

A weapon intermediate between the pistol and the submachine gun is the United States carbine in several models, listed as the M1 and variations, and the M2. This was a cooperative development of the Winchester Repeating Arms Company and the United States Ordnance Department shortly before our entry into World War II. Its original form was a 15-shot semi-automatic weapon, gas-operated, with a bolt similar to that of the Garand rifle but with an intermediate gas piston action which is a basic Winchester development. It used a straight cased .30 caliber cartridge, muzzle velocity of about 2000 feet per second, 110 grain bullet. With a weight of less than five pounds, it was much shorter than the rifle. An M2 model was adopted in September, 1944, that fired either full or semiautomatic and used a 30-shot magazine. The carbine provides accurate fire up to about 300 yards. It was used by many special troops not commonly equipped with rifles, including officers up to the rank of Major, by direction, and was frequently seen in newsreels in the hands of officers of much higher rank.

The standard pistol of our armed forces since 1911 has been, and still is, the famous Colt .45 automatic. This is another invention of John Browning, developed by the Colt Company between 1900 and 1911 and adopted in that year. This is an 8-shot, powerful, compact pistol using a .45 caliber bullet with a striking force of over 300 foot pounds. To augment this pistol during the First World War, Colt and Smith & Wesson revolvers were chambered for the same cartridge, which was held in 3-shot clips for the revolvers. Many of these revolvers were still in use during World War II. They are designated as Model 1917 revolvers.

In addition, both Colt and Smith & Wesson revolvers, chambered for the .38 special cartridge, have been in extensive use during World War II by the Navy and Coast Guard and were standard issue for these branches of the Service. The cartridge supplied to them was a .38 Special revolver cartridge with a metal jacketed bullet which was also supplied in tracer type for signalling purposes. While this might seem to be a reversion to the old .38 caliber which was unsuccessful about the turn of the century, the present .38 caliber cartridge is a far more accurate, more powerful load than the one proved unsatisfactory at that time.

These are the weapons of our fighting forces, normally called Small Arms, which went with the Infantryman as he locked in hand to hand combat with the Japs and the Nazis.

Weapons of Our Allies

The small arms of the rest of the world follow the same general trends reflected in those used by the United States.

Great Britain employed the famous Short Magazine Lee Enfield rifle, originally developed and adopted about 1890. This is a turning bolt rifle with a 10-shot charger loaded magazine and a very fast, smooth bolt action.

In line with the streamlining of equipment for production, a modification of the Pattern 14 Enfield was manufactured in this country for the British by the Savage Arms Company. It was listed as the rifle No. 4, Mark I. Simplified construction throughout for easy machine manufacture included such features as a simple spike bayonet with no handle as we know it, and two groove rifling instead of the original British five grooves.

In the light machine gun field, the principal British weapon is the famous Bren. This is a gas-operated, bipod mounted light machine gun, weighing about twenty pounds and feeding from an overhead box magazine inserted in the magazine holder in the top of the gun. It was used by the Infantry in the field and also in a light, mechanized vehicle designated as the Bren gun carrier.

The British also used a slightly different gun, listed as the Vickers Berthier, which, in common with the Bren, was developed from the original Czechoslovakian weapon of the middle 1920's. The Lewis machine gun, similar to those used in this country, except that it is chambered for the .303 British cartridge, was also in use in the various British services, both in the radiator fitted model and in the stripped down aircraft type. Multiple Lewis gun mounts, with as many as six or eight firing at once, were used in anti-aircraft work.

All British rifles and light machine guns are chambered for the standard .303 British cartridge which uses a flat based, pointed bullet with a muzzle velocity slightly less than a United States cartridge but otherwise generally similar to it, except that it is a rimmed cartridge instead of rimless and not as convenient for feeding in most types of automatic weapons.

It should be noted, by those who have either British guns or ammunition as souvenirs, that this cartridge bears no resemblance whatever to the .303 Savage cartridge as made in this country. This latter is a sporting cartridge very similar to the Winchester .30–30 and is about as far away from a military type as is the .30–30. It will not interchange with any military cartridge.

The British also, particularly in their commando units, were great users of the submachine gun, employing all models of the U. S. Tommy gun in the original .45 caliber and several British submachine guns designed on the five and ten cent store principal. Most of these guns were designed and manufactured for not much more than ten dollars and look like the results of a collaboration of Rube Goldberg and the late Mr. Woolworth. Commonest among them is the Sten submachine gun in several models or Marks, and also the Lanchester, all chambered for the 9 mm. Luger cartridge in its higher power loadings.

The British have never relied extensively on the pistol, always considering the side arm as very much a secondary weapon. The standard British pistol for many years was the .455 caliber Webley revolver. It used a .45 caliber bullet of 250 grains but of a very low velocity in comparison to American loadings.

A .455 Webley & Scott automatic pistol, issued to the British Navy at the time of the First World War, was a very square, awkward looking weapon, although excellently made. It was chambered for a .455 auto-pistol cartridge which is again weaker in power, although with about the same bullet, as our .45 ACP.

The standard British service pistol of World War II was the .380 pistol No. II Mark I. This was a tip-up hinged frame revolver similar to the Webley but chambered for a .380 or .38 caliber cartridge somewhat less in power than our .38 special, and far below anything we have used as a service cartridge since 1909. This cartridge uses a case exactly the same as our .38 Colt New Police or .38 Smith & Wesson revolver cartridge and different types of bullets, including a 172 and a 200 grain of low velocity. In addition, great quantities of both Colt and Smith & Wesson revolvers chambered for this cartridge were made in this country for sale to the British. Any of these weapons will also take the standard .38 Colt New Police or .38 S & W regular cartridges. They will not chamber a .38 short or long Colt, or .38 S&W Special.

Many American weapons of all types have been supplied to our Allies under lend-lease. After Dunkirk, hundreds of thousands of U. S. rifles Model 1917 and other small arms were sent to Great Britain. Newsreel shots of British soldiers often showed them equipped with these arms.

Among our other Allies, Russia has made great strides in weapons of all types since World War I. A number of models of the original Russian Moisin-Nagant turning bolt rifle, 7.62 mm. caliber, were in use during World War II. These included the original models (some made in the U. S. during World War I) and a number of modifications developed in the 1920s and '30s. In addition, Russia used three semiautomatic rifles. The first was the Simonov Model 1936, a gas operated rifle; some models were capable of full as well as semi-automatic fire from a 15-shot detachable magazine. The later and better semi-automatic rifles were the Tokarev, Models 1938 and 1940, both relatively similar to each other except for details and modifications. These guns tap their gas through ports in the top of the barrel to drive rearward an operating rod, which in turn sends back the bolt cover and unlocks the bolt by camming up its locking surface from engagement with an abutment that crosses the entire receiver. The action, although automatic, is very similar to the old hand operated Lee straight pull rifle and a very positive and excellent design.

The standard Russian light machine gun is the Dektyarov which weighs slightly over twenty pounds. It is a gas-operated weapon, fired from a bipod and shoulder stock and fed by a flat pan magazine of somewhat similar appearance to that of the Lewis gun.

All Russian rifle caliber weapons use the standard rimmed 7.62 Russian cartridge which has been loaded in this country for hunting purposes since unused stocks of Russian type rifles manufactured by American makers were sold in this country after the collapse of the Imperial Russian Government during World War I. The cartridge is an excellent hunting cartridge of a power comparable to our .30-'06.

The Russians used a number of types of submachine guns, including a modified Bergmann, known as the Fedorou, plus adaptations of the Finnish Suomi and captured German models. While the captured weapons and the Finnish gun are chambered for the 9 mm. Luger cartridge, truly Russian submachine guns are unique in that they are chambered for the 7.63 mm. Mauser pistol cartridge, which is most uncommon in submachine guns.

The latest Russian submachine gun, a "5 & 10c store" type, is similar to the U.S. M3 and the Sten. Listed as the Russian model 1942, it has a stock which folds upward over the barrel and a pistol grip and magazine holder which is used for a forward hand support.

The Russian hand gun of the First World War was a peculiar weapon known as the Nagant revolver. It has a cylinder which moves backward and forward to form a gas seal by inserting the cartridge case into the breech of the barrel at the time the gun is fired. It is of relatively small caliber (7.5 mm.) and low stopping power. This gun was also used in World War II to some extent, as were German Luger pistols and particularly the German Model of 1898, 7.63 mm. Mauser, which has been very popular in Russia for a number of years. Russia also used an automatic pistol, the Tokarev, designed by the Russian arms inventor of that name from the basic Browning Model 1911 type action. It had an outside hammer, locked breech, short recoil type, but was unusual in that this, like the standard Russian submachine gun, is chambered for the 7.63 mm. Mauser cartridge, and handles the cartridge very excellently in this strong type of locked breech action. The Tokarev pistol can be used with standard 7.63 mm. Mauser pistol cartridges as manufactured in the U.S.

Among our other Allies, the Dutch used a turning-bolt Mannlicher rifle in the 6.5 mm. caliber and the Danish-Madsen light machine gun. The Dutch also adopted, during World War II, the Johnson semi-automatic rifle and the Johnson light machine gun in U. S 30-'06 caliber, as described under United States weapons, to replace and augment their earlier arms. The standard Dutch side arm is a

Luger pistol, originally manufactured in England and chambered for the standard 9 mm. Luger cartridge.

French Infantry rifles of the earlier models include the 1886 tubular magazine, turning-bolt Lebel rifle and several models in use during the First World War, which were turning-bolt Lebel rifles of very much modified Mannlicher types but resembling a Mannlicher in that they took their cartridges in three or five shot clips which entered and became part of the action. All of these were chambered for the original 8 mm. Lebel cartridge, which has a rimmed case of relatively poor shape. An improvement in French ammunition for later type weapons occurred between 1925 and 1929, culminating in the 7.5 mm. rimless cartridge of modern type. This is used in two French rifles, the MAS and the Lebel Model 1934, and also in the latest French machine gun — the Chatellerault Model 1929, a weapon similar in general type to the Bren but using the unusual feature of two triggers, one for semi- and one for full automatic fire. Some few of the early Chauchat long recoil French automatic rifles of the First World War, chambered for the original 8 mm. Lebel cartridge, were also used in World War II, but this weapon is practically obsolete.

One French submachine gun, the Pistolet Mitrailleuse, Model 1938, was developed as of that date to take the 7.65 mm. long pistol cartridge. This was a simple blowback weapon with no special features of interest.

French pistols and revolvers are also relatively poor according to our standards. The 8 mm. Lebel revolver dates back to the 1890's and uses a metal jacketed bullet with a muzzle energy well below our small .38 caliber pocket revolver. The latest French sidearm is the MAS automatic pistol Model 1935A, chambered for a 7.65 mm. long cartridge. This has no duplicate in this country and is a relatively poor cartridge.

Another French automatic pistol which, although not officially used by the French government, has been manufactured there since 1928 is the Le Francais, chambered for the 9 mm. Browning long cartridge and consequently not useable with any ammunition available in this country. This is a peculiar double action weapon with a straight drive firing pin which is not cocked by the automatic action. The barrel breaks upward to load by releasing a catch at the right side above the trigger guard and it is not necessary to draw the slide back at any time. It is not a weapon that we would consider particularly desirable from American military

standards.

Among the small nations, either fighting on our side or overrun by the Germans, the Belgians used a turning-bolt Mauser type rifle of 7.65 mm. caliber and standard Mauser characteristics. Belgium is, however, the seat of the famous Fabrique Nationale d'Armes de Guerre plant, manufacturers of Browning's automatic weapons and particularly automatic pistols. The earliest of the Browning military pistols is the Model 1903, 9 mm. Browning long, a straight blowback weapon, chambered for a cartridge that is not manufactured in this country and not interchangeable with any cartridge made here. It looks like an overgrown model of our .380 Colt, slightly longer but otherwise very similar. The Browning pistols, Model of 1910 and military Model of 1922, which is an enlargement of the 1910 pocket, are chambered for the 7.65 mm. and 9 mm. short or .380 pistol cartridges common in this country. These are straight blowback weapons characterized by a mainspring around the barrel and of hammerless design.

The latest of the Browning military pistols has been particularly popular throughout Europe and was extensively used by the Germans after their capture of the F. N. plant. This is the M1935 Browning pistol, chambered for the 9 mm. Luger cartridge — in appearance somewhat similar to our .45 Model of 1911. It uses, however, a simplified and modernized version of the locked breech action and a double column magazine holding 13 cartridges. It is also sometimes fitted with a shoulder stock.

Another Browning modification is found in the Radom pistol, manufactured at the Government Armory at Radom on the Vistula river in Poland for the Polish Army since 1935. This plant was also overrun by the Germans and the Radom is commonly found as manufactured for them there. It is chambered for the 9 mm. Luger cartridge and is of generally Browning locked breech characteristics somewhat simplified for modern production. It is an excellent weapon in the examples made by the Polish, but some very crude German manufactured models are encountered. The Polish also used a Mauser rifle of the standard German type.

The Czechoslovakians, the originators of the ZB gas-operated light machine gun which was widely copied throughout Europe and listed by the Germans as the Model 1926 gun, also used the Mauser type rifle in the standard German 7.92 mm. caliber, and have made three small military type pistols. The first, the Model of 1924, is a turning barrel, locked breech

action chambered for the 9 mm. short or .380 automatic Colt pistol cartridge. The Model 1927 is similar to the Model 1924 except that it is chambered for the .32 cartridge and is a straight blowback. Both of these models have a small outside hammer and are of single action design. A model 1938, the latest of the Czech pistols, is very different from either of the others. It is one of the few pistols that uses a double action system entirely as the hammer follows the slide down and is not cocked by the automatic action. This is chambered for the .380 cartridge, is a straight blowback, but with an exceptionally strong retractor spring. These are all well made weapons in the models made by the Czechs. Rougher copies of them were turned out by the Germans during the latter part of the war.

Weapons of the Axis

Of the arms of our enemies, those of Germany were, of course, the largest number which we encountered and also the most numerous to return to the United States as souvenirs and relics. Germany's standard Infantry rifle of the past 50 years or so has been the Gewehr '98, invented by Paul Mauser and commonly called the Mauser rifle. This is a turning-bolt, staggered column magazine repeater — the ancestor of most military rifles used in the world since the turn of the century, including our Model 1903 Springfield. The most common Mauser in use during World War II was a carbine model closely approximating the Springfield in general size and shape. Earlier, longer barrel models are also still met occasionally. This, in common with the other German rifle caliber small arms, uses the 7.92 or "8 mm." rifle cartridge described in the first part of this article. A simplified model was made after 1942 that is of very doubtful quality.

The standard Mauser was augmented during the war by four models of semi-automatic rifles which were developed and put into service as the war progressed. These were the Gewehr '41, '41M, '41W and '43. They were all gas operated rifles, three of which used a bolt with folding lugs similar to the Russian Dektyarov light machine gun. Gas was tapped either at the muzzle or, in the latest model, about three quarters of the way up the barrel to drive operating rods positioned on top of the barrel instead of below as in our Garand. These weapons, particularly those made in the latter part of the war, were very cheaply made of castings and stampings; some give evidences of not standing up very well. It is advisable to be careful of these weapons; they are not suitable for conversion to sporting arms as little change in the shape of the stock can be made on account of the gas system. They should not be altered to any other cartridge and should be tested and watched very carefully even with a German load before using them.

The Germans also used a number of special weapons of rifle or carbine size and weight which included the Fallschirmjaeger Gewehr '42, or paratroopers rifle — in effect a light machine gun with the unusual feature of semi-automatic fire with the bolt closed between shots. This was a very poorly constructed weapon weighing only a little over ten pounds-, which is very light for an arm of this type. It probably didn't stand up too well.

The Germans developed a cartridge as an answer to our carbine cartridge — the 7.92 short. It had a lighter bullet of the same diameter as their standard rifle cartridge but in a short, bottle-necked case. This was used in a machine carbine, capable of either full or semi-automatic fire. Manufactured from stamped parts, it was exceptionally well made for an arm of this type. It was listed as the machine pistol '43, or carbine '44. As it is a full or semi-automatic weapon, it falls into the machine pistol class, gas operated by a piston on the top of the barrel which seems to be a very popular arrangement in Germany.

Austrian and Hungarian troops were armed with the straight pull Mannlicher rifle of bolt action repeating type, using a rimmed 8 mm. cartridge and the breech system of Ferdinand Ritter Von Mannlicher, second in popularity only to that of Mauser among military rifles.

The German army was extensively supplied with submachine guns, ranging all the way from the original Bergmann Muskette up through the Neuhausen, Solothurn S1-100, Erma and a number of others, to the latest Schmeisser folding stock paratroopers submachine gun, Model of 1940. These follow the general pattern of submachine guns all over the world — for the most part simple blowback weapons weighing 8 or 10 pounds, cocked with the bolt open and utilizing the 9 mm. Luger pistol ammunition. There was one exception and that was the Steyr-Solothurn Sl-100, which is listed by the Germans as the Austrian Model 34 chambered for the 9 mm. Mauser pistol cartridge, which is much less common than the Luger.

The use of great quantities of storm troopers, secret police, SS Corps members, etc., gave rise to the need of enormous quantities of handguns by the German military establishment. The original German official pistol was the Luger Model 1908, which is a short recoil, locked

breech automatic originally designed as the Borchardt by an American who came from Connecticut. German troops have always used, more or less unofficially, the Mauser Model of 1898, chambered for the original Mauser 7.63 pistol cartridge, relatively rarely for the Mauser 9 mm. pistol cartridge and more commonly for the Luger 9 mm. cartridge, as considerable quantities were made chambered in the latter load for the Prussian Army during World War I. Pistols chambered for 9 mm. Luger cartridges can always be identified by a large figure 9 cut into the grip and painted RED. Otherwise they will be smaller caliber, approximately .30, and chambered for the bottlenecked Mauser cartridge. A .35 caliber pistol, not marked 9 is chambered for the 9 mm. Mauser cartridge, which is very hard to obtain; it will not use the 9 mm. Luger cartridge satisfactorily.

Shortly before World War II, in 1938, the German Army adopted the Walther Model 1936 HP, or Heeres Pistole, meaning army pistol. This is designated officially by the Germans as the Pistole 38, and has been a very popular souvenir weapon. It is a well designed short recoil, locked breech action pistol, but has the very dangerous drawback that it can be assembled without its locking yoke in place and will fire that way at least once. It will not, however, do the firer or the pistol any good if it is so fired. This feature should be checked before the pistol is fired. It is chambered for the standard 9 mm. Luger cartridge, but its locking action is such that it is particularly dangerous to use the high velocity submachine gun loads in it — this should never be done.

In addition to these standard weapons, the Germans have used the Austrian pistols of World War I and later improvements, which include the Steyr Model 1911, an outside hammer, short recoil pistol, chambered for the 9 mm. Steyr cartridge (which is NOT the same as any of the other 9 mms.), and the Hungarian Model of 1937, a simple blowback pistol of small size made with an outside hammer and chambered for the 9 mm. Kurz or Colt .380 cartridge. This is an excellent little pistol and usually very well made.

The Czechoslovakian pistols in all three models were commonly found in use by the Germans, as was the Polish Radom after the capture of Poland. Weapons made in captured plants, under German supervision, particularly toward the latter part of the war, are all extremely crude and very roughly machined. Their material may also be questioned in some cases and it is advisable to be pretty careful of them.

In addition to standard military types, nearly all the pocket pistols in use in Europe for the last 30 odd years have been found with official German army marks on them and apparently were issued to all kinds of special troops, police, etc. Nearly all of these are chambered for one of three cartridges which are commonly available for this type of pistol. Those marked 9 mm. Kurz or 9 mm. Corto, are chambered for the .380 ACP cartridge. Those marked 7.65 mm. or 7.65 Browning, are chambered for .32 ACP, and those marked 6.35 mm. or 6.35 mm. Browning, are chambered for the .25 ACP. They range in types from simple blow-back to some curious and complicated locked breech systems. Many of them are good, some of them not so good; it is advisable to have an expert check them.

The universal light machine gun of the German army consists of a series of progressive models of what was originally the Dreyse MG 1913 of the First World War. These are all recoil operated, air-cooled light machine guns, weighing in the neighsborhood of 25 pounds, and normally fired from a bipod mount with a shoulder stock. They can also be attached to an elaborate tripod and fed with a belt for use as a light-heavy machine gun. The first improvement of the Dreyse, listed as the Dreyse-Solo-thurn Model of 1934, is one of the guns supposed to be manufactured in Switzerland but was actually made out of parts which were classed as "baby carriages" and other household items and made in Germany and shipped to Switzerland for assembly. This also uses a round radiator and a crutch-like shoulder stock with a bipod.

The next improved version of the Model 34 is similar in general appearance but different in a number of details, especially in that it uses a turning-bolt head instead of a turning barrel sleeve in its action.

The last version of this gun, the MG42, is made almost entirely of stampings and is notable for its extremely high cyclic rate of fire. The gun fires at a rate of nearly 1500 shots a minute and sounds like a ripping sheet as it goes off. This is higher than any other ground gun — higher than most military authorities consider practical. All these models are chambered for the standard German Infantry rifle cartridge.

Italy used a Mannlicher type, turning-bolt rifle of 6.5 mm. (.25) caliber which has the usual characteristics of these weapons. It is called the Mannlicher-Carcano and uses a rimless .25 caliber cartridge similar in general appearance to the Mannlicher-Schoenauer cartridge as manufactured in this country for sporting rifles, but different in a number of characteristics. As Italian rifles are not particularly well made, it would be extremely unsafe to use in them any ammunition manufactured in this country. They should be used only with Italian ammunition made for them; some of those that have come over here look as though they should not be used with any ammunition at all, as the workmanship is extremely poor and the materials are soft.

The most common Italian light machine gun was the Breda. This was made in several models and is a typical bipod mounted, shoulder stock, light machine gun with, however, some unusual features. It has a box magazine on the right hand side of the gun. The action is a combination of recoil and blowback which requires the use of greased ammunition. Some of these guns were made in the 6.5 caliber and some in a caliber similar to, 30-'06, listed as the 7.35 mm. Italian cartridge. There were some Italian rifles also chambered for this cartridge and they should by no means be used with any such cartridge as our .30-'06 even though the bore appears to be about the same size as they were not intended to stand pressures such as our ammunition develops.

The standard Italian submachinegun was the 9 mm. Beretta Model of 1938, a blowback gun, fed from a box magazine inserted from the bottom. One uncommon feature of this machine gun is the bayonet which is fitted to it for close fighting. It also uses the system of two triggers, one for semi- and one for full automatic fire. This is one of the better made Italian weapons. It uses the Italian 9 mm. Luger type cartridge, but with the Italian loading of lower power.

The Italian handgun of the First World War, the Glisenti, looks somewhat like the Luger but is entirely different from it in action. It is a short recoil action with a breechblock of relatively weak application of what is sometimes called the "prop up" locking system. The Italian variation is so pivoted that it is really only a rotating wedge and the pistol might almost be classed as a straight blowback. While the cartridge is the same case size as the 9 mm. Luger, Italian loadings are at least 25% lighter in power and pressure, so the Glisenti pistol should not be fired with anything except Italian ammunition. In fact, this is another one of the weapons that it is better not to fire at all, although it has an interesting automatic action and is a very desirable relic for design study.

This pistol was augmented in World War II by the Beretta pistol Model of 1934, adopted by the Italian army in that year. This is a pocket size, straight blowback with an outside hammer, chambered for the 9 mm. Corto or .380 pistol cartridge and is excellently designed for this cartridge. Beretta's arms are all much better made than most other Italian weapons; Beretta pistols, made up to the last year or two of the Italian participation in the war, are of excellent workmanship. The last production was relatively poorer in finish but still good in design. This pistol was also chambered for the 7.65 mm. or .32 ACP cartridge and. issued in this caliber for military purposes. Some of them were supplied to the German army by the Italian makers before the surrender of Italy.

Japanese infantry weapons have been publicized as being of very small caliber and, consequently, of extremely low power. The Arisaka rifle, year '38, is to. all intents and purposes a model 1907 Mauser with the exception of a very clever light metal action cover which travels back and forth with the bolt and keeps dirt and sand out of the action when the bolt is closed. The caliber is 6.5 mm. or .25 caliber; actually, the cartridge is on paper only about 10% less effective than our standard .30-'06 ammunition. The weight of the bullet is 139 grains, velocity 2500 feet per second. It is by no means the next thing to a shooting gallery .22, as frequent news accounts implied. It is apparent, however, that the Japanese did not entirely trust the power of a .25 caliber cartridge as they changed in 1939 to a 7.7 cartridge very similar to the British .303; as they were at that time at war with China, such a change in the middle of hostilities indicates serious doubts as to the quality of ammunition then in use. However, they continued to use .25 caliber as well, for our troops ran into rifles and light machine guns chambered for it all during the war.

The Japanese Ordnance must have been a very complicated business and owners of Japanese souvenirs will find themselves in nearly as much trouble as Japanese Ordnance men on account of the bewildering variations in Japanese ammunition. In addition to the rifles, the Japanese used several machine guns of rifle caliber. These were the 1922 hopper fed Nambu, a light bipod mounted gun in .25 caliber, the 1936 Type 96, a top magazine light bipod mounted gun somewhat similar to the Bren, in .25 caliber, and the 7.7 caliber version of it listed as the type 99 or 1939. Japanese rifles are of very poor quality and workmanship — they should be considered as *relics only!*

The Japanese rifle chambered for the 7.7 cartridge is also listed as the model 1939 rifle. To complicate matters further, rifles and machine guns did not take the same type of ammunition in all cases. In the 6.5 there was a full charge load for rifles and the old fashioned heavy machine guns, and a reduced charge load for the Nambu Model 1922 gun and the 1936, Type 96 gun. This could also be used in the rifles but rifle type ammunition would probably jam in the machine guns. In the 7.7 caliber there were three different types of cartridges, rimmed, semi-rimmed and rimless. Rimmed cartridges were used only in aircraft guns, the semi-rimmed in heavy machine guns of the Hotchkiss type and the rimless in Model 1939 rifles and machine guns.

The Japanese also are the only ones who departed from the standard bullet markings for AP, tracer, etc. Their markings are very light lacquered bands at the mouth of the case: pink for ball ammunition, green for tracer and black for AP.

Japan designed no sub-machine guns of her own, but did develop three automatic pistols which are definitely of native design. The first of these, the Model of 1914 Nambu invented by General Kijiru Nambu, looks like the Luger but with a locked breech, short recoil prop-up action more closely resembles the Mauser. It is distinguishable by a recoil spring on the left hand side of the frame only. The next model is a modification listed as the Model 1925 and distinguishable by two recoil springs, one on each side of the bolt. The third pistol is an entirely different one, the Type 94. It uses a slide and spring around the barrel and pivoted inside hammer.

All three pistols are chambered for the 8 mm. Nambu pistol cartridge, a bottlenecked rimless cartridge similar in appearance to 7.65 mm. Luger but by no means the same. *NO* Japanese pistol should be fired with any other cartridge as, particularly in the case of the Model 94, the action is not strong enough to handle cartridges of American or European type for the workmanship is relatively poor.

These are the Infantry weapons with which World War II has been fought by the United States, their Allies and their enemies. The trend has been toward better automatic and semi-automatic weapons and a great many more of them. The firepower of the average Infantry Battalion has increased in the last 25 years by geometric rather than arithmetic progression, and this trend may well be reflected in sporting arms over the next few years. The First World War changed the hunting arms in this country from the lever action to the bolt action, and while the manufacturers are not yet in a position to announce any quantity of new designs, it is probable that some new sporting automatics will appear on the market as the result of World War II.

MILITARY SMALL ARMS-PISTOLS ¼ ACTUAL SIZE

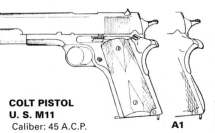

COLT PISTOL
U. S. M11
 Caliber: 45 A.C.P.
Length: 8½"
Shots: 7
Weight: 39 oz.
Action: Short Recoil — Semi Auto
UNITED STATES — BRITISH EMPIRE

A1

WEBLEY PISTOL
M 1913
 Caliber: 455
Length: 8½"
Shots: 7
Weight: 36 oz.
Action: Short Recoil — Semi Auto
BRITISH NAVY

TOKAREV PISTOL
Caliber: 7.62 MM
Length: 7¾"
Shots: 8
Weight: 30 oz.
Action: Short Recoil — Semi Auto
RUSSIA

WALTHER M'38 (P. 38)
Caliber: 9 MM
Length: 8½"
Shots: 8
Weight: 34 oz.
Action: Short Recoil — Semi Auto
GERMANY

MAUSER PISTOL M'98
Caliber: 7.63 MM
Length: 12"
Shots: 10
Weight: 45 oz.
Action: Short Recoil — Semi Auto
GERMANY — RUSSIA, ETC.

LUGER PISTOL M'08
Caliber: 9 MM
Length: 8¾"
Shots: 7
Weight: 30 oz.
Action: Short Recoil — Semi Auto
GERMANY, ETC

F. N. BROWNING
M 1935
Caliber: 9 MM
Length: 7¾"
Shots: 10-15
Weight: 32 oz,
Action: Short Recoil — Semi Auto
BELGIUM — FRANCE
GERMANY

PISTOL M'35 A
Caliber: 7.65MM Long
Length: 7½"
Shots: 8
Weight: 26 oz.
Action: Short Recoil — Semi Auto
FRANCE

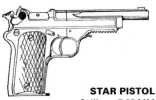

STAR PISTOL
Caliber: 7.65 MM
Length: 7¼"
Shots 7
Weight:
Action: Blowback — Semi Auto
FRANCE

GLISENTI PISTOL M'10
Caliber: 9 MM
Length: 8¼"
Shots: 7
Weight: 32 oz,
Action: Short Recoil — Semi Auto
ITALY

BERETTA PISTOL M'34
Caliber: 9 MM Corto
Length: 6"
Shots: 7
Weight: 23½ oz.
Action: Blowback — Semi Auto
ITALY

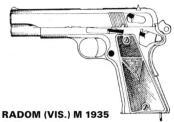

RADOM (VIS.) M 1935
Caliber: 9 MM
Length: 8"
Shots: 8
Weight: 36 oz.
Action: Short Recoil — Semi Auto
POLAND — GERMANY

MILITARY PISTOLS and REVOLVERS ¼ ACTUAL SIZE

NAMBU PISTOL M'14
Caliber: 8 MM
Length: 9"
Shots: 8
Weight: 31 oz.
Action: Short Recoil — Semi Auto
JAPAN

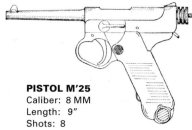

PISTOL M'25
Caliber: 8 MM
Length: 9"
Shots: 8
Weight: 32 oz.
Action: Short Recoil — Semi Auto
JAPAN

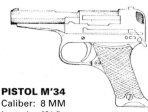

PISTOL M'34
Caliber: 8 MM
Length: 6⅝"
Shots: 6
Weight: 27 oz.
Action: Short Recoil — Semi Auto
JAPAN

ZECH M 1938
Cal.: 9mmShort(380)
Length: 7⅝"
Shots: 8
Weight: 32 oz.
Action: Blowback — Semi Auto
CZECHOSLOVAKIA — GERMANY

STEYR PISTOL M'11
Caliber: 9 MM
Length: 8½"
Shots: 8
Weight: 38½ oz.
Action: Short Recoil — Semi Auto
AUSTRIA

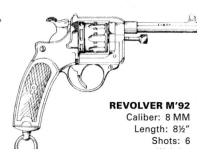

REVOLVER M'92
Caliber: 8 MM
Length: 8½"
Shots: 6
Weight:
Action: Double Action Revolver
FRANCE

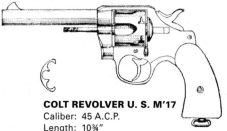

COLT REVOLVER U. S. M'17
Caliber: 45 A.C.P.
Length: 10¾"
Shots: 6
Weight: 40 oz.
Action: ouble Action Revolver
UNITED STATES

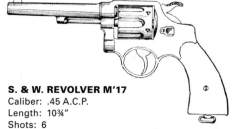

S. & W. REVOLVER M'17
Caliber: .45 A.C.P.
Length: 10¾"
Shots: 6
Weight: 36 oz.
Action: Double Action Revolver
UNITED STATES

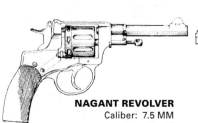

NAGANT REVOLVER
Caliber: 7.5 MM
Length: 9"
Shots: 7
Weight: 28 oz,
Action: Double Action Revolver
RUSSIA

ENFIELD NO. 2 MK 1
Caliber: 380
Length: 9½"
Shots: 6
Weight: 27½ OZ.
Action: Double Action Revolver
BRITISH EMPIRE

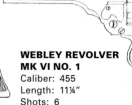

**WEBLEY REVOLVER
MK VI NO. 1**
Caliber: 455
Length: 11¼"
Shots: 6
Weight: 38 oz.
Action: Double Action Revolver
BRITISH EMPIRE

MILITARY SMALL ARMS-RIFLES ⅛ ACTUAL SIZE

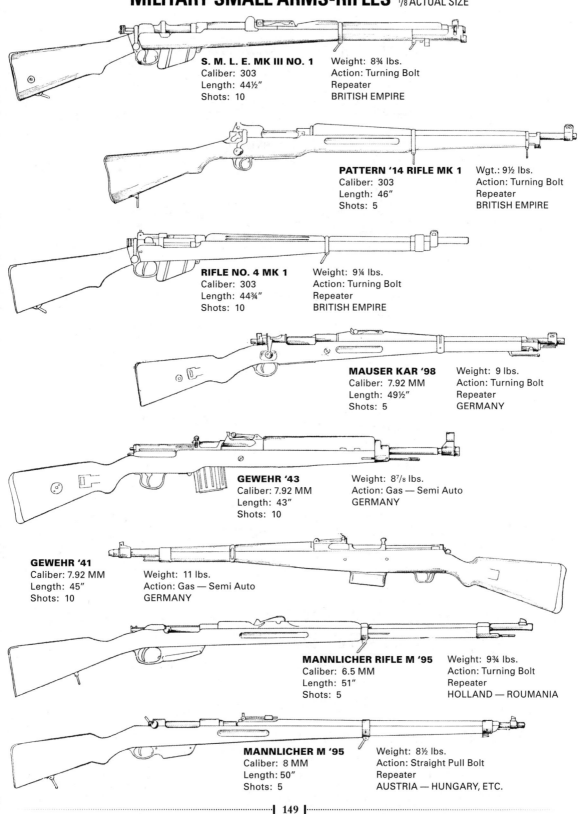

S. M. L. E. MK III NO. 1
Caliber: 303
Length: 44½"
Shots: 10

Weight: 8¾ lbs.
Action: Turning Bolt
Repeater
BRITISH EMPIRE

PATTERN '14 RIFLE MK 1
Caliber: 303
Length: 46"
Shots: 5

Wgt.: 9½ lbs.
Action: Turning Bolt
Repeater
BRITISH EMPIRE

RIFLE NO. 4 MK 1
Caliber: 303
Length: 44¾"
Shots: 10

Weight: 9¼ lbs.
Action: Turning Bolt
Repeater
BRITISH EMPIRE

MAUSER KAR '98
Caliber: 7.92 MM
Length: 49½"
Shots: 5

Weight: 9 lbs.
Action: Turning Bolt
Repeater
GERMANY

GEWEHR '43
Caliber: 7.92 MM
Length: 43"
Shots: 10

Weight: $8^7/_8$ lbs.
Action: Gas — Semi Auto
GERMANY

GEWEHR '41
Caliber: 7.92 MM
Length: 45"
Shots: 10

Weight: 11 lbs.
Action: Gas — Semi Auto
GERMANY

MANNLICHER RIFLE M '95
Caliber: 6.5 MM
Length: 51"
Shots: 5

Weight: 9¾ lbs.
Action: Turning Bolt
Repeater
HOLLAND — ROUMANIA

MANNLICHER M '95
Caliber: 8 MM
Length: 50"
Shots: 5

Weight: 8½ lbs.
Action: Straight Pull Bolt
Repeater
AUSTRIA — HUNGARY, ETC.

MILITARY SMALL ARMS-RIFLES ⅛ ACTUAL SIZE

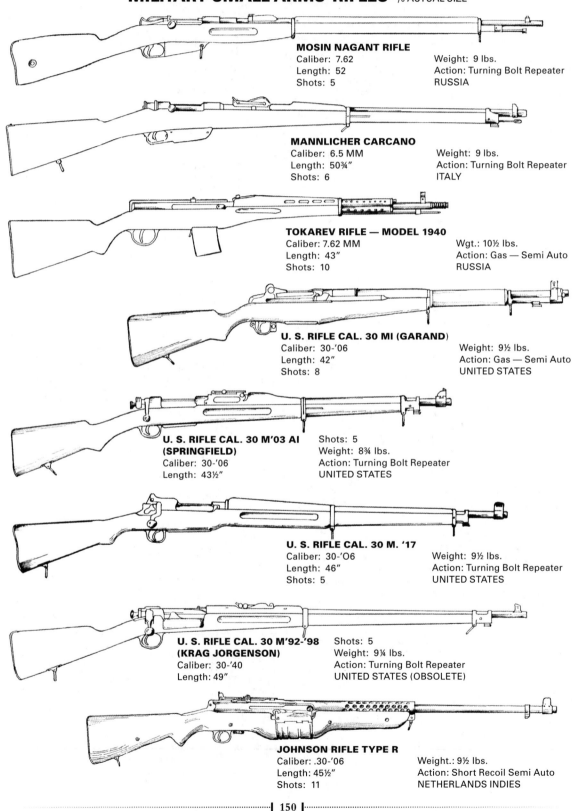

MOSIN NAGANT RIFLE
Caliber: 7.62
Length: 52
Shots: 5

Weight: 9 lbs.
Action: Turning Bolt Repeater
RUSSIA

MANNLICHER CARCANO
Caliber: 6.5 MM
Length: 50¾"
Shots: 6

Weight: 9 lbs.
Action: Turning Bolt Repeater
ITALY

TOKAREV RIFLE — MODEL 1940
Caliber: 7.62 MM
Length: 43"
Shots: 10

Wgt.: 10½ lbs.
Action: Gas — Semi Auto
RUSSIA

U. S. RIFLE CAL. 30 MI (GARAND)
Caliber: 30-'06
Length: 42"
Shots: 8

Weight: 9½ lbs.
Action: Gas — Semi Auto
UNITED STATES

U. S. RIFLE CAL. 30 M'03 AI (SPRINGFIELD)
Caliber: 30-'06
Length: 43½"

Shots: 5
Weight: 8¾ lbs.
Action: Turning Bolt Repeater
UNITED STATES

U. S. RIFLE CAL. 30 M. '17
Caliber: 30-'06
Length: 46"
Shots: 5

Weight: 9½ lbs.
Action: Turning Bolt Repeater
UNITED STATES

U. S. RIFLE CAL. 30 M'92-'98 (KRAG JORGENSON)
Caliber: 30-'40
Length: 49"

Shots: 5
Weight: 9¼ lbs.
Action: Turning Bolt Repeater
UNITED STATES (OBSOLETE)

JOHNSON RIFLE TYPE R
Caliber: .30-'06
Length: 45½"
Shots: 11

Weight.: 9½ lbs.
Action: Short Recoil Semi Auto
NETHERLANDS INDIES

MILITARY RIFLES and CARBINES ⅛ ACTUAL SIZE

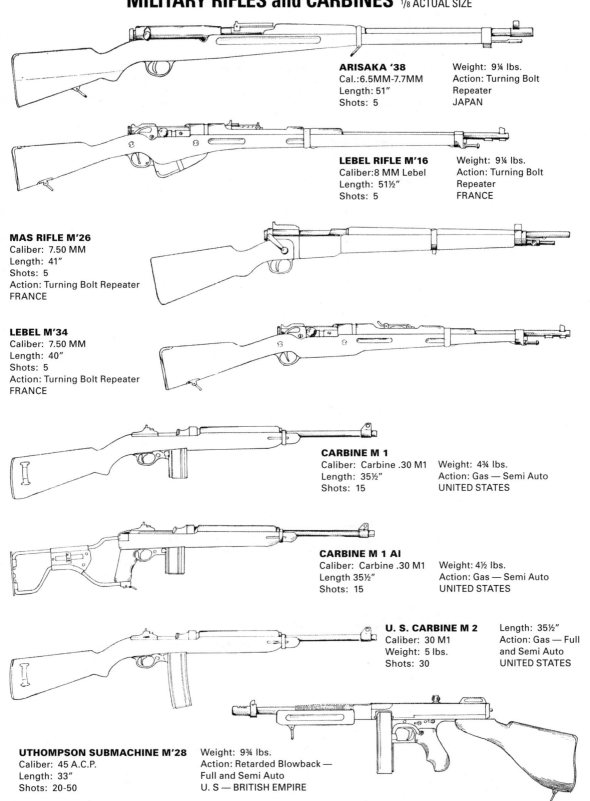

ARISAKA '38
Cal.:6.5MM-7.7MM
Length: 51"
Shots: 5

Weight: 9¼ lbs.
Action: Turning Bolt
Repeater
JAPAN

LEBEL RIFLE M'16
Caliber:8 MM Lebel
Length: 51½"
Shots: 5

Weight: 9¼ lbs.
Action: Turning Bolt
Repeater
FRANCE

MAS RIFLE M'26
Caliber: 7.50 MM
Length: 41"
Shots: 5
Action: Turning Bolt Repeater
FRANCE

LEBEL M'34
Caliber: 7.50 MM
Length: 40"
Shots: 5
Action: Turning Bolt Repeater
FRANCE

CARBINE M 1
Caliber: Carbine .30 M1
Length: 35½"
Shots: 15

Weight: 4¾ lbs.
Action: Gas — Semi Auto
UNITED STATES

CARBINE M 1 AI
Caliber: Carbine .30 M1
Length 35½"
Shots: 15

Weight: 4½ lbs.
Action: Gas — Semi Auto
UNITED STATES

U. S. CARBINE M 2
Caliber: 30 M1
Weight: 5 lbs.
Shots: 30

Length: 35½"
Action: Gas — Full
and Semi Auto
UNITED STATES

UTHOMPSON SUBMACHINE M'28
Caliber: 45 A.C.P.
Length: 33"
Shots: 20-50

Weight: 9¾ lbs.
Action: Retarded Blowback —
Full and Semi Auto
U. S — BRITISH EMPIRE

AMERICAN and ENGLISH SUBMACHINE GUNS ⅛ ACTUAL SIZE

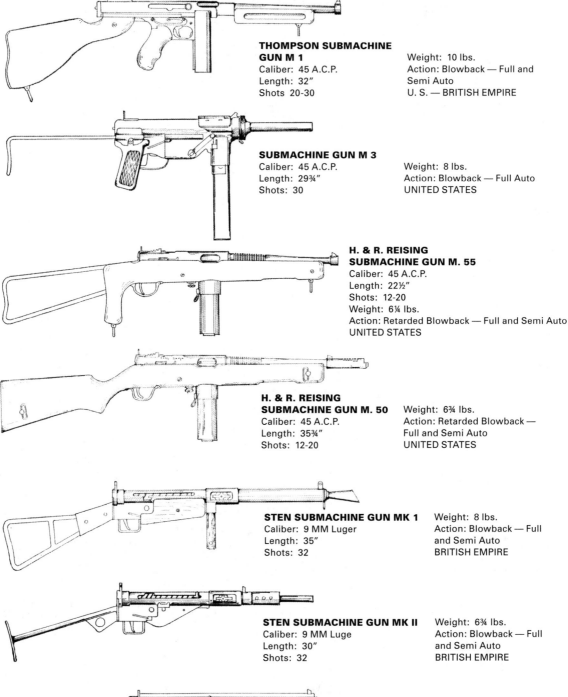

THOMPSON SUBMACHINE GUN M 1
Caliber: 45 A.C.P.
Length: 32"
Shots 20-30
Weight: 10 lbs.
Action: Blowback — Full and Semi Auto
U. S. — BRITISH EMPIRE

SUBMACHINE GUN M 3
Caliber: 45 A.C.P.
Length: 29¾"
Shots: 30
Weight: 8 lbs.
Action: Blowback — Full Auto
UNITED STATES

H. & R. REISING SUBMACHINE GUN M. 55
Caliber: 45 A.C.P.
Length: 22½"
Shots: 12-20
Weight: 6¼ lbs.
Action: Retarded Blowback — Full and Semi Auto
UNITED STATES

H. & R. REISING SUBMACHINE GUN M. 50
Caliber: 45 A.C.P.
Length: 35¾"
Shots: 12-20
Weight: 6¾ lbs.
Action: Retarded Blowback — Full and Semi Auto
UNITED STATES

STEN SUBMACHINE GUN MK 1
Caliber: 9 MM Luger
Length: 35"
Shots: 32
Weight: 8 lbs.
Action: Blowback — Full and Semi Auto
BRITISH EMPIRE

STEN SUBMACHINE GUN MK II
Caliber: 9 MM Luge
Length: 30"
Shots: 32
Weight: 6¾ lbs.
Action: Blowback — Full and Semi Auto
BRITISH EMPIRE

STEN SUBMACHINE GUN MK III
Caliber: 9 MM Luger
Length: 30"
Shots: 32
Weight: 6¾ lbs.
Action: Blowback — Full and Semi Auto
BRITISH EMPIRE

GERMAN SUBMACHINE GUNS ⅛ ACTUAL SIZE

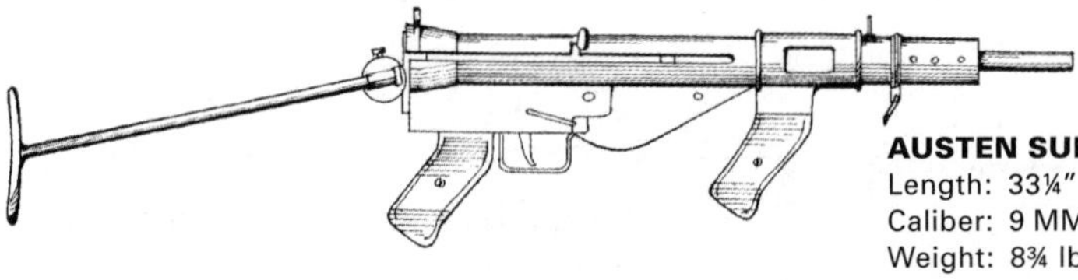

AUSTEN SUBMACHINE GUN
Length: 33¼"
Caliber: 9 MM Luger
Weight: 8¾ lbs.

Shots: 32
Action: Blowback — Full
and Semi Auto
BRITISH EMPIRE

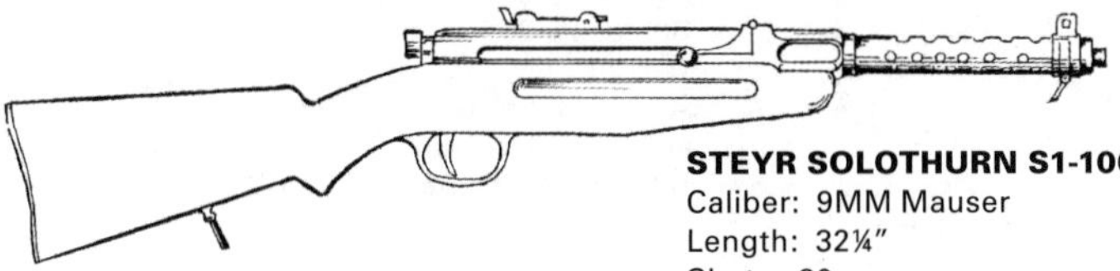

STEYR SOLOTHURN S1-100 SUBMACHINE GUN
Caliber: 9MM Mauser
Length: 32¼"
Shots: 30

Weight: 9⅞ lbs.
Action: Blowback — Full
and Semi Auto
GERMANY

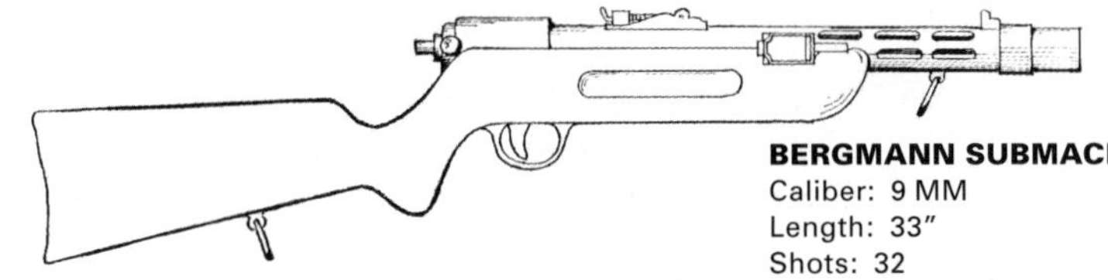

BERGMANN SUBMACHINE GUN M'34
Caliber: 9 MM
Length: 33"
Shots: 32

Weight: 9 lbs.
Action: Blowback — Full
and Semi Auto
GERMANY

SCHMEISSER M'38 SUBMACHINE GUN
Caliber: 9 MM Luger
Length: 35"
Shots: 32
Weight: 9 lbs.
Action: Blowback — Full Auto
GERMANY

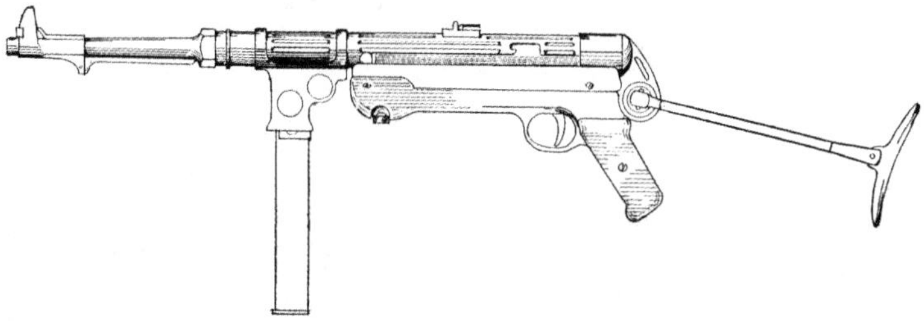

M. P. 43 (KAR 44)
Caliber: 7.92 MM Short
Length: 38"
Shots: 32
Weight: 10½ lbs.
Action: Gas — Full
and Semi Auto
GERMANY

NEUHAUSEN SUBMACHINE GUN
Caliber: 9 MM Luger
Shots: 40
Weight: 9 lbs.
Action: Blowback — Full Auto
GERMANY

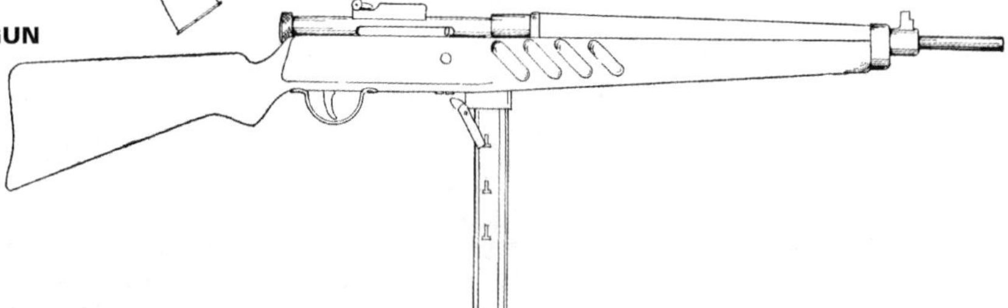

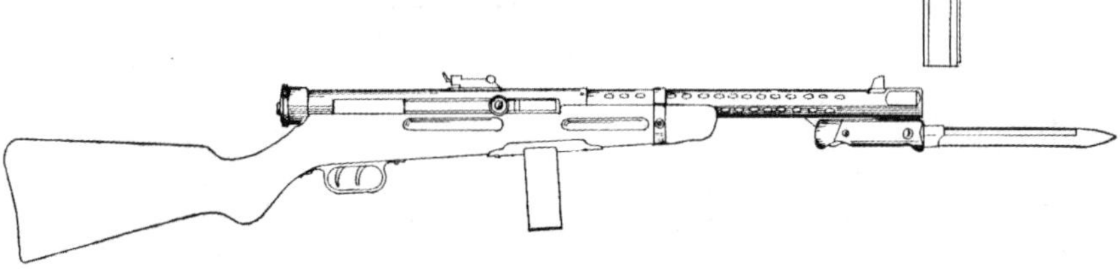

BERETTA SUBMACHINE GUN
Caliber: 9 MM Luger
Shots 10-40
Weight: 9¾ lbs.
Action: Blowback — Full
and Semi Auto
ITALY

LIGHT MACHINE GUNS _{1/8} ACTUAL SIZE

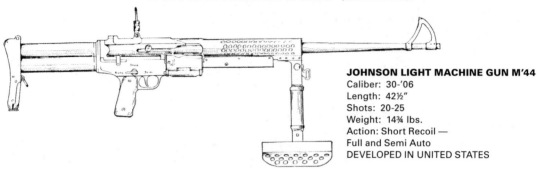

JOHNSON LIGHT MACHINE GUN M'44
Caliber: 30-'06
Length: 42½"
Shots: 20-25
Weight: 14¾ lbs.
Action: Short Recoil —
Full and Semi Auto
DEVELOPED IN UNITED STATES

BREN LIGHT MACHINE GUN
Caliber: .303
Lgth.: 49½"
Shots: 30

Weight: 23 lbs.
Action: Gas — Full
and Semi Auto
BRITISH EMPIRE

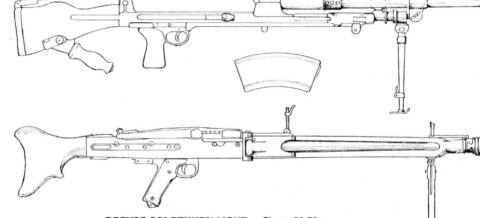

**DREYSE-SOLOTHURN LIGHT
MACHINE GUN M.G. '42**
Caliber: 7.92 MM
Length: 48"

Shots: 50-75
Weight: 25 lbs.
Action: Short Recoil — Full Auto
GERMANY

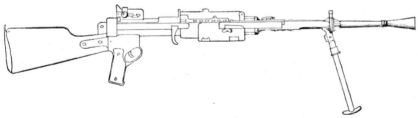

BREDA LIGHT MACHINE GUN
Caliber: 6.50 MM and 7.35MM
Length: 40"
Shots: 20
Weight: 23½ lbs.
Action: Short Recoil — Full Auto
ITALY

DEGTYAROV LIGHT MACHINE GUN
Caliber: 7.62 MM
Length: 50"
Shots: 47

Weight: 18½ lbs.
Action: Gas — Full Auto
RUSSIA

EUROPEAN MILITARY CARTRIDGES ACTUAL SIZE

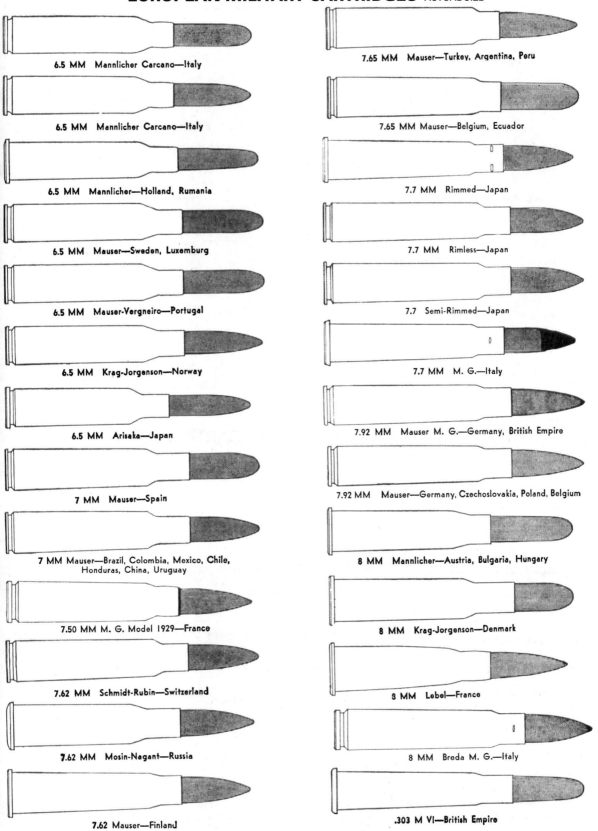

6.5 MM   Mannlicher Carcano—Italy

6.5 MM   Mannlicher Carcano—Italy

6.5 MM   Mannlicher—Holland, Rumania

6.5 MM   Mauser—Sweden, Luxemburg

6.5 MM   Mauser-Vergneiro—Portugal

6.5 MM   Krag-Jorgenson—Norway

6.5 MM   Arisaka—Japan

7 MM   Mauser—Spain

7 MM Mauser—Brazil, Colombia, Mexico, Chile,
Honduras, China, Uruguay

7.50 MM M. G. Model 1929—France

7.62 MM   Schmidt-Rubin—Switzerland

7.62 MM   Mosin-Nagant—Russia

7.62 Mauser—Finland

7.65 MM   Mauser—Turkey, Argentina, Peru

7.65 MM Mauser—Belgium, Ecuador

7.7 MM   Rimmed—Japan

7.7 MM   Rimless—Japan

7.7 Semi-Rimmed—Japan

7.7 MM   M. G.—Italy

7.92 MM   Mauser M. G.—Germany, British Empire

7.92 MM   Mauser—Germany, Czechoslovakia, Poland, Belgium

8 MM   Mannlicher—Austria, Bulgaria, Hungary

8 MM   Krag-Jorgenson—Denmark

8 MM   Lebel—France

8 MM   Breda M. G.—Italy

.303 M VI—British Empire

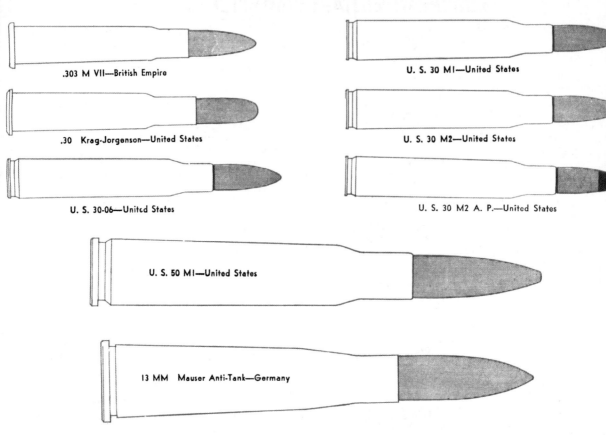

.303 M VII—British Empire

U. S. 30 MI—United States

.30 Krag-Jorgenson—United States

U. S. 30 M2—United States

U. S. 30-06—United States

U. S. 30 M2 A. P.—United States

U. S. 50 MI—United States

13 MM   Mauser Anti-Tank—Germany

MILITARY PISTOL and REVOLVER CARTRIDGES ACTUAL SIZE

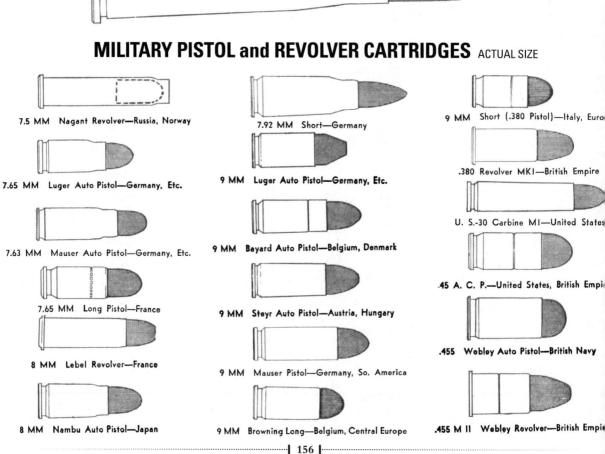

7.5 MM   Nagant Revolver—Russia, Norway

7.92 MM   Short—Germany

9 MM   Short (.380 Pistol)—Italy, Euro

7.65 MM   Luger Auto Pistol—Germany, Etc.

9 MM   Luger Auto Pistol—Germany, Etc.

.380 Revolver MKI—British Empire

7.63 MM   Mauser Auto Pistol—Germany, Etc.

9 MM   Bayard Auto Pistol—Belgium, Denmark

U. S.-30 Carbine MI—United States

7.65 MM   Long Pistol—France

9 MM   Steyr Auto Pistol—Austria, Hungary

.45 A. C. P.—United States, British Empi

8 MM   Lebel Revolver—France

9 MM   Mauser Pistol—Germany, So. America

.455   Webley Auto Pistol—British Navy

8 MM   Nambu Auto Pistol—Japan

9 MM   Browning Long—Belgium, Central Europe

.455 M II   Webley Revolver—British Empi

The 30 Carbine

...smaller than some, but big enough most... ■ David L. Ward

THE 30 M-1 Carbine has been around now for some fifty years. During that time, it has been called any number of nasty things from worthless to impotent. Other diatribes are simply unprintable here. But if the carbine was so utterly useless and totally disliked, why were so many made (in excess of six million — more than any other weapon in WWII) and why has it seen so much use in combat? And most of all, why is it still so popular even in this day of the more sophisticated and more powerful assault rifle?

The answers to those questions lie in plain view for those who wish to look. The M-l Carbine performs very well indeed within the parameters for which it was designed. That's the key. It was designed as a light shoulder weapon to replace the 45 ACP and the submachine gun. At distances inside one hundred yards, it handles that task admirably. It is more powerful and more accurate than the 45. Now before you choke on that, look at the energy figures. From an 18-inch barrel, the 30 Carbine musters more than 1950 fps and 900 foot pounds of energy; the 45 manages a little more than 500 fpe, even if you give it 1000 fps from the Thompson SMG.

There's no contest in the accuracy department, either. My IBM Carbine, manufactured in September of 1943, keeps Military Specifications Ball in six to eight inches at 100 yards with iron sights. Try and match that with your issue 45 pistol or Tommy gun.

It is important to keep the M-1 Carbine in perspective. If you wish to compare it to the M-1 Garand or any semiautomatic rifle, assault or otherwise, it fails miserably. It's underpowered and relatively inaccurate, shooting too light a bullet. And that, I suspect, is most of the problem with the carbine for those who used (or maybe never used) it. It started out on the wrong foot, or they did.

Could it be possible that the U.S. Ordnance

Author and target shot at 50 yards with 1943 IBM Carbine and 110-grain Hornady SP in front of 14.8 grains of IMR 4227. Rifle was capable of respectable accuracy with the right loads.

Department did not provide an adequate explanation of the exact purpose of the carbine for the grunt in the field? I know an inadequate explanation of any topic by our government is hard to fathom, but it could be true. In which case, we begin to see the reason no one could understand why he was issued such a puny toy instead of a Garand. The carbine was never intended to shoot targets at two hundred or three hundred yards, a distance at which many were used, especially in Korea. However, in the up-close-and-personal arena, it offered a lot of controllable firepower and performed as well or better than anything else. Men who fought with them in such a manner generally agree with that statement.

The whole concept that finally emerged as the 30 M-1 Carbine for the U.S. military began after WWI. In the 1920s, both the United States and Germany concluded independently that their main battle cartridges were overly powerful for most combat conditions. The majority of infantry fire-fights occurred at less than two hundred yards, usually much less. A smaller, less powerful round would offer numerous advantages in weight, cost, and accuracy during rapid-fire and still give adequate killing power in most military situations.

Two possible avenues for development were considered at the time: Increase the power of the submachine gun round to lengthen its useful range or shorten the main battle cartridge and chamber it in a smaller automatic rifle. The Germans opted for the latter and by 1934 had a prototype cartridge based on their full-sized 8mm, but with a case only 33mm long. It delivered a 125-grain bullet at 2247 fps from a 16-inch barrel. Called the 7.92 Kurz, it and the rifle that chambered it were the forerunners of all modern assault weapons. The U.S., meanwhile, opted to do nothing because of the logistics and cost of replacing its whole inventory of shoulder weapons. "Use up what we got" — that's what I always say. Progressive thinking.

By 1940, the idea was resurrected in the U.S. However, the Ordnance Department decided to take a step in the direction of a more powerful pistol cartridge to fit into a lightweight carbine rather than drop the recently developed M-1 Garand. What they got is better than the issue pistol and SMG, while smaller and easier to shoot than the full-sized rifle. Looking at how things developed, this probably was the wrong choice, but not necessarily a *bad* choice. The Germans' work on their 7.92 Kurz was kept secret, expecially from

(Right) Loads for the 30 Carbine: Left to right—Mil. Spec. Ball, Speer 100-grain Plinker, Hornady 110-grain SP, Speer 110-grain HP and Sierra 110-grain HP.

(Left) Standard U.S. WWI small arms cartridges and those that were conceived later. Left to right: 30-06, 45 ACP, 30 Carbine, 7.62 NATO and 5.56 NATO.

those who signed the Treaty of Versailles, so the U.S. Ordnance Department was pretty much on its own in the development stages.

Designs were submitted by a number of companies, but the short piston, locked-bolt prototype from Winchester won out and became the Caliber 30 M-1 Carbine as we know it. Winchester based the new cartridge on the obsolete 32 Self-Loading, a nearly worthless semi-rimmed round that sent a 165-grain slug out the barrel at a modest 1450 fps. The bullet was lightened to 100 grains, the pressure bumped, and the velocity consequently increased to 1970 fps from the new rimless case in an 18-inch barrel, a substantial boost in horsepower. The 30 Carbine case measures 32.77mm in length, almost the same as the Kurz, but the smaller diameter and smaller powder capacity force it to give up 300 fps to the German cartridge.

When I asked veterans from WWII or Korea about the performance of the M-1 Carbine in combat, their answers were both interesting and quite similar. Inevitably, the first words out were something like "not worth much" or "didn't kill very well" or, for Korea, "it jammed a lot." But the more they talked, the more they mentioned that for close-in work or night patrols or repelling mass infantry charges it worked pretty well — lots of firepower when you needed it. And at shorter rang-

es, the little bullet knocked 'em down quite regularly, multiple hits being somewhat easier to accomplish with the 30 Carbine than with the 45 ACP for the average GI. As for jamming, everything jams when it's frozen or dirty, or both.

Today, the 30 M-1 Carbine is long since retired, at least from the U.S. military, though I expect it is still getting used as a combat arm in a few out-of-the-way places. You could look at the 30 Carbine as a kind of dead end in the evolution of military small arms, much like the woolly mammoth of the Ice Age. It was a good idea at the time, but something better came along and displaced it.

Today, most of the applications for the 30 Carbine are recreational and, as you'll see, for home or self-defense. Currently, AM AC (formerly Iver Johnson) is the only company manufacturing new 30 Carbines for the commercial market. They bought out the Universal people in the mid-1980s and have all of their equipment and materials. AMAC turns out four to five hundred new carbines a month along with one hundred or so improved and revamped Enforcers, a 10.5-inch barreled semi-automatic pistol formerly produced by Universal. They hope to get a stainless steel carbine with a synthetic stock on the market soon. Great for boats and airplanes.

On the used market, there are a pleth-

Hollowpoints available for 30 Carbine: Speer 110-grain (left), and Sierra 110-grain. Speer offers lots of exposed lead and gaping hollow area, great for home defense or close-in varmints, while the Sierra is ideal for longer-range varmints.

The 45 ACP at left and 30 Carbine, with 41 and 44 magnums to the right. From an 18-inch barrel, the Carbine round is easily more powerful than the 45 and is very close to the revolver magnums when they are fired in a 6-inch barrel.

ora of carbines, often at very good prices. Buyer beware, however, as some have seen rough duty in the past forty or so years. Others have been refurbished at the factory (or armory, which one I have no idea) and might make pretty nice shooters.

Also, there are carbines in very fine shape selling at a collector's price. Some folks are willing to pay a premium price for a particular manufacturer, often for one with the Winchester headstamp. But Rock-Ola made the fewest carbines at 228,500; followed by Standard Products with 247,155; IBM with 346,500; Quality Hardware with 359,662; National Postal Meter 413,017; Underwood Elliot Fisher 545,616; Saginaw 739,136; Winchester up there with 828,059; and Inland Division of General Motors topping out with 2,625,000 carbines of all types. Prices will vary according to condition, obviously.

Prices also will vary according to the model or variation. The M-1A had the paratrooper folding wire stock. An original in fine condition will set you back a substantial amount. M-2s, designed for select-fire, are around but are subject to federal registration and taxation. For a select-fire weapon, however, they aren't overly expensive, but they do confuse the collector values. Also, there is an M-3 variation that was an M-2 with a receiver grooved for an infra-red sniper scope. I've never run across one, but for the right amount of cash, I'm sure they're available.

Of all the makes and models out there, the one thing they have in common is they are all shooters in the most basic sense. That is probably the reason the car-

bine is so popular today: It's fun to shoot and doesn't cost you an arm and a leg to do so. Military Specifications Ball is relatively cheap, as long as you don't burn up several hundred rounds per session.

When I was young, my dad would take my brother and me down to the

Light recoil of the 30 Carbine lets everyone enjoy shooting it. Here, author's wife draws a bead on an unsuspecting tin can.

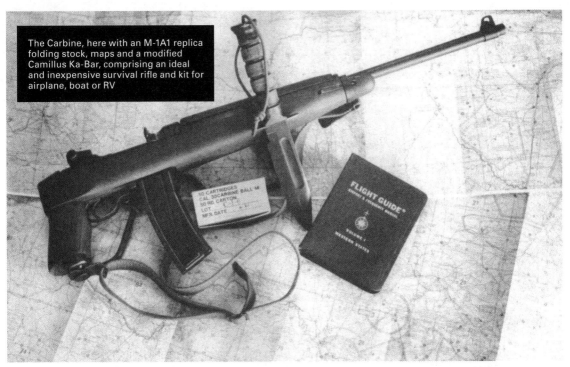

The Carbine, here with an M-1A1 replica folding stock, maps and a modified Camillus Ka-Bar, comprising an ideal and inexpensive survival rifle and kit for airplane, boat or RV

Missouri River outside Kansas City every so often to do some shooting. We'd bang away with the 22s, having lots of fun but always keeping an eye on the stubby bundle wrapped in an oily, old bedsheet. Finally, Dad would take out the carbine (brought back from Guadalcanal, or was it New Britain?) which seemed to us like the most powerful rifle in the world. We got to touch off a few rounds, but ammo was limited then, and we never got to shoot it enough. I decided then that I would have one someday. Finally, after waiting too long, I bought the IBM and have enjoyed it ever since.

These days, nearly every major manufacturer of ammo offers a soft-point load in 30 Carbine. That tells you something about this puny round. A lot of folks use it for a lot of hunting. For shooting small game and varmints, there's no question it is very effective out to around one hundred fifty yards — assuming you have mounted the appropriate sights to allow accurate shooting out that far. And I expect quite a few use it for medium game hunting like deer and black bear-sometimes legal, sometimes not. I understand a number of carbines get toted into the swamps in southern states, looking for bear, alligators, and the like.

And why not? Look at the numbers again. The carbine makes 1900+ fps and 900 + fpe of energy with an expanding bullet. A 44 Magnum in a six-inch barrel is similarly potent, and no one hesitates to hunt deer or bear with a 44 Magnum handgun, do they? So what's the matter with the 30 Carbine? As long as it's legal

for hunting big game where you are, *not one thing*. Just remember to treat it like a long, two-handed pistol and keep your shots less than one hundred yards, preferably less than seventy-five yards. Hunting in the woods or swamp makes that fairly easy.

Legality brings up two points. First, each state has its own set of rules on minimums for big-game hunting with firearms. Here in Colorado, things are divided into two categories for modern arms: rifles and handguns. Within the rifle category, the poor 30 Carbine is eliminated by a requirement of 1000 fps residual energy at one hundred yards. No way. It does, however, meet all other requirements. For handguns, though, if you stuff a 120-grain soft-point into it, then it meets the minimums, since there is no downrange energy requirement. Ironic, eh? In all fairness to the Division of Wildlife, all handgun hunters must qualify at a range under state supervision before they may get a big-game license. Still, they would seem to have things backwards.

The second point concerning legality is the assault rifle classification. A straightforward look at the old carbine would seem to place it right in that category. But that is not always the case. Again in Colorado, and Denver in particular, a law was recently passed banning assault-type rifles. It targets weapons designed for magazines of greater than 20-round capacity. AK-15s, AKs, and Uzis, etc. are out. Mini-14s, Auto-Ordnance Thompson semi-automatics, and carbines are ok. Well, almost. For some reason known

only to the Denver City Council, Plainfield Carbines are not legal. All others are. But the 30-round magazines aren't. Unless you're in the suburbs. Or merely passing through the Denver city limits — with it in a case. Anyway, you had best check with your local police department about the whole thing.

Back to ammunition. If you handload, there is considerable flexibility in the 30 Carbine. Besides the full metal jackets and the softpoints, three other very useful bullets out there will add to the carbine's versatility. The Speer 100-grain Plinker is a round-nose, half-jacket bullet designed for moderate velocities. It can be loaded down to near rimfire speeds and still work the action. Great for rabbits, although so is the Military Specifications full metal jacket stuff. Speer also offers its 110-grain Varminter, which has a round-nose style with lots of lead exposed and a huge hollowpoint. If it feeds in your rifle, it would make an outstanding home-defense bullet in front of 14 or 15 grains of WW 296 or IMR 4227. The third bullet is a 110-grain pointed hollowpoint, ideal for varmints of any persuasion. This last bullet is longer than the round-noses and requires deeper seating, thereby cutting back some on the available powder space. I lost about .5-grain and seated it right on top of the powder. Velocity loss is not bad. This bullet is well worth working up a load or two. It shoots well and definitely damages prairie dogs.

Handloading is pretty straightforward for the 30 Carbine. It headspaces on the case mouth, so there's no crimping allowed. Otherwise, load it just like any straight-walled pistol case. Trim no shorter than 1.286 inches, again because of the headspace. Speaking of trimming, brass is everywhere, some commercial and hordes of G.I. The commercial is a bit lighter with my batch of W-W averaging 69.3 grains and G.I. weighing in at an average of 71.1 grains. It will affect your loads some, so keep an eye on it and don't mix 'em. Also, stick with small-rifle primers; the 30 Carbine pressures are too high for pistol primers.

A number of the faster burning powders work fine for the little 30. The highest velocities come from H110, IMR 4227,296, and 680.I worked with all but the latter and got good results. I don't see any great need to work up a dozen or so loads for your carbine; I ended up with three, all of which shoot about two inches at 50 yards. If you're interested, they are here.

Loaded with expanding bullets, the 30 Carbine will make an excellent home-defense weapon. With a 15- or 30-round magazine, the question of adequate firepower becomes moot. Almost any member of the family can be taught to shoot it well, unlike a handgun of similar power. And unlike a magnum handgun, the light, expanding bullet in a 30 Carbine will lose its momentum more rapidly than a heavy, large-caliber bullet, meaning less penetration should you miss your target — perish the thought! As for the big bullet vs. little bullet controversy, if you don't hit a vital spot, the size or weight of the bullet makes little difference, and the carbine is easier to shoot well than a 44 or 45 ACP.

While on the topic of reloading the 30 Carbine, I should mention that some twenty-five years ago there was considerable interest in wildcatting the little case. Remember, this was before the true assault weapons became so popular or even widely available. Everyone liked the carbine but often found the cartridge disappointing.

Enter Melvin Johnson and son Ed. Melvin developed and marketed the 5.7 MMJ Spitfire, a carbine chambered for a 30 Carbine case necked to 22. It advertised 3000 fps with a 40-grain full-jacketed bullet, which is not too far from M-16 ballistics. The whole thing could be had in

a package with two barrels, one in 30 and one in 22, and at a modest price. Unfortunately, Melvin died as things were getting moving. And according to rumor, his son Ed was killed later in an automobile accident. Either way, the company is out of business, bought out by Plain-field which was bought out by Iver Johnson which was bought out by AM AC. The AM AC people say they could build carbines in 22 or 25 if there was enough demand. On the other hand, how do you know what the demand will be without a rifle to shoot? It's too bad, the rig would have been a dandy. RCBS still offers dies for the 5.7 MMJ, however.

Many others also experimented with necking down the 30 Carbine case. Harold Tucker, of St. Louis, worked with both 22 and 25 calibers. He's out of the business now and was somewhat surprised to have me call and inquire about his work. Apparently, everyone else experimenting with the carbine also has dropped it, since no one I spoke with knew of anyone really working with it. Guy Neil at Hornady has been interested in the 22 version and a 25 version, possibly for silhouette work, but hasn't gotten very far. For everything else, though, modern assault rifles seem to have taken over. Some are about as light and handy, and some are considerably more accurate. Yet the old carbine still has a lot of appeal, and mine is plenty potent and accurate enough for my demands.

Recently, I added a replica of the M-1A1 folding stock to my collection of add-on goodies for the carbine. Although not the answer to a perfect folder, it is well-made (careful, some are not) and makes the carbine even more easily stowable in a car, boat, airplane, or RV. It also just plain looks good. Ram-Line in Wheat Ridge, Colorado, is considering bringing out a synthetic folder for the carbine. If you think that's a good idea, then call 'em and bug 'em about it. While on the topic of stocks, the original on my carbine was quite thick in the area of the grip, just behind the trigger housing. Some judicious wood removal and contouring makes the weapon considerably more comfortable to shoot.

One other use for the old carbine: It may be one of the best outdoor survival rifles around. It's light; the ammo is light;

M-1A folding stock turns the 30 Carbine into a compact rifle for boat, trail or RV, or just for a walk around the place.

and it's adequately powerful with soft-points for harvesting food up to the deer class, should you need to. With the folding stock, it is quite compact — measuring about 26 inches folded. Such modest weight and dimensions take up little space in an RV boat, or airplane.

So it seems that there are a number of uses today for a rifle and cartridge designed fifty years ago. Just remem ber to look at the 30 M-l Carbine as a powerful pistol, not as a wimpy rifle. You'll be much happier with it.

HANDLOADING YOUR M-1 CARBINE

Use	Bullet Gr. Wgt.	Type	Powder Type	Grains	MV (fps)
Small Game	100	Speer Plinker	4227	13.8	1756
Varmints	100	Sierra Hollowpoint	H110	13.5	1842
Home Defense	100	Hornady Softpoint	4227	14.8	1923

World War II's Snipers and Sniper Rifles

■ Konrad F. Schreier, Jr.

THERE ARE MANY stories about the various exploits of U.S. Army and Marine Corps snipers of World War II. A surprising number of them are true.

This is remarkable since there were relatively few of these precision combat riflemen. The U.S. armed forces' attitude toward the special skill was that, while unquestionably a useful combat skill, sniping was nowhere near as important as others ranging from leadership to the ability to carry out orders quickly and effectively.

In World War II, the basic requirement of the Army and Marine Corps was for as many "average" riflemen as they could train, and there was little time available for the extensive marksmanship training required by snipers. Adequate sniper rifles were provided, however, and the riflemen who used them were usually those who had shown superior marksmanship skills during regular training. This situation had been true as long as there had been soldiers and Marines. In the Revolutionary War, skilled American riflemen took their toll of the enemy. In the Civil War, Col. Hiram Berdan organized a U.S. Volunteer Regiment, the "Corps of Rifle Sharpshooters," whose marksmanship was feared and respected by the enemy.

In the 1898 Spanish-American War, U.S. Army sharpshooters did some very effective sniping. They did it with the Army-issue 30-caliber Krag rifle or, in a

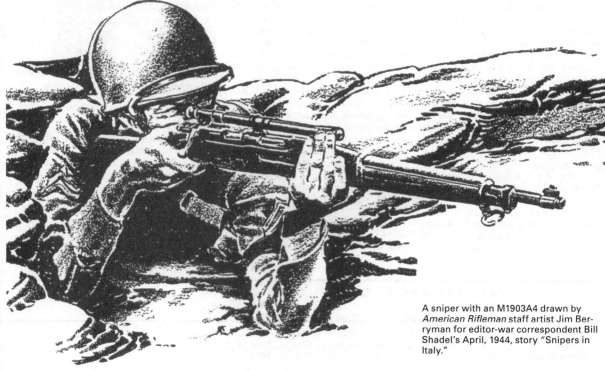

A sniper with an M1903A4 drawn by *American Rifleman* staff artist Jim Berryman for editor-war correspondent Bill Shadel's April, 1944, story "Snipers in Italy."

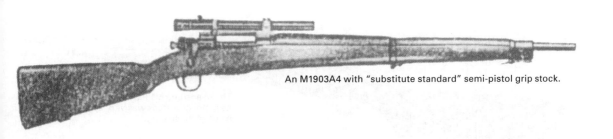

An M1903A4 with "substitute standard" semi-pistol grip stock.

few cases, with civilian target rifles firing the standard Krag ammunition. By this time, Army rifle marksmanship training had been much improved, but there was no such thing as special sniper training.

When the Army adopted the caliber 30 Rifle Model of 1903, the 30-06 Springfield, it proved to be very accurate, and the "Telescopic Musket Sight Model of 1908" was developed for "sharpshooting" with it. Although this sight was later improved and then re-issued as the Model of 1913, it was a primitive periscopic rifle design. It did, however, improve the ability of sharpshooters to hit targets at longer ranges than with the rifle's regular iron sights.

U.S. Army General Orders 23 of 1909 authorized the issue of two Model of 1903 rifles with telescopic musket sights per infantry company, and this order remained in effect through World War II! These rifles were to be issued to soldiers who made the highest scores in training exercises, but no special training regulations for their use were ever published. Unit commanders could decline the issue of these scoped rifles if they felt their unit's assignment would not require them, and this also held true through World War II!

Records indicate that by the end of World War I, at least 1550 Model of 1908 and 5041 Model of 1913 Telescopic Musket sights had been procured. They saw service with U.S. Army units in France in World War I. Unfortunately, their vulnerability to the dirt and moisture conditions of World War I trench warfare severely limited their combat use.

The Army adopted the term "sniping" from the British in World War I, and it was a very important element of the trench warfare tactics of that war. However, in actual World War I combat, most sniping was done by the units' most proficient riflemen using standard-issue iron-sighted rifles. The ranges were short, less than a dozen yards to no more than a couple hundred yards. A sniper had to be an expert marksman who could make the best use of camouflage, cover and con-

cealment. Although they were used, telescopic sights were not required for that.

During World War I, the Army found the two-man sniper team was the most effective. While one man did the shooting, the other was the observer who located targets. Both had to be proficient marksmen since they traded roles. Sniper teams were also expected to observe enemy activities. This was the beginning of the scout-sniper teams much used in World War II and since.

During World War I, troop dissatisfaction with the old Model of 1908 and Model of 1913 scope sights caused the Army to procure some 5000 commercial Winchester A5 scopes to replace them. These were also 6x and mounted on '03 Springfields with standard commercial mounts. The Winchester A5 remained in the inventory until early World War II, but it never satisfactorily met the military requirement for resistance to moisture and dirt.

In the early 1920s, Army Ordnance did some experimenting with sniper sights. While none was adopted, the work led the way to the development of much improved commercial telescopic sights.

Improved commercial scopes led to long-range target shooting with military-caliber rifles. All through the 1920s and 1930s, long-range matches were popular among both civilian and military riflemen, and they were a major event at the Camp Perry National Matches and at many other rifle events.

Although the armed forces had no standard sniper rifle at the time, the following training regulations for snipers were published in 1940:

19. Snipers a. *Purpose and use. Snipers are expert riflemen stationed in the forward areas of a defensive position for the purpose of firing on enemy soldiers who expose themselves. Specifically, their duties are: (1) to fire on enemy scouts or patrols who attempt to approach or observe the positions; (2) to protect observers and sentinels by firing at hostile snipers who are firing at them; (3) in case of attack by the*

enemy; (a) to fire on the leaders of the attack, thus compelling deployment at long range and possibly delaying it; (b) to fire on individuals who are especially active in filtering to the front, and also upon machine gunners. In the attack, when the platoon halts for any purpose, as for example to reorganize following a successful assault, snipers are placed in favorable locations to the front and flanks in order to prevent hostile reconnaissance and delay counterattacks. When a force withdraws from a battle front snipers are usually left in position in order to keep back hostile scouts or patrols. Snipers operate in pairs when sufficient men are available, and scouts are habitually employed and trained for this duty.

b. The sniper's post; location; concealment. *(1) Sniper's posts or nests are generally located in the same terrain as advanced observation points. In fact sniping and observation posts are sometimes combined, and snipers always observe and report what they see. Usually, the observation posts proper occupy the highest ground favorable for observation, while the sniper's posts are on somewhat lower ground, more favorable for fire. Sniper's posts are, in general, similar to small observation posts.*

(2) Temporary posts may be located in trees (preferably trees with plenty of foliage), behind rocks, stumps, hedges or bushes, or in shell holes. More permanent posts are dug into the ground, camouflaged, and provided with overhead cover.

(3) When a sniper's post is manned by a single individual, he performs the duties of both observer and sniper. When there are two men, one acts as observer and the other as sniper.

c. Organizing the sector. *As soon as the post is occupied the scouts proceed to organize their sector.*

d. Duties of the rifleman. *The scout acting as sniper must be able to fire quickly and accurately on moving or still targets. As the sniper fires, the observer watches the effect. Long-range sniping may be carried on with rifles equipped with telescopic sights.*

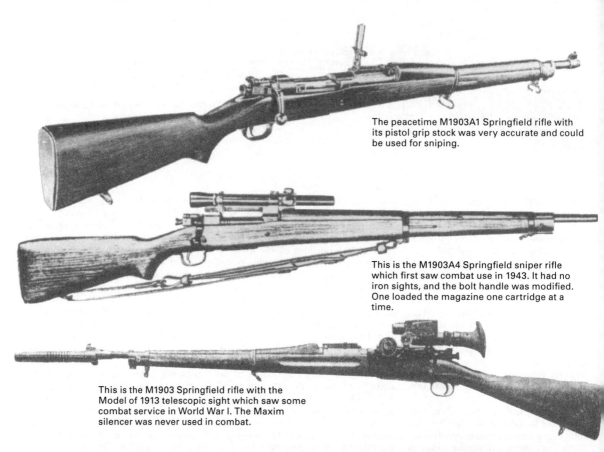

The peacetime M1903A1 Springfield rifle with its pistol grip stock was very accurate and could be used for sniping.

This is the M1903A4 Springfield sniper rifle which first saw combat use in 1943. It had no iron sights, and the bolt handle was modified. One loaded the magazine one cartridge at a time.

This is the M1903 Springfield rifle with the Model of 1913 telescopic sight which saw some combat service in World War I. The Maxim silencer was never used in combat.

20. Platoon Scouts. *Each rifle squad includes two men designated as scouts. These men should be good rifle shots, especially trained in the use of cover and concealment, in movements, and in the methods taught in this chapter. At least one, and preferably both, should be equipped with compasses. Both are equipped with tracer ammunition for designating targets.*

While this training regulation mentions the use of rifles with telescopic sights, it was basically intended for sniping with standard iron-sighted guns. However, at the time, the Army often issued the most accurate available issue rifle to riflemen designated as scout-snipers. These could be peacetime '03 Springfields in the "National Match target grade" or the beautifully made M1903A1 Springfield which had a special pistol grip stock and alloy steel action. These were standard issue with iron sights, but capable of superior accuracy.

World War II regulations recognized that the maximum range at which any rifleman could expect to hit a man-size target with any '03 Springfield rifle was about 600 yards. They also recognized that the longer the range, the harder it was to find a man-size target, let alone hit it. In

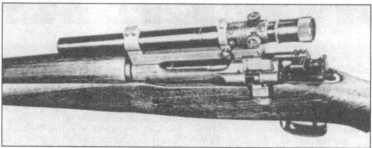

This is the Weaver 330C mounted on the M1903A4 — a sniper mainstay in service.

combat, it was found the longest range at which a rifleman could find and hit man-size targets regularly was 300 to 400 yards. This would become a principal reason the U.S. armed forces adopted scoped sniper rifles in World War II.

Another problem that combat riflemen had was estimating the range to a man-sized target so they could set their iron sights for maximum accuracy at ranges past a couple of hundred yards. Training targets were shot at known ranges, but combat riflemen had to estimate the distance by eye, with no instruments or range-finders to help them.

World War II riflemen received train-ing in range estimation by eye. The scout-snipers had to be experts at this task, and some received considerable training.

There was no standard-issue telescopic-sighted sniper rifle in the U.S. armed forces when we entered World War II. During the 1930s, practically every Army and Marine Corps regular, reserve or National Guard unit had a rifle team. These teams regularly had scope-sighted '03 Spring-fields privately purchased for use in matches, and these often went into combat with the units and riflemen who had them.

The most popular of these were match-grade '03s with commercial 6X to

Pre-World War II rifle marksmanship training included this prone sandbag rest position recommended for sniping and/or long-range accurate firing.

This 1943 ad shows a Winchester Model 70 target rifle with a high-power telescopic sight. Many such became sniper rifles used in combat.

UNERTL TARGET SCOPES

To Shooter Friends, Unertl Optical Co. wishes to advise that for the duration of the National Emergency they cannot furnish target scopes but hope that their friends will keep in contact by writing for Free Booklet.

3551-3555 East St.　　J. UNERTL OPTICAL CO.　　Pittsburgh (14), Pa.

This Weaver ad featuring their telescopic sight for the M1903A4 Springfield sniper rifle appeared in 1943 magazines.

Here's where your Weaver Scope has gone!

This official Signal Corps photo shows Pfc. Edward J. Foley, American sniper with the 36th Division in Italy, checking his rifle before going up to the front. The telescope sight is a Weaver 330.

★ ★ Maybe you've been wanting a Weaver Scope, and couldn't find one. Well, this is the answer. Your scope is on a fighting front somewhere in the world, helping American snipers to do a better job. The sniper has a tricky job on his hands — not only because he has to maneuver into position to get a long range shot, but because his "game" can shoot back! Surely he deserves the best there is!

The WEAVER SCOPE

Still in stock at most dealers; If you don't find the model you want, write us.

The WEAVER-CHOKE

Six interchangeable choke tubes make your shotgun an all-purpose gun, everything from skeet to long range ducks.

$9.75

Complete with any 2 choke tubes

WEAVER

Scopes and Chokes

Made in El Paso, Texas by W. R. WEAVER CO.

8X sights in commercial mounts. These found limited combat use throughout World War II, though they were never officially adopted.

Another popular prewar rifle, particularly in the U.S. Marine Corps, was the Winchester Model 70 30-06 target rifle. Most such had sights in the 6X to 8X range, though some had 10x or even more powerful. This was a superb outfit for long ranges. It wasn't officially adopted until after World War II, and a number of them were purchased and remained in use until the Vietnam War!

As soon as the U.S. forces were committed to ground combat in World War II, urgent requests for scoped sniper rifles were submitted from the field. Ordnance immediately tested '03 Springfields with commercial 2.5X sights. The reason the 2.5X types were selected for testing is they seemed best for the sniping ranges up to 600 or so yards, which tactically proved best in combat.

By the fall of 1942, Ordnance selected peacetime Springfield '03s or '03Als with a 2.2X Weaver sight in Redfield Junior mounts. The rifle had its regular iron sights removed and the bolt handle bent to clear the scope. While a few of these were assembled and issued, it was impossible to locate enough selected '03s to build enough sniper rifles to meet the ever-increasing requirement.

Ordnance turned to Remington, who was manufacturing the '03A3 Springfield, and had them equip it with the same Weaver 330 telescopic sight in Redfield

Junior mounts, with the bolt handle bent to clear the scope. The Springfield's regular iron sights were omitted, and either a full-or semi-pistol grip stock was used. The Army adopted this as the Cal. 30 Rifle M1903A4 (Sniper's); the scope was designated the Telescopic Rifle Sight M73 in December, 1942, and it was immediately put in production. The model was first issued to troops in early 1943.

Some 30,000 '03A4 Springfield sniper rifles were built during World War II. They have been frequently criticized by many people. The rough wartime finish and stamped metal parts did not satisfy many riflemen who expected a sniper rifle to have the precision finish and look of a commercial long-range target rifle, but the gun's performance in combat was satisfactory.

U.S. Army records show that the '03A4 Springfield performed as well or better than any other World War II military-issue sniper rifle. An "as issued" '03A4 with its telescopic sight properly zeroed was deadly accurate at ranges out to at least 400 yards. When given a gunsmith-style, target-shooter's fine-tuning, it could shoot very well out to 600 yards and farther, and many gunsmiths who had joined the Army Ordnance Department worked them over. There are records of '03A4 sniper Springfields making effective shots at ranges as long as 1000 yards. This, however, required perfect light and weather conditions.

The '03A4 Springfield remained sniper standard in the U.S. armed forces until the change to 7.62mm NATO-caliber rifles in the late 1950s. They remained in "war reserve" until some were used in the Vietnam War, and there may still be some stored.

At the time the '03A4 sniper Springfield was being developed, the Army Ground Forces Command issued a request for a study of a sniper rifle based on the M-1 Garand. A series of experimental prototypes were built and tested in 1943, but the availability and combat performance of the '03A4 Springfield made this a low-priority project for Ordnance.

This testing did establish several characteristics an M-l sniper rifle would need to have. One was that the telescopic sight would have to be offset to the left so the Garand's regular iron sights could be used, and so it could be clip-loaded in the usual manner. To do this, a buttstock cheekrest would be required.

The Army adopted two M-l Garand sniper rifles in mid 1944. The experimental M-1E7 version was adopted as the

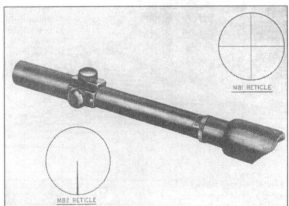

M81 and M82 2.2x sights for the Garand M-1C and M-1D sniper rifles. The M84 with a different reticle was adopted too late to see combat.

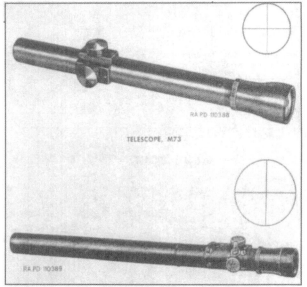

At top is the Lyman Alaskan 2.2X designated the M73; the bottom is the Weaver 330C 2.2X designated the M73B1. The Weaver was the model most commonly issued with the M1903A4 Springfield sniper rifle.

Cal. 30 Rifle M-1C (Sniper's) and went into production at Springfield Armory. It used a Griffin & Howe commercial scope mount on the left side of the rifle's receiver, which would suit any of the several models of standard 2.5X scopes then available.

The M-1C Sniper Garand was the model which first reached troops in World War II. They were some of the best M-l Garands that Springfield Armory produced and were carefully selected for the modification. Unfortunately, they lacked the accuracy beyond 500 yards that snipers wanted. Garand accuracy was adversely affected by its muzzle-mounted gas cylinder and its multi-piece stock. Some 8,000

M-1C Garand sniper rifles had been built by the end of World War II.

The second sniper M-1 was designed by Springfield Armory to eliminate the need for the threaded holes in the left side of the receiver required by the M-1C model. Designated the Cal. 30 Rifle M-1D (Sniper's), its scope mount attached to the left side of the breech end of the rifle's barrel. A number of M-1D Garand sniper rifles were issued to troops and used in combat in the last months of World War II.

By the end of the war, the U.S. Army had adopted five sniper rifle scopes which could be used interchangeably on any sniper rifle. The M73 was the original

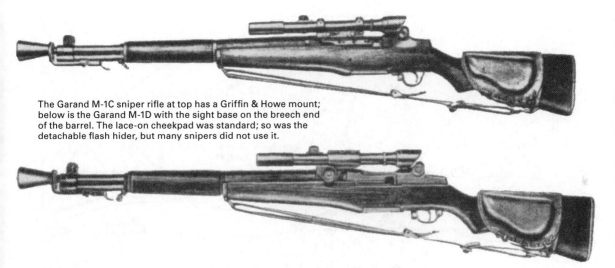

The Garand M-1C sniper rifle at top has a Griffin & Howe mount; below is the Garand M-1D with the sight base on the breech end of the barrel. The lace-on cheekpad was standard; so was the detachable flash hider, but many snipers did not use it.

model, and it was used on most of the '03A4 Springfields. The M73B1, a commercial 2.2x Lyman Alaskan, was adopted as an alternate standard for the M73, but it saw little combat use.

The M81, M82 and M84 scopes were all special models designed to have better resistance to dirt and moisture. The Army described them as 2.5X scopes, but they were all actually 2.2X. During World War II, these sights were mostly assembled on the M-1C and M-1D Garand sniper rifles, and they, along with the M73 and M73B1 scopes, remained in use long after the end of the war.

No matter what kind of sniper rifle a World War II GI or Marine had, he always had problems finding accurate ammunition for it. Many trained with the superbly accurate match target ammunition the Army Ordnance Department had been providing since 1908. However, under wartime or combat conditions, there was no way the Service of Supply could distribute this special ammunition to combat troops with any assurance it would reach the snipers who could use it. The quanities of 30-caliber rifle ammunition in the supply lines were just too vast. Even so, some units departing for combat from the United States did manage to take supplies of this special target-grade ammunition along for their snipers.

Another way World War II Army and Marine Corps snipers found the accurate ammunition they wanted sounds impractical, but it was done. The huge amount of ammo was made in batches known as "lots," some of which had superior accuracy to others. In fact, some of the match target ammunition the Ordnance Department provided was simply the result

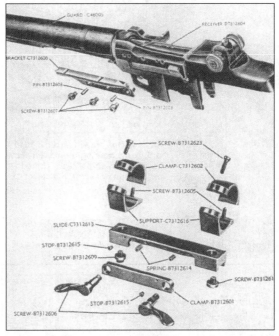

The Griffin & Howe side mount for the M-1C was pretty complex.

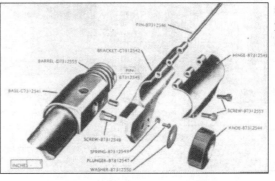

Springfield Armory's mount for the M-1D was hardly simpler.

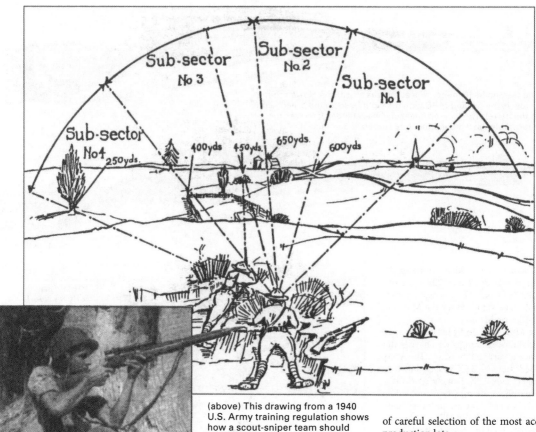

(above) This drawing from a 1940 U.S. Army training regulation shows how a scout-sniper team should organize their sector and select its probable targets.

(left) A Marine Corps sniper in the Pacific with an M1903A4 Springfield. (U.S. Marine Corps photo)

of careful selection of the most accurate production lots.

Snipers could, and did, testfire ammunition from the many lots available in their supplies to find the one which had the best accuracy. Then they would draw a supply of that lot to meet their needs. This was another unauthorized but effective procedure.

After World War II, the effectiveness of Army and Marine Corps snipers was well recognized, but ignored. An unsigned article in the February-March issue of *Army Ordnance* magazine was titled: "Sniping — A Neglected Art." Snipers were among the most resourceful, determined soldiers in the U.S. armed forces, but they seldom received recognition. However, they did get the rifles they needed.

This drawing from a pre-World War II training regulation shows how to set up a training range for eye range estimation. Their use declined when replacement training had to be accelerated, but they always existed at World War II training facilities.

Guns of Vietnam

A lot of years have passed since Korea and WW II — and many more since the Big War. So many that veterans of those bloody affairs would have a hard time recognizing the weapons now serving in Vietnam. Here's a look at most of them. ∎ Col. Jim Crossman

For Vietnam use, even the bayonet has been changed.

T HE WHITE-HAIRED old gentleman sank into the chair and unbuttoned the choker collar of his worn tunic with a sigh of relief. As he leaned down to unwrap his roll leggings, he said ruefully, "This uniform doesn't seem as comfortable as it was back in the Big War. Something has changed! Which is why I'm here — I had special arrangements made so I could come down here and watch you fellows train and see if there has been any change in the weapons since I was fighting. I brought my young friend here along to see what he could learn."

The "young friend" patted his bulging "Ike jacket." "Don't stand in front of me," he said, "I seem to have put on a little weight recently and I'm afraid one of these buttons will pop off and hurt you! Now I don't expect to see anything new, because

it really wasn't so very long ago when I was in World War Two — less than 25 years ago when I was drafted."

The young man in the green beret nodded respectfully. "Fine, gentlemen, we're glad to have you here and to show you our weapons. I'll try to relate them to the things you knew, but I may miss, because I wasn't born when you were fighting World War II, and my folks hadn't been born when you, sir, were fighting your Big War in 1917! We won't have time to get into all the weapons this afternoon, so we'll skip the artillery and tanks and start right out with something I think you'll recognize."

As he laid the 45 pistol on the table in front of him, delighted smiles of recognition broke out on the faces of the two veterans. John Browning's design has been with us since about 1911. Not

that we couldn't make something lighter than that 2½-lb. beauty, and not that we couldn't go to a more modern cartridge than the 45 Auto, with its 220-gr. bullet at 830 feet per second. In fact, we had agreed with the British and Canadians that we would change to the 9mm cartridge if we changed pistols. But the cost of replacing existing guns with something better seemed to be much greater than the benefit to be gained. The pistol is considered a badge of authority and an emergency weapon, not really a basic combat weapon, so it looks as if Mr. Browning's 45 will be with us for a long time — until something remarkably better comes along.

Another gun the old timers will recognize is also a John Browning design — the 50-cal. M2 machine gun. Although not developed until after WW I, the mechanism follows the same scheme as the 30 cal. M1917, of which we made over 40,000 in 1918. In addition to the M1917A1 — water-cooled — we used the Browning M1919A4 and M1919A6 30-cal. guns in WW II, both air-cooled versions of the older gun. The M1919 gun was most recently used in tanks, although with the change to the 7.62mm cartridge they're probably pretty well gone. But the 50-cal. still goes merrily along as secondary armament — primarily anti-aircraft — on tanks, armored personnel carriers and other vehicles. The 50 cartridge looks like a big '06, and feels like a real big one, with the 660-gr. bullet at a velocity of 2900 fps. The gun is proportionately big, weighing around 82 lbs. without mount.

These are about the only two old-timers left. You'll recall that even between WW I and the end of WW II we had a lot of guns replaced or new weapons introduced — including the M1 rifle, the Thompson submachine gun, the M3 "grease gun," the 2.3" bazooka, the 57mm and 75mm recoilless rifles, the tubular rifle grenade, the 60mm mortar, 37mm, 57mm and other anti-tank guns and many others.

While there was a major change between the two "Big Wars," there has been even more change in the past 20 years and

The 4.2" mortar, unusual in that it has a rifled barrel, started life as a chemical mortar, with HE shells became a popular Infantry support weapon during WW II, still serves in that role.

our ground troops in Viet Nam are using many new weapons — their first use in anger. Unless you have been following these developments carefully, you may well be surprised at the assortment of new weapons.

The New Weapons

Now that we have gotten the venerable Browning guns out of the way, we can move on to some of the interesting new things. A good way to start is by trying to sort out the rather confusing rifle picture. The fine M14 rifle was developed after WW II, as a result of combat experience. It is patterned after the basic and successful M1 rifle mechanism, but with a better gas system and other improvements for more reliability. It weighs about a pound less than the M1, has a 20-round detachable box magazine, selective semi- or full-automatic fire, and represents a considerable net gain over the M1. It is chambered for the 7.62mm (30-cal.) cartridge, which is shorter and lighter than the 30-06 cartridge, although having the same power — 150-gr. bullet at 2800 fps. This was adopted by many nations as the 7.62mm NATO cartridge.

In the original plan, another rifle, the M15, was to move into the spot which had been held by the Browning Automatic Rifle — the respected old BAR of WW I and II. The M15 was merely the M14 action with a heavy barrel and other minor changes to make it a good, bipod-mounted, sustained-fire rifle. Weighing more than the M14, it still hefted many pounds less than the BAR, and was to serve as the squad base of fire. Unfortunately, it was killed before it ever got in production. It came as no surprise to some of us when, a few years later, it was found that the light M14 couldn't handle the sustained-fire role. The M14E2 has now been devised to handle this job, and some 8000 have recently been made. Essentially it is the M14 action and barrel with a straight line stock, muzzle stabilizer, modified bipod, long sling and a few other changes. Weight has gone up to nearly 13 lbs., but the M14E2 is much more effective in the sustained fire role.

The Air Force was concerned with a defensive weapon for protecting air fields. They didn't need the power of the M14 but were not too happy with the 30-cal. M1 carbine. Finally they settled on the commercial AR15 rifle, which was developed by Armalite and is being made by Colt. Some AR15s were used experimentally in Viet Nam, and suddenly caught the popular fancy partly through their recognized virtues, but mostly because of some grossly exaggerated and inaccurate reporting. After a series of tests, the Army adopted the rifle for certain units

where weight was a major factor. While the Air Force bought the rifle pretty much off-the-shelf, the Army requested some changes to meet their tougher requirements, thus the Army version is known as the XM16E1, while the Air Force model is the M16.

Both, of course, shoot the 5.56mm cartridge. In civilian clothes this is known as the 223 Remington, a slightly larger edition of the 222 Remington. With a 50- or 55-gr. bullet at 3200–3300 fps, the 222 (and the 222 Remington Mag.) is well-known by varmint hunters and bench rest shooters. The 5.56mm cartridge is much smaller and lighter than the 7.62mm, so more of them can be carried in a given weight. Since the muzzle energy is about 50% of the 7.62, the rifle can be made lighter and is easier to handle in full automatic fire. Additional rifles have been ordered for use in Vietnam, so it is apparently proving popular, as would be expected, since it is short, light, compact and easy to shoot. The more powerful M14 is also making a good name for itself and is being used by the Marines and some Army units.

The ground machine gun role is being adequately filled by the M60 air-cooled gun, which was developed as part of the 7.62mm family. With a weight of 23 pounds, a quick-change barrel and the good cut-off gas expansion system, it apparently is doing very well. Using a metallic link belt, it fires from the open bolt position, and will handle the ball, tracer and all the other 7.62mm cartridges, a rate of fire of around 600 rounds per minute. With the sights and some other unnecessary parts removed, the M60C becomes helicopter armament, about which more later.

The M73 and M85 machine guns were the first we've had specially designed for tank use. Both (the M73 in 7.62mm, and the M85 in 50-cal.) have short receivers and are easier to use inside the tank. Both use push-through type metallic-link belts

The 45 ACP — still used by U.S. fighting men.

The Davy Crockett, a big recoilless rocket designed to give the Infantry nuclear capability. So far it has been used with high explosive shells.

and shoot the usual variety of cartridges. They're usually used only in tanks.

The WWII 30-cal. carbine was designed to largely replace the pistol for personal protection. Unfortunately it looked like a rifle and was used as a rifle — but it just didn't have the stuff. It acquired a bad reputation in some circles and was replaced by the M14 in the changeover. The 45 caliber submachine gun — originally the Thompson but later replaced by the M3 "grease gun" — was also mostly replaced by the M14, with its full-auto fire capability.

Sniper Rifles

We're in the same position right now as we were at the start of each World War as far as a sniper rifle is concerned — we don't have one. We used the Warner and Swasey low-magnification prismatic scope on the WWI Springfield, a low-power hunting scope on the WWII Springfield (which became the M1903A4), and finally a low-power scope on the M1 rifle — the M1C or M1D. These have all been dropped, in line with the usual Army custom of paying little attention to sniping. But according to the reports, the Marines brought over a batch of Winchester 30-06 M70 target rifles and target scopes, set up a sniper school and then proceeded to show they could make hits at long range. They've decided to go to the Remington 40X in 7.62mm with one of the good variable-power varmint type scopes mounted on it. This oughta teach the VC to keep out of sight!

When the Swiss inventor Mohaupt presented the U.S. with the shaped charge in 1940, this was a real revolution in armor piercing ammunition. This development was based on the Neumann-Monroe principle of "focusing" an explo-

sive charge to give great penetration in steel. While this was an old principle, no one really knew what to do with it until Mohaupt came along. Prior to that time, armor penetration was based on a big projectile at high velocity — the bigger and faster the better. But with the shaped charge, it was merely necessary to put the charge against the plate anyway you could and velocity did not matter. It had one disadvantage — penetration was greatly reduced if the projectile was rotated. We used the 2.36" rocket launcher with a shaped charge in WWII, but swapped it for the 3.5" launcher during the Korea shooting. The Army has now dropped this, but the Marines are using it effectively. In addition to having something like 12 inches of armor penetration, it is a good antipersonnel and anti-materiel weapon. The 12-lb. shoulder-fired launcher shoots a 7½-lb. rocket at a velocity near 500 fps, to a range of about 1300 yards.

The Army is using the M72 LAW — Light Anti-tank Weapon — for anti-tank use, not that there has been much urgent need for this in Vietnam. The LAW is a rocket weapon, with the projectile being fired from its collapsible carrying case, which is a throw-away. In the collapsed position, this 66mm launcher is short and compact, and the assembly weighs only 4½ lbs. When the tube is extended, it provides a guide for the rocket and protection for the shooter. Sights and firing mechanism come into use in the extended position.

One of the remarkable developments of WWII was the recoilless rifle. First used in the shoulder-fired 57mm and followed by the bigger and heavier 75mm, the recoilless principle went back to the crude Davis gun of WW I. By letting gas

blast out of ports in the back end of the rifle, heavy projectiles could be fired at fair velocity with no recoil. Rockets had the same virtue, but at that time were very inaccurate. As rocket accuracy increases, they may well take over the role of the recoilless rifle, since the rocket launcher can be made considerably lighter.

The 57mm and 75mm recoilless rifles, and a later 105mm size, have been dropped, leaving two in use. The 90mm M67 rifle fires a fin-stabilized HEAT (High Explosive Anti-Tank) round at a velocity of 700 fps. The 35-lb. weight of the rifle makes it a bit on the heavy side, but like all recoilless rifles, it puts rifle accuracy and cannon power on a man's shoulder.

The other recoilless rifle being used in Vietnam is the 106mm M40 type, a very powerful weapon designed for anti-tank use but formidable against any target. Normally mounted on a jeep, the 106 can be man-carried for short distances, although its 288 lbs. get tiresome pretty quickly. It fires a HEAT round capable of penetrating a foot-and-a-half of armor, at the respectable velocity of over 1600 fps. It carries a coaxially mounted 50-cal. semiauto rifle, which fires a cartridge with a moderate velocity bullet whose trajectory closely matches that of the big projectile. The gunner ranges and determines lead on moving targets with the 50 cal. spotting rifle and promptly switches to the big gun for a first round hit — the very best kind of hit!

A light, fast, tracked vehicle was designed to carry 6 of these rifles and to be a very mobile and very dangerous anti-tank weapon. The Marines adopted and are using this "Ontos," but the Army hasn't so far.

New/Old Mortars

While the veteran of 1917 might have trouble believing the recoilless rifles, he wouldn't have a bit of trouble with the 81mm mortar. Some improvements in metallurgy, in ballistics and in operating details are about the only changes. The present M29 mortar weighs less than 100 pounds with the new lightweight, corrugated tube, the new bipod and the light metal baseplate. Accuracy has improved and range has been increased to around 4000 yards, with the 9-lb. shell, which gets a velocity of nearly 800 fps.

Where we started out adopting the 3", 4" and 6" Stokes mortars from the British and the 240mm (10") job from the French, the only other big mortar we have now is the 4.2" M30. This started life as a chemical mortar, but during WW II there was much need for high explosive rounds and little need for chemicals, so the 4.2" shifted its main responsibility. With a 25-lb. shell holding nearly 8 lbs.

(continued on page 174)

(top left) The M14 rifle handles the efficient 7.62mm NATO cartridge. Note how the soldier has taped two magazines together so a full one can be inserted fast.

(top right) M67 90mm recoilless rifle, operated by a two man crew, fires a fin-stabilized explosive anti-tank round — puts rifle accuracy and cannon power on a man's shoulder.

(left) M79 40mm grenade launcher is deadly against VC personnel to almost quarter-mile ranges.

(bottom left) Sustained fire capability is provided by M60 air-cooled machine gun, caliber 7.62mm. With sights and other parts removed, it becomes helicopter armament.

(bottom right) M70 Winchester 30-06 target rifle topped by Unertl scope serves this sniper well. Also in use now is the Remington 40X in 7.62mm with a variable power scope.

(above) The Entac tank-destroying missile is guided after launching by the gunner's directions, transmitted from his joy-stick control through connecting wires.

(upper right) Though dropped by the Army, the 60mm mortar is used by Marines, who like its light weight.

(right) Scoped M1 sniper rifle still sees some use.

(below) The 5.56mm rifle is popular with some troops in Viet (continued on page 174)nam because of its light weight, though it's not as effective as numerous inaccurate and exaggerated newspaper reports have claimed.

(lower right) Slide action 12-ga. riot-type shotgun is a favorite jungle weapon. Bandoliers of ammo are for 7.62mm machine gun.

Claymore anti-personnel mine; it can be fired by remote control.

(continued from page 171)

of HE, shooting to 6,000 yards, this is a flexible and powerful weapon. Weighing around 700 lbs., it is mobile to a degree but not exactly a one-man weapon. Unlike its smaller smoothbore brother, the 4.2" mortar is rifled. The shell has an expanding plate on the bottom which sets up under the powder gas pressure and engages the rifling. Where the fin-stabilized 81mm mortar can be used at any high angle, the spin-stabilized 4." is limited to about 65 degrees, since at higher angles the shell will not turn over.

During various reorganizations, the Army dropped the little 60mm company mortar, but the Marines have always had an affection for it. They are using it in Vietnam, where its 45-lb. weight and 2,000-yard range with a 3-lb. shell work out just right.

Even such a simple and unglamorous weapon as the grenade has changed in recent years. We originally adopted the British "Mills" type (circa WWI), with its serrated cast iron body filled with HE. Somewhere along the way, we changed the HE filling to EC Blank Fire Powder. This very fast burning powder burst the grenade along the serrations quite neatly. While the few big fragments didn't give very good area coverage, they were still dangerous at a considerable distance, but we went back to HE, which increased the effectiveness. This old Mk II type has been passed by progress and the new M26 is being used. This is about the same size and shape, but has a smooth exterior. It has the same old pull ring and safety lever, but there the similarity stops. The body of the M26 is made of square, notched wire, wound into shape, and covered with a thin metal shell. The 6 ounces of Composition B filler breaks it up into a thousand or more fragments, at velocities over 4000 fps.

Although the time delay fuze has been standard for many years, it has some disadvantages — like bounding merrily back in your lap when you throw it so as to accidently hit a tree! Although the present time fuze is noiseless and smokeless in operation, the 4–5 second delay often afforded the other guy a little chance to duck. The latest fuze, now going into production, has an additional impact element so that the grenade will usually go off when it hits something solid. If it doesn't, the time fuze will still fire it. To avoid unpleasantness too close to home the impact element has a delayed-arming feature, which will keep it from going off at your feet if you drop it, and will get it through the nearby brush before the impact element is armed.

A related, but unglamorous, weapon is the new "Claymore" mine. This in effect consists of a block of HE, about 9" long, 3" wide, and an inch thick, slightly curved around the long side. On the outside of the curve, steel balls are imbedded in the HE. The mine is provided with built-in tripod legs and a sight, and can be fired by remote control. When fired, the steel balls are blasted out and cover the area in front like a shotgun pattern.

The rifle grenade is not in fashion in the Army right now, although the Marines are finding it useful. We started with a grenade which had a long rod extending down in the barrel, shifted to the French V-B type with the cup discharger as well as the grenade with the hole down the middle to let the bullet through, then ended up in WW II with the tubular launcher. Designed by Mohaupt for use with the shaped charge antitank grenade, the grenade body was fastened to a hollow tube, which fitted over a tubular extension on the barrel. The grenade tube had stabilizing fins on the outside, thus with the special blank cartridge and an additional booster cartridge, a 1¼-lb. grenade could be thrown over 350 yards. In addition to anti-tank grenades, a wide variety of pyrotechnic signals, smokes, and anti-personnel grenades was developed.

In the Army, hand-held rocket-propelled pyrotechnics have taken over the signaling function from the grenade, while the LAW and 90mm recoilless have taken over the close-range anti-tank work. The fine M79 new 40mm grenade launcher has taken over the anti-personnel role.

The 40mm grenade cartridge looks like a very short, stubby, conventional cartridge. The business end contains a fuze, a streamlined cover and the grenade itself. The grenade is a small ball, about 1½" in diameter, made of flat serrated wire, much like the M26 grenade. It holds a few ounces of the very powerful explosive RDX. The grenade body breaks up into several hundred fragments, at velocities over 4000 fps. The fuze is armed by a combination of spin and setback when the cartridge is fired, and it has a delayed arming feature. Small as the grenade may seem, it is very potent.

The M79 grenade launcher looks much like a short and chubby single-barrel break-open shotgun. The aluminum barrel is rifled. The launcher weighs about 6 lbs. and with the 6-oz. grenade fired at a velocity of 250 feet per second, it is not too unpleasant to shoot — certainly far more comfortable than that abusive rifle grenade. The cartridge uses the high-low principle, where a small charge of powder is burned in a small chamber at high pressure, but is metered out into large chamber where it works against the projectile at low pressure. The powder burns at a pressure of around 35,000 psi, but works against the projectile at only about 3,500 psi. The M79 is one of the really new weapons in Vietnam and has been making a name for itself. With good accuracy, good effectiveness and a range of nearly 400 yards, it is a comforting thing to have in the rifle squad.

Airborne Ground Weapons

Some 20 years ago I was involved in testing the helicopter for Infantry use, and a year or two later I did a lot of flying for an article on fox hunting from the chopper. However, we were all so interested in them as a means of transportation that we didn't think about arming

105mm howitzer — proved in WW II and Korea — continues its outstanding performance in Viet Nam.

them. Now one of the real surprises of the Vietnam affair has been the effectiveness of the armed helicopter and the rather surprising toughness of the chopper in withstanding enemy fire. Although this article is about ground weapons, much of the armament used on the chopper has been adapted from ground weapons, and since the chopper is used right with the ground troops, we'll sneak in a word or two about it.

Just about everything you can think of has been hung on the helicopter and used experimentally, but the VC have been getting the worst end of four major standardized weapons systems. Two M6OC 7.62mm machine guns have been mounted on outriggers on each side of the aircraft. With power elevation and traverse slaved to the gunner's sight, this is a very effective system, with a rate of fire of 2,000 shots a minute.

The M5 weapons system is based on the 40mm grenade launcher M75. This is a motor-driven automatic launcher, with a rate of fire of 250 shots a minute. The 40mm grenade is descended from the foot soldier's 40mm, but is heavier, holds more HE and has higher velocity and therefore more range. The same high-low principle is used, but the change is from 35,000 to 12,000 psi, giving the heavier grenade a velocity of nearly 800 fps. The launcher is carried in a nose-mounted turret, giving considerable flexibility in elevation and deflection. The turret is slaved to the gunner's sight, much as the machine guns are. The 40mm grenade cartridges are connected by links and feed from the storage area through flexible chuting into the turret.

The ground pounders have been us-ing the SS-10 or "Entac" wire-guided missile as a flexible, effective antitank weapon. This is a rocket which is launched at moderate velocity and which has a long-burning sustainer motor to maintain or slightly increase the speed. The gunner, with a small joy-stick control, actually flies the missile from the launching site. Commands are passed to the missile over two fine wires which pay out of its back end, while a brilliant flare in the tail of the missile helps the gunner keep it in sight.

The chopper people have adopted a four-missile mount, along with sights and other controls, for use on the Bell HU-1 "Huey" series. The SS-11 used on this has a usable range of 500 to 3500 yards, and with 3½ lbs. of HE, is something to be feared.

The fourth standardized weapon system is based on the 2.75" Navy rocket. This rocket is 4 feet long, weighs 18 lbs., carries 1½ lbs. of HE and has a burn-out velocity of 2300 fps. A Huey can carry a couple of 24-tube rocket launchers, which gives considerable firepower. While these are the main systems, there have been many other combinations tried, such as a couple of 7-tube rocket launchers with the machine guns, etc. Although not listed formally in the standard books, one of the very useful systems consists of two eager soldiers "riding shotgun" — standing in the open doorway clutching a light machine gun!

Even the big "Vulcan," the 20mm Gatling gun, has been used experimentally in the chopper. Developed by Army Ordnance, this gun is standard armament on some Air Force planes. The Vulcan is the motor-driven, 6-barreled gun, with the barrels rotating together and never stopping during firing. Each barrel has a rate of fire — depending on how fast you want to drive the gun — of better than 1000 shots a minute, so the combination can get up to 7,000 or better. This is a mighty big gun for the chopper and a more likely version seems to be the "Minigun." This, another Gatling like the big gun, was developed by General Electric, but the Minigun is in 7.62mm caliber.

At the other end of the scale, the tank has had some rather tough going in Vietnam. Between jungle and marsh, this really isn't the best tank country. But on occasions tanks have been used with good results. We have one battalion of M48's in the country, plus smaller units of M60's. Both run about 50 tons and use 7.62mm coaxial M73 machine guns and 50-cal. M85 machine guns in the cupola. Main armament of the M48 is the 90mm gun, while the M60 tank carries the big 105mm gun.

The artillery has been kept busy, starting with the workhorse of WWII — the 105mm towed howitzer. Other old and new artillery weapons have been used, including some of the later self-propelled weapons. Among these are the 105mm and 155mm howitzers, the 8" howitzer and the big long-range 175mm gun, which is seeing its first combat. With a firing range of around 20 miles, plus good mobility on its tracks, this gun can cover a lot of area.

There are many other weapons which have been used to a greater or lesser extent, and some of those noted as having passed out of the picture may have found limited use. Take the shotgun, for example — it is not on the equipment list of a rifle outfit, but it has been used considerably in the jungle, where its short range is no major handicap. The M3 45-cal. "grease gun" is being used by the Marines in some cases, and even the much-castigated M1 carbine probably has seen some use.

The armament on Air Force, Navy and Marine aircraft has been used very extensively and effectively — but that is another story.

As the Green Beret finished, the two veterans struggled back into their uniforms and, after many thanks, headed for their car. The World War I vet was heard to say to his companion, "These kids just don't know what a real war is like! With all these fancy weapons — say, if we'd had weapons like this, we'd have licked the Kaiser in a few weeks!"

Marines like this Ontos, a light tracked carrier, because of the fire power its six 106mm recoilless rifles provide.

The M14 Rifle
... HAIL AND FAREWELL

▌ John Lachuk

THE MUCH MALIGNED M14 is being quietly phased out of production. It has apparently been abandoned by the Pentagon brass, though not yet openly repudiated. A search is in progress to find a worthy replacement for the rifle which proved to be modern in name only and has had, the way things look, the shortest life in history from production to obsolescence.

The Army hopes to leapfrog adoption of another conventional shoulder rifle by a crash program to develop exotic weapons such as the SPIW (Special Purpose Individual Weapon), a superposed barreled weapon, firing both grenades and high velocity dart-like bullets; or the Gyrojet, which fires small self-contained plastic rocket projectiles from cheaply cast smoothbore guns. Slanted orifices, in the tail, spin the rockets to impart stability. Even Laser "ray guns" are receiving serious considerations as future weapons.

Despite this feverish activity, it appears likely that such Buck Rogers weapons will be on the drawing board for some time yet. A more familiar but *modern* arm is certainly needed to fill the gap, and possibly to back up eventual use of the far-out types contemplated.

Your editor suggested that I "test-fire" some likely successors to the M14. Considering the immense stockpiles of NATO 7.62 ammo scattered throughout the world, we may end up with yet another 30-cal. rifle. Some promising candidates in this size are the ArmaLite AR-10 and their brand new AR-16. A marginal contender (I feel) is the Belgian FN Browning Light Assault Rifle. In line with the effort to lighten both weapon and ammo, we come up with the 223 caliber rifles, the AR-15 and newly unveiled AR-18.

First, however, let's try to learn where the M14 failed its great promise. The M14 represents a political victory but a monumental mechanical failure for the U.S. Army Ordnance. In 1955 we literally bludgeoned the 15-nation North Atlantic Treaty Organization into accepting the T65 (now 7.62 NATO), a boiled-down version of the half-century old 30-06, as the standard NATO cartridge. This course was pursued despite the insistence of countries like England that a smaller caliber, such as their 280, could perform as well and provide lighter ammunition.

The U.S. also wanted a common rifle for NATO, but Atlantic Treaty Alliance members baulked at accepting the American T44 (experimental M14), a rifle that was far from proven and is still years away from truly mass production.

Several NATO countries adopted the FN rifle. In 1954, it was designated the T48 and tested by our Ordnance, alongside the M14. Both guns were adjudged superior to the M1 Garand, but the FN was rejected in favor of the home-grown rifle. Among other advantages, the M14 was said to be, "better suited for American transition to mass production." Delays of over a year in delivery of the first M14 rifles touched off a stir in Congress in 1961. At that time, Iron Curtain countries were estimated to possess some 35 million modern, 30-shot "Avtomat Kalashnikov" AK-47 full automatic rifles, with production going full tilt in Russia, China and Czechoslovakia. Meanwhile, Belgium, England, Germany and Canada had adopted and were in full production of the FN assault rifles.

The sudden end to orders for the M14 at just under 1.4 million units has caught several major producers flatfooted, yet it comes as no real surprise. Early obsolescence of the M14 was candidly predicted in March of 1960, when General Trudeau, Chief of Army Research and Development, testified before a Congressional hearing that a replacement was already being sought for the M14. The date of expected obsolescence was 1965. He elaborated, "I think that a new-type, shorter range ammunition is possible. We should consider the design of the best weapon to fire it. I believe the weapon should be light and simple to operate."

The M14, which was originally projected as a "light rifle," eventually trimmed less than a pound from the unwieldly Garand. There is little apparent difference between the M14 that resulted from 20 years of development and $130 million in expenditures, and the original Garand prototypes of 1920. Early publicity heralded the M14 as a full-automatic rifle that would replace such special purpose weapons as the sub-machine gun and light machine gun. The M14's major failing is its lack of control-ability in full-automatic fire. Trained rifleman have told me the gun climbs so badly they can't keep 3 shots in a silhouette at 25 yards. Current issue M14's are semi-automatic. Officers control a supply of full automatic selectors, which, it is said, could be placed in the guns when needed.

Apologists for this policy say that full-automatic rifles in the hands of infantrymen pose an impossible logistical problem, the supplying of a steady stream of leaden "water" to the soldier's lethal "hoses." Statistics point up that it required

50,000 rounds of ammunition to produce one "good Commie" in Korea. Compare this with the average 29 round balls the Colonials fired per British Redcoat killed in the Revolutionary War, using muzzle-loading rifles and muskets.

Apparently the soldier values his shots more if they come one at a time. Still full-auto fire has its uses, if we can but train our GIs to recognize them. It can keep enemy heads down during flanking maneuvers, and provide small outnumbered groups with superior fire power for short periods. Air Force Manual 50-12 lists maximum rate of fire at 150 to 200 rounds per minute. USAF Tech Sergeant Vern Duchek tells me he can pour out 240 to 280 rounds per minute, including reloading time, using the AR-15. Even a squad could lay down a nearly impenetrable rain of fire at that rate — assuming they had ample ammo!

In Russia, during World War II, the vaunted Wehrmacht faced death charges lasting for hours. Eventual breakthrough often resulted in the collapse of entire

German defense perimeters. At Stalingrad, such a marathon suicide charge led to the capture of 400,000 Germans. Infantry armed with full-automatic rifles could well make such an attack too costly to continue.

M14 Rivals

The Belgian FN rifle that we rejected in favor of the M14 was designed by M. Dieudonné Siave, engineer with Fabrique Nationale d'Arms de Guerre, in Liége, and a protégé of the late John M. Browning. Originally chambered for a short 7mm cartridge, the FN was converted to fire the 7.62 NATO. A number of NATO members adopted the FN, including Germany. Germany later took in, or was taken in by, the CETME, or Gew C3, a rifle designed by German engineers, working in Spain. The CETME uses a delayed blowback action, and boasts all of the failings of that system as applied to heavy rifle calibers, especially the problem of overly violent extraction, to prevent case head separations, the chamber is fluted and ammo lubricated. No CETME was available for testing, but a semi-automatic version of the FN came to hand.

It seems remarkable that *all* of the other likely M14 replacements were designed by ArmaLite, Inc., a small independent development company in Costa Mesa, Calif. It began in 1954 with three dedicated gun buffs who believed that stable, lightweight missile-age plastics and alloys could be applied to firearms. Metallurgist George Sullivan was president, plastics expert Chuck Dorchester, vice-president, and ballistician Gene Stoner, chief engineer. ArmaLite, then a division of Fairchild Engine and Airplane Corp., soon received an R and D (research and development) contract from the Air Force for the AR-5, the 22 Hornet survival rifle.

Later, the ArmaLite trio turned their attention to regular military rifles. Uninhibited by preconceived notions of what a rifle should look like, they made their objective the producing of a practical weapon of the least possible weight. The AR-10, a 7½-pound 7.62 NATO caliber full- and semi-automatic rifle resulted. It has a European style machine gun configuration. Major metal parts such as the receiver and magazine are anodized aluminum alloy. Even the barrel of the original model was aluminum with a steel liner. Handguard and butt-stock are molded of fiberglass. To operate the action, gas is routed from a port near the muzzle through a tube atop the barrel, to enter a massive steel bolt carrier and start it rearward. As it

(above) Don Egger found the AR-15 could be readily aimed and controlled from the shoulder during full-automatic fire. Note two ejected cases in the air, one behind his ear and the other just leaving the action.

(left) The original onus laid on the AR-15 by Gen. Wm. G. Wyman was that it must "penetrate both sides of a GI helmet at 500 yards." Here's physical proof that the gun fullfills that requirement.

moves back, the carrier cuts off entry of gases and bleeds off the pressure within through escape vents. Kinetic energy carries it back, camming open the 7-lug bolt and extracting the case.

In 1956, the AR-10 was submitted to an Ordnance Board for testing at the Springfield Armory, but failed to pass the criteria set up for it. At that time, Chuck Dorchester pleaded in vain that the M14 be fired alongside, as a control. Recently released test data on the M14 show it to be markedly inferior to the AR-10 performance.

correct artillery projectile. The AR-15, a scaled-down version of the AR-10, was developed to fire the new centerfire 22.

The AR-15 went through months of Ordnance testing, alongside the Winchester 224 rifle, a modification of the M1 carbine in 1958–59. Afterwards, a review board under General Powell recommended the purchase of at least 700 AR-15s for extended field testing. Ordnance countered with a proposal to work for an "optimum round of 25 caliber," which could then be incorporated into the new rifle.

had not Air Force Chief of Staff, General Curtis LeMay come across it in 1960, recommended the Air Force test the gun as a replacement for their antiquated M1 carbines. In a new test at Lackland AF Base, the AR-15 easily outshot both the M14 and the Russian AK-47.

Tests indicated further that training time could be cut in half with the AR-15. In a 3-week period, almost half the trainees made Expert with the AR-15 (now labeled the 5.56mm M16 by Army Ordnance), while less than one-quarter made it with the M14.

USAF Orders AR-15 Rifles

Many of the initial AF order for 8,500 AR-15s went with Special Services to Vietnam, where they racked up an incredible record for dependability and effectiveness. An AF armorer returned to Lackland in 1963 to provide first-hand knowledge on battle maintenance problems. When asked what replacement parts were most needed, he replied, "I don't know. We haven't broken anything yet!"

The revolution in concept represented

(left) ArmaLite lineup, top to bottom; brand new AR-18, 223; prototype AR-16, 7.62 with wooden stocks — to be replaced with polycarbonate; famed AR-15, 223; note absence of openings for entrance of dirt and mud; AR-10, a truly fine military rifle, 7.62 NATO.

(below) AR-15; a trim and deadly military rifle. Bayonet and quick detachable bipod add to gun's versatility. It can fire grenades without any added attachments.

Fairchild licensed the AR-10 to Artillerie-Inrichtingen of Holland in 1957 and to Colt's Patent Fire Arms Mfg. Co. a year later. It was a Netherlands gun, with a steel barrel boosting the weight to a hair over 9 pounds, that we had for testing.

Despite Ordnance turndown, the AR-10 brought ArmaLite a reputation for functional innovation. It also brought General Wm. G. Wyman, Chief of the Continental Army Command at Fort Monroe, Va., to California in mid-1957 with a suggestion that a 22-caliber automatic rifle that could "penetrate both sides of a GI helmet at 500 yards," might prove interesting to the Army. Gene Stoner tried the 222 Remington cartridge, but found it lacking the energy required. He reamed the chamber deeper and fire-formed 222 cases to hold more powder, then designed a 55-gr. boat-tail bullet for his new "223" cartridge by scaling down a ballistically

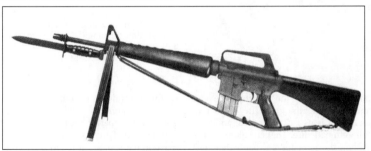

No 25 caliber cartridge ever materialized.

Eventually, a discouraged Fair-child Corp. began hurting from the $1,450,000 development cost of the AR-15, and licensed it to Colt's. Colt's found a good reception with emerging nations of the Far East, where small statured Asiatic soldiers discovered at last a rifle that made them all at least 10 feet tall. The AR-15 might have been relegated to this oriental limbo

by the AR-15 lies not so much in the rifle as in using a small-bore for a military weapon. Chuck hunters have long known the explosive destruction of high velocity small-bores, but the idea of shooting combatants with them just never caught on before. The Army made quite a fuss about not reducing lethality in adopting the AR-15. They needn't have worried. Reports from Vietnam tell of men beheaded or with arms and legs nearly shot off. Wounds that would prove minor with the 7.62 mean certain death with the 223, it is claimed, but there has been no incontrovertible proof of that flat statement. There could hardly be, by the nature of things.

Various articles have ascribed this devastating effect to the 223 bullet "tumbling" in tissue. ArmaLite Vice-President Burton T. Miller, (Col., USAF, ret.) helped conduct the original AR-15 tests. He discounts the tumbling theory, though he agrees the 223 may yaw in tissue. "There's really no mystery about the killing power of the 223," says Col. Miller. "Any varmint shooter knows that hydrostatic shock does the damage. Soon after we got the AR-15, gun buffs at Lackland AF Marksmanship School had sporting rifles chambered to the 223. During deer season, they shot numerous whitetails, with seldom a second shot required, even with full jacketed military ammo. Low neck shots invariably bloodshot meat on the off front shoulder."

Col. Miller says that exit wounds on most of the animals were relatively small, indicating the bullets stayed together. The 223 may disintegrate, though, on close range shots. During testing, I shot into gallon paint cans of water, which blew up most impressively. The lack of exit holes was explained when I found bits of jacket and core inside several of the cans.

Colonel Miller also refutes the hoary contention that light, high velocity bullets are more easily deflected than heavy, slow bullets. "I understand that the Marines constructed a deflection range at Quantico," he says, "with 50 yards of brush between the firing line and the targets.

It was virtually impossible for bullets to avoid encountering limb of varying sizes. Over a period of weeks, the AR-15 and M14 were fired side by side through this brush. The 223 scored as many hits, with no more apparent keyholes than the 7.62. At Aberdeen Proving Grounds, wooden dowels of given size and position, provide an absolutely controlled deflection test. Here, the 223 actually got more hits than the 7.62."

The 223 easily meets the original criterion laid on it, to penetrate both sides of a GI helmet at 500 yards. It also penetrates 5/16" steel plate with a 200 Brinell rating at 200 yards. During our testfiring the 223 penetrated ⅜" boiler plate at 50 yards, right alongside the 7.62, and almost got through ½" plate, cratering as deeply as the NATO round.

The 223 has the inherent accuracy that delights bench rest and varmint shooters. Col. Van Dueson, CO at the Lackland AFB Marksmanship School, has a lightweight sporter in 223 that consistently shoots under 1 inch at 200 yards. Armed forces use opens the door to cheap and plentiful 223 ammo. The 223 may not fare as well as the 7.62 in high winds, but 1000-yard tests of light machine guns in both calibers developed 50% more hits with the small-bore, perhaps because the 223 was less disrupted by recoil.

The AR-15 proved more accurate with a twist of 1–12 rather than with the bench resters' favored 1–14 twist. Colt's changed the twist to 1–12 because cold tests at 65° indicated the heavier air unstabilized 55-gr. 223 bullets from a 1–14 twist.

AR-15 Accuracy Test

A USAF Operational Suitability Test run last year describes accuracy testing

of 40 random-chosen AR-15s, with some 10,000 rounds fired from a Mann rest, through a 100-yard tunnel. Results indicated that GI AR-15s using issue ammo could outshoot most match grade M1s and M14s. To top this, the 223 ammo used was considered inferior by its manufacturer, who promised marked improvement in future lots. Over-all average of all of the 223 guns tested with 1–12 twist was 3.21" AES (at extreme spread), in Part A of the test, and 2.85" AES in part B. Reloads of 26 grains of BL-C and 52-gr. Sierra bullets reduced groups 1 to 2 inches. Merely pulling the GI bullets and substituting Sierras cut groups 1 inch.

The AR-15 and AR-10 were products of early ArmaLite genius. They have recently come up with a couple of new weapons, the AR-16 (7.62 NATO) and the AR-18 (223), sharing the same general conformation — squarish pressed-steel receiver and trigger groups, with low-lying barrels to avoid climbing in full-automatic fire. The new AR team uses a piston and tappet rod, situated above the barrel to energize the bolt carrier, which disengages 7 locking lugs by rotating them 22.5°. Both guns sport manual charging handles.

Army Ordnance objected to the lack of a manual charging handle on the AR-15, but ArmaLite had a good reason for its absence. The AR-15 is sealed against dirt and mud by a hinged cover over the ejection port and a hollow polyethelyne muzzle plug. A charging handle slot would destroy this seal. The AR-15 goes from "buttoned up" condition into action with the first shot, camming open the ejection port cover and blowing off the plastic muzzle plug.

Don Egger fired all of the rifles prone as well as on the bench, as did the author. Guns, left to right: AR-18 with open sight, AR-15, AR-10 (firing is AR-16), FN, and another AR-18 with peep sight. All handled well.

(As we go to press, Colt's informs us that they have added a new manual bolt-forward-assist to all AR-15s going to the Army. The assist is a small knob projecting back from the right of the receiver. It can be struck with the palm. It moves only about ½". It engages one or another of 28 notches in the bolt carrier, a la ratchet, to force the bolt closed at any point where it might conceivably stick in its forward travel. The USAF has not asked for this device, considering the 8-pound forward thrust of the recoil spring sufficient to close the bolt.)

ArmaLite designed its two new rifles to attack the dirt problem from another angle. They exclude dirt and mud where feasible, but if some does get into an action, it literally chews up the foreign material and spits it back out through openings around the trigger and bolt. The bolt carrier slides on two guide rods that also carry the recoil springs, making for a self-cleaning action. So long as the ammunition remains clean, the guns will function through unbelievable sand or mud baths. In H.P. White lab tests, the AR-16 and AR-18 continued to fire with the trigger groups completely full of mud.

A recent demonstration of the AR-18 at Lorton, Va., turned out numerous interested military observers, domestic and foreign. It developed later that there was even a Communist agent in the group! After the tests, General Curtis LeMay remarked, "If you can hold the price, I think you've got something there!" Such curt praise from the General could be likened to 6 choruses of Handel's "Messiah" from the average man.

The AR-16 and AR-18 are already licensed to the West German firm Erma-Werke GMBH, of Dachau, for European distribution. Estimated tooling costs run $1.2 million, about 25% of tooling-up money for the M14 or AR-15. In 10,000 lots, unit cost will be under $60, less than half that for the M14 in like quantities. "Their low cost and ease of manufacture helps make these guns the finest military rifles of all time," says Chuck Dorchester, current ArmaLite president. "Every Free World nation, large or small, is determinend to produce its own small arms. Both guns combine the extensive use of sheet metal stampings with automatic screw machine parts, designed to require a minimum of close tolerances. Small nations can virtually produce these guns in ordinary machine shops; and when the military need is met, this same tooling can literally be converted back from making swords to plowshares."

The AR-16 and AR-18 boast another military advantage, a folding stock that is practical in use and locks securely out of the way when not wanted. With the stock folded, the guns measure about 28 inches, for use in tanks, personnel carriers, etc., or for jump troops. They can be fired like machine pistols. The stock material is a new, virtually unbreakable plastic called polycarbonate. "You could drive a truck over that stock, says Chuck Dorchester, "and not hurt it any." Contrast this with the rash of broken stocks whenever paratroops jump carrying the M14s.

Test Firing and Evaluations

Evaluating all of these rifles presented a formidable project. Actual firing required several days and over 2,000 rounds of ammo. To give GUN DIGEST readers an educated analysis of their military capabilities, I enlisted Don Egger, of Los Angeles, a skilled rifleman and hunter. Don completed his hitch in the Marines, where he trained with both semi- and full-automatic weapons, and was rated a Sharpshooter.

Three basic criteria determine the combat effectiveness of any military rifle. First, the weapon must function dependably, often under extremely adverse conditions. Also, it must be accurate and lethal. We tested the guns for malfunctions by deliberately firing them full-automatic until they were badly overheated, except for the civilian model FN, which was fired rapidly semi-auto. Accuracy was checked from a bench rest. Lethality of the two cartridges involved is beyond question, but we tested for penetration and disruptive effect in cans of water.

Since the AR-18 was a brand new gun, we tried it out first. We demonstrated its destructive force by reducing a concrete block wall to a rubble in a matter of minutes, using full-auto fire. In my first experience with a full-automatic rifle, I took a death grip on the AR-18. It was about like using the touch of a Mack truck driver on a power steering Cadillac. I overcontrolled grossly. Finally, I loosened my clutch on the pistol grip and let the fore-end rest on my open palm, where it vibrated gently like a foot massage machine. The effect was miraculous. I could direct a steady stream of fire wherever desired.

We tested three AR-18 rifles, one the No. 2 prototype and two chosen at random from the first production lot. All 3 functioned full-auto without a hitch, through half a case of ammo. The handguard on the prototype got too hot to hold, but chief engineer Art Miller said more vents would be added to the alumi-

num heat deflector, next to the barrel, to carry off excess heat.

The first prototype AR-18 taken to the range by Col. Miller worked at full-auto straight off, which is in itself a pretty fair testimonial for the slip-stick boys at ArmaLite. A few stoppages occurred when cases spun back into the action. Moving the ejection port back slightly eliminated this problem, and the gas port was opened a little to increase the cycling rate.

Well-engineered though it was, the AR-18 did develop one bug. The flash-hider doubles as a grenade launcher, as on the AR-15, so no added attachments are required to fire the bomblike grenades. However, in test firing dummy grenades, we found the recoil shock jarred the gun open. ArmaLite added a spring-loaded crossbolt to lock the latch in place.

We then turned our attention to the AR-15, firing the same 223 round. In firing, the AR-15 matched all of the talents of the AR-18. It has a less boxy but bulkier silhouette. Handling qualities were similar with the two guns. I rather preferred the lower sights on the AR-18. The rear sight on the AR-15 provides a built in handle, but the AR-18 carries easily at the balance point, just ahead of the receiver. The AR-15 has the edge in resistance to corrosion, with its milled alloy receiver. It also has a fold-down trigger guard that allows its use with mittens. Windage adjustment on the AR-15 is effected by turning a drum with the point of a cartridge, similar to the AR-18. There were more similarities than differences between the two.

Test Fire Report

All the guns tested had many points in common. All were gas-operated and fired from closed bolts. All had vertical pistol grips and 20-shot clips jutting down from the receivers, and safety-selectors above the pistol grips on the left side for full or semi-auto. Front sights on all of the guns were round posts, threaded so they could be rotated for elevation adjustment. Don Egger preferred the FN sight because it was the dullest and blackest of the lot. He would have liked all of the posts 1/32" wider and the peeps enlarged about the same amount. The AR-10 and AR-15 can be equipped with a special scope designed to fit a mount built into the handle. The FN has a special bolt cover for scope mounting. The AR-16 and AR-18 are being fitted with a heavy-duty 3X scope developed by Lyman, in a QD mount that will not obscure the iron sights when the scope is removed.

Bench rest accuracy with these 223 rifles was about equal, with groups running from 3 to 4½ inches. The AR-18 is potentially as accurate as the already proven AR-15. They both feature a new style of construction, using a barrel extension within the receiver to provide locking surfaces for the bolt lugs. The receiver acts merely to join the stock and barrel, and carry the bolt, being subjected to no stress. Accuracy is based almost wholly upon the barrel-ammunition combination, not on such tenuous factors as stock bedding.

Of the 7.62 rifles, the AR-10 seemed to have the best all around handling qualities, but both the AR-10 and AR-16 handled well in full-automatic fire; certainly not with the ease of the 223 rifles, but they were readily controlled for short bursts. Bench rests groups were surprisingly close to the small bores. We fired three 10-shot groups with each rifle. The averages are shown in the accompanying chart. We fired into gallon paint cans and old ammo boxes full of water with the 7.62s, and they punched neat little holes on both sides. The 223's exploded the same cans for a convincing demonstration of greater shock. It appears that 21 rounds of 223 could do far more damage than their scale balance of 10 NATO cartridges. They also cost the government 2¢ less apiece.

The FN provided some remarkable bench rest groups, using GI ammo. At 3 to 3½ inches, they were within Army standards for match guns and ammo. Prone firing with the bipod gave groups almost as good, but lowered the point of impact about 4 inches. The bipod arms fold, to nest neatly within the steel handguard on the model tested. Standard is a wooden fore-end and buttstock. I can only surmise the rifle's handling characteristics under full auto-fire, but it has a low barrel and straight line recoil, and proved controllable during very rapid semi-auto firing. An adjustable gas regulator allows the gun to be adapted to adverse conditions of cold and mud. Also, the cycling rate could be varied at will. The lower receiver is a stamping, the upper section apparently forged and milled. Two opposing screws adjust windage on the rear sight. It has a sliding ramp for ranges of 200 to 600 yards. I liked the husky charging handle on the left side.

Using my accuracy-proven Avtron chronograph, we found that American- and German-made 7.62 ammo gave about identical velocity figures. Complaints that foreign NATO ammo was not up to pressure standards, and that U.S. issue would not function in foreign guns

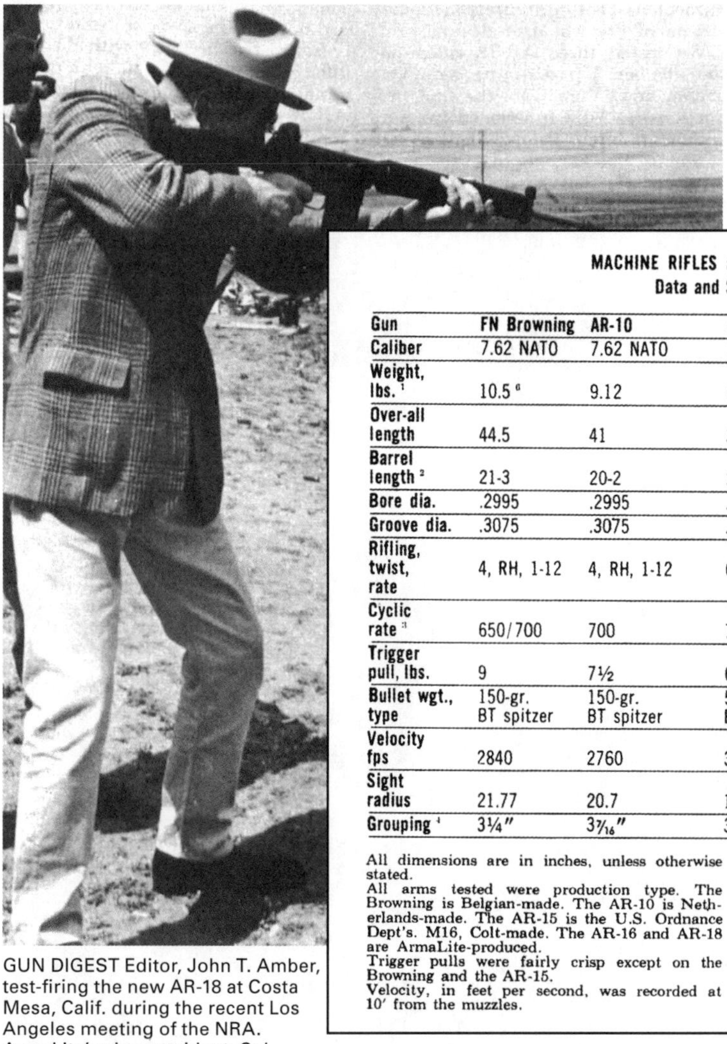

GUN DIGEST Editor, John T. Amber, test-firing the new AR-18 at Costa Mesa, Calif. during the recent Los Angeles meeting of the NRA. ArmaLite's vice president, Col. Miller, is explaining the operation of the weapon.

MACHINE RIFLES and PISTOL CARBINES
Data and Specifications

Gun	FN Browning	AR-10	AR-15	AR-16	AR-18
Caliber	7.62 NATO	7.62 NATO	223 (5.56mm)	7.62 NATO	223 (5.56mm)
Weight, lbs. [1]	10.5 [6]	9.12	6.62	8.75	6.3
Over-all length	44.5	41	39	41.5 (27) [5]	38 (28¾) [5]
Barrel length [2]	21-3	20-2	20-1	20-2	18¼-1
Bore dia.	.2995	.2995	.220	.2995	.2190
Groove dia.	.3075	.3075	.2245	.3075	.2235
Rifling, twist, rate	4, RH, 1-12	4, RH, 1-12	6, RH, 1-12	4, RH, 1-12	6, RH, 1-12
Cyclic rate [3]	650/700	700	700/800	650	750
Trigger pull, lbs.	9	7½	6½	7¾	7½
Bullet wgt., type	150-gr. BT spitzer	150-gr. BT spitzer	55-gr. BT spitzer	150-gr. BT spitzer	55-gr. BT spitzer
Velocity fps	2840	2760	3199	2764	3182
Sight radius	21.77	20.7	19.94	22.5	20.125
Grouping [4]	3¼″	3⁷⁄₁₆″	3⅝″	4¼″	3¾″

All dimensions are in inches, unless otherwise stated.
All arms tested were production type. The Browning is Belgian-made. The AR-10 is Netherlands-made. The AR-15 is the U.S. Ordnance Dept's. M16, Colt-made. The AR-16 and AR-18 are ArmaLite-produced.
Trigger pulls were fairly crisp except on the Browning and the AR-15.
Velocity, in feet per second, was recorded at 10′ from the muzzles.

[1] With magazine empty.
[2] Second figure gives length of flash hider.
[3] Rounds per minute.
[4] The average for three 10-shot groups, center-to-center of farthest shots, at 100 yds. Slow fire, from a rest.
[5] With stock folded.
[6] Weight of standard Browning. Light version runs 8¼ lbs., bipod type 10½.

were unfounded in this instance. The FN, with its extra inch of barrel, chronographed 80 fps faster than the AR-10 and AR-16.

The Colt-made AR-15 also surprised us with 129 fps more than the AR-18. We guessed that the original chamber configuration in the AR-15, rather than its 1–14 twist was the cause. To be certain, we took the gun back to ArmaLite, reamed the chamber to the new SAAMI standard, and chronographed it again. Velocity fell off to nearly equal the AR-18. The original chamber was changed when pressures ran to as high as 58,000 psi instead of Army specs of 52,000 psi. The new chamber, with 2°27' angle and a .060" lead, dropped pressures to 50,000 psi, with a corresponding drop in velocity. During AF tests, AR-15s dropped 8 primers in 1000 rounds with the old chamber, and only 1 primer in 10,000 rounds with the new chamber.

The 223 is notably easy on barrels. NATO specs call for 6,000 rounds minimum barrel life. After firing 11,000 rounds in one AR-18, most of it full-auto, ArmaLite removed and sectioned the barrel. The completely erosion-free chamber came as a surprise. Usually, gas leaks around the case and erodes the chamber neck. Rifling was scorched near the chamber, but the barrel was still shooting 3½-inch groups when it was dissected. I noted a chamfer in the front edge of the gas port, where it entered the bore. Art Miller explained that the gases speed past the port, strike the base of the bullet, and bounce back to enter the port. The hole is too small to chamfer after drilling, but the gases cut their own chamfer, stepping up the cyclic rate as much as 50 rounds per minute during the life of the barrel.

I timed field stripping and reassembly for each gun, but found little to choose between them. All were swift and easy to take down, breaking open like shotguns, with a latch or pin release. The innards literally spilled out of all of them. Average takedown time was 20 to 30 seconds, reassembly 30 to 45. The only tool required was a single cartridge.

For whatever it's worth, I'll list the guns in order of my preference: AR-18, AR-15, AR-10, AR-16 and FN. Don Egger rated them: AR-15, AR-18, AR-16, FN and AR-10. The choices were hard to make! Both Don and I thought the 223 outrated the 7.62 for over-all combat effectiveness by 2 to 1.

Among the NATO caliber rifles, I rated the FN last because of its 11½ lb. weight when loaded. A lightweight model with "Hyduminium" receiver trims about a pound. Don preferred the sights on the FN, and found its weight no handicap, thus he judged it ahead of the AR-10.

To me, the AR-10 is in a class by itself. I can't understand its rejection by Army Ordnance. The weapon provides match accuracy, and is controllable full automatic, from the shoulder or hip. On a bipod, it doubles ably as a light machine gun. The AR-10 is a steeping giant that may yet awaken.

The AR-16 retains the AR-10's favorable qualities and adds an unheard of compactness in a weapon for this potent a cartridge. Add ease and economy of manufacture, and you have an ideal rifle for Alliance nations still committed to the NATO caliber.

The AR-18 has the assets of the AR-16, with the added effectiveness of the 223 cartridge. The AR-15 has already proved its capabilities in actual battle. The FN is recognized throughout the world as a fine military weapon. Any one of the guns tested could profitably be substituted for the discredited M14.

All new Army AR-15s have Colt's new manual bolt-forward assist. 28 notches are cut on the right side of the bolt carrier. The assist moves about ½-inch, and it is used to force the bolt closed if it should stick at any point in its forward travel.

Col. Miller inspects remains of concrete block wall shot to shreds with full automatic fire from the 223 cal. AR-18. Such a wall would offer no defense to an enemy soldier.

The Story of
AR-10

■ Wm. B. Edwards

T HE "GREAT RIFLE CONTRO-
VERSY" is still a controversy.
It was called just that years ago
by military analyst Hanson W.
Baldwin, in reference to the inability of
the U.S. Ordnance Department to decide
on a new infantry rifle to replace the Garand, and the term is still apt. A new rifle
has stirred up the controversy again in the
sacred halls of Washington, in the concrete ranges of Springfield Armory, and
on the firing fronts at Aberdeen Proving
Ground. This promising contender for
adoption as our service rifle is the AR-10,
designed by the west coast Armalite Division of Fairchild Engine & Airplane
Corp., with headquarters in Hagerstown,
Maryland. AR-10, weighing 6.85 pounds,
is the first actually light rifle to be tested
since the start of the Army's light rifle development program over a decade ago. It
is the only rifle in existence which would
meet the recent *Futurarmy* requirements of a seven-pound or less shoulder
weapon. The Garand weighs well over
nine pounds; various recent test weapons
range up to 12 pounds.

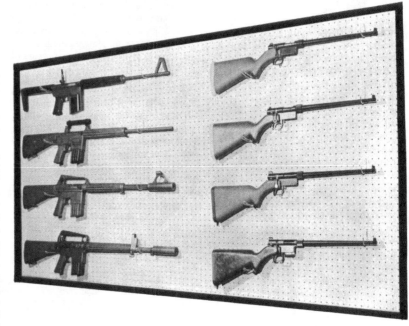

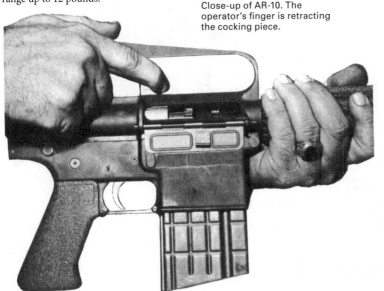

Close-up of AR-10. The
operator's finger is retracting
the cocking piece.

Junking the Ml Garand is long overdue. Since the first American soldier died
with an empty Garand in his hands, the
enemy charge signalled by the characteristic twanging sound as the Ml's clip was
ejected on the last shot, this rifle has been
recognized as obsolete The search for a
weapon to replace it has been conducted
by the small arms research and development branch of the Office of Chief of
Ordnance, in cooperation with Springfield Armory and foreign and U. S. contractors. First in line was a modified Ml
Garand, with a 20-shot detachable box
magazine and selector switch for full-auto
fire. But the modification weighed more
than its prototype. Lightweight, plus firepower, and the ability to hit what was
aimed at, were alt desirable. A succession
of "T" (test) rifles proceeded through the
model shops, from T-25, a modified Ml to
T-44, a still-further modified box-maga-
zine Ml, and the ill-fated T-47. Then came
the T-48, a full-auto weapon heralded as

"light" even though it weighed as much as 12 pounds in some versions. The T-44 was a Springfield Armory design; the T-48 one borrowed from Fabrique Nationale in Belgium. All the while Ordnance could not settle on a weapon for production and first-line issue. Other nations did not have so much trouble in their search.

Britain, Canada and Belgium adopted the FN T-48 in a lightning move disconcerting to the U.S. We had thumbed-down Britain's own rotary-lock EM-2 rifle, tested here several years ago. Since then the U.S. has adopted a medium machine gun (the M60) embodying similar rotary bolt and gas-operating systems to that used in the EM-2. France, after four years of playing games with U.S. Research and Development, adopted their gas-operated Mdle. 1949 rifle. Switzerland, unwilling to bear with the U.S. lead in NATO arms designing, has just adopted the roller-locked Neuhausen AM-55 assault rifle. The AM-55 was studied by Springfield Armory last summer but the decision was against adopting it.

Major nations like Russia completed their re-arming with new light infantry weapons, a series of light rifle, machine carbine, light belt-fed machine gun, adapted to various tactical uses, cheaply manufactured, and employing their new short-case cartridge. Even so undeveloped a nation as Egypt, after field experience with the Belgian FN rifle, adopted a modification of Swedish design and is manufacturing it in their new arms factory.

Meanwhile nearly $40,000,000 worth of Ml rifles have been procured since 1945 by the U. S. Army from American contractors. Abroad, Breda and Beretta in Italy are both manufacturing the Ml Garand for Italian service and export government sales to other NATO countries. Austria is equipped with Garands. These are admittedly better than their 1895-model Steyr rifles, but not much more so in a fire-fight. Denmark has adopted the Ml Garand as their Model 1950, a good, workable, but tactically obsolete weapon using the unnecessarily long 30-06 cartridge. This, then, was the stage prepared when the Armalite AR-10 rifle entered the scene last fall at Springfield Armory.

Tests of the Armalite at Springfield are classified. One observer declared that upon reading the test reports "I laughed, and laughed, and laughed — the report was that absurd. All the good points of the AR-10 were minimized, and the bad features were emphasized in careful detail."

From the public relations office of Armalite the only word available was "It did some rather remarkable things (at Springfield) but, as you can appreciate, the matter is at a delicate stage. Quite naturally, we encountered some technical difficulties, but these were such that the solution was obvious.

(above) AR-10, the Armalite Corporation's full automatic, gas-operated, ultra light combat rifle — a potent package of steel, alloys and plastics.

(left) George Sullivan, initiator of the Armalite's weapons program, ready to insert the MA-1 barrel and action into the plastic buttstock.

I can say that the gun passed tests which no other gun has undergone." What these specific tests are cannot be said until the report is published. Meanwhile, what sort of a gun is this new focal point of Ordnance controversy?

It is light — a full-scale automatic machine-rifle weighing 6.85 pounds compared with, for example, the BAR's 18–20 pounds heft. It is simple in design. Although nominally gas operated, the gas piston and tubes associated with most gas guns are dispensed with. Operating pressure is tapped from near the muzzle and conducted through a small tube to the breech. Inside the receiver, the tube passes into a channel cut in a bolt-operating slide at the rear of the actual breech bolt. The bolt, a multi-lug affair reminiscent of the Johnson short-recoil guns, locks inside a barrel collar. A stud on the bolt is cammed in a rotary fashion by a slot in the bolt operating slide. As the slide is blown to the rear by gas pressure, the bolt rotates, then withdraws, extracting the fired case and compressing the recoil spring contained in the butt stock.

The simplicity of this gas system, a decided improvement on any now in use by any army for a military rifle, accounts in part for the ridiculously low cost of the AR-10. "In mass production we could make these to sell for about $40" was the claim of one Armalite man.

A straight-line weapon, with very high sights because the top line of the stock is on the same axis as the barrel, the AR-10 is topped by a handle big enough for Arctic mittens, moulded integral with the receiver. At the handle's rear is an adjustable aperture sight. The handle allows the gun to be held up like a big pot of coffee, and there is more similarity than that: the weight of gun complete with loaded aluminum clip magazine and 20 7.62 NATO or 308 cartridges, is just the same as a two-quart pot of coffee!

I've fired this new rifle, and it's a dream. The light weight does not cause any pronounced recoil. A light titanium can is hung on the front for a muzzle brake, and on full-auto fire the gun simply does not have any objectionable rearward motion or muzzle rise. Even without the muzzle brake, kick is much less than with some other full-auto shoulder rifles. Yet the caliber is "full power," not reduced to ease kick in any way. In spite of the fact that I am left handed, the gun is very easy to use since the operating handle is placed vertically above the receiver, like the old model Thompson, and below the sight line.

At the right, a spring loaded cover seals the ejection port from dirt, mud and rain. It flips open instantly on firing when the first shot is snapped off, but can be easily closed by the soldier during a lull in combat.

The first time I saw the AR-10 was on a wintry, raw wet day late in November, last year. In company with machine gun dealers Sam Cummings of Interarmco, Val Forgett of "Ma Hunter's," and Col. George M. Chinn, USMC, author of that monumental work, *The Machine Gun*. I had driven up from Washington to the home of Richard Boutelle, president of Fairchild Aircraft, in Hagerstown, Md.

As we stamped in Boutelle's lodge-like home, shaking rain from our coats, Col. Chinn's eyes lit on the AR-10 and several prototype rifles spread out in anticipation of our visit. "Boy," he said in his Kentucky drawl, "I'd have walked up here to see these." In working the action and noting the unusual gas operating system, Chinn observed considerable gas smudges on the left locking lugs. "You might get some pretty bad gas fouling from this," he commented. "But it would be an easy matter to take your gas off a little farther to the rear," he agreed with Boutelle, who had pointed out that this gun had been fired

(above) Iso-Cyanate foam, the plastic filter that makes the stocks light and strong, overflows the mold.

(center) Removing the AR-10 stock from the mold.

(right) MA-1, the Survival Gun, floats — barrel, action, etc., are held watertight within the hollow buttstock.

over 600 times without cleaning, and that the need for cleaning was not unknown in other gas-operated guns.

The sensational thing immediately noticed about the AR-10 was its light weight. Aluminum, magnesium, titanium, and small amounts of stainless steel plus plastic are the ingredients of AR-10. Originally planned as a stamped sheet-aluminum receiver, the AR-10 was finalized with a forged and machined receiver of high-strength alloy, possible because all the locking surfaces which take most of the beating in firing were on the stainless steel bolt head, or in the small barrel collar.

The barrel itself is a steel liner swaged in an aluminum tube fluted on the outside. Surrounding this is a thin shell of tough plastic, the front tubular handguard. Air circulates freely through this cover, keeping it cool in hot firing.

We had a chance to get AR-10 hot a few minutes later, in the back yard of Boutelle's home. Shortly the stillness of the Sabbath was shattered by the repeated "bruuup" fire of light machine guns. Cummings had brought along his FG-42 German paratroop machine rifle, a well-designed but heavy 9-pound shoulder weapon, outmoded now by light-alloy

guns. Boutelle had an automatic sporting rifle of a different design, but very light weight, using plastics and aluminum. These three — the AR-10, FG-42, and the experimental sporter, performed in what may prove to be a history-making test, the first "press showing" of the Armalite weapons.

The gun has no built-in inaccuracies — it will shoot true. In every respect the AR-10 behaved well. In one test it performed better than expected — the use of too-short ammunition in full-auto fire. Loaded with 110-grain Winchester 308 stuff, the AR-10 slammed twenty shots through the chamber in one easy burst. In practically any other automatic weapon on full auto, the short-bullet rounds would have made failure to feed a certainty. The ability to use sporting ammunition in an emergency is one factor not to be over-looked in developing arms for a nation where the citizen is the soldier. Kick was negligible.

In handling, the "feel" of both AR-10 and the experimental sporter was something definitely pleasant. Reams of copy have been ground out by gun writers on the advantages of a light rifle or shotgun in the field. But the AR-10's basic principles, its alloy and plastic construction,

offer the first chance ever presented to American sportsmen to get a truly light weapon. Though both Armalite weapons bulked as large as standard commercial arms, they weighed hardly as much as a boy's 22. Needless to say, Armalite got my order for the first production gun sold, right then.

There are some more gadgets in Armalite's bag of tricks. One neat trick is the MA-1 survival rifle, a stubby 22 Hornet caliber clip-fed bolt action using the alloy and plastic construction pioneered by Armalite. A sub-caliber barrel insert for 22 Long Rifle adapts the weapon to small game, while the 22 Hornet will do for some animals a little bigger. The weapon can be completely dismounted without using tools, and packed into its own buttstock, it's a mere 14" in over-all length. With the rubber cap "butt plate" in place, the whole package will *float*.

Adopted by the Air Force, the MA-1 is not in quantity production because large stocks of less efficient models of survival rifle are on hand. But Armalite feels that with 2" added to the barrel, and 2" more to the butt stock to hold it, they can sell the gun to sportsmen. The next time you capsize a canoe in white water, think how nice it would be to find your rifle, neatly put up in a watertight parcel, floating beside you.

Also almost ready for the sportsman are prototype models of conventional bolt-action sporting rifles and repeating shotguns. With barrels of the high-strength aluminum alloy developed for Armalite by Alcoa, the new rainbow-hued autoloading shotguns weigh less than 5½ pounds. Full-sized sporting rifles, built on Mauser and M722 Remington actions, with steel-lined Armalite aluminum barrels in bright anodized gold, blue and red, weigh as little as six pounds complete with 4X scopes.

The creative engineering, designing, and production of such a variety of futuristic weapons has been the result of teamwork at Armalite. Under the guidance of George Sullivan, a Los Angeles aeronautical engineer and gun hobbyist, the Armalite Division was set up as a research branch of the Fairchild Engine & Airplane Corp., in 1953. Sullivan had been experimenting with aircraft manufacturing methods in his home workshop, and believed that lighter weight guns would be better guns. His work was brought to the attention of Richard S. Boutelle, president of Fairchild, in 1953. Boutelle is a member of the "One-Shot" antelope club, and has for years enjoyed guns as a

Richard Boutelle, head of Fairchild Aircraft, submerges the MA-1 but it pops surface-ward and floats!

(above) Warren Runnals, gunsmith at Armalite, test firing the AR-10 at the company's indoor range.

(below) AR-10 in the test cradle, just after firing 600 rounds in 30 minutes.

(bottom) Stoner (left) and Dorchester waiting for the gun to cool enough for removal from the cradle.

hobby. Once when a friend asked his wife "Why don't you buy Dick a gun cabinet?" she looked around the room with its walls hung with trophies and rifles, and witheringly replied "Because we keep house in one." Sullivan's ideas and Boutelle's coincided from the first, and Fairchild funds have backed the project since then.

To work with Sullivan came Eugene Stoner, another gun crank with experience in the Marine Corps and with U.S. Army Ordnance. Stoner's design philosophy dovetailed right in with Sullivan's lightweight ideas, and the ex-Marine became Armalite's chief engineer. Coordinating all was Charles Dorchester, another member of Sullivan's team, experienced in engineering matters.

These men and their associates in the Armalite Los Angeles shop have created a new concept of weapons that is already making its effect felt throughout the world. Since their work first became known, a leading Swiss small-arms firm has become interested in the new Armalite-Alcoa alloy. Within the past few months (this past spring) the AR-10 rifle has been demonstrated with commendable success to South American countries which have wanted to obtain first-class, light, infantry rifles of modern model. The government of Israel, interested in the greatest economy with the greatest fire-power and durability in a rifle, is studying the AR-10. Meanwhile, what will its effect be with our Army Ordnance?

"We don't really want the T-48 Belgian rifle," one top Springfield Armory department head told me, "since it would mean a 100% retooling." But the T-44 is not entirely satisfactory, either. A stalemate between T-44 and T-48 has now been broken. With the Armalite entry in the great rifle controversy, the need for a decision can be postponed a little longer. Last

summer, for instance, the Swiss AM-55 assault carbine delayed the decision for a few months. Now the AR-10 must be considered. Even if no decision is made, Ordnance need not be unhappy. In the offing is a radically new system of firearm, a combination revolver-automatic with jam-proof feed and triangular cartridges, the Dardick gun. "The army is all steamed up about our gun," Dardick Corporation's ordnance consultant said.

Can it be that the Ordnance Dept. welcomes these new gun developments, welcomes them because they permit postponing any decision to adopt a new weapon? Could be. Meanwhile, we still have plenty of the Garands.

(top) Left to right — Dorchester, Stoner and Runnals checking over the AR-10 after test firing.

(bottom) Left, chief engineer Gene Stoner, and Charles Dorchester, super-intendent at Armalite. The Survival Gun, broken down, left in foreground.

The M16A2

New World Standard For Infantry Rifles...

■ C. E. Harris

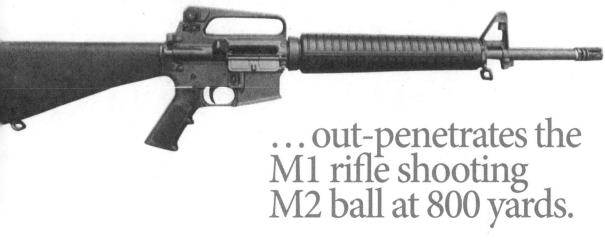

...out-penetrates the M1 rifle shooting M2 ball at 800 yards.

THE M16A2 is the new standard to which past and future military rifles will be compared. This second-generation 5.56mm rifle is the product of cooperation between industry and U.S. forces to develop, test and field a product-improved rifle which should meet their needs to the end of this century. The M16A2, standardized in November, 1983, is a wonderful example of how the military development and procurement system is *supposed* to work. The efficiency with which this work proceeded from concept to production and fielding is a tribute to military-industrial cooperation.

When the M16A1 rifle was first adopted by U.S. troops in 1967, the Marines were the most vocal opponent of a "small

caliber" rifle. At that time there were valid complaints about the reliability of the M16 and its M193 ammunition and its range and lethality. Although changes in the rifle and ammunition corrected the functional problems, by 1970 it was apparent the sights and the ballistics of the 55-gr. M193 cartridge reached their limits in combat at about 500 yards. To many critics, even 500 yards pushed credibility.

Adopting the 5.56mm NATO SS109/M855 cartridge in 1977 brought ammunition effective to well beyond 600 yards in lethality and accuracy and penetration. Standardization of this NATO cartridge brought a need to adapt the M16 rifle to it, and provided the opportunity to correct the known tactical deficiencies in the M16A1. The USMC Firepower Division, at Quantico, VA, was tasked with this development in cooperation with Colt Industries, under supervision of the Joint Services Small Arms Program (JSSAP).

The product-improved rifle was identified as M16A1E1 during operational testing which preceded formal type classification. Operational testing of 30 M16A1E1 rifles served to evaluate the changes and provide input for further refinements which would be incorporated

M16A2 barrel marking gives caliber and twist as "1/7."

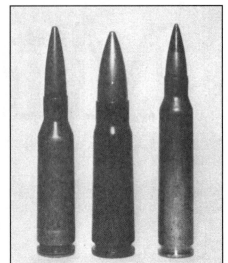

The AK74 5.45mm cartridge and the AK47 7.62mm cartridge — the competitors — are shown to the left of the 5.56mm NATO M855 cartridge, our new standard.

Production version of Colt M16A2: Obvious changes visible are heavier barrel, new muzzle-brake/compensator, improved sights and hand guard, integral brass deflector on receiver and contoured pistol grip.

in the production version of the M16A2. The Modified Operation Test (MOT) began on November 23, 1981, and was completed on December 11, 1981. Supplemental tests continued through August, 1982, to confirm the validity of some proposed improvements and to confirm their production feasibility.

The M16A2 is now in full production, having been adopted by the U.S. Marines to replace their entire complement of M16A1 rifles within the next five years. The Army has also decided to adopt the M16A2. The Canadians are also adopting it, but without the new sights or burst control, as the C7.

The test findings summarized in the MOT Final Report conclude the M16A2 performs as well or better than the M16A1 in all areas. The advantages of the M16A2 over the M16A1 are listed below:

• *Increased effectiveness:* higher hit probability, greater lethality and penetration, improved range through use of NATO standard SS109/M855 ammunition.

• *Better durability and handling* with improved, stronger handguard, and buttstock, longer buttstock, new buttcap, contoured pistol grip.

• *Reduced barrel jump and muzzle climb* during full automatic or sustained semi-automatic fire with new muzzle-brake-compensator.

• *Reduced dust signature* as well when fired over sandy or dusty ground.

• *Heavier, stronger barrel,* to resist bending, with 7-inch twist to exploit advantages of new NATO ammunition.

• *Better sights:* improved contrast and less glare with square post front sight, faster target acquisition of moving targets, better detection of targets in low light, and improved accuracy at long range by use of two optimized rear sight apertures.

• *Better fire control* and more effective use of ammunition with 3-shot burst option.

Operational firepower effectiveness was evaluated by comparing the M16A1 and M16A2 in tactical scenarios. These included base of fire, assault and coun-

terattack, ambush, long range and mid-range defensive fires, final protective fires, defense against ambush, area target suppression, and night firing.

There was no appreciable difference in base of fire effectiveness between the M16A1 and M16A2, but in the assault and counterattack, test results from the Small Arms Remoted Target System (SARTS) showed the A2 obtained a significantly greater percentage of hits in burst fire. When fired semi-automatic on the field range and Infantry Tactical Training (ITT) course simulations, no significant difference was noted. In the ambush scenario, using high volume semi-automatic fire no appreciable difference was noted. Firing in the burst mode at night the data were inconclusive, but when the same course of fire was fired in daylight on the area target suppression test, the A2 delivered 7 percent more hits at 100 meters than did the M16A1.

When firing in the burst mode at multiple targets at 100 meters the A2 gave a significantly higher number of hits, but at

Right side of receiver shows the integral brass deflector on the receiver behind the ejection port which prevents lefthanders from being struck by ejected cases. Aluminum device sandwiched between pistol grip and lower receiver inhibits inadvertent automatic in non-combat situations, such as marksmanship training, where this photo was taken.

50 meters this difference was not apparent. All persons firing the M16A1 used for comparison were firing short bursts of 2 or 3 rounds, which may or may not be what would happen in the high stress of actual combat. In the simulation of a patrol being ambushed, requiring quick reaction, immediate action and firing in bursts or automatic fire, the A2 obtained 19 percent hits, compared to only 12 percent for the M16A1.

The A2's increased ruggedness was evaluated through user assessments and inspection of rifles for damage after an exercise in which several squads conducted an operation clearing seven buildings in "combat town." Rifles were used as steps and to gain access to second stories of buildings. Each participant attacked a rubber dummy stabilized by ropes, ex-

ecuting the vertical butt stroke, smash, parry and horizontal butt stroke, in the same sequence with each weapon. Participants also fixed bayonets and attacked a simulated enemy, bayonetting and slashing it twice. The handguards of the A2 were more durable and appeared to offer better control in close combat, and for urban or builtup area operations.

Portability of each weapon was compared for tactical and non-tactical methods of carry, including the manual of arms while marching. Test participants marched to and from the range with both weapons, and carried them through the combat town course, day movement course and other subtests which included a forced march. User comments indicated no preference for carrying either the M16A1 or A2.

Vulnerability of the weapons to detection and countermeasures were assessed by comparing the noise generated when being carried, and while being operated, as well as the muzzle flash and/or dust signature produced when each weapon fired in day or night conditions. Photographic presentations of the muzzle flash or dust produced were obtained to provide an accurate assessment. Personnel in the butts also answered questionnaires assessing their ability to identify which weapons were being fired based on sounds heard in the butts.

Conclusions indicated no difference in the amount of noise generated by either weapon when being carried or operated. No difference was indicated in muzzle flash in day or night conditions. No significant dust signature was noted due to

The contoured pistol grip is intended to provide more secure grasping; backstrap is deeply grooved, and frontstrap has deep finger groove to provide secure hold. Selector lever offers choice of semi-auto or 3-shot bursts. Rear sight has minute of angle clicks for windage and elevation, matched to M855 or SS109 ammunition.

cold weather conditions, although when firing over new snow less disturbance was noted under the muzzles of the A2s. No essential difference in shape that could be used as a characteristic to identify units can be noted at any distance without the aid of binoculars or a telescope. Personnel in the butts could distinguish which ammunition was being fired at ranges beyond 600 meters, because the NATO SS109 and M855 ammunition remains supersonic to a far greater range, producing a distinct crack as it passes overhead, whereas the 55-grain M193 bullet goes subsonic shortly beyond 600 meters, producing only a muffled pop.

A limited test compared the M16A1 and the new A2 as to any interference generated while carrying the weapons caused by changes in center of gravity, or meth-

ods of carry when engaged in airborne, amphibious or helicopter operations. Participants carried both rifles in operation scenarios wearing full combat gear. There was no meaningful difference between weapons regarding their compatibility or suitability while entering or exiting landing craft, vehicles or aircraft.

The human factors evaluation, or "man-machine interface" characteristics of the two rifles were compared as they might affect operating safety (including hot or sharp parts), useability and adjustability of sights and controls in terms of speed, accessibility, and accuracy of adjustment; and recoil, as it affects recovery time, in burst fire or sustained rapid semi-automatic fire, accuracy in precision fire, comfort and confidence. The effects of the redesigned handguard and buttstock

were also evaluated as they affected accuracy, control in automatic fire and hand to hand combat.

Test participants preferred the sights on the M16A2 to those on the M16A1 because they were easier to adjust and provided a greater range of adjustment, which effectively doubles the useful engagement range of this rifle with SS109-M855-type ammunition compared to the M16A1 with M193-type ammunition. The sights on the A2 are safer to adjust when the weapon is loaded than those on the M16A1, because the front sight is not used for routine sight changes. Ranging adjustments are made on the elevation dial of the rear sight after the front sight is initially adjusted to obtain a battlesight zero. Refinements were made in the size of the front sight post and rear sight ap-

M16A2 front sight is square in cross-section with parallel sides to provide a more distinct sight picture. After first zero adjustment, rear sight offers all adjustments normally required.

The small aperture leg is used for precision daylight fire at ranges beyond 200 meters. The large aperture is used for snap shooting at ranges less than 200 meters and for low light level use near dawn or dusk. Elevation drum moves sight in minute of angle clicks.

ertures based on these tests to optimize precision of fire in daylight conditions, and target acquisition for close range snap shooting and firing in morning or evening nautical twilight conditions.

The M16A2 production sight is adjustable from 300 to 800 meters and has indexing marks on the dial and receiver which align when the sight is turned all the way down or within one click. The 300- and 800-meter settings are co-located on the same position, marked with an indexing line on the top of the dial. Remaining ranges are marked on the dial in 100m increments, i.e., 4, 5, 6, and 7. Range markings on the elevation dial align with the following detents 8/3 (800/300 meters) at 0 or 25th click, 4–3rd click, 5–7th click, 6–12th click, 7–18th click. The short range rear sight aperture is used for ranges up to 200m, has an outside diameter of .375-in. and an inside diameter of .20-in. It is marked "0–2" at the base and has a windage reference point at the top which is used for precision fire with the long range aperture.

The long range aperture is used for firing beyond 200m and has an outside diameter of .375-in. with an inside diameter of .070-in. It is marked "3–8" at the base. The rear faces of both sight apertures are concave and heavily phosphated to reduce glare. One quarter-revolution (one movement/detent) of the front sight moves point of impact approximately 1.4 MOA, one click of the elevation dial on the rear sight moves point of impact approximately 1 MOA, and one click of the windage knob on the rear sight moves point of impact approximately ½ MOA. Firing tests indicate that point of impact is not significantly different with M193 or SS109/M855 ammunition when using the same sight settings at ranges less than 500 meters.

Accuracy and penetration of the M16A1 with M193, the A2 with M193 and SS109/M855 and the Soviet AK-74 with 5.45mm Type PS ammunition were compared at ranges from 100 to 900 meters. The Soviet AK-74 was found to be reliable and accurate at short ranges, but its sights were a limiting factor beyond about 200 meters — it has a short sighting radius, open rear notch sight and no windage adjustments. The M193 ammunition was found most accurate at ranges less than 300 meters, but the SS109 most accurate at ranges beyond 500 meters. The most accurate rifle overall was the M16A2 with SS109 ammunition; the next most accurate was the M16A2 with M193, followed by the M16A1 with M193 and finally the

Table I
Accuracy Comparison of M16A2 vs. AK-74

Weapon/Ammunition	Range (yds.)				
	100	300	600	800	1000
M16A2 with 55-gr. M193					
Mean Radius (ins.)	1.87	4.18	13.2	18.3	no hits
Extreme Spread (ins.)	5.25	13.4	31.4	46.5	no hits
Hits On "E" Silhouette 39" high x 19" wide	20x20	20x20	11x20	10x20	no hits
Score on NRA decimal target SR and MR	99-6X	93-1X	81-1X	79	no hits
M16A2 with M855/SS109					
Mean Radius (ins.)	1.95	5.22	10.98	11.78	15.95
Extreme Spread (ins.)	5.5	15.75	32.75	43.0	73.9
Hits on "E" Silhouette	20x20	20x20	15x20	12x20	6x10
Score on NRA decimal target SR and MR	99-5X	90-1X	91-2X	82-1X	79-1X
AK-74 with 5.45 mm PS					
Mean Radius (ins.)	1.87	8.47	15.9	20.3	no hits
Extreme Spread (ins.)	7.25	21.6	44.0	74.5	no hits
Hits on "E" Silhouette	20x20	17x20	9x20	7x20	no hits
Score on NRA decimal target SR and MR	99-6X	79-0X	69-0X	57	no hits

AK-74 with Type PS ammunition. Accuracy results for the various weapons and types of ammunition tested are summarized in the accompanying tables.

In penetration tests the M16A1 rifle with M193 ammunition, the M16A2 with SS109, M855, M193 and Olin Penetrator (commercial approximation of the SS109), and the AK-74 with Type PS ammunition were fired against 3.5mm thick mild steel plates at various ranges. In addition, the 7.62mm M40A1 Remington sniper rifle with M118 Special Ball (Match, 175-2.0 gr. bullet at 2575 fps) and M80 standard Ball (148.0-2.0 bullet at 2750 fps) were fired for comparison. Maximum ranges at which penetrations of the test plate occurred were 500 yards for the M193, 600 for the AK-74 and 7.62mm M80, and 800 for the 7.62mm M118, 5.56mm SS109, M855 and Olin Penetrator. Results are summarized in an accompanying table.

The question of lethality and effectiveness of the M193 cartridge fired from the fast twist rifling in the M16A2 was of concern because existing stocks of M193 ammunition will be used until sufficient supplies of type M855 ammunition can be produced to replace it. Previous testing had already established there was no loss of precision when M193 ammunition was fired in the M16A2. However, since some nations had adopted faster twists of rifling for supposed humanitarian reasons, this factor had to be investigated. Test firings were conducted with M193 ammunition in both the M16A2 and M16A1 at ranges of 100, 300 and 500 yards, shooting into 20 percent gelatin blocks of U.S. DoD standards, 50cm thick. Testing indicated there was no significant difference in the lethality of M193 ammunition in the M16A2 as compared to the M16A1 at any range fired. The SS109/M855 was equivalent to the M193 at ranges up to 300 yards, and it was significantly more effective at longer ranges, such as 500 yards.

Brief tests were conducted to determine the compatibility of the M16A2 barrel with 22 rimfire ammunition used in the M261 Conversion Unit. This sub-caliber training device is used by Army and Air Force units for preliminary training and by reserve units not having year-round ranges. The conversion unit replaces the standard bolt carrier assembly and converts the weapon to blowback operation, firing 22 LR ammunition from 10-round magazine inserts which are loaded into standard M16 magazines. The device is made under contract to the U.S. Army by Saco Defense Systems, Inc., Saco, ME.

Familiar M16A1 features such as take-down mechanism and bolt-assist knob coexist with new things like brass deflector at right on M16A2.

New muzzle-brake/compensator has a closed bottom to reduce dust signature produced when rifle is fired from prone position. It also dramatically improves hit probability in burst fire by reducing muzzle climb.

Table II

Performance Of Typical Military Rifles Against NATO 3.5mm Thick Mild Steel Test Plate

Weapon	Cartridge	Range (yds.)	Performance*
Carbine, M1	Ball, M1	100	CP
		200	FP
AKM	7.62x39 PS	300	CP
	(steel core)	400	50% CP, 50% PP
M16A1	Ball, M193	400	CP
		500	50% CP, 50% PP
		600	FP
M16A2	Ball, M855	600	CP
		700	CP
		800	50% CP, 50% PP
		1000	FP
AK-74	5.45x39 PS	600	CP
		800	FP
Rifle, M1	Ball M2	500	CP
		600	FP
Rifle, M14	Ball M80	700	CP
		800	FP
Rifle, M21/M40	Ball M118	800	CP
		900	50% CP, 50% PP
		1000	FP

*Explanation of terms:
    CP - complete perforation in which major portion of the projectile exits the armor
    PP - partial penetration in which a hole is generated but the major portion of the projectile does not exit the armor
    FP - failure to penetrate, the plate may be dented but is intact

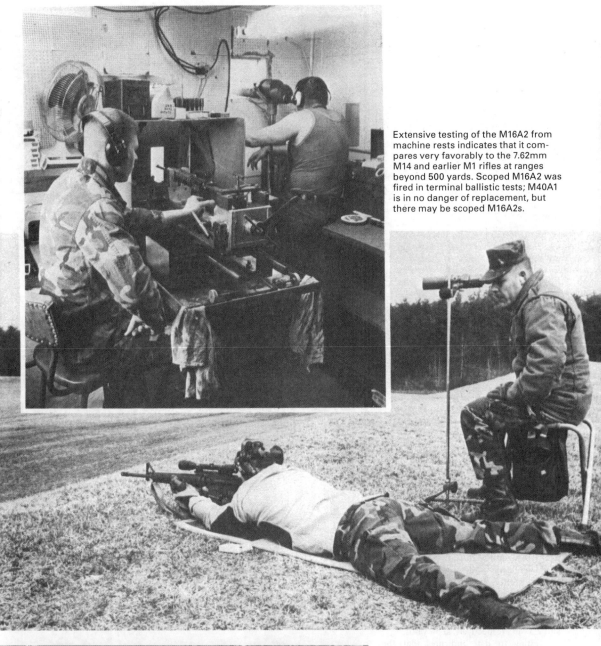

Extensive testing of the M16A2 from machine rests indicates that it compares very favorably to the 7.62mm M14 and earlier M1 rifles at ranges beyond 500 yards. Scoped M16A2 was fired in terminal ballistic tests; M40A1 is in no danger of replacement, but there may be scoped M16A2s.

(left) Writer Harris is well-known as a shooter who will shoot all of what's handy anytime there's a chance. Here he shoots an Egyptian AKM; he has fired the AR-15 and the various M16 options in about all the variations there are and created some of them himself. Indeed, the USMC officially commended Harris for his work with them on the M16A2.

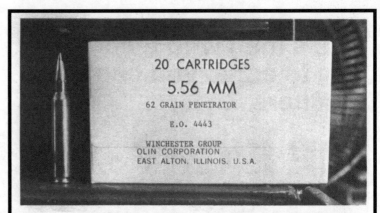

NATO 5.56mm ammunition is made in the U.S. by Olin Corp. and by Lake City Ammunition Plant. FN production is the standard by which others are compared. Ballistics are approximately 3100 fps for a 62-gr. steel core bullet from the M16A2, capable of perforating a 3.5mm steel plate at 700 yards, and capable of defeating soft body armor to 1000 yards. Accuracy of this ammunition from the M16A2 is approximately 2 minutes of angle at ranges less than 300, and about 3 minutes to 1000 yards.

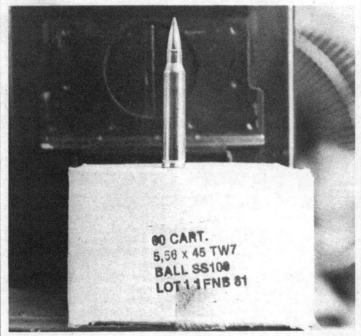

The normal accuracy expected of 10-shot groups with 22 rimfire ammunition fired from the M16A1 with M261 Conversion unit is about 4 MOA at ranges up to 50 meters. Although this is about twice the dispersion of M193 or SS109 type ammunition, it is deemed adequate for training purposes. Side-by-side comparisons with two M16A2 and M16A1 upper receivers, used alternately on the same lower receivers, firing the same M261 unit showed no significant difference in precision, the mean extreme spread of ten consecutive 10-shot groups with each being 2.25-in. and 2.37-in., respectively, at 50 yards.

Testing to date indicates that the M16A2 preserves the strong points of the M16A1 system, while correcting most, if not all of its deficiencies. Since the M16A2 has been adopted by the U.S. Army and U.S. Marine Corps, as well as by the Canadian Forces, it is sure to become a new standard against which future gen erations of small caliber weapons will be compared.

All the old infantry hardware is present — sling swivel and bayonet lug — on the M16A2 but the barrel is noticeably heavier than the M16A1 and the new muzzle brake is a boon.

The AR-15/M16:
The rifle that was never supposed to be

How the "Mattel Toy" became America's Assault Rifle.

▌ Chrstopher R. Bartocci

Photos by Lawrence Ventura. Property of the Wisconsin Department of Justice, State Crime Laboratory-Milwaukee.

The M16-series rifles have served the U.S. military, law enforcement and sportsman with distinction for nearly 40 years. They have become the world's standard for comparison. Here is the latest, the M16A2 assault rifle.

IN MARCH OF 1965, the first U.S. troops landed in Vietnam. They were carrying the M14 rifle, chambered for the 7.62×51mm NATO (M80 Ball) cartridge, which had a detachable 20-round magazine and was capable of semi- and full-automatic fire. The military soon learned the M14 on full auto was extremely difficult to control; most burst fire was ineffective. As a result, many M14 rifles were issued with the selector levers removed, making the rifle effectively, an M1 Garand with a 20-round magazine. The M14 was accurate but heavy, weighing nearly nine pounds, empty. As U.S. involvement in the Vietnam War escalat-

ed, our troops encountered North Vietnamese as well as the Vietcong carrying the Soviet-designed AK47 (Avtomat Kalashnikova model 47), chambered for the 7.62×39mm Soviet cartridge, and had a 30-round magazine. The AK's light recoil permitted controllable, accurate full-auto bursts and American troops began to feel outgunned. The United States needed it's own assault rifle — and needed it fast.

During the early 1950s, ArmaLite, a division of Fairchild Engine and Airplane Corporation of Hollywood, California, was working on a new assault rifle. The chief engineer was Eugene M. Stoner (1922–1997), described by many as the

most gifted firearms designer since John Browning. His first attempt to create a new assault rifle was designated the AR10 (ArmaLite Rifle model 10).

The AR-10 was the first weapon to incorporate Gene Stoner's patented (U. S. Patent No. 2,951,424) gas system. This system uses a port in the barrel to bleed gas from the fired cartridge into a tube that runs under the hand-guard, from the front sight assembly to the upper receiver and into the carrier key on the bolt carrier. The pressure gives a hammer-like blow to the bolt carrier, pushing it rearward while simultaneously unlocking the eight-lug bolt from the barrel extension. The bolt and bolt carrier, continuing to move rearward, extract and eject the spent cartridge case and the buffer and recoil/buffer spring return the bolt assembly forward, stripping a cartridge off the magazine, chambering it and locking the bolt into the barrel extension. Using expertise gained in the aircraft industry, Stoner designed the upper and lower receivers of the AR-10 to be made of lightweight aircraft aluminum.

The first AR-10 prototype, chambered for the 7.62×5 1mm NATO cartridge carried in a 20-round magazine, was completed in 1955. The rifle proved extremely accurate for a gas-operated weapon. In December 1955, the first AR10 was presented to the Infantry Board and School at Fort Benning, Georgia, by Gene Stoner and George Sullivan, an ArmaLite executive. Stoner demonstrated his new weapon concept to General William Wyman at Fort Benning on May 6th, just five days after the announcement of the adoption of the M14. Subsequently, the Board recommended further investigation into the AR-10. In 1957 General Wyman, impressed by the merits and performance of the AR-10, went to the ArmaLite Company and asked

Gene Stoner to join a weapons program, offering ArmaLite financial support for future development of ArmaLite rifles in exchange for proprietary rights to the final product. Subsequently, ArmaLite introduced a totally new concept for the modern battlefield, a 22-caliber battle rifle. As a result, the 30-caliber AR-10 was to have a short history with the U.S. military.

The AR-10, scaled down to fire the popular 222 Remington cartridge, had little recoil in semi-auto mode and was amazingly controllable on full-auto. There was heavy resistance to the radical new design from the Ordnance Corps, especially from Dr. Frederick Carten. Doctor Carten was adamantly opposed to weapons developed by commercial companies outside the Ordnance Corps and Springfield Armory, as well as guns made of aluminum and plastic.

General Wyman ordered 10 of these new rifles, along m with 100,000 rounds of ammunition, for Infantry M Board trials. ArmaLite's W focus was thus changed to the 22-caliber rifle and the AR-15 M (ArmaLite Rifle model 15) was born. In 1958, General Wyman ordered the Army to conduct the first tests on the new AR-15.

Among the changes from the AR-10 to the AR-15 were revised sights to accommodate the flatter-shooting 22-caliber cartridge; elevation to be adjusted via a threaded front post sight rather than within the rear sight, where a less expensive L-shaped peep sight was substituted. The resulting rifle was 37½ inches long and weighed an incredible 6 pounds empty; 6.12 pounds with a loaded 25-round magazine. The AR-15 made use of high-impact fibrite stocks, pistol grips and handguards. A selector lever on the left side of the rifle could be manipulated with the shooter's right thumb without removing the hand from the pistol grip. The magazine release, on the right side of

The original AR15; the weapon configuration that Colt bought from ArmaLite. Notice the three-prong suppressor, the fibrite stock/ pistol/grip/firearm grips, the absent forward assist and the smooth bolt carrier without forward-assist grooves. This was the model used in the Department of Defense testing which launched the weapon's reputation for durability, reliability and accuracy.

The Army/Marine version adopted towards the middle of the Vietnam War to serve the U.S. Marines (until 1983) and the Army (until 1986). Note the forward assist, magazine release fence "Boss" and the "bird cage" flash suppressor. Note the 25-meter zeroing target.

the receiver, could be operated with the trigger finger; when pressed, the magazine would drop free. A fresh magazine, requiring no camming — or 'rocking' — could be inserted straight into the magazine well. This attribute contributed significantly to speedy reloading in combat situations compared to its closest rival, the AK47/AKM. These are two of the main reasons why the AR-15/M16-series rifles are considered the finest human-engineered assault rifles in the world.

A bolt catch mechanism is located on the left side of the rifle. When the last round was fired, the magazine follower would elevate the bolt catch and lock the bolt to the rear. After inserting a full magazine, the rifleman would push in on the upper portion of the bolt catch to release the bolt and load the rifle. The receivers, produced from 7075 T6 aircraft aluminum, which helps keep the rifle lightweight and dissipates heat better than conventional metals, are hard-anodized with a non-reflective matte gray weather-resistant finish.

Stoner went to Aberdeen Proving Ground for ammunition assistance. He enlisted the expertise of Robert Hutton, known as the father of the 5.56×45mm round. The pressures involved were more than the 222 Remington case could handle, so the 222 Special was developed. Sierra Bullet Co. made the 55-grain full metal jacket boat-tail bullet and the first "222 Special" ammunition was loaded by Remington Arms. This cartridge, with a muzzle velocity of 3250 fps and a maximum effective range of 460 meters, became the 5.56×45mm Ball M193/223 Remington.

Tests by the Infantry Board and School at Fort Benning went very well for the AR-15. Stoner personally delivered the weapons and conducted training and familiarization classes for all involved in the testing. In March of 1958, the Board found some "bugs" in the AR-15 system. Some of the resultant changes incorporated in the first rifles were reduction of the trigger pull to seven pounds; replacement of the one-piece handguard with a two-piece triangular handguard; magazine capacity reduced from 25 to 20 rounds and the switching of the selector lever settings. The Board found the AR-15 to be nearly three times more reliable than the M14 in the development stages. Despite the positive conclusion of the

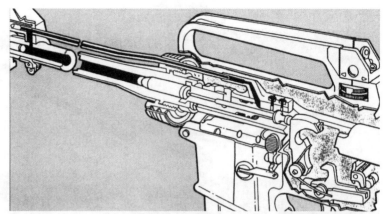

The firing sequence of Gene Stoner's design. After the hammer strikes the primer and fires the round, the bullet travels down the barrel and reaches the gas port where gas is bled into the gas tube and back into the bolt carrier assembly. The diverted gas delivers a hammer-like blow and moves the carrier to the rear, unlocking the bolt, extracting and ejecting the fired cartridge. The buffer spring returns the bolt carrier forward, chambering a fresh round and locking the bolt into the barrel extension — the rifle is now ready to fire again. *Printed with permission of Colt Firearms.*

test, Dr. Carten's report stated the AR-15 had not demonstrated sufficient technical merit and should not be developed by the Army. Accordingly, the Ordnance Corps lost interest in the AR-15.

When Bill Davis, at the time Chief of the Small Arms Branch at Aberdeen Proving Ground, first encountered the AR-15, he was quite impressed and found it had no shortcomings that would not be worked out in the normal course of development. Davis thought Carten's decision to drop the AR-15 rifle was a bad one and that the weapon held great promise.

On February 19, 1959, Colt's Patent Firearms Manufacturing Company of Hartford, Connecticut purchased the rights to the AR-15 and AR-10 from Fairchild Stratos (ArmaLite) for a lump sum of $75,000 plus a royalty of four and a half percent on all further production of the AR-15 and AR-10. Colt also paid Cooper & Macdonald (a sales group who did a lot of work in Southeast Asia) $250,000 and a one percent royalty on all production of AR-15 and AR-10 rifles.

In July of 1960, Air Force General Curtis LeMay attended a Fourth of July celebration where a Colt salesman placed three watermelons on a firing range at distances of 50, 100 and 150 yards — then gave General LeMay an AR-15 and load-

The forward assist bolt closure mechanism. The M16A1 (shown) had the *"tear drop"* style while the new M16A2 has a round button style.

Tlution of the M16 to the M16A1 is very evident when the rifles are compared side by side. The M16 (top) and the M16A1 (bottom). Note the addition of the forward bolt assist, magazine fence guard "BOSS" and the "birdcage" flash suppressor on the M16A1.

ed magazines. Following this hands-on range evaluation, General LeMay ordered 80,000 rifles on the spot. However, Congress put the General's order on hold.

Concurrently, Colt had requested a retrial from the Ordnance Corps to demonstrate improvements to the rifle. Initially the request was denied, the Ordnance Corps saying the military had no use for such a weapon. However, a request arrived at the Pentagon from Lackland Air Force Base requesting the AR-15 be qualified as a candidate to replace M2 carbines.

The combat 5.56×45mm. The M193 Ball Cartridge (left), 55-grain full metal jacket boattail bullet. The M855/SS109 Ball Cartridge (right), 62-grain full metal Jacket boattail with a hardened steel penetrator core. Identified by the green tip.

This turn of events caused Congress to investigate why the Ordnance Corps had boycotted the AR-15. Subsequently, the Ordnance Corps set up the test without delay.

The test was concluded in November 1960. Three rifles were subjected to a light machine-gun test and two to accuracy tests. There were a total of 24,443 rounds fired. One rifle in the accuracy test delivered an amazing 10-round group at 100 yards that measured only 1.5 inches; any group under six inches at 100 yards being acceptable for an assault rifle. The rifle also performed admirably in the unlubricated, dust, extreme cold and rain tests. The final results indicated the AR-15 was superior to all competitors, including the M14. The rifle was then approved for Air Force trial.

It took General LeMay three tries before his request was approved. In the summer of 1961, the Deputy Defense Secretary approved 8,500 AR-15 rifles for the Air Force, pending congressional approval … which Congress withheld. General LeMay then brought the issue to President Kennedy, without success. Finally, in May of 1962, the purchase was approved. With things warming up in Southeast Asia, the AR-15 was about to meet the Army.

Many of the U.S. advisors in Vietnam were equipped with the new AR-15 rifle. Rifles began to surface throughout Vietnam, totally outside the normal small arms procurement process. The first troops using the AR-15 under combat conditions were very enthusiastic, pre-

ferring it to all other weapons. The South Vietnamese were impressed with the rifle, as well. In December 1961, Secretary of Defense Robert McNamara authorized a purchase of 1,000 AR-15s. There was further testing (Project AGILE) to explore the compatibility of the AR-15 rifle to the smaller Vietnamese. The results indicated the AR-15 was more suitable for the South Vietnamese military than the M2 carbine. In actual combat, the new 5.56×45mm cartridge was found to be more lethal than its 30-caliber counterparts. while Project AGILE testing was being conducted, the Army completed the Hitch Report, which was a comparison of the AR-15, AK47, M14 and Ml Garand. The report concluded that the AR-15 was superior to the weapons to which it was compared.

Testing of the AR-15 weapon system had met with contempt from the Ordnance Corps. In one test in the Arctic, weapons were malfunctioning at alarming rates. As soon as Gene Stoner heard, he was on the next plane to Fort Greeley, Alaska. He found parts misaligned, front sights removed (front sights held in with taper pins have no reason to ever be removed) and replaced with pieces of welding rod. With missing and damaged parts, there was no way the weapons would function properly and, with welding rod replacing the front sight, accuracy suffered. The arctic test was, in fact, rigged to make the AR-15 look inadequate. Gene Stoner repaired all the weapons; the test resumed and the weapons performed admirably.

Fortunately, Defense Secretary Mc-

Namara was fond of the AR-15, knew the Ordnance Corps was dragging its feet on the weapon and on January 23, 1963, halted all procurements of the M14. Finally, in 1964, Defense Secretary McNamara ordered the Ordnance Corps to work with all branches of the armed forces to get the AR-15 ready for issue to all military personnel...one rifle for all branches. The Army purchased 100,000 rifles for issue to the Air Assault, Airborne, Ranger and Special Forces units.

After the AR15 — now, the M16 rifle — went into circulation, more was learned about how to improve the rifle. The rifling twist was changed from 1:14 inches to 1:12 inches. The Army wanted a manual bolt closure device added so, if the bolt failed to lock, it could be manually closed — and the forward assist assembly was born. The firing pin was lightened to prevent slam-fires (caused by the inertia of the firing pin when the bolt closed on a round). The buffer was changed from the original hollow version to one with weights in it to prevent the bolt from bouncing back when it slammed into the barrel extension.

On November 4, 1963, Colt was awarded a contract worth $13.5 million dollars for the procurement of 104,000 rifles ... the legendary "One Time Buy." Of those rifles, 19,000 were M16s for the Air Force and 85,000 were the XM16E1 (with the bolt closure device/forward assist assembly) for the Army and Marines. The XM16E1 was adopted as the M16A1 rifle. Steps were taken to procure ammunition.

Procurement of the ammunition is one of the main factors in the rifle's performance early in the Vietnam War. The initial ammunition used by DOD was made to Armalite/Colt specifications that called for IMR 4475 propellant. The weapon's

The M16A1 field-stripped. The ease and simplicity of disassembly made cleaning easy. All AR-15/M16-series weapons disassemble in the same manner.

reputation for durability and reliability was based on this ammo/extruded propellant combination. However, the military wanted to standardize propellants and the propellant used in the established 7.62×51mm NATO cartridge was Ball powder manufactured by Olin Corporation. So, when ammunition was ordered, Olin's Ball powder was used for the new 5.56×45mm M193 Ball cartridge. Both powders created the desired 50,750 psi.

Ball (spherical) powder reaches its peak pressure significantly faster than extruded IMR powder. Ball powder generates larger amounts of carbon residue that clogs the gas tube and barrel port, causing the firearm to malfunction. The most serious malfunctions, during the early use of Ball powder, involved extraction problems and a significant increase in the cyclic rate of fire. Despite having this information, the Department Of Defense still approved use of Ball powder. Gene Stoner was approached by Frank Vee of the OSD Comptrol-

lers office after the package was approved and asked what he (Gene Stoner) thought of the use of Ball powder. Stoner asked, "Why are you asking me now?" Vee said, "I would have felt better if you would have approved the package." Stoner replied, "Well, now we both don't feel so good."

The "one-time buy" was now a thing of the past. The original $13.5 million contract turned into a $17,994,694.23 contract. There were an additional 33,500 rifles that went to the Air Force, 240 to the Navy and 82 to the Coast Guard. Over $517,000 worth of spare parts was ordered.

The first field performance reports, from the 5th Special Forces in Vietnam, were excellent. The rifle had been well received and was very popular, although instruction manuals were in "short supply." During the investigation by the Ichord Subcommittee of the M16 Rifle Program, Honorable Richard Ichord said — regarding the rifle's reputation with the North Vietnamese Army and Vietcong — "I understand that they refer to this rifle as 'black rifle',...I have heard their motto is 'Beware of the units with the black rifles'... they have been possessed with deadly fear." In September 1965, General Westmoreland ordered an additional 100,000 rifles and requested all U.S. ground

The battle cartridges of the 20th Century (left to right): 7.62×63mm (30-06 Springfield); 8mm Mauser; 7.62×54mm Russian; 7.92×33mm Kurtz; 30 US Carbine; 7.62×51 mm NATO (308 Winchester); 7.62×39mm Soviet; 5.56×45mm NATO (223 Remington) and the 5.45×39mm Soviet.

Which is the better assault rifle? The M16A1 (top) or the AKM/AK47 (bottom)? Both are the most prolific military rifles of the last half of the 20th century; the most tested and most produced all over the world. Author feels hands-down winner is the M16 series.

forces in Vietnam be equipped with the new M16A1 rifles. Colt now signed an additional contract to deliver 25,000 rifles a month by December 1966. In 1968, GM Hydramatic Division and Harrington & Richardson were awarded second-source contracts from the Department of Defense.

Letters from the field began reporting the rifles were malfunctioning at an alarming rate, with U.S. troops found dead next to jammed M16 rifles. Spent cartridge cases were becoming lodged in the chamber and the only way to remove them was to knock them out with a cleaning rod. Requests were made for Colt to send a representative to the field to solve this problem. This turn of events was highly publicized by the media.

A representative from Colt, Mr. Kanemitsu Ito, went to Vietnam and claimed to be shocked, having never seen equipment in such poor shape. He claimed to have looked down the barrel of one rifle and not seen 'daylight' due to severe rusting and pitting. Many of the troops he spoke to said they were never trained to maintain their rifle, that the rifle was "self-cleaning" and that they had not handled an M16/M16A1 rifle until they arrived "*in-country.*" Subsequently, Mr. Ito gave classes on maintenance all over South Vietnam.

Seeking an independent, unbiased report of the true field performance situation, the Ichord Congressional Subcom-

mittee selected a retired officer, Colonel Crossman, as their representative and sent him to Vietnam. In the course of his investigation, he interviewed 250 soldiers and Marines throughout South Vietnam, fully 50 percent of whom reported malfunctions with their M16/M16A1 rifles. Of these malfunctions, 90 percent were failures to extract. Colonel Crossman found 22-caliber cleaning kits in short supply and concluded many of the problems were due to lack of maintenance and cleaning. He also felt there was room for improvement in the rifle. He concluded, "It was not possible to correlate ammunition make or type with malfunctions." His findings report, dated June 16, 1967, included the statement that the rifle needed a complete overhaul in design and manufacture.

According to Gene Stoner, there were hardly any 22-caliber cleaning kits in Vietnam — and no instruction manuals. The "cleanup" began: The military developed bore and chamber cleaning brushes and began to distribute 22-caliber cleaning kits, firearm maintenance cards and instruction manuals, for the M16/M16A1 rifles.

From May 15th through August 22nd, 1967, the much-publicized Ichord Congressional Subcommittee (Honorable Richard Ichord, Chairman) investigated the history, development, testing, procurement and foreign sales of the M16 rifle. During the investigation, the subcommit-

tee visited U.S. military training installations of all branches where the committee members interviewed hundreds of Vietnam returnees on their experiences with the M16/ M16A1 rifle. They also visited South Vietnam to interview troops in combat zones. Several people were called to testify before the subcommittee. Two topics, not identified until after the subcommittee returned from Vietnam, were the propellant and high cyclic rate issues. The subcommittee would focus most of their attention on these two aspects.

Reports from Vietnam of failures to extract in the field caused the subcommittee great concern. They investigated, finding the major contributor to malfunctions was ammunition assembled using Ball powder. The change from IMR extruded powder to Ball powder in 1964 for the 5.56mm ammunition was neither justified nor supported by test data, they found. The subcommittee also found the Ball propellant sole-source position enjoyed by Olin Mathieson for many years — and their close relationship with the Army — may have influenced Army Materiel Command. They felt the AR-15/M16 rifle, as initially developed, was an excellent and reliable weapon. Further, certain modifications made to the rifle at the insistence of the Army — also unsupported by test data — were unnecessary. For example, both the Air Force and the Marine Corps found no evidence to support the expense and possible problems of the manual bolt closure (forward assist) device.

Gene Stoner was called to testify at the congressional hearings to explain the extraction problem; he explained the failure to extract was due to the use of Ball powder.

Gene Stoner [To Mr. Bray]: "Well, the cartridge tends to stick under high residual pressure in the barrel, and of course with this too-soon action you also have a higher bolt velocity. In other words, your bolt is trying to open at higher speeds, so you have an aggravated condition where the cartridge is tending to stick in there a little longer or a little harder, and you are also giving it a harder jerk by driving the bolt faster."

Mr. Bray [To Gene Stoner]: "Then a faster rate of fire could cause that situation (failure to extract)?"

Gene Stoner [To Mr. Bray]: "This is probably one of the worst conditions you can get, by increasing the cyclic rate."

Basically, Ball propellant causes the bolt to open prematurely, before the spent cartridge case has had sufficient time to contract. The result is the extractor shears off the rim of the spent cartridge case — which sticks in the chamber. Ball and IMR powders create the same peak pressure but the Ball powder reaches its peak much faster than IMR powder, causing a significant increase in the cyclic rate of fire. Ball powder leaves significantly more fouling in the chamber and bolt assembly. Gene Stoner also pointed out the rifle had gone through more than 22 changes from his original design and neither Colt nor the Department of Defense consulted him on how some changes would impact his design.

The forward assist was one of the changes on which he was not consulted and Mr. Ichord asked Gene Stoner his opinion of the device.

Gene Stoner [To Mr. Ichord]: "I wasn't in on that, except I was told the Army insisted on it. There were reasons for it. One reason was that they felt that due to the fact that the M1, and the M14 rifle, and the carbine had always had something for a soldier to push on; that maybe this would be a comforting feeling to him, or something. I could never quite get it through my mind that it was necessary. I did not really advise it. I thought it was a mistake, myself. But I made my thought known to the people."

He explained the last thing you want to do is force a round into a dirty chamber, which quickly leads to function failures. The chamber fouling tends to embed

Specifications Table

	M16/M16A1 Rifles	M16A2 Rifles
Caliber	5.56×45mm NATO	5.56×45mm NATO
	M193 Ball	M855Ball/M 193 Ball
Method of Operation	Gas	Gas
Locking System	Rotating Bolt	Rotating Bolt
Type of Fire	Selective	Semi/ 3-Shot Burst
Weight Empty	7 pounds	7.9 pounds
Magazine Capacity	20 & 30 Rounds	20 & 30 Rounds
Barrel Length	20 inches	20 inches
Overall Length	39 inches	39.624 inches
Technical Data	Rifling: 6 grooves, right hand twist, 1 turn in 12 inches	Rifling: 6 grooves, right hand twist, 1 turn in 7 inches
Sights	**Front;** post with elevation adj. **Rear;** L-type aperture windage adj. only.	**Front;** post with elevation adj. **Rear;** L-type aperture adj. windage and elevation
Cyclic Rate	750 to 950 RPM	750 to 950 RPM
Practical Rate of Fire	150–200 RPM, Automatic	150–200 RPM, Automatic
Muzzle Velocity	M193 Ball-3,250 fps.	M193 Ball-3,250 fps. M855 Ball-3,100 fps.
Muzzle Energy	M193 Ball- 1,270 ft/lb	M193 Ball-1,270 ft/lb M855 Ball-1,302 ft/lb
Cooling	Air	Air
Maximum Effective	460 Meters/ 503 yards	M193 Ball-460 meters/ 503 yards
Range (Individual / Point Targets)		M855 Ball-550 meters/ 600 yards
(Area Target)		M855 Ball-800 meters/ 875 yards
Maximum Range	2,653 Meters/ 2,902 yards	M193Ball-2, 653 meters/ 2,902 yards
		M855 Ball-3, 600 meters/ 3,935 yards

in the soft brass cartridge case and lock it in, causing a fired cartridge case to be — literally — locked into the chamber at the moment of extraction. Gene Stoner was able to prove the rifle and ammunition combination he furnished to Armalite/ Colt was a totally reliable weapon system and the change the military made, without his consent, caused the malfunctions. He told the committee he expressed these concerns to the OSD Comptrollers office and was ignored. The subcommittee ac-

cepted this as the reason for the condition.

M16 rifle project manager, Col. Yout, was of particular interest to the subcommittee. Throughout the hearing he was accused of making irresponsible decisions as to the direction of the program.

Mr. Ichord [to Col. Yout]: "We have evidence and are advised by our experts … that Ball propellant, which you apparently speak so highly of, does have an adverse affect upon the operation of the

M16 rifle. It speeded up the cyclic rate. It is dirtier burning … . When we are also advised that the Army was cautioned against making this change from IMR to Ball propellant … Naturally, we would be quite concerned. Apparently you aren't so concerned. I don't understand your explanation. I just haven't been able to understand you — but perhaps you haven't offered the information in words I can understand. Would you care to say something?" He never replied to the question.

The Army made a statement on July 27, 1967: "From the vantage point of retrospect, it has sometimes been suggested that the particular behavior of Ball propellant should have been predicted … Had the Army anticipated these developments, it is most unlikely that the course chosen in January, 1964, would have been the same. A decision to reduce the velocity requirement, and continue loading IMR4475 propellant would probably have been made instead, and development of alternate propellants could have been pursued more deliberately."

This is the closest to an admission of negligence by the Army for the decision to use Ball powder. Gene Stoner warned them long before it got to this point; who would know more about the rifle's performance and design intent than the man who designed it? In the end, the rifle was not the problem; instead, this was an ammunition-driven problem that altered the design intent of the rifle.

In August 1967, the hearings ended, and in October 1967, the subcommittee concluded, "Grave mismanagement, errors of judgment

The CAR15 (Colt Automatic Rifle 15) gained major popularity with the development of the new M4 and M4A1 carbine. Note the telescoping stock and the shorter barrel. Most CAR15 rifles were issued with a 14-inch barrel.

and lack of responsibility had characterized the Army's handling of the entire M16 program." They stated the officials in the Department of the Army were aware of the adverse affect of Ball propellant on

the cyclic rate of the M16 rifle as early as March 1964, yet continued to accept delivery of additional thousands of rifles that were not subjected to acceptance or endurance tests using Ball propellant. All Colt endurance testing was done using IMR 4475. The subcommittee also concluded, "The failure on the part of officials with authority in the Army to cause action to be taken to correct the deficiencies of the 5.56mm ammunition borders on criminal negligence."

The cyclic rate of the rifle was increased 10 to 15 percent (approximately 200 rounds per minute), resulting in higher stress on certain components caused by the higher velocity of the bolt carrier assembly. As a result, there were parts driven beyond their working parameters - as well as the bolt opening prematurely. Many parts were changed to more stringent specifications to help deal with the higher pressure curve and harder impact. To solve the chamber corrosion and failure-to-extract issues, all future production rifle barrels would be chrome-lined. Even though chrome-lining barrels is a military specification, Ordinance failed to require this basic requirement on the AR-15/M16 rifle system.

Chrome-lining the barrels gave three major improvements to the standard barrel. First, the chrome-lined barrel was corrosion resistant. Second, chrome is slippery in nature and assists in extraction and ejection. When chromed, the walls of the chamber are harder; sand and mud don't "iron" into them. Thirdly, chrome is 2 to 3 times harder than standard barrel steel so the barrel lasts significantly longer. The new, improved M16/M16A1

barrel assemblies would have stamped on the barrel, in front of the front sight assembly: "**C**" (Chrome Chamber Only), "**C MP B**" (Chrome Chamber, Barrel & Magnetic Resonance Tested) or "**C MP Chrome Bore**"(Chrome Chamber, Barrel & Magnetic Resonance Tested). Many experts, including Bill Davis, felt the failure to chrome the chamber was responsible for many of the early malfunctions in Vietnam.

The flash hider was changed from the early three-prong to the new "bird cage" style. The three-prong suppressor was superior to the new design, but was snagprone in the field. With these modifications in place, the M16/M16A1 rifle was "perfected" and performing to the Department of Defense acceptance standards.

The AR15/M16 Carbines

Soon there was a demand for a smaller, more compact, version of the rifle. Early in 1966, the Army expressed interest for a carbine for its special operation units, placing an order totaling some 2,050 carbines. Lieutenant Col. Yout later ordered an additional 765 Colt "Commandos" — and a new name was coined for the carbine project. The first carbines were known as CAR15 (Colt Automatic Rifle). These first designs incorporated a 10-inch barrel and a sliding butt stock. Later the barrel was changed to 11.4 inches to permit the weapon to launch grenades. The Army signed a contract for 2,815 "Commando model" submachine guns on June 28, 1966.

As expected, the CAR15 — now the XM177E2 — successfully passed all testing phases at Aberdeen Proving Ground. However, a new problem appeared: the deafening noise and large fireball from the muzzle, thanks to the CAR15's higher cyclic rate of 700 to 1,000 rounds per minute. As a remedy, many of these rifles were equipped with 14.5-inch barrels, a practice that carried over to the M4 project of the early 1980s.

Product Improvement (PIP)

On October 28, 1980, there was a new 5.56×45mm cartridge on the block. NATO (Northern Atlantic Treaty Organization) had adopted the Belgian-made SS109. This new bullet had two major differences from the GI 5.56×45mm M193 Ball cartridge. First, the bullet weighed 62 grains instead of 55 grains. Second, this new bullet had a hardened steel penetrator core, giving this new 5.56×45mm round better penetration at all distances than the 7.62×51mm NATO (M80 Ball) round. This new SS109 round penetrated three 3.5mm mild steel plates at 640 meters and a U.S. issue helmet at 1,300 meters.

The new 5.56×45mmNATO round revolutionized military small arms ammunition all over the world. In 1974, the Soviet Union switched from the 7.62×39mm (AK47/AKM) to the 5.45×39mm Soviet round of the new AK74 rifle. This new round was a .221-inch diameter 52-grain full metal jacket boat-tail armor-piercing bullet with a velocity of 3000fps.

The new SS109 round was more lethal than the original M193 Ball round due to the faster "spin" and fragmentation upon impact with soft tissue.

Military surgeons all over the world have asked the United Nations to ban small caliber high-velocity rounds in combat — including the 5.56×45mm and the 5.45×39mm cartridges — which they believe cause unnecessary pain and suffering.

Switzerland re-designed the M855/SS109 round with a thicker jacket to stop fragmentation upon impact.

The SR25, perhaps the most accurate autoloader on the face of the earth. Gene Stoner revives his original AR10 design, with some added features of the M16A2, to build this semi-automatic 7.62×51 mm sniper rifle.

This new cartridge, however, was significantly more accurate at longer ranges than the M193 Ball cartridge, boosting the maximum effective range to 800 meters. To accommodate this new cartridge, a new barrel twist — from 1:12 inches to 1:7 inches — was required to stabilize the heavier 62-grain bullet.

There was a catch: the SS109 ammunition could not be fired accurately in an M16/M16A1 rifle due to its slower rifling twist. The bullet would not stabilize and would "keyhole" in flight. This new cartridge was about to be adopted as the M855 Ball cartridge of the U.S. military and the new PIP project would redesign the M16A1 rifle around this cartridge.

The United States Marine Corps began negotiations with Colt in January of 1980, asking for three modified rifles that would make use of the new FN SS109/XM855 cartridge and would incorporate four Marine-designated changes:

1. The sights must be adjustable to 800 meters.

2. The bullet must be accurate to 800 meters and possess the capability to penetrate all known steel helmets and body armor at 800 meters.

3. The strength of the plastic stock, pistol grip and handguards — as well as the strength of the exposed portion of the barrel — must be improved.

4. The rifle must have the full-auto capability replaced with a 3-shot burst mode.

The Joint Services Small Arms Program (JSSAP) PIP

The first rifles arrived from Colt in November of 1981. The USMC Firepower Division at Quantico, Virginia, would lead the PIP project. On November 11th, 20 Marines and 10 soldiers from the 197th Infantry Brigade at Fort Benning, Georgia, would take 30 M16A1 rifles and 30 M16A1E1 (PIP rifles) and test them for a month. The test report was issued on December 11th and the conclusions were as follows:

• The sights were easily adjusted in the field by hand rather than with a bullet tip.

• Increased the effectiveness at long range, more so than the M16A1.

• More durable plastic furniture on the M16A1E1, for hand-to-hand combat.

• Sights were better for low-light conditions thanks to a larger-diameter (5mm) close-range aperture in the rear sight.

• Increased ammunition conservation and more effective fire with the 3-round burst than with full-auto fire.

• Utilized the XM855 NATO (SS109) ammunition, which improves the accuracy and penetration at all ranges. The product-improvement (PIP) "M16A1E1" was classified as the M16A2 in September of 1982 and was adopted by the United States Marine Corps in November of 1983. The Marines ordered 76,000 M16A2 rifles from Colt.

The Army did not adopt the M16A2 until 1986.

The M16A2 Rifle

There were twelve major changes from the M16A1 to the M16A2 and, although the rifles seem similar at first glance, they are two totally different weapons. Many improvements were necessary to accommodate the new M855 Ball and M856 tracer rounds. The twelve major variances between the A1 and A2 are as follows:

1. The flash suppresser of the M16A1 is now a muzzle brake/ compensator on the M16A2. Instead of having vents all around the flash suppresser, the bottom has been left solid, which reduces muzzle climb and prevents dust from flying when firing from the prone position.

2. The barrel, from the front sight assembly to the flash suppressor/compensator, is heavier. The M16A1 rifles barrels were known to bend when paratroopers landed and the barrels hit the ground. When the A1 barrels would heat up, sling tension could bend them. The new M16A2 barrels had a rifling twist of 1:7 inches to accommodate the SS109/M855 cartridge.

3.The front sight post on the M16A2 is square, contrasted to the round post of the M16A1.

4. The M16A2 handguard was redesigned to have an interchangeable, upper and lower, round ribbed handguard.

5. The slip-ring "delta ring" was redesigned and is now canted for easier removal of the hand-guards.

6. A spent shell deflector was added to the upper receiver behind the ejection port of the M16A2 to accommodate left-hand shooters and, as well, the pivot pin area of the upper receiver has been

The M16A2 is mechanically identical to the M16 and the M16A1. The only difference is the 3-round burst selector setting in lieu of full-auto. All the changes were improvements to accuracy, more durable stock and grips as well as some structural reinforcements.

strengthened. The area around the buffer tube extension (takedown pin area) was strengthened to prevent cracking during hand-to-hand combat or from impact on the butt of the weapon while cushioning one's fall.

7. The rear sight was redesigned. The 1.75mm and 5mm apertures made adjustable for windage as well as elevation. The maximum elevation setting is 800 meters. There is still an "L-shaped" sight aperture, and there is a 5mm aperture battle sight effective to 200 meters.

8. The forward assist assembly was changed from the "tear drop" style of the M16A1 to the new round "button" style forward assist assembly of the M16A2.

9. The pistol grip is now made of a stronger plastic (™Zytel), and incorporates a "swell" below the middle finger position.

10. The three-shot Burst selector lever setting of the M16A2 replaced the Auto setting of the M16A1.

11. The ⅝-inch longer M16A2 stock is made from foam-filled nylon, said to be ten to twelve times stronger than the fibrite stocks of the M16 /M16A1.

12. The buttplate has been made stronger (™Zytel), and the entire buttplate is checkered. The trapdoor can be opened by hand rather requiring the tip of a cartridge.

Critics Attack the M16A2

There were critics who still found problems with the M16A2. One of the greatest criticisms was the substitution of

the Burst mode for the Automatic mode selector option. The critics reasoned the M16 rifle was adopted because U.S. troops felt outgunned by the North Vietnamese Army/Viet Cong who were equipped with full-auto AK47s. While, theoretically, the 3-round burst was more effective than full-auto fire, there was no substitute for a well-trained automatic rifleman. More recently, infantry units have noticed it takes more time to clear rooms and buildings in the MOUT (Military Operations in Urban Terrain) environment with the 3-round burst versus the full-auto mode and feel the full-auto option is desirable in those circumstances.

Not only was the conceptual validity of the three-round Burst under scrutiny, but the mechanical design as well. The burst mechanism does not recycle. If only two rounds were fired — because the trigger was not held long enough or the weapon ran out of ammunition — the next time the trigger was pulled only one round would fire.

Further, some critics found the sighting system too complex. The Canadian military addressed many of the issues brought up by American military critics. When Canada replaced their aging FN FAL 7.62mmNATO rifles, they modeled the new rifle after the M16A2. Their Diemaco-manufactured C7 was, virtually, an M16A2 that retained the rear sight and the full-auto setting of the M16A1. Some critics did not like the fact that the new M855 cartridge could not be fired in the current issue M16 /M16A1 rifles without

raising concerns that the fast l:7-inch rifling twist would more quickly burn out barrels during extended rapid fire.

The "Shorty" Program Revisited: The M4 Carbine.

In 1994, the Army adopted the second carbine of the 20th century and the first general issue carbine since 1941, the M4, perhaps the finest carbine ever developed. They were, at first, to be used by special operation units, but then were selected for use in many other units. Deliveries began in August of 1994, from Colt's Manufacturing, for 24,000 M4 carbines contracted at $11 million; another contract followed in 1995 for 16,217 M4A1 carbines.

The M4 is basically an M16A2 with a telescoping butt stock and a 14.5-inch barrel. The barrel has the heavy profile of the M16A2 barrel with a modified groove to accommodate the M203 grenade launcher. With its 14.5-inch barrel, the M4 fires the M855 Ball round at 2900 fps. The M4 incorporates the M16A2 fully adjustable rear sight. Colt's Manufacturing claims there is little, if any, difference in accuracy at ranges up to 500-600 meters. M4 carbines can be found with either full-auto or burst settings. The M4 duplicates the reliability and accuracy of the full-size rifle and weighs only 5.65 pounds.

The M4 has two variants, the standard M4 and the M4A1. The M4A1 is identical to the M4 with the exception of its removable carrying handle, which is attached to a Picatinny Weaver rail system. This arrangement enables easy attachment of

The latest in the M16 family, the M16A2. The standard by which all assault rifles are judged. Note major changes: fully adjustable rear sight, round handguards, longer stock, finger swell on pistol grip and cartridge case deflector. Note the 25-meter zeroing target.

optical sighting systems or, by reattaching the carrying handle, use of the iron sights.

Rebirth of the AR-10, Further Developments by Gene Stoner

The legacy of the ArmaLite rifles is far from over. The great weapons designer, Eugene Stoner, never stopped working on his AR-10 design. He, along with C. Reed Knight of Knight's Manufacturing, perfected the AR-10 and added many design features of the M16A2, to build the SR25 (Stoner Rifle Model 25). The model number comes from adding the 10 from the AR-10 and the 15 from the AR-15. Basically the SR25 looks like an M16 on steroids, beefed up to accommodate the 30-caliber round. The SR25 Match rifle is a 7.62×51mm NATO sniper rifle. Knight's Manufacturing is one of the only manufacturers that guarantee their rifle will shoot one minute of angle at 100 yards using factory 168-grain Match 7.62×51mm NATO/308 Winchester ammunition. This rifles incorporates the 5R rifling sniper barrel manufactured by Remington Arms for the M24 sniper rifle. Knight's Manufacturing is the only company to which Remington has ever sold these precision barrel blanks. The 5R rifling is designed to optimize the use of 168-grain Match 7.62×51mm NATO/308 Winchester ammunition. Many firearms experts claim the SR25 is the most accurate semi-automatic rifle in the world.

In May of 2000, the U.S. Navy SEALS adopted the SR25 — now classified as the Mk 11 Mod 0 — as a full weapons system: rifle, Leupold scope, back-up pop-up iron sights and a sound suppresser. This is a modified SR25 Match rifle, which has a 20-inch barrel instead of 24-inch barrel. Following this sale, the U.S. Army Rangers also purchased SR25 rifles.

Production Sources of Civilian/ Military Versions of the AR-15/M16

The AR-15 rifle has been copied all over the world, in military and sporting configurations. The Canadian military adopted the C7 as its main battle rifle. The C7, literally a modified M16A2 rifle, is manufactured by Diemaco of Ontario, Canada, an unknown company to most of the world but a large player in this weapons system. Diemaco has supplied their C7 and C8 weapons systems to Denmark, Norway, New Zealand and the Netherlands. They also equip the legendary British SAS and SBS with their SFW (Special Forces Weapon), designated the British L119A1 Assault Rifle. There have also been other military copies of the M16-series rifle made by Elisco Tool Company of the Philippines and Chartered Industries of Singapore.

Currently manufacturing the M16A2 and M4 carbines for the U.S. military are Colt's Manufacturing Inc, Hartford, Connecticut, and FN Manufacturing of Columbia, South Carolina. Quality Parts/Bushmaster Firearms of Windham,

Maine, have manufactured approximately 400 complete M4 carbines for the United States Department of Defense as well as an additional (approximately) 400 complete M4 upper receivers assemblies.

The semi-automatic Colt AR-15/ Sporter-series rifles have become very popular in the world of competitive shooters. Colt's Manufacturing Company, Inc., manufactures more civilian versions of the rifle than any other manufacturer, even though there are many other semi-auto clones produced. One of the finest is the XM15E2S, made by Quality Parts-Bushmaster Firearms. Some other manufacturers are Olympic Arms of Olympia, Washington, and ArmaLite, Inc., a division of Eagle Arms of Coal Valley, Illinois.

The AR-15/M16 rifle has come a long way, surviving political opposition and its troubles in Vietnam to become one of the finest military rifles ever produced, with more than 9 million M16-series rifles in service throughout the world, equipping the troops of more than 20 nations. The U.S. military has always been a military of marksmen, and the M16A2 complements this philosophy, setting a standard of accuracy very few assault rifles can match while enjoying the reputation of being the finest human-engineered assault rifle in the world. The M16-series rifle continues to be the rifle of choice of SWAT teams and police departments all over the country, and it will be the main battle rifle of the United States well into the new millennium. ━━━━►